About the Cover Image

Armenian woman from Isfahan, painting, 20th century

In this painting by an unknown artist from the early twentieth century, an Armenian woman wearing an elaborate headdress and brocade jacket gazes serenely at the viewer. Her clothing is what became defined as "Armenian national dress," one of many national and ethnic costumes largely invented during the period of growing nationalism in the nineteenth century but claimed as part of much older traditions. Armenia was a kingdom in southwest Asia that adopted Christianity in the fourth century. Conquered by various empires over the centuries, Armenians scattered and developed global trading networks that for a time centered on Isfahan (now in Iran), where this painting is located. Many Armenians remained in Armenia, which became part of the Ottoman Empire, until Ottoman authorities during World War I ordered their mass deportation to the Syrian Desert, a genocidal policy through which hundreds of thousands died from exhaustion, starvation, or massacre.

Armenian Woman from Isfahan, painting, 20th century/Armenian Cathedral and Museum, Julfa, Isfahan, Iran/De Agostini Picture Library/G. Dagli Orti/Bridgeman Images

THE CONTEMPORARY WORLD

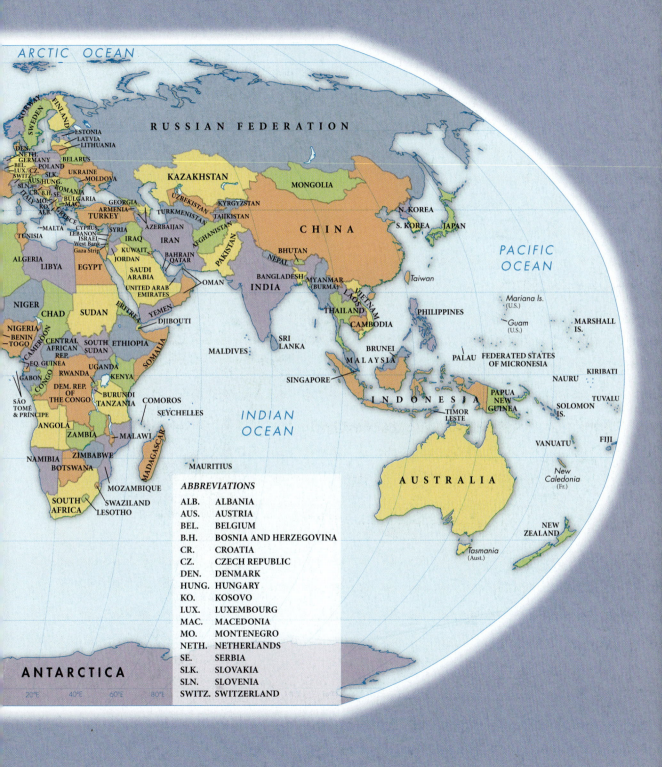

ARCTIC OCEAN

RUSSIAN FEDERATION

NORWAY
SWEDEN
FINLAND
ESTONIA
LATVIA
LITHUANIA
DEN.
NETH.
GERMANY
BELARUS
BEL.
LUX.
POLAND
SWITZ.
CZ.
SLK.
UKRAINE
AUS.
HUNG.
MOLDOVA
SLN.
ITALY
CR.
B.H.
SE.
ROMANIA
MO.
BULGARIA
KO.
MAC.
ALB.
GREECE
GEORGIA
MALTA
ARMENIA
AZERBAIJAN
TUNISIA
CYPRUS
SYRIA
TURKEY
LEBANON
ISRAEL
West Bank
IRAQ
IRAN
Gaza Strip
KUWAIT
BAHRAIN
QATAR
JORDAN

KAZAKHSTAN
MONGOLIA
UZBEKISTAN
KYRGYZSTAN
TURKMENISTAN
TAJIKISTAN
AFGHANISTAN
CHINA
PAKISTAN

N. KOREA
S. KOREA
JAPAN

PACIFIC OCEAN

ALGERIA
LIBYA
EGYPT
SAUDI
ARABIA
UNITED ARAB
EMIRATES
OMAN

BHUTAN
NEPAL
BANGLADESH
INDIA
MYANMAR
(BURMA)
LAOS
VIETNAM

Taiwan

Mariana Is.
(U.S.)

MARSHALL
IS.

NIGER
CHAD
SUDAN
YEMEN
ERITREA
DJIBOUTI
THAILAND
CAMBODIA

PHILIPPINES

Guam
(U.S.)

NIGERIA
BENIN
TOGO
CAMEROON
CENTRAL
AFRICAN
REP.
SOUTH
SUDAN
ETHIOPIA
SOMALIA
MALDIVES
SRI
LANKA
BRUNEI
MALAYSIA

PALAU

FEDERATED STATES
OF MICRONESIA

NAURU

KIRIBATI

EQ. GUINEA
GABON
CONGO
RWANDA
UGANDA
KENYA
DEM. REP.
OF THE CONGO
BURUNDI
TANZANIA
SINGAPORE

INDONESIA

PAPUA
NEW
GUINEA

SOLOMON
IS.

TUVALU

SÃO
TOMÉ
& PRÍNCIPE
COMOROS
SEYCHELLES

TIMOR
LESTE

ANGOLA
ZAMBIA
MALAWI
MADAGASCAR

INDIAN
OCEAN

VANUATU

FIJI

NAMIBIA
ZIMBABWE
BOTSWANA

New
Caledonia
(Fr.)

AUSTRALIA

MAURITIUS

SOUTH
AFRICA
SWAZILAND
LESOTHO
MOZAMBIQUE

NEW
ZEALAND

Tasmania
(Aust.)

ABBREVIATIONS

ALB.   ALBANIA
AUS.   AUSTRIA
BEL.   BELGIUM
B.H.   BOSNIA AND HERZEGOVINA
CR.   CROATIA
CZ.   CZECH REPUBLIC
DEN.   DENMARK
HUNG.   HUNGARY
KO.   KOSOVO
LUX.   LUXEMBOURG
MAC.   MACEDONIA
MO.   MONTENEGRO
NETH.   NETHERLANDS
SE.   SERBIA
SLK.   SLOVAKIA
SLN.   SLOVENIA
SWITZ. SWITZERLAND

ANTARCTICA

20°E   40°E   60°E   80°E

A History of
World Societies

CONCISE EDITION

CONCISE EDITION

A History of
World Societies

ELEVENTH EDITION

MERRY E. WIESNER-HANKS
University of Wisconsin–Milwaukee

PATRICIA BUCKLEY EBREY
University of Washington

ROGER B. BECK
Eastern Illinois University

JERRY DÁVILA
University of Illinois at Urbana-Champaign

CLARE HARU CROWSTON
University of Illinois at Urbana-Champaign

JOHN P. McKAY
University of Illinois at Urbana-Champaign

bedford/st.martin's
Macmillan Learning

Boston | New York

FOR BEDFORD/ST. MARTIN'S

Vice President, Editorial, Macmillan Learning Humanities: Edwin Hill

Program Director for History: Michael Rosenberg

Senior Program Manager for History: William J. Lombardo

History Marketing Manager: Melissa Rodriguez

Director of Content Development: Jane Knetzger

Senior Developmental Editor: Heidi L. Hood

Senior Content Project Manager: Christina M. Horn

Senior Workflow Manager: Jennifer Wetzel

Production Assistant: Brianna Lester

Senior Media Project Manager: Michelle Camisa

Media Editor: Tess Fletcher

Associate Editor: Mary Posman Starowicz

Copy Editor: Jennifer Brett Greenstein

Indexer: Leoni Z. McVey

Composition: Jouve

Cartographer: Mapping Specialists, Ltd.

Photo Editor: Christine Buese

Photo Researcher: Bruce Carson

Permissions Editor: Eve Lehmann

Senior Art Director: Anna Palchik

Text Design: Boynton Hue Studio

Cover Design: William Boardman

Cover Art: Armenian Woman from Isfahan, painting, 20th century/Armenian Cathedral and Museum, Julfa, Isfahan, Iran/De Agostini Picture Library/ G. Dagli Orti/Bridgeman Images

Printing and Binding: LSC Communications

Manufactured in the United States of America.

2 1 0 9 8 7
f e d c b a

For information, write: Bedford/St. Martin's, 75 Arlington Street, Boston, MA 02116

ISBN 978-1-319-07011-3 (Combined Edition)

ISBN 978-1-319-07015-1 (Volume 1)

ISBN 978-1-319-07014-4 (Volume 2)

ACKNOWLEDGMENTS

Acknowledgments and copyrights appear on the same page as the text and art selections they cover; these acknowledgments and copyrights constitute an extension of the copyright page.

We are pleased to introduce the first Concise Edition of our popular textbook *A History of World Societies*. The Concise Edition provides the social and cultural focus, comprehensive regional organization, and global perspective that have long been hallmarks of *A History of World Societies* in a smaller, more affordable trim size. Featuring the full narrative of the eleventh edition of the comprehensive parent text plus select features, images, maps, and pedagogical tools, the Concise Edition incorporates the latest and best scholarship in the field in an accessible, student-friendly manner. Each of the authors on our collaborative team is a regional expert with deep experience in teaching world history, who brings insights into the text from the classroom, as well as from new secondary works and his or her own research in archives and libraries. In response to the growing emphasis on historical thinking skills in the teaching of history at all levels, the book's primary source program offers a wide variety of sources, both written and visual, presented in different ways to allow students to practice different skills. The rich primary sources and innovative tools of the Concise Edition—both print and digital—have been carefully designed to help students think historically and master the material.

The Story of *A History of World Societies*

In this age of global connections, with their influence on the economy, migration patterns, popular culture, and climate change, among other aspects of life, the study of world history is more vital and urgent than ever before. An understanding of the broad sweep of the human past helps us comprehend today's dramatic changes and enduring continuities. People now migrate enormous distances and establish new lives far from their places of birth, yet migration has been a constant in history since the first humans walked out of Africa. Satellites and cell phones now link nearly every inch of the planet, yet the expansion of communication networks is a process that is thousands of years old. Children who speak different languages at home now sit side by side in schools and learn from one another, yet intercultural encounters have long been a source of innovation, transformation, and at times, unfortunately, conflict.

This book is designed for twenty-first-century students who will spend their lives on this small interconnected planet and for whom an understanding of only local or national history will no longer be sufficient. We believe that the study of world history in a broad and comparative context is an exciting, important, and highly practical pursuit. It is our conviction, based on considerable experience in introducing large numbers of students to world history, that a book reflecting current trends in scholarship can excite readers and inspire an enduring interest in the long human experience.

Our strategy has been twofold. First, we have made social and cultural history the core elements of our narrative. We know that engaging students' interest in the past is often a challenge, but we also know that the emphasis on individual experience in its social and cultural dimensions connects with students and makes the past vivid and accessible. We seek to re-create the lives of ordinary people in appealing human terms and also to highlight the interplay between men's and women's lived experiences and the ways they reflect on these to create meaning. Thus, in addition to foundational works of philosophy and literature, we include popular songs and stories. We present objects along with texts as important sources for studying history, and this has allowed us to incorporate the growing emphasis on material culture in the work of many historians. At the same time, we have been mindful of the need to give great economic, political, and intellectual developments the attention they deserve. We want to give individual students and instructors an integrated perspective so that they can pursue—on their own or in the classroom—the themes and questions that they find particularly exciting and significant.

Second, we have made every effort to strike an effective global and regional balance. The whole world interacts today, and to understand the interactions and what they mean for today's citizens, we must study the whole world's history. Thus we have adopted a comprehensive regional organization with a global perspective that is clear and manageable for students. For example, Chapter 7 introduces students in depth to East Asia, and at the same time the chapter highlights the cultural connections that occurred via the Silk Road and the spread of Buddhism. We study all geographical areas, conscious of the separate histories of many parts of the world, particularly in the earliest millennia of human development. We also stress the links among cultures, political units, and economic systems, for these connections have made the world what it is today. We make comparisons and connections across time as well as space, for understanding the unfolding of the human story in time is the central task of history. We further students' understanding of these connections with the addition of new timelines in each chapter that put regional developments into a global context.

Primary Sources for Historical Thinking

A History of World Societies offers an extensive program of primary source assignments to help students master a number of key learning outcomes, among them **critical thinking**, **historical thinking**, **analytical thinking**, and **argumentation**, as well as learning about the **diversity of world cultures**.

To encourage comparisons across chapters and across cultures, we offer the **Global Viewpoints** feature, which provides students with perspectives from two cultures on a key issue. This feature offers a pair of primary documents on a topic that illuminates the human experience, allowing us to provide more concrete examples of differences in the ways people thought. Anyone teaching world history has to emphasize larger trends and developments, but students sometimes get the wrong impression that everyone in a society thought alike. We hope that teachers can use these passages to get students thinking about diversity within and across societies. The 33 Global Viewpoints assignments—one in each chapter—introduce students to working with sources, encourage critical analysis, and extend the narrative while giving voice to the people of the past. Each includes a brief introduction and questions for analysis. Carefully chosen for accessibility, each pair of documents presents views on a diverse range of topics such as "Roman and Chinese Officials in Times of Disaster" (Chapter 6), "Early Descriptions of Africa from Egypt" (Chapter 10), "Aztec and Spanish Views on Christian Conversion in New Spain" (Chapter 16), "Declarations of Independence: The United States and Venezuela" (Chapter 22), and "Gandhi and Mao on Revolutionary Means" (Chapter 29).

A second type of original source feature, **Analyzing the Evidence** (one in each chapter), features an individual visual or written source, longer and more substantial than those in other features, chosen to extend and illuminate a major historical issue considered in each chapter, with headnotes and questions that help students understand the source and connect it to the information in the rest of the chapter. Selected for their interest and carefully integrated into their historical context, these in-depth looks at sources provide students with firsthand encounters with people of the past and should, we believe, help students "hear" and "see" the past. Topics include "The Teachings of Confucius" (Chapter 4), "Sufi Collective Ritual" (Chapter 9), "The Abduction of Women in *The Secret History of the Mongols*" (Chapter 12), "Courtly Love Poetry" (Chapter 14), "Duarte Barbosa on the Swahili City-States" (Chapter 20), "*Rain, Steam and Speed—the Great Western Railway*" (Chapter 23), "Slaves Sold South from Richmond, 1853" (Chapter 27), "A Member of China's Red Guards on Democratic Reform" (Chapter 32), and "Protest Against Genetically Modified Foods" (Chapter 33).

Taken together, the primary source features in this book offer the tools for building historical skills, including **chronological reasoning**, **explaining causation**, **evaluating context**, and **assessing perspective**. In LaunchPad these features are each accompanied by autograded questions that test students on their basic understanding of the sources so instructors can ensure students read the sources, quickly identify and help students who may be struggling, and focus more class time on thoughtful discussion and instruction.

In addition, our **primary source documents collection**, *Sources of World Societies*, includes written and visual sources that closely align the readings with the chapter topics and themes of this edition. The documents are available in a fully assignable and assessable electronic format within each chapter in LaunchPad, and the multiple-choice questions—now accompanying each source—measure comprehension and hold students accountable for their reading.

Finally, our new **Bedford Document Collections** modules in LaunchPad, which are also available for customizing the print text, provide a flexible repository of discovery-oriented primary source projects ready to assign. Each curated project—written by a historian about a favorite topic—poses a historical question and guides students through analysis of the sources. Examples include "The Silk Road: Travel and Trade in Premodern Inner Asia"; "The Spread of Christianity in the Sixteenth and Early Seventeenth Centuries"; "The Singapore Mutiny of 1915: Understanding World War I from a Global Perspective"; and "Living Through Perestroika: The Soviet Union in Upheaval, 1985–1991."

Student Engagement with Biography

In our years of teaching world history, we have often noted that students come alive when they encounter stories about real people in the past. To give students a chance to see the past through ordinary people's lives, each chapter includes one of the popular **Individuals in Society** biographical essays, each of which offers a brief study of an individual or group, informing students about the societies in which the individuals lived. This feature grew out of our long-standing focus on people's lives and the varieties of historical experience, and we believe that readers will empathize with these human beings who themselves were seeking to define their own identities. The spotlighting of individuals, both famous and obscure, perpetuates the book's continued attention to cultural and intellectual developments, highlights human agency, and reflects changing interests within the historical profession as well as the development of "micro-history." These features include essays on people such as Sudatta, a lay follower of the Buddha (Chapter 3); Queen Cleopatra of Egypt (Chapter 6); Ibn Battuta, the famous Muslim traveler (Chapter 9); Catarina de San Juan, an Indian woman who had been enslaved by Portuguese traders and transported to Mexico (Chapter 16); Toussaint L'Ouverture, leader of the Haitian Revolution (Chapter 22); Samuel Crompton, inventor of the spinning mule (Chapter 23); and Ning Lao, a Chinese working woman (Chapter 29).

Geographic Literacy

We recognize students' difficulties with geography, so our text offers **Mapping the Past map activities**. Included in each chapter, these activities ask students to analyze a map and make connections to the larger processes discussed in the narrative, giving them valuable practice in reading and interpreting maps. In LaunchPad, these maps come with new assignable activities. Throughout the textbook and online in LaunchPad, nearly **100 full-size maps** illustrate major developments in the chapters.

In addition, **75 spot maps** are embedded in the narrative to show specific areas under discussion.

Chronological Literacy in a Global Context

The attention to global connections and comparisons that marks this Concise Edition can also be seen in new timelines at the end of each chapter. Along with graphically displaying major events and developments from the chapter, they also include key developments in other regions with cross-references to the chapters in which they are discussed. These comparisons situate events in the global story and help students identify similarities and differences among regions and societies.

Helping Students Understand the Narrative

We know firsthand and take seriously the challenges students face in understanding, retaining, and mastering so much material that is often unfamiliar. With the goal of making this the most student-centered edition yet, we continued to enhance the book's pedagogy on many fronts. To focus students' reading, each chapter opens with a chapter preview with focus questions keyed to the main chapter headings. These questions are repeated within the chapter and again in the "Review and Explore" section at the end of each chapter that provides helpful guidance for reviewing key topics. "Review and Explore" also includes "Make Comparisons and Connections" questions that prompt students to assess larger developments across chapters, thus allowing them to develop skills in evaluating change and continuity, making comparisons, and analyzing context and causation.

Within the narrative, a chapter summary reinforces key chapter events and ideas for students. This is followed by the chapter-closing **Connections** feature, which synthesizes main developments and makes connections and comparisons between countries and regions to explain how events relate to larger global processes, such as the influence of the Silk Road, the effects of the transatlantic slave trade, and the ramifications of colonialism. This also serves as a bridge to the subsequent chapters.

Key terms are bolded in the text, defined in the margin, and listed in the "Review and Explore" section to promote clarity and comprehension, and **phonetic**

spellings are located directly after terms that readers are likely to find hard to pronounce.

The chapter ends with **Suggested Resources**, which includes up-to-date readings on the vast amount of new work being done in many fields, as well as recommended documentaries, feature films, television dramas, and websites.

The high-quality art and map program has been thoroughly revised and features **hundreds of contemporaneous illustrations**. To make the past tangible, and as an extension of our attention to cultural history, we include numerous artifacts—from weapons and armor to dishes, furnishings, and figurines. As in earlier editions, all illustrations have been carefully selected to complement the text, and all include captions that inform students while encouraging them to read the text more deeply. **Numerous high-quality full-size maps** illustrate major developments in the narrative, and helpful spot maps are embedded in the narrative to locate areas under discussion.

In addition, whenever an instructor assigns the **LaunchPad e-Book** (which can be bundled for free with the print book), students get not only access to all of the additional special features and primary sources of the comprehensive edition but also full access to **Learning-Curve**, an online adaptive learning tool that promotes mastery of the book's content and diagnoses students' trouble spots. With this adaptive quizzing, students accumulate points toward a target score as they go, giving the interaction a game-like feel. Feedback for incorrect responses explains why the answer is incorrect and directs students back to the text to review before they attempt to answer the question again. The end result is a better understanding of the key elements of the text. Instructors who actively assign LearningCurve report their students come to class prepared for discussion and their students enjoy using it. In addition, Learning-Curve's reporting feature allows instructors to quickly diagnose which concepts students in their classes are struggling with so they can adjust lectures and activities accordingly. The LaunchPad e-Book with Learning-Curve is thus an invaluable asset for instructors who need to support students in all settings, from traditional lectures to hybrid, online, and newer "flipped" classrooms. In LaunchPad, instructors can also assign the **Guided Reading Exercise** for each chapter, which prompts students to read actively to collect information that answers a broad analytic question central to

the chapter as a whole. Through these tools and more, LaunchPad can make the textbook even easier for students to understand and use. To learn more about the benefits of LearningCurve and LaunchPad's other features, see the "Versions and Supplements" section on page xv.

All the features and tools in the book, large and small, are intended to give students and instructors an integrated perspective so that they can pursue—on their own or in the classroom—the historical questions that they find particularly exciting and significant.

Helping Instructors Teach with Digital Resources

As noted, *A History of World Societies* is offered in Macmillan's premier learning platform, **LaunchPad**, an intuitive and interactive e-Book and course space. Free when packaged with the print book or available at a low price when used on its own, LaunchPad grants students and teachers access to a wealth of online tools and resources built specifically for this text to enhance reading comprehension and promote in-depth study. LaunchPad's course space and interactive e-Book are ready to use as is (or can be edited and customized with your own material) and can be assigned right away.

Developed with extensive feedback from history instructors and students, **LaunchPad for *A History of World Societies*** includes the complete narrative and special features of the comprehensive edition print book; the companion reader, *Sources of World Societies*; and **LearningCurve**, an adaptive learning tool designed to get students to read before they come to class. With **an expanded set of source-based questions in the test bank and in LearningCurve**, instructors now have more ways to test students on their understanding of sources and narrative in the book. The addition of the **new Bedford Document Collections modules in LaunchPad** means instructors have a flexible repository of discovery-oriented primary source projects to assign and to extend the text, making LaunchPad for *A History of World Societies* a one-stop shop for working with sources and thinking critically in a multitude of modes.

LaunchPad also offers several other distinctly useful assignment options to help students get the most from their reading, including **Guided Reading Exercises** that prompt students to be active readers of the chapter narrative and autograded **primary source quizzes** to test comprehension of written and visual sources in the book, the companion reader, and the Bedford Document Collections modules. These features, plus **additional primary source documents**, **video sources and tools for making video assignments**, **map activities**, **flashcards**, and **customizable test banks**, make Launchpad a great asset for any instructor who wants to enliven world history for students.

With training and support just a click away, LaunchPad can help you take your teaching into a new era. To learn more about the benefits of LearningCurve and LaunchPad, see "Versions and Supplements" on page xv.

Acknowledgments

It is a pleasure to thank the many instructors who critiqued the book in preparation for this revision: Gene Barnett, Calhoun Community College; Amanda Carr-Wilcoxson, Pellissippi State Community College; Ted Cohen, Lindenwood University; Fiona Foster, Tidewater Community College; Paul J. Fox, Kennesaw State University; Duane Galloway, Rowan-Cabarrus Community College; Margaret Genvert, Salisbury University; Richard Bach Jensen, Northwestern State University; Kelly Kennington, Auburn University; Alex Pavuk, Morgan State University; Franklin Rausch, Lander University; Ryan L. Ruckel, Pearl River Community College; Dr. Anthony R. Santoro, Christopher Newport University; Chuck Smith, University of the Cumberlands; Molly E. Swords, University of Idaho; Scott N. West, University of Dayton; Dr. Kari Zimmerman, University of St. Thomas; and Michael Andrew Žmolek, University of Iowa.

It is also a pleasure to thank the many editors who have assisted us over the years, first at Houghton Mifflin and now at Bedford/St. Martin's (Macmillan Learning). At Bedford/St. Martin's, these include senior development editor Heidi Hood, associate editor Mary Posman Starowicz, program manager Laura Arcari, director of development Jane Knetzger, senior program director Michael Rosenberg, photo researcher Bruce Carson, text permissions editor Eve Lehmann, and senior content project manager Christina Horn, with the guidance of senior managing editor Michael Granger. Other key contributors were designer Cia Boynton, copy editor Jennifer Brett Greenstein, proofreaders Angela Morrison and Susan Zorn, indexer Leoni McVey, and cover designer William Boardman.

Many of our colleagues at the University of Illinois, the University of Washington, the University of Wisconsin–Milwaukee, and Eastern Illinois University continue to provide information and stimulation, often without even knowing it. We thank them for it. The authors recognize John P. McKay, Bennett D. Hill, and John Buckler, the founding authors of this textbook, whose vision set a new standard for world history textbooks. The authors also thank the many students over the years with whom we have used earlier editions of this book. Their reactions and opinions helped shape our revisions to this edition, and we hope it remains worthy of the ultimate praise they bestowed, that it is "not boring like most textbooks." Merry Wiesner-Hanks would, as always, like to thank her husband, Neil, without whom work on this project would not be possible. Patricia Ebrey thanks her husband, Tom. Clare Haru Crowston thanks her husband, Ali, and her children, Lili, Reza, and Kian, who are a joyous reminder of the vitality of life that we try to showcase in this book. Roger Beck thanks Ann for supporting him through five editions now, and for sharing his love of history. He is also grateful to the World History Association for all past, present, and future contributions to his understanding of world history. Jerry Dávila thanks Liv, Ellen, and Alex, who are reminders of why history matters.

Each of us has benefited from the criticism of his or her coauthors, although each of us assumes responsibility for what he or she has written. Merry Wiesner-Hanks has written Chapters 1, 2, 5, 6, 8, 14, and 15; Patricia Buckley Ebrey has written Chapters 3, 4, 7, 9, 12, 13, 17, 21, and 26; Roger B. Beck has written Chapters 10, 20, 25, and 28–30; Clare Haru Crowston has written Chapters 16, 18, 19, and 22–24; and Jerry Dávila has written Chapters 11, 27, and 31–33.

MERRY E. WIESNER-HANKS
PATRICIA BUCKLEY EBREY
ROGER B. BECK
JERRY DÁVILA
CLARE HARU CROWSTON

Adopters of *A History of World Societies* and their students have access to abundant print and digital resources and tools, the acclaimed *Bedford Series in History and Culture* volumes, and much more. The LaunchPad course space for *A History of World Societies* provides access to the narrative as well as a wealth of primary sources and other features, along with assignment and assessment opportunities at the ready. See below for more information, visit the book's catalog site at **macmillanlearning .com**, or contact your local Bedford/St. Martin's sales representative.

Get the Right Version for Your Class

To accommodate different course lengths and course budgets, *A History of World Societies* is available in several different versions and formats to best suit your course needs. The comprehensive *A History of World Societies* includes a full-color art program and a robust set of features. Offered now for the first time, *A History of World Societies*, Concise Edition, also provides the full narrative, with a streamlined art and feature program, at a lower price. *A History of World Societies*, Value Edition, offers a trade-sized two-color option with the full narrative and selected art and maps at a steeper discount. The Value Edition is also offered at the lowest price point in loose-leaf, and all versions are available as e-Books. For the best value of all, package a new print book with LaunchPad at no additional charge to get the best each format offers—a print version for easy portability with a LaunchPad interactive e-Book and course space with LearningCurve and loads of additional assignment and assessment options.

- **Combined Volume** (Chapters 1–33): available in paperback, Concise, Value, loose-leaf, and e-Book formats and in LaunchPad
- **Volume 1: To 1600** (Chapters 1–16): available in paperback, Concise, Value, loose-leaf, and e-Book formats and in LaunchPad
- **Volume 2: Since 1450** (Chapters 16–33): available in paperback, Concise, Value, loose-leaf, and e-Book formats and in LaunchPad

As noted below, any of these volumes can be packaged with additional titles for a discount. To get ISBNs for discount packages, visit **macmillanlearning.com** or contact your Bedford/St. Martin's representative.

Assign LaunchPad—an Assessment-Ready Interactive e-Book and Course Space

Available for discount purchase on its own or for packaging with new books at no additional charge, LaunchPad is a breakthrough solution for history courses. Intuitive and easy to use for students and instructors alike, Launch-Pad is ready to use as is, and can be edited, customized with your own material, and assigned quickly. Launch-Pad for *A History of World Societies* includes Bedford/St. Martin's high-quality content all in one place, including the full interactive e-Book and the companion reader *Sources of World Societies*, plus LearningCurve formative quizzing, guided reading activities designed to help students read actively for key concepts, autograded quizzes for each primary source, and chapter summative quizzes. Through a wealth of formative and summative assessments, including the adaptive learning program of LearningCurve (see the full description ahead), students gain confidence and get into their reading before class. Through the Bedford Document Collections for World History (see full description ahead), embedded within LaunchPad, instructors get a flexible repository of discovery-oriented primary source projects ready to assign. These features, plus additional primary source documents, video sources and tools for making video assignments, map activities, flashcards, and customizable test banks, make LaunchPad an invaluable asset for any instructor.

LaunchPad easily integrates with course management systems, and with fast ways to build assignments, rearrange chapters, and add new pages, sections, or links, it lets teachers build the courses they want to teach and hold students accountable. For more information, visit **launchpadworks.com** or to arrange a demo, contact us at **history@macmillan.com**.

Assign LearningCurve So Your Students Come to Class Prepared

Students using LaunchPad receive access to Learning-Curve for *A History of World Societies*. Assigning Learning-Curve in place of reading quizzes is easy for instructors, and the reporting features help instructors track overall class trends and spot topics that are giving students trouble so they can adjust their lectures and class activities. This online learning tool is popular with students because it was designed to help them rehearse content at their own pace in a nonthreatening, game-like environment. The feedback for wrong answers provides instructional coaching and sends students back to the book for review. Students answer as many questions as necessary to reach a target score, with repeated chances to revisit material they haven't mastered. When LearningCurve is assigned, students come to class better prepared.

iClicker, Active Learning Simplified

iClicker offers simple, flexible tools to help you give students a voice and facilitate active learning in the classroom. Students can participate with the devices they already bring to class using our iClicker Reef mobile apps (which work with smartphones, tablets, or laptops) or iClicker remotes. We've now integrated iClicker with Macmillan's LaunchPad to make it easier than ever to synchronize grades and promote engagement — both in and out of class. iClicker Reef access cards can also be packaged with LaunchPad or your textbook at a significant savings for your students. To learn more, talk to your Macmillan Learning representative or visit us at **www.iclicker.com**.

Take Advantage of Instructor Resources

Bedford/St. Martin's has developed a rich array of teaching resources for this book and for this course. They range from lecture and presentation materials and assessment tools to course management options. Most can be found in LaunchPad or can be downloaded or ordered at **macmillanlearning.com**.

Bedford Coursepack for Blackboard, Canvas, Brightspace by D2L, or Moodle. We can help you integrate our rich content into your course management

system. Registered instructors can download coursepacks that include our popular free resources and book-specific content for *A History of World Societies*. Visit **macmillanlearning.com** to find your version or download your coursepack.

Instructor's Resource Manual. The instructor's manual offers both experienced and first-time instructors tools for presenting textbook material in engaging ways. It includes content learning objectives, annotated chapter outlines, and strategies for teaching with the textbook, plus suggestions on how to get the most out of LearningCurve and a survival guide for first-time teaching assistants.

Guide to Changing Editions. Designed to facilitate an instructor's transition from the earlier edition of *Understanding World Societies* to this new Concise Edition, this guide presents an overview of major changes as well as of changes in each chapter.

Online Test Bank. The test bank includes a mix of fresh, carefully crafted multiple-choice, matching, short-answer, and essay questions for each chapter. Many of the multiple-choice questions feature a map, an image, or a primary source excerpt as the prompt. All questions appear in Microsoft Word format and in easy-to-use test bank software that allows instructors to add, edit, resequence, filter by question type or learning objective, and print questions and answers. Instructors can also export questions into a variety of course management systems.

The Bedford Lecture Kit: Lecture Outlines, Maps, and Images. Look good and save time with *The Bedford Lecture Kit*. These presentation materials include fully customizable multimedia presentations built around chapter outlines that are embedded with maps, figures, and images from the textbook and are supplemented by more detailed instructor notes on key points and concepts.

Print, Digital, and Custom Options for More Choice and Value

For information on free packages and discounts up to 50%, visit **macmillanlearning.com**, or contact your local Bedford/St. Martin's sales representative.

NEW *Sources of World Societies*, Third Edition. Designed to accompany *A History of World Societies*, each chapter of this primary source collection contains approximately five written and visual sources that present history from the perspectives of well-known figures and ordinary individuals alike. *Sources of World Societies* provides a broad selection of 165 primary source documents and images as well as editorial apparatuses to help students understand the sources. Each chapter also includes a selection of sources dedicated to varied viewpoints on a specific topic. This companion reader is an exceptional value for students and offers plenty of assignment options for instructors. Available free when packaged with the print text and included in the LaunchPad e-Book with autograded quizzes for each source. Also available on its own as a downloadable e-Book.

NEW The Bedford Document Collections for World History. Found in the LaunchPad for *A History of World Societies* and available to customize the print text, this collection provides a flexible repository of discovery-oriented primary source projects ready to assign. Each curated project—written by a historian about a favorite topic—poses a historical question and guides students through analysis of the sources. Examples include "The Silk Road: Travel and Trade in Premodern Inner Asia"; "The Spread of Christianity in the Sixteenth and Early Seventeenth Centuries"; "The Singapore Mutiny of 1915: Understanding World War I from a Global Perspective"; and "Living Through Perestroika: The Soviet Union in Upheaval, 1985–1991." For more information, visit **macmillanlearning.com**.

NEW The Bedford Document Collections for World History Custom Print Modules. Choose one or two document projects from the collection (see above) and add them in print to a Bedford/St. Martin's title, or select several to be bound together in a custom reader created specifically for your course. Either way, the modules are affordably priced. For more information, contact your Bedford/St. Martin's representative.

NEW Bedford Tutorials for History. Designed to customize textbooks with resources relevant to individual courses, this collection of brief units, each 16 pages long and loaded with examples, guides students through basic skills such as using historical evidence effectively, working with primary sources, taking effective notes, avoiding plagiarism and citing sources, and more. Up to two tutorials can be added to a Bedford/St. Martin's history survey title at no additional charge, freeing you to spend your class time focusing on content and interpretation. For more information, visit **macmillanlearning .com/historytutorials**.

The Bedford Series in History and Culture. More than 100 titles in this highly praised series combine first-rate scholarship, historical narrative, and important primary documents for undergraduate courses. Each book is brief, inexpensive, and focused on a specific topic or period. New titles in the series include *Apartheid in South Africa: A Brief History with Documents* by David M. Gordon; *Politics and Society in Japan's Meiji Restoration: A Brief History with Documents* by Anne Walthall and M. William Steele; and *The Congo Free State and the New Imperialism: A Brief History with Documents* by Kevin Grant. For a complete list of titles, visit **macmillanlearning.com**. Package discounts are available.

Rand McNally Atlas of World History. This collection of almost 70 full-color maps illustrates the eras and civilizations in world history from the emergence of human societies to the present. Free when packaged.

The Bedford Glossary for World History. This handy supplement for the survey course gives students historically contextualized definitions for hundreds of terms—from *abolitionism* to *Zoroastrianism*—that they will encounter in lectures, reading, and exams. Free when packaged.

Trade Books. Titles published by sister companies Hill and Wang; Farrar, Straus and Giroux; Henry Holt and Company; St. Martin's Press; Picador; and Palgrave Macmillan are available at a 50% discount when packaged with Bedford/St. Martin's textbooks. For more information, visit **macmillanlearning.com/tradeup**.

A Pocket Guide to Writing in History. Updated to reflect changes made in the 2017 *Chicago Manual of Style* revision, this portable and affordable reference tool by Mary Lynn Rampolla provides reading, writing, and research advice useful to students in all history courses. Concise yet comprehensive advice on approaching typical history assignments, developing critical reading skills, writing effective history papers, conducting research, using and documenting sources, and avoiding plagiarism—enhanced with practical tips and examples throughout—has made this slim reference a bestseller. Package discounts are available.

A Student's Guide to History. This complete guide to success in any history course provides the practical help students need to be successful. In addition to introducing students to the nature of the discipline, author Jules Benjamin teaches a wide range of skills, from preparing for exams to approaching common writing assignments, and explains the research and documentation process with plentiful examples. Package discounts are available.

BRIEF CONTENTS

CONTENTS

1 The Earliest Human Societies
TO 2500 B.C.E.   2

photo: National Museum of Art of Romania, Bucharest, Romania/Bridgeman
Images

photo: Louvre, Paris, France/Erich Lessing/Art Resource, NY

photo: De Agostino Picture Library/G. Nimatallah/Bridgeman Images

4 China's Classical Age
TO 221 B.C.E. 88

5 The Greek Experience
3500–30 B.C.E. 114

photo: Chinese, bronze and jade figure: Eastern Zhou, Warring States, 4th–3rd century B.C./Museum of Fine Arts, Boston/Maria Antoinette Evans Fund, 31.976/Bridgeman Images

photo: Glyptothek, Stalliche Antikensammlung, Munich, Germany/© Vanni Archive/Art Resource, NY

6 The World of Rome
CA. 1000 B.C.E.–400 C.E.   144

7 East Asia and the Spread of Buddhism
221 B.C.E.–845 C.E.   174

photo: Detail of the Initiate, from the Catechism Scene, North Wall, fresco/
Villa dei Misteri, Pompeii, Italy/Bridgeman Images

photo: © Panorama/The Image Works

8 Continuity and Change in Europe and Western Asia
250–850   204

9 The Islamic World
600–1400   234

photo: Private Collection/Photo © Tallandier/Bridgeman Images

photo: Islamic Art Museum, Cairo, Egypt/De Agostini Picture Library/ Gianni Dagli Orti/Bridgeman Images

12 Cultural Exchange in Central and Southern Asia

300–1400 330

13 States and Cultures in East Asia

800–1400 362

14 Europe and Western Asia in the Middle Ages
800–1450   388

photo: Court workshop of Duke Ludwig I of Liegnitz and Brieg, 1364–1398.
Tempera colors, colored washes and ink on parchment/Liszt Collection/Quint
& Lox akg-images

15 Europe in the Renaissance and Reformation
1350–1600   422

photo: Louvre, Paris, France/Bridgeman Images

16 The Acceleration of Global Contact
1450–1600   454

17 The Islamic World Powers
1300–1800   488

photo: From *Codex Ixtlilxochitl*, 1582, pigment on European paper/Bibliothèque Nationale, Paris, France/De Agostini Picture Library/akg-images

photo: Chehel Sotoun, or *The 40 Columns*, Isfahan, Iran/Bridgeman Images

18 European Power and Expansion
1500–1750   518

photo: *Peace Treaty of Nijmegen*, 1678/Museum of Fine Arts, Budapest, Hungary/Erich Lessing/Art Resource, NY

19 New Worldviews and Ways of Life
1540–1790   556

photo: *Portrait of a Young Woman*, by an unknown artist, previously attributed to Jean-Etienne Liotard (1702–1789) (pastel on paper)/Saint Louis Art Museum/Bridgeman Images

photo: Hip Ornament: Portuguese Face, 16th–19th century. Brass, iron. Gift of Mr. and Mrs. Klaus G. Perls, 1991 (1991.162.9)/The Metropolitan Museum of Art, New York/Image copyright © The Metropolitan Museum of Art/Image source: Art Resource, NY

photo: Detail, *Portrait of the Imperial Bodyguard Zhanyinbao*, China, 18th century, Qing Dynasty (1644–1911). Hanging scroll; ink and color on silk. Purchase, The Dillon Fund Gift, 1986 (1986.206)/The Metropolitan Museum of Art, New York/Image copyright © The Metropolitan Museum of Art/Image source: Art Resource, NY

photo: *Jean-Baptiste Belley (1747–1805), Deputy of Santo Domingo at the French
Convention*, 1797, by Anne-Louis Girodet de Roussy-Trioson (1767–1824) (oil
on canvas). Inv. MV4616. Photo: Gerard Blot/Château de Versailles, France/
© RMN–Grand Palais/Art Resource, NY

photo: *Interior of a Furnace*, 1865 (oil on canvas) (detail) by Charles Housez
(1822–1888)/BOURNE GALLERY ARCHIVE/© Bourne Gallery, Reigate,
Surrey, UK/ Bridgeman Images

26 Asia and the Pacific in the Era of Imperialism
1800–1914   794

27 The Americas in the Age of Liberalism
1810–1917   826

photo: Victoria and Albert Museum, London, UK/V&A Images/Art Resource, NY

photo: Edward S. Curtis Collection/Library of Congress, Prints and Photographs Division, Washington, D.C./LC-USZ62-1044492

28 World War and Revolution
1914–1929   858

29 Nationalism in Asia
1914–1939   896

photo: Private Collection/Archives Charmet/Bridgeman Images

photo: © Dinodia Photo Library/The Image Works

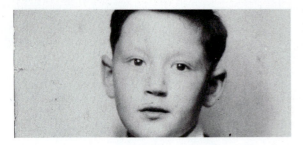

30 The Great Depression and World War II
1929–1945   928

photo: United States Holocaust Memorial Museum, courtesy of Israel Lichtenstein

31 Decolonization, Revolution, and the Cold War
1945–1968   968

photo: Pictures from History/Bridgeman Images

32 Liberalization
1968–2000s   1006

33 The Contemporary World in Historical Perspective   1044

photo: Thalia Watmough/aliki image library/Alamy Stock Photo

photo: Masterfile/Royalty-Free

MAPS, FIGURES, AND TABLES

Maps

Figures and Tables

SPECIAL FEATURES

GLOBAL VIEWPOINTS

ANALYZING THE EVIDENCE

INDIVIDUALS IN SOCIETY

MAPPING THE PAST

A History of
World Societies

CONCISE EDITION

1

The Earliest Human Societies

to 2500 B.C.E.

When does history begin? Previous generations of historians generally answered that question with "when writing begins." Thus they started their histories with the earliest-known invention of writing, which happened about 3500–3200 B.C.E. in the Tigris and Euphrates River Valleys of Mesopotamia, in what is now Iraq. Anything before that was "prehistory." That focus on only the last five thousand years leaves out most of the human story, however, and today historians no longer see writing as such a sharp dividing line. They explore all eras of the human past through many different types of sources, and some push the beginning of history back to the formation of the universe, when time itself began. This very new conceptualization of "big history" is actually similar in scope to the world's oldest histories, because for thousands and perhaps tens of thousands of years many peoples have narrated histories of their origins that also begin with the creation of the universe.

Exploring the entire human past means beginning in Africa, where millions of years ago humans evolved from a primate ancestor. They migrated out of Africa in several waves, walking along coasts and over land, eventually spreading across much of the earth. Their tools were initially multipurpose sharpened stones and sticks, but gradually they invented more specialized tools that enabled them to obtain food more easily, make clothing, build shelters, and decorate their surroundings. Environmental changes, such as the advance and retreat of the glaciers, shaped life dramatically and may have led to the most significant change in all of human history, the domestication of plants and animals.

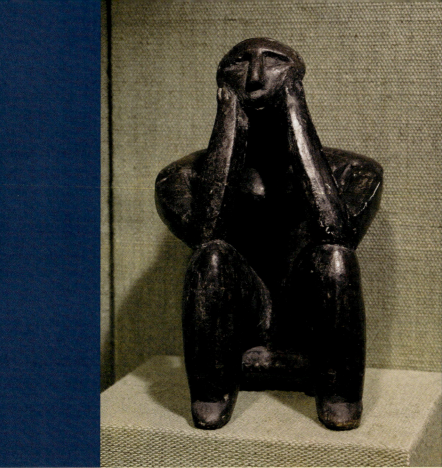

The Thinker of Cernavoda

This small terra-cotta figure, created about 5000 B.C.E. and unearthed at Cernavoda in Romania, is the oldest known sculpture to show human introspection, the distinction that led archaeologists to give it its name. The figure sits on a low stool, head in hands, in what looks like deep thought or perhaps grief, as it was deposited in a grave beside the body.

National Museum of Art of Romania, Bucharest, Romania/Bridgeman Images

CHAPTER PREVIEW

EVOLUTION AND MIGRATION
How did humans evolve, and where did they migrate?

LATER PALEOLITHIC SOCIETY, CA. 200,000–9000 B.C.E.
What were the key features of Paleolithic society?

THE DEVELOPMENT OF AGRICULTURE IN THE NEOLITHIC ERA, CA. 9000 B.C.E.
How did plant and animal domestication develop, and what effects did it have on human society?

NEOLITHIC SOCIETY
How did growing social and gender hierarchies and expanding networks of trade increase the complexity of human society in the Neolithic period?

How did humans
evolve, and where
did they migrate?

Evolution and Migration

Studying the earliest era of human history involves methods that seem simple—looking carefully at an object—as well as new high-tech procedures, such as DNA analysis. Through such research, scholars have examined early human evolution, traced the expansion of the human brain, and studied migration out of Africa and across the planet. Combined with spoken language, that larger brain enabled humans to adapt to many different environments and to be flexible in their responses to new challenges.

Understanding the Early Human Past

People throughout the world have developed systems of classification that help them understand things: earth and sky; seen and unseen; animal, vegetable, and mineral; past, present, and future. Among these systems of classification was one invented in eighteenth-century Europe that divided all living things on earth into groups. Each of these divisions—such as that between plants and animals—is further subdivided into smaller and smaller groups, such as class, order, family, and genus. The final important division is the species, which is generally defined as a group of organisms that can interbreed with one another and produce fertile offspring of both sexes.

In their natural state, members of a species resemble one another, but over time they can become increasingly dissimilar. (Think of Chihuahuas and Great Danes, both members of the same species.) Ever since humans began shaping the world around them, this process has often been the result of human action. But in the long era before humans, the increasing dissimilarity resulted, in the opinion of most scientists, from the process of natural selection. Small variations within individuals in one species enabled them to acquire more food and better living conditions and made them more successful in breeding, thus allowing them to pass their genetic material on to the next generation. When a number of individuals within a species became distinct enough that they could no longer interbreed successfully with others, they became a new species. Species also become extinct, particularly during periods of mass extinctions such as the one that killed the dinosaurs about 65 million years ago. Natural processes of species formation and extinction continue, although today changes in the biosphere—the living matter in the world—result far more from human action than from natural selection.

The scientists who developed this system of organizing the world placed humans within it, using the same means of classification that they used for all other living things. Humans were in the animal kingdom, the order of Primates, the family Hominidae, and the genus *Homo*. Like all classifications, this was originally based on externally visible phenomena: humans were placed in the Primates order because, like other primates, they have hands that can grasp, eyes facing forward to allow better depth perception, and relatively large brains; they were placed in the **hominid** (HOM-uh-nid) family along with chimpanzees, gorillas, and orangutans because they shared even more features with these great apes. Over 98 percent of human DNA is the same as that of chimpanzees, which indicates to most scientists that humans and chimpanzees share a common ancestor. That common ancestor probably lived between 5 million and 7 million years ago.

hominids Members of the family Hominidae that contains humans, chimpanzees, gorillas, and orangutans.

Physical remains were the earliest type of evidence studied to learn about the distant human past, and scholars used them to develop another system of classification, one that distinguished between periods of time rather than types of living creatures. (Constructing models of time is called "periodization.") They gave labels to eras according to the primary materials out of which tools that survived were made. Thus the earliest human era became the Stone Age, the next era the Bronze Age, and the next the Iron Age. They further divided the Stone Age into the Old Stone Age, or **Paleolithic era**, the long period that began when hominids first made tools about 2.5 million years ago, during which people used stone, bone, and other natural products to make their tools and gained food largely by **foraging**—that is, by gathering plant products, trapping or catching small animals and birds, and hunting larger prey. This was followed by the New Stone Age, or **Neolithic era**, which saw the beginning of agricultural and animal domestication. People around the world adopted agriculture at various times, and some never did, but the transition between the Paleolithic (pay-lee-oh-LITH-ik) and the Neolithic (nee-oh-LITH-ik) is usually set at about 9000 B.C.E., the point at which agriculture was first developed.*

Geologists refer to the last twelve thousand years as the Holocene (meaning very recent) epoch. The entire history of the human species fits well within the Holocene and the previous geologic epoch, the Pleistocene (PLIGH-stuh-seen), which began about 2.5 million years ago.

The Pleistocene was marked by repeated advances in glaciers and continental ice sheets. Glaciers tied up huge quantities of the earth's water, leading to lower sea levels, making it possible for animals and eventually humans to walk between places that were separated by oceans during interglacial times. Animals and humans were also prevented from migrating to other places by the ice sheets themselves, however, and the colder climate made large areas unfit to live in. Climate thus dramatically shaped human cultures.

Hominid Evolution

Using many different pieces of evidence from all over the world, archaeologists, paleontologists, and other scholars have developed a view of human evolution whose basic outline is widely shared, though there are disagreements about details. Most primates, including other hominids such as chimpanzees and gorillas, have lived primarily in trees, but at some point a group of hominids in East Africa began to spend more time on the ground, and between 6 and 7 million years ago they began to walk upright at least some of the time.

Over many generations, the skeletal and muscular structure of some hominids evolved to make upright walking easier, and they gradually became fully bipedal.

Paleolithic era Period before 9000 B.C.E. during which humans used tools of stone, bone, and wood and obtained food by gathering and hunting.

foraging A style of life in which people gain food by gathering plant products, trapping or catching small animals and birds, and hunting larger prey.

Neolithic era Period beginning in 9000 B.C.E. during which humans obtained food by raising crops and animals and continued to use tools primarily of stone, bone, and wood.

---

*A note on dates:** This book generally uses B.C.E. (Before the Common Era) and C.E. (Common Era) when giving dates, a system of chronology based on the Christian calendar and now used widely around the world. Scholars who study the very earliest periods of hominid and human history usually use the phrase "years ago" to date their subjects, as do astrophysicists and geologists; this is often abbreviated as B.P. (Before the Present). Because the scale of time covered in Chapter 1 is so vast, a mere two thousand years does not make much difference, and so B.C.E. and "years ago" have similar meaning in this chapter.

The Great Rift Valley

Site of human fossils

- Australopithecine
- Homo habilis
- Homo erectus

Fossil Footprints from Laetoli in Tanzania About 3.5 million years ago, several australopithecines walked in wet ash from a volcanic eruption. Their footprints, discovered by the archaeologist Mary Leakey, indicate that they walked fully upright and suggest that they were not solitary creatures, for they walked close together. (John Reader/Science Source)

The earliest fully bipedal hominids, whom paleontologists place in the genus *Australopithecus* (aw-strah-loh-PITH-uh-kuhs), lived in southern and eastern Africa between 2.5 and 4 million years ago. Walking upright allowed australopithecines (aw-strah-loh-PITH-uh-seens) to carry and use things, which allowed them to survive better and may have also spurred brain development.

About 3.4 million years ago some hominids began to use naturally occurring objects as tools, and sometime around 2.5 million years ago one group of australopithecines in East Africa began to make and use simple tools, evolving into a different type of hominid that later paleontologists judged to be the first in the genus *Homo*. Called *Homo habilis* (HOH-moh HAB-uh-luhs) ("handy human"), they made sharpened stone pieces, which archaeologists call hand axes, and used them for various tasks. This suggests greater intelligence, and the skeletal remains support this, for *Homo habilis* had a larger brain than did the australopithecines.

About 2 million years ago, another species, called *Homo erectus* (HOH-moh ee-REHK-tuhs) ("upright human"), evolved in East Africa. *Homo erectus* had still larger brains and made tools that were slightly specialized for various tasks, such as handheld axes, cleavers, and scrapers. Archaeological remains indicate that *Homo erectus* lived in larger groups than had earlier hominids and engaged in cooperative gathering, hunting, and food preparation. The location and shape of the larynx suggest that members of this species were able to make a wider range of sounds than were earlier hominids, so they may have relied more on vocal sounds than on gestures to communicate ideas to one another.

One of the activities that *Homo erectus* carried out most successfully was moving (Map 1.1). Gradually small groups migrated out of East Africa onto the open plains of central Africa, and from there into northern Africa. From 1 million to 2 million years ago, the earth's climate was in a warming phase, and these hominids ranged still farther, moving into western Asia by as early as 1.8 million years ago. Bones and other materials from China and the island of Java in Indonesia indicate that *Homo erectus* had reached there by about 1.5 million years ago, migrating over large landmasses as well as along the coasts. (Sea levels were lower than they are today, and Java could be reached by walking.) *Homo erectus* also walked north, reaching what is now Spain by at least 800,000 years ago and what is now Germany by 500,000 years ago. In each of these places, *Homo erectus* adapted gathering and hunting techniques to the local environment, learning how to find new sources of plant food and how to best catch local animals. Although the climate was warmer than it is today, central Europe was not balmy, and these hominids may have used fire to provide light and heat, cook food, and keep away predators. Many lived in the open or in caves, but some built simple shelters, another indication of increasing flexibility and problem solving.

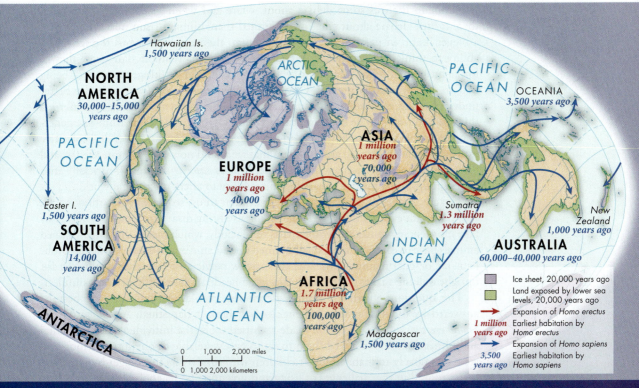

The map shows:

Hawaiian Is.
1,500 years ago

NORTH
AMERICA
30,000–15,000
years ago

ARCTIC
OCEAN

PACIFIC
OCEAN

OCEANIA
3,500 years ago

PACIFIC
OCEAN

ASIA
1 million
years ago
70,000
years ago

EUROPE
1 million
years ago
40,000
years ago

Easter I.
1,500 years ago

SOUTH
AMERICA
14,000
years ago

Sumatra
1.3 million
years ago

New
Zealand
1,000 years ago

INDIAN
OCEAN

AUSTRALIA
60,000–40,000 years ago

ATLANTIC
OCEAN

ANTARCTICA

AFRICA
1.7 million
years ago
100,000
years ago

Madagascar
1,500 years ago

0   1,000   2,000 miles
0 1,000 2,000 kilometers

Legend:
- Ice sheet, 20,000 years ago
- Land exposed by lower sea levels, 20,000 years ago
- Expansion of Homo erectus
- 1 million years ago Earliest habitation by Homo erectus
- Expansion of Homo sapiens
- 3,500 years ago Earliest habitation by Homo sapiens

MAPPING THE PAST

MAP 1.1 Human Migration in the Paleolithic and Neolithic Eras

ANALYZING THE MAP What were the major similarities and differences between the migrations of *Homo erectus* and those of *Homo sapiens*? How did environmental factors shape human migration?

CONNECTIONS What types of technology were required for the migration patterns seen here? What do these migration patterns suggest about the social organization of early people?

Homo Sapiens, "Thinking Humans"

Homo erectus was remarkably adaptable, but another hominid proved still more so: *Homo sapiens* (HOH-moh SAY-pee-enz) ("thinking humans"). A few scientists think that *Homo sapiens* evolved from *Homo erectus* in a number of places in Afroeurasia, but the majority think that, like hominid evolution from earlier primates, this occurred only in East Africa. The evidence is partly archaeological, but also genetic. One type of DNA, called mitochondrial DNA, indicates that modern humans are so similar genetically that they cannot have been evolving for the last 1 million or 2 million years. This evidence suggests that the evolution of *Homo sapiens* has instead taken place for only about 200,000 years. Because there is greater human genetic variety today in Africa than in other parts of the world, the evidence also suggests that *Homo sapiens* have lived there the longest, so that Africa is where they first emerged.

Although there is some debate about where and when *Homo sapiens* emerged, there is little debate about what distinguished these humans from earlier hominids: a bigger brain, in particular a bigger forebrain, the site of conscious thought. The ability to think reflectively allowed for the creation of symbolic language, that is, for language that follows certain rules and that can refer to things or states of being that are not necessarily present. Greater intelligence allowed *Homo sapiens* to better understand and manipulate the world around them, and symbolic language allowed this understanding to be communicated within a group and passed from one generation to the next. Through spoken language *Homo sapiens* began to develop collective explanations for the world around them that we would now call religion, science, and philosophy. Spoken language also enabled *Homo sapiens* to organize socially into larger groups, thus further enhancing their ability to affect the natural world.

The advantages of a larger brain seem evident to us, so we may not think to ask why hominids evolved this way. Large brains also bring disadvantages, however. They take more energy to run than other parts of the body, which means that large-brained animals have to eat more than small-brained ones. Large brains create particular problems for bipedal mammals because the narrow pelvic structure that works best for upright walking makes giving birth to a large-headed infant difficult and painful.

The question of why hominids developed ever-larger brains might best be answered by looking at how paleontologists think it happened. As *Homo habilis*, *Homo erectus*, and *Homo sapiens* made and used tools, the individuals whose mental and physical abilities allowed them to do so best were able to obtain more food and were more likely to mate and have children who survived. Thus bigger brains led to better tools, but the challenges of using and inventing better tools also created selective pressure that led to bigger brains.

The same thing may have happened with symbolic language and thought. A slightly bigger brain allowed for more complex thought and better language skills. These thinking and speaking skills enabled individuals to better attract mates and fend off rivals, which meant a greater likelihood of passing on the enhanced brain to the next generation. As we know from contemporary research on the brain, learning language promotes the development of specific areas of the brain.

The growth in brain size and complexity may also have been linked to social organization. Individuals who had better social skills were more likely to mate than those who did not—this has been observed in chimpanzees and, of course, in modern humans—and thus to pass on their genetic material. Social skills were particularly important for females because the combination of bipedalism and growing brain size led to selective pressure for hominid infants to be born at an even earlier stage in their development than other primate infants were. Thus the period when human infants are dependent on others is very long, and mothers with good social networks to assist them were more likely to have infants who survived. Humans are unique in the duration and complexity of their care for children. Cooperative child rearing, along with the development of social skills and the adaptability this encouraged, may have been an impetus to brain growth.

All these factors operated together in processes that promoted bigger and better brains. In the Paleolithic period, *Homo sapiens'* brains invented highly specialized tools made out of a variety of materials that replaced the more general-purpose stone tools made by *Homo erectus*: barbed fishhooks and harpoons, snares and traps for catching small animals, bone needles for sewing clothing, awls for punching holes in leather, nets for catching fish, sharpened flint pieces bound to wooden or bone handles for hunting or cutting, and slings for carrying infants. By 25,000 years ago, and perhaps earlier, humans in some parts of the world were weaving cloth, nets, and baskets out of bark, rushes, grasses, and other natural materials, and by 17,000 years ago they were using bows and atlatls (AHT-lah-tuhlz) — notched throwing sticks made of bone, wood, or antler — to launch arrows and barbs with flint points bound to wooden shafts. The archaeological evidence for increasingly sophisticated language and social organization is less direct than that for tool use, but it is hard to imagine how humans could have made the tools they did — or would have chosen to decorate so many of them — without both of these.

Migration and Differentiation

Like *Homo erectus* had earlier, groups of *Homo sapiens* moved. By 200,000 years ago they had begun to spread across Africa, and by 120,000 years ago they had begun to migrate out of Africa to Eurasia (see Map 1.1). They most likely walked along the coasts of India and Southeast Asia, and then migrated inland. At the same time, further small evolutionary changes led to our own subspecies of anatomically modern humans, *Homo sapiens sapiens* (which literally translates as "thinking thinking humans"). *Homo sapiens sapiens* moved into areas where there were already *Homo erectus* populations, eventually replacing them and leaving *Homo sapiens* as the only survivors and the ancestors of all modern humans.

The best-known example of interaction between *Homo erectus* and *Homo sapiens sapiens* is that between Neanderthals (named after the Neander Valley in Germany, where their remains were first discovered) and a group of anatomically modern humans called Cro-Magnons. **Neanderthals** (nee-AHN-der-tals) lived throughout Europe and western Asia beginning about 200,000 years ago, had brains as large as those of modern humans, and used tools, including spears and scrapers for animal skins, that enabled them to survive in the cold climate of Ice Age central Europe and Russia. They built freestanding houses and decorated objects and themselves with red ochre, a form of colored clay. They sometimes buried their dead carefully with tools, animal bones, and perhaps flowers, which suggests that they understood death to have a symbolic meaning.

Cro-Magnon peoples had moved into parts of western Asia where Neanderthals lived by about 70,000 years ago, and into Europe by about 45,000 years ago. The two peoples appear to have lived side by side for millennia, hunting the same types of animals and gathering the same types of plants. The last evidence of Neanderthals as a separate species comes from about 30,000 years ago, and it is not clear exactly how they died out. They may have been killed by Cro-Magnon peoples, or they simply may have lost the competition for food as the climate worsened around 30,000 years ago and the glaciers expanded.

Homo erectus migrated great distances, but *Homo sapiens sapiens* made use of greater intelligence and better toolmaking capabilities to migrate still farther. They had used simple rafts to reach Australia by at least 50,000 years ago, and by 35,000 years ago had reached New Guinea. By at least 15,000 years ago, humans had walked across the land bridges then linking Siberia and North America at the Bering Strait and had crossed into the Americas. Because by 14,000 years ago

Neanderthals Group of *Homo erectus* with brains as large as those of modern humans that lived in Europe and western Asia between 200,000 and 30,000 years ago.

Land Bridge Across the Bering Strait, ca. 15,000 B.C.E.

Polynesian Oceangoing Sailing Canoe This is a Hawaiian replica of the type of large double-hulled canoe in which Polynesians sailed around the Pacific as they settled many different island groups. This canoe, called the Hokule'a, has taken many voyages using traditional Pacific techniques of celestial navigation. The two hulls provided greater stability, and canoes designed like this sailed thousands of miles over the open ocean. (© 2015 Polynesian Voyaging Society, photo: OIWI TV)

humans were already in southern South America, ten thousand miles from the land bridges, many scholars now think that people came to the Americas much earlier. They think humans came from Asia to the Americas perhaps as early as 20,000 or even 30,000 years ago, walking or using rafts along the coasts. (See Chapter 11 for a longer discussion of this issue.)

With the melting of glaciers, sea levels rose, and parts of the world that had been linked by land bridges, including North America and Asia as well as many parts of Southeast Asia, became separated by water. This cut off migratory paths but also spurred innovation. Humans designed and built ever more sophisticated boats and learned how to navigate by studying wind and current patterns, bird flights, and the position of the stars. They sailed to increasingly remote islands, including those in the Pacific, the last parts of the globe to be settled. The western Pacific islands were inhabited by about 2000 B.C.E., Hawaii by about 500 C.E., and New Zealand by about 1000 C.E. (For more on the settlement of the Pacific islands, see "The Settlement of the Pacific Islands" in Chapter 12.)

Once humans had spread out over much of the globe, groups often became isolated from one another, and people mated only with other members of their own group or those who lived nearby, a practice anthropologists call **endogamy**. Thus, over thousands of generations, although humans remained one species, *Homo sapiens sapiens* came to develop differences in physical features, including skin and hair color, eye and body shape, and amount of body hair. Language also changed over generations, so that thousands of different languages were eventually spoken. Groups created widely varying cultures and passed them on to their children, further increasing diversity among humans.

Beginning in the eighteenth century, European natural scientists sought to develop a system that would explain human differences at the largest scale. They divided people into very large groups by skin color and other physical characteristics and termed these groups "races," a word that had originally meant lineage. They first differentiated these races by continent of origin—Americanus, Europaeus, Asiaticus, and Africanus—and then by somewhat different geographic areas. The word *Caucasian* was first used by the German anatomist and naturalist Johann Friedrich

endogamy The practice of marrying within a certain ethnic or social group.

Blumenbach (1752–1840) to describe light-skinned people of Europe and western Asia because he thought that their original home was most likely the Caucasus Mountains on the border between Russia and Georgia. He thought that they were the first humans and the most attractive. This meaning of *race* has had a long life, though biologists and anthropologists today do not use it, as it has no scientific meaning or explanatory value. All humans are one species with less genetic variety than chimpanzees.

Later Paleolithic Society, ca. 200,000–9000 B.C.E.

What were the key features of Paleolithic society?

Eventually human cultures became widely diverse, but in the Paleolithic period people throughout the world lived in ways that were similar to one another. Archaeological evidence and studies of modern foragers suggest that people lived in small groups of related individuals and moved throughout the landscape in search of food. Most had few material possessions, only what they could carry, although in areas where food resources were especially rich, such as along seacoasts, they built structures and lived more permanently in one place. In the later Paleolithic, people in many parts of the world created art and music and developed religious ideas that linked the natural world to a world beyond.

megafaunal extinction Die-off of large animals in many parts of the world, 45,000–10,000 B.C.E., caused by climate change and most likely human hunting.

Foraging for Food

Paleolithic peoples have often been called hunter-gatherers, but recent archaeological and anthropological research indicates that both historical and contemporary hunter-gatherers have depended much more on gathered foods than on hunted meat. Thus most scholars now call them foragers, a term that highlights the flexibility and adaptability in their search for food. Most of the foods foragers ate were plants, and much of the animal protein in their diet came from foods gathered or scavenged rather than hunted directly: insects, shellfish, small animals caught in traps, fish and other sea creatures caught in weirs and nets, and animals killed by other predators.

Paleolithic peoples did hunt large game. Groups working together forced animals over cliffs, threw spears, and, beginning about 15,000 B.C.E., used bows and atlatls to shoot projectiles so that they could stand farther away from their prey while hunting. The final retreat of the glaciers also occurred between about 13,000 and 8000 B.C.E., and the warming climate was less favorable to the very large mammals that had roamed the open spaces of many parts of the world. Wooly mammoths, mastodons, and wooly rhinos all died out in Eurasia in this **megafaunal extinction**, as did camels, horses, and sloths in the Americas and giant kangaroos and wombats in Australia. In many places, these extinctions occurred just about the time that modern humans migrated into an area, and increasing numbers of scientists think that they were at least in part caused by human hunting, as many types of large animals vanished in Australia about 45,000 B.C.E., shortly after humans arrived, long before the final climate warming.

Paleolithic Hand Axes Like most Paleolithic stone tools, these two hand axes from Libya in northern Africa were made by chipping flakes off stone to form a sharpened edge. Although they are traditionally called axes, they were used for a variety of purposes, including skinning, cutting, and chopping. (Robert Harding Images/Masterfile)

division of labor
Differentiation of tasks by gender, age, training, status, or other social distinction.

Most foraging societies that exist today, or did so until recently, have some type of **division of labor** by sex, and also by age, with children and older people responsible for different tasks than adult men and women are. Men are more often responsible for hunting and women for gathering plant and animal products. This has led scholars to assume that in Paleolithic society men were also responsible for hunting, and women for gathering, although this may not have been the case. The stone and bone tools that remain from the Paleolithic period give no clear evidence of who used them, and the division of labor may have been somewhat flexible, particularly during periods of scarcity.

Obtaining food was a constant preoccupation, but it was not a constant job. Studies of recent foragers indicate that, other than in times of environmental disasters such as prolonged droughts, people need only about ten to twenty hours a week to gather food and carry out the other tasks needed to survive, such as locating water and building shelters. Moreover, the diet of foragers is varied and nutritious; it is low in fat and salt, high in fiber, and rich in vitamins and minerals. The slow pace of life and healthy diet did not mean that Paleolithic life spans approached those of the modern world, however. People avoided such contemporary killers as heart disease and diabetes, but they often died at young ages from injuries, infections, animal attacks, and interpersonal violence. Mothers and infants died in childbirth, and many children died before they reached adulthood.

Total human population thus grew very slowly during the Paleolithic, from perhaps half a million humans in the world about 30,000 years ago to about 5 million 10,000 years ago. Moreover, the population was widely scattered, with small bands of people occupying very large territories. The low population density meant that human impact on the environment was relatively small, although still significant. In addition to contributing to the extinction of some large animals, Paleolithic people may have also shaped their environments by setting fires, which encouraged the growth of new plants and attracted animals that fed on them, making hunting or snaring game easier. This practice was a factor in the spread of plants that thrived best with occasional burning, such as the eucalyptus in Australia.

Family and Kinship Relationships

Small bands of humans — twenty or thirty people was a standard size for foragers in harsh environments — were scattered across broad areas, but this did not mean that each group lived in isolation. Their travels in search of food brought them into contact with one another, not simply for talking and celebrating, but also for providing opportunities for the exchange of sexual partners, which was essential to group survival. Mating arrangements varied in their permanence, but many groups seem to have developed a somewhat permanent arrangement whereby a man or woman left his or her original group and joined the group of his or her mate, what would later be termed marriage.

Within each band, and within the larger kin groups, individuals had a variety of identities; they were simultaneously fathers, sons, husbands, and brothers, or mothers, daughters, wives, and sisters. Each of these identities was relational (parent to child, sibling to sibling, spouse to spouse), and some of them, especially parent to child, gave one power over others. Paleolithic people were not differentiated by wealth, for in a foraging society accumulating material goods was not advantageous.

But they were differentiated by such factors as age, gender, and position in a family, and no doubt by personal qualities such as intelligence, courage, and charisma.

Stereotypical representations of Paleolithic people often portray men going off to hunt while women and children crouched around a fire, waiting for the men to bring back meat. Studies of the relative importance of gathering to hunting, women's participation in hunting, and gender relations among contemporary foraging peoples have led some analysts to turn these stereotypes on their heads. They see Paleolithic bands as egalitarian groups in which the contributions of men and women to survival were recognized and valued, and in which both men and women had equal access to the limited amount of resources held by the group. Other scholars argue that this is also a stereotype, overly romanticizing Paleolithic society. They note that, although social relations among foragers were not as hierarchical as they were in other types of societies, many foraging groups had one person who held more power than others, and that person was almost always a man. This debate about gender relations is often part of larger discussions about whether Paleolithic society — and by implication, "human nature" — was primarily peaceful and nurturing or violent and brutal, and whether these qualities are gender related. Like much else about the Paleolithic, sources about gender and about violence are fragmentary and difficult to interpret; there may simply have been a diversity of patterns, as there is among more modern foragers.

Whether peaceful and egalitarian or violent and hierarchical, heterosexual relations produced children, who were cared for as infants by their mothers or other women who had recently given birth. Breast milk was the only food available that infants could easily digest, so mothers nursed their children for several years. Along with providing food for infants, extended nursing brings a side benefit: it suppresses ovulation and thus acts as a contraceptive. Foraging groups needed children to survive, but too many could tax scarce food resources. Other than for feeding, children were most likely cared for by other male and female members of the group as well as by their mothers during the long period of human childhood.

Cultural Creations and Spirituality

Beginning in the Paleolithic, human beings expressed themselves through what we would now term the arts or culture: painting and decorating walls and objects, making music with their voices and a variety of instruments, imagining and telling stories, dancing alone or in groups. Evidence from the Paleolithic, particularly from after about 50,000 years ago, includes flutes, carvings, jewelry, and paintings done on cave walls and rock outcroppings that depict animals, people, and symbols. In many places these paintings also show the outline of a human hand — often done by blowing pigment around it — or tracings of the fingers.

At the same time that people marked and depicted the world around them, they also appear to have developed ideas about supernatural forces that controlled some aspects of the natural world and the place of humans in it, what we now term spirituality or religion. Paleolithic burials, paintings, and objects suggest that people may have thought of their world as extending beyond the visible. People, animals, plants, natural occurrences, and other things around them had spirits, an idea called **animism**. The only evidence of Paleolithic animism that survives is physical, of course, but more recent animist traditions carry on this understanding of the spiritual nature and interdependence of all things.

animism Idea that people, animals, plants, natural occurrences, and other parts of the physical world have spirits.

Death took people from the realm of the living, but for Paleolithic groups people continued to inhabit an unseen world, along with spirits and deities, after death; thus kin groups included deceased as well as living members of a family. The unseen world regularly intervened in the visible world, for good and ill, and the actions of dead ancestors, spirits, and gods could be shaped by living people. Concepts of the supernatural pervaded all aspects of life; hunting, birth, death, and natural occurrences such as eclipses, comets, and rainbows all had religious meaning. Supernatural forces were understood to determine the basic rules for human existence, and upsetting these rules could lead to chaos.

Ordinary people learned about the unseen world through dreams and portents, and messages and revelations were also sent more regularly to **shamans**, spiritually adept men and women who communicated with the unseen world. Shamans created complex rituals through which they sought to ensure the health and prosperity of an individual, family, or group. Many cave paintings show herds of prey animals, and several include a masked human figure usually judged to be a shaman performing some sort of ritual. (See "Analyzing the Evidence: Bison and Human in Lascaux Cave," at right.) Objects understood to have special power, such as carvings or masks in the form of an animal or person, could give additional protection, as could certain plants or mixtures eaten, sniffed, or rubbed on the skin. Shamans thus also operated as healers, with cures that included what we would term natural medicines and religious healing.

shamans Spiritually adept men and women who communicated with the unseen world.

The Development of Agriculture in the Neolithic Era, ca. 9000 B.C.E.

How did plant and animal domestication develop, and what effects did it have on human society?

Foraging remained the basic way of life for most of human history. In a few especially fertile areas, however, the natural environment provided enough food that people could become more settled. As they remained in one place, they began to plant seeds as well as gather wild crops, to raise certain animals instead of hunting them, and to selectively breed both plants and animals to make them more useful to humans. This seemingly small alteration was the most important change in human history;

Grinding Stones from a Neolithic Village in Jordan, occupied 7200–6500 B.C.E. Paleolithic people used stone tools to crush and grind ochre, nuts, grains, and other materials, but as crops were domesticated in the Neolithic, grinding stones such as these from Jordan in the Fertile Crescent became even more common. Grinding maximizes the amount of digestible food and caloric content derived from grain, providing important nutritional benefits as increasingly sedentary populations relied on limited areas of cultivation for most of their food. Wear patterns in women's wrist bones indicate that hand grinding was often a woman's task, a gender division of labor that continued for millennia in many parts of the world. (Gerard Degeorge/akg-images)

Bison and Human in Lascaux Cave

The interconnected series of caves in the Lascaux region of southwestern France has paintings (dating from about 15,000 B.C.E.) of nearly two thousand figures on its walls, including animals that would have been hunted and eaten, such as deer, bulls, bison, and horses, and those that would have been feared as predators, such as lions, other big cats, and bears, as well as geometric and abstract designs. Most of the paintings, made with colored minerals on surfaces smoothed by the artist, are located far from the cave entrance and are not easily accessible, suggesting they were made for ceremonial or ritual purposes, not as decorations for living spaces. Amid the amazing animals is a depiction, painted near the bottom of a 20-foot shaft in a remote part of the cave, of a human next to a bison spilling its guts out onto the ground. Scholars first interpreted this enigmatic scene as a hunting accident but more recently have proposed that the human is a shaman with a bird mask and a bird-head staff in a state of trance, as his body and limbs are rigid. The figure has what looks like a penis, and is usually described as a man, although some anthropologists have suggested it could have been a woman wearing an artificial penis along with a mask, as gender inversions were often part of rituals and performances. Thus the person may have been biologically female but culturally understood to be male in this ritual. Or the figure — and the actual shaman whom it may have represented — could have been understood as a third gender, neither male nor female, or both at the same time, just as the shaman may have been thought to take on the qualities of the bird represented by the mask but still remain human. Shamans regarded as a third gender could be found in the more recent past than the Paleolithic in many parts of the world, including various regions of Asia, North and South America, and Australia.

(Universal History Archive/UIG via Getty Images)

QUESTIONS FOR ANALYSIS

1. Shamans in Paleolithic and more recent societies were understood to harness power that crossed various types of boundaries, including those between the seen and unseen worlds, life and death, animal and human, and sometimes male and female. Why might this be advantageous in hunting rituals or other types of ceremonies? If the person depicted here is a shaman, what boundaries might the shaman depicted here be seen as crossing?
2. Why might Paleolithic people have made cave paintings? What do these paintings suggest about Old Stone Age culture and society?

Agricultural Revolution
Dramatic transformation in human history resulting from the change from foraging to raising crops and animals.

because of its impact it is often termed the **Agricultural Revolution**. Plant and animal domestication marked the transition from the Paleolithic to the Neolithic. It allowed the human population to grow far more quickly than did foraging, but it also required more labor, which became increasingly specialized.

The Development of Horticulture

Areas of the world differed in the food resources available to foragers. In some, acquiring enough food to sustain a group was difficult, and groups had to move constantly. In others, moderate temperatures and abundant rainfall allowed for verdant plant growth; or seas, rivers, and lakes provided substantial amounts of fish and shellfish. Groups in such areas were able to become more settled. About 15,000 years ago, the earth's climate entered a warming phase, and the glaciers began to retreat. As the earth became warmer, the climate became wetter, and more parts of the world were able to support sedentary or semi-sedentary groups of foragers.

In several of these places, foragers began planting seeds in the ground along with gathering wild grains, roots, and other foodstuffs. By observation, they learned the optimum times and places for planting. They removed unwanted plants through weeding and selected the seeds they planted in order to get crops that had favorable characteristics, such as larger edible parts. Through this human intervention, certain crops became **domesticated**, that is, modified by selective breeding so as to serve human needs, in this case to provide a more reliable source of food. Archaeologists trace the development and spread of plant raising by noting when the seeds and other plant parts they discover show evidence of domestication.

domesticated Plants and animals modified by selective breeding so as to serve human needs; domesticated animals will behave in specific ways and breed in captivity.

horticulture Crop raising done with hand tools and human power.

This early crop planting was done by individuals using hoes and digging sticks, and it is often termed **horticulture** to distinguish it from the later agriculture using plows. Intentional crop planting developed first in the part of southwest Asia archaeologists call the Fertile Crescent, which runs from present-day Lebanon, Israel, and Jordan north to Turkey and then south along the Tigris and Euphrates Rivers to the Iran-Iraq border (Map 1.2). About 9000 B.C.E. people there began to plant seeds of the wild wheat and barley they had already been harvesting, along with seeds of legume crops, such as peas and lentils, and of the flax with which they made linen cloth. By about 8000 B.C.E. people were growing sorghum and millet in parts of the Nile River Valley, and perhaps yams in western Africa. By about 7000 B.C.E. they were growing domesticated rice, millet, and legumes in China; yams and taro in Papua New Guinea; and perhaps squash in Mesoamerica. In each of these places, the development of horticulture occurred independently, and it may have happened in other parts of the world as well.

Nowhere do archaeological remains alone answer the question of who within any group first began to cultivate crops, but the fact that, among foragers, women were primarily responsible for gathering plant products suggests that they may also have been the first to plant seeds in the ground. In many parts of the world, crops continued to be planted with hoes and digging sticks for millennia, and crop raising remained primarily women's work, while men hunted or later raised animals.

Why, after living successfully as foragers for tens of thousands of years, did humans in so many parts of the world all begin raising crops at about the same

The Fertile Crescent

Fertile Crescent

time? The answer to this question is not clear, but crop raising may have resulted from population pressures in those parts of the world where the warming climate provided more food. More food meant lower child mortality and longer life spans, which allowed communities to grow. When population growth outstripped the local food supply, people had a choice: they could move to a new area—the solution that foragers had relied on when faced with the problem of food scarcity—or they could develop ways to increase the food supply to keep up with population growth, a solution that the warming climate was making possible. They chose the latter and began to plant more intensively, beginning cycles of expanding population and intensification of land use that have continued to today.

A recent archaeological find at Göbekli Tepe (gyeh-BEHK-lee TEH-peh) in present-day Turkey, at the northern edge of the Fertile Crescent, suggests that cultural factors may have played a role in the development of agriculture. Here, around 9000 B.C.E. hundreds of people came together to build rings of massive, multi-ton, elaborately carved limestone pillars and then covered them with dirt and built more. The people who created this site lived some distance away, where archaeological evidence indicates they first carved the pillars. The evidence also reveals that they ate wild game and plants, not crops. The project may have unintentionally spurred the development of new methods of food production that would allow the many workers to be fed efficiently. Indeed, it is very near here that evidence of the world's oldest domesticated wheat has been discovered. Archaeologists speculate that the symbolic, cultural, or perhaps religious importance of the structure can help explain why the people building it changed from foraging to agriculture.

Whatever the reasons for the move from foraging to crop raising, within several centuries of initial crop planting, people in the Fertile Crescent, parts of China, and the Nile Valley were relying on domesticated food products alone. They built permanent houses near one another in villages surrounded by fields, and they invented new ways of storing foods, such as in pottery made from clay. (See "Global Viewpoints: Stone Age Houses in Chile and China," page 20.) Villages were closer together than were the camps of foragers, so population density as well as total population grew.

A field of planted and weeded crops yields ten to one hundred times as much food—measured in calories—as the same area of naturally occurring plants. It also requires much more labor, however, which was provided both by the greater number of people in the community and by the longer hours those people worked. Farming peoples were often in the fields from dawn to dusk. Early farmers were also less healthy than foragers were. Their narrower range of foodstuffs made them more susceptible to disease and nutritional deficiencies such as anemia.

Foragers who lived at the edge of horticultural communities appear to have recognized the negative aspects of crop raising, for they did not immediately adopt this new way of life. Instead farming spread when a village became too large and some residents moved to a new area. Because the population of farming communities grew so much faster than that of foragers, however, horticulture quickly spread into fertile areas. By about 6500 B.C.E. farming had spread northward from the Fertile Crescent into Greece, and by 4000 B.C.E. farther northward all the way to Britain; by 4500 B.C.E. it had spread southward into Ethiopia. At the same time, crop raising spread

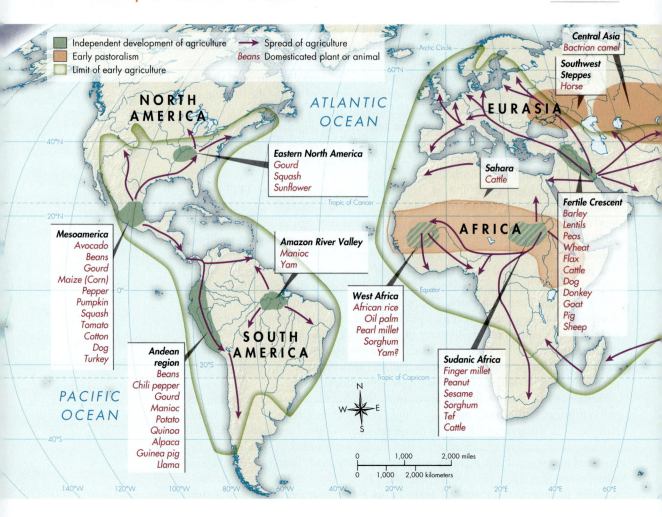

Independent development of agriculture ⟶ Spread of agriculture
Early pastoralism *Beans* Domesticated plant or animal
Limit of early agriculture

Central Asia
Bactrian camel

Southwest Steppes
Horse

NORTH AMERICA

ATLANTIC OCEAN

EURASIA

Arctic Circle

60°N

40°N

Eastern North America
Gourd
Squash
Sunflower

Tropic of Cancer

20°N

Mesoamerica
Avocado
Beans
Gourd
Maize (Corn)
Pepper
Pumpkin
Squash
Tomato
Cotton
Dog
Turkey

Amazon River Valley
Manioc
Yam

Sahara
Cattle

AFRICA

Fertile Crescent
Barley
Lentils
Peas
Wheat
Flax
Cattle
Dog
Donkey
Goat
Pig
Sheep

West Africa
African rice
Oil palm
Pearl millet
Sorghum
Yam?

Equator

0°

SOUTH AMERICA

Andean region
Beans
Chili pepper
Gourd
Manioc
Potato
Quinoa
Alpaca
Guinea pig
Llama

20°S

Tropic of Capricorn

Sudanic Africa
Finger millet
Peanut
Sesame
Sorghum
Tef
Cattle

PACIFIC OCEAN

N
W · E
S

40°S

0   1,000   2,000 miles
0   1,000   2,000 kilometers

140°W 120°W 100°W 80°W 60°W 40°W 20°W 0° 20°E 40°E 60°E

out from other areas in which it was first developed, and slowly larger and larger parts of China, South and Southeast Asia, and East Africa became home to horticultural villages.

People adapted crops to their local environments, choosing seeds that had qualities that were beneficial, such as drought resistance. They also domesticated new kinds of crops. In the Americas, for example, by about 3000 B.C.E. corn was domesticated in southern Mexico and potatoes and quinoa in the Andes region of South America, and by about 2500 B.C.E. squash and beans in eastern North America. These crops then spread, so that by about 1000 B.C.E. people in much of what is now the western United States were raising corn, beans, and squash. In the Indus Valley of South Asia, people were growing dates, mangoes, sesame seeds, and cotton along with grains and legumes by 4000 B.C.E. Accordingly, crop raising led to dramatic human alteration of the environment.

Certain planted crops eventually came to be grown over huge areas of land, so that some scientists describe the Agricultural Revolution as a revolution of codependent

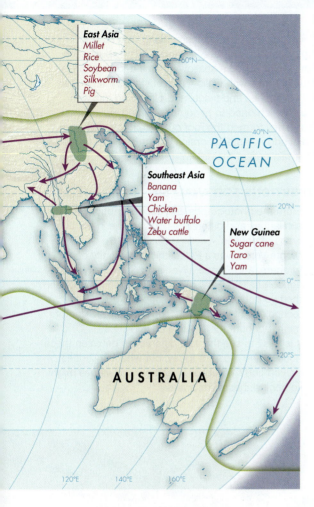

MAP 1.2 The Spread of Agriculture and Pastoralism
Local plants and animals were domesticated in many different places. Agriculturalists and pastoralists spread the knowledge of how to raise them, and spread the plants and animals themselves through migration, trade, and conquest.

domestication: humans domesticated crops, but crops also "domesticated" humans so that they worked long hours spreading particular crops around the world. Of these, corn has probably been the most successful; more than half a million square miles around the world are now planted in corn.

In some parts of the world horticulture led to a dramatic change in the way of life, but in others it did not. Horticulture can be easily combined with gathering and hunting, as plots of land are usually small; many cultures, including some in Papua New Guinea and North America, remained mixed foragers and horticulturists for thousands of years. Especially in deeply wooded areas, people cleared small plots by chopping and burning the natural vegetation, and planted crops in successive years until the soil eroded or lost its fertility, a method termed "slash and burn." They then moved to another area and began the process again, perhaps returning to the first plot many years later, after the soil had rejuvenated itself. Groups using shifting slash-and-burn cultivation remained small and continued to rely on the surrounding forest for much of their food.

Stone Age Houses in Chile and China

One of the central issues facing most human groups has been shelter from the elements. People's varying solutions to this issue reflect the environmental challenges and opportunities offered by their particular surroundings. Not only are houses physical structures, but they also reflect, communicate, and shape cultural and social values. The photographs on this page show the remains of houses built during the Paleolithic and Neolithic periods in two parts of the world very far from one another.

Monte Verde in Chile (right) dates from about 12,000 B.C.E. The archaeologists who have studied this site have concluded that here, along a creek, a small group of perhaps twenty to thirty people built a 20-foot-long structure of wooden poles covered by animal skins. Within the structure were smaller living quarters separated by skins, each with its own small fire pit, around which archaeologists have found stone tools, rope made of reeds, and many different types of foraged food, including wild potatoes and seaweed that came from coastal areas far away.

The village of Banpo near Xi'an in China (below) dates from about 4500 B.C.E. Archaeologists have concluded that a group of several hundred people built fifty or so houses there, along with kilns for making pottery and cellars for storage. They built each house by digging a shallow hole as a foundation, surrounding this with walls made of stakes interwoven with branches and twigs, and plastering this with mud, which dried to become wind and water resistant. They formed the roof out of thatch made from millet and rice stalks, grains they raised that formed the main part of their diet.

QUESTIONS FOR ANALYSIS

1. From the photographs and the descriptions, what similarities and differences do you see in the two types of houses?
2. Monte Verde was a Paleolithic community of foragers, and Banpo a Neolithic community of agriculturalists. How might the differences between the two houses have been shaped by the technology of food production? What other factors might account for the differences?
3. It is easy to see the vast differences between these houses and those of today, but what similarities do you find? What social and cultural values might lie behind these similarities?

Monte Verde, Chile, ca. 12,000 B.C.E.
(Courtesy of Tom D. Dillehay)

Banpo, China, ca. 4500 B.C.E. (JTB Photo/SuperStock)

Animal Domestication and the Rise of Pastoralism

At roughly the same time that they domesticated certain plants, people also domesticated animals. The earliest animal to be domesticated was the dog, which separated genetically as a subspecies from wolves at least 15,000 years ago and perhaps much earlier. The relationship provided both humans and dogs with benefits: humans gained dogs' better senses of smell and hearing and their body warmth, and dogs gained new food sources and safer surroundings. Not surprisingly, humans and domestic dogs migrated together, including across the land bridges to the Americas and on boats to Pacific islands.

Dogs fit easily into a foraging lifestyle, but humans also domesticated animals that led them to completely alter their way of life. In about 9000 B.C.E., at the same time they began to raise crops, people in the Fertile Crescent domesticated wild goats and sheep, probably using them first for meat, and then for milk, skins, and eventually fleece (see Map 1.2). They learned from observation and experimentation that traits are passed down from generation to generation, and they began to breed the goats and sheep selectively for qualities that they wanted. Sometimes they trained dogs to assist them in herding, and then selectively bred the dogs for qualities that were advantageous for this task.

Head of a Sheep Carved in sandstone at the southern end of the Tigris and Euphrates Valleys about 3200 B.C.E., this head was originally part of a full sculpture of a sheep. By this time, meat, milk, skins, and fleece from domesticated sheep were essential to settled agriculturalists and nomadic pastoralists in much of southwest Asia, and their importance came to be reflected in material culture. (Kimbell Art Museum, Fort Worth/Bridgeman Images)

Sometime after goats and sheep, pigs were domesticated in both the Fertile Crescent and China, as were chickens in southern Asia. Like domesticated crops, domesticated animals eventually far outnumbered their wild counterparts. Animal domestication also shaped human evolution; groups that relied on animal milk and milk products for a significant part of their diet tended to develop the ability to digest milk as adults, while those that did not remained lactose intolerant as adults, the normal condition for mammals.

Sheep and goats allow themselves to be herded, and people developed a new form of living, **pastoralism**, based on herding and raising livestock. In areas with sufficient rainfall and fertile soil, pastoralism can be relatively sedentary and thus is easily combined with horticulture; people built pens for animals, or in colder climates constructed special buildings or took them into their houses. They learned that animal manure increases crop yields, so they gathered the manure from enclosures and used it as fertilizer.

pastoralism An economic system based on herding flocks of goats, sheep, cattle, or other animals.

Increased contact with animals and their feces also increased human contact with various sorts of disease-causing pathogens. This was particularly the case where humans and animals lived in tight quarters. Thus pastoralists and agriculturalists developed illnesses that had not plagued foragers, and the diseases became endemic, that is, widely found within a region without being deadly. Ultimately people who lived with animals developed resistance to some of these illnesses, but foragers' lack of resistance to many illnesses meant that they died more readily after coming into contact with new endemic diseases, as was the case when Europeans brought small-pox to the Americas in the sixteenth century.

In drier areas, flocks need to travel long distances from season to season to obtain enough food, so some pastoralists became nomadic. Nomadic pastoralists often gather wild plant foods as well, but they tend to rely primarily on their flocks of ani-mals for food. Pastoralism was well suited to areas where the terrain or climate made crop planting difficult, such as mountains, deserts, dry grasslands, and tundras. Even-tually other grazing animals, including cattle, camels, horses, yak, and reindeer, also became the basis of pastoral economies in Central and West Asia, many parts of Africa, and far northern Europe.

Plow Agriculture

Horticulture and pastoralism brought significant changes to human ways of life, but the domestication of certain large animals had an even bigger impact. Cattle and water buffalo were domesticated in some parts of Asia and North Africa in which they occurred naturally by at least 7000 B.C.E., and horses, donkeys, and camels by about 4000 B.C.E. All these animals can be trained to carry people or burdens on their backs and to pull loads dragged behind them. The domestication of large ani-mals dramatically increased the power available to humans to carry out their tasks, which had both an immediate effect in the societies in which this happened and a long-term effect when these societies later encountered societies in which human labor remained the only source of power.

The pulling power of animals came to matter most, because it could be applied to food production. Sometime in the seventh millennium B.C.E., people attached wooden sticks to frames that animals dragged through the soil, thus breaking it up and allowing seeds to sprout more easily. These simple scratch plows were modified over millennia to handle different types of soil and other challenges. Using plows, Neolithic people produced a significant amount of surplus food, which meant that some people in the community could spend their days performing other tasks, increasing the division of labor. Surplus food had to be stored, and some began to specialize in making products for storage, such as pots, bas-kets, and other kinds of containers. Others specialized in making tools, houses, and other items needed in village life, or in producing spe-cific types of food, including alcoholic beverages made from fermented fruits and grains. Families and households became increasingly interdependent, trading food for other com-modities or services. In the same way that foragers had

Neolithic Pot, from China, ca. 2600–2300 B.C.E.
This two-handled pot, made in the Yellow River Valley of baked ceramics, is painted in a swirling red and black geometric design. Neolithic agricultural communities produced a wide array of storage containers for keeping food and other commodities from one season to the next. (Museum purchase, Fowler McCormack, Class of 1921. Fund. Y1979-94. Photo: Bruce M. White/Princeton University Art Museum/Art Resource, NY)

continually improved their tools and methods, people improved the processes through which they made things. Sometime between 4000 and 3500 B.C.E. pot makers in Mesopotamia invented the potter's wheel. Between 3500 and 3000 B.C.E. people in several parts of the world adapted wheels for use on carts and plows pulled by animals, combining wheels with axles to allow them to spin freely. Wheeled vehicles led to road building, and wheels and roads together made it possible for people and goods to travel long distances more easily, whether for settlement, trade, or conquest.

Stored food was also valuable and could become a source of conflict, as could other issues in villages where people lived close together. Villagers needed more complex rules than did foragers about how food was to be distributed and how different types of work were to be valued. Certain individuals began to specialize in the determination and enforcement of these rules, and informal structures of power gradually became more formalized as elites developed. These elites then distributed resources to their own advantage, often using force to attain and maintain their power.

Neolithic Society

The division of labor that plow agriculture allowed led to the creation of **social hierarchies**, the divisions between rich and poor, elites and common people that have been a central feature of human society since the Neolithic era. Plow agriculture also strengthened differentiation based on gender, with men becoming more associated with the world beyond the household and women with the domestic realm. Social hierarchies were reinforced over generations as children inherited goods and status from their parents. People increasingly communicated ideas within local and regional networks of exchange, just as they traded foodstuffs, tools, and other products.

Social Hierarchies and Slavery

Within foraging groups, some individuals already had more authority because of their links with the world of gods and spirits, positions as heads of kin groups, or personal characteristics. These three factors gave individuals advantages in agricultural societies, and the advantages became more significant over time as there were more resources to control. Priests and shamans became full-time religious specialists, exchanging their services in interceding with the gods for food. In many communities, religious specialists were the first to work out formal rules of conduct that later became oral and written codes of law. The codes often required people to accord deference to priests as the representatives of the gods, so that they became an elite group with special privileges.

Individuals who were the heads of large families or kin groups had control over the labor of others, and this power became more significant when that labor brought material goods that could be stored. Material goods—plows, sheep, cattle, sheds, pots, carts—gave one the ability to amass still more material goods, and the gap between those who had them and those who did not widened. Storage also allowed wealth to be retained over long periods of time and handed down from one family member to another, so that over generations small differences in wealth grew larger. The ability to control the labor of others could also come from physical strength, a charismatic personality, or leadership talents, and such traits may have also led to greater wealth.

> **How did growing social and gender hierarchies and expanding networks of trade increase the complexity of human society in the Neolithic period?**

> **social hierarchies**
> Divisions between rich and poor, elites and common people that have been a central feature of human society since the Neolithic era.

Wealth itself could command labor, as individuals or families could buy the services of others to work for them or impose their wishes through force, hiring soldiers to threaten or carry out violence. Eventually some individuals bought others outright. Slavery predates written records, but it developed in almost all agricultural societies. Like animals, slaves were a source of physical power for their owners, providing them an opportunity to amass still more wealth and influence.

Gender Hierarchies and Inheritance

patriarchy Social system in which men have more power and access to resources than women, and some men are dominant over other men.

Along with hierarchies based on wealth and power, the development of agriculture was intertwined with a hierarchy based on gender. The system in which men have more power and access to resources than women, and some men are dominant over other men, is called **patriarchy**. Every society in the world that has left written records has been patriarchal, but as patriarchy came before writing, we can conclude that it originated in the early Neolithic, the Paleolithic, or perhaps even in the hominid past.

Plow agriculture heightened patriarchy. Although farming with a hoe was often done by women, plow agriculture came to be a male task, perhaps because of men's upper-body strength or because plow agriculture was more difficult to combine with care for infants and small children than was horticulture. At the same time that cattle began to be raised for pulling plows and carts rather than for meat, sheep began to be raised primarily for wool. Spinning thread and weaving cloth became primarily women's work. Spinning and weaving were generally done indoors and involved simpler and cheaper tools than did plowing; they could also be taken up and put down easily, and so could be done at the same time as other tasks.

Though in some ways this arrangement seems complementary, with each sex doing some of the necessary labor, plow agriculture increased gender hierarchy. Men's responsibility for plowing and other agricultural tasks took them outside the household more often than women's duties did, enlarging their opportunities for leadership. This role may have led to their being favored as inheritors of family land and the right to farm communally held land. Accordingly, over generations, women's independent access to resources decreased, and it became increasingly difficult for women to survive without male support.

As inherited wealth became more important, men wanted to make sure that their sons were theirs, so they restricted their wives' movements and activities. This was especially the case among elite families. Among foragers and horticulturalists, women needed to be mobile for the group to survive; their labor outdoors was essential. Among agriculturalists, the labor of animals, slaves, and hired workers could substitute for that of women in families that could afford them. Thus in some Neolithic societies, there is evidence that women spent more and more of their time within the household. Social norms and ideals gradually reinforced this pattern, so that by the time written laws and other records emerged in the second millennium B.C.E., elite women were expected to work at tasks that would not take them beyond the household or away from male supervision. Non-elite women also tended to do work that could be done within or close by the household, such as cooking, cloth production, and the care of children, the elderly, and small animals.

Social and gender hierarchies were enhanced over generations as wealth was passed down unequally, and they were also enhanced by rules and norms that shaped sexual relationships, particularly heterosexual ones. However their power originated, elites began to think of themselves as a group set apart from the rest by some element that made them distinctive—such as military prowess, natural superiority, or connections with a deity. They increasingly understood this distinctive quality to be hereditary and tended to marry within their group, a social endogamy we might think of as the selective breeding of people. They developed traditions—later codified as written laws—that stipulated how such marriages would pass status and wealth to the next generation. Relationships between elite men and non-elite women generally did not function in this way, or did so to a lesser degree; the women were defined as concubines or mistresses, or simply as sexual outlets for powerful men. Relations between an elite woman and a non-elite man generally brought shame and dishonor to the woman's family and sometimes death to the man. (Early rules and laws about sex generally did not pay much attention to same-sex relations because these did not produce children who could threaten systems of inheritance.)

No elite can be completely closed to newcomers, however, because the accidents of life and death, along with the genetic problems caused by repeated close intermarriage, make it difficult for any small group to survive over generations. Thus mechanisms were developed in many cultures to adopt boys into elite families, to legitimate the children of concubines and slave women, or to allow elite girls to marry men lower on the social hierarchy. All systems of inheritance also need some flexibility. The inheritance patterns in some cultures favored male heirs exclusively, but in others close relatives were favored over those more distant, even if this meant allowing daughters to inherit. The drive to keep wealth and property within a family or kin group often resulted in women's inheriting, owning, and in some cases managing significant amounts of wealth, a pattern that continues today. Hierarchies of wealth and power thus intersected with hierarchies of gender in complex ways.

Trade and Cross-Cultural Connections

The increase in food production brought by the development of plow agriculture allowed Neolithic villages to grow ever larger. By 7000 B.C.E. or so, some villages in the Fertile Crescent may have had as many as ten thousand residents. One of the best known of these, Çatal Hüyük (cha-TAHL hoo-YOOK) in what is now modern Turkey, shows evidence of trade as well as of the specialization of labor. Çatal Hüyük's residents lived in mud-brick houses whose walls were covered in white plaster. The men and women of the town grew wheat, barley, peas, and almonds and raised sheep and perhaps cattle, though they also seem to have hunted. They made textiles, pots, figurines, baskets, carpets, copper and lead beads, and other goods. They gathered, sharpened, and polished obsidian, a volcanic rock that could be used for knives, blades, and mirrors, and then traded it with neighboring towns. From here the obsidian was exchanged still farther away, for Neolithic societies slowly developed local and then regional networks of exchange and communication.

Among the goods traded in some parts of the world was copper. Pure copper occurs close to the surface in some areas, and people, including those at Çatal Hüyük, hammered it into shapes for jewelry and tools. More often, copper, like most metals, occurs mixed with other materials in a type of rock called ore, and by about 5500 B.C.E. people in the Balkans had learned that copper could be extracted from ore by heating it in a smelting process. (See "Individuals in Society: The Iceman," page 26.)

The Iceman

ON SEPTEMBER 19, 1991, TWO GERMAN vacationers climbing in the Italian Alps came upon a corpse lying facedown and covered in ice. Scientists determined that the Iceman, as the corpse is generally known, died 5,300 years ago. He was between twenty-five and thirty-five years old at the time of his death, and he stood about five feet two inches tall. An autopsy revealed much about the man and his culture. The bluish tinge of his teeth showed a diet of milled grain, which proves that he came from an environment where crops were grown. The Iceman hunted as well as farmed: he was found with a bow and arrows and shoes of straw, and he wore a furry cap and a robe of animal skins that had been stitched together with thread made from grass.

The equipment discovered with the Iceman demonstrates that his people mastered several technologies. He carried a hefty copper ax, made by someone with a knowledge of metallurgy. In his quiver were numerous wooden arrow shafts and two finished arrows. The arrows had sharpened flint heads and feathers attached to the ends of the shafts with resin-like glue. Apparently the people of his culture knew the value of feathers to direct the arrow and thus had mastered the basics of ballistics. His bow was made of yew, a relatively rare wood in central Europe that is among the best for archers.

Yet a mystery still surrounds the Iceman. When his body was first discovered, scholars assumed that he was a hapless traveler overtaken in a fierce snowstorm. But the autopsy found an arrowhead lodged under his left shoulder. The Iceman was not alone on his last day. Someone was with him, and that someone had shot him from below and behind. The Iceman is the victim in the first murder mystery in Europe, and the case will never be solved.

The artifacts found with the body tell scientists much about how the Iceman lived. The Iceman's shoes, made with a twine framework stuffed with straw and covered with skin, indicate that he used all parts of the animals he hunted.

(discovery: Paul Hanny/Gamma-Rapho via Getty Images; shoes: South Tyrol Museum of Archaeology — www.iceman.it)

QUESTIONS FOR ANALYSIS

1. What does the autopsy of the corpse indicate about the society in which the Iceman lived?
2. How do the objects found with the Iceman support the generalizations about Neolithic society in this chapter?

Stone Circle at Nabta Playa, Egypt, ca. 4800 B.C.E. This circle of stones, erected when the Egyptian desert received much more rainfall than it does today, may have been a type of calendar marking the summer solstice. Circular arrangements of stones or ditches were constructed in many places during the Neolithic era, and most no doubt had calendrical, astronomical, and/or religious purposes. (© Mike P. Shepherd/Alamy Stock Photo)

Smelting techniques were discovered independently in many places around the world, including China, Southeast Asia, West Africa, and the Andes region. Pure copper is soft, but through experimentation artisans learned that it would become harder if they mixed it with other metals such as arsenic, zinc, or tin during heating, creating an alloy called bronze.

Because it was stronger than copper, bronze had a far wider range of uses, so much so that later historians decided that its adoption marked a new period in human history, the Bronze Age. It began about 3000 B.C.E. in some places, and by about 2500 B.C.E. bronze technology was having an impact in many parts of the world, especially in weaponry. The end of the Bronze Age came with the adoption of iron technology, which also varied in its beginnings from 1200 B.C.E. to 300 B.C.E. All metals were expensive and hard to obtain, however, which meant that stone, wood, bone, leather, bark, and grasses remained important materials for tools and weapons long into the Bronze Age, and the only materials in the vast parts of the world where metals were unobtainable.

Objects were not the only things traded over increasingly long distances during the Neolithic period, for people also carried ideas as they traveled. Knowledge about the seasons and the weather was vitally important for those who depended on crop raising, and agricultural peoples in many parts of the world began to calculate recurring patterns in the world around them, slowly developing calendars. Scholars have demonstrated that people built circular structures of mounded earth or huge upright stones to help them predict the movements of the sun and stars.

The rhythms of the agricultural cycle and patterns of exchange also shaped religious beliefs and practices. Shamans and priests developed ever more elaborate rituals designed to assure fertility, in which the gods were often given something from a community's goods in exchange for their favor. In many places gods came to be associated with patterns of birth, growth, death, and regeneration. Like humans, the gods came to have a division of labor and a social hierarchy. Thus, as human society was becoming more complex, so was the unseen world.

Chapter Summary

Through studying the physical remains of the past, sometimes with very new high-tech procedures such as DNA analysis, scholars have determined that human evolution involved a combination of factors, including bipedalism, larger brain size, spoken symbolic language, and longer periods of infancy. Humans invented ever more complex tools, many of which were made of stone, from which later scholars derived the name for this earliest period of human history, the Paleolithic era. These tools allowed Paleolithic peoples to shape the world around them. During this era, humans migrated out of Africa, adapting to many different environments and developing diverse cultures. Early humans lived in small groups of related individuals, moving through the landscape as foragers in the search for food.

Beginning about 9000 B.C.E. people living in southwest Asia, and then elsewhere, began to plant seeds as well as gather wild crops, raise certain animals, and selectively breed both plants and animals to make them more useful to humans. This domestication of plants and animals was the most important change in human history and marked the beginning of the Neolithic era. The domestication of large animals led to plow agriculture, through which humans could raise much more food, and the world's population grew. Plow agriculture allowed for a greater division of labor, which strengthened social hierarchies based on wealth and gender. Neolithic agricultural communities developed technologies to meet their needs and often traded with one another for products that they could not obtain locally. Religious ideas came to reflect the new agricultural society.

CONNECTIONS

The human story is often told as a narrative of unstoppable progress toward greater complexity. The small kin groups of the Paleolithic gave way to Neolithic villages that grew ever larger until they became cities. Egalitarian foragers became stratified by divisions of wealth and power that were formalized as aristocracies, castes, and social classes. Oral rituals of worship, healing, and celebration in which everyone participated grew into a dizzying array of religions, philosophies, and branches of knowledge presided over by specialists. The rest of this book traces this story and explores the changes over time that are the central thread of history.

As you examine what can seem to be a staggering number of developments, it is also important to remember that many things were slow to change and that some aspects of human life in the Neolithic, or even the Paleolithic, continued. Foraging, horticulture, pastoralism, and agriculture have been the primary economic activities of most people throughout the entire history of the world. Though today there are only a few foraging groups in very isolated areas, there are significant numbers of horticulturalists and pastoralists, and their numbers were much greater just a century ago. At that point the vast majority of the world's people still made their living directly through agriculture. The social patterns set in early agricultural societies — with most of the population farming the land and a small number of elite who lived off their labor — lasted for millennia. You have no doubt recognized other similarities between the early peoples discussed in this chapter and the people you see around you, and it is important to keep these continuities in mind as you embark on your examination of human history.

CHAPTER 1   Review and Explore

Identify Key Terms

Identify and explain the significance of each item below.

hominids (p. 4)	**megafaunal extinction** (p. 11)	**horticulture** (p. 16)
Paleolithic era (p. 5)	**division of labor** (p. 12)	**pastoralism** (p. 21)
foraging (p. 5)	**animism** (p. 13)	**social hierarchies** (p. 23)
Neolithic era (p. 5)	**shamans** (p. 14)	**patriarchy** (p. 24)
Neanderthals (p. 9)	**Agricultural Revolution** (p. 16)	
endogamy (p. 10)	**domesticated** (p. 16)	

Review the Main Ideas

Answer the focus questions from each section of the chapter.

1. How did humans evolve, and where did they migrate? (p. 4)

2. What were the key features of Paleolithic society? (p. 11)

3. How did plant and animal domestication develop, and what effects did it have on human society? (p. 14)

4. How did growing social and gender hierarchies and expanding networks of trade increase the complexity of human society in the Neolithic period? (p. 23)

Make Comparisons and Connections

Analyze the larger developments and continuities within and across chapters.

1. Why is the Agricultural Revolution called the most important change in human history?

2. What continuities persisted between the Paleolithic and Neolithic eras?

3. Why and how did social hierarchies develop?

4. Along with basic ways of life such as foraging, horticulture, pastoralism, and agriculture, what other aspects of society that developed in the Neolithic do you see around you today? What might account for these continuities stretching across millennia?

TIMELINE

Suggested Resources

BOOKS

Christian, David. *Maps of Time: An Introduction to Big History*. 2002. An elegant examination of the story of the cosmos, from the Big Bang to today.

Diamond, Jared. *Guns, Germs, and Steel: The Fates of Human Societies*, 2d ed. 2005. Extremely influential and wide-ranging examination of the long-term impact of agriculture, animal domestication, and the environment on differing rates of development around the world.

Ehrlich, Paul R., and Anne H. Ehrlich. *Dominant Animal: Human Evolution and the Environment*. 2009. By two of today's leading biologists; traces the impact of humans on the planet from the Paleolithic to today.

Fagan, Brian M. *World Prehistory: A Brief Introduction*, 8th ed. 2010. A thorough survey that presents up-to-date scholarship, designed for students.

Flannery, Kent, and Joyce Marcus. *The Creation of Inequality: How Our Prehistoric Ancestors Set the Stage for Monarchy, Slavery, and Empire*. 2012. Traces the development of hierarchies in many cultures around the world.

Gamble, Clive. *Timewalkers: The Prehistory of Global Colonization*. 2006. A lively examination of how and why humans came to be everywhere in the world.

Hawkes, Kristen, and Richard R. Paine. *The Evolution of Human Life History*. 2006. A series of articles that examine the ways in which the distinctions between humans and other animals came to be.

Hrdy, Sarah Blaffer. *Mothers and Others: The Evolutionary Origins of Human Understanding*. 2009. Provides the new, more egalitarian perspective on evolution.

Lewis-Williams, David, and David Pearce. *Inside the Neolithic Mind: Consciousness, Cosmos, and the Realm of the Gods*. 2005. An analysis of Neolithic belief systems and the cultural products that resulted from them.

McCarter, Susan Foster. *Neolithic*. 2007. An introductory survey of the development and impact of agriculture, with many illustrations.

Pinker, Steven. *How the Mind Works*, 2d ed. 2009. An insightful examination of how the mind evolved, along with a survey of modern brain science.

Pollan, Michael. *The Omnivore's Dilemma: A Natural History of Four Meals*. 2007. A witty and thoughtful look at the way food is produced today, and how this contrasts with our foraging past.

Timeline

- ◆ **ca. 25,000** B.C.E. Earliest evidence of woven cloth and basket
- ◆ **ca. 9000** B.C.E. Beginning of the Neolithic; horticulture; domestication of sheep and goats
- ◆ **ca. 2500** B.C.E. Bronze technology common; beginning of the Bronze Age
- ◆ **ca. 7000** B.C.E. Domestication of cattle; plow agriculture
- **ca. 13,000–8000** B.C.E. Final retreat of glaciers
- **ca. 4500–4000** B.C.E. Invention of pottery wheel
- **ca. 3500–3200** B.C.E. Earliest known writing; development of wheeled transport
- ◆ **ca. 3800** B.C.E. First cities in Sumer **(Ch. 2)**
- **2800–1800** B.C.E. Harappan civilization in India **(Ch. 3)**
- **ca. 20,000–30,000 years ago** Possible human migration from Asia to the Americas
- ◆ **ca. 15,000** B.C.E. Earliest evidence of bows and atlatls
- ◆ **ca. 15,000** B.C.E. Humans cross the Bering Strait land bridge to the Americas

25,000 B.C.E.	10,000 B.C.E.	5000 B.C.E.	1000 B.C.E.

Richerson, Peter J., and Robert Boyd. *Not by Genes Alone: How Culture Transformed Human Evolution.* 2005. Examines the role of culture in evolution, drawing on many different fields.

Stringer, Chris. *The Complete World of Human Evolution,* 2d ed. 2012. A relatively compact and nicely illustrated introduction that includes the newest archaeological and chemical evidence.

Tattersall, Ian. *Masters of the Planet: The Search for Our Human Origins.* 2012. An up-to-date survey of how humans evolved and how people have studied this, in a lively narrative written for general readers.

DOCUMENTARIES

Becoming Human (*Nova,* 2011). Three-part series that examines the latest research on hominid evolution from 6 million years ago to today, using computer-generated animation and prosthetics.

Cave of Forgotten Dreams (Werner Herzog, 2010). Renowned director Werner Herzog goes inside the newly discovered Chauvet caves of southern France to film the oldest-known human artwork from around 32,000 years ago.

Decoding Neanderthals (*Nova,* 2013). One-hour documentary that presents newest genetic and archaeological evidence about Neanderthals.

The Incredible Human Journey (BBC, 2009). Five-part documentary and accompanying book that examine human migrations out of Africa; each episode examines a different continent.

WEBSITES

Art History Resources: Prehistoric Art. This section of Art History Resources, designed and run by art historian Christopher Witcombe, contains many links to sites on prehistoric art. **arthistoryresources .net/ARTHprehistoric.html**

Becoming Human. Presented by the Institute of Human Origins at Arizona State University, this site explores human evolution with video, articles, news, and debates. **www.becominghuman.org**

Evolution. The PBS Evolution website, which complements an eight-hour television broadcast series, offers video clips from the series, simulations, animations, interactive timelines, expert commentary, and primary sources. **www.pbs.org/wgbh/evolution/**

2

Complex Societies in Southwest Asia and the Nile Valley
3800–500 B.C.E.

Five thousand years ago, humans were living in most parts of the planet. They had designed technologies to meet the challenges presented by deep forests and jungles, steep mountains, and blistering deserts. As the climate changed, they adapted, building boats to cross channels created by melting glaciers and finding new sources of food when old sources were no longer plentiful. In some places the new sources included domesticated plants and animals, which allowed people to live in much closer proximity to one another than they had as foragers.

That proximity created opportunities, as larger groups of people pooled their knowledge to deal with life's challenges, but it also created problems. Human history from that point on can be seen as a response to these opportunities, challenges, and conflicts. As small villages grew into cities, people continued to develop technologies and systems to handle new issues. To control their more complex societies, people created governments, militaries, and taxation systems. In some places they invented writing to record taxes, inventories, and payments, and they later put writing to other uses. The first places where these new technologies and systems were introduced were the Tigris and Euphrates River Valleys of southwest Asia and the Nile Valley of northeast Africa, areas whose histories became linked through trade, military conquests, and migrations.

Persian Archers

In this colorful decorative frieze made of glazed brick, men wearing long Persian robes and laced ankle boots carry spears, bows, and quivers. This reconstruction in the Louvre Museum in Paris was made from material found in the palace of King Darius I of Persia in Susa, built about 510 B.C.E. Enough bricks were found there to suggest that there were originally many archers, perhaps representing Darius's royal guards or symbolizing the entire Persian people.

Louvre, Paris, France/Erich Lessing/Art Resource, NY

CHAPTER PREVIEW

Writing, Cities, and States

The remains of buildings, burial sites, weapons, tools, artwork, and other handmade objects provide our only evidence of how people lived, thought, felt, and died during most of the human past. Beginning about 5,000 years ago, however, people in some parts of the world developed a new technology, writing. Writing developed to meet the needs of more complex urban societies that are often referred to as "civilizations." In particular, writing met the needs of the state, a new political form that developed during the time covered in this chapter.

Written Sources and the Human Past

Historians who study human societies that developed systems of writing continue to use many of the same types of physical evidence as do those who study societies without writing. For some cultures, the writing or record-keeping systems have not yet been deciphered, so our knowledge of these people also depends largely on physical evidence. Scholars can read the writing of a great many societies, however, adding greatly to what we can learn about them.

Much ancient writing survives only because it was copied and recopied, sometimes years after it was first produced. The survival of a work means that someone from a later period—and often a long chain of someones—judged it worthy of the time, effort, and resources needed to produce copies. The copies may not be completely accurate. Historians studying ancient works thus often try to find as many early copies as they can and compare them to arrive at the version they think is closest to the original.

The works considered worthy of copying tend to be those that are about the political and military events involving major powers, those that record religious traditions, or those that come from authors who were later regarded as important. By contrast, written sources dealing with the daily life of ordinary men and women were few to begin with and were rarely saved or copied because they were not considered significant.

Some early written texts survive in their original form because people inscribed them in stone, shells, bone, or other hard materials, intending them to be permanent. Stones with inscriptions were

Clay Letter Written in Cuneiform and Its Envelope, ca. 1850 B.C.E.
In this letter from a city in Anatolia, located on the northern edge of the Fertile Crescent in what is now southern Turkey, a Mesopotamian merchant complains to his brother at home, hundreds of miles away, that life is hard and comments on the trade in silver, gold, tin, and textiles. Correspondents often enclosed letters in clay envelopes and sealed them by rolling a cylinder seal across the clay, leaving the impression of a scene, just as you might use a stamped wax seal today. Here the very faint impression of the sender's seal at the bottom shows a person, probably the owner of the seal, being led in a procession toward a king or god. (© The Trustees of the British Museum/Art Resource, NY)

often erected in the open in public places for all to see, so they include text that leaders felt had enduring importance, such as laws, religious proclamations, decrees, and treaties. (The names etched in granite on the Vietnam Veterans Memorial in Washington, D.C., are perhaps the best-known modern example, but inscriptions can be found on nearly every major public building.) Sometimes this permanence was accidental: in ancient Mesopotamia (in the area of modern Iraq), all writing was initially made up of indentations on soft clay tablets, which then hardened. Hundreds of thousands of these tablets have survived, the oldest written in cuneiform (see "Writing, Mathematics, and Poetry") and dating to about 3200 B.C.E. From these written records historians have learned about many aspects of everyday life. By contrast, writing in Egypt at the same time was often done in ink on papyrus sheets, made from a plant that grows abundantly in Egypt. Some of these papyrus sheets have survived, but papyrus is much more fragile than hardened clay, so most have disintegrated. In China, the oldest surviving writing is on bones and turtle shells from about 1200 B.C.E., but it is clear that writing was done much earlier on less permanent materials such as silk and bamboo. (For more on the origins of Chinese writing, see "The Development of Writing" in Chapter 4.)

Cities and the Idea of Civilization

Along with writing, the growth of cities has often been a way that scholars mark the increasing complexity of human societies. In the ancient world, residents of cities generally viewed themselves as more advanced and sophisticated than rural folk—a judgment still made today by urban dwellers. They saw themselves as more "civilized," a word that comes from the Latin adjective *civilis*, which refers to either a citizen of a town or of a larger political unit such as an empire.

This depiction of people as either civilized or uncivilized was gradually extended to whole societies. Beginning in the eighteenth century European scholars described those societies in which political, economic, and social organizations operated on a large scale as "civilizations." Civilizations had cities; laws that governed human relationships; codes of manners and social conduct that regulated how people were to behave; and scientific, philosophical, and theological ideas that explained the larger world. Generally only societies that used writing were judged to be civilizations.

Until the middle of the twentieth century, historians often referred to the earliest places where writing and cities developed as the "cradles of civilization," proposing a model of development for all humanity patterned on that of an individual person. However, the idea that all human societies developed (or should develop) in a uniform process from a "cradle" to a "mature" civilization has now been largely discredited, and some world historians choose not to use the word *civilization* at all because it could imply that some societies are superior to others. But they have not rejected the idea that about 5,000 years ago a new form of human society appeared.

The Rise of States, Laws, and Social Hierarchies

Cities concentrated people and power, and they required more elaborate mechanisms to make them work than had small agricultural villages and foraging groups. These mechanisms were part of what political scientists call "the state," an organization in which a share of the population is able to coerce resources out of everyone else in order to gain and then maintain power. In the earliest states, the interest that gained power was often one particular family or kin group, a set of religious leaders, or even a charismatic or talented individual able to handle the problems of dense urban communities. These same types of states continue to today as monarchies, theocracies, and dictatorships, joined by types of states that developed more recently, such as democracies, in which power is understood to reside in "the people."

However they were and are established, states coerce people through violence, or the threat of violence, and develop armies and police forces for this purpose; even in democracies, people can be forced to do things they do not want to do with the threat of imprisonment or other punishment. Using armed force to gain resources is not very efficient, however, so states developed other ways to do this, such as bureaucracies and systems of taxation. States also need to keep track of people and goods, so they sometimes developed systems of recording information and accounting, usually through writing, though not always. In the Inca Empire of the Andes, for example, information about money, goods, and people was recorded on collections of colored knotted strings called *khipus* (see "Societies of the Americas in a Global Context" in Chapter 11). These systems allowed for the creation of more elaborate rules of behavior, often written down in the form of law codes, which facilitated further growth in state power, or in the form of religious traditions, which specified what sort of behavior is pleasing to the gods or other supernatural forces and thus convinced people to act in certain ways.

Written laws and traditions generally create more elaborate social hierarchies, in which divisions between elite groups and common people are established more firmly. They also generally heighten gender hierarchies. Those who gain power in states are most often men, so they tend to establish laws and norms that favor males in marriage, property rights, and other areas.

Whether we choose to call the process "the birth of civilization," or "the development of complex society," or "the growth of the state," in the fourth millennium B.C.E. Neolithic agricultural villages expanded into cities that depended largely on food produced by the surrounding countryside while people living in cities carried out other tasks. The organization of a more complex division of labor was undertaken by an elite group, which enforced its will through laws, taxes, and bureaucracies backed up by armed force or the threat of it. Social and gender hierarchies became more complex and rigid. All this happened first in Mesopotamia, then in Egypt, and then in India and China.

How did the peoples of Mesopotamia form states and develop new technologies and institutions?	# Mesopotamia from Sumer to Babylon

States first developed in Mesopotamia, where sustained agriculture reliant on irrigation from the Euphrates (you-FRAY-teez) and Tigris Rivers resulted in larger populations, a division of labor, and the growth of cities. Priests and rulers developed ways to control and organize these complex societies. Conquerors from the north unified Mesopotamian city-states into larger empires and spread Mesopotamian culture over a large area.

Environmental Challenges, Irrigation, and Religion

Mesopotamia was part of the Fertile Crescent, where settled agriculture first developed (see "The Development of Horticulture" in Chapter 1). The earliest agricultural

Sumerian Harpist This small clay tablet, carved between 2000 B.C.E. and 1500 B.C.E., shows a seated woman playing a harp. Her fashionable dress and hat suggest that she is playing for wealthy people, perhaps at the royal court. Images of musicians are common in Mesopotamian art, which indicates that music was important in Mesopotamian culture and social life. (Louvre, Paris, France/Erich Lessing/Art Resource, NY)

villages in Mesopotamia were in the northern, hilly parts of the river valleys, where there is abundant rainfall for crops. Farmers had brought techniques of crop raising southward by about 5000 B.C.E., to the southern part of Mesopotamia known as Sumer (SOO-mer). In this arid climate farmers developed large-scale irrigation, which required organized group effort but allowed the population to grow. By about 3800 B.C.E. one of these agricultural villages, Uruk (OO-rook), had expanded significantly, becoming what many historians view as the world's first city. Over the next thousand years, other cities emerged in Sumer, trading with one another and creating massive hydraulic projects including reservoirs, dams, and dikes to prevent major floods. These cities built defensive walls, marketplaces, and large public buildings; each came to dominate the surrounding countryside, becoming city-states independent from one another, though not very far apart.

The city-states of Sumer relied on irrigation systems that required cooperation and at least some level of social and political cohesion. The authority to run this system was, it seems, initially assumed by Sumerian priests. Encouraged and directed by their religious leaders, people built temples on tall platforms in the center of their cities. Temples grew into elaborate complexes of buildings with storage space for grain and other products and housing for animals. (Much later, by about 2100 B.C.E., some of the major temple complexes were embellished with a huge stepped pyramid, called a ziggurat, with a shrine on the top.) Surrounding the temple and other large buildings were the houses of ordinary citizens, each constructed around a central courtyard.

To Sumerians, and to later peoples in Mesopotamia as well, many different gods and goddesses controlled the world, a religious idea later scholars called **polytheism**. Each deity represented cosmic forces such as the sun, moon, water, and storms. The gods judged good and evil and would punish humans who lied or cheated. People believed that humans had been created to serve the gods and generally anticipated being well treated by the gods if they honored them through rituals and temples.

polytheism The worship of many gods and goddesses.

Sumerian Politics and Society

Exactly how kings emerged in Sumerian society is not clear. Scholars have suggested that during times of crisis a chief priest or sometimes a military leader assumed what was supposed to be temporary authority over a city. He established an army, trained it, and led it into battle. Temporary power gradually became permanent kingship, and kings in some Sumerian city-states began to hand down the kingship to their sons, establishing patriarchal hereditary dynasties in which power was handed down through the male line. The symbol of royal status was the palace, which came to rival the temple in its grandeur.

Kings made alliances with other powerful individuals, often through marriage. Royal family members were responsible for many aspects of government. Kings worked closely with religious authorities and relied on ideas about their connections with the gods, as well as the kings' military might, for their power. Royal children, both sons and daughters, were sometimes priests and priestesses in major temples. Acting together, priests, nobles, and kings in Sumerian cities used force, persuasion, and threats of higher taxes to maintain order, keep the irrigation systems working, and keep food and other goods flowing.

The king and the nobles held extensive tracts of land, as did the temple; these lands were worked by the palace's or the temple's clients—free men and women who were dependent on the palace or the temple. They received crops and other goods in return for their labor. Although this arrangement assured the clients of a livelihood, the land they worked remained the possession of the palace or the temple. Some individuals and families owned land outright and paid their taxes in the form of agricultural products or items they made. At the bottom rung of society were slaves. Like animals, slaves were a source of physical power for their owners, providing them an opportunity to amass more wealth and influence.

Each of these social categories included both men and women, but their experiences were not the same, for Sumerian society made distinctions based on gender. Most elite landowners were male, but women who held positions as priestesses or as queens ran their own estates independently of their husbands and fathers. Some women owned businesses and took care of their own accounts. They could own property and distribute it to their offspring. Sons and daughters inherited from their parents, although a daughter received her inheritance in the form of a dowry, which technically remained hers but was managed by her husband or husband's family after marriage. The Sumerians established the basic social, economic, and intellectual patterns of Mesopotamia and influenced their neighbors to the north and east.

Writing, Mathematics, and Poetry

The origins of writing probably date back to the ninth millennium B.C.E., when people in southwest Asia used clay tokens as counters for record keeping. By the fourth millennium people had realized that impressing the tokens on soft clay, or drawing pictures of the tokens on clay, was simpler than making tokens. This breakthrough in turn suggested that more information could be conveyed by adding pictures of other objects, and slowly the new technology of writing developed. The result was a complex system of pictographs in which each sign pictured an object, such as "star" (line A of Figure 2.1). These pictographs were the forerunners of the Sumerian form of writing known as **cuneiform** (kyou-NEE-uh-form), for which the first surviving examples date from about 3200 B.C.E.

Pictographs were initially limited in that they could not represent abstract ideas, but the development of ideograms—signs that represented ideas—made writing more versatile. Thus the sign for "star" could also be used to indicate "heaven," "sky,"

cuneiform Sumerian form of writing; the term describes the wedge-shaped marks made by a stylus.

or even "god." The real breakthrough came when scribes started using signs to represent sounds. For instance, the symbol for "water" (two parallel wavy lines) could also be used to indicate "in," which sounded the same as the spoken word for "water" in Sumerian.

The development of the Sumerian system of writing was piecemeal, with scribes making changes and additions as they were needed. The system became so complicated that the Sumerians established scribal schools, which by 2500 B.C.E. flourished throughout the region. Students at the schools were all male, and most came from families in the middle range of urban society. Scribal schools were primarily intended to produce individuals who could keep records of the property of temple officials, kings, and nobles. Thus writing first developed as a way to enhance the growing power of elites, not to record speech.

Sumerians wrote numbers as well as words on clay tablets, and some surviving tablets show multiplication and division problems. The Sumerians and later Mesopotamians made significant advances in mathematics using a numerical system based on units of sixty, ten, and six, from which we derive our division of hours into sixty minutes and minutes into sixty seconds. They also developed the concept of place value—that the value of a number depends on where it stands in relation to other numbers.

Written texts were not an important part of Sumerian religious life, nor were they central to the religious practices of most of the other peoples in this region. Stories about the gods circulated orally and traveled with people when they moved up and down the rivers. Sumerians also told stories about heroes and kings, many of which were eventually reworked into the world's first **epic poem**, the *Epic of Gilgamesh* (GIL-guh-mesh), which was later written down. (See "Analyzing the Evidence: Gilgamesh's Quest for Immortality," page 40.)

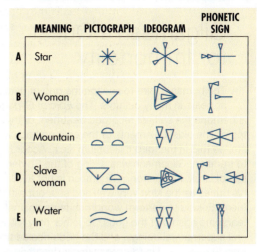

FIGURE 2.1 Sumerian Writing

(Source: Information from S. N. Kramer, *The Sumerians: Their History, Culture, and Character* [Chicago: University of Chicago Press, 1963].)

epic poem An oral or written narration of the achievements and sometimes the failures of heroes that embodies peoples' ideas about themselves.

Empires in Mesopotamia

The wealth of Sumerian cities also attracted conquerors from the north. Around 2300 B.C.E. Sargon, the king of a region to the north of Sumer, conquered a number of Sumerian cities with what was probably the world's first permanent army and created a large state. The symbol of his triumph was a new capital, the city of Akkad (AH-kahd). Sargon also expanded the newly established Akkadian empire westward to northern Syria, which became the breadbasket of the empire. He encouraged trading networks that brought in goods from as far away as the Indus River in South Asia and what is now Turkey (Map 2.1). Sargon spoke a different language than did the Sumerians, one of the many languages that scholars identify as belonging to the Semitic language family, which includes modern-day Hebrew and Arabic. Akkadians adapted cuneiform writing to their own language, and Akkadian became the diplomatic language used over a wide area.

Sargon tore down the defensive walls of Sumerian cities and appointed his own sons as their rulers to help him cement his power. He also appointed his daughter, Enheduana (en-hoo-DWANN-ah) (2285–2250 B.C.E.), as high priestess in the city

Gilgamesh's Quest for Immortality

The human desire to escape the grip of death appears in many cultures. The *Epic of Gilgamesh* is perhaps the earliest recorded treatment of this topic. The oldest elements of the epic go back to stories told in the third millennium B.C.E. According to tradition, Gilgamesh was a king of the Sumerian city of Uruk. In the story, Gilgamesh is not fulfilling his duties as the king very well and sets out with his friend Enkidu to perform wondrous feats against fearsome agents of the gods. Together they kill several supernatural beings, and the gods decide that Enkidu must die. He foresees his own death in a dream.

■ Listen again, my friend [Gilgamesh]! I had a dream in the night.
The sky called out, the earth replied,
I was standing in between them.
There was a young man, whose face was obscured.
His face was like that of an Anzu-bird.
He had the paws of a lion, he had the claws of an eagle.
He seized me by my locks, using great force against me. . . .
He seized me, drove me down to the dark house, dwelling of Erkalla's god [the underworld], . . .
On the road where travelling is one way only,
To the house where those who stay are deprived of light. . . .

[Enkidu sickens and dies. Gilgamesh is distraught and determined to become immortal. He decides to journey to Ut-napishtim and his wife, the only humans who have eternal life. Everyone he meets along the way asks him about his appearance, and Gilgamesh always answers with the same words.]

How could my cheeks not be wasted, nor my face dejected,
Nor my heart wretched, nor my appearance worn out,
Nor grief in my innermost being,
Nor my face like that of a long-distance traveller,
Nor my face weathered by wind and heat
Nor roaming open country clad only in a lionskin?
My friend was the hunted mule, wild ass of the mountain, leopard of open country,
Enkidu my friend was the hunted mule, wild ass of the mountain, leopard of open country.
We who met, and scaled the mountain,
Seized the Bull of Heaven [the sacred bull of the goddess Ishtar] and slew it,
Demolished Humbaba [the ogre who guards the forest of the gods] who dwelt in the Pine Forest,
Killed lions in the passes of the mountains,
My friend whom I love so much, who experienced every hardship with me,
Enkidu my friend whom I love so much, who experienced every hardship with me—
The fate of mortals conquered him!
For six days and seven nights I wept over him: I did not allow him to be buried
Until a worm fell out of his nose.
I was frightened and
I am afraid of Death, and so I roam open country.

of Ur. Here she wrote a number of hymns, becoming the world's first author to put her name to a literary composition.

Sargon's dynasty appears to have ruled Mesopotamia for about 150 years, and then collapsed, in part because of a period of extended drought. Various city-states then rose to power, one of which was centered on the city of Babylon. Babylon was in an excellent position to dominate trade on both the Tigris and Euphrates Rivers, and it was fortunate in having a very able ruler in Hammurabi (hahm-moo-RAH-bee) (r. 1792–1750 B.C.E.). Initially a typical king of his era, he unified Mesopotamia later in his reign by using military force, strategic alliances with the rulers of smaller territories, and religious ideas. As had earlier rulers, Hammurabi linked his success with the will of the gods. He connected himself with the sun-god Shamash, the god of law and justice, and encouraged the spread of myths that explained how Marduk, the primary god of Babylon, had been elected king of the gods by the other deities in

The words of my friend weigh upon me. . . .
I roam open country on long journeys.
How, O how could I stay silent, how, O how could I
  keep quiet?
My friend whom I love has turned to clay: Enkidu my
  friend whom I love has turned to clay.
Am I not like him? Must I lie down too,
Never to rise, ever again?

[Gilgamesh finally reaches Ut-napishtim, to whom he
tells his story, and who says to him:]

Why do you prolong grief, Gilgamesh?
Since [the gods made you] from the flesh of gods and
  mankind,
Since [the gods] made you like your father and mother
[Death is inevitable] . . . ,
Nobody sees the face of Death,
Nobody hears the voice of Death.
Savage Death just cuts mankind down.
Sometimes we build a house, sometimes we make a nest,
But then brothers divide it upon inheritance.
Sometimes there is hostility in [the land],
But then the river rises and brings flood-water. . . .
The Anunnaki, the great gods, assembled;
Mammitum [the great mother goddess] who creates fate
  decreed destinies with them.
They appointed death and life.
They did not mark out days for death,
But they did so for life.

[Gilgamesh asks Ut-napishtim how he and his wife
can be immortal like the gods, if death is inevitable.
Ut-napishtim tells him the story of how they survived

a flood sent by the gods and the chief god Enlil
blessed them with eternal life. Gilgamesh wants this
as well, but fails two opportunities Ut-napishtim provides for him to achieve it. At the end of the epic, he
simply returns to Uruk with the boatman Ur-shanabi,
to whom he points out the glories of the city.]

Go up on to the wall of Uruk, Ur-shanabi, and walk
  around,
Inspect the foundation platform and scrutinize the
  brickwork! Testify that its bricks are baked bricks,
And that the Seven Counsellors must have laid its
  foundations!
One square mile is city, one square mile is orchards, one
  square mile is claypits, as well as the open ground of
  Ishtar's temple.
Three square miles and the open ground comprise
  Uruk.

QUESTIONS FOR ANALYSIS

1. What does the *Epic of Gilgamesh* reveal about attitudes toward friendship in ancient Mesopotamia?
2. What does the epic tell us about views of the nature of human life? Where do human beings fit into the cosmic world?
3. Although Gilgamesh did not achieve personal immortality at the end of his quest, how can his final words to Ur-shanabi be seen as a tribute to long-lasting human endeavors?

Source: *Myths from Mesopotamia: Creation, the Flood, Gilgamesh, and Others*, trans. Stephanie Dalley (Oxford: Oxford University Press, 1989), pp. 88–89, 103–104, 107, 108–109, 120. Used by permission of Oxford University Press.

Mesopotamia. Babylonian ideas and beliefs thus became part of the cultural mixture of Mesopotamia, which spread far beyond the Tigris and Euphrates Valleys to the shores of the Mediterranean Sea and the Harappan cities of the Indus River Valley (see "The Land and Its First Settlers, ca. 3000–1500 B.C.E." in Chapter 3).

Life Under Hammurabi

Hammurabi's most memorable accomplishment was the proclamation of an extensive law code, introduced about 1755 B.C.E. **Hammurabi's law code** set a variety of punishments for breaking the law, including fines and physical punishment such as mutilation, whipping, and burning. It demanded that the punishment fit the crime, calling for "an eye for an eye and a tooth for a tooth," at least among social equals, although higher-ranking people could pay a fine to lower-ranking victims instead of having an arm broken or losing an eye.

Hammurabi's law code
A proclamation issued by Babylonian king Hammurabi to establish laws regulating many aspects of life.

MAP 2.1 Spread of Cultures in Southwest Asia and the Nile Valley, ca. 3000–1640 B.C.E. This map illustrates the spread of the Mesopotamian and Egyptian cultures through the semicircular stretch of land often called the Fertile Crescent. From this area, the knowledge and use of agriculture spread throughout western Asia, northern Africa, and Europe.

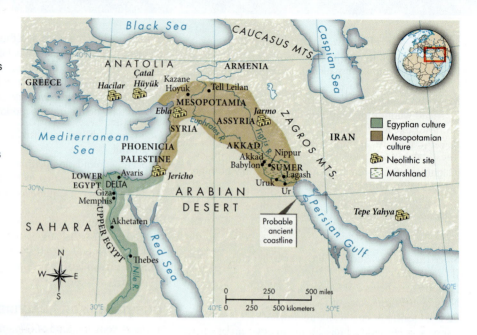

Hammurabi's code provides a wealth of information about daily life in Mesopotamia, although, like all law codes, it prescribes what the lawgivers hope will be the situation rather than providing a description of real life. We cannot know if its laws were enforced, but we can use it to see what was significant to people in Hammurabi's society. Because of farming's fundamental importance, the code dealt extensively with agriculture. Tenants faced severe penalties for neglecting the land or not working it at all. The code also regulated other trades, and artisans had to guarantee the quality of their goods and services to consumers. Hammurabi gave careful attention to marriage and the family. As elsewhere in the area, marriage had aspects of a business agreement. The groom or his father offered the prospective bride's father a gift, and if this was acceptable, the bride's father provided his daughter with a dowry, which technically remained hers. A father could not disinherit a son without just cause, and the code ordered the courts to forgive a son for his first offense. On family matters and other issues, Hammurabi's code influenced other law codes, including those later written down in Hebrew Scripture (see "The Jewish Religion").

Law Code of Hammurabi Hammurabi ordered his code to be inscribed on stone pillars and set up in public throughout the Babylonian empire. At the top of the pillar Hammurabi (left) is depicted receiving the rod and ring of authority from Shamash, the god of law and justice. (Louvre, Paris, France/© RMN–Grand Palais/Art Resource, NY)

The Egyptians

How did the Egyptians create a prosperous and long-lasting society?

At about the same time that Sumerian city-states expanded and fought with one another in the Tigris and Euphrates Valleys, a more cohesive state under a single ruler grew in the valley of the Nile River in North Africa. This was Egypt, which for long stretches of history was prosperous and secure. At various times groups invaded and conquered Egypt or migrated into Egypt seeking better lives. Often these newcomers adopted aspects of Egyptian culture, and Egyptians also carried their traditions with them when they established an empire and engaged in trade.

The Nile and the God-King

No other single geographical factor had such a fundamental and profound impact on Egyptian life, society, and history as the Nile River (see Map 2.2). The Nile flooded once a year for a period of several months, bringing fertile soil and moisture for farming. Through the fertility of the Nile and their own hard work, Egyptians produced an annual agricultural surplus, which in turn sustained a growing and prosperous population. The Nile also unified Egypt, serving as a highway that promoted easy communication.

The political power structures that developed in Egypt came to be linked with the Nile. Somehow the idea developed that a single individual, a king, was responsible for the rise and fall of the Nile. The king came to be viewed as a descendant of the gods and thus a god himself. This belief came about before the development of writing in Egypt, so the precise details of its origins have been lost. Political unification most likely proceeded slowly, but stories told about early kings highlighted one who had united Upper Egypt (the upstream valley in the south) and Lower Egypt (the delta area of the Nile that empties into the Mediterranean Sea) into a single kingdom around 3100 B.C.E. Historians later divided Egyptian history into dynasties, or families, of kings, and more recently into periods with distinctive characteristics (see the chronology "Periods of Egyptian History"). The political unification of Egypt in the Archaic Period (3100–2660 B.C.E.) ushered in the period known as the Old Kingdom (2660–2180 B.C.E.).

The focal point of religious and political life in the Old Kingdom was the king, who commanded the wealth, resources, and people of Egypt. The king's surroundings had to be worthy of a god, and only a magnificent palace was suitable for his home; in fact, the word **pharaoh**, which during the New Kingdom (1570–1070 B.C.E.) came to be used for the king, originally meant "great house." Just as the kings occupied a great house in life, so they reposed in great pyramids after death. Built during the Old Kingdom, these massive stone tombs contained all the things needed by the king in his afterlife and also symbolized the king's power and his connection with the sun-god.

pharaoh The title given to the king of Egypt in the New Kingdom, from a word that meant "great house."

Like the Mesopotamians, the Egyptians were polytheistic, worshipping many gods of all types, some mightier than others. They developed complex ideas of their gods that reflected the world around them, and these views changed over the many centuries of Egyptian history as gods took on new attributes and often merged with one another. During the Old Kingdom, Egyptians considered the sun-god Ra the creator of life. Much later, during the New Kingdom (see "Migrations, Revivals, and Collapse"), the pharaohs of a new dynasty favored the worship of a different sun-god,

PERIODS OF EGYPTIAN HISTORY

PERIOD	DATES	SIGNIFICANT EVENTS
Archaic	3100–2660 B.C.E.	Unification of Egypt
Old Kingdom	2660–2180 B.C.E.	Construction of the pyramids
First Intermediate	2180–2080 B.C.E.	Political chaos
Middle Kingdom	2080–1640 B.C.E.	Recovery and political stability
Second Intermediate	1640–1570 B.C.E.	Instability resulting from struggles for power and Hyksos migrations
New Kingdom	1570–1070 B.C.E.	Creation of an Egyptian empire; growth in wealth
Third Intermediate	1100–653 B.C.E.	Political fragmentation and conquest by outsiders

Amon. As his cult grew, Amon came to be identified with Ra, and eventually the Egyptians combined them into one sun-god, Amon-Ra.

The Egyptians likewise developed views of an afterlife that reflected the world around them and that changed over time. During the later part of the Old Kingdom, the walls of kings' tombs were carved with religious texts that provided spells that would bring the king back to life and help him ascend to heaven. Toward the end of the Old Kingdom, the tombs of powerful nobles also contained such inscriptions, an indication that more people expected to gain everlasting life. In the Middle Kingdom (2080–1640 B.C.E.), new types of spells appeared on the coffins of even more people, a further expansion in admissions to the afterlife. During the New Kingdom, a time when Egypt came into greater contact with the cultures of the Fertile Crescent, Egyptians developed even more complex ideas about the afterlife, recording these in written funerary manuscripts that have come to be known as the *Book of the Dead*. These texts explained that the soul left the body to become part of the divine after death and told of the god Osiris (oh-SIGH-ruhs), who died each year and was then brought back to life by his wife Isis (IGH-suhs) when the Nile flooded. Osiris eventually became king of the dead, weighing dead humans' hearts to determine whether they had lived justly enough to deserve everlasting life. Egyptians also believed that proper funeral rituals, in which the physical body was mummified, were essential for life after death, so Osiris was assisted by Anubis, the jackal-headed god of mummification.

To ancient Egyptians, the king embodied justice and order—harmony among people, nature, and the divine. Kings did not always live up to this ideal, of course. The two parts of Egypt were difficult to hold together, and several times in Egypt's long history there were periods of civil war and political fragmentation, which scholars term the First (2180–2080 B.C.E.) and Second (1640–1570 B.C.E.) Intermediate Periods. Yet the monarchy survived, and in each period a strong warrior-king arose to restore order and expand Egyptian power.

Egyptian Society and Work

Egyptian society reflected the pyramids that it built. At the top stood the pharaoh, who relied on a circle of nobles, officials, and priests to administer his kingdom. All of them were assisted by scribes, who used a writing system perhaps adapted from Mesopotamia or perhaps developed independently. Egyptian scribes actually created two writing systems: one called hieroglyphics for engraving important religious or political texts on stone or writing them on papyrus made from reeds growing in the Nile Delta, and a much simpler system called hieratic that allowed scribes to write more quickly and was used for the documents of daily life. The cities of the Nile Valley were also home to artisans of all types, along with merchants and other trades-people. A large group of farmers made up the broad base of the social pyramid.

For Egyptians, the Nile formed an essential part of daily life. During the flooding season—from June to October—farmers worked on the pharaoh's building programs and other tasks away from their fields. When the water began to recede, they diverted some of it into ponds for future irrigation and began planting wheat and barley, using plows pulled by oxen or people. From October to February farmers planted and tended crops, and from February until the next flood they harvested them. As in Mesopotamia, common people paid their obligations to their superiors in products and in labor. People's labor obligations in the Old Kingdom may have included forced work on the pyramids and canals, although recent research suggests that most people who built the pyramids were paid for their work. Some young men were drafted into the pharaoh's army, which served as both a fighting force and a labor corps.

The lives of all Egyptians centered around the family. Just as in Mesopotamia, marriage was a business arrangement. A couple's parents arranged the marriage, which seems to have taken place at a young age. Once couples were married, having children, especially sons, was a high priority, as indicated by surviving charms to promote fertility and prayers for successful childbirth. Boys continued the family line, and only they could perform the proper burial rites for their father.

Most Egyptian men had only one wife, but among the wealthy some had several wives or concubines. Ordinary women were expected to obey their fathers, husbands, and other men, but they possessed considerable economic and legal rights. They could own land in their own names, operate businesses, and testify in court. Literature and art depict a world in which ordinary husbands and wives enjoyed each other's company.

Migrations, Revivals, and Collapse

While Egyptian civilization flourished in the Nile Valley, various groups migrated throughout the Fertile Crescent and then accommodated themselves to local cultures (Map 2.2). Some settled in the Nile Delta, including a group the Egyptians called Hyksos. Although they were later portrayed as a conquering horde, the Hyksos were actually migrants looking for good land, and their entry into the delta, which began around 1800 B.C.E., was probably gradual and generally peaceful. The newcomers began to worship Egyptian deities and modeled their political structures on those of the Egyptians.

The Hyksos brought with them methods of making bronze that had become common in the eastern Mediterranean by about 2500 B.C.E. (see "Trade and Cross-Cultural

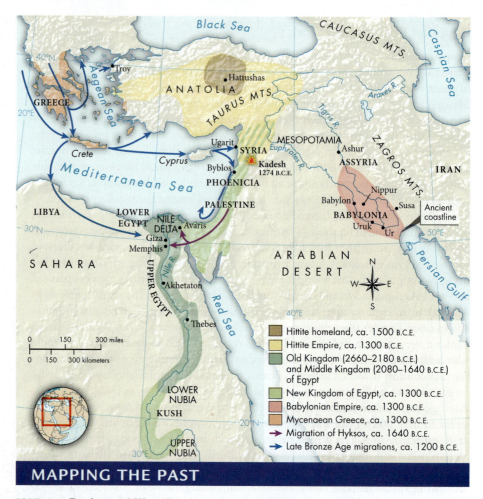

MAPPING THE PAST

MAP 2.2 Empires and Migrations in the Eastern Mediterranean The rise and fall of empires in the eastern Mediterranean were shaped by internal developments, military conflicts, and the migration of peoples to new areas.

ANALYZING THE MAP At what point was the Egyptian empire at its largest? The Hittite Empire? What were the other major powers in the eastern Mediterranean at this time?

CONNECTIONS What were the major effects of the migrations of the Hyksos? Of the late Bronze Age migrations? What clues does the map provide as to why the late Bronze Age migrations had a more powerful impact than those of the Hyksos?

Connections" in Chapter 1) and techniques for casting it into weapons that became standard in Egypt. They thereby brought Egypt fully into the Bronze Age culture of the Mediterranean world. The Hyksos also introduced horse-drawn chariots and the composite bow, made of multiple materials for greater strength, which along with bronze weaponry revolutionized Egyptian warfare. The migration of the Hyksos, combined with a series of famines and internal struggles for power, led Egypt to fragment politically in what later came to be known as the Second Intermediate Period.

In about 1570 B.C.E. a new dynasty of pharaohs arose, pushing the Hyksos out of the delta and conquering territory to the south and northeast. These warrior-pharaohs inaugurated what scholars refer to as the New Kingdom, a period characterized not only by enormous wealth and conscious imperialism but also by a greater sense of insecurity because of new contacts and military engagements. By expanding Egyptian power beyond the Nile Valley, the pharaohs created the first Egyptian empire, and they celebrated their triumphs with giant statues and rich tombs on a scale unparalleled since the pyramids of the Old Kingdom.

The New Kingdom pharaohs include a number of remarkable figures. Among these was Hatshepsut (haht-SHEP-soot) (r. ca. 1479–ca. 1458 B.C.E.), one of the few female pharaohs in Egypt's long history. (See "Individuals in Society: Hatshepsut and Nefertiti," page 48.) Amenhotep III (ah-men-HOE-tep) (r. ca. 1388–ca. 1350 B.C.E.) corresponded with other powerful kings in Babylonia and other kingdoms in the Fertile Crescent. Amenhotep III was succeeded by his son, who took the name Akhenaton (ah-keh-NAH-tuhn) (r. 1351–1334 B.C.E.). He renamed himself as a mark of his changing religious ideas, choosing to worship a new sun-god, Aton, instead of the traditional Amon or Ra. Akhenaton's wife Nefertiti (nehf-uhr-TEE-tee) supported his religious ideas, but this new religion, imposed from above, failed to find a place among the people, and after his death traditional religious practices returned.

One of the key challenges facing the pharaohs after Akhenaton was the expansion of the kingdom of the Hittites. At about the same time that the Sumerians were establishing city-states, speakers of **Indo-European languages** migrated into Anatolia, modern-day Turkey. Indo-European is a large family of languages that includes English, most of the languages of modern Europe, ancient Greek, Latin, Persian, Hindi, Bengali, and Sanskrit (for more on Sanskrit, see "The Aryans During the Vedic Age, ca. 1500–500 B.C.E." in Chapter 3). It also includes Hittite, the language of one of the peoples who migrated into this area. Information about the Hittites comes from archaeological sources and also from written cuneiform tablets that provide details about politics and economic life. These records indicate that beginning about 1600 B.C.E. Hittite kings began to conquer more territory (see Map 2.2). As the Hittites expanded southward, they came into conflict with the Egyptians, who were establishing their own larger empire. There were a number of battles, but both sides seem to have recognized the impossibility of defeating the other, and in 1258 B.C.E. the Egyptian king Ramesses II (r. ca. 1290–1224 B.C.E.) and the Hittite king Hattusili III (hah-too-SEE-lee) (r. ca. 1267–1237 B.C.E.) concluded a peace treaty.

The treaty brought peace between the Egyptians and the Hittites for a time, but this stability did not last. Within several decades of the treaty, groups of seafaring peoples whom the Egyptians called "Sea Peoples" raided, migrated, and marauded in the eastern Mediterranean, disrupting trade and in some cases looting and destroying cities. These raids, combined with the expansion of

Indo-European languages A large family of languages that includes English, most of the languages of modern Europe, ancient Greek, Latin, Persian, Hindi, Bengali, and Sanskrit.

Hittite Archer in a Chariot In this stylized stone carving made about 1000 B.C.E. in Anatolia (modern-day Turkey), a Hittite archer driven in a chariot shoots toward his foes, while a victim of an earlier shot is trampled beneath the horse's hooves. The arrows might have been tipped with iron, which was becoming a more common material for weapons and tools.

(Dagli Orti/REX/Shutterstock)

Hatshepsut and Nefertiti

Granite head of Hatshepsut.

(bpk Bildagentur/Aegyptisches Museum und Paprussammkung, Staatliche Museen, Berlin, Germany/Photo: Margarete Büsing/Art Resource, NY)

Painted limestone bust of Nefertiti.

(bpk Bildagentur/Aegyptisches Museum und Paprussammkung, Staatliche Museen, Berlin, Germany/Photo: Margarete Büsing/Art Resource, NY)

EGYPTIANS UNDERSTOOD THE PHARAOH TO be the living embodiment of the god Horus, the source of law and morality, and the mediator between gods and humans. The pharaoh's siblings and children were also viewed as in some ways divine. Because of this, a pharaoh often took his sister or half-sister as one of his wives, a practice that imitated the behavior of the gods in Egyptian mythology. This concentrated divine blood set the pharaonic family apart from other Egyptians (who did not marry close relatives). A pharaoh chose one of his wives to be the "Great Royal Wife," or principal queen. Often this was a relative, though sometimes it was one of the foreign princesses who married pharaohs to establish political alliances.

The familial connection with the divine allowed a handful of women to rule in their own right in Egypt's long history. We know the names of four female pharaohs, of whom the most famous was Hatshepsut. She was the sister and wife of Thutmose II and, after he died, served as regent—as adviser and co-ruler—for her young stepson Thutmose III, who was the son of another woman. Hatshepsut sent trading expeditions and sponsored artists and architects, ushering in a period of artistic creativity and economic prosperity. She built one of the world's great buildings, an elaborate terraced temple at Deir el Bahri, which eventually served as her tomb. Hatshepsut's status as a powerful female ruler was difficult for Egyptians to conceptualize, and she is often depicted in male dress or with a false beard, thus looking more like the male rulers who were the norm. After her death, Thutmose III tried to destroy all evidence that she had ever ruled, smashing statues and scratching her name off inscriptions, perhaps because of personal animosity and perhaps because he wanted to erase the fact that a woman had once been pharaoh.

Though female pharaohs were very rare, many royal women had power through their position as Great Royal Wives. The most famous was Nefertiti (ca. 1370–1330 B.C.E.), the wife of Akhenaton. Her name means "the perfect (or beautiful) woman has come." Nefertiti used her position to spread the new religion of the sun-god Aton. Together she and Akhenaton built a new palace at Akhetaten, the present-day Amarna, away from the old centers of power. There they developed the cult of Aton to the exclusion of the traditional deities. Nearly the only literary survivor of their religious belief is the "Hymn to Aton," which declares Aton to be the only god. It describes Nefertiti as "the great royal consort whom he, Akhenaton, loves. The mistress of the Two Lands, Upper and Lower Egypt."

Nefertiti is often shown as being the same size as her husband, and in some inscriptions she is performing religious rituals that would normally have been carried out only by the pharaoh. The exact details of her power are hard to determine, however. An older theory held that her husband removed her from power, though there is also speculation that she may have ruled secretly in her own right after his death. Her tomb has long since disappeared, though some scholars believe that an unidentified mummy discovered in 2003 in Egypt's Valley of the Kings may be Nefertiti's.

QUESTIONS FOR ANALYSIS

1. Why might it have been difficult for Egyptians to accept a female ruler?
2. What opportunities do hereditary monarchies such as that of ancient Egypt provide for women? How does this fit with gender hierarchies in which men are understood as superior?

the Assyrians (see "Assyria, the Military Monarchy"), led to the collapse of the Hittite Empire and the fragmentation of the Egyptian empire. There is evidence of drought, and some scholars have suggested that a major volcanic explosion in Iceland cooled the climate for several years, leading to a series of poor harvests. All of these developments are part of a general "Bronze Age Collapse" in the period around 1200 B.C.E. that historians see as a major turning point.

The political and military story of battles, waves of migrations, and the rise and fall of empires can mask striking continuities in the history of Egypt and its neighbors. Disrupted peoples and newcomers shared practical concepts of agriculture and metallurgy with one another, and wheeled vehicles allowed merchants to transact business over long distances. Merchants, migrants, and conquerors carried their gods and goddesses with them, and religious beliefs and practices blended and changed. Cuneiform tablets, wall inscriptions, and paintings testify to commercial exchanges and cultural accommodation, adoption, and adaptation, as well as war and conquest.

Iron Age Period beginning about 1100 B.C.E. when iron became the most important material for weapons and tools in some parts of the world.

Iron and the Emergence of New States

The Bronze Age Collapse was a time of massive political and economic disruption, but it was also a period of the spread of new technologies, especially iron. Iron is the most common element in the earth, but most iron on or near the earth's surface occurs in the form of ore, which must be smelted at high temperatures to extract the metal. This process was invented independently during the second millennium B.C.E. in several parts of the world, including Anatolia (modern-day Turkey), Nigeria, and most likely southern India. Early iron was too brittle to be of much use, but iron-workers continued to experiment and improve their products, and iron weapons gradually became stronger and cheaper than their bronze counterparts. Thus, in the schema of dividing history into periods according to the main material out of which tools are made (see "Understanding the Early Human Past" in Chapter 1), the **Iron Age** began in about 1100 B.C.E. Iron weapons became important items of trade around the Mediterranean and throughout the Tigris and Euphrates Valleys, and the technology for making them traveled as well.

The decline of Egypt allowed new powers to emerge. South of Egypt along the Nile was a region called Nubia, which as early as 2000 B.C.E. served as a conduit of trade through which a variety of products flowed north from sub-Saharan Africa. As Egypt expanded during the New Kingdom, it took over northern Nubia, incorporating it into the growing Egyptian empire. The Nubians adopted many features of Egyptian culture, including Egyptian gods, the use of hieroglyphs, and the building of pyramids. Many Nubians became officials in the Egyptian bureaucracy and officers in the army, and there was significant intermarriage between the two groups.

Nubian Cylinder Sheath This small silver sheath made about 520 B.C.E., perhaps for holding rolled papyrus, shows a winged goddess on one side and the Egyptian god Amon-Ra (not visible in this photograph) on the other. It and others like it were found in the tombs of the king of Kush and suggest ways that Egyptian artistic styles and religious ideas influenced cultures farther up the Nile.

(Cylinder sheath of Amani-natake-lebte, Napatan Period, reign of King Amani-natake-lebte, 538–519 B.C. [gilded silver & colored paste], Nubian/Museum of Fine Arts, Boston, Massachusetts, USA/Bridgeman Images)

With the contraction of the Egyptian empire, an independent kingdom, Kush, rose to power in Nubia, with its capital at Napata in what is now Sudan. The Kushites conquered southern Egypt, and in 727 B.C.E. the Kushite king Piye (PIGH) (r. ca. 747–716 B.C.E.) swept through the entire Nile Valley to the delta in the north. United once again, Egypt enjoyed a brief period of peace during which the Egyptian culture continued to influence that of its conquerors. In the seventh century B.C.E. invading Assyrians pushed the Kushites out of Egypt, and the Kushite rulers moved their capital farther up the Nile to Meroë (MER-oh-ee), where they built hundreds of pyramids. Meroë became a center of iron production, exporting iron goods to much of Africa and across the Red Sea and the Indian Ocean to India. Gold and cotton textiles also provided wealth to the Kushite kingdom, which in the third century B.C.E. developed its own alphabet.

While Kush expanded in the southern Nile Valley, another group rose to prominence along the Mediterranean coast of modern Lebanon. These people established the prosperous commercial centers of Tyre (TIRE), Sidon, and Byblos. They were master shipbuilders, and from about 1100 B.C.E. to 700 B.C.E. many of the residents of these cities became the seaborne merchants of the Mediterranean. Their most valued products were purple and blue textiles, from which originated their Greek name, **Phoenicians** (fih-NEE-shuhns), meaning "Purple People." They also worked bronze and iron, which they shipped processed or as ore, and made and traded glass products, gold, ivory, and other types of rare goods. Phoenician ships often carried hundreds of jars of wine, and the Phoenicians introduced grape growing to new regions around the Mediterranean, dramatically increasing the amount of wine available for consumption and trade.

Phoenicians People of the prosperous city-states in what is now Lebanon who traded and founded colonies throughout the Mediterranean and spread the phonetic alphabet.

The variety and quality of the Phoenicians' trade goods generally made them welcome visitors. They established colonies and trading posts throughout the Mediterranean and as far west as the Atlantic coast of modern-day Portugal. The Phoenicians' voyages brought them into contact with the Greeks, to whom they introduced many aspects of the older and more urbanized cultures of Mesopotamia and Egypt.

The Phoenicians' overwhelming cultural achievement was the spread of a completely phonetic system of writing—that is, an alphabet (Figure 2.2). Writers of cuneiform and hieroglyphics had developed signs that were used to represent sounds, but these were always used with a much larger number of ideograms. Sometime around 1800 B.C.E. workers in the Sinai Peninsula, which was under Egyptian control, began to use only phonetic signs to write, with each sign designating one sound. This system vastly simplified writing and reading and spread among common people as a practical means of record keeping and communication. Egyptian scribes and officials continued to use hieroglyphics, but the Phoenicians adapted the simpler system for their own language and spread it around the Mediterranean. The Greeks modified this alphabet for their own language, and the Romans later based their alphabet—the script we use to write English today—on Greek. Alphabets based on the Phoenician alphabet were also created in the Persian Empire and formed the basis of Hebrew, Arabic, and various alphabets of South and Central Asia.

Phoenician Settlements in the Mediterranean

Phoenicia, ca. 750 B.C.E.
Area of Phoenician settlement
• Settlement
→ Phoenician trade route

SPAIN
ITALY
ANATOLIA
Carthage
Mediterranean Sea
Byblos
Sidon
Tyre

HIEROGLYPHIC	REPRESENTS	UGARITIC	PHOENICIAN	GREEK	ROMAN
〉	Throw stick	T	𐤀	Γ	G
𓀠	Man with raised arms	E	𐤄	E	E
⌒	Basket with handle	▷	✓	K	K
∿∿∿	Water	⊢	⌇	M	M
୧	Snake	⊶	丶	N	N
◉	Eye	◁	O	O	O
⌒	Mouth	⊨	?	Π	P
𓁹	Head	⊟	9	P	R
𓆳	Pool with lotus flowers	⊲⊺⊳	W	Σ	S
⊏⊐	House	⊥⊥	9	B	B
𓄤	Ox-head	⊶	K	A	A

FIGURE 2.2 Origins of the Alphabet List of hieroglyphic, Ugaritic, Phoenician, Greek, and Roman sign forms.

(Source: A. B. Knapp, *The History and Culture of Ancient Western Asia and Egypt.* Reproduced with permission of Wadsworth Publishing Company in the format Educational/Instructional Program via Copyright Clearance Center.)

The Hebrews

How did the Hebrews create an enduring written religious tradition?

The legacy of another people who took advantage of Egypt's collapse to found an independent state may have been even more far-reaching than that of the Phoenicians. For a period of several centuries, the Hebrews controlled first one and then two small states on the western end of the Fertile Crescent. The Hebrews created a new form of religious belief, a monotheism based on the worship of an all-powerful god they called **Yahweh** (YAH-way). Beginning in the late seventh century B.C.E. the Hebrews began to write down their religious ideas, traditions, laws, advice literature, prayers, hymns, history, and prophecies in a series of books. These were gathered together centuries later to form the Hebrew Bible, which Christians later adopted and termed the "Old Testament" to parallel specific Christian writings in the "New Testament." The Hebrew Bible later became the core of the Hebrews' religion, Judaism, named after Judah, the southern of the two Hebrew kingdoms. Jews today revere these texts, as do many Christians, and Muslims respect them, all of which gives them particular importance.

Yahweh All-powerful god of the Hebrew people and the basis for the enduring religious traditions of Judaism.

The Hebrew State

The Hebrews were nomadic pastoralists who may have migrated into the Nile Delta from the east seeking good land for their herds of sheep and goats. According to the Hebrew Bible, they were enslaved by the Egyptians but were led out of Egypt by a charismatic leader named Moses. The Hebrews settled in the area between the Mediterranean and the Jordan River known as Canaan and were organized into tribes, each tribe consisting of numerous families who thought of themselves as related to one another. They slowly adopted agriculture and, not surprisingly, at times worshipped

Mediterranean Sea
Samaria
Jerusalem
Dead Sea
EGYPT
SINAI
Gulf of Suez
Possible location of Mt. Sinai

➤ Possible route of the Exodus, ca. 1250 B.C.E.
☐ Solomon's kingdom, ca. 950 B.C.E.
☐ Israel, ca. 800 B.C.E.
☐ Judah, ca. 800 B.C.E.

The Hebrew Exodus and State, ca. 1250–800 B.C.E.

the agricultural gods of their neighbors. In this they followed the common historical pattern of newcomers by adapting the culture of an older, well-established people.

The Bible reports that the greatest danger to the Hebrews came from a group known as the Philistines (FIH-luh-steenz), who migrated to and established a kingdom in Canaan. The Hebrews found a leader in Saul, who with his men fought the Philistines. Saul subsequently established a monarchy over the Hebrew tribes, an event conventionally dated to about 1025 B.C.E. Saul's work was carried on by David of Bethlehem, who captured the city of Jerusalem, which he made the religious and political center of the realm. David's son Solomon (r. ca. 965–925 B.C.E.) launched a building program that the biblical narrative describes as including cities, palaces, fortresses, and roads. The most symbolic of these projects was the Temple of Jerusalem. The Temple of Jerusalem was intended to be the religious heart of the kingdom, a symbol of Hebrew unity and of Yahweh's approval of the Hebrew state.

This state did not last long. At Solomon's death his kingdom broke into political halves. The northern part became Israel, with its capital at Samaria, and the southern half was Judah, with Jerusalem remaining its center. War broke out between the northern and southern halves, and the Assyrians wiped out the northern kingdom in 722 B.C.E. Judah survived numerous invasions until the Babylonians crushed it in 587 B.C.E. The survivors were sent into exile in Babylonia, a period commonly known as the Babylonian Captivity. In 538 B.C.E. the Persian king Cyrus the Great conquered the Babylonians and permitted some forty thousand exiles to return to Jerusalem (see "The Rise and Expansion of the Persian Empire" and "Global Viewpoints: Rulers and Divine Favor for Babylonians and Hebrews," page 56). They rebuilt the temple, although politically the area was simply part of the Persian Empire.

The Jewish Religion

During and especially after the Babylonian Captivity, the most important Hebrew texts of history, law, and ethics were edited and brought together in the Torah, the first five books of the Hebrew Bible. Fundamental to an understanding of the Jewish religion is the concept of the Covenant, an agreement that people believed to exist between themselves and Yahweh. According to the Bible, Yahweh appeared to the tribal leader Abraham, promising him that he would be blessed, as would his descendants, if they followed Yahweh. (Because Judaism, Christianity, and Islam all regard this event as foundational, they are referred to as the "Abrahamic religions.") Yahweh next appeared to Moses when he was leading the Hebrews out of Egypt, and Yahweh made a covenant with the Hebrews: if they worshipped Yahweh as their only god, he would consider them his chosen people and protect them from their enemies. Individuals such as Abraham and Moses who acted as intermediaries between Yahweh and the Hebrew people were known as "prophets." Much of the Hebrew Bible consists of writings in the prophets' voices, understood as messages from Yahweh to the Hebrews.

Worship was embodied in a series of rules of behavior, the Ten Commandments, which Yahweh gave to Moses; these required certain kinds of religious observances and forbade the Hebrews to steal, kill, lie, or commit adultery, thus creating a system of ethical absolutes. From the Ten Commandments a complex system of rules of conduct was created and later written down as Hebrew law. The later prophets such as Isaiah created a system of ethical monotheism, in which goodness was understood to come from a single transcendent god whom the Hebrews were to worship, and in which religious obligations included fair and just behavior toward other people as well as rituals.

Like Mesopotamian deities, Yahweh punished people, but the Hebrews also believed he would protect them all, not simply kings and powerful priests, and make them prosper if they obeyed his commandments. The religion of the Hebrews was thus addressed to not only the elites but also the individual. Because kings or other political leaders were not essential to its practice, the rise or fall of a kingdom was not crucial to the religion's continued existence. Religious leaders were important in Judaism, but personally following the instructions of Yahweh was the central task for observant Jews in the ancient world.

Hebrew Society

The Hebrews were originally nomadic, but they adopted settled agriculture in Canaan, and some lived in cities. Over time, communal use of land gave way to family or private ownership, and devotions to the traditions of Judaism replaced tribal identity.

Family relationships reflected evolving circumstances. Marriage and the family were fundamentally important in Jewish life. Celibacy was frowned upon, and almost all major Jewish thinkers and priests were married. As in Mesopotamia and Egypt, marriage was a family matter, too important to be left solely to the whims of young people. The bearing of children was seen in some ways as a religious function. Sons were especially desired because they maintained the family bloodline while keeping ancestral property in the family. A firstborn son became the head of the household upon his father's death. Mothers oversaw the early education of the children, but as boys grew older, their fathers provided more of their education.

The development of urban life among Jews created new economic opportunities, especially in crafts and trade. People specialized in certain occupations, and, as in most ancient societies, these crafts were family trades.

The Assyrians and the Persians

Small kingdoms like those of the Phoenicians and the Jews could exist only in the absence of a major power. In the ninth century B.C.E. one major power arose in the form of the Assyrians, who starting in northern Mesopotamia created an empire through often-brutal military conquests. And from a base in what is now southern Iran, the Persians established an even larger empire, developing effective institutions of government.

> **How did the Assyrians and the Persians consolidate their power and control the subjects of their empires?**

Assyria, the Military Monarchy

Starting from a base in northern Mesopotamia around 900 B.C.E., the Assyrians began a campaign of expansion and domination, conquering, exacting tribute, and building new fortified towns, palaces, and temples. By means of almost constant warfare, the Assyrians created an empire that stretched from their capital of Nineveh on the Tigris River to central Egypt. Revolt against the Assyrians inevitably promised the rebels bloody battles and cruel sieges followed by surrender, accompanied by systematic torture and slaughter, and sometimes deportations.

Assyrian methods were certainly harsh, but in practical terms Assyria's success was due primarily to the size of its army and to the army's sophisticated and effective

Assyrian Warriors Attack a City In this Assyrian carving from a royal throne room made about 865 B.C.E., warriors cross a river on inflated skins, which both support them and provide air for breathing underwater. Such innovative techniques, combined with a large army and effective military organization, allowed the Assyrians to establish a large empire. (British Museum, London, UK/© 2004 Werner Forman/TopFoto/The Image Works)

military organization. In addition, the Assyrians developed a wide variety of siege machinery and techniques, including excavations to undermine city walls and battering rams to knock down walls and gates. Never before in this area had anyone applied such technical knowledge to warfare. The Assyrians also knew how to coordinate their efforts, both in open battle and in siege warfare. Not only did the Assyrians know how to win battles, but they also knew how to take advantage of their victories. As early as the eighth century B.C.E., the Assyrian kings began to organize their conquered territories into an empire. The lands closest to Assyria became provinces governed directly by Assyrian officials. Kingdoms beyond the provinces were not annexed but became dependent states.

By the seventh century B.C.E. Assyrian power seemed firmly established. Yet the downfall of Assyria was swift and complete. Babylon won its independence in 626 B.C.E. and joined forces with a new group, the Medes, an Indo-European-speaking people from Persia. Together the Babylonians and the Medes destroyed the Assyrian Empire in 612 B.C.E., paving the way for the rise of the Persians.

The Rise and Expansion of the Persian Empire

As we have seen, Assyria rose to power from a base in the Tigris and Euphrates River Valleys of Mesopotamia, which had seen many earlier empires. The Assyrians were defeated by a coalition that included not only a Mesopotamian power—Babylon—but also a people with a base of power in a part of the world that had not been the site of earlier urbanized states: Persia (modern-day Iran) (Map 2.3).

Iran's geographical position and topography explain its traditional role as the highway between western and eastern Asia. Nomadic peoples migrating south from the broad steppes of Russia and Central Asia have streamed into Iran throughout much of history. (For an in-depth discussion of these groups, see Chapter 12.) Confronting the uncrossable salt deserts, most have turned either westward or eastward, moving on until they reached the advanced and wealthy urban centers of Mesopotamia and India. Cities did emerge along these routes, however, and Iran became the area where nomads met urban dwellers.

MAP 2.3 The Assyrian and Persian Empires, ca. 1000–500 B.C.E. The Assyrian Empire at its height around 650 B.C.E. included almost all of the old centers of power in the ancient Near East. By 500 B.C.E., however, the Persian Empire was far larger, extending from the Mediterranean Sea to the Indus River.

Among these nomads were Indo-European-speaking peoples who migrated into this area about 1000 B.C.E. with their flocks and herds. They were also horse breeders, and the horse gave them a decisive military advantage over those who already lived in the area. One of these groups was the Medes, who settled in northern Iran. With the rise of the Medes, the balance of power in western Asia shifted east of Mesopotamia for the first time.

In 550 B.C.E. Cyrus the Great (r. 559–530 B.C.E.), king of the Persians (another Indo-European-speaking group) and one of the most remarkable statesmen of antiquity, conquered the Medes. Cyrus then set out to win control of the shore of the Mediterranean and thus of the terminal ports of the great trade routes that crossed Iran and Anatolia and to secure eastern Iran from the threats of nomadic invasions. In a series of major campaigns Cyrus achieved both goals, thereby consolidating the Persian Empire, though he ultimately died on the battlefield in eastern Iran.

After his victories, Cyrus made sure the Persians were portrayed as liberators, and in some cases he was more benevolent than most conquerors. According to his own account, he freed all the captive peoples, including the Hebrews, who were living in forced exile in Babylon. He returned the Hebrews' sacred objects to them and allowed those who wanted to do so to return to Jerusalem, where he paid for the rebuilding of their temple. (See "Global Viewpoints: Rulers and Divine Favor for Babylonians and Hebrews," page 56.)

Cyrus's successors continued the Persian conquests, creating the largest empire the world had yet seen. Darius (r. 521–486 B.C.E.) conquered Scythia in Central Asia, along with much of Thrace and Macedonia, areas north of the Aegean Sea (see Map 2.3). Darius began to call himself "King of Kings." Invasions of Greece by Darius and his son Xerxes were unsuccessful, but the Persian Empire lasted another two hundred years, until it became part of the empire of Alexander the Great (see "From Polis to Monarchy, 404–200 B.C.E." in Chapter 5).

Rulers and Divine Favor for Babylonians and Hebrews

In the ancient world, individuals who established large empires through conquest often subsequently proclaimed that their triumph was the result of divine favor, and they honored the gods of the regions they conquered. King Cyrus the Great of Persia appears to have followed this tradition in at least some of his conquests. A text written in cuneiform on a sixth-century-B.C.E. Babylonian clay cylinder presents Cyrus describing the way in which the main Babylonian god, Marduk, selected him to conquer Babylon and restore proper government and worship. Cyrus is also portrayed as divinely chosen in the book of Isaiah in Hebrew Scripture, probably written sometime in the late sixth century B.C.E., after Cyrus allowed the Jews to return to Jerusalem. Here it is mainly the Hebrew god Yahweh who speaks, explaining why he has made Cyrus victorious even though Cyrus is not a Jew.

The Cyrus Cylinder

■ I am Cyrus, king of the universe, the great king, the powerful king, king of Babylon, king of Sumer and Akkad, king of the four quarters of the world. . . .

When I went as harbinger of peace i[nt]o Babylon I founded my sovereign residence within the palace amid celebration and rejoicing. Marduk, the great lord, bestowed on me as my destiny the great magnanimity of one who loves Babylon, and I every day sought him out in awe. My vast troops marched peaceably in Babylon, and the whole of [Sumer] and Akkad had nothing to fear. I sought the welfare of the city of Babylon and all its sanctuaries. As for the population of Babylon, . . . [w]ho as if without div[ine intention] had endured a yoke not decreed for them, I soothed their weariness, I freed them from their bond. . . . Marduk, the great lord, rejoiced at [my good] deeds, and he pronounced a sweet blessing over me, Cyrus, the king who fears him, and over Cambyses, the son [my] issue, [and over] all my troops, that we might proceed further at his exalted command.

The Book of Isaiah, Chapter 45

■ Thus said the Lord to Cyrus, His anointed one— whose right hand He has grasped, Treading down nations before him, Ungirding the loins of kings, Opening doors before him, and letting no gate stay shut: I will march before you, and level the hills that loom up; I will shatter doors of bronze and cut down iron bars. I will give you treasures concealed in the dark and secret hoards—So that you may know that it is I the LORD, the God of Israel, who call you by name. For the sake of My servant Jacob, Israel My chosen one, I call you by name, I hail you by title, though you have not known Me. I am the LORD, and there is none else; beside Me, there is no God. I engird you, though you have not known Me. . . .

It was I who roused him [that is, Cyrus] for victory, and who level all roads for him. He shall rebuild My city, and let My exiled people go, without price and without payment—said the LORD of hosts.

QUESTIONS FOR ANALYSIS

1. How would you compare the portrayal of Cyrus and the balance between divine and human actions in the two texts?
2. The Babylonians were polytheistic, and the Hebrews were monotheistic. How does this shape the way divine actions and favor are portrayed in the texts?
3. Both of these texts have been very influential in establishing the largely positive historical view of Cyrus. What limitations might there be in using these as historical sources?

Sources: Cylinder inscription translation by Irving Finkel, curator of Cuneiform Collections at the British Museum, www.britishmuseum.org. © The Trustees of the British Museum. All rights reserved. Used by permission of The British Museum; "The Book of Isaiah" in *Tanakh: A New Translation of The Holy Scriptures According to the Traditional Hebrew Text*.

The Persians also knew how to preserve the peace they had won on the battlefield. To govern the empire, they created an efficient administrative system based in their newly built capital city of Persepolis. Under Darius, they divided the empire into districts and appointed either Persian or local nobles as administrators called satraps to head each one. The satrap controlled local government, collected taxes, heard legal cases, and maintained order. He was assisted by a council and also by officials and army leaders sent from Persepolis who made sure that he knew the will of the king and that the king knew what was going on in the provinces. The Persians allowed the peoples they conquered to maintain their own customs and beliefs as long as they paid the proper amount of taxes and did not rebel, thus creating a culture that blended older and newer religious traditions and ways of seeing the world. Because Persian art depicted both Persians and non-Persians realistically, it is an excellent source of information about the weapons, tools, clothing, and even hairstyles of many peoples of the area.

Communication and trade were eased by a sophisticated system of roads linking the empire from the coast of Asia Minor to the valley of the Indus River. These roads meant that the king was usually in close touch with officials and subjects, and they simplified the defense of the empire by making it easier to move Persian armies. The roads also aided the flow of trade, which Persian rulers further encouraged by building canals, including one that linked the Red Sea and the Nile.

The Religion of Zoroaster

Persian religion was originally polytheistic and tied to nature, with Ahuramazda (ah-HOOR-uh-MAZ-duh) as the chief god. Around 600 B.C.E. the ideas of Zoroaster (zoh-roh-ASS-tuhr), a thinker and preacher whose dates are uncertain, began to gain prominence. Zoroaster is regarded as the author of key religious texts, which were later gathered together in a collection of sacred texts called the Avesta. He introduced new spiritual concepts, stressing devotion to Ahuramazda alone and emphasizing the individual's responsibility to choose between the forces of creation, truth, and order and those of nothingness, chaos, falsehood, and disorder. Zoroaster taught that people possessed free will and that they must rely on their own consciences to guide them through an active life in which they focused on "good thoughts, good words, and good deeds." Their decisions were crucial, he warned, for there would come a time of reckoning. At the end of time, the forces of order would win, and the victorious Ahuramazda, like the Egyptian god Osiris, would preside over a last judgment to determine each person's eternal fate.

Zoroaster's writings were communicated by teachers, and King Darius began to use Zoroastrian language and images. Under the protection of the Persian kings, Zoroastrian ideas spread throughout Iran and the rest of the Persian Empire, and then into central China. **Zoroastrianism** survived the fall of the Persian Empire to influence Christianity, Islam, and Buddhism, largely because of its belief in a just life on earth and a happy afterlife. Good behavior in the world, even though unrecognized at the time, would receive ample reward in the hereafter. Evil, no matter how powerful a person had been in life, would be punished after death. In some form or another, Zoroastrian concepts still pervade many modern religions, and Zoroastrianism still exists as a religion.

Zoroastrianism Religion based on the teachings of Zoroaster that emphasized the individual's responsibility to choose between good and evil.

Chapter Summary

Beginning about 5,000 years ago, people in some parts of the world invented writing, in large part to meet the needs of the state. States first developed in the southern part of Mesopotamia known as Sumer, where priests and rulers invented ways to control and organize people who lived in cities reliant on irrigation. Conquerors from the north unified Mesopotamian city-states into larger empires and spread Mesopotamian culture over a large area.

During the third millennium B.C.E. Egypt grew into a cohesive state under a single ruler. For long stretches of history, Egypt was prosperous and secure in the Nile Valley, although at times various groups migrated into or invaded and conquered this kingdom. During the period known as the New Kingdom, warrior-kings created a large Egyptian empire. After the collapse of the New Kingdom, the Nubian rulers of Kush conquered Egypt, and another group, the Phoenicians, came to dominate trade in the Mediterranean, spreading a letter alphabet. Another group, the Hebrews, created a new form of religious belief based on the worship of a single all-powerful god.

In the ninth century B.C.E. the Assyrians used a huge army and sophisticated military tactics to create an empire from a base in northern Mesopotamia. The Persians established an even larger empire, developing effective institutions of government and building roads. The Persians generally allowed their subjects to continue their own customs, traditions, and religions. Around 600 B.C.E. a new religion grew in Persia based on the teachings of the prophet Zoroaster.

CONNECTIONS

"History is written by the victors" goes a common saying often incorrectly attributed to British prime minister Winston Churchill, who led Britain during World War II. This is not always true; people who have been vanquished in wars or devastated by oppression have certainly made their stories known. But in other ways it is always true, for writing created records and therefore was the origin of what many people understand as history. Writing was invented to serve the needs of people who lived close to one another in cities and states, and almost everyone who could write lived in states. Because most written history, including this book, concentrates on areas with states and complex societies, the next two chapters examine the societies that were developing in India and China during the period discussed in this chapter. In Chapter 5 we pick up on developments in the Mediterranean that link to those in Mesopotamia, Egypt, and Persia discussed in this chapter.

It is important to remember that, as was the spread of agriculture, the growth of the state was a slow process. States became the most powerful and most densely populated forms of human society, and today almost everyone on the planet is at least hypothetically a citizen of a state or, as we now call them, nation (or sometimes of more than one, if he or she has dual citizenship). Just three hundred years ago, however, only about a third of the world was governed by states; in the rest of the world, people lived in bands of foragers, villages led by kin leaders, family groups of pastoralists, chiefdoms, confederations of tribes, or other forms of social organization. In 500 B.C.E. perhaps only a little over 5 percent of the world's population lived in states.

The first inquiries into the past in the West were written at just about this time, by the Greek writer Herodotus (heh-ROD-duh-tuhs) (ca. 484–ca. 425 B.C.E.), who used the word *historia* to describe them, from which we get the word *history*. In his histories, Herodotus pays primary attention to the Persians and the Greeks, both of whom had writing and states, but he also discusses many peoples who had neither. In their attempts to provide a balanced account of all the world's peoples, not just those who lived in places where writing developed, historians today are also looking beyond written sources. Those sources invariably present only part of the story, as Winston Churchill — a historian as well as a political leader — noted in something he actually *did* say: "History will bear me out, particularly as I shall write that history myself."

CHAPTER 2   Review and Explore

Identify Key Terms

Identify and explain the significance of each item below.

polytheism (p. 37)   **pharaoh** (p. 43)   **Yahweh** (p. 51)

cuneiform (p. 38)   **Indo-European languages** (p. 47)   **Zoroastrianism** (p. 57)

epic poem (p. 39)   **Iron Age** (p. 49)

Hammurabi's law code (p. 41)   **Phoenicians** (p. 50)

Review the Main Ideas

Answer the focus questions from each section of the chapter.

1. How does writing shape what we can know about the past, and how did writing develop to meet the needs of cities and states? (p. 34)

2. How did the peoples of Mesopotamia form states and develop new technologies and institutions? (p. 36)

3. How did the Egyptians create a prosperous and long-lasting society? (p. 43)

4. How did the Hebrews create an enduring written religious tradition? (p. 51)

5. How did the Assyrians and the Persians consolidate their power and control the subjects of their empires? (p. 53)

Make Comparisons and Connections

Analyze the larger developments and continuities within and across chapters.

1. Thinking about continuities, as well as change, what aspects of life in the Neolithic period continued with little change in the states of Mesopotamia and Egypt? What were the most important differences?

2. Most peoples in the ancient world gained influence over others and became significant in history through military conquest and the establishment of states and empires. By contrast, how did the Phoenicians and the Hebrews shape the development of world history? What does this suggest about the importance of cultural as well as political developments in world history?

3. How were the empires that developed in Mesopotamia, Egypt, and Persia similar to one another? Which of the characteristics you have identified as a similarity do you predict will also be found in later empires, and why?

TIMELINE

| | SOUTHWEST ASIA | AFRICA | AMERICAS | ASIA | EUROPE |

SOUTHWEST ASIA

← ca. 3800 B.C.E. Establishment of first cities in Sumer

◆ ca. 3200 B.C.E. Earliest surviving cuneiform writing

◆ ca. 2500 B.C.E. Bronze weaponry becomes common in Mesopotamia

◆ ca. 2300 B.C.E. Establishment of Akkadian empire

AFRICA

ca. 2660–2180 B.C.E. Old Kingdom in Egypt

AMERICAS

ca. 2500 B.C.E. First cities in Peru **(Ch. 11)**

ASIA

ca. 2800–1800 B.C.E. Harappan civilization in India **(Ch. 3)**

EUROPE

| 3000 B.C.E | 2500 B.C.E. | 2000 B.C.E. |

Suggested Resources

BOOKS

Briant, Pierre. *From Cyrus to Alexander: A History of the Persian Empire*. 2002. A superb treatment of the entire Persian Empire.

Edwards, David N. *The Nubian Past*. 2004. Studies the history of Nubia and the Sudan, incorporating archaeological evidence to supplement historical sources.

Goldenberg, Robert. *The Origins of Judaism: From Canaan to the Rise of Islam*. 2007. Examines the development of Jewish ideas and traditions.

Kriwaczek, Paul. *In Search of Zarathustra: Across Iran and Central Asia to Find the World's First Prophet*. 2004. An award-winning BBC journalist follows the legacy of Zoroaster back through time.

Leick, Gwendolyn. *The Babylonians*. 2002. An introduction to all aspects of Babylonian life and culture.

Markoe, Glenn E. *The Phoenicians*. 2000. Presents these seafarers at home and abroad in the Mediterranean.

McDowell, A. G. *Village Life in Ancient Egypt: Laundry Lists and Love Songs*. 1999. A fascinating study of the basic social and economic factors of Egyptian life.

Podany, Amanda. *Brotherhood of Kings: How International Relations Shaped the Ancient Near East*. 2010. Examines a thousand years of diplomacy among rulers.

Provan, Iain, V. Philips Long, and Tremper Longman III. *A Biblical History of Israel*, 2d ed. 2015. A history of ancient Israel that relies primarily on the biblical text.

Van de Mieroop, Marc. *A History of the Ancient Near East, 3000–332 B.C.E.* 2010. A concise history from Sumerian cities to Alexander the Great.

Visicato, Giuseppe. *The Power and the Writing: The Early Scribes of Mesopotamia*. 2000. Studies the practical importance of early Mesopotamian scribes.

Vivante, Bella. *Daughters of Gaia: Women of the Ancient World*. 2008. Explores the political, religious, and economic activities of actual women, and also examines ideas about gender.

ca. 1200 B.C.E. Bronze Age Collapse; destruction and drought

722 B.C.E. Kingdom of Israel destroyed by the Assyrians

1792–1750 B.C.E. Hammurabi rules Babylon

ca. 1100 B.C.E. Beginning of the Iron Age; Phoenicians begin to trade in the Mediterranean

ca. 1600 B.C.E. Hittites begin to expand their empire

ca. 965–925 B.C.E. Hebrew kingdom ruled by Solomon

587 B.C.E. Kingdom of Judah destroyed by the Babylonians

ca. 900–612 B.C.E. Assyrian Empire

550 B.C.E. Cyrus the Great consolidates the Persian Empire

ca. 1570–1070 B.C.E. New Kingdom in Egypt

ca. 1500–300 B.C.E. Olmec civilization in Mexico (Ch. 11)

ca. 1500–1050 B.C.E. Shang Dynasty in China (Ch. 4)

800–500 B.C.E. Rise of Sparta and Athens in Greece (Ch. 5)

1500 B.C.E.	1000 B.C.E.	500 B.C.E.

DOCUMENTARIES

Ancient Worlds: Come Together (BBC, 2010). Archaeologist and historian Richard Miles explores the beginning of civilization in the cities of Mesopotamia.

The Bible's Buried Secrets (*Nova*, 2008). In this two-hour special, *Nova* examines the ancient Israelites through biblical and other ancient texts and archaeological artifacts.

Egypt's Golden Empire (PBS, 2002). This three-part series on the era of the New Kingdom examines the lives of pharaohs, nobles, and ordinary people in Egypt's expanding empire.

Engineering an Empire: The Persians (History Channel, 2006). This hour-long documentary focuses on the engineering of the Persian Empire, especially its canals and roads.

The Kings: From Babylon to Baghdad (History Channel, 2004). This feature-length documentary surveys the rulers of Mesopotamia, from Sargon of Akkad to Saddam Hussein, with special attention to military matters.

WEBSITES

Ancient Civilizations, Mesopotamia, and Egypt. Three interactive sites from the British Museum highlight objects in the museum's fabulous collection, with maps, essays, and other resources.
www.ancientcivilizations.co.uk
www.mesopotamia.co.uk
www.ancientegypt.co.uk

Cuneiform Digital Library Initiative. CDLI offers scholars tens of thousands of pictures of cuneiform texts, many with transcriptions in English, plus a useful wiki written by scholars about Mesopotamian history. The site is run by UCLA and the Max Planck Institute of the History of Science.
cdli.ucla.edu

Israel Antiquities Authority. The official website of the Israel Antiquities Authority features a huge collection of artifacts from many periods in the "National Treasures" section.
www.antiquities.org.il/default_en2.aspx

3

The Foundation of Indian Society
to 300 C.E.

During the centuries when the peoples of ancient Mesopotamia and Egypt were developing urban civilizations, people in India were wrestling with the same challenges — food production, building of cities, political administration, and questions about human life and the cosmos. Like the civilizations of the Nile River Valley and southwestern Asia, the earliest Indian civilization centered on a great river, the Indus. From about 2800 B.C.E. to 1800 B.C.E., the Harappan culture thrived and expanded over a huge area.

A very different Indian society emerged after the decline of this civilization. It was dominated by the Aryans, warriors who spoke an early version of Sanskrit. The Indian caste system and the Hindu religion, key features of Indian society that continued into modern times, had their origins in early Aryan society. By the middle of the first millennium B.C.E., the Aryans had set up numerous small kingdoms throughout north India. This was the great age of Indian religious creativity, when Buddhism and Jainism were founded and the early Brahmanic religion of the Aryans developed into Hinduism.

The first major Indian empire, the Mauryan Dynasty, emerged in the wake of the Greek invasion of north India in 326 B.C.E. This dynasty reached its peak under King Ashoka, who actively promoted Buddhism both within his realm and beyond it. Not long after his reign, however, the empire broke up, and for several centuries India was politically divided. Although India never had a single language and only periodically had a centralized government, cultural elements dating back to the ancient period — the core ideas of Brahmanism, the caste system, and the early epics — spread through trade and other contact, even when the subcontinent was divided into competing kingdoms.

Female Spirit from an Indian Stupa

Royal patronage aided the spread of Buddhism in India, especially the patronage of King Ashoka, who sponsored the construction of numerous Buddhist monuments. This head of a female spirit (called a *yakshini*) is from the stupa that Ashoka had built at Bharhut in central India.

De Agostino Picture Library/G. Nimatallah/Bridgeman Images

CHAPTER PREVIEW

THE LAND AND ITS FIRST SETTLERS, CA. 3000–1500 B.C.E.
What does archaeology tell us about the Harappan civilization in India?

THE ARYANS DURING THE VEDIC AGE, CA. 1500–500 B.C.E.
What kind of society and culture did the Indo-European Aryans create?

INDIA'S GREAT RELIGIONS
What ideas and practices were taught by the founders of Jainism, Buddhism, and Hinduism?

WESTERN CONTACT AND THE MAURYAN UNIFICATION OF NORTH INDIA, CA. 513–185 B.C.E.
What was the result of Indian contact with the Persians and Greeks, and what were the consequences of unification under the Mauryan Empire?

SMALL STATES AND TRADING NETWORKS, 185 B.C.E.–300 C.E.
How was India shaped by political disunity and contacts with other cultures during the five centuries from 185 B.C.E. to 300 C.E.?

The Land and Its First Settlers, ca. 3000–1500 B.C.E.

The subcontinent of India, a landmass as large as western Europe, juts southward into the warm waters of the Indian Ocean. Today this region is divided into the separate countries of Pakistan, Nepal, India, Bangladesh, and Sri Lanka, but these divisions are recent, and for this discussion of premodern history, the entire subcontinent will be called India.

In India, as elsewhere, the possibilities for both agriculture and communication have always been shaped by geography. Most areas in India are warm all year, with average temperatures ranging from 79°F in the north to 85°F in the south. Monsoon rains sweep northward from the Indian Ocean each summer. The lower reaches of the Himalaya Mountains in the northeast are covered by dense forests. Immediately to the south are the fertile valleys of the Indus and Ganges Rivers. These lowland plains, which stretch all the way across the subcontinent, were tamed for agriculture over time, and India's great empires were centered there. To their west are the deserts of Rajasthan and southeastern Pakistan, historically important in part because their flat terrain enabled invaders to sweep into India from the northwest. South of the great river valleys rise the jungle-clad Vindhya Mountains and the dry, hilly Deccan Plateau. Only along the western coast of this part of India do the hills give way to narrow plains where crop agriculture flourished (see Map 3.2, page 79). India's long coastlines and predictable winds fostered maritime trade with other countries bordering the Indian Ocean.

Agriculture was well established in India by about 7000 B.C.E. Wheat and barley were the early crops, probably having spread in their domesticated form from what is today the Middle East. Farmers also domesticated cattle, sheep, and goats and learned to make pottery.

The story of the first civilization in India is one of the most dramatic in the ancient world. From the Bible, people knew about ancient Egypt and Sumer for centuries, but it was not until 1921 that archaeologists found astonishing evidence of a thriving and sophisticated Bronze Age urban culture dating to about 2500 B.C.E. at Mohenjo-daro in what is now Pakistan. Since 1921 thousands of additional sites of this **Harappan** (huh-RAH-puhn) civilization have been found in both India and Pakistan.

Harappan The first Indian civilization; also known as the Indus Valley civilization.

Harappan civilization extended over a vast area and evolved over a period of nearly a millennium (Map 3.1). It extended over nearly five hundred thousand square miles in the Indus Valley, making it more than twice as large as ancient Egypt or Sumer. Yet Harappan civilization was marked by striking uniformity in the layout and construction of towns. Figurines of pregnant women have been found throughout the area, suggesting common religious ideas and practices. It was a literate civilization, like those of Egypt and Mesopotamia, but its script has not yet been deciphered.

Like Mesopotamian cities, Harappan cities were centers for crafts and trade and were surrounded by extensive farmland. Craftsmen produced ceramics decorated with geometric designs. The Harappans were the earliest known manufacturers of cotton cloth, and this cloth was so abundant that goods were wrapped in it for shipment. Trade was extensive. As early as the reign of Sargon of Akkad in the third millennium b.c.e. (see "Empires in Mesopotamia" in Chapter 2), trade between India and Mesopotamia carried goods and ideas between the two cultures, probably by way of the Persian Gulf. The Harappan port of Lothal had a stone dock 700 feet long, next to which were massive granaries and bead-making factories.

The cities of Mohenjo-daro in southern Pakistan, and Harappa, some 400 miles to the north, were huge for this period, more than 3 miles in circumference, with populations estimated at 35,000 to 40,000. Both were defended by great citadels that towered 40 to 50 feet above the surrounding plain. The cities, with their straight streets, had obviously been planned and built before being settled—they were not the outcomes of villages that grew and sprawled haphazardly. The houses were substantial, many two stories tall, some perhaps three. The focal point of a house was a central courtyard onto which the rooms opened.

Perhaps the most surprising aspect of the elaborate planning of these cities was their complex system of drainage. Each house had a bathroom with a drain connected to brick-lined sewers located under the major streets. Openings allowed the refuse to be collected, probably to be used as fertilizer on nearby fields. No other ancient city had such an advanced sanitation system.

Both Mohenjo-daro and Harappa also contained numerous large structures, which archaeologists think were public buildings. One of the most important was the large ventilated storehouse for the community's grain. Mohenjo-daro also had a marketplace or place of assembly, a palace, and a huge pool some 39 feet long by 23 feet wide by 8 feet deep, thought by some to have been used for ritual purification. In contrast to ancient Egypt and Mesopotamia, no great tombs have been discovered in Harappa, making it more difficult to envision the life of the elite.

The prosperity of the Indus civilization depended on constant and intensive cultivation of the rich river valley. Although rainfall seems to have been greater than in recent times, the Indus, like the Nile, flowed through a relatively dry region made fertile by annual floods and irrigation. And as in Egypt, agriculture was aided by a long, hot growing season and near-constant sunshine.

Because no one has yet deciphered the written language of the Harappan people, their political, intellectual, and religious life is largely unknown. There clearly was a political structure with the authority to organize city planning and facilitate trade, but we do not even know whether there were hereditary kings.

Soon after 2000 b.c.e., the Harappan civilization mysteriously declined, with people leaving the cities to live in rural villages. The decline cannot be attributed to the arrival of powerful invaders, as was once thought. Rather it was internally generated. Some scholars suspect an environmental crisis, perhaps a severe drought, an earthquake that led to a shift in the course of the river, or a buildup of salt and alkaline in the soil until they reached levels toxic to plants. Others speculate that long-distance commerce collapsed, leading to an economic depression. Yet others theorize

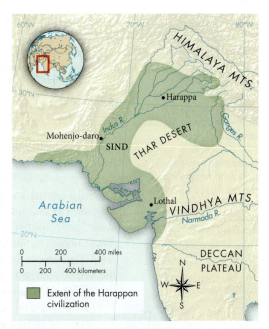

MAP 3.1 Harappan Civilization, ca. 2500 b.c.e. The earliest civilization in India developed in the Indus River Valley in the west of the subcontinent.

that the population fell prey to diseases, such as malaria, that caused people to flee the cities.

After the Harappan cities were abandoned, for the next thousand years India had no large cities, no kiln-fired bricks, and no written language.

The Aryans During the Vedic Age, ca. 1500–500 B.C.E.

What kind of society and culture did the Indo-European Aryans create?

Aryans The dominant people in north India after the decline of the Indus Valley civilization; they spoke an early form of Sanskrit.

After the decline of the Harappan civilization, a people who called themselves **Aryans** became dominant in north India. They were speakers of an early form of Sanskrit, an Indo-European language closely related to ancient Persian and more distantly related to Latin, Greek, Celtic, and their modern descendants, such as English. For example, the Sanskrit *nava*, "ship," is related to the English word *naval*; *deva*, "god," to *divine*; and *raja*, "ruler," to *regal*. The word *Aryan* itself comes from *Arya*, "noble" or "pure" in Sanskrit, and has the same linguistic root as *Iran* and *Ireland*. The Aryans flourished during the Vedic Age (ca. 1500–500 B.C.E.). Named for the Vedas, a large and significant body of ancient sacred works written in Sanskrit, this period witnessed the Indo-Aryan development of the caste system and the Brahmanic religion and the writing of the great epics that represent the earliest form of Indian literature.

Aryan Dominance in North India

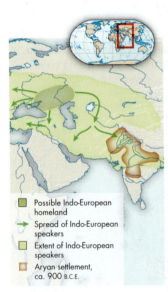

Possible Indo-European homeland
→ **Spread of Indo-European speakers**
Extent of Indo-European speakers
Aryan settlement, ca. 900 B.C.E.

Indo-European Migrations and the Vedic Age

Until relatively recently, the dominant theory was that the Aryans came into India from outside, perhaps as part of the same movements of people whereby the Hittites occupied parts of Anatolia, the Achaeans entered Greece, and the Kassites conquered Sumer—all in the period from about 1900 B.C.E. to 1750 B.C.E. Some scholars, however, have proposed that the Indo-European languages spread to this area much earlier; to them it seems possible that the Harappan people were speakers of an early Indo-European language. If that was the case, the Aryans would be one of the groups descended from this early population.

Modern politics complicates analysis of the appearance of the Aryans and their role in India's history. Europeans in the eighteenth and nineteenth centuries developed the concept of Indo-European languages, and they did so in an age both highly conscious of race and in the habit of identifying races with languages. The racist potential of the concept was exploited by the Nazis, who glorified the Aryans as a superior race. Even in less politicized contexts, the notion of a group of people who entered India from outside and made themselves its rulers is troubling to many. Does it mean that the non-Aryans are the true Indians? Does it add legitimacy to those who in later times conquered India from outside? Does it justify or undermine the caste system? One of the difficulties faced by scholars who wish to take a dispassionate view of these issues is that the evidence for the earlier Harappan culture is entirely archaeological, while the evidence for the Aryans is almost entirely based on linguistic analysis of modern languages and orally transmitted texts of uncertain date.

Rig Veda The earliest collection of Indian hymns, ritual texts, and philosophical treatises, it is the central source of information on early Aryans.

The central source of information on the early Aryans is the ***Rig Veda***, the earliest of the Vedas, originally an oral collection of hymns, ritual texts, and philosophical

Earthenware Horse Figurines The Aryans were great horsemen, perhaps explaining the inclusion of these models of horses in a tomb in north India during the Vedic period.

(American Museum of Natural History, New York/Photo © Boltin Picture Library/ Bridgeman Images)

treatises composed in Sanskrit between 1500 B.C.E. and 500 B.C.E. Like Homer's epics in Greece, which were written in the same period (see "The 'Dark Age'" in Chapter 5), these texts were transmitted orally. They portray the Aryans as warrior tribes who glorified military skill and heroism; loved to drink, hunt, race, and dance; and counted their wealth in cattle. The Aryans did not sweep across India in a quick campaign, nor were they a disciplined army led by one conqueror. Rather they were a collection of tribes that frequently fought with each other and only over the course of several centuries came to dominate north India. (See "Global Viewpoints: Divine Martial Prowess in India and Sumer," page 68.)

The key to the Aryans' success probably lay in their superior military technology. Those they fought often lived in fortified towns and put up a strong defense against them, but Aryan warriors had superior technology, including two-wheeled chariots, horses, and bronze swords and spears. Their epics present the struggle for north India in religious terms, describing their chiefs as godlike heroes and their opponents as irreligious savages who did not perform the proper sacrifices. In time, however, the Aryans clearly absorbed much from those they conquered, such as agricultural techniques and foods.

At the head of each Aryan tribe was a chief, or raja (RAH-juh), who led his followers in battle and ruled them in peacetime. The warriors in the tribe elected the chief for his military skills. Next in importance to the chief was the priest. In time, priests evolved into a distinct class possessing precise knowledge of complex rituals and of the invocations and formulas that accompanied them, rather like the priest classes in ancient Egypt, Mesopotamia, and Persia. Below them in the pecking order was a warrior nobility who rode into

Bronze Sword This bronze sword, with a rib in the middle of the blade for strength, is a striking example of the quality of Aryan arms. Superior weapons gave the Aryans military advantage. (© The Trustees of the British Museum/Art Resource, NY)

Divine Martial Prowess in India and Sumer

Depictions of heroic military leaders and their interactions with their closest followers are found in the literature of many early societies. Sometimes the closest followers had once been opponents but were won over after recognizing the victor's strength and courage. In India, one of the documents recounting such heroes is the *Rig Veda*, a collection of hymns that is the best source of information about the early Aryans. In the excerpt that follows, Indra, the king of the gods, boasts of his might to a band of fighters. It can be compared to the second document, from the Sumerian *Epic of Gilgamesh*, which describes how Enkidu became a follower of Gilgamesh after being defeated by him in hand-to-hand combat.

"Indra and the Maruts" from the *Rig Veda*

■ [*Maruts:*] "Indra, where are you coming from, all alone though you are so mighty? What is your intention, true lord? Will you make a pact with us, now that you have met us in our finery? Master of bay horses, tell us what your purpose is for us.". . .

[*Indra:*] "Where was that independent spirit of yours, Maruts, when you left me all alone in the fight with the dragon? *I* was the one, fierce and strong and mighty, who bent aside the lethal weapons of every enemy with my own weapons."

[*Maruts:*] "You did much with us as allies, with our many powers yoked in common, O bull. . . ."

[*Indra:*] "*I* killed Vritra, O Maruts, by my Indra-power, having grown strong through my own glorious rage. With the thunderbolt on my arm I made these all-luminous waters move well for man."

[*Maruts:*] "No one can overcome your power, generous Indra; no one your equal is known to exist among the gods; no one being born now or already born could get such power. Do the things you will do, as you have grown strong."

[*Indra:*] "Even when I am alone, my formidable power must be vast; whatever I boldly set out to do, I do. For I am known as terrible, O Maruts; whatever I set in motion, Indra himself is master of that. Your praise has made me rejoice, lordly Maruts, the sacred chant worthy of hearing that you made here for me — for Indra the bull, the good fighter."

battle in chariots and perhaps on horseback. The warrior class met at assemblies to reach decisions and advise the raja. The common tribesmen tended herds and worked the land. To the conquered non-Aryans fell the drudgery of menial tasks. It is difficult to define precisely their social status. Though probably not slaves, they were certainly subordinate to the Aryans and worked for them in return for protection.

Over the course of several centuries, the Aryans pushed farther east into the valley of the Ganges River, at that time a land of thick jungle populated by aboriginal forest peoples. The tremendous challenge of clearing the jungle was made somewhat easier by the introduction of iron around 1000 B.C.E., probably by diffusion from Mesopotamia.

As Aryan rulers came to dominate large settled populations, the style of political organization changed from tribal chieftainship to territorial kingship. In other words, the ruler now controlled an area with people living in permanent settlements, not a nomadic tribe that moved as a group. Moreover, kings no longer needed to be elected by the tribe; it was enough to be invested by priests and to perform the splendid royal ceremonies they designed. The priests, or **Brahmins**, supported the growth of royal power in return for royal confirmation of their own power and status. The Brahmins

Brahmins Priests of the Aryans; they supported the growth of royal power in return for royal confirmation of their own religious rights, power, and status.

"Enkidu and Gilgamesh" from the *Epic of Gilgamesh*

■ [Enkidu said,] "I will go to the place where Gilgamesh lords it over the people, I will challenge him boldly, and I will cry aloud in Uruk, 'I have come to change the old order, for I am the strongest here.'" . . .

He entered Uruk, that great market, and all the folk thronged round him where he stood in the street in strong-walled Uruk. The people jostled; speaking of him they said, "He is the spit of Gilgamesh." "He is shorter." "He is bigger of bone." "This is the one who was reared on the milk of wild beasts. His is the greatest strength." The men rejoiced: "Now Gilgamesh has met his match. This great one, this hero whose beauty is like a god, he is a match even for Gilgamesh."

In Uruk the bridal bed was made, fit for the goddess of love. The bride waited for the bridegroom, but in the night Gilgamesh got up and came to the house. Then Enkidu stepped out, he stood in the street and blocked the way. Mighty Gilgamesh came on and Enkidu met him at the gate. He put out his foot and prevented Gilgamesh from entering the house, so they grappled, holding each other like bulls. They broke the doorposts and the walls shook, they snorted like bulls locked

together. They shattered the doorposts and the walls shook. Gilgamesh bent his knee with his foot planted on the ground and with a turn Enkidu was thrown. Then immediately his fury died. When Enkidu was thrown he said to Gilgamesh, "There is not another like you in the world. Ninsun, who is as strong as a wild ox in the byre, she was the mother who bore you, and now you are raised above all men, and [the god] Enlil has given you the kingship, for your strength surpasses the strength of men." So Enkidu and Gilgamesh embraced and their friendship was sealed.

QUESTIONS FOR ANALYSIS

1. In what ways do Indra and Gilgamesh resemble each other?
2. As works of literature, what do these two selections have in common?

Sources: *The Rig Veda: An Anthology of the One Hundred and Eight Hymns*, selected, translated, and annotated by Wendy Doniger O'Flaherty (London: Penguin Classics, 1981); *The Epic of Gilgamesh*, translated with an introduction by N. K. Sandars (London: Penguin Classics, 1960, Third Edition 1972). Copyright © N. K. Sandars, 1960, 1964, 1972. Reproduced by permission of Penguin Books Ltd.

also served as advisers to the kings. In the face of this royal-priestly alliance, the old tribal assemblies of warriors withered away. By the time Persian armies reached the Indus around 513 B.C.E., there were sixteen major Aryan kingdoms in north India.

Life in Early India

Caste was central to the social life of these north Indian kingdoms. Early Aryan society had distinguished among the warrior elite, the priests, ordinary tribesmen, and conquered subjects. These distinctions gradually evolved into the **caste system**, which divided society into strictly defined hereditary groups. Society was conceived of as four hierarchical strata whose members did not eat with or marry each other. These strata, or varnas, were Brahmin (priests), Kshatriya (KSHAT-tree-ya) (warriors and officials), Vaishya (VIGH-sha) (merchants), and Shudra (peasants and laborers). The caste system allowed the numerically outnumbered Aryans to maintain dominance over their subjects and not be culturally absorbed by them.

Social and religious attitudes supported the caste system. Aryans considered the work of artisans impure. They left all such work to the local people, who were probably superior to them in these arts anyway. Trade, by contrast, was not viewed as

caste system The Indian system of dividing society into hereditary groups whose members interacted primarily within the group, and especially married within the group.

demeaning. Brahmanic texts of the period refer to trade as equal in value to farming, serving the king, or being a priest.

In the *Rig Veda*, the caste system is attributed to the gods:

> When they divided [the primeval man], into how many different portions did they arrange him? What became of his mouth, what of his two arms? What were his two thighs and his two feet called?
> His mouth became the brahman, his two arms was made into the [kshatriya]; his two thighs became the vaishyas, of his two feet the shudra was born.[1]

As priests, the Brahmins were expected to memorize every syllable and tone of the Vedas so that their rituals would please the gods. They not only conducted the traditional ceremonies but also developed new ones for new circumstances. As agriculture became more important to the Aryans, for example, Brahmins acted as agents of Agni, the god of fire, to purify the land for crops. The Brahmins also knew the formulas and spells that were effective against diseases and calamities.

Those without places in the four varnas—that is, newly conquered peoples and those who had lost their caste status through violations of ritual—were outcastes. That simply meant that they belonged to no caste. In time, some of them became "untouchables" because they were "impure." They were scorned because they earned their living by performing such "polluting" jobs as slaughtering animals and dressing skins.

Slavery was a feature of early social life in India, as it was in Egypt, Mesopotamia, and elsewhere in antiquity. People captured in battle often became slaves, but captives could also be ransomed by their families. At birth, slave children automatically became the slaves of their parents' masters. Indian slaves could be bought, used as collateral, or given away. At the same time, a clever, hard-working, or fortunate slave could buy his and his family's way out of slavery.

Like most nomadic tribes, the Aryans were patrilineal and patriarchal (tracing descent through males and placing power in the senior men of the family). Thus the roles of women in Aryan society probably were more subordinate than were the roles of women in the cultures of south India, many of which were matrilineal (tracing descent through females). But even in Aryan society women were treated somewhat more favorably than in later Indian society. They were not yet given in child-marriage, and widows had the right to remarry. In epics such as the *Ramayana*, women are often portrayed as forceful personalities, able to achieve their goals both by using feminine ploys to cajole men and by direct action.

Brahmanism

The Aryans recognized a multitude of gods who shared some features with the gods of other early Indo-European societies such as the Persians and Greeks. Ordinary people dealt with these gods through priests who made animal sacrifices to them. By giving valued things to the gods, people strengthened both the power of the gods and their own relationships with them. Gradually, under the priestly monopoly of the Brahmins, correct sacrifice and proper ritual became so important that most Brahmins believed that a properly performed ritual would force a god to grant a worshipper's wish. Ordinary people could watch a ceremony, such as a fire ritual, which was often held outdoors, but could not perform the key steps in the ritual.

The *Upanishads* (oo-PAH-nih-shadz), composed between 750 B.C.E. and 500 B.C.E., record speculations about the mystical meaning of sacrificial rites and about cosmological questions of man's relationship to the universe. They document a gradual shift from the mythical worldview of the early Vedic Age to a deeply philosophical one. Associated with this shift was a movement toward asceticism (uh-SEH-tuh-sihz-uhm) — severe self-discipline and self-denial.

Ancient Indian cosmology (theories of the universe) focused not on a creator who made the universe out of nothing, but rather on endlessly repeating cycles. Key ideas were **samsara**, the reincarnation of souls by a continual process of rebirth, and **karma**, the tally of good and bad deeds that determined the status of an individual's next life. Good deeds led to better future lives, evil deeds to worse future lives — even to reincarnation as an animal. Reward and punishment worked automatically; there was no all-knowing god who judged people and could be petitioned to forgive a sin, and each individual was responsible for his or her own destiny in a just and impartial world.

> **samsara** The transmigration of souls by a continual process of rebirth.

> **karma** The tally of good and bad deeds that determines the status of an individual's next life.

To most people, especially those on the low end of the economic and social scale, these ideas were attractive. By living righteously and doing good deeds, people could improve their lot in the next life. Yet there was another side to these ideas: the wheel of life could be seen as a treadmill, giving rise to a yearning for release from the relentless cycle of birth and death. One solution offered in the *Upanishads* was moksha, or release from the wheel of life. Brahmanic mystics claimed that life in the world was actually an illusion and that the only way to escape the wheel of life was to realize that ultimate reality was unchanging.

The unchanging ultimate reality was called **brahman**. Brahman was contrasted to the multitude of fleeting phenomena that people consider important in their daily lives. The individual soul or self was ultimately the same substance as the universal brahman, in the same way that each spark is in substance the same as a large fire.

> **brahman** The unchanging ultimate reality, according to the *Upanishads*.

The *Upanishads* gave the Brahmins a high status to which the poor and lowly could aspire in a future life. The rulers of Indian society also encouraged the new trends, since the doctrines of samsara and karma encouraged the poor and oppressed to labor peacefully and dutifully. Thus, although the new doctrines were intellectually revolutionary, in social and political terms they supported the existing power structure.

India's Great Religions

> **What ideas and practices were taught by the founders of Jainism, Buddhism, and Hinduism?**

By the sixth and fifth centuries B.C.E., cities had reappeared in India, and merchants and trade were thriving. Bricks were again baked in kilns and used to build ramparts around cities. One particular kingdom, Magadha, had become much more powerful than any of the other states in the Ganges plain, defeating its enemies by using war elephants and catapults for hurling stones. Written language had also reappeared.

This was a period of intellectual ferment throughout Eurasia — the period of the early Greek philosophers, the Hebrew prophets, Zoroaster in Persia, and Confucius and the early Daoists in China. In India it led to numerous sects that rejected various elements of Brahmanic teachings. The two most influential were Jainism and Buddhism. Their founders were contemporaries living in the Ganges plain. Hinduism emerged in response to these new religions but at the same time was the most direct descendant of the old Brahmanic religion.

Jainism

The key figure of Jainism, Vardhamana Mahavira (flourished ca. 520 B.C.E.), was the son of the chief of a small state and a member of the warrior class. Like many ascetics of the period, he left home to become a wandering holy man. For twelve years, from ages thirty to forty-two, he traveled through the Ganges Valley until he found enlightenment and became a "completed soul." Mahavira taught his doctrines for about thirty years, founding a disciplined order of monks and gaining the support of many lay followers, male and female.

Jainism Indian religion whose followers consider all life sacred and avoid destroying other life.

Mahavira accepted the Brahmanic doctrines of karma and rebirth but developed these ideas in new directions, founding the religion referred to as **Jainism**. He asserted that human beings, animals, plants, and even inanimate objects all have living souls enmeshed in matter, accumulated through the workings of karma. The souls conceived by the Jains float or sink depending on the amount of matter with which they are enmeshed. The ascetic, who willingly undertakes suffering, can dissipate some of the accumulated karma and make progress toward liberation. If a soul at last escapes from all the matter weighing it down, it becomes lighter than ordinary objects and floats to the top of the universe, where it remains forever in bliss.

Mahavira's followers pursued such liberation by living ascetic lives and avoiding evil thoughts and actions. The Jains considered all life sacred and tried to live without destroying other life. A Jain who wished to avoid violence to life became a vegetarian and took pains not to kill any creature, even tiny insects in the air and soil. Farming was impossible for Jains, who tended instead to take up trade. Among the most conservative Jains, priests practiced nudity, for clinging to clothes, even a loincloth, was a form of attachment. Lay Jains could pursue Jain teachings by practicing nonviolence and not eating meat.

Although Jainism never took hold as widely as Hinduism and Buddhism (discussed below), over the next few centuries it became an influential strand in Indian thought, and it has several million adherents in India today. Fasting and nonviolence as spiritual practices in India owe much to Jain teachings. In the twentieth century Mohandas Gandhi, leader of the Indian independence movement, was influenced by these ideas through his mother, and the American civil rights leader Dr. Martin Luther King, Jr., was in turn influenced by Gandhi.

Bronze Jain Altarpiece This ninth- or tenth-century bronze sculpture, 10 inches tall, was probably commissioned by a Jain layman or laymen. The central figure is a Jain saint seated in lotus posture, surrounded by other Jain holy men and minor deities. Elephants and lions hold up the base, and there are devotees kneeling below the throne on either side.
(Victoria and Albert Museum/V & A Images, London, UK/Art Resource, NY)

Siddhartha Gautama and Buddhism

Siddhartha Gautama (fl. ca. 500 B.C.E.), also called Shakyamuni ("sage of the Shakya tribe"), is best known as the Buddha ("enlightened one"). He was a contemporary of Mahavira and came from the same warrior social class. He was born the son of a chief of one of the tribes in the Himalayan foothills in what is now Nepal. At age twenty-nine, unsatisfied with his life of comfort and troubled by the suffering he saw around him, he left home to become a wandering ascetic. He traveled south to the kingdom of Magadha, where he studied with yoga masters, but later took up extreme asceticism. According to tradition, while meditating under a bo tree at Bodh Gaya, he reached enlightenment—that is, perfect insight into the processes of the universe. After several weeks of meditation, he preached his first sermon, urging a "middle way" between asceticism and worldly life. For the next forty-five years, the Buddha traveled through the Ganges Valley, propounding his ideas, refuting his adversaries, and attracting followers. To reach as wide an audience as possible, the Buddha preached in the local language, Magadhi, rather than in Sanskrit, which was already becoming a priestly language. Probably because he refused to recognize the divine authority of the Vedas and dismissed sacrifices, he attracted followers mostly from among merchants, artisans, and farmers, rather than Brahmins. (See "Analyzing the Evidence: Gandharan Frieze Depicting the Buddha's Enlightenment," page 74.)

In his first sermon the Buddha outlined his main message, summed up in the **Four Noble Truths** and the **Eightfold Path**. The Four Noble Truths are as follows: (1) pain and suffering, frustration, and anxiety are ugly but inescapable parts of human life; (2) suffering and anxiety are caused by human desires and attachments; (3) people can understand these weaknesses and triumph over them; and (4) this triumph is made possible by following a simple code of conduct, the Eightfold Path. The basic insight of Buddhism is thus psychological. The deepest human longings can never be satisfied, and even those things that seem to give pleasure cause anxiety because we are afraid of losing them. Attachment to people and things causes sorrow at their loss.

Buddhism differed from Brahmanism and later Hinduism in that it ignored the caste system. Everyone, noble and peasant, educated and ignorant, male and female, could follow the Eightfold Path. Moreover, the Buddha was extraordinarily nondogmatic. Convinced that each person must achieve enlightenment on his or her own, he emphasized that the path was important only because it led the traveler to enlightenment, not for its own sake. He compared it to a raft, essential to cross a river but useless once the traveler reaches the far shore. There was no harm in honoring local gods or observing traditional ceremonies, as long as one remembered the goal of enlightenment and did not let sacrifices become snares or attachments. The willingness of Buddhists to tolerate a wide variety of practices aided the spread of the religion.

The Buddha's followers transmitted his teachings orally until they were written down in the second or first century B.C.E. These scriptures are called sutras. The form of monasticism that developed among the Buddhists was less strict than that of the Jains. Buddhist monks moved about for eight months of the year (except the rainy season), begging for their one meal a day, but they could bathe and wear clothes. Within a few centuries Buddhist monks began to overlook the rule that they should travel. They set up permanent monasteries, generally on land donated by kings or other patrons. Orders of nuns also appeared, giving women the opportunity to seek truth in ways men had traditionally used. The main ritual that monks and nuns

Four Noble Truths The Buddha's message that pain and suffering are inescapable parts of life; suffering and anxiety are caused by human desires and attachments; people can understand and triumph over these weaknesses; and this triumph is made possible by following a simple code of conduct.

Eightfold Path The eight-step code of conduct set forth by the Buddha in his first sermon.

Gandharan Frieze Depicting the Buddha's Enlightenment

Gandhara is the region in modern Afghanistan and Pakistan encompassing the Swat and Peshawar Valleys. It became a major center of Buddhism during the era when the Kushans were kings, especially the first and second centuries C.E. Greek artistic styles had been brought to the region by successors of Alexander the Great, and during the Kushan period these styles were adopted to depict the Buddha in stone sculpture. The rulers and other well-to-do patrons commissioned hundreds of Buddhist monuments as a way to acquire merit, and many survive today. Depictions of episodes from the life of the Buddha are common. Gandharan images of the Buddha usually show him with garments draped over a shoulder and his wavy hair drawn up in a bun.

The sculpture shown here, from the Gandharan region and probably dating to about 200 C.E., is one of a set of four that depicts the four major events in the life of the Buddha: his birth, his enlightenment, his first sermon, and his abandonment of his physical body for nirvana. These stones are 26 inches tall and probably originally decorated the walls of a stupa (a monument holding relics).

Buddhist tradition holds that after sitting for forty days under a bo tree, the Buddha became enlightened — that is, attained perfect understanding. This occurred in Bodh Gaya, a small city in north India that in time became a major pilgrimage site for Buddhists.

In this sculpture, the Buddha sits cross-legged under a canopy of tree leaves. Two toppled soldiers, possibly representing evil demons, are depicted under his seat. Looking on are both human beings in a variety of costumes and several sorts of animals, some with seemingly human features. In Buddhist cosmology, animals are part of the circle of life. In their next incarnation, they might be born as a human being or even a god, in the same way that human beings, if their tally of good and bad deeds leads to rebirth at a lower level, can be reincarnated as animals or insects.

(Freer Gallery, Smithsonian Institution/Bridgeman Images)

QUESTIONS FOR ANALYSIS

1. What are the people around the Buddha doing? How are they dressed?
2. How many different kinds of animals are depicted in the frieze? Do they have any human traits? Why would they be attracted to the Buddha?
3. What do you think the patron or the sculptor hoped to achieve by creating this piece?
4. Does this piece successfully convey any Buddhist teachings? If so, which ones?

Palace Life As Buddhism developed, many stories were told of the prior lives of the Buddha. This scene is from a story of Prince Mahajanaka, whose uncle usurped his throne, leading him to become a merchant and have many adventures before returning to marry the daughter of his uncle and retake the throne. This scene, from the Ajanta caves, shows him enjoying the pleasures of palace life. (Pictures from History/Bridgeman Images)

performed in their monastic establishments was the communal recitation of the sutras. Lay Buddhists could aid the spread of Buddhist teachings by providing food for monks and support for their monasteries, and they could pursue their own spiritual progress by adopting practices such as abstaining from meat and alcohol. (See "Individuals in Society: Sudatta, Lay Follower of the Buddha," page 76.)

Because Buddhism had no central ecclesiastical authority like the Christian papacy, early Buddhist communities developed several divergent traditions and came to stress different sutras. One of the most important of these, associated with the monk-philosopher Nagarjuna (fl. ca. 100 C.E.), is called **Mahayana**, or "Great Vehicle," because it was a more inclusive form of the religion. One branch of Mahayana taught that reality is empty (that is, nothing exists independently of itself). Another branch held that ultimate reality is consciousness, that everything is produced by the mind.

Just as important as the metaphysical literature of Mahayana Buddhism was its devotional side, influenced by the religions then prevalent in Central Asia, such as Zoroastrianism (see "The Religion of Zoroaster" in Chapter 2). The Buddha became deified and was placed at the head of an expanding pantheon of other Buddhas and **bodhisattvas** (boh-dih-SUHT-vuhz). Bodhisattvas were Buddhas-to-be who had stayed in the world after enlightenment to help others on the path to salvation. The Buddhas and bodhisattvas became objects of veneration. With the growth of Mahayana, Buddhism attracted more and more laypeople.

Buddhism remained an important religion in India until about 1200 C.E. By that time it had spread widely through East, Central, and Southeast Asia. After 1200 C.E. Buddhism declined in India, losing out to both Hinduism and Islam, and the number of Buddhists in India today is small. Buddhism never lost its hold in Nepal and Sri Lanka, however, and today it is also a major religion in Southeast Asia, Tibet, China, Korea, and Japan.

Mahayana The "Great Vehicle," a tradition of Buddhism that aspires to be more inclusive.

bodhisattvas Buddhas-to-be who stayed in the world after enlightenment to help others on the path to salvation.

Sudatta, Lay Follower of the Buddha

AS HE TAUGHT, THE BUDDHA ATTRACTED both disciples and lay followers. Stories of his interactions with them were passed down orally for centuries, and undoubtedly were elaborated over time. Still, these accounts give us a sense of what life was like in early India. The wealthy banker or merchant Sudatta is a good example of an ardent lay follower. He was so generous to others that he is normally referred to by his epithet, Anathapindada, which means "benefactor of the needy."

In one conversation with the Buddha, Sudatta asks if he must leave the world to attain nirvana:

> Now, I have heard thy disciples praise the bliss of the hermit and denounce the unrest of the world. "The Holy One," they say, "has given up his kingdom and his inheritance, and has found the path of righteousness, thus setting an example to all the world how to attain Nirvana." My heart yearns to do what is right and to be a blessing unto my fellows. Let me then ask you, Must I give up my wealth, my home, and my business enterprises, and, like you, go into homelessness in order to attain the bliss of a religious life?

The Buddha replied that the individual's approach to wealth was crucial. Anyone who cleaves to wealth needs to cast it aside, but anyone who, "possessing riches, uses them rightly, will be a blessing unto his fellows." It is cleaving to wealth and power that enslaves people, not the mere possession of wealth. "If they live in the world not a life of self but a life of truth, then surely joy, peace, and bliss will dwell in their minds."*

The people depicted here are performing the Buddhist ritual of circumambulating a stupa (a mound containing the ashes or other relics of a monk). (British Museum, London, UK/Erich Lessing/Art Resource, NY)

Sudatta purchased a large park to provide a place where the Buddha and his disciples could live during the rainy season and had many buildings built there. The Buddha returned to this Jetavana Monastery many times. Sudatta also gave generously to the poor and needy. As a result of his generosity, Sudatta gradually grew poor. Then, through divine intervention, those who owed him money returned it, making him wealthy once again.

Stories recounted that Sudatta's family, including his son and three daughters, became pious followers. The Buddha himself helped convert Sudatta's unpleasant daughter-in-law. After hearing Sudatta's son's wife scolding the servants, the Buddha instructed her on the proper conduct of wives. There were three types of bad wives, he told her: the destructive wife, who is pitiless, fond of other men, and contemptuous of her husband; the thievish wife, who squanders the family wealth; and the mistress wife, who is rude, lazy, and domineering. These he contrasted with the four kinds of good wives: the motherly wife, who cares for her husband as a mother for her son; the sisterly wife, who defers to her husband as a younger sister defers to her older brother; the friend wife, who loves her husband as if he were her best friend; and the handmaiden wife, who is calm, patient, and obedient. Deeply moved by these teachings, the daughter-in-law determined to be a handmaiden wife.

Sudatta died before the Buddha. On his deathbed, Sudatta was advised to face death by deciding not to cling to what is seen, heard, sensed, thought, attained, sought after, or pondered by the intellect.

QUESTIONS FOR ANALYSIS

1. What can you infer about the circumstances of the early followers of the Buddha from the life of Sudatta?
2. What insights does the life of Sudatta provide into the ways faith in Buddhism was spread?

*Paul Carus, *The Gospel of Buddha* (Chicago: Open Court, 1894/1915), pp. 61–63, slightly modified.

Hinduism

Both Buddhism and Jainism were direct challenges to the old Brahmanic religion. Both rejected animal sacrifice, which by then was a central element in the rituals performed by Brahmin priests. Even more important, both religions tacitly rejected the caste system, accepting people of any caste into their ranks. Over the next several centuries (ca. 400 B.C.E.–200 C.E.), in response to this challenge, the Brahmanic religion evolved in a more devotional direction, developing into the religion commonly called Hinduism. In Hinduism Brahmins retained their high social status, but it became possible for individual worshippers to have more direct contact with the gods, showing their devotion without using priests as intermediaries.

The bedrock of Hinduism is the belief that the Vedas are sacred revelations and that a specific caste system is implicitly prescribed in them. Hinduism is a guide to life, the goal of which is to reach union with brahman, the unchanging ultimate reality. There are four steps in this search, progressing from study of the Vedas in youth to complete asceticism in old age. In their quest for brahman, people are to observe **dharma** (DAHR-muh), the moral law.

> **dharma** The Sanskrit word for moral law, central to both Buddhist and Hindu teachings.

Hinduism assumes that there are innumerable legitimate ways of worshipping brahman, including devotion to personal gods. After the third century B.C.E. Hinduism began to emphasize the roles and personalities of thousands of powerful gods. These gods were usually represented by images, either small ones in homes or larger ones in temples. People could show devotion to their personal gods by reciting hymns or scriptures and by making offerings of food or flowers before these images. A worshipper's devotion to one god did not entail denial of other deities; ultimately all were manifestations of brahman, the ultimate reality. Hinduism's embrace of a large pantheon of gods enabled it to incorporate new sects, doctrines, beliefs, rites, and deities.

A central ethical text of Hinduism is the *Bhagavad Gita* (BAH-guh-vahd GEE-tuh), a part of the world's longest ancient epic, the *Mahabharata*. It was passed down orally for centuries before being recorded in its present form, perhaps as late as the fourth century C.E. The *Bhagavad Gita* offers guidance on the most serious problem facing a Hindu—how to live in the world and yet honor dharma and thus achieve release from the wheel of life. The heart of the *Bhagavad Gita* is the spiritual conflict confronting Arjuna, a human hero about to ride into battle against his kinsmen. As he surveys the battlefield, struggling with the grim notion of killing his relatives, Arjuna voices his doubts to his charioteer, none other than the god Krishna. When at last Arjuna refuses to spill his family's blood, Krishna then clarifies the relationship between human reality and the eternal spirit. He explains compassionately to Arjuna the duty to act—to live in the world and carry out his duties as a warrior. Indeed, the *Bhagavad Gita* emphasizes the

The God Vishnu Vishnu is depicted here coming to the rescue of an elephant in the clutches of a crocodile. It comes from the fifth-century-C.E. Dasavatara Temple in Uttar Pradesh. (© akg-images/Jean-Louis Nou/The Image Works)

necessity of action, which is essential for the welfare of the world. For Arjuna the warrior's duty is to wage war in compliance with his dharma. Only those who live within the divine law without complaint will be released from rebirth. One person's dharma may be different from another's, but both individuals must follow their own dharmas.

Hinduism provided a complex and sophisticated philosophy of life and a religion of enormous emotional appeal that was attractive to ordinary Indians. Over time it grew to be the most common religion in India. Hinduism validated the caste system, adding to the stability of everyday village life, since people all knew where they stood in society. Hinduism also inspired the preservation of literary masterpieces in Sanskrit and the major regional languages of India. Among these are the *Puranas*, which are stories of the gods and great warrior clans, and the *Mahabharata* and *Ramayana*, which are verse epics of India's early kings.

What was the result of Indian contact with the Persians and Greeks, and what were the consequences of unification under the Mauryan Empire?

Western Contact and the Mauryan Unification of North India, ca. 513–185 B.C.E.

In the late sixth century B.C.E., with the creation of the Persian Empire that stretched from the west coast of Anatolia to the Indus River (see "The Rise and Expansion of the Persian Empire" in Chapter 2), west India was swept up in events that were changing the face of the ancient Near East. A couple of centuries later, by 322 B.C.E., the Greeks had supplanted the Persians in northwest India. Chandragupta saw this as an opportunity to expand his territories, and he successfully unified all of north India. The Mauryan (MAWR-ee-uhn) Empire that he founded flourished under the reign of his grandson, Ashoka, but after Ashoka's death the empire declined.

Encounters with the West

India became involved in the turmoil of the sixth century B.C.E. when the Persian emperor Darius conquered the Indus Valley and Kashmir in northwest India about 513 B.C.E. Persian control did not reach eastward beyond the Punjab, but even so, it fostered increased contact between India and the Near East and led to the introduction of new ideas, techniques, and materials into India—including the minting of silver coins and writing in the Aramaic script to keep records.

The Persian Empire in turn succumbed to Alexander the Great, and in 326 B.C.E. Alexander led his Macedonian and Greek troops through the Khyber Pass into the Indus Valley (see "From Polis to Monarchy, 404–200 B.C.E." in Chapter 5). The India

Hellenistic Influences in Gandharan Art Because Alexander the Great's army had reached Gandhara and Hellenistic states subsequently controlled it for more than a century, the art of this region was strongly influenced by Greek artistic styles. This stucco figure was excavated from a site in eastern Afghanistan where some twenty-three thousand Greco-Buddhist sculptures were found. Hellenistic influence, as evidenced by the drape of the clothing and the modeling of the head, is particularly easy to recognize in this piece. (Musée des Arts Asiatiques–Guimet, Paris, France/Erich Lessing/Art Resource, NY)

that Alexander encountered was composed of many rival states. He defeated some of these states in the northwest and heard reports of others.

The Greeks were intrigued by the Indian culture they encountered. Alexander had heard of the sophistication of Indian philosophers and summoned some to instruct him or debate with him. The Greeks were also impressed with Indian cities, most notably Taxila, a major center of trade in the Punjab. From Taxila, Alexander followed the Indus River south, hoping to find the end of the world. His men, however, mutinied and refused to continue. When Alexander turned back, he left his general Seleucus (suh-LOO-kuhs) in charge of his easternmost region.

Chandragupta and the Founding of the Mauryan Empire

The one to benefit most from Alexander's invasion was Chandragupta, the ruler of a growing state in the Ganges Valley. He took advantage of the crisis caused by Alexander's invasion to expand his territories, and by 322 B.C.E. he had made himself sole master of north India (Map 3.2). In 304 B.C.E. he defeated the forces of Seleucus.

With stunning effectiveness, Chandragupta applied the lessons learned from Persian rule. He adopted the Persian practice of dividing the area into provinces. Each province was assigned a governor, usually drawn from Chandragupta's own family. He established a complex bureaucracy to see to the operation of the state and a bureaucratic taxation system that financed public services through taxes on agriculture. He also built a regular army, complete with departments for everything from naval matters to the collection of supplies.

For the first time in Indian history, one man governed most of the subcontinent, exercising control through delegated power. From his capital at Pataliputra in the Ganges Valley, Chandragupta sent agents to the provinces to oversee the workings of government and to keep him informed of conditions in his realm. In designing his bureaucratic system, Chandragupta enjoyed the able assistance of his great minister Kautilya, who wrote a treatise called the *Arthashastra* on how a king should seize, hold, and manipulate power. Kautilya urged the king to use propaganda to gain support, and stressed the importance of seeking the enemies of his enemies, who would make good allies. When a neighboring prince was in trouble, that was the perfect time to attack him.

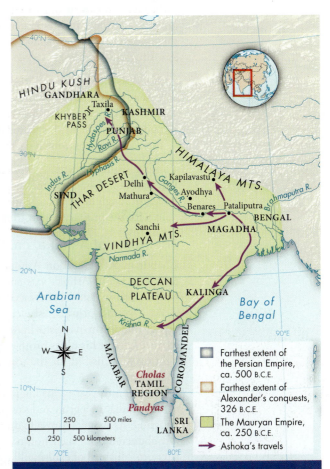

MAPPING THE PAST

MAP 3.2 The Mauryan Empire, ca. 250 B.C.E. The Ganges River Valley was the heart of the Mauryan Empire. Although India is protected from the cold by mountains in the north, mountain passes in the northwest allowed both migration and invasion.

ANALYZING THE MAP Where are the major rivers of India? How close are they to mountains?

CONNECTIONS Can you think of any reasons that the Persian Empire and Alexander's conquests both reached into the same region of northwest India?

Megasthenes, a Greek ambassador sent by Seleucus, spent fourteen years in Chandragupta's court. He left a lively description of life there. He described the city as square and surrounded by wooden walls, 22 miles on each side, with 570 towers and 64 gates. It had a university, a library, and magnificent palaces, temples, gardens, and parks. The king personally presided over court sessions where legal cases were heard and petitions received. The king claimed for the state all mines and forests, and there were large state farms, granaries, shipyards, and spinning and weaving factories. Even prostitution was controlled by the state. Only a portion of the empire was ruled so directly, according to Megasthenes. In outlying areas, local kings were left in place if they pledged loyalty. Megasthenes described Chandragupta's fear of treachery and assassination attempts:

> Nor does the king sleep during the day, and at night he is forced at various hours to change his bed because of those plotting against him. . . . When he leaves to hunt, he is thickly surrounded by a circle of women, and on the outside by spear-carrying bodyguards. The road is fenced off with ropes, and to anyone who passes within the ropes as far as the women death is the penalty.[2]

Those measures apparently worked, as Chandragupta lived a long life. According to Jain tradition, Chandragupta became a Jain ascetic and died a peaceful death in 298 b.c.e. Although he personally adopted a nonviolent philosophy, he left behind a kingdom with the military might to maintain order and defend India from invasion.

The Reign of Ashoka, ca. 269–232 B.C.E.

Chandragupta's grandson Ashoka proved to be one of India's most remarkable figures. The era of Ashoka was enormously important in the religious history of the world, because Ashoka embraced Buddhism and promoted its spread beyond India.

As a young prince, Ashoka served as governor of two prosperous provinces where Buddhism flourished. At the death of his father about 274 b.c.e., Ashoka rebelled against his older brother, who had succeeded as king, and after four years of fighting won his bid for the throne. Crowned king, Ashoka ruled intelligently and energetically.

In the ninth year of his reign, 261 b.c.e., Ashoka conquered Kalinga, on the east coast of India. In a grim and savage campaign, Ashoka reduced Kalinga by wholesale slaughter. As Ashoka himself admitted, "One hundred and fifty thousand were forcibly abducted from their homes, 100,000 were killed in battle, and many more died later on."[3] Instead of exulting like a conqueror, however, Ashoka was consumed with remorse and revulsion at the horror of war. He embraced Buddhism and used the machinery of his empire to spread Buddhist teachings throughout India. He supported the doctrine of not hurting humans or animals that was then spreading among religious people of all sects in India. He banned animal sacrifices, and in place of hunting expeditions he took pilgrimages. Two years after his conversion, he undertook a 256-day pilgrimage to all the holy sites of Buddhism, and on his return he sent missionaries to all known countries. Ashoka's remarkable crisis of conscience changed the way he ruled. He emphasized compassion, nonviolence, and adherence to dharma. He appointed officials to oversee the moral welfare of the realm and required local officials to govern humanely. Ashoka erected stone pillars, on the Persian model, with inscriptions to inform the people of his policies. He also had long inscriptions carved

The North Gate at Sanchi This is one of four ornately carved gates guarding the stupa at Sanchi in the state of Madhya Pradesh in India. Containing the relics of the Buddha, this Buddhist memorial shrine was originally commissioned by Ashoka, but the gateways were added later. (Olaf Kruger/Robert Harding)

into large rock surfaces near trade routes. In his last important inscription he spoke of his efforts to encourage his people toward the path of righteousness:

> I have had banyan trees planted on the roads to give shade to man and beast; I have planted mango groves, and I have had ponds dug and shelters erected along the roads at every eight kos. Everywhere I have had wells dug for the benefit of man and beast. But this benefit is but small, for in many ways the kings of olden time have worked for the welfare of the world; but what I have done has been done that men may conform to righteousness.[4]

These inscriptions are the earliest fully dated Indian texts. (Until the script in which they were written was deciphered in 1837, nothing was known of Ashoka's achievements.)

Ashoka felt the need to protect his new religion and to keep it pure. He warned Buddhist monks that he would not tolerate schism—divisions based on differences of opinion about doctrine or ritual. According to Buddhist tradition, a great council of Buddhist monks was held at Pataliputra, where the earliest canon of Buddhist texts was codified. At the same time, Ashoka honored India's other religions, even building shrines for Hindu and Jain worshippers.

Despite his devotion to Buddhism, Ashoka never neglected his duties as ruler of the **Mauryan Empire**. He tightened the central government of the empire and kept a close check on local officials. He built roads and rest spots to improve communication within the realm. These measures also facilitated the march of armies and the armed enforcement of Ashoka's authority.

Ashoka ruled for thirty-seven years. After he died in about 232 B.C.E., the Mauryan Dynasty went into decline, and India broke up into smaller units, much like those in existence before Alexander's invasion. Even though Chandragupta had instituted bureaucratic methods of centralized political control and Ashoka had vigorously pursued the political and cultural integration of the empire, the institutions they created were not entrenched enough to survive periods with weaker kings.

Mauryan Empire The first Indian empire, founded by Chandragupta.

How was India shaped by political disunity and contacts with other cultures during the five centuries from 185 B.C.E. to 300 C.E.?

Small States and Trading Networks, 185 B.C.E.–300 C.E.

After the end of the Mauryan Dynasty in 185 B.C.E. and for much of subsequent Indian history, political unity would be the exception rather than the rule. By this time, however, key elements of Indian culture—the caste system; the religious traditions of Hinduism, Buddhism, and Jainism; and the great epics and legends—had given India a cultural unity strong enough to endure even without political unity.

In the years after the fall of the Mauryan Dynasty, a series of foreign powers dominated the Indus Valley and adjoining regions. The first were hybrid Indo-Greek states ruled by the inheritors of Alexander's defunct empire stationed in what is now Afghanistan. The city of Taxila became a major center of trade, culture, and education, fusing elements of Greek and Indian culture.

The Kushan Empire, ca. 200 C.E.

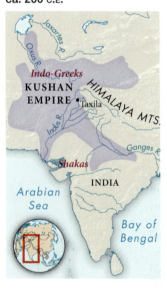

The great, slow movement of nomadic peoples out of East Asia that brought the Scythians to the Near East brought the Shakas to northwest India. They controlled the region from about 94 B.C.E. to 20 B.C.E., when they were displaced by a new nomadic invader, the Kushans, who ruled the region of today's Afghanistan, Pakistan, and west India as far south as Gujarat.

During the Kushan period, which lasted to about 250 C.E., Greek culture had a considerable impact on Indian art. Indo-Greek artists and sculptors working in India adorned Buddhist shrines, modeling the earliest representation of the Buddha on Hellenistic statues of Apollo. Another contribution from the Indo-Greek states was coin cast with images of the king, which came to be widely adopted by Indian rulers, aiding commerce and adding evidence of rulers' names and sequence to the historical record. Places where coins are found also show patterns of trade.

Cultural exchange also went in the other direction. Old Indian animal folktales were translated into Syriac and Greek, and these translated versions eventually made their way to Europe. South India in this period was also the center of active seaborne trade, with networks reaching all the way to Rome. Indian sailing technology was highly advanced, and much of this trade was in the hands of Indian merchants. Roman traders based in Egypt followed the routes already used by Arab traders, sailing with the monsoon from the Red Sea to the west coast of India in about two weeks, and returning about six months later when the direction of the winds reversed. In the first century C.E. a Greek merchant involved in this trade reported that the traders sold coins, topaz, coral, crude glass, copper, tin, and lead and bought pearls, ivory, silk (probably originally from China), jewels of many sorts (probably many from Southeast Asia), and above all cinnamon and pepper. More Roman gold coins of the first and second centuries C.E. have been found near the southern tip of India than in any other area.

During these centuries there were significant advances in science, mathematics, and philosophy. Indian astronomers charted the movements of stars and planets and recognized that the earth was spherical. In the realm of physics, Indian scientists, like their Greek counterparts, conceived of matter in terms of five elements: earth, air, fire, water, and ether. This was also the period when Indian law was codified. The *Code of Manu*, which lays down family, caste, and commercial law, was compiled in the second or third century C.E., drawing on older texts.

Code of Manu The codification of early Indian law that lays down family, caste, and commercial law.

Lotus Gatherer This image of a woman gathering lotuses is from Sittanavasal Cave, a second-century-c.e. rock-cut temple in Tamil Nadu near the south end of India. (Pictures from History/Bridgeman Images)

Regional cultures tend to flourish when there is no dominant unifying state, and the Tamils of south India were one of the major beneficiaries of the collapse of the Mauryan Dynasty. The period from 200 b.c.e. to 200 c.e. is considered the classical period of Tamil culture, when many great works of literature were written under the patronage of the regional kings. Some of the poems written then provide evidence of lively commerce, mentioning bulging warehouses, ships from many lands, and complex import-export procedures. From contact of this sort, the south came to absorb many cultural elements from the north, but also retained differences. Castes were present in the south before contact with the Sanskrit north, but took distinct forms, as the Kshatriya (warrior) and Vaishya (merchant) varnas were hardly known in the far south.

Chapter Summary

Civilization first emerged in the Indus River Valley of India in the third millennium b.c.e. The large cities of this Harappan civilization were carefully planned, with straight streets and sewers; buildings were of kiln-dried brick. Harappan cities were largely abandoned by 1800 b.c.e. for unknown reasons.

A few centuries later, the Aryans, speakers of an early form of the Indo-European language Sanskrit, rose to prominence in north India, marking the beginning of the Vedic Age. Aryan warrior tribes fought using chariots and bronze swords and spears, gradually expanding into the Ganges River Valley. The first stages of the Indian caste system date to this period, when warriors and priests were ranked above merchants, artisans, and farmers. The Vedas document the religious ideas of this age, such as the importance of sacrifice and the notions of karma and rebirth.

Beginning around 500 b.c.e. three of India's major religions emerged. Mahavira, the founder of the Jain religion, taught his followers to live ascetic lives, avoid harming any living thing, and renounce evil thoughts and actions. The founder of

Buddhism, Siddhartha Gautama, or the Buddha, similarly taught his followers a path to liberation that involved freeing themselves from desires, avoiding violence, and gaining insight. Hinduism developed in response to the popularity of Jainism and Buddhism, both of which rejected animal sacrifice and ignored the caste system. Hindu traditions validated sacrifice and caste and developed devotional practice, giving individuals a more personal relationship with the gods they worshipped.

From contact with the Persians and Greeks in the sixth century B.C.E. and fourth century B.C.E., respectively, new political techniques, ideas, and art styles and the use of money entered the Indian repertoire. Shortly after the arrival of the Greeks, much of north India was politically unified by the Mauryan Empire under Chandragupta. His grandson Ashoka converted to Buddhism and promoted its spread inside and outside of India.

After the decline of the Mauryan Empire, India was politically fragmented for several centuries. Indian cultural identity remained strong, however, because of shared literature and religious ideas. In the northwest, new nomadic groups, the Shakas and the Kushans, emerged. Cultural interchange was facilitated through trade both overland and by sea.

NOTES

1. *Rig Veda 10.90*, in *Sources of Indian Tradition* by Ainslie Thomas Embree, Stephen N. Hay, and William Theodore De Bary. Reproduced with permission of COLUMBIA UNIVERSITY PRESS in the format Book via Copyright Clearance Center.
2. *Strabo* 15.1.55, trans. John Buckler.
3. Quoted in H. Kulke and D. Rothermund, *A History of India*, 3d ed. (London: Routledge, 1998), p. 62.
4. Embree et al., *Sources of Indian Tradition*, p. 148. Reproduced with permission of COLUMBIA UNIVERSITY PRESS in the format Book via Copyright Clearance Center.

CONNECTIONS

India was a very different place in the third century C.E. than it had been in the early phase of Harappan civilization more than two thousand years earlier. The region was still divided into many different polities, but people living there in 300 shared much more in the way of ideas and traditions. The great epics such as the *Mahabharata* and the *Ramayana* provided a cultural vocabulary for groups that spoke different languages and had rival rulers. New religions had emerged, notably Buddhism and Jainism, and Hinduism was much more a devotional religion. Contact with ancient Mesopotamia, Persia, Greece, and Rome had brought new ideas, practices, and products.

During this same time period, civilization in China underwent similar expansion and diversification. China was farther away than India from other Eurasian centers of civilization, and its developments were consequently not as closely linked. In China, writing with a symbol for each word appeared with the Bronze Age Shang civilization and was preserved into modern times, in striking contrast to India and lands to its west, which developed alphabetical writing systems. Still, some developments affected both India and China, such as the appearance of chariots and horseback riding. The next chapter takes up the story of these developments in early China. In Chapter 12, after considering early developments in Europe, Asia, Africa, and the Americas, we return to the story of India.

Identify Key Terms

Identify and explain the significance of each item below.

Harappan (p. 64)　　　　**karma** (p. 71)　　　　**bodhisattvas** (p. 75)

Aryans (p. 66)　　　　**brahman** (p. 71)　　　　**dharma** (p. 77)

Rig Veda (p. 66)　　　　**Jainism** (p. 72)　　　　**Mauryan Empire** (p. 81)

Brahmins (p. 68)　　　　**Four Noble Truths** (p. 73)　　　　*Code of Manu* (p. 82)

caste system (p. 69)　　　　**Eightfold Path** (p. 73)

samsara (p. 71)　　　　**Mahayana** (p. 75)

Review the Main Ideas

Answer the focus questions from each section of the chapter.

1. What does archaeology tell us about the Harappan civilization in India? (p. 64)

2. What kind of society and culture did the Indo-European Aryans create? (p. 66)

3. What ideas and practices were taught by the founders of Jainism, Buddhism, and Hinduism? (p. 71)

4. What was the result of Indian contact with the Persians and Greeks, and what were the consequences of unification under the Mauryan Empire? (p. 78)

5. How was India shaped by political disunity and contacts with other cultures during the five centuries from 185 B.C.E. to 300 C.E.? (p. 82)

Make Comparisons and Connections

Analyze the larger developments and continuities within and across chapters.

1. In what ways did ancient India follow patterns of development similar to those seen elsewhere?

2. What are the similarities and differences between the religious ideas and practices of early India and those that emerged in the Nile River Valley and southwest Asia?

3. How was the development of India's material culture affected by developments elsewhere?

TIMELINE

Suggested Resources

BOOKS

Basham, A. L. *The Wonder That Was India,* 3d rev. ed. 1968. Classic appreciative account of early Indian civilization by a scholar deeply immersed in Indian literature.

Dehejia, Vidya. *Indian Art.* 1997. Well-illustrated introduction to the visual feast of Indian art.

Embree, Ainslee, ed. *Sources of Indian Tradition,* 2d ed. 1988. An excellent introduction to Indian religion, philosophy, and intellectual history through translations of major sources.

Koller, John M. *The Indian Way,* 2d ed. 2004. An accessible introduction to the variety of Indian religions and philosophies.

Kulke, Hermann, and Dietmar Rothermund. *A History of India,* 3d ed. 1998. A good balanced introduction to Indian history.

Lopez, Donald S., Jr. *The Story of the Buddha: A Concise Guide to Its History and Teachings.* 2001. Emphasizes Buddhist practice, drawing examples from many different countries and time periods.

Miller, Barbara, trans. *The Bhagavad-Gita: Krishna's Counsel in Time of War.* 1986. One of several excellent translations of India's classical literature.

Possehl, Gregory L. *The Indus Civilization.* 2002. Overview of Harappan civilization, by one of the on-site researchers.

Renfew, Colin. *Archaeology and Language: The Puzzle of Indo-European Origins.* 1987. In-depth analysis of the question of the origins of the Aryans.

Scharff, Harmut. *The State in Indian Tradition.* 1989. Scholarly analysis of the period from the Aryans to the Muslims.

Thapar, Romila. *Early India to 1300.* 2002. Overview by a leading Indian historian.

Wright, Rita P. *The Ancient Indus: Urbanism, Economy, and Society.* 2010. Broad-ranging overview that brings in Mesopotamian sources.

ca. 1500–500 B.C.E. Vedic Age: Aryans dominate in north India; caste system develops; *Rig Veda*

ca. 400 B.C.E.–200 C.E. Brahmanic religion develops into Hinduism

750–500 B.C.E. *Upanishads,* foundation of Brahmanic religion

ca. 520 B.C.E. Founding of Jainism

513 B.C.E. Persian conquest of parts of northwest India

ca. 500 B.C.E. Founding of Buddhism

326 B.C.E. Alexander the Great invades northwest India

ca. 322–185 B.C.E. Mauryan Empire

269–232 B.C.E. Reign of Ashoka; Buddhism spreads in Central Asia

500–400 B.C.E. Flowering of Greek art and philosophy **(Ch. 5)**

ca. 3 B.C.E.–29 C.E. Life of Jesus **(Ch. 6)**

336–324 B.C.E. Conquests of Alexander the Great **(Ch. 5)**

403–221 B.C.E. China's Warring States Period, golden age of Chinese philosophy **(Ch. 4)**

| 1000 B.C.E. | 500 B.C.E. | 1 C.E. |

DOCUMENTARIES

Ancient India: A Journey Back in Time (Cromwell Productions, 2006). This fifty-minute documentary provides particularly strong coverage of Harappan civilization.

The Soul of India (Rick Ray Films, 2001). This ninety-minute film introduces both India's geography and its religions.

FEATURE FILMS

Ashoka (Alchemy/Millennium, 2002). A heavily fictionalized account of the third-century-B.C.E. ruler; in Hindi with English subtitles.

Ramayana: The Epic (Maya Entertainment, 2011). An animated film, praised for its special effects.

WEBSITES

Ancient India. An interactive site with summaries of history, maps, and photos; part of the Ancient History Encyclopedia. **www.ancient.eu/india/**

Know India: Ancient History. An extensive survey of Indian history on an Indian government site, with many links to different periods and monuments. **www.archive.india.gov.in/knowindia/culture_heritage.php?id=2**

Science, Medicine, Technology in Ancient India. A site offering good treatment of ancient Indian science, mathematics, engineering, medicine, shipping, and other technical subjects. **www.crystalinks.com/indiascience.html**

4

China's Classical Age
to 221 B.C.E.

In comparison to India and Mesopotamia, China developed in relative isolation. Communication with West and South Asia was very difficult, impeded by high mountains and vast deserts. Though there was some trade, the distances were so great that they did not allow the kind of cross-fertilization that occurred in western Eurasia. Moreover, there were no cultural breaks comparable to the rise of the Aryans in India or the Assyrians in Mesopotamia to introduce new peoples and languages. The impact of early China's relative isolation is found in many distinctive features of its culture. Perhaps the most important is its writing system; unlike the other major societies of Eurasia, China retained a logographic writing system with a symbol for each word. This writing system shaped not only Chinese literature and thought but also key social and political processes, such as the nature of the ruling class and interactions with non-Chinese peoples.

Chinese history is commonly discussed in terms of a succession of dynasties. The Shang Dynasty (ca. 1500–1050 B.C.E.) was the first to have writing, metalworking, cities, and chariots. The Shang kings played priestly roles, serving as intermediaries with both their royal ancestors and the high god Di. The Shang were overthrown by one of their vassal states, which founded the Zhou Dynasty (ca. 1050). The Zhou rulers set up a decentralized feudal governmental structure that evolved over centuries into a multistate system, with the Zhou Dynasty itself not abolished until 256 B.C.E. As warfare between the states intensified in the sixth century B.C.E., social and cultural change quickened. Aristocratic privileges declined, and China entered one of its most creative periods, when the philosophies of Confucianism, Daoism, and Legalism were developed.

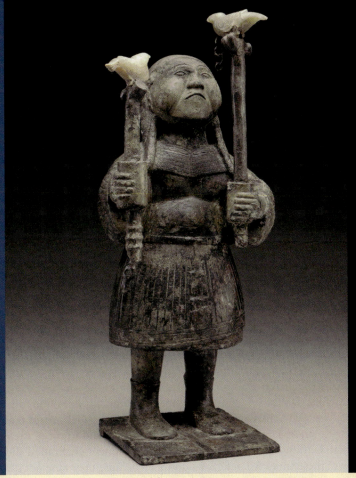

Attendant with Birds

This bronze lamp stand from the region of the Zhou royal tombs dates to the Warring States Period.

Chinese, bronze and jade figure: Eastern Zhou, Warring States, 4th–3rd century B.C./
Museum of Fine Arts, Boston/Maria Antoinette Evans Fund, 31.976/Bridgeman Images

CHAPTER PREVIEW

**What was the impact
of China's geography
on the development of
Chinese societies?**

The Emergence of Civilization in China

The term *China*, like the term *India*, does not refer to the same geographical entity at all points in history. The historical China, also called China proper, was smaller than present-day China, not larger like the historical India. The contemporary People's Republic of China includes Tibet, Inner Mongolia, Turkestan, Manchuria, and other territories that in premodern times were neither inhabited by Chinese nor ruled directly by Chinese states.

The Impact of Geography

China proper, about a thousand miles north to south and east to west, occupies much of the temperate zone of East Asia (Map 4.1). The northern part, drained by the Yellow River, is colder, flatter, and more arid than the south. Rainfall in many areas is less than twenty inches a year, making the land well suited to crops like wheat and millet. The dominant soil is **loess** (LUHS) — fine wind-driven earth that is fertile and easy to work even with simple tools. Because so much of the loess ends up as silt in the river, the riverbed rises and easily floods unless diked. Drought is another perennial problem for farmers in the north. The Yangzi (YANG-zuh) River is the dominant feature of the warmer, wetter, and more lush south, a region well suited to rice cultivation. The Yangzi and its many tributaries are navigable, so boats were traditionally the preferred means of transportation in the south.

loess Soil deposited by wind; it is fertile and easy to work.

Mountains, deserts, and grasslands separated China proper from other early civilizations. Between China and India lay Tibet, with its vast mountain ranges and high plateaus. North of Tibet are great expanses of desert, and north of the desert, grasslands stretch from Ukraine to eastern Siberia. Chinese civilization did not spread into any of these Inner Asian regions, above all because they were not suited to growing crops. Inner Asia, where raising animals is a more productive use of land than planting crops, became the heartland of China's traditional enemies, such as the nomadic tribes of the Xiongnu (SHUHNG-noo) and Mongols.

Early Agricultural Societies of the Neolithic Age

From about 9000 B.C.E. agriculture was practiced in China beginning in the Yellow River Valley. It apparently originated independently of somewhat earlier developments in Egypt and Mesopotamia but was perhaps influenced by developments in Southeast Asia, where rice was also cultivated very early. By 7000 B.C.E. cattle had been domesticated and plow agriculture

Neolithic Jade Plaque This small plaque (2½ inches by 3¼ inches), dating from about 2000 B.C.E., is similar to others of the Liangzhu area near modern Shanghai. It is incised to depict a human figure that merges into a monster mask. The lower part could be interpreted as the figure's arms and legs but at the same time resembles a monster mask with bulging eyes, prominent nostrils, and a large mouth. (Zhejiang Provincial Institute of Cultural Relics and Archeology/Uniphoto Press, Japan/Ancient Art & Architecture Collection, Ltd.)

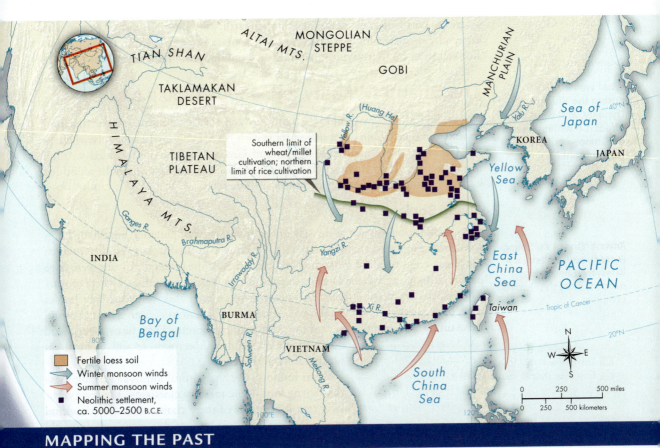

MAPPING THE PAST

MAP 4.1 **The Geography of Historical China** Chinese civilization developed in the temperate regions drained by the Yellow and Yangzi Rivers.

ANALYZING THE MAP Trace the routes of the Yellow and Yangzi Rivers. Where are the areas of loess soil? Where are the Neolithic sites concentrated?

CONNECTIONS Does China's geography explain much about its history? (See also Map 4.2.) What geographical features had the greatest impact in the Neolithic Age? How might the fact that the Yellow and Yangzi Rivers flow west to east, rather than north to south, have influenced the development of Chinese society?

began. By 5000 B.C.E. there were Neolithic village settlements in several regions of China. The primary Neolithic crops were drought-resistant millet, grown in the loess soils of the north, and rice, grown in the wetlands of the lower reaches of the Yangzi River, where inhabitants supplemented their diet with fish. In both areas pigs, dogs, and cattle were domesticated, and by 3000 B.C.E. sheep had become important in the north and water buffalo in the south. Silk production can also be traced back to this period.

Over the course of the fifth to third millennia B.C.E., many distinct regional Neo-lithic cultures emerged. These Neolithic societies left no written records, but we know from the material record that over time they came to share more social and cultural practices. Fortified walls made of rammed earth were built around settlements in many places, suggesting not only increased contact between Neolithic societies but also increased conflict. (For more on life in Neolithic societies, see Chapter 1.)

What was life like during the Shang Dynasty, and what effect did writing have on Chinese culture and government?

The Shang Dynasty, ca. 1500–1050 B.C.E.

Archaeological evidence indicates that after 2000 B.C.E. a Bronze Age civilization appeared in north China that shared traits with Bronze Age civilizations elsewhere in Eurasia, such as Mesopotamia, Egypt, and Greece. These traits included writing, metalworking, class stratification, and cult centers. This civilization can be identified with the Shang Dynasty, long known from early texts.

Shang Society

Anyang One of the Shang Dynasty capitals from which the Shang kings ruled for more than two centuries.

Shang civilization was not as densely urban as that of Mesopotamia, but Shang kings ruled from large settlements (Map 4.2). The best excavated is **Anyang**, from which the Shang kings ruled for more than two centuries. At the center of Anyang were large palaces, temples, and altars. Outside the central core were industrial areas where bronze-workers, potters, stone carvers, and other artisans lived and worked. Many homes were built partly below ground level, probably as a way to conserve heat. Beyond these urban settlements were farming areas and large forests. Deer, bears, tigers, wild boars, elephants, and rhinoceros were still plentiful in north China in this era.

Texts found in the Shang royal tombs at Anyang show that Shang kings were military chieftains. The king regularly sent out armies of three thousand to five thousand men on campaigns, and when not at war they would go on hunts lasting for months. They fought rebellious vassals and foreign tribes, but the situation constantly changed as vassals became enemies and enemies accepted offers of alliance. War booty was an important source of the king's revenue, especially the war captives who could be enslaved. Bronze-tipped spears and battle axes were widely used by Shang warriors, giving them an advantage over less technologically advanced groups. Bronze was also used for the fittings of the chariots that came into use around 1200 B.C.E. Chariot technology apparently spread by diffusion across Eurasia, passing from one society to the next.

Shang power did not rest solely on military supremacy. The Shang king was also the high priest, the one best qualified to offer sacrifices to the royal ancestors and the high god Di. Royal ancestors were viewed as able to intervene with Di, send curses, produce dreams, assist the king in battle, and so on. The king divined his ancestors' wishes by interpreting the cracks made in heated cattle bones or tortoise shells prepared for him by professional diviners.

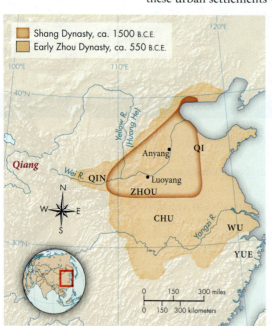

MAP 4.2 The Shang and Early Zhou Dynasties, ca. 1500–400 B.C.E. The early Zhou government controlled larger areas than the Shang did, but the independent states of the Warring States Period were more aggressive about pushing out their frontiers, greatly extending the geographical boundaries of Chinese civilization.

Shang palaces were undoubtedly splendid but were constructed of perishable material like wood, and nothing of them remains today, giving China none of the ancient stone buildings and monuments so characteristic of the West. What has survived are the lavish underground tombs built for Shang kings and their consorts.

The one royal tomb not robbed before it was excavated was for Lady Hao, one of the many wives of the king Wu Ding (ca. 1200 B.C.E.). The tomb was filled with almost 500 bronze vessels and weapons, over 700 jade and ivory ornaments, and 16 people who would tend to Lady Hao in the afterlife. Human sacrifice did not occur only at funerals. Inscribed bones report sacrifices of war captives in the dozens and hundreds.

Shang society was marked by sharp status distinctions. The king and other noble families had family and clan names transmitted along patrilineal lines, from father to son. Kingship similarly passed along patrilineal lines. The kings and the aristocrats owned slaves, many of whom had been captured in war. In the urban centers there were substantial numbers of craftsmen who worked in stone, bone, and bronze.

Shang farmers were obligated to work for their lords (making them essentially serfs). Their lives were not that different from the lives of their Neolithic ancestors, and they worked the fields with similar stone tools. They usually lived in small, compact villages surrounded by fields. Some new crops became common in Shang times, most notably wheat, which had spread from western Asia.

Royal Burials at Anyang Eleven large tombs and more than a thousand small graves have been excavated at the royal burial ground at Anyang. In 2005 seven pits were discovered in which horses and chariots had been buried to accompany a king in the afterlife. (China Newsphoto/Reuters/Newscom)

Bronze Metalworking

As in Egypt, Mesopotamia, and India, the development of more complex forms of social organization in Shang China coincided with the mastery of metalworking, specifically bronze. The bronze industry required the coordination of a large labor force and skilled artisans. Most surviving Shang bronze objects are vessels such as cups, goblets, steamers, and cauldrons that would have originally been used during sacrificial ceremonies.

The decoration on Shang bronzes seems to say something interesting about Shang culture, but scholars do not agree about what that is. In the art of ancient Egypt, Assyria, and Babylonia, representations of agriculture (domesticated plants and animals) and of social hierarchy (kings, priests, scribes, and slaves) are very common, matching our understandings of the social, political, and economic development of those societies. In Shang China, by contrast, images of wild animals predominate. Some animal images readily suggest possible meanings. Birds, for example, suggest to many the idea of messengers that can communicate with other realms, especially realms in the sky. More problematic is the most common image, the stylized animal face called the **taotie** (taow-tyeh). To some it is a monster—a fearsome image that would scare away evil forces. Others imagine a dragon—an animal whose vast powers had more positive associations. Some hypothesize that it reflects masks used in rituals. Others associate it with animal sacrifices, totemism, or shamanism. Without new evidence, scholars can only speculate.

taotie A stylized animal face commonly seen in Chinese bronzes.

The Development of Writing

The survival of divination texts inscribed on bones from Shang tombs demonstrates that writing was already a major element in Chinese culture by 1200 B.C.E. Writing must have been developed earlier, but the early stages cannot be traced, probably because writing was done on wood, bamboo, silk, or other perishable materials.

The invention of writing had profound effects on China's culture and government. A written language made possible a bureaucracy capable of keeping records and corresponding with commanders and governors far from the palace. Hence literacy became the ally of royal rule, facilitating control over a wide realm. Literacy also preserved the learning, lore, and experience of early Chinese society and facilitated the development of abstract thought.

Like ancient Egyptian and Sumerian scripts, the Chinese script was **logographic**: each word was represented by a single symbol. In western Eurasia logographic scripts were eventually modified or replaced by phonetic scripts, but that never happened in China. Because China retained its logographic writing system, many years were required to gain full mastery of reading and writing, which added to the prestige of education.

Why did China retain a logographic writing system even after encounters with phonetic ones? Although phonetic systems have many real advantages, especially with respect to ease of learning to read, there are some costs to dropping a logographic system. Since characters did not change when the pronunciation changed, educated Chinese could read texts written centuries earlier without the need for translation. Moreover, as the Chinese language developed regional variants, readers of Chinese could read books and letters by contemporaries whose oral language they could not comprehend. Thus the Chinese script played a large role in holding China together and fostering a sense of connection with the past. In addition, many of China's neighbors (Japan, Korea, and Vietnam, in particular) adopted the Chinese script, allowing communication through writing between people whose languages were totally unrelated. In this regard, Chinese characters were like Arabic numerals, which have the same meaning however they are pronounced (Table 4.1).

logographic A system of writing in which each word is represented by a single symbol, such as the Chinese script.

TABLE 4.1 Pronouncing Chinese Words
Phonetic equivalents for the vowels and especially perplexing consonants are given here.

LETTER	PHONETIC EQUIVALENT IN CHINESE
a	ah
e	uh
i	ee; except after *z*, *c*, and *ch*, when the sound is closer to *i* in *it*
u	oo; as in English *food*
c	ts (*ch*, however, is like English *ch*)
q	ch
z	dz
zh	j
x	sh

How was China governed, and what was life like during the Zhou Dynasty?

The Early Zhou Dynasty, ca. 1050–400 B.C.E.

West of the Shang capital was the domain of Zhou (JOE), which had inherited cultural traditions from the Neolithic cultures of the northwest and absorbed most of the material culture of the Shang. In about 1050 B.C.E. the Zhou rose against the Shang and defeated them in battle. Their successors maintained the cultural and political advances that the Shang rulers had introduced.

Zhou Politics

The early Zhou period is the first one for which transmitted texts exist in some abundance. The ***Book of Documents*** (ca. 900 B.C.E.) describes the Zhou conquest of the Shang as the victory of just and noble warriors over decadent courtiers led by an irresponsible and sadistic king.

Like the Shang kings, the Zhou kings sacrificed to their ancestors, but they also sacrificed to Heaven. The *Book of Documents* assumes a close relationship between Heaven and the king, who was called the Son of Heaven. In this book, Heaven gives the king a mandate to rule only as long as he rules in the interests of the people. Because the last king of the Shang had been decadent and cruel, Heaven took the mandate away from him and entrusted it to the virtuous Zhou kings. This theory of the **Mandate of Heaven** was probably developed by the early Zhou rulers as a kind of propaganda to win over the former subjects of the Shang. It remained a central feature of Chinese political ideology from the early Zhou period on.

Rather than attempt to rule all their territories directly, the early Zhou rulers set up a decentralized feudal system. They sent relatives and trusted subordinates with troops to establish walled garrisons in the conquered territories. Such a vassal was generally able to pass his position on to a son, so that in time the domains became hereditary. By 800 B.C.E. there were about two hundred lords with domains large and small.

As generations passed and ties of loyalty and kinship grew more distant, regional lords became so powerful that they no longer obeyed the commands of the king. In 771 B.C.E. the Zhou king was killed by an alliance of non-Chinese tribesmen and Zhou vassals. One of his sons was put on the throne, and then for safety's sake the capital was moved east to modern Luoyang, just south of the Yellow River in the heart of the central plains (see Map 4.2). However, the revived Zhou Dynasty never fully regained control over its vassals, and China entered a prolonged period without a strong central authority and with nearly constant conflict (the later Zhou Dynasty, also called the Warring States Period).

Life During the Early Zhou Dynasty

During the early Zhou period, aristocratic attitudes and privileges were strong. Inherited ranks placed people in a hierarchy ranging downward from the king to the rulers of states with titles like duke and marquis, to the hereditary great officials of the states, to the lower ranks of the aristocracy—men who could serve in either military or civil capacities, known as **shi**—and finally to the ordinary people (farmers, craftsmen, and traders). Patrilineal family ties were very important in this society, and at the upper reaches, at least, sacrifices to ancestors were one of the key rituals used to forge social ties.

Glimpses of what life was like at various social levels in the early Zhou Dynasty can be found in the ***Book of Songs*** (ca. 900 B.C.E.), which contains the earliest Chinese poetry. Some of the songs are hymns used in court religious ceremonies, such as offerings to ancestors. Others clearly had their origins in folk songs. The seasons set the pace for rural life, and the songs contain many references to seasonal changes, such as the appearance of insects like grasshoppers and crickets. Some of these songs depict farmers clearing fields, plowing and planting, gathering mulberry leaves for silkworms, and spinning and weaving. Farming life involved not merely cultivating crops like millet, hemp (for cloth), beans, and vegetables but also hunting small animals

Book of Documents One of the earliest Chinese books, containing documents, speeches, and historical accounts about early Zhou rule.

Mandate of Heaven The theory that Heaven gives the king a mandate to rule only as long as he rules in the interests of the people.

shi The lower ranks of Chinese aristocracy; these men could serve in either military or civil capacities.

Book of Songs The earliest collection of Chinese poetry; it provides glimpses of what life was like in the early Zhou Dynasty.

The Inglorious Side of War in the *Book of Songs* and the *Patirruppattu*

The *Book of Songs*, the earliest collection of Chinese poetry, dating back to around 900 B.C.E., includes not only poems that glorify the valiant military victor, but also ones that look at war from the side of ordinary soldiers forced to march and fight. These poems can be compared to others written by poets at court in south India, which were preserved in *Patirruppattu*, an anthology from the classical period of Tamil literature, about 200 B.C.E.–200 C.E.

Soldiers' Complaints in the *Book of Songs*

Hear, minister of war, the charge we bring!
We are the teeth and talons of the king;
   Close to his person is our place.
Why have you sent us to this homeless life,
Where far from court we roam, 'mid miseries rife?
   Why are we doomed to this disgrace

Hear, minister of war, the accusing word!
We are the taloned soldiers of our lord,
   And near his person should have rest.
But you from court have sent us far away,
Where ceaselessly we toil from day to day,
   By constant misery oppressed.

Hear, minister of war, whose erring deed
Has paid our valor with a sorry meed,
   When we should near the court reside.
Why have you sent us far to suffer grief,
And leave our mothers longing for relief,
   With all their cooking labors tried?

The Waste of War from *Patirruppattu*

HARVEST OF WAR

Great king
you shield your men from ruin,
so your victories, your greatness
are bywords.

Loose chariot wheels
lie about the battleground
with the long white tusks
of bull-elephants.

Flocks of male eagles
eat carrion
with their mates.

Headless bodies
dance about
before they fall
to the ground.

Blood glows,
like the sky before nightfall,
in the red center
of the battlefield.

and collecting grasses and rushes to make rope and baskets. (See "Global Viewpoints: The Inglorious Side of War in the *Book of Songs* and the *Patirruppattu*," above.)

   Many of the folk songs are love songs that depict a more informal pattern of courtship than the one that prevailed in later China. One stanza reads:

> I pray you, Zhongzi,
> Do not come leaping over my wall,
> Do not break my mulberry trees.
> It's not that I care about them,
> But I fear the words of my brothers.
> You, Zhongzi, are to be loved,
> But my brothers' words —
> are to be feared.[1]

Demons dance there.
And your kingdom
is an unfailing harvest
of victorious wars.

BATTLE SCENE

You might ask,
      "This Porai, so fierce in war,
      how big
      are his armies, really?"
Listen,
new travelers on the road!

As the enemy mob scampers and flees
and kings die on the field,

I've no body count
of those who kill as they fall,
and falling,
dance the victory dance
with lifted hands.

I've no count of the well-made chariots
that run all over them,
wheel-rims hardly worn,

nor of the horses, the men,
numberless,
I've not counted them.

And those elephants of his,
they cannot be pegged down,
they twist goads out of shape,

they stamp even on the moving shadows
of circling eagles,
and stampede like the cattle
of the Konkars
with pickax troops on a wasteland of pebbles, they
      really move, those elephants in his army:
I can see them but I cannot count them.

QUESTIONS FOR ANALYSIS

1. Who is speaking in these poems?
2. What can you infer about warfare of the periods from these pieces?
3. How significant do you think it is that the Chinese poems were composed seven centuries or more before the Indian ones?

Sources: *The Book of Poetry: Book IV, The Decade of Chi Fu*, trans. James Legge (1876), at www.sacred-texts.com; A. K. Ramanujan, ed. and trans., *Poems of Love and War: From the Eight Anthologies and the Ten Long Poems of Classical Tamil* (New York: Columbia University Press, 1985), pp. 115–117. Copyright 1985 by Columbia University Press. Reproduced by permission of Columbia University Press in the format Textbook via Copyright Clearance Center.

There were also songs of complaint, such as this one in which the ancestors are rebuked for failing to aid their descendants:

The drought is extreme,
And it cannot be stopped.
More fierce and fiery,
it is leaving me no place.
My end is near; —
I have none to look up to, none to look round to.
The many dukes and their ministers of the past
Give me no help.
Oh parents and ancestors,
How can you bear to see us like this?[2]

Bells of the Marquis of Zeng Music played a central role in court life in ancient China, and bells are among the most impressive bronze objects of the period. The tomb of a minor ruler who died about 400 B.C.E. contained 124 musical instruments, including drums, flutes, mouth organs, pan pipes, zithers, a set of 32 chime stones, and this 64-piece bell set. The bells bear inscriptions that name the two tones each bell could make, depending on where it was struck. Five men, using poles and mallets and standing on either side of the set of bells, would have played the bells by hitting them from outside. (Hubei Provincial Museum/Uniphoto Press, Japan/Ancient Art & Architecture Collection, Ltd.)

Social and economic change quickened after 500 B.C.E. Cities began appearing all over north China. Thick earthen walls were built around the palaces and ancestral temples of the ruler and other aristocrats, and often an outer wall was added to protect the artisans, merchants, and farmers who lived outside the inner wall. Accounts of sieges launched against these walled citadels, with scenes of the scaling of walls and the storming of gates, are central to descriptions of military confrontations in this period.

The development of iron technology in the early Zhou Dynasty promoted economic expansion and allowed some people to become very rich. By 500 B.C.E. iron was being widely used for both farm tools and weapons. Late Zhou texts frequently mention trade across state borders in goods such as furs, copper, dyes, hemp, salt, and horses. People who grew wealthy from trade or industry began to rival rulers for influence. Rulers who wanted trade to bring prosperity to their states welcomed traders and began casting coins to facilitate trade.

Social mobility increased over the course of the Zhou period. Rulers often sent out their own officials rather than delegate authority to hereditary lesser lords. This trend toward centralized bureaucratic control created opportunities for social advancement for the *shi* on the lower end of the old aristocracy. Competition among such men guaranteed rulers a ready supply of able and willing subordinates, and competition among rulers for talent meant that ambitious men could be selective in deciding where to offer their services. (See "Individuals in Society: Lord Mengchang," at right.)

Religion in Zhou times was not simply a continuation of Shang practices. The practice of burying the living with the dead—so prominent in the royal tombs of the Shang—steadily declined in the middle Zhou period. New deities and cults also

Lord Mengchang

DURING THE WARRING STATES PERIOD, MEN could rise to high rank on the basis of talent. Lord Mengchang rose on the basis of his people skills: he treated his retainers so well that he attracted thousands of talented men to his service, enabling him to rise to prime minister of his native state of Qi in the early third century B.C.E.

Lord Mengchang's beginnings were not promising. His father, a member of the Qi royal family, already had more than forty sons when Mengchang was born, and he ordered the mother, one of his many concubines, to leave the baby to die. She, however, secretly reared him, and while still a child he was able to win his father's approval through his cleverness.

At his father's death Mengchang succeeded him. Because Mengchang would provide room and board to men who sought to serve him, he soon attracted a few thousand retainers, many of humble background, some fleeing justice. Every night, we are told, he ate with them all in his hall, treating them equally no matter what their social origins.

Most of the stories about Mengchang revolve around retainers who solved his problems in clever ways. Once, when Mengchang had been sent as an envoy to Qin, the king of Qin was persuaded not to let so talented a minister return to help Qi. Under house arrest, Mengchang was able to ask one of the king's consorts to help him, but in exchange she wanted a fur coat kept in the king's treasury. A former thief among Mengchang's retainers stole it for him, and Mengchang was soon on his way. By the time he reached the barrier gate, Qin soldiers were pursuing him, and he knew that he had to get through quickly. One of his retainers imitated the crowing of a cock, which got the other cocks to crow, making the guards think it was dawn, so they opened the gates and let his party through.

When Mengchang served as prime minister of Qi, his retainers came up with many clever stratagems that convinced the nearby states of Wei and Han to join Qi in resisting Qin. Several times, one of his retainers of modest origins, Feng Xuan (FUNG SCHWAN), helped Mengchang withstand the political vicissitudes of the day. When sent to collect debts owed to Mengchang in his fief of Xue, Feng Xuan instead forgave all the debts of those too poor to repay their loans. Later, when Lord Mengchang lost his post at court and returned to his fief, most of his retainers deserted him, but he found himself well loved by the local residents, all because of Feng Xuan's generosity in his name. After Mengchang reattained his court post and was traveling back to Qi, he complained to Feng Xuan about those who had deserted him. Feng Xuan, we are told, got down from the carriage and bowed to Lord Mengchang, and when pressed said that the lord should accept the retainers' departures as part of the natural order of things:

> Wealth and honor attract while poverty and lowliness repel; such is the nature of things. Think of it like the market. In the morning it is crowded and in the evening it is deserted. This is not because people prefer the morning to the evening, but rather because what they want can not be found there [in the evening]. Do not let the fact that your retainers left when you lost your position lead you to bar them from returning. I hope that you will treat them just the way you did before.*

QUESTIONS FOR ANALYSIS

1. How did Mengchang attract his many retainers, and how did their service benefit him?
2. Who in this story benefited from hereditary privilege, and who advanced because of ability? What does this suggest about social mobility during the Warring States Period?
3. Many of the stories about Mengchang are included in *Intrigues of the Warring States*, a book that Confucians disapproved of. What do you think they found objectionable?

*Shi ji 75.2362. Translated by Patricia Buckley.

Menchang promoted trade by issuing bronze coins. Some Zhou coins, like the ones cast in the mold shown here, were shaped liked minature knives. (© The Trustees of the British Museum/Art Resource, NY)

appeared, especially in the southern state of Chu, where areas that had earlier been considered barbarian were being incorporated into the cultural sphere of the Central States, as the core region of China was called. By the late Zhou period, Chu was on the forefront of cultural innovation and produced the greatest literary masterpiece of the era, the *Songs of Chu*, a collection of fantastical poems full of images of elusive deities and shamans who could fly through the spirit world.

How did advances in military technology contribute to the rise of independent states?

The Warring States Period, 403–221 B.C.E.

By 400 B.C.E. advances in military technology were undermining the old aristocratic social structure of the Zhou. Large, well-drilled infantry armies able to withstand and defeat chariot-led forces became potent military forces in the **Warring States Period**, which lasted from 403 B.C.E. to 221 B.C.E. Fueled by the development of new weaponry and war tactics, the Chinese states destroyed each other one by one until only one state was left standing—the state of Qin (CHIN).

Warring States Period
The period of Chinese history between 403 B.C.E. and 221 B.C.E., when states fought each other and one state after another was destroyed.

New Technologies for War

By 300 B.C.E. states were sending out armies of a few hundred thousand drafted foot soldiers, usually accompanied by horsemen. Adding to their effectiveness was the development of the **crossbow** around 350 B.C.E. The intricate bronze trigger of the crossbow allowed a foot soldier to shoot farther than could a horseman carrying a light bow. One text of the period reports that a skilled soldier with a powerful crossbow and a sharp sword was the match of a hundred ordinary men. To defend against crossbows, soldiers began wearing armor and helmets.

crossbow A powerful mechanical bow developed during the Warring States Period.

The introduction of cavalry in this period further reduced the need for a chariot-riding aristocracy. Shooting bows and arrows from horseback was first perfected by non-Chinese peoples to the north of China proper, who at that time were making the transition to a nomadic pastoral economy. The northern state of Jin developed its own cavalry to defend itself from the attacks of these horsemen. Once it started using cavalry against other Chinese states, they too had to master the new technology. From this time on, acquiring and pasturing horses was a key component of military preparedness.

The Warring States, 403–221 B.C.E.

☐ Final seven states, ca. 235 B.C.E.

As military competition intensified, rulers wanted to increase their populations, to have more commoners to serve as foot soldiers and more craftsmen to supply weapons. To increase agricultural output, they brought new land into cultivation, drained marshes, and dug irrigation channels. They wanted to undermine the power of lords over their subjects in order to get direct access to the peasants' labor power. Serfdom thus gradually declined. Registering populations led to the extension of family names to commoners at an earlier date than anywhere else in the world.

The development of infantry armies also created the need for a new type of general, and rulers became less willing to let men lead troops merely because of aristocratic birth. In *The Art of War* (453–403 B.C.E.), Sun Wu described the ideal general as a master of maneuver, illusion, and deception. He argued that heroism is a useless virtue that leads to needless deaths. Discipline, however, is essential, and he insisted that the entire army had to be trained to follow the orders of its commanders without questioning them. He also explicitly called for use of deceit:

War is the Way of deceit. Thus one who is competent pretends to be incompetent; one who uses [his army] pretends not to use it; one who draws near pretends to be distant; one who is distant pretends to draw near. If [the enemy desires] some advantage, entice him [with it]. . . . Attack where he does not expect it and go where he has not imagined. This is how military experts are victorious.[3]

The Victorious States

During the Warring States Period, states on the periphery of the Zhou realm had more room to expand than did states in the center. With access to more resources, they were able to pick off their neighbors, one after the other. Still, for two centuries the final outcome was far from clear, as alliances among states were regularly made and nearly as regularly broken.

By the third century B.C.E. there were only seven important states remaining. These states were much more centralized than their early Zhou predecessors. Their kings had eliminated indirect control through vassals and in their place dispatched royal officials to remote cities, controlling them from a distance through the transmission of documents and dismissing them at will. Before the end of the third century B.C.E. one state, Qin, conquered all of the others, a development discussed in Chapter 7.

Hunters This depiction of men attacking an animal is found on a late Zhou bronze ritual vessel covered with incised images of people and their activities.

Confucius and His Followers

The Warring States Period was the golden age of Chinese philosophy, the era when the "Hundred Schools of Thought" were in competition. During the same period in which Indian sages and mystics were developing religious speculation about karma, souls, and ultimate reality (see "India's Great Religions" in Chapter 3), Chinese thinkers were arguing about the ideal forms of social and political organization and man's connections to nature.

> **What ideas did Confucius teach, and how were they spread after his death?**

Confucius

As a young man, Confucius (traditional dates: 551–479 B.C.E.) had served in the court of his home state of Lu without gaining much influence. After leaving Lu, he set out with a small band of students and wandered through neighboring states in search of a ruler who would take his advice. We know what he taught from the *Analects*, a collection of his sayings put together by his followers after his death. (See "Analyzing the Evidence: The Teachings of Confucius," page 102.)

The thrust of Confucius's thought was ethical rather than theoretical or metaphysical. He talked repeatedly of an ideal age in the early Zhou Dynasty when everyone was devoted to fulfilling his or her role: superiors looked after those dependent on them; inferiors devoted themselves to the service of their superiors; parents and children, husbands and wives all wholeheartedly embraced what was expected of

The Teachings of Confucius

Confucius's ideas are known to us primarily through the sayings recorded by his disciples in the *Analects*. Although these sayings seem to have been haphazardly arranged, several themes emerge clearly from them. The passages here were selected to show Confucius's ideas on the morally superior gentleman, filial piety, and the best way to govern.

The Superior Man

■ Confucius said, "If the superior man is not grave, he will not inspire awe, and his learning will not be on a firm foundation. Hold loyalty and faithfulness to be fundamental. Have no friends who are not as good as yourself. When you have made mistakes, don't be afraid to correct them." (1:8)

Confucius said, "The superior man does not seek fulfillment of his appetite nor comfort in his lodging. He is diligent in his duties and careful in his speech. He associates with men of moral principles and thereby realizes himself. Such a person may be said to love learning." (1:14)

Confucius said, "The superior man is not an implement [tool or utensil]." (2:12)

Zigong asked about the superior man. Confucius said, "He acts before he speaks and then speaks according to his action." (2:13)

Confucius said, "The superior man understands righteousness; the inferior man understands profit." (4:16)

Confucius said, "The superior man wants to be slow in word but diligent in action." (4:24)

Confucius said, "The superior man is conciliatory but does not identify himself with others; the inferior man identifies with others but is not conciliatory." (13:23)

Confucius said, "The superior man understands the higher things [moral principles]; the inferior man understands the lower things [profit]." (14:24)

Filial Piety

■ Young men should be filial when at home and respectful to their elders when away from home. They should be earnest and faithful. They should love all extensively and be intimate with men of humanity. When they have any energy to spare after the performance of moral duties, they should use it to study literature and the arts. (1:6)

Confucius said, "When a man's father is alive, look at the bent of his will. When his father is dead, look at his conduct. If for three years [of mourning] he does not change from the way of his father, he may be called filial." (1:11)

Meng Yizi asked about filial piety. Confucius said, "Never disobey." [Later,] when Fan Chi was driving him, Confucius told him, "Mengsun asked me about filial piety, and I answered him, 'Never disobey.'" Fan Chi said, "What does that mean?" Confucius said, "When parents are alive, serve them according to the rules of propriety. When they die, bury them according to the rules of propriety and sacrifice to them according to the rules of propriety." (2:5)

Ziyu asked about filial piety. Confucius said, "Filial piety nowadays means to be able to support one's parents. But we support even dogs and horses. If there is no feeling of reverence, wherein lies the difference?" (2:7)

Confucius said, "In serving his parents, a son may gently remonstrate with them. When he sees that they

them. Confucius saw five relationships as the basis of society: between ruler and subject; between father and son; between husband and wife; between elder brother and younger brother; and between friend and friend.

A man of moderation, Confucius was an earnest advocate of gentlemanly conduct. He redefined the term *gentleman* (*junzi*) to mean a man of moral cultivation rather than a man of noble birth. He repeatedly urged his followers to aspire to be gentlemen rather than petty men intent on personal gain. The Confucian gentleman found his calling in service to the ruler. Confucius asserted that loyal advisers should encourage their rulers to govern through ritual, virtue, and concern for the

are not inclined to listen to him, he should resume an attitude of reverence and not abandon his effort to serve them. He may feel worried, but does not complain." (4:18)

Confucius said, "When his parents are alive, a son should not go far abroad; or if he does, he should let them know where he goes." (4:19)

On Governing

■ Confucius said, "A ruler who governs his state by virtue is like the north polar star, which remains in its place while all the other stars revolve around it." (2:1)

Confucius said, "Lead the people with governmental measures and regulate them by law and punishment, and they will avoid wrongdoing but will have no sense of honor and shame. Lead them with virtue and regulate them by the rules of propriety (*li*) and they will have a sense of shame and, moreover, set themselves right." (2:3)

Confucius said, "The common people may be made to follow it [the Way] but may not be made to understand it." (8:9)

Zigong asked about government. Confucius said, "Sufficient food, sufficient armament, and sufficient confidence of the people." Zigong said, "Forced to give up one of these, which would you abandon first?" Confucius said, "I would abandon the armament." Zigong said, "Forced to give up one of the remaining two, which would you abandon first?" Confucius said, "I would abandon food. There have been deaths from time immemorial, but no state can exist without the confidence of the people." (12:7)

Duke Jing of Qi asked Confucius about government. Confucius replied, "Let the ruler *be* a ruler, the minister *be* a minister, the father *be* a father, and the son *be* a

son." The duke said, "Excellent! Indeed when the ruler is not a ruler, the minister not a minister, the father not a father, and the son not a son, although I may have all the grain, shall I ever get to eat it?" (12:11)

Ji Kangzi asked Confucius about government, saying, "What do you think of killing the wicked and associating with the good?" Confucius replied, "In your government what is the need of killing? If you desire what is good, the people will be good. The character of a ruler is like wind and that of the people is like grass. In whatever direction the wind blows, the grass always bends." (12:19)

The Duke of She asked about government. Confucius said, "[There is good government] when those who are near are happy and those far away desire to come." (13:16)

The Duke of She told Confucius, "In my country there is an upright man named Gong. When his father stole a sheep, he bore witness against him." Confucius said, "The upright men in my community are different from this. The father conceals the misconduct of the son and the son conceals the misconduct of the father. Uprightness is to be found in this." (13:18)

QUESTIONS FOR ANALYSIS

1. What can you infer about Confucius's opinion of rulers of his day? What were their shortcomings?
2. Which of the virtues Confucius advocates are the hardest to achieve?

Source: Wing-tsit Chan, *A Source Book in Chinese Philosophy* (Princeton, N.J.: Princeton University Press, 1963), pp. 20–24, 28, 33, 39–42, slightly modified. Reproduced with permission of PRINCETON UNIVERSITY PRESS in the format Book via Copyright Clearance Center.

welfare of their subjects, and much of the *Analects* concerns the way to govern well. To Confucius the ultimate virtue was **ren** (humanity). A person of humanity cares about others and acts accordingly:

> **ren** Humanity, the ultimate Confucian virtue.

[The disciple] Zhonggong asked about humanity. Confucius said, "When you go abroad, behave to everyone as if you were receiving a great guest. Employ the people as though you were assisting at a great sacrifice. Do not do unto others what you would not have them do to you. Then neither in your country nor in your family will there be complaints against you."[4]

In the Confucian tradition, studying texts came to be valued over speculation, meditation, and mystical identification with deities. Confucius encouraged the men who came to study with him to master the poetry, rituals, and historical traditions that we know today as Confucian classics.

The Spread of Confucian Ideas

The eventual success of Confucian ideas owes much to Confucius's followers in the three centuries following his death. The most important of them were Mencius (ca. 370–300 B.C.E.) and Xunzi (SHOON-dzuh) (ca. 310–215 B.C.E.).

Mencius, like Confucius, traveled around offering advice to rulers of various states. Over and over he tried to convert them to the view that the ruler able to win over the people through benevolent government would succeed in unifying "all under Heaven." Mencius proposed concrete political and financial measures to ease tax burdens and otherwise improve the people's lot. Men willing to serve an unworthy ruler earned his contempt, especially when they worked hard to fill the ruler's coffers or expand his territory. In one conversation, the king of Qi (CHEE) asked if it was true that the founder of the Zhou Dynasty had taken up arms against his lord, the last king of Shang. Mencius replied that that was what the histories said. The king then asked whether it was permissible for a subject to assassinate his lord, and Mencius replied that the ruler in question was a villain and a criminal, making killing him the right thing to do.

With his disciples and fellow philosophers, Mencius also discussed other issues in moral philosophy, arguing strongly, for instance, that human nature is fundamentally good, as everyone is born with the capacity to recognize what is right and act on it. Anyone who saw a baby about to fall into a well would immediately come to its rescue. This would not be because he wanted a good reputation among his friends and neighbors or because he disliked hearing the child cry, but rather because of his inborn feeling of commiseration from which other virtues can grow.

Xunzi, a half century later, took the opposite view of human nature, arguing that people are born selfish and that only through education and ritual do they learn to put moral principle above their own interest. Much of what is desirable is not inborn but must be taught:

> The son yielding to or taking over the work of his father, or a younger brother yielding to or taking over the work of his elder brother—these two lines of action are contrary to original nature and violate natural feelings. Nevertheless, the way of filial piety is the pattern and order of propriety and righteousness.[5]

Neither Confucius nor Mencius had had much actual political or administrative experience, but Xunzi had worked for many years in the court of his home state. Not surprisingly, he showed more consideration than either Confucius or Mencius for the difficulties a ruler might face in trying to rule through ritual and virtue. Xunzi was also a more rigorous thinker than his predecessors and developed the philosophical foundations of many ideas merely outlined by Confucius and Mencius. Although he did not think gods respond to rituals, he did not propose abandoning rituals, because the rites themselves have positive effects on performers and observers. Not only do they let people express feelings and satisfy desires in an orderly way, but because they specify graduated ways to perform the rites according to social rank, ritual traditions

Serving Parents with Filial Piety This twelfth-century-C.E. illustration of a passage in the *Classic of Filial Piety* shows how commoners should serve their parents: by working hard at productive jobs such as farming and tending to their parents' daily needs. The married son and daughter-in-law offer food or drink to the older couple as their own children look on, thus learning how they should treat their own parents after they become aged. (The Art Archive/REX/Shutterstock)

sustain the social hierarchy. Xunzi compared and contrasted ritual and music: music shapes people's emotions and creates feelings of solidarity, while ritual shapes people's sense of duty and creates social differentiation.

The Confucian vision of personal ethics and public service found a small but ardent following during the Warring States Period. In later centuries rulers came to see men educated in Confucian virtues as ideal advisers and officials. Neither revolutionaries nor flatterers, Confucian scholar-officials opposed bad government and upheld the best ideals of statecraft. Confucian political ideals shaped Chinese society into the twentieth century.

The Confucian vision also provided a moral basis for the Chinese family that continues into modern times. Repaying parents and ancestors came to be seen as a sacred duty. Because people owe their very existence to their parents, they should reciprocate by respecting their parents, making efforts to please them, honoring their memories, and placing the interests of the family line above personal preferences, all of which were aspects of **filial piety**. Since the family line is a patrilineal line from father to son to grandson, placing great importance on it has had the effect of devaluing women.

filial piety Reverent attitude of children to their parents extolled by Confucius.

Daoism, Legalism, and Other Schools of Thought

How did the teachings of Daoism, Legalism, and other schools of thought differ from those of Confucianism?

During the Warring States Period, rulers took advantage of the destruction of states to recruit newly unemployed men to serve as their advisers and court assistants. Lively debate often resulted as these strategists proposed policies and refuted opponents.

Followers took to recording their teachers' ideas, and the circulation of these "books" (rolls of silk, or strips of wood or bamboo tied together) served to stimulate further debate.

Many of these schools of thought directly opposed the ideas of Confucius and his followers. Most notable were the Daoists, who believed that the act of striving to improve society only made it worse, and the Legalists, who argued that a strong government depended not so much on moral leadership as on effective laws and procedures.

Daoism

Confucius and his followers believed in moral action. They thought men of virtue should devote themselves to making the government work to the benefit of the people. Those who came to be labeled Daoists disagreed. They thought striving to make things better generally made them worse. They sought to go beyond everyday concerns and to let their minds wander freely. Rather than making human beings and human actions the center of concern, they focused on the larger scheme of things, the whole natural order identified as the Way, or **Dao** (DOW).

Early Daoist teachings are known from two surviving books, the *Laozi* and the *Zhuangzi*, both dating to the third century B.C.E. Laozi (LOU-dzuh), the putative author of the *Laozi*, may not be a historical figure, but the text ascribed to him has been of enduring importance. A recurrent theme in this brief, aphoristic text is the mystical superiority of yielding over assertion and silence over words: "The Way that can be discussed is not the constant Way." Because purposeful action is counterproductive, the ruler should let people return to a natural state of ignorance and contentment:

Dao The Way, a term used by Daoists to refer to the natural order.

> Do not exalt the worthy, so that the people shall not compete.
> Do not value rare treasures, so that the people shall not steal.
> Do not display objects of desire, so that the people's hearts shall not be disturbed.
> Therefore in the government of the sage,
> He keeps their hearts vacuous,
> Fills their bellies,
> Weakens their ambitions,
> And strengthens their bones.
> He always causes his people to be without knowledge or desire,
> And the crafty to be afraid to act.
> By acting without action, all things will be in order.[6]

In the philosophy of the *Laozi*, the people would be better off if they knew less, gave up tools, renounced writing, stopped envying their neighbors, and lost their desire to travel or engage in war.

Zhuangzi (JWANG-dzuh) (369–286 B.C.E.), the author of the book of the same name, shared many of the central ideas of the *Laozi*. The *Zhuangzi* is filled with parables, flights of fancy, and fictional encounters between historical figures, including Confucius and his disciples. A more serious strain of Zhuangzi's thought concerned death. He questioned whether we can be sure life is better than death. When a friend expressed shock that Zhuangzi was not weeping at his wife's death but rather singing, Zhuangzi explained:

> When she died, how could I help being affected? But as I think the matter over, I realize that originally she had no life; and not only no life; she had no form; not only no form, she had no material force. In the limbo of existence and non-existence, there was transformation and the material force was evolved. The material force was transformed to be form, form was transformed to become life, and now birth has transformed to become death. This is like the rotation of the four seasons, spring, summer, fall, and winter. Now she lies asleep in the great house [the universe]. For me to go about weeping and wailing would be to show my ignorance of destiny. Therefore I desist.[7]

Zhuangzi was similarly iconoclastic in his political philosophy. In one parable a wheelwright insolently tells a duke that books are useless because all they contain are the dregs of men long dead. The duke, offended, threatens execution unless the wheelwright can explain his remark. The wheelwright responds by arguing that truly skilled craftsmen respond to situations spontaneously; they do not analyze or reason or even keep in mind the rules they have mastered. The most important truths they know cannot be written down or even explained to others. This strain of Daoist thought denies the validity of verbal reasoning and the sorts of knowledge conveyed through words.

Daoism can be seen as a response to Confucianism, a rejection of many of its basic premises. Nevertheless, over the course of Chinese history, many people felt the pull of both Confucian and Daoist ideas and studied the writings of both schools. Even Confucian scholars who had devoted much of their lives to public service might find that the teachings of the *Laozi* or *Zhuangzi* helped to put their frustrations in perspective.

Legalism

Over the course of the fourth and third centuries B.C.E., one small state after another was conquered, and the number of surviving states dwindled. Rulers fearful that their states might be next were ready to listen to political theorists who claimed expertise in the accumulation of power. These theorists, labeled **Legalists** because of their emphasis on the need for rigorous laws, argued that strong government depended not on the moral qualities of the ruler and his officials, as Confucians claimed, but on the establishment of effective laws and procedures. Legalism, though eventually discredited, laid the basis for China's later bureaucratic government.

In the fourth century B.C.E. the western state of Qin radically reformed itself along Legalist lines. The king of Qin abolished the aristocracy. Social distinctions were to be based on military ranks determined by the objective criterion of the number of enemy heads cut off in battle. In place of the old fiefs, the Qin king created counties and appointed officials to govern them according to the laws he decreed at court. To increase the population, Qin recruited migrants from other states with offers of land and houses. To encourage farmers to work hard and improve their land, they were allowed to buy and sell it. Ordinary farmers were thus freed from serf-like obligations to the local nobility, but direct control by the state could be even more

Legalists Political theorists who emphasized the need for rigorous laws and laid the basis for China's later bureaucratic government.

Inlaid Wine Flask In the same period when the Hundred Schools of Thought competed, bronze craftsmen developed new and imaginative ways to decorate bronze vessels. The lively diagonal design on this bronze wine flask was created by pounding silver into planned spaces.

(Wine flask [bianhu], Late Warring States [bronze with silver inlay], Eastern Zhou Dynasty [770–221 B.C.]/Freer Gallery, Smithsonian Institution/Bridgeman Images)

onerous. Taxes and labor service obligations were heavy. Travel required a permit, and vagrants could be forced into penal labor service. All families were grouped into mutual responsibility groups of five and ten families; whenever anyone in the group committed a crime, all the others were equally liable unless they reported it.

Legalism found its greatest exponent in Han Feizi (ca. 280–233 B.C.E.), who had studied with the Confucian master Xunzi but had little interest in Confucian values of goodness or ritual. In his writings he warned rulers of the political pitfalls awaiting them. They had to be careful where they placed their trust, for "when the ruler trusts someone, he falls under that person's control." Given subordinates' propensities to pursue their own selfish interests, the ruler should keep them ignorant of his intentions and control them by manipulating competition among them. Warmth, affection, or candor should have no place in his relationships with others.

In Han Feizi's view, if rulers would make the laws and prohibitions clear and the rewards and punishments automatic, then the officials and common people would be easy to govern. Uniform laws get people to do things they would not otherwise be inclined to do, such as work hard and fight wars; such laws are thus essential to the goal of establishing hegemony over all the other states.

The laws of the Legalists were designed as much to constrain officials as to regulate the common people. The third-century-B.C.E. tomb of a Qin official has yielded statutes detailing the rules for keeping accounts, supervising subordinates, managing penal labor, conducting investigations, and many other responsibilities of officials. Infractions were generally punishable through the imposition of fines.

Legalism saw no value in intellectual debate or private opinion. Divergent views of right and wrong lead to weakness and disorder. The ruler should not allow others to undermine his laws by questioning them. In Legalism, there were no laws above or independent of the wishes of the rulers, no laws that might set limits on rulers' actions in the way that natural or divine laws did in Greek thought.

Rulers of several states adopted some Legalist ideas, but only the state of Qin systematically followed them. The extraordinary but brief success Qin had with these policies is discussed in Chapter 7.

Yin and Yang

Confucians, Daoists, and Legalists had the greatest long-term impact on Chinese civilization, but the Hundred Schools of Thought also included everyone from logicians, hedonists, and utopians to natural philosophers who analyzed the workings of nature.

Phoenix and Tigers Divine animals, such as dragons and phoenixes, are often portrayed in the art of the Warring States Period, especially in the south, where the art of lacquered wood was perfected. (Werner Forman/akg-images)

A key idea developed by the natural philosophers was the concept of **yin and yang**, first described in the divination manual called the *Book of Changes* (ca. 900 B.C.E.), and developed into much more elaborate theories by late Zhou theorists. Yin is the feminine, dark, receptive, yielding, negative, and weak; yang is the masculine, bright, assertive, creative, positive, and strong. Yin and yang are complementary poles rather than distinct entities or opposing forces. The movement of yin and yang accounts for the transition from day to night and from summer to winter. These models based on observation of nature were extended to explain not only phenomena we might classify as natural, such as illness, storms, and earthquakes, but also social phenomena, such as the rise and fall of states and conflict in families. In all these realms, unwanted things happen when the balance between yin and yang gets disturbed.

In recent decades archaeologists have further complicated our understanding of early Chinese thought by unearthing records of the popular religion of the time—astrological manuals, handbooks of lucky and unlucky days, medical prescriptions, exercises, and ghost stories. The tomb of an official who died in 316 B.C.E., for example, has records of divinations showing that illness was seen as the result of unsatisfied spirits or malevolent demons, best dealt with through performing exorcisms or offering sacrifices to the astral god Taiyi (Grand One).

yin and yang A concept of complementary poles, one of which represents the feminine, dark, and receptive, and the other the masculine, bright, and assertive.

Chapter Summary

After several thousand years of Neolithic cultures, Bronze Age civilization developed in China, with cities, writing, and sharp social distinctions. Shang kings led armies and presided at sacrifices to the high god Di and the royal ancestors. The Shang armies' bronze-tipped weapons and chariots gave them technological superiority over their neighbors. War booty, including slaves who were often sacrificed to the gods, provided the Shang king with revenue.

The Zhou Dynasty, which overthrew the Shang in about 1050 B.C.E., parceled out its territory to hereditary lords. The earliest Chinese books date to this period. The *Book of Documents* provides evidence of the belief in the Mandate of Heaven, which justified Zhou rule. The *Book of Songs* offers glimpses into what life was like for elites and ordinary people alike in the early Zhou.

By the Warring States Period, which began in 403 B.C.E., the old domains had become independent states. As states destroyed each other, military technology made many advances, including the introduction of cavalry, infantry armies, and the crossbow. This was also the golden age of Chinese philosophy. Confucius and his followers promoted the virtues of sincerity, loyalty, benevolence, filial piety, and duty. Mencius urged rulers to rule through goodness and argued that human nature is good. Xunzi stressed the power of ritual and argued that human nature is selfish and must be curbed through education. Daoists and Legalists rejected all these ideas. The Daoists Laozi and Zhuangzi looked beyond the human realm to the entire cosmos and spoke of the relativity of concepts such as good and bad and life and death. Legalists heaped ridicule on the Confucian idea that a ruler could get his people to be good by being good himself and proposed instead rigorous laws with strict rewards and punishments. Natural philosophers explained the changes of seasons and health and illness in terms of the complementary forces of yin and yang.

NOTES

1. James Legge, trans. and ed., *The Chinese Classics* (Oxford: Oxford University Press, 1865–1895), p. 126, slightly modified.
2. Ibid., p. 531.
3. Victor H. Mair, Nancy S. Steinhardt, and Paul R. Goldin, eds., *Hawai'i Reader in Traditional Chinese Culture* (Honolulu: University of Hawai'i Press, 2005), p. 117.
4. Wing-tsit Chan, trans. and ed., *A Sourcebook in Chinese Philosophy* (Princeton, N.J.: Princeton University Press, 1963), p. 39. Reproduced with permission of PRINCETON UNIVERSITY PRESS in the format Book via Copyright Clearance Center.
5. Ibid., p. 129.
6. Ibid., pp. 140–141.
7. Ibid., p. 209.

CONNECTIONS

China's transition from Neolithic farming villages to a much more advanced civilization with writing, metalworking, iron coinage, crossbows, philosophical speculation, and competing states occurred centuries later than in Mesopotamia or India, but by the Warring States Period China was at much the same stage of development as other advanced societies in Eurasia. Although many elements of China's civilization were clearly invented in China — such as its writing system, its method of casting bronze, and its Confucian philosophy — it also adopted elements that diffused across Asia, such as the cultivation of wheat, the horse-driven chariot, and riding horseback.

Greece, the subject of the next chapter, is located very close to the ancient Near Eastern civilizations, so it developed more rapidly, as it was able to borrow many elements of civilization from its neighbors. It was also much smaller than China, yet in time had enormous impact on the wider world. If we keep India and China in mind, the originality of the political forms and ideas of early Greece will stand out more clearly. We return to China's history in Chapter 7, after looking at Greece and Rome.

CHAPTER 4   Review and Explore

Identify Key Terms

Identify and explain the significance of each item below.

loess (p. 90)	**Mandate of Heaven** (p. 95)	**ren** (p. 103)
Anyang (p. 92)	**shi** (p. 95)	**filial piety** (p. 105)
taotie (p. 93)	***Book of Songs*** (p. 95)	**Dao** (p. 106)
logographic (p. 94)	**Warring States Period** (p. 100)	**Legalists** (p. 107)
Book of Documents (p. 95)	**crossbow** (p. 100)	**yin and yang** (p. 109)

Review the Main Ideas

Answer the focus questions from each section of the chapter.

1. What was the impact of China's geography on the development of Chinese societies? (p. 90)

2. What was life like during the Shang Dynasty, and what effect did writing have on Chinese culture and government? (p. 92)

3. How was China governed, and what was life like during the Zhou Dynasty? (p. 94)

4. How did advances in military technology contribute to the rise of independent states? (p. 100)

5. What ideas did Confucius teach, and how were they spread after his death? (p. 101)

6. How did the teachings of Daoism, Legalism, and other schools of thought differ from those of Confucianism? (p. 105)

Make Comparisons and Connections

Analyze the larger developments and continuities within and across chapters.

1. Which features of early China's history seem closest to developments in other early civilizations, such as Mesopotamia, Egypt, and India?

2. Why do we refer to the ideas developed in India in the second half of the first millennium B.C.E. as religion and to those developed in China during the same period as philosophy? Is this a useful distinction? Why or why not?

3. Do Chinese Legalist ideas resemble ideas developed by other societies, including much more modern societies?

TIMELINE

CHINA

← **ca. 9000** B.C.E. Farming begins in Yellow River Valley
← **ca. 7000** B.C.E. Domestication of cattle; plow agriculture begins

SOUTH ASIA

MEDITERRANEAN WORLD

◆ **ca. 2500** B.C.E. Bronze Age begins in Mesopotamia **(Ch. 2)**

| 2500 B.C.E. | 2000 B.C.E. | 1500 B.C.E. |

Suggested Resources

BOOKS

Chang, Kwang-chih, and Xu Pingfang. *The Formation of Chinese Civilization: An Archaeological Perspective.* 2005. Essays by leading archaeologists in China.

de Bary, William Theodore, and Irene Bloom. *Sources of Chinese Tradition.* 1999. Large collection of primary sources for Chinese intellectual history, with lengthy introductions.

Ebrey, Patricia Buckley. *Cambridge Illustrated History of China,* 2d ed. 2010. Well-illustrated brief overview of Chinese history.

Feng, Li. *Early China: A Social and Cultural History.* 2013. Draws extensively on recent archaeological discoveries.

Graham, A. C. *Disputers of the Tao: Philosophical Argument in Ancient China.* 1989. A philosophically rich overview of the intellectual flowering of the Warring States Period.

Ledderose, Lothar. *Ten Thousand Things: Module and Mass Production in Chinese Art.* 2000. A new interpretation of Chinese culture in terms of modules; offers fresh perspectives on the Chinese script and the production of bronzes.

Lewis, Mark. *Writing and Authority in Early China.* 1999. An examination of early Chinese thought in terms of the ways that texts create authority.

Loewe, Michael, and Edward Shaughnessy, eds. *The Cambridge History of Ancient China: From the Origins of Civilization to 221 B.C.* 1999. An authoritative collection of chapters, half by historians, half by archaeologists.

Mote, F. W. *Intellectual Foundations of China.* 1989. Brief but stimulating introduction to early Chinese thought.

Puett, Michael. *To Become a God: Cosmology, Sacrifice, and Self-Divinization in Early China.* 2004. Brings an anthropological perspective to the development of early Chinese thought.

ca. 1500–1050 B.C.E. Shang Dynasty; first writing in China

551–479 B.C.E. Life of Confucius

◆ **ca. 500 B.C.E.** Iron technology in wide use

ca. 1050–256 B.C.E. Zhou Dynasty

403–221 B.C.E. China's Warring States Period, golden age of Chinese philosophy **(Ch. 4)**

ca. 370–300 B.C.E. Mencius

369–286 B.C.E. Zhuangzi and the development of Daoism

◆ **ca. 350 B.C.E.** Infantry armed with crossbows

ca. 1500–500 B.C.E. Vedic Age in India; caste system develops **(Ch. 3)**

◆ **ca. 1250 B.C.E.** Moses leads Hebrews out of Egypt **(Ch. 2)**

◆ **ca. 500 B.C.E.** Founding of Buddhism and Jainism in India **(Ch. 3)**

◆ **509 B.C.E.** Roman Republic founded **(Ch. 6)**

ca. 500–338 B.C.E. Classical period in Greece; development of drama and philosophy and major building projects in Athens **(Ch. 5)**

336–324 B.C.E. Conquests of Alexander the Great **(Ch. 5)**

1000 B.C.E.	**500 B.C.E.**	**1 C.E.**

Shankman, Steven, and Stephen W. Durrant. *Early China / Ancient Greece: Thinking Through Comparisons.* 2002. A collection of articles that encourage cross-cultural comparisons.

Sterckx, Roel, ed. *Of Tripod and Palate: Food, Politics, and Religion in Traditional China.* 2005. Provides a fresh look at many elements in early Chinese culture.

Thorp, Robert. *China in the Early Bronze Age: Shang Civilization.* 2005. Clear synthesis based on recent research.

Thorp, Robert, and Richard Vinograd. *Chinese Art and Culture.* 2001. Broad coverage of all of China's visual arts.

Yang, Xin, ed. *The Golden Age of Chinese Archaeology.* 1999. The well-illustrated catalogue of a major show of Chinese archaeological finds.

DOCUMENTARY

Ancient China (Films for the Humanities and Sciences, 1996). A broad overview of China through the Han Dynasty.

FEATURE FILMS

The Emperor and the Assassin (Beijing Film Studio, 1999). A film on the attempted assassination of the king of Qin; in Chinese with English subtitles.

Hero (Zhang Yimou Studio, 2002). A fictional reimaging of an attempted assassination of the king of Qin; in Chinese with English subtitles.

The Warring States (Beijing Starlit Movie and TV Culture Co., 2011). Focuses on the rivalry between two generals; in Chinese with English subtitles.

WEBSITE

Warring States Period. Wikipedia offers useful maps and a detailed history. **en.wikipedia.org/wiki /Warring_States_period**

5

The Greek Experience
3500–30 B.C.E.

Humans came into Greece over many thousands of years, in waves of migrants whose place of origin and cultural characteristics have been the source of much scholarly debate. The people of ancient Greece built on the traditions and ideas of earlier societies to develop a culture that fundamentally shaped the civilization of the western part of Eurasia, much as the Chinese culture shaped the civilization of the eastern part. The Greeks were the first in the Mediterranean and neighboring areas to explore many of the questions about the world around them and the place of humans in it that continue to concern thinkers today. Drawing on their day-to-day experiences as well as logic and empirical observation, they developed ways of understanding and explaining the world around them, which grew into modern philosophy and science. They also created new political forms and new types of literature and art.

Historians, archaeologists, and classicists divide the history of the Greeks into three broad periods: the Helladic period, which covered the Bronze Age, roughly 3000 B.C.E. to 800 B.C.E.; the Hellenic period, from the Bronze Age Collapse to the death of Alexander the Great, the ruler of Macedonia who conquered Greece, in 323 B.C.E.; and the Hellenistic period, stretching from Alexander's death to the Roman conquest in 30 B.C.E. of the kingdom established in Egypt by Alexander's successors. During the Hellenic period, Greeks developed a distinctive form of city-state known as the polis and made lasting cultural and intellectual achievements. During the Hellenistic period, Macedonian and Greek armies defeated the Persian Empire and built new cities and kingdoms, spreading Greek ideas as far as India (see "Western Contact and the Mauryan Unification of North India" in Chapter 3). During their conquests they blended their ideas and traditions with those of the societies they encountered, creating a vibrant culture.

Greek Boy with Goose

In the Hellenistic culture that developed across a huge area after Alexander the Great's conquests, wealthy urban residents wanted art that showed real people rather than gods. This statue of a little boy wrestling a goose, originally carved about 200 B.C.E., no doubt found an eager buyer.

Glyptothek, Stalliche Antikensammlung, Munich, Germany/© Vanni Archive/Art Resource, NY

CHAPTER PREVIEW

How did the geography of Greece shape its earliest history?

Greece in the Bronze Age, ca. 3000–800 B.C.E.

Hellas, as the Greeks call their land, encompasses the Greek peninsula with its southern peninsular extension, known as the Peloponnesus (peh-luh-puh-NEE-suhs), and the islands surrounding it, an area known as the Aegean (ah-JEE-uhn) basin (Map 5.1). During the Bronze Age, which for Greek history is called the "Helladic period," early settlers in Greece began establishing small communities contoured by the mountains and small plains that shaped the land. The geographical fragmentation of Greece encouraged political fragmentation. Early in Greek history several kingdoms did emerge—including the Minoan on the island of Crete and the Mycenaean on the mainland—but the rugged terrain prohibited the growth of a great empire like those of Mesopotamia or Egypt.

The Minoans and Mycenaeans

On the large island of Crete, Bronze Age farmers and fishermen began to trade their surpluses with their neighbors, and cities grew, housing artisans and merchants. Beginning about 2000 B.C.E. Cretans voyaged throughout the eastern Mediterranean and the Aegean, carrying the copper and tin needed to make bronze as well as many other goods. Social hierarchies developed, and in many cities certain individuals came to hold power. The Cretans began to use writing about 1900 B.C.E., in a form later

MAP 5.1 Classical Greece, ca. 450 B.C.E. In antiquity the home of the Greeks included the islands of the Aegean and the western shore of Turkey as well as the Greek peninsula itself. Crete, the home of Minoan civilization, is the large island at the bottom of the map. The Peloponnesian peninsula, where Sparta is located, is connected to the rest of mainland Greece by a very narrow isthmus at Corinth.

Mycenaean Dagger Blade This scene in gold and silver on the blade of an iron dagger depicts hunters armed with spears and protected by shields defending themselves against charging lions. The Mycenaeans were a robust, warlike people who enjoyed the thrill and the danger of hunting.

(National Archaeological Museum, Athens, Greece/Ancient Art & Architecture Collection, Ltd./Bridgeman Images)

scholars called Linear A, a script with hundreds of signs believed to be pictographs and syllables. (For more on writing, see "Writing, Mathematics, and Poetry" in Chapter 2.) The few extant examples of this writing have not been deciphered. At about the same time that writing began, rulers in several cities of Crete began to build large structures with hundreds of interconnected rooms. The archaeologists who discovered these huge structures called them palaces, and they named the flourishing and vibrant culture of this era Minoan, after the mythical king of Crete, Minos.

Few specifics are known about Minoan political life except that a king and a group of nobles stood at its head. Minoan society was long thought to have been relatively peaceful, but new excavations are revealing more and more walls around cities, which has called the peaceful nature of Minoan society into question. In terms of their religious life, Minoans appear to have worshipped goddesses far more than gods. Whether this translated into more egalitarian gender roles for real people is unclear, but surviving Minoan art, which shows women as well as men leading religious activities, watching entertainment, and engaging in athletic competitions, such as leaping over bulls, suggests that it might have.

As Minoan culture was flourishing on Crete, a different type of society developed on the mainland. This society was founded by groups who had migrated in during the period after 2000 B.C.E. By about 1650 B.C.E. one group of these immigrants had raised palaces and established cities at Thebes, Athens, Mycenae (migh-SEE-nee), and elsewhere. These palace-centers ruled by local kings formed a loose hegemony under the authority of the king of Mycenae, and the archaeologists who first discovered traces of this culture called it the Mycenaean (migh-see-NEE-ahn).

As in Crete, the political unit was the kingdom, and the king and his warrior aristocracy stood at the top of society. The seat and symbol of the king's power was his palace, which was also the economic center of the kingdom. Palace scribes kept records with a script known as Linear B, which used roughly two hundred ideographic and syllabic signs. This script appears to have descended from Linear A, but unlike the earlier script, Linear B has been deciphered, and it is the earliest documented form of written Greek.

The available written and archaeological evidence suggests a society in which war was common. Mycenaean cities were all fortified by thick stone walls, and graves contain spears, javelins, swords, helmets, and the first examples of metal armor known in the world.

Contacts between the Minoans and Mycenaeans were originally peaceful, and Minoan culture and trade goods flooded the Greek mainland. But most scholars think that around 1450 B.C.E., possibly in the wake of an earthquake that left Crete vulnerable, the Mycenaeans attacked Crete, destroying many towns and occupying

Knossos (NOH-sohs), Crete's leading city. For about the next fifty years, the Myce-naeans ruled much of the island. Then, between about 1300 B.C.E. and 1100 B.C.E., various kingdoms in and beyond Greece ravaged one another in a savage series of wars that destroyed both the Minoan and Mycenaean civilizations.

The fall of the Minoans and Mycenaeans was part of what some scholars see as a general collapse of Bronze Age civilizations in the eastern Mediterranean, including the end of the Egyptian New Kingdom and the fall of the Hittite Empire (see "Migra-tions, Revivals, and Collapse" in Chapter 2). This collapse appears to have had a number of causes: internal economic and social problems; invasions and migrations by outsiders; changes in warfare and weaponry, particularly the adoption of iron weapons, which made foot soldiers the most important factor in battles and reduced the power of kings and wealthy nobles fighting from chariots; and natural disasters such as volcanic eruptions, earthquakes, and droughts.

The "Dark Age"

In Greece these invasions, migrations, disasters, and social problems worked together to usher in a period of poverty and disruption that historians have traditionally called the "Dark Age" of Greece (ca. 1100–800 B.C.E.). Cities were destroyed, population declined, villages were abandoned, and trade decreased. Even writing, which was not widespread before this period, was a casualty of the chaos.

The Bronze Age Collapse led to the widespread and prolonged movement of Greek peoples, both within Greece itself and beyond. They dispersed beyond main-land Greece farther south to the islands of the Aegean Sea and in greater strength across the Aegean to the shores of Anatolia in modern-day Turkey (see Map 5.1). By the conclusion of the Dark Age, the Greeks had spread their culture throughout the Aegean basin, and like many other cultures around the Mediterranean and the Near East, they had adopted iron.

Archaeological sources from the Dark Age are less rich than those from the peri-ods that came after, so they are often used in conjunction with literary sources writ-ten in later centuries to give us a more complete picture of the era. These included tales of the heroic deeds of legendary heroes similar to the epic poems of Mesopota-mia and the *Ramayana* in India. Sometime in the eighth or seventh century B.C.E. many of these were gathered together in two long epic poems: the *Iliad*, which tells the story of the Trojan War, a war similar to those fought by Mycenaean kings, and the *Odyssey*, which records the adventures of one of the heroes of that war. These poems were recited orally, and once writing was reintroduced to Greece, they were written down and attributed to a poet named Homer, though scholars debate whether Homer was an actual historical individual. The two poems present human and divine characters who are larger than life but also petty, vindictive, pouting, and deceitful, flaws that drive the action forward, usually with tragic results.

Greeks also learned about the gods and goddesses of their polytheistic system from another poet, Hesiod (HEH-see-uhd), who most scholars think lived sometime between 750 and 650 B.C.E. Hesiod's *Theogony* combines Mesopotamian and Hittite myths with a variety of Greek oral traditions to tell a coherent story of the origin of the gods, and his *Works and Days* portrays the gods watching over the earth, looking for justice and injustice, while leaving the great mass of men and women to live lives of hard work and endless toil.

The Development of the Polis in the Archaic Age, ca. 800–500 B.C.E.

What was the role of the polis in Greek society?

Homer lived in the era after the Dark Age, which later historians have termed the Archaic age (800–500 B.C.E.). The most important political change in this period was the development of the **polis** (PAH-lihs) (plural *poleis [pah-LEH-is]*), a word generally translated as "city-state." During the Archaic period, poleis established colonies throughout much of the Mediterranean, spreading Greek culture, and two particular poleis rose to prominence on the Greek mainland: Sparta and Athens.

polis Generally translated as "city-state," it was the basic political and institutional unit of ancient Greece.

Organization of the Polis

The Greek polis was not the first form of city-state to emerge. The earliest states in Sumer were also city-states, as were many of the small Mycenaean kingdoms. What differentiated the new Greek model from older city-states was that the polis was more than a political institution — it was a community of citizens with their own customs and laws. With one exception, the poleis that emerged after 800 B.C.E. did not have kings but instead were self-governing. The physical, religious, and political forms of the polis varied from place to place, but everywhere it was relatively small, reflecting the fragmented geography of Greece. The very smallness of the polis, however, enabled Greeks to see how they fit individually into their city and thus how the individual parts made up the social whole.

hoplites Heavily armed citizens who served as infantrymen and fought to defend the polis.

The polis included a city and its surrounding countryside. The countryside was essential to the economy of the polis and provided food to sustain the entire population. The people of the polis typically lived in a compact group of houses within the city, which by the fifth century B.C.E. was generally surrounded by a wall. Another feature was a usually elevated area called the acropolis, where the people erected temples, altars, and public monuments. The polis also contained a public square or marketplace, the agora (EH-gohr-ah), where there were porticoes, shops, public buildings, and courts. The agora was the political center of the polis.

All poleis, with one exception, did not have standing armies. Instead they relied on their citizens for protection. Very rich citizens often served as cavalry, which was, however, never as important as the heavily armed infantrymen known as **hoplites**. These commoners were the backbone of the army, just as foot soldiers were in China during the Warring

Spartan Hoplite This bronze figurine portrays an armed foot soldier about to strike an enemy. His massive helmet with its full crest gives his head nearly complete protection, while a metal corselet covers his chest and back, and greaves (similar to today's shin guards) protect his shins. In his right hand he carries a thrusting spear (now broken off), and in his left a large round shield.
(bpk Bildagentur/Antikensammlung, Staatliche Museen, Berlin, Germany/Photo: Johannes Laurentius/Art Resource, NY)

States Period (see "The Warring States Period" in Chapter 4). Hoplites wore bronze helmets and leather and bronze body armor, which they purchased themselves.

Greek poleis had several different types of government. Sporadic periods of violent political and social upheaval often led to the takeover of power by one man, a type of government the Greeks called tyranny. Tyrants were not always oppressive rulers, however, and sometimes used their power to benefit average citizens. **Democracy** was rule by citizens, not the people as a whole. Almost all Greek cities defined a citizen as an adult man with at least one citizen parent. Thus citizens shared ancestry as well as a place of residence. Women were citizens for religious and reproductive purposes, but their citizenship did not give them the right to participate in government. Free men who were not children of a citizen, known as resident foreigners, and slaves were not citizens and had no political voice.

Oligarchy was government by a small group of wealthy citizens. Many Greeks preferred oligarchy because it provided more political stability than did democracy. Although oligarchy was the government of the prosperous, it left the door open for political and social advancement. If members of the polis could meet property or money qualifications, they could enter the governing circle.

> **democracy** A type of Greek government in which all citizens administered the workings of government.

> **oligarchy** A type of Greek government in which citizens who owned a certain amount of property ruled.

Overseas Expansion

The development of the polis coincided with the growth of the Greek world in both wealth and numbers, bringing new problems. The increase in population created more demand for food than the land could supply. The resulting social and political tensions drove many people to seek new homes outside of Greece (Map 5.2).

Greeks traveled throughout the Mediterranean, sailing in great numbers to Sicily and southern Italy, where there was ample space for expansion. Some adventurous Greeks sailed farther west to Sardinia, France, Spain, and perhaps even the Canary Islands. From these new outposts Greek influence extended to southern France.

In contrast to earlier military invasions and migrations of peoples, these were very often intentional colonizing ventures, organized and planned by a specific polis seeking new land for its residents, or by the losers in a political conflict within a polis who were forced to leave. Colonization changed the entire Greek world, both at home and abroad. In economic terms the expansion of the Greeks created a much larger market for agricultural and manufactured goods.

The Growth of Sparta

During the Archaic period Sparta became the leading military power in Greece. To expand their polis, the Spartans did not establish colonies but instead conquered Messenia (muh-SEE-nee-uh), a region in the southwestern Peloponnesus. They turned the Messenians into helots (HEH-luhts), unfree residents forced to work state lands. The helots soon rose in a revolt that took the Spartans thirty years to crush. Afterward, non-nobles who had shared in the fighting as foot soldiers appear to have demanded rights equal to those of the nobility and a voice in the government. Under intense pressure the aristocrats agreed to remodel the state into a new system.

The plan for the new system in Sparta was attributed to the lawgiver Lycurgus (ligh-KUHR-guhs), who may or may not have been an actual person. Political distinctions among Spartan men were eliminated, and all citizens became legally equal. Two kings, who were primarily military leaders, and a council of nobles shared exec-

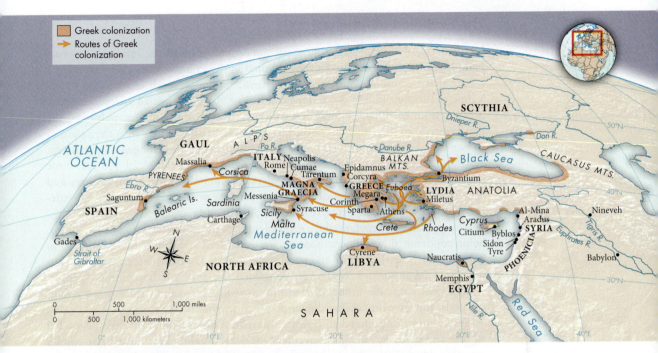

MAP 5.2 Greek Colonization, ca. 750–550 B.C.E. The Greeks established colonies along the shores of the Mediterranean and Black Seas, spreading Greek culture and creating a large trading network.

utive power with five ephors (EH-fuhrs), overseers elected by the citizens. Helots worked the land, while Spartan citizens devoted their time to military training, and Sparta became extremely powerful.

In the system attributed to Lycurgus, every citizen owed primary allegiance to Sparta. Suppression of the individual along with an emphasis on military prowess led to a barracks state. Even family life was sacrificed to the polis. After long, hard military training that began at age seven, citizens became lifelong soldiers. Because men often did not see their wives or other women for long periods, not only in times of war but also in times of peace, their most meaningful relations were same-sex ones. The Spartan military leaders may have viewed such relationships as militarily advantageous because they believed that men would fight even more fiercely for lovers and comrades. An anecdote frequently repeated about one Spartan mother sums up Spartan military values. As her son was setting off to battle, the mother handed him his shield and advised him to come back either victorious and carrying the shield, or dead and being carried on it. Spartan men were expected to train vigorously, do with little, and like it, qualities reflected even today in the word *spartan*.

Spartans expected women in citizen families to be good wives and strict mothers of future soldiers. With men in military service much of their lives, women in citizen families ran the estates and owned land in their own right, and they were not physically restricted or secluded.

The Evolution of Athens

Like Sparta, Athens faced pressing social and economic problems during the Archaic period, but instead of creating a state devoted to the military, the Athenians created a state that became a democracy. For Athens, the late seventh century B.C.E. was a time of turmoil. In 621 B.C.E. Draco (DRAY-koh), an Athenian aristocrat, under pressure from small landholders and with the consent of the nobles, published the first law code of the Athenian polis. His code was harsh—and is thus the origin of the word *draconian*—but it embodied the ideal that the law belonged to all citizens. Yet the aristocracy still governed Athens oppressively, and the social and economic situation remained dire. Noble landholders continued to force small farmers and artisans into economic dependence. Many families were sold into slavery as settlement for debts, while others were exiled and their land mortgaged to the rich.

One person who recognized these problems was the aristocrat Solon (SOH-luhn). Solon condemned his fellow aristocrats for their greed and dishonesty. According to later sources, Solon's sincerity and good sense convinced other aristocrats that he was no crazed revolutionary. Moreover, he gained the trust of the common people. Around 594 B.C.E. the nobles elected him *archon* (AHR-kahn), chief magistrate of the polis, and gave him extraordinary power to reform the state.

Solon immediately freed all people enslaved for debt, recalled all exiles, canceled all debts on land, and made enslavement for debt illegal. Solon allowed non-nobles into the old aristocratic assembly, where they could vote in the election of magistrates. Later sixth-century-B.C.E. leaders further broadened the opportunities for commoners to take part in government, transforming Athens into a democracy.

The democracy functioned on the ideal that all full citizens should play a role in government. In 487 B.C.E. the election of the city's nine archons was replaced by reappointment by lot, which meant that any citizen with a certain amount of property had a chance of becoming an archon. Making laws was the responsibility of two bodies, the *boule* (BOO-lee), or council, composed of five hundred members, and the *ecclesia* (ee-KLEE-zhee-uh), the assembly of all citizens. By supervising the various committees of government and proposing bills and treaties to the ecclesia, the boule guided Athenian political life. Nonetheless, the ecclesia, open to all male citizens over eighteen years of age, had the final word through its votes.

<aside>In the classical period, how did war influence Greece, and how did the arts, religion, and philosophy develop?</aside>

Turmoil and Culture in the Classical Period, 500–338 B.C.E.

From the time of the Mycenaeans, violent conflict was common in Greek society, and this did not change in the fifth century B.C.E., the beginning of what scholars later called the classical period of Greek history. First, the Greeks beat back the armies of the Persian Empire. Then, turning their spears against one another, they destroyed their own political system in a century of warfare that began with the Peloponnesian War. Although warfare was one of the hallmarks of the classical period, intellectual and artistic accomplishments were as well.

The Deadly Conflicts, 499–404 B.C.E.

In 499 B.C.E. the Greeks who lived on the western coast of what is now Turkey, an area then known as Ionia, unsuccessfully rebelled against the Persian Empire, which had ruled the area for fifty years (see "The Rise and Expansion of the Persian Empire" in Chapter 2). The Athenians provided halfhearted help to the Ionians, and in retaliation the Persians struck at Athens, only to be surprisingly defeated by the Athenian hoplites at the Battle of Marathon. In 480 B.C.E. the Persian king Xerxes (ZUHRK-seez) personally led a massive invasion of Greece. Under the leadership of Sparta, many Greek poleis, though not all, united to fight the Persians in what later historians termed the Persian wars. The larger Persian army enjoyed early success, but the tide of the war quickly turned and the invasion ended in failure.

The victorious Athenians and their allies then formed the Delian League, a military alliance intended to liberate Ionia from Persian rule and keep the Persians out of Greece. The Athenians, however, turned the league into an Athenian empire. They reduced their allies to the status of subjects. Athenian ideas of freedom and democracy did not extend to the citizens of other cities, and cities that objected to or revolted over Athenian actions were put down.

Under their great leader Pericles (PEHR-uh-kleez) (ca. 494–429 B.C.E.), the Athenians grew so powerful and aggressive that they alarmed Sparta and its allies. In 431 B.C.E. Athenian imperialism finally drove Sparta into the conflict known as the Peloponnesian War. The Peloponnesian War lasted a generation (431–404 B.C.E.) and brought in its wake disease, widespread civil wars, destruction, famine, and huge loss of life. In 404 B.C.E. the Athenians finally surrendered to Sparta and its allies, and Sparta stripped it of its empire. Conflicts among the states of Greece continued, however.

Athenian Arts in the Age of Pericles

In the midst of the warfare of the fifth century B.C.E., Pericles turned Athens into the showplace of Greece. He appropriated Delian League money to pay for a huge building program to rebuild the city that had been destroyed during the Persian occupation in 480 B.C.E. and to display to all Greeks the glory of the Athenian polis. Workers erected temples and other buildings as patriotic memorials housing statues and carvings, often painted in bright colors, showing the gods in human form and celebrating the Athenian victory over the Persians. (The paint later washed away, leaving the generally white sculpture that we think of as "classical.") The Acropolis in the center of the city was crowned by the Parthenon, a temple that celebrated the greatness of Athens and its patron goddess, Athena, who was represented by a huge statue. (See "Analyzing the Evidence: The Acropolis of Athens," page 124.) Sculptors in Athens increasingly based their statues of gods and heroes on studies of actual human anatomy. Accordingly, the statues showed realistic musculature, although the figures were always depicted in the prime form of young adulthood and with a noble facial expression, as befit a deity. Most large-scale Greek paintings have been lost, but Greek pottery was frequently decorated with painted figures and scenes that sometimes show more ordinary humans as well as divine figures. These men and women also had realistic musculature and expressions, and they are going about the ordinary tasks of daily life—working, cooking, going in and out of doors.

Other aspects of Athenian culture were also rooted in the life of the polis. The polis sponsored plays as part of the city's religious festivals and required wealthy citizens to pay the expenses of their production. Many plays were highly controversial,

The Persian Wars, 499–479 B.C.E.

Areas of Persian control
Greek states at war with Persia
Neutral Greek states

Thermopylae 480 B.C.E.   Artemisium 480 B.C.E.
Plataea 479 B.C.E.   Marathon 490 B.C.E.
Salamis 480 B.C.E.
Crete

The Delian League, ca. 478–431 B.C.E.

Delian League
Allied with Delian League, 446 B.C.E.
Athenian military settlement

Thasos
Corcyra
BOEOTIA
Megara   Athens
Corinth   Delos
Sparta
PERSIAN EMPIRE

The Acropolis of Athens

The natural rock formation of the Acropolis probably had a palace on top as early as the Mycenaean period, when it was also surrounded by a defensive wall. Temples were constructed beginning in the sixth century B.C.E., and after the Persian wars Pericles ordered the reconstruction and expansion of many of these, as well as the building of new and more magnificent temples and an extension of the defensive walls. The largest building is the Parthenon, a temple dedicated to the goddess Athena, which originally housed a 40-foot-tall statue of Athena made of ivory and gold sheets attached to a wooden frame. Near it were smaller temples built to commemorate the victory over the Persians. Much of the Parthenon was damaged when it was shelled during a war between Venice and the Ottoman Empire in the seventeenth century, and air pollution continues to eat away at the marble.

The Athenians normally hiked up the long approach to the Acropolis only for religious festivals, of which the most important and joyous was the Great Panathenaea, held every four years to honor the virgin goddess Athena and perhaps offer sacrifices to older deities as well. For this festival, Athenian citizens and legal noncitizen residents formed a huge procession to bring the statue of Athena in the Parthenon an exquisite robe, richly embroidered by the citizen women of Athens with mythological scenes. After the religious ceremonies, all the people joined in a feast.

(Marie Mauzy/Art Resource, NY)

QUESTIONS FOR ANALYSIS

1. Look at the Parthenon in the center of the photograph. What words would you use to describe the building and its style?
2. Imagine yourself as an Athenian walking up the hill toward the Parthenon. What impression would the setting and the building itself convey?

with overt political and social commentary, but they were neither suppressed nor censored. Not surprisingly, given the incessant warfare, conflict was a constant element in Athenian drama, and playwrights used their art in attempts to portray, understand, and resolve life's basic conflicts.

Aeschylus (EHS-kuh-luhs) (525–456 B.C.E.) was the first dramatist to explore such basic questions as the rights of the individual, the conflict between the individual and society, and the nature of good and evil. In his trilogy of plays, *The Oresteia*, he treats the themes of betrayal, murder, and reconciliation, urging the use of reason and justice to reconcile fundamental conflicts.

The plays of Sophocles (SAH-fuh-kleez) (496–406 B.C.E.) also deal with matters personal, political, and divine. In *Antigone*—which tells of how a king's mistakes in judgment lead to the suicides of his son, his son's fiancée, and his wife—Sophocles emphasizes the precedence of divine law over political law and family custom. In *Oedipus the King*, Sophocles tells the story of a good man doomed by the gods to kill his father and marry his mother. When Oedipus fails to avoid his fate, he blinds himself in despair and flees into exile. In *Oedipus at Colonus*, Sophocles treats the last days of the broken man, whose patient suffering and uncomplaining piety ultimately win the blessings and honor of the gods.

Euripides (yoo-RIH-puh-deez) (ca. 480–406 B.C.E.) likewise explored the theme of personal conflict within the polis and sounded the depths of the individual. With Euripides drama entered a new and more personal phase. To him the gods mattered far less than people.

Athens also produced writers of comedies, who used humor as political commentary in an effort to suggest and support the best policies for the polis. Best known of the comedians is Aristophanes (eh-ruh-STAH-fuh-neez) (ca. 445–386 B.C.E.), a merciless critic of cranks, quacks, and fools. He used his art of sarcasm to dramatize his ideas on the right conduct of citizens and their leaders for the good of the polis.

Families and Sexual Relations

The Athenians, like other Greeks, lived with comparatively few material possessions in houses that were rather simple. A typical Athenian house consisted of a series of rooms opening onto a central courtyard that contained a well, an altar, and a washbasin. Larger houses often had a front room where the men of the family ate and entertained guests, as well as women's quarters at the back. Meals consisted primarily of various grains, especially wheat and barley, as well as lentils, olives, figs, grapes, fish, and a little meat, foods that are now part of the highly touted "Mediterranean diet."

In the city a man might support himself as a craftsman, or he could contract with the polis to work on public buildings. Certain crafts, including spinning and weaving, were generally done by women. Men and women without skills worked as paid laborers. Slavery was commonplace in Greece, as it was throughout the ancient world. Slaves, who were paid for their work, were usually foreigners.

Citizenship was the basis of political power for men in ancient Athens and was inherited. After the middle of the fifth century, only those whose parents were both citizens were citizens, except for a few men given citizenship as a reward for service to the city. Adult male citizens were expected to take part in political decisions and be active in civic life, no matter what their occupation. They were also in charge of relations between the household and the wider community.

Women in Athens and elsewhere in Greece, like those in Mesopotamia, brought dowries to their husbands upon marriage, which went back to their fathers in cases of divorce. Women did not play a public role in classical Athens, and we know the names of no female poets, artists, or philosophers. Women in wealthier citizen families probably spent most of their time at home, leaving the house only to attend some religious festivals, and perhaps occasionally plays. The main function of women from citizen families was to bear and raise children. In their quarters of the house women

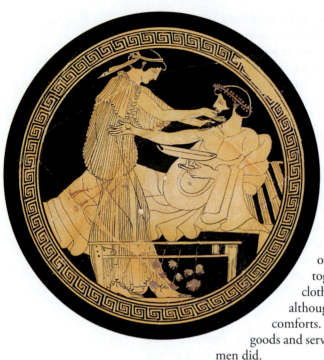

Hetaera and Man at a Dinner Party In this scene painted on the inside of a drinking cup, a hetaera (one of Athens's sophisticated courtesans known for their intellectual accomplishments as well as sexual allure) strokes the beard of a man who holds a drinking cup. Sexual and comic scenes were common on Greek pottery, particularly on objects that would have been used at a private dinner party hosted by a citizen, known as a symposium. Wives did not attend symposia, but hetaerae and entertainers were often hired to perform for the male guests.

(Symposium scene, interior, drinking cup, Late Archaic Period, c. 490–480 B.C. [kylix], Makron Painter [fl. c. 490–480 B.C.] Museum of Fine Arts, Boston/Henry Lillie Pierce Fund/Bridgeman Images)

oversaw domestic slaves and hired labor, and together with servants and friends worked wool into cloth. Women from noncitizen families lived freer lives, although they worked harder and had fewer material comforts. They performed manual labor in the fields or sold goods and services in the agora, going about their affairs much as men did.

Same-sex relations were generally accepted in all of ancient Greece. In classical Athens part of a male adolescent citizen's training might entail a hierarchical sexual and tutorial relationship with an older man, who most likely was married and may have had female sexual partners as well. These relationships between young men and older men were often celebrated in literature and art, in part because Athenians regarded perfection as possible only in the male. Women were generally seen as inferior to men, dominated by their bodies rather than their minds. A small number of sources refer to female-female sexual desire, the most famous of which are a few of the poems of Sappho (SEH-foh), a female poet of the sixth century B.C.E.

Same-sex relations did not mean that people did not marry, for Athenians saw the continuation of the family line as essential. Sappho, for example, appears to have been married and had a daughter. Sexual desire and procreation were both important aspects of life, but ancient Greeks did not necessarily link them.

Public and Personal Religion

Like most peoples of the ancient world, the Greeks were polytheists, worshipping a variety of gods and goddesses who were immortal but otherwise acted just like people. As elsewhere, Greek religion was primarily a matter of ritual, with rituals designed to appease the divinities believed to control the forces of the natural world. Processions, festivals, and sacrifices offered to the gods were frequently occasions for people to meet together socially. Migration, invasion, and colonization brought the Greeks into contact with other peoples and caused their religious beliefs to evolve.

By the classical era, the primary gods were understood to live metaphorically on Mount Olympus, the highest mountain in Greece. Besides these Olympian gods, each polis had its own minor deities, each with his or her own local group of worshippers. The polis administered the cults and religious festivals, and everyone was expected to participate in these civic rituals. In contrast to Mesopotamia, Egypt, and Vedic India, priests held little power in Greece; their purpose was to care for temples and sacred property and to conduct the proper rituals, but not to make religious or political rules or doctrines. Much religion was local and domestic, and individual families honored various deities privately in their homes.

Along with public and family forms of honoring the gods, some Greeks also participated in what later historians have termed **mystery religions**, in which participants underwent an initiation ritual and gained secret knowledge that they were forbidden to reveal to the uninitiated. Many of these religions promised rebirth or an afterlife to adherents.

The Greeks also shared some Pan-Hellenic festivals, the chief of which were held at Olympia to honor the god Zeus and at Delphi to honor the god Apollo. The festivities at Olympia included athletic contests that inspired the modern Olympic games. Held every four years after they started in 776 B.C.E., the contests attracted visitors from all over the Greek world and lasted until the fourth century C.E., when they were banned by a Christian emperor because they were pagan. The Pythian games at Delphi were also held every four years, and these contests included musical and literary competitions.

mystery religions Belief systems that were characterized by secret doctrines, rituals of initiation, and sometimes the promise of rebirth or an afterlife.

The Flowering of Philosophy

Just as the Greeks developed rituals to honor gods, they spun myths and epics to explain the origins of the universe. Over time, however, some Greeks began to question their old gods and myths, and they sought rational rather than supernatural explanations for natural phenomena. These Greek thinkers, based in Ionia, are called the Pre-Socratics because their rational efforts preceded those of the better-known Socrates. Taking individual facts, they wove them into general theories that led them to conclude that, despite appearances, the universe is actually simple and subject to natural laws.

Drawing on their observations, the Pre-Socratics speculated about the basic building blocks of the universe, and most decided that all things were made of four simple substances: fire, air, earth, and water. Democritus (dih-MAW-kruh-tuhs) (ca. 460–370 B.C.E.) broke this down further and created the atomic theory that the universe is made up of invisible, indestructible particles. The stream of thought started by the Pre-Socratics branched into several directions. Hippocrates (hih-PAW-kruh-teez) (ca. 470–400 B.C.E.) became the most prominent physician and teacher of medicine of his time. He sought natural explanations for diseases and natural means to treat them. Illness was caused not by evil spirits, he asserted, but by physical problems in the body, particularly by imbalances in what he saw as four basic bodily fluids: blood, phlegm, black bile, and yellow bile. In a healthy body these fluids, called humors, were in perfect balance, and medical treatment of the ill sought to help the body bring them back into balance. Hippocrates seems to have advocated letting nature take its course and not intervening too much, though later medicine based on the humoral theory would be much more interventionist, with bloodletting emerging as the central treatment for many illnesses.

Religious Procession in Hellenic Greece This painted wooden slab from about 540 B.C.E., found in a cave near Corinth, shows adults and children about to sacrifice a sheep to the deities worshipped in this area. The participants are dressed in their finest clothes and crowned with garlands. Music adds to the festivities. Rituals such as this were a common part of religious life throughout Greece. The boys are shown with tanned skin and women with white, reflecting the ideal that men's lives took place largely outside in the sun-filled public squares, and women's in the shaded interiors of homes. The woman at the front of the procession has her hair up, indicating her married status, while the women at the rear have the long uncovered hair of unmarried women. (National Archaeological Museum, Athens, Greece/Gianni Dagli Orti/De Agostini Picture Library/Bridgeman Images)

The Sophists (SOFF-ihsts), a group of thinkers in fifth-century-B.C.E. Athens, applied philosophical speculation to politics and language, questioning the beliefs and laws of the polis to understand their origin. They believed that excellence in both politics and language could be taught, and they provided lessons for the young men of Athens who wished to learn how to persuade others.

Socrates (SOK-ruh-teez) (ca. 470–399 B.C.E.), whose ideas are known only through the works of others, also applied philosophy to politics and to people. His approach when exploring ethical issues and defining concepts was to start with a general topic or problem and to narrow the matter to its essentials. He did so by continuously questioning participants in a discussion or argument rather than lecturing, a process known as the Socratic method. Many Athenians viewed Socrates with suspicion because he challenged the traditional beliefs and values of Athens. His views brought him into conflict with the government. The leaders of Athens tried him for corrupting the youth of the city, and for impiety, that is, for not believing in the gods honored in the city. In 399 B.C.E. they executed him.

Most of what we know about Socrates comes from his student Plato (427–347 B.C.E.), who wrote dialogues in which Socrates asks questions and who also founded the Academy, a school dedicated to philosophy. Plato developed the theory that there are two worlds: the impermanent, changing world that we know through our senses, and the eternal, unchanging realm of "forms" that constitute the essence of true reality. According to Plato, true knowledge and the possibility of living a virtuous life come from contemplating ideal forms—what later came to be called **Platonic ideals**—not from observing the visible world.

Platonic ideals In Plato's thought, the eternal unchanging ideal forms that are the essence of true reality.

Plato's student Aristotle (384–322 B.C.E.) believed that true knowledge came from observation of the world, analysis of natural phenomena, and logical reasoning, not contemplation. Aristotle thought that everything had a purpose, so that to know something, one also had to know its function. The range of Aristotle's thought is staggering. His interests embraced logic, ethics, natural science, physics, politics, poetry, and art. He studied the heavens as well as earth and judged the earth to be the center of the universe, with the stars and planets revolving around it. Plato's idealism profoundly shaped Western philosophy, but Aristotle came to have an even wider influence. For many centuries in Europe, the authority of his ideas was second only to the Bible's, and his ideas had a great impact in the Muslim world as well.

The philosophers of ancient Athens lived at roughly the same time as major thinkers in religious and philosophical movements in other parts of the world, including Mahavira (the founder of Jainism), the Buddha, Confucius, and several prophets in Hebrew Scripture. All of these individuals thought deeply about how to live a moral life, and all had tremendous influence on later intellectual, religious, and social developments. There is no evidence that they had any contact with one another, but the parallels among them are strong enough that some historians describe the period from about 800 B.C.E. to 200 B.C.E. as the "Axial Age," by which they mean that this was a pivotal period of intellectual and spiritual transformation.

Hellenistic Society, 323–30 B.C.E.

How did Alexander the Great's conquests shape society in the Hellenistic period?

The Greek city-states wore themselves out fighting one another, and Philip II, the ruler of Macedonia, a kingdom in the north of Greece, gradually conquered one after another and took over their lands. He then turned against the Persian Empire but was killed by an assassin. His son Alexander continued the fight. Alexander conquered the entire Persian Empire from Libya in the west to Bactria in the east (see Map 5.3). He also founded new cities in which Greek and local populations mixed, although he died while planning his next campaign. Alexander left behind an empire that quickly broke into smaller kingdoms, but more important, his death in 323 B.C.E. ushered in an era, the **Hellenistic**, in which Greek culture, the Greek language, and Greek thought spread as far as India, blending with local traditions.

Hellenistic Literally means "like the Greek"; describes the period from the death of Alexander the Great in 323 B.C.E. to the Roman conquest of Egypt in 30 B.C.E., when Greek culture spread.

From Polis to Monarchy, 404–200 B.C.E.

Immediately after the Peloponnesian War, Sparta began striving for empire over all the Greeks but could not maintain its hold. In 371 B.C.E. an army from the polis of Thebes destroyed the Spartan army, but the Thebans were unable to bring peace to Greece. Philip II (r. 359–336 B.C.E.), ruler of the kingdom of Macedonia on the northern border of Greece, turned the situation to his advantage. By clever use of his wealth and superb army, Philip won control of the northern Aegean, and in 338 B.C.E. he defeated a combined Theban-Athenian army, conquering Greece.

After his victory, Philip united the Greek states with his Macedonian kingdom and got the states to cooperate in a crusade to liberate the Ionian Greeks from Persian rule. Before he could launch his crusade, Philip fell to an assassin's dagger in 336 B.C.E. His son Alexander vowed to carry on Philip's mission and led an army of Macedonians and Greeks into western Asia. He won major battles against the Persians and seized Egypt from them without a fight. He ordered the building of a

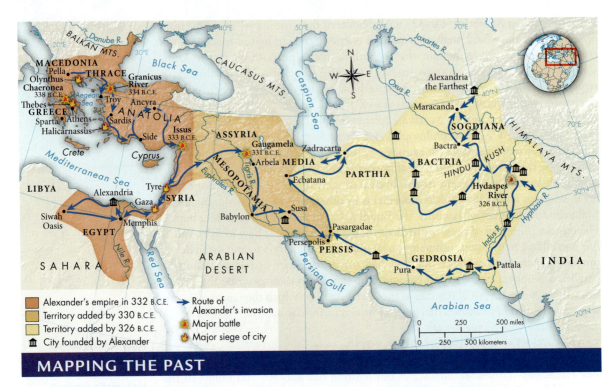

MAPPING THE PAST

MAP 5.3 Alexander's Conquests, 336–324 B.C.E. Alexander's campaign of conquest was extensive and speedy. More important than the great success of his military campaigns was his founding of Hellenistic cities.

ANALYZING THE MAP Where are most of the cities founded by Alexander located in relation to Greece? What does this suggest about his aims?

CONNECTIONS Compare this map with Map 5.2, which shows Greek colonization in the Hellenic period. What are the major differences between the two processes of expansion?

new city where the Nile meets the Mediterranean, a city that would soon be called Alexandria and that within a century would grow into an enormous city, rivaling Chang-an in China and Pataliputra in the Mauryan Empire of India.

By 330 B.C.E. the Persian Empire had fallen, but Alexander had no intention of stopping, and he set out to conquer much of the rest of Asia. After four years of fighting his soldiers crossed the Indus River (in the area that is now Pakistan), and finally, at the Hyphasis River, the troops refused to go farther. Alexander was enraged by the mutiny, but the army stood firm. Still eager to explore the limits of the world, Alexander turned south to the Arabian Sea and then back west (Map 5.3).

Alexander died in Babylon in 323 B.C.E. from fever, wounds, and excessive drinking. In just thirteen years he had created an empire that stretched from his homeland of Macedonia to India, gaining the title "the Great" along the way. His campaign swept away the Persian Empire, and in its place he established a Macedonian monarchy, although this fell apart with his death. Several of the chief Macedonian generals aspired to become sole ruler, which led to civil wars that lasted for decades and tore Alexander's empire apart. By the end of these conflicts in about 300 B.C.E., the most successful generals had carved out their own smaller monarchies, although these monarchies continued to be threatened by internal splits and external attacks.

Ptolemy (TAH-luh-mee) seized Egypt, and his descendants, the Ptolemies, ruled Egypt for nearly three hundred years, until the death of the last Ptolemaic ruler, Cleopatra VII, in 30 B.C.E. Antigonus and his descendants, the Antigonids (an-TIH-guh-nuhds), gained control of the Macedonian kingdom in Europe, which they held until they were overthrown by the Romans in 168 B.C.E. (see "Roman Expansion and Its Repercussions" in Chapter 6). Seleucus won the bulk of Alexander's empire; his monarchy initially

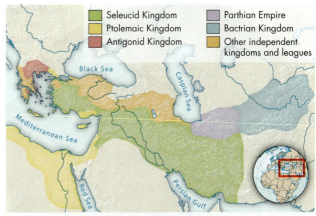

The Hellenistic World, ca. 263 B.C.E.

extended from western Asia to India, although it gradually broke into smaller states. In terms of political stability and peace, these monarchies were no improvement on the Greek polis.

To encourage obedience, Hellenistic kings often created ruler cults that linked the king's authority with that of the gods, or they adopted ruler cults that already existed. This created a symbol of unity within kingdoms ruling different peoples who at first had little in common. Kings sometimes gave the cities in their territory all the external trappings of a polis, such as a council or an assembly of citizens, but these had no power. The city was not autonomous, as the polis had been, but had to follow royal orders. Hellenistic rulers generally relied on paid professionals to staff their bureaucracies and on trained, paid, full-time soldiers rather than citizen hoplites to fight their wars.

Building a Hellenized Society

Alexander's most important legacy was the spread of Greek ideas and traditions across a wide area, a process scholars later called **Hellenization**. To maintain contact with the Greek world as he moved farther eastward, Alexander founded new cities and military colonies and settled Greek and Macedonian troops and veterans in them. This practice continued after his death. These cities and colonies became powerful instruments in the spread of Hellenism and in the blending of Greek and other cultures. Wherever it was established, the Hellenistic city resembled a modern city. It was a cultural center with theaters, temples, and libraries—a seat of learning and a place for amusement. The Hellenistic city was also an economic center—a marketplace and a scene of trade and manufacturing.

The ruling dynasties of the Hellenistic world were Macedonian in origin, and Greeks and Macedonians initially filled all important political, military, and diplomatic positions. The prevailing institutions and laws were Greek, and Greek became the common spoken language of the entire eastern Mediterranean. Everyone who wanted to find an official position or compete in business had to learn it. Those who did gained an avenue of social mobility, and as early as the third century B.C.E. local people in some Greek cities began to rise in power and prominence. Cultural influences in the other direction occurred less frequently because they brought fewer

Hellenization The spread of Greek ideas, culture, and traditions to non-Greek groups across a wide area.

Metal Plate from Ay Khanoum This spectacular metal plate, made in the Bactrian city of Ay Khanoum on the Oxus River in the second century B.C.E., probably depicts the goddess Cybele being pulled in a chariot by lions with the sun-god above. Worship of Cybele, an earth-mother goddess, spread into Greece from the east, and was then spread by her Greek followers as they traveled and migrated. (National Museum of Afghanistan, Kabul/ Photo by Thierry Ollivier/Musée Guimet/Getty Images)

advantages. Few Greeks learned a non-Greek language unless they were required to because of their official position. Greeks did begin to worship local deities, but often these were somewhat Hellenized and their qualities blended with those of an existing Greek god or goddess.

In the booming city of Alexandria, the Ptolemies generally promoted Greek culture over that of the local Egyptians. This favoritism eventually led to civil unrest, but it also led the Ptolemies to support anything that enhanced Greek learning or traditions. Ptolemaic kings established what became the largest library in the ancient world. Alexandria was also home to the largest Jewish community in the ancient world, and here Jewish scholars translated the Hebrew Bible into Greek for the first time.

The kings of Bactria and Parthia (see the map "The Hellenistic World") spread Greek culture far to the east, and their kingdoms became outposts of Hellenism. Some Bactrian and Parthian rulers converted to Buddhism, and the Buddhist ruler of the Mauryan Empire in northern India, Ashoka, may have ordered translations of his laws into Greek for the Greek-speaking residents of Bactria and Parthia. In the second century B.C.E., after the collapse of the Mauryan Empire, Bactrian armies conquered part of northern India, establishing several small Indo-Greek states where the mixing of religious and artistic traditions was particularly pronounced (see "Western Contact and the Mauryan Unification of North India" in Chapter 3).

Yet the spread of Greek culture was wider than it was deep, as it generally did not extend far beyond the reaches of the cities. Many urban residents adopted the aspects of Hellenism that they found useful, but people in the countryside generally did not embrace it, nor were they encouraged to.

The Growth of Trade and Commerce

Not only did Alexander's conquests change the political face of the ancient world, but the spread of Greeks eastward also created new markets, causing trade to flourish. The economic connections of the Hellenistic world later proved valuable to the Romans, allowing them to trade products and ideas more easily over a broad area.

Alexander used the wealth of the Persian Empire to finance the building of roads, the development of harbors, and especially, as noted earlier, the founding of new cities. These cities opened whole new markets to merchants. Whenever possible, merchants sent their goods by water, but overland trade also became more prominent in the Hellenistic era. This period also saw the development of standardized business customs, so that merchants of different nationalities communicated in a way understandable to them all. Trade was further facilitated by the coining of money, which provided merchants with a standard way to value goods as well as a convenient method of payment.

The increased volume of trade helped create prosperity that made luxury goods affordable to more people. As a result, overland traders brought easily transportable luxuries such as gold, silver, and precious stones to market. They extended their networks into China, from which the most prominent good in terms of volume was silk. The trade in silk later gave the major east-west route its name: the Great Silk Road. In return the peoples of the eastern Mediterranean sent east manufactured or extracted goods, especially metal weapons, cloth, wine, and olive oil. (For more on the Silk Road in East Asia, see "Inner Asia and the Silk Road" in Chapter 7.)

More economically important than trade in exotic goods were commercial dealings in essential commodities like raw materials and grain and industrial products such as pottery. Most trade in bulk commodities like grain and wood was seaborne.

For the cities of Greece and the Aegean, the trade in grain was essential because many of them could not grow enough in their mountainous terrain. Fortunately for them, abundant wheat supplies were available nearby in Egypt and in the area north of the Black Sea. The Greek cities often paid for their grain by exporting olive oil, wine, honey, dried fruit, nuts, and vegetables. Another significant commodity supplied by the Greeks was fish, which for export was salted, pickled, or dried.

Slaves were a staple of Hellenistic trade, traveling in all directions on both land and sea routes. War provided prisoners for the slave market; to a lesser extent, so did kidnapping and capture by pirates, although the origin of most slaves is unknown. Both old Greek states and new Hellenistic kingdoms were ready slave markets, and throughout the Mediterranean world slaves were almost always in demand for work in shops, fields, farms, mines, and the homes of wealthier people.

Despite the increase in trade, the Hellenistic period did not see widespread improvements in the way most people lived and worked. Cities flourished, but many people who lived in rural areas were actually worse off than they had been before, because of higher levels of rents and taxes. Technology was applied to military needs, but not to the production of food or other goods. Manual labor, not machinery, continued to turn out the agricultural produce, raw materials, and manufactured goods the Hellenistic world used.

Hellenistic Religion, Philosophy, and Science

How did religion, philosophy, and science develop in the Hellenistic world?

The mixing of peoples in the Hellenistic era influenced religion, philosophy, and science. The Hellenistic kings built temples to the old Olympian gods and promoted rituals and ceremonies like those in earlier Greek cities, but new deities also gained prominence. More people turned to mystery religions that blended Greek and non-Greek elements. Others turned to practical philosophies that provided advice on how to live a good life. In the scholarly realm, Hellenistic thinkers made advances in mathematics, astronomy, and mechanical design. Additionally, physicians used observation and dissection to better understand the way the human body works.

Religion in the Hellenistic World

When Hellenistic kings founded cities, they also built temples for the old Olympian gods. In this way they spread Greek religious beliefs throughout the Hellenistic world. Greeks and non-Greeks in the Hellenistic world also honored and worshipped deities that had not been important in the Hellenic period or that were a blend of imported Greek and indigenous gods and goddesses. Tyche (TIGH-kee), for example, was a new deity, the goddess and personification of luck, fate, chance, and fortune. Many people also believed that magic rituals and spells that invoked Tyche along with other Greek and non-Greek deities were effective, and they sought the assistance of individuals reputed to have special knowledge or powers in convincing supernatural forces to help them or to leave them alone. (See "Global Viewpoints: Hellenistic and Chinese Spells," at right.)

Increasingly, many people were attracted to mystery religions, which in the Hellenic period had been linked to specific gods in particular places, which meant that people who wished to become members had to travel. But new mystery religions, like Hellenistic culture in general, were not tied to a particular place; instead they were spread throughout the Hellenistic world, and temples of the new deities sprang up wherever Greeks lived.

Mystery religions incorporated aspects of both Greek and non-Greek religions and claimed to save their adherents from the worst that fate could do. Most taught that by the rites of initiation, in which the secrets of the religion were shared, devotees became united with a deity who had also died and risen from the dead. The sacrifice of the god and his victory over death saved the devotee from eternal death. Similarly, mystery religions demanded a period of preparation in which the converts strove to become pure and holy, that is, to live by the religion's precepts. Once aspirants had prepared themselves, they went through the initiation, usually a ritual of great emotional intensity symbolizing the entry into a new life.

Among the mystery religions, the Egyptian cult of Isis took the Hellenistic world by storm. In Egyptian mythology Isis brought her husband, Osiris, back to life (see "The Nile and the God-King" in Chapter 2), and during the Hellenistic era this power came to be understood by her followers as extending to them as well. She promised to save any mortal who came to her, and her priests asserted that she had bestowed on humanity the gift of civilization and founded law and literature. Isis was understood to be a devoted mother as well as a devoted wife, and she became the goddess of marriage, conception, and childbirth. She became

Isis and Horus In this small statue from Egypt, the goddess Isis is shown suckling her son, Horus. Worship of Isis spread throughout the Hellenistic world; her followers believed that Isis offered them life after death, just as she had brought Horus's father, Osiris, back to life. (Louvre, Paris, France/Peter Willi/Bridgeman Images)

Hellenistic and Chinese Spells

Throughout the ancient world, people carried out rituals and ceremonies to attract good spirits and drive away bad ones, and in many places they also sought to use the spirits and gods to accomplish tasks for them. Most of these rituals were oral, but sometimes they were written down. The first text is from a Hellenistic spell inscribed on a lead tablet and is directed toward Anubis, the dog-headed Egyptian god of the underworld; by means of this spell, a woman named Sophia seeks to attract a woman named Gorgonia. With the religious mixing common in the Hellenistic world, the text mentions a number of Egyptian and Greek deities of the underworld and was most likely written by a professional spell caster. The second text is from a third-century-B.C.E. Chinese manuscript written on bamboo slips and discovered in a tomb. It provides a series of spells designed to identify demons and instruct people in how to lessen the demons' power.

Hellenistic Spell of Attraction

■ "Fundament of the gloomy darkness, jagged-toothed dog, covered with coiling snakes, turning three heads, traveler in the recesses of the underworld, come, spirit-driver, with the Erinyes [or Furies, Greek goddesses of vengeance, often shown with snake hair and whips], savage with their stinging whips; holy serpents, maenads [frenzied female followers of Dionysus], frightful maidens, come to my wroth incantations. Before I persuade by force this one and you, render him immediately a fire-breathing daemon. Listen and do everything quickly, in no way opposing me in the performance of this action; for you are the governors of the earth." . . . By means of this corpse-daemon inflame the heart, the liver [which people also saw as a location of emotions], the spirit of Gorgonia, whom Nilogenia bore, with love and affection for Sophia, whom Isara bore. . . . Drive Gorgonia, whom Nilogenia bore, drive her, torment her body night and day, force her to rush forth from every place and every house, loving Sophia, whom Isara bore, she, surrendered like a slave, giving herself and all her possessions to her, because this is the will and command of the great god. . . . "Blessed lord of the immortals, holding the scepters of Tartaros and

of terrible, fearful Styx [?] and of life-robbing Lethe, the hair of Kerberos trembles in fear of you, you crack the loud whips of the Erinyes; the couch of Persephone delights you, when you go to the longed bed, whether you be the immortal Sarapis, whom the universe fears, whether you be Osiris, star of the land of Egypt; your messenger is the all-wise boy; yours is Anubis, the pious herald of the dead. Come hither, fulfill my wishes, because I summon you by these secret symbols."

Chinese Spells to Repel Demons

■ Spellbinding to inflict odium on demons. The Wanghang [demons who live underground] who injure people treat people unpropitiously. Let the way for how to spellbind them be declared, to enable the people to not encounter the baleful and calamitous. What demons detest are namely reclining in a crouch, sitting like a winnowing basket, interlinked motion [with the legs apart and extended], and the leaning stand [all postures thought to make the body resistant to demons]. . . .

The dwelling places of the great spirits cannot be passed through. They like to injure people. Make pellets from dog excrement and carry them when passing through. Throw them at the spirit when it appears, and it will not injure people. . . .

If human or birds or beasts as well as the six domestic animals constantly roam through a person's domicile, these are spirits from above who like to descend and take pleasure in entering. Have boys and girls who have never entered the domicile beat drums, ring bells with clappers, and screech at them, and they will not come.

QUESTIONS FOR ANALYSIS

1. In the Hellenistic spell, what feelings does Sophia direct Anubis and the other spirits to create in Gorgonia, and what behavior is the expected result of these feelings?
2. In the Chinese spell, what actions are people to take to drive away demons?
3. Belief in the power of spirits is sometimes viewed as making people feel helpless and fatalistic. Do these sources provide evidence of this? Why or why not?

Sources: Bernadette J. Brooten, *Love Between Women: Early Christian Responses to Female Homoeroticism* (Chicago: University of Chicago Press, 1996), pp. 83–87; Donald Harper, "A Chinese Demonography of the Third Century B.C.," *Harvard Journal of Asiatic Studies*, 45, no. 2 (December 1985): 480, 495, 496.

Hellenistic Married Life This small terra-cotta figurine from Myrina in what is now Turkey, made in the second century B.C.E., shows a newly married couple sitting on a bridal bed. The groom is drawing back the bride's veil, and she is exhibiting the modesty that was a desired quality in young women. Figurines representing every stage of life became popular in the Hellenistic period and were used for religious offerings in temples and sacred places. This one was found in a tomb. (Louvre, Paris, France/Erich Lessing/Art Resource, NY)

the most important goddess of the Hellenistic world. Devotion to Isis, and to many other mystery religions, spread to the Romans as well as the Greeks when the two civilizations came into greater contact.

Philosophy and Its Guidance for Life

While some people turned to mystery religions to overcome Tyche and provide something permanent in a world that seemed unstable, others turned to philosophy. Several new schools of philosophical thought emerged in the Hellenistic period. One of these was **Epicureanism**, a practical philosophy of serenity in an often-tumultuous world. Epicurus (340–270 B.C.E.) decided that the principal goods of human life were contentment and pleasure, which he defined as the absence of pain, fear, and suffering. By encouraging the pursuit of pleasure, he was not advocating drunken revels or sexual excess, which he thought caused pain, but promoting moderation. Epicurus also taught that individuals could most easily attain peace and serenity by ignoring the outside world and looking instead into their personal feelings. His followers ignored politics because it led to tumult, which would disturb the soul.

Epicureanism A system of philosophy based on the teachings of Epicurus, who viewed a life of contentment, free from fear and suffering, as the greatest good.

Zeno (335–262 B.C.E.), a philosopher from Cyprus, advanced a different concept of human beings and the universe. Zeno first came to Athens to form his own school, the Stoa. His philosophy, **Stoicism** (STOH-uh-sih-zuhm), in turn, came to be named for his school. Zeno and his followers considered nature an expression of divine will; in their view, people could be happy only when living in accordance with nature. They stressed the unity of humans and the universe, stating that all people were obliged to help one another.

The Stoics' most lasting practical achievement was the creation of the concept of natural law. They concluded that as all people were kindred, partook of divine reason, and were in harmony with the universe, one natural law governed them all.

Stoicism A philosophy, based on the ideas of Zeno, that held that people could only be happy when living in accordance with nature and accepting whatever happened.

Hellenistic Science and Medicine

Hellenistic thinkers made advances in mathematics, astronomy, and mechanical design. The most notable of the Hellenistic astronomers was Aristarchus of Samos (ca. 310–230 B.C.E.). Aristarchus rightly concluded that the sun is far larger than the earth and that the stars are enormously distant from the earth. He also argued against Aristotle's view that the earth is the center of the universe, instead propounding the heliocentric theory—that the earth and planets revolve around the sun.

In geometry Euclid (YOO-kluhd) (fl. ca. 300 B.C.E.), a mathematician living in Alexandria, compiled a valuable textbook of existing knowledge. His *Elements of Geometry* became the standard introduction to the subject.

The greatest thinker of the Hellenistic period was Archimedes (ahr-kuh-MEE-deez) (ca. 287–212 B.C.E.). A clever inventor, he devised new artillery for military purposes. In peacetime he created the water screw to draw water from a lower to a higher level. (See "Individuals in Society: Archimedes, Scientist and Inventor," page 138.) He also invented the compound pulley to lift heavy weights. His chief interest, however, lay in pure mathematics. He founded the science of hydrostatics (the study of fluids at rest) and discovered the principle that the weight of a solid floating in a liquid is equal to the weight of the liquid displaced by the solid.

Eratosthenes (ehr-uh-TOSS-thuh-neez) (285–ca. 204 B.C.E.), who was the librarian of the vast Ptolemaic royal library in Alexandria, used mathematics to further the geographical studies for which he is most famous. He concluded that the earth is a spherical globe and calculated the circumference of the earth geometrically with remarkable accuracy.

As the new artillery devised by Archimedes indicates, Hellenistic science was used for purposes of war as well as peace. Theories of mechanics were applied to build military machines. The catapult became the most widely used artillery piece. As the Assyrians had earlier, engineers built siege towers, large wooden structures that served as artillery platforms, and put them on wheels so that soldiers could roll them up to a town's walls. Generals added battering rams to bring down large portions of walls. If these new engines made warfare more efficient, they also added to the misery of the people, as war often directly involved the populations of cities. War and illness fed the need for medical advances, and doctors as well as scientists combined observation with theory during the Hellenistic period. Herophilus, who lived in the first half of the third century B.C.E., worked in Alexandria and studied the writings attributed to Hippocrates. He approached the study of medicine in a systematic,

Archimedes, Scientist and Inventor

ARCHIMEDES WAS BORN IN THE GREEK CITY of Syracuse in Sicily, an intellectual center in which he pursued scientific interests. He was the most original thinker of his time and a practical inventor. In his book *On Plane Equilibriums*, he dealt for the first time with the basic principles of mathematics, including the principle of the lever. He once said that if he were given a lever and a suitable place to stand, he could move the world. He also demonstrated how easily his compound pulley could move huge weights with little effort, as reported by the Roman biographer Plutarch:

> A three-masted merchant ship of the royal fleet had been hauled on land by hard work and many hands. Archimedes put aboard her many men and the usual freight. He sat far away from her; and without haste, but gently working a compound pulley with his hand, he drew her towards him smoothly and without faltering, just as though she were running on the surface.

He likewise invented the Archimedian screw, a pump to bring subterranean water up to irrigate fields, which quickly came into common use. In his treatise *On Floating Bodies*, Archimedes founded the science of hydrostatics. He concluded that an object will float if it weighs less than the water it displaces, and that whenever a solid floats in a liquid, the weight of the solid equals the weight of the liquid displaced. A story told later by the Roman architect Vitruvius recounts that Archimedes discovered this when he climbed into a public bath and noticed the water flowing out because of the bulk of his body, which enabled him to prove that a king's gold crown was really part silver. He sprang out of the tub and rushed through the streets naked, yelling in a loud voice, "Eureka, eureka" ("I have found it, I have found it").

War between Rome and Syracuse unfortunately interrupted Archimedes's scientific life. In 213 B.C.E., during the Second Punic War, the Romans besieged the city. Hiero, its king and Archimedes's friend, asked the scientist for help in repulsing Roman attacks. Archimedes began to build remarkable devices, including weapons that threw stones to break up infantry attacks. For use against Roman warships he is said to have designed a machine with beams from which large claws dropped onto the hulls of enemy warships, hoisted them into the air, and dropped them back into the sea. Later Greek authors reported that he destroyed Roman ships with a series of polished mirrors that focused sunlight and caused the ships to catch fire. Modern

scientific fashion: he dissected dead bodies and measured what he observed. His students carried on his work, searching for the causes and nature of illness and pain.

Medical study did not lead to effective cures for the infectious diseases that were the leading cause of death for most people, however, and people attempted to combat illness in a variety of ways. Medicines prescribed by physicians or prepared at home often included natural products blended with materials understood to work magically. People in the Hellenistic world may have thought that fate determined what would happen, but they also actively sought to make their lives longer and healthier.

Chapter Summary

Greece's mountainous terrain encouraged the development of small, independent communities and political fragmentation. Sometime after 2000 B.C.E. two kingdoms—the Minoan on Crete and the Mycenaean on the mainland—did emerge,

experiments re-creating Archimedes's weapons have found that the claw may have been workable, but the mirrors probably were not, as they required a ship to remain stationary for the fire to ignite. It is not certain whether his war machines were actually effective, but later people recounted tales that the Romans became so fearful that whenever they saw a bit of rope or a stick of timber projecting over one of the walls protecting Syracuse, they shouted, "There it is—Archimedes is trying some engine on us," and fled. After many months the Roman siege was successful, however, and Archimedes was killed by a Roman soldier.

QUESTIONS FOR ANALYSIS

1. How did Archimedes combine theoretical mathematics and practical issues in his work?
2. What applications do you see in the world around you of the devices Archimedes improved or invented, such as the lever, the pulley, and artillery?

Several of Archimedes's treatises were found on a palimpsest, a manuscript that has been scraped and washed so that another text can be written over it, thus reusing the expensive parchment. Reusing parchment was a common practice in the Middle Ages, but the original text can sometimes be reconstructed. Using digital processing with several types of light and X-rays to study this thirteenth-century-C.E. prayer book, scientists were slowly able to decipher the texts by Archimedes that were underneath, including one that had been completely lost.

(Image by the Rochester Institute of Technology. Copyright resides with the owner of the Archimedes Palimpsest, but digital images of the entire manuscript can be found at www.archimedespalimpsest.org.)

but these remained smaller than the great empires of Mesopotamia, India, and China. The fall of these kingdoms led to a period of disruption and decline known as the Greek Dark Age (ca. 1100–800 B.C.E.). However, Greek culture survived, and Greeks developed the independent city-state, known as the polis. Greeks also established colonies and traveled and traded as far east as the Black Sea and as far west as the Atlantic Ocean. Two poleis became especially powerful: Sparta, which created a military state in which men remained in the army most of their lives, and Athens, which created a democracy in which male citizens had a direct voice. In the classical period, between 500 B.C.E. and 338 B.C.E., Greeks engaged in war with the Persians and with one another, but they also created drama, philosophy, and magnificent art and architecture.

In the middle of the fourth century B.C.E. the Greek city-states were conquered by the Macedonians under King Philip II and his son Alexander. Alexander conquered the entire Persian Empire and founded new cities in which Greek and local populations mixed. His successors continued to build cities and colonies, which were centers of trade and spread Greek culture over a broad area, extending as far east as India. The mixing of peoples in the Hellenistic era influenced religion, philosophy, and science. New deities gained prominence, and many people turned to mystery religions that blended Greek and non-Greek elements as they offered followers secret knowledge and eternal life. Others turned to practical philosophies that provided advice on how to live a good life. Advances were made in technology, mathematics, science, and medicine, but these were applied primarily to military purposes, not to improving the way ordinary people lived and worked.

CONNECTIONS

The ancient Greeks built on the achievements of earlier societies in the eastern Mediterranean, but they also added new elements, including drama, philosophy, science, and realistic art. Eventually the Greek world was largely conquered by the Romans, as you will learn in the following chapter, and the various Hellenistic monarchies became part of the Roman Empire. In cultural terms the lines of conquest were reversed: the Romans derived their alphabet from the Greek alphabet, though they changed the letters somewhat. Roman statuary was modeled on Greek and was often, in fact, made by Greek sculptors, who found ready customers among wealthy Romans. Furthermore, the major Roman gods and goddesses were largely the same as Greek ones, though they had different names. Although the Romans did not seem to have been particularly interested in the speculative philosophy of Socrates and Plato, they were drawn to the more practical philosophies of the Epicureans and Stoics. And like the Hellenistic Greeks, many Romans turned to mystery religions that offered secret knowledge and promised eternal life.

The influence of the ancient Greeks was not limited to the Romans, of course. The cities and military colonies founded in the wake of Alexander's conquests spread Greek ideas and culture around the entire eastern Mediterranean and eastward to Central and South Asia — today's Afghanistan, Pakistan, and Tajikistan. As discussed in Chapter 3, art and thought in northern India were shaped by the blending of Greek and Buddhist traditions. And as you will see in Chapter 15, European thinkers and writers made conscious attempts to return to classical ideals in art, literature, and philosophy during the Renaissance. In the United States political leaders from the Revolutionary era on decided that important government buildings should be modeled on the Parthenon or other temples. In some ways, capitol buildings in the United States are good symbols of the legacy of Greece — gleaming ideals of harmony, freedom, democracy, and beauty that (as with all ideals) do not always correspond with realities.

CHAPTER 5   Review and Explore

Identify Key Terms

Identify and explain the significance of each item below.

polis (p. 119)   **mystery religions** (p. 127)   **Epicureanism** (p. 136)
hoplites (p. 119)   **Platonic ideals** (p. 128)   **Stoicism** (p. 137)
democracy (p. 120)   **Hellenistic** (p. 129)
oligarchy (p. 120)   **Hellenization** (p. 131)

Review the Main Ideas

Answer the focus questions from each section of the chapter.

1. How did the geography of Greece shape its earliest history? (p. 116)

2. What was the role of the polis in Greek society? (p. 119)

3. In the classical period, how did war influence Greece, and how did the arts, religion, and philosophy develop? (p. 122)

4. How did Alexander the Great's conquests shape society in the Hellenistic period? (p. 129)

5. How did religion, philosophy, and science develop in the Hellenistic world? (p. 133)

Make Comparisons and Connections

Analyze the larger developments and continuities within and across chapters.

1. Philosophers and religious thinkers in ancient India, China, and Greece, such as Mahavira and the Buddha (Chapter 3), Confucius and Zhuangzi (Chapter 4), and Socrates and Zeno (this chapter), all developed ideas about the ultimate aim of human life. What similarities and differences do you see among them?

2. The Persian Empire (Chapter 2) first brought India and the Mediterranean in contact with one another, and these contacts increased with the conquests of Alexander (Chapter 3 and this chapter). What were the major results of these contacts in terms of politics, culture, and economics?

3. Cities had existed in the areas conquered by Alexander long before his conquests. What would the residents of Sumer or Babylon (Chapter 2), the early cities of the Indus River Valley (Chapter 3), and a Hellenistic city find unusual about one another's cities? What would seem familiar?

4. Looking at your own town or city, what evidence do you find of the cultural legacy of ancient Greece?

TIMELINE

EURASIA

ca. 1200–323 B.C.E. Hellenic period

← ca. 3000–800 B.C.E. Helladic period (Bronze Age) in Greece

← ca. 2000–1100 B.C.E. Minoan and Mycenaean civilizations

ca. 1100–800 B.C.E. Greece's Dark Age; population declines, trade decreases, writing disappears

AFRICA

ca. 1570–1070 B.C.E. New Kingdom in Egypt **(Ch. 2)**

AMERICAS

ca. 1500–300 B.C.E. Olmec civilization in Mexico **(Ch. 11)**

ASIA

ca. 1500–1050 B.C.E. Shang Dynasty in China **(Ch. 4)**

ca. 1500–500 B.C.E. Vedic Age in India **(Ch. 3)**

1500 B.C.E.	1250 B.C.E.	1000 B.C.E.

Suggested Resources

BOOKS

Beard, Mary. *The Parthenon.* 2010. A cultural history of Athens's most famous building, including the many controversies that surround it.

Bowden, Hugh. *Mystery Cults of the Ancient World.* 2010. Examines the main mystery religions of the ancient Mediterranean, using artistic and literary evidence.

Davidson, James. *Courtesans and Fishcakes: The Consuming Passions of Classical Athens.* 1999. A witty examination of sex, wine, food, and other objects of desire, based on plays, poems, speeches, and philosophical treatises.

Errington, R. Malcolm. *A History of the Hellenistic World, 323–30 B.C.* 2008. Easily the best coverage of the period: full, scholarly, and readable.

Freeman, Philip. *Alexander the Great.* 2010. Designed for general readers, this excellent biography portrays Alexander as both ruthless and cultured.

Hansen, Mogens Herman. *Polis: An Introduction to the Ancient Greek City-State.* 2006. The authoritative study of the polis.

Kagan, Donald. *The Peloponnesian War.* 2003. A comprehensive yet accessible study that focuses on not only leaders and battles, but also the human costs.

Manning, J. G. *The Last Pharaohs: Egypt Under the Ptolemies, 305–30 B.C.* 2009. Examines the impact of the Ptolemies on Egyptian society and the way their state blended Greek and Egyptian elements.

Patterson, Cynthia B. *The Family in Greek History.* 2001. Treats public and private family relations.

Roochnik, David. *Retrieving the Ancients: An Introduction to Greek Philosophy.* 2004. A sophisticated and well-written narrative of ancient Greek thought designed for students.

Waterfield, Robin. *Dividing the Spoils: The War for Alexander the Great's Empire.* 2011. A cultural and political narrative of this turbulent period, based on up-to-date research.

323–30 B.C.E. Hellenistic period

ca. 700–500 B.C.E. Sparta and Athens develop distinctive political institutions

323–ca. 300 B.C.E. Civil wars lead to the establishment of the Ptolemaic, Antigonid, and Seleucid dynasties

ca. 800–500 B.C.E. Archaic age; rise of the polis; Greek colonization of the Mediterranean

ca. 500–338 B.C.E. Classical period; development of drama, philosophy, and major building projects in Athens

168 B.C.E. Roman overthrow of the Antigonid dynasty

30 B.C.E. Roman conquest of Egypt; Ptolemaic dynasty ends

499–404 B.C.E. Persian and Peloponnesian wars

336–324 B.C.E. Alexander the Great's military campaigns

| 750 B.C.E. | 500 B.C.E. | 250 B.C.E. | 1 C.E. |

DOCUMENTARIES

Athens: The Truth About Democracy (BBC, 2007). Historian Bettany Hughes takes a critical look at classical Athens, with attention to slavery, imperialism, the flow of money, and restrictions on women.

In the Footsteps of Alexander the Great (BBC, 2010). Michael Wood follows Alexander's two-thousand-mile journey from Greece to India, tracing his conquests and the meaning these have for the peoples of these areas today.

The Rise and Fall of the Spartans (History Channel, 2003). Examines the creation, maintenance, and end of Sparta's distinctive military/political system.

FEATURE FILMS

The Odyssey (Andrey Konchalovskiy, 1997). Originally made as a television miniseries, this film portrays many of Odysseus's adventures much as Homer wrote them. Shot on location in the Mediterranean.

Troy (Wolfgang Petersen, 2004). A fairly decent Hollywood film that focuses, as did Homer in his epic, on the personalities and motivations of the characters as well as on the Trojan War itself.

WEBSITES

Diotima: Materials for the Study of Women and Gender in the Ancient World. Contains an extensive anthology of translated Greek, Latin, Egyptian, and Coptic texts, along with articles, book reviews, databases, and images. **www.stoa.org/diotima/**

Internet Ancient History Sourcebook. Well-organized collection of ancient Mediterranean texts and art and archaeological sources. Organized chronologically and topically, with materials from 2000 B.C.E. to 500 C.E. **www.fordham.edu/Halsall/ancient/asbook .html**

Perseus Digital Library. The premier site for accessing the literature and archaeology of ancient Greek culture and now Roman as well, with hundreds of primary texts in Greek, Latin, and English translation, and thousands of images from museum collections and archaeological sites. **www.perseus.tufts .edu/hopper/**

6

The World of Rome
ca. 1000 B.C.E.–400 C.E.

Like the Persians under Cyrus, the Mauryans under Chandragupta, and the Macedonians under Alexander, the Romans conquered vast territories. With a republican government under the leadership of the Senate, a political assembly whose members were primarily wealthy landowners, the Romans conquered all of Italy, then the western Mediterranean basin, and then areas in the East that had been part of Alexander the Great's empire. As they did, they learned about and incorporated Greek art, literature, philosophy, and religion, but the wars of conquest also led to serious problems that the Senate proved unable to handle. After a grim period of civil war that ended in 31 B.C.E., the emperor Augustus restored peace and expanded Roman power and law as far east as the Euphrates River, creating the institution that the modern world calls the "Roman Empire." Later emperors extended Roman authority farther still, so that at its largest the Roman Empire stretched from England to Egypt and from Portugal to Persia.

Roman history is generally divided into three periods: the monarchical period, traditionally dated from 753 B.C.E. to 509 B.C.E., in which the city of Rome was ruled by kings; the republic, traditionally dated from 509 B.C.E. to 27 B.C.E., in which it was ruled by the Senate; and the empire, from 27 B.C.E. to 476 C.E., in which Roman territories were ruled by an emperor.

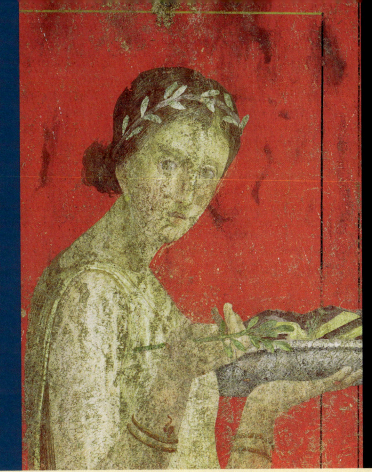

Woman from Pompeii

This brightly painted fresco from a villa in Pompeii shows a young woman carrying a tray in a religious ritual. Pompeii was completely buried in ash in a volcanic explosion in 79 c.e., and excavations have revealed life in what was a vacation spot for wealthy Romans.

Detail of the Initiate, from the Catechism Scene, North Wall, fresco/Villa dei Misteri, Pompeii, Italy/Bridgeman Images

CHAPTER PREVIEW

THE ROMANS IN ITALY
How did the Romans come to dominate Italy, and what political institutions did they create?

ROMAN EXPANSION AND ITS REPERCUSSIONS
How did Rome expand its power beyond Italy, and what were the effects of this expansion?

ROME AND THE PROVINCES
What was life like in Rome, and what was it like in the provinces?

THE COMING OF CHRISTIANITY
What was Christianity, and how did it affect life in the Roman Empire?

TURMOIL AND REFORM
How did the emperors respond to political, economic, and religious issues in the third and fourth centuries?

How did the Romans come to dominate Italy, and what political institutions did they create?

The Romans in Italy

The colonies established by Greek poleis (city-states) in the Hellenic era included a number along the coast of southern Italy and Sicily. So many Greek settlers came to this area that it later became known as Magna Graecia—Greater Greece. These Greek colonies transmitted much of their culture to people who lived farther north in the Italian peninsula. These included the Etruscans (ih-TRUHS-kuhns), who built the first cities north of Magna Graecia, and then the Romans, who eventually came to dominate the peninsula. In addition to allying with conquered peoples and granting them citizenship, the Romans established a republic ruled by a Senate. However, social conflicts over the rights to power eventually erupted and had to be resolved.

The Etruscans

The Etruscans, ca. 500 B.C.E.

Etruscan homeland
Areas of expansion
• Etruscan city

ALPS

Adriatic Sea

Corsica
Rome

Sardinia
Tyrrhenian
Sea

Sicily

The culture that is now called Etruscan developed in north-central Italy about 800 B.C.E. The Etruscans most likely originated in Turkey or elsewhere in southwest Asia, although when they migrated to Italy is not clear. The Etruscans spoke a language that was very different from Greek and Latin, but they adopted the Greek alphabet to write their language.

The Etruscans established permanent settlements that evolved into cities resembling the Greek city-states (see "Organization of the Polis" in Chapter 5) and thereby built a rich cultural life, full of art and music, that became the foundation of civilization in much of Italy. They spread their influence over the surrounding countryside, which they farmed and mined for its rich mineral resources. From an early period the Etruscans began to trade natural products, especially iron, with their Greek neighbors to the south and with other peoples throughout the Mediterranean in exchange for luxury goods. Etruscan cities appear to have been organized in leagues, and beginning about 750 B.C.E. the Etruscans expanded southward into central Italy through military actions and through the establishment of colony cities. In the process they encountered a small collection of villages subsequently called Rome.

The Founding of Rome

Archaeological evidence indicates that the ancestors of the Romans began to settle on the hills east of the Tiber during the early Iron Age, around 1000 B.C.E. to 800 B.C.E. Later Romans told a number of stories about the founding of Rome. These mix legend and history, but they illustrate the traditional ethics, morals, and ideals of Rome.

According to legend, Romulus and Remus founded the city of Rome, an event later Roman authors dated precisely to 753 B.C.E. These twin brothers were the sons of the war god Mars, and their mother, Rhea Silvia, was a descendant of Aeneas, a brave and pious Trojan who left Troy after it was destroyed by the Greeks in the Trojan War. The brothers, who were left to die by a jealous uncle, were raised by a female wolf. When they were grown they decided to build a city, but quarreled over its location; Romulus killed Remus and named the city after himself. He also established a council of advisers later called the Senate. He and his mostly male followers expanded their power over neighboring peoples, in part by abducting and marrying their women. The women then arranged a peace by throwing themselves between their brothers and their husbands, convincing them that killing kin would make the men cursed. The Romans, favored by the gods, continued their rise to power. This founding myth ascribes positive traits to the Romans: they are descended from gods and heroes, can thrive in wild and tough settings, will defend their boundaries at all costs, and mix with other peoples rather than simply conquering them. Also, the story portrays women who were ancestors of Rome as virtuous and brave.

Later Roman historians continued the story by describing a series of kings after Romulus, each elected by the Senate. According to tradition, the last three kings were Etruscan, and another tale about female virtue was told to explain why the Etruscan kings were overthrown. In this story, the son of King Tarquin, the Etruscan king who ruled Rome, raped Lucretia, a virtuous Roman wife, in her own home. She demanded that her husband and father seek vengeance and then committed suicide in front of them. Her father and husband and the other Roman nobles swore to avenge Lucretia's death by throwing out the Etruscan kings, and they did. The Romans generally accepted this story as historical fact and dated the expulsion of the Etruscan kings to 509 B.C.E. They thus saw this year as marking the end of the monarchical period and the dawn of the republic, which had come about because of a wronged woman and her demands.

Most historians today view the idea that Etruscan kings ruled the city of Rome as legendary, but they stress the influence of the Etruscans on Rome. The Etruscans transformed Rome into a real city with walls, temples, a drainage system, and other urban structures. The Romans adopted the Etruscan alphabet, which the Etruscans themselves had adopted from the Greeks. Even the toga came from the Etruscans, as did gladiatorial combat honoring the dead. In engineering and architecture the Romans adopted some design elements and the basic plan of their temples, along with paved roads, from the Etruscans.

In this early period the city of Rome does appear to have been ruled by kings. A hereditary aristocracy advised the kings and may have played a role in choosing them. And sometime in the sixth century B.C.E. a group of aristocrats revolted against these kings and established a government in which the main institution of power would be the **Senate**, an assembly of aristocrats, rather than a single monarch. Executive power was in the hands of leaders called **consuls**, who commanded the army in battle, administered state business, and supervised financial affairs, but there were always two of them and they were elected for one-year terms only, not for life. Rome thereby became a republic, not a monarchy. Thus at the core of the myths is a bit of history.

The Roman Conquest of Italy

In the years following the establishment of the republic, the Romans fought numerous wars with their neighbors on the Italian peninsula. The Roman army was made up primarily of citizens of Rome, who were organized for military campaigns into legions. War also involved diplomacy, at which the Romans became masters.

In 387 B.C.E. the Romans suffered a major setback when the Celts—or Gauls, as the Romans called them—invaded the Italian peninsula from the north and sacked the city of Rome. The Celts agreed to abandon Rome in return for a thousand pounds of gold. In the century that followed, the Romans rebuilt their city and recouped their losses. They brought Latium and their Latin allies fully under their control and conquered Etruria. In a series of bitter wars the Romans also subdued southern Italy

Senate The assembly that was the main institution of power in the Roman Republic, originally composed only of aristocrats.

consuls Primary executives in the Roman Republic, elected for one-year terms, who commanded the army in battle, administered state business, and supervised financial affairs.

and then turned north. Their superior military institutions, organization, and manpower allowed them to conquer or bring under their influence most of Italy by about 265 B.C.E. (Map 6.1).

As they expanded their territory, the Romans spread their religious traditions throughout Italy, blending them with local beliefs and practices. Religion for the Romans was largely a matter of honoring one's own ancestors and kin, and showing loyalty to the state. The main goal of religion was to secure the peace of the gods and

MAP 6.1 Roman Italy and the City of Rome, ca. 218 B.C.E. As Rome expanded, it built roads linking major cities and offered various degrees of citizenship to the territories it conquered or with which it made alliances. The territories outlined in green that are separate from the Italian peninsula were added by 218 B.C.E., largely as a result of the Punic Wars.

to harness divine power for public and private enterprises. Religious rituals were an important way of expressing common civic values, which for Romans meant those evident in their foundation myths: bravery, morality, seriousness, family, and home. Victorious generals made sure to honor the gods of people they had conquered and by doing so transformed them into gods they could also call on for assistance in their future campaigns. As the Romans conquered the cities of Magna Graecia, the Greek deities were absorbed into the Roman pantheon.

Once they had conquered an area, the Romans did what the Persians had earlier done to help cement their new territory: they built roads. Roman roads facilitated the flow of communication, trade, and armies from the capital to outlying areas.

In politics the Romans shared full Roman citizenship with many of their oldest allies, particularly the inhabitants of the cities of Latium. In other instances they granted citizenship without the franchise, that is, without the right to vote or hold Roman office. These allies were subject to Roman taxes and calls for military service but ran their own local affairs.

The Roman State

Along with citizenship, the republican government was another important institution of Roman political life. The Romans summed up their political existence in a single phrase: *senatus populusque Romanus*, "the Senate and the Roman people," which they abbreviated "SPQR." This phrase stands for the beliefs, customs, and laws of the republic—its unwritten constitution that evolved over two centuries to meet the demands of the governed.

In the early republic, social divisions determined the shape of politics. Political power was in the hands of a hereditary aristocracy—the **patricians**, whose privileged legal status was determined by their birth as members of certain families. The common people of Rome, the **plebeians** (plih-BEE-uhns), were free citizens with a voice in politics, but they had few of the patricians' political and social advantages. While some plebeian merchants rivaled the patricians in wealth, most plebeians were poor artisans, small farmers, and landless urban dwellers.

The Romans created several assemblies through which men elected high officials and passed ordinances. The most important of these was the Senate. During the republic, the Senate advised the consuls and other officials about military and political matters and handled government finances. Because the Senate sat year

patricians The Roman hereditary aristocracy, who held most of the political power in the republic.

plebeians The common people of Rome, who were free but had few of the patricians' advantages.

Coin Showing a Voter This coin from 63 B.C.E. shows a citizen dropping a tablet into a voting urn, the Roman equivalent of today's ballot box. The *V* on the tablet means a yes vote, and an inscription on the coin identifies the moneyer, the official who controlled coin production and decided what would be shown on the coins. This moneyer, Lucius Cassius Longinus, depicted a vote held fifty years earlier about whether an ancestor of his should be named prosecutor in a trial charging three vestal virgins with unchastity. As was common among moneyers, Longinus chose this image as a way to advance his political career, in this case by suggesting his family's long history of public office. (Bibliothèque Nationale de France [BnF]/Snark/Art Resource, NY)

after year with the same members, while the consuls changed annually, it provided stability, and its advice came to have the force of law. Another responsibility of the Senate was to handle relations between Rome and other powers.

The highest officials of the republic were the two consuls, positions initially open only to patrician men. The consuls commanded the army in battle, administered state business, and supervised financial affairs. When the consuls were away from Rome, praetors (PREE-tuhrz) could act in their place. After the age of overseas conquests (see "Roman Expansion and Its Repercussions"), the Romans divided their lands in the Mediterranean into provinces governed by ex-consuls and ex-praetors.

A lasting achievement of the Romans was their development of law. Roman civil law, the *ius civile*, consisted of statutes, customs, and forms of procedure that regulated the lives of citizens. As the Romans came into more frequent contact with foreigners, the praetors applied a broader *ius gentium*, the "law of the peoples," to such matters as peace treaties, the treatment of prisoners of war, and the exchange of diplomats. In the ius gentium, all sides were to be treated the same regardless of their nationality. By the late republic, Roman jurists had widened this still further into the concept of *ius naturale*, "natural law" based in part on Stoic beliefs (see "Philosophy and Its Guidance for Life" in Chapter 5). Natural law, according to these thinkers, is made up of rules that govern human behavior that come from applying reason rather than customs or traditions, and so apply to all societies. In reality, Roman officials generally interpreted the law to the advantage of Rome, of course, at least to the extent that the strength of Roman armies allowed them to enforce it. But Roman law came to be seen as one of Rome's most important legacies.

Social Conflict in Rome

Inequality between plebeians and patricians led to a conflict known as the Struggle of the Orders. In this conflict the plebeians sought to increase their power by taking advantage of the fact that Rome's survival depended on its army, which needed plebeians to fill the ranks of the infantry. According to tradition, in 494 B.C.E. the plebeians literally walked out of Rome and refused to serve in the army. Their general strike worked, and the patricians made important concessions. They allowed the plebeians to elect their own officials, the tribunes, who could bring plebeian grievances to the Senate for resolution and could also veto the decisions of the consuls. Thus, as in Archaic age Greece (see "The Development of the Polis in the Archaic Age" in Chapter 5), political rights were broadened because of military needs for foot soldiers.

The law itself was the plebeians' primary target. Only the patricians knew what the law was, and only they could argue cases in court. All too often they used the law for their own benefit. The plebeians wanted the law codified and published. After much struggle, in 449 B.C.E. the patricians surrendered their legal monopoly and codified and published the Laws of the Twelve Tables. The patricians also made legal procedures public so that plebeians could argue cases in court. Several years later the patricians passed a law that for the first time allowed patricians and plebeians to marry one another.

After a ten-year battle, the Licinian-Sextian laws passed in 367 B.C.E. gave wealthy plebeians access to all the offices of Rome, including the right to hold one of the two consulships. Once plebeians could hold the consulship, they could also sit in the

Senate and advise on policy. Though decisive, this victory did not automatically end the Struggle of the Orders. That happened only in 287 B.C.E. with the passage of the *lex Hortensia*, which gave the resolutions of the *concilium plebis*, the plebeian assembly, the force of law for patricians and plebeians alike.

Roman Expansion and Its Repercussions

How did Rome expand its power beyond Italy, and what were the effects of this expansion?

As the republican government was developing, Roman territory continued to expand. The Romans conquered lands all around the Mediterranean, bringing them unheard-of power and wealth. As a result, many Romans became more cosmopolitan and comfortable, and they were especially influenced by the culture of one conquered land: Greece. Yet social unrest also came in the wake of the wars, opening unprecedented opportunities for ambitious generals who wanted to rule Rome like an empire. A series of civil wars ensued, wars that republican government did not survive.

Overseas Conquests and the Punic Wars, 264–133 B.C.E.

The Romans did not map out grandiose strategies to conquer the world. Rather they responded to situations as they arose. This meant that they sought to eliminate any state they saw as a military threat.

Their presence in southern Italy brought the Romans to the island of Sicily, where they confronted another great power in the western Mediterranean, Carthage (CAHR-thij). The city of Carthage had been founded by Phoenicians as a trading colony in the eighth century B.C.E. (see "Iron and the Emergence of New States" in Chapter 2). By the fourth century B.C.E. the Carthaginians began to expand their holdings. At the end of a long string of wars, the Carthaginians had created a mercantile empire that stretched from western Sicily to beyond Gibraltar.

The Carthaginian Empire and the Roman Republic, 264 B.C.E.

The conflicting ambitions of the Romans and Carthaginians led to the first of the three **Punic Wars**. During the course of the first war, which lasted from 264 B.C.E. to 241 B.C.E., Rome built a navy and defeated Carthage in a series of sea battles. Sicily became Rome's first province, but despite a peace treaty, the conflict was not over.

Punic Wars A series of three wars between Rome and Carthage in which Rome emerged the victor.

Carthaginian armies moved into Spain, where Rome was also claiming territory. The brilliant Carthaginian general Hannibal (ca. 247–183 B.C.E.) marched an army of tens of thousands of troops—and, more famously, several dozen war elephants—from Spain across what is now France and over the Alps into Italy, beginning the Second Punic (PYOO-nik) War (218–201 B.C.E.). Hannibal won three major victories, including a devastating blow at Cannae in southeastern Italy in 216 B.C.E. He then spread devastation throughout Italy. Yet Hannibal was not able to win areas near Rome in central Italy.

The Roman general Scipio Africanus (ca. 236–ca. 183 B.C.E.) took Spain from the Carthaginians and then struck directly at Carthage itself, prompting the Carthaginians to recall Hannibal from Italy to defend the homeland. In 202 B.C.E., near the town of Zama, Scipio defeated Hannibal in one of the world's truly decisive battles.

Scipio's victory meant that the world of the western Mediterranean would henceforth be Roman. Roman language, law, and culture, fertilized by Greek influences, would in time permeate this entire region.

The Second Punic War contained the seeds of still other wars. Unabated fear of Carthage led to the Third Punic War (149–146 B.C.E.), a needless, unjust, and savage conflict that ended with obliteration of the city of Carthage itself.

After the Second Punic War, the Romans turned east. Roman victory in Macedonia turned Antigonid Macedonia into a Roman province. Then they moved farther east and defeated the Seleucid monarchy. In 133 B.C.E. the king of Pergamum in Asia Minor willed his kingdom to Rome when he died. The Ptolemies of Egypt retained formal control of their kingdom, but they obeyed Roman wishes in terms of trade policy. Declaring the Mediterranean *mare nostrum*, "our sea," the Romans began to create a political and administrative machinery to hold the Mediterranean together under a system of provinces ruled by governors sent from Rome.

New Influences and Old Values in Roman Culture

With the conquest of the Mediterranean world, Rome became a great city. The spoils of war went to build theaters, stadiums, and other places of amusement, and Romans and Italian townspeople began to spend more of their time in leisure pursuits. This new urban culture reflected Hellenistic influences. Romans developed a liking for Greek literature and art, and it became common for an educated Roman to speak both Latin and Greek. Furthermore, the Roman conquest of the Hellenistic East resulted in wholesale confiscation of Greek paintings and sculpture to grace Roman temples, public buildings, and private homes.

The Greek custom of bathing also gained popularity in the Roman world. Increasingly, Romans built large public buildings containing pools supplied by intricate systems of aqueducts. These structures were more than just places to bathe. Baths included gymnasia where men exercised, snack bars and halls where people chatted and read, and even libraries and lecture halls. Women had opportunities to bathe, generally in separate facilities or at separate times, and both women and men went to the baths to see and be seen. Conservative commentators objected to these new pastimes as a corruption of traditional Roman values, but most Romans saw them as a normal part of urban life.

paterfamilias The oldest dominant male of the family, who held great power over the lives of family members.

New customs did not change the core Roman social structures. The male head of the household was called the **paterfamilias**, and he had great power over his children. Fathers had the power to decide how family resources should be spent, and sons did not inherit until after their fathers had died. Women could inherit and own property, though they generally received a smaller portion of any family inheritance than their brothers did. The Romans praised women, like Lucretia of old, who were virtuous and loyal to their husbands and devoted to their children. Very young children were under their mother's care, and most children learned the skills they needed from their own parents. For children from wealthier urban families, opportunities for formal education increased in the late republic. Boys and girls might be educated in their homes by tutors, and boys also might go to a school, paid for by their parents.

An influx of slaves from Rome's conquests provided labor for the fields, mines, and cities. To the Romans slavery was a misfortune that befell some people, but it did not entail any racial theories. For loyal slaves the Romans always held out the possibility of freedom, and manumission—the freeing of individual slaves by their masters—became common. Nonetheless, slaves rebelled from time to time in large-scale revolts, which were put down by Roman armies.

Membership in a family did not end with death, as the spirits of the family's ancestors were understood to remain with the family. They and other gods regarded as protectors of the household were represented by small statues that were kept in a special cupboard, honored at family celebrations, and taken with the family when they moved.

The Late Republic and the Rise of Augustus, 133–27 B.C.E.

The wars of conquest eventually created serious political problems for the Romans. When the soldiers returned home, they found their farms practically in ruins. Many were forced to sell their land to ready buyers who had grown rich from the wars. These wealthy men created huge estates called latifundia. Now landless, veterans moved to the cities, especially Rome, but could not find work. These developments not only created unrest in the city but also threatened Rome's army by reducing its ranks, because landless men, even if they were Romans and lived in Rome, were forbidden to serve in the Roman army. The landless veterans found a leader in Tiberius Gracchus (163–133 B.C.E.), an aristocrat who was appalled by the situation. He proposed dividing public land among the poor. But a group of wealthy senators murdered him, launching a long era of political violence that would destroy the republic. Still, Tiberius's brother Gaius Gracchus (153–121 B.C.E.) passed a law providing the urban poor with cheap grain and urged practical reforms. Once again senators tried to stem the tide of reform by murdering him.

The next reformer, Gaius Marius (ca. 157–86 B.C.E.), recruited landless men into the army to put down a rebel king in Africa. He promised them land for their service. But after his victory, the Senate refused to honor his promise. From then on, Roman soldiers looked to their commanders, not to the Senate or the state, to protect their interests. Rome was also dividing into two political factions, both of which wanted political power. Both factions named individuals as supreme military commander, and each led Roman troops against an external enemy but also against each other. One of these generals, Sulla, gained power in Rome, and in 81 B.C.E. the Senate made him dictator, an official office in the Roman Republic given to a man who was granted absolute power temporarily to handle emergencies such as war. Dictators were supposed to step down after six months, but Sulla held this position for nine years, and after that it was too late to restore the republican constitution.

The history of the late republic is the story of power struggles among many famous Roman figures against a background of unrest at home and military campaigns abroad. Pompey (PAHM-pee) used military victories in Spain to force the Senate to allow him to run for consul. In 59 B.C.E. he was joined in a political alliance called the First Triumvirate by Crassus, another ambitious politician and the wealthiest man in Rome, and by Julius Caesar (100–44 B.C.E.). Born of a noble family, Caesar, an able general, was also a brilliant politician with unbridled ambition and a superb orator with immense literary ability. Recognizing that military success led to power, Caesar led his troops to victory in Spain and Gaul, modern France. The First Triumvirate fell apart after Crassus was killed in battle in 53 B.C.E. while trying to conquer Parthia, leaving Caesar and Pompey in competition with each other for power. The result was civil war. The Ptolemaic rulers of Egypt became mixed up in this war, particularly Cleopatra VII, who allied herself with Caesar and had a son by him. (See "Individuals in Society: Queen Cleopatra," page 154.) Caesar emerged

Queen Cleopatra

CLEOPATRA VII (69–30 B.C.E.) WAS A PTOLEMY, a member of the dynasty of Hellenistic rulers of Egypt who had established power in the third century B.C.E. Although she was a Greek, she was passionately devoted to her Egyptian subjects and was the first in her dynasty who could speak Egyptian as well as Greek. Just as ancient pharaohs had linked themselves with the gods, she had herself portrayed as the goddess Isis and may have seen herself as a reincarnation of Isis (see "The Nile and the God-King" in Chapter 2).

At the same time that civil war was raging in the late Roman Republic, Cleopatra and her brother Ptolemy XIII were in a dispute over who would be supreme ruler in Egypt. Julius Caesar captured the Egyptian capital of Alexandria, Cleopatra arranged to meet him, and the two became lovers, although Cleopatra was much younger and Caesar was married. The two apparently had a son, Caesarion, and Caesar's army defeated Ptolemy's army, ending the power struggle. In 46 B.C.E. Cleopatra arrived in Rome, where Caesar put up a statue of her as Isis in one of the city's temples. The Romans hated her because they saw her as a decadent Eastern queen and a threat to what were considered traditional Roman values.

After Caesar's assassination, Cleopatra returned to Alexandria. There she became involved in the continuing Roman civil war that now pitted Octavian, Caesar's heir, against Marc Antony, who commanded the Roman army in the East. When Antony visited Alexandria in 41 B.C.E. he met Cleopatra, and though he was already married to Octavian's sister, he became her lover. He abandoned (and later divorced) his Roman wife, married Cleopatra in 37 B.C.E., and changed his will to favor his children by Cleopatra. Antony's wedding present to Cleopatra was a huge grant of territory, much of it Roman, that greatly increased her power and that of all her children, including Caesarion. Antony also declared Caesarion to be Julius Caesar's rightful heir.

Octavian used the wedding gift as the reason to declare Antony a traitor. He and other Roman leaders described Antony as a romantic fool captivated by the seductive Cleopatra. Roman troops turned against Antony and joined with Octavian, and at the Battle of Actium in 31 B.C.E. Octavian defeated the army and

The only portraits of Cleopatra that date from her own lifetime are on the coins that she issued. This one, made at the mint of Alexandria, shows her as quite plain, reinforcing the point made by Cicero that her attractiveness was based more on intelligence and wit than physical beauty. The reverse of the coin shows an eagle, a symbol of rule. (© The Trustees of the British Museum/Art Resource, NY)

navy of Antony and Cleopatra. Antony committed suicide, as did Cleopatra shortly afterward. Octavian ordered the teenage Caesarion killed, but the young children of Antony and Cleopatra were allowed to go back to Rome, where they were raised by Antony's widow. In another consequence of Octavian's victory, Egypt became a Roman province.

Roman sources are viciously hostile to Cleopatra, and she became the model of the alluring woman whose sexual attraction led men to their doom. Stories about her beauty, sophistication, lavish spending, desire for power, and ruthlessness abounded and were retold for centuries. The most dramatic story was that she committed suicide through the bite of a poisonous snake, which may have been true and which has been the subject of countless paintings. Her tumultuous relationships with Caesar and Antony have been portrayed in plays, novels, movies, and television programs.

QUESTIONS FOR ANALYSIS

1. How did Cleopatra benefit from her relationships with Caesar and Antony? How did they benefit from their relationships with her?
2. How did ideas about gender and Roman suspicion of the more sophisticated Greek culture combine to shape Cleopatra's fate and the way she is remembered?
3. "Individuals in Society: Hatshepsut and Nefertiti" in Chapter 2 also focuses on leading female figures in Egypt, but these two women lived more than a thousand years before Cleopatra. How would you compare their situation with hers?

victorious, and he began to make a number of legal and economic reforms, acting on his own authority, though often with the approval of the Senate, which he packed with his supporters. He issued laws about debt, the collection of taxes, and the distribution of grain and land. Roman allies in Italy were to have full citizenship. He founded new colonies, which were to be populated by veterans and the poor.

Caesar was wildly popular with most people in Rome, but some senators opposed his rise to what was becoming absolute power. In 44 B.C.E. a group of conspirators assassinated him and set off another round of civil war. His grandnephew, the eighteen-year-old Octavian (63 B.C.E.–14 C.E.), joined with two of Caesar's followers, Marc Antony and Lepidus, in the Second Triumvirate. After defeating Caesar's murderers, they had a falling-out. Octavian forced Lepidus out of office and waged war against Antony, who had now also become allied with Cleopatra. In 31 B.C.E. Octavian defeated the combined forces of Antony and Cleopatra at the Battle of Actium in Greece. His victory ended the age of civil war. For his success, in 27 B.C.E. the Senate gave Octavian the name Augustus, meaning "revered one." Although the Senate did not mean this to be a decisive break, that date is generally used to mark the end of the Roman Republic and the start of the Roman Empire.

The Successes of Augustus

After Augustus ended the civil wars, he faced the monumental problems of reconstruction. He had to rebuild effective government, pay his army for its services, care for the welfare of the provinces, and address the danger of various groups on Rome's frontiers. Augustus was highly successful in meeting these challenges.

Augustus claimed that he was restoring the republic, but he was actually transforming the government into one in which all power was held by a single ruler. Augustus fit his own position into the republican constitution not by creating a new office for himself but by gradually taking over many of the offices that traditionally had been held by separate people.

The Senate named him often as both consul and tribune. He was also named imperator (ihm-puh-RAH-tuhr), a title given to victorious commanders, and held control of the army, which he made a permanent standing organization. Furthermore, recognizing the importance of religion, he had himself named *pontifex maximus*, or chief priest. The Senate also gave him the honorary title *princeps civitatis*, "first citizen of the state."

Augustus as Imperator In this marble statue, found in the villa of Augustus's widow, Augustus is dressed in a military uniform and in a pose usually used to show leaders addressing their troops. This emphasizes his role as imperator, the head of the army. The figures on his breastplate show various peoples the Romans had defeated or with whom they had made treaties, along with assorted deities. Although Augustus did not declare himself a god — as later Roman emperors would — this statue shows him barefoot, just as gods and heroes were in classical Greek statuary, and accompanied by Cupid riding a dolphin, both symbols of the goddess Venus, whom he claimed as an ancestor. (Vatican Museum and Galleries, Vatican State/Bridgeman Images)

Considering what had happened to Julius Caesar, Augustus wisely wielded all this power in the background, and his period of rule is officially called the "principate." The Senate continued to exist as a court of law and deliberative body. Without specifically saying so, however, Augustus created the office of emperor. The English word *emperor* is derived from the Latin word *imperator*, an origin that reflects the fact that Augustus's command of the army was the main source of his power. In other reforms, Augustus made provincial administration more orderly and improved its functioning. He further professionalized the army and awarded grants of land in the frontier provinces to veterans. He encouraged local self-government and the development of cities. As a spiritual bond between the provinces and Rome, Augustus encouraged the cult of *Roma et Augustus* (Rome and Augustus) as the guardian of the state. The cult spread rapidly and became a symbol of Roman unity, part of Roman civic religion. Augustus had himself portrayed on coins standing alongside the goddess Victory and on celebratory stone arches built to commemorate military victories. In addition, he had temples, stadiums, marketplaces, and public buildings constructed in Rome and other cities.

In the social realm, Augustus promoted marriage and childbearing through legal changes that released free women and freedwomen (female slaves who had been freed) from male guardianship if they had given birth to a certain number of children. Men and women who were unmarried or had no children were restricted in the inheritance of property.

Aside from addressing legal issues and matters of state, Augustus actively encouraged poets and writers. For this reason the period of his rule is known as the "golden age" of Latin literature. Roman poets and prose writers celebrated human accomplishments in works that were highly polished, elegant in style, and intellectual in conception.

Rome's greatest poet was Virgil (70–19 B.C.E.), whose masterpiece is the *Aeneid* (uh-NEE-id), an epic poem that is the Latin equivalent of the Greek *Iliad* and *Odyssey* (see "The 'Dark Age'" in Chapter 5). Virgil's account of the founding of Rome and the early years of the city gave final form to the legend of Aeneas, the Trojan hero (and ancestor of Romulus and Remus; see "The Founding of Rome") who escaped to Italy at the fall of Troy. As Virgil told it, Aeneas became the lover of Dido (DIGH-doh), the widowed queen of Carthage, but left her because his destiny called him to found Rome. Swearing the destruction of Rome, Dido committed suicide, and, according to Virgil, her enmity helped cause the Punic Wars. In leaving Dido, an "Eastern" queen, Aeneas put the good of the state ahead of marriage or pleasure. The parallels between this story and the real events involving Antony and Cleopatra were not lost on Augustus, who encouraged Virgil to write the *Aeneid* and made sure it was circulated widely immediately after Virgil died.

One of the most significant aspects of Augustus's reign was Roman expansion into northern and western Europe (Map 6.2). Augustus completed the conquest of Spain, founded twelve new towns in Gaul, and saw that the Roman road system linked new settlements with one another and with Italy. After hard fighting, he made the Rhine River the Roman frontier in Germania (Germany). Meanwhile, generals conquered areas as far as the Danube River, and Roman legions penetrated the areas of modern Austria, southern Bavaria, and western Hungary. The regions of modern Serbia, Bulgaria, and Romania also fell. Within this area the legionaries built fortified camps. Roads linked these camps with one another, and settlements grew up around

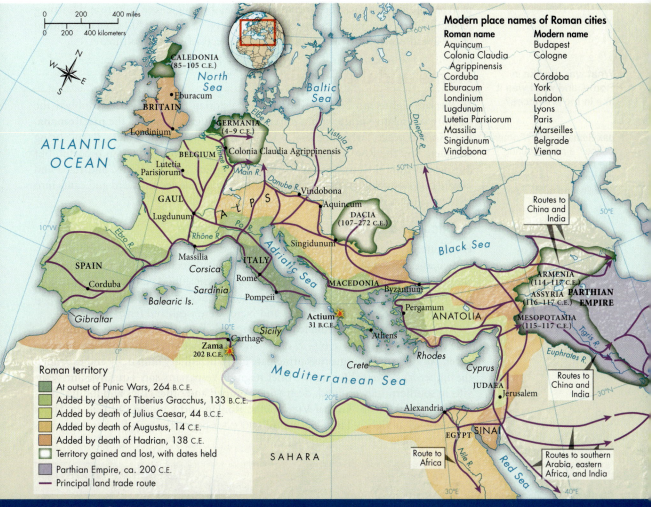

Modern place names of Roman cities

Roman name	Modern name
Aquincum	Budapest
Colonia Claudia Agrippinensis	Cologne
Corduba	Córdoba
Eburacum	York
Londinium	London
Lugdunum	Lyons
Lutetia Parisiorum	Paris
Massilia	Marseilles
Singidunum	Belgrade
Vindobona	Vienna

Roman territory

- At outset of Punic Wars, 264 B.C.E.
- Added by death of Tiberius Gracchus, 133 B.C.E.
- Added by death of Julius Caesar, 44 B.C.E.
- Added by death of Augustus, 14 C.E.
- Added by death of Hadrian, 138 C.E.
- Territory gained and lost, with dates held
- Parthian Empire, ca. 200 C.E.
- — Principal land trade route

MAPPING THE PAST

MAP 6.2 Roman Expansion, 262 B.C.E.–180 C.E. Rome expanded in all directions, eventually controlling every shore of the Mediterranean and vast amounts of land.

ANALYZING THE MAP How would you summarize the pattern of Roman expansion — that is, which areas were conquered first and which later? How long was Rome able to hold on to territories at the outermost boundaries of its empire?

CONNECTIONS Many of today's major cities in these areas were founded as Roman colonies. Why do you think so many of these cities were founded along the northern border of Roman territory?

the camps, eventually becoming towns. Traders began to frequent the frontier and to do business with the people who lived there; as a result, for the first time, central and northern Europe came into direct and continuous contact with Mediterranean culture.

Romans did not force their culture on native people in Roman territories. However, just as earlier ambitious people in the Hellenistic world knew that the surest path to political and social advancement lay in embracing Greek culture and learning to speak Greek (see "Building a Hellenized Society" in Chapter 5), those determined to get ahead now learned Latin and adopted aspects of Roman culture.

What was life like in Rome, and what was it like in the provinces?

Rome and the Provinces

pax Romana The "Roman peace," a period during the first and second centuries C.E. of political stability and relative peace.

In the late eighteenth century the English historian Edward Gibbon dubbed the stability and relative peace within the empire that Augustus created the **pax Romana**, the "Roman peace," which he saw as lasting about two hundred years. People being conquered by the Romans might not have agreed that things were so peaceful, but during this time the growing city of Rome saw great improvements, and trade and production flourished in the provinces. Rome also expanded eastward and came into indirect contact with China.

Political and Military Changes in the Empire

For about fifty years after Augustus's death in 14 C.E. the dynasty that he established — known as the Julio-Claudians because all were members of the Julian and Claudian clans — provided the emperors of Rome. Two of the Julio-Claudians, Tiberius and Claudius, were sound rulers and created a bureaucracy of able administrators to help them govern. Two of them, Caligula and Nero, were weak and frivolous.

In 68 C.E. Nero's inept rule led to military rebellion and widespread disruption. Two years later Vespasian (r. 69–79 C.E.), who established the Flavian dynasty, restored order. He also turned Augustus's principate into a hereditary monarchy and expanded the emperor's powers. During the brief reign of Vespasian's son Titus, Mount Vesuvius in southern Italy erupted, destroying Pompeii and other cities and killing thousands of people. (See "Global Viewpoints: Roman and Chinese Officials in Times of Disaster," at right.) The Flavians (69–96 C.E.) paved the way for the Antonines

Gladiator Mosaic Made in the first half of the fourth century C.E., this mosaic from an estate outside Rome includes the name of each gladiator next to the figure. At the top a gladiator stands in a victory pose, while the fallen gladiator at the bottom is marked with the symbol Ø, indicating that he has died in combat. Many of the gladiators in this mosaic, such as those at the left, appear less fit and fearsome than the gladiators depicted in movies, more closely reflecting the reality that gladiatorial combat was a job undertaken by a variety of people. (Galleria Borghese, Rome, Italy/Scala/Art Resource, NY)

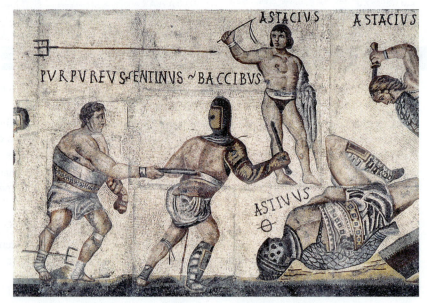

Roman and Chinese Officials in Times of Disaster

Government officials in ancient empires were often confronted with natural disasters, and their response to them was seen as a mark of their character and capabilities, just as it is today. In the first text below, the Roman author Pliny the Younger describes the actions of his uncle Pliny the Elder during the eruption of Mount Vesuvius in 79 C.E. In the second text, the Chinese historian Sima Qian (145–ca. 85 B.C.E.) (see Chapter 7) describes the actions of the official Ji An during a famine.

Pliny the Younger on Pliny the Elder

■ My uncle was stationed at Misenum, in active command of the fleet. On 24 August, in the early afternoon, my mother drew his attention to a cloud of unusual size and appearance. . . . My uncle's scholarly acumen saw at once that it was important enough for a closer inspection, and he ordered a boat to be made ready, . . . [but] what he had begun in a spirit of inquiry he completed as a hero. He gave orders for the warships to be launched and went on board himself with the intention of bringing help to many more people. . . . He hurried to the place which everyone else was hastily leaving, steering his course straight for the danger zone. He was entirely fearless, describing each new movement and phase of the portent to be noted down exactly as he observed them. Ashes were already falling, hotter and thicker as the ships drew near, followed by bits of pumice and blackened stones, charred and cracked by the flames. . . . He was able to bring his ship in. . . .

Meanwhile on Mount Vesuvius broad sheets of fire and leaping flames blazed at several points, their bright glare emphasized by the darkness of night. . . . The buildings were now shaking with violent shocks, and seemed to be swaying to and fro as if they were torn from their foundations. . . . My uncle decided to go down to the shore and investigate on the spot the possibility of any escape by sea, but he found the waves still wild and dangerous. . . . He stood leaning on two slaves and then suddenly collapsed, I imagine because the dense fumes choked his breathing. . . . His body was found intact and uninjured, still fully clothed and looking more like sleep than death.

Sima Qian on Ji An

■ During the reign of Emperor Jing, Ji An, on the recommendation of his father, was appointed as a mounted guard to the heir apparent. . . . When a great fire broke out in Henei and destroyed over 1,000 houses, the emperor . . . sent Ji An to observe the situation. On his return he reported, "The roofs of the houses were so close together that the fire spread from one to another; that is why so many homes were burned. It is nothing to worry about. As I passed through Henan on my way, however, I noted that the inhabitants were very poor, and over 10,000 families had suffered so greatly from floods and droughts that fathers and sons were reduced to eating each other. I therefore took it upon myself to use the imperial seals to open the granaries of Henan and relieve the distress of the people. I herewith return the seals and await punishment for overstepping my authority in this fashion."

The emperor, impressed with the wisdom he had shown, overlooked the irregularity of his action and transferred him to the post of governor. . . . Ji An studied the doctrines of the Yellow Emperor and Lao Zi. . . . He was sick a great deal of the time, confined to his bed and unable to go out, and yet after only a year or so as governor of Donghai he had succeeded in setting the affairs of the province in perfect order and winning the acclaim of the people.

QUESTIONS FOR ANALYSIS

1. How do the two officials respond to the disasters, and how do the authors of these works judge their responses?
2. What cultural ideals do the authors convey in their descriptions of these officials?

Sources: *The Letters of Pliny the Younger*, translated with an introduction by Betty Radice (London: Penguin Classics, 1963, reprinted 1969); *Records of the Grand Historian: Han Dynasty II*, by SIMA QIAN. Reproduced with permission of COLUMBIA UNIVERSITY PRESS in the format Book via Copyright Clearance Center.

(96–192 C.E.), a dynasty of emperors under whose leadership the Roman Empire experienced a long period of prosperity and the height of the pax Romana. Wars generally ended victoriously and were confined to the frontiers. Second-century emperors made further changes in government that helped the empire run more efficiently while increasing the authority of the emperor.

The Roman army also saw changes, transforming from a mobile unit to a much larger defensive force, with more and more troops who were noncitizens. Because army service could lead to citizenship, non-Romans joined the army willingly to gain citizenship, receive a salary, and learn a trade. The frontiers became firmly fixed and were defended by a system of forts and walls. Behind these walls, the network of roads was expanded and improved, both to supply the forts and to reinforce them in times of trouble.

Life in Imperial Rome

The expansion and stabilization of the empire created great wealth, much of which flowed into Rome. The city, with a population of over a million, may have been the largest city in the world at that time. Although Rome could boast of stately palaces, noble buildings, and beautiful residential areas, most people lived in shoddily constructed houses and took whatever work was available. Many residents of the city of Rome were slaves, who ranged from highly educated household tutors or government officials or widely sought sculptors to workers who engaged in hard physical tasks.

Fire and crime were perennial problems even in Augustus's day, and sanitation was poor. In the second century urban planning and new construction greatly improved the situation. For example, engineers built an elaborate system that collected sewage from public baths, the ground floors of buildings, and public latrines. They also built hundreds of miles of aqueducts, most of them underground, to bring fresh water into the city from the surrounding hills.

Rome grew so large that it became ever more difficult to feed its residents. Emperors solved the problem by providing citizens with free oil, wine, and grain for bread. By doing so, they also stayed in favor with the people. They and other sponsors also entertained the people with gladiatorial contests in which participants fought using swords and other weapons. Some gladiators were criminals or prisoners of war, but by the imperial period increasing numbers were volunteers, often poor immigrants who saw gladiatorial combat as a way to support themselves. All gladiators were trained in gladiatorial schools and were legally slaves, although they could keep their winnings and a few became quite wealthy. The Romans were even more addicted to chariot racing than to gladiatorial shows. Winning charioteers were idolized just as sports stars are today.

Prosperity in the Roman Provinces

As the empire grew and stabilized, many Roman provinces grew prosperous through the growth of agriculture, trade, and industry, among other factors. Peace and security opened Britain, Gaul, and the lands of the Danube to settlers from other parts of the Roman Empire. Veterans were given small parcels of land in the provinces, becoming tenant farmers. The garrison towns that grew up around provincial military camps became the centers of organized political life, and some grew into major cities.

Roman Architecture These three structures demonstrate the beauty and utility of Roman architecture. The Coliseum in Rome (below), a sports arena that could seat fifty thousand spectators, built between 70 C.E. and 80 C.E., was the site of gladiatorial games, animal spectacles, and executions. The Pantheon in Rome (right), a temple dedicated to all the gods, was built in its present form about 130 C.E., after earlier temples on the site had burned down. Its dome, 140 feet in diameter, remains the largest unreinforced concrete dome in the world. Romans also used concrete for more everyday purposes. The Pont du Gard at Nîmes in France (above) is a bridge over a river that carried an aqueduct supplying millions of gallons of water per day to the Roman city of Nîmes in Gaul; the water flowed in a channel at the very top. Although this bridge was built largely without mortar or concrete, many Roman aqueducts and bridges relied on concrete and sometimes iron rods for their strength.

(Pont du Gard: De Agostini Picture Library/ O. Geddo/Bridgeman Images; Pantheon: Dagli Orti/ REX/Shutterstock; Coliseum: Bridgeman Images)

The rural population throughout the empire left few records, but the inscriptions that remain point to a melding of cultures. Latin blended with the original language of an area and with languages spoken by those who came into the area later. Slowly what would become the Romance languages of Spanish, Italian, French, Portuguese, and Romanian evolved. Religion was another site of cultural exchange and mixture. Romans moving into an area learned about and began to venerate local gods, and local people learned about Roman ones. Gradually hybrid deities and rituals developed.

The Romans were the first to build cities in northern Europe, but in the eastern Mediterranean they ruled cities that had existed before Rome itself was even a village. Here there was much continuity in urban life from the Hellenistic period. There was less construction than in the Roman cities of northern and western Europe because existing buildings could simply be put to new uses.

The expansion of trade during the pax Romana made the Roman Empire an economic as well as a political force. Britain and Belgium became prime grain producers, and Britain's wool industry probably got its start under the Romans. Italy and southern Gaul produced huge quantities of wine. Roman colonists introduced the olive to southern Spain and northern Africa, which soon produced most of the oil consumed in the western part of the empire. In the East the olive oil production of Syrian farmers reached an all-time high, and Egypt produced tons of wheat that fed the Roman populace.

The growth of industry in the provinces was another striking development of this period, as cities in Gaul and Germany eclipsed the old Mediterranean manufacturing centers. Lyons in Gaul and later Cologne in Germany became the new centers of the glassmaking industry, and the cities of Gaul were nearly unrivaled in the manufacture of bronze and brass. Soldiers in the Roman army brought new methods of pottery-making northwards, setting up facilities to make roof tiles, amphoras, and dishes for their units. Some of these grew into industrial-scale kilns that were large enough to fire tens of thousands of pots at once. Fancier pottery often portrayed Greco-Roman gods and heroes, thus spreading Mediterranean myths and stories throughout the empire and beyond. Aided by all this growth in trade and industry, Europe and western Asia were linked in ways they had not been before.

Eastward Expansion and Contacts Between Rome and China

As the Romans drove farther eastward, they encountered the Parthians, who had established a kingdom in what is now Afghanistan and Iran in the Hellenistic period (see "Building a Hellenized Society" in Chapter 5). In the second century the Romans tried unsuccessfully to drive out the Parthians, who came to act as a link between Roman and Chinese merchants. Chinese merchants sold their wares to the Parthians, who then carried the goods overland to Mesopotamia or Egypt, from which they were shipped throughout the Roman Empire. In 226 C.E. the Parthians were defeated by the Sassanids, a new dynasty in the area (see "The Sassanid Empire and Conflicts with Byzantium" in Chapter 8). When the Romans continued their attacks against this new enemy, the Sassanid king Shapur conquered the Roman legions of the emperor Valerian, whom he took prisoner. Shapur employed the captured Roman soldiers and engineers to build roads, bridges, dams, and canals, and their designs and methods were later used throughout the Sassanid empire.

Although warfare disrupted parts of western Asia, it did not stop trade that had prospered from Hellenistic times (see "The Growth of Trade and Commerce" in Chapter 5). Silk was still a major commodity from east to west, along with other luxury goods. In return the Romans traded glassware, precious gems, and slaves. The Parthians added exotic fruits, rare birds, rugs, and other products.

The pax Romana was also an era of maritime trade, and Roman ships sailed from Egyptian ports to the mouth of the Indus River, where Romans purchased local merchandise and wares imported by the Parthians. Some hardy mariners pushed down the African coast and into the Indian Ocean. Roman coins have been found in Sri Lanka and Vietnam, clear evidence of trade connections, although most likely no merchant traveled the entire distance.

The period of this contact coincided with the era of Han greatness in China (see "China and Rome" in Chapter 7). During the reign of the Roman emperor Nerva (r. 96–98 C.E.), a Han emperor sent an ambassador, Gan Ying, to make contact with the Roman Empire. Gan Ying made it as far as the Persian Gulf ports, where he heard about the Romans from Parthian sailors and reported back to his emperor that the Romans were wealthy, tall, and strikingly similar to the Chinese. His report became part of a group of accounts about the Romans and other "western" peoples that circulated widely among scholars and officials in Han China. Educated Romans did not have a corresponding interest in China. For them, China remained more of a mythical than a real place, and they never bothered to learn more about it.

The Coming of Christianity

> **What was Christianity, and how did it affect life in the Roman Empire?**

During the reign of the emperor Tiberius (r. 14–37 C.E.), in the Roman province of Judaea a Jewish man named Jesus of Nazareth preached, attracted a following, and was executed on the order of the Roman prefect Pontius Pilate. Christianity, the religion created by Jesus's followers, came to have an enormous impact first in the Roman Empire and later throughout the world.

Factors Behind the Rise of Christianity

The civil wars that destroyed the Roman Republic left their mark on Judaea, where Jewish leaders had taken sides in the conflict. The turmoil created a climate of violence throughout the area, and among the Jews movements in opposition to the Romans spread. Many Jews came to believe that a final struggle was near and that it would lead to the coming of a savior, or **Messiah**, who would destroy the Roman legions and inaugurate a period of happiness and plenty for Jews. This apocalyptic belief was an old one among Jews, but by the first century C.E. it had become more widespread than ever.

The pagan world also played its part in the story of early Christianity. The term **pagan**, which originally referred to those who lived in the countryside, came to refer to those who practiced religions other than Judaism or Christianity. This included the traditional Roman civic religion devoted to the gods of the hearth, home, and countryside, which had often blended with the worship of other local deities as the Roman Empire expanded. The cult of the emperor, spread through the erection of statues, temples, and monuments, had been added to this, and for some people mystery religions offered the promise of life after death (see Chapter 5). Many people in

Messiah In Jewish belief, a savior who would bring a period of peace and happiness for Jews; many Christians came to believe that Jesus was that Messiah.

pagan Originally referring to those who lived in the countryside, the term came to mean those who practiced religions other than Judaism or Christianity.

the Roman Empire practiced all of these religions, combining them in whatever way seemed most beneficial or satisfying to them.

The Life and Teachings of Jesus

Into this climate of Messianic hope and Roman religious blending came Jesus of Nazareth (ca. 3 B.C.E.–29 C.E.). According to Christian Scripture, he was born to deeply religious Jewish parents and raised in Galilee. His ministry began when he was about thirty, and he taught by preaching and telling stories.

Like Socrates and the Buddha, Jesus left no writings. Accounts of his sayings and teachings first circulated orally among his followers and were later written down. The principal evidence for his life and deeds are the four Gospels of the Bible (Matthew, Mark, Luke, and John). These Gospels are records of Jesus's teachings, written sometime in the late first century to build a community of faith. Their authors had probably heard many different people talk about what Jesus said and did, and there are discrepancies among the four accounts. These differences indicate that early followers had a diversity of beliefs about Jesus's nature and purpose.

However, almost all the early sources agree on certain aspects of Jesus's teachings: he preached of a heavenly kingdom of eternal happiness in a life after death and of the importance of devotion to God and love of others. His teachings were based on Hebrew Scripture and reflected a conception of God and morality that came from Jewish tradition. The Greek translation of the Hebrew word *Messiah* is *Christus*, the origin of the English word *Christ*. Was Jesus the Messiah, the Christ? A small band of followers thought so, and Jesus claimed that he was. Yet Jesus had his own conception of the Messiah. He would establish a spiritual kingdom, not an earthly one.

The Roman official Pontius Pilate knew little about Jesus's teachings. He was concerned with maintaining peace and order. According to the New Testament, crowds followed Jesus into Jerusalem at the time of Passover, a highly emotional point in the Jewish year that marked the Jewish people's departure from Egypt under the leadership of Moses (see "The Hebrew State" in Chapter 2). The prospect that these crowds would spark violence alarmed Pilate. Some Jews believed that Jesus was the long-awaited Messiah. Others hated and feared him because they thought him religiously dangerous. To avert riot and bloodshed, Pilate condemned Jesus to death, and his soldiers carried out the sentence. On the third day after Jesus's crucifixion, some of his followers claimed that he had risen from the dead. For his earliest followers and for generations to come, the resurrection of Jesus became a central element of faith.

Depiction of Jesus This mural, from a Roman camp at Dura-Europos on the Euphrates River, may be the earliest known depiction of Jesus. Dating to 235 C.E., it depicts Jesus healing a paralytic man, an incident described in the New Testament. Early Christians used art to spread their message. (Yale University Art Gallery, Dura-Europos Collection)

The Spread of Christianity

Believers in Jesus's divinity met in small assemblies or congregations, often in one another's homes, to discuss the meaning of Jesus's message and to celebrate a ritual (later called the Eucharist or Lord's Supper) commemorating his last meal with his disciples before his arrest. Because they expected Jesus to return to the world very soon, they regarded earthly life and institutions as unimportant. Only later did these congregations evolve into what came to be called the religion of Christianity, with a formal organization and set of beliefs.

The catalyst in the spread of Jesus's teachings and the formation of the Christian Church was Paul of Tarsus, a well-educated Hellenized Jew. Paul traveled all over the Roman Empire and wrote letters of advice to many groups. These letters were copied and widely circulated, transforming Jesus's ideas into more specific moral teachings. As a result of his efforts, Paul became the most important figure in changing Christianity from a Jewish sect into a separate religion, and many of his letters became part of Christian Scripture.

The breadth of the Roman Empire was another factor behind the spread of Christianity. If all roads led to Rome, they also led outward to the provinces. This enabled early Christians to spread their faith easily throughout the world known to them, as Jesus had told his followers to do. The Romans also considered their empire universal, and the early Christians combined the two concepts of universalism.

Though most of the earliest converts seem to have been Jews, Paul urged that Gentiles, or non-Jews, be accepted on an equal basis. The earliest Christian converts included people from all social classes. These people were reached by missionaries and others who spread the Christian message through family contacts, friendships, and business networks. Many women were active in spreading Christianity. Paul greeted male and female converts by name in his letters and noted that women often provided financial support for his activities. The growing Christian communities differed over the extent to which women should participate in the workings of the religion; some favored giving women a larger role in church affairs, while others were more restrictive.

People were attracted to Christian teachings for a variety of reasons. Christianity was in many ways a mystery religion, offering its adherents special teachings that would give them immortality. But in contrast to traditional mystery religions, Christianity promised this immortality widely, not only to a select few. Christianity also offered the possibility of forgiveness, for believers accepted that human nature is weak and that even the best Christians could fall into sin. But Jesus loved sinners and forgave those who repented. Christianity was also attractive to many because it gave the Roman world a cause. By spreading the word of Christ, Christians played their part in God's plan for the triumph of Christianity on earth. Christianity likewise gave its devotees a sense of identity and community. To stress the spiritual kinship of this new type of community, Christians often called one another brother and sister. Also, many Christians took Jesus's commandment to love one another as a guide and provided support for widows, orphans, and the poor, just as they would for family members.

The Growing Acceptance and Evolution of Christianity

At first, most Roman officials largely ignored the followers of Jesus, viewing them simply as one of the many splinter groups within Judaism, but slowly some came to oppose Christian practices and beliefs. They considered Christians to be subversive dissidents because they stopped practicing traditional rituals and they objected to the cult of the emperor. Some Romans thought that Christianity was one of the worst of the mystery cults, with immoral and indecent rituals. Pagans also feared that the Greco-Roman gods would withdraw their favor from the Roman Empire because of the Christian insistence that the pagan gods either did not exist or were evil spirits. And many worried that Christians were trying to destroy the Roman family with their insistence on a new type of kinship.

Persecutions of Christians, including torture and executions, were organized by governors of Roman provinces and sometimes by the emperor, beginning with Nero. Most persecutions were, however, local and sporadic in nature. Responses to Christianity on the part of Roman emperors varied. Some left Christians in peace, while others ordered them to sacrifice to the emperor and the Roman gods or risk death.

By the second century Christianity was changing. The belief that Jesus was soon coming again gradually waned, and as the number of converts increased, permanent institutions were established. These included buildings and a hierarchy of officials often modeled on those of the Roman Empire. **Bishops**, officials with jurisdiction over a certain area, became especially important. They began to assert that they had the right to determine the correct interpretation of Christian teachings and to choose their successors.

bishop A Christian Church official with jurisdiction over a certain area and the power to determine the correct interpretation of Christian teachings.

Christianity also began to attract more highly educated individuals who developed complex theological interpretations of issues that were not clear in scripture. Often drawing on Greek philosophy and Roman legal traditions, they worked out understandings of such issues as how Jesus could be both divine and human and how God could be both a father and a son (and later a spirit as well, a Christian doctrine known as the Trinity). Bishops and theologians often modified teachings that seemed upsetting to Romans, such as Jesus's harsh words about wealth and family ties. Given all these changes, Christianity became more formal in the second century, with power more centralized.

How did the emperors respond to political, economic, and religious issues in the third and fourth centuries?

Turmoil and Reform

The prosperity and stability of the second century gave way to a period of domestic upheaval and foreign invasion in the Roman Empire that historians have termed the "crisis of the third century." Trying to repair the damage was the major work of the emperors Diocletian (r. 284–305) and Constantine (r. 306–337). They enacted political and religious reforms that dramatically changed the empire.

Political Measures

During the crisis of the third century the Roman Empire was stunned by civil war, as different individuals, generally military commanders from the border provinces, claimed rights to leadership of the empire. Beginning in 235, emperors often ruled for only a few years or even months. Army leaders in the provinces declared their loyalty to one faction or another, or they broke from the empire entirely, thus ceasing to supply troops or taxes. Non-Roman groups on the frontiers took advantage of the chaos to invade Roman-held territory along the Rhine and Danube, occasionally even crossing the Alps to maraud in Italy. In the East, Sassanid armies advanced all the way to the Mediterranean. By the time peace was restored, the empire's economy was shattered, cities had shrunk in size, and many farmers had left their lands.

Diocletian, who had risen through the ranks of the military to become emperor in 284, ended the period of chaos. Under Diocletian the princeps became *dominus*, "lord," reflecting the emperor's claim that he was "the elect of god." To underscore the emperor's exalted position, Diocletian and his successor, Constantine, adopted the court ceremonies and trappings of the Persian Empire.

Diocletian recognized that the empire had become too large for one man to handle and so in 293 divided it into a western and an eastern half. He assumed direct control of the eastern part, giving a colleague the rule of the western part along with the title *augustus*. Diocletian and his fellow augustus further delegated power by appointing two men to assist them. Each man was given the title *caesar* to indicate his exalted rank.

The Division of the Roman World, 293 C.E.

After a brief civil war following Diocletian's death, Constantine eventually gained authority over the entire empire but ruled from the East. Here he established a new capital for the empire at Byzantium, an old Greek city on the Bosporus, a strait on the boundary between Europe and Asia. He named it "New Rome," though it was soon called Constantinople. In his new capital Constantine built palaces, warehouses, public buildings, and even a hippodrome for horse racing, modeling them on Roman buildings. In addition, he built defensive works along the borders of the empire, trying hard to keep it together, as did his successors. Despite their efforts, however, the eastern and the western halves drifted apart.

The emperors ruling from Constantinople could not provide enough military assistance to repel invaders in the western half of the Roman Empire, and Roman authority there slowly disintegrated. In 476 a Germanic chieftain, Odoacer, deposed the Roman emperor in the West. This date thus marks the official end of the Roman Empire in the West, although the Roman Empire in the East, later called the Byzantine Empire, would last for nearly another thousand years.

Economic Issues

Along with political challenges, major economic problems also confronted Diocletian and Constantine, including inflation and declining tax revenues. In an attempt to curb inflation, Diocletian issued an edict that fixed maximum prices and wages throughout the empire. He and his successors dealt with the tax system just as strictly and inflexibly. Taxes became payable in kind, that is, in goods and services instead of money. All those involved in the growing, preparation, and transportation of food and other essentials were locked into their professions, as the emperors tried to assure a steady supply of these goods. In this period of severe depression, many localities could not pay their taxes. In such cases local tax collectors, who were themselves locked into service, had to make up the difference from their own funds. This system soon wiped out a whole class of moderately wealthy people and set the stage for the lack of social mobility that was a key characteristic of European society for many centuries to follow.

The emperors' measures did not really address Rome's central economic problems. During the turmoil of the third and fourth centuries, many free farmers and their families were killed by invaders or renegade soldiers, or abandoned farms ravaged in the fighting. Consequently, large tracts of land lay untended. Landlords with ample

The Edict of Toleration and the Edict of Milan

The emperor Diocletian's persecution of Christians, the last, longest, and harshest official persecution, ended shortly after his death, and the emperors who succeeded him decided instead to tolerate Christianity. In 311 Galerius, senior emperor in the multiheaded late empire, who had been a leading figure in the Diocletian persecutions, issued an edict of toleration legalizing Christianity. In 313 Constantine and Licinius, co-emperors and rivals for power, agreed in a letter to governors of Roman provinces that all religions should be tolerated and property taken from Christians should be returned to them. This letter later became known as the Edict of Milan, but there probably was never a formal edict.

Edict of Toleration (311 C.E.)

■ Among other arrangements which we are always accustomed to make for the prosperity and welfare of the republic, we had desired formerly to bring all things into harmony with the ancient laws and public order of the Romans, and to provide that even the Christians who had left the religion of their fathers should come back to reason; since, indeed, the Christians themselves, for some reason, had followed such a caprice and had fallen into such a folly that they would not obey the institutes of antiquity, which perchance their own ancestors had first established; but at their own will and pleasure, they would thus make laws unto themselves which they should observe and would collect various peoples in diverse places in congregations. Finally when our law had been promulgated to the effect that they should conform to the institutes of antiquity, many were subdued by the fear of danger, many even suffered death. And yet since most of them persevered in their determination, and we saw that they neither paid the reverence and awe due to the gods nor worshipped the God of the Christians, in view of our most mild clemency and the constant habit by which we are accustomed to grant indulgence to all, we thought that we ought to grant our most prompt indulgence also to these, so that they may again be Christians and may hold their conventicles [religious services], provided they do nothing contrary to good order.

Edict of Milan (313 C.E.)

■ When I, Constantine Augustus, as well as I, Licinius Augustus, fortunately met near Mediolanurn [Milan], and were considering everything that pertained to the public welfare and security, we thought, among other things which we saw would be for the good of many, those regulations pertaining to the reverence of the Divinity ought certainly to be made first, so that we

resources began at once to claim as much of this land as they could. The huge estates that resulted, called villas, were self-sufficient and became islands of stability in an unsettled world. In return for the protection and security landlords could offer, many small landholders gave over their lands and their freedom. To guarantee a supply of labor, landlords denied them the freedom to move elsewhere. Free men and women were becoming tenant farmers bound to the land, who would later be called serfs.

The Acceptance of Christianity

The crisis of the third century seemed to some emperors, including Diocletian, to be the punishment of the gods. Diocletian increased persecution of Christians, hoping that the gods would restore their blessing on Rome. Yet his persecutions were never very widespread or long-lived, and by the early fourth century most Romans tolerated Christianity, even if they did not practice it. In several edicts, emperors reversed Diocletian's policy and instead ordered toleration of all religions. (See "Analyzing the Evidence: The Edict of Toleration and the Edict of Milan," above.) Constantine went beyond toleration to favoring Christianity, expecting in return the support of church officials in maintaining order, and late in his life he was baptized as a Chris-

might grant to the Christians and others full authority to observe that religion which each preferred; whence any Divinity whatsoever in the seat of the heavens may be propitious and kindly disposed to us and all who are placed under our rule. And thus by this wholesome counsel and most upright provision we thought to arrange that no one whatsoever should be denied the opportunity to give his heart to the observance of the Christian religion, or that religion which he should think best for himself, so that the Supreme Deity, to whose worship we freely yield our hearts may show in all things His usual favor and benevolence. Therefore, your Worship [the governor to whom this letter is directed] should know that it has pleased us to remove all conditions whatsoever, which were in the rescripts formerly given to you officially, concerning the Christians and now any one of these who wishes to observe Christian religion may do so freely and openly, without molestation. . . .

Moreover, in the case of the Christians especially we esteemed it best to order that if it happens anyone heretofore has bought from our treasury from anyone whatsoever, those places where they were previously accustomed to assemble, concerning which a certain decree had been made and a letter sent to you officially, the same shall be restored to the Christians without payment or any claim of recompense and without any kind of fraud or deception. . . . And since these Christians are known to have possessed not only those places in which they were accustomed to assemble, but also other property, namely the churches, belonging to them as a corporation and not as individuals, all these things which we have included under the above law, you will order to be restored, without any hesitation or controversy at all, to these Christians. . . . Let this be done so that, as we have said above, Divine favor towards us, which, under the most important circumstances we have already experienced, may, for all time, preserve and prosper our successes together with the good of the state.

QUESTIONS FOR ANALYSIS

1. How does Galerius explain his persecution of Christians? His decision to now tolerate them?
2. Why have Constantine and Licinius decided to allow everyone to practice his or her own religion?
3. How do the statements of the emperors fit with Roman ideas about harnessing divine power for the public good, and about the proper role of religion in the state?

Source: Lactantius, *De Mortibus Persecutorum*, Chs. 34, 35, 48, in *Opera*, ed. O. F. Fritzsche, II, p. 288 sq. (Bibl. Patr. Ecc. Lat. XI). Translated in University of Pennsylvania, Dept. of History, *Translations and Reprints from the Original Sources of European History* (Philadelphia: University of Pennsylvania Press, 1897?–1907?), vol. 4:1, pp. 28–30. Accessed from Internet History Sourcebook Project, Fordham University.

tian. Constantine also freed the clergy from imperial taxation and endowed the building of Christian churches.

Helped in part by its favored position in the empire, Christianity slowly became the leading religion, and emperors after Constantine continued to promote it. In 380 the emperor Theodosius (r. 379–395) made Christianity the official religion of the empire. He allowed the church to establish its own courts and to use its own body of law, called "canon law." With this he laid the foundation for later growth in church power (see "The Growth of the Christian Church" in Chapter 8).

Chapter Summary

The Italian peninsula was settled by many different groups, including Greeks in the south and Etruscans in the north. The Etruscans expanded southward into central Italy, where they influenced the culture of the small town that was growing into the city of Rome. Rome prospered and expanded its own territories, establishing a republican government led by the Senate. In a series of wars the Romans conquered the Mediterranean, creating an overseas empire that brought them unheard-of power and wealth, but also social unrest and civil war. The meteoric rise to power of Julius Caesar in the first century B.C.E. led to his assassination, but his grandnephew Augustus finally restored peace and order to Rome. Under Augustus, the republic became an empire.

Augustus and his successors further expanded Roman territories. The city of Rome became the magnificent capital of the empire. The Roman provinces and frontiers also saw extensive prosperity through the growth of agriculture, industry, and trade connections. Christianity, a religion created by the followers of Jesus of Nazareth, spread across the empire, beginning in the first century C.E. Initially some Roman officials and emperors persecuted Christians, but gradually hostility decreased. Emperors in the fourth century first allowed Christianity and then made it the official religion of the empire, one of many measures through which they attempted to solve the problems created by invasions and political turmoil. Their measures were successful in the East, where the Roman Empire lasted for another thousand years, but not in the West, where the Roman Empire ended in the fifth century.

CONNECTIONS

The Roman Empire, with its powerful — and sometimes bizarre — leaders, magnificent buildings, luxurious clothing, and bloody amusements, has long fascinated people. Politicians and historians have closely studied the reasons for its successes and have even more closely analyzed the weaknesses that led to its eventual collapse. Despite the efforts of emperors and other leaders, the Western Roman Empire slowly broke apart and by the fifth century C.E. no longer existed. By the fourteenth century European scholars were beginning to see the fall of the Roman Empire as one of the great turning points in Western history, the end of the classical era. That began the practice of dividing Western history into different periods — eventually, the ancient, medieval, and modern eras. Those categories still shape the way that Western history is taught and learned.

This three-part conceptualization also shapes the periodization of world history. As you saw in Chapter 4 and will see in Chapter 7, China is also understood to have had a classical age. As you will read in Chapter 11, the Maya of Mesoamerica did as well, stretching from 300 C.E. to 900 C.E. South Asia is often described as having a classical period, which developed during the Mauryan Empire that lasted from 322 B.C.E. to 185 B.C.E. as discussed in Chapter 3 and extended to the Gupta Empire that ruled northern India from ca. 320 C.E. to 480 C.E., which will be discussed in Chapter 12. The dates of these ages are different from those of the classical period in the Mediterranean, but there are striking similarities among all these civilizations: successful large-scale administrative bureaucracies were established, trade flourished, cities grew, roads were built, and new cultural forms developed. In all these civilizations this classical period was followed by an era of decreased prosperity and increased warfare and destruction.

CHAPTER 6   # Review and Explore

Identify Key Terms

Identify and explain the significance of each item below.

Senate (p. 147)

consuls (p. 147)

patricians (p. 149)

plebeians (p. 149)

Punic Wars (p. 151)

paterfamilias (p. 152)

pax Romana (p. 158)

Messiah (p. 163)

pagan (p. 163)

bishop (p. 166)

Review the Main Ideas

Answer the focus questions from each section of the chapter.

1. How did the Romans come to dominate Italy, and what political institutions did they create? (p. 146)

2. How did Rome expand its power beyond Italy, and what were the effects of this expansion? (p. 151)

3. What was life like in Rome, and what was it like in the provinces? (p. 158)

4. What was Christianity, and how did it affect life in the Roman Empire? (p. 163)

5. How did the emperors respond to political, economic, and religious issues in the third and fourth centuries? (p. 166)

Make Comparisons and Connections

Analyze the larger developments and continuities within and across chapters.

1. What allowed large empires in the ancient world, including the Persian (Chapter 2), the Mauryan (Chapter 3), and the Roman, to govern vast territories and many different peoples successfully?

2. Looking over the long history of Rome, do interactions with non-Romans or conflicts among Romans themselves appear to be the most significant drivers of change? Why? How is this different from other classical civilizations?

3. No classical Chinese thinkers knew about Roman political developments, but the issues they considered, such as how to achieve order and what made government strong, could also be applied to Rome. How do you think Confucians, Daoists, and Legalists (Chapter 4) would have assessed the Roman Republic? The Roman Empire?

TIMELINE

ROMAN WORLD

← **753 B.C.E.** Traditional founding of the city of Rome

◆ **509 B.C.E.** Traditional date of the establishment of the Roman Republic

264–241 B.C.E.
218–201 B.C.E.
149–146 B.C.E. Punic Wars

◆ **ca. 265 B.C.E.** Romans control most of Italy

ASIA

ca. 322–185 B.C.E. Mauryan Empire in India **(Ch. 3)**

AMERICAS

EUROPE

ca. 500–338 B.C.E. Classical period in Athens **(Ch. 5)**

500 B.C.E.   **250 B.C.E.**

Suggested Resources

BOOKS

Aldrete, Gregory S. *Daily Life in the Roman City.* 2004. Reveals the significance of ordinary Roman life in the city of Rome, its port Ostia, and Pompeii.

Canfora, Luciano. *Julius Caesar: The Life and Times of the People's Dictator.* 2007. Provides a new interpretation of Caesar that puts him fully in the context of his times.

Clark, Gillian. *Christianity and Roman Society.* 2004. Surveys the evolution of Christian life among Christians and with their pagan neighbors.

Evans, J. K. *War, Women, and Children in Ancient Rome.* 2000. Provides a concise survey of how war affected the home front in wartime.

Everitt, Anthony. *The Rise of Rome: The Making of the World's Greatest Empire.* 2012. An engaging and thorough narrative written for general readers.

Freeman, Charles. *A New History of Early Christianity.* 2010. A survey of the first four centuries of Christianity, written for a general audience.

Haynes, Sybille. *Etruscan Civilization: A Cultural History.* 2005. Deals with cultural history, with special emphasis on Etruscan women.

Holland, Tom. *Rubicon: The Triumph and Tragedy of the Roman Republic.* 2003. A lively account of the disintegration of the republic from the Gracchi to Caesar's death.

Joshel, Sandra R. *Slavery in the Roman World.* 2010. An overview of Roman slavery, designed for students.

Knapp, Robert. *Invisible Romans.* 2011. A view of Roman life that focuses on ordinary men and women: soldiers, slaves, laborers, housewives, gladiators, and outlaws.

Kyle, Donald G. *Sport and Spectacle in the Ancient World.* 2007. Deals in grim detail with the ritualized violence of the gladiatorial games.

Warrior, Valerie. *Roman Religion.* 2006. A relatively brief study that examines the actual practices of Roman religion in their social contexts.

DOCUMENTARIES

From Jesus to Christ: The First Christians (PBS, 1998). A four-part documentary exploring the life and death of Jesus and the transformation of Christianity from a small group to an established church. With commentary by theologians, archaeologists, and historians on many key issues.

◆ **44 B.C.E.** Assassination of Julius Caesar

◆ **31 B.C.E.** Octavian (Augustus) defeats Antony and Cleopatra

◆ **27 B.C.E.** Senate grants Octavian the title "Augustus," marking the beginning of the Roman Empire

14 B.C.E.–68 C.E. Julio-Claudian emperors; expansion into northern and western Europe

ca. 3 B.C.E.–29 C.E. Life of Jesus

96–192 C.E. Antonine emperors; Roman Empire at its greatest extent

69–96 C.E. Flavian emperors; restoration of order after civil wars

284–337 C.E. Diocletian and Constantine attempt to reconstruct the empire

235–284 C.E. Third-century crisis; civil war; invasions; economic decline

◆ **311 and 313 C.E.** Edicts of Toleration and Milan, allowing practice of Christianity

◆ **380 C.E.** Theodosius makes Christianity the official religion of the empire

476 C.E. ◆ Odoacer deposes last Roman emperor in the West

206 B.C.E.–220 C.E. Han dynasty in China **(Ch. 7)**

224–651 C.E. Sassanid dynasty in Persia **(Ch. 8)**

100–800 C.E. Moche civilization in Peru **(Ch. 11)**

1 C.E.   **250 C.E.**   **500 C.E.**

Great Generals of the Ancient World: Alexander the Great, Hannibal, Julius Caesar (History Channel, 2006). Three-part examination of the military careers, battles, and personalities of the most successful generals in the ancient world.

Rome: The Rise and Fall of an Empire (History Channel, 2008). A thirteen-part documentary, with re-enactments—especially of battle scenes, power struggles, and lavish banquets—that traces Rome from the second century B.C.E. to the fifth century C.E.

FEATURE FILMS AND TELEVISION

Gladiator (Ridley Scott, 2000). The Academy Award–winning historical epic about a Roman general who becomes a gladiator and avenges the murder of his family by a power-crazy emperor.

Rome (HBO and BBC, 2005, 2007). British-American historical-drama television series set in the transition from republic to empire, with real historical figures and invented characters, that succeeds in presenting a grittier and more realistic Rome than do most Hollywood epics.

Spartacus (Stanley Kubrick, 1960). An Oscar-winning epic that tells the story of the slave revolt led by

Spartacus; starring and produced by Kirk Douglas, who considered the movie in part a response to McCarthy-era blacklisting.

WEBSITES

LacusCurtius: Into the Roman World. Primary and secondary resources on ancient Rome, including photographs, inscriptions, maps, and links to other Roman websites. **penelope.uchicago.edu/Thayer /E/Roman/home.htm**

Rome Reborn: A Digital Model of Ancient Rome. Three-dimensional digital models by an international team of scholars illustrating the urban development of ancient Rome; includes a fascinating video tour of the streets of Rome in 320 C.E. **www.romereborn.virginia.edu/**

Vindolanda Tablets Online. A highly unusual find of wooden writing tablets from the second century C.E., discovered at the Roman fortress of Vindolanda behind Hadrian's Wall in Britain, reveals many aspects of non-elite Roman society and military life. The site includes text images, transliterated texts, English translations, and historical background. **vindolanda.csad.ox.ac.uk/**

7

East Asia and the Spread of Buddhism
221 B.C.E.–845 C.E.

East Asia was transformed over the millennium from 221 B.C.E. to 800 C.E. At the beginning of this era, China had just been unified into a single state upon the Qin defeat of all the rival states of the Warring States Period, but it still faced major military challenges with the confederation of the nomadic Xiongnu to its north. At the time China was the only place in East Asia with writing, large cities, and complex state organizations. Over the next several centuries, East Asia changed dramatically as new states emerged. To protect an emerging trade in silk and other valuables, Han China sent armies far into Central Asia. War, trade, diplomacy, missionary activity, and the pursuit of learning led the Chinese to travel to distant lands and people from distant lands to go to China. Among the results were the spread of Buddhism from India and Central Asia to China and the adaptation of many elements of Chinese culture by near neighbors, especially Korea and Japan. Buddhism came to provide a common set of ideas and visual images to all the cultures of East Asia, much the way Christianity linked societies in Europe.

Increased communication stimulated state formation among China's neighbors: Tibet, Korea, Manchuria, Vietnam, and Japan. Written Chinese was increasingly used as an international language by the ruling elites of these countries, and the new states frequently adopted political models from China as well. By 800 C.E. each of these regions was well on its way to developing a distinct political and cultural identity.

Palace Maid

Ceramic models of attractive young women were often placed in Chinese tombs, reflecting hopes for the afterlife.

© Panorama/The Image Works

CHAPTER PREVIEW

THE AGE OF EMPIRE IN CHINA: THE QIN AND HAN DYNASTIES
What were the social, cultural, and political consequences of the unification of China under the strong centralized governments of the Qin and Han empires?

THE SPREAD OF BUDDHISM OUT OF INDIA
How did Buddhism find its way into East Asia, and what was its appeal and impact?

THE CHINESE EMPIRE RE-CREATED: SUI (581–618) AND TANG (618–907)
What were the lasting accomplishments of the Sui and Tang Dynasties?

THE EAST ASIAN CULTURAL SPHERE
What elements of Chinese culture were adopted by Koreans, Vietnamese, and Japanese, and how did they adapt them to their own circumstances?

What were the social, cultural, and political consequences of the unification of China under the strong centralized governments of the Qin and Han empires?

The Age of Empire in China: The Qin and Han Dynasties

In much the same period in which Rome created a huge empire, the Qin and Han rulers in China created an empire on a similar scale. Like the Roman Empire, the Chinese empire was put together through force of arms and held in place by sophisticated centralized administrative machinery. The governments created by the Qin and Han Dynasties affected many facets of Chinese social, cultural, and intellectual life.

The Qin Unification, 221–206 B.C.E.

In 221 B.C.E., after decades of constant warfare, Qin (CHIN), the state that had adopted Legalist policies during the Warring States Period (see "Legalism" in Chapter 4), succeeded in defeating the last of its rivals, and China was unified for the first time in many centuries. Deciding that the title "king" was not grand enough, the king of Qin invented the title "emperor" (*huangdi*) (hwang-dee). He called himself the First Emperor in anticipation of a long line of successors. His state, however, did not long outlast him.

Once he ruled all of China, the First Emperor and his shrewd Legalist minister Li Si embarked on a sweeping program of centralization that touched the lives of nearly everyone in China. To cripple the nobility of the defunct states, who could have posed serious threats, the First Emperor ordered the nobles to leave their lands and move to the capital. The private possession of arms was outlawed to make it more difficult for subjects to rebel. The First Emperor dispatched officials to administer the territory that had been conquered and controlled the officials through a long list of regulations, reporting requirements, and penalties for inadequate performance.

Army of the First Emperor
The thousands of life-size ceramic soldiers buried in pits about a half mile from the First Emperor's tomb help us imagine the Qin military machine. It was the Qin emperor's concern with the afterlife that led him to construct such a lifelike guard. The soldiers were originally painted in bright colors, and they held real bronze weapons. (Rolf_42/Getty Images)

To harness the enormous human resources of his people, the First Emperor ordered a census of the population. Census information helped the imperial bureaucracy to plan its activities: to estimate the labor force available for military service and building projects and the tax revenues needed to pay for them. To make it easier to administer all regions uniformly, the Chinese script was standardized, outlawing regional variations in the ways words were written. The First Emperor also standardized weights, measures, coinage, and even the axle lengths of carts. To make it easier for Qin armies to move rapidly, thousands of miles of roads were built, which indirectly facilitated trade. Most of the labor on the projects came from drafted farmers or convicts working out their sentences.

Some modern Chinese historians have glorified the First Emperor as a bold conqueror who let no obstacle stop him, but traditionally he was castigated as a cruel, arbitrary, impetuous, suspicious, and superstitious megalomaniac. Hundreds of thousands of subjects were drafted to build the **Great Wall** (ca. 230–208 B.C.E.), a rammed-earth fortification along the northern border between the Qin realm and the land controlled by the nomadic Xiongnu. After Li Si complained that scholars (especially Confucians) used records of the past to denigrate the emperor's achievements and undermine popular support, the emperor had all writings other than useful manuals on topics such as agriculture, medicine, and divination collected and burned. As a result of this massive book burning, many ancient texts were lost.

> **Great Wall** A rammed-earth fortification built along the northern border of China during the reign of the First Emperor.

Like Ashoka in India a few decades earlier (see "The Reign of Ashoka" in Chapter 3), the First Emperor erected many stone inscriptions to inform his subjects of his goals and accomplishments. He had none of Ashoka's modesty, however. On one stone he described his conquest of the other states this way (referring to himself in the third person, as was customary): "He wiped out tyrants, rescued the common people, brought peace to the four corners of the earth. His enlightened laws spread far and wide as examples to All Under Heaven until the end of time. Great is he indeed!"[1]

Assassins tried to kill the First Emperor three times, and perhaps as a consequence he became obsessed with discovering the secrets of immortality. He spent lavishly on a tomb designed to protect him in the afterlife. After he died in 210 B.C.E., the Qin state unraveled. The Legalist institutions designed to concentrate power in the hands of the ruler made the stability of the government dependent on his strength and character, and his heir proved ineffective. The heir was murdered by his younger brother, and uprisings soon followed.

The Han Dynasty, 206 B.C.E.–220 C.E.

The eventual victor in the struggle for power that ensued in the wake of the collapse of the Qin Dynasty was Liu Bang, known in history as Emperor Gaozu (gow-dzoo) (r. 202–195 B.C.E.). The First Emperor of Qin was from the Zhou aristocracy. Gaozu was, by contrast, from a modest family of commoners, so his elevation to emperor is evidence of how thoroughly the Qin Dynasty had destroyed the old order.

Gaozu did not disband the centralized government created by the Qin, but he did remove its most unpopular features. Harsh laws were canceled, taxes were sharply reduced, and a policy of noninterference was adopted in an effort to promote economic recovery. With policies of this sort, relative peace, and the extension of China's frontiers, the Chinese population grew rapidly, reaching 58 million in the census of

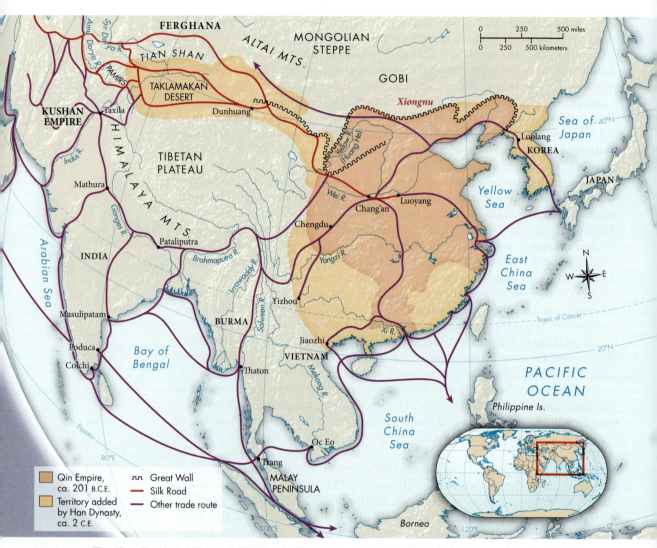

MAP 7.1 The Han Empire, 206 B.C.E.–220 C.E. The Han Dynasty asserted sovereignty over vast regions from Korea in the east to Central Asia in the west and Vietnam in the south. Once garrisons were established, traders were quick to follow, leading to considerable spread of Chinese material culture in East Asia. Chinese goods, especially silk, were in demand far beyond East Asia, promoting long-distance trade across Eurasia.

2 C.E. (Map 7.1). Few other societies kept such good records, making comparisons difficult, but high-end estimates for the Roman Empire are in a similar range (50–70 million).

The Han government was largely supported by the taxes and forced labor demanded of farmers, but this revenue regularly fell short of the government's needs. To pay for his military campaigns, Emperor Wu, the "Martial Emperor" (r. 141–87 B.C.E.), took over the minting of coins, confiscated the land of nobles, sold offices and titles, and increased taxes on private businesses. In 119 B.C.E. government monopolies were established in the production of iron, salt, and liquor. These enterprises had previously been sources of great profit for private entrepreneurs. Large-scale grain dealing also had been a profitable business, and the government now took that over as well.

Han Intellectual and Cultural Life

In contrast to the Qin Dynasty, which favored Legalism, the Han came to promote Confucianism. The Han government's efforts to recruit men trained in the Confucian classics marked the beginning of the Confucian scholar-official system, one of the most distinctive features of imperial China.

However, the Confucianism that made a comeback during the Han Dynasty was a changed Confucianism. Although Confucian texts had fed the First Emperor's bonfires, some dedicated scholars had hidden their books, and others had memorized whole works. The ancient books recovered in this way—called the **Confucian classics**—were revered as repositories of the wisdom of the past. Confucian scholars treated these classics with piety and attempted to make them more useful as sources of moral guidance by writing commentaries on them. Other Han Confucians developed comprehensive cosmological theories that explained the world in terms of cyclical flows of yin and yang (see "Yin and Yang" in Chapter 4) and the five phases (fire, water, earth, metal, and wood). Natural disasters such as floods or earthquakes were viewed as signs that the emperor had failed in his role of maintaining the proper balance among the forces of Heaven and earth.

Confucian classics The ancient texts recovered during the Han Dynasty that Confucian scholars treated as sacred scriptures.

Han art and literature reveal a fascination with omens, portents, spirits, immortals, and occult forces. Emperor Wu tried to make contact with the world of gods and immortals through elaborate sacrificial offerings of food and wine, and he welcomed astrologers, alchemists, seers, and shamans to his court.

A major intellectual accomplishment of the Han Dynasty was history writing. Sima Qian (SIH-mah chyen) (145–ca. 85 B.C.E.) wrote a comprehensive history of China from the time of the mythical sage-kings of high antiquity to his own day, dividing his account into a chronology recounting political events, biographies of key individuals, and treatises on subjects

Bronze Mirror The backs of bronze mirrors were frequently decorated with images of deities and animals and with auspicious words. As viewers turned the mirrors, they saw different scenes. This Han mirror features an outer border with semicircles decorated with cloud patterns and squares with words written on them. In the center are deities.

(Mirror [bronze]. Eastern Han Dynasty [25–220]/Cleveland Museum of Art, Ohio, USA/ Gift of Drs. Thomas and Martha Carter in Honor of Sherman E. Lee/Bridgeman Images)

such as geography, taxation, and court rituals. As an official of the emperor, he had access to important people and to the imperial library. Sima Qian believed fervently in visiting the sites where history was made, examining artifacts, and questioning people about events. The result of his research, ten years or more in the making, was ***Records of the Grand Historian***, a massive work of literary and historical genius. In the chapter devoted to moneymakers, he wrote of families that grew rich from trade or manufacturing, concluding that wealth has no permanent master: "It finds its way to the man of ability like the spokes of a wheel converging upon the hub, and from the hands of the worthless it falls like shattered tiles."[2] For centuries to come, Sima Qian's work set the standard for Chinese historical writing, although most of the histories modeled after it covered only a single dynasty. The first of these was the work of three members of the Ban family in the first century C.E. (See "Individuals in Society: The Ban Family," page 184.)

Records of the Grand Historian A comprehensive history of China written by Sima Qian.

The circulation of books like Sima Qian's was made easier by the invention of paper, which the Chinese traditionally date to 105 C.E. Scribes had previously written on strips of bamboo and wood or rolls of silk. Cai Lun, to whom the Chinese attribute the invention of paper, worked the fibers of rags, hemp, bark, and other scraps into sheets of paper. Though less durable than wood, paper was far lighter and became a convenient means of conveying the written word.

Inner Asia and the Silk Road

The difficulty of defending against the nomadic pastoral peoples to the north in the region known as Inner Asia is a major reason China came to favor a centralized bureaucratic form of government. Resources from the entire subcontinent were needed to maintain control of the northern border.

Chinese civilization did not spread easily to the grasslands north of China proper, because those lands were too dry and cold to make good farmland. Herding sheep, horses, camels, and other animals made better economic use of those lands. By the third century B.C.E. several different peoples practicing nomadic pastoralism lived in those regions, moving with their herds north in summer and south in winter. Families lived in tents that could be taken down and moved to the next camp. Herds were tended on horseback, and everyone learned to ride from a young age. The differences in their ways of life led Chinese farmers and Inner Asian herders to look down on each other. For most of the imperial period, Chinese farmers looked on the northern non-Chinese horsemen as gangs of bullies who thought robbing was easier than working for a living. The nomads identified glory with military might and viewed farmers as contemptible weaklings.

In the late third century B.C.E. the Xiongnu (shyuhng-new) (possibly the same group that was known in the West as the Huns) formed the first great confederation of nomadic tribes (see Map 7.1). The Qin's Great Wall was built to defend against the Xiongnu, and the Qin sent out huge armies in pursuit of them. The early Han emperors tried to make peace with them, offering generous gifts of silk, rice, cash, and even imperial princesses as brides, but to little avail. Xiongnu power did not wane, and in 166 B.C.E. 140,000 Xiongnu raided to within a hundred miles of the Chinese capital.

Emperor Wu then decided that China had to push the Xiongnu back. He sent several armies of 100,000 to 300,000 troops deep into Xiongnu territory. These

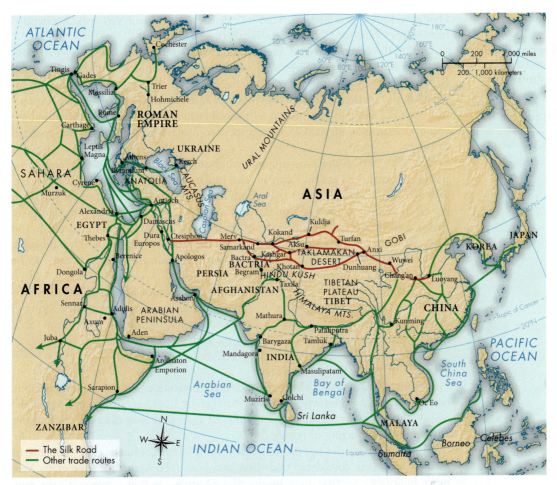

MAP 7.2 The Silk Trade in the Seventh Century C.E. Silk — made from the cocoons of silkworms — was highly valued for the light, colorful, and supple cloth that could be made from it. For centuries all the silk that reached the non-Chinese world came from China, but in time other countries learned how to make it.

costly campaigns were of limited value because the Xiongnu were a moving target. If the Xiongnu did not want to fight the Chinese troops, they simply moved their camps. To try to find allies and horses, Emperor Wu turned his attention west, toward Central Asia. From an envoy he sent into Bactria, Parthia, and Ferghana in 139 B.C.E., the Chinese learned for the first time of other civilized states comparable to China. These regions, he reported, were familiar with Chinese products, especially silk, and did a brisk trade in them.

In 114 B.C.E. Emperor Wu sent an army into Ferghana and gained recognition of Chinese overlordship in the area, thus obtaining control over the trade routes across Central Asia commonly called the **Silk Road** (Map 7.2).

At the same time, Emperor Wu sent troops into northern Korea to establish military districts that would flank the Xiongnu on their eastern border. By 111 B.C.E. the

Silk Road The trade routes across Central Asia linking China to western Eurasia.

tributary system A system first established during the Han Dynasty to regulate contact with foreign powers. States and tribes beyond its borders sent envoys bearing gifts and received gifts in return.

Han government also had extended its rule south into Nam Viet, which extended from south China into what is now northern Vietnam.

During the Han Dynasty, China developed a **tributary system** to regulate contact with foreign powers. States and tribes beyond its borders sent envoys bearing gifts and received gifts in return. Over the course of the dynasty, the Han government's outlay on these gifts was huge, perhaps as much as 10 percent of state revenue. Although the tributary system was a financial burden to the Chinese, it reduced the cost of defense and offered China confirmation that it was the center of the civilized world.

The silk given to the Xiongnu and other northern tributaries often entered the trading networks of Persian, Parthian, and Indian merchants, who carried it by caravans across Asia. There was a market both for skeins of silk thread and for silk cloth woven in Chinese or Syrian workshops. Caravans returning to China carried gold, horses, and occasionally handicrafts of West Asian origin, such as glass beads and cups. Through the trade along the Silk Road, the Chinese learned of new foodstuffs, including walnuts, pomegranates, sesame, and coriander, all of which came to be grown in China.

Maintaining a military presence so far from the center of China was expensive. To cut costs, the government set up self-supporting military colonies, recruited Xiongnu tribes to serve as auxiliary forces, and established vast government horse farms. Still, military expenses threatened to bankrupt the Han government.

Life in Han China

How were ordinary people's lives affected by the creation of a huge Han bureaucratic empire? The lucky ones who lived in Chang'an or Luoyang, the great cities of the empire, got to enjoy the material benefits of increased long-distance trade and a boom in the production of luxury goods.

The government did not promote trade per se. The Confucian elite, like ancient Hebrew wise men, considered trade necessary but lowly. Agriculture and crafts were more honorable because they produced something, but merchants merely took advantage of others' shortages to make profits as middlemen. This attitude justified the government's takeover of the grain, iron, and salt businesses.

Markets were the liveliest places in the cities. Besides stalls selling goods of all kinds, markets offered fortune-tellers, jugglers, acrobats, and puppet shows. The markets were also used for the execution of criminals, to serve as a warning to onlookers.

Government patronage helped maintain the quality of craftsmanship in the cities. By the beginning of the first century C.E. China also had about fifty state-run iron-working factories. In contrast to Roman blacksmiths, who hammered heated iron to make wrought iron tools, the Chinese knew how to liquefy iron and pour it into molds, producing tools with a higher carbon content that were harder and more durable. Iron was replacing bronze in tools, but bronzeworkers still turned out a host of goods, including jewelry and mirrors. Bronze was also used for coins and for precision tools such as carpenters' rules and adjustable wrenches.

The bulk of the population in Han times and even into the twentieth century consisted of peasants living in villages of a few hundred households. Because the Han empire, much like the contemporaneous Roman Empire, drew its strength from

Ceramic Model of a Pigsty Chinese farmers regularly raised pigs, keeping them in walled-off pens and feeding them scraps. This Han Dynasty model of such a pigsty was placed in a tomb to represent the material goods one hoped the deceased would enjoy in the afterlife.

(Funerary model of a pigsty [earthenware], Western Han Dynasty [206 B.C.–A.D. 24]/Minneapolis Institute of Arts. Minnesota, USA/Gift of Alan and Dena Naylor in memory of Thomas E. Leary/Bridgeman Images)

a large population of free peasants who contributed both taxes and labor services to the state, the government had to try to keep peasants independent and productive. To fight peasant poverty, the government kept land taxes low (one-thirtieth of the harvest), provided relief in times of famine, and promoted up-to-date agricultural methods. Still, many hard-pressed peasants were left to choose between migration to areas where new lands could be opened and quasi-servile status as the dependents of a magnate. Throughout the Han period, Chinese farmers in search of land to till pushed into frontier areas, expanding Chinese domination at the expense of other ethnic groups, especially in central and south China.

The Chinese family in Han times was much like Roman and Indian families. In all three societies senior males had great authority, parents arranged their children's marriages, and brides normally joined their husbands' families. Other practices were more distinctive to China, such as the universality of patrilineal family names, the practice of dividing land equally among the sons in a family, and the great emphasis placed on the virtue of filial piety. The brief *Classic of Filial Piety*, which claimed that filial piety was the root of all virtue, gained wide circulation in Han times. The virtues of loyal wives and devoted mothers were extolled in *Biographies of Exemplary Women*, which told the stories of women from China's past. One of the most commonly used texts for the education of women was *Admonitions for Women* by Ban Zhao, in which she extols the feminine virtues, such as humility. (See "Individuals in Society: The Ban Family," page 184.)

China and Rome

The empires of China and Rome were large, complex states governed by monarchs, bureaucracies, and standing armies. Both lasted for centuries and reached the people directly through taxation and conscription policies. Both invested in infrastructure such as roads and waterworks. Both saw their civilization as better than any other and were open to others' learning their ways. The two empires faced the similar challenge of having to work hard to keep land from becoming too concentrated in the hands of hard-to-tax wealthy magnates. In both empires people in neighboring areas that

The Ban Family

BAN BIAO (3–54 C.E.), A SUCCESSFUL OFFICIAL from a family with an envied library, had three highly accomplished children: his twin sons, the general Ban Chao (32–102) and the historian Ban Gu (32–92); and his daughter, Ban Zhao (ca. 45–120). After distinguishing himself as a junior officer in campaigns against the Xiongnu, Ban Chao was sent in 73 C.E. to the western regions to see about the possibility of restoring Chinese overlordship there, which had been lost several decades earlier. Ban Chao spent most of the next three decades in Central Asia. Through patient diplomacy and a show of force, he re-established Chinese control over the oasis cities of Central Asia, and in 92 he was appointed protector general of the area.

His twin brother, Ban Gu, was one of the most accomplished writers of his age, excelling in a distinctive literary form known as the rhapsody (*fu*). His "Rhapsody on the Two Capitals" is in the form of a dialogue between a guest from Chang'an and his host in Luoyang. It describes the palaces, spectacles, scenic spots, local products, and customs of the two great cities. Emperor Zhang (r. 76–88) was fond of literature and often had Ban Gu accompany him on hunts or travels. He also had him edit a record of the court debates he held on issues concerning the Confucian classics.

Ban Biao was working on the *History of the Former Han Dynasty* when he died in 54. Ban Gu took over this project, modeling it on Sima Qian's *Records of the Grand Historian*. He added treatises on law, geography, and bibliography, the last a classified list of books in the imperial library.

Because of his connection to a general out of favor, Ban Gu was sent to prison in 92, where he soon died. At that time the *History of the Former Han Dynasty* was still incomplete. The emperor called on Ban Gu's widowed sister, Ban Zhao, to finish it. She came to the palace, where she not only worked on the history but also became a teacher of the women of the palace. According to the *History of the Later Han*, she taught them the classics, history, astronomy, and mathematics. In 106 an infant succeeded to the throne, and the widow of an earlier emperor became regent. This empress frequently turned to Ban Zhao for advice on government policies.

Ban Zhao credited her own education to her learned father and cultured mother and became an advocate of

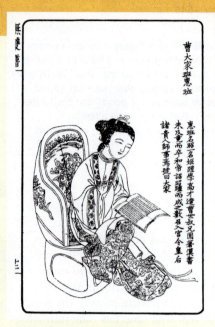

Ban Zhao, Han Dynasty writer. (© Fotoe/Uniphoto Press, Japan/Ancient Art & Architecture Collection, Ltd.)

the education of girls. In her *Admonitions for Women*, Ban Zhao objected that many families taught their sons to read but not their daughters. She did not claim girls should have the same education as boys; after all, "just as yin and yang differ, men and women have different characteristics." Women, she wrote, will do well if they cultivate womanly virtues such as humility. "Humility means yielding and acting respectful, putting others first and oneself last, never mentioning one's own good deeds or denying one's own faults, enduring insults and bearing with mistreatment, all with due trepidation."* In subsequent centuries Ban Zhao's *Admonitions* became one of the most commonly used texts for the education of Chinese girls.

QUESTIONS FOR ANALYSIS

1. What inferences can you draw from the fact that a leading general had a brother who was a literary man?
2. What does Ban Zhao's life tell us about women in her society? How do you reconcile her personal accomplishments with the advice she gave for women's education?

*Patricia Buckley Ebrey, ed., *Chinese Civilization: A Sourcebook*, 2d ed., revised and expanded (New York: Free Press, 1993), p. 75.

came under political domination were attracted to the conquerors' material goods, productive techniques, and other cultural products, resulting in gradual cultural assimilation. China and Rome also had similar frontier problems and tried similar solutions, such as recruiting "barbarian" soldiers and settling soldier-colonists.

Nevertheless, the differences between Rome and Han China are also worth noting. The Roman Empire was linguistically and culturally more diverse than China. In China there was only one written language; people in the Roman Empire still wrote in Greek and several other languages, and people in the eastern Mediterranean could claim more ancient civilizations. China did not have comparable cultural rivals. Politically the dynastic principle was stronger in China than in Rome, and there was no institution comparable to the Roman Senate. In contrast to the graduated forms of citizenship in Rome, citizenship in Han China made no distinctions between original and added territories. The social and economic structures also differed in the two empires. Slavery was much more important in Rome than in China, and merchants were more favored.

The Fall of the Han and the Age of Division

In the second century C.E. the Han government suffered a series of blows. A succession of child emperors required regents to rule in their place until they reached maturity, allowing the families of empresses to dominate the court. Emperors, once grown, turned to **eunuchs** (castrated palace servants) for help in ousting the empresses' families, only to find that the eunuchs were just as difficult to control. In 166 and 169 scholars who had denounced the eunuchs were arrested, killed, or banished from the capital and official life. Then in 184 a millenarian religious sect rose in massive revolt. The armies raised to suppress the rebels soon took to fighting among themselves. After years of fighting, a stalemate was reached, with three warlords each controlling distinct territories in the north, the southeast, and the southwest. In 220 one of them forced the last of the Han emperors to abdicate, formally ending the Han Dynasty.

The period after the fall of the Han Dynasty is often referred to as the **Age of Division** (220–589). A brief reunification from 280 to 316 came to an end when non-Chinese who had been settling in north China since Han times attempted to take power. For the next two and a half centuries, north China was ruled by one or more non-Chinese dynasties (the Northern Dynasties), and the south was ruled by a sequence of four short-lived Chinese dynasties (the Southern Dynasties) centered in the area of the present-day city of Nanjing.

In the south a hereditary aristocracy entrenched itself in the higher reaches of officialdom. These families saw themselves as maintaining the high culture of the Han and looked on the emperors of the successive dynasties as upstarts—as military men rather than men of culture. In this aristocratic culture the arts of poetry and calligraphy flourished, and people began collecting writings by famous calligraphers.

Establishing the capital at Nanjing, south of the Yangzi River, had a beneficial effect on the economic development of the south. The south, with its temperate climate and ample supply of water, offered nearly unlimited possibilities for such development.

The Northern Dynasties are interesting as the first case of alien rule in China. Ethnic tensions flared from time to time. In the late fifth century the Northern Wei (way) Dynasty (386–534) moved the capital from near the Great Wall to the ancient city of Luoyang, adopted Chinese-style clothing, and made Chinese the official language.

eunuchs Castrated males who played an important role as palace servants.

Age of Division The period after the fall of the Han Dynasty, when China was politically divided.

But the armies remained in the hands of the non-Chinese Xianbei tribesmen. Soldiers who saw themselves as marginalized by the pro-Chinese reforms rebelled in 524. For the next fifty years north China was torn apart by struggles for power.

How did Buddhism find its way into East Asia, and what was its appeal and impact?

The Spread of Buddhism Out of India

In much the same period that Christianity was spreading out of its original home in ancient Israel, Buddhism was spreading beyond India. Buddhism came to Central, East, and Southeast Asia with merchants and missionaries along the overland Silk Road, by sea from India and Sri Lanka, and also through Tibet. Like Christianity, Buddhism was shaped by its contact with cultures in the different areas into which it spread, leading to several distinct forms.

Buddhism's Path Through Central Asia

Under Ashoka in India (see "The Reign of Ashoka" in Chapter 3), Buddhism began to spread to Central Asia. This continued under the Kushan empire (ca. 50–250 C.E.). Over the next several centuries most of the city-states of Central Asia became centers of Buddhism, from Bamiyan northwest of Kabul, to Kucha, Khotan, Loulan, Turfan, and Dunhuang (Map 7.3).

The form of Buddhism that spread from Central Asia to China, Japan, and Korea was called Mahayana, which means "Great Vehicle," reflecting the claims of its adherents to a more inclusive form of the religion. Influenced by the Iranian religions then prevalent in Central Asia, Buddhism became more devotional. The Buddha came to be treated as a god, the head of an expanding pantheon of other Buddhas and bodhisattvas (Buddhas-to-be). With the growth of this pantheon, Buddhism became as much a religion for laypeople as for monks and nuns.

The Appeal and Impact of Buddhism in China

Why did Buddhism find so many adherents in China during the three centuries from 200 to 500 C.E.? There were no forced conversions, but still the religion spread rapidly. In the unstable political environment, many people were open to new ideas. To Chinese scholars the Buddhist concepts of the reincarnation of souls, karma, and nirvana posed a stimulating intellectual challenge. To rulers the Buddhist religion offered a source of magical power and a political tool to unite Chinese and non-Chinese. In a tumultuous age Buddhism's emphasis on kindness, charity, and eternal bliss was deeply comforting. As in India, Buddhism posed no threat to the social order, and the elite who were drawn to Buddhism encouraged its spread to people of all classes.

The monastic establishment grew rapidly in China. Like their Christian counterparts in medieval Europe, Buddhist monasteries played an active role in social, economic, and political life. Given the importance of family lines in China, becoming a monk was a major decision, since a man had to give up his surname and take a vow of celibacy, thus cutting himself off from the ancestral cult. Those not ready to become monks or nuns could pursue Buddhist goals as pious laypeople by performing devotional acts and making contributions to monasteries.

In China women turned to Buddhism as readily as men. Although birth as a female was considered lower than birth as a male, it was also viewed as temporary, and women were encouraged to pursue salvation on terms nearly equal to those of men.

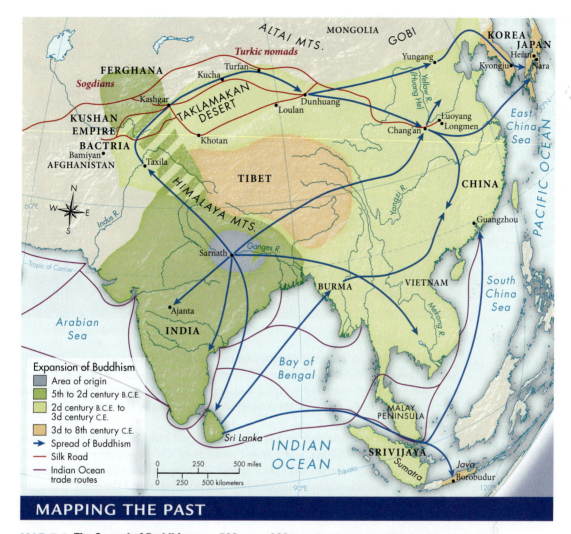

MAPPING THE PAST

MAP 7.3 The Spread of Buddhism, ca. 500 B.C.E.–800 C.E. Buddhism spread throughout India in Ashoka's time and beyond India in later centuries. The different forms of Buddhism found in Asia today reflect this history. The Mahayana Buddhism of Japan came via Central Asia, China, and Korea, with a secondary later route through Tibet. The Theravada Buddhism of Southeast Asia came directly from India and indirectly through Sri Lanka.

ANALYZING THE MAP Trace the routes of the spread of Buddhism by time period. How fast did Buddhism spread?

CONNECTIONS Why do you think Buddhism spread more to the east of India than to the west?

Joining a nunnery became an alternative for a woman who did not want to marry or did not want to stay with her husband's family in widowhood. Later, the only woman ruler of China, Empress Wu, invoked Buddhist principles to justify her role (see "The Tang Dynasty"), further evidence of how Buddhism brought new understandings of gender.

Monumental Rock-Cut Buddha at Yungang

The Xianbei rulers of the Northern Wei funded the carving of Buddhist statues at Yungang in the late fifth century. The tallest of these statues, shown here, is about 45 feet high; it is one of about fifty-one thousand Buddha images at the site. The massive stone Buddha at Bamiyan in Afghanistan provided a model for cave temples like this one in China. (1970s/Getty Images)

Buddhism had an enormous impact on the visual arts in China, especially sculpture and painting. Before Buddhism, Chinese had not set up statues of gods in temples, but now they decorated temples with a profusion of images. Inspired by the cave temples of India and Central Asia, Buddhists in China, too, carved caves into rock faces to make temples.

Not everyone was won over by Buddhist teachings. Critics of Buddhism labeled it immoral, unsuited to China, and a threat to the state since monastery land was not taxed and monks did not perform labor service. Although twice rulers closed monasteries, no attempt was made to suppress belief in Buddhism, and the religion continued to thrive in the subsequent Sui and Tang periods.

What were the lasting accomplishments of the Sui and Tang Dynasties?

The Chinese Empire Re-created: Sui (581–618) and Tang (618–907)

Political division was finally overcome when the Sui Dynasty conquered its rivals to reunify China in 589. Although the dynasty lasted only thirty-seven years, it left a lasting legacy in the form of political reform, the construction of roads and canals, and the institution of written merit-based exams for the appointment of officials. The Tang Dynasty that followed would last for centuries and would build upon the Sui's accomplishments to create an era of impressive cultural creativity and political power.

The Sui Dynasty, 581–618

In the 570s and 580s the long period of division in China was brought to an end under the leadership of the Sui (SWAY) Dynasty. The conquest of the south involved naval as well as land battles, with thousands of ships on both sides contending for control of the Yangzi River. The Sui reasserted Chinese control over northern Vietnam and campaigned into Korea and against the new force on the steppe, the Turks. The Sui strengthened central control of the government by curtailing the power of local officials to appoint their own subordinates and by instituting in 605 C.E. competitive written examinations for the selection of officials.

The crowning achievement of the Sui Dynasty was the construction of the **Grand Canal**, which connected the Yellow and Yangzi River regions. Henceforth the rice-growing Yangzi Valley and south China played an ever more influential role in the country's economic and political life, strengthening China's internal cohesion and facilitating maritime trade with Southeast Asia, India, and areas farther west.

Despite these accomplishments, the Sui Dynasty lasted for only two reigns. The ambitious projects of the two Sui emperors led to exhaustion and unrest, and in the ensuing warfare Li Yuan, a Chinese from the same northwest aristocratic circles as the founder of the Sui, seized the throne.

Grand Canal A canal, built during the Sui Dynasty, that connected the Yellow and Yangzi Rivers. It was notable for strengthening China's internal cohesion and economic development.

The Tang Dynasty, 618–907

The dynasty founded by Li Yuan, the Tang, was one of the high points of traditional Chinese civilization. Especially during this dynasty's first century, its capital, Chang'an, was the cultural center of East Asia, drawing in merchants, pilgrims, missionaries, and students to a degree never matched before or after. This position of strength gave the Chinese the confidence to be open to learning from the outside world, leading to a more cosmopolitan culture than in any other period before the twentieth century.

The first two Tang rulers, Gaozu (Li Yuan, r. 618–626) and Taizong (tie-dzuhng) (r. 626–649), were able monarchs. Adding to their armies auxiliary troops composed of Turks, Tanguts, Khitans, and other non-Chinese led by their own chieftains, they campaigned into Korea, Vietnam, and Central Asia. In 630 the Chinese turned against their former allies, the Turks, gaining territory from them and winning for Taizong the title of Great Khan.

Tang China, ca. 750 C.E.

In the civil sphere the Tang emperors built on the Sui precedent of using written examinations to select officials. Candidates had to master the Confucian classics and the rules of poetry, and they had to be able to analyze practical administrative and political matters. Government schools were founded to prepare the sons of officials and other young men for service as officials.

The mid-Tang Dynasty saw two women—Empress Wu and Consort Yang Guifei (yahng gway-fay)—rise to positions of great political power. Empress Wu was the consort of the weak and sickly emperor Gaozong. After Gaozong suffered a stroke in 660, she took full charge. She continued to rule after Gaozong's death, summarily deposing her own two sons and dealing harshly with all opponents. In 690 she proclaimed herself emperor, becoming the only woman to take that title in Chinese history. To gain support, she circulated a Buddhist sutra that predicted the imminent reincarnation of the Buddha Maitreya as a female monarch, during whose reign the world would be free of illness, worry, and disaster. Although despised by later Chinese historians as an evil usurper, Empress Wu was an effective leader. It was not until she was over eighty that members of the court were able to force her out in favor of her son.

Chang'an

Urban Planning Chang'an in Tang times attracted merchants, pilgrims, and students from all over East Asia. The city was laid out on a square grid (left) and divided into walled wards, the gates to which were closed at night. Temples were found throughout the city, but trade was limited to two government-supervised markets. In the eighth and ninth centuries the Japanese copied the general plan of Chang'an in designing their capitals — first at Nara, then at Heian, shown on the right. (Visual Connection Archive)

Her grandson, the emperor Xuanzong (r. 713–756), presided over a brilliant court and patronized leading poets, painters, and calligraphers. In his later years, after he became enamored of his consort Yang Guifei, he did not want to be bothered by the details of government and allowed her to place friends and relatives in important positions in the government. One of her favorites was the general An Lushan, who rebelled in 755. Xuanzong had to flee the capital, and the troops that accompanied him forced him to have Yang Guifei executed.

The rebellion of An Lushan was devastating to the Tang Dynasty. Peace was restored only by calling on the Uighurs (WEE-gurz), a Turkish people allied with the Tang, who looted the capital after taking it from the rebels. The rebellion was finally suppressed in 763, but Tang strength was never fully re-established. Many military governors came to treat their provinces as hereditary kingdoms. In addition, palace eunuchs gained increasing power at court.

Tang Culture

The reunification of north and south led to cultural flowering. The Tang capital cities of Chang'an and Luoyang became great metropolises. In these cosmopolitan cities, knowledge of the outside world was stimulated by the presence of envoys, merchants, pilgrims, and students who came from neighboring states in Central Asia, Japan, Korea, Tibet, and Southeast Asia. Because of the presence of foreign merchants, many religions were practiced, including Nestorian Christianity, Manichaeism, Zoroastrianism, Judaism, and Islam, although none of them spread into the Chinese population the way Buddhism had a few centuries earlier. Foreign fashions in hair and clothing were often copied, and foreign amusements such as the Persian game of polo found followings among the well-to-do. The introduction of new musical instruments and tunes from India, Iran, and Central Asia brought about a major transformation in Chinese music.

The Tang Dynasty was the great age of Chinese poetry. Skill in composing poetry was tested in the civil service examinations, and educated men had to be able to compose poems at social gatherings. The pain of parting, the joys of nature, and the pleasures of wine and friendship were all common poetic topics. One of Li Bo's (701–762) most famous poems describes an evening of drinking with only the moon and his shadow for company:

Five-Stringed Pipa/Biwa
This musical instrument, decorated with fine wood marquetry, was probably presented by the Tang court to a Japanese envoy. It was among the objects placed in a Japanese royal storage house (Shōsōin) in 756.
(Kyodo News International, Inc.)

> A cup of wine, under the flowering trees;
> I drink alone, for no friend is near.
> Raising my cup I beckon the bright moon,
> For he, with my shadow, will make three men.
> The moon, alas, is no drinker of wine;
> Listless, my shadow creeps about at my side.
> . . .
> Now we are drunk, each goes his way.
> May we long share our odd, inanimate feast,
> And we meet at last on the cloudy River of the sky.[3]

In Tang times Buddhism fully penetrated Chinese daily life. Stories of Buddhist origin became widely known, and Buddhist festivals became among the most popular holidays. Buddhist monasteries ran schools for children and in remote areas provided lodging for travelers. Merchants entrusted their money and wares to monasteries for safekeeping, in effect transforming the monasteries into banks and warehouses.

At the intellectual and religious level, Buddhism was developing in distinctly Chinese directions. Two schools that thrived were Pure Land and Chan. **Pure Land** appealed to laypeople because the simple act of calling on the Buddha Amitabha and his chief helper, the compassionate bodhisattva Guanyin, could lead to rebirth in Amitabha's paradise, the Pure Land. Among the educated elite the **Chan** school (known in Japan as Zen) also gained popularity. Chan teachings rejected the authority of the sutras and claimed the superiority of mind-to-mind transmission of Buddhist truths.

Opposition to Buddhism re-emerged in the late Tang period. In addition to concerns about the fiscal impact of removing so much land from the tax rolls and so many men from government labor service, there were concerns about Buddhism's foreign origins. As China's international position weakened, xenophobia surfaced. During the persecution of 845, more than 4,600 monasteries and 40,000 temples and shrines were destroyed, and more than 260,000 Buddhist monks and nuns were

Pure Land A school of Buddhism that taught that by calling on the Buddha Amitabha, one could achieve rebirth in Amitabha's Pure Land paradise.

Chan A school of Buddhism (known in Japan as Zen) that rejected the authority of the sutras and claimed the superiority of mind-to-mind transmission of Buddhist truths.

forced to return to secular life. Although this ban was lifted after a few years, the monastic establishment never fully recovered. Buddhism retained a strong hold among laypeople, and basic Buddhist ideas like karma and reincarnation had become fully incorporated into everyday Chinese thinking. But Buddhism was never again as central to Chinese life.

What elements of Chinese culture were adopted by Koreans, Vietnamese, and Japanese, and how did they adapt them to their own circumstances?

The East Asian Cultural Sphere

During the millennium from 200 B.C.E. to 800 C.E., China exerted a powerful influence on its immediate neighbors, who began forming states of their own. By Tang times China was surrounded by independent states in Korea, Manchuria, Tibet, the area that is now Yunnan province, Vietnam, and Japan. All of these states were much smaller than China in area and population, making China by far the dominant force politically and culturally until the nineteenth century. Nevertheless, each of these separate states developed a strong sense of its independent identity.

The earliest information about each of these countries is found in Chinese sources. Han armies brought Chinese culture to Korea and Vietnam, but even in those cases much cultural borrowing was entirely voluntary as the elite, merchants, and craftsmen adopted the techniques, ideas, and practices they found appealing. In Japan much of the process of absorbing elements of Chinese culture was mediated via Korea. In Korea, Japan, and Vietnam the fine arts—painting, architecture, and ceramics in particular—were all strongly influenced by Chinese models. Tibet, though a thorn in the side of Tang China, was as much in the Indian sphere of influence as in the Chinese and thus followed a somewhat different trajectory. Most significantly, it never adopted Chinese characters as its written language, nor was it as influenced by Chinese artistic styles as were other areas. Moreover, the form of Buddhism that became dominant in Tibet came directly from India, not through Central Asia and China.

In each area Chinese-style culture was at first adopted by elites, but in time many Chinese products and ideas, ranging from written language to chopsticks and soy sauce, became incorporated into everyday life. By the eighth century the written Chinese language was used by educated people throughout East Asia. The books that educated people read included the Chinese classics, histories, and poetry, as well as Buddhist sutras translated into Chinese. The great appeal of Buddhism known primarily through Chinese translation was a powerful force promoting cultural borrowing.

Vietnam

Vietnam's climate is much like that of southernmost China—subtropical, with abundant rain and rivers. The Vietnamese first appear in Chinese sources as a people of south China called the Yue, who gradually migrated farther south as the Chinese state expanded. The people of the Red River Valley in northern Vietnam had achieved a relatively advanced level of Bronze Age civilization by the first century B.C.E. The bronze heads of their arrows were often dipped in poison to facilitate killing large animals such as elephants, whose tusks were traded to China for iron. Power was held by hereditary tribal chiefs who served as civil, religious, and military leaders, with the king as the most powerful chief.

The collapse of the Qin Dynasty in 206 B.C.E. had an impact on this area because a former Qin general, finding himself in the far south, set up his own kingdom of Nam Viet. This kingdom covered much of south China and was ruled by the king from his capital near the present site of Guangzhou. Its population consisted chiefly of the Viet people. After killing all officials loyal to the Chinese emperor, the king adopted the customs of the Viet and made himself the ruler of a vast state that extended as far south as modern-day Da Nang.

After almost a hundred years of diplomatic and military duels between the Han Dynasty and the Nam Viet king and his successors, Nam Viet was conquered in 111 B.C.E. by Chinese armies. Chinese administrators were assigned to replace the local nobility. Chinese political institutions were imposed, and Confucianism was treated as the official ideology. The Chinese language was introduced as the medium of official and literary expression, and Chinese characters were adopted as the written form for the Vietnamese spoken language. The Chinese built roads, waterways, and harbors to facilitate communication within the region and to ensure that they maintained administrative and military control over it.

The Kingdom of Nam Viet, ca. 150 B.C.E.

Chinese innovations that were beneficial to the Vietnamese were readily integrated into the indigenous culture, but the local elite were not reconciled to Chinese political domination. The most famous early revolt took place in 39 C.E., when two widows of local aristocrats, the Trung sisters, led an uprising against foreign rule. After overwhelming Chinese strongholds, they declared themselves queens of an independent Vietnamese kingdom. Three years later a powerful army sent by the Han emperor re-established Chinese rule.

China retained at least nominal control over northern Vietnam through the Tang Dynasty, and there were no real borders between China proper and Vietnam during this time. The local elite became culturally dual, serving as brokers between the Chinese governors and the native people.

Korea

Korea is a mountainous peninsula some 600 miles long extending south from Manchuria and Siberia. At its tip it is about 120 miles from Japan (Map 7.4). Archaeological, linguistic, and anthropological evidence indicates that the Korean people share a common ethnic origin with other peoples of North Asia, including those of Manchuria, Siberia, and Japan. Linguistically, Korean is not related to Chinese.

Korea began adopting elements of technology from China in the first millennium B.C.E., including bronze and iron technology. Chinese-Korean contact expanded during the Warring States Period, when the state of Yan extended into part of Korea. In about 194 B.C.E. Wiman, an unsuccessful rebel against the Han Dynasty, fled to Korea and set up a state called Choson in what is now northwest Korea and southern Manchuria. In 108 B.C.E. this state was overthrown by Han armies and four prefectures were established there.

The impact of the Chinese prefectures in Korea was similar to that of the contemporaneous Roman colonies in Britain in encouraging the spread of culture and political forms. The Chinese never controlled the entire Korean peninsula, however. The Han commanderies coexisted with the native Korean kingdom of Koguryŏ, founded in the first century B.C.E. Chinese sources describe this kingdom as a society

Hunting Scene in Goguryeo Tomb This lively scene of hunters pursuing deer and tigers was painted on the wall of a sixth-century tomb near the Goguryeo capital, north of the Yalu River. (Pictures from History/Bridgeman Images)

of aristocratic tribal warriors who had under them a mass of serfs and slaves, mostly from conquered tribes. After the Chinese colonies were finally overthrown, the kingdoms of Paekche and Silla emerged farther south on the peninsula in the third and fourth centuries C.E., leading to what is called the Three Kingdoms Period (313–668 C.E.). In all three Korean kingdoms Chinese was used as the language of government and learning. Each of the three kingdoms had hereditary kings, but their power was curbed by the existence of very strong hereditary elites.

Buddhism was officially introduced in Koguryŏ from China in 372 and in the other states not long after. Buddhism connected Korea to societies across Asia. Buddhist monks went back and forth between China and Korea.

When the Sui Dynasty finally reunified China in 589, it tried to establish control of at least a part of Korea. But the Korean kingdoms were much stronger than their predecessors in Han times, and they repeatedly repulsed Chinese attacks. The Tang government then tried allying itself with one state, Silla, to fight the others. Silla and Tang jointly destroyed Paekche in 660 and Koguryŏ in 668. With its new resources Silla was able to repel Tang efforts to make Korea a colony but agreed to vassal status. The unification under Silla marked the first political unification of Korea.

For the next century Silla embarked on a policy of wholesale borrowing of Chinese culture and institutions. Annual embassies were sent to Chang'an, and large numbers of students studied in China.

Japan

The heart of Japan is four mountainous islands off the coast of Korea (see Map 7.4). Since the land is rugged and lacking in navigable waterways, the Inland Sea, like the Aegean in Greece, was the easiest avenue of communication in early times. Hence the land bordering the Inland Sea—Kyushu, Shikoku, and Honshu—developed as the political and cultural center of early Japan. Geography also blessed Japan with a moat to protect it from external interference—the Korea Strait and the Sea of Japan.

Japan's early development was closely tied to that of the mainland, especially to Korea. Anthropologists have discerned several major waves of immigrants into Japan. People of the Jōmon (joh-mohn) culture, established by about 10,000 B.C.E. after an influx of people from Southeast Asia, practiced hunting and fishing and fashioned clay pots. New arrivals from northeast Asia brought agriculture and a distinct culture called Yayoi (yah-yoh-ee) (ca. 300 B.C.E.–300 C.E.). During the Han Dynasty, objects of Chinese and Korean manufacture found their way into Japan, an indication that people were traveling back and forth as well. In the third century C.E. Chinese histories begin to report on the land called Wa made up of mountainous islands. It had numerous communities with markets, granaries, tax collection, and class distinctions. The people liked liquor, ate with their fingers, used body paint, and purified themselves by bathing after a funeral.

One of the most distinctive features of early Japan was its female rulers. A Chinese historian of the time wrote:

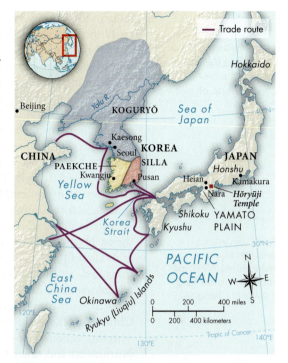

MAP 7.4 Korea and Japan, ca. 600 C.E. Korea and Japan are of similar latitude, but Korea's climate is more continental, with harsher winters. Of Japan's four islands, Kyushu is closest to Korea and mainland Asia.

> The country formerly had a man as ruler. For some seventy or eighty years after that there were disturbances and warfare. Thereupon the people agreed upon a woman for their ruler. Her name was Pimiko [pee-mee-koe]. She occupied herself with magic and sorcery, bewitching the people. Though mature in age, she remained unmarried. She had a younger brother who assisted her in ruling the country. After she became the ruler, there were few who saw her. She had one thousand women as attendants, but only one man. He served her food and drink and acted as a medium of communication. . . .
>
> When Pimiko passed away, a great mound was raised, more than a hundred paces in diameter. Over a hundred male and female attendants followed her to the grave. Then a king was placed on the throne, but the people would not obey him. Assassination and murder followed; more than one thousand were thus slain.
>
> A relative of Pimiko named Iyo, a girl of thirteen, was then made queen and order was restored.[4]

During the fourth through sixth centuries new waves of migrants from Korea brought the language that evolved into Japanese as well as sericulture (silkmaking), bronze swords, crossbows, iron plows, and the Chinese written language. In this period a social order similar to Korea's emerged, dominated by a warrior aristocracy organized into clans. Clad in helmets and armor, these warriors wielded swords, battle-axes, and often bows, and some rode into battle on horseback. Those vanquished in battle were made slaves. Each clan had its own chieftain, who marshaled clansmen for battle and served as chief priest. By the fifth century the chief of the clan that claimed descent from the sun-goddess, located in the Yamato plain around

Shinto The Way of the Gods, Japan's native religion.

Nara Japan's capital and first true city; it was established in 710 and modeled on the Tang capital of Chang'an.

modern Osaka, had come to occupy the position of monarch. These Yamato rulers established the chief shrine of the sun-goddess near the seacoast, where she could catch the first rays of the rising sun. This native religion was later termed **Shinto**, the Way of the Gods, and it coexisted with Buddhism, formally introduced in 538 C.E.

Beginning in the sixth century Prince Shōtoku (show-toe-coo) (574–622) undertook a sweeping reform of the state designed to strengthen Yamato rule by adopting Chinese-style bureaucratic practices (though not the recruitment of officials by examination). In 604 he instituted a ladder of official ranks similar to China's, admonished the nobility to avoid strife and opposition, and urged adherence to Buddhist precepts. Near his seat of government, Prince Shōtoku built the magnificent Hōryūji (hoe-ryou-jee) Temple and staffed it with monks from Korea. (See "Analyzing the Evidence: Hōryūji Temple," at right.) He also opened direct relations with China, sending four missions during the brief Sui Dynasty.

State-building efforts continued through the seventh century and culminated in the establishment in 710 of Japan's first long-term true city, the capital at **Nara**, north of modern Osaka. Nara, which was modeled on the Tang capital of Chang'an, gave its name to an era that lasted until 794 and was characterized by the avid importation of Chinese ideas and methods. As Buddhism developed a stronghold in Japan, it inspired many trips to China to acquire sources and to study at Chinese monasteries. Chinese and Korean craftsmen were often brought back to Japan, especially to help with the decoration of the many Buddhist temples then under construction. Musical instruments and tunes were imported as well, many originally from Central Asia. Chinese practices were instituted, such as the compilation of histories and law codes, the creation of provinces, and the appointment of governors to collect taxes from them. By 750 some seven thousand men staffed the central government.

Increased contact with the mainland had unwanted effects as well. In contrast to China and Korea, both part of the Eurasian landmass, Japan had been relatively isolated from many deadly diseases, so when diseases arrived with travelers, people did not have immunity. The great smallpox epidemic of 735–737 is thought to have reduced the population of about 5 million by 30 percent. (See "Global Viewpoints: Coping with Epidemics in Japan and Byzantium," page 198.)

The Buddhist monasteries that ringed Nara were both religious centers and wealthy landlords, and the monks were active in the political life of the capital. Copying the policy of the Tang Dynasty in China, the government ordered every province to establish a Buddhist temple with twenty monks and ten nuns to chant sutras and perform other ceremonies on behalf of the emperor and the state. When an emperor abdicated in 749 in favor of his daughter, he became a Buddhist monk, a practice many of his successors would later follow.

Many of the temples built during the Nara period still stand, the wood, clay, and bronze statues in them exceptionally well preserved. The largest of these temples was the Tōdaiji, with its huge bronze statue of the Buddha, which stood fifty-three feet tall and was made from more than a million pounds of metal. When the temple and statue were completed in 752, an Indian monk painted the eyes. Objects from the dedication ceremony were placed in a special storehouse, and about ten thousand of them are still there, including books, weapons, mirrors, screens, and objects of gold, lacquer, and glass—most made in China but some coming from Central Asia and Persia via the Silk Road.

Hōryūji Temple

Japanese Buddhist temples, like those in China and Korea, consisted of several buildings within a walled compound. The buildings of the Hōryūji Temple (built between 670 and 711, after Prince Shōtoku's original temple burned down) include the oldest wooden structures in the world and house some of the best early Buddhist sculpture in Japan. Craftsmen were sent from Korea to aid in the construction and decoration of the temple, and they brought with them styles that originated in China and India.

(Michael Hitoshi/The Image Bank/Getty Images)

The Hōryūji compound is surrounded by a wall lined with covered arcades. Visitors entered through the gate, visible here as a multistory building in the wall on the right. After entering, they saw the five-story pagoda on the left, which is 122 feet tall. It houses what is thought to be a fragment of a bone of the Buddha. To its right is the main hall, built to house the temple's principal images. Originally, these images had included both statues of Buddhas and bodhisattvas and paintings of them on the walls, but a fire in 1949 destroyed the wall paintngs. The statues were preserved, however, and are today classed as national treasures (as are the buildings). Behind the pagoda and main hall is the lecture hall where the monks would assemble for sermons.

The five-story pagoda could be seen from far away, much like the steeples of cathedrals in medieval Europe. Most of the buildings outside this main compound are of later date, and the outer buildings include monks' quarters, libraries, and dining halls.

QUESTIONS FOR ANALYSIS

1. How does this temple complex compare to the great churches of Europe? What are the most signifcant differences?
2. Was this temple laid out primarily for the convenience of monks who resided there or for lay believers coming to worship? How would their needs differ?
3. What is interesting about the roofs?

197

Coping with Epidemics in Japan and Byzantium

Major epidemics struck across Eurasia many times, but Japan was far enough from the mainland to escape most of them. The first text below is an order issued by the Japanese central government to the provincial governments in 737 after the arrival of a devastating epidemic, probably smallpox. The second text is an account from the Byzantine historian Procopius of a deadly plague that hit Constantinople in 542.

Japanese Proclamation of 737

■ One: This infection is called "red swellings." When it first begins, it is similar to autumnal fevers. Suffering in bed lasts for three or four days in some cases, five or six in others, before the blotches appear. For three or four days as the swellings appear, the limbs and internal organs become hot as if on fire. . . .

Two: Wrap the victim's abdomen and hips thoroughly in hemp cloth or floss silk. Without fail, keep the patient warm. Never let him become chilled.

Three: When there is no floor, do not lie directly on the earth. Spread a straw mat on the ground and lie down to rest.

Four: We recommend the drinking of rice gruel, either thick or thin, and broth made from boiled rice or millet. But do not eat raw fish or fresh fruits and vegetables. Also do not drink water or suck ice. . . .

Five: In general, people with this illness have no appetite. Force the patient to eat. . . .

Six: For twenty days after the illness passes do not carelessly eat raw fish or fresh fruit or vegetables; do not drink water, take a bath, have sex, force yourself to do anything, or walk in wind and rain. If you overdo it, a relapse will begin immediately. . . .

Seven: In general, if you want to bring this illness under control, do not use pills or powders. If a fever arises, take only a little ginseng boiled in water.

Concerning the above, since the 4th month all in the capital and Kinai have been bedridden with this disease. Many have died. We are also aware that people in the provinces have been afflicted with this distress. So we have written up this set of instructions. Each provincial governor should send it along to his neighbor. When it arrives, make a copy and designate one official at the district office who holds the position of secretary or higher to act as the messenger. The messenger should go quickly to the next place without delaying. The provincial office shall make a tour of its jurisdiction and announce these instructions to the people. If they have no rice for gruel, the province shall make an estimate, grant grain relief from government stores, and report to the Council. When the order arrives, carry it out.

Chapter Summary

After unifying China in 221 B.C.E., the Qin Dynasty created a strongly centralized government that did away with noble privilege. The First Emperor standardized script, coinage, weights, and measures. He also built roads, the Great Wall, and a huge tomb for himself. During the four centuries of the subsequent Han Dynasty, the harsher laws of the Qin were lifted, but the strong centralized government was preserved. The Han government promoted internal peace by providing relief in cases of floods, droughts, and famines and by keeping land taxes low for the peasantry. The Han government sent huge armies against the nomadic Xiongnu, whose confederation threatened them in the north, but the Xiongnu remained a potent foe. Still, Han armies expanded Chinese territory in many directions.

For nearly four centuries after the fall of the Han Dynasty, China was divided among contending states. After 316 the north was in the hands of non-Chinese rul-

Procopius on the Plague of Justinian

■ [542 C.E.] During these times there was a pestilence, by which the whole human race came near to being annihilated. . . . In the second year it reached Byzantium in the middle of spring, where it happened that I was staying at that time. . . .

Those who were attending [the victims] were in a state of constant exhaustion and had a most difficult time of it throughout. . . . [The patients] had also great difficulty in the matter of eating, for they could not easily take food. And many perished through lack of any man to care for them, for they were either overcome by hunger, or threw themselves down from a height. . . . Death came in some cases immediately, in others after many days; and with some the body broke out with black pustules about as large as a lentil and these did not survive even one day, but all succumbed immediately. With many also a vomiting of blood ensued without visible cause and straightway brought death. . . .

And it fell to the lot of the emperor, as was natural, to make provision for the trouble. He therefore detailed soldiers from the palace and distributed money, commanding Theodorus to take charge of this work. . . . Theodorus, by giving out the emperor's money and by making further expenditures from his own purse, kept burying the bodies which were not cared for. And when it came about that all the tombs which had existed previously were filled with the dead, then they dug up all the places about the city one after the other, laid the dead there, each one as he could, and departed; but later on those who were making these trenches, no longer able to keep up with the number of the dying, mounted the towers of the fortifications in Sycae, and tearing off the roofs threw the bodies in there in complete disorder; and they piled them up just as each one happened to fall, and filled practically all the towers with corpses, and then covered them again with their roofs. . . . Indeed in a city which was simply abounding in all good things starvation almost absolute was running riot.

QUESTIONS FOR ANALYSIS

1. The first document is a decree issued during an epidemic, and the second is a narrative looking back on an epidemic that has already run its course. What differences in these accounts reflect the nature of the documents?
2. What differences in the understanding of disease can you detect in these accounts?
3. What clues do these accounts provide about the identity of the diseases in the epidemics?

Sources: Reprinted by permission of the Harvard Asia Society from William Farris, *Population and Epidemic Disease in Early Japan, 645–900* (Harvard University Asia Center, 1985), pp. 60–61. © The President and Fellows of Harvard College, 1985; Procopius, *History of the Wars*, trans. H. B. Dewing, Loeb Classical Library (Cambridge, Mass.: Harvard University Press, 1914), pp. 451–473.

ers, while the south had Chinese rulers. In this period merchants and missionaries brought Buddhism to China. Many elements of Buddhism were new to China—a huge body of scriptures, celibate monks and nuns, traditions of depicting Buddhas and bodhisattvas in statues and paintings, and a strong proselytizing tradition. Rulers became major patrons in both north and south.

Unlike the Roman Empire, China was successfully reunified in 589 C.E. The short Sui Dynasty was followed by the longer Tang Dynasty. Tang China regained overlordship of the Silk Road cities in Central Asia. The Tang period was one of cultural flowering, with achievements in poetry especially notable. Music was enriched with instruments and tunes from Persia. Tang power declined after 755, when a powerful general turned his army against the government. Although the rebellion was suppressed, the government was not able to regain its strong central control. Moreover, powerful states were formed along Tang's borders. At court, eunuchs gained power at the expense of civil officials.

Over the ten centuries covered in Chapter 7, Korea, Japan, and Vietnam developed distinct cultures while adopting elements of China's material, political, and religious culture, including the Chinese writing system. During the Tang era, ambitious Korean and Japanese rulers sought Chinese expertise and Chinese products, including Chinese-style centralized governments and the Chinese written language.

NOTES

1. Li Yuning, ed., *The First Emperor of China* (White Plains, N.Y.: International Arts and Sciences Press, 1975), pp. 275–276, slightly modified.
2. Burton Watson, trans., *Records of the Grand Historian of China*, vol. 2 (New York: Columbia University Press, 1961), p. 499.
3. Arthur Waley, trans., *More Translations from the Chinese* (New York: Knopf, 1919), p. 27.
4. *Sources of Japanese Tradition*, by William Theodore de Bary, Donald Keene, George Tanabe, and Paul Varley, eds. Reproduced with permission of COLUMBIA UNIVERSITY PRESS in the format Book via Copyright Clearance Center.

CONNECTIONS

East Asia was transformed in the millennium between the Qin unification in 221 B.C.E. and the end of the eighth century C.E. The Han Dynasty and four centuries later the Tang Dynasty proved that a centralized, bureaucratic monarchy could bring peace and prosperity to populations of 50 million or more spread across China proper. By 800 C.E. neighboring societies along China's borders, from Korea and Japan on the east to the Uighurs and Tibetans to the west, had followed China's lead, forming states and building cities. Buddhism had transformed the lives of all of these societies, bringing new ways of thinking about life and death and new ways of pursuing spiritual goals.

In the same centuries that Buddhism was adapting to and simultaneously transforming the culture of much of eastern Eurasia, comparable processes were at work in western Eurasia, where Christianity continued to spread. The spread of these religions was aided by increased contact between different cultures, facilitated in Eurasia by the merchants traveling the Silk Road or sailing the Indian Ocean. Where contact between cultures wasn't as extensive, as in Africa (discussed in Chapter 10), religious beliefs were more localized. The collapse of the Roman Empire in the West during this period was not unlike the collapse of the Han Dynasty, but in Europe the empire was never put back together at the level that it was in China, where the Tang Dynasty by many measures was more splendid than the Han. The story of these centuries in western Eurasia is taken up in Chapters 8 and 9, which trace the rise of Christianity and Islam and the movement of peoples throughout Europe and Asia. Before returning to the story of East Asia after 800 in Chapter 13, we will also examine the empires in Africa (Chapter 10) and the Americas (Chapter 11).

CHAPTER 7   Review and Explore

Identify Key Terms

Identify and explain the significance of each item below.

Great Wall (p. 177)

Confucian classics (p. 179)

Records of the Grand Historian (p. 180)

Silk Road (p. 181)

tributary system (p. 182)

eunuchs (p. 185)

Age of Division (p. 185)

Grand Canal (p. 189)

Pure Land (p. 191)

Chan (p. 191)

Shinto (p. 196)

Nara (p. 196)

Review the Main Ideas

Answer the focus questions from each section of the chapter.

1. What were the social, cultural, and political consequences of the unification of China under the strong centralized governments of the Qin and Han empires? (p. 176)

2. How did Buddhism find its way into East Asia, and what was its appeal and impact? (p. 186)

3. What were the lasting accomplishments of the Sui and Tang Dynasties? (p. 188)

4. What elements of Chinese culture were adopted by Koreans, Vietnamese, and Japanese, and how did they adapt them to their own circumstances? (p. 192)

Make Comparisons and Connections

Analyze the larger developments and continuities within and across chapters.

1. What philosophies or other cultural elements in pre-imperial China (see Chapter 4) help explain China's development after 221 B.C.E.?

2. How did Buddhism in early India compare to Buddhism in Tang China?

3. How did the influence of Han and Tang China on neighboring regions compare to the influence of Rome on its neighbors?

TIMELINE

221–206 B.C.E. China unified under Qin Dynasty

206 B.C.E.–220 C.E. Han Dynasty

145–ca. 85 B.C.E. Sima Qian, Chinese historian

114–111 B.C.E. Under Emperor Wu, Han Dynasty extends its borders into Central Asia, Korea, and Nam Viet

MEDITERRANEAN WORLD

◆ **44 B.C.E.** Julius Caesar killed **(Ch. 6)**

ca. 3 B.C.E.–29 C.E. Life of Jesus **(Ch. 6)**

EURASIA

200 B.C.E	1 C.E.	200 C.E.

Suggested Resources

BOOKS

Barfield, Thomas. *Perilous Frontier: Nomadic Empires and China, 221 B.C.–A.D. 1757*. 1989. A bold interpretation of the relationship between the rise and fall of dynasties in China and the rise and fall of nomadic confederations that derived resources from them.

Elvin, Mark. *The Pattern of the Chinese Past*. 1973. Analyzes the military dimensions of China's unification.

Farris, Wayne. *Population, Disease, and Land in Early Japan, 645–900*. 1985. Shows the impact of the eighth-century introduction of smallpox to Japan on the government and rural power structure.

Hardy, Grant. *Worlds of Bronze and Bamboo: Sima Qian's Conquest of History*. 1999. An excellent introduction to the methods of China's earliest historian. Although Sima Qian seems to present just the facts, Hardy shows how he brings out different perspectives and interpretations in different chapters.

Holcomb, Charles. *The Genesis of East Asia, 221 B.C.–A.D. 907*. 2001. A thought-provoking analysis of the connections between China and Korea, Japan, and Vietnam that emphasizes the use of the Chinese script.

Lee, Peter H. *Sourcebook of Korean Civilization*. 1993. Excellent collection of primary sources.

Lewis, Mark Edward. *China's Cosmopolitan Empire: The Tang Dynasty*. 2009. This accessible and lively survey complements the author's works on the Han Dynasty (*The Early Chinese Empires*) and the period of division (*China Between Empires*).

Schafer, Edward. *The Golden Peaches of Samarkand*. 1963. Draws on Tang literature to show the place of the western regions in Tang life and imagination.

Scheidel, Walter, ed. *Rome and China: Comparative Perspectives on Ancient World Empires*. 2009. Contributors compare legal and military institutions, trade, money, and charity.

Seth, Michael J. *A Concise History of Korea: From the Neolithic Period Through the Nineteenth Century.* 2006. An up-to-date and well-balanced introduction to Korean history.

Totman, Conrad. *A History of Japan.* 1999. A broad and up-to-date history of Japan.

Varley, H. Paul. *Japanese Culture.* 2000. An accessible introduction to Japanese history and culture.

Waley, Arthur. *The Life and Times of Po Chu-i, 772–846 A.D.* 1949. A lively biography of a Tang official, which draws heavily on his poetry.

Watt, James C. Y. *China: Dawn of a Golden Age, 200–750 A.D.* 2004. A well-illustrated catalogue of a major art and archaeological exhibition.

Wright, Arthur. *Buddhism in Chinese History.* 1959. This short book remains a good introduction to China's encounter with Buddhism and the ways Buddhism was adapted to China.

DOCUMENTARIES

Emperor's Ghost Army (*Nova*, 2014). *Nova* special on the terra-cotta army buried with the First Emperor of Qin.

Yungang Grottos (NHK, 2003). A documentary on the Buddhist caves carved in the fifth century, from a series on World Heritage Sites in China.

FEATURE FILM

Hero (Zhang Yimou, 2002). A fictional reimaging of an attempted assassination of the king of Qin.

WEBSITE

Asian Topics: An Online Resource for Asian History and Culture. This website run by Columbia University offers a good overview of Confucianism, Chinese poetry, classical Japan, and other topics covered in this chapter. Short videos introduce the material. **afe.easia.columbia.edu/at/**

8

Continuity and Change in Europe and Western Asia
250–850

From the third century onward the Western Roman Empire slowly disintegrated, and in 476 the Ostrogothic chieftain Odoacer deposed the Roman emperor in the West and did not take on the title of emperor. This date thus marks the official end of the Roman Empire in the West, although much of the empire had come under the rule of various barbarian tribes well before that. Scholars have long seen this era as one of the great turning points in Western history, but during the last several decades the focus has shifted to continuities as well as changes. What is now usually termed "late antiquity" has been recognized as a period of creativity and adaptation in Europe and western Asia, not simply of decline and fall.

The two main agents of continuity were the Eastern Roman (or Byzantine) Empire and the Christian Church. The Byzantine (BIZ-uhn-teen) Empire lasted until 1453, a thousand years longer than the Western Roman Empire, and it preserved and transmitted much of Greco-Roman law and philosophy. Missionaries and church officials spread Christianity within and far beyond the borders of what had been the Roman Empire, carrying Christian ideas and institutions west to Ireland and east to Central and South Asia. The main agent of change in late antiquity was the migration of barbarian groups throughout much of Europe and western Asia. They brought different social, political, and economic structures with them, but as they encountered Roman and Byzantine culture and became Christian, their own ways of doing things were also transformed.

LOOH
ANRI
REX DUX
ALAMAN
NORUM

A Germanic Ruler

This Germanic ruler appears in an early-ninth-century collection of laws, made in present-day southern France, which includes portraits of rulers, bishops, and nobles along with legal texts such as the Breviary of Alaric, a Visigothic law code based on Roman law and issued in 506. This ruler is identified here as Lodhanri, king of the Alemanni, a confederation of tribes that fought the Romans and were then conquered by the Franks.

Private Collection/Photo © Tallandier/Bridgeman Images

CHAPTER PREVIEW

How did the Byzantine Empire preserve the legacy of Rome?

The Byzantine Empire

The Byzantine (or Eastern Roman) Empire (Map 8.1) preserved the forms, institutions, and traditions of the old Roman Empire, and its people even called themselves Romans. Most important, however, is how Byzantium protected the intellectual heritage of Greco-Roman civilization and then passed it on.

Sources of Byzantine Strength

While the western parts of the Roman Empire gradually succumbed to barbarian invaders, the Byzantine Empire survived Germanic, Persian, and Arab attacks. In 540 a force of Xiongnu (whom the Greeks and Romans called Huns) and Bulgars reached the gates of Constantinople. In 583 the Avars, a mounted Mongol people who had swept across Russia and the Balkans, seized Byzantine forts along the Danube and also reached the walls of Constantinople. Between 572 and 630 the Greeks were repeatedly at war with the Sassanid Persians (see "The Sassanid Empire and Conflicts with Byzantium"). Beginning in 632 Muslim forces pressured the Byzantine Empire (see "Islamic States and Their Expansion" in Chapter 9).

Why didn't one or a combination of these enemies capture Constantinople? The answer lies in strong military leadership and even more in the city's location and excellent fortifications. During the long reign of the emperor Justinian (r. 527–565), Byzantine generals were able to reconquer much of Italy and North Africa. The Byzantines ruled most of Italy from 535 to 572 and the southern part of the peninsula

MAP 8.1 The Byzantine and Sassanid Empires, ca. 600 Both the Byzantine and Sassanid Empires included territory that had earlier been part of the Roman Empire. The Sassanid Persians fought Roman armies before the founding of the Byzantine Empire. Later Byzantium and the Sassanids engaged in a series of wars that weakened both and brought neither lasting territorial acquisitions.

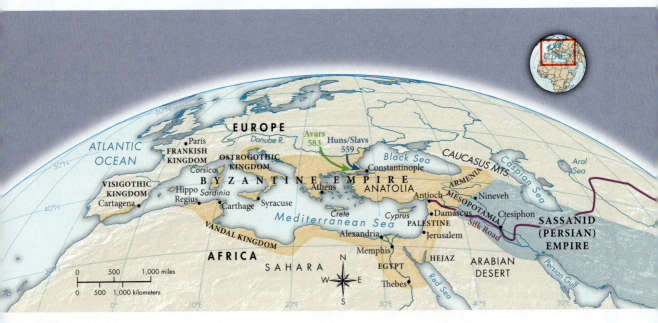

until the eleventh century. They ruled North Africa until it was conquered by Muslim forces in the late seventh century. Massive triple walls, built by the emperors Constantine and Theodosius II (r. 408–450) and kept in good repair by later emperors, protected Constantinople from sea invasion. Within the walls huge cisterns provided water, and vast gardens and grazing areas supplied food so the defending people could hold out far longer than the besieging army. Attacking Constantinople by land posed greater geographical and logistical problems than a seventh- or eighth-century government could solve. Because the city survived, the empire, though reduced in territory, endured.

The Sassanid Empire and Conflicts with Byzantium

For several centuries the Sassanid empire of Persia was Byzantium's most regular foe. Ardashir I (r. 224–243), the ruler of a small state and the first of the Sassanid dynasty, conquered the Parthian empire in 226 (see Map 6.2). Ardashir kept expanding his holdings to the east and northwest. Like all empires, the Sassanid depended on agriculture for its economic prosperity, but its location also proved well suited for commerce (see Map 8.1). A lucrative caravan trade linked the Sassanid empire to the Silk Road and China. This trade brought about considerable cultural contact between the Sassanids and the Chinese.

Whereas the Parthians had tolerated many religions, the Sassanid Persians made Zoroastrianism (see "The Religion of Zoroaster" in Chapter 2) the official state religion. The king's power rested on the support of nobles and Zoroastrian priests who monopolized positions in the court and in the imperial bureaucracy. A highly elaborate court ceremonial and ritual exalted the status of the king and emphasized his semidivine pre-eminence over his subjects. (The Byzantine monarchy, the Roman papacy, and the Muslim caliphate subsequently copied aspects of this Persian ceremonial.) Adherents to religions other than Zoroastrianism, such as Jews and Christians, faced discrimination.

An expansionist foreign policy brought Persia into frequent conflict with Rome and then with Byzantium. Neither side was able to achieve a clear-cut victory until the early seventh century, when the Sassanids advanced all the way to the Mediterranean and even took Egypt in 621. Their victory would be very short-lived, however, as the taxes required to finance the wars and conflicts over the succession to the throne had weakened the Persians. The Byzantines crushed the Persians

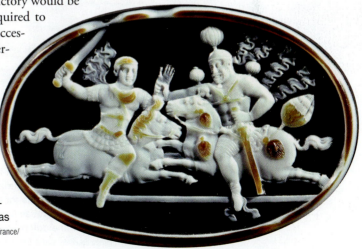

Sassanid Cameo In this cameo — a type of jewelry made by carving into a multicolored piece of rock — the Sassanid king Shapur and the Byzantine emperor Valerian, each identifiable by his distinctive clothing and headgear, fight on horseback. This image does not record an actual hand-to-hand battle, but uses the well-muscled rulers as symbols of their empires. (Bibliothèque Nationale, Paris, France/ Erich Lessing/Art Resource, NY)

in a series of battles ending with one at Nineveh in 627. Just five years later, the first Arabic forces inspired by Islam entered Persian territories, and by 651 the Sassanid dynasty had collapsed (see "Islam's Spread Beyond Arabia" in Chapter 9).

Justinian's Code of Law

Byzantine emperors organized and preserved Roman law, making a lasting contribution to the medieval and modern worlds. By the fourth century Roman law had become a huge, bewildering mass. Its sheer bulk made it almost unusable. The emperor Justinian appointed a committee of eminent jurists to sort through and organize the laws. The result was the *Corpus Juris Civilis* (Body of Civil Law), a multipart collection of laws and legal commentary issued from 529 to 534 that is often simply termed **Justinian's Code** and formed the backbone of Byzantine jurisprudence from that point on.

Justinian's Code Multipart collection of laws and legal commentary issued in the sixth century by the emperor Justinian.

Like so much of classical culture, Justinian's Code was lost in western Europe with the end of the Roman Empire, but it was rediscovered in the eleventh century and came to form the foundation of law for nearly every modern European nation.

Byzantine Intellectual Life

Just as they valued the law, the Byzantines prized education. As a result, many masterpieces of ancient Greek literature survived to influence the intellectual life of the modern world. Among members of the large reading public, history was a favorite subject. The most remarkable Byzantine historian was Procopius (ca. 500–ca. 562), who wrote the *Secret History*, a vicious and uproarious attack on Justinian and his wife, the empress Theodora. (See "Individuals in Society: Theodora of Constantinople," page 210.)

Greek Fire In this illustration from a twelfth-century manuscript, sailors shoot Greek fire toward an attacking ship from a pressurized tube that looks strikingly similar to a modern flamethrower. The exact formula for Greek fire has been lost, but it was probably made from a petroleum product because it continued burning on water. Greek fire was particularly important in Byzantine defenses of Constantinople from Muslim forces in the late seventh century. (Museo del Prado, Madrid, Spain/Bridgeman Images)

Although the Byzantines discovered little that was new in mathematics and geometry, they made advances in military applications. For example, they invented an explosive liquid that came to be known as "Greek fire." The liquid was heated and propelled by a pump through a bronze tube, and as the jet left the tube, it was ignited—somewhat like a modern flamethrower.

The Byzantines devoted a great deal of attention to medicine, and their general level of medical competence was far higher than that of western Europeans. Yet their physicians could not cope with the terrible disease, often called "the Justinian plague," that swept through the Byzantine Empire and parts of western Europe between 542 and 560. In 2013 scientists studying ancient teeth confirmed that this disease was bubonic plague caused by the bacillus *Yersinia pestis*, probably originating in northwestern India and carried to the Mediterranean region by ships. The epidemic had profound political as well as social consequences. It weakened Justinian's military resources, thus hampering his efforts to restore unity to the Mediterranean world.

Life in Constantinople

By the seventh century Constantinople was the greatest city in the Christian world: a large population center, the seat of the imperial court and administration, and the pivot of a large volume of international trade. Given that the city was a natural geographical connecting point between East and West, its markets offered goods from many parts of the world. Furs and timber flowed across the Black Sea from the Rus (Russia) to the capital, as did slaves across the Mediterranean from northern Europe and the Balkans via Venice. Spices, silks, jewelry, and other luxury goods came to Constantinople from India and China by way of Arabia, the Red Sea, and the Indian Ocean. In return, the city exported glassware, mosaics, gold coins, silk cloth, carpets, and a host of other products, with much foreign trade in the hands of Italian merchants. At the end of the eleventh century Constantinople may have been the world's third-largest city, with only Córdoba in Spain and Kaifeng in China larger.

Constantinople did not enjoy constant political stability. Between the accession of Emperor Heraclius in 610 and the fall of the city to Western Crusaders in 1204 (see "The Crusades" in Chapter 14), four separate dynasties ruled at Constantinople. Imperial government involved such intricate court intrigue, assassination plots, and military revolts that the word *byzantine* is sometimes used in English to mean extremely entangled and complicated politics.

The typical household in the city included family members and servants, some of whom were slaves. Artisans lived and worked in their shops, while clerks, civil servants, minor officials, and business people commonly dwelled in multistory buildings perhaps comparable to the apartment complexes of modern American cities. Wealthy aristocrats resided in freestanding mansions that frequently included interior courts, galleries, large reception halls, small sleeping rooms, reading and writing rooms, baths, and chapels.

In the homes of the upper classes, the segregation of women seems to have been the first principle of interior design. As in ancient Athens, private houses contained a *gynaeceum* (guy-neh-KEE-uhm), or women's apartment, where women were kept strictly separated from the outside world. The fundamental reason for this segregation was the family's honor.

Theodora of Constantinople

THE MOST POWERFUL WOMAN IN BYZANTINE history was the daughter of a bear trainer for the circus. Theodora (ca. 497–548) grew up in what her contemporaries regarded as an undignified and morally suspect atmosphere, and she worked as a dancer and actress, both dishonorable occupations in the Roman world. Despite her background, she caught the eye of Justinian, who was then a military leader and whose uncle (and adoptive father) Justin had himself risen from obscurity to become the ruler of the Byzantine Empire. Under Justinian's influence, Justin changed the law to allow an actress who had left her disreputable life to marry whom she liked, and Justinian and Theodora married in 525. When Justinian was proclaimed co-emperor with his uncle Justin on April 1, 527, Theodora received the rare title of *augusta*, empress. Thereafter her name was linked with Justinian's in the exercise of imperial power.

Most of our knowledge of Theodora's early life comes from the *Secret History*, a tell-all description of the vices of Justinian and his court written by Procopius around 550. Procopius was the official court historian and thus spent his days praising those same people. In the *Secret History*, however, he portrays Theodora and Justinian as demonic, greedy, and vicious, killing court-

iers to steal their property. In scene after detailed scene, Procopius portrays Theodora as particularly evil, sexually insatiable, and cruel, a temptress who used sorcery to attract men, including the hapless Justinian.

In one of his official histories, *The History of the Wars of Justinian*, Procopius presents a very different Theodora. Riots between the supporters of two teams in chariot races had turned deadly, and Justinian wavered in his handling of the perpetrators. Both sides turned against the emperor, besieging the palace while Justinian was inside it. Shouting "*Nika!*" (Victory), the rioters swept through the city, burning and looting. Justinian's counselors urged flight, but, according to Procopius, Theodora rose and declared:

> For one who has reigned, it is intolerable to be an exile. . . . If you wish, O Emperor, to save yourself, there is no difficulty: we have ample funds and there are the ships. Yet reflect whether, when you have once escaped to a place of security, you will not prefer death to safety. I agree with an old saying that the purple [that is, the color worn only by emperors] is a fair winding sheet [to be buried in].

Justinian rallied, ordered more than thirty thousand men and women executed, and crushed the revolt.

Other sources describe or suggest Theodora's influence on imperial policy. Justinian passed a number of laws that improved the legal status of women, such as allowing women to own property and to be guardians

---

As it was throughout the world, marriage was part of a family's strategy for social advancement. Both the immediate family and the larger kinship group participated in the selection of a bride or a groom, choosing a spouse who might enhance the family's wealth or prestige.

How did the Christian Church become a major force in Europe?

The Growth of the Christian Church

As the Western Roman Empire disintegrated, the Christian Church survived and grew, becoming the most important institution in Europe. The administrators of the church developed permanent institutions that drew on the Greco-Roman tradition but also expressed Christian values.

The Evolution of Church Leadership and Orthodoxy

Believers in early Christian communities chose their own leaders, but over time appointment by existing church leaders or secular rulers became the common practice. During the reign of Diocletian (die-oh-KLEE-shun) (r. 284–305), the Roman

over their own children. He forbade the exposure of unwanted infants, which happened more often to girls than to boys because boys were valued more highly. Theodora presided at imperial receptions for Arab sheiks, Persian ambassadors, Germanic princesses from the West, and barbarian chieftains from southern Russia. When Justinian fell ill from the bubonic plague in 542, Theodora took over his duties. Justinian is reputed to have consulted her every day about all aspects of state policy, including religious policy regarding the doctrinal disputes that continued throughout his reign.

Theodora's influence over her husband and her power in the Byzantine state continued until she died, perhaps of cancer, twenty years before Justinian. Her influence may have even continued after death, for Justinian continued to pass reforms favoring women and, at the end of his life, accepted an interpretation of Christian doctrine she had favored. Institutions that she established, including hospitals and churches, continued to be reminders of her charity and piety.

Theodora has been viewed as a symbol of the use of beauty and cleverness to attain position and power, and also as a strong and capable co-ruler who held the empire together during riots, revolts, and deadly epidemics. Just as she fascinated Procopius, she continues to intrigue writers today, who make her a character not only in historical works, but also in science fiction and fantasy.

A sixth-century mosaic of the empress Theodora, made of thousands of tiny cubes of glass, shows her with a halo — a symbol of power — and surrounded by officials, priests, and court ladies. (San Vitale, Ravenna, Italy/Bridgeman Images)

QUESTIONS FOR ANALYSIS

1. How would you assess the complex legacy of Theodora?
2. Since Procopius's public and private views of the empress are so different, should he be trusted at all as a historical source? Why or why not?

Empire had been divided for administrative purposes into geographical units called **dioceses**, and Christianity adopted this pattern. Each diocese was headed by a bishop, who was responsible for organizing preaching, overseeing the community's goods, maintaining orthodox (established or correct) doctrine, and delegating responsibilities for preaching and teaching. The center of a bishop's authority was his cathedral, a word deriving from the Latin *cathedra*, meaning "chair."

The early Christian Church benefited from the administrative abilities of church leaders. Bishop Ambrose of Milan (339–397) was typical of the Roman aristocrats who held high public office, converted to Christianity, and subsequently became bishops. Like many bishops, Ambrose had a solid education in classical law and rhetoric, which he used to become an eloquent preacher. He had a strong sense of his authority and even successfully resisted Emperor Theodosius's (r. 379–395) efforts to take control of church property. Ambrose's assertion that the church was supreme in spiritual matters and the state in secular issues was to serve as the cornerstone of the church's position on church-state relations for centuries. Because of his strong influence, Ambrose came to be regarded as one of the "fathers of the church," that is, early

dioceses Geographic administrative districts of the church, each under the authority of a bishop and centered on a cathedral.

Christian thinkers whose authority was regarded as second only to the Bible in later centuries.

Although conflicts between religious and secular leaders were frequent, the church also received support from the emperors. In 380 Theodosius made Christianity the official religion of the empire, and later in his reign he authorized the closure or destruction of temples and holy sites dedicated to the traditional Roman and Greek gods. In return for such support, the emperors expected the Christian Church's assistance in maintaining order and unity.

Christians disagreed with one another about many issues. In the fourth and fifth centuries disputes arose over the nature of Christ. For example, Arianism, developed by Arius (ca. 250–336), a priest of Alexandria, held that Jesus was created by the will of God the Father and thus was not co-eternal with him. Emperor Constantine, who legalized Christianity in 312, rejected the Arian interpretation. In 325 he summoned a council of church leaders to Nicaea (nigh-SEE-uh) in Asia Minor and presided over it personally. The council produced the Nicene (nigh-SEEN) Creed, which defined the position that Christ is "eternally begotten of the Father" and of the same substance as the Father. Arius and those who refused to accept Nicene Christianity were banished. Their interpretation of the nature of Christ was declared a **heresy**, that is, a belief that contradicted the interpretation the church leaders declared was correct, which was termed orthodoxy. These actions did not end Arianism, however. Several later emperors were Arian Christian, and Arian missionaries converted many barbarian tribes, who were attracted by the idea that Jesus was God's second-in-command, which fit well with their own warrior hierarchies and was less complicated than the idea of two persons with one substance. The Nicene interpretation eventually became the most widely held understanding of the nature of Christ, however, and is accepted today by the Roman Catholic Church, the Eastern Orthodox Churches, and most Protestant Churches.

The Nicene Creed says little specifically about the Holy Spirit, but in the following centuries the idea that the Father, Son, and Holy Spirit are "one substance in three persons" — the Trinity — became a central doctrine in Christianity, though again there were those who disagreed. Disputes about the nature of Christ also continued, with factions establishing themselves as separate Christian groups. The Nestorians, for example, regarded the divine and human natures in Jesus as distinct from one another, whereas the orthodox opinion was that they were united. The Nestorians split from the rest of the church in the fifth century after their position was outlawed and settled in Persia. Nestorian Christian missionaries later founded churches in Central Asia, India, and China.

The Western Church and the Eastern Church

The leader of the church in the West, the bishop of Rome, became more powerful than his counterpart in the Byzantine East for a variety of reasons. Most significantly, bishops of Rome asserted that Rome had a special place in Christian history. According to tradition, Saint Peter, chief of Jesus's disciples, had lived in Rome and been its first bishop. Thus, as successors of Peter, the bishops of Rome — known as **popes** — claimed a privileged position in the church hierarchy, an idea called the Petrine Doctrine. They urged other churches to appeal to Rome for the resolution of disputed issues and sent letters of guidance to other bishops. (The Christian Church headed

heresy A religious practice or belief judged unacceptable by church officials.

popes Heads of the Roman Catholic Church, who became political as well as religious authorities. The period of a pope's term in office is called a pontificate.

by the pope in Rome was generally called the Roman Church in this era, and later the Roman Catholic Church.)

The popes also expanded the church's secular authority. They made treaties with barbarian leaders, charged taxes, enforced laws, and organized armies. The Western Christian Church headed by the pope in Rome would become the most enduring nongovernmental institution in world history.

By contrast, in the East the emperor's jurisdiction over the church was fully acknowledged. As in Rome, there was a head of the church in Constantinople, called the patriarch, but he did not develop the same powers that the pope did in the West because there was never a similar power vacuum into which he needed to step. He and other high church officials were appointed by the emperor. The Eastern emperors looked on religion as a branch of the state, and they considered it their duty to protect the faith not only against heathen outsiders but also against heretics within the empire. Following the pattern set by Constantine, the emperors summoned councils of bishops and theologians to settle doctrinal disputes. They and the Eastern bishops did not accept Rome's claim to primacy, and gradually the Byzantine Christian Church, generally called the **Orthodox Church**, and the Roman Church began to diverge. In addition, other branches of Christianity in the East, including the Nestorians, Maronites, and Copts, developed their own distinctive theological ideas and patterns of organization, which have continued to today.

Orthodox Church Another name for the Eastern Christian Church, over which emperors continued to have power.

Christian Monasticism

Christianity began and spread as a city religion. With time, however, some especially pious Christians started to feel that a life of asceticism (extreme material sacrifice, including fasting and the renunciation of sex) was a better way to show their devotion to Christ's teachings, just as followers of Mahavira or the Buddha had centuries earlier in South Asia (see "India's Great Religions" in Chapter 3).

Ascetics often separate themselves from their families and normal social life, and this is what Christian ascetics did. Individuals and small groups withdrew from cities and moved to the Egyptian desert, where they sought God through prayer in caves and shelters in the desert or mountains. These individuals were called hermits or monks. Gradually, large groups of monks emerged in the deserts of Upper Egypt, creating a style of life known as monasticism. Many devout women were also attracted to this type of monasticism, becoming nuns. Although monks and nuns led isolated lives, ordinary people soon recognized them as holy people and sought them as spiritual guides.

Church leaders did not really approve of the solitary life. Hermits sometimes claimed to have mystical experiences—direct communications with God. If hermits could communicate directly with the Lord, what need had they for priests, bishops, and the institutional church? The church hierarchy instead encouraged those who wanted to live ascetic lives of devotion to do so in communities. Consequently, in the fourth, fifth, and sixth centuries many different kinds of communal monasticism developed in Gaul, Italy, Spain, Anglo-Saxon England, and Ireland.

In 529 Benedict of Nursia (ca. 480–547) wrote a brief set of regulations for the monks who had gathered around him at Monte Cassino, between Rome and Naples. Benedict's guide for monastic life, known as *The Rule of Saint Benedict*, slowly replaced all others, and it has influenced all forms of organized religious life in the Roman

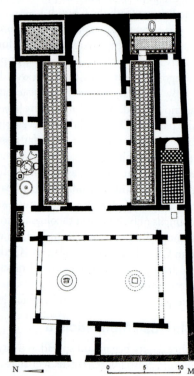

Floor Plan and Foundation of Kursi Monastery Church Built on the eastern shore of the Sea of Galilee in the fifth century at a major pilgrimage site, this walled monastery had living quarters for the monks, a guesthouse, and a bath for pilgrims. It contained a church modeled on the type of Roman public building known as a basilica, with an open courtyard with two wells (at the bottom in the pictures), mosaic floors, and a central nave separated from side aisles by rows of arched columns. In one side chapel (on the left in the pictures) was a small baptismal font, and in another a press for olive oil, a major source of income for the monastery. The skeletons of thirty monks were found in a crypt when the site was uncovered during road construction in 1970. (Private Collection/Photo © Zev Radovan/Bridgeman Images)

Church. The guide outlined a monastic life of regularity, discipline, and moderation in an atmosphere of silence. Under Benedict's regulations, monks spent part of each day in formal prayer, chanting psalms and other prayers from the Bible. The rest of the day was passed in manual labor, study, and private prayer. The monastic life as conceived by Saint Benedict provided opportunities for men of different abilities and talents—from mechanics to gardeners to literary scholars. The Benedictine form of religious life also appealed to women, because it allowed them to show their devotion and engage in study. Benedict's twin sister, Scholastica (480–543), adapted the *Rule* for use by her community of nuns.

Benedictine monasticism also succeeded partly because it was so materially successful. In the seventh and eighth centuries Benedictine monasteries pushed back forests and wastelands, drained swamps, and experimented with crop rotation, making a significant contribution to the agricultural development of Europe. Monasteries also conducted schools for local young people. Some learned about prescriptions and herbal remedies and went on to provide medical treatment for their localities. Others copied manuscripts and wrote books. Local and royal governments drew on the services of the literate men and able administrators the monasteries produced.

Because all monasteries followed rules, men who lived a communal monastic life came to be called regular clergy, from the Latin word *regulus* (rule). In contrast, priests and bishops who staffed churches in which people worshipped and who were not cut off from the world were called secular clergy. According to official church doctrine, women were not members of the clergy, but this distinction was not clear to most people, who thought of nuns as members of the clergy.

Monasticism in the Orthodox world differed in fundamental ways from the monasticism that evolved in western Europe. First, while *The Rule of Saint Benedict* gradually became the universal guide for all western European monasteries, each monastic house in the Byzantine world developed its own set of rules for organization and behavior. Second, education never became a central feature of the Orthodox houses. Since bishops and patriarchs of the Orthodox Church were recruited only from the monasteries, however, these institutions did exercise cultural influence.

Christian Ideas and Practices

The growth of Christianity was tied not just to institutions such as the papacy and monasteries but also to ideas. Initially, Christians rejected Greco-Roman culture. Gradually, however, Christian leaders and thinkers developed ideas that drew on classical influences, though there were also areas of controversy that differed in the Western and Eastern Churches.

How did Christian thinkers adapt classical ideas to Christian teachings, and what new religious concepts and practices did they develop?

Christianity and Classical Culture

In the first century Christians believed that Christ would soon fulfill his promise to return and that the end of the world was near; therefore, they saw no point in devoting time to learning. By the second century, however, these apocalyptic expectations were diminishing, and church leaders began to incorporate elements of Greek and Roman philosophy and learning into Christian teachings (see "The Growing Acceptance and Evolution of Christianity" in Chapter 6). They found support for this incorporation in the written texts that circulated among Christians. In the third and fourth centuries these texts were brought together as the New Testament of the Bible, with general agreement about most of what should be included but sharp disputes about some books. Although some of Jesus's sermons as recorded in the Gospels (see "The Life and Teachings of Jesus" in Chapter 6) urged followers to avoid worldly attachments, other parts of the Bible advocated acceptance of existing social, economic, and political structures. Christian thinkers built on these, adapting Christian teachings to fit with Roman realities and Roman ideas to fit with Christian aims, just as Buddhist thinkers adapted Buddhist teachings when they spread them to Central Asia, China, Korea, and Japan (see "The Spread of Buddhism Out of India" in Chapter 7).

Saint Jerome (340–419), a theologian and linguist regarded as a father of the church, translated the Old Testament and New Testament from Hebrew and Greek, respectively, into vernacular Latin. Called the Vulgate, his edition of the Bible served as the official translation until the sixteenth century. Familiar with the writings of classical authors such as Cicero and Virgil, Saint Jerome believed that Christians should study the best of ancient thought because it would direct their minds to God. He maintained that the best ancient literature should be interpreted in light of the Christian faith.

Christian attitudes toward gender and sexuality provide a good example of the ways early Christians first challenged and then largely adopted the views of their contemporary world. In his plan of salvation Jesus considered women the equal of men. Women were among the earliest converts to Christianity and took an active role in its spread, preaching, acting as missionaries, being martyred alongside men, and perhaps even baptizing believers. Some women embraced the ideal of virginity and either singly or in monastic communities declared themselves "virgins in the service of Christ." All this initially made Christianity seem dangerous to many Romans who viewed marriage as the foundation of society and the proper patriarchal order.

Not all Christian teachings about gender were radical, however. In the first century male church leaders began to place restrictions on female believers. Women were forbidden to preach and were gradually excluded from holding official positions in Christianity other than in women's monasteries. In so limiting the activities of female believers, Christianity was following well-established social patterns, just as it modeled its official hierarchy after that of the Roman Empire.

Christian teachings about sexuality also built on and challenged classical models. The rejection of sexual activity involved an affirmation of the importance of a spiritual life, but it also incorporated hostility toward the body found in some Hellenistic philosophies. Just as spirit was superior to matter, the thinking went, the mind was superior to the body. Though Christian teachings affirmed that God had created the material world and sanctioned marriage, most Christian thinkers also taught that celibacy was the better life and that anything that distracted one's attention from the spiritual world performed an evil function. For most clerical writers (who were themselves male), this temptation came from women, and in some of their writings women themselves are portrayed as evil, the "devil's gateway." Thus the writings of many church fathers contain a strong streak of misogyny (hatred of women), which was passed down to later Christian thinkers.

The Marys at Jesus's Tomb This late-fourth-century ivory panel tells the biblical story of Mary Magdalene and another Mary who went to Jesus's tomb to anoint the body (Matthew 28:1–7). At the top guards collapse when an angel descends from Heaven, and at the bottom the Marys listen to the angel telling them that Jesus has risen. Here the artist uses Roman artistic styles to convey Christian subject matter, synthesizing classical form and Christian teaching. (Castello Sforzesco Milan, Italy/Scala/Art Resource, NY)

Saint Augustine on Sin, Grace, and Redemption

One thinker had an especially strong role in shaping Christian views about sexual activity and many other issues: Saint Augustine of Hippo (354–430). Augustine was born into an urban family in what is now Algeria in North Africa. His father was a pagan; his mother, Monica, was a devout Christian. He gained an excellent education, fathered a son, and experimented with various religious ideas. In adulthood he converted to his mother's religion, eventually becoming bishop of the city of Hippo Regius.

Augustine's autobiography, *The Confessions*, is a literary masterpiece and one of the most influential books in Western history. Written in the rhetorical style and language of late Roman antiquity, it marks a synthesis of Greco-Roman forms and Christian thought. *The Confessions* describes Augustine's moral struggle, the conflict between his spiritual aspirations and his sensual self. Many Greek and Roman philosophers had taught that knowledge would lead to virtue. Augustine came to reject this idea, claiming that people do not always act on the basis of rational knowledge. Instead the basic or dynamic force in any individual is the will. When Adam ate the fruit forbidden by God in the Garden of Eden (Genesis 3:6), he committed the "original sin" and corrupted the will, wrote Augustine. Adam's sin did not simply remain his own but was passed on to all later humans through sexual intercourse; even infants were tainted. Original sin thus became a common social stain, in Augustine's opinion, transmitted by sexual desire. By viewing sexual desire as the result of Adam and Eve's disobedience to divine instructions, Augustine linked sexuality even more clearly with sin than had earlier church fathers. According to Augustine, because Adam disobeyed God, all human beings have an innate tendency to sin: their will is weak. But Augustine held that God restores the strength of the will through grace, which is transmitted in certain rituals that the church defined as **sacraments**, such as baptism. Augustine's ideas on sin, grace, and redemption became the foundation of all subsequent Western Christian theology, Protestant as well as Catholic.

sacraments Certain rituals of the church believed to act as a conduit of God's grace, such as baptism.

The Iconoclastic Controversy

Augustine's ideas about original sin did not become important in the Eastern Orthodox Church, where other issues seemed more significant. In the centuries after Constantine, the most serious dispute within the Orthodox Church concerned icons — images or representations of God the Father, Jesus, and the saints in painting, bas-relief, or mosaic. Icons were important tools in conversion and in people's devotional lives, but some church leaders and emperors came to feel that the veneration of images had gone too far.

The result of this dispute was a terrible theological conflict, the **iconoclastic controversy**, that split the Byzantine world for a century. In 730 the emperor Leo III (r. 717–741) ordered the destruction of icons. The removal of these images from Byzantine churches provoked a violent reaction: entire provinces revolted, and the Byzantine Empire and the Roman papacy severed relations. Since Eastern monasteries were the fiercest defenders of icons, Leo's son Constantine V (r. 741–775) seized their property, executed some of the monks, and forced other monks into the army. Theological disputes and civil disorder over the icons continued intermittently until 843, when the icons were restored.

iconoclastic controversy The conflict over the veneration of religious images in the Byzantine Empire.

The implications of the iconoclastic controversy extended far beyond strictly theological issues. Iconoclasm raised the question of the right of the emperor to intervene in religious disputes. Iconoclasm antagonized the pope and served to encourage him in his quest for an alliance with the Frankish monarchy (see "The Warrior-Ruler Charlemagne"), which further divided the two parts of Christendom. The ultimate acceptance of icons profoundly influenced subsequent art within both Eastern and Western Christianity.

How did the barbarians shape social, economic, and political structures in Europe and western Asia?

Migrating Peoples

The word *barbarian* comes from the Greek *barbaros*, meaning someone who did not speak Greek. (To the Greeks, others seemed to be speaking nonsense syllables; *barbar* is the Greek equivalent of "blah-blah" or "yada-yada.") The Greeks used this word to include people such as the Egyptians, whom the Greeks respected. The Romans usually used the Latin version of *barbarian* to mean the peoples who lived beyond the northeastern boundary of Roman territory, whom they regarded as unruly, savage, and primitive. (See "Global Viewpoints: Roman and Byzantine Views of Barbarians," page 220.) That value judgment is generally also present when we use *barbarian* in English, but there really is no other word to describe the many different peoples who lived to the north of the Roman Empire. Thus historians of late antiquity use the word *barbarian* to designate these peoples, who spoke a variety of languages but had similarities in their basic social, economic, and political structures (Map 8.2). Many of these historians find much to admire in barbarian society.

Barbarians included many different ethnic groups with social and political structures, languages, laws, and beliefs developed in central and northern Europe and western Asia over many centuries. Among the largest barbarian groups were the Celts (KELTS) (whom the Romans called Gauls) and Germans; Germans were further subdivided into various tribes, such as Ostrogoths, Visigoths, Burgundians, and Franks. *Celt* and *German* are often used as ethnic terms, but they are better understood as linguistic terms, a Celt being a person who spoke a Celtic language and a German one who spoke a Germanic language. Celts, Germans, and other barbarians brought their customs and traditions with them when they moved south and west, and these gradually combined with classical and Christian customs and beliefs to form new types of societies. From this cultural mix the Franks emerged as an especially strong and influential force, and they built a lasting empire (see "The Warrior-Ruler Charlemagne").

Social and Economic Structures

Barbarian groups usually resided in small villages, and climate and geography determined the basic patterns of agricultural and pastoral life. Many groups settled on the edges of clearings where they raised barley, wheat, oats, peas, and beans. Men and women tilled their fields with simple scratch plows and harvested their grain with small iron sickles. The kernels of grain were eaten as porridge, ground up for flour, or fermented into strong, thick beer. Most of people's caloric intake came from grain in some form.

Within the villages, there were great differences in wealth and status. Free men and their families constituted the largest class, and the number of cattle these men

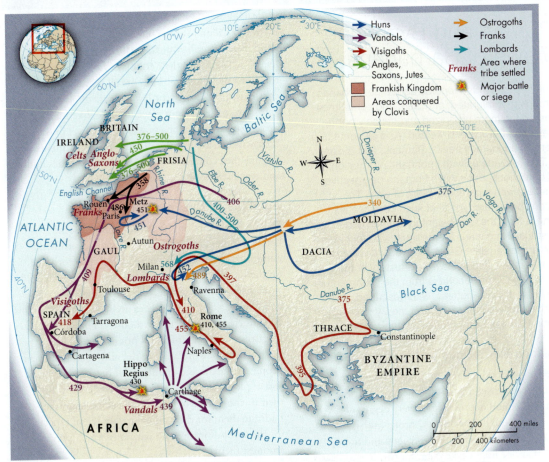

MAP 8.2 The Barbarian Migrations, ca. 340–500 Various barbarian groups migrated throughout Europe and western Asia in late antiquity, pushed and pulled by a number of factors. Many of them formed loosely structured states, of which the Frankish kingdom would become the most significant.

possessed indicated their wealth and determined their social status. Free men also took part in tribal warfare. Slaves acquired through warfare worked as farm laborers, herdsmen, and household servants. Barbarian society was patriarchal: within each household the father had authority over his wife, children, and slaves. Some wealthy and powerful men had more than one wife, a pattern that continued even after they became Christian, but polygamy was not widespread among ordinary people. Once women were widowed, they sometimes assumed their husbands' rights over family property and took guardianship of their children.

Tribes, Warriors, and Laws

The basic social and political unit among barbarian groups was the tribe or confederation, made up of kin groups whose members believed they were all descended from a common ancestor. Tribes were led by chieftains, who were elected from among

Roman and Byzantine Views of Barbarians

The earliest written records about the barbarian groups that migrated, attacked, and sometimes conquered the more urbanized and densely populated areas of Europe and western Asia all come from the pens of educated Greeks, Romans, and Byzantines. They provide us with important information about barbarians, but always from the perspective of outsiders with a particular point of view. The selections below are typical of such commentary. The first is from the fourth-century Roman general and historian Ammianus Marcellinus, who fought in Roman armies against Germanic tribes, the Huns, and the Persians and later wrote a history of the Roman Empire. The second is from the sixth-century Byzantine historian Agathias, who described recent encounters between the forces of the Byzantine emperor Justinian and various Germanic tribes.

Ammianus Marcellinus on the Huns, ca. 380

■ The people of the Huns, but little known from ancient records, dwelling beyond the Maeotic Sea near the ice-bound ocean, exceed every degree of savagery. . . . They all have compact, strong limbs and thick necks, and are so monstrously ugly and misshapen, that one might take them for two-legged beasts or for the stumps, rough-hewn into images, that are used in putting sides to bridges. But although they have the form of men, however ugly, they are so hardy in their mode of life that they have no need of fire nor of savory food, but eat the roots of wild plants and the half-raw flesh of any kind of animal whatever, which they put between their thighs and the backs of their horses, and thus warm a little. They are never protected by any buildings, but they avoid these like tombs. . . . They are not at all adapted to battles on foot, but they are almost glued to their horses, which are hardy, it is true, but ugly. . . . They fight from a distance with missiles having sharp bone [points], instead of the usual (metal) parts, joined to the shafts with wonderful skill;

then they gallop over the intervening spaces and fight hand to hand with swords, regardless of their own lives. . . . No one in their country ever plows a field or touches a plow-handle. They are all without fixed abode, without hearth, or law, or settled mode of life, and keep roaming from place to place, like fugitives, accompanied by wagons in which they live; in wagons their wives weave for them their hideous garments, in wagons they cohabit with their husbands, bear children, and rear them to the age of puberty.

Agathias on the Franks

■ The Franks are not nomads, as indeed some barbarian peoples are, but their system of government, administration and laws are modelled more or less on the Roman pattern, apart from which they uphold similar standards with regard to contracts, marriage, and religious observance. They are in fact all Christians and adhere to the strictest orthodoxy. They also have magistrates in their cities and priests and celebrate the feasts in the same way we do, and, for a barbarian people, strike me as extremely well-bred and civilized and as practically the same as ourselves except for their uncouth style of dress and peculiar language. I admire them for their other attributes and especially for the spirit of justice and harmony which prevails amongst them.

QUESTIONS FOR ANALYSIS

1. What qualities of the Huns does Ammianus Marcellinus find admirable? What does he criticize?
2. What qualities of the Franks does Agathias praise? Why does he find these qualities admirable?
3. How does the fact that both Ammianus Marcellinus and Agathias come from agricultural societies with large cities shape their views of barbarians?

Sources: *Ammianus Marcellinus: Volume I*, Loeb Classical Library Volume 331, with an English translation by John C. Rolfe (Cambridge, Mass.: Harvard University Press), pp. 383, 385. First published 1939. Loeb Classical Library® is a registered trademark of the President and Fellows of Harvard College; Agathias, *The Histories*, trans. Joseph D. Frendo (Berlin: Walter de Gruyter, 1975), p. 10.

Visigothic Work and Play This page comes from one of the very few manuscripts from the time of the barbarian invasions to have survived, a copy of the first five books of the Old Testament — the Pentateuch — made around 600, perhaps in Visigothic Spain or North Africa. The top shows biblical scenes, while the bottom shows people engaged in everyday activities: building a wall, drawing water from a well, and trading punches. (The Art Archive/REX/Shutterstock)

the male members of the most powerful family. The chief led the tribe in war, settled disputes among its members, conducted negotiations with outside powers, and offered sacrifices to the gods. As barbarian groups migrated into and conquered parts of the Western Roman Empire, their chiefs became even more powerful. Often chiefs adopted the title of king.

Closely associated with the chief in some tribes was the comitatus (kuhm-ee-TAH-tuhs), or war band. The warriors swore loyalty to the chief and fought alongside him in battle. Warriors may originally have been relatively equal to one another, but during the migrations and warfare of the second through the fourth centuries, the war band was transformed into a system of stratified ranks. When tribes settled down, warriors also began to acquire land as both a mark of prestige and a means to power. Social inequalities emerged and gradually grew stronger. These inequalities help explain the origins of the European noble class.

Early barbarian tribes had no written laws, but beginning in the late fifth century some chieftains began to collect, write, and publish lists of their customs and laws. Barbarian law codes often included clauses designed to reduce interpersonal violence. Any crime that involved a personal injury, such as assault, rape, and murder, was given a particular monetary value, called the **wergeld** (WUHR-gehld) (literally "man-money") that was to be paid by a person accused of a crime to the victim or the victim's family. The wergeld varied according to the severity of the crime and also the social status and gender of the victim, and was designed to prevent an act of violence from escalating into a blood-feud between families.

wergeld Compensatory payment for death or injury set in many barbarian law codes.

Like most people of the ancient world, barbarians worshipped hundreds of gods and goddesses with specialized functions. They regarded certain mountains, lakes, rivers, or groves of trees as sacred because these were linked to deities. Among the Celts, religious leaders called druids had legal and educational as well as religious functions, orally passing down laws and traditions from generation to generation. Bards singing poems and ballads also passed down myths and stories of heroes and gods, which were written down much later.

Migrations and Political Change

Migrating groups that the Romans labeled barbarians had moved southward and eastward off and on since about 100 C.E. (see "Migrating Peoples"). Why did the barbarians migrate? In part, they were searching for more regular supplies of food, better farmland, and a warmer climate. Conflicts within and among barbarian groups also led to war and disruption, which motivated groups to move. Roman expansion led to further movement of barbarian groups but also to the blending of cultures.

The spread of the Celts presents a good example of both conflict and assimilation. Celtic-speaking peoples had lived in central Europe since at least the fifth century B.C.E. and had spread out from there to the Iberian Peninsula in the west, Hungary in the east, and the British Isles in the north. As Julius Caesar advanced northward into what he termed Gaul (present-day France), he defeated many Celtic tribes (see Map 6.2). Celtic peoples conquered by the Romans often assimilated to Roman ways, intermarrying with Romans and adopting the Latin language and many aspects of Roman culture. By the fourth century C.E., however, Gaul and Britain were under pressure from Germanic groups moving westward. Roman troops withdrew from Britain, and Celtic-speaking peoples clashed with Germanic-speaking invaders, of whom the largest tribes were the Angles and the Saxons. Some Celtic-speakers moved farther west. Others remained and intermarried with Germanic peoples, their descendants forming a number of small Anglo-Saxon kingdoms.

In eastern Europe, a significant factor in barbarian migration and the merging of various Germanic groups was pressure from nomadic steppe peoples from central Asia, most prominently the Huns, who attacked the Black Sea area and the Eastern Roman Empire beginning in the fourth century. Under the leadership of their warrior-king Attila, the Huns attacked the Byzantine Empire in 447 and then turned westward, allying with some Germanic groups and moving into what is now France. After Attila turned his army southward and crossed the Alps into Italy, a papal delegation, including Pope Leo I himself, asked him not to attack Rome. Though papal diplomacy was later credited with stopping the advance of the Huns, their dwindling food supplies and a plague that spread among their troops were probably much more important factors. The Huns retreated from Italy, and within a year Attila was dead. The Huns never again played a significant role in European history. Their conquests had pushed many Germanic groups together, however, which transformed smaller bands of people into larger, more unified peoples who could more easily pick the Western Roman Empire apart.

Anglo-Saxon Helmet This ceremonial bronze helmet from seventh-century England was found inside a ship buried at Sutton Hoo. The nearly 100-foot-long ship was dragged overland before being buried completely. It held one body and many grave goods, including swords, gold buckles, and silver bowls made in Byzantium. The unidentified person who was buried here was clearly wealthy and powerful, and so was very likely a chief. (© The Trustees of the British Museum/Art Resource, NY)

After they conquered an area, barbarians generally established states ruled by kings. However, the kingdoms did not have definite geographical borders, and their locations shifted as tribes moved. Eventually, barbarian kingdoms came to include Italy itself. The Western Roman emperors increasingly relied on barbarian commanders and their troops to maintain order, and, as we saw in Chapter 6, in 476 the barbarian chieftain Odoacer (oh-doh-AY-suhr) deposed Romulus Augustus, the last person to have the title of Roman emperor in the West. Odoacer did not take the title of emperor, calling himself instead the king of Italy, so this date marks the official end of the Roman Empire in the West. From Constantinople, Eastern Roman emperors such as Justinian (see "Sources of Byzantine Strength") worked to reconquer at least some of the West from barbarian tribes. They were occasionally successful but could not hold the empire together for long.

Christian Missionaries and Conversion

How did the church convert barbarian peoples to Christianity?

The Mediterranean served as the highway over which Christianity spread to the cities of the Roman Empire. Christian teachings were often spread into the countryside and into areas beyond the borders of the empire by those who had dedicated their lives to the church, such as monks. Such missionaries were often sent by popes specifically to convert certain groups.

Missionaries' Actions

Throughout barbarian Europe, religion was not a private or individual matter; it was a social affair, and the religion of the chieftain or king determined the religion of the people. Thus missionaries concentrated their initial efforts not on ordinary people but on kings or tribal chieftains and the members of their families. Because they had more opportunity to spend time with missionaries, queens and other female members of the royal family were often the first converts in an area, and they influenced their husbands and brothers. Germanic kings sometimes accepted Christianity because they came to believe that the Christian God was more powerful than pagan gods and that the Christian God—in either its Arian or Roman version—would deliver victory in battle.

Many barbarian groups were converted by Arian missionaries (see "The Evolution of Church Leadership and Orthodoxy"), who also founded dioceses. Bishop Ulfilas (ca. 310–383), for example, an Ostrogoth himself, translated the Bible from Greek into the Gothic language even before Jerome wrote the Latin Vulgate, creating a new Gothic script in order to write it down. In the sixth and seventh centuries most Goths and other Germanic tribes converted to Roman Christianity, sometimes peacefully and sometimes as a result of conquest. Ulfilas's Bible—and the Gothic script he invented—were forgotten and rediscovered only a thousand years later.

Tradition identifies the conversion of Ireland with Saint Patrick (ca. 385–461). After a vision urged him to Christianize Ireland, Patrick studied in Gaul and in 432 was consecrated a bishop. He then returned to Ireland, where he converted the Irish tribe by tribe, first baptizing the king.

The Christianization of the English began in earnest in 597, when Pope Gregory I (pontificate 590–604) sent a delegation of monks to England. The conversion of the

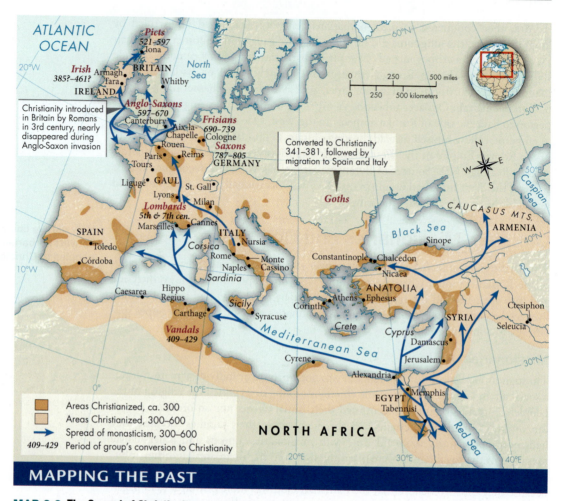

MAPPING THE PAST

MAP 8.3 The Spread of Christianity, ca. 300–800 Originating in the area near Jerusalem, Christianity spread throughout and then beyond the Roman world.

ANALYZING THE MAP Based on the map, how did the roads and sea-lanes of the Roman Empire influence the spread of Christianity?

CONNECTIONS How does the map support the conclusion that Christianity began as an urban religion and then spread into more rural areas?

English had far-reaching consequences because Britain later served as a base for the Christianization of Germany and other parts of northern Europe (Map 8.3). In eastern Europe Byzantine missionaries gained converts among the Bulgars and Slavs. Between the fifth and tenth centuries the majority of people living in Europe accepted the Christian religion—that is, they received baptism, though baptism in itself did not automatically transform people into Christians.

The Process of Conversion

When a ruler marched his people to the waters of baptism, the work of Christianization had only begun. Churches could be built, and people could be required to attend services and belong to parishes, but the process of conversion was a gradual one.

How did missionaries and priests get masses of pagan and illiterate peoples to understand Christian ideals and teachings? They did it through preaching, assimilation of pagan customs, the ritual of penance, and veneration of the saints. Those who preached aimed to present the basic teachings of Christianity and strengthen the newly baptized in their faith through stories about the lives of Christ and the saints.

Deeply ingrained pagan customs and practices, however, could not be stamped out by words alone. Thus Christian missionaries often pursued a policy of assimilation, easing the conversion of pagan men and women by stressing similarities between their customs and beliefs and those of Christianity and by mixing barbarian pagan ideas and practices with Christian ones. For example, bogs and lakes sacred to Germanic gods became associated with saints, as did various aspects of ordinary life, such as traveling, planting crops, and worrying about a sick child. Aspects of existing midwinter celebrations were assimilated into celebrations of Christmas. Spring rituals involving eggs and rabbits (both symbols of fertility) were added to celebrations of Easter. People joined with family members, friends, and neighbors to celebrate these holidays, and also baptisms, weddings, and funerals, presided over by a priest.

The ritual of **penance** was also instrumental in teaching people Christian ideas. Christianity taught that certain actions and thoughts were sins. Only by confessing sins and asking forgiveness could a sinning believer be reconciled with God. Confession was initially a public ritual, but by the fifth century individual confession to a parish priest was more common. During this ritual the individual knelt before the priest, who questioned him or her about sins he or she might have committed. The priest then set a penance such as fasting or saying specific prayers to allow the person to atone for the sin. Penance gave new converts a sense of the behavior expected of Christians, encouraged the private examination of conscience, and offered relief from the burden of sinful deeds.

> **penance** Ritual in which Christians asked a priest for forgiveness for sins and the priest set certain actions to atone for the sins.

Veneration of **saints**, people who had lived (or died) in a way that was spiritually heroic or noteworthy, was another way that Christians formed stronger connections with their religion. Saints were understood to provide protection and assistance to worshippers, and parish churches often housed saints' relics, that is, bones, articles of clothing, or other objects associated with them. The relics served as links between the material world and the spiritual, and miracle stories about saints and their relics were an important part of Christian preaching and writing.

> **saints** People who were venerated for having lived or died in a way that was spiritually heroic or noteworthy.

Christians came to venerate the saints as powerful and holy. They prayed to saints or to the Virgin Mary to intercede with God, or they simply asked the saints to assist and bless them. The entire village participated in processions marking saints' days or important points in the agricultural year, often carrying images of saints or their relics around the houses and fields. The decision to adopt Christianity was often made first by an emperor or king, but actual conversion was a local matter, as people came to feel that the parish priest and the saints provided them with benefits in this world and the world to come.

How did the Franks build and govern a European empire?

Frankish Rulers and Their Territories

Most barbarian kingdoms did not last very long, but one that did—and that came to have a decisive role in history—was that of the confederation of Germanic peoples known as the Franks. In the fourth and fifth centuries the Franks settled within the empire and allied with the Romans, some attaining high military and civil positions. Though at that time the Frankish kingdom was simply one barbarian kingdom among many, rulers after the influential Clovis used a variety of tactics to expand their holdings, enhance their authority, and create a stable system. Charles the Great (r. 768–814), generally known by the French version of his name, Charlemagne (SHAHR-luh-mayne), created the largest state in western Europe since the Roman Empire.

The Merovingians and Carolingians

Merovingian A dynasty of rulers that decisively unified the Franks under the reign of Clovis (ca. 481–511) and ruled the Frankish kingdom until the seventh century.

The Franks believed that Merovech, a semi-legendary figure, founded their ruling dynasty, which was thus called **Merovingian** (mehr-uh-VIHN-jee-uhn). The reign of Clovis (r. ca. 481–511) was decisive in the development of the Franks as a unified people. Through military campaigns, Clovis acquired the central provinces of Roman Gaul and began to conquer southern Gaul from other Germanic tribes. His wife, Clotild, a Roman Christian, pressured him to convert, but he refused. His later biographer Gregory of Tours, a bishop in the Frankish kingdom in the sixth century, attributed his conversion to a battlefield vision, just as Emperor Constantine's biographers had reported about his conversion.

Most historians today conclude that Clovis's conversion to Roman Christianity was a pragmatic choice: it brought him the crucial support of the bishops of Gaul in his campaigns against tribes that were still pagan or had accepted the Arian version of Christianity. As the defender of Roman Christianity against heretical tribes, Clovis went on to conquer the Visigoths, extending his domain to include much of what is now France and southwestern Germany.

Following Frankish traditions in which property was divided among male heirs, at Clovis's death his kingdom was divided among his four sons. For the next two centuries rulers of the various kingdoms fought one another in civil wars, and other military leaders challenged their authority.

Merovingian kings based some aspects of their government on Roman principles. For example, they adopted the Roman concept of the *civitas*—Latin for a city and its surrounding territory. A count presided over the civitas, raising troops, collecting royal revenues, and providing justice. Within the royal household, Merovingian politics provided women with opportunities, and some queens not only influenced but occasionally also dominated events. Because the finances of the kingdom were merged with those of the royal family, queens often had control of the royal treasury just as more ordinary women controlled household expenditures.

Carolingian A dynasty of rulers that took over the Frankish kingdom from the Merovingians in the seventh century; *Carolingian* derives from the Latin word for "Charles," the name of several members of this dynasty.

At the king's court an official called the mayor of the palace supervised legal, financial, and household officials; the mayor of the palace also governed in the king's absence. In the seventh century the position as mayor was held by members of an increasingly powerful family, the **Carolingians** (ka-ruh-LIHN-jee-uhns), who advanced themselves through advantageous marriages, a well-earned reputation for military strength, and the help of the church. *Carolingian* derives from the Latin word for "Charles," the name of several members of this dynasty.

Eventually the Carolingians replaced the Merovingians as rulers of the Frankish kingdom, cementing their authority when the Carolingian Charles Martel defeated Muslim invaders in 732 at the Battle of Poitiers (pwah-tee-AY) in central France. Muslims and Christians have interpreted the battle differently. Muslims considered it a minor skirmish and attributed the Frankish victory to Muslim difficulties in maintaining supply lines over long distances and to ethnic conflicts and unrest in Islamic Spain. Charles Martel and later Carolingians used the victory to portray themselves as defenders of Christendom against the Muslims.

The Battle of Poitiers helped the Carolingians acquire more support from the church, perhaps their most important asset. They further strengthened their ties to the church by supporting the work of missionaries who preached Christian principles — including the duty to obey secular authorities — to pagan peoples and by allying themselves with the papacy against other Germanic tribes.

The Warrior-Ruler Charlemagne

The most powerful of the Carolingians was Charlemagne. Through brutal military expeditions that brought wealth and by peaceful travel, personal appearances, shrewd marital alliances, and the sheer force of his personality, Charlemagne sought to awe newly conquered peoples and rebellious domestic enemies. By around 805 the Frankish kingdom included all of continental Europe except Spain, Scandinavia, southern Italy, and the Slavic fringes of the East.

For administrative purposes, Charlemagne divided his entire kingdom into counties. Each of the approximately six hundred counties was governed by a count. As a link between local authorities and the central government, Charlemagne appointed officials called *missi dominici*, "agents of the lord king." Each year beginning in 802 two missi, usually a count and a bishop or abbot, visited assigned districts. They checked up on the counts and their districts' judicial, financial, and clerical activities. (See "Analyzing the Evidence: The Capitulary de Villis," page 228.)

In the autumn of the year 800 Charlemagne visited Rome, where on Christmas Day Pope Leo III crowned him emperor. The event had momentous consequences. In taking as his motto *Renovatio romani imperi* (Revival of the Roman Empire), Charlemagne was deliberately perpetuating old Roman imperial ideas while identifying with the new Rome of the Christian Church. From Baghdad, the Abbasid Empire's caliph, Harun al-Rashid (r. 786–809), congratulated Charlemagne on his coronation with the gift of an elephant. The elephant survived for nearly a decade, though like everyone else at Charlemagne's capital of Aachen (AH-ken) on the western border of modern Germany, it lived in a city that was far less sophisticated, healthy, and beautiful than Abbasid Baghdad. Although the Muslim caliph recognized Charlemagne as a fellow sovereign, the Byzantines regarded his papal coronation as rebellious and Charlemagne as a usurper. His crowning as emperor thus marked a decisive break between Rome and Constantinople and gave church authorities in the West proof that the imperial title could be granted only by the pope.

Charlemagne's Conquests, ca. 768–814

- ▇ Frankish Kingdom, 768
- ▢ Areas conquered by Charlemagne
- ▇ Tributary peoples
- ▇ Byzantine Empire

The Capitulary de Villis

Charlemagne and other Frankish rulers issued sets of instructions and decisions, called capitularies, to their officials on legal, military, political, and economic matters. Like all instructions or sets of rules, capitularies describe an ideal, not the way things really were, but we can still use them as sources for many aspects of life. The Capitulary de Villis, issued in about 800, describes the wide variety of activities envisioned for royal manors, which were run by individuals called stewards.

■ We desire that each steward shall make an annual statement of all our income, giving an account of our lands cultivated by the oxen which our own plowmen drive and of our lands which the tenants of farms ought to plow; of the pigs, of the rents, of the obligations and fines; of the game taken in our forests without our permission; of the various compositions [things that have been made]; of the mills, of the forest, of the fields, of the bridges and ships; of the free men and the districts under obligations to our treasury; of markets, vineyards, and those who owe wine to us; of the hay, firewood, torches, planks, and other kinds of lumber; of the waste lands; of the vegetables, millet, panic [a type of millet]; of the wool, flax, and hemp; of the fruits of the trees; of the nut trees, larger and smaller; of the grafted trees of all kinds; of the gardens; of the turnips; of the fish ponds; of the hides, skins, and horns; of the honey and wax; of the fat, tallow [fat used for candles], and soap; of the mulberry wine, cooked wine, mead, vinegar, beer, and wine, new and old; of the new grain and the old; of the hens and eggs; of the geese; of the number of fishermen, workers in metal, sword makers, and shoemakers; of the bins and boxes; of the turners and saddlers; of the forges and mines, — that is, of iron, lead, or other substances; of the colts and fillies. They shall make all these known to us, set forth separately and in order, at Christ-

mas, so that we may know what and how much of each thing we have.

The greatest care must be taken that whatever is prepared or made with the hands, — that is, bacon, smoked meat, sausage, partially salted meat, wine, vinegar, mulberry wine, cooked wine, garum [fermented fish sauce], mustard, cheese, butter, malt, beer, mead, honey, wax, flour, — all should be prepared and made with the greatest cleanliness.

Each steward on each of our domains shall always have, for the sake of ornament, peacocks, pheasants, ducks, pigeons, partridges, and turtle-doves. . . .

For our women's work they are to give at the proper time, as has been ordered, the materials [for cloth-making], — that is, the linen, wool, woad [for making blue dye], vermilion [for making red dye], madder [for making yellow dye], wool combs, teasels, soap, grease, vessels, and the other objects which are necessary. . . .

Each steward shall have in his district good workmen, namely, blacksmiths, a goldsmith, a silversmith, shoemakers, turners, carpenters, sword makers, fishermen, fowlers, soap makers, men who know how to make beer, cider, perry [pear cider], or other kind of liquor good to drink, bakers to make pastry for our table, net makers who know how to make nets for hunting, fishing, and fowling, and other sorts of workmen too numerous to be designated.

QUESTIONS FOR ANALYSIS

1. What tasks were men expected to do on Charlemagne's estates? What tasks were seen as women's work?
2. How does this listing of the work on medieval estates support the idea that the Carolingian economy was more localized than the economy of the Roman Empire had been? (See "Rome and the Provinces" in Chapter 6.)

Source: James Harvey Robinson, ed., *Readings in European History*, vol. 1 (Boston: Ginn and Company, 1904), pp. 137–139.

As he built an empire through conquest and strategic alliances, Charlemagne also set in motion a cultural revival that later historians called the "Carolingian Renaissance." The Carolingian Renaissance was a rebirth of interest in, study of, and preservation of the language, ideas, and achievements of classical Greece and Rome. Scholars at Charlemagne's capital of Aachen copied Greco-Roman and Christian books and manuscripts and created libraries housed in churches and monasteries. Furthermore, Charlemagne urged monasteries to promote Christian learning.

Charlemagne and His Wife This illumination from a ninth-century manuscript portrays Charlemagne with one of his wives. Marriage was an important tool of diplomacy for Charlemagne, and he had a number of wives and concubines. (Abbey Library, Sankt Paul im Lavanttal, Austria/Erich Lessing/Art Resource, NY)

Charlemagne left his vast empire to his sole surviving son, Louis the Pious (r. 814–840), who attempted to keep the empire intact. This proved to be impossible. Members of the nobility engaged in plots and open warfare against the emperor, often allying themselves with one of Louis's three sons. In 843, shortly after Louis's death, those sons agreed to the **Treaty of Verdun**, which divided the empire into three parts: Charles the Bald received the western part, Lothair the middle and the title of emperor, and Louis the eastern part, from which he acquired the title "the German." Though of course no one knew it at the time, this treaty set the pattern for political boundaries in Europe that have been maintained through today, including the modern states of Germany, France, and Italy. Other than in brief periods under Napoleon and Hitler, Europe would never again see as large a unified state as it had under Charlemagne, which is one reason he has become a symbol of European unity in the twenty-first century.

The weakening of central power was hastened by invasions and migrations from the north, south, and east. Thus Charlemagne's empire ended in much the same way that the Roman Empire had earlier, from a combination of internal weakness and external pressure.

The Treaty of Verdun, 843

Treaty of Verdun A treaty ratified in 843 that divided Charlemagne's territories among his three surviving grandsons; their kingdoms set the pattern for the modern states of Germany, France, and Italy.

Chapter Summary

During the sixth and seventh centuries the Byzantine Empire survived waves of attacks, owing to effective military leadership and to fortifications around Constantinople. Byzantine emperors organized and preserved Roman institutions, and the Byzantine Empire survived until 1453. The emperor Justinian oversaw creation of a new uniform code of Roman law. The Byzantines prized education, and because of them many aspects of ancient Greek thought survived to influence the intellectual life of the Muslim world and eventually that of western Europe.

Christianity gained the support of the fourth-century emperors, and the church gradually adopted the Roman system of hierarchical organization. The church possessed able administrators and leaders. Bishops expanded their activities, and in the fifth century the bishops of Rome, taking the title "pope," began to stress their supremacy over other Christian communities. Monasteries offered opportunities for individuals to develop deeper spiritual devotion and also provided a model of Christian living and places for education and learning. Christian thinkers reinterpreted the classics in a Christian sense, incorporating elements of Greek and Roman philosophy into Christian teachings.

Barbarian groups migrated throughout Europe and Central Asia beginning in the second century. Among barbarians, the basic social unit was the tribe, made up of kin groups and led by a tribal chieftain. Missionaries and priests persuaded pagan and illiterate peoples to accept Christianity. Most barbarian kingdoms were weak and short-lived, though the kingdom of the Franks was relatively more unified and powerful. Rulers first in the Merovingian dynasty, and then in the Carolingian, used military victories, carefully calculated marriage alliances, and the help of the church to enhance their authority. Carolingian government reached the peak of its power under Charlemagne, who brought much of Europe under his authority through military conquest and strategic alliances.

CONNECTIONS

For centuries the end of the Roman Empire in the West was seen as a major turning point in history: the fall of the sophisticated and educated classical world to uncouth and illiterate tribes, and the beginning of a "Dark Ages" that would last for centuries. Over the last several decades, however, many historians have put a greater emphasis on continuities. Barbarian kings relied on officials trained in Roman law, and Latin remained the language of scholarly communication and the Christian Church. Greco-Roman art and architecture still adorned the land, and people continued to use Roman roads, aqueducts, and buildings. In eastern Europe and western Asia, the Byzantine Empire preserved the traditions of the Roman Empire and protected the intellectual heritage of Greco-Roman culture for another millennium.

In the middle of the era covered in this chapter, a new force emerged that had a dramatic impact on much of Europe and western Asia — Islam. In the seventh and eighth centuries Sassanid Persia, much of the Byzantine Empire, and the barbarian kingdoms in the Iberian Peninsula fell to Arab forces motivated by this new religion. As we have seen in this chapter, a reputation as victors over Islam helped the Franks establish the most powerful state in Europe. As we will see when we pick up the story of Europe again in Chapter 14, Islam continued to shape European culture and politics in subsequent centuries. In terms of world history, the expansion of Islam may have been an even more dramatic turning point than the fall of the Roman Empire. Here, too, however, there were continuities, as the Muslims adopted and adapted Greek, Byzantine, and Persian political and cultural institutions.

CHAPTER 8   Review and Explore

Identify Key Terms

Identify and explain the significance of each item below.

Justinian's Code (p. 208)

dioceses (p. 211)

heresy (p. 212)

popes (p. 212)

Orthodox Church (p. 213)

sacraments (p. 217)

iconoclastic controversy (p. 217)

wergeld (p. 221)

penance (p. 225)

saints (p. 225)

Merovingian (p. 226)

Carolingian (p. 226)

Treaty of Verdun (p. 229)

Review the Main Ideas

Answer the focus questions from each section of the chapter.

1. How did the Byzantine Empire preserve the legacy of Rome? (p. 206)

2. How did the Christian Church become a major force in Europe? (p. 210)

3. How did Christian thinkers adapt classical ideas to Christian teachings, and what new religious concepts and practices did they develop? (p. 215)

4. How did the barbarians shape social, economic, and political structures in Europe and western Asia? (p. 218)

5. How did the church convert barbarian peoples to Christianity? (p. 223)

6. How did the Franks build and govern a European empire? (p. 226)

Make Comparisons and Connections

Analyze the larger developments and continuities within and across chapters.

1. The end of the Roman Empire in the West in 476 has long been viewed as one of the most important turning points in history. Do you agree with this idea? Why or why not?

2. How did the Christian Church adapt to Roman and barbarian society? How was it different in 850 than it had been in 100, as discussed in Chapter 6?

3. In what ways were the spread of Buddhism (Chapter 7) and the spread of Christianity similar? In what ways were they different?

TIMELINE

Suggested Resources

BOOKS

Barbero, Allesandro. *Charlemagne: Father of a Continent.* 2004. A wonderful biography of Charlemagne and a study of the times in which he lived that argues for the complexity of his legacy.

Brown, Peter. *Augustine of Hippo*, rev. ed. 2000. The definitive biography of Saint Augustine, who is viewed here as a symbol of change.

Burns, Thomas S. *Rome and the Barbarians, 100 B.C.–400 A.D.* 2003. Argues that Germanic and Roman cultures assimilated more than they conflicted.

Clark, Gillian. *Late Antiquity: A Very Short Introduction.* 2011. A compact survey of the era, portraying it as a period of great transformation rather than simply decline.

Dunn, Marilyn. *The Emergence of Monasticism: From the Desert Fathers to the Early Middle Ages.* 2003. Focuses on the beginnings of monasticism.

Fletcher, Richard. *The Barbarian Conversion: From Paganism to Christianity.* 1998. A superbly written analysis of conversion to Christianity.

Heather, Peter. *Empires and Barbarians: The Fall of Rome and the Birth of Europe.* 2010. Evaluates the dynamics of migration and the social, economic, and ethnic interactions that created Europe.

Herrin, Judith. *The Formation of Christendom.* 1987. The best synthesis of the development of the Christian Church from the third to the ninth centuries.

Todd, Malcolm. *The Early Germans*, 2d ed. 2004. Uses archaeological and literary sources to analyze Germanic social structure, customs, and religion and to suggest implications for an understanding of migration and ethnicity.

Ward-Perkins, Bryan. *The Fall of Rome and the End of Civilization.* 2006. Uses material evidence to trace the physical destruction and economic dislocation that accompanied the barbarian migrations.

730–843 Iconoclastic controversy

768–814 Reign of Charlemagne

843 ◆
Treaty of Verdun divides
Carolingian kingdom

535–572 Byzantines reconquer and rule Italy

527–565 Reign of Justinian

ca. 500–700 Ascendency of Kingdom of Aksum **(Ch. 10)**

◆ **ca. 600** Christian missionaries convert Nubian rulers **(Ch. 10)**

◆ **639–642** Islam introduced to Africa **(Ch. 10)**

ca. 600–900 Peak of Maya civilization **(Ch. 11)**

632–750 Expansion of Islam **(Ch. 9)**

618–907 Tang Dynasty in China **(Ch. 7)**

| 600 | 700 | 800 |

Wells, Peter S. *The Barbarians Speak: How the Conquered Peoples Shaped Roman Europe.* 1999. Presents extensive evidence of Celtic and Germanic social and technical development.

Wickham, Chris. *Framing the Early Middle Ages: Europe and the Mediterranean, 400–800.* 2007. A massive yet accessible survey of economic and social changes in many regions, with great attention to ordinary people.

DOCUMENTARIES

The Dark Ages (History Channel, 2007). A blood-and-gore-filled documentary of the violence and instability of the early Middle Ages that also looks at Charlemagne and others as heroic creators of new institutions.

The Germanic Tribes: The Complete Four-Part Saga (Kultur, 2003). Using computer graphics and re-enactments, this documentary examines the settlements and religion of the German tribes as well as their warfare, and argues that they actually preserved much of the Roman legacy.

Terry Jones' Barbarians (BBC, 2006). A witty and lively four-part documentary by a member of the Monty Python comedy troupe that sees the barbarians as less important for Rome's fall than other factors.

WEBSITES

Christian Classics Ethereal Library. Hosted by Calvin College, this site has hundreds of primary sources in the public domain on all aspects of the history of Christianity and is especially strong in the writings of the church fathers, including Jerome, Ambrose, Augustine, and Benedict. **www.ccel.org**

Internet Medieval Sourcebook. The definitive location for primary sources from the Middle Ages. Most of the texts are in English and are organized chronologically and thematically.
www.fordham.edu/halsall/sbook.html

The Labyrinth: Resources for Medieval Studies. Run by Georgetown University, this site provides free access to electronic resources in medieval studies, which are organized thematically. **labyrinth.georgetown.edu**

9

The Islamic World
600–1400

Around 610 in the city of Mecca in what is now Saudi Arabia, a merchant called Muhammad had a religious vision that inspired him to preach God's revelations to the people of Mecca. By the time he died in 632, he had many followers in Arabia, and a century later his followers controlled what is now Syria, Palestine, Egypt, Iraq, Iran, northern Africa, Spain, and southern France. Within another century Muhammad's beliefs had been carried across Central Asia to the borders of China and India. The speed with which Islam spread is one of the most amazing stories in world history, and scholars have pointed to many factors that must have contributed to its success. Military victories were rooted in strong military organization and the practice of establishing garrison cities in newly conquered territories. The religious zeal of new converts certainly played an important role. So too did the political weakness of many of the governments then holding power in the lands where Islam extended, such as the Byzantine government centered in Constantinople. Commerce and trade also spread the faith of Muhammad.

Although its first adherents were nomads, Islam developed and flourished in a mercantile milieu. By land and sea, Muslim merchants transported a rich variety of goods across Eurasia. On the basis of the wealth that trade generated, a gracious, sophisticated, and cosmopolitan culture developed with centers at Baghdad and Córdoba. During the ninth, tenth, and eleventh centuries, the Islamic world witnessed enormous intellectual vitality and creativity. Muslim scholars produced important work in many disciplines, especially mathematics, medicine, and philosophy. This brilliant civilization profoundly influenced the development of both Eastern and Western civilizations.

Egyptian Man

Life remained gracious in the great cities of North Africa and the Middle East even as Islam brought new traditions. This image of a man wearing a turban and holding a cup is from a wall painting. Found in Egypt, it dates to the eleventh century, during the Fatimid caliphate.

Islamic Art Museum, Cairo, Egypt/De Agostini Picture Library/Gianni Dagli Orti/Bridgeman Images

CHAPTER PREVIEW

THE ORIGINS OF ISLAM
From what kind of social and economic environment did Muhammad arise, and what did he teach?

ISLAMIC STATES AND THEIR EXPANSION   What made possible the spread of Islam, and what forms of government were established to rule Islamic lands?

FRAGMENTATION AND MILITARY CHALLENGES, 900–1400
How were the Islamic lands governed from 900 to 1400, and what new challenges did rulers face?

MUSLIM SOCIETY: THE LIFE OF THE PEOPLE   What social distinctions were important in Muslim society?

TRADE AND COMMERCE   Why did trade thrive in Islamic lands?

CULTURAL DEVELOPMENTS
What new ideas and practices emerged in the arts, sciences, education, and religion?

MUSLIM-CHRISTIAN ENCOUNTERS   How did Muslims and Christians come into contact with each other, and how did they view each other?

235

From what kind of
social and economic
environment did
Muhammad arise, and
what did he teach?

The Origins of Islam

Much of the Arabian peninsula is desert. Outside the oasis towns were Bedouin (BEH-duh-uhn) nomadic tribes who grazed sheep, goats, and camels. Though always small in number, Bedouins were politically dominant because of their toughness, solidarity, fighting traditions, possession of horses and camels, and ability to control trade and lines of communication. Mecca became the economic and cultural center of western Arabia, in part because pilgrims came to visit the Ka'ba, a temple containing a black stone thought to be a god's dwelling place. Muhammad's roots were in this region.

Arabian Social and Economic Structure

The basic social unit of the Bedouins and other Arabs was the tribe. Consisting of people connected through kinship, tribes provided protection and support and in turn expected members' total loyalty. Like the Germanic peoples in the age of their migrations (see "Migrating Peoples" in Chapter 8), Arab tribes were not static entities but rather continually evolving groups. A particular tribe might include both nomadic and sedentary members.

In northern and central Arabia in the early seventh century, tribal confederations led by their warrior elite were dominant. In the southern parts of the peninsula, however, priestly aristocracies tended to hold political power. Many oasis or market towns had a shrine to their guardian deity where the priest would try to settle disputes among warring tribes. All Arabs respected the shrines because they served as neutral places for such arbitration.

The power of the northern warrior tribes rested on their fighting skills. The southern religious aristocracy, by contrast, depended on its religious and economic power. The political genius of Muhammad was to bind together these different tribal groups into a strong, unified state.

Muhammad's Rise as a Religious Leader

Much like the earliest accounts of Jesus and the Buddha, the earliest account of the life of Muhammad (ca. 570–632) comes from oral traditions passed down among followers. According to these traditions, Muhammad was a merchant in the caravan trade who later married a wealthy widow. At about age forty Muhammad had a vision of an angelic being who commanded him to preach the revelations that God would be sending him. Muhammad began to preach to the people of Mecca, urging them to give up their idols and to submit to the one indivisible God. After his death, scribes organized the revelations jotted down or memorized by followers. In 651 they published the version of them that Muslims consider authoritative,

Page from Arabic Manuscript The aesthetic appeal of Arabic calligraphy is easy to recognize in this page from a fourteenth-century manuscript. (Edinburgh University Library, Scotland/With kind permission of the University of Edinburgh/Bridgeman Images)

Dome of the Rock, Jerusalem
Completed in 691 and revered by Muslims as the site where Muhammad ascended to Heaven, the Dome of the Rock is the oldest surviving Islamic sanctuary and, after Mecca and Medina, the holiest place in Islam. Although influenced by Byzantine and Persian architecture, it also has distinctly Arab features, such as the 700 feet of carefully selected Qur'anic inscriptions and vegetal motifs that grace the top of the outer walls. (ImageBROKER/SuperStock)

the **Qur'an** (kuh-RAHN). Muslims revere the Qur'an for its sacred message and for the beauty of its Arabic language.

For the first two or three centuries after the death of Muhammad, there was considerable debate about theological and political issues. Likewise, religious scholars had to sort out and assess the **hadith** (huh-DEETH), collections of the sayings and anecdotes about Muhammad. Muhammad's example as revealed in the hadith became the legal basis for the conduct of every Muslim. The life of Muhammad provides the "normative example," or **Sunna** (SOON-ah), for the Muslim believer.

The Tenets of Islam

Islam, the strict monotheistic faith that is based on the teachings of Muhammad, rests on the principle of the oneness and omnipotence of God (Allah). The word *Islam* means "surrender to God," and *Muslim* means "a person who submits." Muslims believe that Muhammad was the last of the prophets, completing the work begun by Abraham, Moses, and Jesus. Islam appropriates much of the Old and New Testaments of the Bible but often retells the narratives with significant shifts in meaning. Islam recognizes Moses's laws about circumcision, ritual bathing, and restrictions on eating pork and shellfish, and the Qur'an calls Christians "nearest in love" to Muslims. Muhammad insisted that he was not preaching a new message; rather, he was calling people back to the one true God, urging his contemporaries to reform their lives and return to the faith of Abraham, the first monotheist.

Unlike the Old Testament, much of which is historical narrative, or the New Testament, which is a collection of essays on the example and teachings of Jesus, the Qur'an is a collection of directives issued in God's name. Its organization is not strictly topical or chronological. To deal with seeming contradictions, later commentators explained the historical circumstances behind each revelation.

Qur'an The sacred book of Islam.

hadith Collections of the sayings of and anecdotes about Muhammad.

Sunna An Arabic term meaning "trodden path." The term refers to the deeds and sayings of Muhammad, which constitute the obligatory example for Muslim life.

The Qur'an prescribes a strict code of moral behavior. A Muslim must recite the profession of faith in God and in Muhammad as his prophet: "There is no God but God, and Muhammad is his Prophet." A believer must also pray five times a day, fast and pray during the sacred month of Ramadan, make a pilgrimage (hajj) to the holy city of Mecca once during his or her lifetime, and give alms to the Muslim poor. These fundamental obligations are known as the **Five Pillars of Islam**.

Islam forbids alcoholic beverages and gambling. It condemns usury in business — that is, lending money and charging the borrower interest — and taking advantage of market demand for products to raise prices. Muslim jurisprudence condemned licentious behavior by both men and women and specified the same punishments for both.

As on the Christian Judgment Day, on the Islamic Judgment Day God will separate the saved and the damned. The Qur'an describes in detail the frightful tortures with which God will punish the damned and the heavenly rewards of the saved and the blessed.

What made possible the spread of Islam, and what forms of government were established to rule Islamic lands?

Islamic States and Their Expansion

According to Muslim tradition, Muhammad's preaching at first did not appeal to many people — for the first three years he attracted only fourteen believers. In preaching a transformation of the social order and calling for the destruction of the idols in the Ka'ba, Muhammad challenged the power of the local elite and the pilgrimage-based economy. As a result, the townspeople of Mecca turned against him, and he and his followers were forced to flee to Medina. This *hijra* (hih-JIGH-ruh), or emigration, occurred in 622, and Muslims later dated the beginning of their era from it.

At Medina, Muhammad attracted increasing numbers of believers, many of whom were Bedouins who supported themselves by raiding caravans en route to Mecca, setting off a violent conflict between Mecca and Medina. After eight years of strife, Mecca capitulated. In this way, by the time Muhammad died in 632, he had welded together all the Bedouin tribes.

Muhammad displayed genius as both political strategist and religious teacher. He gave Arabs the idea of a unique and unified **umma** (UH-muh), or community, that consisted of all those whose bond was a common religious faith. The umma was to be a religious and political community led by Muhammad for the achievement of God's will on earth. The Islamic notion of an absolute higher authority transcended the boundaries of individual tribal units and fostered political consolidation. All authority came from God through Muhammad.

Islam's Spread Beyond Arabia

After the Prophet's death, Islam quickly spread far beyond Arabia. In the sixth century two powerful empires divided the Middle East: the Greek-Byzantine empire centered at Constantinople and the Persian-Sassanid empire concentrated at Ctesiphon (near Baghdad in present-day Iraq). The Byzantine Empire stood for Hellenistic culture and championed Christianity (see Chapter 8). The Sassanid empire espoused Persian cultural traditions and favored the religious faith known as Zoroastrianism (see "The Religion of Zoroaster" in Chapter 2). From the fourth through sixth centuries the Byzantines and Sassanids fought each other fiercely, each trying to

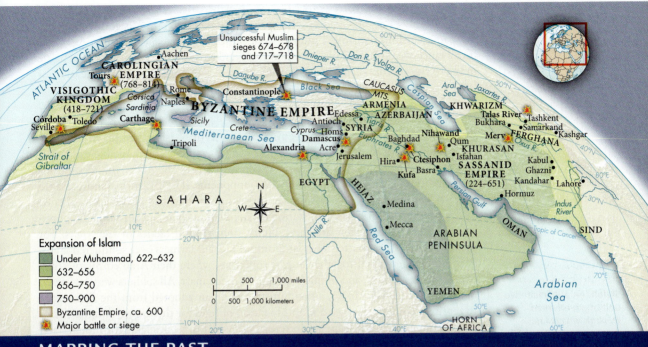

MAPPING THE PAST

MAP 9.1 The Expansion of Islam, 622–900 The rapid expansion of Islam in a relatively short span of time testifies to the Arabs' superior fighting skills, religious zeal, and economic ambition as well as to their enemies' weakness. Plague, famine, and political troubles in Sassanid Persia contributed to Muslim victory there.

ANALYZING THE MAP Trace the routes of the spread of Islam by time period. How fast did it spread? How similar were the climates of the regions that became Muslim?

CONNECTIONS Which were the most powerful and populous of the societies that were absorbed into the Islamic world? What regions or societies were more resistant?

expand its territories at the expense of the other and to control and tax the rich trade coming from Arabia and the Indian Ocean region. Many peripheral societies were drawn into the conflict. The resulting disorder facilitated the growth of Islamic states.

　　The second and third successors of Muhammad, Umar (r. 634–644) and Uthman (r. 644–656), launched a two-pronged attack against the Byzantine and Sassanid Empires. One force moved north from Arabia against the Byzantine provinces of Syria and Palestine (see Map 8.1, page 206). From Syria, the Muslims conquered the rich province of Egypt. Simultaneously, Arab armies swept into the Sassanid empire. The Muslim defeat of the Persians at Nihawand in 642 signaled the collapse of this empire (Map 9.1).

　　The Muslims continued their drive eastward and in the mid-seventh century occupied the province of Khurasan. By 700 the Muslims had crossed the Oxus River and swept toward Kabul, today the capital of Afghanistan. They then penetrated Kazakhstan and seized Tashkent. From southern Persia, a Muslim force marched into the Indus Valley in northwest India in 713 and founded an Islamic community there.

To the west, Arab forces moved across North Africa and crossed the Strait of Gibraltar. In 711 at the Guadalete River they easily defeated the Visigothic kingdom of Spain. Muslims controlled most of Spain until the thirteenth century. Advances into France were stopped in 732 when the Franks defeated Arab armies in a battle near the city of Tours, and Muslim occupation of parts of southern France did not last long.

Reasons for the Spread of Islam

By the beginning of the eleventh century the crescent of Islam had flown from the Iberian heartlands to northern India. How can this rapid and remarkable expansion be explained? Most historians point to a combination of the Arabs' military advantages and the political weaknesses of their opponents. The Byzantine and Sassanid Empires had just fought a grueling century-long war and had also been weakened by the plague, which hit urban, stationary populations harder than nomadic populations. Equally important are the military strength and tactics of the Arabs. For example, rather than scattering as landlords of peasant farmers over conquered lands, Arab soldiers remained together in garrison cities, where their Arab ethnicity, tribal organization, religion, and military success set them apart. All soldiers were registered in the **diwān** (dih-WAHN), an administrative organ adopted from the Persians or Byzantines. Soldiers received a monthly ration of food for themselves and their families and an annual cash stipend. In return, they had to be available for military service. Fixed salaries, regular pay, and the lure of battlefield booty attracted rugged tribesmen from Arabia.

diwān An administrative unit of government through which Arab soldiers were registered during the early years of the spread of Islam.

The Caliphate and the Split Between Shi'a and Sunni Alliances

When Muhammad died in 632, he left a large Muslim umma, but this community stood in danger of disintegrating into separate tribal groups. Neither the Qur'an nor the Sunna offered guidance concerning the succession.

In this crisis, according to tradition, a group of Muhammad's ablest followers elected Abu Bakr (573–634), the Prophet's father-in-law and close supporter, and hailed him as caliph (KAY-lihf), a term combining the ideas of leader, successor, and deputy (of the Prophet). In the two years of his rule (632–634), Abu Bakr governed on the basis of his personal prestige within the Muslim umma. He sent out military expeditions, collected taxes, dealt with tribes on behalf of the entire community, and led the community in prayer.

Gradually, under Abu Bakr's first three successors, Umar (r. 634–644), Uthman (r. 644–656), and Ali (r. 656–661), the caliphate (KAL-uh-fate) emerged as an institution. Umar succeeded in exerting his authority over the Bedouin tribes involved in ongoing conquests. Uthman asserted the right of the caliph to protect the economic interests of the entire umma. Also, Uthman's publication of the definitive text of the Qur'an showed his concern for the unity of the umma. However, Uthman was from a Mecca family that had resisted the Prophet until the capitulation of Mecca in 630, and he aroused resentment when he gave favors to members of his family. Opposition to Uthman coalesced around Ali, and when Uthman was assassinated in 656, Ali was chosen to succeed him.

Uthman's cousin Mu'awiya, a member of the Umayyad family who had built a power base as governor of Syria, refused to recognize Ali as caliph. In the ensuing civil

Ivory Chest of Pamplona, Spain The court of the Spanish Umayyads prized small, intricately carved ivory chests, often made in a royal workshop and used to store precious perfumes. This exquisite side panel depicts an eleventh-century caliph flanked by two attendants. An inscription on the front translates as "In the Name of God. Blessings from God, goodwill, and happiness." (Museo de Navarra, Pamplona, Spain/photo: Markus Bassler, © Bildarchiv Monheim GmbH/Alamy Stock Photo)

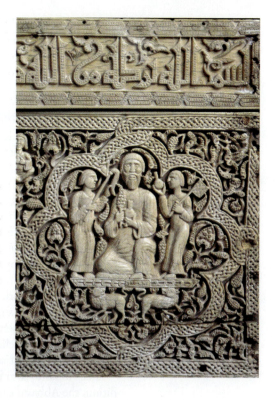

war Ali was assassinated, and Mu'awiya (r. 661–680) assumed the caliphate. Mu'awiya founded the Umayyad Dynasty and shifted the capital of the Islamic state from Medina in Arabia to Damascus in Syria. Although electing caliphs remained the Islamic ideal, beginning with Mu'awiya, the office of caliph increasingly became hereditary. Two successive dynasties, the Umayyad (661–750) and the Abbasid (750–1258), held the caliphate.

From its inception the caliphate rested on the theoretical principle that Muslim political and religious unity transcended tribalism. Mu'awiya sought to enhance the power of the caliphate by making tribal leaders dependent on him for concessions and special benefits. At the same time, his control of a loyal and well-disciplined army enabled him to take the caliphate in an authoritarian direction. Through intimidation he forced the tribal leaders to accept his son Yazid as his heir, thereby establishing the dynastic principle of succession.

The assassination of Ali and the assumption of the caliphate by Mu'awiya had another profound consequence. It gave rise to a fundamental division in the umma and in Muslim theology. Ali had claimed the caliphate on the basis of family ties — he was Muhammad's cousin and son-in-law. When Ali was murdered, his followers argued that Ali had been the Prophet's designated successor — partly because of the blood tie, partly because Muhammad had designated Ali **imam** (ih-MAHM), or leader in community prayer. These supporters of Ali were called **Shi'a** (SHEE-uh), meaning "supporters" or "partisans" of Ali (Shi'a are also known as Shi'ites). In succeeding generations, opponents of the Umayyad Dynasty emphasized their blood descent from Ali and claimed to possess divine knowledge that Muhammad had given them as his heirs.

Those who accepted Mu'awiya as caliph insisted that the central issue was adhering to the practices and beliefs of the umma based on the precedents of the Prophet. They came to be called **Sunnis** (SOO-neez), which derived from *Sunna* (examples from Muhammad's life). When a situation arose for which the Qur'an offered no solution, Sunni scholars searched for a precedent in the Sunna, which gained an authority comparable to that of the Qur'an itself.

Both Sunnis and Shi'a maintain that authority within Islam lies first in the Qur'an and then in the Sunna. Who interprets these sources? Shi'a claim that the imam does, for he is invested with divine grace and insight. Sunnis insist that interpretation comes from the consensus of the **ulama**, the group of religious scholars.

imam The leader in community prayer.

Shi'a Arabic term meaning "supporters of Ali"; they make up one of the two main divisions of Islam.

Sunnis Members of the larger of the two main divisions of Islam; the division between Sunnis and Shi'a began in a dispute about succession to Muhammad, but over time many differences in theology developed.

ulama A group of religious scholars whom Sunnis trust to interpret the Qur'an and the Sunna.

Throughout the Umayyad period, the Shi'a constituted a major source of discontent. They condemned the Umayyads as worldly and sensual rulers, in contrast to the pious true successors of Muhammad. A rival Sunni clan, the Abbasid (uh-BA-suhd), exploited the situation, agitating the Shi'a and encouraging dissension among tribal factions.

The Abbasid Caliphate

In 747 the Abbasid leader Abu' al-Abbas led a rebellion against the Umayyads, and in 750 he won general recognition as caliph. Damascus had served as the headquarters of Umayyad rule. Abu' al-Abbas's successor, al-Mansur (r. 754–775), founded the city of Baghdad in 762 and made it his capital. Thus the geographical center of the caliphate shifted eastward to former Sassanid territories. The first three Abbasid caliphs crushed their opponents, turned against many of their supporters, and created a new ruling elite drawn from newly converted Persian families that had traditionally served the ruler. The Abbasid revolution established a basis for rule and citizenship more cosmopolitan and Islamic than the narrow, elitist, and Arab basis that had characterized Umayyad government.

The Abbasids worked to identify their rule with Islam. They patronized the ulama, built mosques, and supported the development of Islamic scholarship. Although at first Muslims represented only a small minority of the conquered peoples, Abbasid rule provided the religious-political milieu in which Islam gained, over time, the allegiance of the vast majority of the populations from Spain to Afghanistan.

The Abbasids also borrowed heavily from Persian culture. Following Persian tradition, the Abbasid caliphs claimed to rule by divine right, as reflected in the change of their title from "successor of the Prophet" to "deputy of God." A majestic palace with hundreds of attendants and elaborate court ceremonies deliberately isolated the caliph from the people he ruled. Subjects had to bow before the caliph and kiss the ground, symbolizing his absolute power.

Under the third caliph, Baghdad emerged as a flourishing commercial, artistic, and scientific center. Its population of about a million people created a huge demand for goods and services, and Baghdad became an entrepôt (trading center) for textiles, slaves, and foodstuffs coming from Oman, East Africa, and India. The city also became intellectually influential. Harun al-Rashid organized the translation of Greek medical and philosophical texts. As part of this effort the Christian scholar Hunayn Ibn Ishaq (808–873) translated Galen's medical works into Arabic and made Baghdad a center for the study and practice of medicine. Likewise, impetus was given to the study of astronomy, as Muslim astronomers sought to correct and complement Ptolemaic astronomy. Above all, studies in Qur'anic textual analysis, history, poetry, law, and philosophy—all in Arabic—reflected the development of a distinctly Islamic literary and scientific culture.

An important innovation of the Abbasids was the use of slaves as soldiers. The caliph al-Mu'tasim (r. 833–842) acquired several thousand Turkish slaves who were converted to Islam and employed in military service. Scholars have offered varied explanations for this practice: that the use of slave soldiers was a response to a manpower shortage; that as highly skilled horsemen, the Turks had military skills superior to those of the Arabs and other peoples; and that al-Mu'tasim felt he could trust the Turks more than the Arabs, Persians, Khurasans, and other recruits. In any case, slave soldiers—later including Slavs, Indians, and sub-Saharan blacks—became a standard feature of Muslim armies in the Middle East until the twentieth century.

Administration of the Islamic Territories

The Islamic conquests brought into being a new imperial system. At the head stood the caliph, who led military campaigns against unbelievers. Theoretically, he had the ultimate responsibility for the interpretation of the sacred law. In practice, however, the ulama interpreted the law as revealed in the Qur'an and the Sunna. In the course of time, the ulama's interpretations constituted a rich body of law, the **shari'a** (shuh-REE-uh), which covered social, criminal, political, commercial, and religious matters. The *qadis* (KAH-dees), or judges, who were well versed in the sacred law, carried out the judicial functions of the state. Nevertheless, Muslim law prescribed that all people have access to the caliph, and he set aside special times for hearing petitions and for directly redressing grievances.

shari'a Muslim law, which covers social, criminal, political, commercial, and religious matters.

The central administrative organ was the diwān, which collected the taxes that paid soldiers' salaries and financed charitable and public works, such as aid to the poor and the construction of mosques, irrigation works, and public baths. Another important undertaking was a relay network established to rapidly convey letters and intelligence reports between the capital and distant outposts.

The early Abbasid period witnessed considerable economic expansion and population growth, complicating the work of government. New and specialized departments emerged, each with a hierarchy of officials. The most important new official was the vizier (vuh-ZEER), a position that the Abbasids adopted from the Persians. The vizier was the caliph's chief assistant. Depending on the caliph's personality, viziers could acquire extensive power, and some used their offices for personal gain. Away from the capital, **emirs**, or governors, were given overall responsibility for public order, maintenance of the armed forces, and tax collection. Below them, experienced native officials often remained in office.

emirs Arab governors who were given overall responsibility for public order, maintenance of the armed forces, and tax collection.

Fragmentation and Military Challenges, 900–1400

In theory, the caliph and his central administration governed the whole empire, but in practice, the many parts of the empire enjoyed considerable local independence. At the same time, the enormous distance between many provinces and the imperial capital made it difficult for the caliph to prevent provinces from breaking away. Consequently, regional dynasties emerged in much of the Islamic world, including Spain, Persia, Central Asia, northern India, and Egypt. None of these states repudiated Islam, but they did stop sending tax revenues to Baghdad. Moreover, states frequently fought costly wars against their neighbors in their attempts to expand. Sometimes these conflicts were worsened by Sunni-Shi'a antagonisms. All these developments, as well as invasions by Turks and Mongols, posed challenges to central Muslim authority.

How were the Islamic lands governed from 900 to 1400, and what new challenges did rulers face?

Breakaway Territories and Shi'a Gains

One of the first territories to break away from the Baghdad-centered caliphate was Spain. In 755 an Umayyad prince who had escaped death at the hands of the Abbasids

The Patio of the Lions at Alhambra, Fourteenth Century The fortress that the Moorish rulers of Spain built at Granada is considered one of the masterpieces of Andalusian art, notable for the fine carving of geometrical designs and Arabic calligraphy. (George Holton/Science Source)

and fled to Spain set up an independent regime at Córdoba (see Map 9.1). Other territories soon followed. In 800 the emir in Tunisia in North Africa set himself up as an independent ruler and refused to place the caliph's name on the local coinage. And in 820 Tahir, the son of a slave, was rewarded with the governorship of Khurasan because he had supported the caliphate. Once he took office, Tahir ruled independently of Baghdad.

In 946 a Shi'a Iranian clan overran Iraq and occupied Baghdad. The caliph was forced to recognize the clan's leader as commander in chief and to allow the celebration of Shi'a festivals—though the caliph and most of the people were Sunnis. A year later the caliph was accused of plotting against his new masters, snatched from his throne, dragged through the streets, and blinded. Blinding was a practice adopted from the Byzantines as a way of rendering a ruler incapable of carrying out his duties. This incident marked the practical collapse of the Abbasid caliphate. Abbasid caliphs, however, remained as puppets of a series of military commanders and symbols of Muslim unity until the Mongols killed the last Abbasid caliph in 1258 (see "The Mongol Invasions").

The Fatimid Caliphate, 909–1171

In another Shi'a advance, the Fatimids, a Shi'a dynasty that claimed descent from Muhammad's daughter Fatima, conquered North Africa and then expanded into the Abbasid province of Egypt, founding the city of Cairo as their capital in 969. For the next century or so, Shi'a were in ascendancy in much of the western Islamic world.

The Ascendancy of the Turks

In the mid-tenth century the Turks began to enter the Islamic world in large numbers. First appearing in Mongolia in the sixth century, groups of Turks, such as the Seljuks, gradually appeared across the grasslands of Eurasia. Skilled horsemen, they became prime targets for Muslim slave raids, as they made good slave soldiers. Once the Turks understood that Muslims could not be captured for slaves, more and more of them converted to Sunni Islam and often became *ghazi*, frontier raiders, who attacked unconverted Turks to capture slaves.

In the 1020s and 1030s Seljuk Turks overran Persia and then pushed into Iraq and Syria. Baghdad fell to them on December 18, 1055, and the caliph became a puppet of the Turkish sultan. The Turkish elite rapidly gave up pastoralism and took up the sedentary lifestyle of the people they governed.

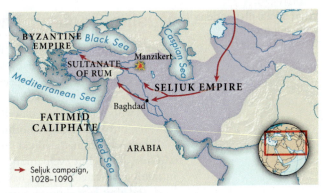

The Seljuk Empire in 1000

The Turks brought badly needed military strength to the Islamic world. They played a major part in recovering Jerusalem after it was held for nearly a century, from 1099 to 1187, by the European Crusaders (who had fought to take Christian holy lands back from the Muslims; see "The Course of the Crusades" in Chapter 14). The influx of Turks from 950 to 1100 also helped provide a new expansive dynamic. At the Battle of Manzikert in 1071, Seljuk Turks broke through Byzantine border defenses, opening Anatolia to Turkish migration. Over the next couple of centuries, perhaps a million Turks entered the area — including bands of ghazis and dervishes (Sufi brotherhoods; see "The Mystical Tradition of Sufism").

The Mongol Invasions

In the early thirteenth century the Mongols arrived in the Middle East. Originally from the grasslands of Mongolia, in 1206 they proclaimed Chinggis Khan (ca. 1162–1227) as their leader, and he welded Mongol, Tartar, and Turkish tribes into a strong confederation that rapidly subdued neighboring settled societies (see "Chinggis Khan and the Mongol Empire" in Chapter 12).

In 1219–1221, when the Mongols first reached the Islamic lands, the areas from Persia through the Central Asian cities of Herat and Samarkand were part of the kingdom of Khwarizm. The ruler—the son of a Turkish slave who had risen to governor of a province—had the audacity to execute Chinggis's envoy, and Chinggis retaliated with a force of a hundred thousand soldiers that sacked city after city, often slaughtering the residents or enslaving them and sending them to Mongolia. Millions are said to have died. The irrigation systems that were needed for agriculture in this dry region had been neglected for some time, and with the Mongol invasions they suffered a fatal blow.

Not many Mongol forces were left in Persia after the campaign of 1219–1221, and another army, sent in 1237, captured the Persian city of Isfahan. In 1251 the decision was taken to push farther west, taking Baghdad in 1258 and killing the last Abbasid caliph. Mamluk soldiers from Egypt, however, were able to withstand the Mongols and prevent them from taking Egypt and the Islamic lands in North Africa. The desert ecology of the region did not provide suitable support for the Mongol armies, which required five horses for each soldier.

The Mongols ruled the central Muslim lands (referred to as the Il-khanate) for eighty years. In 1295 the Mongol ruler Ghazan embraced Islam and worked for the revival of Muslim culture. As the Turks had done earlier, the Mongols, once converted, injected new vigor into the faith and spirit of Islam. In the Il-khanate the Mongols governed through Persian viziers and native financial officials.

Muslim Society: The Life of the People

When the Prophet appeared, Arab society consisted of independent Bedouin tribal groups loosely held together by loyalty to a strong leader and by the belief that all members of a tribe were descended from a common ancestor. Heads of families elected the sheik, or tribal chief. He was usually chosen from among elite warrior families who believed their bloodlines made them superior. According to the Qur'an, however, birth counted for nothing; piety was the only criterion for honor.

When Muhammad defined social equality, he was thinking about equality among Muslims alone. But even among Muslims, a sense of pride in ancestry could not be instantly eradicated. Claims based on birth remained strong among the first Muslims, and after Islam spread outside of Arabia, full-blooded Arab tribesmen regarded themselves as superior to foreign converts.

The Social Hierarchy

In the Umayyad period, Muslim society was distinctly hierarchical. At the top of the hierarchy were the caliph's household and the ruling Arab Muslims who constituted the ruling elite. It was a relatively small group, greatly outnumbered by Muslim villagers and country people.

Converts constituted the second class in Islamic society, one that grew slowly over time. Converts to Islam had to attach themselves to one of the Arab tribes in a subordinate capacity. From the Muslim converts eventually came the members of the commercial and learned professions—merchants, traders, teachers, doctors, artists, and interpreters of the shari'a. Over the centuries, Berber, Copt, Persian, Aramaean, and other converts to Islam intermarried with their Muslim conquerors. Gradually, assimilation united peoples of various ethnic backgrounds.

dimmis A term meaning "protected peoples"; they included Jews, Christians, and Zoroastrians.

Dhimmis (zih-MEEZ)—including Jews, Christians, and Zoroastrians—formed the third stratum. Considered "protected peoples" because they worshipped only one God, they were allowed to practice their religions, maintain their houses of worship, and conduct their business affairs as long as they gave unequivocal recognition to Muslim political supremacy and paid a small tax. Because many Jews and Christians were well educated, they were often appointed to high positions in provincial capitals as well as in Damascus and Baghdad. However, their social position deteriorated during the Crusades and the Mongol invasions, when there was a general rise of religious loyalties. At those times, Muslims suspected the dhimmis, often rightly, of collaborating with the enemies of Islam.

How did the experience of Jews under Islam compare with that of Jews living in Christian Europe? Recent scholarship shows that in Europe Jews were first marginalized in the Christian social order and then completely expelled from it. In Islam Jews, though marginalized, participated fully in commercial and professional activities, some attaining economic equality with their Muslim counterparts. Islamic culture was urban and commercial and gave merchants considerable respect.

Slavery

Slavery had long existed in the ancient Middle East, and Muslim expansion ensured a steady flow of slaves captured in war. The Qur'an accepted slavery much the way the Old and New Testaments did. But the Qur'an prescribes just and humane treatment of slaves, explicitly encourages the freeing of slaves, and urges owners whose slaves ask for their freedom to give them the opportunity to buy it. In fact, the freeing of slaves was thought to pave the way to paradise.

Women slaves worked as cooks, cleaners, laundresses, and nursemaids. A few performed as singers, musicians, dancers, and reciters of poetry. Many female slaves also served as concubines. Not only rulers but also high officials and rich merchants owned many concubines. Down the economic ladder, artisans and tradesmen often had concubines who assumed domestic as well as sexual duties.

According to tradition, the seclusion of women in a harem protected their virtue, and when men had the means the harem was secured by eunuch (castrated) guards. Muslims also employed eunuchs as secretaries, tutors, and commercial agents, possibly because eunuchs were said to be more manageable and dependable than men with ordinary desires. Male slaves, eunuchs or not, were also set to work as longshoremen on the docks, as oarsmen on ships, in construction crews, in workshops, and in gold and silver mines. Male slaves also fought as soldiers.

Slavery in the Islamic world differed in at least two fundamental ways from the slavery later practiced in the Americas. First, race had no particular connection to slavery among Muslims, who were as ready to take slaves from Europe as from Africa. Second, slavery in the Islamic world was not the basis for plantation agriculture, as it was in the southern United States, the Caribbean, and Brazil in the eighteenth and nineteenth centuries. Slavery was rarely hereditary in the Islamic world. Most slaves who were taken from non-Muslim peoples later converted, which often led to emancipation. To give Muslim slavery the most positive possible interpretation, one could say that it provided a means to fill certain socioeconomic and military needs and that it assimilated rather than segregated outsiders.

Slaves Dancing A few women slaves performed as dancers, singers, and musicians, usually before an elite audience of rulers, officials, and wealthy merchants. This reconstructed wall painting from the ninth century adorned a harem in a royal palace in Samarra. (bpk Bildagentur/Art Resource, NY)

Women in Classical Islamic Society

Before Islam, Arab tribal law gave women virtually no legal powers. Parents accepted payments for their daughters, and their husbands could terminate the union at will. Also, women had virtually no property or succession rights. Seen from this perspective, the Qur'an sought to improve the social position of women.

The Qur'an, like the religious scriptures of other traditions, emphasizes moral precepts, not descriptions of social practice, and the text is open to different interpretations. Modern scholars tend to agree that the Islamic sacred book intended women to be the spiritual equals of men and gave them considerable economic rights. In the early Umayyad period, moreover, women played active roles in the religious, economic, and political life of the community. They owned property, traveled widely,

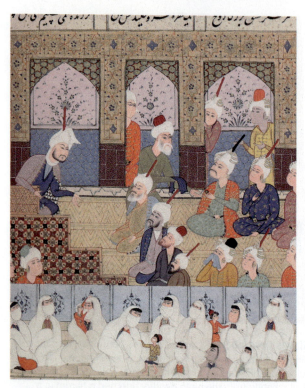

Separating Men and Women in a Mosque In this mid-sixteenth-century illustration of the interior of a mosque, a screen separates the women, who are wearing veils and tending children, from the men. The women can hear what is being said, but the men cannot see them. (© Bodleian Libraries 2017, Ouseley Add 24 folio 55v/The University of Oxford, UK/Art Resource, NY)

and participated with men in public religious rituals and observances.

The Islamic ideal of women and men having equal value to the community did not last. In the Abbasid period the practices of the Byzantine and Persian lands that had been conquered, including seclusion of women, were absorbed. The supply of slave women increased substantially. Some scholars speculate that as wealth replaced ancestry as the main criterion of social status, men more and more viewed women as possessions, as a form of wealth. As society changed, the precepts of the Qur'an were interpreted in more patriarchal ways.

Men were also seen as dominant in their marriages. The Qur'an states that "men are in charge of women because Allah hath made the one to excel the other, and because they (men) spend of their property (for the support of women). So good women are obedient, guarding in secret that which Allah hath guarded."[1] A thirteenth-century commentator on this passage argued from it that women are incapable of and unfit for any public duties, such as participating in religious rites, giving evidence in the law courts, or being involved in any public political decisions.

The practices of veiling and seclusion of women have their roots in pre-Islamic times, and they took firm hold in classical Islamic society. As Arab conquerors subjugated various peoples, they adopted some of the vanquished peoples' customs. Veiling was probably of Byzantine or Persian origin. The practice of secluding women also derives from Arab contacts with Persia and other Eastern cultures. By 800 women in more prosperous households stayed out of sight. The harem became another symbol of male prestige and prosperity, as well as a way to distinguish upper-class from lower-class women.

Marriage, the Family, and Sexuality

As in medieval Europe and traditional India and China, marriage in Muslim society was considered too important an undertaking to be left to the romantic emotions of the young. Families or guardians, not the prospective bride and groom, identified suitable partners and finalized the contract. Because it was absolutely essential that the bride be a virgin, marriages were arranged shortly after puberty. Husbands were commonly ten to fifteen years older. Youthful marriages ensured a long period of fertility.

A wife's responsibilities depended on the wealth and occupation of her husband. A farmer's wife helped in the fields, ground the corn, carried water, prepared food, and did the myriad tasks necessary in rural life. Shopkeepers' wives in the cities sometimes helped in business. In an upper-class household, the wife supervised servants, looked after all domestic arrangements, and did whatever was needed for her husband's comfort.

In every case, children were the wife's special domain. A mother exercised authority over her children and enjoyed their respect. A Muslim tradition asserts that "paradise is at the mother's feet." Thus, as in Chinese culture, the prestige of the young wife depended on the production of children—especially sons—as rapidly as possible. A wife's failure to have children was one of the main reasons for a man to divorce his wife or take a second wife.

Like the Jewish tradition, Muslim law permits divorce. Although divorce is allowed, it is not encouraged. One commentator cited the Prophet as saying, "The lawful thing which God hates most is divorce."[2]

In contrast to the traditional Christian view of sexual activity as inherently shameful and only a cure for lust even within marriage, Islam maintains a healthy acceptance of sexual pleasure for both males and females. The Qur'an permits a man to have four wives, provided that all are treated justly. Still, the vast majority of Muslim males were monogamous because only the wealthy could afford to support more than one wife.

Trade and Commerce

Why did trade thrive in Islamic lands?

Unlike the Christian West or the Confucian East, the Islamic world looked favorably on profit-making enterprises. According to the sayings of the Prophet: "The honest, truthful Muslim merchant will stand with the martyrs on the Day of Judgment. I commend the merchants to you, for they are the couriers of the horizons and God's trusted servants on earth."[3] The Qur'an, moreover, has no prohibition against trade with Christians or other unbelievers. In fact, non-Muslims, including the Jews of Cairo and the Armenians in the central Islamic lands, were prominent in mercantile networks.

Waterways served as the main commercial routes of the Islamic world (Map 9.2). They included the Mediterranean and Black Seas; the Caspian Sea and the Volga River, which gave access deep into Russia; the Aral Sea, from which caravans departed for China; the Gulf of Aden; and the Arabian Sea and the Indian Ocean, which linked the Persian Gulf region with eastern Africa, the Indian subcontinent, and eventually Indonesia and the Philippines.

Cairo was a major Mediterranean entrepôt for intercontinental trade. Foreign merchants sailed up the Nile to the Aswan region, traveled east from Aswan by caravan to the Red Sea, and then sailed down the Red Sea to Aden, where they entered the Indian Ocean on their way to India. They exchanged textiles, glass, gold, silver, and copper for Asian spices, dyes, and drugs and for Chinese silks and porcelains. Muslim and Jewish merchants dominated the trade with India, and all spoke and wrote Arabic. Their commercial practices included the *sakk* (the Arabic word is the root of the English *check*), an order to a banker to pay money held on account to a third party. Muslims also developed other business innovations, such as the bill of exchange, a written order from one person to another to pay a specified sum of money to a designated person or party, and the idea of the joint stock company, an

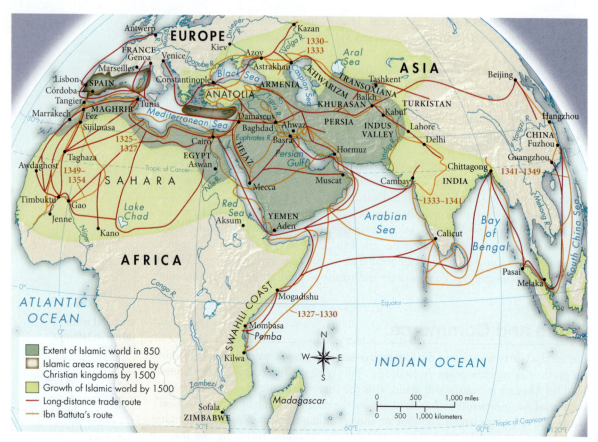

MAP 9.2 The Expansion of Islam and Its Trading Networks in the Thirteenth and Fourteenth Centuries
By 1500 Islam had spread extensively in North and East Africa, and into the Balkans, the Caucasus, Central Asia, India, and the islands of Southeast Asia. Muslim merchants played a major role in bringing their religion as they extended their trade networks. They were active in the Indian Ocean long before the arrival of Europeans.

arrangement that lets a group of people invest in a venture and share its profits (and losses) in proportion to the amount each has invested.

Trade also benefited from improvements in technology. The adoption from the Chinese of the magnetic compass, an instrument for determining directions at sea by means of a magnetic needle turning on a pivot, greatly helped navigation of the Arabian Sea and the Indian Ocean. The construction of larger ships led to a shift in long-distance cargoes from luxury goods such as pepper, spices, and drugs to bulk goods such as sugar, rice, and timber. The teak forests of western India supplied the wood for Arab ships.

Beginning in the late twelfth century Persian and Arab seamen sailed down the east coast of Africa and established trading towns between Somalia and Sofala (see "The East African City-States" in Chapter 10). These thirty to fifty urban centers controlled by merchants linked Zimbabwe in southern Africa with the Indian Ocean trade and the Middle Eastern trade.

A private ninth-century list mentions a great variety of commodities transported into and through the Islamic world by land and by sea:

Imported from India: tigers, leopards, elephants, leopard skins, red rubies, white sandal-wood, ebony, and coconuts

From China: aromatics, silk, porcelain, paper, ink, peacocks, fiery horses, saddles, felts, cinnamon

From the Byzantines: silver and gold vessels, embroidered cloths, fiery horses, slave girls, rare articles in red copper, strong locks, lyres, water engineers, specialists in plowing and cultivation, marble workers, and eunuchs

From Egypt: ambling donkeys, fine cloths, papyrus, balsam oil, and, from its mines, high-quality topaz

From the Khazars [a people living on the northern shore of the Black Sea]: slaves, slave women, armor, helmets, and hoods of mail

From Ahwaz [a city in southwestern Persia]: sugar, silk brocades, castanet players and dancing girls, kinds of dates, grape molasses, and candy.[4]

One byproduct of the extensive trade through Islamic lands was the spread of useful plants. Cotton, sugarcane, and rice spread from India to other places with suitable climates. Citrus fruits made their way to Muslim Spain from Southeast Asia and India. The value of this trade contributed to the prosperity of the Abbasid era.

Cultural Developments

Long-distance trade provided the wealth that made possible a gracious and sophisticated culture in the cities of the Islamic world. (See "Individuals in Society: Ibn Battuta," page 252.) Education helped foster achievements in the arts and sciences, and Sufism brought a new spiritual and intellectual tradition.

> **What new ideas and practices emerged in the arts, sciences, education, and religion?**

The Cultural Centers of Baghdad and Córdoba

Although cities and mercantile centers dotted the entire Islamic world, the cities of Baghdad and Córdoba, at their peak in the tenth century, stand out as the finest examples of cosmopolitan Muslim civilization. On Baghdad's streets thronged a kaleidoscope of races, creeds, costumes, and cultures. Shops and marketplaces offered a dazzling and exotic array of goods from all over the world.

The caliph Harun al-Rashid presided over a glamorous court. He invited writers, dancers, musicians, poets, and artists to live in Baghdad, and he is reputed to have rewarded one singer with one hundred thousand silver pieces for a single song. This brilliant era provided the background for the tales that appear in *The Thousand and One Nights*.

The central story of this fictional collection concerns the attempt of a new bride, Scheherazade, to keep her husband, Shahyar, legendary king of Samarkand, from killing her out of certainty that she will be unfaithful like his first wife. In efforts to delay her execution, she entertains him with one tale a night for 1,001 nights. In the end, Scheherazade's efforts succeed, and her husband pardons her. Among the tales

Ibn Battuta

IN 1354 THE SULTAN OF MOROCCO
appointed a scribe to write an account of the travels of Abu 'Abdallah Ibn Battuta (1304–1368), who between 1325 and 1354 had traveled through most of the Islamic world. The two men collaborated. The result was a travel book written in Arabic and later hailed as the richest eyewitness account of fourteenth-century Islamic culture.

Ibn Battuta was born in Tangiers to a family of legal scholars. As a youth, he studied Muslim law, gained fluency in Arabic, and acquired the qualities considered essential for a civilized Muslim gentleman: courtesy, manners, and the social polish that eases relations among people.

At age twenty-one he left Tangiers to make the hajj (pilgrimage) to Mecca. He crossed North Africa and visited Alexandria, Cairo, Damascus, and Medina. Reaching Mecca in October 1326, he immediately praised God for his safe journey, kissed the Holy Stone at the Ka'ba, and recited the ritual prayers. There he decided to see more of the world.

In the next four years Ibn Battuta traveled to Iraq and to Basra and Baghdad in Persia, then returned to Mecca before sailing down the coast of Africa as far as modern Tanzania. On the return voyage he visited Oman and the Persian Gulf region, then traveled by land across central Arabia to Mecca. Strengthened by his stay in the holy city, he decided to go to India by way of Egypt, Syria, and Anatolia; across the Black Sea to the plains of western Central Asia, detouring to see Constantinople; back to the Asian steppe; east to Khurasan and Afghanistan; and down to Delhi in northern India.

For eight years Ibn Battuta served as a judge in the service of the sultan of Delhi. In 1341 the sultan chose him to lead a diplomatic mission to China. After the expedition was shipwrecked off the southeastern coast of India, Ibn Battuta traveled through southern India, Sri Lanka, and the Maldive Islands. Then he went to China, stopping in Bengal and Sumatra before reaching the southern coast of China, then under Mongol rule. Returning to Mecca in 1346, he set off for home, getting to Morocco in 1349. After a brief trip across the Strait of Gibraltar to Granada, he undertook his last journey, by camel caravan across the Sahara to Mali

Travelers to Baghdad would have seen slave markets like this one. (Bibliothèque Nationale, Paris, France/Art Resource, NY)

in the West African Sudan (see "The Kingdom of Mali, ca. 1200–1450" in Chapter 10), returning home in 1354. Scholars estimate that he had traveled about seventy-five thousand miles.

Ibn Battuta had a driving intellectual curiosity to see and understand the world. At every stop, he sought the learned jurists and pious men at the mosques and madrasas. He marveled at the Lighthouse of Alexandria, then in ruins; at the vast harbor at Kaffa (in southern Ukraine on the Black Sea), whose two hundred Genoese ships were loaded with silks and slaves for the markets at Venice, Cairo, and Damascus; and at the elephants in the sultan's procession in Delhi, which carried machines that tossed gold and silver coins to the crowds.

Ibn Battuta must have had an iron constitution. He endured fevers, dysentery, malaria, the scorching heat of the Sahara, and the freezing cold of the steppe. His thirst for adventure was stronger than his fear of nomadic warriors and bandits on land and the dangers of storms and pirates at sea.

QUESTIONS FOR ANALYSIS

1. Trace the routes of Ibn Battuta's travels on Map 9.2.
2. How did a common Muslim culture facilitate Ibn Battuta's travels?

Source: R. E. Dunn, *The Adventures of Ibn Battuta: A Muslim Traveler of the Fourteenth Century* (Berkeley: University of California Press, 1986).

she tells him are such famous ones as "Aladdin and His Lamp," "Sinbad the Sailor," and "Ali Baba and the Forty Thieves." Though filled with folklore, the *Arabian Nights* (as it is also called) has provided many of the images through which Europeans have understood the Islamic world.

Córdoba in southern Spain competed with Baghdad for the cultural leadership of the Islamic world. With a population of about 1 million, Córdoba contained 1,600 mosques, 900 public baths, 213,177 houses for ordinary people, and 60,000 mansions for generals, officials, and the wealthy. In its 80,455 shops, 13,000 weavers produced silks, woolens, and brocades that were internationally famous. Córdoba was also a great educational center with 27 free schools and a library containing 400,000 volumes. (By contrast, the renowned Benedictine abbey of Saint-Gall in Switzerland had about 600 books.) Moreover, Córdoba's scholars made contributions in chemistry, medicine and surgery, music, philosophy, and mathematics. It was through Córdoba and Persia that the Indian game of chess entered western Europe. The contemporary Saxon nun Hroswitha of Gandersheim (d. 1000) described Córdoba as the "ornament of the world."[5]

Education and Intellectual Life

Muslim culture valued learning, especially religious learning, because knowledge provided the guidelines by which men and women should live. From the eighth century onward, formal education for young men involved reading, writing, and the study of the Qur'an, believed essential for its religious message and for its training in proper grammar and syntax.

Islam is a religion of the law, taught at **madrasas** (muh-DRA-suhs), schools for the study of Muslim law and religion. Schools were urban phenomena. Wealthy merchants endowed them, providing salaries for teachers, stipends for students, and living accommodations for both. All Islamic higher education rested on a close relationship between teacher and students, so in selecting a teacher, the student (or his father) considered the character and intellectual reputation of the teacher, not that of the institution. Students built their subsequent careers on the reputation of their teachers.

madrasa A school for the study of Muslim law and religion.

Learning depended heavily on memorization. In primary school a boy began his education by memorizing the entire Qur'an. In adolescence a student learned by heart an introductory work in one of the branches of knowledge, such as jurisprudence or grammar. Later he analyzed the texts in detail. Every class day, the teacher examined the student on the previous day's learning and determined whether the student fully understood what he had memorized. Students, of course, learned to write, for they had to record the teacher's commentary on a particular text. But the overwhelming emphasis was on the oral transmission of knowledge.

Because Islamic education focused on particular books, when the student had mastered a text to his teacher's satisfaction, the teacher issued the student a certificate stating that he had studied the book or collection of traditions with his teacher. The certificate allowed the student to transmit a text to the next generation on the authority of his teacher.

As the importance of books suggests, the Muslim transmission and improvement of papermaking techniques had special significance to education. After Chinese

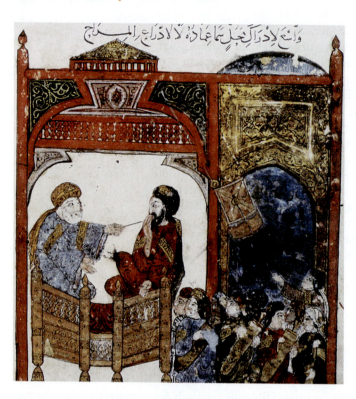

ويقول لا يزال الرجل يما عاد ولا يزاج المنهج

Teachers Disputing in a Madrasa Although Islamic education relied heavily on memorization of the Qur'an, religious scholars frequently debated the correct interpretation of a particular text. Listening to this lively disputation, the students illustrated in this 1222 book are learning to think critically and creatively. (Bibliothèque Nationale, Paris, France/Roland and Sabrina Michaud/akg-images)

papermaking techniques spread westward, Muslim papermakers improved on them by adding starch to fill the pores in the surfaces of the sheets. Even before the invention of printing, papermaking had a revolutionary impact on the collection and diffusion of knowledge.

Muslim higher education, apart from its fundamental goal of preparing men to live wisely and in accordance with God's law, aimed at preparing them to perform religious and legal functions as Qur'an — or hadith — readers; as preachers in the mosques; as professors, educators, or copyists; and especially as judges. Judges issued fatwas, or legal opinions, in the public courts; their training was in the Qur'an, hadith, or some text forming part of the shari'a.

On the issue of female education, Islamic culture was ambivalent. Tradition holds that Muhammad said, "The seeking of knowledge is a duty of every Muslim," but, because of the basic Islamic principle that "men are the guardians of women, because God has set the one over the other," the law excluded women from participating in the legal, religious, or civic occupations for which the madrasa prepared young men. Moreover, educational theorists insisted that men should study in a sexually isolated environment. Nevertheless, many young women were educated at home. According to one biographical dictionary covering the lives of 1,075 women, 411 of them had memorized the Qur'an, studied with a particular teacher, and received a certificate.

In comparing Islamic higher education during the twelfth through fourteenth centuries with that available in Europe or China at the same time (see "The Scholar-Officials and Neo-Confucianism" in Chapter 13 and "Universities and Scholasticism" in Chapter 14), there are some striking similarities and some major differences. In both Europe and the Islamic countries religious authorities ran most schools, while in China the government, local villages, and lineages ran schools, and private tutoring was very common. In the Islamic world, as in China, the personal relationship of teacher and student was seen as key to education. In Europe the reward for satisfactorily completing a course of study was a degree granted by the university. In China, at the very highest levels, the state ran a civil service examination system that rewarded achievement with appointments in the state bureaucracy. In Muslim culture, by contrast, it was not the school or the state but the individual teacher whose evaluation mattered and who granted certificates.

Still, there were also some striking similarities in the practice of education. Students in all three cultures had to master a sacred language (Latin, Arabic, or classical Chinese). In all three cultures education rested heavily on the study of basic religious, legal, or philosophical texts. Also, in all three cultures memorization played a large role in the acquisition and transmission of learning. Furthermore, teachers in all three societies lectured on particular passages, and leading teachers might disagree fiercely about the correct interpretations of a particular text, forcing students to question, to think critically, and to choose among divergent opinions. In all three societies these educational practices contributed to cultural cohesion and ties among the educated living in scattered localities.

In the Islamic world the spread of the Arabic language, not only among the educated classes but also among all the people, was the decisive element in the creation of a common culture. Recent scholarship demonstrates that after the establishment of the Islamic empire, the spread of the Arabic language was more important than religion in fostering cultural change. Whereas conversion to Islam was gradual, linguistic conversion occurred much faster. Arabic became the official language of the state and its bureaucracies in former Byzantine and Sassanid territories. Islamic rulers required tribute from monotheistic peoples—the Persians and Greeks—but they did not force them to change their religions. Conquered peoples were, however, compelled to adopt the Arabic language. In time Arabic produced a cohesive and "international" culture over a large part of the Eurasian world. Among those who wrote in Arabic was the erudite Gregory Bar-Hebraeus (1226–1286), a bishop of the Syrian Orthodox Church. He wrote widely on philosophy, poetry, language, history, and theology, sometimes in Syriac, sometimes in Arabic. (See "Global Viewpoints: Amusing Animal Stories by Syrian and Greek Authors," page 256.)

As a result of Muslim creativity and vitality, modern scholars consider the years from 800 to 1300 to be one of the most brilliant periods in the world's history. Near the beginning of this period the Persian scholar al-Khwarizmi (d. ca. 850) harmonized Greek and Indian findings to produce astronomical tables that formed the basis for later Eastern and Western research. Al-Khwarizmi also studied mathematics, and his textbook on algebra (from the Arabic *al-jabr*) was the first work in which the word *algebra* is used to mean the "transposing of negative terms in an equation to the opposite side."

Muslim medical knowledge far surpassed that of the West in this era. The Baghdad physician al-Razi (865–925), the first physician to make the clinical distinction between measles and smallpox, produced an encyclopedic treatise on medicine that was translated into Latin and circulated widely in the West. In Córdoba the great surgeon al-Zahrawi (d. 1013) produced an important work in which he discussed the cauterization of wounds (searing them with a branding iron) and the crushing of stones in the bladder. Muslim science reached its peak in the work of Ibn Sina of Bukhara (980–1037), known in the West as Avicenna. His *al-Qanun* codified all Greco-Arab medical thought, described the contagious nature of tuberculosis and the spreading of diseases, and listed 760 drugs.

Amusing Animal Stories by Syrian and Greek Authors

In thirteenth-century Syria, Gregory Bar-Hebraeus wrote not only on serious subjects such as religion and philosophy but also on more playful subjects, and his works include a large collection of amusing stories. Persian, Hebrew, Indian, and Christian wise men appear in these tales, as do animals, clowns, and thieves. The stories that feature talking animals are reminiscent of Aesop's *Fables*, an older set of stories in which animals have distinct humanlike character traits. Aesop's *Fables* can be traced back to Greek and Latin versions, but tales were added over time, so all cannot have been written by the Greek storyteller Aesop. Two of his fables are included here for comparison with Bar-Hebraeus's tales.

Bar-Hebraeus's *Laughable Stories*

■ A wolf, a fox, and a lion having banded themselves together snared a goat, a stag, and a hare. And the lion said to the wolf, "Divide these among us." The wolf said, "The goat is for you, the stag is for me, and the hare is for the fox." When the lion heard these words he became furious and leaped upon the wolf and choked him. Then he said to the fox, "You divide them." The fox said to him, "The goat is for your breakfast, the hare for your lunch, and the stag for your supper." The lion then asked him, "Where have you learned to make such an equitable division?" The fox replied, "From this wolf which lies before you, O my lord the king."

A wolf, a fox, and a hare found a lamb, and they said to each other, "He who is the oldest among us shall eat him." The hare said, "I was born before God created the heavens and the earth," and the fox said, "You are right indeed, for I was present when you were born," and the wolf, at the same time seizing the lamb, said, "My stature and capacity are witnesses that I am older than you both," so he ate the lamb.

Aesop's *Fables*

■ The Birds waged war with the Beasts, and each were by turns the conquerors. A Bat, fearing the uncertain issues of the fight, always fought on the side which he felt was the strongest. When peace was proclaimed, his deceitful conduct was apparent to both combatants. Therefore being condemned by each for his treachery, he was driven forth from the light of day, and henceforth concealed himself in dark hiding-places, flying always alone and at night.

A Wolf, having stolen a lamb from a fold, was carrying him off to his lair. A Lion met him in the path, and seizing the lamb, took it from him. Standing at a safe distance, the Wolf exclaimed, "You have unrighteously taken that which was mine from me!" To which the Lion jeeringly replied, "It was righteously yours, eh? The gift of a friend?"

QUESTIONS FOR ANALYSIS

1. What makes stories with animal characters interesting?
2. Could Bar-Hebraeus have been inspired by Aesop's *Fables*? What is your evidence?
3. What are the moral messages in each of these stories, and what can you learn about each culture from these messages?

Sources: Gregory Bar Hebraeus, *The Laughable Stories*, trans. E. A. W. Budge (London: Luzac, 1897), pp. 90–91, slightly modified; *Aesop's Fables*, trans. G. F. Townsend (London: G. Routledge and Sons, 1882), pp. 45, 73.

Muslim scholars also wrote works on geography, jurisprudence, and philosophy. Al-Kindi (d. ca. 870) was the first Muslim thinker to try to harmonize the principles of ethical and social conduct discussed by Plato and Aristotle and the religious precepts of the Qur'an. Inspired by Plato's *Republic* and Aristotle's *Politics*, the distinguished philosopher al-Farabi (d. 950) wrote a political treatise describing an ideal city whose ruler is morally and intellectually perfect and who has as his goal the citizens' complete happiness. Ibn Rushid, or Averroës (1126–1198), of Córdoba, a judge in Seville and later the royal court physician, paraphrased and commented on the works of Aristotle. He insisted on the right to subject all knowledge, except the dogmas of faith, to the test of reason and on the essential harmony of religion and philosophy.

The Mystical Tradition of Sufism

Like the world's other major religions—Buddhism, Hinduism, Judaism, and Christianity—Islam also developed a mystical tradition: Sufism (SOO-fih-zuhm). It arose in the ninth and tenth centuries as a popular reaction to the materialism and worldliness of the later Umayyad regime. Sufis sought a personal union with God—divine love and knowledge through intuition rather than through rational deduction and study of the shari'a. The earliest of the Sufis followed an ascetic routine (denial of physical desires to achieve a spiritual goal), dedicating themselves to fasting, prayer, meditation on the Qur'an, and the avoidance of sin.

The woman mystic Rabi'a (717–801) epitomized this combination of renunciation and devotion. An attractive woman who refused marriage so that nothing would distract her from a total commitment to God, Rabi'a attracted followers, for whom she served as a spiritual guide. One of her poems captures her deep devotion: "O my lord, if I worship thee from fear of hell, and if I worship thee in hope of paradise, exclude me thence, but if I worship thee for thine own sake, then withhold not from me thine eternal beauty."[6]

Between the tenth and the thirteenth centuries groups of Sufis gathered around prominent leaders called *shaykhs*; members of these groups were called *dervishes*. Dervishes entered hypnotic or ecstatic trances, either through the constant repetition of certain prayers or through physical exertions such as whirling or dancing (hence the English phrase "whirling dervish" for one who dances with abandonment). (See "Analyzing the Evidence: Sufi Collective Ritual," page 258.)

Some Sufis acquired reputations as charismatic holy men to whom ordinary Muslims came seeking healing, charity, spiritual consolation, or political mediation between tribal and factional rivals. Other Sufis became known for their writings. Probably the most famous medieval Sufi was the Spanish mystic-philosopher Ibn al'Arabi (1165–1240). He traveled widely in Spain, North Africa, and Arabia seeking masters of Sufism. In Mecca he received a "divine commandment" to begin his major work, *The Meccan Revelation*, which evolved into a personal encyclopedia of 560 chapters. Also at Mecca, the wisdom of a beautiful young girl inspired him to write a collection of love poems, *The Interpreter of Desires*, for which he composed a mystical commentary. In 1223, after visits to Egypt, Anatolia, Baghdad, and Aleppo, Ibn al'Arabi concluded his pilgrimage through the Islamic world at Damascus, where he produced *The Bezels [Edges] of Wisdom*, considered one of the greatest works of Sufism.

Sufi Collective Ritual

The collective rituals in which Sufis try through ecstatic experiences to come closer to God have always fascinated outsiders, including non-Sufi Muslims. The work of art shown here has connections both to religion and to literature: it is a sixteenth-century Persian miniature painting illustrating the work of a fourteenth-century Persian poet whose poems had a place in Sufi rituals.

The Sufi movement originally emerged in response to the increasing worldliness of the expanding Muslim community and flourished in Safavid Persia. As a way to draw closer to God, Sufis engaged in ascetic practices and performed group rituals, which could involve music, singing, dancing, and recitation of prayers. While performing the rituals, Sufis experienced sensations of happiness, fear, hope, longing, and bliss. Because it is difficult to convey ecstatic or mystical experiences in normal language, writers commonly employed the language of love poetry to articulate these feelings.

The fourteenth-century poet Hafiz (1325–1389), whose work is illustrated here, is one of the most influential poets in the Persian language. He wrote tributes to the joys of love and wine, as well as satires on court politics of the period. His lyric poetry excels at conveying the intoxication of love and mystical experience.

More than a century after Hafiz's death, the painter Sultan Muhammad (active 1500–1550) employed the conventions of Persian miniature painting to illustrate Sufis inspired by Hafiz's poetry. Persian miniatures were first developed as an art form to illustrate luxury books and are generally the size of a page. The colors are bright and pure because the artists used mineral pigments that do not fade. Faces are often shown in three-quarters view, and the lighting is even, with no shadows or shading shown. Viewers of these works look down on the scene as though they were situated at a higher spot. The paintings often combine interior elements with exterior elements, which are visible through windows. Despite the small size of the paintings, numerous figures are often depicted, with those

(Edinburgh University Library, Scotland/With kind permission of the Edinburgh University/ Bridgeman Images)

farther away shown higher on the page. The clothing of the figures, the patterns on the floor and wall tiles, and even the plants seen through the windows are commonly rendered in fine detail.

QUESTIONS FOR ANALYSIS

1. Which features of this painting conform to the conventions of Persian miniature painting?
2. How are people dressed? Are distinctions among people expressed through their dress?
3. What musical instruments do you see?
4. What sort of ritual activity is depicted? Are any of the people mere observers, or are they all participating in one way or another?

Muslim-Christian Encounters

During the early centuries of its development, Islam came into contact with the other major religions of Eurasia—Hinduism in India, Buddhism in Central Asia, Zoroastrianism in Persia, and Judaism and Christianity in western Asia and Europe. However, the relationship that did the most to define Muslim identity was the one with Christianity. To put this another way, the most significant "other" to Muslims in the heartland of Islam was Christendom. The close physical proximity and the long history of military encounters undoubtedly contributed to making the Christian-Muslim encounter so important to both sides.

European Christians and Middle Eastern Muslims shared a common Judeo-Christian heritage. In the classical period of Islam, Muslims learned about Christianity from the Christians they met in conquered territories; from the Old and New Testaments; from Jews; and from Jews and Christians who converted to Islam. Before 1400 there was a wide spectrum of Muslim opinion about Jesus and Christians. At the time of the Crusades and the Christian reconquest of Muslim Spain (the *reconquista*, 722–1492), polemical anti-Christian writings appeared. In other periods, Muslim views were more positive.

In the Middle Ages, Christians and Muslims met frequently in business and trade. Commercial contacts, especially when European merchants resided for a long time in the Muslim East, gave them familiarity with Muslim art and architecture. Also, Christians very likely borrowed aspects of their higher education system from Islam.

In the Christian West, Islam had the greatest cultural impact in Andalusia in southern Spain. Between roughly the eighth and twelfth centuries Muslims, Christians, and Jews lived in close proximity in Andalusia, and some scholars believe the period represents a remarkable era of interfaith harmony. Many Christians adopted Arab patterns of speech and dress, gave up the practice of eating pork, and developed a special appreciation for Arab music and poetry. Some Christian women of elite status chose the Muslim practice of going out in public with their faces veiled. These

Playing Chess This page from a thirteenth-century book on chess and other games depicts a Moor and a Christian playing chess together. (Biblioteca Monasterio del Escorial, Madrid, Spain/Index/Bridgeman Images)

Mozarabs Christians who adopted some Arab customs but did not convert.

assimilated Christians, called **Mozarabs** (moh-ZAR-uhbz), did not attach much importance to the doctrinal differences between the two religions.

However, Mozarabs soon faced the strong criticism of both Muslim scholars and Christian clerics. Muslim teachers feared that close contact between people of the two religions would lead to Muslim contamination and become a threat to the Islamic faith. Christian bishops worried that a knowledge of Islam would lead to confusion about essential Christian doctrines. Both Muslim scholars and Christian theologians argued that assimilation led to moral decline.

Thus, beginning in the late tenth century Muslim regulations closely defined what Christians and Muslims could do. A Christian, however much assimilated, remained an unbeliever, a word that carried a pejorative connotation. Mozarabs had to live in special sections of cities; could not learn the Qur'an, employ Muslim workers or servants, or build new churches; and had to be buried in their own cemeteries. A Muslim who converted to Christianity was sentenced to death. By about 1250 the Christian reconquest of Muslim Spain had brought most of the Iberian Peninsula under Christian control. With their new authority, Christian kings set up schools that taught both Arabic and Latin to train missionaries.

Beyond Andalusian Spain, mutual animosity limited contact between people of the two religions. The Muslim assault on Christian Europe in the eighth and ninth centuries—with villages burned, monasteries sacked, and Christians sold into slavery—left a legacy of bitter hostility. Christians felt threatened by a faith that acknowledged God as creator of the universe but denied the Trinity and that accepted Jesus as a prophet but denied his divinity. Europeans' perception of Islam as a menace helped inspire the Crusades of the eleventh through thirteenth centuries (see "The Crusades" in Chapter 14).

Despite the conflicts between the two religions, Muslim scholars often wrote sympathetically about Jesus. For example, Ikhwan al-Safa, an eleventh-century Islamic brotherhood, held that in his preaching Jesus deliberately rejected the harsh punishments reflected in the Jewish Torah and tried to be the healing physician, teaching by parables and trying to touch people's hearts by peace and love. The prominent theologian and qadi (judge) of Teheran, Abd al-Jabbar (d. 1024), though not critical of Jesus, argued that Christians had rejected Jesus's teachings: they failed to observe the ritual purity of prayer, substituting poems by Christian scholars for scriptural prayers; they gave up circumcision, the sign of their covenant with God and Abraham; they moved the Sabbath from Saturday to Sunday; they allowed the eating of pork and shellfish; and they adopted a Greek idea, the Trinity, defending it by quoting Aristotle. Thus, al-Jabbar maintained, Christians failed to observe the laws of Moses and Jesus and distorted Jesus's message.

In the Christian West, both positive and negative views of Islam appeared in literature. The Bavarian knight Wolfram von Eschenbach's *Parzival* and the Englishman William Langland's *Piers the Plowman*—two medieval poems that survive in scores of manuscripts, suggesting that they circulated widely—reveal broad-mindedness and tolerance toward Muslims. Some travelers in the Middle East were impressed by the kindness and generosity of Muslims and with the strictness and devotion with which Muslims observed their faith. Frequently, however, Christian literature portrayed Muslims as the most dreadful of Europe's enemies, guilty of every kind of crime. In his *Inferno*, for example, the great Florentine poet Dante (1265–1321) placed the Muslim philosophers Avicenna and Averroës with other virtuous "heathens," among them Socrates and Aristotle, in the first circle of Hell, where they endured only moderate punishment. Muhammad, however, Dante consigned to the ninth circle, near Satan himself, where he was condemned as a spreader of discord and scandal and suffered perpetual torture.

Even when they rejected each other most forcefully, the Christian and Islamic worlds had a significant impact on each other. Art styles, technology, and even institutional practices spread in both directions. During the Crusades Muslims adopted Frankish weapons and methods of fortification. Christians in contact with Muslim scholars recovered ancient Greek philosophical texts that survived only in Arabic translation.

Chapter Summary

Muhammad, born in the Arabian peninsula, experienced a religious vision, after which he preached to the people to give up their idols and submit to the one indivisible God. He believed in the same God as the Christians and Jews and taught strict monotheism. Islam, the religion based on Muhammad's teachings, appropriated much of the Old and New Testaments of the Bible. After Muhammad's death, his followers gathered his revelations, eventually producing the Qur'an.

Within the span of a century, Muslims carried their faith from the Arabian peninsula through the Middle East, to North Africa and Spain, and to the borders of India. Successors to Muhammad established the caliphate, which through two successive dynasties coordinated rule over Islamic lands. A key challenge faced by the caliphate was a fundamental division in Muslim theology between the Sunnis and the Shi'a.

Over time, many parts of the Muslim empire gained considerable local independence. Far-flung territories such as Spain began to break away from the Baghdad-centered caliphate. By the tenth century Turks played a more important role in the armies and came to be the effective rulers in much of the Middle East. They were succeeded by the Mongols, who invaded the Middle East in the thirteenth century and ruled the central Islamic lands for eighty years.

Muslim society was distinctly hierarchical. In addition to a structure that privileged the ruling Arab Muslims over converts to Islam, then over Jews, Christians, and Zoroastrians, there were also a substantial number of slaves, generally war captives. Slaves normally were converted to Islam and might come to hold important positions, especially in the army. Distinctions between men's and women's roles in Islamic society were strict. Over time, the seclusion and veiling of women became common practices, especially among the well-to-do.

Islam did not discourage trade and profitmaking. By land and sea Muslim merchants transported a rich variety of goods across Asia, the Middle East, Africa, and western Europe. As trade thrived, innovations such as money orders, bills of exchange, and joint stock companies aided the conduct of business.

Wealth from trade made possible a gracious and sophisticated culture in the cities of the Islamic world, especially Baghdad and Córdoba. During this period Muslim scholars produced important work in many disciplines, especially mathematics, medicine, and philosophy. A new spiritual and intellectual tradition arose in the mystical practices of Sufism. Muslims, Christians, and Jews interacted in many ways during this period. At the time of the Crusades and of the Christian reconquest of Islamic Spain, polemical anti-Christian writings appeared, but in other periods Islamic views were more positive. Many Christians converted in the early centuries of the spread of Islam. Others such as the Mozarabs assimilated into Muslim culture while retaining their religion.

NOTES

1. Quoted in B. F. Stowasser, "The Status of Women in Early Islam," in *Muslim Women*, ed. F. Hussain (New York: St. Martin's Press, 1984), p. 25.
2. F. E. Peters, *A Reader on Classical Islam* (Princeton, N.J.: Princeton University Press, 1994), p. 250.
3. Quoted in B. Lewis, ed. and trans., *Islam from the Prophet Muhammad to the Capture of Constantinople*. Vol. 2: *Religion and Society*, 35w from p. 126. © 1974 by Bernard Lewis. Used by permission of Oxford University Press, USA.
4. Ibid., pp. 154–157.
5. R. Hillenbrand, "Cordoba," in *Dictionary of the Middle Ages*, vol. 3, ed. J. R. Strayer (New York: Scribner's, 1983), pp. 597–601.
6. Margaret Smith, *Readings from the Mystics of Islam* (London: Luzac and Co., 1950), p. 11.

CONNECTIONS

During the five centuries that followed Muhammad's death, his teachings came to be revered in large parts of the world, from Spain to Afghanistan. Although in some ways similar to the earlier spread of Buddhism out of India and Christianity out of Palestine, the spread of Islam occurred largely through military conquests that extended Islamic lands. Still, conversion was never complete; both Christians and Jews maintained substantial communities within Islamic lands. Moreover, cultural contact among Christians, Jews, and Muslims was an important element in the development of each culture.

Muslim civilization in these centuries drew from many sources, including Persia and Byzantium, and in turn had broad impact beyond its borders. Muslim scholars preserved much of early Greek philosophy and science through translation into Arabic. Trade connected the Muslim lands both to Europe and to India and China.

During the first and second centuries after Muhammad, Islam spread along the Mediterranean coast of North Africa, which had been part of the Roman world. The next chapter explores other developments in the enormous and diverse continent of Africa during this time. Many of the written sources that tell us about the African societies of these centuries were written in Arabic by visitors from elsewhere in the Islamic world. Muslim traders traveled through many of the societies in Africa north of the Congo, aiding the spread of Islam to the elites of many of these societies. Ethiopia was an exception, as Christianity spread there from Egypt before the time of Muhammad and retained its hold in subsequent centuries. Africa's history is introduced in the next chapter.

CHAPTER 9   **Review and Explore**

Identify Key Terms

Identify and explain the significance of each item below.

Qur'an (p. 237)	**diwān** (p. 240)	**shari'a** (p. 243)
hadith (p. 237)	**imam** (p. 241)	**emirs** (p. 243)
Sunna (p. 237)	**Shi'a** (p. 241)	**dhimmis** (p. 246)
Five Pillars of Islam (p. 238)	**Sunnis** (p. 241)	**madrasa** (p. 253)
umma (p. 238)	**ulama** (p. 241)	**Mozarabs** (p. 260)

Review the Main Ideas

Answer the focus questions from each section of the chapter.

1. From what kind of social and economic environment did Muhammad arise, and what did he teach? (p. 236)

2. What made possible the spread of Islam, and what forms of government were established to rule Islamic lands? (p. 238)

3. How were the Islamic lands governed from 900 to 1400, and what new challenges did rulers face? (p. 243)

4. What social distinctions were important in Muslim society? (p. 246)

5. Why did trade thrive in Islamic lands? (p. 249)

6. What new ideas and practices emerged in the arts, sciences, education, and religion? (p. 251)

7. How did Muslims and Christians come into contact with each other, and how did they view each other? (p. 259)

Make Comparisons and Connections

Analyze the larger developments and continuities within and across chapters.

1. How does the spread of Islam compare to the spread of earlier universal religions, such as Buddhism (Chapter 7) and Christianity (Chapters 6, 8)?

2. In what ways was the development of culture in the Islamic lands shaped by trade and thriving cities?

3. What are the similarities in the role of teachers and holy books in Islamic lands, Europe (Chapter 8), and China (Chapter 7)? What are the differences?

TIMELINE

Suggested Resources

BOOKS

Ahmed, Leila. *Women and Gender in Islam.* 1993. Links modern issues to their historical roots.

Allen, Roger. *An Introduction to Arabic Literature.* 2000. Excellent treatment of literature from the Qur'an to the *Arabian Nights.*

Berkey, Jonathan P. *The Formation of Islam: Religion and Society in the Near East, 600–1800.* 2003. A compact but broad-ranging overview.

Bulliet, Richard W. *Cotton, Climate, and Camels in Early Islamic Iran.* 2009. Links a cooling of the climate to a decline in the Iranian cotton industry and crossbreeding of one- and two-humped camels.

Cohen, Mark R. *Under Crescent and Cross: The Jews in the Medieval Ages.* 1994. Argues that Jews were less marginalized and persecuted under Islamic states than under Christian states.

Constable, Olivia Remie. *Trade and Traders in Muslim Spain: The Commercial Realignment of the Iberian Peninsula, 900–1500.* 1994. An excellent study of Muslim trade and commerce, drawing on a wide range of both Western and Arab sources.

Ettinghausen, Richard, Oleg Grabar, and Marilyn Jenkins-Madina. *The Art and Architecture of Islam, 650–1250.* 2001. A stunningly illustrated overview of Islamic art.

Fletcher, Richard. *The Cross and the Crescent.* 2003. A balanced, fascinating, and lucidly written short account of the earliest contacts between Christians and Muslims.

Hourani, Albert, and Malise Ruthven. *A History of the Arab Peoples,* 2d ed. 2003. An important synthesis.

Lewis, Bernard, ed. and trans. *Islam from the Prophet Muhammad to the Capture of Constantinople: Religion and Society.* 1987. A collection of original sources on many topics.

Long, Pamela O. *Technology and Society in the Medieval Centuries: Byzantium, Islam, and the West, 500–1300.* 2003. A useful survey of Arab scientific and military developments.

Peters, F. E. *The Hajj: The Muslim Pilgrimage to Mecca and the Holy Places.* 1994. Covers the social, commercial, and political significance of the obligatory Muslim pilgrimage to Mecca.

950–1100 Turks enter Middle East on a large scale

1258 ◆
Mongols capture Baghdad,
kill last Abbasid caliph

◆ **1055** Baghdad falls to Seljuk Turks

1099–1187 Christian Crusaders hold Jerusalem

ca. 1100–1150 Construction of Angkor Wat
temple in the Khmer Empire of Cambodia **(Ch. 12)**

◆ **1054** Latin, Greek churches split **(Ch. 14)**

◆ **1066** Norman Conquest of England **(Ch. 14)**

| 900 | 1000 | 1100 | 1200 |

Sells, Michael. *Approaching the Qur'an.* 2007. Includes selected translations set in historical and cultural context.

Stowasser, Barbara Freyer. *Women in the Qur'an: Traditions and Interpretation.* 1994. A fine analysis of the Qur'an's statement on women.

Turner, Howard R. *Science in Medieval Islam: An Illustrated Introduction.* 1995. A fascinating exploration of Islamic science with chapters on astronomy, medicine, geography, alchemy, mathematics, and other topics.

DOCUMENTARIES

Journey to Mecca (Vivendi, 2011). The story of Ibn Battuta and his extensive travels.

The Life of Muhammad (PBS, 2013). A three-part series on Muhammad's life and philosophy.

Muhammad: Legacy of a Prophet (KQED, 2002). A two-hour documentary with extensive footage from the Middle East and interviews with present-day followers.

FEATURE FILMS

Destiny (Youssef Chahine, 1997). A historical story centered on the political struggles of the philosopher Averroës in twelfth-century Andalusia.

El Naser Salah el Dine (Youssef Chahine, 1963). An Arabic fictionalization of the Crusades.

Muhammad: The Messenger of God (Majid Majidi, 2015). An Iranian film about Muhammad's childhood, filmed without directly showing Muhammad.

WEBSITES

Archnet. A rich collection of photos and videos on the architecture of Islamic societies, with a useful timeline. **archnet.org**

Jewel of Muscat. Detailed information on the design, construction, and voyage of the *Jewel of Muscat*, the ship built to replicate the ninth-century Middle Eastern ship that was wrecked at Belitung. The site includes links to films made about the reconstructed ship. **jewelofmuscat.tv/home/**

10

African Societies and Kingdoms
1000 B.C.E.–1500 C.E.

Until fairly recently, much of the outside world knew little about the African continent, its history, or its people. The continent's sheer size, along with tropical diseases and the difficulty of navigating Africa's rivers inland, limited travel to a few intrepid Muslim adventurers such as Ibn Battuta. (See "Individuals in Society: Ibn Battuta" in Chapter 9.) Ethnocentrism and racism became critical factors with the beginning of the Atlantic slave trade in the 1500s, followed in the nineteenth century by European colonialism, which distorted and demeaned knowledge and information about Africa. More recent scholarship has allowed us to learn more about early African civilizations and to appreciate the richness, diversity, and dynamism of those cultures. We know now that between about 400 and 1,500 civilizations, some highly centralized, bureaucratized, and socially stratified, developed in Africa alongside communities with looser forms of social organization often held together through common kinship bonds.

In West Africa several large empires closely linked to the trans-Saharan trade in salt, gold, cloth, ironware, ivory, and other goods arose during this period. After 700 this trade connected West Africa with Muslim societies in North Africa and the Middle East. Vast stores of new information, contained in books and carried by visiting scholars, arrived from an Islamic world that was experiencing a golden age.

Meanwhile, Bantu-speaking peoples spread ironworking and domesticated crops and animals from modern Cameroon to Africa's southern tip. They established kingdoms, such as Great Zimbabwe, in the interior. At the same time, the Swahili established large and prosperous city-states along the Indian Ocean coast.

Ife Ruler

West African rulers, such as the one shown in this bronze head of a Yoruban king, or *oni*, from the thirteenth or fourteenth century, were usually male.

Pictures from History/Bridgeman Images

CHAPTER PREVIEW

267

How did Africa's geography shape its history and contribute to its diverse population?

The Land and Peoples of Africa

The world's second-largest continent after Asia, Africa covers 20 percent of the earth's land surface, and African cultures are enormously diverse both within and across regions. It is difficult and mistaken to make broad generalizations about African life—statements that begin "African culture is . . ." or "African people are . . ." are virtually meaningless. African peoples are not and never have been homogeneous, and this rich diversity makes the study of African history both exciting and challenging.

Five main climatic zones roughly divide the African continent (Map 10.1). Fertile land with unpredictable rainfall borders parts of the Mediterranean in the north and the southwestern coast of the Cape of Good Hope in the south. Inland from these areas are dry steppes with little plant life. These steppes gradually give way to Africa's great deserts: the vast Sahara in the north—3.5 million square miles—and the Namib (NAH-mihb) and Kalahari in the south. The Sahara's southern sub-desert fringe is called the Sahel (SA-hihl), from the Arabic word for "shore." The savannas (flat grasslands) extend in a swath across the continent's widest part—parts of south-central Africa and along the eastern coast—and account for some 55 percent of the African continent. Dense, humid tropical rain forests stretch along coastal West Africa and on both sides of the equator in central Africa. Africa's climate is mostly tropical, with subtropical climates limited to the northern and southern coasts and the regions of high elevation. Rainfall is seasonal on most of the continent and is very sparse in desert and semidesert areas.

Geography and climate have significantly shaped African economic development. In the eastern African plains, the earliest humans hunted wild animals. The drier steppe regions favored herding. Wetter savanna regions, like the Nile Valley, encouraged grain-based agriculture. Tropical forests favored hunting and gathering and, later, root-based agriculture. Rivers and lakes supported economies based on fishing.

Africa's peoples are as diverse as the continent's topography. In North Africa contacts with Asian and European civilizations date back to the ancient Phoenicians (fi-NEE-shuhns), Greeks, and Romans (see "Building a Hellenized Society" in Chapter 5 and "Overseas Conquests and the Punic Wars, 264–133 B.C.E." in Chapter 6). Groups living on the coast or along trade routes had the greatest degree of contact with outside groups. The Berbers of North Africa, living along the Mediterranean, intermingled with many different peoples—with Muslim Arabs, who first conquered North Africa in the seventh and eighth centuries C.E. (see "Trade and Commerce" in Chapter 9); with Spanish Muslims and Jews, many of whom settled in North Africa following their expulsion from Spain in 1492 (see "Politics and the State in the Renaissance" in Chapter 15); and with sub-Saharan peoples, with whom they traded across the Sahara Desert. The Swahili (swah-HEE-lee) peoples along the East African coast developed a maritime civilization and had rich commercial contacts with southern Arabia, the Persian Gulf, India, China, and the Malay Archipelago (ahr-kuh-PEL-uh-goh).

The ancient Greeks called the peoples who lived south of the Sahara *Ethiopians*, which means "people with burnt faces." The Berbers also described this region based on its inhabitants, coining the term *Akal-n-Iquinawen*, which survives today as

Nok Woman Hundreds of terra-cotta sculptures such as the figure of this woman survive from the Nok culture, which originated in the central plateau of northern Nigeria in the first millennium B.C.E.

(Private Collection/Photo © Heini Schneebeli/Bridgeman Images)

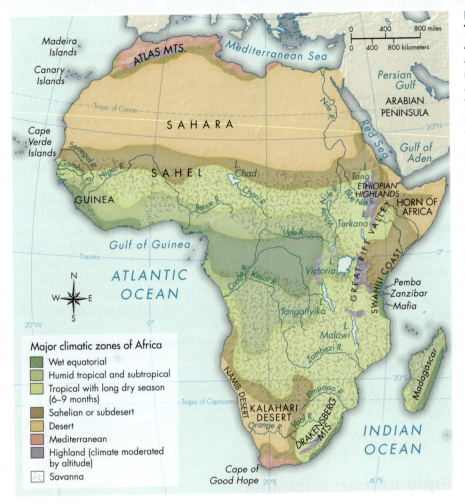

MAP 10.1
The Geography of Africa
Africa's climate zones have always played a critical role in the history of the continent and its peoples. These zones mirror each other north and south of the equator: tropical forest, savanna, sub-desert, desert, and Mediterranean climate.

Guinea (GIN-ee). The Arabs used the term *Bilad al-Sudan*, which survives as *Sudan*. The Berber and Arab terms both mean "land of the blacks." South of the Sahara, short-statured peoples, sometimes inaccurately referred to as Pygmies, inhabited the equatorial rain forests. South of those forests, in the continent's southern third, lived the Khoisan (KOI-sahn), people who were primarily hunters but also had domesticated livestock.

Ancient Egypt, at the crossroads of three continents, was a melting pot of different cultures, peoples, and languages. This diverse and cosmopolitan population contributed to the great achievements of Egyptian culture. Many scholars believe that Africans originating in the sub-Sahara resided in ancient Egypt, primarily in Upper Egypt (south of what is now Cairo), but that other ethnic groups constituted the majority of the population. Merchants based in the capital, Alexandria, carried on trade with East Asia, India, Arabia, East Africa, and across the Mediterranean Sea. (See "Global Viewpoints: Early Descriptions of Africa from Egypt," page 270.)

Early Descriptions of Africa from Egypt

The Rosetta Stone is a stone slab engraved with three sets of inscriptions: one in ancient Egyptian hieroglyphics; one in a demotic, or common, Egyptian script used in everyday writing; and one in Greek as used by the Ptolemaic rulers (see "Building a Hellenized Society" in Chapter 5). The identical texts contain a Ptolemaic decree honoring Ptolemy V. By comparing the Greek and demotic texts against the hieroglyphics, scholars for the first time could decipher the hieroglyphs. The first excerpt comes from these texts.

The *Periplus of the Erythraean Sea* is the earliest known document describing the East African coast and the Indian Ocean trade. Written in Greek around 50 C.E., probably by an Egyptian merchant from Alexandria, the *Periplus* provides a detailed account of the author's sea voyage for use by future travelers. The excerpt here describes the East African coast.

The Rosetta Stone

■ With good fortune! It has seemed fitting to the priests of all the temples of Egypt, as to the honours which are due to King Ptolemy, living forever, the Manifest God . . . , and those . . . due to the Father-loving Gods, who brought him into being, and those . . . due to the Beneficent Gods, . . . and those . . . due to the Brother-and-Sister Gods, . . . and those . . . due to the Saviour Gods, the ancestors of his ancestors, to increase them; and that a statue should be set up for King Ptolemy, . . . which should be called "Ptolemy who has protected the Bright Land," the meaning of which is "Ptolemy who has preserved Egypt." . . .

And there should be produced a cult image for King Ptolemy, . . . son of Ptolemy and Queen Arsinoe, the Father-loving Gods, . . . and a procession festival should be held in the temples and the whole of Egypt for King Ptolemy, . . . each year, . . . for five days, with garlands being worn, burnt offerings and libations being performed . . . ; and the priests . . . in each of the temples of Egypt should be called "The Priests of the Manifest God." . . .

And the decree should be written on a stela of hard stone, in sacred writing, document writing, and Greek writing, and . . . set up in the first-class temples, the second-class temples and the third-class temples, next to the statue of the King, living forever.

How did agriculture affect life among the early societies in the western Sudan and among the Bantu-speaking societies of central and southern Africa?

Early African Societies

The introduction of new crops from Asia and the establishment of settled agriculture profoundly changed many African societies, although the range of possibilities largely depended on local variations in climate and geography. Bantu-speakers took the knowledge of domesticated livestock and agriculture, along with the ironworking skills that had developed in northern and western Africa, and spread them south across central and southern Africa. The most prominent feature of early West African society was a strong sense of community based on blood relationships and religion.

Agriculture and Its Impact

Agriculture began very early in Africa. Knowledge of plant cultivation moved west from the Levant (leh-VANT) (modern Israel and Lebanon), arriving in the Nile Delta in Egypt about the fifth millennium B.C.E. Settled agriculture then traveled down the Nile Valley and moved west across the Sahel to the central and western Sudan. West Africans were living in agricultural communities by the first century B.C.E. From there plant cultivation spread to the equatorial forests. African farmers learned to domesticate plants. Cereal-growing people probably taught forest people to plant grains on plots of land cleared by a method known as "slash and burn." Gradually

Periplus of the Erythraean Sea

■ 15. After two courses of a day and night along the Ausanitic coast [coast of modern Zanzibar], is the island Menuthias, about three hundred stadia from the mainland, low and wooded, in which there are rivers and many kinds of birds and the mountain-tortoise. There are no wild beasts except the crocodiles; but there they do not attack men. In this place there are sewed boats, and canoes hollowed from single logs, which they use for fishing and catching tortoise. In this island they also catch them in a peculiar way, in wicker baskets, which they fasten across the channel-opening between the breakers.

16. Two days' sail beyond, there lies the very last market-town of the continent of Azania, which is called Rhapta. . . . Along this coast live men of piratical habits, very great in stature, and under separate chiefs for each place. The . . . chief governs . . . under some ancient right. . . . And the people of Muza now . . . send thither many large ships; using Arab captains and agents, who are familiar with the natives and intermarry with them, and who know the whole coast and understand the language.

17. There are imported into these markets the lances made at Muza especially for this trade, and hatchets and daggers and awls, and various kinds of glass; and at some places a little wine, and wheat, not for trade, but to serve for getting the good-will of the savages. There are exported from these places a great quantity of ivory, but inferior to that of Adulis, and rhinoceros-horn and tortoise-shell (which is in best demand after that from India), and a little palm-oil.

QUESTIONS FOR ANALYSIS

1. What information about Ptolemaic Egypt is contained in the Rosetta Stone texts?
2. Who are the various gods, besides the manifest god, Ptolemy, in the Rosetta Stone texts?
3. What aspects of the East African coast did the author of the *Periplus* write about, and how might these details benefit future travelers to the region?

Sources: Richard Parkinson, *Cracking Codes: The Rosetta Stone and Decipherment* (Berkeley: University of California Press, 1999), pp. 199–200; W. H. Schoff, trans. and ed., *The Periplus of the Erythraean Sea: Travel and Trade in the Indian Ocean by a Merchant of the First Century* (London, 1912), pp. 27–29.

most Africans evolved a sedentary way of life: living in villages, clearing fields, relying on root crops, and fishing. Hunting-and-gathering societies survived only in scattered parts of Africa, particularly in the central rain forest region and in southern Africa.

Between 1500 B.C.E. and 1000 B.C.E. agriculture also spread southward from Ethiopia along the Great Rift Valley of present-day Kenya and Tanzania. Archaeological evidence reveals that the peoples of East Africa grew cereals, raised cattle, and used wooden and stone tools. Cattle raising spread more quickly than did planting, the herds prospering on the open savannas that are free of tsetse (SEHT-see) flies, which are devastating to cattle. Early East African peoples prized cattle highly. Many trading agreements, marriage alliances, political compacts, and treaties were negotiated in terms of cattle.

Cereals such as millet and sorghum are indigenous to Africa. Scholars speculate that traders brought bananas, plantains, taros (a type of yam), sugarcane, and coconut palms to Africa from Southeast Asia between 900 and 1100 C.E. Because tropical forest conditions were ideal for banana plants, their cultivation spread rapidly. Throughout sub-Saharan Africa native peoples also domesticated donkeys, pigs, chickens, geese, and ducks, although all these came from outside Africa. The guinea fowl appears to be the only animal native to Africa that was domesticated, despite the wide varieties of animal species in Africa. All the other large animals—elephants, hippopotamuses, giraffes, rhinoceros, and zebras—were simply too temperamental to domesticate. The evolution from a hunter-gatherer life to a settled life had profound effects. In contrast to nomadic societies, settled societies made shared or common needs more apparent, and those needs strengthened ties among extended families. Agricultural and pastoral populations also increased, though scholars speculate that this increase did not remain steady, but rather fluctuated over time. Nor is it clear that population growth was accompanied by a commensurate increase in agricultural output.

Early African societies were similarly influenced by the spread of ironworking, though scholars dispute the route by which this technology spread to sub-Saharan Africa. Some believe the Phoenicians brought the iron-smelting technique to northwestern Africa, from which it spread southward. Others insist it spread westward from the Meroë (MEHR-oh-ee) region of the Nile. The great trans-Saharan trade routes may have carried ironworking south from the Mediterranean coast. In any case, ancient iron tools found at the village of Nok on the Jos Plateau in present-day Nigeria seem to prove that ironworking industries existed in West Africa by at least 700 B.C.E. The Nok culture, which enjoys enduring fame for its fine terra-cotta sculptures, flourished from about 800 B.C.E. to 200 C.E.

Bantu Migrations

The spread of ironworking is linked to the migrations of Bantu-speaking peoples. Today the overwhelming majority of the 70 million people living south and east of the Congo River speak a **Bantu** language. Lacking written sources, modern scholars have tried to reconstruct the history of Bantu-speakers on the basis of linguistics, oral traditions, archaeology, and anthropology. Botanists and zoologists have played particularly critical roles in providing information about early diets and environments. The word *Bantu* is a linguistic classification, and linguistics (the study of the nature, structure, and modification of human speech) has helped scholars explain the migratory patterns of African peoples east and south of the equatorial forest.

Bantu-speaking peoples originated in the Benue (BEY-nwey) region, the borderlands of modern Cameroon and Nigeria. Between the first and second millennium B.C.E. they began to spread south and east into the equatorial forest zone. Historians still debate why they began this movement. Some hold that rapid population growth sent people in search of land. Others believe that the evolution of centralized kingdoms allowed rulers to expand their authority, while causing newly subjugated peoples to flee in the hope of regaining their independence.

Because the earliest Bantu-speakers lacked words for grains and cattle herding, they probably were not initially involved in grain cultivation or livestock domestication. During the next fifteen hundred years, Bantu-speakers migrated throughout the savanna, adopted mixed agriculture, and learned ironworking. Mixed agriculture (cultivating cereals and raising livestock) and ironworking were practiced in western East Africa (the region of modern Burundi) in the first century B.C.E. In the first millennium C.E. Bantu-speakers migrated into eastern and southern Africa. Here the Bantu-speakers, with their iron weapons, either killed, drove off, or assimilated the hunting-gathering peoples they met. Some of the assimilated inhabitants gradually adopted a Bantu language, contributing to the spread of Bantu culture.

Bantu Speakers of a Bantu language living south and east of the Congo River.

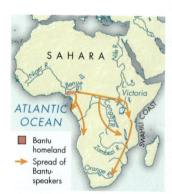

Bantu Migrations, ca. 1000 B.C.E.–1500 C.E.

The settled cultivation of cereals, the keeping of livestock, and the introduction of new crops such as the banana—together with Bantu-speakers' intermarriage with indigenous peoples—led over a long period to considerable population increases and the need to migrate farther. The so-called Bantu migrations should not be seen as a single movement sweeping across Africa from west to east to south and displacing all peoples in its path. Rather, those migrations were an extended series of group interactions between Bantu-speakers and pre-existing peoples in which bits of culture, languages, economies, and technologies were shared and exchanged to produce a wide range of cultural variation across central and southern Africa.[1]

The Bantu-speakers' expansion and subsequent land settlement that dominated eastern and southern African history in the first fifteen hundred years of the Common Era were uneven. Significant environmental differences determined settlement patterns. Some regions had plenty of water, while others were very arid. These differences resulted in very uneven population distribution. The greatest population density seems to have been in the region bounded on the west by the Congo River and on the north, south, and east by Lakes Edward and Victoria and Mount Kilimanjaro (kil-uh-muhn-JAHR-oh). The rapid growth of the Bantu-speaking population led to further migration southward and eastward. By the eighth century the Bantu-speaking people had crossed the Zambezi River and had begun settling in the region of present-day Zimbabwe (zim-BAHB-wey). By the fifteenth century they had reached Africa's southeastern coast.

Life in the Kingdoms of the Western Sudan, ca. 1000 B.C.E.– 800 C.E.

The **Sudan** (soo-DAN) is the region bounded by the Sahara to the north, the Gulf of Guinea to the south, the Atlantic Ocean to the west, and the mountains of Ethiopia to the east (see Map 10.1). In the western Sudan savanna a series of dynamic kingdoms emerged in the millennium before European intrusion began in the 1400s and 1500s.

Sudan The African region surrounded by the Sahara, the Gulf of Guinea, the Atlantic Ocean, and the mountains of Ethiopia.

Between 1000 B.C.E. and 200 C.E. the peoples of the western Sudan made the momentous shift from nomadic hunting to settled agriculture. The rich savanna proved ideally suited to cereal production, especially rice, millet, and sorghum. People situated near the Senegal River and Lake Chad supplemented their diet with fish. Food supply affects population, and the region's inhabitants increased dramatically in number. By 400 C.E. the entire savanna, particularly around Lake Chad, the Niger (NIGH-juhr) River bend, and present-day central Nigeria, had a large population.

Families and clans affiliated by blood kinship lived together in villages or small city-states. The extended family formed the basic social unit. A chief, in consultation with a council of elders, governed a village. Some villages seem to have formed kingdoms. In this case, village chiefs were responsible to regional heads, who answered to provincial governors, who in turn were responsible to a king. The kings and their families formed an aristocracy.

Kingship in the Sudan may have emerged from the priesthood. African kings always had religious sanction or support for their authority, as they had the ability to negotiate with the gods, and were often considered divine. In this respect, early African kingship bears a strong resemblance to Germanic kingship of the same period (see "Political Developments" in Chapter 14).

Although the Mende (MEN-dee) in modern Sierra Leone was one of the few African societies to be led by female rulers, women exercised significant power and autonomy in many African societies. Among the Asante (uh-SAN-tee) in modern-day Ghana, one of the most prominent West African peoples, the king was considered divine but shared some royal power with the Queen Mother. She was a full member of the governing council and enjoyed full voting power in various matters of state. The Queen Mother initially chose the future king from eligible royal candidates. He then had to be approved by both his elders and the commoners. Among the Yoruba in modern Nigeria, the Queen Mother held the royal insignia and could refuse it if the future king did not please her. The institutions of female chiefs, known as *iyalode* among the Yoruba (YOHR-uh-buh) and *omu* among the Igbo (IG-boh) in modern Nigeria, were established to represent women in the political process. The *omu* was even considered a female co-ruler with the male chief.

Western Sudanese religions, like African religions elsewhere, were animistic and polytheistic. Most people believed that a supreme being had created the universe and was the source of all life. Nearly all African religions also recognized ancestral spirits, which might seek God's blessings for families' and communities' prosperity and security as long as these groups behaved appropriately. If not, the ancestral spirits might not protect them from harm, and illness and misfortune could result. Some African religions believed as well that nature spirits lived in such things as the sky, forests, rocks, and rivers. These spirits controlled natural forces and had to be appeased. Because special ceremonies were necessary to satisfy the spirits, special priests with the knowledge and power to communicate with them through sacred rituals were needed. Family and village heads were often priests. Each family head was responsible for ceremonies honoring the family's dead and living members.[2]

In some West African societies, oracles who spoke for the gods were particularly important. Some of the most famous were the Igbo oracles in modern Nigeria. These were female priestesses who were connected with a particular local deity that resided in a sacred cave or other site. Inhabitants of surrounding villages would come to the priestess to seek advice about such matters as crops and harvests, war, marriage, legal issues, and religion. Clearly, these priestesses held much power and authority, even over the local male rulers.

Kinship patterns and shared religious practices helped bind together the early western Sudan kingdoms. Islam's spread across the Sahara by at least the ninth century C.E., however, created a north-south religious and cultural divide in the western Sudan. Islam advanced across the Sahel but halted when it reached the West African savanna and forest zones. Societies in these southern zones maintained their traditional animistic religious practices. Muslim empires along the Niger River's great northern bend evolved into formidable powers ruling over sizable territory as they seized control of the southern termini of the trans-Saharan trade. What made this long-distance trade possible was the "ship of the desert," the camel.

What characterized trans-Saharan trade, and how did it affect West African society?

The Trans-Saharan Trade

"Trans-Saharan trade" refers to the north-south trade across the Sahara (Map 10.2). The camel had an impact on this trade comparable to the very important impact of horses and oxen on European agriculture. Although scholars dispute exactly when the camel was introduced from Central Asia—first into North Africa, then into the

Sahara and the Sudan—they agree that it was before 200 C.E. The trans-Saharan trade brought lasting economic and social change to Africa, facilitating the spread of Islam via Muslim Arab traders, and affected the development of world commerce.

The Berbers of North Africa

Sometime in the fifth century C.E. the North African **Berbers** (BUHR-buhrs) fashioned a saddle for use on the camel. The saddle gave the Berbers and later the region's Arabian inhabitants maneuverability on the animal and thus a powerful political and military advantage: they came to dominate the desert and to create lucrative routes across it. The Berbers determined who could enter the desert, and they extracted large sums of protection money from merchant caravans in exchange for a safe trip.

> **Berbers** North African peoples who controlled the caravan trade between the Mediterranean and the Sudan.

Between 700 C.E. and 900 C.E. the Berbers developed a network of caravan routes between the Mediterranean coast and the Sudan (see Map 10.2). The long expedition across the Sahara testifies to the traders' spirit and to their passion for wealth. Ibn Battuta, an Arab traveler in the fourteenth century, when the trade was at its height, left one of the best descriptions of the trans-Saharan traffic. (See "Individuals in Society: Ibn Battuta" in Chapter 9.)

Nomadic raiders, the Tuareg (TWAH-rehg), posed a serious threat to trans-Saharan traders. The Tuareg were Berbers who lived in the desert uplands and preyed on the caravans as a way of life. To avoid being victimized, merchants made safe-conduct agreements with them and selected guides from among them. Large numbers of merchants crossed the desert together to discourage attack; caravans of twelve thousand camels were reported in the fourteenth century.

Berber merchants from North Africa controlled the caravan trade that carried dates, salt (essential in tropical climates to replace the loss from perspiration) from the Saharan salt mines, and some manufactured goods—silk and cotton cloth, beads, mirrors—to the Sudan. These products were exchanged for the much-coveted commodities of the West African savanna—gold, ivory, gum, kola nuts (eaten as a stimulant), and enslaved West African men and women who were sold to Muslim slave markets in Morocco, Algiers, Tripoli, and Cairo.

Effects of Trade on West African Society

The steady growth of trans-Saharan trade (Table 10.1) had three important effects on West African society. First, trade stimulated gold mining. Parts of modern-day Senegal, Nigeria, and Ghana contained rich veins of gold, and scholars estimate that by the eleventh century nine tons of gold were exported to the Mediterranean coast and Europe annually—a prodigious amount for the time, since even with modern machinery and sophisticated techniques, total gold exports from the same region in 1937 amounted to only twenty-one tons. Some of this metal went to Egypt. From there it was transported down the Red Sea and eventually to India (see Map 9.2) to pay for the spices and silks demanded by Mediterranean commerce. In this way, African gold linked the entire world, exclusive of the Western Hemisphere.

Tuareg Berber Camel Rider Berbers such as this man on his camel near Timbuktu in Mali have crossed the Sahara Desert for hundreds of years, transporting primarily salt from the north and returning with gold and other items from West Africa. The Tuareg are often referred to as the "Blue Men of the Sahara" because of their distinctive deeply dyed blue robes and turbans, which they still wear today.
(© A. Van Zandbergen/Africa Imagery/Africa Media Online/The Image Works)

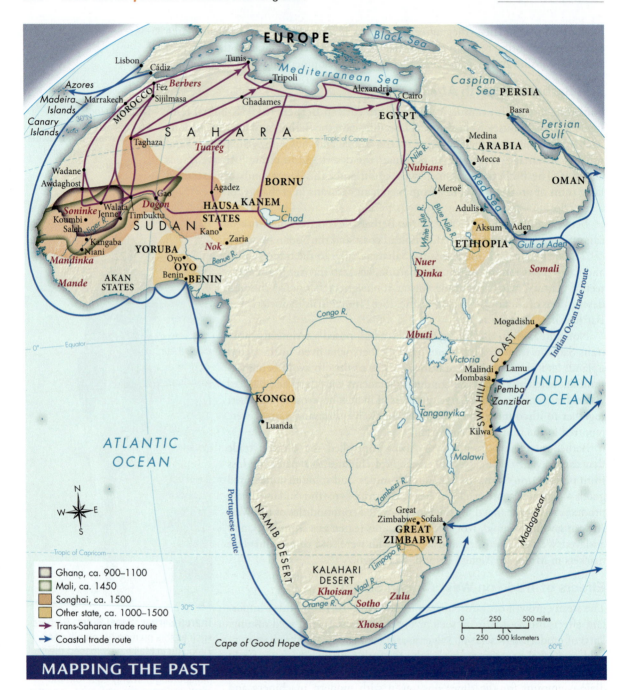

MAPPING THE PAST

MAP 10.2 African Kingdoms and Trade, ca. 800–1500 Throughout world history powerful kingdoms have generally been closely connected to far-flung trade networks.

ANALYZING THE MAP Which kingdoms, empires, and city-states were linked to the trans-Saharan trade network? Which were connected to the Indian Ocean trade network? To the Portuguese route?

CONNECTIONS How were the kingdoms, empires, and city-states shown on this map shaped by their proximity to trade routes?

Second, trade in gold and other goods created a desire for slaves. Slaves were West Africa's second-most-valuable export (after gold). Slaves worked the gold and salt mines, and in Muslim North Africa, southern Europe, and southwestern Asia there was a high demand for household slaves among the elite. African slaves, like their early European and Asian counterparts, seem to have been peoples captured in war. Recent research suggests, moreover, that large numbers of black slaves were also recruited for Muslim military service through the trans-Saharan trade. Table 10.1 shows the scope of the trans-Saharan slave trade. The total number of blacks enslaved over an 850-year period between 650 and 1500 C.E. may be tentatively estimated at more than 4 million.[3]

Slavery in Muslim societies, as in European and Asian countries before the fifteenth century, was not based on skin color. Muslims also enslaved Caucasians who had been purchased, seized in war, or kidnapped from Europe. Wealthy Muslim households in Córdoba, Alexandria, and Tunis often included slaves of a number of races, all of whom had been completely cut off from their cultural roots. Likewise, West African kings who sold blacks to northern traders also bought a few white slaves — Slavic, British, and Turkish — for their own domestic needs. Race had little to do with the phenomenon of slavery.

The third important effect of trans-Saharan trade on West African society was its role in stimulating the development of urban centers. Scholars date the growth of African cities from around the early ninth century. Families that had profited from trade tended to congregate in the border zones between the savanna and the Sahara. They acted as middlemen between the miners to the south and the Muslim merchants from the north. By the early thirteenth century these families had become powerful merchant dynasties. Muslim traders from the Mediterranean settled permanently in the trading depots, from which they organized the trans-Saharan caravans. The concentration of people stimulated agriculture and the craft industries. Gradually cities of sizable population emerged. Jenne (JENN-ay), Gao (GAH-oh), and Timbuktu (tim-buhk-TOO), which enjoyed commanding positions on the Niger River bend, became centers of the export-import trade. Sijilmasa (sih-jil-MAS-suh) grew into a thriving market center. Koumbi Saleh, with between fifteen thousand and twenty thousand inhabitants, was probably the largest city in the western Sudan in the twelfth century. (By European standards, Koumbi Saleh was a metropolis; London and Paris achieved this size only in the late thirteenth century.) Between 1100 and 1400 these cities played a dynamic role in West Africa's commercial life and became centers of intellectual creativity.

The Spread of Islam in Africa

Perhaps the most influential consequence of the trans-Saharan trade was the introduction of Islam to West Africa. In the eighth century Arab invaders overran all of coastal North Africa. They introduced the Berbers living there to Islam (see "Trade and Commerce" in Chapter 9), and gradually the Berbers became Muslims. As

TABLE 10.1 Estimated Magnitude of Trans-Saharan Slave Trade, 650–1500

YEARS	ANNUAL AVERAGE OF SLAVES TRADED	TOTAL
650–800	1,000	150,000
800–900	3,000	300,000
900–1100	8,700	1,740,000
1100–1400	5,500	1,650,000
1400–1500	4,300	430,000

Source: R. A. Austen, "The Trans-Saharan Slave Trade: A Tentative Census," in *The Uncommon Market: Essays in the Economic History of the Atlantic Slave Trade*, ed. H. A. Gemery and J. S. Hogendorn (New York: Academic Press, 1979).

Spread of Islam
— Southern extent of Islam, ca. 1300
▨ Rain forest
▨ Savanna
▨ Desert

The Spread of Islam in Africa

traders, these Berbers carried Islam to sub-Saharan West Africa. From the eleventh century onward militant Almoravids (al-MAWR-uh-vids), a coalition of fundamentalist western Saharan Berbers, preached Islam to the rulers of Ghana, Mali, Songhai, and Kanem-Bornu. These rulers, admiring Muslim administrative techniques and wanting to protect their kingdoms from Muslim Berber attacks, converted to Islam. Some merchants also sought to preserve their elite mercantile status with the Berbers by adopting Islam. Muslims quickly became integral to West African government and society. Hence, from roughly 1000 to 1400, Islam in West Africa was a class-based religion with conversion inspired by political or economic motives. Rural people in the Sahel region and the savanna and forest peoples farther south, however, largely retained their traditional animism.

Conversion to Islam introduced West Africans to a rich and sophisticated culture. By the late eleventh century Muslims were guiding the ruler of Ghana in the operation of his administrative machinery. Because efficient government depends on keeping and preserving records, Islam's arrival in West Africa marked the advent of written documents there. Arab Muslims also taught Ghana's rulers how to manufacture bricks, and royal palaces and mosques began to be built of brick. African rulers corresponded with Arab and North African Muslim architects, theologians, and other intellectuals, who advised them on statecraft and religion. Islam accelerated the development of the West African empires of the ninth through fifteenth centuries.

After the Muslim conquest of Alexandria, Egypt, in 641 (see "Islamic States and Their Expansion" in Chapter 9), Islam spread southward from Egypt up the Nile Valley and west to Darfur (dahr-FOOR) and Wadai (wah-digh). This Muslim penetration came not suddenly by military force but, as in the trans-Saharan trade routes in West Africa, gradually through commercial networks.

Muslim expansion from the Arabian peninsula across the Red Sea to the Horn of Africa, then southward along the coast of East Africa, represents a third direction of Islam's growth in Africa. From ports on the Red Sea and the Gulf of Aden (AHD-en), maritime trade carried Islam to East Africa and the Indian Ocean. Between the eighth and tenth centuries Muslims founded the port city of **Mogadishu** (maw-gah-DEE-shoo), today Somalia's capital. In the twelfth century Mogadishu developed into a Muslim sultanate. Archaeological evidence, confirmed by Arabic sources, reveals a rapid Islamic expansion along Africa's east coast in the thirteenth century as far south as Kilwa (KILL-wa), where Ibn Battuta visited a center for Islamic law in 1331.

Mogadishu A Muslim port city in East Africa founded between the eighth and tenth centuries; today it is the capital of Somalia.

How were the East African city-states, Aksum, and Great Zimbabwe different from and similar to the kingdoms of the western Sudan?

African Kingdoms and Empires, ca. 800–1500

All African societies shared one basic feature: a close relationship between political and social organization. Ethnic or blood ties bound clan members together. What scholars call **stateless societies** were culturally homogeneous ethnic societies, generally organized around kinship groups. The smallest ones numbered fewer than a hundred people and were nomadic hunting groups. Larger stateless, or decentralized, societies, such as the Tiv in modern central Nigeria, consisted of perhaps several thousand people who lived a settled and often agricultural and/or herding life. These societies lacked a central authority figure, such as a king, capital city, or military. A village or group of villages might recognize a chief who held very limited powers and

stateless societies African societies bound together by ethnic or blood ties rather than by being political states.

whose position was not hereditary, but more commonly they were governed by local councils, whose members were either elders or persons of merit. Although stateless societies functioned successfully, their weakness lay in their inability to organize and defend themselves against attack by the powerful armies of neighboring kingdoms or by the European powers of the colonial era.

While stateless societies were relatively common in Africa, the period from about 800 to 1500 is best known as the age of Africa's great empires (see Map 10.2). This period witnessed the flowering of several powerful African states. In the western Sudan the large empires of Ghana, Mali (MAH-lee), and Songhai (song-GAH-ee) developed, complete with sizable royal bureaucracies. On the east coast emerged thriving city-states based on sophisticated mercantile activities and, like the western Sudan, heavily influenced by Islam. In Ethiopia, in central East Africa, kings relied on their peoples' Christian faith to strengthen political authority. In southern Africa the empire of Great Zimbabwe, built on the gold trade with the east coast, flourished.

The Kingdom of Ghana, ca. 900–1100

So remarkable was the kingdom of **Ghana** (GAH-nuh) during the age of Africa's great empires that Arab and North African visitors praised it as a model for other rulers. Even in modern times, ancient Ghana holds a central place in Africa's historical consciousness. When the British Gold Coast colony gained its independence in 1957, its new leaders paid tribute to their heritage by naming their new country Ghana. Although modern Ghana lies far from the site of the old kingdom, the name was selected to signify the rebirth of ancient Ghana's illustrious past.

The Soninke (so-NING-kee) people inhabited the nucleus of the territory that became the Ghanaian kingdom. They called their ruler *ghana*, or war chief. By the late eighth century Muslim traders and other foreigners applied the king's title to the region where the Soninke lived, the kingdom south of the Sahara. The Soninke themselves called their land Wagadou (WAH-guh-doo). Only the southern part of Wagadou received enough rainfall to be agriculturally productive, and it was here that the civilization of Ghana developed (see Map 10.2). Skillful farming and efficient irrigation systems led to abundant crop production, which eventually supported a population of as many as two hundred thousand.

In 992 Ghana captured the Berber town of Awdaghost (OW-duh-gost), strategically situated on the trans-Saharan trade route. Thereafter Ghana controlled the southern portion of a major caravan route. Before the year 1000 Ghana's rulers had extended their influence almost to the Atlantic coast and had captured a number of small kingdoms in the south and east. By the early eleventh century the Ghanaian king exercised sway over a territory approximately the size of Texas. No other power in the western Sudan could successfully challenge him.

Throughout this vast West African territory, all authority sprang from the king. Religious ceremonies and court rituals emphasized the king's sacredness and were intended to strengthen his authority. The king's position was hereditary in the matrilineal line—that is, the ruling king's heir was one of the king's sister's sons (presumably the eldest or fittest for battle). According to the eleventh-century Spanish Muslim geographer al-Bakri (1040?–1094), "This is their custom . . . the kingdom is inherited only by the son of the king's sister. He the king has no doubt that his successor is a son of his sister, while he is not certain that his son is in fact his own."[4]

Ghana From the word for "war chief," the name of a large and influential African kingdom inhabited by the Soninke people.

A council of ministers assisted the king in the work of government, and from the ninth century on most of these ministers were Muslims. The royal administration was well served by ideas, skills, and especially literacy brought from the North African and Arab Muslim worlds. The king and his people, however, clung to their ancestral religion and basic cultural institutions.

The Ghanaian king held court in the large and vibrant city of **Koumbi Saleh** (KOOM-bi SA-lah), which was actually two towns, one inhabited by the king and his royal court and the other by Muslims. Al-Bakri provides a valuable description of the Muslim part of the town in the eleventh century:

Koumbi Saleh The city in which the king of Ghana held his court.

> The city of Ghana consists of two towns lying on a plain, one of which is inhabited by Muslims and is large, possessing twelve mosques—one of which is a congregational mosque for Friday prayer; each has its imam, its muezzin and paid reciters of the Quran. The town possesses a large number of jurisconsults and learned men.[5]

Either to protect themselves or to preserve their special identity, the Muslims of Koumbi Saleh lived separately from the African artisans and tradespeople. Ghana's Muslim community was large and prosperous, and Muslim religious leaders exercised civil authority over their fellow Muslims. The presence of religious leaders and other learned Muslims suggests that Koumbi Saleh was a city of vigorous intellectual activity.

Al-Bakri also described the royal court:

> The town inhabited by the king is six miles from the Muslim one and is called Al Ghana. . . . The residence of the king consists of a palace and a number of dome-shaped dwellings, all of them surrounded by a strong enclosure, like a city wall. In the town . . . is a mosque, where Muslims who come on diplomatic missions to the king pray.[6]
>
> The king adorns himself, as do the women here, with necklaces and bracelets; on their heads they wear caps decorated with gold, sewn on material of fine cotton stuffing. When he holds court in order to hear the people's complaints and to do justice, he sits in a pavilion around which stand ten horses wearing golden trappings; behind him ten pages stand, holding shields and swords decorated with gold; at his right are the sons of the chiefs of the country, splendidly dressed and with their hair sprinkled with gold. . . . When the king's coreligionists appear before him, they fall on their knees and toss dust on their heads—this is their way of greeting their sovereign. Muslims show respect by clapping their hands.[7]

Justice derived from the king, who heard cases at court or on his travels throughout his kingdom. As al-Bakri recounts:

> When a man is accused of denying a debt or of having shed blood or some other crime, a headman (village chief) takes a thin piece of wood, which is sour and bitter to taste, and pours upon it some water which he then gives to the defendant to drink. If the man vomits, his innocence is recognized and he is congratulated. If he does not vomit and the drink remains in his stomach, the accusation is accepted as justified.[8]

This appeal to the supernatural for judgment was similar to the justice by ordeal that prevailed among the Germanic peoples of western Europe at the same time (see "Law and Justice" in Chapter 14).

The king's elaborate court, the administrative machinery he built, and the extensive territories he governed were all expensive. To support the kingdom, the royal estates—some hereditary, others conquered in war—produced annual revenue, mostly in the form of foodstuffs for the royal household. The king also received tribute annually from subordinate chieftains. Customs duties on goods entering and leaving the country generated revenues as well. Salt was the largest import. Berber merchants paid a tax to the king on the cloth, metalwork, weapons, and other goods they brought into the country from North Africa; in return these traders received royal protection from bandits. African traders bringing gold into Ghana from the south also paid the customs duty.

Finally, the royal treasury held a monopoly on the export of gold. The gold industry was undoubtedly the king's largest source of income. Medieval Ghana's fame rested on gold. The ninth-century Persian geographer al-Ya-qubi wrote, "Its king is mighty, and in his lands are gold mines. Under his authority are various other kingdoms—and in all this region there is gold."[9] The governing aristocracy—the king, his court, and Muslim administrators—occupied the highest rung on the Ghanaian social ladder. On the next rung stood the merchant class. Considerably below the merchants stood the farmers, cattle breeders, gold mine supervisors, and skilled craftsmen and weavers—what today might be called the middle class. Some merchants and miners must have enjoyed great wealth, but, as in all aristocratic societies, money alone did not grant prestige. High status was based on blood and royal service. On the social ladder's lowest rung were slaves, who worked in households, on farms, and in the mines. As in Asian and European societies of the time, slaves accounted for only a small percentage of the population.

Apart from these social classes stood the army. Ghana's king maintained at his palace a standing force of a thousand men, comparable to the bodyguards of the Roman emperors. These thoroughly disciplined, well-armed, totally loyal troops protected the king and the royal court. They lived in special compounds, enjoyed the king's favor, and sometimes acted as his personal ambassadors to subordinate rulers. In wartime this regular army was augmented by levies of soldiers from conquered peoples and by the use of slaves and free reserves.

The reasons for ancient Ghana's decline are still a matter of much debate. The most commonly accepted theory for Ghana's rapid decline is that the Berber Almoravid dynasty of North Africa invaded and conquered Ghana around 1100 and forced its rulers and people to convert to Islam. Some historians examining this issue have concluded that while Almoravid and Islamic pressures certainly disrupted the empire, weakening it enough for its incorporation into the rising Mali empire, there was no Almoravid military invasion and subsequent forced conversion to Islam.[10]

The Kingdom of Mali, ca. 1200–1450

Ghana and its capital of Koumbi Saleh were in decline between 1100 and 1200. The old empire split into several small kingdoms that feuded among themselves. One people, the Mandinka (man-DING-goh), from the kingdom of Kangaba on the upper Niger River, gradually asserted their dominance over these kingdoms. The Mandinka had long been part of the Ghanaian empire, and the Mandinka and Soninke belonged to the same language group. Kangaba formed the core of the new empire of Mali. Building on Ghanaian foundations, Mali developed into a better-organized and more powerful state than Ghana.

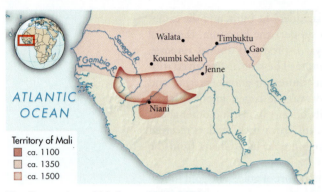

ATLANTIC
OCEAN

Territory of Mali
■ ca. 1100
□ ca. 1350
□ ca. 1500

The Expansion of Mali, ca. 1200–1450

Mali owed its greatness to two fundamental assets. First, its strong agricultural and commercial base supported a large population and provided enormous wealth. Second, Mali had two rulers, Sundiata (soon-JAH-tuh) and Mansa Musa, who combined military success with exceptionally creative personalities.

The earliest surviving evidence about the Mandinka, dating from the early eleventh century, indicates that they were extremely successful at agriculture. Consistently large harvests throughout the twelfth and thirteenth centuries meant a plentiful food supply, which encouraged steady population growth. Kangaba's geographical location also ideally positioned the Mandinka in the heart of the West African trade networks. Earlier, during the period of Ghanaian hegemony, the Mandinka had acted as middlemen in the gold and salt traffic flowing north and south. In the thirteenth century Mandinka traders formed companies, traveled widely, and gradually became a major force in the entire West African trade.

Mali's founder, Sundiata (r. ca. 1230–1255), set up his capital at Niani, transforming the city into an important financial and trading center. He then embarked on a policy of imperial expansion. Through a series of military victories, Sundiata and his successors absorbed into Mali other territories of the former kingdom of Ghana and established hegemony over the trading cities of Gao, Jenne, and Walata.

These expansionist policies were continued in the fourteenth century by Sundiata's descendant Mansa Musa (MAHN-sa MOO-sa) (r. ca. 1312–1337), early Africa's most famous ruler. In the language of the Mandinka, *mansa* means "emperor." Ultimately Mansa Musa's influence extended northward to several Berber cities in the Sahara, eastward to the trading cities of Timbuktu and Gao, and westward to the Atlantic Ocean. Throughout his territories, he maintained strict royal control over the flourishing trans-Saharan trade. Thus this empire, roughly twice the size of the Ghanaian kingdom and containing perhaps 8 million people, brought Mansa Musa fabulous wealth.

Mansa Musa built on the foundations of his predecessors. Malian society's stratified aristocratic structure perpetuated the pattern set in Ghana, as did the system of provincial administration and annual tribute. The emperor took responsibility for the territories that formed the heart of the empire and appointed governors to rule the outlying provinces and dependent kingdoms. But Mansa Musa made a significant innovation: in a practice strikingly similar to a system used in both China and France at the time, he appointed royal family members as provincial governors.

In another aspect of administration, Mansa Musa also differed from his predecessors. He became a devout Muslim. Although most of the Mandinka remained animists, Islamic practices and influences in Mali multiplied.

The most celebrated event of Mansa Musa's reign was his pilgrimage to Mecca in 1324–1325, during which he paid a state visit to the Egyptian sultan. Mansa Musa's entrance into Cairo was magnificent. Preceded by five hundred slaves, each carrying a six-pound staff of gold, he followed with a huge host of retainers, including one hundred elephants each bearing one hundred pounds of gold. The emperor

The Great Friday Mosque, Jenne The mosque at Jenne was built in the form of a parallelogram. Inside, nine long rows of adobe columns run along a north-south axis and support a flat roof of palm logs. A pointed arch links each column to the next in its row, forming nine east-west archways facing the *mihrab*, the niche in the wall of the mosque indicating the direction of Mecca, and from which the imam speaks. This mosque (rebuilt in 1907 based on the original thirteenth-century structure) testifies to the considerable wealth, geometrical knowledge, and manpower of Mali. (Gerard Degeorge/akg-images)

lavished his wealth on the citizens of the Egyptian capital. Writing twelve years later, al-Omari, one of the sultan's officials, recounts:

> This man Mansa Musa spread upon Cairo the flood of his generosity: there was no person, officer of the court, or holder of any office of the Sultanate who did not receive a sum of gold from him. The people of Cairo earned incalculable sums from him, whether by buying and selling or by gifts. So much gold was current in Cairo that it ruined the value of money.[11]

As a result of this pilgrimage, for the first time the Mediterranean world learned firsthand of Mali's wealth and power, and the kingdom began to be known as one of the world's great empires. Mali retained this international reputation into the fifteenth century. Musa's pilgrimage also had significant consequences within Mali. He gained some understanding of the Mediterranean countries and opened diplomatic relations with the Muslim rulers of Morocco and Egypt. His zeal for the Muslim faith and Islamic culture increased. Musa brought back from Arabia the distinguished architect al-Saheli, whom he commissioned to build new mosques in Timbuktu and other cities. These mosques served as centers for African conversion to Islam.

Timbuktu began as a campsite for desert nomads, but under Mansa Musa it grew into a thriving entrepôt (trading center), attracting merchants and traders from North Africa and all parts of the Mediterranean world. They brought with them cosmopolitan attitudes and ideas. In the fifteenth century Timbuktu developed into a great center for scholarship and learning. Architects, astronomers, poets, lawyers, mathematicians, and theologians flocked there. One hundred fifty schools, for men only,

Timbuktu Originally a campsite for desert nomads, it grew into a thriving city under Mansa Musa, king of Mali and Africa's most famous ruler.

were devoted to Qur'anic studies. The school of Islamic law enjoyed a distinction comparable to the prestige of the Cairo school (see "Education and Intellectual Life" in Chapter 9). The vigorous traffic in books that flourished in Timbuktu made them the most common items of trade. Timbuktu's tradition and reputation for African scholarship lasted until the eighteenth century.

Moreover, in the fourteenth and fifteenth centuries many Arab and North African Muslim intellectuals and traders married native African women. The necessity of living together harmoniously, the traditional awareness of diverse cultures, and Timbuktu's cosmopolitan atmosphere contributed to a rare degree of racial tolerance and understanding. After visiting the court of Mansa Musa's successor in 1352–1353, Ibn Battuta observed:

> [T]he Negroes possess some admirable qualities. They are seldom unjust, and have a greater abhorrence of injustice than any other people. Their sultan shows no mercy to anyone who is guilty of the least act of it. There is complete security in their country. Neither traveler nor inhabitant in it has anything to fear from robbers. . . . They do not confiscate the property of any white man who dies in their country, even if it be uncounted wealth. On the contrary, they give it into the charge of some trustworthy person among the whites.[12]

The third great West African empire, Songhai, succeeded Mali in the fifteenth century. It encompassed the old empires of Ghana and Mali and extended its territory farther north and east to become one of the largest African empires in history (see Map 10.2).

The Kingdom of Aksum, ca. 600

Aksum A kingdom in northwestern Ethiopia that was a sizable trading state and the center of Christian culture.

Ethiopia: The Christian Kingdom of Aksum

Just as the ancient West African empires were significantly affected by Islam and the Arab culture that accompanied it, the African kingdoms that arose in modern Sudan and Ethiopia in northeast Africa were heavily influenced by Egyptian culture, and they influenced it in return. This was particularly the case in ancient Nubia (NOO-bee-uh). Nubia's capital was at Meroë (see Map 10.2); thus the country is often referred to as the Nubian kingdom of Meroë.

As part of the Roman Empire, Egypt was subject to Hellenistic and Roman cultural forces, and it became an early center of Christianity. Nubia, however, was never part of the Roman Empire; its people retained ancient Egyptian religious ideas. Christian missionaries traveled to the Upper Nile region and successfully converted the Nubian rulers around 600 C.E. By that time, there were three separate Nubian states, of which the kingdom of Nobatia, centered at Dongola, was the strongest. The Christian rulers of Nobatia had close ties with the **Aksum** (AHK-soom) kingdom in Ethiopia, and through this relationship Egyptian culture spread to Ethiopia.

Two-thirds of Ethiopia consists of the Ethiopian highlands, the rugged plateau region of East Africa. The Great Rift Valley divides this territory into two massifs (mountain masses), of which the Ethiopian Plateau is the larger. Sloping away from each side of the Great Rift Valley are a series of mountains and valleys. Together with this mountainous environment, the three Middle Eastern religions—Judaism, Christianity, and Islam—have all influenced Ethiopian society.

By the first century C.E. the Aksum kingdom in northwestern Ethiopia was a sizable trading state. Merchants at Adulis (ah-DUL-uhs), its main port on the Red Sea, sold ivory, gold, emeralds, rhinoceros horns, shells, and slaves to the Sudan, Arabia, Yemen, and various cities across the Indian Ocean in exchange for glass, ceramics, fabrics, sugar, oil, spices, and precious gems. Adulis contained temples, stone-built houses, and irrigated agriculture. Between the first and eighth centuries Aksum served as the capital of an empire extending over much of what is now northern Ethiopia. The empire's prosperity rested on trade.

Islam's expansion into northern Ethiopia in the eighth century weakened Aksum's commercial prosperity. The Arabs first ousted the Greek Byzantine merchants who traded on the Dahlak Archipelago (in the southern Red Sea) and converted the islands' inhabitants. Then Muslims attacked and destroyed Adulis. Some Aksumites converted to Islam; many others found refuge in the rugged mountains north of the kingdom, where they were isolated from outside contacts. Thus began the insularity that characterized later Ethiopian society.

Tradition ascribes to Frumentius (froo-MEN-shee-uhs) (ca. 300–380 C.E.), a Syrian Christian trader, the introduction of Coptic (KAHP-tik) Christianity, an Orthodox form of Christianity that originated in Egypt, into Ethiopia. Kidnapped as a young boy en route from India to Tyre (in southern Lebanon), Frumentius was taken to Aksum, given his freedom, and appointed tutor to the future king, Ezana (ee-ZAHN-ah). Upon Ezana's accession to the throne, Frumentius went to Alexandria, Egypt, where he was consecrated the first bishop of Aksum around 328 C.E. He then returned to Ethiopia with some priests to spread Christianity. Shortly after members of the royal court accepted Christianity in about 350 C.E., it became the Ethiopian state religion. Ethiopia's future was to be inextricably linked to Christianity, a unique situation in sub-Saharan Africa.

Ethiopia's acceptance of Christianity led to the production of ecclesiastical documents and royal chronicles, making Ethiopia the first sub-Saharan African society that can be studied from written records. The Scriptures were translated into Ge'ez (gee-EHZ), an ancient language and script used in Ethiopia and Aksum. Pagan temples were dedicated to Christian saints, and, as in early medieval Ireland and in the Orthodox Church of the Byzantine world, monasteries were the Christian faith's main cultural institutions in Ethiopia. As the Ethiopian state expanded, vibrant monasteries provided inspiration for the establishment of convents for nuns, as in medieval Europe (see "Monastic Life" in Chapter 14).

Monastic records provide fascinating information about early Ethiopian society. Settlements were formed on the warm and moist plateau lands. Farmers used a scratch plow (unique in sub-Saharan Africa) to cultivate wheat and barley, and they regularly rotated these cereals. Plentiful rainfall seems to have helped produce abundant crops, which in turn led to population growth. Because of ecclesiastical opposition to polygyny (the practice of having multiple wives), monogamy was the norm, other than for kings and the very rich. An abundance of land meant that young couples could establish independent households. Widely scattered farms, with the parish church as the central social unit, seem to have been the usual pattern of existence.

Above the broad class of peasant farmers stood warrior-nobles. Their wealth and status derived from their fighting skills, which kings rewarded with grants of estates and with the right to collect tribute from the peasants. To acquire lands and to hold warriors' loyalty, Ethiopian kings pursued a policy of constant territorial expansion. (See "Individuals in Society: Amda Siyon," page 287.) Nobles maintained order in their regions, supplied kings with fighting men, and displayed their superior status

Christianity and Islam in Ethiopia The prolonged contest between the two religions in Ethiopia was periodically taken to the battlefield. This drawing from the eighteenth century by an Ethiopian artist shows his countrymen (left) advancing victoriously and celebrates national military success. (© The British Library Board/The Image Works)

by the size of their households and their generosity to the poor.

Sometime in the fourteenth century six scribes in the Tigrayan (tee-GREY-uhn) highlands of Ethiopia combined oral tradition, Jewish and Islamic commentaries, apocryphal (noncanonical) Christian texts, and the writings of the early Christian Church fathers to produce the *Kebra Nagast* (The Glory of Kings). This history served the authors' goals: it became an Ethiopian national epic, glorifying a line of rulers descended from the Hebrew king Solomon (see "The Hebrews" in Chapter 2), arousing patriotic feelings, and linking Ethiopia's identity to the Judeo-Christian tradition. The book deals mostly with the origins of Emperor Menilek I (MEN-uh-lik) of Ethiopia in the tenth century B.C.E.

The *Kebra Nagast* asserts that Queen Makeda (ma-KAY-da) of Ethiopia (called Sheba in the Jewish tradition) had little governmental experience when she came to the throne. So she sought the advice and wise counsel of King Solomon (r. ca. 965–925 B.C.E.) in Jerusalem. Makeda learned Jewish statecraft, converted to Judaism, and expressed her gratitude to Solomon with rich gifts of spices, gems, and gold. During this visit, Solomon tricked Makeda into allowing him into her bed. Their son, Menilek, was born some months later. When Menilek reached maturity, he visited Solomon in Jerusalem. There Solomon anointed him crown prince of Ethiopia and sent a retinue of young Jewish nobles to accompany him home as courtiers. Unable to face life without the Hebrews' Ark of the Covenant, the courtiers stole the cherished wooden chest, which the Hebrews believed contained the Ten Commandments. God apparently approved the theft, for he lifted the youths, pursued by Solomon's army, across the Red Sea and into Ethiopia. Thus, according to the *Kebra Nagast*, Menilek avenged his mother's shame, and God gave his legal covenant to Ethiopia, Israel's successor.[13] Although written around twenty-three hundred years after the events, the myths and legends contained in the *Kebra Nagast* effectively served the purpose of building nationalistic fervor.

Based on this lineage, from the tenth to the sixteenth centuries, and even in the Ethiopian constitution of 1955, Ethiopia's rulers claimed they belonged to the Solomonic line of succession. Thus the church and state in Ethiopia were inextricably linked.

In the later thirteenth century the dynasty of the Solomonic kings witnessed a literary and artistic renaissance particularly notable for works of hagiography (biographies of saints), biblical exegesis (critical explanation or interpretation of the Bible), and manuscript illumination. The most striking feature of Ethiopian society from 500 to 1500 was the close relationship between the church and the state. Christianity inspired fierce devotion and equated doctrinal heresy with political rebellion, thus reinforcing central monarchical power.

Amda Siyon

SCHOLARS CONSIDER AMDA SIYON (r. 1314–1344) the greatest ruler of Ethiopia's Solomonic dynasty. Yet we have no image or representation of him. We know nothing of his personal life, though if he followed the practice of most Ethiopian kings, he had many wives and children. Nor do we know anything about his youth and education. The evidence of what he did, however, suggests a tough military man who personified the heroic endurance and physical pain expected of warriors. According to a chronicle of Siyon's campaign against the Muslim leader of Ifat,

> [Siyon] clove the ranks of the rebels and struck so hard that he transfixed two men as one with the blow of his spear, through the strength of God. Thereupon the rebels scattered and took to flight, being unable to hold their ground in his presence.

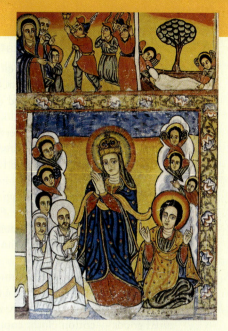

Colorful biblical scenes adorn the interior of the Urai Kidane Miharet Church, one of the many monasteries established by Amda Siyon.

(De Agostini Picture Library/akg-images)

Amda Siyon reinforced control over his kingdom's Christian areas. He then expanded into the neighboring regions of Shewa, Gojam, and Damot. Victorious there, he gradually absorbed the Muslim states of Ifat and Hedya to the east and southeast. These successes gave him effective control of the central highlands and also the Indian Ocean trade routes to the Red Sea (see Map 10.2). He governed in a quasi-feudal fashion. Theoretically the owner of all land, he assigned *gults*, or fiefs, to his ablest warriors. In return for nearly complete authority in their regions, these warrior-nobles conscripted soldiers for the king's army, required agricultural services from the farmers working on their land, and collected taxes in kind.

Ethiopian rulers received imperial coronation at Aksum, but their kingdom had no permanent capital. Rather, the ruler and court were peripatetic. They constantly traveled around the country to crush revolts, to check the warrior-nobles' management of the gults, and to impress ordinary people with royal dignity.

Territorial expansion had important economic and religious consequences. Amda Siyon concluded trade agreements with Muslims by which they were allowed to trade with his country in return for Muslim recognition of his authority and their promise to accept his administration and pay taxes. Economic growth followed. As a result of these agreements, the flow of Ethiopian gold, ivory, and slaves to Red Sea ports for export to the Islamic heartlands and to South Asia accelerated. Profits from commercial exchange improved people's lives, or at least the lives of the upper classes.

Monk-missionaries from traditional Christian areas flooded newly conquered regions, stressing that Ethiopia was a new Zion, or a second Israel—a Judeo-Christian nation defined by religion. Ethiopian Christianity focused on the divinity of the Old Testament Yahweh, rather than on the humanity of the New Testament Jesus. Jewish dietary restrictions, such as the avoidance of pork and shellfish, shaped behavior, and the holy Ark of the Covenant had a prominent place in the liturgy. But the monks also taught New Testament values, especially the importance of charity and spiritual reform. Following the Byzantine pattern, the Ethiopian priest-king claimed the right to summon church councils and to issue doctrinal degrees. Christianity's stress on monogamous marriage, however, proved hard to enforce. As in other parts of Africa (and in Islamic lands, China, and South Asia), polygyny remained common, at least among the upper classes.

QUESTIONS FOR ANALYSIS

1. What features mark Ethiopian culture as unique and distinctive among early African societies?
2. Referring to Solomonic Ethiopia, assess the role of legend in history.

Sources: G. W. B. Huntingford, ed., *The Glorious Victories of Amda Seyon* (Oxford: Oxford University Press, 1965), pp. 89–90; H. G. Marcus, *A History of Ethiopia*, updated ed. (Berkeley: University of California Press, 2002); J. Iliffe, *Africans: The History of a Continent*, 2d ed. (New York: Cambridge University Press, 2007).

The East African City-States

Like Ethiopia, the East African city-states were shaped by their proximity to the trade routes of the Red Sea and Indian Ocean. In the first century C.E. a merchant seaman from Alexandria in Egypt sailed down the Red Sea and out into the Indian Ocean, where he stopped at seaports along the coasts of East Africa, Arabia, and India. He took careful notes on all he observed, and the result, the *Periplus of the Erythraean Sea* (*erythraean* comes from the Greek word meaning "red," which was used to designate the Red Sea as well as the Indian Ocean), is the earliest surviving literary evidence of the city-states of the East African coast. (See "Global Viewpoints: Early Descriptions of Africa from Egypt," page 270.) Although primarily preoccupied with geography and navigation, the *Periplus* includes accounts of the local East African peoples and their commercial activities. Since the days of the Roman emperors, the *Periplus* testifies, the East African coast had strong commercial links with India and the Mediterranean.

Greco-Roman ships sailed from Adulis on the Red Sea around the tip of the Gulf of Aden and down the portion of the East African coast that the Greeks called Azania, in modern-day Kenya and Tanzania (see Map 10.2). These ships carried manufactured goods — cotton cloth, copper and brass, iron tools, and gold and silver plate. At the African coastal emporiums, Mediterranean merchants exchanged these goods for cinnamon, myrrh and frankincense, captive slaves, and animal byproducts such as ivory, rhinoceros horns, and tortoise shells. The ships then headed back north and, somewhere around Cape Guardafui (gwahr-duh-FWEE) on the Horn of Africa, caught the monsoon winds eastward to India, where ivory was in great demand. In the early centuries of the Common Era many merchants and seamen from the Mediterranean settled in East African coastal towns. Succeeding centuries saw the arrival of more traders. The great emigration from Arabia after the death of Muhammad accelerated Muslim penetration of the area, which the Arabs called the Zanj, "land of the blacks," a land inhabited by Bantu-speaking peoples whom they also called the Zanj. Along the coast, Arabic Muslims established small trading colonies whose local peoples were ruled by kings and practiced various animistic religions. Eventually — whether through Muslim political hegemony or gradual assimilation — the coastal peoples slowly converted to Islam. Indigenous African religions, however, remained strong in the continent's interior. (See "Analyzing the Evidence: A Tenth-Century Muslim Traveler Describes Parts of the East African Coast," page 290.)

Migrants from the Arabian peninsula and the Malay Archipelago had a profound influence on the lives of the East African coastal people. Beginning in the late twelfth century fresh waves of Arabs and of Persians from Shiraz poured down the coast, first settling at Mogadishu, then pressing southward to Kilwa. Everywhere they landed, they introduced Islamic culture to the indigenous population. Similarly, from the first to the fifteenth centuries Indonesians crossed the Indian Ocean and settled on the African coast and on the large island of Madagascar. All these immigrants intermarried with Africans, and the resulting society combined Asian, African, and especially Islamic traits. The East African coastal culture was called **Swahili**, after a Bantu language whose vocabulary and poetic forms exhibit a strong Arabic influence.

By the late thirteenth century **Kilwa** had become the most powerful Swahili coastal city, exercising political hegemony as far north as Pemba and as far south as Sofala (see Map 10.2). In the fourteenth and fifteenth centuries the coastal cities

Swahili The East African coastal culture, named after a Bantu language whose vocabulary and poetic forms exhibit strong Arabic influences.

Kilwa The most powerful city on the east coast of Africa by the late thirteenth century.

Great Mosque at Kilwa Built between the thirteenth and fifteenth centuries to serve the Muslim commercial aristocracy of Kilwa on the Indian Ocean, the mosque attests to the wealth and power of the East African city-states. (© Ulrich Doering/Alamy Stock Photo)

were great commercial empires, comparable to the Italian city-state of Venice (see Chapter 14). Like Venice, Swahili cities such as Kilwa, Mombasa (mohm-BAHS-uh), and Pemba were situated on offshore islands. The tidal currents that isolated them from the mainland also protected them from landside attack.

Much current knowledge about life in the East African trading societies rests on the account of Ibn Battuta. He described Kilwa as "one of the finest and most substantially built towns; all the buildings are of wood, and the houses are roofed with al-dis [reeds]."[14] On the mainland were fields and orchards of rice, millet, oranges, mangoes, and bananas and pastures and yards for cattle, sheep, and poultry. Yields were apparently high; Ibn Battuta noted that the rich enjoyed three enormous meals a day and were very fat.

From among the rich mercantile families that controlled the coastal cities arose rulers who governed both the main city and surrounding territory. Such was the case with the island city of Kilwa and the nearby mainland. These rulers took various titles, including king, sultan, and sheik.

Approaching the East African coastal cities in the late fifteenth century, Portuguese traders were astounded at their enormous wealth and prosperity. This wealth rested on the ruler's monopolistic control of all trade in the area. Some coastal cities manufactured goods for export, such as cloth and iron tools. The bulk of the cities' exports, however, consisted of animal products—leopard skins, tortoise shell, ambergris, ivory—and gold. The gold originated in the Mutapa region south of the Zambezi River, where the Bantu mined it. As in tenth-century Ghana, gold was a royal monopoly in the fourteenth-century coastal city-states. Kilwa's prosperity rested on its traffic in gold.

African goods satisfied the global aristocratic demand for luxury goods. In Arabia leopard skins were made into saddles, shells were made into combs, and ambergris was used in the manufacture of perfumes. Because African elephants' tusks were larger and more durable than those of Indian elephants, African ivory was in great demand in India for sword and dagger handles, carved decorative objects, and the ceremonial bangles used in Hindu marriage rituals. Wealthy Chinese also valued African ivory for use in sedan chair construction. In exchange for these natural products, the Swahili cities brought in, among many other items, incense, glassware, glass beads, and carpets from Arabia; textiles, spices, rice, and cotton from India; and grains, fine porcelain, silk, and jade from China.

A Tenth-Century Muslim Traveler Describes Parts of the East African Coast

Other than Ethiopia, early African societies left no written accounts, so modern scholars rely on the chronicles of travelers and merchants. These outsiders, however, come with their own preconceptions, attitudes, and biases. They tend to measure what they visit and see by the conditions and experiences with which they are familiar.

In the early tenth century the Muslim merchant-traveler Al Mas'udi (d. 945), in search of African ivory, visited Oman, the southeast coast of Africa, and Zanzibar. He referred to all the peoples he encountered as Zanj, a term that he also applied to the maritime Swahili culture of the area's towns. Al Mas'udi's report, excerpted here, offers historians a wealth of information about these peoples and places.

■ Omani seamen cross the strait [of Berbera, off northern Somalia] to reach Kanbalu island [perhaps modern Pemba], located in the Zanj sea. The island's inhabitants are a mixed population of Muslims and idolatrous Zanj. . . . I have sailed many seas, the Chinese sea, the Rum sea [Mediterranean], the Khazar [Caspian Sea], the Kolzom [Red Sea], and the sea of Yemen. I have encountered dangers without number, but I know no sea more perilous than the Zanj. Here one encounters a fish called el-Owal [whale]. . . . The sailors fear its approach, and both day and night strike pieces of wood together or beat drums to drive it away. . . . Ambergris* is found in great quantities along the Zanj coast. . . . The best ambergris is found in the islands and on the shores of the Zanj sea: it is round, of a pale blue tint, sometimes the size of an ostrich egg. Lumps of it are swallowed by the whale. . . .

When the sea becomes very rough the whale vomits up large rock size balls of ambergris. When it tries to gulp them down again it chokes to death and its body floats to the surface. Quickly the Zanj, . . . having waited for such a favorable moment, draw the fish near with harpoons and tackle, cut open its stomach, and extract the ambergris. The pieces found in its intestines emit a nauseating odor, . . . but the fragments found near the back are much purer as these have been longer inside the body. . . .

The lands of the Zanj provide the people with wild leopard skins that they wear and that they export to Muslim countries. These are the largest leopard skins and make the most beautiful saddles. The Zanj also export tortoise-shell for making combs, and ivory . . . likewise. . . . The giraffe is the most common animal found in these lands. . . . They [the Zanj] settled in this country and spread south to Sofala, which marks the most distant frontier of this land. . . . Just as the China sea ends with Japan, the limits of the Zanj sea are Sofala and the Waqwaq, a region with a warm climate and fertile soil that produces gold in abundance and many other marvelous things. Here the Zanj built their capital and chose their king, whom they call *Mfalme*, the traditional title for their sovereigns. The *Mfalme* rules over all other Zanj kings and commands 300,000 cavalrymen. The Zanj employ the ox as a beast of burden, for their country contains no horses, mules, or camels, and they do not even know of these animals. Nor do they know of snow or hail. . . . The territory of the Zanj commences where a branch diverts from the upper Nile and continues to Sofala and the Waqwaq. Their villages extend for about 700 parasangs in length and breadth along the coast. The country is divided into valleys, mountains, and sandy deserts. Wild elephants abound, but you will not see a single tame one. The Zanj employ them neither for war nor for anything else. . . . When they want to catch them, they throw into the water the leaves, bark, and branches of a particular tree; then they hide in ambush until the elephants come to drink.

Slaves were another export from the East African coast. Reports of East African slave trading began with the publication of the *Periplus*. The trade accelerated with the establishment of Muslim settlements in the eighth century and continued up through the arrival of the Portuguese in the late fifteenth century, which provided a market for African slaves in the New World (see Chapter 15). In fact, the global slave market fueled the East African coastal slave trade until at least the beginning of the twentieth century.

The tainted water burns them and makes them drunk, causing them to fall down and be unable to get up. The Zanj then rush upon them, armed with very long spears, and kill them for their tusks. Indeed, the lands of the Zanj produce tusks each weighing fifty pounds and more. They generally go to Oman, and are then sent on to China and India. These are the two primary destinations, and if they were not, ivory would be abundant in Muslim lands.

In China the kings and military and civil officers ride in ivory palanquins:† no official or dignitary would dare to enter the royal presence in an iron palanquin. Thus they prefer straight tusks to curved. . . . They also burn ivory before their idols and incense their altars with its perfume, just as Christians use the Mary incense and other scents in their churches. The Chinese derive no other benefit from the elephant and believe it brings bad fortune when used for domestic purposes or war. In India ivory is much in demand. There dagger handles, as well as curved sword-scabbards, are fashioned from ivory. But ivory is chiefly used in the manufacture of chessmen and backgammon pieces. . . .

Although the Zanj are always hunting the elephant and collecting its ivory, they still make no use of ivory for their own domestic needs. For their finery they use iron rather than gold and silver, and oxen, as we mentioned above, as beasts of burden or for war, as we use camels or horses. The oxen are harnessed like horses and run at the same speed.

To return to the Zanj and their kings, these are known as *Wfalme*, meaning son of the Great Lord. They refer thus to their king because he has been selected to govern them fairly. As soon as he exerts tyrannical power or strays from the rule of law they put him to death and exclude his descendants from accession to the throne. They claim that through his wrongful actions he ceases to be the son of the Master, that is, the King of Heaven and Earth. They give God the name *Maliknajlu*, meaning the Sovereign Master.

The Zanj express themselves eloquently and have preachers in their own language. Often a devout man will stand in the center of a large crowd and exhort his listeners to render themselves agreeable to God and to submit to his commands. He depicts for them the punishments their disobedience exposes them to, and recalls the example of their ancestors and former kings. These people possess no religious code: their kings follow custom and govern according to traditional political practices.

The Zanj eat bananas, as abundant here as they are in India; but their dietary staples are millet and a plant called *kalari*, which is pulled from the earth like truffles. It is similar to the cucumber of Egypt and Syria. They also eat honey and meat. Every man worships what he pleases, be it a plant, an animal or a mineral.‡ The coconut grows on many of the islands: its fruit is eaten by all the Zanj peoples. One of these islands, situated one or two days' sail off the coast, contains a Muslim population and a hereditary royal family. This is the island of Kanbalu, which we have already mentioned.

QUESTIONS FOR ANALYSIS

1. What does Al Mas'udi's report tell us about the Zanj peoples and their customs? How would you describe his attitude toward them?
2. What commodities were most sought after by Muslim traders? Why? Where were they sold?

Source: Al Mas'udi, *Les Prairies d'Or*, trans. Arab to French by C. Barbier de Meynard and Pavet de Courteille (Paris: Imperial Printers, 1861, 1864), vol. 1: pp. 231, 234, 333–335; vol. 3: pp. 2, 3, 5–9, 26–27, 29, 30–31. Trans. French to English by Roger B. Beck.

*A solid, waxy, flammable substance, produced in the digestive system of sperm whales, not swallowed as Mas'udi purports. Ambergris was principally used in perfumery and should not be confused with amber, the fossil resin used in the manufacture of ornamental objects such as beads and women's combs.

†An enclosed litter attached to poles that servants supported on their shoulders.

‡These are forms of animism.

As in West Africa, traders obtained slaves primarily through raids and kidnapping. The Arabs called the northern Somalia coast *Ras Assir* (Cape of Slaves). From there, Arab traders transported slaves northward up the Red Sea to the markets of Arabia and Persia. Muslim dealers also shipped blacks from the Zanzibar (ZAN-zuh-bahr) region across the Indian Ocean to markets in India.

As early as the tenth century sources mention persons with "lacquer-black bodies" in the possession of wealthy families in Song China.[15] In 1178 a Chinese official noted in a memorial to the emperor that Arab traders were shipping thousands of blacks from East Africa to the Chinese port of Guangzhou (Canton) by way of the Malay Archipelago.

It appears, however, that in Indian, Chinese, and East African markets, slaves were never as valuable a commodity as ivory. Thus the volume of the Eastern slave trade did not approach that of the trans-Saharan slave trade.[16]

Southern Africa and Great Zimbabwe

Southern Africa, bordered on the northwest by the Kalahari Desert and on the northeast by the Zambezi (zam-BEE-zee) River (see Map 10.2), enjoys a mild and temperate climate. Desert conditions prevail along the Atlantic coast. Eastward toward the Indian Ocean rainfall increases, amounting to fifty to ninety inches a year in some places. Temperate grasslands characterize the interior highlands. Considerable variations in climate occur throughout much of southern Africa from year to year.

Southern Africa has enormous mineral resources: gold, copper, diamonds, platinum, and uranium. Preindustrial peoples mined some of these deposits in open excavations down several feet, but fuller exploitation required modern technology.

Southern Africa has a history that is very different from those of West Africa, the Nile Valley, and the East African coast. Unlike the rest of coastal Africa, southern Africa remained far removed from the outside world until the Portuguese arrived in the late fifteenth century—with one important exception. Bantu-speaking people reached southern Africa in the eighth century. They brought skills in ironworking and mixed farming (settled crop production plus cattle and sheep raising) and immunity to the kinds of diseases that later decimated the Amerindians of South America (see Chapter 16).

The earliest residents of southern Africa were hunters and gatherers. In the first millennium C.E. new farming techniques from the north arrived. Lack of water and timber (both needed to produce the charcoal used in iron smelting) slowed the spread of iron technology and tools and thus of crop production in southwestern Africa. These advances reached the western coastal region by 1500. By that date, Khoisan-speakers were tending livestock in the arid western regions. To the east, descendants of Bantu-speaking immigrants grew sorghum, raised cattle and sheep, and fought with iron-headed spears.

The nuclear family was the basic social unit among early southern African peoples, who practiced polygyny and traced descent in the male line. Several families formed bands numbering between twenty and eighty people. Such bands were not closed entities; people in neighboring territories identified with bands speaking the same language. As in most preindustrial societies, a division of labor existed whereby men hunted and women cared for children and raised edible plants. People lived in caves or in camps made of portable material, and they moved from one watering or hunting region to another as seasonal or environmental needs required.

Mapungubwe Golden Rhino The kingdom of Mapungubwe (1075–1220), in modern South Africa on the Limpopo River, was a precursor to the great kingdom of Great Zimbabwe to its north. Like that kingdom, it traded gold and ivory to the coast that eventually reached Egypt, India, and China. Several golden objects have been found at the site, including this famous gold foil rhinoceros, which displays the superb craftsmanship of Mapungubwe goldsmiths a thousand years ago.
(Africa 24 Media/Melita Moloney/University of Pretoria, South Africa/Newscom)

In 1871 a German explorer came upon the ruined city of **Great Zimbabwe** southeast of what is now Masvingo (mahz-VING-goh) in Zimbabwe. The ruins consist of two vast complexes of dry-stone buildings, a fortress, and an elliptically shaped enclosure commonly called the Temple. Stone carvings, gold and copper ornaments, and Asian ceramics once decorated the buildings. The ruins extend over sixty acres and are encircled by a massive wall. The entire city was built from local granite between the eleventh and fifteenth centuries without any outside influence. Archaeologists consider Great Zimbabwe the most impressive monument in Africa south of the Nile Valley and the Ethiopian highlands.

These ruins tell a remarkable story. Great Zimbabwe was the political and religious capital of a vast empire. During the first millennium C.E. settled crop cultivation, cattle raising, and work in metal led to a steady buildup in population in the Zambezi-Limpopo region. The area also contained a rich gold-bearing belt. Gold ore lay near the surface; alluvial gold lay in the Zambezi River tributaries. In the tenth century the inhabitants collected the alluvial gold by panning and washing; after the year 1000 the gold was worked in open mines with iron picks. Traders shipped the gold eastward to Sofala (see Map 10.2). Great Zimbabwe's wealth and power rested on this gold trade.

Great Zimbabwe declined in the fifteenth century, perhaps because the area had become agriculturally exhausted and could no longer support the large population. Some people migrated northward and settled in the Mazoe River Valley, a tributary of the Zambezi. This region also contained gold, and the settlers built a new empire in the tradition of Great Zimbabwe. This empire's rulers were called Mwene Mutapa (m-WEY-nee muh-TUH-pa), and their power was also based on the gold trade down the Zambezi River to Indian Ocean ports. It was this gold that the Portuguese sought when they arrived on the East African coast in the late fifteenth century.

Great Zimbabwe A ruined southern African city five hundred to a thousand years old; it is considered the most impressive monument south of the Nile Valley and Ethiopian highlands.

Chapter Summary

Africa is a huge continent with many different climatic zones and diverse geography. The African peoples are as varied as the topography. North African peoples were closely connected with the Middle Eastern and European civilizations of the Mediterranean basin. New crops introduced from Asia and the adoption of agriculture profoundly affected early societies across western and northeastern Africa as they transitioned from hunting and gathering in small bands to settled farming communities. Beginning in modern Cameroon and Nigeria, Bantu-speakers spread across central and southern Africa over a period of more than two thousand years. Possessing iron tools and weapons, domesticated livestock, and a knowledge of agriculture, these Bantu-speakers assimilated, killed, or drove away the region's previous inhabitants.

Africans in the West African Sahel participated in the trans-Saharan trade, which affected West African society in three important ways: it stimulated gold mining; it increased the demand for West Africa's second-most-important commodity, slaves; and it stimulated the development of large urban centers in West Africa.

Similarly, the Swahili peoples in city-states along the East African coast traded with Arabia, the Persian Gulf, India, China, and the Malay Archipelago. They depended on Indian Ocean commercial networks, which they used to trade African products for luxury items from Arabia, Southeast Asia, and East Asia. Great Zimbabwe, in southern Africa's interior, traded gold to the coast for the Indian Ocean trade.

The Swahili city-states and the Western Sudan kingdoms were both part of the Islamic world. Arabian merchants brought Islam with them as they settled along the East African coast, and Berber traders brought Islam to West Africa. Differing from its neighbors, Ethiopia formed a unique enclave of Christianity in the midst of Islamic societies. The majority of Bantu-speaking peoples of Great Zimbabwe and central and southern Africa were neither Islamic nor Christian.

NOTES

1. T. Spear, "Bantu Migrations," in *Problems in African History: The Precolonial Centuries*, ed. R. O. Collins et al. (New York: Markus Weiner Publishing, 1994), p. 98.
2. J. S. Trimingham, *Islam in West Africa* (Oxford: Oxford University Press, 1959), pp. 6–9.
3. R. A. Austen, "The Trans-Saharan Slave Trade: A Tentative Census," in *The Uncommon Market: Essays in the Economic History of the Atlantic Slave Trade*, ed. H. A. Gemery and J. S. Hogendorn (New York: Academic Press, 1979), pp. 1–71, esp. p. 66.
4. Quoted in J. O. Hunwick, "Islam in West Africa, A.D. 1000–1800," in *A Thousand Years of West African History*, ed. J. F. Ade Ajayi and I. Espie (New York: Humanities Press, 1972), pp. 244–245.
5. Quoted in A. A. Boahen, "Kingdoms of West Africa, c. A.D. 500–1600," in *The Horizon History of Africa* (New York: American Heritage, 1971), p. 183.
6. Al-Bakri, *Kitab al-mughrib fdhikr bilad Ifriqiya wa'l-Maghrib (Description de l'Afrique Septentrionale)*, trans. De Shane (Paris: Adrien-Maisonneuve, 1965), pp. 328–329.
7. Quoted in R. Oliver and C. Oliver, eds., *Africa in the Days of Exploration* (Englewood Cliffs, N.J.: Prentice-Hall, 1965), p. 10.
8. Quoted in Boahen, "Kingdoms of West Africa," p. 184.
9. This quotation and the next appear in E. J. Murphy, *History of African Civilization* (New York: Delta, 1972), pp. 109, 111.
10. Pekka Masonen and Humphrey J. Fisher, "Not Quite Venus from the Waves: The Almoravid Conquest of Ghana in the Modern Historiography of Western Africa," *History in Africa* 23 (1996): 197–232.
11. Quoted in Murphy, *History of African Civilization*, p. 120.
12. Quoted in Oliver and Oliver, *Africa in the Days of Exploration*, p. 18.
13. See H. G. Marcus, *A History of Ethiopia*, updated ed. (Berkeley: University of California Press, 2002), pp. 17–20.
14. Ibn Battuta, *The Travels of Ibn Battuta, A.D. 1325–1354*, vol. 1, ed. H. A. R. Gibb (London: University Press, 1972), pp. 379–380.
15. Austen, "The Trans-Saharan Slave Trade," p. 65; J. H. Harris, *The African Presence in Asia* (Evanston, Ill.: Northwestern University Press, 1971), pp. 3–6, 27–30; P. Wheatley, "Analecta Sino-Africana Recensa," in Neville Chittick and Robert Rotberg, *East Africa and the Orient* (New York: Africana Publishing, 1975), p. 109.
16. I. Hrbek, ed., *General History of Africa*. Vol. 3: *Africa from the Seventh to the Eleventh Century* (Berkeley: University of California Press; New York: UNESCO, 1991), pp. 294–295, 346–347.

CONNECTIONS

Africa was an integral part of the vast trans-Saharan and Indian Ocean trading networks that stretched from Europe to China. This trade brought wealth to African kingdoms, empires, and city-states that developed alongside the routes. But the trade in ideas more profoundly connected the growing African states to the wider world, most notably through Islam, which had arrived by the seventh century, and Christianity, which developed a foothold in Ethiopia.

Prior to the late fifteenth century Europeans had little knowledge about African societies. All this would change during the European Age of Discovery. Chapter

16 traces the expansion of Portugal from a small, poor European nation to an overseas empire, as it established trading posts and gained control of the African gold trade. Portuguese expansion led to competition, spurring Spain and then England to strike out for gold of their own in the Americas. The acceleration of this conquest would forever shape the history of Africa and the Americas (see Chapters 11 and 15) and intertwine them via the African slave trade that fueled the labor needs of the colonies in the Americas.

CHAPTER 10   Review and Explore

Identify Key Terms

Identify and explain the significance of each item below.

Bantu (p. 272)	**stateless societies** (p. 278)	**Aksum** (p. 284)
Sudan (p. 273)	**Ghana** (p. 279)	**Swahili** (p. 288)
Berbers (p. 275)	**Koumbi Saleh** (p. 280)	**Kilwa** (p. 288)
Mogadishu (p. 278)	**Timbuktu** (p. 283)	**Great Zimbabwe** (p. 293)

Review the Main Ideas

Answer the focus questions from each section of the chapter.

1. How did Africa's geography shape its history and contribute to its diverse population? (p. 268)

2. How did agriculture affect life among the early societies in the western Sudan and among the Bantu-speaking societies of central and southern Africa? (p. 270)

3. What characterized trans-Saharan trade, and how did it affect West African society? (p. 274)

4. How were the East African city-states, Aksum, and Great Zimbabwe different from and similar to the kingdoms of the western Sudan? (p. 293)

Make Comparisons and Connections

Analyze the larger developments and continuities within and across chapters.

1. How did the geography and size of Africa affect African societies and their contact with the rest of the world?

2. What different cultures influenced the African people living along the continent's eastern coast?

3. Based on the discussion in Chapter 9 on the spread of Islam and what you learned in this chapter, how did Islam influence the different societies of West and East Africa?

4. How might the Bantu migrations compare with earlier migrations, such as the Indo-European migrations discussed in Chapter 2 or the Barbarian migrations discussed in Chapter 8?

TIMELINE

Suggested Resources

BOOKS

Austen, Ralph. *African Economic History*. 1987. Classic study of Africa's economic history.

Austen, Ralph. *Trans-Saharan Africa in World History*. 2010. Excellent new introduction to the Sahara region and the trans-Saharan trade that gave it life.

Beck, Roger B. *The History of South Africa*, 2d ed. 2014. Introduction to this large and important country.

Bouvill, E. W., and Robin Hallett. *The Golden Trade of the Moors: West African Kingdoms in the Fourteenth Century*. 1995. Classic description of the trans-Saharan trade.

Ehret, Christopher. *An African Classical Age: Eastern and Southern Africa in World History, 1000 B.C. to A.D. 400*. 2001. Solid introduction by a renowned African scholar.

Ehret, Christopher. *The Civilizations of Africa: A History to 1800*, 2d ed. 2013. The best study of pre-1800 African history.

Gilbert, Erik, and Jonathan Reynolds. *Africa in World History*, 3d ed. 2011. Groundbreaking study of Africa's place in world history.

Iliffe, John. *Africans: The History of a Continent*, 2d ed. 2007. Thoughtful introduction to African history.

Klieman, Kairn A. *The Pygmies Were Our Compass: Bantu and Batwa in the History of West Central Africa, Early Times to c. 1900 C.E.* 2003. A unique study of Bantu and forest people in precolonial African history.

Levtzion, Nehemia, and Randall L. Pouwels. *History of Islam in Africa*. 2000. Comprehensive survey of Islam's presence in Africa.

Marcus, H. G. *A History of Ethiopia*, updated ed. 2002. Standard introduction to Ethiopian history.

Middleton, John. *African Merchants of the Indian Ocean: Swahili of the East African Coast*. 2004. A brief but solid introduction to the Swahili people.

ca. 900–1100 C.E. Kingdom of Ghana;
bananas and plantains arrive in Africa from Asia

1314–1344 C.E. Reign of Amda
Siyon in Ethiopia

ca. 1200–1450 C.E. Kingdom of Mali

ca. 1100–1450 C.E. Great Zimbabwe built, flourishes

ca. 1312–1337 C.E.
Reign of Mansa Musa in Mali

1324–1325 C.E. Mansa Musa's
pilgrimage to Mecca

1095–1270 C.E. Christian Crusades in western Asia and North Africa (Ch. 14)

1206–1360s C.E. Mongol Empire rules across
Central and East Asia (Ch. 12)

900   1200   1500

Mitchell, Peter. *African Connections: Archaeological Perspectives on Africa and the Wider World*. 2005. Places ancient Africa and its history in a global context.

Newman, J. L. *The Peopling of Africa: A Geographic Interpretation*, rev. ed., 1997. Explores population distribution and technological change up to the late nineteenth century.

Schmidt, Peter R. *Historical Archaeology in Africa: Representation, Social Memory, and Oral Traditions*. 2006. An excellent introduction to archaeology and the reconstruction of Africa's history.

DOCUMENTARY

Africa: A Voyage of Discovery with Basil Davidson (Home Vision, 1984). An eight-part series about African history and society. See particularly episode 2, "Mastering the Continent"; episode 3, "Caravans of Gold"; and episode 4, "Kings and Cities." Run times are about fifty minutes for each program.

WEBSITES

The Story of Africa. Some of the world's top Africanists have contributed to this BBC website's discussion of African history from an African perspective. **www.bbc.co.uk/worldservice/africa/features /storyofafrica/index.shtml**

Internet African History Sourcebook. A valuable reference site for historical sources on African history. **sourcebooks.fordham.edu/halsall/africa /africasbook.asp**

11

The Americas
3200 B.C.E.–1500 C.E.

When peoples of the Americas first came into sustained contact with peoples from Europe, Africa, and Asia at the turn of the sixteenth century, their encounters were uneven. Isolation from other world societies made peoples of the Americas vulnerable to diseases found elsewhere in the world. When indigenous peoples were exposed to these diseases through contact with Europeans, the devastating effects of epidemics facilitated European domination. But this exchange also brought into global circulation the results of thousands of years of work by peoples of the Americas in plant domestication that changed diets worldwide, making corn, potatoes, and peppers into the daily staples of many societies.

Domestication of these crops intensified farming across the Americas that sustained increasingly complex societies. At times these societies grew into vast empires built on trade, conquest, and tribute. Social stratification and specialization produced lands not just of subjects and kings, but of priests, merchants, artisans, scientists, and engineers who achieved extraordinary feats.

In Mesoamerica (MAY-so-america) — the region stretching from present-day central Mexico to Nicaragua — the dense urban centers of Maya, Teotihuacan (TAY-oh-tee-hwa-can), Toltec, and Aztec city-states and empires featured great monuments, temples, and complex urban planning. Roadways and canals extended trade networks that reached from South America to the Great Lakes region of North America. Precise calendars shaped religious, scientific, medical, and agricultural knowledge.

In the Andes, the mountain range that extends from southernmost present-day Chile north to Colombia and Venezuela, peoples adapted to the mountain range's stark vertical stratification of climate and ecosystems to produce agricultural abundance similar to that of Mesoamerica. Andean technological, agricultural, and engineering innovations allowed people to make their difficult mountain terrain a home rather than a boundary.

Werner Forman/Universal Images Group/Getty Images

Peruvian Burial Figure

This figure of a woman, wrapped in a shawl, was typical of representations of people that were placed in the burial sites in the Andes. The figure depicts an Inca emperor's concubine, a social and ceremonial role that symbolized Mamacona, the Virgin of the Sun.

CHAPTER PREVIEW

SOCIETIES OF THE AMERICAS IN A GLOBAL CONTEXT
How did ancient peoples of the Americas adapt to, and adapt, their environment?

ANCIENT SOCIETIES
What patterns established by early societies shaped civilization in Mesoamerica and the Andes?

THE INCAS
What were the sources of strength and prosperity, and of problems, for the Incas?

THE MAYA AND TEOTIHUACAN
How did the Maya and Teotihuacan develop prosperous and stable societies in the classical era?

THE AZTEC EMPIRE
How did the Mexica build on the achievements of earlier Mesoamerican cultures and develop new traditions to create their large empire?

AMERICAN EMPIRES AND THE ENCOUNTER
What did the European encounter mean for peoples of the major American empires?

How did ancient peoples of the Americas adapt to, and adapt, their environment?

Societies of the Americas in a Global Context

Like people everywhere, civilizations of the Americas interpreted the meaning of the world and their place in the cosmos. They organized societies stratified not just by gender, class, and ethnicity but also by professional roles and wealth, and they adapted to and reshaped their physical and natural world. But they did all this on their own, without outside influences and within a distinct environment.

If the differences between the civilizations in the Americas and other world regions are remarkable, the similarities are even more so. By studying the peoples of the Americas before their encounters with other world societies, we gain a clearer view of universal aspects of the human experience.

Trade and Technology

The domestication of crops and animals created an abundance of food and livestock, which allowed people to take on new social roles and to develop specialized occupations. As cities emerged, they became hubs of a universal human activity: trade. These cities were home to priests who interpreted the nature of the world, as well as a nobility from which kings emerged, some of whom forged vast empires.

The differences in the development and application of three different kinds of technologies — the wheel, writing and communications systems, and calendars — capture this essential nature of human adaptability.

Because of conditions specific to the Americas, societies in Mesoamerica and the Andes did not use wheels for transportation before their encounters with other world peoples that began in 1492. In Mesoamerica there were no large animals like horses or oxen to domesticate as beasts of burden, so there was no way to power wagons or chariots. In the Andes, domesticated llamas and alpacas served as pack animals and were a source of wool and meat. But in the most densely settled, cultivated, and developed areas, the terrain was too difficult for wheeled transportation. Instead Andean peoples developed extensive networks of roads that navigated steep changes in altitude, supported by elaborate suspension bridges made from woven vegetable fibers.

Peoples of the Americas also did not develop alphabetical writing systems, but this did not mean they did not communicate in writing or record information. If we separate our understanding of the alphabetical reading you are doing right now from its functions — communicating and storing information — we can appreciate the ways in which Andean and **Mesoamerican** civilizations accomplished both. Peoples of the Americas spoke thousands of languages (hundreds are still spoken today). Mesoamericans, beginning with the Olmecs (1500–300 B.C.E.), used phonograms, characters that represent sound, and logograms, characters that represent words or ideas, similar to those of ancient Egyptian hieroglyphs or Japanese kanji. Later civilizations wrote books on paper and deerskin, some of which have survived to the present.

The Andean innovation for recording information was particularly remarkable. The **khipu** (KEY-pooh) was an assemblage of colored and knotted strings. Differences in color and type of knot, as well as the knots' order and placement, served as a binary system akin to a contemporary computer database. Khipus were used to record demographic, economic, and political information that allowed imperial rulers and local leaders to understand and manage complex data across a vast empire.

Mesoamerica The term used to designate the area spanning present-day central Mexico to Nicaragua.

khipu An intricate system of knotted and colored strings used by early Andean cultures to store information such as census and tax records.

Mesoamerican peoples used a sophisticated combination of calendars. These were based on a Calendar Round that combined a 365-day solar calendar with a 260-day lunar calendar based on the numbers thirteen and twenty, which were sacred to peoples of Mesoamerica. Annual cycles were completed when twenty 13-day bundles converged with thirteen 20-day bundles. Together with the solar calendar, these formed a 52-year cycle whose precision was unsurpassed in the premodern world. It also provided an incredibly intricate mechanism not only for following the solar and lunar years but also for connecting these to aspects of daily life and religion. The calendars helped users interpret their world.

Settlement and Environment

The ancient settlers of the Americas migrated from Asia, though their timing and their route are debated. One possibility is that the first settlers migrated across the Bering Strait from what is now Russia to Alaska and gradually migrated southward sometime between 15,000 and 13,000 B.C.E. But archaeological excavations have identified much earlier settlements, perhaps dating to up to 20,000–30,000 years ago, along the Andes in South America than they have for Mesoamerica or North America. Evidence from some settlements suggest the possibility that seafaring migration may have also occurred.

Like early settlers elsewhere in the world, populations of the Americas could be divided into three categories: nomadic peoples, semi-sedentary farming communities, and dense agricultural communities capable of sustaining cities. Over time, urban settlement and empire formation centered on two major regions. The first area was the region around Lake Titicaca, where the Inca Empire (1438–1532) originated. Located at the present-day border between Peru and Bolivia, Lake Titicaca is the highest lake in the world (12,500 feet high) and the largest lake in South America (3,200 square miles). The second area was the Valley of Mexico on the central plateau of Mesoamerica, where empires such as the Aztec Empire (1428–1521) formed cities around Lake Texcoco. Access to these large freshwater lakes allowed agriculture to expand through irrigation, which in turn supported growing urban populations.

The earliest farming settlements emerged around 10,000 B.C.E. when communities began the long process of domesticating and modifying plants, including squash, maize (corn), potatoes, peppers, and beans. The origins of maize in Mesoamerica are unclear, though it became a centerpiece of the Mesoamerican diet and spread across the Americas. Eaten together with beans, maize provided Mesoamerican peoples with a diet sufficient in protein despite the scarcity of meat. Mesoamericans processed kernels through **nixtamalization**, boiling the maize in a solution of water and mineral lime. The process broke down compounds in the kernels, increasing their nutritional value, while enriching the resulting *masa*, or paste, with dietary minerals including calcium, potassium, and iron.

nixtamalization Boiling maize in a solution of water and mineral lime to break down compounds in the kernels, increasing their nutritional value.

The masa could be cooked with beans, meat, or other ingredients to make tamales. It could also be rolled flat on a stone called a *metate* (MAY-tah-teh) and baked into tortillas. Tortillas played roles similar to those of bread in wheat-producing cultures: they could be stored, they were light and easy to transport, and they were used as the basic building block of meals. Aztec armies of the fifteenth century could travel long distances because they carried tortillas for sustenance. Along an army's route, communities were obligated to provide tribute in tortillas.

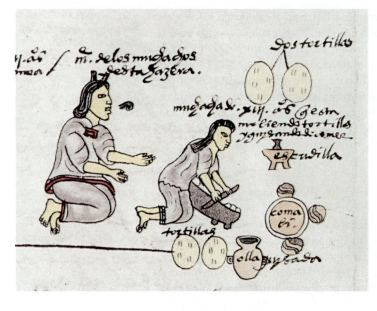

Making Tortillas A mother teaches her daughter to roll tortillas on a metate. The dough at the right of the metate was masa made with maize and lime. The preparation process, known as nixtamalization, enriched the maize paste by adding calcium, potassium, and iron.

(From the *Codex Mendoza*, Mexico, c. 1541–1542 [pen and ink on paper]/Bodleian Library, Oxford, UK/Bridgeman Images)

Andean peoples cultivated another staple of the Americas, the potato. Potatoes first grew wild, but selective breeding produced many different varieties. For Andean peoples, potatoes became an integral part of a complex system of cultivation at varying altitudes. Communities created a system of "vertical archipelagos" through which they took advantage of the changes of climate along the steep escarpments of the Andes. Different crops could be cultivated at different altitudes, allowing communities to engage in intense and varied farming in what would otherwise have been inhospitable territory.

Communities raised multiple crops and engaged in year-round farming by working at different altitudes located within a day's journey from home. Some of these zones of cultivation were so distant—sometimes over a week's journey—that they were tended by temporary or permanent colonies, called *mitmaq*, of the main settlement.

At higher elevations, members of these communities cultivated potatoes. Arid conditions across much of the altiplano (AL-tee-plan-oh), or high-plains plateau, meant that crops of potatoes could sometimes be planted only every few years. But the climate—dry with daily extremes of heat and cold—could be used to freeze-dry potatoes that could be stored indefinitely. Above the potato-growing zone, shepherds tended animals such as llamas and alpacas, which provided wool and dried meat, or *ch'arki* (the origin of the word *jerky*). They also served as pack animals that helped farmers bring in the crops from their high- and low-altitude plots. The animals' manure served as fertilizer for farming at lower altitudes.

At middle altitudes, communities used terraces edged by stone walls to extend cultivation along steep mountainsides to grow corn. In the lowlands, communities cultivated the high-protein grain quinoa, as well as beans, peppers, and coca. Farmers chewed coca (the dried leaves of a plant native to the Andes from which cocaine is derived) to alleviate the symptoms of strenuous labor at extremely high altitudes. Coca also added nutrients such as calcium to the Andean diet and played an important role in religious rituals. In the lowlands communities also grew cotton, and in coastal areas they harvested fish and mussels. Fishermen built inflatable rafts made of sealskin. Communities specialized in the types of production their ecosystems allowed.

Ancient Societies

What patterns established by early societies shaped civilization in Mesoamerica and the Andes?

Between 1500 and 1200 B.C.E. emerging civilizations in Mesoamerica and the Andes established lasting patterns of production, culture, and social organization that would long influence societies of the Americas. In Mesoamerica, Olmec civilization laid the foundation for future empires. The imprint of Olmec civilization spread across long networks of trade that would one day extend from Central America to the Mississippi Valley and the Great Lakes of North America. In the Andes, Chavín and Moche civilizations formed the early part of a long cycle of centralization and decentralization. This political and economic centralization helped spread technology, culture, and religion.

Olmec Agriculture, Technology, and Religion

The **Olmecs** were an early civilization that shaped the religion, trade practices, and technology of later civilizations in Mesoamerica. They flourished in the coastal lowlands of Mexico from 1500 to 300 B.C.E. The Olmecs formed the first cities of Mesoamerica, and these cities served as centers of agriculture, trade, and religion (Map 11.1). Through long-distance trade, the Olmecs spread their culture and technology across Mesoamerica, establishing beliefs and practices that became common to the civilizations that followed.

Olmec The earliest advanced Mesoamerican civilization.

The Olmecs settled along rivers in the coastal lowlands, where they cultivated maize, squash, beans, and other plants. They supplemented their diet with wild game and fish. But they lacked many other resources. In particular, they carried stone for many miles for the construction of temples and for carving massive monuments, many in the shape of heads. Across far-flung networks the Olmecs traded rubber, cacao (from which chocolate is made), pottery, and jaguar pelts, as well as the services of artisans such as painters and sculptors, in exchange for obsidian, a volcanic glass that could be carved to a razor-sharp edge and used for making knives, tools, spear tips, and other weapons.

These ties between the Olmecs and other communities spread religious practices, creating a shared framework of beliefs among later civilizations. These practices included the construction of large pyramid temples, as well as sacrificial rituals. Olmec deities, like those of their successors, were combinations of gods and humans, included merged animal and human forms, and had both male and female identities. People practicing later religions based their gods on a fusion of human and spirit traits along the lines of the Olmec were-jaguar: a half-man, half-jaguar figure.

The Olmecs also used a solar calendar with a 365-day year. This calendar begins with the year 3114 B.C.E., though its origins and the significance of this date are unclear. Archaeologists presume that the Olmecs combined the solar calendar

MAP 11.1 The Olmecs, ca. 1500–300 B.C.E. Olmec civilization flourished in the coastal lowlands of southern Mexico along the Caribbean coast. Olmec patterns of settlement, culture, religion, organization, and trade are known almost solely through excavation of archaeological sites.

with a 260-day lunar calendar, to form the combined Calendar Round. All the later Mesoamerican civilizations used at least one of these calendars, and most used both of them.

Hohokam, Hopewell, and Mississippian Societies

Mesoamerican trading networks extended into southwestern North America, where by 300 B.C.E. the Hohokam people and other groups were using irrigation canals, dams, and terraces to enhance their farming of arid lands (Map 11.2). Like the Olmecs and other Mesoamerican peoples, the Hohokam built ceremonial platforms and played games with rubber balls that were traded over a long distance in return for turquoise and other precious stones. Along with trade goods came religious ideas, including the belief in local divinities who created, preserved, and destroyed. The Mesoamerican Feathered Serpent god became important to desert peoples. They

MAP 11.2 Major North American Agricultural Societies, ca. 600–1500 C.E. Many North American groups used agriculture to increase the available food supply and allow greater population density and the development of urban centers. This map shows three of these cultures: the Mississippian, Anasazi, and Hohokam.

Cahokia Mounds in Illinois Monks Mound is located in Cahokia, the largest Mississippian settlement. The pyramid is nearly 100 feet tall and 1,000 feet long, making it the largest constructed structure north of Mesoamerica.

(Ira Block/National Geographic Creative)

planted desert crops such as agave, as well as cotton and maize that came from Mexico. Other groups, including the Anasazi (ah-nah-SAH-zee), the Yuma, and later the Pueblo and Hopi, also built settlements in this area using large sandstone blocks and masonry to construct thick-walled houses that offered protection from the heat. Mesa Verde, the largest Anasazi town, had a population of about twenty-five hundred living in houses built into and on cliff walls. Roads connected Mesa Verde to other Anasazi towns, allowing timber and other construction materials to be brought in more easily. Eventually drought, deforestation, and soil erosion led to decline in both the Hohokam and Anasazi cultures.

In eastern North America, mound building began around 5500 B.C.E. One of the most important mound-building cultures was the Hopewell (200 B.C.E.–600 C.E.), named for a town in Ohio near the site of the most extensive mounds. Some mounds were burial chambers. Other mounds formed animal or geometric figures. Hopewell earthworks also included canals that enabled trading networks to expand, bringing products from the Caribbean far into the interior. Those trading networks also carried maize, allowing more intensive agriculture to spread throughout the eastern woodlands of North America.

At Cahokia (kuh-HOE-kee-uh), near the confluence of the Mississippi and Missouri Rivers in Illinois, archaeologists have identified the largest mound complex in North America, part of a ceremonial center and city that may have housed nearly forty thousand people. Work on this complex of mounds, plazas, and houses—which covered 5½ square miles—began about 1050 C.E. and was completed about 1250 C.E. A fence of wooden posts surrounded the center of the complex. Several hundred mounds inside and outside the fence served as tombs and as the bases for temples and palaces. The largest mound rose in four stages to a height of one hundred feet and was nearly one thousand feet long. On its top stood a large building, used perhaps as a temple.

Cahokia trade reached far across North America. Mississippian mound builders relied on agriculture to support their complex cultures, and by the time Cahokia was built, maize agriculture had spread to the Atlantic coast. Particularly along riverbanks and the coastline, fields of maize, beans, and squash surrounded large, permanent villages containing many houses, all encompassed by walls made of earth and timber.

At its peak in about 1150 Cahokia was the largest city north of Mesoamerica. However, its construction stripped much of the surrounding countryside of trees, which made spring floods worse and eventually destroyed much of the city. An earthquake in the thirteenth century furthered the destruction, and the city never recovered. The worsening climate of the fourteenth century, which brought famine to Europe, probably also contributed to Cahokia's decline, and its population dispersed.

Kinship and Ancestors in the Andes

In the Andes social organization and religion shaped ideas of spiritual kinship as well as patterns of production and trade. The *ayllu* (IGH-you), or clan, served as the fundamental social unit of Andean society. Kinship was based on a shared ancestor and on worship of *huaca*, sacred spaces or things that had spiritual characteristics and were sometimes linked to ancestors. Huaca were often a part of the landscape, such as a spring or stone. Members of an ayllu considered their huaca as more than a spirit: it owned the lands the ayllu's farmers tended, and it served as the center of community obligations such as the pooling of labor.

Ancestor worship provided the foundations of Andean religion and spirituality, served as the basis of authority, and guided food production. All members of the ayllu owed allegiance to *kurakas*, or clan leaders, who typically traced the most direct lineage to an ancestor identified with a huaca. This lineage made them both temporal and spiritual leaders of their ayllu. An Andean family's identity came from membership in an ayllu's ancestral kinship, and its subsistence came from participation in the broader community's shared farming across vertical climate zones. People often labored collectively and reciprocally.

Archaeologists periodize Andean history in cycles of centralization and decentralization. There were three great periods of centralization, which archaeologists call the Early, Middle, and Late Horizon. The Late Horizon, which included the Inca Empire, was the briefest, cut short by the Spanish conquest (see "Conquest and Settlement" in Chapter 16). The first period, the Early Horizon (ca. 1200–200 B.C.E.), centered on the people of Chavín (chah-VEEN), upland from present-day Lima. The Chavín spread their religion along with technologies for the weaving and dyeing of wool and cotton. Weaving became the most widespread means of recording and representing information in the Andes.

After the end of the Early Horizon, regional states emerged, including **Moche** (MOH-cheh) civilization, which flourished along a 250-mile stretch of Peru's northern coast between 100 and 800 C.E. The Moche people developed complex irrigation systems, with which they raised food crops and cotton. Each Moche valley contained a large ceremonial center with palaces and pyramids surrounded by settlements of up to ten thousand people. Their dazzling gold and silver artifacts, as well as elaborate headdresses, display great skill in pottery and metalwork.

Moche A Native American culture that thrived along Peru's northern coast between 100 and 800 C.E.

Politically, the Moche were organized into a series of small city-states rather than one unified state, and warfare was common among them. Beginning about 500 the Moche suffered several severe El Niños, changes in ocean current patterns in the Pacific that bring searing drought and flooding. They were not able to respond effectively to the devastation, and their urban population declined.

Pan-Andean cultures re-emerged during the Middle Horizon (500–1000 C.E.), centered to the south in Tiwanaku (TEE-wan-ah-kooh), in Lake Titicaca, and to the north at Wari, near present-day southern Peru. The city-state of Wari's dominion stretched from the altiplano north of Lake Titicaca to the Pacific coast, drawing on Moche culture. Its reach between mountain and coastal regions led to extensive exchanges of goods and beliefs. The city-state of Tiwanaku extended its influence in the other direction, south of the lake. Both Wari and Tiwanaku practiced ancestor worship, and Tiwanaku religion centered on the figure of Viracocha, the god creator and father of humanity, who was identified with the sun and storms.

Storms and climate shifts were central to Andean people's worldview because changes in climate, particularly abrupt changes brought by El Niño, could devastate whole civilizations. El Niño disrupted Moche culture and contributed to the decline of Wari and Tiwanaku. As the Middle Horizon ended, the cities of Tiwanaku and Wari endured on a smaller scale, but between 1000 and 1200 C.E. they lost their regional influence. The eras between the Early, Middle, and Late Horizon, known as Intermediate Periods, were times of decentralization in which local cultures and practices re-emerged. It was out of these local developments that new centralizing empires would over time emerge.

The Incas

What were the sources of strength and prosperity, and of problems, for the Incas?

Inca was the name of the governing family of the largest and last Andean empire. The empire, whose people we will call the Incas, was called Tawantinsuyu (TAH-want-een-soo-you), meaning "from the four parts, one," expressing the idea of a unified people stretching in all directions.

Inca The name of the dynasty of rulers who built the largest and last indigenous empire across the Andes.

The Inca Model of Empire

In the Late Intermediate Period (1200–1470), the Pan-Andean influences of Wari and Tiwanaku waned. City-states around Lake Titicaca competed and fought. The strongest ones again emerged. To the north, the Chimu claimed the legacy of the Moche and Wari. To the south, the city of Cuzco became the hub of a growing kingdom under the hereditary control of the Incas (Map 11.3). The ways Inca rulers adapted techniques of statecraft from Wari and religious practices from Titicaca gave them powerful tools that helped them build their empire.

In the 1420s Viracocha Inca emerged as the first Inca leader to attempt permanent conquest. Unlike the *sinchis* (SEEN-cheese), or kings, of other city-states, Viracocha Inca fashioned himself an emperor and, in adopting the name Viracocha, connected himself to the god of creation. Around 1438 rivals invaded Viracocha Inca's territories and he fled. His son, Pachacuti, remained in Cuzco and fended off the invaders. He crowned himself emperor and embarked on a campaign of conquest. Pachacuti Inca conquered the Chimu and incorporated beliefs and practices from this northern civilization.

Machu Picchu The Inca ruins of Machu Picchu rise spectacularly above the steep valley of the Urubamba River. The site was built around 1450 as a royal estate and abandoned after the Spanish conquest. (Tony Camacho/Science Source)

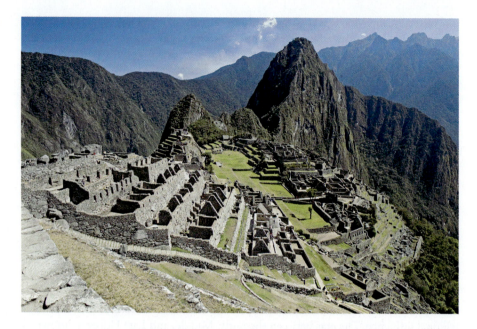

After conquering the Chimu, Pachacuti instituted practices that expanded the empire across the Andes. He combined Andean ancestor worship with the Chimu system of a split inheritance, a combination that drove swift territorial expansion and transformed Tawantinsuyu into one of the largest empires in the world. Under the system of ancestor worship, the Incas believed the dead emperor's spirit was still present, and they venerated him through his mummy. Split inheritance meant that the dead emperor retained all the lands he had conquered, commanded the loyalty of all his subjects, and continued to receive tribute. A *panaqa* (pan-AH-kah), a trust formed by his closest relatives, managed both the cult of his mummy and his temporal affairs. Chimu split inheritance became a basic structure of the empire's organization.

When the ruler died, his corpse was preserved as a mummy in elaborate clothing and housed in a sacred and magnificent chamber. A sixteenth-century account of the death of Pachacuti Inca in 1471 described the practices for burying and honoring him:

> He was buried by putting his body in the earth in a large new clay urn, with him very well dressed. Pachacuti Inca [had] ordered that a golden image made to resemble him be placed on top of his tomb. And it was to be worshiped in place of him by the people who went there. . . . [He had] ordered those of his own lineage to bring this statue out for the feasts that were held in Cuzco. When they brought it out like this, they sang about the things that the Inca did in his life, both in the wars and in his city. Thus they served and revered him, changing its garments as he used to do, and serving it as he was served when he was alive.[1]

The panaqa of descendants of each dead ruler managed his lands and used his income to care for his mummy, maintain his cult, and support themselves, all at great

MAPPING THE PAST

MAP 11.3 The Inca Empire, 1532 Andean peoples turned their stark mountain landscape to their advantage by settling and farming in vertical archipelagos. Settlements were located at temperate altitudes, while farming and herding took place at higher and lower altitudes.

ANALYZING THE MAP In what ways did Andean peoples turn their mountain landscape from an obstacle into a resource?

CONNECTIONS What types of geographic features did other peoples of the Americas, or peoples in other regions of the world, adapt to their advantage? How did adaptation to their geography shape those societies?

expense. When a ruler died, one of his sons was named the new Inca emperor. He received the title, but not the lands and tribute—nor, for that matter, the direct allegiance of the nobility, bound as it was to the deceased ruler. The new emperor built his own power and wealth by conquering new lands.

Inca Imperial Expansion

The combination of ancestor worship and split inheritance provided the logic and impulse for expanding Inca power. The desire for conquest provided incentives for courageous (or ambitious) nobles: those who succeeded in battle and gained new territories for the state could expect to receive lands, additional wives, servants, herds of llamas, gold, silver, and other status symbols. Common soldiers who distinguished themselves could be rewarded and raised to noble status. Under Pachacuti Inca and his successors, Inca domination was extended by warfare to the frontier of present-day Ecuador and Colombia in the north and to present-day Chile in the south, an area of about 350,000 square miles. Eighty provinces, scores of ethnic groups, and 16 million people came under Inca control.

The Incas integrated regions they conquered by spreading their language and their gods. Magnificent temples housed images of these gods. Priests led prayers and elaborate rituals, and during occasions such as natural disasters or military victories they sacrificed humans. The Incas' official language, **Quechua** (KEH-chuh-wah), spread across the empire. Along with another major Andean language, Aymara, it is still spoken by millions in Peru, Bolivia, and regions of Ecuador, Argentina, and Chile.

Pressure for growth strained the Inca Empire. Conquerable lands became scarce, so the Incas directed their attentions to the tropical Amazon forest east of the Andes—an effort that led to military disasters. Inca armies traditionally waged combat in massed formation, often engaging in hand-to-hand combat. But in dense jungles armies could not maneuver or maintain order against enemies who used guerrilla

Quechua The official language of the Incas, it is still spoken by most Peruvians today.

tactics. Another source of stress came from revolts among subject peoples in conquered territories. Even the system of roads and message-carrying runners couldn't keep up with the administrative needs of the empire. The average runner could cover about 175 miles per day—a remarkable feat of physical endurance, especially at a high altitude—but as the empire grew, so did the distances communication needed to cover. The round trip from the capital at Cuzco to Quito in Ecuador, for example, took ten to twelve days, so an emperor might have to base urgent decisions on incomplete or out-of-date information. The empire was overextended.

Imperial Needs and Obligations

At its height, the Inca Empire extended over 2,600 miles. The challenges of sustaining an empire with that reach, not to mention one built so fast, required extraordinary resourcefulness. The Inca Empire met these demands by adapting aspects of local culture to meet imperial needs. For instance, the empire demanded that the ayllus, the local communities with shared ancestors, include imperial tribute in the rotation of labor and the distribution of harvested foods. In return, community leaders received goods from the empire.

As each Inca emperor conquered new lands and built his domain, he mobilized people and resources by drawing on local systems of labor and organization. Much as ayllus developed satellite communities called mitmaq to take advantage of remote farming areas, the emperor relocated families or even whole villages over long distances to consolidate territorial control or quell unrest. What had been a community practice became a tool of imperial expansion. The emperor sent mitmaq settlers, known as *mitmaquisuna*, far and wide, creating diverse ethnic enclaves. Inca rulers and nobles also married the daughters of elite families among the peoples they conquered.

The reciprocal labor carried out within ayllus expanded into a labor tax called the *mit'a* (MEE-tuh), which rotated among households in an ayllu throughout the year. Tribute paid in labor provided the means for building the infrastructure of empire. Rotations of laborers carried out impressive engineering projects, allowing the vast empire to extend over the most difficult and inhospitable terrain. An excellent system of roads facilitated the movement of armies and the rapid communication of royal orders by runners.

Like Persian and Roman roads, these feats of engineering linked an empire. On these roads Inca officials, tax collectors, and accountants traveled throughout the empire, using elaborate khipus to record financial and labor obligations, the output of fields, population levels, land transfers, and other numerical records. Only around 650 khipus are known to survive today, because colonial Spaniards destroyed them, believing khipus might contain religious messages that conflicted with their efforts to impose Christianity.

Weaving for Tribute Felipe Guaman Poma de Ayala's line drawing shows a woman weaving fine cloth on a back-strap loom. The drawing indicates that the woman is "weaving for tribute," which in Poma de Ayala's time would have been paid to the Spaniards, continuing a traditional obligation of providing tribute to Inca rulers.

(Museo Nacional de Antropologia, Arqueologia y Historia, Lima, Peru/ De Agostini Picture Library/Bridgeman Images)

The Maya and Teotihuacan

In Mesoamerica the classical period (300 C.E.–900 C.E.) saw major advances in religion, art, architecture, and farming, akin to those of the classical civilizations of the Mediterranean. Long-lasting city-states rose in **Maya** regions between 300 C.E. and 900 C.E. City-states also developed in the Valley of Mexico, where **Teotihuacan** emerged as a major center of trade between 300 C.E. and 650 C.E. The classical period was followed by the postclassical Toltec Empire (900–1174 C.E.), which adapted the cultural, ritual, and aesthetic practices that influenced later empires like the Aztecs.

Maya Agriculture and Trade

The Maya inhabited the highlands of Guatemala and the Yucatán peninsula in present-day Mexico and Belize. Their physical setting shaped two features of Maya society. First, the abundance of high-quality limestone allowed them to build monumental architecture. Second, limestone formations created deep natural wells called *cenotes* (say-NOH-tehs), which became critical sources of water in an often-arid environment. Cenotes were essential to farming and also became important religious and spiritual sites. The staple crop of the Maya was maize, often raised in small remote plots called *milpas* in combination with other foodstuffs, including beans, squash, chili peppers, root crops, and fruit trees.

The entire Maya region may have had as many as 14 million inhabitants. Sites like Uxmal, Uaxactún, Copán, Piedras Negras, Tikal, Palenque, and Chichén Itzá (Map 11.4) emerged as independent city-states, each ruled by a hereditary king. These cities featured ornate temples, engraved pillars, palaces for nobles, pyramids where nobles were buried, and courts for ball games. A hereditary nobility owned land, exercised political power, and directed religious rituals. Artisans and scribes made up the social level below. Other residents were farmers, laborers, and slaves, the latter including prisoners of war.

At Maya markets, jade, obsidian, beads of red spiny oyster shell, lengths of cloth, and cacao beans—all in high demand in the Mesoamerican world—served as media of exchange. The extensive trade among Maya communities, plus a common language, promoted unity among the peoples of the region. Merchants traded beyond Maya regions, particularly with the Zapotecs of Monte Albán, in the Valley of Oaxaca, and with the Teotihuacanos of the central valley of Mexico. Since this long-distance trade played an important part in international relations, the merchants conducting it were high nobles or even members of the royal family.

Maya Science and Religion

The Maya developed the most complex writing system in the Americas, a script with nearly a thousand glyphs. They recorded important events and observations in books

How did the Maya and Teotihuacan develop prosperous and stable societies in the classical era?

Maya A highly developed Mesoamerican culture centered in the Yucatán peninsula of Mexico. The Maya created the most intricate writing system in the Western Hemisphere.

Teotihuacan The monumental city-state that dominated trade in classical era Mesoamerica.

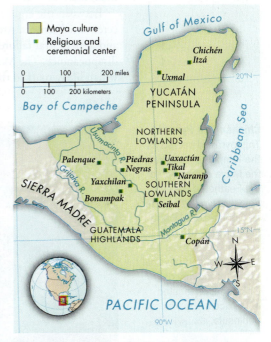

MAP 11.4 The Maya World, 300–900 C.E. The Maya built dozens of cities linked together in trading networks of roads and rivers. Only the largest of them are shown here.

made of bark paper and deerskin, on pottery, on stone pillars called steles, and on buildings. The inscriptions include historical references that record events in the lives of Maya kings and nobles. As was common for elites everywhere, Maya leaders stressed the ancient ancestry of their families. (See "Analyzing the Evidence: The Maya Calendar," at right.)

Few Maya books survived the wrath of sixteenth-century Spanish religious authorities, who viewed the books as heretical and ordered them destroyed. A handful survived, offering a window into religious rituals and practices, as well as Maya astronomy. From observation of the earth's movements around the sun, the Maya used a calendar of eighteen 20-day months and one 5-day month, for a total of 365 days, along with the 260-day lunar calendar based on 20 weeks of 13 days. When these calendars coincided every 52 years, the Maya celebrated with feasting, ball-game competitions, and religious observances that included blood sacrifice by kings to honor the gods.

The Maya devised a form of mathematics based on the vigesimal (20) rather than the decimal (10) system. More unusual was their use of the number zero, which allows for more complex calculations. The Maya's proficiency with numbers made them masters of abstract knowledge—notably in astronomy and mathematics.

Between the eighth and tenth centuries the Maya abandoned their cultural and ceremonial centers. Archaeologists attribute their decline to a combination of warfare and agricultural failures due to drought and land exhaustion. Decline did not mean disappearance. The Maya ceased building monumental architecture around 900 C.E., which likely marked the end of the era of rule by powerful kings who could mobilize

Chichén Itzá Pyramid

This pyramid served as the temple to Kukulkan, the Maya expression of the Feathered Serpent deity known to the Aztecs as Quetzalcoatl. Eighty feet tall and 180 feet across, it served as the ceremonial and physical center of the city of Chichén Itzá, located in Mexico's Yucatán peninsula. (Courtesy of Jerry Dávila)

The Maya Calendar

The Maya, like other Mesoamerican peoples, used a 365-day solar calendar and a 260-day lunar calendar. They recorded dates by using both calendars, expressed either in a 52-year cycle, known as a Calendar Round, or using a linear calendar beginning in a year corresponding with 3114 B.C.E. The carving here records a date using the Long Count calendar that is equivalent to February 11, 526 C.E.

The date appears as part of a carving that formed part of the ceremonial complex in the classical period Maya city of Yaxchilan, located in present-day Chiapas in southern Mexico. Towering over the Usumacinta River, Yaxchilan was the home to powerful kings who ordered the story of their dynasty told through exquisitely engraved lintels above doorways, like this one, and on stone slabs known as steles.

The lintel date marks the beginning of a king's reign. The date is rendered through the images of animals and deities that correspond with the Maya Long Count calendar. The monkey (right column, second from top) signals a day date. The day is defined by the god's head in its hand, which means 6, and the skull beneath the hand, which means 10: or 16 days. Above the monkey is Hun Hunaphu, the god of maize. To the left of the monkey is Yax Balam, deity of the moon, and below Yax Balam is Hun Ahau, a hero tied to the underworld. Beneath the monkey figure, the two dots correspond with the number 2. Numbers were expressed though a system of bars and dots in which a single bar equals 5 and a single dot equals 1. The chart here shows the Maya means of representing numbers 1 to 19. The buildings of Maya cities were densely inscribed with such carvings that celebrated the reign of kings, depicted their ancestry, and commemorated feats in battle.

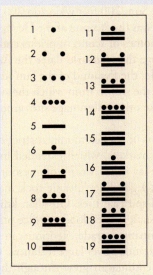

(Otis Imboden/National Geographic Creative)

QUESTIONS FOR ANALYSIS

1. Calendars show not only dates but also the sense of time of the people who used them. What do the figures in this calendar show you about the Maya and their world?

2. How does the Maya system of numbers resemble other numerical systems with which you are familiar?

3. What does this carving show us about the kinds of uses the calendar served?

the labor required to build it. The Maya persisted in farming communities, a pattern of settlement that helped preserve their culture and language in the face of external pressures.

Maya communities resisted invasions from warring Aztec armies by dispersing from their towns and villages and residing in their milpas during invasions. When Aztec armies entered the Yucatán peninsula or the highlands of what is today Guatemala, communities vanished, leaving Aztec armies with nothing to conquer. This tactic continued to serve Maya communities under Spanish colonial rule. Though Spaniards claimed the Yucatán, the Maya continued to use the strategy that had served them so well in resisting the Aztecs. Many communities avoided Spanish domination for generations. The last independent Maya kingdom succumbed only in 1697, and resistance continued well into the nineteenth century.

Teotihuacan and the Toltecs

The most powerful city in classical Mesoamerica emerged at Teotihuacan, northwest of the lands of the Maya. At its height, between 300 and 600 C.E., its population reached as high as 250,000, making it one of the largest cities in the world at that time. The heart of Teotihuacan was a massive ceremonial center anchored by a colossal Pyramid of the Sun, 700 feet wide and 200 feet tall, and a Pyramid of the Moon. Connecting them was the Avenue of the Dead, 150 feet wide and 2 miles long, along which stood the homes of scores of priests and lords. The monuments of Teotihuacan were so massive that centuries later the Aztecs thought they had been built by giants. A cave under the Pyramid of the Sun suggests the ceremonial center's origins. Caves symbolized the womb from which the sun and moon were born. It is possible that it emerged like other pilgrimage sites around the world that became important marketplaces.[2]

The monuments of the ceremonial district of Teotihuacan were matched in grandeur by the city's markets, which extended its influence across Mesoamerica. The city's trade empire lay in its control of a resource vital to Mesoamerican society and religion: obsidian, a glasslike volcanic rock that could be worked into objects with both material and spiritual uses. Obsidian knives were used for daily tasks and for important rituals such as the blood sacrifice practiced by the Maya.[3]

Religion accompanied trade. Teotihuacan was a religious and cultural center whose influence extended over large distances. One factor in the city's success was its ethnic diversity. Teotihuacan grew through the migration of outsiders along trade networks, and these groups built separate ethnic neighborhoods. Two gods that were particularly important to classical period civilizations were Tlaloc (Chac in Maya), the god of rain, and Quetzalcoatl, the plumed serpent. The worship of these deities became an enduring aspect of Mesoamerican religion that the Toltecs and the Aztecs embraced.[4]

Teotihuacan thrived as a commercial and religious hub because it controlled trade of the most valuable goods. This combination helped Teotihuacan grow, and in turn the trade networks it sustained helped other regions in Mesoamerica develop through contact with other groups and the spread of technologies. Over time, improvements in other regions decreased Teotihuacan's comparative advantage, as its trading partners produced increasingly valuable goods, spurring competition. By 600 its influence had begun to decline, and in 650 the residents of the city seem to have burned its ceremonial center in what may have been a revolt against the city's leadership. The city had ceased to be a major trade center by 900 C.E.[5]

The Toltecs (900–1200 C.E.) filled the void created by Teotihuacan's decline. The Toltecs inaugurated a new era, the postclassical, which ended with the Spanish conquest of the Aztec Empire. The postclassical period saw fewer technological or artistic advances. Instead it was a time of intensified warfare in Mesoamerica and a time of rapid and bold imperial expansion through conquest. After the decline of Teotihuacan, the Toltecs entered the Valley of Mexico and settled in Tula. The Toltecs' legend of their origins held that in 968 C.E. their people were led into the valley by a charismatic king, Topiltzin. He assumed the name of Quetzalcoatl, the Feathered Serpent god, with whom he later became merged in Aztec mythology. In 987, amid infighting, Topiltzin-Quetzalcoatl and his followers were expelled from Tula. They marched south, where they conquered and settled in a Maya region.

The Toltecs, ca. 900–1200 C.E.

The Toltec origin myth later merged with the mythology of the Aztecs, who fashioned themselves modern Toltecs, and in turn these myths continued to evolve after the Spanish conquest in the sixteenth century to explain their defeat. Through this long and distorted course, the legend went like this: Topiltzin-Quetzalcoatl and his followers marked their journey into exile by shooting arrows into saplings, forming crosslike images. Settled in the east, he sent word that he would return to take back his rightful throne in the Mesoamerican calendar year Ce Acatl. And by tradition, the god Quetzalcoatl's human manifestation was bearded and light skinned. Ce Acatl corresponded to the European year 1519, when Hernán Cortés marched into the Aztec capital Tenochtitlan (light skinned, bearded, and coming from the east bearing crosses). In this retelling of the myth of Quetzalcoatl among the generations that followed the conquest, the demise of the Aztec Empire at the hands of a vengeful god had been foretold by half a millennium.

Nahuatl The language of the Aztecs, which they inherited from the Toltecs.

The Toltecs built a military empire and gradually absorbed the culture, practices, and religion of their neighbors in the Valley of Mexico. Their empire declined amid war, drought, and famine over the eleventh and twelfth centuries. The last Toltec king died in 1174. After the demise of the Toltec Empire, city-states in the Valley of Mexico competed with each other militarily and to cast themselves as the legitimate descendants and heirs of the Toltecs.

Mexica The dominant ethnic group of what is now Mexico, who created an empire based on war and religion that reached its height in the fifteenth century.

The Aztec Empire

Aztec is the modern name given to the empire created by a **Nahuatl**-speaking people, the **Mexica**, who settled on Lake Texcoco in the Valley of Mexico between 1300 and 1345 (Map 11.5). They formed a vast and rapidly expanding empire ruled by the twin cities of Tenochtitlan (tay-nawch-TEET-lahn) and Tlatelolco, which by 1500 were probably larger than any city in Europe except Istanbul. This was the Aztec Empire, a network of alliances and tributary states with the Mexica at its core. Examining the means by which they formed and expanded their empire, as well as the vulnerabilities of that empire, can help us build a rich understanding of Mesoamerican society.

How did the Mexica build on the achievements of earlier Mesoamerican cultures and develop new traditions to create their large empire?

MAP 11.5 The Aztec (Mexica) Empire in 1519 The Mexica migrated into the central valley of what is now Mexico from the north, conquering other groups and establishing an empire, later called the Aztec Empire. The capital of the Aztec Empire was Tenochtitlan, built on islands in Lake Texcoco.

The Mexica: From Vassals to Masters

In the early fourteenth century the seminomadic Mexica migrated to the crowded and highly cultured Valley of Mexico. They found an environment that, since the collapse of the Toltec Empire in the twelfth century, had divided into small, fragile alliances that battled to claim the legacy of the Toltecs. At the time of their arrival, control over much of the valley lay in the hands of the Tepanec Alliance. The Mexica negotiated the right to settle on a swampy island on Lake Texcoco in exchange for military service to the Tepanecs. Here, in 1325, they founded the city of Tenochtitlan, which would become the capital of the Aztec Empire.

The Mexica adopted the customs of their new region, organizing clan-based communities called *calpolli*, incorporating the deities of their new neighbors, and serving the Tepanecs. They gradually reclaimed land around their island to form the two urban centers, Tenochtitlan and Tlatelolco. Mexica farmers adopted a technique used in parts of Lake Texcoco called *chinampa* (chee-NAHM-pah) agriculture. Under this system, farmers built up reeds and mud along the margins of Lake Texcoco to gradually extend farming well into the lake.

At its peak, the chinampa farming system formed vast areas of tidy rectangular plots divided by canals that allowed for canoe transportation of people and crops.

When the Spanish entered **Tenochtitlan** (which they called Mexico City) in November 1519, they were amazed at this city, which seemed to rise straight out of the lake.

Over time, the Mexica improved their standing by asking a powerful neighboring city-state to name a prince considered to be of noble Toltec descent to rule them, forming a dynasty that would become the most powerful in Mesoamerica. The new ruler, or *tlatoani* (tlah-TOH-annie), Acamapichtli (ah-cama-PITCH-lee), increased the Mexica's social rank and gave them the ability to form alliances.

By the end of Acamapichtli's reign (1372–1391), the Mexica had adapted to their new environment and had adopted the highly stratified social organization that would encourage the ambitions of their own warrior class. Under the rule of Acamapichtli's successors Huitzilihuitl (r. 1391–1417) and Chimalpopoca (r. 1417–1427), the Mexica remained subordinate to the Tepanec Alliance. But in 1427 a dispute over the succession of the Tepanec king created an opportunity for the Mexica. The Mexica formed a coalition with other cities in the Valley of Mexico, besieged the Tepanec capital for nearly three months, and then defeated it. A powerful new coalition had emerged: the Triple Alliance, with the Mexica as its most powerful partner. The Aztec Empire was born.

To consolidate the new political order, Tlatoani Itzcoatl, guided by his nephew Tlacaelel, burned his predecessors' books and drafted a new history. This history placed the warrior cult and its religious pantheon at the center of Mexica history, making the god of war, Huitzilopochtli, the patron deity of the empire. Huitzilopochtli, "Hummingbird of the South," was a god unique to the Mexica who, according to the new official origin stories of the Mexica people, had ordered them to march south until they found an island where he gave them the sign of an eagle eating a serpent, which appeared to them in Tenochtitlan. (See "Individuals in Society: Tlacaelel," page 318.)

Under the new imperial order, government offices combined military, religious, and political functions. Eventually, tlatoanis formalized these functions into distinct noble and common classes. The Valley of Mexico had sustained itself through chinampa agriculture, but as the empire grew, tribute from distant conquered peoples increasingly fed the valley's rapidly growing population. The Mexica sustained themselves through military conquest, imposing their rule over a vast part of modern Mexico.

Life in the Aztec Empire

Few social distinctions existed among the Aztecs during their early migrations, but by the early sixteenth century Aztec society changed as the warrior aristocracy asserted great authority. Men who had distinguished themselves in war occupied the highest military and social positions in the state. Generals, judges, and governors of provinces were appointed by the emperor from among his servants who had earned reputations as war heroes. These great lords, or *tecuhtli* (teh-COOT-lee), dressed luxuriously and lived in palaces.

Beneath the aristocracy of military leaders and imperial officials was the class of warriors. Theoretically, every free man could be a warrior, and parents dedicated their male children to war, burying a male child's umbilical cord with arrows and a shield on the day of his birth. In practice, the sons of nobles were more likely to become

Tenochtitlan The largest Aztec city, built starting in 1325. The Spanish admired it when they entered in 1519.

Tlacaelel

THE HUMMINGBIRD GOD HUITZILOPOCHTLI was originally a somewhat ordinary god of war and of young men, but in the fifteenth century he was elevated in status among the Mexica. He became increasingly associated with the sun and gradually became the most important Mexica deity. This change appears to have been primarily the work of Tlacaelel, the very long-lived chief adviser to the emperors Itzcoatl (r. 1427–1440), Moctezuma I (r. 1440–1469), and Axayacatl (r. 1469–1481). Tlacaelel first gained influence during wars in the 1420s in which the Mexica defeated the rival Tepanecs, after which he established new systems of dividing military spoils and enemy lands. At the same time, he advised the emperor that new histories were needed in which the destiny of the Mexica people was made clearer. Tlacaelel ordered the destruction of older historical texts, and under his direction the new chronicles connected Mexica fate directly to Huitzilopochtli. Mexica writing was primarily pictographic, drawn and then read by specially trained scribes who used written records as an aid to oral presentation, especially for legal issues, historical chronicles, religious and devotional poetry, and astronomical calculations.

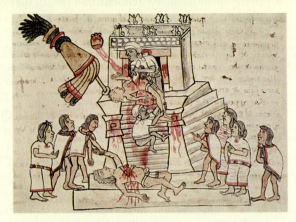

Tlacaelel emphasized human sacrifice as one of the Aztecs' religious duties. (Biblioteca Nazionale Centrale, Florence, Italy/ Bridgeman Images)

According to these new texts, the Mexica had been guided to Lake Texcoco by Huitzilopochtli; there they saw an eagle perched on a cactus, which a prophecy foretold would mark the site of their new city. Huitzilopochtli kept the world alive by bringing the sun's warmth, but to do this he required the Mexica, who increasingly saw themselves as the "people of the sun," to provide a steady offering of human blood.

warriors because of their fathers' positions and influence in the state. At the age of six, boys entered a school that trained them for war. They were taught to fight with a *ma-cana*, a paddle-shaped wooden club edged with bits of obsidian, and learned to live on little food and sleep and to accept pain without complaint. When a man reached adulthood, he fought his first campaign. If he captured a prisoner for ritual sacrifice, he acquired the title *iyac*, or warrior. If he continued to succeed in later campaigns, he became a *tequiua*—one who shared in the booty and was thus a member of the nobility. If a young man failed in several campaigns to capture the required four prisoners, he became a *macehualli* (plural *macehualtin*), a commoner.

The macehualtin were the ordinary citizens—the backbone of Aztec society and the vast majority of the population. The word *macehualli* means "worker" and implies boorish speech and vulgar behavior. Macehualtin performed agricultural, military, and domestic services and carried heavy burdens not required of noble warriors. They were assigned to work on the temples, roads, and bridges. Unlike nobles, priests, orphans, and slaves, macehualtin paid taxes. Macehualtin in the capital, however, possessed certain rights: they held their plots of land for life, and they received a share of the tribute paid by the provinces to the emperor.

The worship of Huitzilopochtli became linked to cosmic forces as well as daily survival. In Nahua tradition, the universe was understood to exist in a series of five suns, or five cosmic ages. Four ages had already passed, and their suns had been destroyed; the fifth sun, the age in which the Mexica were now living, would also be destroyed unless the Mexica fortified the sun with the energy found in blood. Warfare thus brought new territory under Mexica control and provided sacrificial victims to nourish the sun-god. With these ideas, Tlacaelel created what Miguel León-Portilla, a leading contemporary scholar of Nahua religion and philosophy, has termed a "mystico-militaristic" conception of Aztec destiny.

Human sacrifice was practiced in many cultures of Mesoamerica, including the Olmec and the Maya as well as the Mexica, before the changes introduced by Tlacaelel, but historians believe the number of victims increased dramatically during the last period of Mexica rule. A huge pyramid-shaped temple in the center of Tenochtitlan, dedicated to Huitzilopochtli and Tlaloc, the god of rain, was renovated and expanded many times, the last in 1487. To dedicate each expansion, priests sacrificed war captives. Similar ceremonies were held regularly throughout the year on days dedicated to Huitzilopochtli and were attended by many observers, including representatives from neighboring states as well as masses of Mexica. According to many accounts, victims were placed on a stone slab, and their hearts were cut out with an obsidian knife; the officiating priest then held the heart up as an offering to the sun. Sacrifices were also made to other gods at temples elsewhere in Tenochtitlan, and perhaps in other cities controlled by the Mexica.

Estimates of the number of people sacrificed to Huitzilopochtli and other Mexica gods vary enormously and are impossible to verify. Both Mexica and later Spanish accounts clearly exaggerated the numbers, but most historians today assume that between several hundred and several thousand people were killed each year.

QUESTIONS FOR ANALYSIS

1. How did the worship of Huitzilopochtli contribute to Aztec expansion? To hostility toward the Aztecs?
2. Why might Tlacaelel have believed it was important to destroy older texts as he created this new Aztec mythology?

Sources: Miguel León-Portilla, *Pre-Columbian Literatures of Mexico* (Norman: University of Oklahoma Press, 1969); Inga Clendinnen, *Aztecs: An Interpretation* (Cambridge: Cambridge University Press, 1991).

Beneath the macehualtin were the *tlalmaitl*, the landless workers or serfs who provided agricultural labor, paid rents, and were bound to the soil—they could not move off the land. In many ways the tlalmaitl resembled European serfs, but unlike serfs they performed military service when called. Slaves were the lowest social class. Most were prisoners captured in war or kidnapped from enemy tribes. People convicted of crimes could be sentenced to slavery, and people in serious debt sometimes sold themselves. Female slaves often became their masters' concubines. Mexica slaves could save money, buy property or slaves of their own, and purchase their freedom. If a male slave married a free woman, their offspring were free. Most slaves eventually gained their freedom.

Women of all social classes operated within the domestic sphere. As the little hands of the newborn male were closed around a tiny bow and arrow indicating his warrior destiny, so the infant female's hands were wrapped around miniature weaving instruments and a small broom: weaving was a sacred and exclusively female art, and the broom signaled a female's responsibility for the household shrines and for keeping the home swept and free of contamination. Save for the few women vowed to the service of the temple, marriage and the household were a woman's fate, and marriage

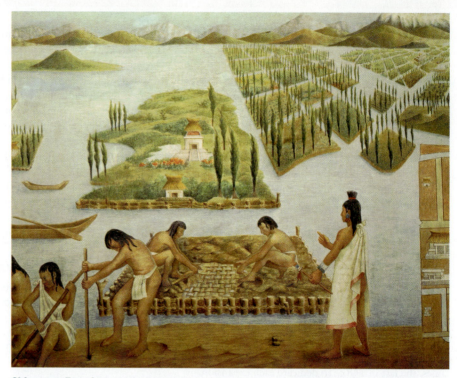

Chinampa Farming This modern illustration shows farmers in the Aztec Empire building chinampa farming plots by reclaiming land from Lake Texcoco. Farmers created the plots by packing them with vegetation and mud from the lake, supporting their boundaries by planting willow trees. Chinampas allowed for intensive farming in a region that had limited rainfall, and the canals between them permitted easy transportation. (Museo de la Ciudad de Mexico, Mexico City/De Agostini Picture Library/Gianni Dagli Orti/Bridgeman Images)

represented social maturity for both sexes. Pregnancy became the occasion for family and neighborhood feasts, and a successful birth launched celebrations lasting from ten to twenty days.

The Limits of the Aztec Empire

Mesoamerican empires like that of the Aztecs were not like modern nation-states that consolidate control of the territory within their borders. Instead the Aztec Empire was a syndicate in which the Mexica, their allies, and their subordinates thrived on trade and tribute backed by the threat of force.

When a city succumbed, its captive warriors were marched to Tenochtitlan to be sacrificed. The defeated city was obligated to provide tribute including corn, flowers, feathers, gold, and hides. But conquest stopped short of assimilation. Rulers and nobles remained in place. Subjects were not required to adopt Mexica gods, and local communities and their leaders remained intact.

The death of a ruler is always a time of uncertainty, and this was especially true in Mesoamerica under the Aztec Empire. For peoples of the Valley of Mexico and beyond, this meant war was sure to arrive. The council of high nobles who served the deceased ruler chose the new tlatoani, who was often the commander of the army. Once the new tlatoani was named, he would embark on a military campaign in order to answer the questions his succession raised: Would he bring sacrificial victims to the gods and thus ensure prosperity and fertility during his reign? Could he preserve and strengthen the alliances that composed the empire? Could he keep rivals at bay?

A success in the tlatoani's inaugural military campaign provided new tribute-paying subjects, produced a long train of sacrificial victims captured in battle, maintained the stability of the empire's alliances, warned off potential foes, and kept conquered areas in subordination. After the successful campaign, the new tlatoani invited the rulers of allied, subject, and enemy city-states alike to his coronation ceremony—a pageant of gifts, feasts, and bloody sacrifice that proclaimed Tenochtitlan's might.

But success was not always possible, as the troubled rule of Tizoc (r. 1481–1486) demonstrated. After a series of wars that produced few sacrifices, he was poisoned by his own subjects. His successor, Ahuitzotl (r. 1486–1502), faced the challenge of reinvigorating the empire through renewed displays of strength. To symbolize the restoration of Tenochtitlan's power, he waged wars of conquest that exceeded anything ever seen, culminating in two coronation ceremonies, the second of which involved sacrificing over eighty thousand captive warriors.

Blood sacrifice was not new to the Aztecs. For centuries Mesoamerican peoples had honored their gods this way, but the Aztecs elevated the warrior cult as their central observance. They believed the earth had been destroyed and re-created four times. The end of creation loomed after their age, the fifth sun. Since the apocalypse might be forestalled through divine intervention, their sacrifice could show that humans were worthy of divine intervention. If ancient deities had given their lives to save the sun, how could mortals refuse to do the same?

The ceremony observing the end of each fifty-two-year bundle reflected the worldview of the Mexica. Had humans sacrificed enough for the gods to intercede and ensure the sun would rise again? In preparation for the end, families broke their earthenware vessels, cleansed their homes, and extinguished all fires. Upon the new dawn, priests made a fire on the chest of a living, powerful captive warrior. Noble warriors lit torches from this new fire and relayed the flame of creation into each hearth in the empire. For the next fifty-two years, all would know the fire in their hearth, like the rising of the sun itself, was the fruit of a sacred warrior sacrifice.

Quetzalcoatl Bleeding Himself to Create Man This image reflects Quetzalcoatl in his human form, carrying out the sacrifice that created humanity. The combination of spiritual and human forms allowed rulers such as Topiltzin to also claim identities as gods. (akg-images)

The need for sacrifice, as well as the glorification of the warriors who provided it through battle, was a powerful rationale for the expansion of the Aztec Empire. The role of the Aztecs' sacrifice-based religious system is the subject of scholarly debate: Did the religious system guide imperial expansion? Or did imperial expansion guide the religious system? These views are by no means incompatible: for the Aztecs, the peoples who came under their rule, and the peoples who resisted them, the twin goals of empire building and service to the gods were inseparable.

What did the European encounter mean for peoples of the major American empires?

American Empires and the Encounter

By 1500 the Incas and Aztecs strained under the burdens of managing the largest empires the Americas had seen. Both faced the challenges of consolidating their gains, bearing the costs of empire and of the swelling nobility, and waging war in increasingly distant and difficult conditions.

The Last Day of the Aztecs

In 1502 the last Mexica to rule before the arrival of the Spaniards, Moctezuma II, was named tlatoani. Moctezuma inherited a strained empire. His predecessors had expanded the empire's reach from the Caribbean coast to the Pacific. At the margins of the empire the Aztecs encountered peoples who were seminomadic or who, like the Maya, had abandoned their cities to resist conquest. An empire that had expanded rapidly through conquest found itself with little room to grow.

Aztec leaders had sought targets for conquest that were easy to overpower or that produced goods that made for valuable tribute. This created an empire riddled with independent enclaves that had resisted conquest. The most powerful of these was Tlaxcala (tlah-SKAH-lah), at the edge of the Valley of Mexico. In addition, even areas under Aztec rule retained local leadership and saw themselves as subjected peoples, not as Aztecs.

Finally, the costs of empire had become onerous. Generations of social mobility through distinction in war had produced a bloated nobility both exempt from and sustained by tribute. Tenochtitlan became dependent on tributary maize in order to feed itself. The lack of new peoples to conquer meant the empire had little promise of increased prosperity. The dwindling flow of sacrificial victims meant the Mexica might be losing the great cosmic struggle to keep creation from ending.

Faced with these challenges, Moctezuma II introduced reforms, reducing the privileges (and thus the costs to the empire) of the lesser nobility and narrowing the pathways of social mobility. However, the austerity he imposed caused unrest. He also attempted to conquer the autonomous enclaves left by his predecessors. As Moctezuma targeted these enclaves, their ability to resist sapped their resources and strained their morale without producing a corresponding reward for the empire in sacrifice or tribute.

By the time he reached the gates of Tenochtitlan in 1519, the Spanish conquistador Hernán Cortés had forged alliances with foes of the Aztecs, particularly Tlaxcala, which had so ably resisted conquest. The Tlaxcalans saw in the foreigners an opportunity to fight the Mexica. Cortés's band of six hundred Spaniards arrived in Tenochtitlan accompanied by tens of thousands of Tlaxcalan soldiers. In Tlaxcala the defeat of Tenochtitlan would be seen as the Tlaxcalans' victory, not that of the handful of Spaniards.

Whatever Moctezuma made of the strangers, he received them as guests while he sought to understand the nature of this encounter and its significance for his empire. Perhaps he hesitated, losing the opportunity to act against them. Perhaps he concluded that he had no chance of defeating them, since at that moment most of the men he could count on in battle were tending to their crops and the capital had been so riddled with resentment of his reforms that he was powerless to act.

Either way, Cortés and his men managed the encounter skillfully and succeeded in taking Moctezuma prisoner. When the residents of Tenochtitlan rose up to expel the Spaniards, Moctezuma was killed. Though the Spaniards were expelled from the city, they left an unwelcome guest, smallpox. The first epidemic of the disease swept through the city in 1520, killing Moctezuma's successor within a matter of months. Cuauhtemoc, the last tlatoani of the Mexica, was named that same year.

The Aztec Empire and the Mexica people were not defeated by technology, cultural superiority, or a belief that the Europeans were gods. Instead they suffered a political defeat: their fall was owed more than anything to the willingness of allies and enemies alike to join with the Spaniards against them when they perceived an opportunity.

Through the lens of history, the destruction of the Aztec Empire seems swift, but Tenochtitlan resisted for two years. During this time the Spaniards and Tlaxcalans brokered alliances leaving the Mexica virtually alone in their fight. In this sense, the end of the Aztec Empire looked a lot like its beginning: people who had obeyed the Mexica now took advantage of the opportunity to defeat them, just as the Mexica had done with the Tepanec Alliance. Even so, abandoned by their allies, the besieged Mexica fought on through famine and disease, defending their city street by street until Cuauhtemoc surrendered to Cortés on August 13, 1521.

The Fall of the Incas

In 1525 Huayna Capac Inca, the grandson of Pachacuti Inca, became ill while carrying out a military campaign in present-day Ecuador, at the northern frontier of the empire. His illness was likely smallpox, introduced by Europeans waging wars of conquest in Mesoamerica, and it would kill him. But as he waged war, he also received news of the foreigners—Spaniards—in the north and anticipated that they would come southward.

Huayna Capac's death unleashed civil war between two of his sons over succession to the throne. Huascar claimed it as the firstborn. Atahualpa (ah-tuh-WAHL-puh), Huayna Capac's favorite and an experienced commander who had accompanied him in his Ecuadorean campaign, claimed it as well. Atahualpa asserted that Huayna Capac's dying wish was that Atahualpa succeed him. The brothers fought until 1532, when Atahualpa vanquished and imprisoned Huascar and consolidated his rule in Cuzco. That same year a group of Spaniards led by Francisco Pizarro landed on the Peruvian coast, pursuing rumors of a city of gold in the mountains.

Atahualpa agreed through emissaries to meet the Spaniards at the city of Cajamarca in northern Peru. In a demonstration of his imperial authority, he entered Cajamarca carried on a golden litter, accompanied by four military squadrons totaling twenty-four thousand soldiers. Members of the nobility followed, carried on their own litters. Their procession was preceded by a multitude of servants who cleared the ground, removing all stones, pebbles, and even bits of straw. Atahualpa met the

Inca and Spanish Views on Religion, Authority, and Tribute

In 1532 Atahualpa Inca met with a band of Spaniards led by Francisco Pizarro, who ambushed him and took him prisoner. At the beginning of their meeting, a priest accompanying Pizarro read to Atahualpa, through a translator, a document prepared in Spain in 1513 called the *Requerimiento*. The document presented Roman Christianity and the Spaniards' religious right to conquest. Conquistadors were obligated to read the *Requerimiento* in front of witnesses before waging a war of conquest. Spanish colonial sources and the 1609 account by chronicler Garcilaso de la Vega, son of an Andean woman and a Spanish soldier, describe the remarkable exchange.

Friar Vicente de Valverde Presents the *Requerimiento*

■ It is proper that you should know, most famous and most powerful king, that it is necessary that Your Highness and all your subjects should not only learn the true Catholic faith but that you should hear and believe the following. . . .

Therefore the holy pope of Rome . . . has conceded the conquest of these parts to Charles V, . . . the most powerful king of Spain and monarch of all the earth. . . . The great emperor Charles V has chosen as his lieutenant and ambassador Don Francisco Pizarro, who is now here, . . . so that Your Highness and all your realms will become tributaries; that is to say, you will pay tribute to the emperor, and will become his vassal and deliver your kingdom wholly into his hands, renouncing the administration of it, as other kings and lords have done. . . . If you seek obstinately to resist, you may rest assured that God will suffer that you and all your Indians shall be destroyed by our arms.

The Inca Atahualpa Responds

■ I will be no man's tributary. I am greater than any prince upon the earth. Your emperor may be a great prince . . . and I am willing to hold him as a brother. As for the pope of whom you speak, he must be crazy to talk of giving away countries that do not belong to him. For my faith, I will not change it. Your own God,

Spanish intending to understand them and hear them out. However, the meeting between Atahualpa and Pizarro reflected deeply different worldviews. (See "Global Viewpoints: Inca and Spanish Views on Religion, Authority, and Tribute," above.)

Though Atahualpa had not planned to fight, Pizarro planned an ambush, using the city walls to trap Atahualpa's soldiers and kill a large number of them. The Spaniards took Atahualpa prisoner and eventually executed him. The Spaniards named a new indigenous leader, Manco Capac, whom they hoped to control. But Manco Capac turned against the Spaniards. He, and later his son Tupac Amaru, led resistance against the Spaniards until 1567. Each time the Inca forces besieged a Spanish-controlled city or town, however, their proximity to the Spaniards exposed them to European diseases. They were more successful in smaller-scale attacks, which delayed and limited Spanish colonization, but did not undo it.

Chapter Summary

The civilizations of the Andes and Mesoamerica from which the Incas and Aztecs emerged had remarkable similarities with, and differences from, other ancient and premodern civilizations in other regions of the world. Indigenous societies of the

as you say, was put to death by the very men he created. But mine . . . [pointing to the sun] still lives in the heavens, and looks down upon his children. . . .

You threaten us with war and death . . . and say that I must renounce my kingdom and become the tributary of another, either willingly or by force. Whence I deduce one of two things: either your prince and you are tyrants who are destroying the world, depriving others of their realms, slaying and robbing those who have done you no harm and owe you nothing, or you are ministers of God, whom we call Pachacámac, who has chosen you to punish and destroy us. . . .

You have mentioned five great men I should know. The first is God . . . : he is perchance the same as our Pachacámac and Viracocha. The second is he whom you say is the father of all other men on whom they have all heaped their sins. The third you call Jesus Christ . . . , but he was killed. The fourth you call pope. The fifth is Charles. . . . If this Charles is prince and lord of the whole world, why should he need the pope to give him a new grant and concession to make war on me and usurp these kingdoms? If he has to ask the pope's permission, is not the pope a greater lord than

he, and more powerful, and prince of all the world? Also, I am surprised that you say that I must pay tribute to Charles and not to the others, for you give no reason for paying the tribute, and I have certainly no obligation whatever to pay it.

QUESTIONS FOR ANALYSIS

1. According to Atahualpa, what is the source of his authority? According to him, what is the source of the Spaniards' authority?
2. Why does Atahualpa believe that the Spaniards have more gods than the Incas do?
3. How does Atahualpa perceive the Spaniards and their intentions?

Sources: Excerpts "It is proper that you should know" and "You threaten us with war" from Garcilaso de la Vega, *Royal Commentaries of the Incas, and General History of Peru*, translated by H. V. Livermore (Austin: University of Texas Press, 1989), pp. 679–81, 685–86. Used by permission of the University of Texas Press; excerpt "I will be no man's tributary" from William Prescott, *History of the Conquest of Peru*, vol. 1. (1847, repr., 1892), p. 370.

Americas developed extensive networks of trade. In Mesoamerica and the Andes, the domestication of crops led to the kind of bountiful production that allowed for diversification of labor among farmers, priests, nobles, merchants, and artisans. In these environments, cycles of centralization occurred in which powerful city-states emerged and embarked on campaigns of conquest, bringing vast regions under their political, religious, and cultural influence.

But civilizations of the Americas developed in unique ways as well. This was particularly true in the Andes, where peoples developed specialized patterns of farming in vertical archipelagos in their inhospitable mountain environment. Similarly, though Andean peoples did not develop writing, they instead developed the khipu into a sophisticated system of recording and communicating information.

Ultimately, the history of the peoples of the Americas was defined by their diverse experiences as they coped with varied climates, ecology, and geography. And peoples' experiences of adapting to their environments, and of transforming those environments to meet their needs, shaped the ways they understood their world. These experiences led them to produce precise calendars, highly detailed readings of the stars, and an elaborate architecture of religious beliefs through which they interpreted their relationships to their world and their place in the cosmos.

NOTES

1. *Narrative of the Incas by Juan de Betanzos*, trans. and ed. Roland Hamilton and Dana Buchanan from the Palma de Mallorca manuscript, p. 138.
2. Michael Coe, *Mexico from the Olmecs to the Aztecs*, 5th ed. (New York: Thames and Hudson, 2002), p. 107.
3. Ross Hassig, *War and Society in Ancient Mesoamerica* (Berkeley: University of California Press, 1992), p. 56.
4. Ibid., p. 49.
5. Ibid., pp. 81, 85.

CONNECTIONS

The early sixteenth century marked the end of independent empires of the Americas and the gradual integration of American peoples into global empires seated in Europe. Spaniards were the most motivated and had their greatest success when they encountered dense, organized urban areas. Here they displaced existing overlords as the recipients of tribute in goods and labor. The Spanish were less interested in sparsely settled areas that did not have well-established systems of trade and tribute and were harder to subdue. As a result, European conquest was a surprisingly drawn-out process. Peoples of the Americas resisted conquest until well into the nineteenth century.

The incidental companion of conquest — disease — was also uneven in its effects. Over the course of the sixteenth century, epidemics shrank the population of the Americas from 50 million to just 5 million. But epidemic diseases spread through human contact, such as measles and smallpox, are primarily urban phenomena: these diseases emerged as ancient cities grew large enough that the diseases could spread quickly among dense populations. As a result, the impact of the diseases brought by Europeans was the most severe and the most destructive in the cities of the Americas.

Since cities faced the brunt of both disease and wars of conquest, the disruptions caused by the encounter were disproportionally felt there. Whole systems of knowledge, sets of artisanal skills, political cultures, and religious thought resided in cities. Thus, as epidemics erupted, many of the most remarkable aspects of American civilizations were lost. Rural peoples and cultures were much more resilient. It was in rural areas that languages, foodways, farming practices, and approaches to healing — indeed whole worldviews — endured and evolved. By contrast, Spanish colonial towns and cities were protected from indigenous attacks because they bore diseases that could afflict their attackers. The Americas were rapidly integrated with the rest of the world in the sixteenth century, but the combination of conquest, colonization, and disease ensured the unevenness of this exchange.

CHAPTER 11   Review and Explore

Identify Key Terms

Identify and explain the significance of each item below.

Mesoamerica (p. 300)   **Moche** (p. 306)   **Teotihuacan** (p. 311)

khipu (p. 300)   **Inca** (p. 307)   **Nahuatl** (p. 315)

nixtamalization (p. 301) **Quechua** (p. 309)   **Mexica** (p. 315)

Olmec (p. 303)   **Maya** (p. 311)   **Tenochtitlan** (p. 317)

Review the Main Ideas

Answer the focus questions from each section of the chapter.

1. How did ancient peoples of the Americas adapt to, and adapt, their environment? (p. 300)

2. What patterns established by early societies shaped civilization in Mesoamerica and the Andes? (p. 303)

3. What were the sources of strength and prosperity, and of problems, for the Incas? (p. 307)

4. How did the Maya and Teotihuacan develop prosperous and stable societies in the classical era? (p. 311)

5. How did the Mexica build on the achievements of earlier Mesoamerican cultures and develop new traditions to create their large empire? (p. 315)

6. What did the European encounter mean for peoples of the major American empires? (p. 322)

Make Comparisons and Connections

Analyze the larger developments and continuities within and across chapters.

1. What are some examples of unique ways in which peoples of the Americas adapted to their environment?

2. How did the connection between religion and imperial expansion among the Aztecs and Incas resemble the role of religion in the expansion of the Roman Empire (Chapter 6) or of Islamic states (Chapter 9)?

3. Much of what we know about ancient societies of the Americas is based on archaeological data rather than written sources. How does the reliance on archaeological data shape our understanding of history? What does it help us understand? What is hard for us to interpret from it?

4. What aspects of life in the Americas were most vulnerable to change after the arrival of Europeans?

TIMELINE

AMERICAS

← **ca. 20,000–30,000 years ago** Initial human migration to the Americas

← **ca. 10,000 B.C.E.** Farming begins with the cultivation of squash in the Andes and Mesoamerica

← **ca. 5500 B.C.E.** Earliest mound building in North America

ca. 1500–300 B.C.E. Olmec culture

◆ **ca. 1200 B.C.E.** Emergence of Chavín culture in the Andes

ROMAN WORLD

AFRICA

ISLAMIC WORLD

EAST ASIA

1500 B.C.E.	1000 B.C.E.	500 B.C.E.

Suggested Resources

BOOKS

Carassco, David, and Scott Sessions. *Daily Life of the Aztecs: People of the Sun and Earth.* 2008. An overview of Aztec culture designed for general readers.

Clendinnen, Inga. *Aztecs: An Interpretation.* 1992. Pays particular attention to the role that rituals and human sacrifice played in Aztec culture.

Coe, Michael D. *The Maya.* 2011. A new edition of a classic survey that incorporates the most recent scholarship.

Coe, Michael D. *Mexico: From the Olmecs to the Aztecs.* 2013. A rich examination of Mesoamerican peoples with the exception of the Maya.

Hassig, Ross. *Mexico and the Spanish Conquest.* 2006. A study of indigenous participation in the conquest by a leading historical anthropologist.

Kehoe, Alice Beck. *America Before the European Invasion.* 2002. An excellent survey of North America before the coming of the Europeans, by an eminent anthropologist.

León-Portilla, Miguel. *The Aztec Image of Self and Society: An Introduction to Nahua Culture.* 1992. A rich appreciation of Aztec religious ritual and symbolism.

Mann, Charles C. *1491: New Revelations of the Americas Before Columbus.* 2006. A thoroughly researched overview of all the newest scholarship, written for a general audience.

Mumford, Jeremy Ravi. *Vertical Empire: The General Resettlement of Indians in the Colonial Andes.* 2012. A study of Andean mountain life between Inca and Spanish rule.

ca. 1325 C.E. ◆
Construction of Mexica
city of Tenochtitlan begins

ca. 100–800 C.E. Moche culture

ca. 300–650 C.E. Peak of Teotihuacan's influence

ca. 1050–1250 C.E.
Construction of mounds at Cahokia

ca. 600–900 C.E. Peak of
Maya civilization

ca. 1428–1521 C.E.
Aztec Empire dominates Mesoamerica

ca. 1438–1532 C.E.
Inca Empire dominates the Andes

509 B.C.E.–476 C.E.
Roman Republic and Empire (Ch. 6)

ca. 1100–1450 C.E. Great
Zimbabwe built, flourishes (Ch. 10)

632–1100 C.E. Early spread of Islam in
Asia, Africa, and Europe (Chs. 9, 10, 12)

200–538 C.E. Spread of Buddhism in China, Korea, and Japan (Ch. 7)

| 1 C.E. | 500 C.E. | 1000 C.E. | 1500 C.E. |

Pauketat, Timothy, R. *Cahokia: Ancient America's Great City on the Mississippi.* 2009. Surveys the major North American archaeological site.

Ramirez, Susan. *To Feed and Be Fed: The Cosmological Bases of Authority and Identity in the Andes.* 2008. Examines the relationships between ancestors, the spiritual world, and the physical world that shaped Andean societies.

Restall, Matthew, and Amara Solari. *2012 and the End of the World: The Western Roots of the Maya Apocalypse.* 2011. Reflects on popular interpretations of the Maya calendar and cosmology.

Schele, Linda, and Peter Matthews. *The Code of Kings: The Language of Seven Sacred Maya Temples and Tombs.* 1998. A landmark study of ancient Maya language.

WEBSITES

Cahokia Mounds. Resource on the largest ancient settlement site north of Mexico in the Americas. **cahokiamounds.org/learn/**

Khipu Database Project. A database of Andean khipus and resources on the research conducted on them. **khipukamayuq.fas.harvard.edu**

Living Maya Time: Calendar. The Smithsonian National Museum of the American Indian's site provides information on interpreting the Maya calendar. **maya.nmai.si.edu/calendar**

Mesolore. A rich site for interpreting indigenous documents from ancient Mexico. **www.mesolore.org**

12

Cultural Exchange in Central and Southern Asia
300–1400

The large expanse of Asia treated in this chapter underwent profound changes during the centuries examined here. The north saw the rise of nomadic pastoral societies, first the Turks, then more spectacularly the Mongols. The nomads' mastery of the horse and mounted warfare gave them a military advantage that agricultural societies could rarely match. From the fifth century on, groups of Turks appeared along the fringes of the settled societies of Eurasia, from China and Korea to India and Persia. Often Turks were recruited as auxiliary soldiers; sometimes they gained the upper hand. By the tenth century many were converting to Islam (see "The Ascendancy of the Turks" in Chapter 9).

Much more dramatic was the rise of the Mongols under the charismatic leadership of Chinggis Khan in the late twelfth and early thirteenth centuries. A military genius with a relatively small army, Chinggis subdued one society after another from Byzantium to the Pacific. For a century Mongol hegemony fostered unprecedented East-West trade and contact. More Europeans made their way east than ever before, and Chinese inventions such as printing and the compass made their way west.

Over the course of several centuries, Arab and Turkish armies brought Islam to India, but the Mongols never gained power there. In the Indian subcontinent during these centuries, regional cultures flourished. Although Buddhism declined, Hinduism continued to flourish. India continued to be the center of a very active seaborne trade, and this trade helped carry Indian ideas and practices to Southeast Asia. Buddhism was adopted in much of Southeast Asia, along with other ideas and techniques from India. The maritime trade in spices and other goods brought increased contact with the outside world to all but the most isolated of islands in the Pacific.

Mongol Woman

Women played influential roles among the Mongols. The Mongol woman portrayed in this painting is Chabi, wife of Khubilai Khan. Like other Mongols, she maintained Mongol dress even though she spent much of her time in China.

CHAPTER PREVIEW

CENTRAL ASIAN NOMADS
What aspects of nomadic life gave the nomads of Central Asia military advantages over nearby settled civilizations?

CHINGGIS KHAN AND THE MONGOL EMPIRE
How did Chinggis Khan and his successors conquer much of Eurasia, and how did the Mongol conquests change the regions affected?

EAST-WEST COMMUNICATION DURING THE MONGOL ERA
How did the Mongol conquests facilitate the spread of ideas, religions, inventions, and diseases?

INDIA, ISLAM, AND THE DEVELOPMENT OF REGIONAL CULTURES, 300–1400
What was the result of India's encounters with Turks, Mongols, and Islam?

SOUTHEAST ASIA, THE PACIFIC ISLANDS, AND THE GROWTH OF MARITIME TRADE
How did states develop along the maritime trade routes of Southeast Asia and beyond?

What aspects of nomadic life gave the nomads of Central Asia military advantages over nearby settled civilizations?

nomads Groups of people who move from place to place in search of food, water, and pasture for their animals, usually following the seasons.

steppe Grasslands that are too dry for crops but support pasturing animals; they are common across much of the center of Eurasia.

Central Asian Nomads

One experience Rome, Persia, India, and China all shared was conflict with **nomads** who came from the very broad region referred to as Central Asia. This region was dominated by the **steppe**, arid grasslands that stretched from modern Hungary to Mongolia and parts of present northeast China. Initially small in number, the nomadic peoples of this region used their military superiority to conquer first other nomads, then the nearby settled societies. In the process they created settled empires of their own that drew on the cultures they absorbed.

Nomadic Society

Easily crossed by horses but too dry for crop agriculture, the grasslands could support only a thin population of nomadic herders who lived off their sheep, goats, camels, horses, or other animals. Following the seasons, they would break camp at least twice a year and move their animals to new pastures, going north in the spring and south in the fall.

In their search for water and good pastures, nomadic groups often came into conflict with other nomadic groups pursuing the same resources, which the two would then fight over. Groups on the losing end, especially if they were small, faced the threat of extermination or slavery, which prompted them to make alliances with other groups or move far away. Groups on the winning end of intertribal conflicts could exact tribute from those they defeated.

To get the products of nearby agricultural societies, especially grain, woven textiles, iron, tea, and wood, nomadic herders would trade their own products, such as horses and furs. When trade was difficult, they would turn to raiding to seize what they needed. Much of the time nomadic herders raided other nomads, but nearby agricultural settlements were common targets as well. The nomads' skill as horsemen and archers made it difficult for farmers and townsmen to defend against them.

Political organization among nomadic herders was generally very simple. Clans— members of an extended family—had chiefs, as did tribes (coalitions of clans). Leadership within a group was based on military prowess and was often settled by fighting. Occasionally a charismatic leader would emerge who was able to extend alliances to form confederations of tribes. From the point of view of the settled societies, which have left most of the records about these nomadic groups, large confederations were much more of a threat, since they could plan coordinated attacks on cities and towns. Large confederations rarely lasted more than a century or so, however, and when they broke up, tribes again spent much of their time fighting with each other.

The three most wide-ranging and successful confederations were those of the Xiongnu—Huns, as they were known in the West—who emerged in the third century B.C.E. in the area near China; the Turks, who had their origins in the same area in the fourth and fifth centuries C.E.; and the Mongols, who did not become important until the late twelfth century. In all three cases, the entire steppe region was eventually swept up in the movement of peoples and armies.

The Turks

The Turks were the first of the Inner Asian peoples to have left a written record in their own language; the earliest Turkish documents date from the eighth century.

Turkic languages today are spoken by the Uighurs in western China; the Uzbeks, Kazakhs, Kyrghiz (KIHR-guhz), and Turkmens of Central Asia; and the Turks of modern Turkey.

In 552 a group called Turks who specialized in metalworking rebelled against their overlords, the Rouruan, whose empire dominated the region from the eastern Silk Road cities of Central Asia through Mongolia. The Turks quickly supplanted the Rouruan as overlords of the Silk Road in the east. When the first Turkish khagan (ruler) died a few years later, the Turkish empire was divided between his younger brother, who took the western part (modern Central Asia), and his son, who took the eastern part (modern Mongolia). In 576 the Western Turks captured the Byzantine city of Bosporus in the Crimea.

The Eastern Turks frequently raided China and just as often fought among themselves. A seventh-century Chinese history records that "the Turks prefer to destroy each other rather than to live side-by-side. They have a thousand, nay ten thousand clans who are hostile to and kill one another. They mourn their dead with much grief and swear vengeance."[1] In the early seventh century the empire of the Eastern Turks ran up against the growing military might of the Tang Dynasty in China and soon broke apart.

In the eighth century a Turkic people called the Uighurs (WEE-gurs) formed a new empire based in Mongolia that survived about a century. During this period many Uighurs adopted religions then current along the Silk Road, notably Buddhism, Nestorian Christianity, and Manichaeism. In the ninth century this Uighur empire collapsed, but some Uighurs fled west, setting up their capital city in Kucha, where they created a remarkably stable and prosperous kingdom that lasted four centuries (ca. 850–1250).

Farther west in Central Asia other groups of Turks rose to prominence. Often local Muslim forces would try to capture them, employ them as slave soldiers, and convert them. By the mid- to late tenth century many were serving in the armies of the Abbasid caliphate. Also in the tenth century Central Asian Turks began converting to Islam (which protected them from being abducted as slaves). Then they took to raiding unconverted Turks.

In the mid-eleventh century Turks had gained the upper hand in the caliphate, and the caliphs became little more than figureheads. From there Turkish power was extended into Syria, Palestine, and Asia Minor. In 1071 Seljuk (SEHL-jook) Turks inflicted a devastating defeat on the Byzantine army in eastern Anatolia.

In India, Persia, and Anatolia the formidable military skills of nomadic Turkish warriors made it possible for them to become overlords of settled societies. Often Persian was used as the administrative language of the states they formed. Nevertheless, despite the presence of Turkish overlords all along the southern fringe of the steppe, no one group of Turks was able to unite them all into a single political unit. That feat had to wait for the next major power on the steppe, the Mongols.

Seljuk Turk Attendant
At 47 inches tall, this figure wears an elaborate headdress and fine garments. He is thought to represent a member of a ruler's personal guard. The work is thought to date to about 1200 and to have come from Iran.

(Attributed to Iran or Afghanistan. Late 12th–early 13th century C.E. Stucco; incised, painted gilt. Cora Timken Burnett Collection of Persian Miniatures and Other Persian Art Objects, Bequest of Cora Timken Burnett, 1956 [57.51.18]/ The Metropolitan Museum of Art, New York/Image copyright © The Metropolitan Museum of Art/Image source: Art Resource, NY)

The Mongols

In the twelfth century ambitious Mongols did not aspire to match the Turks or other groups that had migrated west, but rather wanted to be successors to the Khitans and Jurchens, nomadic groups that had stayed in the east and mastered ways to extract resources from China. The Khitans and Jurchens had formed hybrid nomadic-urban states, with northern sections where tribesmen continued to live in the traditional way and southern sections politically controlled by the non-Chinese rulers but settled largely by taxpaying Chinese. The Khitans and Jurchens had scripts created to record their languages and adopted many Chinese governing practices. They built cities in pastoral areas that served as trading centers and places to enjoy their newly acquired wealth. In both the Khitan and Jurchen cases, their elite became culturally dual, adept in Chinese ways as well as in their own traditions.

yurts Tents in which the pastoral nomads lived; they could be quickly dismantled and loaded onto animals or carts.

The Mongols lived north of these hybrid nomadic-settled societies and maintained their traditional ways. They lived in tents called **yurts** rather than in houses. The yurts, about twelve to fifteen feet in diameter, were constructed of light wooden frames covered by layers of wool felt, greased to make them waterproof. The floor of a yurt was covered first with dried grass or straw, then with felt, skins, or rugs. In the center, directly under the smoke hole, was the hearth. Goat horns attached to the frame of the yurt were used as hooks to hang joints of meat, cooking utensils, bows, quivers of arrows, and the like. A group of families traveling together would set up their yurts in a circle open to the south and draw up their wagons in a circle around the yurts for protection.

The Mongol diet consisted mostly of animal products. The most common meat was mutton, supplemented with wild game. When grain or vegetables could be obtained through trade, they were added to the diet. The Mongols milked sheep, goats, cows, and horses and made cheese and fermented alcoholic drinks from the milk.

Because of the intense cold of the winter, the Mongols made much use of furs and skins for clothing. Hats were of felt or fur, boots of felt or leather. Men wore leather belts to which their bows and quivers could be attached. Women of high rank wore elaborate headdresses decorated with feathers.

Mongol women had to work very hard and had to be able to care for the animals when the men were away hunting or fighting. They normally drove the carts and set up and dismantled the yurts. They also milked the sheep, goats, and cows and made the butter and cheese. Because water was scarce, clothes were not washed with water, nor were dishes. Women, like men, had to be expert riders, and many also learned to shoot. They participated actively in family decisions, especially as wives and mothers. In *The Secret History of the Mongols*, the mother and wife of the Mongol leader Chinggis Khan frequently make impassioned speeches on the importance of family loyalty. (See "Analyzing the Evidence: The Abduction of Women in *The Secret History of the Mongols*," page 336.)

Mongol men kept as busy as the women. They made the carts and wagons and the frames for the yurts. They also made harnesses for the horses and oxen, leather saddles, and the equipment needed for hunting and war, such as bows and arrows. Men also had charge of the horses, and they milked the mares. One specialist among the nomads was the blacksmith, who made stirrups, knives, and other metal tools.

Kinship underlay most social relationships among the Mongols. Normally each family occupied a yurt, and groups of families camping together were usually related along the male line. More distant patrilineal relatives were recognized as members of the same clan and could call on each other for aid. People from the same clan could not marry each other, so men had to get wives from other clans. When a woman's husband died, she would be inherited by another male in the family, such as her husband's brother. Tribes were groups of clans, often distantly related. Both clans and tribes had chiefs who would make decisions on where to graze and when to retaliate against another tribe that had stolen animals or people. Women were sometimes abducted for brides. When tribes stole men from each other, they normally made them into slaves, and slaves were forced to do much of the heavy work.

Even though population was sparse in the regions where the Mongols lived, conflict over resources was endemic, and each camp had to be on the alert for attacks. Defending against attacks and retaliating against raids was as much a part of the Mongols' daily life as caring for their herds and trading with nearby settlements.

Mongol children learned to ride at a young age. The Mongols' horses were small but nimble and able to endure long journeys and bitter cold. The prime weapon boys had to learn to use was the compound bow, which had a pull of about 160 pounds and a range of more than 200 yards; it was well suited for using on horseback, giving Mongol soldiers an advantage in battle. Other commonly used weapons were small battle-axes and lances fitted with hooks to pull enemies off their saddles.

As with the Turks and other steppe nomads, religious practices centered around the shaman, a religious expert believed to be able to communicate with the gods. The high god of the Mongols was Heaven/Sky, but they recognized many other gods as well. Some groups of Mongols, especially those closer to settled communities, converted to Buddhism, Nestorian Christianity, or Manichaeism (man-uh-KEY-an-ism).

Chinggis Khan and the Mongol Empire

How did Chinggis Khan and his successors conquer much of Eurasia, and how did the Mongol conquests change the regions affected?

In the mid-twelfth century the Mongols were just one of many peoples in the eastern grasslands, neither particularly numerous nor especially advanced. Why then did the Mongols suddenly emerge as an overpowering force on the historical stage? One explanation is ecological. A drop in the mean annual temperature created a subsistence crisis. As pastures shrank, the Mongols and other nomads had to look beyond the steppe to get more of their food from the agricultural world. A second reason for their sudden rise was the appearance of a single individual, the brilliant but utterly ruthless Temujin (ca. 1162–1227), later and more commonly called Chinggis Khan (sometimes spelled Genghis or Ghengis).

Chinggis Khan

In Temujin's youth, his father had built a modest tribal following. When Temujin's father was poisoned by a rival, his followers, not ready to follow a boy of twelve, drifted away, leaving Temujin and his mother and brothers in a vulnerable position. Temujin slowly collected followers. In 1182 Temujin was captured and carried in a cage to a rival's camp. After a daring midnight escape, he led his followers to join a stronger chieftain whom his father had once aided. With the chieftain's help, Temujin began avenging the insults he had received.

Temujin proved to be a natural leader, and as he subdued the Tartars, Kereyids, Naimans, Merkids, and other Mongol and Turkish tribes, he built up an army of loyal followers. He mastered the art of winning allies through displays of personal courage in battle and generosity to his followers. To those who opposed him, he could be merciless. He once asserted that nothing gave more pleasure than massacring one's

The Abduction of Women in *The Secret History of the Mongols*

Within a few decades of Chinggis Khan's death, oral traditions concerning his rise were written down in the Mongolian language in *The Secret History of the Mongols*. The account begins with the cycles of revenge among the tribes in Mongolia, many of which began when women were abducted for wives. The following passages relate how Temujin's (Chinggis Khan's) father, Yesugei, seized Hogelun, Temujin's future mother, from a passing Merkid tribesman; how twenty years later three Merkids in return seized women from Temujin; and how Temujin got revenge.

■ That year Yesugei the Brave was out hunting with his falcon on the Onan. Yeke Chiledu, a nobleman of the Merkid tribe, had gone to the Olkhunugud people to find himself a wife, and he was returning to the Merkid with the girl he'd found when he passed Yesugei hunting by the river. When he saw them riding along Yesugei leaned forward on his horse. He saw it was a beautiful girl. Quickly he rode back to his tent and just as quick returned with his two brothers, Nekun Taisi and Daritai Odchigin. When Chiledu saw the three Mongols coming he . . . cut back around the far side of the hill and rode to Lady Hogelun, the girl he'd just married, who stood waiting for him at the front of their cart. "Did you see the look on the faces of those three men?" she asked him. "From their faces it looks like they mean to kill you. As long as you've got your life there'll always be girls for you to choose from. There'll always be women to ride in your cart. As long as you've got your life you'll be able to find some girl to marry. When you find her, just name her

Hogelun for me, but go now and save your own life!" Then she pulled off her shirt and held it out to him, saying: "And take this to remember me, to remember my scent." . . .

The three Mongols chased him across seven hills before turning around and returning to Hogelun's cart. . . . As they rode her back toward their camp, Hogelun began to cry, . . . and she cried till she stirred up the waters of the Onan River, till she shook the trees in the forest and the grass in the valleys. But as the party approached their camp Daritai, riding beside her, warned her to stop: "This fellow who held you in his arms, he's already ridden over the mountains. This man who's lost you, he's crossed many rivers by now. You can call out his name, but he can't see you now even if he looks back. If you tried to find him now you won't even find his tracks. So be still now," he told her. Then Yesugei took Lady Hogelun to his tent as his wife. . . .

[Some twenty years later] one morning just before dawn Old Woman Khogaghchin, Mother Hogelun's servant, woke with a start, crying: "Mother! Mother! Get up! The ground is shaking, I hear it rumble. The Tayichigud must be riding back to attack us. Get up!"

Mother Hogelun jumped from her bed, saying: "Quick, wake my sons!" They woke Temujin and the others and all ran for the horses. Temujin, Mother Hogelun, and Khasar each took a horse. . . . Mother Hogelun lifted the baby Temulun onto her saddle. They saddled the last horse as a lead and there was no horse left for [Temujin's wife] Lady Borte. . . .

Old Woman Khogaghchin, who'd been left in the camp, said: "I'll hide Lady Borte." She made her get into a black covered cart. Then she harnessed the cart to a speckled ox. Whipping the ox, she drove the cart away from the camp down the Tungelig. As the first light of day hit them, soldiers rode up and told them

Chinggis Khan The title given to the Mongol ruler Temujin in 1206; it means Great Ruler.

enemies, seizing their horses and cattle, and ravishing their women. Sometimes Temujin would kill all the men in a defeated tribe to prevent later vendettas. At other times he would take them on as soldiers in his own armies.

In 1206, at a great gathering of tribal leaders, Temujin was proclaimed **Chinggis Khan** (JING-gus kahn), or Great Ruler. Chinggis decreed that Mongol, until then an unwritten language, be written down in the script used by the Uighur Turks. With this script a record was made of the Mongol laws and customs, ranging from the rules for the annual hunt to punishments of death for robbery and adultery. Another meato stop. "Who are you?" they asked her, and Old Woman Khogaghchin answered: "I'm a servant of Temujin's. I've just come from shearing his sheep. I'm on my way back to my own tent to make felt from the wool." Then they asked her: "Is Temujin at his tent? How far is it from here?" Old Woman Khogaghchin said: "As for the tent, it's not far. As for Temujin, I couldn't see whether he was there or not. I was just shearing his sheep out back." The soldiers rode off toward the camp, and Old Woman Khogaghchin whipped the ox. But as the cart moved faster its axle-tree snapped. "Now we'll have to run for the woods on foot," she thought, but before she could start the soldiers returned. They'd made [Temujin's half brother] Belgutei's mother their captive, and had her slung over one of their horses with her feet swinging down. They rode up to the old woman shouting: "What have you got in that cart!" "I'm just carrying wool," Khogaghchin replied, but an old soldier turned to the younger ones and said, "Get off your horses and see what's in there." When they opened the door of the cart they found Borte inside. Pulling her out, they forced Borte and Khogaghchin to ride on their horses, then they all set out after Temujin. . . .

The men who pursued Temujin were the chiefs of the three Merkid clans, Toghtoga, Dayin Usun, and Khagatai Darmala. These three had come to get their revenge, saying: "Long ago Mother Hogelun was stolen from our brother, Chiledu." When they couldn't catch Temujin they said to each other: "We've got our revenge. We've taken their wives from them," and they rode down from Mount Burkhan Khaldun back to their homes. . . .

Having finished his prayer Temujin rose and rode off with Khasar and Belgutei. They rode to [his father's sworn brother] Toghoril Ong Khan of the Kereyid camped in the Black Forest on the Tula River. Temujin spoke to Ong Khan, saying: "I was attacked by surprise by the three Merkid chiefs. They've stolen my wife from me. We've come to you now to say, 'Let my father the Khan save my wife and return her.'" . . .

[Temujin and his allies] came down on [the Merkid chief] as if through the smoke-hole of his tent, beating down the frame of his tent and leaving it flat, capturing and killing his wives and his sons. They struck at his door-frame where his guardian spirit lived and broke it to pieces. They completely destroyed all his people until in their place there was nothing but emptiness. . . .

As the Merkid people tried to flee from our army running down the Selenge with what they could gather in the darkness, as our soldiers rode out of the night capturing and killing the Merkid, Temujin rode through the retreating camp shouting out: "Borte! Borte!" . . .

When [Lady Borte] recognized Temujin's voice, Borte leaped from her cart. Lady Borte and Old Woman Khogaghchin saw Temujin charge through the crowd and they ran to him, finally seizing the reins of his horse. All about them was moonlight. As Temujin looked down to see who had stopped him he recognized Lady Borte. In a moment he was down from his horse and they were in each other's arms, embracing.

QUESTIONS FOR ANALYSIS

1. What do you learn from these stories about the Mongol way of life?
2. "Marriage by capture" has been practiced in many parts of the world. Can you infer from these stories why such a system would persist? What was the impact of such practices on kinship relations?
3. Can you recognize traces of the oral origins of these stories?

Source: Paul Kahn, trans., *The Secret History of the Mongols: The Origin of Chinghis Khan.* Copyright © 1984. Reprinted with permission of Paul Kahn.

sure adopted at this assembly was a postal relay system to send messages rapidly by mounted courier, suggesting that Chinggis already had ambitions to rule a vast empire.

With the tribes of Mongolia united, the energies previously devoted to infighting and vendettas were redirected to exacting tribute from the settled populations nearby, starting with the Jurchen (Jin) state that extended into north China (see Map 13.1). Because of his early experiences with intertribal feuding, Chinggis mistrusted traditional tribal loyalties, and as he fashioned a new army, he gave it a new, nontribal decimal structure (based on units of ten). He conscripted soldiers from all the tribes

The Tent of Chinggis Khan In this fourteenth-century Persian illustration from Rashid al-Din's *History of the World*, two guards stand outside while Chinggis is in his tent. (Bibliothèque Nationale, Paris, France/ Bridgeman Images)

and assigned them to units that were composed of members from different tribes. He selected commanders for each unit whom he could remove at will, although he allowed commanders to pass their posts on to their sons.

After Chinggis subjugated a city, he would send envoys to cities farther out to demand submission and threaten destruction. Those who opened their city gates and submitted without fighting could join the Mongols, but those who resisted faced the prospect of mass slaughter. He despised city dwellers and would sometimes use them as living shields in the next battle. After the Mongol armies swept across north China in 1212–1213, ninety-odd cities lay in rubble. Not surprisingly many governors of cities and rulers of small states hastened to offer submission.

Chinggis preferred conquest to administration and did not stay in north China to set up an administrative structure. He left that to subordinates and turned his attention westward, to Central Asia and Persia, then dominated by different groups of Turks. In 1218 Chinggis proposed to the Khwarizm (QUAHR-uh-zim) shah of Persia that he accept Mongol overlordship and establish trade relations. The shah, to show his determination to resist, ordered the envoy and the merchants who had accompanied him killed. The next year Chinggis led an army of one hundred thousand soldiers west to retaliate. Mongol forces destroyed the shah's army and sacked one Persian city after another.

After returning from Central Asia, Chinggis died in 1227 during the siege of a city in northwest China. Before he died, he instructed his sons not to fall out among themselves but instead to divide the spoils.

Chinggis's Successors

khanates The states ruled by a khan; the four units into which Chinggis divided the Mongol Empire.

Although Mongol leaders traditionally had had to win their positions, after Chinggis died the empire was divided into four states called **khanates**, with one of the lines of his descendants taking charge of each (Map 12.1). Chinggis's third son, Ögödei, assumed the title of khan, and he directed the next round of invasions.

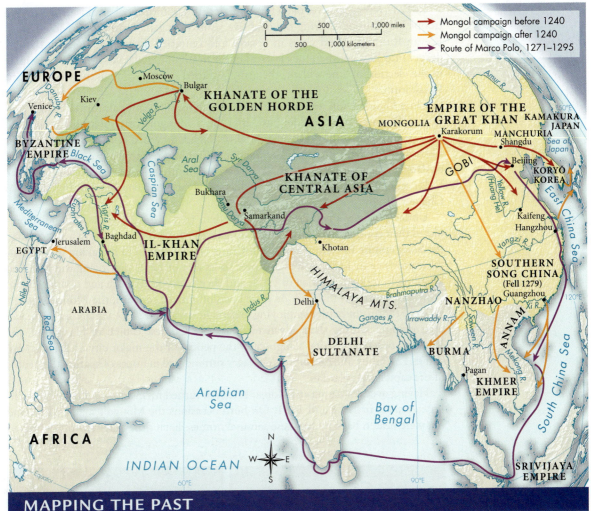

MAPPING THE PAST

MAP 12.1 The Mongol Empire The creation of the vast Mongol Empire facilitated communication across Eurasia and led to both the spread of deadly plagues and the transfer of technical and scientific knowledge. After the death of Chinggis Khan in 1227, the empire was divided into four khanates ruled by different lines of his successors. In the 1270s the Mongols conquered southern China, but most of their subsequent campaigns did not lead to further territorial gains.

ANALYZING THE MAP Trace the campaigns of the Mongols. Which ones led to acquisition of territory, and which ones did not?

CONNECTIONS Would the division of the Mongol Empire into separate khanates have made these areas easier for the Mongols to rule? What drawbacks might it have had from the Mongols' point of view?

In 1237 representatives of all four lines led 150,000 Mongol, Turkish, and Persian troops into Europe. During the next five years, they gained control of Moscow and Kievan Rus and looted cities in Poland and Hungary. They were poised to attack deeper into Europe when they learned of the death of Ögödei in 1241. To participate in the election of a new khan, the army returned to the Mongols' new capital city, Karakorum.

Once Ögödei's son was certified as his successor, the Mongols turned their attention to Persia and the Middle East. In 1256 a Mongol army took northwest Iran, then pushed on to the Abbasid capital of Baghdad. When it fell in 1258, the last Abbasid caliph was murdered, and the population was put to the sword. The Mongol onslaught was successfully resisted, however, by both the Delhi sultanate (see "The Delhi Sultanate") and the Mamluk rulers in Egypt (see "The Mongol Invasions" in Chapter 9).

Under Chinggis's grandson Khubilai Khan (r. 1260–1294), the Mongols completed their conquest of China. Proceeding deliberately, the Mongols first surrounded the Song empire in central and south China (see Chapter 13) by taking its westernmost province in 1252, as well as Korea to its east in 1258; destroying the Nanzhao kingdom in modern Yunnan in 1254; and then continuing south and taking Annam (northern Vietnam) in 1257. As their invasion moved forward, the Mongols used a variety of forms of battle, employing experts in naval and siege warfare from all over their empire. During their advance toward the Chinese capital of Hangzhou, the Mongols ordered the total slaughter of the people of the major city of Changzhou, and in 1276 the Chinese empress dowager surrendered in hopes of sparing the people of the capital a similar fate.

Having overrun China and Korea, Khubilai turned his eyes toward Japan, launching invasions in 1274 and 1281. On both occasions the Mongols managed to land but were beaten back by Japanese samurai armies. Each time fierce storms destroyed

Mongols Conquer Baghdad The siege of Baghdad in 1258 is depicted in this illustration from Rashid al-Din's *History of the World*, which was published in Persia in the fourteenth century. (Pictures from *History*/Bridgeman Images)

the Mongol fleets. The Japanese claimed that they had been saved by the *kamikaze*, the "divine wind" (which later lent its name to the thousands of Japanese aviators who crashed their airplanes into American warships during World War II). Twelve years later, in 1293, Khubilai tried sending a fleet to the islands of Southeast Asia, including Java, but it met with no more success than the fleets sent to Japan.

Why were the Mongols so successful against so many different types of enemies? Even though their population was tiny compared to the populations of the large agricultural societies they conquered, their tactics, their weapons, and their organization all gave them advantages. Like other nomads before them, they were superb horsemen and excellent archers. Their horses were extremely nimble, able to change direction quickly, thus allowing the Mongols to maneuver easily and ride through infantry forces armed with swords, lances, and javelins.

The Mongols were also open to trying new military technologies. To attack walled cities, they learned how to use catapults and other engines of war. At first they employed Chinese catapults, but when they learned that those used by the Turks in Afghanistan were more powerful, they adopted the better model. The Mongols also used exploding arrows and gunpowder projectiles developed by the Chinese.

The Mongols made good use of intelligence and tried to exploit internal divisions in the countries they attacked. Thus in north China they appealed to the Khitans, who had been defeated by the Jurchens a century earlier, to join them in attacking the Jurchens. In Syria they exploited the resentment of Christians against their Muslim rulers.

MONGOL CONQUESTS

1206	Temujin made Chinggis Khan
1215	Fall of Beijing (Jurchens)
1219–1220	Fall of Bukhara and Samarkand in Central Asia
1227	Death of Chinggis
1237–1241	Raids into eastern Europe
1257	Conquest of Annam (northern Vietnam)
1258	Conquest of Abbasid capital of Baghdad; conquest of Korea
1260	Khubilai succeeds to khanship
1274	First attempt at invading Japan
1276	Surrender of Song Dynasty (China)
1281	Second attempt at invading Japan
1293	Mongol fleet unsuccessful in invasion of Java
mid-14th century	Decline of Mongol power

The Mongols as Rulers

The success of the Mongols in ruling vast territories was due in large part to their willingness to incorporate other ethnic groups into their armies and governments. Whatever their original country or religion, those who served the Mongols loyally were rewarded. Uighurs, Tibetans, Persians, Chinese, and Russians came to hold powerful positions in the Mongol governments.

Since, in Mongol eyes, the purpose of fighting was to gain riches, the Mongols would regularly loot the settlements they conquered, taking whatever they wanted, including the residents. Land would be granted to military commanders, nobles, and army units to be governed and exploited as the recipients wished. Those working the land would be given to them as serfs. The Mongols built a capital city called Karakorum in modern Mongolia, and to bring it up to the level of the cities they conquered, they transported skilled workers from those cities. For instance, after Bukhara and Samarkand were captured in 1219–1220, some thirty thousand artisans were enslaved and transported to Mongolia.

The traditional nomad disdain for farmers led some commanders to suggest turning north China into a gigantic pasture after it was conquered. In time, though, the Mongols came to realize that simply appropriating the wealth and human resources of the settled lands was not as good as extracting regular revenue from them. The Mongols gave Chinese methods of taxation a try, but soon political rivals convinced the khan that he would gain even more by letting Central Asian Muslim merchants bid against each other for licenses to collect taxes any way they could, a system called **tax-farming**. Ordinary Chinese found this method of tax collecting much more oppressive than traditional Chinese methods, since there was little to keep the tax collectors from seizing everything they could.

tax-farming Assigning the collection of taxes to whoever bids the most for the privilege.

By the second half of the thirteenth century there was no longer a genuine pan-Asian Mongol Empire. Much of Asia was in the hands of Mongol successor states, but these were generally hostile to each other. Khubilai was often at war with the khanate of Central Asia, then held by his cousin Khaidu, and he had little contact with the khanate of the Golden Horde in south Russia. The Mongols adapted their methods of government to the existing traditions of each place they ruled, and the regions went their separate ways.

In China the Mongols resisted assimilation and purposely avoided many Chinese practices. The rulers conducted their business in the Mongol language and spent their summers in Mongolia. Khubilai discouraged Mongols from marrying Chinese and took only Mongol women into the palace. Chinese were treated as legally inferior not only to the Mongols but also to all other non-Chinese.

In Central Asia, Persia, and Russia the Mongols tended to merge with the Turkish groups already there and, like them, converted to Islam. Russia in the thirteenth century was not a strongly centralized state, and the Mongols allowed Russian princes and lords to continue to rule their territories as long as they turned over adequate tribute. The city of Moscow became the center of Mongol tribute collection and grew in importance. In the Middle East the Mongol Il-khans (as they were known in Persia) were more active as rulers, again continuing the traditions of the caliphate. In Mongolia itself, however, Mongol traditions were maintained.

Mongol control in each of the khanates lasted about a century. In the mid-fourteenth century the Mongol dynasty in China deteriorated into civil war, and in the 1360s the Mongols withdrew back to Mongolia. There was a similar loss of Mongol power in Persia and Central Asia. Only on the south Russian steppe did the Golden Horde maintain its hold for another century.

As Mongol rule in Central Asia declined, a new conqueror emerged, Timur, also known as Tamerlane (Timur the Lame). Not a nomad but a highly civilized Turkish noble, Timur in the 1360s struck out from his base in Samarkand into Persia, north India (see "The Delhi Sultanate"), southern Russia, and beyond. His armies used the terror tactics that the Mongols had perfected, massacring the citizens of cities that resisted. In the decades after his death in 1405, however, Timur's empire went into decline.

East-West Communication During the Mongol Era

How did the Mongol conquests facilitate the spread of ideas, religions, inventions, and diseases?

The Mongol governments did more than any earlier political entities to encourage the movement of people and goods across Eurasia. With these vast movements came cultural accommodation as the Mongols, their conquered subjects, and their trading partners learned from one another. This cultural exchange involved both physical goods and the sharing of ideas, including the introduction of new religious beliefs and the adoption of new ways to organize and rule the Mongol Empire. It also facilitated the spread of the plague and the unwilling movement of enslaved captives.

The Movement of Peoples

The Mongols had never looked down on merchants the way the elites of many traditional states did, and they welcomed the arrival of merchants from distant lands. Even when different groups of Mongols were fighting among themselves, they usually allowed caravans to pass without harassing them.

The Mongol practice of transporting skilled people from the lands they conquered also brought people into contact with each other in new ways. Besides those forced to move, the Mongols recruited administrators from all over. Especially prominent were the Uighur Turks of Chinese Central Asia, whose familiarity with Chinese civilization and fluency in Turkish were extremely valuable in facilitating communication.

One of those who served the Mongols was Rashid al-Din (ca. 1247–1318). A Jew from Persia and the son of an apothecary, Rashid al-Din converted to Islam at the age of thirty and entered the service of the Mongol Il-khan of Persia as a physician. He rose in government service, traveled widely, and eventually became prime minister. Rashid al-Din became friends with the ambassador from China, and together they arranged for translations of Chinese works on medicine, agronomy, and statecraft. Aware of the great differences between cultures, he believed that the Mongols should try to rule in accord with the moral principles of the majority in each land. On that basis he convinced the Mongol khan of Persia to convert to Islam. Rashid al-Din undertook to explain the great variety of cultures by writing a world history more comprehensive than any previously written. (See "Global Viewpoints: Explaining the Workings of Paper Money in China, Persia, and Europe," page 345.)

The Mongols were remarkably open to religious experts from all the lands they encountered. More Europeans made their way as far as Mongolia and China in the Mongol period than ever before. Popes and kings sent envoys to the Mongol court in the hope of enlisting the Mongols on their side in their long-standing conflict with Muslim forces over the Holy Land. European visitors were also interested in finding Christians who had been cut off from the West by the spread of Islam, and in fact there were considerable numbers of Nestorian Christians in Central Asia.

The most famous European visitor to the Mongol lands was the Venetian Marco Polo (ca. 1254–1324). In his famous *Description of the World*, Marco Polo described all the places he visited or learned about during his seventeen years away from home. He reported being warmly received by Khubilai, who impressed him enormously. He was also awed by the wealth and splendor of Chinese cities and spread the notion of Asia as a land of riches.

Planting Trees The illustrations in early copies of Marco Polo's book show the elements that Europeans found most interesting. This page illustrates Khubilai's order that trees be planted along the main roads. (Bibliothèque Nationale, Paris/akg-images)

The Spread of Disease, Goods, and Ideas

The rapid transfer of people and goods across Central Asia spread more than ideas and inventions. It also spread diseases, the most deadly of which was the plague known in Europe as the Black Death, which scholars identify today as the bubonic plague. In the early fourteenth century, transmitted by rats and fleas, the plague began to spread from Central Asia into West Asia, the Mediterranean, and western Europe. The confusion of the mid-fourteenth century that led to the loss of Mongol power in China, Iran, and Central Asia undoubtedly owes something to the effect of the spread of the plague and other diseases. (For more on the Black Death, see Chapter 14.)

Traditionally, the historians of each of the countries conquered by the Mongols portrayed them as a scourge. Among contemporary Western historians, it is now more common to celebrate the genius of the Mongol military machine and treat the spread of ideas and inventions as an obvious good. There is no reason to assume, however, that people benefited equally from the improved communications and the new political institutions of the Mongol era. Merchants involved in long-distance trade prospered, but those enslaved and transported hundreds or thousands of miles from home would have seen themselves not as the beneficiaries of opportunities to encounter cultures different from their own but rather as the most pitiable of victims. Moreover, the places that were ruled by Mongol governments for a century or more—China, Central Asia, Persia, and Russia—do not seem to have advanced at a more rapid rate during that century than they did in earlier centuries, either economically or culturally.

In terms of the spread of technological and scientific ideas, Europe seems to have been by far the main beneficiary of increased communication, largely because in 1200 it lagged farther behind than the other areas. Chinese inventions such as printing, gunpowder, and the compass spread westward. Persian and Indian expertise in astronomy and mathematics also spread. In terms of the spread of religions, Islam probably gained the most. It came to dominate in Chinese Central Asia, which had previously been Buddhist.

Explaining the Workings of Paper Money in China, Persia, and Europe

In China the Mongols maintained the established practice of circulating paper money (see "The Medieval Chinese Economic Revolution" in Chapter 13), which amazed visitors from other parts of Eurasia. The three texts below give different perspectives on the use of paper money. The first is a legal ruling issued in 1291 by the Mongols in China, the second is Marco Polo's description of the practice as he witnessed it in the 1290s, and the third is Rashid al-Din's account of the failed attempt to introduce the practice in Mongol-ruled Persia in 1294.

The Yuan Code of 1291

■ At any Treasury for Note Circulation, when a person comes to exchange worn-out notes for new notes, the responsible official shall oversee the counting of the notes in the presence of the owner. If none of the notes are patched or counterfeited, the official shall apply the stamp "Exchanged" to them and place them in the treasury and hand over new notes to the owner. The supervising authorities shall send inspectors to make frequent inspections. Any violator of these provisions shall be investigated and punished.

Marco Polo

■ The coinage of this paper money is authenticated with as much form and ceremony as if it were actually pure gold or silver; for to each note a number of officers, specially appointed, not only subscribe their names, but affix their seals also. . . . This paper currency is circulated in every part of the Great Khan's dominions; nor dares any person, at the peril of his life, refuse to accept it in payment. All his subjects receive it without hesitation, because, wherever their business may call them, they can dispose of it again in the purchase of merchandise they may require. . . .

When any person happens to be possessed of paper money which from long use has become damaged, they carry it to the mint, where, upon the payment of only three per cent, they receive fresh notes in exchange.

Should any be desirous of procuring gold or silver for the purpose of manufacture, such as of drinking-cups, girdles, or other articles wrought of these metals, they in like manner apply to the mint, and for their paper obtain the bullion they require.

Rashid al-Din

■ On Friday [July 27, 1294], Akbuka, Togachar, Sadr al-Din, and Tamachi-Inak went to Tabriz to launch the paper money [*chao*]. They arrived there on [August 13], promulgated the decree, and prepared a great quantity of paper money. On Saturday [September 12, 1294], in the city of Tabriz, they put the paper money into circulation. The decree laid down that any person who refused to accept it would be summarily executed. For one week, in fear of the sword, they accepted it, but they gave very little in return. Most of the people of Tabriz perforce chose to leave, taking the textiles and foodstuffs from the bazaars with them, so that nothing was available, and people who wanted to eat fruit went secretly to the orchards. The city, which had been so populous, was completely emptied of people. Vagabonds and ruffians looted whatever they found in the streets. Caravans ceased to go there. . . .

Sadr al-Din, affected by the words [of a dervish], and with the assent of the retainers after this ruination, obtained a decree authorizing the sale of foodstuffs for gold. Because of this people became bold and transacted business openly in gold, and the absent returned to the city, and within a short time it was flourishing again. In the end, the attempt to introduce paper money did not succeed.

QUESTIONS FOR ANALYSIS

1. What do you learn about the processes of cultural borrowing from these sources?
2. What features of paper money most impressed Marco Polo?
3. What made it difficult to introduce paper money in Tabriz?

Sources: *Dayuan tongzhi tiaoge* (Taipei: Huasheng shuju, 1980), 14.1b–2a, trans. Patricia Ebrey; Manuel Komroff, ed., *The Travels of Marco Polo* (New York: Boni and Liveright, 1926), pp. 159–161; Bernard Lewis, ed. and trans., *Islam from the Prophet Muhammad to the Capture of Constantinople.* Vol. 2: *Religion and Society* (New York: Oxford University Press, 1987), 292w from p. 192, slightly modified. © 1974 by Bernard Lewis. Used by permission of Oxford University Press, USA.

What was the result of India's encounters with Turks, Mongols, and Islam?

India, Islam, and the Development of Regional Cultures, 300–1400

After the Mauryan Empire broke apart in 185 B.C.E. (see "The Reign of Ashoka" in Chapter 3), India was politically divided into small kingdoms for several centuries. Only the Guptas in the fourth century would emerge to unite much of north India, though their rule was cut short by the invasion of the Huns in about 450. A few centuries later, India was profoundly shaped by Turkish nomads from Central Asia who brought their culture and, most important, Islam to India. Despite these events, the lives of most Indians remained unchanged, with the majority of the people living in villages in a society defined by caste.

The Gupta Empire, ca. 320–480

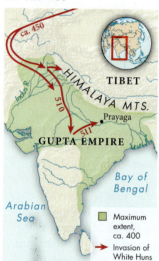

The Gupta Empire, ca. 320–480

TIBET

HIMALAYA MTS.

Prayaga

GUPTA EMPIRE

Bay of Bengal

Arabian Sea

☐ Maximum extent, ca. 400

→ Invasion of White Huns

The Gupta Empire, ca. 320–480

In the early fourth century a state emerged in the Ganges plain that was able to bring large parts of north India under its control. The rulers of this Indian empire, the Guptas, consciously modeled their rule after that of the Mauryan Empire, and the founder took the name of the founder of that dynasty, Chandragupta. The Guptas united north India and received tribute from states in Nepal and the Indus Valley, thus giving large parts of India a period of peace and political unity.

The Guptas' administrative system was not as centralized as that of the Mauryans. In the central regions they drew their revenue from a tax on agriculture of one-quarter of the harvest and maintained monopolies on key products such as metals and salt (reminiscent of Chinese practice). They also exacted labor service for the construction and upkeep of roads, wells, and irrigation systems. More distant areas were assigned to governors who were allowed considerable leeway, and governorships often became hereditary. Areas still farther away were encouraged to become vassal states.

The Gupta kings were patrons of the arts. Poets composed epics for the courts of the Gupta kings, and other writers experimented with prose romances and popular tales. India's greatest poet, Kalidasa (ca. 380–450), like Shakespeare, wrote poems as well as plays in verse.

In mathematics, too, the Gupta period could boast of impressive intellectual achievements. The so-called Arabic numerals are actually of Indian origin. Indian mathematicians developed the place-value notation system, with separate columns for ones, tens, and hundreds, as well as a zero sign to indicate the absence of units in a given column. This system greatly facilitated calculation and had spread as far as Europe by the seventh century.

The Gupta rulers were Hindus, but they tolerated all faiths. Buddhist pilgrims from other areas of Asia reported that Buddhist monasteries with hundreds or even thousands of monks and nuns flourished in the cities. The success of Buddhism did not hinder Hinduism with its many gods, which remained popular among ordinary people.

The great crisis of the Gupta Empire was the invasion of the Huns in about 450. Mustering his full might, the Gupta ruler Skandagupta (r. ca. 455–467) threw back the invaders, but they had dealt the dynasty a fatal blow.

India's Medieval Age and the First Encounter with Islam

After the decline of the Gupta Empire, India once again broke into separate kingdoms that were frequently at war with each other. Most of the dynasties of India's medieval age (ca. 500–1400) were short-lived, but a balance of power was maintained between the major regions of India, with none gaining enough of an advantage to conquer the others. Particularly notable are the Cholas, who dominated the southern tip of the peninsula, Sri Lanka, and much of the eastern Indian Ocean to the twelfth century (see Map 12.2, page 353).

Political division fostered the development of regional cultures. Literature came to be written in India's regional languages, among them Marathi, Bengali, and Assamese. Commerce continued as before, and the coasts of India remained important in the sea trade of the Indian Ocean.

The first encounters with Islam occurred in this period. In 711 the Umayyad governor of Iraq seized the Sind area in western India (modern Pakistan). The western part of India remained part of the caliphate for centuries, but Islam did not spread much beyond this foothold. During the ninth and tenth centuries Turks from Central Asia moved into the region of today's northeastern Iran and western Afghanistan, then known as Khurasan. Converts to Islam, they first served as military forces for the caliphate in Baghdad, but as its authority weakened, they made themselves rulers of an effectively independent Khurasan and frequently sent raiding parties into north India. Beginning in 997 Mahmud of Ghazni (r. 997–1030) led seventeen annual forays into India from his base in modern Afghanistan. He systematically looted Indian palaces and temples, viewing religious statues as infidels' idols. Eventually the Arab conquerors of the Sind fell to the Turks. By 1030 the Indus Valley, the Punjab, and the rest of northwest India were in the grip of the Turks.

Kandariyâ Mahâdeva Hindu Temple Built around 1050 by a local king in central India, this is one of the best-preserved Hindu temples from the medieval period. The main spire rises 100 feet, and the sides are decorated with more than six hundred stone statues. (Yvan Travert/akg-images)

The new rulers encouraged the spread of Islam, but the Indian caste system (see "Life in Early India" in Chapter 3) made it difficult to convert higher-caste Indians. Notions of purity were fundamental, as a Persian scholar explained:

> They totally differ from us in religion, as we believe in nothing in which they believe, and vice versa. On the whole, there is very little disputing about theological topics among them; at the utmost they fight with words, but they will never stake their soul or body or property on religious controversy. . . . They call foreigners impure and forbid having any connection with them, be it by intermarriage or any kind of relationship, or by sitting, eating, and drinking with them, because thereby, they think, they would be polluted.[2]

protected people The Muslim classification used for Hindus, Christians, and Jews; they were allowed to follow their religions but had to pay a special tax.

After the initial period of raids and destruction of temples, the Muslim Turks came to an accommodation with the Hindus, who were classed as a **protected people**, like the Christians and Jews, and allowed to follow their religion. They had to pay a special tax but did not have to perform military service. Local chiefs and rajas were often allowed to remain in control of their domains as long as they paid tribute. Most Indians looked on the Muslim conquerors as a new ruling caste, capable of governing and taxing them but otherwise peripheral to their lives. The myriad castes largely governed themselves, isolating the newcomers.

Nevertheless, over the course of several centuries Islam gained a stronghold on north India, especially in the Indus Valley (modern Pakistan) and in Bengal at the mouth of the Ganges River (modern Bangladesh). Moreover, the sultanate seems to have had a positive effect on the economy. Much of the wealth confiscated from temples was put to more productive use, and India's first truly large cities emerged. The Turks also were eager to employ skilled workers, giving new opportunities to low-caste manual and artisan labor.

The Muslim rulers were much more hostile to Buddhism than to Hinduism, seeing Buddhism as a competitive proselytizing religion. In 1193 a Turkish raiding party destroyed the great Buddhist university at Nalanda in Bihar. Buddhist monks were killed or forced to flee to Buddhist centers in Southeast Asia, Nepal, and Tibet. Buddhism, which had thrived for so long in peaceful and friendly competition with Hinduism, subsequently went into decline in its native land.

Hinduism, however, remained as strong as ever. South India was largely unaffected by these invasions, and traditional Hindu culture flourished there under native kings ruling small kingdoms. (See "Individuals in Society: Bhaskara the Teacher," at right.) Devotional cults and mystical movements flourished. This was a great age of religious art and architecture in India. Extraordinary temples covered with elaborate bas-relief were built in many areas.

The Delhi Sultanate

In the twelfth century a new line of Turkish rulers arose in Afghanistan, led by Muhammad of Ghur (d. 1206). Muhammad captured Delhi and extended his control nearly throughout north India. When he fell to an assassin in 1206, one of his generals, the former slave Qutb-ud-din, seized the reins of power and established a government at Delhi, separate from the government in Afghanistan. This sultanate of Delhi lasted for three centuries, even though dynasties changed several times.

A major accomplishment of the Delhi sultanate was holding off the Mongols. Chinggis Khan and his troops entered the Indus Valley in 1221 in pursuit of the shah

Bhaskara the Teacher

IN INDIA, AS IN MANY OTHER SOCIETIES, astronomy and mathematics were closely linked, and many of the most important mathematicians served their rulers as astronomers. Bhaskara (1114–ca. 1185) was such an astronomer-mathematician. For generations his Brahmin family had been astronomers at the Ujjain astronomical observatory in north-central India, and his father had written a popular book on astrology.

Bhaskara was a highly erudite man. A disciple wrote that he had thoroughly mastered eight books on grammar, six on medicine, six on philosophy, five on mathematics, and the four Vedas. Bhaskara eventually wrote six books on mathematics and mathematical astronomy. They deal with solutions to simple and quadratic equations and show his knowledge of trigonometry, including the sine table and relationships between different trigonometric functions, and even some of the basic elements of calculus.

A court poet who centuries later translated Bhaskara's book titled *The Beautiful* explained its title by saying Bhaskara wrote it for his daughter named Beautiful (Lilavati) as consolation when his divination of the best time for her to marry went awry. Whether Bhaskara did or did not write this book for his daughter, many of the problems he provides in it have a certain charm:

> On an expedition to seize his enemy's elephants, a king marched two yojanas the first day. Say, intelligent calculator, with what increasing rate of daily march did he proceed, since he reached his foe's city, a distance of eighty yojanas, in a week?*
>
> Out of a heap of pure lotus flower, a third part, a fifth, and a sixth were offered respectively to the gods Siva, Vishnu, and the Sun; and a quarter was presented to Bhavani. The remaining six lotuses were given to the venerable preceptor. Tell quickly the whole number of lotus.†
>
> If eight best variegated silk scarfs, measuring three cubits in breadth and eight in length, cost a hundred nishkas, say quickly, merchant, if thou understand trade, what a like scarf, three and a half cubits long and half a cubit wide will cost.‡

Bhaskara had a long career. His first book on mathematical astronomy, written in 1150 when he was thirty-six, used mathematics to calculate solar and lunar eclipses or planetary conjunctions. Thirty-three years later he was still writing on the subject, this time providing simpler ways to solve problems encountered before. Bhaskara wrote his books in Sanskrit, already a literary language rather than a vernacular language, but even in his own day some of them were translated into other Indian languages.

The observatory where Bhaskara worked in Ujjain today stands in ruins. (© Anirudha Cheoolkar/Dinodia Photo/age-fotostock)

QUESTIONS FOR ANALYSIS

1. What might have been the advantages of making occupations like astronomer hereditary in India?
2. Are the problems posed by Bhaskara ones that people would face in ordinary life?

*Quotations from Haran Chandra Banerji, *Colebrooke's Translation of the Lilavati*, 2d ed. (Calcutta: The Book Co., 1927), pp. 80–81, 30, 51, 200. The answer is that each day he must travel 22/7 yojanas farther than the day before.

†The answer is 120.

‡The answer, from the formula $x = (1 \times 7 \times 1 \times 100) / (8 \times 3 \times 8 \times 2 \times 2)$, is given in currencies smaller than the nishka: 14 drammas, 9 panas, 1 kakini, and 6⅔ cowry shells. (20 cowry shells = 1 kakini, 4 kakini = 1 pana, 16 panas = 1 dramma, and 16 drammas = 1 nishka.)

of Khurasan. The sultan wisely kept out of the way, and when Chinggis Khan left some troops in the area, the sultan made no attempt to challenge them. Two generations later, in 1299, a Mongol khan launched a campaign into India with two hundred thousand men, but the sultan of the time was able to defeat them. Two years later the Mongols returned and camped at Delhi for two months, but they eventually left without taking the sultan's fort. Another Mongol raid in 1306–1307 also was successfully repulsed.

During the fourteenth century, however, the Delhi sultanate was in decline and proved unable to ward off the armies of Timur, who took Delhi in 1398. Timur's invasion left a weakened sultanate. The Delhi sultanate endured under different rulers until 1526, when it was conquered by the Mughals, a Muslim dynasty that would rule over most of northern India from the sixteenth into the nineteenth century.

Life in Medieval India

Local institutions played a much larger role in the lives of people in medieval India than did the state. Craft guilds oversaw conditions of work and trade, local councils handled law and order at the town or village level, and local castes gave members a sense of belonging and identity.

Like peasant societies elsewhere, including in China, Japan, and Southeast Asia, agricultural life in India ordinarily meant village life. The average farmer worked a small plot of land outside the village. All the family members pooled their resources — human, animal, and material — under the direction of the head of the family. These joint efforts strengthened family solidarity.

The agricultural year began with spring plowing. The traditional plow, drawn by two oxen wearing yokes and collars, had an iron-tipped share and a handle with which the farmer guided it. Rice, the most important grain, was sown at the beginning of the long rainy season. Beans, lentils, and peas were the farmer's friends, for they grew during the cold season and were harvested in the spring, when fresh food was scarce. Cereal crops such as wheat, barley, and millet provided carbohydrates and other nutrients. Some families cultivated vegetables, spices, fruit trees, and flowers in their gardens. Sugarcane was another important crop.

Farmers also raised livestock. Most highly valued were cattle, which were raised for plowing and milk, hides, and horns, but Hindus did not slaughter them for meat. Like the Islamic and Jewish prohibition on the consumption of pork, the eating of beef was forbidden among Hindus.

Local craftsmen and tradesmen were frequently organized into guilds, with guild heads and guild rules. The textile industries were particularly well developed. Textiles were produced in large quantities and traded throughout India and beyond. The cutting and polishing of precious stones was another industry associated closely with foreign trade.

In the cities shops were open to the street; families lived on the floors above. The busiest tradesmen dealt in milk and cheese, oil, spices, and perfumes. In addition to these tradesmen and merchants, a host of peddlers shuffled through towns and villages selling everything from needles to freshly cut flowers.

During the first millennium C.E., the caste system reached its mature form. Within the broad division into the four varnas (strata) of Brahmin, Kshatriya, Vaishya, and Shudra (see "Life in Early India" in Chapter 3), the population was subdivided into

Men at Work This stone frieze from the Buddhist stupa in Sanchi depicts Indian men doing a variety of everyday jobs. Although the stone was carved to convey religious ideas, we can use it as a source for such details of daily life as the sort of clothing men wore while working and how they carried loads. (DEA/G. Nimatallah/De Agostini Picture Library/Getty Images)

numerous castes, or **jati**. Each caste had a proper occupation. In addition, its members married only within the caste and ate only with other members. Members of high-status castes feared pollution from contact with lower-caste individuals and had to undertake rituals of purification to remove the taint.

Eventually Indian society comprised perhaps as many as three thousand castes. Each caste had its own governing body, which enforced the rules of the caste. Those incapable of living up to the rules were expelled, becoming outcastes. These unfortunates lived hard lives, performing tasks that others considered unclean or lowly.

Villages were often walled, as in north China and the Middle East. Cattle and sheep roamed as freely as people. Some families kept pets, such as cats or parrots. Half-wild mongooses served as effective protection against snakes. The pond outside the village was its main source of water and also a spawning ground for fish, birds, and mosquitoes. After the farmers returned from the fields in the evening, the village gates were closed until morning.

For all members of Indian society regardless of caste, marriage and family were the focus of life. As in China, the family was under the authority of the eldest male, who might take several wives, and ideally sons stayed home with their parents after they married. The family affirmed its solidarity by the religious ritual of honoring its dead ancestors—a ritual that linked the living and the dead, much like ancestor worship in China (see "Shang Society" in Chapter 4). People commonly lived in extended families: grandparents, uncles and aunts, cousins, and nieces and nephews all lived together in the same house or compound.

Children in poor households worked as soon as they were able. Children in wealthier households faced the age-old irritations of learning reading, writing, and arithmetic. Less attention was paid to daughters than to sons, though in more prosperous families they were often literate. Because girls who had lost their virginity could seldom hope to find good husbands, daughters were customarily married as children, with consummation delayed until they reached puberty.

A wife was expected to have no life apart from her husband. A widow was expected to lead the hard life of the ascetic: sleeping on the ground; eating only one simple meal a day, without meat, wine, salt, or honey; wearing plain, undyed clothes without jewelry; and shaving her head. She was viewed as inauspicious to everyone but her children, and she did not attend family festivals. Among high-caste Hindus,

jati The thousands of Indian castes.

sati A practice whereby a high-caste Hindu woman would throw herself on her husband's funeral pyre.

a widow would be praised for throwing herself on her husband's funeral pyre. Buddhist sects objected to this practice, called **sati**, but some Hindu religious authorities declared that by self-immolation a widow could expunge both her own and her husband's sins, so that both would enjoy eternal bliss in Heaven.

Within the home the position of a wife depended on her own intelligence and strength of character. Wives were supposed to be humble, cheerful, and diligent, even toward worthless husbands. As in other patriarchal societies, however, occasionally a woman ruled the household. For women who did not want to accept the strictures of married life, the main way out was to join a Buddhist or Jain religious community.

How did states develop along the maritime trade routes of Southeast Asia and beyond?

Southeast Asia, the Pacific Islands, and the Growth of Maritime Trade

Much as Roman culture spread to northern Europe and Chinese culture spread to Korea, Japan, and Vietnam, in the first millennium C.E. Indian learning, technology, and material culture spread to the mainland and islands of Southeast Asia. The spread of Indian culture was facilitated by the growth of maritime trade, but this interchange did not occur uniformly, and by 1400 there were still isolated societies in this region, most notably in the Pacific Islands east of Indonesia.

Southeast Asia is a tropical region that is more like India than China. The topography of mainland Southeast Asia is marked by north-south mountain ranges separated by river valleys (Map 12.2). It was easy for people to migrate south along these rivers but harder for them to cross the heavily forested mountains that divided the region into areas that had limited contact with each other. The indigenous population was originally mostly Malay, but migrations over the centuries brought many other peoples, including speakers of Austro-Asiatic (such as Vietnamese and Cambodian), Austronesian (such as Malay and Polynesian), and Sino-Tibetan-Burmese (such as Burmese and possibly Thai) languages, some of whom moved to the islands offshore and farther into the Pacific Ocean.

State Formation and Indian Influences

Southeast Asia was long a crossroads. Traders from China, India, Africa, and Europe either passed through the region when traveling from the Indian to the Pacific Ocean or came for its resources, notably spices (Map 12.3).

The northern part of modern Vietnam was under Chinese political control off and on from the second century B.C.E. to the tenth century C.E. (see "Vietnam" in Chapter 7), but Indian influence was of much greater significance for the rest of Southeast Asia. The first state to appear in historical records, called Funan by Chinese visitors, had its capital in southern Vietnam. In the first to sixth centuries C.E. Funan extended its control over much of Indochina and the Malay Peninsula. Merchants from northwest India would offload their goods and carry them across the narrowest part of the Malay Peninsula. The ports of Funan offered food and lodging to the merchants as they waited for the winds to shift to continue their voyages. Brahmin priests and Buddhist monks from India settled along with the traders, serving the Indian population and attracting local converts. Rulers often invited Indian priests and monks to serve under them.

Sixth-century Chinese sources report that the Funan king lived in a multistory palace and the common people lived in houses built on piles with roofs of bamboo

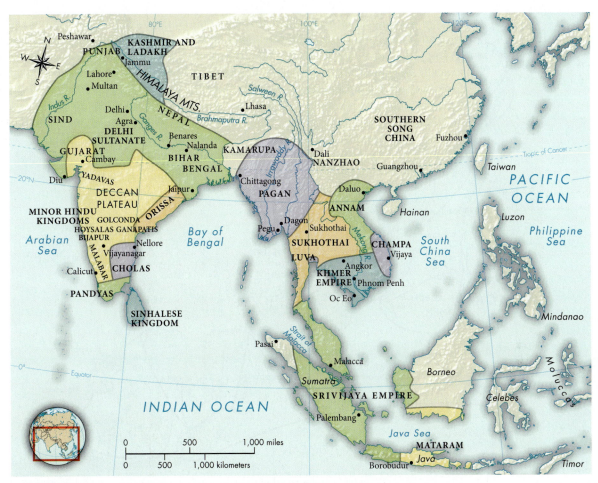

MAP 12.2 South and Southeast Asia in the Thirteenth Century The extensive coastlines of South and Southeast Asia and the predictable monsoon winds aided seafaring in this region. Note the Strait of Malacca, through which most East-West sea trade passed.

leaves. The king rode around on an elephant, but narrow boats measuring up to ninety feet long were a more important means of transportation. The people enjoyed both cockfighting and pig fighting. Instead of drawing water from wells, as the Chinese did, they made pools, from which dozens of nearby families would draw water.

After the decline of Funan, maritime trade continued to grow, and petty kingdoms appeared in many places. Indian traders frequently established small settlements, generally located on the coast. Contact with the local populations led to intermarriage and the creation of hybrid cultures. Local rulers often adopted Indian customs and values, embraced Hinduism and Buddhism, and learned **Sanskrit**, India's classical literary language. Sanskrit gave different peoples a common mode of written expression, much as Chinese did in East Asia and Latin did in Europe.

When Indian traders, migrants, and adventurers entered mainland Southeast Asia, they encountered both long-settled peoples and migrants moving southward

Sanskrit India's classical literary language.

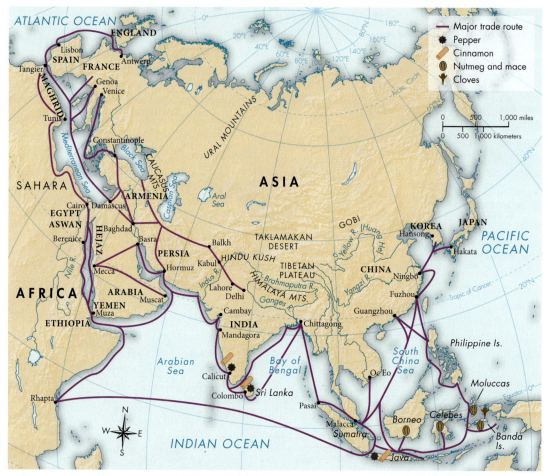

MAP 12.3 **The Spice Trade, ca. 100 B.C.E.–1500 C.E.** From ancient times on, the high demand for spices was a major reason for both Europeans and Chinese to trade with South and Southeast Asia. Spices were used not only for flavor in food but also for medicinal purposes. The spice trade was largely a maritime one, conducted through a series of middlemen who shipped between ports.

from the frontiers of China. As in other extensive migrations, the newcomers fought one another as often as they fought the native populations. In 939 the north Vietnamese became independent of China and extended their power southward along the coast of present-day Vietnam. The Thais had long lived in what is today southwest China and north Myanmar. In the eighth century the Thai tribes united in a confederacy and expanded northward against Tang China. Like China, however, the Thai confederacy fell to the Mongols in 1253. Still farther west another tribal people, the Burmese, migrated to the area of modern Myanmar in the eighth century. They also established a state, which they ruled from their capital, Pagan, and came into contact with India and Sri Lanka.

The most important mainland state was the Khmer (kuh-MAIR) Empire of Cambodia (802–1432), which controlled the heart of the region. The Khmers were indigenous to the area. Their empire eventually extended south to the sea and the northeast Malay Peninsula. Indian influence was pervasive; the impressive temple complex at Angkor Wat built in the early twelfth century was dedicated to the Hindu god Vishnu. Social organization, however, was modeled not on the Indian caste system but on indigenous traditions of social hierarchy. A large part of the population was of slave status, many descended from non-Khmer mountain tribes defeated by the Khmers. Generally successful in a long series of wars with the Vietnamese, the Khmers reached the peak of their power in 1219 and then gradually declined.

The Srivijayan Maritime Trade Empire

Far different from these land-based states was the maritime empire of **Srivijaya** (SCHREE-vuh-jie-uh), based on the island of Sumatra in modern Indonesia. From about 500 on, it held the important Strait of Malacca, through which most of the sea traffic between China and India passed. This state, held together as much by alliances as by direct rule, was in many ways like the Gupta state of the same period in India, securing its prominence and binding its vassals and allies through its splendor and the promise of riches through trade.

Srivijaya A maritime empire that held the Strait of Malacca and the waters around Sumatra and adjacent islands.

Much as the Korean and Japanese rulers adopted Chinese models (see "The East Asian Cultural Sphere" in Chapter 7), the Srivijayan rulers drew on Indian traditions to justify their rule and organize their state. The Sanskrit writing system was used for government documents, and Indians were often employed as priests, scribes, and administrators. Indian mythology took hold, as did Indian architecture and sculpture. Kings and their courts, the first to embrace Indian culture, consciously spread it to their subjects.

After several centuries of prosperity, Srivijaya suffered a stunning blow in 1025. The Chola state in south India launched a large naval raid and captured the Srivijayan king and capital. Unable to hold their gains, the Indians retreated, but the Srivijayan Empire never regained its vigor.

During the era of the Srivijayan kingdom, other kingdoms flourished as well in island Southeast Asia. Borobudur, the magnificent Buddhist temple complex, was begun under patronage of Javan rulers around 780. This stone monument depicts the ten tiers of Buddhist cosmology. When pilgrims made the three-mile-long winding ascent, they passed numerous sculpted reliefs depicting the journey from ignorance to enlightenment.

Buddhism became progressively more dominant in Southeast Asia after 800. Mahayana Buddhism became important in Srivijaya and Vietnam, but Theravada Buddhism, closer to the original Buddhism of early India, became the dominant form in the rest of mainland Southeast Asia. Buddhist missionaries from India and Sri Lanka played a prominent role in these developments. Local converts continued the process by making pilgrimages to India and Sri Lanka to worship and to observe Indian life for themselves.

The Spread of Indian Culture in Comparative Perspective

The social, cultural, and political systems developed in India, China, and Rome all had enormous impact on neighboring peoples whose cultures were originally not as technologically advanced. Some of the mechanisms for cultural spread were similar in all three cases, but differences were important as well.

In the case of Rome and both Han and Tang China, strong states directly ruled outlying regions, bringing their civilizations with them. India's states, even its largest empires, such as the Mauryan and Gupta, did not have comparable bureaucratic reach. The expansion of Indian culture into Southeast Asia thus came not from conquest and the extension of direct political control but from the extension of trading networks, with missionaries following along. This made it closer to the way Japan adopted features of Chinese culture, often through the intermediary of Korea. In both cases, the cultural exchange was largely voluntary.

The Settlement of the Pacific Islands

Through most of Eurasia, societies became progressively less isolated over time. But in 1400 there still remained many isolated societies, especially in the islands east of modern Indonesia. As discussed in Chapter 1, *Homo sapiens* began settling the western Pacific Islands very early, reaching Australia by 50,000 years ago and New Guinea by 35,000 years ago. The process did not stop there, however. The ancient Austronesians (speakers of Austronesian languages) were skilled mariners who settled numerous islands of the Pacific in subsequent centuries, generally following the coasts. Their descendants, the Polynesians, learned how to sail into the open ocean with only the stars, currents, wind patterns, paths of birds, and perhaps paths of whales and dolphins to help them navigate. They reached Tahiti and the Marquesas Islands in the central Pacific by about 200 C.E.

After reaching the central Pacific, Polynesians continued to fan out, in some cases traveling a thousand or more miles away. They reached the Hawaiian Islands in about 300 C.E., Easter Island in perhaps 1000, and New Zealand not until about 1000–1300. There even were groups who sailed west, eventually settling in Madagascar between 200 and 500.

In the more remote islands, such as Hawai'i, Easter Island, and New Zealand, the societies that developed were limited by the small range of domesticated plants and animals that the settlers brought with them and those that were indigenous to the place. Easter Island is perhaps the most extreme case. Only 15 miles wide at its widest point (only 63 square miles in total area), it is 1,300 miles from the nearest inhabited island (Pitcairn) and 2,240 miles from the coast of South America. At some point there was communication with South America, as sweet potatoes originally from there made their way to Easter Island. The community that developed on the island raised chickens and cultivated sweet potatoes, taro, and sugarcane. The population is thought to have reached about fifteen thousand at Easter Island's most prosperous period, which began about 1200 C.E. and lasted a couple of centuries. It was then that its people devoted remarkable efforts to fashioning and erecting the large stone statues that still dot the island.

What led the residents of such a small island to erect more than eight hundred statues, most weighing around ten tons and standing twenty to seventy feet tall? One common theory is that they were central to the islanders' religion and that rival clans competed with each other to erect the most impressive statues. The effort they had to expend to carve them with stone tools, move them to the chosen site, and erect them would have been formidable.

Settlement of the Pacific Islands

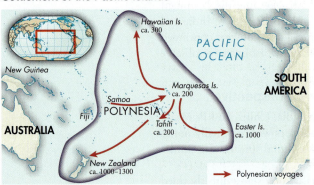

Easter Island Statues
Archaeologists have excavated and restored many of Easter Island's huge statues, which display remarkable stylistic consistency, with the heads disproportionately large and the legs not visible. (Jean-Pierre De Mann/Robert Harding World Imagery)

After its heyday, Easter Island suffered severe environmental stress with the decline of its forests. The islanders could not make boats to fish in the ocean, and bird colonies shrank as nesting areas decreased, also reducing the food supply. Scholars still disagree on how much weight to give the many different elements that contributed to the decline in the prosperity of Easter Island from the age when the statues were erected.

Certainly, early settlers of an island could have a drastic impact on its ecology. When Polynesians first reached New Zealand, they found large birds up to ten feet tall. They hunted them so eagerly that within a century the birds had all but disappeared. Hunting seals and sea lions also led to their rapid depletion. But the islands of New Zealand were much larger than Easter Island, and in time the Maori (the indigenous people of New Zealand) found more sustainable ways to feed themselves, depending more and more on agriculture.

Chapter Summary

The pastoral societies that stretched across Eurasia had the great military advantage of being able to raise horses in large numbers and support themselves from their flocks of sheep, goats, and other animals. Nomadic pastoralists generally were organized on the basis of clans and tribes that selected chiefs for their military talent. Much of the time these tribes fought with each other, but several times in history leaders formed larger confederations capable of coordinated attacks on cities and towns.

From the fifth to the twelfth centuries the most successful nomadic groups on the Eurasian steppes were Turks who gained ascendancy in many of the societies from the Middle East to northern India. In the early thirteenth century, through his charismatic leadership and military genius, the Mongol leader Chinggis Khan conquered much of Eurasia.

After Chinggis's death, the empire was divided into four khanates ruled by four of Chinggis's descendants. For a century the Mongol Empire fostered unprecedented East-West contact. The Mongols encouraged trade and often moved craftsmen and other specialists from one place to another. The Mongols were tolerant of other religions. As more Europeans made their way east, Chinese inventions such as printing and the compass made their way west. Europe especially benefited from the spread of technical and scientific ideas. Diseases also spread, including the Black Death.

India was invaded by the Mongols but not conquered. After the fall of the Gupta Empire in about 480, India was for the next millennium ruled by small kingdoms, which allowed regional cultures to flourish. For several centuries Muslim Turks ruled north India from Delhi. Over time Islam gained adherents throughout South Asia. Hinduism continued to flourish, but Buddhism declined.

Throughout the medieval period India continued to be the center of active seaborne trade, and this trade helped carry Indian ideas and practices to Southeast Asia. Local rulers used experts from India to establish strong states, such as the Khmer kingdom and the Srivijayan kingdom. Buddhism became the dominant religion throughout the region. The Pacific Islands east of Indonesia remained isolated culturally for centuries.

NOTES

1. Trans. in Denis Sinor, "The Establishment and Dissolution of the Türk Empire," in *The Cambridge History of Early Inner Asia*, ed. Denis Sinor (Cambridge: Cambridge University Press, 1990), p. 307.
2. Edward C. Sachau, *Alberuni's India*, vol. 1 (London: Kegan Paul, 1910), pp. 19–20, slightly modified.

CONNECTIONS

The societies of Eurasia became progressively more connected to each other during the centuries discussed in this chapter. One element promoting connection was the military superiority of the nomadic warriors of the steppe: first the Turks, then the Mongols, who conquered many of the settled civilizations near them. Invading Turks brought Islam to India. Connection between societies also came from maritime trade across the Indian Ocean and East Asia. Maritime trade was a key element in the spread of Indian culture to both the mainland and insular Southeast Asia. Other elements connecting these societies included Sanskrit as a language of administration and missionaries who brought both Hinduism and Buddhism far beyond their homelands. Some societies did remain isolated, probably none more than the remote islands of the Pacific, such as Hawai'i, Easter Island, and New Zealand.

East Asia was a key element in both the empires created by nomadic horsemen and the South Asian maritime trading networks. As discussed in Chapter 13, before East Asia had to cope with the rise of the Mongols, it experienced one of its most prosperous periods, during which China, Korea, and Japan became more distinct culturally. China's economy boomed during the Song Dynasty, and the scholar-official class, defined through the civil service examination system, came more and more to dominate culture. In Korea and Japan, by contrast, aristocrats and military men gained ascendancy. Although China, Korea, and Japan all drew on both Confucian and Buddhist teachings, they ended up with elites as distinct as the Chinese scholar-official, the Korean aristocrat, and the Japanese samurai.

CHAPTER 12   Review and Explore

Identify Key Terms

Identify and explain the significance of each item below.

nomads (p. 332)

steppe (p. 332)

yurts (p. 334)

Chinggis Khan (p. 336)

khanates (p. 338)

tax-farming (p. 342)

protected people (p. 348)

jati (p. 351)

sati (p. 352)

Sanskrit (p. 353)

Srivijaya (p. 355)

Review the Main Ideas

Answer the focus questions from each section of the chapter.

1. What aspects of nomadic life gave the nomads of Central Asia military advantages over nearby settled civilizations? (p. 332)

2. How did Chinggis Khan and his successors conquer much of Eurasia, and how did the Mongol conquests change the regions affected? (p. 335)

3. How did the Mongol conquests facilitate the spread of ideas, religions, inventions, and diseases? (p. 343)

4. What was the result of India's encounters with Turks, Mongols, and Islam? (p. 346)

5. How did states develop along the maritime trade routes of Southeast Asia and beyond? (p. 352)

Make Comparisons and Connections

Analyze the larger developments and continuities within and across chapters.

1. How do the states established by Arabs in the seventh and eighth centuries (Chapter 9) compare to those established by Turks in the tenth and eleventh centuries?

2. What similarities and differences are there in the military feats of Alexander the Great (Chapter 5) and Chinggis Khan?

3. How does the slow spread of Buddhism and Indian culture to Southeast Asia compare to the slow spread of Christianity and Roman culture in Europe (Chapters 6 and 8)?

TIMELINE

Suggested Resources

BOOKS

Abu-Lughod, Janet L. *Before European Hegemony: The World System A.D. 1250–1350*. 1989. Examines the period of Mongol domination from a global perspective.

Ali, Daud. *Courtly Culture and Political Life in Early Medieval India*. 2004. Explores the growth of royal households and the development of a courtly world-view in India from 350 to 1200.

Chaudhuri, K. N. *Asia Before Europe*. 1990. Discusses the economy and civilization of cultures within the basin of the Indian Ocean.

Findley, Carter Vaughn. *The Turks in World History*. 2005. Covers both the early Turks and the connections between the Turks and the Mongols.

Fischer, Steven Roger. *A History of the Pacific Islands*. 2002. A broad-ranging history, from early settlement to modern times.

Foltz, Richard. *Religions of the Silk Road: Premodern Patterns of Globalization*. 2010. Considers the spread of religions from the perspective of a region that was home to many universal religions in succession.

Franke, Herbert, and Denis Twitchett, eds. *The Cambridge History of China*. Vol. 6: *Alien Regimes and Border States*. 1994. Clear and thoughtful accounts of the Mongols and their predecessors in East Asia.

Golden, Peter B. *Central Asia in World History*. 2011. Concise and up-to-date account.

Jackson, Peter. *The Delhi Sultanate*. 2003. Provides a close examination of north India in the thirteenth and fourteenth centuries.

Jackson, Peter. *The Mongols and the West, 1221–1410*. 2005. A close examination of many different types of connections between the Mongols and both Europe and the Islamic lands.

Lane, George. *Daily Life in the Mongol Empire*. 2006. Treats many topics, including food, health, dwellings, women, and folktales.

Timeline

- **ca. 1100–1200** Buddhism declines in India
- **1398** Timur takes control of the Delhi sultanate
- **1206** Temujin proclaimed Chinggis Khan
- **1206–1526** Turkish sultanate at Delhi
- **802–1432** Khmer Empire in Cambodia
- **1200–1400** Easter Island society's most prosperous period
- **1276** Mongol conquest of Song China
- **960–1279** Song Dynasty in China (Ch. 13)
- **1258** Mongols conquer Baghdad (Ch. 9)
- **ca. 1000–1100** Islam penetrates sub-Saharan Africa (Ch. 10)
- **1215** Magna Carta (Ch. 14)

1000	1200	1400

Lieberman, Victor. *Strange Parallels: Southeast Asia in Global Context, c. 800–1830*, 2 vols. 2003, 2009. Ambitious and challenging effort to see Southeast Asia as a part of Eurasia.

Ratchnevsky, Paul. *Genghis Khan: His Life and Legacy*. 1992. A reliable account by a leading Mongolist.

Rossabi, Morris. *Khubilai Khan: His Life and Times*. 1988. Provides a lively account of the life of one of the most important Mongol rulers.

Shaffer, Lynda. *Maritime Southeast Asia to 1500*. 1996. A short account of early Southeast Asia from a world history perspective.

DOCUMENTARIES

History of India (BBC, 2007). Episodes 4 and 5 of this series cover the period of Indian history discussed in this chapter.

Secrets of Lost Empires: Easter Island (PBS, 2000). This *Nova* special examines how the huge stone statues could have been moved.

TELEVISION DRAMA

Marco Polo (Netflix, 2014–2016). This multipart, continuing serial dramatization is based loosely on Marco Polo's life.

WEBSITES

Companion Site to Secrets of Lost Empires: Easter Island. This website provides supplementary materials about the creation of the documentary, as well as additional resources. **www.pbs.org/wgbh/nova/lostempires /easter/**

Silk Road Narratives: A Collection of Historical Texts. Part of the Silk Road Seattle Project, this informative website provides descriptions of and links to a variety of interesting historical sources related to the Silk Road. **depts.washington.edu/silkroad/texts /texts.html**

13

States and Cultures in East Asia
800–1400

During the six centuries between 800 and 1400, East Asia was the most advanced region of the world. For several centuries the Chinese economy had grown spectacularly, and China's methods of production were highly advanced in fields as diverse as rice cultivation, the production of iron and steel, and the printing of books. Philosophy and the arts all flourished. China's system of government was also advanced for its time. In the Song period, the principle that the government should be in the hands of highly educated scholar-officials, selected through competitive written civil service examinations, became well established. Song China's great wealth and sophisticated government did not give it military advantage, however, and in this period China had to pay tribute to militarily more powerful northern neighbors, the Khitans (key-tuns), the Jurchens, and finally the Mongols, who conquered all of China in 1279.

During the previous millennium, basic elements of Chinese culture had spread beyond China's borders, creating the East Asian cultural sphere based on the use of Chinese as the language of civilization. Beginning around 800, however, the pendulum shifted toward cultural differentiation as Japan, Korea, and China developed in distinctive ways. In both Korea and Japan, for several centuries court aristocrats were dominant both politically and culturally, and then aristocrats lost out to military men with power in the countryside. By 1200 Japan was dominated by warriors — known as samurai — whose ethos was quite unlike that of China's educated elite. In both Korea and Japan, Buddhism retained a very strong hold, one of the ties that continued to link the countries of East Asia. In addition, China and Korea both had to deal with the same menacing neighbors to the north. Even Japan had to mobilize its resources to fend off two seaborne Mongol attacks.

Song Chancellor

Known for his stern demeanor, Sima Guang (1019–1086) was an eminent historian and a leading official.

CHAPTER PREVIEW

What made possible
the expansion of the
Chinese economy,
and what were the
outcomes of this
economic growth?

The Medieval Chinese Economic Revolution, 800–1100

Chinese historians traditionally viewed dynasties as following a standard cyclical pattern. Founders were vigorous men able to recruit capable followers to serve as officials and generals. Externally they would extend China's borders; internally they would bring peace. Over time, however, emperors born in the palace would get used to luxury and lack the founders' strength and wisdom. Families with wealth or political power would find ways to avoid taxes, forcing the government to impose heavier taxes on the poor. As a result, impoverished peasants would flee, the morale of those in the government and armies would decline, and the dynasty would find itself able neither to maintain internal peace nor to defend its borders.

Viewed in terms of this theory of the **dynastic cycle**, by 800 the Tang Dynasty was in decline (see "The Chinese Empire Re-created: Sui [581–618] and Tang [618–907]" in Chapter 7). It had ruled China for nearly two centuries, and its high point was in the past. A massive rebellion had wracked it in the mid-eighth century, and the Uighur Turks and Tibetans were menacing its borders. Many of the centralizing features of the government had been abandoned, with power falling more and more to regional military governors.

Historically, Chinese political theorists always assumed that a strong, centralized government was better than a weak one or than political division, but, if anything, the Tang toward the end of its dynastic cycle seems to have been both intellectually and economically more vibrant than the early Tang had been. Less control from the central government seems to have stimulated trade and economic growth.

dynastic cycle The theory that Chinese dynasties go through a predictable cycle from early vigor and growth to subsequent decline as administrators become lax and the well-off find ways to avoid paying taxes, cutting state revenues.

A government census conducted in 742 shows that China's population was still approximately 50 million, very close to what it had been in 2 C.E. Over the next three centuries, with the expansion of wet-field rice cultivation in central and south China, the country's food supply steadily increased, and so did its population, which had reached 100 million by 1100. China's population probably already exceeded that of all the Islamic countries of the time or that of all the countries of Europe put together. Urbanization increased, and both literature and the arts thrived. (See "Global Viewpoints: Painters of Uncanny Skill in China and Rome," at right.)

Agricultural prosperity and denser settlement patterns aided commercialization of the economy. Farmers in Song China no longer merely aimed at self-sufficiency. Instead, farmers sold their surpluses and used their profits to buy

Chinese Paper Money Chinese paper currency indicated the unit of currency and the date and place of issue. The Mongols continued the use of paper money, as this note from the Mongol period attests. (National Museum of Chinese History, Beijing, China/Ancient Art & Architecture Collection, Ltd./Bridgeman Images)

Painters of Uncanny Skill in China and Rome

Chinese art critics often expressed astonishment at the ability of exceptional painters to evoke an emotional reaction in viewers. A good example is the account of the eighth-century painter Wu Daozi, written by a ninth-century critic, Zhu Jingxuan, in his *Famous Painters of the Tang Dynasty*. It can be compared to remarks on painters by the Roman man of letters Pliny the Elder (23–79 C.E.).

Zhu Jingxuan on the Painter Wu Daozi

■ A poor orphan, Wu Daozi was so talented by nature that even before he was twenty he had mastered all the subtleties of painting. When he was in Luoyang, the emperor heard of his fame and summoned him to court. . . .

The General Pei Min sent a gift of gold and silk to Wu Daozi and asked him to paint the walls of the Paradise Buddhist monastery. Wu Daozi returned the gold and silk with a note saying, "I have long heard of General Pei. If he would do a sword dance for me, that would be reward enough, and the sight of such vigor will inspire my brush." So the general, even though in mourning, did the sword dance for Wu Daozi, and when the dance was finished Wu made his brush fly with such strength that the painting was done in no time, as though some god was helping him. Wu Daozi also did the laying on of the colors himself. One can still see the painting in the western corridor of the temple. . . .

During the Tianbao period (742–755), the emperor Xuanzong suddenly longed for the Jialing River on the road to Sichuan. So he allowed Wu Daozi the use of post horses and ordered him to go there and make sketches of the scenery. On his return, in response to the emperor's query, Wu said, "I have not brought back a single sketch, but everything is recorded in my mind." He was commanded to depict it on the walls of Great Accord Hall. He painted a landscape of more than 300 *li*, finishing it all in a single day. . . . He also painted five dragons in the Inner Hall whose scales seemed to move. Whenever it was about to rain, mist would emanate from them. . . .

I also heard from an old monk of Scenic Clouds Monastery that when Master Wu painted a Hell scene at the temple, butchers and fishmongers who saw it became so frightened by it that they decided to change their profession and turn to doing good works.

Pliny on the Painters Arellius and Lepidus

■ Not long before the time of the god Augustus, Arellius had earned distinction at Rome, save for the sacrilege by which he notoriously degraded his art. Always desirous of flattering some woman or other with whom he chanced to be in love, he painted goddesses in the person of his mistresses, of whom his paintings are a mere catalogue. The painter Famulus also lived not long ago; he was grave and severe in his person, while his painting was rich and vivid. He painted an Athena whose eyes are turned to the spectator from whatever side he may be looking. . . .

While on the subject of painting I must not omit the well-known story of Lepidus. Once during his triumvirate he had been escorted by the magistrates of a certain town to a lodging in the middle of a wood, and on the next morning complained with threats that the singing of the birds prevented him from sleeping. They painted a snake on an immense strip of parchment and stretched it all round the grove. We are told that by this means they terrified the birds into silence and that this has ever since been a recognized device for quieting them.

QUESTIONS FOR ANALYSIS

1. What assumptions, if any, did the Chinese and Roman authors share about artistic creativity?
2. In what ways did painters gain fame in these two societies?

Sources: Zhu Jingxuan, *Tangchao minghua lu*, in *Tang Wudai hualun* (Changsha: Hunan Meishu Chubanshe, 1997), pp. 83–85, trans. Patricia Ebrey; *The Elder Pliny's Chapters on the History of Art*, trans. K. Jex-Blake (London: Macmillan, 1896), pp. 149–150.

charcoal, tea, oil, and wine. In many places farmers specialized in commercial crops, such as sugar, oranges, cotton, silk, and tea. The need to transport the products of interregional trade stimulated the inland and coastal shipping industries.

As marketing increased, demand for money grew enormously, leading eventually to the creation of the world's first paper money. To avoid the weight and bulk of coins for large transactions, local merchants in late Tang times started trading receipts from deposit shops where they had left money or goods. The early Song authorities awarded a small set of these shops a monopoly on the issuing of these certificates of deposit, and in the 1120s the government took over the system, producing the world's first government-issued paper money.

With the intensification of trade, merchants became progressively more specialized and organized. They set up partnerships and joint stock companies, with a separation of owners (shareholders) and managers. In the large cities merchants were organized into guilds according to the type of product sold, and they arranged sales from wholesalers to shop owners and periodically set prices.

Foreign trade also flourished in the Song period. Chinese ships began to displace Indian and Arab merchants in the South Seas, and ship design was improved in several ways. Watertight bulkheads improved buoyancy and protected cargo. Stern-mounted rudders improved steering. Some of the ships were powered by both oars and sails and were large enough to hold several hundred men.

compass A tool for identifying north using a magnetic needle; it was made useful for sea navigation in Song times when placed in a protective case.

Also important to oceangoing travel was the perfection of the **compass**. The ability of a magnetic needle to point north had been known for some time, but in Song times the needle was reduced in size and attached to a fixed stem (rather than floated in water). In some instances it was put in a small protective case with a glass top, making it suitable for sea travel. The first reports of a compass used in this way date to 1119.

The Song also witnessed many advances in industrial techniques. Heavy industry, especially iron, grew astoundingly. With advances in metallurgy, iron production reached around 125,000 tons per year in 1078, a sixfold increase over the output in 800. Much of the iron was used for military purposes. Mass-production methods were used to make iron armor in small, medium, and large sizes. High-quality steel for swords was made through high-temperature metallurgy. The needs of the army also brought Chinese engineers to experiment with the use of gunpowder. In the twelfth-century wars against the Jurchens, those defending a besieged city used gunpowder to propel projectiles at the enemy.

Economic expansion fueled the growth of cities. Dozens of cities had 50,000 or more residents, and quite a few had more than 100,000, very large populations compared to other places in the world at the time. China's two successive capitals, Kaifeng (kigh-fuhng) and Hangzhou (hahng-joh), each had an estimated 1 million residents. Marco Polo described Hangzhou as the finest and most splendid city in the world. He reported that it had ten marketplaces, each half a mile long, where 40,000 to 50,000 people would shop on any given day. There were also bathhouses; permanent shops selling items such as spices, drugs, and pearls; and innumerable courtesans, whom Marco Polo described as "adorned in much finery, highly perfumed, occupying well-furnished houses, and attended by many female domestics."[1]

The medieval economic revolution shifted the economic center of China south to the Yangzi River drainage area. This area had many advantages over the north China plain. Rice, which grew in the south, provides more calories per unit of land and therefore allows denser settlement. The milder temperatures often allowed two crops to be grown on the same plot of land, first a summer crop of rice and then a winter crop of wheat or vegetables. The abundance of rivers and streams facilitated shipping, which reduced the cost of transportation and thus made regional specialization economically more feasible.

Ordinary people benefited from the Song economic revolution in many ways. There were more opportunities for the sons of farmers to leave agriculture and find work in cities. Those who stayed in agriculture had a better chance of improving their situations by taking up sideline production of wine, charcoal, paper, or textiles. Energetic farmers who grew cash crops such as sugar, tea, mulberry leaves (for silk), and cotton (recently introduced from India) could grow rich. Greater interregional trade led to the availability of more goods at the rural markets held every five or ten days.

Of course, not everyone grew rich. Poor farmers who fell into debt had to sell their land, and if they still owed money they could be forced to sell their daughters as maids, concubines, or prostitutes. The prosperity of the cities created a huge demand for women to serve the rich in these ways, and Song sources mention that criminals would kidnap girls and women to sell in distant cities at huge profits.

China During the Song and Yuan Dynasties, 960–1368

> **How did the civil service examinations and the scholar-official class shape Chinese society and culture, and what impact did the Mongol conquest have on them?**

In the tenth century Tang China broke up into separate contending states, some of which had non-Chinese rulers. The two states that proved to be long lasting were the Song, which came to control almost all of China proper south of the Great Wall, and the Liao (leeow), whose ruling house was Khitan and which held the territory of modern Beijing and areas north (Map 13.1). Although the Song Dynasty had a much larger population, the Liao was militarily the stronger of the two. In the early twelfth century the Liao state was defeated by the Jurchens, another non-Chinese people, who founded the Jin Dynasty and went on to conquer most of north China in 1127, leaving Song to control only the south. After a century the Jurchens' Jin Dynasty was defeated by the Mongols, who extended their Yuan Dynasty to control all of China by 1276.

The Song Dynasty

The founder of the Song Dynasty, Taizu (r. 960–976), was a general whose troops elevated him to emperor (in an act somewhat reminiscent of Roman practice). To make sure that such an act could not happen in the future, Taizu retired or rotated his generals and assigned civil officials to supervise them. In time these civil bureaucrats came to dominate every aspect of Song government and society. The civil service examination system established during the Sui Dynasty (see "The Chinese Empire Re-created: Sui [581–618] and Tang [618–907]" in Chapter 7) was greatly expanded to provide the dynasty with a constant flow of men trained in the Confucian classics.

Curbing the generals' power ended warlordism but did not solve the military problem of defending against the nomadic Khitans' Liao Dynasty to the north. After

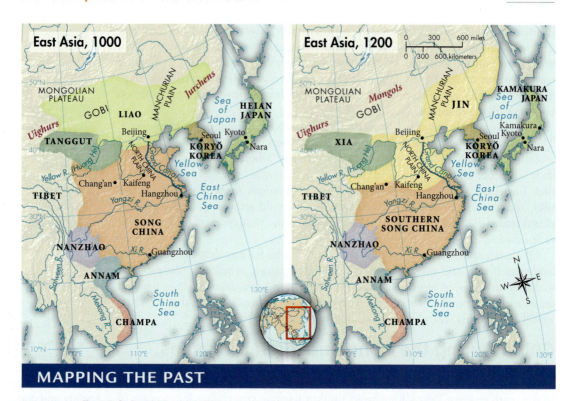

MAPPING THE PAST

MAP 13.1 **East Asia in 1000 and 1200** The Song empire did not extend as far as its predecessor, the Tang, and faced powerful rivals to the north — the Liao Dynasty of the Khitans and the Xia Dynasty of the Tanguts. Koryŏ Korea maintained regular contact with Song China, but Japan, by the late Heian period, was no longer deeply involved with the mainland. By 1200 military families dominated both Korea and Japan, but the borders were little changed. On the mainland the Liao Dynasty had been overthrown by the Jurchens' Jin Dynasty, which also seized the northern third of the Song empire. Because the Song relocated its capital to Hangzhou in the south, this period is called the Southern Song period.

ANALYZING THE MAP What were the countries of East Asia in 1000? What were the major differences in 1200?

CONNECTIONS What connections do you see between the length of their northern borders and the histories of China, Korea, and Japan?

several attempts to push the Liao back beyond the Great Wall, the Song concluded a peace treaty with them. The Song agreed to make huge annual payments of gold and silk to the Khitans, in a sense paying them not to invade. Even so, the Song rulers had to maintain a standing army of more than a million men. By the middle of the eleventh century military expenses consumed half the government's revenues. Song had the industrial base to produce swords, armor, and arrowheads in huge quantities, but had difficulty maintaining enough horses and well-trained horsemen. Even though China was the economic powerhouse of the region, with by far the largest population, the horse was a major weapon of war in this period, and it was not easy to convert wealth to military advantage.

In the early twelfth century the military situation rapidly worsened when the Khitan state was destroyed by another tribal confederation led by the Jurchens, who quickly realized how easy it would be to defeat the Song. After setting siege to the Song capital in 1126, they captured the emperor and former emperor and took them and the entire court into captivity. Song forces rallied around one of the emperor's sons who had escaped capture, and this prince re-established a Song court in the south at Hangzhou (see Map 13.1). This Southern Song Dynasty controlled only about two-thirds of the former Song territories, but the social, cultural, and intellectual life there remained vibrant until the Song fell to the Mongols in 1279.

The Scholar-Officials and Neo-Confucianism

The Song period saw the full flowering of one of the most distinctive features of Chinese civilization, the **scholar-official class** certified through highly competitive civil service examinations. This elite was both broader and better educated than the elites of earlier periods in Chinese history. Once the **examination system** was fully developed, aristocratic habits and prejudices largely disappeared.

To prepare for the examinations, men had to memorize the classics in order to be able to recognize even the most obscure passages. They also had to master specific forms of composition, including poetry, and be ready to discuss policy issues, citing appropriate historical examples. Those who became officials this way had usually tried the exams several times and were on average a little over thirty years of age when they succeeded.

The invention of printing should be given some credit for the trend toward a better-educated elite. Tang craftsmen developed the art of carving words and pictures into wooden blocks, inking the blocks, and pressing paper onto them. Each block held an entire page of text. Such whole-page blocks were used for printing as early as the middle of the ninth century, and in the eleventh century **movable type** (one piece of type for each character) was invented, but it was rarely used because whole-block printing was cheaper. In China, as in Europe a couple of centuries later, the introduction of printing dramatically lowered the price of books, thus aiding the spread of literacy.

Among the upper class the availability of cheaper books enabled scholars to amass their own libraries. Song publishers printed the classics of Chinese literature in huge editions. Works on philosophy, science, and medicine were also avidly consumed, as were Buddhist texts. Han and Tang poetry and historical works became the models for Song writers. One popular literary innovation was the encyclopedia, which first appeared in the Song period.

The life of the educated man involved more than study for the civil service examinations and service in office. Many took to refined pursuits such as collecting antiques or old books and practicing the arts—especially poetry writing, calligraphy, and painting. (See "Analyzing the Evidence: Ma Yuan's Painting *On a Mountain Path in Spring*, page 370.)

The new scholar-official elite produced some extraordinary men able to hold high court offices while pursuing diverse intellectual interests. (See "Individuals in Society: Shen Gua," page 372.) Ouyang Xiu spared time in his busy official career to write love songs, histories, and the first analytical catalogue of rubbings of ancient stone and bronze inscriptions. Sima Guang, besides serving as chancellor, wrote a narrative history of China from the Warring States Period (403–221 B.C.E.) to the founding of the Song Dynasty. Su Shi wrote more than twenty-seven hundred poems and eight hundred letters while active in opposition politics. He was also an esteemed

scholar-official class
Chinese educated elite that included both scholars and officials. The officials had usually gained office by passing the highly competitive civil service examination.

examination system
A system of selecting officials in imperial China based on competitive written examinations.

movable type A system of printing in which one piece of type is used for each unique character.

Ma Yuan's Painting *On a Mountain Path in Spring*

Because competition for the civil service examinations was so fierce, the great majority of those who devoted years to memorizing the classics and preparing for the exams never became officials. But they found many other agreeable ways to fill their time, such as writing poetry, practicing calligraphy, and viewing each other's treasures such as old paintings or calligraphies. A large share of the social life of upper-class men was centered on these refined pastimes: they gathered to compose or criticize poetry, view each other's art treasures, and patronize young talents. Still, they often imagined themselves as solitary figures, walking in the mountains and drawing inspiration from the beauty of the landscape. Paintings of scholars in landscapes became quite common.

It was in fact during the Song period that the art of landscape painting was perfected. In earlier periods, painters had added background to images of people, birds, and buildings, but in Song times they often made the landscape itself the central element in the composition, developing new ways to show depth. Some landscape paintings focused on a large central mountain, but more intimate scenes came to be preferred in the later half of the Song Dynasty (the Southern Song period). Birds and flowers were also a popular subject for paintings. Song painters also developed ways to depict a scene entirely in shades of ink, rather than add colors. In addition, the image was sometimes coupled with a poem, which could be provided by the painter or by someone else, such as the person who requested the painting. In the Southern Song period, painters at court frequently worked closely with members of the court, including empresses and other consorts, who supplied the calligraphy for paintings.

In this painting, the court painter Ma Yuan (ca. 1190–1225) depicts a scholar on an outing accompanied by his boy servant carrying a lute. The scholar gazes into the mist, his eyes attracted by a bird in flight. The poetic couplet was inscribed by Emperor Ningzong (r. 1194–1124), at whose court Ma Yuan served. It reads: "Brushed by his sleeves, wild flowers dance in the wind. / Fleeing from him, hidden birds cut short their songs."

(National Palace Museum, Taipei, Taiwan/photo © AISA/The Everett Collection)

QUESTIONS FOR ANALYSIS

1. Find the key elements in this picture: the scholar, the servant boy, the bird, the willow tree. Are these elements skillfully conveyed? Are there other elements in the painting that you find hard to read?

2. What does the poetic couplet add to this painting? Do you view the painting differently knowing that the poem was supplied by the emperor rather than the painter?

3. If the painter had added more colors, how would this have changed the painting? Would it be better or worse?

painter, calligrapher, and theorist of the arts. Su Song, another high official, constructed an eighty-foot-tall mechanical clock that told not only the time of day but also the day of the month, the phase of the moon, and the position of certain stars and planets in the sky. As in Renaissance Europe a couple of centuries later (see Chapter 15), gifted men made advances in a wide range of fields.

Besides politics, scholars also debated issues in ethics and metaphysics. For several centuries Buddhism had been more vital than Confucianism. Beginning in the late Tang period, Confucian teachers began claiming that the teachings of the Confucian sages contained all the wisdom one needed and that a true Confucian would reject Buddhist teachings. During the eleventh century many Confucian teachers urged students to set their sights not on exam success but on the higher goals of attaining the wisdom of the sages. Metaphysical theories about the workings of the cosmos in terms of *li* (principle) and *qi* (vital energy) were developed in response to the challenge of the sophisticated metaphysics of Buddhism.

Neo-Confucianism, as this movement is generally termed, was more fully developed in the twelfth century by the immensely learned Zhu Xi (joo shee) (1130–1200). Besides serving in office, he wrote, compiled, or edited almost a hundred books; corresponded with dozens of other scholars; and still regularly taught groups of disciples, many of whom stayed with him for years at a time. Although he was treated as a political threat during his lifetime, within decades of his death his writings came to be considered orthodox, and in subsequent centuries candidates for the examinations had to be familiar with his commentaries on the classics.

Neo-Confucianism
The revival of Confucian thinking that began in the eleventh century, characterized by the goal of attaining the wisdom of the sages, not exam success.

Women's Lives in Song Times

Thanks to the spread of printing, more books survive from the Song period than from earlier periods, giving us more glimpses of women's lives. Stories, documents, and legal cases show us widows who ran inns, midwives who delivered babies, pious women who spent their days chanting Buddhist sutras, girls who learned to read with their brothers, farmers' daughters who made money by weaving mats, childless widows

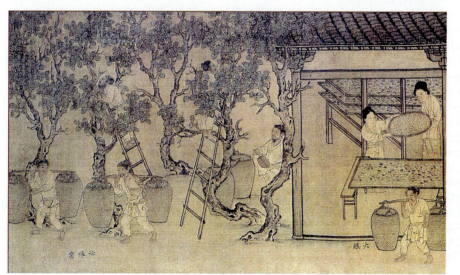

Picking Mulberry Leaves and Feeding Silkworms
This is one scene in a long scroll depicting the work required for the creation of silk textiles. Here we see men climbing ladders to pick mulberry leaves and women feeding the leaves to the silkworms, so that they will spin cocoons from which strands can be separated and twisted into threads. (Pictures from History/Bridgeman Images)

Shen Gua

IN THE ELEVENTH CENTURY IT WAS NOT rare for Chinese men of letters to have broad interests, but few could compare to Shen Gua (1031–1095), a man who tried his hand at everything from mathematics, geography, economics, engineering, medicine, divination, and archaeology to military strategy and diplomacy.

Shen Gua's father was an official, and Shen Gua often accompanied him on his assignments. In 1063 he passed the civil service examinations, and in 1066 he received a post in the capital. He eventually held high astronomical, ritual, and financial posts and became involved in waterworks and the construction of defense walls. He was sent as an envoy to the Khitans in 1075 to try to settle a boundary dispute. When a military campaign that he advised failed in 1082, he was demoted, and he later retired to write.

It is from his book of miscellaneous notes that we know the breadth of his interests. In one note Shen describes how, on assignment to inspect the frontier, he made a relief map of wood and glue-soaked sawdust to show the mountains, roads, rivers, and passes. The emperor was so impressed when he saw it that he ordered all the border prefectures to make relief maps. Elsewhere Shen describes the use of petroleum and explains how to make movable type from clay. Shen Gua often applied a mathematical approach to issues that his contemporaries did not think of in those terms. He once computed the total number of possible situations on a Go board, and another time he calculated the longest possible military campaign given the limits of human carriers, who had to carry their own food as well as food for the soldiers.

Shen Gua is especially known for his scientific explanations. He explained the deflection of the compass from due south. He identified petrified bamboo and from its existence argued that the region where it was found must have been much warmer and more humid in ancient times. He argued against the theory that tides are caused by the rising and setting of the sun, demonstrating that they correlate with the cycles of the moon. He proposed switching from a lunar calendar to a solar one of 365 days, saying that even though his contemporaries would reject his idea, "surely in the future some will adopt my idea." To convince his readers that the sun and the moon were spherical, not flat, he suggested that they cover a ball with fine powder on one side and then look at it obliquely. The powder was the part of the moon illuminated by the sun, and as the viewer looked at it obliquely, the white part would be crescent shaped, like a waxing moon. Shen Gua, however, did not realize that the sun and moon had entirely different orbits, and he explained why they did not collide by positing that both were composed of *qi* (vital energy) and had form but not substance.

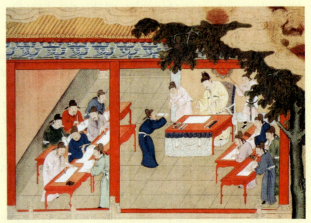

Depicted here are officials reading and discussing examination papers. (Pictures from History/Bridgeman Images)

Shen Gua also wrote on medicine and criticized his contemporaries for paying more attention to old treatises than to clinical experience. Yet he, too, was sometimes stronger on theory than on observation. In one note he argued that longevity pills could be made from cinnabar. He reasoned that if cinnabar could be transformed in one direction, it ought to be susceptible to transformation in the opposite direction as well. Therefore, since melted cinnabar causes death, solid cinnabar should prevent death.

QUESTIONS FOR ANALYSIS

1. In what ways could Shen Gua have used his scientific interests in his work as a government official?
2. How does Shen Gua's understanding of the natural world compare to that of the early Greeks? (See "The Flowering of Philosophy" in Chapter 5.)

Woman Attendant The Song emperors were patrons of a still-extant temple in northern China that enshrined a statue of the "holy mother," the mother of the founder of the ancient Zhou Dynasty. The forty-two maids who attend her, one of whom is shown here, seem to have been modeled on the palace ladies who attended Song emperors. (Taiyuan Jinci/Goddess Hall/Uniphoto Press International Japan/Art and Architecture Collection Ltd.)

who accused their nephews of stealing their property, and wives who were jealous of the concubines their husbands brought home.

Families who could afford it usually tried to keep their wives and daughters within the walls of the house, rather than let them work in the fields or in shops or inns. At home there was plenty for them to do. Not only was there the work of tending children and preparing meals, but spinning, weaving, and sewing were considered women's work as well and took a great deal of time. Families that raised silkworms also needed women to do much of the work of coddling the worms and getting them to spin their cocoons. Within the home women generally had considerable say and took an active interest in issues such as the selection of marriage partners for their children.

Women tended to marry between the ages of sixteen and twenty. Their husbands were, on average, a couple of years older than they were. Marriages were arranged by their parents, who would have either called on a professional matchmaker or turned to a friend or relative for suggestions. Before a wedding took place, written agreements were exchanged, listing the prospective bride's and groom's birth dates, parents, and grandparents; the gifts that would be exchanged; and the dowry the bride would bring.

The young bride's first priority was to try to win over her mother-in-law. One way to do this was to quickly bear a son for the family. Within the patrilineal system, a woman fully secured her position in the family by becoming the mother of one of the men. Every community had older women skilled in midwifery who were called to help when a woman went into labor. If the family was well-to-do, arrangements might be made for a wet nurse to help her take care of the newborn.

Women frequently had four, five, or six children, but likely one or more would die in infancy. If a son reached adulthood and married before the woman herself was widowed, she would be considered fortunate, for she would have always had an adult man who could take care of business for her — first her husband, then her grown son.

A woman with a healthy and prosperous husband faced another challenge in middle age: her husband could bring home a **concubine**. Wives outranked concubines and could give them orders in the house, but a concubine had her own ways of getting back through her hold on the husband. The children born to a concubine were considered just as much children of the family as the wife's children, and if the wife had had only daughters and the concubine had a son, the wife would find herself dependent on the concubine's son in her old age. Moralists insisted that it was wrong for a wife to be jealous of her husband's concubines, but contemporary documents suggest that jealousy was very common.

Neo-Confucianism is sometimes blamed for a decline in the status of women in Song times, largely because one of the best known of the Neo-Confucian teachers, Cheng Yi, once told a follower that it would be better for a widow to die of starvation than to lose her virtue by remarrying. In later centuries this saying was often quoted

concubine A woman contracted to a man as a secondary spouse; although subordinate to the wife, her sons were considered legitimate heirs.

foot binding The practice of binding the feet of girls with long strips of cloth to keep them from growing large.

to justify pressuring widows, even very young ones, to stay with their husbands' families and not remarry. In Song times, however, widows frequently remarried.

It is true that **foot binding** began during the Song Dynasty, but it was not recommended by Neo-Confucian teachers; rather it was associated with the pleasure quarters and with women's efforts to beautify themselves. In this practice, the feet of girls were bound with long strips of cloth to keep them from growing large and to make the feet narrow and arched.

China Under Mongol Rule

As discussed in Chapter 12, the Mongols conquered China in stages, gaining much of north China by 1215 and all of it by 1234, but not taking the south till the 1270s. The north suffered the most devastation. The non-Chinese rulers in the north, the Jin Dynasty of the Jurchen, thought they had the strongest army known to history. Yet Mongol tactics frustrated them. The Mongols would take a city, plunder it, and then withdraw, letting the Jin take it back and deal with the resulting food shortages and destruction. Under these circumstances, Jurchen power rapidly collapsed.

Not until Khubilai was Great Khan was the Song Dynasty defeated and south China brought under the control of the Mongols' Yuan Dynasty. Non-Chinese rulers had gained control of north China several times in Chinese history, but none of them had been able to secure control of the region south of the Yangzi River, which required a navy. By the 1260s Khubilai had put Chinese shipbuilders to work building a fleet, crucial to his victory over the Song (see "Chinggis's Successors" in Chapter 12).

Life in China under the Mongols was much like life in China under earlier alien rulers. Once order was restored, people did their best to get on with their lives. Some were deprived of their land, business, or freedom and suffered real hardship. Yet

Horse and Groom This painting by the Chinese artist Zhao Yong (1291–1361) would likely have appealed to the Mongol rulers, whose way of life was tied closely to their horses. (Pictures from History/ Bridgeman Images)

people still spoke Chinese, followed Chinese customary practices in dividing their family property, made offerings at local temples, and celebrated the new year and other customary festivals. Teachers still taught students the classics, scholars continued to write books, and books continued to be printed.

The Mongols, like other foreign rulers before them, did not see anything particularly desirable in the social mobility of Chinese society. Preferring stability, they assigned people hereditary occupations such as farmer, Confucian scholar, physician, astrologer, soldier, artisan, salt producer, miner, and Buddhist monk; the occupations came with obligations to the state. Besides these occupational categories, the Mongols classified the population into four grades, with the Mongols occupying the top grade. Next came various non-Chinese, such as the Uighurs and Persians. Below them were Chinese former subjects of the Jurchen, called the Han. At the bottom were the former subjects of the Song, called southerners.

The reason for codifying ethnic differences this way was to preserve the Mongols' privileges as conquerors. Chinese were not allowed to take Mongol names, and great efforts were made to keep them from passing as Mongols or marrying Mongols. To keep Chinese from rebelling, they were forbidden to own weapons or congregate in public.

As the Mongols captured Chinese territory, they recruited Chinese into their armies and government. Although some refused to serve the Mongols, others argued that the Chinese would fare better if Chinese were the administrators and could shield Chinese society from the most brutal effects of Mongol rule.

Nevertheless, government service, which had long been central to the identity and income of the educated elite in China, was not as widely available under the Mongols. The Mongols reinstituted the civil service examinations in 1315, but filled only about 2 percent of the positions in the bureaucracy through them and reserved half of those places for Mongols.

The scholar-official elite without government employment turned to alternative ways to support themselves. Those who did not have land to live off of found work as physicians, fortune-tellers, children's teachers, Daoist priests, publishers, booksellers, or playwrights. Many took leadership roles at the local level, such as founding academies for Confucian learning or promoting local charitable ventures. Through such activities, scholars without government offices could assert the importance of civil over military values and see themselves as trustees of the Confucian tradition.

Since the Mongols wanted to extract wealth from China, they had every incentive to develop the economy. They encouraged trade both within China and beyond its borders and tried to keep paper money in circulation. (See "Global Viewpoints: Explaining the Workings of Paper Money in China, Persia, and Europe" in Chapter 12.) They repaired the Grand Canal, which had been ruined during their initial conquest of north China. Chinese industries with strong foreign markets, such as porcelain, thrived. Nevertheless, the economic expansion of late Tang and Song times did not continue under the alien rule of the Jurchens and Mongols.

The Mongols' Yuan Dynasty began a rapid decline in the 1330s as disease, rebellions, and poor leadership led to disorder throughout the country. When a Chinese strongman succeeded in consolidating the south, the Mongol rulers retreated to Mongolia before he could take Beijing. By 1368 the Yuan Dynasty had given way to a new Chinese-led dynasty: the Ming.

Korea Under the Koryŏ Dynasty, 935–1392

During the Silla period, Korea was strongly tied to Tang China and avidly copied China's model (see "Korea" in Chapter 7). This changed along with much else in North Asia between 800 and 1400. In this period Korea lived more in the shadows of the powerful states of the Khitans, Jurchens, and Mongols than in those of the Chinese.

The Silla Dynasty began to decline after the king was killed in a revolt in 780. For the next 155 years, rebellions and coups d'état followed one after the other, as different groups of nobles placed their candidates on the throne and killed as many of their opponents as they could.

The dynasty that emerged from this confusion was called Koryŏ (935–1392). (The English word *Korea* derives from the name of this dynasty.) During this time Korea developed more independently of the China model than it had in Silla times. This was not because the Chinese model was rejected; the Koryŏ (KAWR-yoh) capital was laid out on the Chinese model, and the government was closely patterned on the Tang system. But despite Chinese influence, Korean society remained deeply aristocratic.

The founder of the dynasty, Wang Kon (877–943), was a man of relatively obscure maritime background, and he needed the support of the old aristocracy to maintain control. His successors introduced civil service examinations on the Chinese model, as well as examinations for Buddhist clergy, but because the aristocrats were the best educated and the government schools admitted only the sons of aristocrats, this system served primarily to solidify their control.

At the other end of the social scale, the number of people in the serf-slave stratum seems to have increased. This lowborn stratum included not only privately held slaves but also large numbers of government slaves as well as government workers in mines, porcelain factories, and other government industries. Sometimes entire villages or groups of villages were considered lowborn. There were occasional slave revolts, and some freed slaves did rise in status, but prejudice against anyone with slave ancestors was so strong that the law provided that "only if there is no evidence of lowborn status for eight generations in one's official household registration may one receive a position in the government."[2] In China and Japan, by contrast, slavery was a much more minor element in the social landscape.

The commercial economy declined in Korea during this period. Except for the capital, there were no cities of commercial importance, and in the countryside the use of money declined. One industry that did flourish was ceramics.

Buddhism remained strong throughout Korea, and monasteries became major centers of art and learning. As in Song China and Kamakura Japan, Chan (Zen) and Tiantai (Tendai) were the leading Buddhist teachings. The founder of the Koryŏ Dynasty attributed the dynasty's success to the Buddha's protection, and he and his successors were ardent patrons of the church. The entire Buddhist canon was printed in the eleventh century and again in the thirteenth. As in medieval Europe, aristocrats who entered the church occupied the major abbacies. As in Japan (but not China), some monasteries accumulated military power.

The Koryŏ Dynasty was preserved in name long after the ruling family had lost most of its power. In 1170 the palace guards massacred the civil officials at court

The Koryŏ Dynasty, 935–1392

Map labels:
YUAN DYNASTY
Yalu R.
Kaegyong
1253–1254
1231
1236
1236–1239
1231
KORYŎ KOREA
Sea of Japan
Tonggyang
Yellow Sea
1281
1274
Korea Strait
JAPAN
➤ Mongol invasion
〰 Wall

and placed a new king on the throne. After incessant infighting among the generals and a series of coups, in 1196 the general Ch'oe Ch'ung-hon took control. The domination of Korea by the Ch'oe family was much like the contemporaneous situation in Japan, where warrior bands were seizing power. Moreover, because the Ch'oes were content to dominate the government while leaving the Koryŏ king on the throne, they had much in common with the Japanese shoguns, who followed a similar strategy.

Korea, from early times, recognized China as being in many ways senior to it, but when strong non-Chinese states emerged to its north in Manchuria, Korea was ready to accommodate them as well. Koryŏ's first neighbor to the north was the Khitan state of Liao, which in 1010 invaded and sacked the capital. To avoid destruction, Koryŏ acceded to vassal status, but Liao invaded again in 1018. This time Koryŏ was able to repel the nomadic Khitans. Afterward a defensive wall was built across the Korean peninsula south of the Yalu River. When the Jurchens and their Jin Dynasty supplanted the Khitans' Liao Dynasty, Koryŏ agreed to send them tribute as well.

As mentioned in Chapter 12, Korea was conquered by the Mongols, and the figurehead Koryŏ kings were moved to Beijing, where they married Mongol princesses, their descendants becoming more Mongol than Korean. This was a time of hardship for the Korean people. In the year 1254 alone, the Mongols enslaved two hundred thousand Koreans and took them away. Ordinary people in Korea suffered grievously when their land was used as a launching pad for the huge Mongol invasions of Japan. In this period Korea also suffered from frequent attacks by Japanese pirates, somewhat like the depredations of the Vikings in Europe a little earlier (see "Invasions and Migrations" in Chapter 14).

When Mongol rule in China fell apart in the mid-fourteenth century, it declined in Korea as well. Chinese rebels opposing the Mongols entered Korea and even briefly captured the capital in 1361. When the Ming Dynasty was established in China in 1368, the Koryŏ court was unsure how to respond. In 1388 a general, Yi Song-gye, was sent to oppose a Ming army at the northwest frontier. When he saw the strength of the Ming, he concluded that making an alliance was more sensible than fighting, and he led his troops back to the capital, where in 1392 he usurped the throne, founding the Chosŏn Dynasty.

Japan's Heian Period, 794–1185

How did the Heian form of government contribute to the cultural flowering of Japan in this period?

As described in Chapter 7, during the seventh and eighth centuries the Japanese ruling house pursued a vigorous policy of adopting useful ideas, techniques, and policies from the more advanced civilization of China. The rulers built a splendid capital along Chinese lines in Nara and fostered the growth of Buddhism. Monasteries grew so powerful in Nara, however, that in less than a century the court decided to move away from them and encourage other sects of Buddhism.

The new capital was built about twenty-five miles away at Heian (HAY-ahn) (modern Kyoto). Like Nara, Heian was modeled on the Tang capital of Chang'an. For the first century at Heian the government continued to follow Chinese models, but it turned away from them with the decline of the Tang Dynasty in the late ninth century. During the Heian period (794–1185), Japan witnessed a literary and cultural flowering under the rule of the Fujiwara family.

Fujiwara Rule

Only the first two Heian emperors were much involved in governing. By 860 political management had been taken over by a series of regents from the Fujiwara family, who supplied most of the empresses in this period. The emperors continued to be honored, but the Fujiwaras ruled. Fujiwara dominance represented the privatization of political power and a return to clan politics. Political history thus took a very different course in Japan than in China, where, when a dynasty weakened, military strongmen would compete to depose the emperor and found their own dynasties. In Japan for the next thousand years, political contenders sought to manipulate the emperors rather than supplant them.

The Fujiwaras reached the apogee of their glory under Fujiwara Michinaga (r. 995–1027). Like many aristocrats of the period, he was learned in Buddhism, music, poetry, and Chinese literature and history. He dominated the court for more than thirty years as the father of four empresses, the uncle of two emperors, and the grandfather of three emperors. He acquired great landholdings and built fine palaces for himself and his family. After ensuring that his sons could continue to rule, he retired to a Buddhist monastery, all the while continuing to maintain control.

By the end of the eleventh century several emperors who did not have Fujiwara mothers had found a device to counter Fujiwara control: they abdicated but continued to exercise power by controlling their young sons on the throne. This system of rule has been called **cloistered government** because the retired emperors took Buddhist orders, while maintaining control of the government from behind the scenes.

cloistered government
A system in which an emperor retired to a Buddhist monastery but continued to exercise power by controlling his young son on the throne.

Aristocratic Culture

A brilliant aristocratic culture developed in the Heian period. In the capital at Heian, nobles, palace ladies, and imperial family members lived a highly refined and leisured life. In their society, niceties of birth, rank, and breeding counted for everything. The elegance of one's calligraphy and the allusions in one's poems were matters of intense concern to both men and women at court, as was their dress. Courtiers did not like to leave the capital, and some like the court lady Sei Shonagon shuddered at the sight of ordinary working people. In her *Pillow Book*, she wrote of encountering a group of commoners on a pilgrimage: "They looked like so many basket-worms as they crowded together in their hideous clothes, leaving hardly an inch of space between themselves and me. I really felt like pushing them all over sideways."[3]

In this period a new script was developed for writing Japanese phonetically. Each symbol was based on a simplified Chinese character and represented one of the syllables used in Japanese (such as *ka, ki, ku, ke, ko*). Although "serious" essays, histories, and government documents continued to be written in Chinese, less formal works such as poetry and memoirs were written in Japanese. Mastering the new writing system took much less time than mastering writing in Chinese and this aided the spread of literacy, especially among women in court society.

In the Heian period, women played important roles at all levels of society. Women educated in the arts and letters could advance at court as attendants to the ruler's empress and other consorts. Women could inherit property from their parents, and they would compete with their brothers for shares of the family property. In political life, marrying a daughter to an emperor or shogun was one of the best ways to gain power, and women often became major players in power struggles.

The literary masterpiece of this period is ***The Tale of Genji***, written in Japanese by Lady Murasaki over several years (ca. 1000–1010). This long narrative depicts a cast of characters enmeshed in court life, with close attention to dialogue and personality. Murasaki also wrote a diary that is similarly revealing of aristocratic culture.

Murasaki was one of many women writers in this period. The wife of a high-ranking court official wrote a poetic memoir of her unhappy twenty-year marriage to him and his rare visits. A woman wrote both an autobiography that related her father's efforts to find favor at court and a love story of a hero who travels to China. Another woman even wrote a history that concludes with a triumphal biography of Fujiwara Michinaga.

Buddhism remained very strong throughout the Heian period. A mission sent to China in 804 included two monks in search of new texts. One of the monks, Saichō, spent time at the monasteries on Mount Tiantai and brought back the Buddhist teachings associated with that mountain (called Tendai in Japanese). Tendai's basic message is that all living beings share the Buddha nature and can be brought to salvation. Once back in Japan, Saichō established a monastery on Mount Hiei outside Kyoto, which grew to be one of the most important monasteries in Japan. By the twelfth century this monastery and its many branch temples had vast lands and a powerful army of monk-soldiers to protect its interests.

Kūkai, the other monk on the 804 mission to China, came back with texts from another school of Buddhism — Shingon, or "True Word," a form of **Esoteric Buddhism**. Esoteric Buddhism is based on the idea that teachings containing the secrets of enlightenment had been secretly transmitted from the Buddha. People can gain access to these mysteries through initiation into the mandalas (cosmic diagrams),

The Tale of Genji
A Japanese literary masterpiece about court life written by Lady Murasaki.

Esoteric Buddhism A sect of Buddhism that maintains that the secrets of enlightenment have been secretly transmitted from the Buddha and can be accessed through initiation into the mandalas, mudras, and mantras.

mudras (gestures), and mantras (verbal formulas). On his return to Japan, Kūkai attracted many followers and was allowed to establish a monastery at Mount Kōya, south of Osaka. The popularity of Esoteric Buddhism was a great stimulus to Buddhist art.

What were the causes and consequences of military rule in Japan?

The Samurai and the Kamakura Shogunate, 1185–1333

The gradual rise of a warrior elite over the course of the Heian period finally brought an end to the domination of the Fujiwaras and other Heian aristocratic families. In 1156 civil war broke out between the Taira and Minamoto warrior clans based in western and eastern Japan, respectively. Both clans relied on skilled warriors, later called samurai, who were rapidly becoming a new social class. A samurai and his lord had a double bond: in return for the samurai's loyalty and service, the lord granted him land or income. From 1159 to 1181 a Taira named Kiyomori dominated the court, taking the position of prime minister and marrying his daughter to the emperor. His relatives became governors of more than thirty provinces. Still, the Minamoto clan managed to defeat the Taira, and the Minamoto leader, Yoritomo, became **shogun**, or general-in-chief. With him began the Kamakura Shogunate (1185–1333). This period is often referred to as Japan's feudal period because it was dominated by a military class whose members were tied to their superiors by bonds of loyalty and supported by landed estates rather than salaries.

shogun The Japanese general-in-chief.

The Shogun Minamoto Yoritomo in Court Dress
This wooden sculpture, 27.8 inches tall, was made about a half century after Yoritomo's death for use in a shrine dedicated to his memory. The bold shapes convey Yoritomo's dignity and power. (National Museum, Tokyo, Japan/akg-images)

Military Rule

The similarities between military rule in Japan and feudalism in medieval Europe during roughly the same period have fascinated scholars, as have the very significant differences. In Europe feudalism emerged out of the fusion of Germanic and Roman social institutions and flowered under the impact of Muslim and Viking invasions. In Japan military rule evolved from a combination of the native warrior tradition and Confucian ethical principles of duty to superiors.

The emergence of the samurai was made possible by the development of private landholding. The government land allotment system, copied from Tang China, began breaking down in the eighth century (much as it did in China). By the ninth century local lords had begun escaping imperial taxes and control by commending (formally giving) their land to tax-exempt entities such as monasteries, the imperial family, and high-ranking officials. The local lord then received his land back as a tenant and paid his protector a small rent. The monastery or privileged individual received a steady income from the land, and the local lord escaped imperial taxes and control. By the end of the thirteenth century most land seems to have been taken off the tax rolls this way. Unlike peasants in medieval Europe, where similar practices of commendation occurred, those working the land in Japan never became serfs. More-over, Japanese lords rarely lived on the lands they had rights in, unlike English or French lords, who lived on their manors.

Samurai (SAM-moo-righ) resembled European knights in several ways. Both were armed with expensive weapons, and both fought on horseback. Just as the knight was supposed to live according to the chivalric code, so Japanese samurai were expected to live according to **Bushido** (boo-she-doh), or "way of the warrior." Physical hardship was accepted as routine, and soft living was despised as weak and unworthy. Disloyalty brought social disgrace, which the samurai could avoid only through *seppuku*, ritual suicide by slashing his belly.

Bushido Literally, the "way of the warrior"; the code of conduct by which samurai were expected to live.

The Kamakura Shogunate derives its name from Kamakura, a city near modern Tokyo that was the seat of the Minamoto clan. The founder, Yoritomo, ruled the country much the way he ran his own estates, appointing his retainers to newly created offices. To cope with the emergence of hard-to-tax estates, he put military land stewards in charge of seeing to the estates' proper operation. To bring order to the lawless countryside, he appointed military governors to oversee the military and enforce the law in the provinces. They supervised the conduct of the land stewards in peacetime and commanded the provincial samurai in war.

Yoritomo's wife, Masako, protected the interests of her own family, the Hōjōs, especially after Yoritomo died. She went so far as to force her first son to abdicate when he showed signs of preferring the family of his wife to the family of his mother. She later helped her brother take power away from her father. Thus the process of reducing power holders to figureheads went one step further in 1219 when the Hōjō family reduced the shogun to a figurehead. The Hōjō family held the reins of power for more than a century until 1333.

The Mongols' two massive seaborne invasions in 1274 and 1281 were a huge shock to the shogunate. Although the Hōjō regents, with the help of a "divine wind" (kamikaze), repelled the Mongols, they were unable to reward their vassals in the traditional way because little booty was found among the wreckage of the

Kamakura Shogunate, 1185–1333

Mongol fleets. Discontent grew among the samurai, and by the fourteenth century the entire political system was breaking down. Both the imperial and the shogunate families were fighting among themselves. As land grants were divided, samurai became impoverished.

The factional disputes among Japan's leading families remained explosive until 1331, when the emperor Go-Daigo tried to recapture real power. Go-Daigo destroyed the Kamakura Shogunate in 1333 but soon lost the loyalty of his followers. By 1336 one of his most important military supporters, Ashikaga Takauji, had turned on him and established the Ashikaga Shogunate, which lasted until 1573. Takauji's victory was also a victory for the samurai, who took over civil authority throughout Japan.

Cultural Trends

The cultural distance between the elites and the commoners narrowed a little during the Kamakura period. Buddhism was spread to ordinary Japanese by energetic preachers. Honen (1133–1212) propagated the Pure Land teaching, preaching that paradise could be reached through simple faith in the Buddha and repeating the name of the Buddha Amitabha (ah-mee-tah-bah). His follower Shinran (1173–1263) taught that monks should not shut themselves off in monasteries but should marry and have children. A different path was promoted by Nichiren (1222–1282), a fiery

Night Attack on the Sanjo Palace The twelfth-century civil wars in Japan became the subject of long novels and pictorial handscrolls. This scene from a mid-thirteenth-century painting shows the quick, violent attack on the palace where the retired emperor lived.

(Night Attack on the Sanjo Palace, from the *Illustrated Scrolls of the Events of the Heiji Era* [Heiji monogatari emaki], Kamakura Period, Japan, 2nd half of the 13th century. Detail, ink and color on paper handscroll/Fenollosa-Weld Collection/Museum of Fine Arts, Boston. Photograph © 2017 Museum of Fine Arts, Boston)

and intolerant preacher who proclaimed that to be saved, people had only to invoke sincerely the Lotus Sutra, one of the most important of the Buddhist sutras. These lay versions of Buddhism found a receptive audience among ordinary people in the countryside.

It was also during the Kamakura period that **Zen** came to flourish in Japan. Zen teachings originated in Tang China, where they were known as Chan (see "Tang Culture" in Chapter 7). Rejecting the authority of the sutras, Zen teachers claimed the superiority of mind-to-mind transmission of Buddhist truth. This teaching found eager patrons among the samurai, who were attracted to its discipline and strong master-disciple bonds.

Zen A school of Buddhism that emphasized meditation and truths that could not be conveyed in words.

During the Kamakura period, war tales continued the tradition of long narrative prose works. *The Tale of the Heike* tells the story of the fall of the Taira family and the rise of the Minamoto clan. The tale reached a large and mostly illiterate audience because blind minstrels would chant sections to the accompaniment of a lute. The story is suffused with the Buddhist idea of the transience of life and the illusory nature of glory. Yet it also celebrates strength, courage, loyalty, and pride.

After stagnating in the Heian period, agricultural productivity began to improve in the Kamakura period, and the population grew, reaching perhaps 8.2 million by 1333. Much like farmers in contemporary Song China, Japanese farmers adopted new strains of rice, often double-cropped in warmer regions, made increased use of fertilizers, and improved irrigation for paddy rice. Besides farming, ordinary people made their livings as artisans, traders, fishermen, and entertainers. A vague category of outcasts occupied the fringes of society, in a manner reminiscent of India. Buddhist strictures against killing and Shinto ideas of pollution probably account for the exclusion of butchers, leatherworkers, morticians, and lepers, but other groups, such as bamboo whisk makers, were also traditionally excluded for no obvious reason.

Chapter Summary

The countries of East Asia—China, Japan, and Korea—all underwent major changes in the six centuries from 800 to 1400. In China the loosening of the central government's control of the economy stimulated trade and economic growth. Between 800 and 1100 China's population doubled to 100 million. The economic center of China shifted from the north China plain to the south, the milder region drained by the Yangzi River.

In the Song period, the booming economy and the invention of printing allowed for expansion of the scholar-official class, which came to dominate government and society. Repeatedly, the Song government chose to pay tribute to its militarily powerful neighbors—first the Khitans, then the Jurchens, then the Mongols—to keep the peace. Eventually, however, Song fell to the Mongols.

During the Koryŏ Dynasty, Korea evolved more independently of China than it had previously, in part because it had to placate powerful non-Chinese neighbors. The commercial economy declined, and an increasing portion of the population was unfree, working as slaves for aristocrats or the government. Military strongmen dominated the government, but their armies were no match for the much larger empires to their north. The period of Mongol domination was particularly difficult.

In Heian Japan, a tiny aristocracy dominated government and society. A series of regents, most of them from the Fujiwara family and fathers-in-law of the emperors, controlled political life. The aristocratic court society put great emphasis on taste and refinement. Women were influential at the court and wrote much of the best literature of the period. The Heian aristocrats had little interest in life in the provinces, which gradually came under the control of military clans.

After a civil war between the two leading military clans, a military government, called the shogunate, was established. Two invasions by the Mongols caused major crises in military control. Although both times the invaders were repelled, defense costs were high. During this period culture was less centered on the capital, and Buddhism spread to ordinary people.

NOTES

1. *The Travels of Marco Polo, the Venetian*, ed. Manuel Komroff (New York: Boni and Liveright, 1926), p. 235.
2. Peter H. Lee, ed., *Sourcebook of Korean Civilization* (New York: Columbia University Press, 1993), p. 327.
3. *The Pillow Book of Sei Shonagon*, edited and translated by Ivan Morris, p. 258. Reproduced by permission of COLUMBIA UNIVERSITY PRESS in the format Republish in a book via Copyright Clearance Center.

CONNECTIONS

East Asia faced many internal and external challenges between 800 and 1400, and the ways societies responded to them shaped their subsequent histories. In China the first four centuries of this period saw economic growth, urbanization, the spread of printing, and the expansion of the educated class. In Korea and Japan aristocratic dominance and military rule were more typical of the era. All three areas, but especially China and Korea, faced an unprecedented challenge from the Mongols, with Japan less vulnerable because it did not share a land border. The challenges of the period did not hinder creativity in the literary and visual arts; among the greatest achievements of this era are the women's writings of Heian Japan, such as *The Tale of Genji*, and landscape painting of both Song and Yuan China.

Europe during these six centuries, the subject of the next chapter, also faced invasions from outside; in its case, the pagan Vikings were especially dreaded. Europe had a social structure more like that of Korea and Japan than of China, with less centralization and a more dominant place in society for military men. The centralized church in Europe, however, was unlike anything known in East Asian history. These centuries in Europe saw a major expansion of Christendom, especially to Scandinavia and eastern Europe, through both conversion and migration. Although there were scares that the Mongols would penetrate deeper into Europe, the greatest challenge in Europe was the Black Death and the huge loss of life that it caused.

CHAPTER 13   Review and Explore

Identify Key Terms

Identify and explain the significance of each item below.

dynastic cycle (p. 364)

compass (p. 366)

scholar-official class (p. 369)

examination system (p. 369)

movable type (p. 369)

Neo-Confucianism (p. 371)

concubine (p. 373)

foot binding (p. 374)

cloistered government (p. 378)

The Tale of Genji (p. 379)

Esoteric Buddhism (p. 379)

shogun (p. 380)

Bushido (p. 381)

Zen (p. 383)

Review the Main Ideas

Answer the focus questions from each section of the chapter.

1. What made possible the expansion of the Chinese economy, and what were the outcomes of this economic growth? (p. 364)

2. How did the civil service examinations and the scholar-official class shape Chinese society and culture, and what impact did the Mongol conquest have on them? (p. 367)

3. How did Korean society and culture develop in an age when its northern neighbors were Khitans, Jurchens, and Mongols? (p. 376)

4. How did the Heian form of government contribute to the cultural flowering of Japan in this period? (p. 377)

5. What were the causes and consequences of military rule in Japan? (p. 380)

Make Comparisons and Connections

Analyze the larger developments and continuities within and across chapters.

1. What elements in women's lives in Song China were similar to those in other parts of the world? What elements were more distinctive?

2. How did the impact of Mongol rule on China compare to its impact on Muslim lands (Chapter 9)?

3. How did being an island country affect Japan's history? What other island countries make good comparisons?

4. Did the countries of East Asia have more in common at the end of the Mongol period than they did in the seventh or eighth century (Chapter 7)?

TIMELINE

Suggested Resources

BOOKS

Bowring, Richard. *The Religious Traditions of Japan, 500–1600.* 2005. A wide-ranging study that puts Buddhism in the context of local cults.

Chaffee, John W. *The Thorny Gates of Learning in Sung China: A Social History of Examinations.* 1985. Documents the extensive impact of the examination system and the ways men could improve their chances.

Ebrey, Patricia Buckley. *The Inner Quarters: Marriage and the Lives of Chinese Women in the Sung Period.* 1993. Overview of the many facets of women's lives, from engagements to dowries, child rearing, and widowhood.

Egan, Ronald. *Word, Image, and Deed in the Life of Su Shi.* 1994. A sympathetic portrait of one of the most talented men of the age.

Farris, Wayne W. *Heavenly Warriors.* 1992. Argues against Western analogies in explaining the dominance of the samurai.

Friday, Karl F. *Hired Swords.* 1992. Treats the evolution of state military development in connection with the emergence of the samurai.

Hansen, Valerie. *Changing the Gods in Medieval China, 1127–1276.* 1990. A portrait of the religious beliefs and practices of ordinary people in Song times.

Hansen, Valerie. *The Silk Road: A New History.* 2012. Readers are given a tour of the Silk Road, city by city.

Ko, Dorothy, JaHyun Kim Haboush, and Joan R. Piggott, eds. *Women and Confucian Cultures in Premodern China, Korea, and Japan.* 2003. Addresses both the elements that the East Asian countries shared and the ways they diverged.

Kuhn, Dieter. *The Age of Confucian Rule: The Song Transformation of China.* 2009. An accessible overview that is especially strong on economic history and material culture.

Lorge, Peter. *War, Politics and Society in Early Modern China, 900–1795.* 2009. Examines dynasties as military powers.

1234–1368 Mongols' Yuan Dynasty in China

1130–1200 Zhu Xi, Neo-Confucian philosopher

ca. 1275–1292 Marco Polo travels in China

◆ **1119** First reported use of compass

◆ **1120s** First government-issued paper money in Song China

1185–1333 Kamakura Shogunate in Japan; Zen Buddhism flourishes

◆ **1206** Temujin proclaimed Chinggis Khan **(Ch. 12)**

◆ **1215** Magna Carta **(Ch. 14)**

◆ **1347** Black Death arrives in Europe **(Ch. 14)**

| 1100 | 1200 | 1300 | 1400 |

Morris, Ivan. *The World of the Shining Prince: Court Life in Ancient Japan.* 1964. An engaging portrait of Heian culture based on both fiction and nonfiction sources.

Seth, Michael J. *A Concise History of Korea.* 2006. Readable and engaging overview of Korean history.

Souyri, Pierre François. *The World Turned Upside Down: Medieval Japanese Society.* 2001. A thought-provoking analysis of both the social system and the mentalities of Japan's Middle Ages.

DOCUMENTARIES

China's Age of Invention (PBS, 2000). This *Nova* special draws attention to the many inventions during Song times, including printing and gunpowder.

Samurai Warrior (National Geographic, 2015). This documentary examines a mass grave, probably dating to 1333, whose discovery allowed archaeologists to study the ways samurai fought. It includes many dramatic reimaginations of battles.

FEATURE FILMS

The Men Who Tread on the Tiger's Tail (Akira Kurosawa, 1945). An early film directed by the renowned director Akira Kurosawa, based on traditional stories of the struggle between the Taira and Minamoto clans and the falling-out of the Minamoto brothers.

Musa (*The Warrior*) (Sung-su Kim, 2001). In this historical drama set in 1375, Korean soldiers, escorting an envoy, end up fighting Mongol soldiers. A big production, successful at the box office.

WEBSITE

The Song Dynasty in China. This interactive site devoted to the Song Dynasty covers economic growth, trade, technology, cities, and other topics.
afe.easia.columbia.edu/song/index.html

14

Europe and Western Asia in the Middle Ages
800–1450

By the fifteenth century scholars in the growing cities of northern Italy had begun to think that they were living in a new era, one in which the glories of ancient Greece and Rome were being reborn. What separated their time from classical antiquity, in their opinion, was a long period of darkness and barbarism, to which a seventeenth-century professor gave the name "Middle Ages." In this conceptualization, the history of Europe was divided into three periods — ancient, medieval, and modern — an organization that is still in use today. Later, the history of other parts of the world was sometimes fit into this three-period schema as well, with discussions of the "classical" period in Maya history, of "medieval" India and China, and of "modern" everywhere.

Today historians often question whether labels of past time periods for one culture work on a global scale, and some scholars are uncertain about whether "Middle Ages" is a just term even for European history. They assert that the Middle Ages was not simply a period of stagnation between two high points but rather a time of enormous intellectual energy and creative vitality. While agrarian life continued to dominate Europe, political structures that would influence later European history began to form, and Christianity continued to spread. People at the time did not know that they were living in an era that would later be labeled "middle" or sometimes even "dark," and we can wonder whether they would have shared this negative view of their own times.

Hedwig of Silesia

Noblewomen in medieval Europe played a wide variety of roles. Hedwig of Silesia (a territory now located mostly in Poland) conducted diplomatic negotiations, ruled her husband's territory when he was away, founded monasteries, and worked to expand Christianity in eastern Europe.

Court workshop of Duke Ludwig I of Liegnitz and Brieg, 1364–1398. Tempera colors, colored washes and ink on parchment/Liszt Collection/Quint & Lox akg-images

CHAPTER PREVIEW

POLITICAL DEVELOPMENTS
How did medieval rulers restore order and centralize political power?

THE CHRISTIAN CHURCH
How did the Christian Church enhance its power and create new institutions and religious practices?

THE CRUSADES
What were the causes, course, and consequences of the Crusades?

THE LIFE OF THE PEOPLE
How did the lives of common people, nobles, and townspeople differ, and what new commercial developments increased wealth?

LEARNING AND CULTURE
What were the primary educational and cultural developments in medieval Europe?

CRISES OF THE LATER MIDDLE AGES
Why have the later Middle Ages been seen as a time of calamity and crisis?

How did medieval rulers restore order and centralize political power?

Political Developments

In 800 Charlemagne, the most powerful of the Carolingians, was crowned Holy Roman emperor. After his death his empire was divided among his grandsons, and their kingdoms were weakened by nobles vying for power. In addition, beginning around 800 western Europe was invaded by several different groups. Local nobles were the strongest power, and common people turned to them for protection. By the eleventh century, however, rulers in some parts of Europe had reasserted authority and were slowly building centralized states.

Invasions and Migrations

The Vikings were pagan Germanic peoples from Norway, Sweden, and Denmark. They began to make overseas expeditions, which they themselves called *vikings*, and the word came to be used for people who went on such voyages as well. Viking voyages and attacks began around 800, and by the mid-tenth century the Vikings had brought large sections of continental Europe and Britain under their sway. In the east they sailed the rivers of Russia as far as the Black Sea. In the west they established permanent settlements in Iceland and short-lived ones in Greenland and Newfoundland in Canada (Map 14.1).

Against Viking ships navigated by experienced and fearless sailors, the Carolingian Empire, with no navy, was helpless. At first the Vikings attacked and sailed off laden with booty. Later, on returning, they settled down and colonized the areas they had conquered, often marrying local women and adopting the local languages and some of the customs.

Along with the Vikings, groups of central European steppe peoples known as Magyars (MAG-yahrz) also raided villages in the late ninth century. Moving westward, small bands of Magyars on horseback reached far into Europe. They subdued northern Italy, compelled Bavaria and Saxony to pay tribute, and penetrated into the Rhineland and Burgundy. Western Europeans thought of them as returning Huns, so the Magyars came to be known as Hungarians.

From North Africa, the Muslims also began new encroachments in the ninth century. They already ruled most of Spain and now conquered Sicily, driving northward into central Italy and the south coast of France.

From the perspective of those living in what had been Charlemagne's empire, Viking, Magyar, and Muslim attacks contributed to increasing disorder and violence. Italian, French, and English sources often describe this period as one of terror and chaos. People in other parts of Europe might have had a different opinion. In Muslim Spain and Sicily scholars worked in thriving cities, and new crops such as cotton and sugar enhanced ordinary people's lives. In eastern Europe the Magyars settled in an area that is now Hungary, becoming a strong kingdom. A Viking point of view might be the most positive, for by 1100 descendants of the Vikings not only ruled their homelands in Norway, Sweden, and Denmark but also ruled northern France (a province known as Normandy, or land of the Northmen), England, Sicily, Iceland, and Russia, with an outpost in Greenland and occasional voyages to North America.

"Feudalism" and Manorialism

The large-scale division of Charlemagne's empire into three parts in the ninth century led to a decentralization of power at the local level in western and central Europe.

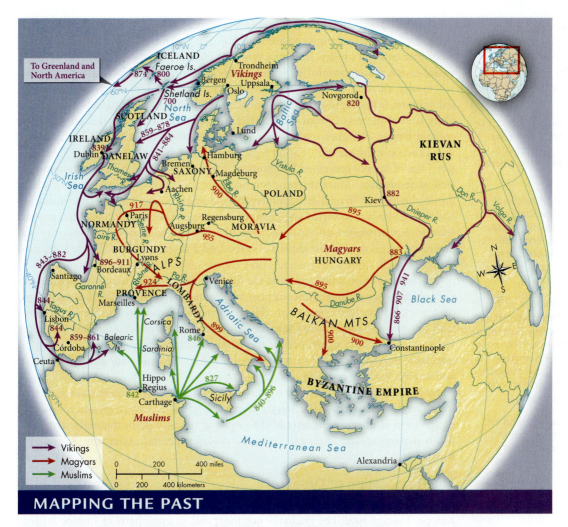

MAPPING THE PAST

MAP 14.1 Invasions and Migrations of the Ninth and Tenth Centuries This map shows the Viking, Magyar, and Muslim invasions and migrations in the ninth and tenth centuries. Compare it with Map 8.2 on the barbarian migrations of late antiquity to answer the following questions.

ANALYZING THE MAP What similarities do you see in the patterns of migration in these two periods? What significant differences?

CONNECTIONS How did the Vikings' expertise in shipbuilding and sailing make their migrations different from those of earlier Germanic tribes? How did this set them apart from the Magyar and Muslim invaders of the ninth century?

Civil wars weakened the power and prestige of kings, who could do little about regional violence. Likewise, the invasions of the ninth century, especially those of the Vikings, weakened royal authority. The Frankish kings were unable to halt the invaders, and the local aristocracy had to assume responsibility for defense. Thus, in the ninth and tenth centuries, aristocratic families increased their authority in their local territories, and distant and weak kings could not interfere. Common people turned for protection to the strongest power, the local nobles.

The most powerful nobles were those who gained warriors' allegiance, often symbolized in an oath-swearing ceremony of homage and fealty that grew out of earlier Germanic oaths of loyalty. In this ceremony a warrior (knight) swore his loyalty as a **vassal** to the more powerful individual, who became his lord. In return for the vassal's loyalty, aid, and military assistance, the lord promised him protection and material support. This support might be a place in the lord's household but was more likely land of the vassal's own, called a **fief** (*feudum* in Latin). The fief, which might contain forests, churches, and towns, technically still belonged to the lord, and the vassal had only the use of it. Earlier legal scholars and historians identified these personal ties of loyalty cemented by grants of land as a political and social system they termed **feudalism**. More recently, increasing numbers of medieval historians have found the idea of "feudalism" problematic, because the word was a later invention and the system was so varied and changed over time. They still point to the personal relationship between lords and vassals as the key way that political authority was organized and note that the church also received and granted land. In the Byzantine Empire as well, nobles, monasteries, and church officials held the most land.

Peasants living on a fief produced the food and other goods necessary to maintain the nobles and churchmen, under a system of **manorialism**, in which they exchanged their work for the lord's protection. They received land to farm, but were tied to the land by various payments and services. Most significantly, a peasant lost his or her freedom and became a **serf**, part of the lord's permanent labor force. Unlike slaves, serfs were personally free, but they were bound to the land and unable to leave it without the lord's permission.

By around 1000 the majority of western Europeans were serfs. In eastern Europe the transition was slower but longer lasting. Western European peasants began to escape from serfdom in the later Middle Ages, at the very point that serfs were more firmly tied to the land in eastern Europe, especially in eastern Germany, Poland, and Russia.

The Restoration of Order

The eleventh century witnessed the beginnings of political stability in much of Europe. Foreign invasions gradually declined, and in some parts of Europe lords in control of large territories built up their power even further, becoming kings over growing and slowly centralizing states. In a process similar to that occurring at the same time in the West African kingdom of Ghana (see "African Kingdoms and Empires" in Chapter 10), rulers expanded their territories and extended their authority by developing larger bureaucracies, armies, judicial systems, and other institutions to maintain control, as well as taxation systems to pay for them. These new institutions and practices laid the foundations for modern national states. Political developments in England, France, Germany, and Hungary provide good examples of the beginnings of the national state in the central Middle Ages.

The Viking Canute (kah-NOOT) (r. 1016–1035) made England the center of his empire, while promoting a policy of assimilation and reconciliation between Anglo-Saxons and Vikings. At the same time, England was divided into local shires, or counties, each under the jurisdiction of a sheriff appointed by the king. When Canute's heir Edward died childless, there were three claimants to the throne. One of these, Duke William of Normandy, crossed the channel and won the English

---

vassal A knight who has sworn loyalty to a particular lord.

fief A portion of land, the use of which was given by a lord to a vassal in exchange for the latter's oath of loyalty.

feudalism A medieval European political system that defines the military obligations and relations between a lord and his vassals and involves the granting of fiefs.

manorialism The economic system that governed rural life in medieval Europe, in which the landed estates of a lord were worked by the peasants under the lord's jurisdiction in exchange for his protection.

serf A peasant who lost his or her freedom and became permanently bound to the landed estate of a lord.

throne by defeating and killing his Anglo-Saxon rival, Harold II, at the Battle of Hastings in 1066. Later dubbed "the Conqueror," William (r. 1066–1087) limited the power of the nobles and church officials and built a unified monarchy. He retained the Anglo-Saxon institution of sheriff, but named Normans to the posts.

In 1128 William's granddaughter Matilda married a powerful French noble, Geoffrey of Anjou. Their son, who became Henry II of England, inherited provinces in northwestern France from his father. When Henry married the great heiress Eleanor of Aquitaine in 1152, he claimed lordship over Aquitaine and other provinces in southwestern France as well. The histories of England and France were thus closely intertwined in the Middle Ages.

In the early twelfth century France consisted of a number of nearly independent provinces, each governed by its local ruler. The work of unifying and enlarging France began under Philip II (r. 1180–1223), also known as Philip Augustus. By the end of his reign Philip was effectively master of northern France, and by 1300 most of the provinces of modern France had been added to the royal domain.

In central Europe the German king Otto I (r. 936–973) defeated many other lords to build up his power, based on an alliance with and control of the church. Under Otto I and his successors, a loose confederation stretching from the North Sea to the Mediterranean developed. In this confederation, later called the Holy Roman Empire, the emperor shared power with princes, dukes, counts, city officials, archbishops, and bishops. Frederick Barbarossa (r. 1152–1190) of the house of Hohenstaufen (HOH-en-shtow-fen) tried valiantly to make the Holy Roman Empire a united state. When he tried to enforce his authority over the cities of northern Italy, however, they formed a league against him in alliance with the pope and defeated him. Germany did not become a unified state.

In eastern Europe, the Hungarians formed a tribal federation and then under Stephen I (r. 1000–1038) created a more centralized kingdom. Stephen became a devout Christian, defeated pagan rivals militarily, and received his crown from the pope as a symbol of their alliance. He further consolidated his power through war, diplomacy, and strategic marriages, and set up an administrative system based on counties. In the middle of the thirteenth century Hungary was invaded by the Mongols (see "Chinggis Khan and the Mongol Empire" in Chapter 12), which led the kings to construct stone castles to defend against further attacks and develop new military tactics.

The Norman Conquest, 1066

Law and Justice

Throughout Europe in the twelfth and thirteenth centuries, the law was a hodge-podge of customs, feudal rights, and provincial practices. Rulers wanted to blend these elements into a uniform system of rules acceptable and applicable to all their peoples, though their success in doing so varied.

The French king Louis IX (r. 1226–1270) was famous for his concern for justice. Each French province, even after being made part of the kingdom of France, retained its unique laws and procedures. But Louis IX created a royal judicial system, establishing the Parlement of Paris, a kind of supreme court that heard appeals from lower courts.

Under Henry II (r. 1154–1189), England developed and extended a common law—a law common to and accepted by the entire country—which was unique in medieval Europe. Henry's son John (r. 1199–1216), however, met with serious disappointment after taking the throne. A combination of royal debt, increased taxation, and military failures fed popular discontent. A rebellion begun by northern barons grew, and in 1215 the barons forced him to attach his seal to the Magna Carta—the "Great Charter," which became the cornerstone of English justice and law. The Magna Carta was simply meant to assert traditional rights enjoyed by nobles, but in time it came to signify the broader principle that everyone, including the king and the government, must obey the law. In 1222 King Andrew II of Hungary was similarly forced by his nobles to agree to the "Golden Bull," affirming their freedom from taxation and right to disobey him if they thought he was acting against the law.

Statements of legal principles such as the Magna Carta or the Golden Bull were not how most people experienced the law in medieval Europe. Instead they were involved in actual cases. Judges determined guilt or innocence in a number of ways. In some cases, they ordered a trial by ordeal, in which the accused might be tied hand and foot and dropped in a lake or river. People believed that water was a pure substance and would reject anything foul or unclean. Thus a person who sank was considered innocent, while a person who floated was found guilty. Trials by ordeal were relatively rare, and courts increasingly favored more rational procedures, in which judges heard testimony, sought witnesses, and read written evidence if it was available. Violent crimes were often punished by public execution. Executioners were feared figures, but they were also well-paid public officials and were a necessary part of the legal structure.

How did the Christian Church enhance its power and create new institutions and religious practices?

The Christian Church

Kings and emperors were not the only rulers consolidating their power in the eleventh and twelfth centuries; the papacy did as well, although the popes' efforts were sometimes challenged by medieval kings and emperors. Despite such challenges, monasteries continued to be important places for learning and devotion, and new religious orders were founded. Christianity expanded into Europe's northern and eastern regions, and Christian rulers expanded their holdings in Muslim Spain.

Papal Reforms

During the ninth and tenth centuries the Western Christian (Roman) Church came under the control of kings and feudal lords, who chose church officials in their territories, granting them fiefs that provided an income and expecting loyalty and service in return. Church offices were sometimes sold outright—a practice called *simony* (SIGH-moh-nee). Although the Western Church encouraged clerical celibacy, many priests were married or living with women. Wealthy families from the city of Rome often chose popes from among their members; thus popes paid more attention to their families' political fortunes or their own pleasures than to the church's institutional or spiritual health. Not surprisingly, clergy at all levels who had bought their positions or had been granted them for political reasons provided little spiritual guidance and were rarely models of high moral standards.

Córdoba Mosque and Cathedral The huge arches of the Great Mosque at Córdoba dwarf the cathedral built in its center after the city was conquered by Christian armies in 1236. During the reconquista (see "The Expansion of Western and Eastern Christianity"), Christian kings often transformed mosques into churches, often by simply adding Christian elements such as crosses and altars to existing structures. (© dbimages/Alamy)

Beginning in the eleventh century a series of popes began to assert their power and also reformed the church. In 1054 the pope sent a delegation to the patriarch of Constantinople demanding that he recognize the pope as the head of the entire Christian Church. The patriarch refused, each side declared the other heretics, and the outcome was a schism between the Roman Catholic and the Orthodox Churches that deepened over the centuries and continues today.

Many popes believed that secular or lay control over the church was largely responsible for the lack of moral leadership, so they proclaimed the church independent from secular rulers. The Lateran Council of 1059 decreed that the authority and power to elect the pope rested solely in the college of cardinals, a special group of priests from the major churches in and around Rome.

Pope Gregory VII (pontificate 1073–1085) vigorously championed reform and the expansion of papal power. He ordered all priests to give up their wives and children or face dismissal, invalidated the ordination of church officials who had purchased their offices, and placed nuns under firmer control of male authorities. He believed that the pope was the vicar of God on earth and that papal orders were the orders of God. He emphasized the political authority of the papacy, ordering that any church official selected or appointed by a layperson should be deposed, and any layperson who appointed a church official should be excommunicated—cut off from the sacraments and the Christian community. European rulers protested this restriction of their power, and the strongest reaction came from Henry IV, the ruler of Germany who later became the Holy Roman emperor. The pope and the emperor used threats and diplomacy against each other, and neither was the clear victor.

Monastic Life

Although they were in theory cut off from the world (see "Christian Monasticism" in Chapter 8), monasteries and convents were deeply affected by issues of money, rank, and power. During the ninth and tenth centuries many monasteries fell under the control and domination of local feudal lords. Powerful laymen appointed themselves or their relatives as abbots, took the lands and goods of monasteries, and spent monastic revenues.

Medieval monasteries also provided noble boys with education and opportunities for ecclesiastical careers. Although a few men who rose in the ranks of church officials were of humble origins, most were from high-status families. Social class also defined the kinds of religious life open to women. Kings and nobles usually established convents for their female relatives and other elite women, and the position of abbess, or head of a convent, became the most powerful position a woman could hold in medieval society. (See "Individuals in Society: Hildegard of Bingen," at right.)

Routines within individual monasteries varied widely from house to house and from region to region. In every monastery, however, daily life centered on the liturgy or Divine Office, psalms, and other prayers, which monks and nuns said seven times a day and once during the night. Praying was looked on as a vital service. Prayers were said for peace, rain, good harvests, the civil authorities, the monks' and nuns' families, and their benefactors. Monastic patrons in turn lavished gifts on the monasteries, which often became very wealthy, controlling large tracts of land and the peasants who farmed them. The combination of lay control and wealth created problems for monasteries as monks and nuns concentrated on worldly issues and spiritual observance and intellectual activity declined.

heresy An idea, belief, or action counter to doctrines that church leaders defined as correct; heretics could be punished by the church.

In the thirteenth century the growth of cities provided a new challenge for the church. Many urban people thought that the church did not meet their spiritual needs. They turned instead to **heresy**—that is, to an idea, belief, or action that ran counter to doctrines that church leaders defined as correct. Various beliefs judged to be heresies had emerged in Christianity since its earliest centuries, and heretics were subject to punishment. In this period, heresies often called on the church to give up its wealth and power. Combating heresy became a principal task of new religious orders, most prominently the Dominicans and Franciscans, who preached and ministered to city dwellers; the Dominicans also staffed the papal Inquisition, a special court designed to root out heresy.

Popular Religion

Religious practices varied widely from country to country and even from province to province. But everywhere, religion permeated everyday life.

For Christians, the village church was the center of community life, with the parish priest in charge of a host of activities. People gathered at the church for services on Sundays and holy days, breaking the painful routine of work. The feasts that accompanied celebrations were commonly held in the churchyard. In everyday life people engaged in rituals and used language heavy with religious symbolism. Everyone participated in village processions to honor the saints and ask their protection. The entire calendar was designed with reference to Christmas, Easter, and Pentecost, events in the life of Jesus and his disciples.

The Christian calendar was also filled with saints' days. Veneration of the saints had been an important tool of Christian conversion since late antiquity (see "Christian Missionaries and Conversion" in Chapter 8), and the cult of the saints was a central feature of popular culture in the Middle Ages. People believed that the saints

Hildegard of Bingen

THE TENTH CHILD OF A LESSER NOBLE FAMILY, Hildegard (1098–1179) was turned over to the care of an abbey in the Rhineland when she was eight years old. There she learned Latin and received a good education. She spent most of her life in various women's religious communities, two of which she founded herself. When she was a child, she began having mystical visions, often of light in the sky, but told few people about them. In middle age, however, her visions became more dramatic: "And it came to pass . . . when I was 42 years and 7 months old, that the heavens were opened and a blinding light of exceptional brilliance flowed through my entire brain. And so it kindled my whole heart and breast like a flame, not burning but warming . . . and suddenly I understood of the meaning of expositions of the books."* She wanted the church to approve of her visions and wrote first to Saint Bernard of Clairvaux, who answered her briefly and dismissively, and then to Pope Eugenius, who encouraged her to write them down. Her first work was *Scivias* (Know the Ways of the Lord), a record of her mystical visions that incorporates extensive theological learning.

Obviously possessed of leadership and administrative talents, Hildegard left her abbey in 1147 to found the convent of Rupertsberg near Bingen. There she produced *Physica* (On the Physical Elements) and *Causa et Curae* (Causes and Cures), scientific works on the curative properties of natural elements; poems; a religious play; and several more works of mysticism. She carried on a huge correspondence with scholars, prelates, and ordinary people. When she was over fifty, she left her community to preach to audiences of clergy and laity, and she was the only woman of her time whose opinions on religious matters were considered authoritative by the church.

Hildegard's visions have been explored by theologians and also by neurologists, who judge that they may have originated in migraine headaches, as she reports many of the same phenomena that migraine sufferers do: auras of light around objects, areas of blindness, feelings of intense doubt and intense euphoria. The interpretations that she develops come from her theological insight and learning, however, not from her illness. That same insight also emerges in her music, which is what she is best known for today. Eighty of her compositions survive—a huge number for a medieval

Inspired by heavenly fire, Hildegard begins to dictate her visions to her scribe. The original of this elaborately illustrated copy of *Scivias* disappeared from Hildegard's convent during World War II, but fortunately a facsimile had already been made. (Private Collection/Bridgeman Images)

composer—most of them written to be sung by the nuns in her convent, so they have strong lines for female voices. Many of her songs and chants have been recorded recently by various artists and are available on compact disk, as downloads, and on several websites.

QUESTIONS FOR ANALYSIS

1. Why do you think Hildegard might have kept her visions secret at first? Why do you think she eventually sought church approval for them?
2. In what ways were Hildegard's accomplishments extraordinary given women's general status in the Middle Ages?

*From *Scivias*, trans. Mother Columba Hart and Jane Bishop, *The Classics of Western Spirituality* (New York/Mahwah: Paulist Press, 1990).

possessed supernatural powers that enabled them to perform miracles, and each saint became the special property of the locality in which his or her relics—remains or possessions—rested. In return for the saint's healing powers and support, peasants would offer prayers, loyalty, and gifts. The Virgin Mary, Christ's mother, became the most important saint, with churches built and special hymns, prayers, and ceremonies created in her honor.

Most people in medieval Europe were Christian, but there were small Jewish communities scattered through many parts of Europe, as well as Muslims in the Iberian Peninsula, Sicily, other Mediterranean islands, and southeastern Europe. Increasing suspicion and hostility marked relations among believers in different religions throughout the Middle Ages, but there were also important similarities in the ways that each group understood and experienced their faiths. In all three traditions, every major life transition was marked by a ceremony that involved religious officials or spiritual elements. In all three faiths, death was marked by religious rituals, and the living had obligations to the dead, including prayers and special mourning periods.

The Expansion of Western and Eastern Christianity

The eleventh and twelfth centuries saw an expansion of Christianity into Scandinavia, the Baltic lands, eastern Europe, and Spain through wars, the establishment of new bishoprics, and the migration of Christian colonists. More and more Europeans began to think of themselves as belonging to a realm of Christianity that was political as well as religious, a realm they called Christendom.

Christian influences entered Scandinavia and the Baltic lands primarily through the creation of dioceses (church districts headed by bishops). This took place in Denmark and Norway in the tenth and eleventh centuries, and then in Sweden and Finland. In all of these areas, Christian missionaries preached, baptized, and built churches. Royal power advanced institutional Christianity, and traditional Norse religions practiced by the Vikings were outlawed. In central and eastern Europe the German emperor Otto I (see "The Restoration of Order") planted a string of dioceses along his northern and eastern frontiers, hoping to pacify the newly conquered Slavs. German nobles built castles, ruthlessly crushed revolts by Slavic peoples, and encouraged German-speaking settlers to move east.

The expansion of Christianity in much of eastern Europe was organized by the Eastern Orthodox Church. King Rastislav of Moravia (r. 846–870)—now part of the Czech Republic—first sent envoys to Rome, but when the pope refused to send missionaries, he turned to the Byzantine emperor Michael III (r. 842–867), who sent the brothers Cyril (826–869) and Methodius (815–885). They invented a Slavic alphabet using Greek characters, later called the Cyrillic alphabet, and translated the Bible into Old Church Slavonic, the first Slavic literary language. Slightly later the rulers of Bulgaria weighed the benefits of Roman and Eastern Christianity, and decided for Eastern Christianity when the Byzantine patriarch agreed the Bulgarian Church could be independent and use Bulgarian as its official language.

In the tenth century other missionaries spread Christianity, the Cyrillic alphabet, and Byzantine art and architecture to what is now Russia. Vladimir I (r. 980–1015), the ruler of the largest state in the area, Kievan Rus, converted to Orthodox Christianity, in part to marry the daughter of the Byzantine emperor. He ordered a mass baptism for the residents of Kiev in a local river, just as western European kings had for their subjects several centuries earlier (see "Christian Missionaries and Conversion" in Chapter 8).

The Iberian Peninsula was another area of Christian expansion. In about 950 Caliph Abd al-Rahman III (912–961) of the Umayyad Dynasty of Córdoba ruled most of the peninsula. Christian Spain consisted of a number of small kingdoms. In the eleventh century divisions and civil wars in the caliphate of Córdoba allowed Christian armies to conquer an increasingly large part of the Iberian Peninsula. By 1248 Christians held all of the peninsula save for the small state of Granada in the south.

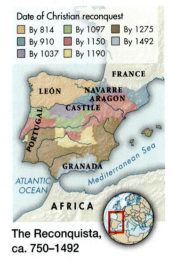

Date of Christian reconquest
- By 814
- By 910
- By 1037
- By 1097
- By 1150
- By 1190
- By 1275
- By 1492

The Reconquista, ca. 750–1492

Fourteenth-century clerical writers would call the movement to expel the Muslims the **reconquista** (ray-kon-KEES-tah) (reconquest)—a sacred and patriotic crusade to wrest the country from "alien" Muslim hands. This religious idea became part of Spanish political culture and of the national psychology. Rulers of the Christian kingdoms of Spain increasingly passed legislation discriminating against Muslims and Jews living under Christian rule, and they attempted to exclude anyone from the nobility who could not prove "purity of blood"—that is, that they had no Muslim or Jewish ancestors.

reconquista A fourteenth-century term used to describe the long Christian crusade to wrest Spain back from the Muslims; clerics believed it was a sacred and patriotic mission.

Spain was not the only place in Europe where "blood" became a way of understanding differences among people and a basis for discriminatory laws. When Germans moved into eastern Europe and English forces took over much of Ireland, they increasingly barred local people from access to legal courts and denied them positions in monasteries or craft guilds. They banned intermarriage between ethnic groups in an attempt to maintain ethnic purity, even though everyone was Christian.

Crusades Holy wars sponsored by the papacy for the recovery of the holy city of Jerusalem from the Muslims.

The Crusades

The expansion of Christianity in the Middle Ages was not limited to Europe but extended to the eastern Mediterranean in what were later termed the **Crusades**. Occurring from the late eleventh to the late thirteenth century, the Crusades were wars sponsored by the papacy to recover the holy city of Jerusalem from the Muslims.

What were the causes, course, and consequences of the Crusades?

Background and Motives

In the eleventh century the papacy had strong reasons for wanting to launch an expedition against Muslims in the East. Such an expedition would strengthen the pope's claim to be the leader of Christian society in the West and would bolster his claims to superiority over the patriarch of the Eastern Orthodox Church (see "The Western Church and the Eastern Church" in Chapter 8).

Popes and other church officials gained support for war in defense of Christianity by promising spiritual benefits to those who joined a campaign or died fighting. Preachers communicated these ideas widely and told stories about warrior-saints who slew hundreds of enemies.

Religious zeal led increasing numbers of people to go on pilgrimages to holy places, including Jerusalem. The Arab Muslims who had ruled Jerusalem and the surrounding territory for centuries generally allowed Christian pilgrims to travel freely, but in the late eleventh century the Seljuk Turks took over Palestine, defeating both Arabic and Byzantine armies and pillaging in Christian and Muslim parts of Asia Minor. They harassed pilgrims and looted churches, and the emperor at Constantinople appealed to the West for support. The emperor's appeal fit well with papal aims, and in 1095 Pope Urban II called for a great Christian holy war. Urban urged Christian knights who had been fighting one another to direct their energies against those he claimed were the true enemies of God, the Muslims.

The Course of the Crusades

Thousands of people of all classes responded to Urban's call, joining what became known as the First Crusade. The First Crusade was successful, mostly because of the dynamic enthusiasm of the participants, who had little more than religious zeal. They knew little of the geography or climate of the Middle East and could never agree on a leader. Adding to these disadvantages, supply lines were never set up, starvation and disease wracked the army, and the Turks slaughtered hundreds of noncombatants. Nevertheless, the army pressed on, besieging and taking several cities, including Antioch. After three years on the road, and a monthlong siege, the Crusaders took Jerusalem in July 1099 (Map 14.2).

With Jerusalem taken, some Crusaders regarded their mission as accomplished and set off for home. Others stayed, setting up institutions to rule local territories and the Muslim population. Four small "Crusader states"—Jerusalem, Edessa, Tripoli, and Antioch—were established, and castles and fortified towns were built in these states to defend against Muslim reconquest. Reinforcements arrived in the form of pilgrims and fighters from Europe, so that there was constant coming and going by land and more often by sea after the Crusaders conquered port cities. Most Crusaders were men, but some women came along as well, assisting in the besieging of towns and castles by providing water to fighting men or foraging for food, working as washerwomen, and providing sexual services.

Between 1096 and 1270 the crusading ideal was expressed in eight papally approved expeditions, though none after the First Crusade accomplished very much. The Muslim states in the Middle East were politically fragmented when the Crusaders first came, and it took them about a century to reorganize. They did so dramatically under Saladin (Salah al-Din), who unified Egypt and Syria. In 1187 the Muslims retook Jerusalem, but the Christians held on to port towns, and Saladin allowed

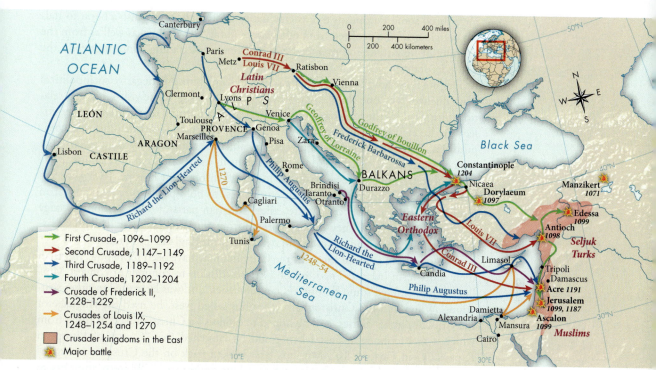

MAP 14.2 The Crusades, 1096–1270 The Crusaders took many different sea and land routes on their way to Jerusalem, often crossing the lands of the Byzantine Empire, which led to conflict with Eastern Christians. The Crusader kingdoms in the East lasted only briefly.

pilgrims safe passage to Jerusalem. From that point on, the Crusader states were more important economically than politically or religiously, giving Italian and French merchants direct access to Eastern products.

After the Muslims retook Jerusalem, the crusading movement faced other setbacks. During the Fourth Crusade (1202–1204), Crusaders stopped in Constantinople, and when they were not welcomed, they sacked the city. The Byzantine Empire splintered into three parts and soon consisted of little more than the city of Constantinople. Moreover, the assault of one Christian people on another made the split between the churches permanent and discredited the entire crusading movement in the eyes of many Christians.

In the late thirteenth century Turkish armies, after gradually conquering all other Muslim rulers, turned against the Crusader states. In 1291 the Christians' last stronghold, the port of Acre, fell. Knights then needed a new battlefield for military actions, which some found in Spain, where the rulers of Aragon and Castile continued fighting Muslims until 1492.

Consequences of the Crusades

The Crusades testified to the religious enthusiasm of the High Middle Ages and the influence of the papacy, gave kings and the pope opportunities to expand their bureaucracies, and provided an outlet for nobles' dreams of glory. The Crusades also introduced some Europeans to Eastern luxury goods. They were also a boon to Italian merchants, who profited from outfitting military expeditions as well as from the opening of new trade routes and the establishment of trading communities in the Crusader states.

Despite these advantages, the Crusades had some seriously negative sociopolitical consequences. For one thing, they proved to be a disaster for Jewish-Christian relations. Inspired by the ideology of holy war, Christian armies on their way to Jerusalem on the First Crusade joined with local mobs to attack Jewish families and communities. Later Crusades brought similar violence, enhanced by accusations that Jews engaged in the ritual murder of Christians to use their blood in religious rites.

Legal restrictions on Jews gradually increased throughout Europe. Jews were forbidden to have Christian servants or employees, to hold public office, to appear in public on Christian holy days, or to enter Christian parts of town without a badge marking them as Jews. They were prohibited from engaging in any trade with Christians except money-lending and were banished from England and France.

The long-term cultural legacy of the Crusades may have been more powerful than their short-term impact. The ideal of a sacred mission to conquer or convert Muslim peoples entered some Europeans' consciousness and was later used in other situations. When in 1492 Christopher Columbus sailed west, he used the language of the Crusades in his diaries, and he hoped to establish a Christian base in India from which a new crusade against Islam could be launched (see "Causes of European Expansion" in Chapter 16). Muslims later looked back on the Crusades as expansionist and imperialist, the beginning of a long trajectory of Western attempts to limit or destroy Islam.

How did the lives of common people, nobles, and townspeople differ, and what new commercial developments increased wealth?

The Life of the People

In the late ninth century medieval intellectuals described Christian society as composed of those who pray (the monks), those who fight (the nobles), and those who work (the peasants). This three-category model does not fully describe medieval society — there were degrees of wealth and status within each group. Also, the model does not take townspeople and the emerging commercial classes into consideration, and it completely excludes those who were not Christian, such as Jews, Muslims, and pagans. Furthermore, those who used the model, generally bishops and other church officials, ignored the fact that each of these groups was made up of both women and men. Despite — or perhaps because of — these limitations, the model of the three categories was a powerful mental construct. Therefore, we can use it to organize our investigation of life in the Middle Ages, broadening it to include groups and issues that medieval authors did not. (See "Christian Monasticism" in Chapter 8 for a discussion of the life of monks and nuns — "those who pray.")

The Life and Work of Peasants

The men and women who worked the land in medieval Europe made up probably more than 90 percent of the population, as they did in China, India, and other parts of the world where agriculture predominated. The evolution of localized systems of authority into more centralized states had relatively little impact on the daily lives of these peasants except when it involved warfare.

Agricultural Work In this scene from a German manuscript written about 1190, men and women of different ages are sowing seeds and harvesting grain. All residents of a village, including children, engaged in agricultural tasks. (Rheinisches Landesmuseum, Bonn, Germany/ Bridgeman Images)

Medieval theologians lumped everyone who worked the land into the category of "those who work," but in fact there were many levels of peasants, ranging from slaves to free and sometimes very rich farmers. In western Europe most peasants were serfs, required to stay in the village and perform labor on the lord's land. Serfs were also often obliged to pay fees on common occurrences, such as marriage or inheritance of property.

Serfdom was a hereditary condition. A person born a serf was likely to die a serf, though many serfs did secure their freedom, and the economic revival that began in the eleventh century (see "Towns, Cities, and the Growth of Commercial Interests") allowed some to buy their freedom. Further opportunities for increased personal freedom came when lords organized groups of villagers to migrate to sparsely settled frontier areas or to cut down forests or fill in swamps so that there was more land available for farming. Those who took on this extra work often gained a reduction in traditional manorial obligations and an improvement of their social and legal conditions.

In the Middle Ages most European peasants, free and unfree, lived in family groups in small villages that were part of a manor, the estate of a lord (see "'Feudalism' and Manorialism"). The manor was the basic unit of medieval rural organization and the center of rural life. Within the manors of western and central Europe, villages were made up of small houses for individual families, a church, and perhaps the large house of the lord, surrounded by land farmed by the villagers. Peasant households consisted of one married couple, their children, and perhaps one or two other relatives, such as a grandparent or unmarried aunt. In southern and eastern Europe, extended families were more likely to live in the same household or very near one another. Between one-third and one-half of children died before age five, though many people lived into their sixties.

The peasants' work was typically divided according to gender. Men and boys were responsible for clearing new land, plowing, and caring for large animals; women and girls were responsible for the care of small animals, spinning, and food preparation. Both sexes harvested and planted crops used for food, worked in the vineyards, and harvested and prepared crops needed by the textile industry—flax and plants used for dyeing cloth. Beginning in the eleventh century water mills and windmills aided in some tasks, especially grinding grain, and an increasing use of horses rather than oxen speeded up plowing.

The mainstay of the diet for peasants everywhere—and for all other classes—was bread. Peasants also ate vegetables; animals were too valuable to be used for food on a regular basis, but weaker animals were often slaughtered in the fall, and their meat was preserved with salt and eaten on great feast days such as Christmas and Easter. Ale was the universal drink of common people, and it provided needed calories and some relief from the difficult and monotonous labor that filled people's lives.

The Life and Work of Nobles

The nobility, though a small fraction of the total population, influenced all aspects of medieval culture. Nobles generally paid few taxes, and they had power over the people living on their lands. They maintained order, resolved disputes, and protected their dependents from attacks. They appointed officials who oversaw agricultural production. The liberty and privileges of the noble were inheritable, perpetuated by blood and not by wealth alone.

The nobles' primary obligation was warfare, just as it was for nobles among the Mexica (see "The Aztec Empire" in Chapter 11) and samurai in Japan (see "The Samurai and the Kamakura Shogunate" in Chapter 13). Nobles were also obliged to attend the lord's court on important occasions.

chivalry A code of conduct that was supposed to govern the behavior of a knight.

Originally, most knights focused solely on military skills, but around 1200 a different ideal of knighthood emerged, usually termed **chivalry**. Chivalry was a code of conduct in which fighting to defend the Christian faith and protecting one's countrymen was declared to have a sacred purpose. Other qualities gradually became part of chivalry: bravery, generosity, honor, graciousness, mercy, and eventually gallantry toward women, which came to be called "courtly love." (See "Analyzing the Evidence: Courtly Love Poetry," page 406.) The chivalric ideal—and it was an ideal, not a standard pattern of behavior—created a new standard of masculinity for nobles, in which loyalty and honor remained the most important qualities, but graceful dancing and intelligent conversation were not considered unmanly.

Noblewomen played a large and important role in the functioning of the estate. They were responsible for managing the household's "inner economy"—cooking, brewing, spinning, weaving, and caring for yard animals. When the lord was away for long periods, his wife became the sole manager of the family properties. Often the responsibilities of the estate fell permanently to her if she became a widow.

Towns, Cities, and the Growth of Commercial Interests

Most people continued to live in villages in the Middle Ages, but the rise of towns and the growth of a new business and commercial class were central to Europe's recovery after the disorders of the tenth century. Several factors contributed to this growth: a rise in population; increased agricultural output, which provided an adequate food supply for new town dwellers; and enough peace and political stability to allow merchants to transport and sell goods. In 1100 the largest cities in Europe were most likely Constantinople and Córdoba, each with several hundred thousand residents; only Kaifeng in China was larger. London and Paris were much smaller: Paris had perhaps 50,000 residents and London 20,000.

Towns in western and eastern Europe were generally enclosed by walls, as were towns in China and India. Most towns were first established as trading centers, with a marketplace in the middle, and they were likely to have a mint for coining money and a court for settling disputes. Residents bargained with lords to make the town politically independent, which gave them the right to hold legal courts, select leaders, and set taxes.

Townspeople also tried to acquire liberties, above all personal freedom, for themselves. It gradually developed that an individual who lived in a town for a year and a day, and was accepted by the townspeople, was free of servile obligations and status. Thus serfs who fled their manors for towns and were able to find work and avoid recapture became free of personal labor obligations. In this way the growth of towns contributed to a slow decline of serfdom in western Europe.

Merchants constituted the most powerful group in most towns, and they were often organized into merchant guilds, which prohibited nonmembers from trading, pooled members' risks, monopolized city offices, and controlled the economy of the town. Towns became centers of production as well, and artisans in particular trades formed their own **craft guilds**. Members of the craft guilds determined the quality, quantity, and price of the goods produced and the number of apprentices and journeymen affiliated with the guild. Formal membership in guilds was generally limited to men, but women often worked in guild shops without official membership.

craft guilds Associations of artisans organized to regulate the quality, quantity, and price of the goods produced as well as the number of affiliated apprentices and journeymen.

Artisans generally made and sold products in their own homes, with production taking place on the ground floor. The family lived above the business on the second or third floor. As the business and the family expanded, additional stories were added.

Most medieval towns and cities developed with little planning or attention to sanitation. Horses and oxen, the chief means of transportation and power, dropped tons of dung on the streets every year. It was universal practice in the early towns to dump household waste, both animal and human, into the road in front of one's house. Despite such unpleasant aspects of urban life, people wanted to get into medieval towns because they represented opportunities for economic advancement, social mobility, and improvement in legal status.

The Expansion of Trade and the Commercial Revolution

The growth of towns went hand in hand with a revival of trade as artisans and craftsmen manufactured goods for local and foreign consumption. As in the city-states of East Africa (see "The East African City-States" in Chapter 10), most trade centered in towns and was controlled by merchants. They began to pool their money to finance trading expeditions, sharing the profits and also sharing the risks.

Italian cities, especially Venice, led the West in trade in general and completely dominated trade with Asia and North Africa, becoming much larger urban communities in the process. Merchants from Florence and Milan were also important traders, and they developed new methods of accounting and record keeping that facilitated the movement of goods and money. The towns of Bruges, Ghent, and Ypres in Flanders were leaders in long-distance trade and built up a vast industry in the manufacture of cloth, aided by ready access to wool from England. The availability of raw wool also encouraged the development of cloth manufacture within England itself.

In much of northern Europe, the Hanseatic League (known as the Hansa for short), a mercantile association of towns formed to achieve mutual security and

The Hanseatic League, 1300–1400

Courtly Love Poetry

Whether female or male, troubadour poets celebrated *fin'amor*, a Provençal word for the pure or perfect love a knight was supposed to feel for his lady, which has in English come to be called "courtly love." In courtly love poetry, the writer praises his or her love object, idealizing the beloved and promising loyalty and great deeds. Most of these songs are written by, or from the perspective of, a male lover who is socially beneath his female beloved; her higher status makes her unattainable, so the lover's devotion can remain chaste and pure, rewarded by her handkerchief, or perhaps a kiss, but nothing more.

Scholars generally agree that poetry praising pure and perfect love originated in the Muslim culture of the Iberian Peninsula, where heterosexual romantic love had long been the subject of poems and songs. Spanish Muslim poets sang at the courts of Christian nobles, and Provençal poets picked up their romantic themes. Other aspects of courtly love are hotly debated. Was it simply a literary convention, or did it shape actual behavior? Did it celebrate adultery, or was true courtly love pure (and unrequited)? How should we interpret medieval physicians' reports of people (mostly young men) becoming gravely ill from "lovesickness"? Were there actually "courts of love" in which women judged lovers based on a system of rules? Did courtly love lead to greater respect for women or toward greater misogyny, as desire for a beloved so often ended in frustration?

It is very difficult to know whether courtly love literature influenced the treatment of real women to any great extent, but it did introduce a new ideal of heterosexual romance into Western literature. Courtly love ideals still shape romantic conventions, and often appear in movies, songs, and novels that explore love between people of different social groups.

The following poem was written by Arnaut Daniel, a thirteenth-century troubadour praised by poets from Dante in the thirteenth century to Ezra Pound in the twentieth. Not much is known about him, but his surviving songs capture courtly love conventions perfectly.

I only know the grief that comes to me,
to my love-ridden heart, out of over-loving,
since my will is so firm and whole
that it never parted or grew distant from her
whom I craved at first sight, and afterwards:
and now, in her absence, I tell her burning words;
then, when I see her, I don't know, so much I have to,
    what to say.

To the sight of other women I am blind, deaf to hearing
    them
since her only I see, and hear and heed,
and in that I am surely not a false slanderer,
since heart desires her more than mouth may say;
wherever I may roam through fields and valleys, plains
    and mountains
I shan't find in a single person all those qualities
which God wanted to select and place in her.

I have been in many a good court,
but here by her I find much more to praise:
measure and wit and other good virtues,
beauty and youth, worthy deeds and fair disport;
so well kindness taught and instructed her
that it has rooted every ill manner out of her:
I don't think she lacks anything good.

No joy would be brief or short
coming from her whom I endear to guess [my
    intentions],
otherwise she won't know them from me,
if my heart cannot reveal itself without words,
since even the Rhone [River], when rain swells it,
has no such rush that my heart doesn't stir
a stronger one, weary of love, when I behold her.

Joy and merriment from another woman seems false and
    ill to me,
since no worthy one can compare with her,
and her company is above the others'.
Ah me, if I don't have her, alas, so badly she has taken
    me!
But this grief is amusement, laughter and joy,
since in thinking of her, of her am I gluttonous and
    greedy:
ah me, God, could I ever enjoy her otherwise!

And never, I swear, I have liked game or ball so much,
or anything has given my heart so much joy
as did the one thing that no false slanderer
made public, which is a treasure for me only.
Do I tell too much? Not I, unless she is displeased:
beautiful one, by God, speech and voice
I'd lose ere I say something to annoy you.

And I pray my song does not displease you
since, if you like the music and lyrics,
little cares Arnaut whether the unpleasant ones like
    them as well.

[Far fewer poems by female trobairitz have survived
than by male troubadours, but those that have survived express strong physical and emotional feelings.
The following song was written in the twelfth century
by the Countess of Dia. She was purportedly the wife
of a Provençal nobleman, though biographies of both
troubadours and trobairitz were often made up to fit
the conventions of courtly love, so we don't know for
sure. The words to at least four of her songs have
survived, one of them with the melody, which is very
rare.]

I've suffered great distress
From a knight whom I once owned.
Now, for all time, be it known:
I loved him—yes, to excess. His jilting I've regretted,
Yet his love I never really returned. Now for my sin I
    can only burn:
Dressed, or in my bed.

O if I had that knight to caress
Naked all night in my arms,
He'd be ravished by the charm
Of using, for cushion, my breast. His love I more deeply
    prize
Than Floris did Blancheor's
Take that love, my core, My sense, my life, my eyes!

Lovely lover, gracious, kind,
When will I overcome your fight?
O if I could lie with you one night!
Feel those loving lips on mine! Listen, one thing sets me
    afire:
Here in my husband's place I want you,
If you'll just keep your promise true: Give me
    everything I desire.

QUESTIONS FOR ANALYSIS

1. Both of these songs focus on a beloved who does
   not return the lover's affection. What similarities
   and differences do you see in them?
2. How does courtly love reinforce other aspects of
   medieval society? What aspects of medieval
   society does it contradict?
3. Can you find examples from current popular music
   that parallel the sentiments expressed in these two
   songs?

Sources: First poem used by permission of Leonardo Malcovati, editor and translator of *Prosody in England and Elsewhere: A Comparative Approach* (London: Gival Press, 2006) and online at http://www.trobar.org/troubadours/arnaut_daniel/arnaut_daniel_17.php; three verses from lyrics by the Countess of Dia, often called Beatritz, the Sappho of the Rhone, in *Lyrics of the Middle Ages: An Anthology*, edited and translated by James J. Wilhelm. Reproduced with per-mission of GARLAND PUBLISHING, INCORPORATED, in the format Republish in a book via Copyright Clearance Center.

exclusive trading rights, controlled trade. During the thirteenth century perhaps two hundred cities from Holland to Poland joined the league. In cities such as Bruges and London, Hanseatic merchants secured special concessions exempting them from all tolls and allowing them to trade at local fairs. Hanseatic merchants also established foreign trading centers.

These developments, which began in the eleventh century, added up to what historians of Europe have called the **commercial revolution**, a direct parallel to the economic revolution going on in Song Dynasty China at the same time (see "The Medieval Chinese Economic Revolution" in Chapter 13). In giving the transformation this name, historians point not only to an increase in the sheer volume of trade and in the complexity and sophistication of business procedures but also to the new attitude toward business and making money. Some even detect a "capitalist spirit" in which making a profit was regarded as a good thing in itself.

The commercial revolution created a great deal of new wealth, which did not escape the attention of kings and other rulers. Wealth could be taxed, and through taxation kings could create strong and centralized states. Through the activities of merchants, Europeans again saw products from Africa and Asia in city marketplaces, as they had in Roman times. The commercial revolution also provided the opportunity for thousands of serfs in western Europe to improve their social position.

commercial revolution
The transformation of the economic structure of Europe, beginning in the eleventh century, from a rural, manorial society to a more complex mercantile society.

What were the primary educational and cultural developments in medieval Europe?

Learning and Culture

The towns that became centers of trade and production in the High Middle Ages also developed into cultural and intellectual centers. Trade brought in new ideas as well as merchandise, and in many cities a new type of educational institution—the university—emerged. As universities appeared, so did other cultural advancements, such as new forms of architecture and literature.

Universities and Scholasticism

Since the time of the Carolingian Empire, monasteries and cathedral schools had offered the only formal instruction available. In the eleventh century in Bologna and other Italian cities, wealthy businessmen established municipal schools; in the twelfth century municipal schools in Italy and cathedral schools in France and Spain developed into much larger universities, a transformation parallel to the opening of madrasas in Muslim cities (see "Education and Intellectual Life" in Chapter 9).

The growth of the University of Bologna coincided with a revival of interest in Roman law. The study of Roman law as embodied in Justinian's Code (see "Justinian's Code of Law" in Chapter 8) had never completely died out in the West, but in the eleventh century the discovery of a complete manuscript of the code in a library in northern Italy led scholars to study and teach Roman law intently.

At the Italian city of Salerno, interest in medicine had persisted for centuries. Greek and Muslim physicians there had studied the use of herbs as cures and had experimented with surgery. The twelfth century ushered in a new interest in Greek medical texts and in the work of Arab and Greek doctors. Ideas from this medical literature spread throughout Europe from Salerno and became the basis of training for physicians at other medieval universities. University training gave physicians high social status and allowed them to charge high fees, although their diagnoses and treatments were based on classical theories, not on interactions with patients.

Although medicine and law were important academic disciplines in the Middle Ages, theology was "the queen of sciences." Paris became the place to study theology, and in the first decades of the twelfth century students from all over Europe crowded into the cathedral school of Notre Dame in that city.

University professors were known as "schoolmen" or **Scholastics**. They developed a method of thinking, reasoning, and writing in which questions were raised and authorities cited on both sides of a question. The goal of the Scholastic method was to arrive at definitive answers and to provide a rational explanation for what was believed on faith.

> **Scholastics** Medieval professors who developed a method of thinking, reasoning, and writing in which questions were raised and authorities cited on both sides of a question.

One of the most famous Scholastics was Peter Abelard (1079–1142). Fascinated by logic, Abelard used a method of systematic doubting in his writing and teaching. Abelard was censured by a church council, but he was highly popular with students.

Thirteenth-century Scholastics devoted an enormous amount of time to collecting and organizing knowledge on all topics. These collections were published as summae (SOO-may), or reference books. Thomas Aquinas (1225–1274), a professor at the University of Paris, produced the most famous collection, the *Summa Theologica*, which deals with a vast number of theological questions.

Students lived in privately endowed residential colleges and were considered to be lower-level members of the clergy, so that any student accused of a crime was tried in church, rather than in city, courts. This clerical status, along with widely held ideas about women's lesser intellectual capabilities, meant that university education was restricted to men.

At all universities the standard method of teaching was the lecture. With this method the professor read a passage from the Bible, Justinian's Code, or one of Aristotle's treatises. He then explained and interpreted the passage. Examinations were given after three, four, or five years of study, when the student applied for a degree. If the candidate passed, he was awarded the first, or bachelor's, degree. Further study enabled the graduate to try for the master's and doctor's degrees. Degrees were technically licenses to teach. Most students, however, did not become teachers. They staffed the expanding royal and papal administrations.

Lecture at the University of Paris Students with somewhat dour expressions take notes while the professor lectures from a book, in this illustration from a history of France made about 1400. (Bibliothèque Nationale, Paris, France/Bridgeman Images)

Cathedrals and a New Architectural Style

Religious devotion was expressed through rituals and institutions, but people also wanted permanent visible representations of their piety, and both church and city leaders wanted physical symbols of their wealth and power. These aims found their outlet in the building of tens of thousands of churches, chapels, abbeys, and, most spectacularly, cathedrals.

In the tenth and eleventh centuries cathedrals were built in a style that resembled ancient Roman architecture, with massive walls, rounded stone arches, and small windows—features later labeled Romanesque. In the twelfth century a new artistic and architectural style spread out from central France. It was dubbed **Gothic** by later Renaissance architects. The basic features of Gothic architecture—pointed arches, high ceilings, and exterior supports called flying buttresses that carried much of the weight of the roof—allowed unprecedented interior light. Stained-glass windows were cut into the stone. Between 1180 and 1270 in France alone, eighty cathedrals, about five hundred abbey churches, and tens of thousands of parish churches were constructed in this new style. They are testimony to the deep religious faith and piety of medieval people and also to the civic pride of urban residents, for towns competed with one another to build the largest and most splendid cathedral. Through its statuary, paintings, and stained-glass windows, the cathedral was designed to teach the people the doctrines of Christian faith through visual images, though these also often showed scenes from the lives of the artisans and merchants who paid for them.

Gothic The term for the architectural and artistic style that began in Europe in the twelfth century and featured pointed arches, high ceilings, and flying buttresses.

Notre Dame Cathedral, Paris, Begun 1163 This view offers a fine example of the twin towers (left), the spire, the great rose window over the south portal (center), and the flying buttresses that support the walls and the vaults. Like hundreds of other churches in medieval Europe, it was dedicated to the Virgin Mary. With a spire rising more than 300 feet, Notre Dame was the tallest building in Europe at the time of its construction. (David R. Frazier/Science Source)

Vernacular Literature and Drama

Latin was the language used in university education, scholarly writing, and works of literature. By the High Middle Ages, however, no one spoke Latin as his or her first language. The barbarian invasions, the mixture of peoples, and the usual changes in language that occurred over time resulted in a variety of local dialects that blended words and linguistic forms in various ways.

In the High Middle Ages, some authors departed from tradition and began to write in their local dialect, that is, in the everyday language of their region, which linguistic historians call the vernacular. This new **vernacular literature** gradually transformed some local dialects into literary languages, such as French, German, Italian, and English, while other local dialects, such as Breton and Bavarian, remained means of oral communication.

Stories and songs in the vernacular were composed and performed at the courts of nobles and rulers. In southern Europe, especially in Provence in southern France, poets who called themselves troubadours wrote and sang lyric verses celebrating love, desire, beauty, and gallantry. Troubadours included a few women, with their poetry often chiding knights who did not live up to the ideal. (See "Analyzing the Evidence: Courtly Love Poetry," page 406.) The songs of the troubadours were widely imitated in Italy, England, and Germany, so they spurred the development of vernacular literature there as well. Drama, derived from the church's liturgy, also emerged as a distinct art form. Actors performed plays based on biblical themes and on the lives of the saints; these dramas were presented in the towns, first in churches and then at the marketplace. By combining comical farce based on ordinary life with serious religious scenes, plays gave ordinary people an opportunity to identify with religious figures and think about their faith.

Beginning in the fourteenth century a variety of evidence attests to the increasing literacy of laypeople. Wills and inventories reveal that many people, not just nobles, possessed books—mainly devotional texts, but also romances, manuals on manners and etiquette, histories, and sometimes legal and philosophical texts. The spread of literacy represents a response to the needs of an increasingly complex society.

vernacular literature
Literature written in the everyday language of a region rather than Latin; this included French, German, Italian, and English.

Crises of the Later Middle Ages

Why have the later Middle Ages been seen as a time of calamity and crisis?

Between 1300 and 1450 Europeans experienced a series of shocks: climate change, economic decline, plague, war, social upheaval, and increased crime and violence. Death and preoccupation with death made the fourteenth century one of the most wrenching periods of history in Europe and western Asia.

The Great Famine and the Black Death

In the first half of the fourteenth century the Northern Hemisphere experienced a series of climate changes, especially the beginning of a period of colder and wetter weather that historical geographers label the "little ice age." Its effects were dramatic and disastrous. Population had steadily increased in the twelfth and thirteenth centuries, but with colder weather, poor harvests led to scarcity and starvation. The costs of grain, livestock, and dairy products rose sharply. Almost all of northern Europe suffered a terrible famine between 1315 and 1322, with dire social consequences: peasants were forced to sell or mortgage their lands for money to buy food, and the number of homeless people greatly increased, as did petty crime. An undernourished

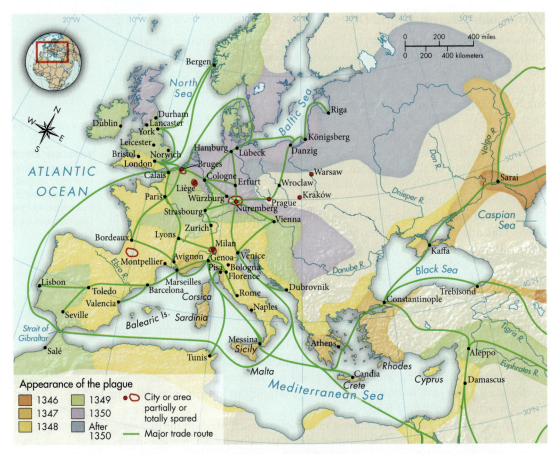

MAP 14.3 The Course of the Black Death in Fourteenth-Century Europe The plague followed trade routes as it spread into and across Europe. A few cities that took strict quarantine measures were spared.

Black Death The plague that first struck Europe in 1347, killing perhaps one-third of the population.

population was dealt a further blow in 1347 in the form of a virulent new disease, later called the **Black Death** (Map 14.3). The symptoms of this disease were first described in 1331 in southwestern China, then part of the Mongol Empire (see "The Spread of Disease, Goods, and Ideas" in Chapter 12). From there it spread across Central Asia by way of Mongol armies and merchant caravans, arriving in the ports of the Black Sea by the 1340s. It then spread to Constantinople and Alexandria, and within a year it was in Mecca, Damascus, Tunis, Genoa, and Venice. From Italy it traveled farther in all directions, in several waves.

DNA evidence taken from the tooth sockets of skeletons in mass graves in England, France, and the Netherlands indicates that the disease that spread in the fourteenth century was the bubonic plague, caused by a variant of the bacillus *Yersinia pestis*, the same bacillus that had caused the Justinian Plague in the sixth century (see "The Byzantine Empire" in Chapter 8). The disease normally afflicts rats. Fleas living on the infected rats drink their blood and pass the bacteria that cause the plague on to the next rat they bite. Usually the disease is limited to rats and other rodents, but at certain points in history the fleas have jumped from their rodent hosts to humans and other animals. The disease had dreadful effects on the body, including growths in the armpit, groin, or neck; black spots or blotches caused by bleeding under the skin; and violent coughing and spitting blood, which were followed by death in two or three days.

At the time, most people believed that the Black Death was caused by poisons or by "corrupted air" that carried the disease from place to place. They sought to keep poisons from entering the body by smelling or ingesting strong-smelling herbs, and they tried to remove the poisons through bloodletting. They also prayed and did penance. Anxiety and fears about the plague caused people to look for scapegoats, and they found them in the Jews, who they believed had poisoned the wells of Christian communities and thereby infected the drinking water. This charge led to the murder of thousands of Jews across Europe.

Historians estimate that across Europe the plague killed about one-third of the population, with some places suffering even higher losses. Of a total English population of perhaps 4.2 million, probably 1.4 million died of the Black Death in its several visits. In Italy densely populated cities endured incredible losses. Florence lost between one-half and two-thirds of its population when the plague visited in 1348. The disease recurred intermittently in the 1360s and 1370s and reappeared many times, as late as the early 1700s in Europe.

In the short term the economic effects of the plague were severe because the death of many peasants disrupted food production. But in the long term the dramatic decline in population eased pressure on the land, and wages and per capita wealth rose for those who survived. The psychological consequences of the plague were profound. (See "Global Viewpoints: Italian and English Views of the Plague," page 414.) Some people sought release in wild living, while others turned to the severest forms of asceticism and frenzied religious fervor.

Procession of Flagellants In this manuscript illumination from 1349, shirtless flagellants, men and women who whipped and scourged themselves as penance for their and society's sins, walk through the Flemish city of Tournai, which had just been struck by the plague. Many people believed that the Black Death was God's punishment for humanity's wickedness. (Private Collection/The Bridgeman Art Library)

Italian and English Views of the Plague

Eyewitness commentators on the plague include the Italian writer Giovanni Boccaccio (1313–1375), who portrayed the course of the disease in Florence in the preface to his book of tales, *The Decameron*, and the English monastic chronicler Henry Knighton (d. 1396), who described the effects of the plague on English towns and villages in his four-volume chronicle of English history.

Giovanni Boccaccio

■ Against this pestilence no human wisdom or fore-sight was of any avail. . . . Men and women in great numbers abandoned their city, their houses, their farms, their relatives, and their possessions and sought other places, going at least as far away as the Florentine countryside—as if the wrath of God could not pursue them with this pestilence wherever they went but would only strike those it found within the walls of the city! . . . Almost no one cared for his neighbor, and relatives hardly ever visited one another—they stayed far apart. This disaster had struck such fear into the hearts of men and women that brother abandoned brother, uncle abandoned nephew, sister left brother, and very often wife abandoned husband, and—even worse, almost unbelievable—fathers and mothers neglected to tend and care for their children as if they were not their own. . . . So many corpses would arrive in front of a church every day and at every hour that the amount of holy ground for burials was certainly insufficient for the ancient custom of giving each body its individual place; when all the graves were full, huge trenches were dug in all the cemeteries of the churches and into them the new arrivals were dumped by the hundreds. . . . Oh how many great palaces, beautiful homes and noble dwellings, once filled with families, gentlemen, and ladies, were now emptied, down to the last servant!

Henry Knighton

■ Then that most grievous pestilence penetrated the coastal regions [of England] by way of Southampton, and came to Bristol, and people died as if the whole strength of the city were seized by sudden death. For there were few who lay in their beds more than three days or two and half days; then that savage death snatched them about the second day. In Leicester, in the little parish of St. Leonard, more than three hundred and eighty died; in the parish of Holy Cross, more than four hundred. . . . And so in each parish, they died in great numbers. . . . At the same time, there was so great a lack of priests everywhere that many churches had no divine services. . . . One could hardly hire a chaplain to minister to the church for less than ten marks. . . . Meanwhile, the king ordered that in every county of the kingdom, reapers and other labourers should not receive more than they were accustomed to receive, under the penalty provided in the statute, and he renewed the statute at this time. The labourers, how-ever, were so arrogant and hostile that they did not heed the king's command, but if anyone wished to hire them, he had to pay them what they wanted, and either lose his fruits and crops or satisfy the arrogant and greedy desire of the labourers as they wished. . . . Similarly, those who received day-work from their tenants throughout the year, as is usual from serfs, had to release them and to remit such service. They either had to excuse them entirely or had to fix them in a laxer manner at a small rent, lest very great and irreparable damage be done to the buildings and the land everywhere remain uncultivated.

QUESTIONS FOR ANALYSIS

1. How did the residents of Florence respond to the plague, as described by Boccaccio?
2. What were some of the effects of the plague in England, as described by Knighton?
3. How might the fact that Boccaccio was writing in an urban setting and Knighton was writing from a rural monastery that owned a large amount of land have shaped their perspectives?

Sources: Giovanni Boccaccio, *The Decameron*, trans. Mark Musa and Peter Bondanella (New York: W. W. Norton, 1982), pp. 7, 9, 12. Copyright © 1982 by Mark Musa and Peter Bondanella. Used by permission of W. W. Norton & Company, Inc.; Henry Knighton, *Chronicon Henrici Knighton*, in *The Portable Medieval Reader*, ed. James Bruce Ross and Mary Martin McLaughlin (New York: Viking, 1949), pp. 218, 220, 222.

The Hundred Years' War

While the plague ravaged populations in Asia, North Africa, and Europe, a long international war in western Europe added further death and destruction. England and France had engaged in sporadic military hostilities from the time of the Norman Conquest in 1066 (see "The Restoration of Order"), and in the middle of the fourteenth century these became more intense. From 1337 to 1453 the two countries intermittently fought one another in what was the longest war in European history, ultimately dubbed the Hundred Years' War, though it actually lasted 116 years.

The Hundred Years' War had a number of causes. Both England and France claimed the duchy of Aquitaine in southwestern France, and the English king Edward III argued that, as the grandson of an earlier French king, he should have rightfully inherited the French throne. Nobles in provinces on the borders of France who were worried about the growing power of the French king supported Edward, as did wealthy wool merchants and clothmakers in Flanders who depended on English wool. The governments of both England and France promised wealth and glory to those who fought, and each country portrayed the other as evil.

The war, fought almost entirely in France, consisted mainly of a series of random sieges and raids. During the war's early stages, England was successful, primarily through the use of longbows fired by well-trained foot soldiers against mounted knights and, after 1375, by early cannon. By 1419 the English had advanced to the walls of Paris. But the French cause was not lost. Though England scored the initial victories, France won the war.

The ultimate French success rests heavily on the actions of Joan, an obscure French peasant girl whose vision and military leadership revived French fortunes and led to victory. Born in 1412 to well-to-do peasants, Joan grew up in a pious household. During adolescence she began to hear voices, which she later said belonged to Saint Michael, Saint Catherine, and Saint Margaret. In 1428 these voices told her that the dauphin of France—Charles VII, who was uncrowned as king because of the English occupation—had to be crowned and the English expelled from France. Joan went to the French court and secured the support of the dauphin to travel, dressed as a knight, with the French army to the besieged city of Orléans.

At Orléans, Joan inspired and led French attacks, and the English retreated. As a result of her successes, Charles made Joan co-commander of the entire army, and she led it to a string of military victories in the summer of 1429. Two months after the victory at Orléans, Charles VII was crowned king at Reims.

Suit of Armor This fifteenth-century suit of Italian armor protected its wearer, but its weight made movement difficult. Both English and French mounted knights wore full armor at the beginning of the Hundred Years' War, but by the end they wore only breastplates and helmets, which protected their vital organs but allowed greater mobility. This suit has been so well preserved that it was most likely never used in battle; it may have been made for ceremonial purposes.

(Armor, Italy, ca. 1400 and later. Steel, brass, textile. Bashford Dean Memorial Collection. Gift of Helen Fahnestock, in memory of her father, Harris C. Fahnestock, 1929 [29.154.3]/The Metropolitan Museum of Art, New York/Image copyright © The Metropolitan Museum of Art/Image source: Art Resource, NY)

Joan and the French army continued their fight against the English. In 1430 England's allies, the Burgundians, captured Joan and sold her to the English, and the French did not intervene. The English wanted Joan eliminated for obvious political reasons, but the primary charge against her was heresy, and the trial was conducted by church authorities. She was interrogated about the angelic voices and about why she wore men's clothing. She apparently answered skillfully, but in 1431 she was condemned as a heretic and burned at the stake in the marketplace at Rouen. The French army continued its victories without her, and demands for an end to the war increased among the English, who were growing tired of the mounting loss of life and the flow of money into a seemingly bottomless pit. Slowly the French reconquered Normandy and finally ejected the English from Aquitaine. At the war's end in 1453, only the town of Calais remained in English hands.

The long war had a profound impact on the two countries. In England and France the war promoted nationalism. It led to technological experimentation, especially with gunpowder weaponry, whose firepower made the protective walls of stone castles obsolete. The war also stimulated the development of the English Parliament. Edward III's constant need for money to pay for the war compelled him to summon it many times, and its representatives slowly built up their powers.

Challenges to the Christian Church

In times of crisis or disaster people of all faiths have sought the consolation of religion, but in the fourteenth century the official Western Christian Church offered little solace. While local clergy eased the suffering of many, a dispute over who was the legitimate pope weakened the church as an institution. In 1309 pressure by the French monarchy led the pope to move his permanent residence to Avignon in southern France. This marked the start of seven successive papacies in Avignon. Not surprising, all these popes were French—a matter of controversy among church followers outside France. Also, the popes largely concentrated on bureaucratic and financial matters to the exclusion of spiritual objectives.

In 1376 one of the French popes returned to Rome, and when he died there several years later Roman citizens demanded an Italian pope who would remain in Rome. The cardinals elected Urban VI, but soon regretted their decision. The cardinals slipped away from Rome and declared Urban's election invalid because it had come about under threats from the Roman mob. They elected a French cardinal who took the name Clement VII (pontificate 1378–1394) and set himself up at Avignon in opposition to Urban. There were thus two popes, a situation that was later termed the Great Schism.

The powers of Europe aligned themselves with Urban or Clement along strictly political lines. France recognized the Frenchman, Clement; England recognized Urban. The rest of Europe lined up behind one or the other. In all European countries the common people were thoroughly confused about which pope was legitimate. In the end the schism weakened the religious faith of many Christians and brought church leadership into serious disrepute.

A first attempt to heal the schism led to the installation of a third pope and a threefold split, but finally a church council meeting at Constance (1414–1418) successfully deposed the three schismatic popes and elected a new leader, who took the name Martin V (pontificate 1417–1431). In the later fifteenth century the papacy concentrated on building up its wealth and political power

■ Allegiance to Rome
■ Allegiance to Avignon
■ Official allegiance to
   Rome but with shifting
   local allegiances

The Great Schism, 1378–1417

in Italy rather than on the concerns of the whole church. As a result, many people decided that they would need to rely on their own prayers and pious actions rather than on the institutional church for their salvation.

The primary challenge facing the Orthodox Church was the expansion of the Turks. In the fourteenth century the Ottoman Turks, who were Sunni Muslim, expanded their rule beyond Anatolia to conquer most of the Balkans, defeating Christian armies (see Map 9.2). They besieged Constantinople many times, and in 1453 were successful, ending the Byzantine Empire. Christianity was no longer the state religion, but the patriarchate of Constantinople actually became more powerful, as the patriarchs were given civil and religious authority over all Christians in the expanding Ottoman Empire. The official religion was Islam, but Christians and Jews were largely free to practice their own religion; they paid higher taxes, however, so there were advantages to converting. The Ottoman Empire was mixed in terms of religion, language, and ethnicity and became a haven for Muslims and Jews fleeing discrimination that resulted from the reconquista in the Iberian Peninsula (see "The Expansion of Western and Eastern Christianity").

Peasant and Urban Revolts

The difficult conditions of the fourteenth and fifteenth centuries spurred a wave of peasant and urban revolts across Europe. In 1358, when French taxation for the Hundred Years' War fell heavily on the poor, the frustrations of the French peasantry exploded in a massive uprising called the Jacquerie (zhah-kuh-REE). Adding to the anger over taxes was the toll taken by the plague and by the famine that had struck some areas. Artisans, small merchants, and parish priests joined the peasants, and residents of both urban and rural areas committed terrible destruction. For several weeks the nobles were on the defensive, until the upper class united to repress the revolt with merciless ferocity.

Taxes and other grievances also led to the 1381 English Peasants' Revolt, involving tens of thousands of people. The Black Death had dramatically reduced the supply of labor, and peasants had demanded higher wages and fewer manorial obligations. Parliament countered with a law freezing wages and binding workers to their manors. The atmosphere of discontent was further enhanced by popular preachers who proclaimed that great disparities between rich and poor went against Christ's teachings. Moreover, decades of aristocratic violence, much of it perpetrated against the weak peasantry, had bred hostility and bitterness.

In 1380 Parliament imposed a poll tax on all citizens to fund the Hundred Years' War. This tax imposed a greater burden on the poor than on wealthier citizens, and it sparked revolt. The boy-king Richard II (r. 1377–1399) met the leaders of the revolt, agreed to charters ensuring the peasants' freedom, tricked them with false promises, and then proceeded to crush the uprising with terrible ferocity. The nobility tried to use this defeat to restore the labor obligations of serfdom, but they were not successful, and the conversion to money rents continued. In Flanders, France, and England peasant revolts often blended with conflicts involving workers in cities. Unrest also occurred in Italian, Spanish, and German cities. In Florence in 1378 the *ciompi*, or poor propertyless wool workers, revolted and briefly shared government of the city with wealthier artisans and merchants. Rebellions and uprisings everywhere revealed deep peasant and worker frustration with the socioeconomic conditions of the time.

Chapter Summary

Invasions by Vikings, Magyars, and Muslims, along with civil wars, created instability in the ninth and tenth centuries. Local nobles became the strongest powers against external threats, establishing a form of decentralized government later known as feudalism. By the twelfth century rulers in some parts of Europe had reasserted authority and were beginning to develop new institutions of government and legal codes that enabled them to assert power over lesser lords and the general population. The papacy also consolidated its power, though these moves were sometimes challenged by kings and emperors. Monasteries continued to be important places for learning and devotion, and new religious orders were founded. A papal call to retake the holy city of Jerusalem led to the Crusades.

The vast majority of medieval Europeans were peasants who lived in small villages and worked their own and their lord's land. Nobles were a tiny fraction of the total population, but they exerted great power over all aspects of life. Medieval towns and cities grew initially as trading centers and then became centers of production.

Towns also developed into cultural and intellectual centers, as trade brought in new ideas as well as merchandise. Universities offered courses of study based on classical models, and townspeople built churches and cathedrals as symbols of their Christian faith and their civic pride. New types of vernacular literature arose in which poems, songs, and stories were written down in local dialects.

In the fourteenth century a worsening climate brought poor harvests, which contributed to an international economic depression and fostered disease. The Black Death caused enormous population losses and social, psychological, and economic consequences. Additional difficulties included the Hundred Years' War, a schism among rival popes that weakened the Western Christian Church, and peasant and worker frustrations that exploded into uprisings.

CONNECTIONS

The Middle Ages continues to fascinate us today. We go to medieval fairs; visit castle-themed hotels; watch movies about knights and their conquests; play video games in which we become warriors, trolls, or sorcerers; and read stories with themes of great quests set in the Middle Ages. Characters from other parts of the world often heighten the exoticism: a Muslim soldier joins the fight against a common enemy, a Persian princess rescues the hero and his sidekick, a Buddhist monk teaches martial arts techniques. These characters from outside Europe are fictional, but they also represent aspects of reality because medieval Europe was not isolated, and political and social structures similar to those in western and eastern Europe developed elsewhere.

In reality few of us would probably want to live in the real Middle Ages, when most people worked in the fields all day and even wealthy lords lived in damp and drafty castles. We do not really want to return to a time when one-third to one-half of all children died before age five and alcohol was the only real pain reliever. But the contemporary appeal of the Middle Ages is an interesting phenomenon, particularly because it stands in such sharp contrast to the attitude of educated Europeans who lived in the centuries immediately afterward. They were the ones who dubbed the period "middle." They saw their own era as the one to be celebrated, and the Middle Ages as best forgotten.

CHAPTER 14   Review and Explore

Identify Key Terms

Identify and explain the significance of each item below.

vassal (p. 392)   **heresy** (p. 396)   **commercial revolution** (p. 408)

fief (p. 392)   **reconquista** (p. 399)   **Scholastics** (p. 409)

feudalism (p. 392)   **Crusades** (p. 399)   **Gothic** (p. 410)

manorialism (p. 392)   **chivalry** (p. 404)   **vernacular literature** (p. 411)

serf (p. 392)   **craft guilds** (p. 405)   **Black Death** (p. 412)

Review the Main Ideas

Answer the focus questions from each section of the chapter.

1. How did medieval rulers restore order and centralize political power? (p. 390)

2. How did the Christian Church enhance its power and create new institutions and religious practices? (p. 394)

3. What were the causes, course, and consequences of the Crusades? (p. 399)

4. How did the lives of common people, nobles, and townspeople differ, and what new commercial developments increased wealth? (p. 402)

5. What were the primary educational and cultural developments in medieval Europe? (p. 408)

6. Why have the later Middle Ages been seen as a time of calamity and crisis? (p. 411)

Make Comparisons and Connections

Analyze the larger developments and continuities within and across chapters.

1. What similarities and differences do you see between the institutions and laws established by medieval European rulers discussed in this chapter and those of the Roman (Chapter 6), Byzantine (Chapter 8), and Chinese (Chapter 13) emperors?

2. What factors over the centuries enabled the Christian Church (Chapters 6, 8, 14) to become the most powerful and wealthy institution in Europe, and what problems did this create?

3. How would you compare the role of trade in economic development in the Islamic world (Chapter 9), Africa (Chapter 10), Southeast Asia (Chapter 12), China (Chapter 13), and Europe in the period from 800 to 1400?

TIMELINE

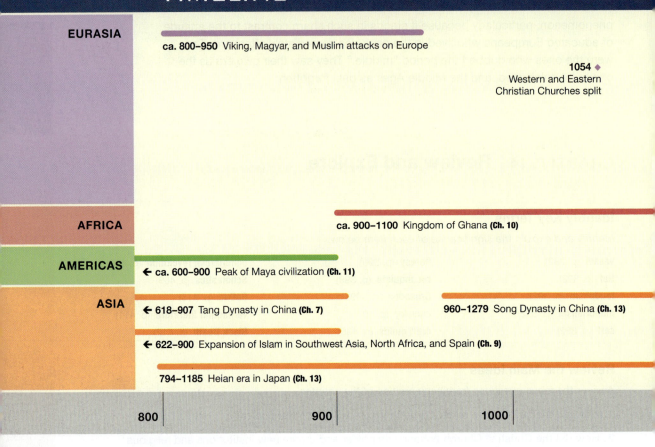

EURASIA

ca. 800–950 Viking, Magyar, and Muslim attacks on Europe

1054 ◆
Western and Eastern
Christian Churches split

AFRICA

ca. 900–1100 Kingdom of Ghana **(Ch. 10)**

AMERICAS

← ca. 600–900 Peak of Maya civilization **(Ch. 11)**

ASIA

← 618–907 Tang Dynasty in China **(Ch. 7)**

960–1279 Song Dynasty in China **(Ch. 13)**

← 622–900 Expansion of Islam in Southwest Asia, North Africa, and Spain **(Ch. 9)**

794–1185 Heian era in Japan **(Ch. 13)**

800　　　　　　900　　　　　　1000

Suggested Resources

BOOKS

Allmand, Christopher. *The Hundred Years War: England and France at War, ca. 1300–1450*, rev. ed. 2005. Designed for students; examines the war from political, military, social, and economic perspectives.

Bennett, Judith M. *A Medieval Life: Cecelia Penifader of Brigstock, c. 1297–1344*. 1998. An excellent brief introduction to all aspects of medieval village life from the perspective of one woman; designed for students.

Epstein, Steven A. *An Economic and Social History of Later Medieval Europe, 1000–1500*. 2009. Examines the most important themes in European social and economic history, with a wide geographic sweep.

Glick, Leonard B. *Abraham's Heirs: Jews and Christians in Medieval Europe*. 1999. Provides information on many aspects of Jewish life and Jewish-Christian relations.

Herlihy, David. *The Black Death and the Transformation of the West*, 2d ed. 1997. A fine treatment of the causes and consequences of the disease that remains the best starting point for study of the epidemic.

Herrin, Judith. *Byzantium: The Surprising Life of a Medieval Empire*. 2008. Portrays the Byzantine Empire as tradition based yet dynamic and discusses its significance for today.

Kaeuper, Richard W. *Chivalry and Violence in Medieval Europe*. 2006. Examines the role chivalry played in promoting violent disorder.

Madden, Thomas. *The New Concise History of the Crusades*. 2005. A highly readable brief survey by the pre-eminent American scholar of the Crusades.

Shahar, Shulamit. *The Fourth Estate: A History of Women in the Middle Ages*, 2d ed. 2003. Analyzes attitudes toward women and provides information on the lives of a variety of women, including nuns, peasants, noblewomen, and townswomen.

Shinners, John. *Medieval Popular Religion, 1000–1500*, 2d ed. 2006. An excellent collection of a wide

1095–1270 Crusades

1309–1376
Papacy in Avignon

1378–1417
Great Schism

1215 Magna Carta

ca. 1337–1453 Hundred Years' War

1358 ♦
Jacquerie peasant uprising in France

♦ **1381** English
Peasants' Revolt

1180–1270 Height of construction of cathedrals in France

♦ **1347** Black Death arrives
in Europe

1453 ♦
Ottomans conquer Constantinople;
end of the Byzantine Empire

ca. 1200–1350 Mongol Empire at the height of its power **(Ch. 12)**

| 1100 | 1200 | 1300 | 1400 |

variety of sources that provide evidence about the beliefs and practices of ordinary Christians.

Spufford, Peter. *Power and Profit: The Merchant in Medieval Europe.* 2003. A comprehensive history of medieval commerce, designed for general readers; includes many illustrations.

Winroth, Anders. *The Age of the Vikings.* 2014. An insightful look at all aspects of Viking society: raiding, trade, religion, art, poetry, and life at home in early medieval Scandinavia.

DOCUMENTARIES

Battle Castle (Parallax, 2012). A six-part interactive documentary that examines sieges and battles involving six formidable castles. Reflects high production values and excellent scholarship, and is accompanied by a website and a computer game.

Terry Jones' Medieval Lives (BBC, 2004). A series that focuses on the real experiences of medieval people often portrayed stereotypically, including the peasant, the damsel, the minstrel, the knight, and the outlaw.

FEATURE FILMS

The Lion in Winter (Anthony Harvey, 1968) (Andrey Konchalovskiy, 2003). Two award-winning film versions of the same play, centering on the intense and hostile relationships among Henry II, his wife Eleanor of Aquitaine, and their sons. The 1968 version stars Katharine Hepburn and Peter O'Toole, and the 2003 version stars Glenn Close and Patrick Stewart.

Monty Python and the Holy Grail (Terry Gilliam and Terry Jones, 1975). A spoof of the King Arthur legend and a send-up of popular views of the Middle Ages. The basis for Eric Idle's 2005 Tony Award–winning musical *Spamalot.*

WEBSITE

Medievalists.net. This medieval-oriented blog provides news, articles, videos, reviews, and general information about the Middle Ages and medieval society. **www.medievalists.net**

15

Europe in the Renaissance and Reformation

1350–1600

While disease, famine, and war marked the fourteenth century in much of Europe, the era also witnessed the beginnings of remarkable changes in many aspects of intellectual and cultural life. First in Italy and then elsewhere, artists and writers thought that they were living in a new golden age, later termed the Renaissance, French for "rebirth." The word *Renaissance* was used initially to describe art that seemed to recapture, or perhaps even surpass, the glories of the classical past and then came to be used for many aspects of life of the period. The new attitude diffused slowly out of Italy, with the result that the Renaissance "happened" at different times in different parts of Europe. It shaped the lives of Europe's educated elites, although families, kin networks, religious beliefs, and the rhythms of the agricultural year still remained important.

Religious reformers carried out even more dramatic changes. Calls for reform of the Christian Church began very early in its history and continued throughout the Middle Ages. In the sixteenth century these calls gained wide acceptance, due not only to religious issues and problems within the church but also to political and social factors. In a movement termed the Protestant Reformation, Western Christianity broke into many divisions, a situation that continues today. The Renaissance and the Reformation were very different types of movements, but both looked back to a time people regarded as purer and better than their own, and both offered opportunities for strong individuals to shape their world in unexpected ways. Both have also been seen as key elements in the creation of the "modern" world.

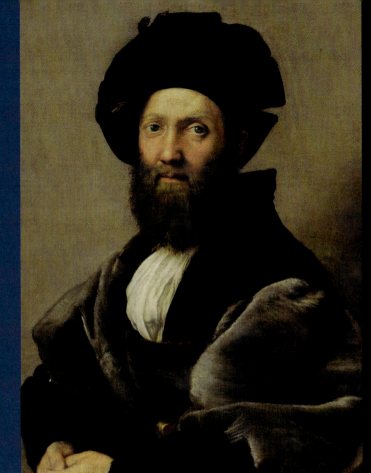

Portrait of Baldassare Castiglione

The author and courtier Baldassare Castiglione directs his calm gaze toward the viewer in this portrait by the renowned Italian Renaissance artist Raphael. Individual portraits like this one expressed the ideals of the Renaissance: elegance, balance, proportion, and self-awareness.

Louvre, Paris, France/Bridgeman Images

CHAPTER PREVIEW

RENAISSANCE CULTURE
What were the major cultural developments of the Renaissance?

SOCIAL HIERARCHIES
What were the key social hierarchies in Renaissance Europe, and how did these hierarchies shape people's lives?

POLITICS AND THE STATE IN THE RENAISSANCE
How did the nation-states of western Europe evolve in this period?

THE PROTESTANT REFORMATION
What were the central ideas of Protestant reformers, and why were they appealing to various groups across Europe?

THE CATHOLIC REFORMATION
How did the Catholic Church respond to the new religious situation?

RELIGIOUS VIOLENCE
What were the causes and consequences of religious violence, including riots, wars, and witch-hunts?

423

What were the major cultural developments of the Renaissance?

Renaissance A French word meaning "rebirth," used to describe a cultural movement that began in fourteenth-century Italy and looked back to the classical past.

patronage Financial support of writers and artists by cities, groups, and individuals, often to produce specific works or works in specific styles.

Italian States, 1494

Renaissance Culture

The **Renaissance** (ca. 1350–1520) was characterized by self-conscious awareness among fourteenth- and fifteenth-century Italians, particularly scholars and writers known as humanists, that they were living in a new era. Their ideas influenced education and were spread through the new technology of the printing press. Interest in the classical past and in the individual also shaped Renaissance art in terms of style and subject matter.

Wealth and Power in Renaissance Italy

Economic growth laid the material basis for the Italian Renaissance and its cultural achievements. Ambitious merchants gained political power to match their economic power and then used their money to buy luxuries and hire talent in a **patronage** system. Through this system, cities, groups, and individuals commissioned writers and artists to produce specific works or works in specific styles. Thus economics, politics, and culture were interconnected.

The Renaissance began in the northern Italian city of Florence, which possessed enormous wealth as a consequence of its domination of European banking. Banking profits allowed elite families to control the city's politics and culture. Although Florence was officially a republic, starting in 1434 the great Medici (MEH-duh-chee) banking family held power almost continually until 1737. They supported an academy for scholars and a host of painters, sculptors, poets, and architects. (See "Individuals in Society: Cosimo and Lorenzo de' Medici," page 426.)

In other Italian cities as well, wealthy merchants and bankers built magnificent palaces and became patrons of the arts, hiring not only architects to design and build these palaces but also artists to fill them with paintings and sculptures, and musicians and composers to fill them with music. Attractions like these appealed to the rich, social-climbing residents of Venice, Florence, Genoa, and Rome, who came to see life more as an opportunity for enjoyment than as a painful pilgrimage to Heaven.

This cultural flowering took place amid political turmoil. In the fifteenth century five powers dominated the Italian peninsula: Venice, Milan, Florence, the Papal States, and the kingdom of Naples. These powers competed furiously for territory and tried to extend their authority over smaller city-states. Whenever one Italian state appeared to gain a predominant position within the peninsula, other states combined to establish a balance of power against the threat, thereby preventing long-term political consolidation.

This division facilitated outside invasions of Italy. These began in 1494 as Italy became the focus of international ambitions and the battleground of foreign armies, and Italian cities suffered severely from continual warfare for decades. Thus the failure of the city-states to form some type of federal system — or at least to establish a common foreign policy — led to centuries of subjugation by outside invaders. Italy was not to achieve unification until 1870.

The Rise of Humanism

The Renaissance was a self-conscious intellectual movement. The realization that something new and unique was happening first came to writers in the fourteenth century, especially to the Italian poet and humanist Francesco Petrarch (frahn-CHEH-skoh PEH-trahrk) (1304–1374). Along with many of his contemporaries, Petrarch sought to reconnect with the classical past, and he believed that such efforts were bringing on a new golden age of intellectual achievement.

Petrarch and other poets, writers, and artists showed a deep interest both in the physical remains of the Roman Empire and in classical Latin texts. The study of Latin classics became known as the *studia humanitates*, usually translated as "liberal studies" or the "liberal arts." People who advocated it were known as *humanists*, and their program as **humanism**. Like all programs of study, humanism contained an implicit philosophy: that human nature and achievements were worthy of contemplation. Humanists did not reject religion; instead they sought to synthesize Christian and classical teachings, pointing out the harmony between them.

Humanists and other Renaissance thinkers emphasized individual achievement. They were especially interested in individuals who had risen above their background to become brilliant, powerful, or unique. Such individuals had the admirable quality of *virtù* (vir-TOO), which is not virtue in the sense of moral goodness, but the ability to shape the world around them according to their will. Humanists thought that their recommended course of study in the classics would provide essential skills for all those who would take on this challenge. Just as Confucian officials did in Song China, they also taught that taking an active role in the world and working for the common good should be the aim of all educated individuals.

Humanists put their educational ideas into practice. They opened schools and academies in which pupils began with Latin grammar and rhetoric, went on to study Roman history and political philosophy, and then learned Greek in order to study Greek literature and philosophy. These classics, humanists taught, would provide models of how to write clearly, argue effectively, and speak persuasively. Gradually humanist education became the basis for intermediate and advanced education for well-to-do urban boys and men.

Humanists disagreed about education for women. Many saw the value of exposing women to classical models of moral behavior and reasoning, but they also wondered whether a program of study that emphasized eloquence and action was proper for women, whose sphere was generally understood to be private and domestic. Through tutors or programs of self-study a few women did become educated in the classics.

Humanists looked to the classical past for political as well as literary models. The best-known political theorist of this era was Niccolò Machiavelli (nih-KOH-loh mah-kee-ah-VEH-lee) (1469–1527), who worked as an official for the city of Florence until he was ousted in a power struggle. He spent the rest of his life writing, and his most famous work is the political treatise *The Prince* (1513). Using the examples of classical and contemporary rulers, *The Prince* argues that the function of a ruler (or a government) is to preserve order and security. To preserve the state, a ruler should use whatever means necessary — brutality, lying, manipulation — but he should not do anything that would make the populace turn against him. *The Prince* is often seen as the first modern guide to politics in the West, though Machiavelli was denounced for writing it, and people later came to use the word *Machiavellian* to mean cunning and ruthless. Machiavelli put a new spin on the Renaissance search for perfection, arguing that ideals needed to be measured in the cold light of the real world.

humanism A program of study designed by Italians that emphasized the critical study of Latin and Greek literature with the goal of understanding human nature.

Cosimo and Lorenzo de' Medici

THE RENAISSANCE IS OFTEN DESCRIBED AS a time of growing individualism, a development evidenced in the era's many personal portraits and individual biographies. But a person's family also remained important, even for those at the very top of society. The Medici of Florence were one of Europe's wealthiest families and used their money to influence politics and culture. The Medici got their start in banking in the late fourteenth century, with smart bets on what would happen politically in turbulent Italy and the adoption of the best new business practices. By the early fifteenth century the Medici bank had branches in Rome, Pisa, London, and other important European cities, and it served as the pope's primary banker.

Cosimo (1389–1464) and his grandson Lorenzo (1449–1492) were the most influential Medici. Not content simply with great wealth, Cosimo operated behind the scenes to gain control of the Florentine political system, although officially the city remained a republic. Worries about his growing power led the dominant faction of the Florentine city council to exile him, but he took his money and his business with him

Botticelli's *Adoration of the Magi* shows many members of the Medici family and their circle, including the artist himself at the far right. (Galleria degli Uffizi, Florence, Italy/Bridgeman Images)

and was soon asked to return. Cosimo supported artists and thinkers, sponsoring what became known as the Platonic Academy, an informal group of Florence's cultural elite named in honor of Plato's famous academy in ancient Athens. Here Marsilio Ficino and other humanists translated Plato's works into Latin, making Greek

Christian Humanism

In the last quarter of the fifteenth century students from the Low Countries, France, Germany, and England flocked to Italy, absorbed the "new learning" of humanism, and carried it back to their own countries. Northern humanists shared the Italians' ideas about the wisdom of ancient texts and felt even more strongly that the best elements of classical and Christian cultures should be combined. These **Christian humanists**, as they were later called, saw humanist learning as a way to bring about reform of the church and to deepen people's spiritual lives.

The Englishman Thomas More (1478–1535) began life as a lawyer, studied the classics, and entered government service. He became best known for his controversial dialogue *Utopia* (1516). *Utopia* describes a community on an island somewhere beyond Europe where all children receive a good humanist education and adults divide their days between manual labor or business pursuits and intellectual activities. The problems that plagued More's fellow citizens, such as poverty and hunger, are solved by a beneficent government. Inequality and greed are prevented because profits from business and property are held in common, not privately. Furthermore, there is religious tolerance, and order and reason prevail.

Christian humanists
Humanists from northern Europe who thought that the best elements of classical and Christian cultures should be combined and saw humanist learning as a way to bring about reform of the church and deepen people's spiritual lives.

learning available to a much wider European audience. Cosimo collected books and manuscripts from all over Europe, assembling an impressive library within the equally impressive Medici palace that he built in the heart of Florence.

Like his grandfather, Lorenzo was the head of the Medici bank and the de facto ruler of Florence. He, too, survived an attempt to oust and even murder him, and the constitution of Florence was modified to favor the Medici. Lorenzo came to be known during his lifetime—with no irony—as "Lorenzo the Magnificent," primarily for his support for learning and the arts. As they had in Cosimo's day, a group of poets, philosophers, and artists spent much of their time at the Medici palace, where Lorenzo patronized writing in Italian as well as humanist scholarship, and himself wrote love lyrics, sonnets, odes, and carnival songs. The group included the humanists Ficino and Giovanni Pico della Mirandola and the artists Michelangelo, Leonardo da Vinci, and Sandro Botticelli, all of them influenced by Platonic concepts of beauty and love. Botticelli's *Adoration of the Magi* shows Cosimo (who was dead by the time the picture was painted) kneeling in front of the Virgin Mary as one of the three kings giving gifts to the infant Jesus, while a black-haired Lorenzo stands with other important Florentines on the right.

In the 1490s many of the Medici bank branches collapsed because of bad loans, and Lorenzo's diplomacy was not successful in maintaining a peaceful balance of power. Like many others in Florence, Lorenzo came under the spell of the charismatic preacher Savonarola, but he died before Savonarola's prediction that God would punish Italy for its vices appeared to come true when the French invaded. The Medici were again ousted, but just as before, they returned, and later became the official and hereditary rulers of Florence and its environs as the Grand Dukes of Tuscany.

QUESTIONS FOR ANALYSIS

1. Renaissance people were fascinated by the quality of virtù, the ability to shape the world around one according to one's will. How did Cosimo and Lorenzo exhibit virtù?

2. The Medici created a model for very wealthy people of how to obtain political and cultural influence. Can you think of more recent examples, including contemporary ones, of those who followed this model?

Better known by contemporaries than Thomas More was the Dutch humanist Desiderius Erasmus (deh-she-DEHR-ee-uhs eh-RAHS-muhs) (1466?–1536) of Rotterdam. His fame rested largely on his exceptional knowledge of Greek and the Bible, as well as his many publications. For Erasmus, education was the key to moral and intellectual improvement, and true Christianity was an inner attitude of the spirit, not a set of outward actions.

Printing and Its Social Impact

The impact of new ideas during this period was magnified by the invention of the printing press with movable metal type. While printing with movable type was invented in China (see "The Scholar-Officials and Neo-Confucianism" in Chapter 13), movable *metal* type was actually developed in the thirteenth century in Korea, though it was tightly controlled by the monarchy and did not have the broad impact there that printing did in Europe. Printing with movable metal type developed in Germany around 1450. Several metal-smiths, most prominently Johann Gutenberg (ca. 1400–1468), transformed the metal stamps used to mark signs on jewelry into type that could be covered with ink and used to mark symbols onto a page. This type could be rearranged for every page and thus could be used over and over. The printing revolution was also enabled by the ready availability of paper, which was made using techniques that had originated in China and spread from Muslim Spain to the rest of Europe.

The effects of the invention of movable-type printing were not felt overnight. Nevertheless, within a half century of the publication of Gutenberg's Bible of 1456, movable type had brought about radical changes. Historians estimate that somewhere between 8 million and 20 million books were printed in Europe between 1456 and 1500, many more than the total number of books that had been produced in the West during the many millennia between the invention of writing and 1456.

Printing transformed both the private and the public lives of Europeans. In the public realm, government and church leaders both used and worried about printing. They printed laws, declarations of war, battle accounts, and propaganda, but they also attempted to censor or ban books and authors whose ideas they thought were wrong. These efforts were rarely effective.

In the private realm, printing enabled people to read identical books so that they could more easily discuss the ideas that the books contained. Although most of the earliest books and pamphlets dealt with religious subjects, printers produced anything that would sell. Illustrations increased a book's sales, so printers published books full of woodcuts and engravings. Additionally, single-page broadsides and fly sheets allowed public events and "wonders" such as comets and two-headed calves to be experienced vicariously. Since books and other printed materials were read aloud to illiterate listeners, print bridged the gap between the written and oral cultures.

Because many laypeople could not read Latin, printers put out works in vernacular languages, fostering standardization in these languages. Works in these languages were also performed on stage. Traveling companies of actors performed before royal courts and in town squares, and in larger cities public theaters offered bawdy comedies and bloody tragedies. In London the works of William Shakespeare (1564–1616) were especially popular.

Art and the Artist

No feature of the Renaissance evokes greater admiration than its artistic masterpieces. In Renaissance Italy wealthy merchants, bankers, popes, and princes spent vast sums to commission art as a means of glorifying themselves and their families. Patrons varied in their level of involvement as a work progressed; some simply ordered a specific subject or scene, while others oversaw the work of the artist or architect very closely.

As a result of patronage, certain artists gained great public acclaim and adulation, leading many historians to view the Renaissance as the beginning of the concept of the artist as genius. In the Middle Ages, people believed that only God created, albeit through individuals, and artistic originality was not particularly valued. By contrast, Renaissance artists and humanists came to think that a work of art was the deliberate creation of a unique personality, of an individual who transcended traditions, rules, and theories.

In terms of artistic themes, religious topics remained popular among both patrons and artists, but frequently the patron had himself and his family portrayed in the scene. As the fifteenth century advanced and humanist ideas spread more widely,

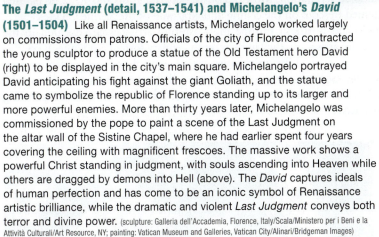

The *Last Judgment* (detail, 1537–1541) and Michelangelo's *David* (1501–1504) Like all Renaissance artists, Michelangelo worked largely on commissions from patrons. Officials of the city of Florence contracted the young sculptor to produce a statue of the Old Testament hero David (right) to be displayed in the city's main square. Michelangelo portrayed David anticipating his fight against the giant Goliath, and the statue came to symbolize the republic of Florence standing up to its larger and more powerful enemies. More than thirty years later, Michelangelo was commissioned by the pope to paint a scene of the Last Judgment on the altar wall of the Sistine Chapel, where he had earlier spent four years covering the ceiling with magnificent frescoes. The massive work shows a powerful Christ standing in judgment, with souls ascending into Heaven while others are dragged by demons into Hell (above). The *David* captures ideals of human perfection and has come to be an iconic symbol of Renaissance artistic brilliance, while the dramatic and violent *Last Judgment* conveys both terror and divine power. (sculpture: Galleria dell'Accademia, Florence, Italy/Scala/Ministero per i Beni e la Attività Culturali/Art Resource, NY; painting: Vatican Museum and Galleries, Vatican City/Alinari/Bridgeman Images)

classical themes and motifs figured increasingly in painting and sculpture. Classical styles also influenced architecture, as architects designed buildings that featured arches and domes modeled on the structures of ancient Rome.

The individual portrait emerged as a distinct genre in Renaissance art. Rather than reflecting a spiritual ideal, as medieval painting and sculpture tended to do, Renaissance portraits showed human ideals, often portrayed in a more realistic style. The Florentine sculptor Donatello (doh-nah-TELL-oh) (1386–1466) revived the classical figure. Leonardo da Vinci (1452–1519) was particularly adept at portraying female grace and beauty. Another Florentine artist, Raphael Sanzio (RAH-feh-ell SAN-zee-oh) (1483–1520), painted hundreds of portraits, becoming the most sought-after artist in Europe (see the portrait at the beginning of this chapter).

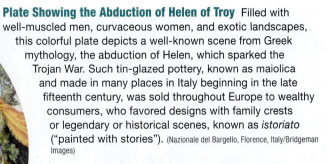

Plate Showing the Abduction of Helen of Troy Filled with well-muscled men, curvaceous women, and exotic landscapes, this colorful plate depicts a well-known scene from Greek mythology, the abduction of Helen, which sparked the Trojan War. Such tin-glazed pottery, known as maiolica and made in many places in Italy beginning in the late fifteenth century, was sold throughout Europe to wealthy consumers, who favored designs with family crests or legendary or historical scenes, known as *istoriato* ("painted with stories"). (Nazionale del Bargello, Florence, Italy/Bridgeman Images)

In the late fifteenth century the center of Renaissance art shifted from Florence to Rome, where wealthy cardinals and popes became active patrons of the arts. To meet this demand, Michelangelo Buonarroti (mee-kell-AN-geh-loh bwa-nah-RAH-tee) (1475–1564) went to Rome from Florence in about 1500 and began the series of statues, paintings, and architectural projects from which he gained an international reputation. Most famously, between 1508 and 1512 he painted religiously themed frescoes on the ceiling and altar wall of the Sistine Chapel.

In both Italy and northern Europe most aspiring artists were educated in the workshops of older artists. By the later sixteenth century formal academies were also established to train artists. Like universities, artistic workshops and academies were male-only settings. Several women did become well known as painters during the Renaissance, but they were trained by their artist fathers and often quit painting when they married.

The Chess Game, **1555** In this oil painting, the Italian artist Sofonisba Anguissola (1532–1625) shows her three younger sisters playing chess, a game that was growing in popularity in the sixteenth century. Each sister looks at the one immediately older than herself, with the girl on the left looking out at her sister, the artist. Anguissola's father, a minor nobleman, recognized his daughter's talent and arranged for her to study with several painters. She became a court painter at the Spanish royal court, where she painted many portraits. Returning to Italy, she continued to be active, painting her last portrait when she was over eighty. (Museum Narodowe, Poznan, Poland/Bridgeman Images)

Women were not alone in being excluded from the institutions of Renaissance culture. Though a few talented artists such as Leonardo and Michelangelo emerged from artisanal backgrounds, most scholars and artists came from families with at least some money. The audience for artists' work was also exclusive, limited mostly to educated and prosperous citizens. Although common people in large cities might have occasionally seen plays such as those of Shakespeare, most people lived in villages with no access to formal schooling or to the work of prominent artists. In general a small, highly educated minority of literary humanists and artists created the culture of and for a social elite. In this way the Renaissance maintained, and even enhanced, a gulf between the learned minority and the uneducated multitude.

Social Hierarchies

The division between the educated and uneducated was one of many social hierarchies evident in the Renaissance. Other hierarchies built on those of the Middle Ages, but also developed new features that contributed to modern social hierarchies, such as those of race, class, and gender.

> **What were the key social hierarchies in Renaissance Europe, and how did these hierarchies shape people's lives?**

Race and Slavery

Renaissance people did not use the word *race* the way we do, but often used *race*, *people*, and *nation* interchangeably for ethnic, national, and religious groups. They did make distinctions based on skin color that were in keeping with later conceptualizations of race, but these distinctions were interwoven with other characteristics when people thought about human differences.

Ever since the time of the Roman Republic, a few black Africans had lived in western Europe. They had come, along with white slaves, as the spoils of war. After the collapse of the Roman Empire and throughout the Middle Ages, Muslim and Christian merchants continued to import black slaves. The black population was especially concentrated in the cities of the Iberian Peninsula. By the mid-sixteenth century blacks, slave and free, constituted roughly 3 percent of the Portuguese population. Slaves and a few free black people could be found in courts and cities in other parts of Europe as well, especially in Italy. (See "Analyzing the Evidence: Titian, *Laura de Dianti*," page 432.)

In Renaissance Portugal, Spain, and Italy, African slaves supplemented the labor force in virtually all occupations. Slaves also formed the primary workforce on the sugar plantations set up by Europeans on the Atlantic islands in the late fifteenth century (see "Sugar and Early Transatlantic Slavery" in Chapter 16).

Until their voyages down the African coast in the late fifteenth century, Europeans had little concrete knowledge of Africans and their cultures. They perceived Africa as a remote place, the home of strange people isolated by heresy and Islam from superior European civilization. Africans' contact, even as slaves, with Christian Europeans would only "improve" the blacks, they believed. The expanding slave trade reinforced negative preconceptions about the inferiority of black Africans.

Wealth and the Nobility

By the thirteenth century, and even more so by the fifteenth, the idea of a hierarchy based on wealth was emerging. This was particularly true in cities, where wealthy

Titian, *Laura de Dianti*

The Venetian artist Titian (1488?–1576) was a master of many types of paintings during his long life, including giant frescoes and oil paintings of religious and historical subjects, classical scenes set in verdant landscapes, and portraits of prominent and wealthy individuals. In the 1520s he was hired by Alfonso d'Este, the duke of Ferrara, to paint large mythological scenes for his private study in the ducal palace, and in 1523 he also painted this portrait of Este's lover, Laura de Dianti, who may have also been Este's third wife. Titian shows her in a gorgeous blue dress and an elaborate pearl and feather headdress, accompanied by a young black page with a gold earring. Wealthy Europeans sometimes had themselves painted with their black servants to indicate their wealth. The boy was most likely a slave, though sometimes free black families lived at courts, in order to produce the young black children who were highly prized as servants. Slaves from Africa and the Ottoman Empire were common in wealthy Italian urban households. Venice served as a major slave-trading hub, with Venetian merchants selling Slavic and Baltic slaves to be transported to Muslim areas, and African and Turkish slaves to be transported to Christian areas. Household slaves in Italian cities, most of whom were girls and women, worked at various tasks, but they were also symbols of the exotic, just as they were at court.

(Photographer: Human Bios GmbH, CH-8280 Kreuzlingen, www.humanbios.com. Courtesy, Kisters Collection)

QUESTIONS FOR ANALYSIS

1. How does Titian convey the message that this woman is wealthy and connected to Venice's overseas trade?
2. How does Titian use the boy's skin color to highlight the woman's fair skin, which was one of the Renaissance ideals of female beauty?
3. What does this painting suggest about Renaissance European attitudes about gender, race, and class?

merchants oversaw vast trading empires, held positions of political power, and lived in splendor rivaling that enjoyed by the richest nobles. (See "Individuals in Society: Cosimo and Lorenzo de' Medici," page 426.)

The development of a hierarchy of wealth did not mean an end to the prominence of nobles, however, and even poorer nobles still had higher status than wealthy commoners did. Thus wealthy Italian merchants enthusiastically bought noble titles in the fifteenth century, and wealthy English and Spanish merchants married their daughters and sons into often-impoverished noble families. The nobility maintained its status in most parts of Europe not by maintaining rigid boundaries, but by taking in and integrating the new social elite created by the hierarchy of wealth.

Gender Roles

Renaissance people would not have understood the word *gender* to refer to categories of people, but they would have easily grasped the concept. Toward the end of the fourteenth century learned men (and a few women) began what was termed the **debate about women**, an argument about women's character, nature, and proper role in society that would last for centuries. Misogynist critiques of women from both clerical and secular authors denounced females as devious, domineering, and demanding. In response, several authors compiled long lists of famous and praiseworthy women. Some writers, including a few women who had gained a humanist education, were interested not only in defending women but also in exploring the reasons behind women's secondary status.

debate about women
An argument about women's character, nature, and proper role in society that began in the later years of the fourteenth century and lasted for centuries.

Beginning in the sixteenth century the debate about women also became a debate about female rulers, because in Spain, England, France, and Scotland women served as advisers to child-kings or ruled in their own right. There were no successful rebellions against female rulers simply because they were women; in part this was because female rulers, especially Queen Elizabeth I of England, emphasized qualities regarded as masculine—physical bravery, stamina, wisdom, duty—whenever they appeared in public.

The dominant notion of the "true" man was that of the married head of household, so men whose class and age would have normally conferred political power but who remained unmarried were sometimes excluded from ruling positions. Actual marriage patterns in Europe left many women unmarried until late in life, but this did not lead to greater equality. Women who worked for wages, as was typical, earned about half to two-thirds of what men did even for the same work. Of all the ways in which Renaissance society was hierarchically arranged—by class, age, level of education, rank, race, occupation—gender was regarded as the most "natural" distinction and therefore the most important one to defend.

Italian City Scene In this detail from a fresco, the Italian painter Lorenzo Lotto captures the mixing of social groups in a Renaissance Italian city. The crowd of men in the left foreground includes wealthy merchants in elaborate hats and colorful coats. Two mercenary soldiers (carrying a sword and a pike) wear short doublets and tight hose stylishly slit to reveal colored undergarments, while boys play with toy weapons at their feet. Clothing like that of the soldiers, which emphasized the masculine form, was frequently criticized for its expense and its "indecency." At the right, women sell vegetables and bread, which would have been a common sight at any city marketplace. (Cappella Suardi, Trescore Balneario, Italy/Scala/Art Resource, NY)

How did the nation-states of western Europe evolve in this period?

Politics and the State in the Renaissance

Beginning in the fifteenth century monarchs used aggressive methods to build up their governments. As they built and maintained power, they emphasized royal majesty and royal sovereignty and insisted on the respect and loyalty of all subjects.

France

The Black Death and the Hundred Years' War left France drastically depopulated, commercially ruined, and agriculturally weak (see "The Hundred Years' War" in Chapter 14). Nonetheless, Charles VII (r. 1422–1461) revived the monarchy and France. He reorganized the royal council, giving increased influence to middle-class men, and strengthened royal finances through taxes on certain products and on land. Moreover, Charles created the first permanent royal army anywhere in Europe.

Two further developments strengthened the French monarchy. The marriage of Louis XII (r. 1498–1515) and Anne of Brittany added Brittany to the state. Louis XII's successor, Francis I (r. 1515–1547), and Pope Leo X reached a mutually satisfactory agreement about church and state powers in 1516 that gave French kings the power to control the appointment and thus the policies of church officials in the kingdom.

England

English society suffered severely in the fourteenth and fifteenth centuries. Between 1455 and 1471 adherents of the ducal houses of York and Lancaster waged civil wars over control of the English throne, commonly called the Wars of the Roses. The chronic disorder hurt trade, agriculture, and domestic industry, and the authority of the monarchy sank lower than it had been in centuries.

The Yorkist Edward IV (r. 1461–1483) succeeded in defeating the Lancastrian forces and after 1471 began to reconstruct the monarchy and consolidate royal power. Henry VII (r. 1485–1509) of the Welsh house of Tudor worked to restore royal prestige, to crush the power of the nobility, and to establish order and law at the local level. Because the government halted the long period of anarchy, it won the key support of the merchant and agricultural upper middle class. Under Henry VII the center of royal authority was the royal council. There Henry VII revealed his distrust of the nobility: very few great lords were among the king's closest advisers, who instead were lesser landowners and lawyers. The royal council handled any business the king put before it — executive, legislative, and judicial.

Secretive, cautious, and thrifty, Henry VII rebuilt the monarchy. He encouraged the cloth industry and built up the English merchant marine. He crushed an invasion from Ireland, secured peace with Scotland, and enhanced English prestige through the marriage of his eldest son, Arthur, to Catherine of Aragon, the daughter of Ferdinand and Isabella of Spain. (Several years after Arthur's death, Catherine would become the wife of his younger brother and the next king of England, Henry VIII; see "England's Shift Toward Protestantism.") When Henry VII died in 1509, he left a country at peace both domestically and internationally, a substantially augmented treasury, and the dignity and role of the Crown much enhanced.

Spain

While England and France laid the foundations of unified nation-states during the Renaissance, Spain remained a conglomerate of independent kingdoms. Even the wedding in 1469 of Isabella of Castile and Ferdinand of Aragon did not bring about administrative unity. Isabella and Ferdinand were, however, able to exert their authority in ways similar to those of the rulers of France and England. They curbed aristocratic power by excluding aristocrats and great territorial magnates from the royal council. They also secured from the Spanish pope Alexander VI the right to appoint bishops in Spain and in the Hispanic territories in America, enabling them to establish the equivalent of a national church. In 1492 their armies conquered Granada, the last territory held by Arabs in southern Spain.

Ferdinand and Isabella's rule also marked the start of greater persecution of the Jews. In the Middle Ages, the kings of France and England had expelled the Jews from their kingdoms, and many had sought refuge in Spain. During the long centuries of the reconquista (see "The Expansion of Western and Eastern Christianity" in Chapter 14), Christian kings in Spain had renewed Jewish rights and privileges; in fact, Jewish industry, intelligence, and money had supported royal power.

In the fourteenth century anti-Semitism in Spain was aggravated by fiery anti-Jewish preaching, by economic dislocation, and by the search for a scapegoat during the Black Death. Anti-Semitic pogroms (violent massacres and riots directed against Jews) swept the towns of Spain, and perhaps 40 percent of the Jewish population was killed or forced to convert. Those who converted were called *conversos* (kuhn-VEHR-sohz) or New Christians. Conversos were often well educated and held prominent positions in government and business.

Such successes bred resentment. Aristocrats resented their financial dependence on conversos, the poor hated the converso tax collectors, and churchmen doubted the sincerity of their conversions. Queen Isabella shared these suspicions, and she and Ferdinand received permission from Pope Sixtus IV to establish an Inquisition to look for conversos who showed any sign of incomplete conversion.

Most conversos identified themselves as sincere Christians; many came from families that had received baptism generations before. In response, officials of the Inquisition developed a new type of anti-Semitism. A person's status as a Jew, they argued, could not be changed by religious conversion, but was in the person's blood and was heritable, so Jews could never be true Christians. Under what were known as "purity of blood" laws, having "pure Christian blood" became a requirement for noble status. Ideas about Jews developed in Spain became important components in European concepts of race, and discussions of "Jewish blood" later expanded into discriminatory definitions of the "Jewish race."

In 1492, shortly after the conquest of Granada, Isabella and Ferdinand issued an edict expelling all practicing Jews from Spain. Of the community of perhaps 200,000 Jews, 150,000 fled. Absolute religious orthodoxy and "purity of blood" served as the theoretical foundation of the Spanish national state.

The Habsburgs

War and diplomacy were important ways that states increased their power in sixteenth-century Europe, but so was marriage. Because almost all of Europe was ruled by hereditary dynasties, claiming and holding resources involved shrewd marital strategies, for it was far cheaper to gain land by inheritance than by war. The benefits of an advantageous marriage stretched across generations, as can be seen most dramatically with the Habsburgs. The Holy Roman emperor Frederick III, a Habsburg who was the ruler of most of Austria, acquired only a small amount of territory—but a great deal of money—with his marriage to Princess Eleanore of Portugal in 1452. He arranged for his son Maximilian to marry Europe's most prominent heiress, Mary of Burgundy. Through this union with the rich and powerful duchy of Burgundy, the Austrian house of Habsburg, already the strongest ruling family in the empire, became an international power. The marriage of Maximilian and Mary angered the French, and it inaugurated centuries of conflict between the Habsburgs and the kings of France. Within the empire, German principalities that resented Austria's pre-eminence began to see that they shared interests with France.

Maximilian learned the lesson of marital politics well, marrying his son and daughter to the children of Ferdinand and Isabella, the rulers of Spain, much of southern Italy, and eventually the Spanish New World empire. His grandson Charles V (1500–1558) fell heir to a vast and incredibly diverse collection of states and peoples (Map 15.1). Charles was convinced that it was his duty to maintain the political and religious unity of Western Christendom. This conviction would be challenged far more than Charles ever anticipated.

The Protestant Reformation

What were the central ideas of Protestant reformers, and why were they appealing to various groups across Europe?

Calls for reform in the church came from many quarters in early-sixteenth-century Europe—from educated laypeople and urban residents, from villagers and artisans, and from church officials themselves. This dissatisfaction helps explain why the ideas of Martin Luther, an obscure professor from a new and not very prestigious German university, found a ready audience. Within a decade of his first publishing his ideas (using the new technology of the printing press), much of central Europe and Scandinavia had broken with the Catholic Church in a movement that came to be known as the **Protestant Reformation**. In addition, even more radical concepts of the Christian message were being developed and linked to calls for social change.

Protestant Reformation
A religious reform movement that began in the early sixteenth century and split the Western Christian Church.

Criticism of the Church

Sixteenth-century Europeans were deeply pious, but many people were also highly critical of the Roman Catholic Church and its clergy. Papal conflicts with rulers and the Great Schism (see "Challenges to the Christian Church" in Chapter 14) badly damaged the prestige of church leaders. Papal tax collection methods were also attacked, and some criticized the papacy itself as an institution.

In the early sixteenth century critics of the church concentrated their attacks on clerical immorality, ignorance, and absenteeism. Charges of immorality were aimed at a number of priests who were drunkards, neglected the rule of celibacy, gambled, or indulged in fancy dress. Charges of ignorance applied to barely literate priests who delivered poor-quality sermons.

In regard to absenteeism, many clerics, especially higher ecclesiastics, held several benefices (offices) simultaneously. However, they seldom visited the communities served by the benefices. Instead they collected revenues from all the benefices assigned to them and hired a poor priest to fulfill their spiritual duties, paying him just a fraction of the income.

There was also local resentment of clerical privileges and immunities. Priests, monks, and nuns were exempt from civic responsibilities, such as defending the city and paying taxes. Yet religious orders frequently held large amounts of urban prop-

MAP 15.1 The Global Empire of Charles V, ca. 1556 Charles V exercised theoretical jurisdiction over more European territory than anyone since Charlemagne. He also claimed authority over large parts of North and South America, although actual Spanish control was weak in much of this area.

erty. City governments were increasingly determined to integrate the clergy into civic life. This brought city leaders into opposition with bishops and the papacy, which for centuries had stressed the independence of the church from lay control.

Martin Luther

By itself, widespread criticism of the church did not lead to the dramatic changes of the sixteenth century. Those resulted from the personal religious struggle of a German Augustinian friar and professor at the University of Wittenberg, Martin Luther (1483–1546).

Martin Luther was a very conscientious friar, but his scrupulous observance of the religious routine, frequent confessions, and fasting gave him only temporary relief from anxieties about sin and his ability to meet God's demands. Through his study of Saint Paul's letters in the New Testament, he gradually arrived at a new understanding of Christian doctrine. His understanding is often summarized as "faith alone, grace alone, scripture alone." He believed that salvation and justification (righteousness in God's eyes) come through faith, and that faith is a free gift of God, not the result of human effort. God's word is revealed only in biblical scripture, not in the traditions of the church.

indulgence A document issued by the pope that substituted for earthly penance or time in purgatory.

At the same time that Luther was engaged in scholarly reflections and professorial lecturing, Pope Leo X authorized a special Saint Peter's indulgence to finance his building plans in Rome. An **indulgence** was a document issued by the pope that substituted for earthly penance or time in purgatory. The archbishop who controlled the area in which Wittenberg was located, Albert of Mainz, also promoted the sale of indulgences, in his case to pay off a debt he had incurred to be named bishop of several additional territories. Albert's sales campaign promised that the purchase of indulgences would bring full forgiveness for one's own sins or buy release from purgatory for a loved one. One of the slogans—"As soon as coin in coffer rings, the soul from purgatory springs"—brought phenomenal success.

Luther was severely troubled that many people believed that they had no further need for repentance once they had purchased indulgences. In October 1517 he wrote a letter to Archbishop Albert on the subject and enclosed in Latin his "Ninety-five Theses on the Power of Indulgences." His argument was that indulgences undermined the seriousness of the sacrament of penance and competed with the preaching of the Gospel. Luther intended his theses for academic debate, but by December of that year they had been translated into German and were being read throughout central Europe. Luther was ordered to go to Rome, but he was able to avoid this because the ruler of the territory in which he lived protected him. The pope nonetheless ordered him to recant many of his ideas, and Luther publicly burned the letter containing the papal order. In this highly charged atmosphere, the twenty-one-year-old emperor Charles V summoned Luther to appear before the **Diet of Worms**, an assembly of representatives from the territories of the Holy Roman Empire meeting in the city of Worms in 1521. Luther, however, refused to give in to demands that he take back his ideas.

Diet of Worms An assembly of representatives from the territories of the Holy Roman Empire convened by Charles V in the city of Worms in 1521. It was here that Martin Luther refused to recant his writings.

Protestant Originally meaning "a follower of Luther," this term came to be generally applied to all non-Catholic western European Christians.

Protestant Thought and Its Appeal

As he developed his ideas, Luther gathered followers, who came to be called Protestants. At first **Protestant** meant "a follower of Luther," but with the appearance of many other reformers, it became a general term applied to all non-Catholic western European Christians.

Catholics and Protestants disagreed on many issues. Catholic teaching held that salvation is achieved by both faith and good works, while Protestants held that salvation comes by faith alone, irrespective of good works or the sacraments. God, not people, initiates salvation. Christian doctrine had long maintained that authority rests both in the Bible and in the traditional teaching of the church, but Protestants asserted that authority rested in the Bible alone. For a doctrine or issue to be valid, they thought, it had to have a scriptural basis. Roman Catholics saw the church as a clerical, hierarchical institution headed by the pope in Rome, while Protestants rejected the authority of the pope and developed various forms of church governance and organization. They also rejected the Catholic idea that monastic religious life was superior, so they closed monasteries and convents and championed marriage as the best Christian life.

Pulpits and printing presses spread the Protestant message all over Germany, and by the middle of the sixteenth century people of all social classes had rejected Catholic teachings and become Protestant. What was the immense appeal of Luther's religious ideas and those of other Protestants?

Educated people and humanists were attracted by Luther's ideas. He advocated a simpler personal religion based on faith, a return to the spirit of the early church, the centrality of the Scriptures in the liturgy and in Christian life, and the abolition of elaborate ceremonies—precisely the reforms the Christian humanists had been calling for. His insistence that everyone should read and reflect on the Scriptures attracted the literate middle classes. Luther's ideas also appealed to townspeople who envied the church's wealth and resented paying for it. After cities became Protestant, the city council taxed the clergy and placed them under the jurisdiction of civil courts.

The printing press also contributed to Luther's fame and success. Many printed works included woodcuts and other illustrations, so that even those who could not read could grasp the main ideas. Hymns were also important means of conveying central points of doctrine, as was Luther's translation of the New Testament into German in 1523.

Luther worked closely with political authorities, viewing them as fully justified in reforming the church in their territories. He instructed all Christians to obey their secular rulers, whom he saw as divinely ordained to maintain order. Individuals may have been convinced of the truth of Protestant teachings on their own, but a territory became Protestant when its ruler brought in reformers to re-educate the territory's clergy, sponsored public sermons, and confiscated church property. This happened in many of the states of the empire during the 1520s and then moved beyond the empire to Denmark-Norway and Sweden.

The Radical Reformation and the German Peasants' War

In the sixteenth century the practice of religion remained a public matter. The ruler determined the official form of religious practice in his (or occasionally her) jurisdiction. Almost everyone believed that the presence of a faith different from that of the majority represented a political threat to the security of the state.

Some individuals and groups rejected the idea that church and state needed to be united, however, and they sought to create a voluntary community of believers as they understood it to have existed in New Testament times. In terms of theology and spiritual practices, these individuals and groups varied widely, though they are generally termed "radicals" for their insistence on a more extensive break with prevailing ideas. Some adopted the custom of baptizing adult believers—for which they were given the title of "Anabaptists" by their enemies—while others saw all outward sacraments or rituals as misguided. Some groups attempted communal ownership of property. Some reacted harshly to members who deviated from the group's accepted practices, but others argued for complete religious tolerance and individualism.

Religious radicals were met with fanatical hatred and bitter persecution, including banishment and execution. Both Protestant and Catholic authorities felt threatened by the social, political, and economic implications of radicals' religious ideas and by their rejection of a state church. Their community spirit and heroism in the face of martyrdom, however, contributed to the survival of radical ideas. In 1787 the authors of the U.S. Constitution, with their opposition to the "establishment of religion" (state churches), would trace the origins of their beliefs, in part, to the radicals of the sixteenth century.

Another group to challenge state authorities was the peasantry. In the early sixteenth century the economic condition of peasants varied from place to place but was generally worse than it had been in the fifteenth century and was deteriorating. Peasants demanded limitations on the new taxes and labor obligations their noble landlords were imposing. They believed that their demands conformed to the Scriptures and cited Luther as a theologian who could prove that they did.

Wanting to prevent rebellion, Luther initially sided with the peasants. But when rebellion broke out, the peasants who expected Luther's support were soon disillusioned. Freedom for Luther meant independence from the authority of the Roman Church, not opposition to legally established secular powers. Firmly convinced that rebellion would hasten the end of civilized society, he wrote the tract *Against the Murderous, Thieving Hordes of the Peasants*. The nobility ferociously crushed the revolt, which became known as the German Peasants' War of 1525.

The Peasants' War greatly strengthened the authority of lay rulers. Because Luther turned against the peasants who revolted, the Reformation lost much of its popular appeal after 1525, though peasants and urban rebels sometimes found a place for their social and religious ideas in radical groups. Peasants' economic conditions did moderately improve, however.

Marriage and Women's Roles

Luther and other Protestants believed that a priest's or nun's vows of celibacy went against human nature and God's commandments. Luther married a former nun, Katharina von Bora (1499–1532), who quickly had several children. Most other Protestant reformers also married, and their wives had to create a new and respectable role for themselves, pastor's wife. They were living demonstrations of their husband's convictions about the superiority of marriage to celibacy, and they were expected to be models of wifely obedience and Christian charity.

Catholics viewed marriage as a sacramental union that, if validly entered into, could not be dissolved. Protestants saw marriage as a contract in which each partner promised the other support, companionship, and the sharing of mutual goods. They believed that spouses who did not comfort or support one another endangered their own souls and the surrounding community; therefore, most Protestants came to allow divorce. Divorce remained rare, however, because marriage was such an important social and economic institution.

Protestants did not break with medieval scholastic theologians in their view that, within marriage, women were to be subject to men. Men were urged to treat their wives kindly and considerately, but also to enforce their authority, through physical coercion if necessary. A few women took the Protestant idea about the priesthood of all believers to heart and wrote religious pamphlets and hymns, but no sixteenth-century Protestants officially allowed women to hold positions of religious authority.

Because the Reformation generally brought the closing of monasteries and convents, marriage became virtually the only occupation for upper-class Protestant

Martin Luther and Katharina von Bora
Lucas Cranach the Elder painted this double marriage portrait to celebrate Luther's wedding in 1525 to Katharina von Bora, a former nun. The artist was one of the witnesses at the wedding and, in fact, had presented Luther's marriage proposal to Katharina. The couple quickly became a model of the ideal marriage, and many churches wanted their portraits. More than sixty similar paintings, with slight variations, were produced by Cranach's workshop and hung in churches and wealthy homes. (Galleria degli Uffizi, Florence, Italy/akg-images)

women. Recognizing this, women in some convents fought the Reformation or argued that they could still be pious Protestants within convent walls. Most nuns left, however, and we do not know what happened to them. The Protestant emphasis on marriage made unmarried women (and men) suspect, for they did not belong to the type of household regarded as the cornerstone of a proper, godly society.

The Reformation and German Politics

Criticism of the church was widespread in Europe in the early sixteenth century. Yet such movements could be more easily squelched by the strong central governments of Spain, France, and England. The Holy Roman Empire, in contrast, included hundreds of largely independent states in which the emperor had far less authority than did the monarchs of western Europe. Thus local rulers of the many states in the empire continued to exercise great power.

Luther's ideas appealed to local rulers within the empire for a variety of reasons. Though Germany was not a nation, people did have an understanding of being German because of their language and traditions. Luther frequently used the phrase "we Germans" in his attacks on the papacy, and his appeal to national feeling influenced many rulers. Also, while some German rulers were sincerely attracted to Lutheran ideas, material considerations swayed many others to embrace the new faith. The rejection of Roman Catholicism and the adoption of Protestantism would mean the legal confiscation of valuable church property. Thus many political authorities in the empire used the religious issue to extend their financial and political power and to enhance their independence from the emperor.

The Habsburg Charles V, elected as emperor in 1521, was a vigorous defender of Catholicism, so it is not surprising that the Reformation led to religious wars. Protestant territories in the empire formed military alliances, and the emperor could not oppose them effectively given other military engagements. In southeastern Europe Habsburg troops were already fighting the Ottoman Turks. Habsburg soldiers were also engaged in a series of wars with the Valois (VAL-wah) kings of France that stretched from 1494 to 1559. The cornerstone of French foreign policy in the sixteenth and seventeenth centuries was the desire to keep the German states divided. Thus Europe witnessed the paradox of the Catholic king of France supporting Lutheran princes in their challenge to his fellow Catholic, Charles V.

Finally, in 1555, Charles agreed to the Peace of Augsburg, which officially recognized Lutheranism and ended religious war in Germany for many decades. Under this treaty, the political authority in each territory of the Holy Roman Empire was permitted to decide whether the territory would be Catholic or Lutheran. His hope of uniting his empire under a single church dashed, Charles V abdicated in 1556, transferring power over his Spanish and Netherlandish holdings to his son Philip II and his imperial power to his brother Ferdinand.

England's Shift Toward Protestantism

As on the continent, the Reformation in England had economic and political as well as religious causes. The impetus for England's break with Rome was the desire of King Henry VIII (r. 1509–1547) for a new wife. When the personal matter of his need to divorce his first wife became enmeshed with political issues, a complete break with Rome resulted.

In 1527, after eighteen years of marriage, Henry's wife Catherine of Aragon had failed to produce a male child, and Henry had also fallen in love with a court lady in waiting, Anne Boleyn. So Henry petitioned Pope Clement VII for an annulment of his marriage to Catherine. When the pope procrastinated in granting the annulment, Henry decided to remove the English Church from papal authority.

Henry used Parliament to legalize the Reformation in England and to make himself the supreme head of the Church of England. Anne had a daughter, Elizabeth, but failed to produce a son, so Henry VIII charged her with adulterous incest and in 1536 had her beheaded. His third wife, Jane Seymour, gave Henry the desired son, Edward, but she died a few days after childbirth. Henry went on to three more wives.

Between 1535 and 1539 Henry decided to dissolve the English monasteries primarily because he wanted their wealth. Hundreds of former church properties were sold to the middle and upper classes, strengthening the upper classes and tying them to the Tudor dynasty, to which Henry belonged. How did everyday people react to Henry's break from the Catholic Church? Recent scholarship points out that people rarely "converted" from Catholicism to Protestantism overnight. Instead they responded to the local consequences of the shift from Catholicism with a combination of resistance, acceptance, and collaboration.

Loyalty to the Catholic Church remained particularly strong in Ireland. Ireland had been claimed by English kings since the twelfth century, but in reality the English had firm control of only the area around Dublin known as the Pale. In 1536, on orders from London, the Irish Parliament, which represented only the English landlords and the people of the Pale, approved the English laws severing the church from Rome. The (English) ruling class adopted the new reformed faith, but most of the Irish people remained Roman Catholic. Irish armed opposition to the Reformation led to harsh repression by the English.

In the short reign of Henry's sickly son Edward VI (r. 1547–1553), strongly Protestant ideas exerted a significant influence on the religious life of the country. The equally brief reign of Mary Tudor (r. 1553–1558), the devoutly Catholic daughter of Catherine of Aragon, witnessed a sharp move back to Catholicism, and many Protestants fled to the continent. Mary's death raised to the throne her half sister Elizabeth (r. 1558–1603) and inaugurated the beginning of religious stability.

Elizabeth had been raised a Protestant, but at the start of her reign sharp differences existed in England. On the one hand, Catholics wanted a Roman Catholic ruler. On the other hand, a vocal number of returning exiles wanted all Catholic elements in the Church of England eliminated. Members of the latter group were called Puritans. Shrewdly, Elizabeth chose a middle course between Catholic and Puritan extremes. The Anglican Church, as the Church of England was called, moved in a moderately Protestant direction.

Calvinism and Its Moral Standards

John Calvin (1509–1564) was born in Noyon in northwestern France. As a young man he studied law, but in 1533 he experienced a religious crisis, as a result of which he converted from Catholicism to Protestantism. Calvin believed that God had specifically selected him to reform the church. Accordingly, he accepted an invitation to assist in the reformation of the city of Geneva. There, beginning in 1541, Calvin worked to establish a Christian society ruled by God through civil magistrates and reformed ministers.

Calvin's ideas are embodied in *The Institutes of the Christian Religion*, first published in 1536 and modified several times afterward. The cornerstone of Calvin's theology was his belief in the absolute sovereignty and omnipotence of God and the total weakness of humanity.

Calvin did not ascribe free will to human beings because that would detract from the sovereignty of God. According to his beliefs, men and women could not actively work to achieve salvation; rather, God decided at the beginning of time who would be saved and who damned. This viewpoint constitutes the theological principle called **predestination**. "This terrible decree," as even Calvin called it, did not lead to pessimism or fatalism. Instead, although Calvinists believed that one's own actions could do nothing to change one's fate, many came to believe that hard work, thrift, and moral conduct could serve as signs that one was among the "elect" chosen for salvation. Any occupation or profession could be a God-given "calling" and should be carried out with diligence and dedication.

predestination Calvin's teaching that God decided at the beginning of time who would be saved and who damned, so people could not actively work to achieve salvation.

Calvin transformed Geneva into a community based on his religious principles. The most powerful organization in the city became the Consistory, a group of laymen and pastors charged with investigating and disciplining deviations from proper doctrine and conduct. (See "Global Viewpoints: Chinese and European Views on Proper Behavior," page 444.)

Religious refugees from France, England, Spain, Scotland, and Italy visited Calvin's Geneva, which became the model of a Christian community for many. Subsequently, the Reformed Church of Calvin served as the model for the Presbyterian Church in Scotland, the Huguenot (HYOO-guh-naht) Church in France, and the Puritan Churches in England and New England. Calvinism became the compelling force in international Protestantism, first in Europe and then in many Dutch and English colonies around the world.

Chinese and European Views on Proper Behavior

Protestant reformers in Europe had clear ideas about virtuous behavior and how to encourage it, and the same was true of Neo-Confucian scholar-officials in China (see "The Scholar-Officials and Neo-Confucianism" in Chapter 13). The reformer John Calvin designed ordinances for the city of Geneva that regulated public and family life, while in China the official and military leader Wang Yangming (1472–1529) called for "community compacts," agreements between community members in which all pledged to act in a moral fashion.

Wang Yangming, Community Compact for Southern Ganzhou, 1520s

■ Nothing can be done to change what has already gone by, but something can still be done in the future. Therefore a community compact is now specially prepared to unite and harmonize all of you.

From now on, all of you who enter into this compact should be filial to your parents and respectful to your elders, teach your children, live in harmony with your fellow villagers, help one another when there is death in the family and assist one another in times of difficulty, encourage one another to do good and warn one another not to do evil, stop litigations and rivalry, cultivate faithfulness and promote harmony, and be sure to be good citizens so that together you may establish the custom of humanity and kindness. . . .

Elect from the compact membership an elderly and virtuous person respected by all to be the compact chief and two persons to be assistant chiefs [and other officials]. . . . Have three record books. One of these is to record the names of compact members and their daily movements and activities, and is to be in the charge of the compact executives. Of the remaining record books, one is for the purpose of displaying good deeds and the other for the purpose of reporting evil deeds. . . . To display good deeds, the language used must be clear and decisive, but in reporting mistakes, the language must be indirect and gentle.

John Calvin, Ecclesiastical Ordinances for the City of Geneva, 1541

■ [The office of the elders appointed to the Consistory] is to keep watch over the lives of everyone, to admonish in love those whom they see in error and leading disorderly lives. Whenever necessary they shall make a report concerning these to the ministers who will be designated to make brotherly corrections. . . .

If the church deems it wise, it will be well to choose two from the Little Council, four from the Council of Two Hundred, honest men of good demeanor, without reproach and free from all suspicion, above all fearing God and possessed of good and spiritual judgment. It will be well to elect them from every part of the city so as to be able to maintain supervision over all. . . .

If there shall be anyone who lays down opinions contrary to received doctrine, he is to be summoned. If he recants, he is to be dismissed without prejudice. If he is stubborn, he is to be admonished from time to time until it shall be evident that he deserves greater severity. . . .

If anyone is negligent in attending worship so that a noticeable offense is evident for the communion of the faithful, or if anyone shows himself contemptuous of ecclesiastical discipline, he is to be admonished. . . .

For the correction of faults, it is necessary to proceed after the ordinance of our Lord. That is, vices are to be dealt with secretly and no one is to be brought before the church for accusation if the fault is neither public nor scandalous, unless he has been found rebellious in the matter. . . .

Let all these measures be moderate; let there not be such a degree of rigor that anyone should be cast down, for all corrections are but medicinal, to bring back sinners to the Lord.

QUESTIONS FOR ANALYSIS

1. What types of actions do Wang and Calvin encourage and discourage?
2. What similarities and differences do you see in the institutions and procedures Wang and Calvin established to enforce proper conduct?
3. How do these documents reflect Confucian and Protestant Christian values and ideals?

Sources: William Theodore de Bary and Irene Bloom, eds., *Sources of Chinese Tradition* (New York: Columbia University Press, 1999), pp. 854–855; *The Protestant Reformation*, ed. Hans J. Hillerbrand (New York: Harper Torchbooks, 1968), pp. 174, 177. Material originally appeared (in slightly modified form) in *The Reformation: A Narrative History Related by Contemporary Observers and Participants*, ed. Hans J. Hillerbrand (New York: Harper and Row, 1964), pp. 192–194. Used by permission of the author.

The Catholic Reformation

How did the Catholic Church respond to the new religious situation?

Between 1517 and 1547 Protestantism made remarkable advances. Nevertheless, the Roman Catholic Church made a significant comeback (Map 15.2). Many historians see the developments within the Catholic Church after the Protestant Reformation as two interrelated movements, one a drive for internal reform, and the other a Counter-Reformation that actively opposed Protestantism. In both movements, papal reforms and new religious orders were important agents.

Papal Reforms and the Council of Trent

Under Pope Paul III (pontificate 1534–1549) the papal court became the center of a reform movement within the Catholic Church. In 1542 he established the Supreme Sacred Congregation of the Roman and Universal Inquisition, often called the Holy Office, with jurisdiction over the Roman Inquisition, a powerful instrument of the Catholic Reformation. The Inquisition had judicial authority over all Catholics and the power to arrest, imprison, and execute.

Pope Paul III also called a general council, which met intermittently from 1545 to 1563 at Trent, an imperial city close to Italy. The decrees of the Council of Trent laid a solid basis for the spiritual renewal of the Catholic Church. It gave equal validity to the Scriptures and to tradition as sources of religious truth and authority. It reaffirmed the seven sacraments and the traditional Catholic teaching on transubstantiation (the transformation of bread and wine into the body and blood of Christ in the Eucharist). It tackled the disciplinary matters that had disillusioned the faithful. The council also required every diocese to establish a seminary for educating and training clergy. Finally, great emphasis was placed on preaching to and instructing the laity, especially the uneducated. For four centuries the doctrinal and disciplinary legislation of Trent served as the basis for Roman Catholic faith, organization, and practice.

New Religious Orders

Just as seminaries provided education, so did new religious orders, which aimed to raise the moral and intellectual level of the clergy and people. The Ursuline (UHR-suh-luhn) order of nuns, founded in 1535 by Angela Merici (1474–1540), attained enormous prestige for its education of women. The Ursulines were the first women's religious order concentrating exclusively on teaching young girls, with the goal of re-Christianizing society by training future wives and mothers. After receiving papal approval in 1565, the Ursulines rapidly spread to France and the New World.

Another important new order was the Society of Jesus, or **Jesuits**. Founded by Ignatius Loyola (1491–1556), and approved by the pope in 1540, this order played a powerful international role in strengthening Catholicism in Europe and spreading the faith around the world. Under Loyola's leadership, the Society of Jesus developed into a highly centralized, tightly knit organization whose professed members vowed to go anywhere the pope said they were needed. They established schools that

Teresa of Ávila In this wood carving from 1625, the Spanish artist Gregorio Fernandez shows Saint Teresa book in hand, actively teaching. The influence of her ideas and actions led the pope to give Teresa the title "Doctor of the Church" in 1970, the first woman to be so honored. (National Museum of Sculpture, Valladolid, Spain/© P. Rotger/Iberfoto/The Image Works)

Jesuits Members of the Society of Jesus, founded by Ignatius Loyola in 1540, whose goal was the spread of the Roman Catholic faith through schools and missionary activity.

Predominant religion in 1555

- Lutheran
- Calvinist (Reformed)
- Church of England
- Roman Catholic
- Eastern Orthodox
- Muslim
- → Spread of Calvinism, from 1541
- ▲ Huguenot center
- — Ottoman Empire, 1566

0   150   300 miles
0   150   300 kilometers

Penetration of Calvinism to England after 1558

Wittenberg: Martin Luther writes Ninety-five Theses 1517

Nantes: Edict of Nantes 1598

Worms: Edict of Worms 1521

Trent: Council of Trent, 1545–1563

Augsburg: Peace of Augsburg 1555

Geneva: Calvin assists in Reformation beginning in 1541

MAPPING THE PAST

MAP 15.2 Religious Divisions in Europe, ca. 1555 The Reformation shattered the religious unity of Western Christendom. The situation was even more complicated than a map of this scale can show. Many cities within the Holy Roman Empire, for example, accepted a different faith than did the surrounding countryside; Augsburg, Basel, and Strasbourg were all Protestant, though surrounded by territory ruled by Catholic nobles.

ANALYZING THE MAP Which countries in Europe were the most religiously diverse? Which were the least diverse?

CONNECTIONS Where was the first arena of religious conflict in Europe, and why did it develop there and not elsewhere? What nonreligious factors contributed to the religious divisions that developed in sixteenth-century Europe, and to what degree can they explain these divisions?

adopted the modern humanist curricula and methods and that educated the sons of the nobility as well as the poor. The Jesuits attracted many recruits and achieved phenomenal success for the papacy and the reformed Catholic Church, carrying Christianity to much of South and Central America, India, and Japan before 1550 and to Brazil, North America, and the Congo in the seventeenth century. Within

Europe the Jesuits brought almost all of southern Germany and much of eastern Europe back to Catholicism. Also, as confessors and spiritual directors to kings, Jesuits exerted great political influence.

Religious Violence

In 1559 France and Spain signed the Treaty of Cateau-Cambrésis (KAH-toh cahm-BREH-sis), which ended the long conflict known as the Habsburg-Valois wars. However, over the next century religious differences led to riots, civil wars, and international conflicts. Especially in France and the Netherlands, Protestants and Catholics opposed one another through preaching, teaching, and violence. Catholics and Protestants alike feared people of other faiths, whom they often saw as agents of Satan. Even more, they feared those explicitly identified with Satan: people believed to be witches. This era also saw the most virulent witch persecutions in European history, as both Protestants and Catholics tried to make their cities and states more godly.

> **What were the causes and consequences of religious violence, including riots, wars, and witch-hunts?**

French Religious Wars

The costs of the Habsburg-Valois wars, waged intermittently through the first half of the sixteenth century, forced the French to increase taxes and borrow heavily. King Francis I's treaty with the pope (see "Politics and the State in the Renaissance") gave the French crown a rich supplement of money and offices and also a vested financial interest in Catholicism. Significant numbers of French people, however, were attracted to Calvinism. Calvinism drew converts from among reform-minded members of the Catholic clergy, the industrious middle classes, and artisan groups. Additionally, some French nobles became Calvinist. By the middle of the sixteenth century perhaps one-tenth of the French population had become **Huguenots**, the name given to French Calvinists.

Huguenots French Calvinists.

Both Calvinists and Catholics believed that the others' books, services, and ministers polluted the community. Preachers communicated these ideas in sermons, triggering religious violence. Armed clashes between Catholic royalist nobles and Calvinist antimonarchical nobles occurred in many parts of France.

Calvinist teachings called the power of sacred images into question, and mobs in many cities destroyed statues, stained-glass windows, and paintings. Catholic mobs responded by defending the sacred images, and crowds on both sides killed their opponents, often in gruesome ways.

A particularly savage Catholic attack on Calvinists took place in Paris on August 24, 1572, Saint Bartholomew's Day. The occasion was the marriage of the king's sister Margaret of Valois to the Protestant Henry of Navarre, which was intended to help reconcile Catholics and Huguenots. Instead Huguenot wedding guests in Paris were massacred, and other Protestants were slaughtered by mobs. Violence spread to the provinces, where thousands were killed. The Saint Bartholomew's Day massacre led to a civil war that dragged on for fifteen years.

What ultimately saved France was a small group of moderates of both faiths called **politiques** (POH-lee-teeks), who believed that only the restoration of a strong monarchy could reverse the trend toward collapse. The politiques also favored officially recognizing the Huguenots. The death of the French queen Catherine de' Medici, followed by the assassination of her son King Henry III, paved the way for the acces-

politiques Catholic and Protestant moderates who sought to end the religious violence in France by restoring a strong monarchy and granting official recognition to the Huguenots.

sion of Henry of Navarre (the unfortunate bridegroom of the Saint Bartholomew's Day massacre), a politique who became Henry IV (r. 1589–1610).

Henry's willingness to sacrifice religious principles to political necessity saved France. He converted to Catholicism but also, in 1598, issued the Edict of Nantes (NAHNT), which granted liberty of conscience (freedom of thought) and liberty of public worship to Huguenots in 150 fortified towns. By helping restore internal peace in France, the reign of Henry IV and the Edict of Nantes paved the way for French kings to claim absolute power in the seventeenth century.

Civil Wars in the Netherlands

In the Netherlands a movement for church reform developed into a struggle for Dutch independence. The Catholic emperor Charles V had inherited the seventeen provinces that compose present-day Belgium and the Netherlands (see "The Habsburgs"). In the Netherlands, as in many other places, Lutheran ideas took root. Charles V had grown up in the Netherlands, however, and he was able to limit the impact of the new ideas. As discussed earlier, Charles V abdicated in 1556 and transferred power over the Netherlands to his son Philip II, who had grown up in Spain. Although Philip, like his father, opposed Protestantism, Protestant ideas spread in the Netherlands.

By the 1560s Protestants in the Netherlands were primarily Calvinists. When Spanish authorities attempted to suppress Calvinist worship and raised taxes, their actions sparked riots and a wave of iconoclasm. In response, Philip II sent twenty thousand Spanish troops, and from 1568 to 1578 civil war raged in the Netherlands between Catholics and Protestants and between the seventeen provinces and Spain. Eventually the ten southern provinces came under the control of the Spanish Habsburg forces. The seven northern provinces, led by Holland, formed the Union of Utrecht (the United Provinces), and in 1581 they declared their independence from Spain. The north was Protestant, and the south remained Catholic. Philip did

Spanish Soldiers Killing Protestants in Haarlem In this 1573 engraving by the Calvinist artist Franz Hogenberg, Spanish soldiers accompanied by priests kill residents of the Dutch city of Haarlem by hanging or beheading, and then dump their bodies in the river. Haarlem had withstood a seven-month siege by Spanish troops in 1572–1573, and after the starving city surrendered, the garrison of troops and forty citizens judged guilty of sedition were executed. Images such as this were part of the propaganda battle that accompanied the wars of religion, but in many cases there were actual atrocities, on both sides. (Private Collection/Bridgeman Images)

not accept the independence of the north, and war continued. England was even drawn into the conflict, supplying money and troops to the United Provinces. (Spain launched the Spanish Armada, an unsuccessful invasion of England, in response.) Hostilities ended in 1609 when Spain agreed to a truce that recognized the independence of the United Provinces.

The Great European Witch-Hunt

Insecurity created by the religious wars contributed to persecution for witchcraft, which actually began before the Reformation in the 1480s but became especially common about 1560. Both Protestants and Catholics tried and executed those accused of being witches.

The heightened sense of God's power and divine wrath in the Reformation era was an important factor in the **witch-hunts**, but other factors were also significant. In the later Middle Ages, scholars and officials added a demonological component to existing ideas about witches. For them, the essence of witchcraft was making a pact with the Devil that required the witch to do the Devil's bidding. Witches were no longer simply people who used magical power to do harm and get what they wanted, but rather people used by the Devil to do what he wanted.

> **witch-hunts** Campaign against witchcraft in Europe and European colonies during the sixteenth and seventeenth centuries in which hundreds of thousands of people, mostly women, were tried, and many of them executed.

Trials involving this new notion of witchcraft as diabolical heresy began in Switzerland and southern Germany in the late fifteenth century; became less numerous in the early decades of the Reformation, when Protestants and Catholics were busy fighting each other; and then picked up again about 1560, spreading to much of western Europe and to European colonies in the Americas. Scholars estimate that during the sixteenth and seventeenth centuries somewhere between 100,000 and 200,000 people were officially tried for witchcraft, and between 40,000 and 60,000 were executed.

Though the gender balance of the accused varied widely in different parts of Europe, between 75 and 85 percent of those tried and executed were women, whom some demonologists viewed as weaker and so more likely to give in to the Devil. Tensions within families, households, and neighborhoods also played a role in witchcraft accusations, as grievances and jealousies led to accusations. Suspects were questioned and tortured by legal authorities, and they often implicated others.

Even in the sixteenth century a few individuals questioned whether witches could ever do harm, make a pact with the Devil, or engage in the wild activities attributed to them. Furthermore, doubts about trial procedures and the use of torture to extract confessions gradually spread among the same type of religious and legal authorities who had so vigorously persecuted witches. By about 1660 prosecutions for witchcraft had become less common.

European ideas about witchcraft traveled across the Atlantic. There were a few trials of European colonists for witchcraft—the most famous of which was at Salem in Massachusetts—but more often indigenous people were accused of being witches.

Chapter Summary

The Renaissance was characterized by self-conscious awareness among educated Europeans, particularly scholars and writers known as humanists, that they were living in a new era. Central to humanists were interest in the Latin classics, belief in individual potential, education for a career of public service, and, in northern Europe, the reform of church and society. Their ideas spread as a result of the development of the printing press with movable metal type, which revolutionized communication. Interest in the classical past and in the individual shaped the style and subject matter of Renaissance art, and patrons provided the money needed for an outpouring of painting, sculpture, and architecture. Social hierarchies in the Renaissance developed new features that contributed to the modern social hierarchies of race, class, and gender. In politics, feudal monarchies gradually evolved into nation-states, as rulers used war, diplomacy, new forms of taxation, centralized institutions, and strategic marital alliances to build up their power.

Many individuals and groups had long called for reforms in the Catholic Church, providing a ready audience in the early sixteenth century for the ideas of Martin Luther. Luther and other reformers, called Protestants, developed a new understanding of Christian doctrine that emphasized faith and grace; Protestant ideas spread rapidly through preaching, hymns, and the printing press; and soon western Europe was split religiously. Local situations influenced religious patterns. In England the king's need for a church-approved divorce triggered the break with Rome, while in France and eastern Europe the ideas of John Calvin gained wide acceptance. By the middle of the sixteenth century the Roman Catholic Church had begun a process of internal reform along with opposing Protestants intellectually, politically, militarily, and institutionally. This reinvigorated Catholic Church would carry Christian ideas around the world, while in Europe religious differences led to riots, witch persecutions, civil wars, and international conflicts.

CONNECTIONS

The Renaissance and the Reformation are often seen as key to the creation of the modern world. The radical changes of these times contained many elements of continuity, however. Artists, humanists, and religious reformers looked back to the classical era and early Christianity for inspiration. Political leaders played important roles in cultural and religious developments, just as they had for centuries in Europe and other parts of the world. Social hierarchies of race, status, and gender built on those of earlier periods. Thinkers highlighted individual achievement, but families, religious brotherhoods, and other groups remained important. The events of the Renaissance and Reformation were thus linked with earlier developments, and they were also closely connected with another important element in the modern world: European exploration and colonization (discussed in Chapter 16). Renaissance monarchs paid for maritime expeditions, expecting a large share of any profits gained and increasingly viewing overseas territory as essential to their own reputations and to a strong state. Moreover, for many, European expansion had a religious dimension and was explicitly linked to the spread of Christianity around the world. The desire for fame, wealth, and power that was central to the Renaissance, and the religious zeal central to the Reformation, were thus key to the European voyages and to colonial ventures as well.

Identify Key Terms

Identify and explain the significance of each item below.

Renaissance (p. 424)   **Protestant Reformation** (p. 436)   **Jesuits** (p. 445)

patronage (p. 424)   **indulgence** (p. 438)   **Huguenots** (p. 447)

humanism (p. 425)   **Diet of Worms** (p. 438)   **politiques** (p. 447)

Christian humanists (p. 426)   **Protestant** (p. 438)   **witch-hunts** (p. 449)

debate about women (p. 433)   **predestination** (p. 443)

Review the Main Ideas

Answer the focus questions from each section of the chapter.

1. What were the major cultural developments of the Renaissance? (p. 424)

2. What were the key social hierarchies in Renaissance Europe, and how did these hierarchies shape people's lives? (p. 431)

3. How did the nation-states of western Europe evolve in this period? (p. 434)

4. What were the central ideas of Protestant reformers, and why were they appealing to various groups across Europe? (p. 436)

5. How did the Catholic Church respond to the new religious situation? (p. 445)

6. What were the causes and consequences of religious violence, including riots, wars, and witch-hunts? (p. 447)

Make Comparisons and Connections

Analyze the larger developments and continuities within and across chapters.

1. The word *Renaissance*, invented to describe the cultural flowering in Italy that began in the fourteenth century, has often been used for other periods of advance in learning and the arts, such as the "Carolingian Renaissance" that you read about in Chapter 8. Can you think of other, more recent "Renaissances" or ways the term is used today?

2. The "debate about women" that you read about in this chapter was not simply a European phenomenon, as educated men (and occasionally a few educated women) in many cultures discussed women's nature and character. How would you compare ideas about women in classical Islamic society (Chapter 9), Song China (Chapter 13), Heian Japan (Chapter 13), Renaissance Italy, and Protestant Germany? How were these ideas reflected (or not reflected) in women's actual lives?

3. Martin Luther is always on every list of the one hundred most influential individuals of all time. Should he be? Why or why not? Who else from this chapter (or other chapters) should be on such a list, and why?

TIMELINE

EUROPE

1508–1512 Michelangelo paints the Sistine Chapel

1450s Development of movable metal type in Germany

1494–1559 Habsburg-Valois Wars

◆ **1521** Diet of Worms

← **1434–1737** Medici family in power in Florence

1525 ◆ Peasant revolts in Germany

◆ **1536** John Calvin publishes *The Institutes of the Christian Religion*

1469 ◆ Marriage of Isabella of Castile and Ferdinand of Aragon

1527 ◆ Henry VIII of England asks Pope Clement VII to annul his marriage to Catherine of Aragon

1540 ◆ Papal approval of the Society of Jesus (Jesuits)

1492 ◆ Spain conquers Granada; practicing Jews expelled from Spain

◆ **1513** Niccolò Machiavelli writes *The Prince*

AFRICA

AMERICAS

← **ca. 1428–1521** Aztec Empire dominates Mesoamerica **(Ch. 11)**

← **ca. 1438–1532** Inca Empire dominates the Andes **(Ch. 11)**

ASIA

← **1368–1644** Ming Dynasty in China **(Ch. 21)**

WORLD

1450–1600 European voyages of discovery and establishment of colonial empires **(Ch. 16)**

1450	1500	1550

Suggested Resources

BOOKS

Bethencourt, Francisco. *The Inquisition: A Global History, 1478–1834.* 2009. A comprehensive study that examines the Inquisition in Spain, Portugal, Italy, and the Iberian empires overseas.

Cameron, Euan. *The European Reformation*, 2d ed. 2012. A thorough analysis of the Protestant and Catholic Reformations throughout Europe.

Earle, T. F., and K. J. P. Lowe, eds. *Black Africans in Renaissance Europe.* 2005. Includes essays discussing many aspects of ideas about race and the experience of Africans in Europe.

Hsia, R. Po-Chia. *The World of Catholic Renewal, 1540–1770*, 2d ed. 2005. Situates the Catholic Reformation in a global context and examines colonial Catholicism.

Johnson, Geraldine. *Renaissance Art: A Very Short Introduction.* 2005. An excellent brief survey that includes male and female artists and sets the art in its cultural and historical context.

Levack, Brian. *The Witch-Hunt in Early Modern Europe*, 3d ed. 2007. A good introduction to the vast literature on witchcraft, with helpful bibliographies.

Man, John. *Gutenberg Revolution: The Story of a Genius and an Invention That Changed the World.* 2002. Presents a rather idealized view of Gutenberg but has good discussions of his milieu and excellent illustrations.

Matheson, Peter, ed. *Reformation Christianity.* 2004. This volume in the People's History of Christianity series explores social issues and popular religion.

Nauert, Charles. *Humanism and the Culture of Renaissance Europe*, 2d ed. 2006. A thorough introduction to humanism throughout Europe.

Waley, Daniel, and Trevor Dean. *The Italian City-Republics*, 4th ed. 2010. Analyzes the rise of independent city-states in northern Italy, including discussion of the artistic and social lives of their inhabitants.

◆ **1598** Edict of Nantes

← ◆ **1555** Peace of Augsburg

← **1545–1563** Council of Trent

1560–1660 Height of European witch-hunt

1558–1603 Reign of Elizabeth I in England

1568–1578 Civil war in the Netherlands

◆ **1572** Saint Bartholomew's Day massacre

ca. 1464–1591
Songhai Empire in West Africa **(Ch. 20)**

ca. 1500–1700 Height of Ottoman, Safavid, and Mughal Empires **(Ch. 17)**

| 1600 | 1650 | 1700 |

Wiesner-Hanks, Merry E. *Women and Gender in Early Modern Europe*, 3d ed. 2008. Discusses all aspects of women's lives as well as ideas about gender.

DOCUMENTARIES

Leonardo da Vinci (BBC, 2004). A three-part documentary telling the life story of Leonardo as an artist, inventor, and engineer. Features tests of his designs for the parachute, tank, diving suit, and glider, and an investigation of the *Mona Lisa*.

The Medici: Godfathers of the Renaissance (PBS, 2004). Surveys the power and patronage of the Medici family, with extensive coverage of art and architecture.

The Protestant Revolution (BBC, 2007). Examines the religious roots and the scientific, cultural, social, economic, and political impact of Protestantism, viewing these as wide-ranging and global in scope.

FEATURE FILMS AND TELEVISION DRAMAS

Luther (Eric Till, 2003). A fairly accurate biopic, starring Joseph Fiennes, which traces Martin Luther's life from his becoming a monk through his break with the church, his marriage, and the German Peasants' War.

Wolf Hall (BBC, 2015). A miniseries based on the award-winning historical novels by Hilary Mantel that focuses on Thomas Cromwell, Henry VIII's chief minister. Praised for its acting and staging, but criticized for its harsh treatment of Thomas More.

WEBSITE

The Medici Archive Project. A database for researching the nearly 3 million letters held by the Medici Granducal Archive Collection in Florence, spanning the years from 1537 to 1743. Includes topical "document highlights" in English and Italian, accompanied by illustrations. **www.medici.org/**

16

The Acceleration of Global Contact
1450–1600

Before 1500 Europeans were relatively marginal players in a centuries-old trading system that linked Africa, Asia, and Europe. The Indian Ocean was the locus of a vibrant cosmopolitan Afroeurasian trade world in which Arab, Persian, Turkish, Indian, African, Chinese, and European merchants and adventurers competed for trade in spices, silks, and other goods. Elites everywhere prized Chinese porcelains and silks, while wealthy members of the Celestial Kingdom, as China called itself, wanted gold, ivory, and rhinoceros horn from Africa and exotic goods and peacocks from India. African people wanted textiles from India and cowrie shells from the Maldives in the Indian Ocean. Europeans craved Asian silks and spices, but they had few desirable goods to offer their trading partners.

By 1550 the European search for better access to Asian trade goods had led to a new overseas empire in the Indian Ocean and the accidental discovery of the Western Hemisphere. With this discovery South and North America were drawn into an international network of trade centers and political empires, which Europeans came to dominate. The era of globalization had begun, creating new political systems and forms of economic exchange as well as cultural assimilation, conversion, and resistance.

Nezahualpilli

At the time of the arrival of Europeans, Nezahualpilli was ruler of the city-state of Texcoco, the second-most-important city in the Aztec Empire after Tenochtitlan.

From *Codex Ixtlilxochitl*, 1582, pigment on European paper/Bibliothèque Nationale, Paris, France/De Agostini Picture Library/akg-images

CHAPTER PREVIEW

THE AFROEURASIAN TRADE WORLD
What was the Afroeurasian trade world prior to the era of European exploration?

THE EUROPEAN VOYAGES OF DISCOVERY
How and why did Europeans undertake ambitious voyages of expansion?

CONQUEST AND SETTLEMENT
What was the impact of Iberian conquest and settlement on the peoples and ecologies of the Americas?

THE ERA OF GLOBAL CONTACT
How was the era of global contact shaped by new commodities, commercial empires, and forced migrations?

CHANGING ATTITUDES AND BELIEFS
How did new encounters shape cultural attitudes and beliefs in Europe and the rest of the world?

What was the Afroeurasian trade world prior to the era of European exploration?

The Afroeurasian Trade World

The Afroeurasian trade world linked the products and people of Europe, Asia, and Africa in the fifteenth century. The West was a marginal player in this trading system. Nevertheless, wealthy Europeans were eager consumers of luxury goods from the East, which they received through Italian middlemen.

The Trade World of the Indian Ocean

The Indian Ocean was the center of the Afroeurasian trade world, serving as a crossroads for commercial and cultural exchanges between China, India, the Middle East, Africa, and Europe (Map 16.1). From the seventh through the fourteenth centuries, the volume of this trade steadily increased, declining only during the years of the Black Death.

Merchants congregated in a series of multicultural, cosmopolitan port cities strung around the Indian Ocean. Most of these cities had some form of autonomous self-government, and mutual self-interest largely limited violence and prevented attempts

MAP 16.1 The Fifteenth-Century Afroeurasian Trading World After a period of decline following the Black Death and the Mongol invasions, trade revived in the fifteenth century. Muslim merchants dominated trade, linking ports in East Africa and the Red Sea with those in India and the Malay Archipelago. The Chinese admiral Zheng He followed the most important Indian Ocean trade routes on his voyages (1405–1433), hoping to impose Ming dominance of trade and tribute.

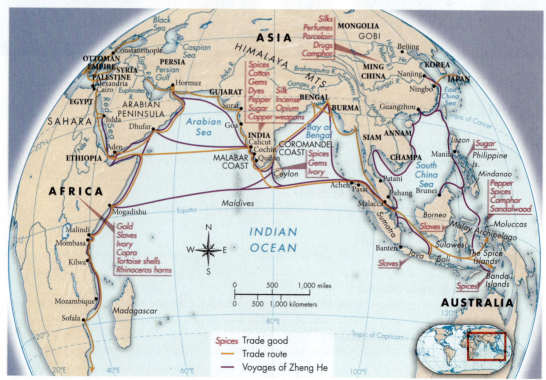

Island of Kilwa   The small island of Kilwa, off the coast of modern-day Tanzania, was a vital center of Indian Ocean trade from the thirteenth to the fifteenth centuries. During this period, the sultanate of Kilwa controlled trade among the Swahili-speaking cities of the east coast of Africa; its merchants dealt in gold, silver, pearls, and porcelain. The arrival of the Portuguese in 1498 led to the loss of Kilwa's autonomy. (Pictures from History/Bridgeman Images)

to monopolize trade. The most developed area of this commercial web was made up of the ports surrounding the South China Sea. In the fifteenth century the port of Malacca became a great commercial entrepôt (AHN-truh-poh), a trading center to which goods were shipped for storage while awaiting redistribution. To Malacca came porcelains, silks, and camphor (used in the manufacture of many medications) from China; pepper, cloves, nutmeg, and raw materials such as sandalwood from the Moluccas; sugar from the Philippines; and textiles, copper weapons, incense, dyes, and opium from India.

The Mongol emperors opened the doors of China to the West, encouraging Europeans like the Venetian trader and explorer Marco Polo to do business there. Marco Polo's tales of his travels from 1271 to 1295 and his encounter with the Great Khan fueled Western fantasies about the Orient. After the Mongols fell to the Ming Dynasty in 1368, China entered a period of agricultural and commercial expansion, population growth, and urbanization (see "Ming China" in Chapter 21). Historians agree that China had the most advanced economy in the world until at least the beginning of the eighteenth century.

China also took the lead in exploration, sending Admiral Zheng He's fleet as far west as Egypt. Each of his seven expeditions from 1405 to 1433 involved hundreds of ships and tens of thousands of men. The purpose of the voyages was primarily diplomatic, to enhance China's prestige and seek tribute-paying alliances. The high expense of the voyages in a period of renewed Mongol encroachment led to the abandonment of the maritime expeditions after the deaths of Zheng He and the emperor. China's turning away from external trade opened new opportunities for European states to expand their role in Asian trade.

Another center of Indian Ocean trade was India, the crucial link between the Persian Gulf and the Southeast Asian and East Asian trade networks. The subcontinent had ancient links with its neighbors to the northwest. Trade among ports bordering the Indian Ocean was revived in the Middle Ages by Arab merchants who circumnavigated India on their way to trade in the South China Sea. The inhabitants of India's Coromandel coast traditionally looked to Southeast Asia, where they had ancient trading and cultural ties. Hinduism and Buddhism arrived in Southeast Asia from India during late antiquity, and a brisk trade between Southeast Asian and Coromandel port cities persisted from that time until the arrival of the Portuguese in the sixteenth century. India itself was an important contributor of goods to the world trading system. Most of the world's pepper was grown in India, and Indian cotton and silk textiles were also highly prized.

Peoples and Cultures of the Indian Ocean

Indian Ocean trade connected peoples from the Malay Peninsula (the southern extremity of the Asian continent), India, China, and East Africa, among whom there was an enormous variety of languages, cultures, and religions. In spite of this diversity, certain sociocultural similarities linked these peoples, especially in Southeast Asia.

In comparison to India, China, or even Europe after the Black Death, Southeast Asia was sparsely populated. People were concentrated in port cities and in areas of intense rice cultivation. Another difference between Southeast Asia and India, China, and Europe was the higher status of women — their primary role in planting and harvesting rice gave them authority and economic power. At marriage, which typically occurred around age twenty, the groom paid the bride (or sometimes her family) a sum of money called **bride wealth**, which remained under her control. This practice was in sharp contrast to the Chinese, Indian, and European dowry, which came under the husband's control. Property was administered jointly, in contrast to the Chinese principle and Indian practice that wives had no say in the disposal of family property. All children, regardless of gender, inherited equally.

bride wealth In early modern Southeast Asia, a sum of money the groom paid the bride or her family at the time of marriage. This practice contrasted with the dowry in China, India, and Europe, which the husband controlled.

Respect for women carried over to the commercial sphere. Women participated in business as partners and independent entrepreneurs. When Portuguese and Dutch men settled in the region and married local women, their wives continued to play important roles in trade and commerce.

In contrast to most parts of the world other than Africa, Southeast Asian peoples had an accepting attitude toward premarital sexual activity and placed no premium on virginity at marriage. Divorce carried no social stigma and was easily attainable if a pair proved incompatible. Either the woman or the man could initiate a divorce.

Trade with Africa and the Middle East

On the east coast of Africa, Swahili-speaking city-states engaged in the Indian Ocean trade, exchanging ivory, rhinoceros horn, tortoise shells, copra (dried coconut), and slaves for textiles, spices, cowrie shells, porcelain, and other goods. The most important cities were Mogadishu, Mombasa, and Kilwa, which had converted to Islam by the eleventh century.

West Africa also played an important role in world trade. In the fifteenth century most of the gold that reached Europe came from the Sudan region in West Africa. Transported across the Sahara by Arab and African traders on camels, the gold was sold in the ports of North Africa. Other trading routes led to the Egyptian cities of Alexandria and Cairo.

Inland nations that sat astride the north-south caravan routes grew wealthy from this trade. In the mid-thirteenth century the kingdom of Mali emerged as an important player on the overland trade route. In later centuries, however, the diversion of gold away from the trans-Sahara routes would weaken the inland states of Africa politically and economically.

Gold was one important object of trade; slaves were another. Long before the arrival of Europeans, Arab and African merchants took West African slaves to the Mediterranean to be sold in European, Egyptian, and Middle Eastern markets and also brought eastern Europeans to West Africa as slaves. In addition, Indian and Arab merchants traded slaves in the coastal regions of East Africa.

The Middle East served as an intermediary for trade between Europe, Africa, and Asia and was also an important supplier of goods for foreign exchange. Two great rival empires, the Persian Safavids and the Turkish Ottomans, dominated the region, competing for control over western trade routes to the East. By the mid-sixteenth century the Ottomans had established control over eastern Mediterranean sea routes to trading centers in Syria, Palestine, Egypt, and the rest of North Africa (see "The Expansion of the Ottoman Empire" in Chapter 17). Their power extended into Europe as far west as Vienna.

Mansa Musa This detail from the Catalan Atlas of 1375, a world map created for the Catalan king, depicts a king of Mali, Mansa Musa, who was legendary for his wealth in gold. European desires for direct access to the trade in sub-Saharan gold helped inspire Portuguese exploration of the west coast of Africa in the fifteenth century. (Bibliothèque Nationale, Paris, France/Bridgeman Images)

Genoese and Venetian Middlemen

Europe constituted a minor outpost in the world trading system, for European craftsmen produced few products to rival those of Asia. However, Europeans desired luxury goods from the East, and in the late Middle Ages such trade was controlled by the Italian city-states of Venice and Genoa. Venice had opened the gateway to Asian trade in 1304, when it established formal relations with the sultan of Mamluk Egypt and started operations in Cairo. Because demand for European goods was low, Venetians funded their purchases through shipping and trade in firearms and slaves.

Venice's ancient trading rival was Genoa. By 1270 Genoa dominated the northern route to Asia through the Black Sea. From then until the fourteenth century the Genoese expanded their trade routes as far as Persia and the Far East.

In the fifteenth century, with Venice claiming victory in the spice trade, the Genoese shifted focus from trade to finance and from the Black Sea to the western Mediterranean. When Spanish and Portuguese voyages began to explore the western Atlantic (see "The European Voyages of Discovery"), Genoese merchants, navigators, and financiers provided their skills and capital to the Iberian monarchs.

A major element of Italian trade was slavery. Merchants purchased slaves in the Balkans of southeastern Europe. After the loss of the Black Sea trade routes—and thus the source of slaves—to the Ottomans, the Genoese sought new supplies of slaves in the West, eventually seizing or buying and selling the Guanches (indigenous peoples from the Canary Islands), Muslim prisoners and Jewish refugees from Spain, and, by the early 1500s, both black and Berber Africans. With the growth of Spanish colonies in the New World, Genoese and Venetian merchants became important players in the Atlantic slave trade.

How and why did Europeans undertake ambitious voyages of expansion?

The European Voyages of Discovery

As Europe recovered after the Black Death, new European players entered the scene with novel technology, eager to spread Christianity and to undo Italian and Ottoman domination of trade with the East. A century after the plague, Iberian explorers began overseas voyages that helped create the modern world, with immense consequences for their own continent and the rest of the planet.

Causes of European Expansion

European expansion had multiple causes. The first was economic. By the middle of the fifteenth century Europe was experiencing a revival of population and economic activity after the lows of the Black Death. This revival created renewed demand for luxuries, especially spices, from the East. Introduced into western Europe by the Crusaders in the twelfth century, spices such as pepper, nutmeg, cinnamon, and cloves added flavor and variety to the monotonous European diet. They were also used in anointing oil and as incense for religious rituals, and as perfumes, medicines, and dyes in daily life. The fall of Constantinople and the subsequent Ottoman control of trade routes created obstacles to fulfilling demands for these precious and prestigious goods. Europeans eager for the profits of trade thus needed to find new sources of precious metal to exchange with the Ottomans or trade routes that bypassed the Ottomans.

Religious fervor and the crusading spirit were the second important catalyst for expansion. Just seven months separated Isabella and Ferdinand's conquest of the emirate of Granada, the last remaining Muslim state on the Iberian Peninsula, and Columbus's departure across the Atlantic. Overseas exploration thus transferred the militaristic religious fervor of the reconquista (reconquest) to new non-Christian territories. As they conquered indigenous empires, Iberians brought the attitudes and administrative practices developed during the reconquista to the Americas.

A third motivation was the dynamic spirit of the Renaissance. Like other men of the Renaissance era, explorers sought to win glory for their exploits and demonstrated a genuine interest in learning more about unknown waters. The detailed journals kept by European voyagers attest to their fascination with the new peoples and places they visited.

The people who stayed at home had a powerful impact on the voyages of discovery. Merchants provided the capital for many early voyages and had a strong say in their course. To gain authorization and financial support for their expeditions, they sought official sponsorship from the Crown. Competition among European monarchs for the prestige and profit of overseas exploration thus constituted another crucial factor in encouraging the steady stream of expeditions that began in the late fifteenth century.

The small number of Europeans who could read provided a rapt audience for tales of fantastic places and unknown peoples. Cosmography, natural history, and geography aroused enormous interest among educated people in the fifteenth and sixteenth centuries. One of the most popular books of the time was the fourteenth-century text *The Travels of Sir John Mandeville*, which purported to be a firsthand account of the author's travels in the Middle East, India, and China.

Technology and the Rise of Exploration

The Iberian powers sought technological improvements in shipbuilding, weaponry, and navigation in order to undertake ambitious voyages of exploration and trade. Medieval European seagoing vessels consisted of open galleys propelled by oars, common in Mediterranean trade, or single-masted sailing ships. Though adequate for short journeys that hugged the shoreline, such vessels were incapable of long-distance journeys or high-volume trade. In the fifteenth century the Portuguese developed the **caravel**, a three-masted sailing ship. Its multiple sails and sternpost rudder made the caravel a more maneuverable vessel that required fewer crewmen to operate. It could carry more cargo than a galley, which meant it could sail farther without stopping for supplies and return with a larger cache of profitable goods. When fitted with cannon, it could dominate larger vessels and bombard port cities.

This period also saw great strides in cartography and navigational aids. Around 1410 a Latin translation reintroduced western Europeans to **Ptolemy's** *Geography*. Written in the second century, the work synthesized the geographical knowledge of the classical world. It represented a major improvement over medieval cartography by depicting the world as round and introducing latitude and longitude markings, but it also contained significant errors. Unaware of the Americas, Ptolemy showed the world as much smaller than it is, so that Asia appeared not very far to the west of Europe.

Originating in China, the magnetic compass was brought to the West in the late Middle Ages. By using the compass to determine their direction and estimating their speed of travel over a set length of time, mariners could determine the course of a ship's voyage. The astrolabe, an instrument invented by the ancient Greeks and perfected by Muslim navigators, was used to determine the altitude of the sun and other celestial bodies. It allowed mariners to plot their latitude, that is, their precise position north or south of the equator.

Much of the new technology that Europeans used on their voyages was borrowed from the East. Gunpowder, the compass, and the sternpost rudder were Chinese inventions. The triangular lateen sail, which allowed caravels to tack against the wind, was a product of the Indian Ocean trade world. Advances in cartography and navigation also drew on the rich tradition of Judeo-Arabic mathematical and astronomical learning in Iberia. In exploring new territories, European sailors thus called

caravel A small, maneuverable, three-masted sailing ship developed by the Portuguese in the fifteenth century that gave the Portuguese a distinct advantage in exploration and trade.

Ptolemy's *Geography* A second-century work translated into Latin around 1410 that synthesized the classical knowledge of geography and introduced latitude and longitude markings.

on techniques and knowledge developed over centuries in China, the Muslim world, and trading centers along the Indian Ocean.

The Portuguese in Africa and Asia

For centuries Portugal was a small and poor nation on the margins of European life whose principal activities were fishing and subsistence farming. Yet Portugal had a long history of seafaring and navigation. Nature favored the Portuguese: winds blowing along their coast offered passage to Africa, its Atlantic islands, and, ultimately, Brazil. Once they had mastered the secret to sailing against the wind to return to Europe (by sailing farther west to catch winds from the southwest), they were poised to lead Atlantic exploration. The objectives of Portuguese exploration included achieving military glory; converting Muslims; and finding gold, slaves, and an overseas route to Asian spice markets.

In the early phases of Portuguese exploration, Prince Henry (1394–1460), a younger son of the king, played a leading role. A nineteenth-century scholar dubbed Henry "the Navigator" because of his support for Portuguese voyages of discovery. Henry participated in Portugal's conquest of Ceuta (sa-OO-tah), an Arab city in northern Morocco, in 1415, an event that marked the beginning of European overseas expansion. In the 1420s, under Henry's direction, the Portuguese began to settle the Atlantic islands of Madeira (ca. 1420) and the Azores (1427). In 1443 they founded their first African commercial settlement at Arguin in North Africa. By the time of Henry's death in 1460, his support for exploration had resulted in thriving sugar plantations on the Atlantic islands, the first arrival of enslaved Africans in Portugal, and new access to African gold.

The Portuguese next established fortified trading posts, called factories, on the gold-rich Guinea coast and penetrated into the African continent all the way to Timbuktu (Map 16.2). By 1500 Portugal controlled the flow of African gold to Europe. In contrast to the Spanish who conquered the Americas (see "Spanish Conquest of the Aztec and Inca Empires"), the Portuguese did not establish large settlements in West Africa or seek to control the political or cultural lives of those with whom they traded. Instead they sought to profit by inserting themselves into existing trading systems. For the first century of their relations, African rulers were equal partners with the Portuguese, benefiting from their experienced armies and European vulnerability to tropical diseases.

In 1487 Bartholomew Diaz (ca. 1451–1500) rounded the Cape of Good Hope at the southern tip of Africa (see Map 16.2), but poor conditions forced him to turn back. A decade later Vasco da Gama (ca. 1469–1524) succeeded in rounding the Cape while commanding a fleet in search of a sea route to India. With the help of an Indian guide, da Gama reached the port of Calicut in India. He returned to Lisbon with spices and samples of Indian cloth, having proved the possibility of lucrative trade with the East via the Cape route. Thereafter, a Portuguese convoy set out for passage around the Cape every March.

Lisbon became the entrance port for Asian goods into Europe, but this was not accomplished without a fight. Muslim-controlled port city-states had long controlled the rich trade of the Indian Ocean, and they did not surrender it willingly. From 1500 to 1515 the Portuguese used a combination of bombardment and diplomatic treaties to establish trading factories at Goa, Malacca, Calicut, and Hormuz, thereby

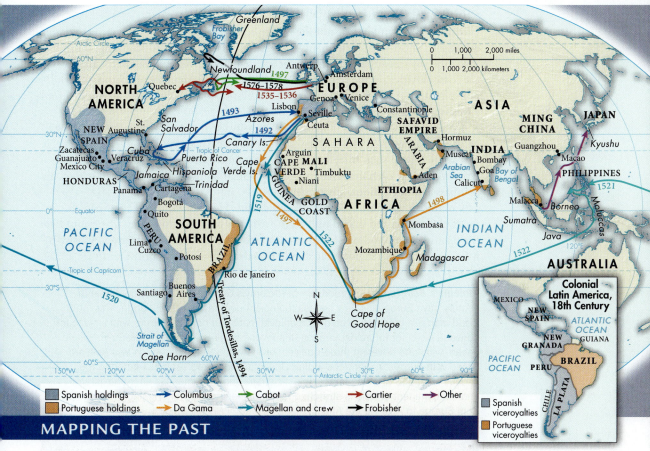

MAP 16.2 Overseas Exploration and Conquest in the Fifteenth and Sixteenth Centuries
The voyages of discovery marked a dramatic new phase in the centuries-old migrations of
European peoples. This map depicts the voyages of the most significant European explorers
of the period.

ANALYZING THE MAP Consider the routes and dates of the voyages shown. How
might the successes of the earlier voyages have contributed to the later expeditions?
Which voyage had the most impact, and why?

CONNECTIONS Do you think the importance of these voyages was primarily economic,
political, or cultural? Why?

laying the foundation for a Portuguese trading empire. The acquisition of port cities
and their trade routes brought riches to Portugal, but, as in Africa, the Portuguese
had limited impact on the lives and religious faith of peoples beyond Portuguese
coastal holdings.

Inspired by the Portuguese, the Spanish had also begun the quest for empire. Theirs
was to be a second, entirely different mode of colonization, leading to the conquest
of existing empires, large-scale settlement, and the forced assimilation of huge indigenous populations.

Spain's Voyages to the Americas

Christopher Columbus was not the first to cross the Atlantic. Ninth-century Vikings established short-lived settlements in Newfoundland, and it is probable that others made the voyage, either on purpose or accidentally, carried by westward currents off the coast of Africa. In the late fifteenth century the achievements of Portugal's decades of exploration made the moment right for Christopher Columbus's attempt to find a westward route across the Atlantic to Asia.

Christopher Columbus, a native of Genoa, was an experienced seaman and navigator. He had worked as a mapmaker in Lisbon and had spent time on Madeira. He was familiar with such fifteenth-century Portuguese navigational aids as *portolans*—written descriptions of the courses along which ships sailed—and the use of the compass as a navigational instrument.

Columbus was also a deeply religious man. He had witnessed the Spanish conquest of Granada and shared fully in the religious fervor surrounding that event. Like the Spanish rulers and most Europeans of his age, Columbus understood Christianity as a missionary religion that should be carried to all places of the earth.

Ptolemy's *Geography* The recovery of Ptolemy's *Geography* in the early fifteenth century gave Europeans new access to ancient geographical knowledge. This 1486 world map is a great advance over medieval maps but contains errors with significant consequences for future exploration. It shows a single continent watered by a single ocean, with land covering three-quarters of the world's surface. Africa and Asia are joined with Europe, making the Indian Ocean a landlocked sea and rendering the circumnavigation of Africa impossible. Australia and the Americas are nonexistent, and the continent of Asia is stretched far to the east, greatly shortening the distance from Europe to Asia via the Atlantic. (Bibliothèque Nationale, Paris, France/Bridgeman Images)

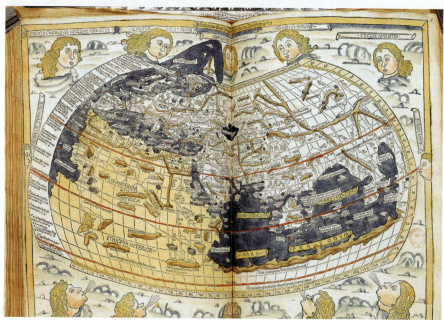

Rejected for funding by the Portuguese in 1483 and by Ferdinand and Isabella in 1486, Columbus finally won the support of the Spanish monarchy in 1492. Buoyed by the success of the reconquista and eager to earn profits from trade, the Spanish crown agreed to make him viceroy over any territory he might discover and to give him one-tenth of the material rewards of the journey.

Columbus and his small fleet left Spain on August 3, 1492. Columbus dreamed of reaching the court of the Mongol emperor, the Great Khan, not realizing that the Ming Dynasty had overthrown the Mongols in 1368. Based on Ptolemy's *Geography* and other texts, he expected to pass the islands of Japan and then land on the east coast of China.

On October 12 Columbus landed in the Bahamas, which he christened San Salvador and claimed for the Spanish crown. In a letter he wrote to Ferdinand and Isabella on his return to Spain, Columbus described the natives as handsome, peaceful, and primitive. Believing he was somewhere off the east coast of Japan, in what he considered the Indies, he called them "Indians," a name that was later applied to all inhabitants of the Americas. Columbus concluded that they would make good slaves and could quickly be converted to Christianity. (See "Analyzing the Evidence: Columbus Describes His First Voyage," page 466.)

Columbus's First Voyage to the New World, 1492–1493

Scholars have identified the inhabitants of the islands as the Taino (TIGH-noh) people. From San Salvador, Columbus sailed southwest, landing on Cuba on October 28. Deciding that he must be on the mainland of China near the coastal city of Quinsay (now Hangzhou), he sent a small embassy inland with letters from Ferdinand and Isabella and instructions to locate the city. Although they found no large settlement, the sight of Taino people wearing gold ornaments on Hispaniola suggested that gold was available in the region. In January, confident that its source would soon be found, he headed back to Spain to report on his discovery.

On his second voyage, Columbus took control of the island of Hispaniola and enslaved its indigenous peoples. On this and subsequent voyages, he brought with him settlers for the new Spanish territories, along with agricultural seed and livestock. Columbus himself, however, had limited skills in governing. Revolt soon broke out against him and his brother on Hispaniola. A royal expedition sent to investigate returned the brothers to Spain in chains, and a royal governor assumed control of the colony.

Spain "Discovers" the Pacific

Columbus never realized the scope of his achievement: that he had found a vast continent unknown to Europeans, except for the fleeting Viking presence centuries earlier. The Florentine navigator Amerigo Vespucci (veh-SPOO-chee) (1454–1512) realized what Columbus had not. Writing about his discoveries on the coast of modern-day Venezuela, Vespucci stated: "Those new regions which we found and explored with the fleet . . . we may rightly call a New World." This letter was the first document to describe America as a continent separate from Asia. In recognition of Amerigo's bold claim, the continent was named for him.

To settle competing claims to the Atlantic discoveries, Spain and Portugal turned to Pope Alexander VI. The resulting **Treaty of Tordesillas** (tawr-duh-SEE-yuhs) in

Treaty of Tordesillas The 1494 agreement giving Spain everything west of an imaginary line drawn down the Atlantic and giving Portugal everything to the east.

Columbus Describes His First Voyage

On his return voyage to Spain in February 1493, Christopher Columbus composed a letter intended for wide circulation and had copies of it sent ahead to Isabella, Ferdinand, and others when his ship docked at Lisbon. Because the letter sums up Columbus's understanding of his achievements, it is considered the most important document of his first voyage.

■ Since I know that you will be pleased at the great success with which the Lord has crowned my voyage, I write to inform you how in thirty-three days I crossed from the Canary Islands to the Indies, with the fleet which our most illustrious sovereigns gave me. I found very many islands with large populations and took possession of them all for their Highnesses; this I did by proclamation and unfurled the royal standard. No opposition was offered.

I named the first island that I found "San Salvador," in honour of our Lord and Saviour who has granted me this miracle. . . . When I reached Cuba, I followed its north coast westwards, and found it so extensive that I thought this must be the mainland, the province of Cathay.* . . . From there I saw another island eighteen leagues eastwards which I then named "Hispaniola."† . . .

Hispaniola is a wonder. The mountains and hills, the plains and meadow lands are both fertile and beautiful. They are most suitable for planting crops and for raising cattle of all kinds, and there are good sites for building towns and villages. The harbours are incredibly fine and there are many great rivers with broad channels and the majority contain gold.‡ The trees, fruits and plants are very different from those of Cuba. In Hispaniola there are many spices and large mines of gold and other metals.§ . . .

The inhabitants of this island, and all the rest that I discovered or heard of, go naked, as their mothers bore them, men and women alike. A few of the women, however, cover a single place with a leaf of a plant or piece of cotton which they weave for the purpose. They have no iron or steel or arms and are not capable of using them, not because they are not strong and well built but because they are amazingly timid. All the weapons they have are canes cut at seeding time, at the end of which they fix a sharpened stick, but they have not the courage to make use of these, for very often when I have sent two or three men to a village to have conversation with them a great number of them have come out. But as soon as they saw my men all fled immediately, a father not even waiting for his son. And this is not because we have harmed any of them; on the contrary, wherever I have gone and been able to have conversation with them, I have given them some of the various things I had, a cloth and other articles, and received nothing in exchange. But they have still remained incurably timid. True, when they have been reassured and lost their fear, they are so ingenuous and so liberal with all their possessions that no one who has not seen them would believe it. If one asks for anything they have they never say no. On the contrary, they offer a share to anyone with demonstrations of heartfelt affection, and they are immediately content with any small thing, valuable or valueless, that is given them. I forbade the men to give them bits of broken crockery, fragments of glass or tags of laces, though if they could get them they fancied them the finest jewels in the world.

I hoped to win them to the love and service of their Highnesses and of the whole Spanish nation and to persuade them to collect and give us of the things which they possessed in abundance and which we needed. They have no religion and are not idolaters; but all believe that power and goodness dwell in the sky and they are firmly convinced that I have come from the sky with these ships and people. In this belief they gave me a good reception everywhere, once they had overcome their fear; and this is not because they are stupid—far from it, they are men of great intelligence, for they navigate all those seas, and give a marvellously good account of everything—but because they have never before seen men clothed or ships like these. . . .

In all these islands the men are seemingly content with one woman, but their chief or king is allowed more than twenty. The women appear to work more than the men and I have not been able to find out if they have private property. As far as I could see whatever a man had was shared among all the rest and this particularly applies to food. . . . In another island, which I am told is larger than Hispaniola, the people have no hair. Here there is a vast quantity of gold, and from here and the other islands I bring Indians as evidence.

In conclusion, to speak only of the results of this very hasty voyage, their Highnesses can see that I will give them as much gold as they require, if they will render me some very slight assistance; also I will give them all the spices and cotton they want. . . . I will also bring them as much aloes as they ask and as many slaves, who will be taken from the idolaters. I believe also that I have found rhubarb and cinnamon and there will be countless other things in addition. . . .

So all Christendom will be delighted that our Redeemer has given victory to our most illustrious King and Queen and their renowned kingdoms, in this great matter. They should hold great celebrations and render solemn thanks to the Holy Trinity with many solemn prayers, for the great triumph which they will have, by the conversion of so many peoples to our holy faith and for the temporal benefits which will follow, for not only Spain, but all Christendom will receive encouragement and profit.

This is a brief account of the facts.

Written in the caravel off the Canary Islands.**

15 February 1493

At your orders
THE ADMIRAL

QUESTIONS FOR ANALYSIS

1. How did Columbus explain the success of his voyage?
2. What was Columbus's view of the Native Americans he met?
3. Evaluate Columbus's statements that the Caribbean islands possessed gold, cotton, and spices.
4. Why did Columbus cling to the idea that he had reached Asia?

Source: J. M. Cohen, ed. and trans., *The Four Voyages of Christopher Columbus* (Penguin Classics, 1969), pp. 115–123. Copyright © J. M. Cohen, 1969, London. Used by permission of Penguin Books Ltd.

*Cathay is the old name for China. In the logbook and later in this letter Columbus accepts the natives' story that Cuba is an island that they can circumnavigate in something more than twenty-one days, yet he insists here and during the second voyage that it is in fact part of the Asiatic mainland.

†Hispaniola is the second-largest island of the West Indies; Haiti occupies the western third of the island, the Dominican Republic the rest.

‡This did not prove to be true.

§These statements are also inaccurate.

**Actually, Columbus was off Santa Maria in the Azores.

1494 gave Spain everything to the west of an imaginary line drawn down the Atlantic and Portugal everything to the east.

The search for profits determined the direction of Spanish exploration. Because its profits from Hispaniola and other Caribbean islands were insignificant compared to Portugal's enormous riches from the Asian spice trade, Spain renewed the search for a western passage to Asia. In 1519 Charles I of Spain (who was also Holy Roman emperor Charles V) commissioned Ferdinand Magellan (1480–1521) to find a direct sea route to Asia. Magellan sailed southwest across the Atlantic to Brazil, and after a long search along the coast he located the strait off the southern tip of South America that now bears his name (see Map 16.2). After passing through the strait into the Pacific Ocean in 1520, his fleet sailed north up the west coast of South America and then headed west into the Pacific.

Terrible storms, disease, starvation, and violence devastated the expedition. Magellan himself was killed in a skirmish in the Malay Archipelago, and only one of the five ships that began the expedition made it back to Spain. This ship returned home in 1522 with only eighteen men aboard, having traveled from the east by way of the Indian Ocean, the Cape of Good Hope, and the Atlantic. The voyage—the first to circumnavigate the globe—had taken close to three years.

Despite the losses, this voyage revolutionized Europeans' understanding of the world by demonstrating the vastness of the Pacific. The earth was clearly much larger than Ptolemy's map had shown. Magellan's expedition also forced Spain's rulers to rethink their plans for overseas commerce and territorial expansion. The westward passage to the Indies was too long and dangerous for commercial purposes. Thus Spain soon abandoned the attempt to oust Portugal from the Eastern spice trade and concentrated on exploiting its New World territories.

Early Exploration by Northern European Powers

Spain's northern European rivals also set sail across the Atlantic during the early days of exploration, searching for a northwest passage to the Indies. In 1497 John Cabot (ca. 1450–1499), a Genoese merchant living in London, landed on Newfoundland. The next year he returned and explored the New England coast. These forays proved futile, and at that time the English established no permanent colonies in the territories they explored.

News of the riches of Mexico and Peru later inspired the English to renew their efforts, this time in the extreme north. Between 1576 and 1578 Martin Frobisher (ca. 1535–1594) made three voyages in and around the Canadian bay that now bears his name. Frobisher brought a quantity of ore back to England, but it proved to be worthless.

Early French exploration of the Atlantic was equally frustrating. Between 1534 and 1541 Frenchman Jacques Cartier (1491–1557) made several voyages and explored the St. Lawrence River of Canada, searching for a passage to the wealth of Asia. When this hope proved vain, the French turned to a new source of profit within Canada itself: trade in beavers and other furs. As had the Portuguese in Asia, French traders bartered with local peoples whom they largely treated as autonomous and equal partners. French fishermen also competed with the Spanish and English for the schools of cod they found in the Atlantic waters around Newfoundland.

Conquest and Settlement

Before Columbus's arrival, the Americas were inhabited by thousands of groups of indigenous peoples with distinct languages and cultures. These groups ranged from hunter-gatherer tribes organized into tribal confederations to settled agriculturalists to large-scale empires containing bustling cities and towns. The best estimate is that the peoples of the Americas numbered between 50 and 60 million in 1492. These numbers were decimated, and the lives of survivors radically altered, by the arrival of Europeans.

> **What was the impact of Iberian conquest and settlement on the peoples and ecologies of the Americas?**

Spanish Conquest of the Aztec and Inca Empires

The first two decades after Columbus's arrival in the New World saw Spanish settlement of Hispaniola, Cuba, Puerto Rico, and other Caribbean islands. Based on rumors of a wealthy mainland civilization, the Spanish governor in Cuba sponsored expeditions to the Yucatán coast of the Gulf of Mexico, including one in 1519 under the command of the **conquistador** (kahn-KEES-tuh-dawr) Hernán Cortés (1485–1547). *Conquistador* was Spanish for "conqueror," a Spanish soldier-explorer who sought to conquer the New World for the Spanish crown. Alarmed by Cortés's

> **conquistador** Spanish for "conqueror"; a Spanish soldier-explorer, such as Hernán Cortés or Francisco Pizarro, who sought to conquer the New World for the Spanish crown.

The Aztec Capital of Tenochtitlan This woodcut map was published in 1524 along with Cortés's letters describing the conquest of the Aztecs. As it shows, Tenochtitlan occupied an island and was laid out in concentric circles. The administrative and religious buildings were at the heart of the city, which was surrounded by residential quarters. Cortés himself marveled at the city in his letters: "The city is as large as Seville or Cordoba. . . . There are bridges, very large, strong, and well constructed, so that, over many, ten horsemen can ride abreast. . . . The city has many squares where markets are held. . . . There is one square . . . where there are daily more than sixty thousand souls, buying and selling. In the service and manners of its people, their fashion of living was almost the same as in Spain, with just as much harmony and order." (Newberry Library, Chicago/Bridgeman Images)

ambition, the governor withdrew his support, but Cortés quickly set sail before being removed from command. Cortés and his party landed on the Mexican coast on April 21, 1519. His camp soon received visits by delegations of Aztec leaders bearing gifts and news of their great emperor.

The **Aztec Empire**, an alliance between the Mexica people and their conquered allies, had risen rapidly in size and power over the fifteenth century. At the time of the Spanish arrival, the empire was ruled by Moctezuma II (r. 1502–1520), from his capital at Tenochtitlan (tay-nawch-TEET-lahn), now Mexico City. The Aztecs were a sophisticated society and culture, with advanced mathematics, astronomy, and engineering. As in European nations at the time, a hereditary nobility dominated the army, the priesthood, and the state bureaucracy and reaped the gains from the agricultural labor of the common people.

Within weeks of his arrival, Cortés acquired translators who provided vital information on the empire and its weaknesses. Through his interpreters, Cortés learned of strong local resentment against the Aztec Empire. The Aztec state practiced brutal warfare against neighboring peoples to secure captives for religious sacrifices and laborers for agricultural and building projects. Once conquered, subject tribes paid continual tribute to the empire through their local chiefs. Realizing that he could exploit dissensions within the empire to his own advantage, Cortés forged an alliance with Tlaxcala (tlah-SKAH-lah), a subject kingdom of the Aztecs. In October a combined Spanish-Tlaxcalan force occupied the Aztec city of Cholula, the second largest in the empire, and massacred thousands of inhabitants. Strengthened by this victory, Cortés formed alliances with other native kingdoms. In November 1519, with a few hundred Spanish men and some six thousand indigenous warriors, he marched on Tenochtitlan.

Unlike other native leaders, Moctezuma refrained from attacking the Spaniards and instead welcomed Cortés and his men into Tenochtitlan. Moctezuma was apparently deeply impressed by Spanish victories and believed the Spanish were invincible. When Cortés took Moctezuma hostage, the emperor's influence crumbled. During the ensuing attacks and counterattacks, Moctezuma was killed. The Spaniards and their allies escaped from the city suffering heavy losses. Cortés quickly began gathering forces and making new alliances against the Aztecs. In May 1521 he led a second assault on Tenochtitlan, leading an army of approximately one thousand Spanish and seventy-five thousand native warriors.[1]

The Spanish victory in late summer 1521 was hard-won and was greatly aided by the effects of smallpox, which had devastated the besieged population of the city. After establishing a new capital in the ruins of Tenochtitlan, Cortés and other conquistadors began the systematic conquest of Mexico, a decades-long and brutal process.

More remarkable than the defeat of the Aztecs was the fall of the remote **Inca Empire** in Peru. Living in a settlement perched more than 9,800 feet above sea level, the Incas were isolated from the Mesoamerican civilization of the Aztecs. Like the Mexica, the Incas had created a polity that rivaled that of the Europeans in population and complexity and that had reached its height in the fifteenth century. The Incas' strength lay largely in their bureaucratic efficiency. Ruled from the capital city of Cuzco, the empire was divided into four major regions, each region into provinces,

Aztec Empire An alliance between the Mexica people and their conquered allies, with its capital in Tenochtitlan (now Mexico City), that rose in size and power in the fifteenth century and possessed a sophisticated society and culture, with advanced mathematics, astronomy, and engineering.

Texcoco
Otumba   Zautla
                        Jalapa
                    Veracruz
        Tlaxcala
Tenochtitlan Cholula

Gulf of Mexico

→ Cortés's original route, 1519
→ Cortés's retreat, 1520
→ Cortés's return route, 1520–1521

Invasion of Tenochtitlan, 1519–1521

Inca Empire The vast and sophisticated Peruvian empire centered at the capital city of Cuzco that was at its peak in the fifteenth century but weakened by civil war at the time of the Spanish arrival.

Inca Women Milking Cows This illustration of Inca women milking cows is from a collection of illustrations by a Spanish bishop that offers a valuable view of life in Peru in the 1780s. (Palacio Real, Madrid, Spain/Photo: Albers Foundation/Art Resource, NY)

and each province into districts. Officials at each level used the extensive network of roads to transmit information and orders. While the Aztecs used a system of glyphs for writing, the Incas had devised a complex system of colored and knotted cords, called khipus, for administrative bookkeeping.

By the time of the Spanish invasion, however, the Inca Empire had been weakened by a civil war over succession and an epidemic of disease, probably smallpox, spread through trade with groups in contact with Europeans. The Spanish conquistador Francisco Pizarro (ca. 1475–1541) landed on the northern coast of Peru on May 13, 1532, the very day the Inca leader Atahualpa (ah-tuh-WAHL-puh) won control of the empire. As Pizarro advanced across the Andes toward Cuzco (KOOS-ko), the capital of the Inca Empire, Atahualpa was also heading there for his coronation.

Like Moctezuma in Mexico, Atahualpa sent envoys to greet the Spanish. Motivated by curiosity about the Spanish, he intended to meet with them to learn more about them and their intentions. Instead the Spaniards ambushed and captured him, extorted an enormous ransom in gold, and then executed him on trumped-up charges in 1533. The Spanish then marched on to Cuzco, profiting, as with the Aztecs, from internal conflicts and forming alliances with local peoples. When Cuzco fell in 1533, the Spanish plundered immense riches in gold and silver.

How was it possible for several hundred Spanish conquistadors to defeat powerful empires commanding large armies, vast wealth, and millions of inhabitants? Historians seeking answers to this question have emphasized a combination of factors: the military superiority provided by Spanish gunpowder, steel swords, and horses; divisions within the Aztec and Inca Empires, which produced many native allies and interpreters for the Spanish; and, most important, the devastating impact of contagious diseases among the indigenous population. Ironically, the well-organized, urban-based Aztec and Inca Empires were more vulnerable to wholesale takeover than were more decentralized and fragmented groups like the Maya in the Yucatán peninsula, whose independence was not wholly crushed until the end of the seventeenth century.

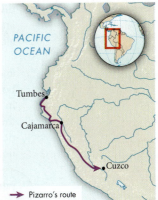

The Conquest of Peru, 1532–1533

Portuguese Brazil

Unlike Mesoamerica or the Andes, the territory of Brazil contained no urban empires but instead had roughly 2.5 million nomadic and settled people divided into small tribes and many different language groups. In 1500 the Portuguese crown named

Pedro Álvares Cabral commander of a fleet headed for the spice trade of the Indies. En route, the fleet sailed far to the west, claiming the coast where they accidentally landed for Portugal under the terms of the Treaty of Tordesillas. The Portuguese soon undertook a profitable trade with local people in brazilwood, a valued source of red dye, which inspired the name of the new colony.

In the 1520s Portuguese settlers brought sugarcane production to Brazil. They initially used enslaved indigenous laborers on sugar plantations, but the rapid decline in the indigenous population soon led to the use of forcibly transported Africans. In Brazil the Portuguese thus created a new form of colonization in the Americas: large plantations worked by enslaved people. This model of slave-worked sugar plantations would spread throughout the Caribbean in the seventeenth century.

Colonial Administration

By the end of the sixteenth century the Spanish and Portuguese had successfully overcome most indigenous groups and expanded their territory throughout modern-day Mexico, the southwestern United States, and Central and South America. In Mesoamerica and the Andes, the Spanish had taken over the cities and tribute systems of the Aztecs and the Incas, basing their control on the prior existence of well-established polities with organized tribute systems.

While early conquest and settlement were conducted largely by private initiatives, the Spanish and Portuguese governments soon assumed more direct control. In 1503 the Spanish granted the port of Seville a monopoly over all traffic to the New World and established the House of Trade to oversee economic matters. In 1523 Spain created the Royal and Supreme Council of the Indies, with authority over all colonial affairs subject to approval by the king. Spanish territories themselves were

viceroyalties The name for the four administrative units of Spanish possessions in the Americas: New Spain, Peru, New Granada, and La Plata.

divided initially into two **viceroyalties**, or administrative divisions: New Spain, created in 1535; and Peru, created in 1542. In the eighteenth century two new viceroyalties, New Granada and La Plata, were created (see Map 16.2).

Within each territory, the viceroy, or imperial governor, exercised broad military and civil authority. The viceroy presided over the *audiencia* (ow-dee-EHN-see-ah), a board of judges that served as his advisory council and the highest judicial body. As in Spain, settlement in the Americas was centered on cities and towns. In each city, the municipal council, or *cabildo*, exercised local authority. Women were denied participation in public life, a familiar pattern from both Spain and precolonial indigenous society.

Portugal adopted similar patterns of rule, with India House in Lisbon functioning much like the Spanish House of Trade and royal representatives overseeing Portuguese possessions in West Africa and Asia. To secure the vast expanse of Brazil, in the

captaincies A system established by the Portuguese in Brazil in the 1530s, whereby hereditary grants of land were given to nobles and loyal officials who bore the costs of settling and administering their territories.

1530s the Portuguese implemented a distinctive system of rule, called **captaincies**, hereditary grants of land given to nobles and loyal officials who bore the costs of settling and administering their territories. Over time, the Crown secured greater power over the captaincies, appointing royal governors to act as administrators. The captaincy of Bahia was the site of the capital, Salvador, home to the governor general and other royal officials.

The Catholic Church played an integral role in Iberian rule. The papacy allowed Portuguese and Spanish officials greater control over the church than was the case at home, allowing them to appoint clerics and collect tithes. This control allowed colonial powers to use the church as an instrument to indoctrinate indigenous people (see "Religious Conversion").

Indigenous Population Loss and Economic Exploitation

From the time of Christopher Columbus in Hispaniola, the Spanish made use of the **encomienda system** to profit from the peoples and territories they encountered in the Americas. This system was a legacy of the methods used to reward military leaders in the time of the reconquista. First in the Caribbean and then on the mainland, conquistadors granted their followers the right to forcibly employ groups of indigenous people as laborers and to demand tribute payments from them in exchange for providing food, shelter, and instruction in the Christian faith. This system was first used in Hispaniola to work gold fields and then in Mexico for agricultural labor and, when silver was discovered in the 1540s, for silver mining.

A 1512 Spanish law authorizing the use of the encomienda (en-ko-me-EN-duh) called for indigenous people to be treated fairly, but in practice the system led to terrible abuses. Spanish missionaries publicized these abuses, leading to debates in Spain about the nature and proper treatment of indigenous people (see "European Debates About Indigenous Peoples"). King Charles I responded to such complaints in 1542 with the New Laws, which set limits on the authority of encomienda holders.

The New Laws provoked a revolt among elites in Peru and were little enforced throughout Spanish territories. Nonetheless, the Crown gradually gained control over encomiendas in central areas of the empire and required indigenous people to pay tributes in cash, rather than in labor. To respond to a shortage of indigenous

encomienda system
A system whereby the Spanish crown granted the conquerors the right to forcibly employ groups of indigenous people as laborers and to demand tribute payments from them in exchange for providing food, shelter, and instruction in the Christian faith.

Spanish Exploitation of Indigenous Labor This image depicts Spanish conquistadors supervising indigenous laborers as they carry arms along the steep road from Veracruz to Tlaxcala in 1520. It was part of a larger painting, produced in the postconquest era and known as the *Lienzo de Tlaxcala*, that tells the story of the alliance between the Tlaxcala kingdom and the Spanish and their defeat of the Aztec Empire. (Sarin Images/Granger, NYC—All rights reserved)

workers, royal officials established a new government-run system of forced labor, called *repartimiento* in New Spain and *mita* in Peru. Administrators assigned a certain percentage of the inhabitants of native communities to labor for a set period each year in public works, mining, agriculture, and other tasks.

Spanish systems for exploiting the labor of indigenous peoples were both a cause of and a response to the disastrous decline in their numbers that began soon after the arrival of Europeans. Some indigenous people died as a direct result of the violence of conquest and the disruption of agriculture and trade caused by warfare. The most important cause of death, however, was infectious disease. Having little or no resistance to diseases brought from the Old World, the inhabitants of the New World fell victim to smallpox, typhus, influenza, and other illnesses.

The pattern of devastating disease and population loss established in the Spanish colonies was repeated everywhere Europeans settled. Overall, population declined by as much as 90 percent or more but with important regional variations. In general, densely populated urban centers were worse hit than rural areas, and tropical, low-lying regions suffered more than cooler, higher-altitude ones.

Colonial administrators responded to native population decline by forcibly combining dwindling indigenous communities into new settlements and imposing the rigors of the encomienda and the repartimiento. By the end of the sixteenth century the search for fresh sources of labor had given birth to the new tragedy of the Atlantic slave trade (see "Sugar and Early Transatlantic Slavery").

Patterns of Settlement

The century after the discovery of silver in 1545 marked the high point of Iberian immigration to the Americas. Although the first migrants were men, soon whole families began to cross the Atlantic, and the European population began to increase through natural reproduction. By 1600 American-born Europeans, called *Creoles*, outnumbered immigrants.

Iberian settlement was predominantly urban in nature. Spaniards settled into the cities and towns of the former Aztec and Inca Empires as the native population dwindled through death and flight. They also established new cities in which settlers were quick to develop urban institutions familiar to them from home: city squares, churches, schools, and universities.

Despite the growing number of Europeans and the rapid decline of the native population, Europeans remained a small minority of the total inhabitants of the Americas. Iberians had sexual relationships with native women, leading to the growth of a substantial population of mixed Iberian and Indian descent known as *mestizos* (meh-STEE-zohz). The large-scale arrival of enslaved Africans, starting in Brazil in the mid-sixteenth century, added new ethnic and racial dimensions to the population.

How was the era of global contact shaped by new commodities, commercial empires, and forced migrations?

The Era of Global Contact

The centuries-old Afroeurasian trade world was forever changed by the European voyages of discovery and their aftermath. For the first time, a truly global economy emerged in the sixteenth and seventeenth centuries, and it forged new links among far-flung peoples, cultures, and societies. The ancient civilizations of Europe, Africa, the Americas, and Asia confronted each other in new and rapidly evolving ways.

Those confrontations often led to conquest, forced migration, and brutal exploitation, but they also contributed to cultural exchange and new patterns of life.

The Columbian Exchange

The travel of people and goods between the Old and New Worlds led to an exchange of animals, plants, and diseases, a complex process known as the **Columbian exchange**. As we have seen, the introduction of new diseases to the Americas had devastating consequences. But other results of the exchange brought benefits not only to the Europeans but also to native peoples.

> **Columbian exchange**
> The exchange of animals, plants, and diseases between the Old and the New Worlds.

Everywhere they settled, the Spanish and Portuguese brought and raised wheat. Grapes and olives brought over from Spain did well in parts of Peru and Chile. Perhaps the most significant introduction to the diet of Native Americans came via the meat and milk of the livestock that the early conquistadors brought with them, including cattle, sheep, and goats. The horse enabled both the Spanish conquerors and native populations to travel faster and farther and to transport heavy loads more easily.

In turn, Europeans returned home with many food crops that became central elements of their diet. Crops originating in the Americas included tomatoes, squash, pumpkins, peppers, and many varieties of beans, as well as tobacco. One of the most important of such crops was maize (corn). By the late seventeenth century maize had become a staple in Spain, Portugal, southern France, and Italy, and in the eighteenth century it became one of the chief foods of southeastern Europe and southern China. Even more valuable was the nutritious white potato, which slowly spread from west to east, contributing everywhere to a rise in population.

While the exchange of foods was a great benefit to cultures across the world, the introduction of European pathogens to the New World had a disastrous impact on the native population. In Europe infectious diseases like smallpox, measles, and influenza—originally spread through contact with domestic animals—killed many people each year. Over centuries of dealing with these diseases, the European population had had time to adapt. Prior to contact with Europeans, indigenous peoples of the New World suffered from insect-borne diseases and some infectious ones, but their lack of domestic livestock spared them the host of highly infectious diseases known in the Old World. The arrival of Europeans spread these microbes among a totally unprepared population, and they fell victim in vast numbers (see "Indigenous Population Loss and Economic Exploitation"). The world after Columbus was thus unified by disease as well as by trade and colonization.

Sugar and Early Transatlantic Slavery

Two crucial and interrelated elements of the Columbian exchange were the transatlantic trade in sugar and slaves. Throughout the Middle Ages, slavery was deeply entrenched in the Mediterranean, but it was not based on race. How, then, did black African slavery enter the European picture and take root in South and then North America? In 1453 the Ottoman capture of Constantinople halted the flow of European slaves from the eastern Mediterranean. Additionally, the successes of the Christian reconquest of the Iberian Peninsula drastically diminished the supply of Muslim captives. Cut off from its traditional sources of slaves, Mediterranean Europe turned to sub-Saharan Africa, which had a long history of slave trading.

Indians Working in a Spanish Sugar Mill Belgian engraver Theodore de Bry published many images of the European exploration and settlement of the New World. De Bry never crossed the Atlantic himself, instead basing his images on travel accounts and other firsthand sources. This image depicts the exploitation of indigenous people in a Spanish sugar mill. (Album/Art Resource, NY)

As Portuguese explorers began their voyages along the western coast of Africa in the 1440s, one of the first commodities they sought was slaves. While the first slaves were simply seized by small raiding parties, Portuguese merchants soon found that it was easier and more profitable to trade with African leaders, who were accustomed to dealing in enslaved people captured through warfare with neighboring powers. In 1483 the Portuguese established an alliance with the kingdom of Kongo. The royal family eventually converted to Christianity, and Portuguese merchants intermarried with Kongolese women, creating a permanent Afro-Portuguese community. From 1490 to 1530 Portuguese traders brought between three hundred and two thousand enslaved Africans to Lisbon each year.

In this stage of European expansion, the history of slavery became intertwined with the history of sugar. In the Middle Ages, sugarcane—native to the South Pacific—was brought to Mediterranean islands. Population increases and greater prosperity in the fifteenth century led to increasing demand for sugar. The establishment of sugar plantations on the Canary and Madeira Islands in the fifteenth century after Iberian colonization testifies to this demand.

Sugar was a particularly difficult crop to produce for profit, requiring constant, backbreaking labor. The invention of roller mills to crush the cane more efficiently meant that yields could be significantly augmented, but only if a sufficient labor force was found to supply the mills. Plantation owners solved the labor problem by forcing first native islanders and then transported Africans to perform the backbreaking work.

The transatlantic slave trade that would ultimately result in the forced transport of over 12 million individuals began in 1518, when Spanish king Charles I authorized traders to bring enslaved Africans to New World colonies. The Portuguese brought the first slaves to Brazil around 1550. After its founding in 1621, the Dutch West India Company transported thousands of Africans to Brazil and the Caribbean, mostly to work on sugar plantations. In the late seventeenth century, with the chartering of the Royal African Company, the English began to bring slaves to Barbados and other English colonies in the Caribbean and mainland North America.

Before 1700, when slavers decided it was better business to improve conditions, some 20 percent of slaves died on the voyage from Africa to the Americas.[2] The most common cause of death was dysentery induced by poor-quality food and water, lack of sanitation, and intense crowding. On sugar plantations, death rates among enslaved people from illness and exhaustion were extremely high. Driven by rising demands for plantation crops, the tragic transatlantic slave trade reached its height in the eighteenth century.

The Transatlantic Slave Trade

Spanish Silver and Its Economic Effects

The sixteenth century has often been called Spain's golden century, but silver mined in the Americas was the true source of Spain's wealth. In 1545, at an altitude of fifteen thousand feet, the Spanish discovered an extraordinary source of silver at Potosí (poh-toh-SEE) (in present-day Bolivia) in unsettled territory captured from the Inca Empire. By 1550 Potosí yielded perhaps 60 percent of all the silver mined in the world. From Potosí and the mines at Zacatecas (za-kuh-TAY-kuhs) and Guanajuato (gwah-nah-HWAH-toh) in Mexico, huge quantities of precious metals poured forth.

Mining became the most important industry in the colonies. Millions of indigenous laborers suffered brutal conditions and death in the silver mines. Demand for new sources of labor for the mines also contributed to the intensification of the African slave trade. Profits for the Spanish crown were immense. The Crown claimed the quinto, one-fifth of all precious metals mined in South America, which represented 25 percent of its total income. Between 1503 and 1650, 35 million pounds of silver and over 600,000 pounds of gold entered Seville's port.

Spain's immense profits from silver paid for the tremendous expansion of its empire and for the large armies that defended it. However, the easy flow of money also dampened economic innovation. It exacerbated the rising inflation Spain was already experiencing in the mid-sixteenth century, a period of growing population and stagnant production. Several times between 1557 and 1647, King Philip II and his successors wrote off the state debt, thereby undermining confidence in the government and destroying the economy. When the profitability of the silver mines diminished in the 1640s, Spain's power was fundamentally undercut.

As Philip II paid his armies and foreign debts with silver bullion, Spanish inflation was transmitted to the rest of Europe. Between 1560 and 1600 prices in most parts of Europe doubled and in some cases quadrupled. Because money bought less, people who lived on fixed incomes, such as nobles, were badly hurt. Those who owed fixed sums of money, such as the middle class, prospered because in a time of rising prices, debts lessened in value each year. Food costs rose most sharply, and the poor fared worst of all.

In many ways, though, it was not Spain but China that controlled the world trade in silver. The Chinese demanded silver for their products and for the payment of imperial taxes. China was thus the main buyer of world silver, absorbing half the world's production. The silver market drove world trade, with New Spain and Japan acting as major sources of the supply of silver and China dominating demand. The world trade in silver is one of the best examples of the new global economy that emerged in this period.

The Birth of the Global Economy

With Europeans' discovery of the Americas and their exploration of the Pacific, the entire world was linked for the first time in history by seaborne trade. The opening of that trade brought into being three successive commercial empires: the Portuguese, the Spanish, and the Dutch.

In the sixteenth century the Portuguese controlled the sea route to India (Map 16.3). From their bases at Goa on the Arabian Sea and at Malacca on the Malay Peninsula, ships carried goods to the Portuguese settlement at Macao. From Macao Portuguese ships loaded with Chinese silks and porcelains sailed to Japan and the Philippines, where Chinese goods were exchanged for Spanish silver from New Spain. Throughout Asia the Portuguese traded in slaves, some of whom were brought all the way across the Pacific to Mexico. (See "Individuals in Society: Catarina de San Juan," page 480.) They also exported horses from Mesopotamia and copper from Arabia to India; from India they exported hawks and peacocks for the Chinese and Japanese markets. Back to Portugal they brought Asian spices that had been purchased with textiles produced in India and with gold and ivory from East Africa. From their colony in Brazil they also shipped back sugar, produced by African slaves whom they had transported across the Atlantic.

Becoming an imperial power a few decades later than the Portuguese, the Spanish were determined to claim their place in world trade. The Spanish Empire in the New World was basically land based, but across the Pacific the Spaniards built a seaborne empire centered at Manila in the Philippines. Established in 1571, the city of Manila served as the transpacific bridge between Spanish America and China. In Manila Spanish traders used silver from American mines to purchase Chinese silk for European markets. The European demand for silk was so huge that in 1597, for example, 12 million pesos of silver, almost the total value of the transatlantic trade, moved from Acapulco in New Spain to Manila.

In the seventeenth century the Dutch challenged the Spanish and Portuguese Empires. The Dutch East India Company was founded in 1602 with the stated intention of capturing the spice trade from the Portuguese. Drawing on their commercial wealth and long experience in European trade, the Dutch emerged by the end of the century as the most powerful worldwide seaborne trading power (see "The Dutch Trading Empire" in Chapter 18).

How did new encounters shape cultural attitudes and beliefs in Europe and the rest of the world?

Changing Attitudes and Beliefs

The age of overseas expansion heightened Europeans' contacts with the rest of the world. These contacts gave birth to new ideas about the inherent superiority or inferiority of different races. Religion became another means of cultural contact, as European missionaries aimed to spread Christianity in both the New World and East Asia. The East-West contacts also led to exchanges of influential cultural and scientific ideas.

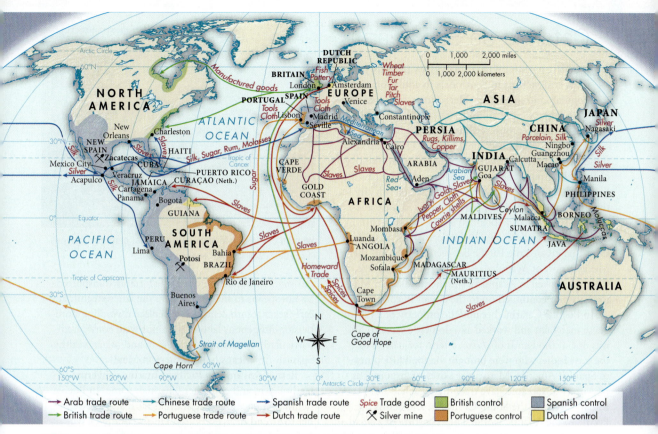

MAP 16.3 Seaborne Trading Empires in the Sixteenth and Seventeenth Centuries By the mid-seventeenth century trade linked all parts of the world except for Australia. Notice that trade in slaves was not confined to the Atlantic but involved almost all parts of the world.

Religious Conversion

Converting indigenous people to Christianity was one of the most important justifications for European expansion. The first missionaries to the New World accompanied Columbus on his second voyage, and more than 2,500 Franciscans, Dominicans, Jesuits, and other friars crossed the Atlantic in the following century. Jesuit missionaries were also active in Japan and China in the sixteenth and seventeenth centuries, until authorities banned their teachings.

Catholic friars were among the first Europeans to seek an understanding of native cultures and languages as part of their effort to render Christianity comprehensible to indigenous people. They were also the most vociferous opponents of abuses committed by Spanish settlers.

Religion had been a central element of pre-Columbian societies, and many, if not all, indigenous people were receptive to the new religion that accompanied the victorious Iberians. (See "Global Viewpoints: Aztec and Spanish Views on Christian Conversion in New Spain," page 482.) In addition to spreading Christianity, missionaries

Catarina de San Juan

A LONG JOURNEY LED CATARINA DE SAN JUAN from enslavement in South Asia to adulation as a popular saint in Mexico. Her journey began on the west coast of India around 1610 when Portuguese traders captured a group of children, including the small girl who would become Catarina. Their ship continued around the southern tip of India, across the Bay of Bengal, through the Strait of Malacca, and across the South China Sea. It docked at Manila, a Spanish city in the Philippines, where the girl was sold at a slave auction. In 1619 Catarina boarded a ship that was part of the Manila Galleon, the annual convoy of Spanish ships that crossed the Pacific between Manila and the Mexican port of Acapulco. After a six-month voyage, Catarina arrived in Acapulco; she then walked to Mexico City and continued on to the city of Puebla.

In Puebla, Catarina became the property of a Portuguese merchant and worked as a domestic servant. She was one of thousands of *chinos*, a term for natives of the East Indies who were brought via the Philippines to Spanish America. Many were slaves, transported as part of a transoceanic slave trade that reached from the Indian Ocean to the South China Sea and across the Pacific to the Atlantic world. They constituted a small

Women of Puebla, Mexico, in traditional clothing. (De Agostini Picture Library/Gianni Dagli Orti/Bridgeman Images)

but significant portion of people forcibly transported by Europeans to the Americas in the late sixteenth and early seventeenth centuries to replace dwindling numbers of indigenous laborers. Chinos were considered particularly apt for domestic labor, and many wealthy Spanish Americans bought them in Manila.

Before crossing the Pacific, Catarina converted to Catholicism and chose her Christian name. In Puebla her master encouraged Catarina's faith and allowed her to attend mass every day. He also drafted a will

taught indigenous peoples European methods of agriculture and instilled obedience to colonial masters. Despite the success of initial conversion efforts, authorities could not prevent the melding together of Catholic teachings with elements of pagan beliefs and practices.

European Debates About Indigenous Peoples

Iberian exploitation of the native population of the Americas began from the moment of Columbus's arrival in 1492. Denunciations of this abuse by Catholic missionaries, however, quickly followed, inspiring vociferous debates in both Europe and the colonies about the nature of indigenous peoples and how they should be treated. Bartolomé de Las Casas (1474–1566), a Dominican friar and former encomienda holder, was one of the earliest and most outspoken critics of the brutal treatment inflicted on indigenous peoples.

Mounting criticism in Spain led King Charles I to assemble a group of churchmen and lawyers to debate the issue in 1550 in the city of Valladolid. One side of the **Valladolid debate**, led by Juan Ginés de Sepúlveda, argued that conquest and forcible conversion were both necessary and justified to save indigenous people from the

Valladolid debate A debate organized by Spanish king Charles I in 1550 in the city of Valladolid that pitted defenders of Spanish conquest and forcible conversion against critics of these practices.

emancipating her after his death, which occurred in 1619. With no money of her own, Catarina became the servant of a local priest. On his advice, Catarina reluctantly gave up her dream of becoming a lay sister and married a fellow chino named Domingo. The marriage was unhappy; Catarina reportedly refused to enter sexual relations with her husband and suffered from his debts, infidelity, and hostility to her faith. She found solace in renewed religious devotion, winning the admiration of priests and neighbors who flocked to her for spiritual comfort and to hear about her ecstatic visions. After fourteen years of marriage, Catarina became a widow and lived out her life in the home of wealthy supporters.

Catarina's funeral in 1688 drew large crowds. Her followers revered her as an unofficial saint, and soon the leaders of Puebla began a campaign to have Catarina beatified (officially recognized by the Catholic church as a saint). Her former confessors published accounts of her life emphasizing her piety, beauty, and exotic Asian origins and marveling at the miraculous preservation of her virginity through the perils of enslavement, long journeys at sea, and marriage. Much of what we know about Catarina derives from these sources and must be viewed as idealized, rather than as strictly historically accurate.

The Spanish Inquisition, which oversaw the process of beatification, rejected Catarina's candidacy and, fearing that popular adulation might detract from the authority of the church, forbade the circulation of images of and texts about her. Despite this ban, popular reverence for Catarina de San Juan continued, and continues to this day in Mexico.

QUESTIONS FOR ANALYSIS

1. Why would the Inquisition react so negatively to popular devotion to Catarina? What dangers did she pose to the Catholic Church in New Spain?
2. What does Catarina's story reveal about the global nature of the Spanish Empire and the slave trade in this period? What does it reveal about divisions within the Catholic Church?

Sources: Tatiana Seijas, *Asian Slaves in Colonial Mexico: From Chinos to Indians* (New York: Cambridge University Press, 2014), pp. 8–26; Ronald J. Morgan, *Spanish American Saints and the Rhetoric of Identity, 1600–1810* (Tucson: University of Arizona Press, 2002), pp. 119–142.

horrors of human sacrifice, cannibalism, and idolatry. To counter these arguments, Las Casas and his supporters depicted indigenous people as rational and innocent children, who deserved protection and tutelage from more advanced civilizations.

Elsewhere in Europe, audiences also debated these questions. Eagerly reading denunciations of Spanish abuses by critics like Las Casas, they derived the **Black Legend** of Spanish colonialism, the notion that the Spanish were uniquely brutal and cruel in their conquest and settlement of the Americas. This legend helped other European powers overlook their own record of colonial violence and exploitation.

Black Legend The notion that the Spanish were uniquely brutal and cruel in their conquest and settlement of the Americas, an idea propagated by rival European powers.

New Ideas About Race

At the beginning of the transatlantic slave trade, most Europeans grouped Africans into the despised categories of pagan heathens or Muslim infidels. As Europeans turned to Africa for new sources of slaves, they drew on myths about Africans' primitiveness and barbarity to defend slavery.

Over time, the institution of slavery fostered a new level of racial inequality. Africans gradually became seen as utterly distinct from and wholly inferior to Europeans. In a transition from rather vague assumptions about Africans' non-Christian religious

Aztec and Spanish Views on Christian Conversion in New Spain

In justifying their violent conquest of the Aztec and Inca civilizations, Spanish conquistadors emphasized the need to bring Christianity to heathen peoples. For the conquered, the imposition of Christianity and the repression of their pre-existing religions were often experienced as yet another form of loss. The first document describes the response of the recently vanquished Aztec leaders of Tenochtitlan to Franciscan missionaries. Despite resistance, missionaries eventually succeeded in converting much of the indigenous population to Catholicism. In the second document, a firsthand account of the Spanish conquest written a few decades after the fall of Tenochtitlan, Bernal Díaz del Castillo expresses great satisfaction at the Catholic piety of some indigenous communities.

Aztec Response to the Franciscans' Explanation of Their 1524 Mission

■ You have told us that we do not know the One who gives us life and being, who is Lord of the heavens and of the earth. You also say that those we worship are not gods. This way of speaking is entirely new to us, and very scandalous. We are frightened by this way of speaking because our forebears who engendered and governed us never said anything like this. On the contrary, they left us this our custom of worshiping our gods, in which they believed and which they worshiped all the time that they lived here on earth. They taught us how to honor them. And they taught us all the ceremonies and sacrifices that we make. They told us that through them [our gods] we live and are, and that we were beholden to them, to be theirs and to serve countless centuries before the sun began to shine and before there was daytime. They said that these gods that we worship give us everything we need for our physical existence: maize, beans, chia seeds, etc. . . . .

All of us together feel that it is enough to have lost, enough that the power and royal jurisdiction have been taken from us. As for our gods, we will die before giving up serving and worshiping them.

beliefs and general lack of civilization, Europeans developed increasingly rigid ideas of racial superiority and inferiority to safeguard the growing profits gained from plantation slavery. Black skin became equated with slavery itself as Europeans at home and in the colonies convinced themselves that blacks were destined by God to serve them as slaves in perpetuity.

Support for this belief went back to the Greek philosopher Aristotle's argument that some people are naturally destined for slavery and to biblical associations between darkness and sin, derived from the biblical story of Noah's curse upon the descendants of his disobedient son Ham to be the "servant[s] of servants." Biblical genealogies listing Ham's sons as those who peopled North Africa and Cush (which includes parts of modern Egypt and Sudan) were read to mean that all inhabitants of those regions bore Noah's curse.

Chapter Summary

Prior to Columbus's voyages, well-developed trade routes linked the peoples and products of Africa, Asia, and Europe. Overall, Europe played a minor role in the Afroeurasian trade world. As the economy and population recovered from the Black

Bernal Díaz del Castillo, from *The True History of the Conquest of New Spain, 1521*

■ It is a thing to be grateful for to God, and for profound consideration, to see how the natives assist in celebrating a holy Mass. . . . There is another good thing they do [namely] that both men, women and children, who are of the age to learn them, know all the holy prayers in their own languages and are obliged to know them. They have other good customs about their holy Christianity, that when they pass near a sacred altar or Cross they bow their heads with humility, bend their knees, and say the prayer "Our Father," which we Conquistadores have taught them, and they place lighted wax candles before the holy altars and crosses, for formerly they did not know how to use wax in making candles. In addition to what I have said, we taught them to show great reverence and obedience to all the monks and priests, and, when these went to their pueblos, to sally forth to receive them with lighted wax candles and to ring the bells, and to feed them very well. . . . Beside the good customs reported by me they have others both holy and good, for when the day of Corpus Christi comes, or that of Our Lady, or other solemn festivals when among us we form processions, most of the pueblos in the neighbourhood of this city of Guatemala come out in procession with their crosses and lighted wax tapers, and carry on their shoulders, on a litter, the image of the saint who is the patron of the pueblo.

QUESTIONS FOR ANALYSIS

1. What reasons do the leaders of Tenochtitlan offer for rejecting the teachings of Franciscan missionaries? What importance do they accord their own religious traditions?

2. What evidence does Díaz provide for the conversion of the indigenous people in the city of Guatemala?

3. How and why do you think the attitudes of indigenous peoples might have evolved from those expressed in the first document to those described in the second? Do you think the second document tells the whole story of religious attitudes under Spanish rule?

Sources: "The Lords and Holy Men of Tenochtitlan Reply to the Franciscans: Bernardino de Sahagún, Coloquios y doctrina Cristiana," ed. Miguel León-Portilla, in *Colonial Spanish America: A Documentary History*, ed. Kenneth Mills and William B. Taylor, pp. 20–21. Reproduced with permission of ROWMAN & LITTLEFIELD PUBLISHERS, INCORPORATED, in the format Republish in a book via Copyright Clearance Center; Bernal Díaz, *The True History of the Conquest of New Spain*, in Stuart B. Schwartz, *Victors and Vanquished: Spanish and Nahua Views of the Conquest of Mexico* (Boston: Bedford/St. Martin's, 2000), pp. 218–219.

Death, Europeans began to seek more direct and profitable access to the Afroeurasian trade world. Technological innovations, many borrowed from the East, enabled explorers to undertake ever more ambitious voyages.

In the aftermath of their conquests of Caribbean islands and the Aztec and Inca Empires, the Spanish established new forms of governance to dominate indigenous peoples and exploit their labor. The arrival of Europeans brought enormous population losses to native communities, primarily through the spread of infectious diseases. Disease was one element of the Columbian exchange, a complex transfer of germs, plants, and animals between the Old and New Worlds. These exchanges contributed to the creation of the first truly global economy. Tragically, a major component of global trade was the transatlantic slave trade, in which Europeans transported Africans to labor in the sugar plantations and silver mines of the New World. European nations vied for supremacy in global trade, with early Portuguese success in India and Asia being challenged first by the Spanish and then by the Dutch.

Increased contact with the outside world led Europeans to develop new ideas about cultural and racial differences. Debates occurred in Spain and its colonies over the nature of the indigenous peoples of the Americas and how they should be treated. Europeans had long held negative attitudes about Africans; as the slave trade grew, they began to express more rigid notions of racial inequality and to claim that Africans were inherently suited for slavery. Religion became another means of cultural contact, as European missionaries aimed to spread Christianity in the New World.

NOTES

1. Thomas Benjamin, *The Atlantic World: Europeans, Africans, Indians and Their Shared History, 1400–1900* (Cambridge: Cambridge University Press, 2009), p. 141.
2. Herbert S. Klein, "Profits and the Causes of Mortality," in *The Atlantic Slave Trade*, ed. David Northrup (Lexington, Mass.: D. C. Heath, 1994), p. 116.

CONNECTIONS

Just two years separated Martin Luther's attack on the Catholic Church in 1517 and Ferdinand Magellan's discovery of the Pacific Ocean in 1520. Within a few short years western Europeans' religious unity and notions of terrestrial geography were shattered. In the ensuing decades Europeans struggled to come to terms with religious differences among Protestants and Catholics at home and with the multitudes of new peoples and places they encountered abroad. Like Muslim forces in the first centuries of Islam, Christian Europeans brought their religion with them and sought to convert conquered peoples to their faith. While some Europeans were fascinated and inspired by this new diversity, too often the result was suffering and violence. Europeans endured decades of religious civil war, and indigenous peoples overseas underwent massive population losses as a result of European warfare, disease, and exploitation. Both Catholic and Protestant religious leaders condoned the trade in slaves that ultimately brought suffering and death to millions of Africans.

Even as the voyages of discovery contributed to the fragmentation of European culture, they also played a role in state centralization and consolidation in the longer term. Henceforth, competition to gain overseas colonies became an integral part of European politics. While Spain's enormous profits from conquest ultimately led to a weakening of its power, over time the Netherlands, England, and France used profits from colonial trade to help build modernized, centralized states.

Two crucial consequences emerged from this era of expansion. The first was the creation of enduring contacts among five of the seven continents of the globe — Europe, Asia, Africa, North America, and South America. From the sixteenth century onward, the peoples of the world were increasingly entwined in divergent forms of economic, social, and cultural exchange. The second was the growth of European power. Europeans controlled the Americas and gradually assumed control over existing trade networks in Asia and Africa. Although China remained the world's most powerful economy until at least 1800, the era of European dominance was born.

CHAPTER 16   Review and Explore

Identify Key Terms

Identify and explain the significance of each item below.

bride wealth (p. 458)

caravel (p. 461)

Ptolemy's *Geography* (p. 461)

Treaty of Tordesillas (p. 465)

conquistador (p. 469)

Aztec Empire (p. 470)

Inca Empire (p. 470)

viceroyalties (p. 472)

captaincies (p. 472)

encomienda system (p. 473)

Columbian exchange (p. 475)

Valladolid debate (p. 480)

Black Legend (p. 481)

Review the Main Ideas

Answer the focus questions from each section of the chapter.

1. What was the Afroeurasian trade world prior to the era of European exploration? (p. 456)

2. How and why did Europeans undertake ambitious voyages of expansion? (p. 460)

3. What was the impact of Iberian conquest and settlement on the peoples and ecologies of the Americas? (p. 469)

4. How was the era of global contact shaped by new commodities, commercial empires, and forced migrations? (p. 474)

5. How did new encounters shape cultural attitudes and beliefs in Europe and the rest of the world? (p. 478)

Make Comparisons and Connections

Analyze the larger developments and continuities within and across chapters.

1. If Europe was at the periphery of the global trading system prior to 1492, where was it situated by the middle of the sixteenth century? What had changed? What had not?

2. How does the spread of Christianity in the aftermath of European conquest in the New World compare with the earlier spread of Christianity under the Roman Empire (Chapter 6) and the spread of Buddhism (Chapter 7) and Islam (Chapters 9, 10, 12)?

3. How did European expansion in the period covered in this chapter draw on earlier patterns of trade and migration in Africa (Chapter 10) and Asia (Chapters 12, 13)?

4. To what extent did the European voyages of expansion and conquest inaugurate an era of global history? Did this era represent the birth of "globalization"? Why or why not?

TIMELINE

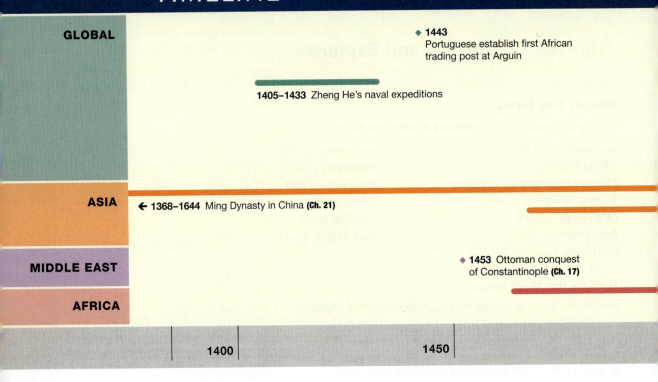

GLOBAL

♦ **1443**
Portuguese establish first African trading post at Arguin

1405–1433 Zheng He's naval expeditions

ASIA

← **1368–1644** Ming Dynasty in China **(Ch. 21)**

MIDDLE EAST

♦ **1453** Ottoman conquest of Constantinople **(Ch. 17)**

AFRICA

1400

1450

Suggested Resources

BOOKS

Crosby, Alfred W. *The Columbian Exchange: Biological and Cultural Consequences of 1492,* 30th anniversary ed. 2003. A lively and highly influential account of the environmental impact of the transatlantic movement of animals, plants, and microbes inaugurated by Columbus.

Elliot, J. H. *Empires of the Atlantic World: Britain and Spain in America, 1492–1830.* 2006. A masterful comparative study of the British and Spanish Empires in the Americas.

Fernández-Armesto, Felipe. *Columbus.* 1992. An excellent biography of Christopher Columbus.

Mann, Charles C. *1491: New Revelations on the Americas Before Columbus,* 2d ed. 2011. A highly readable explanation of the peoples and societies of the Americas before the arrival of Europeans.

Menard, Russell R. *Sweet Negotiations: Sugar, Slavery, and Plantation Agriculture in Early Barbados.* 2006. Explores the intertwined history of sugar plantations and slavery in seventeenth-century Barbados.

Parker, Charles H. *Global Interactions in the Early Modern Age, 1400–1800.* 2010. An examination of the rise of global connections in the early modern period, which situates the European experience in relation to the world's other empires and peoples.

Pomeranz, Kenneth, and Steven Topik. *The World That Trade Created: Society, Culture, and the World Economy, 1400 to the Present.* 1999. The creation of a world market presented through rich and vivid stories of merchants, miners, slaves, and farmers.

Restall, Matthew. *Seven Myths of Spanish Conquest.* 2003. A re-examination of common misconceptions about why and how the Spanish conquered native civilizations in the New World.

Subrahmanyam, Sanjay. *The Portuguese Empire in Asia, 1500–1700: A Political and Economic History,* 2d ed. 2012. A masterful study of the Portuguese overseas empire in Asia that draws on both European and Asian sources.

DOCUMENTARIES

America Before Columbus (National Geographic, 2010). Explores the complex societies and cultures of North America before contact with Europeans and the impact of the Columbian exchange.

Conquistadors (PBS, 2000). Traveling in the footsteps of the Spanish conquistadors, the narrator tells their story while following the paths and rivers they used. Includes discussion of the perspectives and participation of native peoples.

1421: The Year China Discovered America? (PBS, 2004). Investigates the voyages of legendary Chinese admiral Zheng He, exploring the possibility that he and his fleet reached the Americas decades before Columbus.

FEATURE FILMS AND TELEVISION DRAMAS

Black Robe (Bruce Beresford, 1991). A classic film about French Jesuit missionaries among Algonquin and Huron Indians in New France in the seventeenth century.

Marco Polo (Hallmark Channel, 2007). A made-for-television film that follows Italian merchant Marco Polo as he travels to China to establish trade ties with Mongol emperor Khubilai Khan.

The Other Conquest (Salvador Carrasco, 1998). A Mexican film depicting the brutality of the Spanish conquest and its social and religious impact, seen from the perspective of a young Aztec man.

WEBSITES

Discovery and Exploration Collection. A Library of Congress digital collection of maps and manuscripts related to exploration and discovery, many of which relate to the period covered in this chapter. **https://www.loc.gov/collections /discovery-and-exploration/**

Explore Mesolore. A website featuring resources on Mesoamerica, including indigenous documents from the sixteenth century, with helpful explanations of the origins and meaning of the documents. **www.mesolore.org**

The Globalization of Food and Plants. Hosted by the Yale University Center for the Study of Globalization, this website provides information on how various foods and plants — such as spices, coffee, and tomatoes — traveled the world in the Columbian exchange. **yaleglobal.yale.edu/about/food.jsp**

17

The Islamic World Powers

1300–1800

After the decline of the Mongol Empire in the mid-fourteenth century, powerful new Islamic states emerged in south and west Eurasia. By the sixteenth century the Ottoman Empire, centered in Anatolia; the Safavid (SAH-fah-vid) Empire in Persia; and the Mughal (MOO-guhl) Empire in India controlled vast territories from West Africa to Central Asia, from the Balkans to the Bay of Bengal.

Lasting more than six centuries (1299–1922), the Ottoman Empire was one of the largest, best-organized, and most enduring political entities in world history. In Persia (now Iran) the Safavid Dynasty created a Shi'a state and presided over a brilliant culture. In India the Mughal leader Babur and his successors gained control of much of the Indian subcontinent. Mughal rule inaugurated a period of radical administrative reorganization in India and the flowering of intellectual and architectural creativity. Although these three states were often at war with each other, they shared important characteristics and challenges. Their ruling houses all emerged from Turkish tribal organizations, and they all had to adapt their armies to the introduction of firearms. Over time, they became strongly linked culturally, as merchants, poets, philosophers, artists, and military advisers moved relatively easily across their political boundaries. Before the end of this period, Europeans were also active in trade in these empires, especially in India.

Persian Princess

The ruling houses of the Islamic empires were great patrons of art and architecture. This depiction of a princess in a garden is from an early-seventeenth-century palace built by Shah Abbas of the Safavid Dynasty in Persia.

Chehel Sotoun, or *The 40 Columns*, Isfahan, Iran/Bridgeman Images

CHAPTER PREVIEW

How were the three Islamic empires established, and what sorts of governments did they set up?

The Turkish Ruling Houses: The Ottomans, Safavids, and Mughals

Before the Mongols arrived in Central Asia and Persia, another nomadic people from the region of modern Mongolia, the Turks, had moved west, gained control over key territories from Anatolia to Delhi in north India, and contributed to the decline of the Abbasid caliphate in the thirteenth century. As Mongol strength in Persia and Central Asia deteriorated in the late thirteenth to mid-fourteenth centuries, the Turks resumed their expansion. In the late fourteenth century the Turkish leader Timur (1336–1405), also called Tamerlane, built a Central Asian empire from his base in Samarkand that reached into India and through Persia to the Black Sea. After his death, his sons and grandson fought each other for succession, and by 1450 his empire was in rapid decline. Meanwhile, Sufi orders (groups of Islamic mystics) thrived, and Islam became the most important force integrating the region. It was from the many small Turkish chiefs that the founders of the three main empires emerged.

The Expansion of the Ottoman Empire

Ottomans Ruling house of the Turkish empire that lasted from 1299 to 1922.

The **Ottomans** took their name from Osman (r. 1299–1326), the chief of a band of seminomadic Turks that had migrated into western Anatolia while the Mongols still held Persia. The Ottomans gradually expanded at the expense of other small Turkish states and the Byzantine Empire (Map 17.1). Although temporarily slowed by defeat at the hands of Timur in 1402, the Ottomans quickly reasserted themselves after Timur's death in 1405.

Osman's campaigns were intended to subdue, not to destroy. The Ottomans built their empire by absorbing the Muslims of Anatolia and by becoming the protector of the Orthodox Church and of the millions of Greek Christians in Anatolia and the Balkans. A series of victories between 1326 and 1352 made the Ottomans masters of the Balkans. After these victories, the Ottomans made slaves of many captives and trained them as soldiers. These troops were outfitted with guns and artillery and trained to use them effectively.

sultan An Arabic word used by the Ottomans to describe a supreme political and military ruler.

In 1453, during the reign of Sultan Mehmet II (r. 1451–1481), the Ottomans conquered Constantinople, capital of the Byzantine Empire, which had lasted a thousand years. Once Constantinople was theirs, the Ottoman **sultans** (supreme political and military rulers) considered themselves successors to both the Byzantine and Seljuk Turk emperors, and they quickly absorbed the rest of the Byzantine Empire. In the sixteenth century they continued to expand through the Middle East and into North Africa.

To begin the transformation of Constantinople (renamed Istanbul) into an imperial Ottoman capital, Mehmet ordered wealthy residents to build mosques, markets, fountains, baths, and other public facilities. To make up for the loss of population through

Empire of Timur, ca. 1405

war, Mehmet transplanted inhabitants of other territories to the city, granting them tax remissions and possession of empty houses. He wanted them to start businesses, make Istanbul prosperous, and transform it into a microcosm of the empire.

Gunpowder, which was invented by the Chinese and adapted to artillery use by the Europeans, played an influential role in the expansion of the Ottoman state. Mastering this technology, the Ottomans used it to gain control of shipping in the eastern Mediterranean and eliminate the Portuguese from the Red Sea and the Persian Gulf. In 1514, under the superb military leadership of Selim (r. 1512–1520), the Ottomans turned the Safavids back from Anatolia. When the Ottomans acquired Syria and Palestine (1516) and Egypt (1517), they gained control of the holy cities of Islam. Before long the Ottomans had extended their rule across North Africa to Tunisia and Algeria. For the next four centuries a majority of Arabs lived under Ottoman rule.

Suleiman I (r. 1520–1566) extended Ottoman dominion to its widest geographical extent (see Map 17.1). Suleiman's army crushed the Hungarians at Mohács in 1526, killing the king and thousands of his nobles. Three years later the Turks unsuccessfully besieged the Habsburg capital of Vienna. From the late fourteenth to the early seventeenth centuries, the Ottoman Empire was a key player in European politics. In 1525 Francis I of France and Suleiman struck an alliance; both believed that only their collaboration could prevent Habsburg domination of Europe. The Habsburg emperor Charles V retaliated by seeking an alliance with Safavid Persia. Suleiman renewed the French agreement with Francis's son, Henry II (r. 1547–1559), and this accord became the cornerstone of Ottoman policy in western Europe. Ottoman pressure contributed to the official recognition of Lutheran Protestants at the Peace of Augsburg in 1555 and the consolidation of the national monarchy in France.

Sultan Mehmet II Mehmet was called "the Conqueror" because at age twenty-one he captured Constantinople and ended the Byzantine Empire, but he is also known for his patronage of the arts and appreciation of beauty. (Topkapi Palace Museum, Istanbul, Turkey/Bridgeman Images)

Though usually victorious on land, the Ottomans did not enjoy complete dominion on the seas. Competition with the Habsburgs and pirates for control of the Mediterranean led the Ottomans to conquer Cyprus in 1570 and settle thousands of Turks from Anatolia there. In response, Pope Pius V organized a Holy League against the Turks, which won a victory in 1571 at Lepanto off the west coast of Greece with a squadron of more than two hundred Spanish, Venetian, and papal galleys. Still, the Turks remained supreme on land and quickly rebuilt their entire fleet.

To the east, war with Safavid Persia occupied the sultans' attention throughout the sixteenth and well into the seventeenth century. Several issues lay at the root of the long and exhausting conflict: religious antagonism between the Sunni Ottomans and the Shi'a Persians, competition to expand at each other's expense in Mesopotamia, desire to control trade routes, and European alliances. (For more on the Shi'a faith, see "The Safavid Empire in Persia.") Finally, in 1638 the Ottomans captured Baghdad, and the treaty of Kasr-I-Shirim established a permanent border between the two powers.

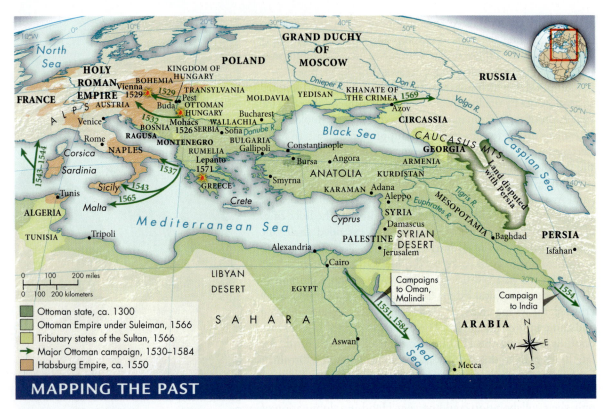

MAPPING THE PAST

MAP 17.1 The Ottoman Empire at Its Height, 1566 The Ottomans, like their great rivals the Habsburgs, rose to rule a vast dynastic empire encompassing many different peoples and ethnic groups. The army and the bureaucracy served to unite the disparate territories into a single state.

ANALYZING THE MAP Trace the coastlines of the Ottoman Empire. What were the major port cities of the empire? Which regions were encompassed within the empire at its height?

CONNECTIONS If the Ottoman Empire is compared to Europe of the same period (see Map 18.2), which had more of its territory near the sea? How did proximity to the Mediterranean shape the politics of Ottoman-European relations in this period?

viziers Chief assistants to caliphs.

The Ottoman political system reached its classic form under Suleiman I. All authority flowed from the sultan to his public servants: provincial governors, police officers, military generals, heads of treasuries, and **viziers** (chief assistants to caliphs). Suleiman ordered Lütfi Paşa (d. 1562), a poet and juridical scholar of slave origin, to draw up a new general code of laws that prescribed penalties for routine criminal acts such as robbery, adultery, and murder. It also sought to reform bureaucratic and financial corruption, such as foreign merchants' payment of bribes to avoid customs duties, imprisonment without trial, and promotion in the provincial administration because of favoritism rather than ability. The legal code also introduced the idea of balanced government budgets. The head of the religious establishment was given the task of reconciling sultanic law with Islamic law.

The Ottomans ruled their more distant lands, such as those in North Africa, relatively lightly. Governors of distant provinces collected taxes and maintained trade routes, but their control did not penetrate deeply into the countryside.

The Ottoman Empire's Use of Slaves

The power of the Ottoman central government was sustained through the training of slaves. Slaves were captured in battle; purchased from Spain, North Africa, and Venice; or drafted through the system known as **devshirme**, by which the sultan's agents compelled Christian families in the Balkans to sell their boys. The slave boys were converted to Islam and trained for the imperial civil service and the standing army. The brightest 10 percent entered the palace school, where they learned to read and write Arabic, Ottoman Turkish, and Persian in preparation for administrative jobs. Other boys were sent to Turkish farms, where they acquired physical toughness in preparation for military service. Known as **janissaries** (Turkish for "recruits"), they formed the elite army corps. Thoroughly indoctrinated and absolutely loyal to the sultan, the janissary corps adapted easily to the use of firearms. The devshirme system enabled the Ottomans to apply merit-based recruitment to military and administrative offices at little cost and provided a means of assimilating Christians living in Ottoman lands.

The Ottoman ruling class included people of varied ethnic origins who rose through the bureaucratic and military ranks, many beginning as the sultan's slaves. In return for their services to the sultan, they held landed estates for the duration of their lives. Because all property belonged to the sultan and reverted to him on the holder's death, Turkish nobles, unlike their European counterparts, did not have a local base independent of the ruler. The absence of a hereditary nobility and of private ownership of agricultural land differentiates the Ottoman system from European feudalism.

Another distinctive characteristic of the Ottomans was the sultan's failure to marry. From about 1500 on, the sultans did not contract legal marriages but perpetuated the ruling house through concubinage. A slave **concubine** (a woman who is a recognized spouse but of lower status than a wife) could not expect to exert power the way a local or foreign noblewoman could. (For a notable exception, see "Individuals in Society: Hürrem," page 494.) When one of the sultan's concubines delivered a boy, she raised him until the age of ten or eleven. Then the child was given a province to govern under his mother's supervision. Because succession to the throne was open to all the sultan's sons, fratricide often resulted upon his death, and the losers were blinded or executed.

Slave concubinage paralleled the Ottoman development of slave soldiers and slave viziers. All held positions entirely at the sultan's pleasure, owed loyalty solely to him, and were thus more reliable than a hereditary nobility. Great social prestige, as well as the opportunity to acquire power and wealth, was attached to being a slave of the imperial household.

The Safavid Empire in Persia

With the decline of Timur's empire after 1450, Persia was controlled by Turkish lords, with no single one dominant until 1501, when fourteen-year-old Isma'il (1487–1524) led a Turkish army to capture Tabriz and declared himself **shah** (Persian word for "king").

The strength of the early **Safavid** state rested on three crucial features. First, the Safavid state utilized the skills of urban bureaucrats and made them an essential part of the civil machinery of government. Second, it secured the loyalty and military support of nomadic Turkish Sufis known as **Qizilbash** (KIH-zihl-bahsh) (a Turkish word meaning "redheads" that was applied to these people because of the red hats

devshirme A process whereby the sultan's agents swept the provinces for Christian youths to be trained as soldiers or civil servants.

janissaries Turkish for "recruits"; they formed the elite army corps.

concubine A woman who is a recognized spouse but of lower status than a wife.

shah Persian word for "king."

Safavid The dynasty that ruled all of Persia and other regions from 1501 to 1722; its state religion was Shi'ism.

Qizilbash Nomadic Turkish Sufis who supplied the early Safavid state with military troops in exchange for grazing rights.

Hürrem

HÜRREM (1505?–1558) WAS BORN IN THE western Ukraine (then part of Poland), the daughter of a Ruthenian priest, and was given the Polish name Aleksandra Lisowska. When Tartars raided, they captured and enslaved her. In 1520 she was given as a gift to Suleiman on the occasion of his accession to the throne. The Venetian ambassador (probably relying on secondhand or thirdhand information) described her as "young, graceful, petite, but not beautiful." She was given the Turkish name Hürrem, meaning "joyful."

Hürrem depicted by a contemporary European artist.

(*Rosa, Consort of Suleiman, Emperor of the Turks*, ca. 1600–1670 [oil on canvas], French School/Royal Collections Trust © Her Majesty Queen Elizabeth II, 2017/Bridgeman Images)

Hürrem apparently brought joy to Suleiman. Their first child was born in 1521. By 1525 they had four sons and a daughter; sources note that by that year Suleiman visited no other woman. But he waited eight or nine years before breaking Ottoman dynastic tradition by making Hürrem his legal wife, the first slave concubine so honored. For the rest of her life, Hürrem played a highly influential role in the political, diplomatic, and philanthropic life of the Ottoman state. First, great power flowed from her position as mother of the prince, the future sultan Selim II (r. 1566–1574). Then, as the intimate and most trusted adviser of the sultan, she was Suleiman's closest confidant. During his frequent trips to the far-flung corners of his multiethnic empire, Hürrem wrote him long letters filled with her love and longing for him and her prayers for his safety in battle. She also shared political information about affairs in Istanbul, the activities of the grand vizier, and the attitudes of the janissaries. At a time when some people believed that the sultan's absence from the capital endangered his hold on the throne, Hürrem acted as his eyes and ears for potential threats.

Hürrem was the sultan's contact with her native Poland, which sent more embassies to Istanbul than any other power. Through her correspondence with King Sigismund I, peace between Poland and the Ottomans was maintained. When Sigismund II succeeded his father in 1548, Hürrem sent congratulations on his accession, along with two pairs of pajamas (originally a Hindu garment but commonly worn in southwestern Asia) and six handkerchiefs. Also, she sent the shah of Persia gold-embroidered sheets and shirts that she had sewn herself, seeking to display the wealth of the sultanate and to keep peace between the Ottomans and the Safavids.

The enormous stipend that Suleiman gave Hürrem permitted her to participate in his vast building program. In Jerusalem (in the Ottoman province of Palestine) she founded a hospice for fifty-five pilgrims that included a soup kitchen that fed four hundred pilgrims a day. In Istanbul Suleiman built and Hürrem endowed the Haseki (meaning "royal favorite concubine") mosque complex and a public bath for women near the Women's Market.

Perhaps Hürrem tried to fulfill two functions hitherto distinct in Ottoman political theory: those of the sultan's favorite and of mother of the prince. She also performed the conflicting roles of slave concubine and imperial wife. Many Turks resented Hürrem's interference at court. They believed she was behind the execution of Suleiman's popular son Mustafa on a charge of treason to make way for her own son to succeed as sultan.

QUESTIONS FOR ANALYSIS

1. How does Hürrem compare to powerful women in other places, such as Empress Wu in China, Isabella of Castile, Catherine de' Medici of France, Elizabeth I of England, or any other you know about?
2. What was Hürrem's "nationality"? What role did it play in her life?

Source: Leslie P. Peirce, *The Imperial Harem: Women and Sovereignty in the Ottoman Empire* (New York: Oxford University Press, 1993).

they wore). In return for the vast grazing lands granted to them, the Qizilbash supplied the shah with troops.

The third source of Safavid strength was the Shi'a faith, which became the compulsory religion of the empire. The Shi'a believed that leadership among Muslims rightfully belonged to the Prophet Muhammad's descendants. Because Isma'il claimed descent from a line of twelve infallible imams (leaders) beginning with Ali (Muhammad's cousin and son-in-law), he was officially regarded as their representative on earth. Isma'il recruited Shi'a scholars to instruct and guide his people, and he persecuted and exiled Sunni **ulama** (religious scholars who interpret the Qur'an and the Sunna, the deeds and sayings of Muhammad). To this day, Iran remains the only Muslim state in which Shi'ism is the official religion.

ulama Religious scholars who interpret the Qur'an and the Sunna, the deeds and sayings of Muhammad.

Safavid power reached its height under Shah Abbas (r. 1587–1629), who moved the capital from Qazvin to Isfahan. His military achievements, support for trade and commerce, and endowment of the arts earned him the epithet "the Great." In the military realm he adopted the Ottoman practice of building an army of slaves, primarily captives from the Caucasus, and used them as a counterweight to the Qizilbash, who had come to be considered a threat. He also increased the use of gunpowder weapons and made alliances with European powers against the Ottomans and Portuguese. In his campaigns against the Ottomans, Shah Abbas captured Baghdad, Mosul, and Diarbakr in Mesopotamia (Map 17.2).

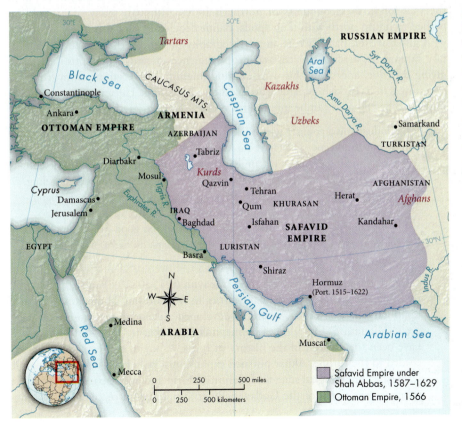

MAP 17.2 The Safavid Empire, 1587–1629 In the late sixteenth century the power of the Safavid kingdom of Persia rested on its strong military force, its Shi'a Muslim faith, and its extraordinarily rich trade in rugs and pottery. Many of the cities on the map, such as Tabriz, Qum, and Shiraz, were great rug-weaving centers.

Conflict between the Ottomans and the Safavids was not an even match. The Safavids did not have as many people or as much wealth as the Ottomans and continually had to defend against encroachments on their western border. Still, they were able to attract some of the Turks in Ottoman lands who felt that their government had shifted too far from its nomadic roots. After Shah Abbas, Safavid power was sapped by civil war between tribal factions vying for control of the court.

The Mughal Empire in India

Mughal A term used to refer to the Muslim empire of India, which was the largest, wealthiest, and most populous of the early modern world.

Of the three great Islamic empires of the early modern world, the **Mughal** Empire of India was the largest, wealthiest, and most populous. Extending over 1.2 million square miles at the end of the seventeenth century, with a population between 100 and 150 million, and with fabulous wealth and resources, the Mughal Empire surpassed the other two by a wide margin. In the sixteenth century only the Ming Dynasty in China could compare.

In 1504 Babur (r. 1483–1530), a Turkish ruler forced out of a small territory in Central Asia, captured Kabul and established a kingdom in Afghanistan. An adventurer who claimed descent from Chinggis Khan and Timur, Babur moved southward in search of resources to restore his fortunes. In 1526, with a force of only twelve thousand men equipped with firearms, Babur defeated the sultan of Delhi at Panipat. Babur's capture of the cities of Agra and Delhi, key fortresses of the north, paved the way for further conquests in northern India. Although many of his soldiers wished to return north with their spoils, Babur decided to stay in India.

A gifted writer, Babur wrote an autobiography in Turkish that recounts his military campaigns, describes places and people he encountered, reports his difficulties giving up wine, and shows his wide-ranging interests in everything from fruit and swimming to a Turkish general who excelled at leapfrog. He was not particularly impressed by India, as can be inferred from this description in his memoirs:

The Mughal Empire, 1526–1857

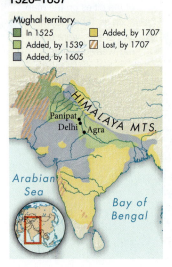

Mughal territory
- In 1525
- Added, by 1539
- Added, by 1605
- Added, by 1707
- Lost, by 1707

HIMALAYA MTS.

Panipat
Delhi
Agra

Arabian Sea

Bay of Bengal

> Hindustan is a country which has few pleasures to recommend it. The people are not handsome. They have no idea of the charms of friendly society, of frankly mixing together, or familiar discourse. They have no genius, no comprehension of mind, no politeness of manner, no kindness or fellow-feeling, no ingenuity or mechanical invention in planning or executing their handicraft works, no skill or knowledge in design or architecture; they have no horses, no good flesh, no grapes or muskmelons, no good fruits, no ice or cold water, no good food or bread in their bazaars, no baths or colleges, no candles, no torches, not a candlestick.[1]

During the reign of Babur's son Humayun (r. 1530–1540 and 1555–1556), the Mughals lost most of their territories in Afghanistan. Humayun went into temporary exile in Persia, where he developed a deep appreciation for Persian art and literature. The reign of Humayun's son Akbar (r. 1556–1605) may well have been the greatest in the history of India. A boy of thirteen when he succeeded to the throne, Akbar pursued expansionist policies. Under his dynamic leadership, the Mughal state took definitive form and encompassed most of the subcontinent north of the Godavari River. No kingdom or coalition of kingdoms could long resist Akbar's armies. The once-independent states of northern India were forced into a centralized political system under the sole authority of the Mughal emperor.

Akbar replaced Turkish with Persian as the official language of the Mughal Empire, and Persian remained the official language until the British replaced it with English in 1835. To govern this vast region, Akbar developed an administrative bureaucracy centered on four co-equal ministers: finance; the army and intelligence; the judiciary and religious patronage; and the imperial household, whose jurisdiction included roads, bridges, and infrastructure throughout the empire. Under Akbar's Hindu finance minister, Raja Todar Mal, a uniform system of taxes was put in place. In the provinces imperial governors were appointed by and responsible solely to the emperor. Whereas the Ottoman sultans and Safavid shahs made extensive use of slaves acquired from non-Muslim lands for military and administrative positions, Akbar used the services of royal princes, nobles, and warrior-aristocrats. Initially these men were Muslims from Central Asia, but to reduce their influence, Akbar vigorously recruited Persians and Hindus. No single ethnic or religious faction could challenge the emperor.

Akbar's descendants extended the Mughal Empire further. His son Jahangir (r. 1605–1628) consolidated Mughal rule in Bengal. (See "Global Viewpoints: Mughal and French Views on Priorities for Monarchs," page 498.) Jahangir's son Shah Jahan (r. 1628–1658) launched fresh territorial expansion. Faced with dangerous revolts by the Muslims in Ahmadnagar and the resistance of the newly arrived Portuguese in Bengal, Shah Jahan not only crushed this opposition but also strengthened his northwestern frontier. Shah Jahan's son Aurangzeb (r. 1658–1707), unwilling to wait for his father to die, deposed him and confined him for years in a small cell. A puritanically devout and strictly orthodox Muslim, as well as a skillful general and a clever diplomat, Aurangzeb ruled more of India than did any previous Mughal emperor, having extended the realm deeper into south India. His reign, however, also marked the beginning of the empire's decline. His non-Muslim subjects were not pleased with his religious zealotry, and his military campaigns were costly. In the south resistance to Mughal rule led to major uprisings. (For more on Aurangzeb's rule, see "Non-Muslims Under Muslim Rule.")

Cultural Flowering

All three Islamic empires presided over extraordinary artistic and intellectual flowering in everything from carpetmaking to architecture and gardening, from geography and astronomy to medicine. At the same time, new religious practices (and conflicts) emerged, and people found new outlets for socializing and exchanging ideas. Artistic and intellectual advances spread from culture to culture, probably because of the common Persian influence on the Turks since the tenth century. This exchange was also aided by shared languages, especially Arabic, Turkish, and Persian. Persian was used as the administrative language by the Mughals in India, and Arabic was a lingua franca of the entire region because of its centrality in Islam. In Ottoman lands both Persian and Arabic were literary languages, but Turkish slowly became the lingua franca of the realm.

> **What cultural advances occurred under the rule of the Ottoman, Safavid, and Mughal Empires?**

Mughal and French Views on Priorities for Monarchs

Jahangir, the fourth Mughal emperor, was as much a patron of the arts as a military commander. Like his great-grandfather Babur, he wrote a memoir. Jahangir's representation of himself and his actions in the memoir can be compared to that of the French king Louis XIV, less than a century later, whose advice to his heir has been preserved.

Jahangir's *Memoirs*

■ At that period when I took my departure from Lahore for Agra, on the occasion recently described, it happily occurred to me to direct that the different land-holders on that route should plant at every town and village, and every stage and halting place, all the way from Lahore to Agra, mulberry and other large and lofty trees affording shade, but particularly those with broad leaves and wide-spreading branches, in order that to all time to come the way-worn and weary traveler might find under their shadow repose and shelter from the scorching rays of the sun during the summer heats. . . . And, lastly, at the passage of every river, whether large or small, convenient bridges were erected, so that the industrious traveler might be able to pursue his objects without obstruction or delay. . . .

With regard to the maxims which should govern the policy of sovereign princes, it has been said, that to resolve without the concurrence of men of experience is the most fallacious of proceedings; but I contend, nevertheless, that there is no safety in council, unless founded in rectitude of mind. I maintain, that if we entrust the concerns of the state to the opinions of another, we give to the Almighty an associate in the secrets of the heart. . . . He that conducts the destinies of his country by the judgment of another, must not forget that he will nevertheless be himself responsible, at the awful day of account, for all the exactions, the tyranny, the unjust decisions, violence, and oppression to which the people may have been exposed, through such imprudent delegation. It is from the reigning sovereign that the awful reckoning will be required, not from those who have been his advisers.

Louis XIV's *Memoirs*

■ The cleverest private individuals take advice from other clever people about their little concerns. What should be the rule for kings who have in their hands the public weal, and whose resolutions harm or benefit the whole earth? Decisions of such importance should never be formed, if possible, without calling upon all the most enlightened, reasonable and wise among our subjects. . . . Besides, our lofty position in some way separates us from our people to whom our ministers are closer, and are consequently able to see a thousand things of which we know nothing, but on which nevertheless we must make up our minds and take measures. Add to this their age, experience, deliberations, and their greater liberty to obtain information and suggestions from their inferiors, who in their turn gather them from others, step by step down to the lowest.

But when on important occasions they have reported to us all the aspects and all the opposing reasons, all that is done elsewhere in similar cases, all that has been done formerly, and all that might be done today, it is incumbent upon us, my son, to choose what must be actually done. And in regard to that choice I will make bold to tell you that if we do not lack good sense or courage there is no other who can make a better one than us.

QUESTIONS FOR ANALYSIS

1. Are you more impressed by the similarities between these two monarchs' comments on consultation with advisers or by the differences? What might account for the similarities and the differences?
2. What can you infer about the personalities of these two monarchs from their remarks?
3. Jahangir describes in great detail the improvements to the roads in his empire. Why would a ruler take pride in the improvement of roads?

Sources: David Price, trans., *Memoirs of the Emperor Jahangueir* (London: The Oriental Translation Committee, 1929), pp. 90–91, slightly modified; Herbert Wilson, trans., *A King's Lessons in Statecraft: Louis XIV: Letters to His Heirs* (New York: Albert and Charles Boni, 1925), pp. 63–64.

The Arts

One of the arts all three empires shared was carpetmaking. Carpet designs and weaving techniques demonstrate both cultural integration and local distinctiveness. Turkic migrants carried their weaving traditions with them as they moved but also readily adopted new motifs, especially from Persia. In Safavid Persia, Shah Abbas was determined to improve his country's export trade and built the small cottage business of carpet weaving into a national industry. In the capital city of Isfahan alone, factories employed more than twenty-five thousand weavers who produced woolen carpets, brocades, and silks of brilliant color, design, and quality. Women and children were often employed as weavers, especially of the most expensive rugs, because their smaller hands could tie tinier knots.

Another art that spread from Persia to both Ottoman and Mughal lands was miniature painting, especially for book illustration. There was an interplay between carpets and miniature painting. Naturalistic depictions of lotus blossoms, peonies, chrysanthemums, tulips, carnations, birds, and even dragons appear in both book illustrations and carpets.

In Mughal India, as throughout the Muslim world, books were regarded as precious objects. Time, talent, and expensive materials went into their production, and they were highly coveted because they reflected wealth, learning, and power. Akbar

Turkish Rug This small carpet (approximately 5½ by 4 feet) was made in seventeenth-century Turkey. Like most other rugs of the region, it is made of hand-knotted wool and features symmetrical geometric designs.

(Lotto type carpet, Ottoman Turkey, 17th-century c.e. Wool [warp, weft and pile]. The James F. Ballard Collection, Gift of James F. Ballard, 1922 [22.100.112]/The Metropolitan Museum of Art, New York, New York, USA/Image copyright © The Metropolitan Museum of Art/Image source: Art Resource, NY)

reportedly possessed twenty-four thousand books when he died. The historian Abu'l-Fazl described Akbar's library and love of books:

> His Majesty's library is divided into several parts. . . . Prose works, poetical works, Hindi, Persian, Greek, Kashmirian, Arabic, are all separately placed. In this order they are also inspected. Experienced people bring them daily and read them before His Majesty, who hears every book from beginning to end . . . and rewards the readers with presents of cash either in gold or silver, according to the number of leaves read out by them. . . . There are no historical facts of past ages, or curiosities of science, or interesting points of philosophy, with which His Majesty, a leader of impartial sages, is unacquainted.[2]

City and Palace Building

In all three empires strong rulers built capital cities and imperial palaces as visible expressions of dynastic majesty. Suleiman "the Magnificent" used his fabulous wealth and thousands of servants to adorn Istanbul with palaces, mosques, schools, and libraries. The building of hospitals, roads, and bridges and the reconstruction of the water systems of the great pilgrimage sites at Mecca and Jerusalem benefited his subjects. Safavid Persia and Mughal India produced rulers with similar ambitions.

The greatest builder under the Ottomans was Mimar Sinan (1491–1588), a Greek-born devshirme recruit who rose to become imperial architect under Suleiman. A contemporary of Michelangelo, Sinan designed 312 public buildings, including mosques, schools, hospitals, public baths, palaces, and burial chapels. His masterpieces, the Shehzade and Suleimaniye Mosques in Istanbul, were designed to maximize the space under the dome.

Shah Abbas made his capital, Isfahan, the jewel of the Safavid Empire. He had his architects place a polo ground in the center and surrounded it with palaces, mosques, and bazaars. In the bazaar one could find splendid rugs, pottery and fine china, metalwork of exceptionally high quality, and silks and velvets of stunning weave and design. A city of perhaps 750,000 people, Isfahan also contained 162 mosques, 48 schools where future members of the ulama learned the sacred Muslim sciences, 273 public baths, and the vast imperial palace. Mosques were richly decorated with blue tile. Private houses had their own garden courts, and public gardens, pools, and parks adorned the wide streets.

Two Masterpieces of Islamic Architecture

Istanbul's Suleimaniye Mosque, designed by Sinan and commissioned by Suleiman I, was finished in 1557. Its interior (below left) is especially spacious. The Taj Mahal (left), built about a century later in Agra in northern India, is perhaps the finest example of Mughal architecture. Its white marble exterior is decorated with Arabic inscriptions and floral designs. (Taj Mahal: Dinodia/Bridgeman Images; mosque: Murat Tander/Lithium Collection/age-fotostock)

Among the Mughal emperors, Shah Jahan had the most sophisticated interest in architecture. Because his capital at Agra was cramped, in 1639 he decided to found a new capital city at Delhi. In the design and layout of the buildings, Persian ideas predominated. The walled palace-fortress alone extended over 125 acres. Built partly of red sandstone, partly of marble, it included private chambers for the emperor; mansions for the wives, widows, and concubines of the imperial household; huge audience rooms for the conduct of public business; baths; and vast gardens filled with flowers, trees, and thirty silver fountains spraying water. In 1650, with living quarters for guards, military officials, merchants, dancing girls, scholars, and hordes of cooks and servants, the palace-fortress housed fifty-seven thousand people. It also boasted a covered public bazaar.

For his palace, Shah Jahan ordered the construction of the Peacock Throne. This famous piece, encrusted with emeralds, diamonds, pearls, and rubies, took seven years to fashion and cost the equivalent of $5 million. It served as the imperial throne of India until 1739, when the Persian warrior Nadir Shah seized it as plunder and carried it to Persia.

Shah Jahan's most enduring monument is the Taj Mahal. Between 1631 and 1648 twenty thousand workers toiled over the construction of this memorial in Agra to Shah Jahan's favorite wife, who died giving birth to their fifteenth child. One of the most beautiful structures in the world, the Taj Mahal is both an expression of love and a superb architectural blending of Islamic and Indian culture.

Gardens

Many of the architectural masterpieces of this age had splendid gardens attached to them. Gardens represent a distinctive and highly developed feature of Persian culture. They commonly were walled, with a pool in the center and geometrically laid-out flowering plants, especially roses. Identified with paradise in Arab tradition, gardens served not only as centers of prayer and meditation but also as places of leisure and revelry. After the incorporation of Persia into the caliphate in the seventh century, formal gardening spread west and east through the Islamic world, as illustrated by the magnificent gardens of Muslim Spain, southern Italy, and, later, southeastern Europe. When Babur established the Mughal Dynasty in India, he adapted the Persian garden to the warmer southern climate. Gardens were laid out near palaces, mosques, shrines, and mausoleums, including the Taj Mahal, which had four water channels symbolizing the four rivers of paradise.

Gardens, of course, are seasonal. To remind themselves of paradise during the cold winter months, rulers, city people, and nomads ordered Persian carpets, most of which feature floral patterns and have formal garden designs.

Intellectual Advances and Religious Trends

Between 1400 and 1800 the culture of the Islamic empires developed in many directions. Particularly notable were new movements within Islam as well as advances in mathematics, geography, astronomy, and medicine. Building on the knowledge of earlier Islamic writers and stimulated by Ottoman naval power, the geographer and cartographer Piri Reis created the *Book of the Sea* (1521), which contained 129 chapters, each with a map incorporating all Islamic (and Western) knowledge of the seas and navigation and describing harbors, tides, dangerous rocks and shores, and storm areas. In the field of astronomy, Takiyuddin Mehmet (1521–1585) built an observatory at Istanbul. His *Instruments of the Observatory* catalogued astronomical instruments and described an astronomical clock that fixed the location of heavenly bodies with greater precision than ever before.

There were also advances in medicine. Under Suleiman the imperial palace itself became a center of medical science, and the large number of hospitals established in Istanbul and throughout the empire testifies to his support for medical research and his concern for the sick. Abi Ahmet Celebi (1436–1523), the chief physician of the empire, produced a study on kidney and bladder stones. Recurrent outbreaks of the plague posed a challenge for physicians in Muslim lands. Muhammad had once said not to go to a country where an epidemic existed but also not to leave a place because an epidemic broke out. As a consequence, when European cities began enforcing quarantines to control the spread of the plague, early Muslim rulers dismissed such efforts. By the sixteenth century, however, a better understanding of contagion led to a redefinition of the proper response to a plague epidemic and allowed for leaving the city in search of clean air.

In the realm of religion, the rulers of all three empires drew legitimacy from their support for Islam. The Sunni-Shi'a split between the Ottomans and Safavids led to efforts to define and enforce religious orthodoxy on both sides. For the Safavids this entailed suppressing Sufi movements and Sunnis, even marginalizing—sometimes massacring—the original Qizilbash warriors, who had come to be seen as politically disruptive. Sectarian conflicts within Islam were not as pronounced in Mughal lands, perhaps because Muslims were greatly outnumbered by non-Muslims, mostly Hindus.

Sufi fraternities thrived throughout the Muslim world in this era, even when the states tried to limit them. In India Sufi orders also influenced non-Muslims. The mystical Bhakti movement among Hindus involved dances, poems, and songs reminiscent of Sufi practice. The development of the new religion of the Sikhs (SEEKS) was also influenced by Sufis. The Sikhs traced themselves back to a teacher in the sixteenth century who argued that God did not distinguish between Muslims and Hindus but saw everyone as his children. Sikhs rejected the caste system (division of society into hereditary groups) and forbade alcohol and tobacco, and men did not cut their hair, covering it instead with a turban. The Sikh

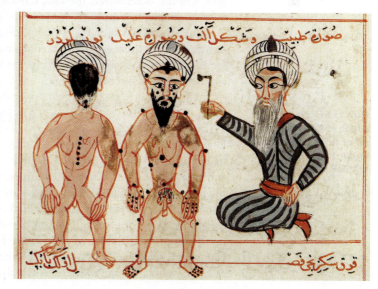

Illustrated Medical Manual The Turkish physician Serafeddin Sabuncuoglu (1385–1470) wrote a treatise of surgery in Turkish, with illustrations, in 1465. This page shows a physician cauterizing leprosy lesions. (Bibliothèque Nationale, Paris, France/Archives Charmet/Bridgeman Images)

movement was most successful in northwest India, where Sikh men armed themselves to defend their communities.

Despite all the signs of cultural vitality in the three Islamic empires, none of them adopted the printing press or went through the sorts of cultural expansion associated with it in China and Europe. Until 1729 the Ottoman authorities prohibited printing books in Turkish or Arabic (Jews, Armenians, and Greeks could establish presses and print in their own languages). Printing was not banned in Mughal India, but neither did the technology spread, even after Jesuit missionaries printed Bibles in Indian languages beginning in the 1550s. The copying of manuscripts was a well-established practice, and those who made their living this way sometimes organized to keep competition at bay. It also needs to be noted that by the end of this period, scientific knowledge was not keeping up with advances made in Europe (see "The Scientific Revolution" in Chapter 19).

Coffeehouses and Their Social Impact

In the mid-fifteenth century a new social convention spread throughout the Islamic world — drinking coffee. Arab writers trace the origins of coffee drinking to Yemen Sufis, who sought a trancelike concentration on God to the exclusion of everything else and found that coffee helped them stay awake. Before long, coffee was being used as a business lubricant — an extension of hospitality to a potential buyer in a shop. Merchants carried the Yemenite practice to Mecca in about 1490. From Mecca, where pilgrims were introduced to it, coffee drinking spread to Egypt and Syria. In 1555 two Syrians opened a coffeehouse in Istanbul. (See "Analyzing the Evidence: Coffee Drinking," at right.)

Coffeehouses provided a place for conversation and male sociability; there a man could entertain his friends cheaply and more informally than at home. But coffeehouses encountered religious and governmental opposition: some people argued that coffee was intoxicating, making it analogous to wine, which was prohibited to Muslims, and others asserted that political discussion in coffeehouses could lead to sedition. On the other hand, the coffee trade was a major source of profit that local notables sought to control.

Although debate over the morality of coffeehouses continued through the sixteenth century, their eventual acceptance represented a revolution in Islamic life: socializing was no longer confined to the home. In the seventeenth century coffee and coffeehouses spread to Europe.

How did Christians, Jews, Hindus, and other non-Muslims fare under these Islamic states?

Non-Muslims Under Muslim Rule

Drawing on Qur'anic teachings, Muslims had long practiced a religious tolerance unknown in Christian Europe. Muslim rulers for the most part guaranteed the lives and property of Christians and Jews in exchange for their promise of obedience and the payment of a poll tax. In the case of the Ottomans, this tolerance was extended not only to the Christians and Jews who had been living under Muslim rule for centuries but also to the Serbs, Bosnians, Croats, and other Orthodox Christians in the newly conquered Balkans. In 1454 Rabbi Isaac Sarfati sent a letter to the Jews in the Rhineland, Swabia, Moravia, and Hungary, urging them to move to Turkey because of the favorable treatment there. A massive migration to Ottoman lands followed.

Coffee Drinking

Coffee beans are native to east Africa and were first grown in Ethiopia. They were brought to Yemen by Sufis in the fifteenth century. There the red beans were boiled in water to produce a hot beverage, which was appreciated for its ability to help participants stay awake during long rituals. By the sixteenth century coffee drinking had spread to other Islamic lands. By then people had learned to roast the beans and grind them finely before adding hot water.

In 1511 some conservative imams in Mecca ruled that coffee should be banned because of its stimulating effects, but the Ottoman sultan Suleiman I overturned their ruling in 1524, helping spread the custom of coffee drinking. As a caffeinated drink, coffee was much like tea. Both proved very popular even though they provided no calories. Because alcohol was forbidden to Muslims, coffee in some ways took its place, providing occasions for socializing either in coffeehouses or in homes or palaces.

This painting by an unknown Ottoman artist is in the Persian miniature style, which is noted for its bright colors and finely drawn details. Part of an album of painting and calligraphy on vellum (fine parchment), the image depicts a banquet where coffee drinking is part of the entertainment. The guests of honor are sitting in a recessed alcove, entertained by three musicians. An attendant in the upper right has a set of cups, and elsewhere in the picture men are shown sipping from cups.

(© The Trustees of the Chester Beatty Library, Dublin, Ireland/Bridgeman Images)

QUESTIONS FOR ANALYSIS

1. How many individuals are shown sipping coffee? What other activities are depicted?
2. How does the artist convey differences in the ages of those drinking coffee?
3. Are there any women in the picture, or are the figures all men? How do you know?
4. Does this picture suggest any reasons why coffee became a popular drink?

When Ferdinand and Isabella of Spain expelled the Jews in 1492 and later, many migrated to the Ottoman Empire.

The Safavid authorities made efforts to convert Armenian Christians in the Caucasus, and many seem to have embraced Islam, some more voluntarily than others. Nevertheless, the Armenian Christian Church retained its vitality, and under the Safavids Armenian Christians were prominent merchants in long-distance trade.

Babur and his successors acquired even more non-Muslim subjects with their conquests in India, which included not only Hindus but also substantial numbers of

Emperor Akbar in the City of Fatehpur Sikri In 1569 Akbar founded the city of Fatehpur Sikri (the City of Victory) to honor the Muslim holy man Sheik Salim Chishti, who had foretold the birth of Akbar's son and heir Jahangir. Akbar is shown here seated on the cushion in the center overseeing the construction of the city. The image is contained in the *Akbarnama*, a book of illustrations Akbar commissioned to officially chronicle his reign. (Victoria & Albert Museum, London, UK/Bridgeman Images)

Jains, Zoroastrians, Christians, and Sikhs. Over time, the number of Indians who converted to Islam increased, but the Mughal rulers did not force conversion. Akbar went the furthest in promoting Muslim-Hindu accommodation. He celebrated important Hindu festivals, such as Diwali, the festival of lights, and he wore his uncut hair in a turban as a concession to Indian practice. Also, Akbar twice married Hindu princesses, one of whom became the mother of his heir, Jahangir, and he appointed the Spanish Jesuit Antonio Monserrate (1536–1600) as tutor to one of his sons. Eventually, Hindus totaled 30 percent of the imperial bureaucracy.

Some of Akbar's successors, above all Aurangzeb, were less tolerant. Aurangzeb appointed censors of public morals in important cities to enforce Islamic laws against gambling, prostitution, drinking, and the use of narcotics. He forbade sati—the self-immolation of widows on their husbands' funeral pyres—and the castration of boys to be sold as eunuchs. He also abolished all taxes not authorized by Islamic law. Aurangzeb's reversal of Akbar's religious tolerance and cultural cosmopolitanism extended further. He ordered the destruction of some Hindu temples and tried to curb Sikhism. He also required Hindus to pay higher customs duties than Muslims. Out of fidelity to Islamic law, he even criticized his mother's tomb, the Taj Mahal: "The lawfulness of a solid construction over a grave is doubtful, and there can be no doubt about the extravagance involved."[3] Aurangzeb's attempts to enforce rigid Islamic norms proved highly unpopular and aroused resistance that weakened Mughal rule.

How were the Islamic empires affected by the gradual shift toward trade routes that bypassed their lands?

Shifting Trade Routes and European Penetration

It has widely been thought that a decline in the wealth and international importance of the Muslim empires could be directly attributed to the long-term shift in trading patterns that resulted from the discoveries of Columbus, Magellan, and other European explorers. The argument is that new sea routes enabled Europeans to acquire goods from the East without using Muslim intermediaries, so that the creation of European colonial powers beginning in the sixteenth century led directly and indirectly to the eclipse of the Ottomans, Safavids, and Mughals. Recent scholars have challenged these ideas as too simplistic. First, it was not until the eighteenth century that political decline became evident in the three Islamic empires. Second, Turkish, Persian, and Indian merchants remained very active as long-distance traders into the eighteenth century and opened up many new routes themselves. It is true that in the Islamic empires New World crops like potatoes and sweet potatoes fueled population increases less rapidly than in western Europe and East Asia. By 1800 the population of India was about 190 million, that of Safavid lands about 8 million, and that of Ottoman lands about 24 million. (By comparison, China's population stood at about 300 million in 1800 and Russia's about 35 million.)

European Rivalry for Trade in the Indian Ocean

Shortly before Babur's invasion of India, the Portuguese had opened the subcontinent to Portuguese trade. In 1510 they established the port of Goa on the west coast of India as their headquarters and through an aggressive policy took control of Muslim shipping in the Indian Ocean and Arabian Sea, charging high fees to let ships through. The Portuguese historian Barrões attempted to justify Portugal's seizure of commercial traffic that the Muslims had long dominated:

> It is true that there does exist a common right to all to navigate the seas and in Europe we recognize the rights which others hold against us; but the right does not extend beyond Europe and therefore the Portuguese as Lords of the Sea are justified in confiscating the goods of all those who navigate the seas without their permission.[4]

In short, the Portuguese decided that Western principles of international law should not restrict them in Asia. As a result, they controlled the spice trade over the Indian Ocean for almost a century.

In 1602 the Dutch formed the Dutch East India Company with the stated goal of wresting the enormously lucrative spice trade from the Portuguese. In 1685 they supplanted the Portuguese in Ceylon (Sri Lanka). The scent of fabulous profits also attracted the English. With a charter signed by Queen Elizabeth, eighty London merchants organized the British East India Company. In 1619 Emperor Jahangir granted a British mission important commercial concessions. Soon, by offering gifts, medical services, and bribes to Indian rulers, the British East India Company was able to set up twenty-eight coastal forts/trading posts. By 1700 the company had founded the cities that became Madras and Calcutta (today called Chennai and Kolkata) and had taken over Bombay (today Mumbai), which had been a Portuguese possession (Map 17.3).

The British called their trading posts factory-forts. The term *factory* did not signify manufacturing; it designated the walled compound containing the residences, gardens, and offices of British East India Company officials and the warehouses where goods were stored before being shipped to Europe. The company president exercised political authority over all residents.

MAP 17.3 India, 1707–1805

In the eighteenth century Mughal power gradually yielded to the Hindu Marathas and to the British East India Company.

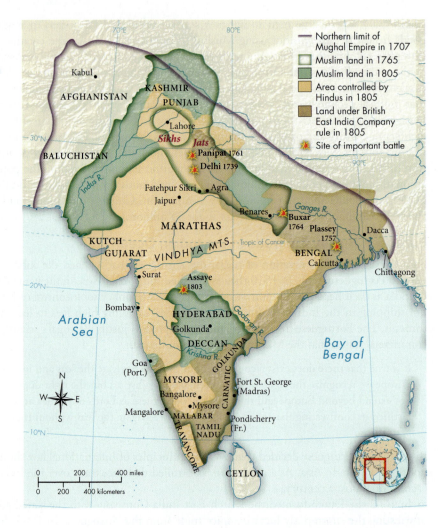

Factory-forts existed to make profits from Asian-European trade, which was robust due to the popularity of Indian and Chinese wares in Europe in the late seventeenth and early eighteenth centuries. The European middle classes wanted Indian textiles, which were colorful, durable, cheap, and washable. The upper classes desired Chinese wallpaper and porcelains and Indian silks and cottons. Other Indian goods in demand included pepper and other spices, sugar, and opium. To pay for these goods, the British East India Company sold silver, copper, zinc, lead, and fabrics to the Indians. Profits grew even larger after 1700, when the company began to trade with China.

Merchant Networks in the Islamic Empires

The shifting trade patterns associated with European colonial expansion brought no direct benefit to the Ottomans and the Safavids, whose merchants could now be bypassed by Europeans seeking goods from India, Southeast Asia, or China. Yet merchants from these Islamic empires often proved adaptable, finding ways to benefit from the new trade networks.

In the case of India, the appearance of European traders led to a rapid increase in overall trade, helping Indian merchants and the Indian economy. Some Indian merchants in Calcutta and Bombay, for instance, made gigantic fortunes from trade within Asia carried on European ships. Block-printed cotton cloth, produced by artisans working at home, was India's chief export.

Within India the demand for cotton cloth, as well as for food crops, was so great that Akbar had to launch a wide-scale road-building campaign. From the Indian region of Gujarat, Indian merchant bankers shipped their cloth worldwide: across the Indian Ocean to Aden and the Muslim-controlled cities on the east coast of Africa; across the Arabian Sea to Muscat and Hormuz and up the Persian Gulf to the cities of Persia; up the Red Sea to the Mediterranean; by sea also to Malacca, Indonesia, China, and Japan; by land across Africa to Ghana on the west coast; and to Astrakhan, Poland, Moscow, and even the Russian cities on the distant Volga River. Indian businessmen had branch offices in many of these places, and all this activity produced fabulous wealth for some Indian merchants. Indian merchants were often devout Hindus, Muslims, Buddhists, or Jains, evidence that undermines the argument of some Western writers, notably Karl Marx (see "The Birth of Socialism" in Chapter 24), that religion retarded Asia's economic development.

Throughout Muslim lands both Jews and Christians were active in commerce. A particularly interesting case involves the Armenian Christians in the sixteenth to eighteenth centuries. Armenian merchants had been trading from their base in Armenia for centuries and were especially known for their trade in Persian silk. When the Portuguese first appeared on the western coast of India in 1498 and began to settle in south India, they found many Armenian merchant communities already there. A few decades later Akbar invited Armenians to settle in his new capital, Agra. In 1603 Shah Abbas captured much of Armenia, taking it from the Ottomans, and forcing the Armenians to move more deeply into Persia.

Armenian merchant networks stretched from Venice and Amsterdam in western Europe, Moscow in Russia, and Ottoman-controlled Aleppo and Smyrna to all the major trading cities of India and even regions farther east, including Guangzhou in southern China and Manila in the Philippines. Many Armenian communities in these cities became quite substantial, built churches,

English Dress Made of Indian Printed Cotton Cloth Early British traders in India were impressed with the quality of the textiles made there and began ordering designs that would be popular with the English. This dress, created around 1770–1780 in England, is made of printed cotton (chintz) from the southeastern part of India. Chintz became so popular in England that it was eventually banned because it was threatening local textile industries. (Victoria and Albert Museum, London, UK/ V & A Images/Art Resource, NY)

and recruited priests. The merchant about to take a journey would borrow a sum of money to purchase goods and would contract to pay it back with interest on his return. Using couriers, these Armenian merchants sent long letters describing the trade environment and the prices that could be realized for given goods.

From the British East India Company to the British Empire in India

Britain's presence in India began with the British East India Company and its desire to profit from trade. Managers of the company in London discouraged all unnecessary expenses and financial risks and thus opposed missionary activities or interference in local Indian politics. Nevertheless, the company responded to political instability in India in the early eighteenth century by extending political control. When warlords appeared or an uprising occurred, people from the surrounding countryside flocked into the company's factory-forts, which gradually came to exercise political authority over the territories around them. The company's factories evolved into defensive installations manned by small garrisons of native troops — known as **sepoys** — trained in Western military weapons and tactics.

sepoys The native Indian troops who were trained as infantrymen.

Britain eventually became the dominant foreign presence in India, despite challenges from the French. From 1740 to 1763 Britain and France were engaged in a tremendous global struggle, and India, like North America in the Seven Years' War (see Chapter 22), became a battlefield and a prize. The French won land battles, but English sea power proved decisive by preventing the landing of French reinforcements. The Treaty of Paris of 1763 recognized British control of much of India, marking the beginning of the British Empire in India.

How was Britain to govern so large a territory? Eventually, the East India Company was pushed out of its governing role because the English Parliament distrusted the company, believing it was corrupt. The Regulating Act of 1773 created the office of governor general to exercise political authority over the territory controlled by the company. The East India Company Act of 1784 required that the governor general be chosen from outside the company, and it made company directors subject to parliamentary supervision.

Implementation of these reforms fell to three successive governors: Warren Hastings (r. 1774–1785), Lord Charles Cornwallis (r. 1786–1794), and the marquess Richard Wellesley (r. 1797–1805). Hastings sought allies among Indian princes, laid the foundations for the first Indian civil service, abolished tolls to facilitate internal trade, placed the salt and opium trades under government control, and planned a codification of Muslim and Hindu laws. Cornwallis introduced the British style of property relations, in which the rents of tenant farmers supported the landlords. Wellesley was victorious over local rulers who resisted British rule, vastly extending British influence in India. Like most nineteenth-century British governors of India, Wellesley believed that British rule strongly benefited the Indians. With supreme condescension, he wrote that British power should be established over the Indian princes in order "to deprive them of the means of prosecuting any measure or of forming any confederacy hazardous to the security of the British empire, and to enable us to preserve the tranquility of India by exercising a general control over the restless spirit of ambition and violence which is characteristic of every Asiatic government."[5]

Political Decline

What common factors led to the decline of central power in the Islamic empires in the seventeenth and eighteenth centuries?

By the end of the eighteenth century all three of the major Islamic empires were on the defensive and losing territory (Map 17.4). They faced some common problems—succession difficulties, financial strain, and loss of military superiority—but their circumstances differed in significant ways as well.

The first to fall was the Safavid Empire. Persia did not have the revenue base to maintain the sort of standing armies that the Ottomans and the Mughals had. Decline in the strength of the army encouraged increased foreign aggression. In 1722 the Afghans invaded from the east, seized Isfahan, and were able to repulse an Ottoman invasion from the west. In Isfahan thousands of officials and members of the shah's family were executed. In the following century no leaders emerged capable of reuniting all of Persia. In this political vacuum, Shi'a religious institutions grew stronger.

MAP 17.4 The Muslim World, ca. 1700 The three great Islamic empires were adjacent to each other and of similar physical size. Many of their other neighbors were Muslim as well.

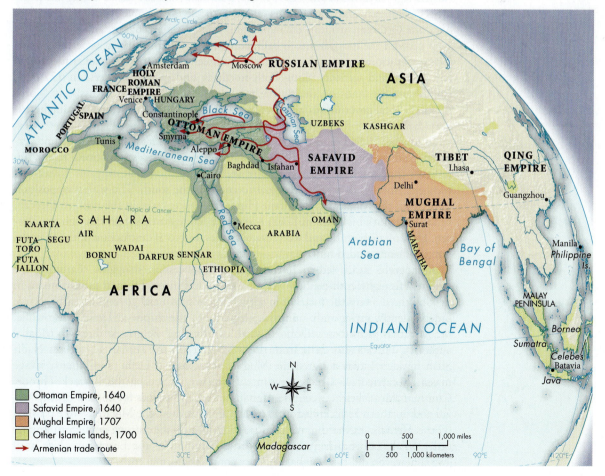

Ottoman Empire, 1640
Safavid Empire, 1640
Mughal Empire, 1707
Other Islamic lands, 1700
Armenian trade route

The Ottoman Empire also suffered from poor leadership. Early Ottoman practice had guaranteed that the sultans would be forceful men. The sultan's sons gained administrative experience as governors of provinces and military experience on the battlefield as part of their education. After the sultan died, any son who wanted to succeed had to contest his brothers to claim the throne, after which the new sultan would have his defeated brothers executed. Although bloody, this system led to the succession of capable, determined men. After Suleiman's reign, however, the tradition was abandoned. To prevent threats of usurpation, sons of the sultan were brought up in the harem, confined there as adults, and denied roles in government. The result was a series of rulers who were minor children or incompetent adults, leaving power in the hands of high officials and the mothers of the heirs. Political factions formed around viziers, military leaders, and palace women. In the contest for political favor, the devshirme was abandoned, and political and military ranks were filled by Muslims.

The Ottoman Empire's military strength also declined. The defeat of the Turkish fleet by the Spanish off the coast of Greece at Lepanto in 1571 marked the loss of Ottoman dominance in the Mediterranean. By the terms of a peace treaty with Austria signed at Karlowitz (1699), the Ottomans lost the major European provinces of Hungary and Transylvania, along with the tax revenues they had provided. Also, the Ottoman armies were depending more on mercenaries, and they did not keep up with the innovations in drill, command, and control that were then transforming European armies. From the late seventeenth century Ottoman armies began losing wars and territory along both northern and eastern borders. In 1774 the empire lost the lands on the northern bank of the Black Sea to Russia. In North Africa the local governors came to act more independently, sometimes starting hereditary dynasties.

In Mughal India the old Turkish practice of letting heirs fight for the throne persisted, leading to frequent struggles over succession, but also to strong rulers. Yet military challenges proved daunting there as well. After defeating his father and brothers, Aurangzeb made it his goal to conquer the south. The stiffest opposition came from the Marathas, a militant Hindu group centered in the western Deccan. From 1681 until his death in 1707, Aurangzeb led repeated sorties through the Deccan. He took many forts and won several battles, but total destruction of the Maratha guerrilla bands eluded him.

Aurangzeb's death led to thirteen years of succession struggles, shattering the empire. His eighteenth-century successors were less successful than the Ottomans in making the dynasty the focus of loyalty. Mughal provincial governors began to rule independently, giving only minimal allegiance to the throne at Delhi. Meanwhile, the Marathas pressed steadily northward, constituting the gravest threat to Mughal authority. Threats also came from the west. In 1739 the Persian adventurer Nadir Shah invaded India, defeated the Mughal army, looted Delhi, and, after a savage massacre, carried off a huge amount of treasure, including the Peacock Throne. Constant skirmishes between the Afghans and the Marathas for control of the Punjab and northern India ended in 1761 at Panipat, where the Marathas were crushed by the Afghans. At that point, India no longer had a state strong enough to impose order on the subcontinent or check the penetration of the Europeans. Not until 1857, however, did the Mughal Dynasty come to a formal end.

In all three empires fiscal difficulties contributed to strain on the state. A long period of peace in the late sixteenth century and again in the mid-eighteenth century, as well as a decline in the frequency of visits of the plague, led to a doubling of the population. Increased population, coupled with the "little ice age" of the mid-seventeenth century, meant that the land could not sustain so many people, nor could the towns provide jobs for the thousands of agricultural workers who fled to them. The return of demobilized soldiers aggravated the problem. Inflation, famine, and widespread uprisings resulted. Power was seized by local notables and military strongmen at the expense of central government officials.

Chapter Summary

After the decline of the Mongols in Central Asia and Persia, many small Turkic-ruled states emerged in the region from Anatolia through Afghanistan. Three of them went on to establish large empires: the Ottomans in Anatolia, the Safavids in Persia, and the Mughals in India. The Ottoman Empire's political system reached its classic form under Suleiman I. All authority flowed from the sultan to his public servants: provincial governors, police officers, military generals, heads of treasuries, and viziers. In Persia for some time Turkish lords competed for power, with no single one dominant until 1501, when a fourteen-year-old military leader declared himself shah. The strength of this Safavid state rested in part on the skills of urban bureaucrats, who were vital to the civil machinery of government. Babur, from his base in Afghanistan, founded the Mughal Empire in India. His grandson Akbar extended Mughal rule far into India. Whereas the Ottoman sultans and Safavid shahs used slaves acquired from non-Muslim lands for military and administrative positions, Akbar relied on the services of royal princes, nobles, and warrior-aristocrats. All three empires quickly adapted to new gunpowder technologies.

Each of the three Islamic empires presided over an extraordinary artistic and intellectual flowering in everything from carpetmaking and book illustration to architecture and gardening, from geography and astronomy to medicine. Each of these empires drew legitimacy from its support for Islam. There were, however, key differences: the Ottomans and Mughals supported the Sunni tradition, the Safavids the Shi'a tradition.

The three Islamic empires all had a substantial number of non-Muslim subjects. The Ottomans ruled over the Balkans, where most of the people were Christian, and Muslims in India were greatly outnumbered by Hindus.

European exploration opened new trade routes and enabled Europeans to trade directly with India and China, bypassing Muslim intermediaries in the Middle East. Within India British merchants increased their political control in politically unstable areas, leading before the end of the eighteenth century to a vast colonial empire in India.

By the end of the eighteenth century all three of the major Islamic empires were losing territory. The first to fall was the Safavid Empire. From the late seventeenth century Ottoman armies began losing wars along the northern and eastern borders, resulting in substantial loss of territory. Military challenges proved daunting in Mughal India as well. In all three empires, as central power declined, local notables and military strongmen seized power.

NOTES

1. *Memoirs of Zehir-Ed-Din Muhammed Baber: Emperor of Hindustan*, trans. John Leyden and William Erskine (London: Longman and Cadell, 1826), p. 333.
2. Quoted in M. C. Beach, *The Imperial Image: Paintings for the Mughal Court* (Washington, D.C.: Freer Gallery of Art, Smithsonian Institution, 1981), pp. 9–10.
3. Quoted in S. K. Ikram, *Muslim Civilization in India* (New York: Columbia University Press, 1964), p. 202.
4. Quoted in K. M. Panikkar, *Asia and Western Domination* (London: George Allen & Unwin, 1965), p. 35.
5. Quoted in W. Bingham, H. Conroy, and F. W. Iklé, *A History of Asia*, vol. 2 (Boston: Allyn and Bacon, 1967), p. 74.

CONNECTIONS

From 1300 to 1800 and from North Africa to India, Islamic civilization thrived under three dynastic houses: the Ottomans, the Safavids, and the Mughals. All three empires had a period of expansion when territory was enlarged, followed by a high point politically and culturally, and later a period of contraction, when territories broke away. Two of the empires had large non-Muslim populations. India, even under Mughal rule, remained a predominantly Hindu land, and the Ottomans, in the process of conquering the Balkans, acquired a population that was largely Greek Orthodox Christians. Though all three states supported Islam, the Safavids took Shi'a teachings as orthodox, while the other two favored Sunni teachings. At the cultural level, the borders of these three states were porous, and people, ideas, art motifs, languages, and trade flowed back and forth.

In East Asia the fifteenth through eighteenth centuries also saw the creation of strong, prosperous, and expanding states, though in the case of China (under the Qing Dynasty) and Japan (under the Tokugawa Shogunate) the eighteenth century was a cultural high point, not a period of decline. The Qing emperors were Manchus, from the region northeast of China proper, reminiscent of the Mughals, who began in Afghanistan. As in the Islamic lands, during these centuries the presence of European powers became an issue in East Asia, though the details were quite different. Although one of the commodities that the British most wanted was the tea produced in China, Britain did not extend political control in China the way it did in India. Japan managed to refuse entry to most European traders after finding their presence and their support for missionary activity disturbing. Chapter 21 takes up these developments in East Asia.

In the next three chapters the focus is on two other regions of the world, Europe and Africa. To fully understand what Britain was doing in India requires more background on what was happening in Europe from 1500 to 1800, a period when religious differences were causing strife between European states that were at the same time beginning to build overseas empires. By the eighteenth century the Scientific Revolution and the Enlightenment were having a major impact on people's lives in Europe, and the slave trade was tying Europe to both Africa and the Americas.

CHAPTER 17 Review and Explore

Identify Key Terms

Identify and explain the significance of each item below.

Ottomans (p. 490)   **shah** (p. 493)

sultan (p. 490)   **Safavid** (p. 493)

viziers (p. 492)   **Qizilbash** (p. 493)

devshirme (p. 493)   **ulama** (p. 495)

janissaries (p. 493)   **Mughal** (p. 496)

concubine (p. 493)   **sepoys** (p. 510)

Review the Main Ideas

Answer the focus questions from each section of the chapter.

1. How were the three Islamic empires established, and what sorts of governments did they set up? (p. 490)

2. What cultural advances occurred under the rule of the Ottoman, Safavid, and Mughal Empires? (p. 497)

3. How did Christians, Jews, Hindus, and other non-Muslims fare under these Islamic states? (p. 504)

4. How were the Islamic empires affected by the gradual shift toward trade routes that bypassed their lands? (p. 506)

5. What common factors led to the decline of central power in the Islamic empires in the seventeenth and eighteenth centuries? (p. 511)

Make Comparisons and Connections

Analyze the larger developments and continuities within and across chapters.

1. In what sense were the states of the Ottomans, Safavids, and Mughals empires rather than large states? Do all three equally deserve the term "empire"? Why or why not?

2. How did the expansion of European presence in the Indian Ocean after 1450 impinge on the societies and economies of each of the Islamic empires?

3. What made it possible for Islamic rulers to tolerate more religious difference than European Christian rulers of the same period did (Chapters 14 and 15)?

TIMELINE

WESTERN AND SOUTH ASIA

1299–1326 Reign of Osman, founder of the Ottoman Dynasty

1299–1922 Ottoman Empire

1336–1405 Life of Timur

♦ **ca. mid-1400s** Coffeehouses become center of Islamic male social life

♦ **1453** Ottoman conquest of Constantinople

EAST ASIA

1368–1644 Ming Dynasty in China **(Ch. 21)**

1405–1433 Zheng He's naval expeditions **(Ch. 21)**

EUROPE

ca. 1350–1520 Italian Renaissance **(Ch. 15)**

AFRICA

AMERICAS

ca. 1428–1521 Aztec Empire dominates Mesoamerica **(Ch. 11)**

ca. 1438–1532 Inca Empire dominates the Andes **(Ch. 11)**

| 1300 | 1400 |

Suggested Resources

BOOKS

Barkey, Karen. *Empire of Difference*. 2008. Places the history of the Ottomans in comparative perspective.

Casale, Giancarlo. *The Ottoman Age of Exploration*. 2011. Lively account of Ottoman rivalry with the Portuguese in the Indian Ocean in the sixteenth century.

Dale, Stephen Frederic. *The Garden of the Eight Paradises: Babur and the Culture of Empire in Central Asia, Afghanistan and India, 1483–1750*. 2004. A scholarly biography that draws on and analyzes Babur's autobiography.

Dale, Stephen Frederic. *The Muslim Empires of the Ottomans, Safavids, and Mughals*. 2010. A comparative study of the three empires, with much on religion and culture.

Findley, Carter Vaughn. *The Turks in World History*. 2005. Takes a macro look at the three Islamic empires as part of the history of the Turks.

Finkel, Caroline. *Osman's Dream: A History of the Ottoman Empire*. 2006. A new interpretation that views the Ottomans from their own perspective.

Inalcik, Halil, and Günsel Renda. *Ottoman Civilization*. 2002. A huge, beautifully illustrated, government-sponsored overview, with an emphasis on the arts and culture.

Lapidus, Ira M. *A History of Islamic Societies*, 2d ed. 2002. A comprehensive yet lucid survey.

Mukhia, Harbans. *The Mughals of India: A Framework for Understanding*. 2004. A short but thoughtful analysis of the Mughal society and state.

Parthasarathi, Prasannan. *Why Europe Grew Rich and Asia Did Not: Global Economic Divergence, 1600–1850*. 2011. Focuses on India and how it compared to Britain in producing cotton and coal and making scientific advances.

Peirce, Leslie P. *The Imperial Harem: Women and Sovereignty in the Ottoman Empire*. 1993. A fresh look at the role of elite women under the Ottomans.

1501–1722 Safavid Empire in Persia

1520–1566 Reign of Ottoman sultan Suleiman I

1631–1648 Construction of Taj Mahal under Shah Jahan in India

1526–1857 Mughal Empire in India

1763 ◆
Treaty of Paris recognizes British control over much of India

1556–1605 Reign of Akbar in Mughal Empire

◆ **1517** Luther's Ninety-five Theses **(Ch. 15)**

ca. 1690–1789
European Enlightenment **(Ch. 19)**

ca. 1464–1591 Songhai kingdom dominates the western Sudan **(Ch. 20)**

◆ **1492** Columbus lands on San Salvador **(Ch. 16)**

1500	1600	1700

Richards, John F. *The Mughal Empire.* 1993. A coherent narrative history of the period 1526–1720.

Ruthven, Malise, and Azim Nanji. *Historical Atlas of Islam.* 2004. Provides numerous maps illustrating the shifting political history of Islamic states.

DOCUMENTARIES

The Great Moghuls (Ecosse Films, 1990). A British documentary (with six episodes) that tells the story of the Mughal Empire.

Ottoman Empire: The War Machine (History Channel, 2006). An overview of the Ottoman Empire, with lots of dramatizations.

Sufi Soul: The Mystic Music of Islam (MWTV/Riverboat, 2005). An introduction to the music to which the whirling dervishes whirl, with footage of many musicians.

Warrior Empire: The Mughals of India (History Channel, 2006). Covers the period from the founder Babar through the death of Aurangzeb in 1707.

FEATURE FILMS

The Day of the Siege: September Eleven 1683 (Renzo Martinelli, 2012). A Polish and Italian film (in English) on the Ottoman attack on Vienna, full of battle scenes.

Jodhaa Akbar (Ashutosh Gowariker, 2008). The story of Mughal emperor Akbar and Rajput princess Jodhaa, who married in the sixteenth century for political reasons and fell in love.

WEBSITES

Archnet. A rich collection of photos and videos on the architecture of Islamic societies, with a useful timeline. **archnet.org**

Gardens of the Mughal Empire. Sites and sounds of many of the major gardens dating to the Mughal period. **www.mughalgardens.org**

The Ottomans. This site on the Ottomans pays special attention to the military and wars, but also covers art and culture. **www.theottomans.org/english /history/index.asp**

18

European Power and Expansion
1500–1750

The two centuries that opened the early modern era witnessed crisis and transformation in Europe. What one historian has described as the long European "struggle for stability" originated with conflicts sparked by the Protestant and Catholic Reformations in the early sixteenth century and continued with economic and social breakdown into the late seventeenth century.[1] To consolidate their authority and expand their territories, European rulers increased the size of their armies, imposed higher taxes, and implemented bureaucratic forms of government. By the end of the seventeenth century they had largely succeeded in restoring order and securing increased power for the state.

The growth of state power within Europe raised a series of questions: Who held supreme power? What made it legitimate? Conflicts over these questions led to rebellions and at times outright civil war. Between roughly 1589 and 1715 two basic patterns of government emerged from these conflicts: absolute monarchy and the constitutional state. Almost all subsequent European governments were modeled on one of these patterns, which have also greatly influenced the rest of the world.

Whether a government was constitutional or absolutist, an important foundation of state power was empire and colonialism. Jealous of the riches and prestige the Iberian powers gained from their overseas holdings, England, France, and the Netherlands vied for territory in Asia and the Americas, while Russia pushed its borders east to the Pacific and west into central Europe. This was a distinctive moment in world history when exchange within and among empires produced constant movement of people, goods, and culture, with no one region or empire able to dominate the others entirely.

Louis XIV

In this painting, King Louis XIV receives foreign ambassadors to celebrate a peace treaty. The king grandly occupied the center of his court, which in turn served as the pinnacle for the French people and, at the height of his glory, for all of Europe.

Peace Treaty of Nijmegen, 1678/Museum of Fine Arts, Budapest, Hungary/Erich Lessing/Art Resource, NY

CHAPTER PREVIEW

THE PROTESTANT AND CATHOLIC REFORMATIONS
How did the Protestant and Catholic Reformations change power structures in Europe and shape European colonial expansion?

SEVENTEENTH-CENTURY CRISIS AND REBUILDING How did seventeenth-century European rulers overcome social and economic crisis to build strong states?

ABSOLUTIST STATES IN WESTERN AND CENTRAL EUROPE
What was absolutism, and how did it evolve in seventeenth-century Spain, France, and Austria?

CONSTITUTIONALISM AND EMPIRE IN ENGLAND AND THE DUTCH REPUBLIC
Why and how did the constitutional state triumph in England and the Dutch Republic?

COLONIAL EXPANSION AND EMPIRE
How did European nations compete for global trade and empire in the Americas and Asia?

THE RUSSIAN EMPIRE How did Russian rulers build a distinctive absolutist monarchy and expand into a vast and powerful empire?

How did the Protestant
and Catholic
Reformations change
power structures in
Europe and shape
European colonial
expansion?

The Protestant and Catholic Reformations

As a result of a movement of religious reform known as the **Protestant Reformation**, Western Christendom broke into many divisions in the sixteenth century. This splintering happened not only for religious reasons but also because of political and social factors. Religious transformation provided a source of power for many rulers and shaped European colonial expansion.

Protestant Reformation
A religious reform movement that began in the early sixteenth century and split the Western Christian Church.

The Protestant Reformation

In early-sixteenth-century western Europe, calls for reform in the church came from many quarters, both within and outside the church. Critics of the church concentrated their attacks on clerical immorality, ignorance, and absenteeism. Charges of immorality were aimed at a number of priests who were drunkards, neglected the rule of celibacy, gambled, or indulged in fancy dress. Charges of ignorance applied to barely literate priests who delivered poor-quality sermons.

In regard to absenteeism, many clerics, especially higher ecclesiastics, held several benefices (offices) simultaneously. However, they seldom visited the communities served by the benefices. Instead they collected revenues from all the benefices assigned to them and hired a poor priest to fulfill their spiritual duties.

There was also local resentment of clerical privileges and immunities. Priests, monks, and nuns were exempt from civic responsibilities, such as defending the city and paying taxes. Yet religious orders frequently held large amounts of urban property. City governments were increasingly determined to integrate the clergy into civic life. This brought city leaders into opposition with bishops and the papacy, which for centuries had stressed the independence of the church from lay control.

This range of complaints helps explain why the ideas of Martin Luther (1483–1546), a priest and professor of theology from the German University of Wittenberg, found a ready audience. Luther and other Protestants—the word comes from a "protest" drawn up by a group of reforming princes in 1529—developed a new understanding of Christian doctrine in which salvation came through God's grace by faith alone and religious authority rested solely in the Bible. These ideas directly contradicted the teachings of the Catholic Church, but they were attractive to educated people and urban residents, and they spread rapidly through preaching, hymns, and the printing press.

Domestic Scene The Protestant notion that the best form of Christian life was marriage and a family helps explain the appeal of Protestantism to middle-class urban men and women, such as those shown in this domestic scene. The large covered bed at the back was both a standard piece of furniture in urban homes and a symbol of proper marital sexual relations. (© Mary Evans Picture Library/The Image Works)

Luther lived in the Holy Roman Empire, a loose collection of largely independent states in which the emperor had far less authority than did the monarchs of western Europe. The Habsburg emperor, Charles V, was a staunch supporter of Catholicism, but the ruler of the territory in which Luther lived protected the reformer. Although Luther appeared before Charles V when he was summoned, he was not arrested and continued to preach and write.

Luther's ideas appealed to the local rulers of the empire for a variety of reasons. Though Germany was not a nation, people did have an understanding of being German because of their language and traditions. Luther frequently used the phrase "we Germans" in his attacks on the papacy, and his appeal to national feeling influenced many rulers. Also, while some German rulers were sincerely attracted to Lutheran ideas, material considerations swayed many others. The adoption of Protestantism would mean the legal confiscation of church properties. Thus many political authorities in the empire used the religious issue to extend their power and to enhance their independence from the emperor. Luther worked closely with political authorities, viewing them as fully justified in reforming the church in their territories. Thus, just as in the Ottoman and Safavid Empires, rulers drew their legitimacy in part from their support for religion. By 1530 many parts of the Holy Roman Empire and Scandinavia had broken with the Catholic Church.

In England the issue of the royal succession triggered that country's break with Rome, and a Protestant Church was established during the 1530s under King Henry VIII (r. 1509–1547) and reaffirmed under his daughter Elizabeth I (r. 1558–1603). Church officials were required to sign an oath of loyalty to the monarch, and people were required to attend services at the state church, which became known as the Anglican Church.

Protestant ideas also spread into France, the Netherlands, Scotland, and eastern Europe. In all these areas, a second generation of reformers built on earlier ideas to develop their own theology and plans for institutional change. The most important of the second-generation reformers was the Frenchman John Calvin (1509–1564), who reformed the city of Geneva, Switzerland. Calvin believed that God was absolutely sovereign and omnipotent and that humans had no free will. Thus men and women could not actively work to achieve salvation, because God had decided at the beginning of time who would be saved and who damned, a theological principle called predestination.

The church in Geneva served as the model for the Presbyterian Church in Scotland, the Huguenot (HYOO-guh-naht) Church in France, and the Puritan Churches in England and New England. Calvinism became the compelling force in international Protestantism, first in Europe and then in many Dutch and English colonies around the world. Calvinism was also the dominant form of Protestantism in France (Map 18.1).

The Catholic Reformation

In response to the Protestant Reformation, by the 1530s the papacy was leading a movement for reform within the Roman Catholic Church. Many historians see the developments within the Catholic Church after the Protestant Reformation as two interrelated movements, one a drive for internal reform linked to earlier reform efforts and the other a Counter-Reformation that opposed Protestantism spiritually, politically, and militarily.

MAP 18.1 Religious Divisions, ca. 1555 In the mid-sixteenth century, much of Europe remained Catholic. The Peace of Augsburg (1555) allowed the ruler of each territory in the Holy Roman Empire to determine the religion of its people. The northern territories of the empire became Lutheran, as did Scandinavia, while much of the southern empire remained Catholic. Sizable Calvinist populations existed in Scotland, the Netherlands, and central Europe. Eastern Europe was dominated by Orthodox Christianity, and the Ottoman Empire to the south and southeast was Muslim.

Pope Paul III (pontificate 1534–1549) established the Supreme Sacred Congregation of the Roman and Universal Inquisition, often called the Holy Office, with judicial authority over all Catholics and the power to imprison and execute. He also called a general council of the church, which met intermittently from 1545 to 1563 at the city of Trent. The Council of Trent laid a solid basis for the spiritual renewal of the Catholic Church. It gave equal validity to the Scriptures and to tradition as sources of religious truth and tackled problems that had disillusioned many Christians. Bishops were required to live in their dioceses and to establish a seminary for educating and training clergy. Finally, it placed great emphasis on preaching to and instructing the laity. For four centuries the Council of Trent served as the basis for Roman Catholic faith, organization, and practice.

Jesuits in China This European image depicts early Jesuit missionaries baptizing converts in south China. (Archiv Gerstenberg—ullstein bild/Granger, NYC—All rights reserved.)

Just as seminaries provided education, so did new religious orders, which aimed to raise the moral and intellectual level of the clergy and people. The Ursuline (UHR-suh-luhn) order of nuns, founded by Angela Merici (1474–1540), attained enormous prestige for its education of women.

Another important new order was the Society of Jesus, or **Jesuits**. Founded by Ignatius Loyola (1491–1556) in 1540, this order played a powerful international role in strengthening Catholicism in Europe and spreading the faith around the world. Recruited primarily from wealthy merchant and professional families, the Society of Jesus developed into a highly centralized organization. It established well-run schools to educate the sons of the nobility as well as the poor. The Jesuits achieved phenomenal success for the papacy and the reformed Catholic Church, carrying Christianity to South and Central America, India, and Japan before 1550 and to Brazil, North America, and the Congo in the seventeenth century. Also, as confessors and spiritual directors to kings, Jesuits exerted great political influence.

Religious Violence

Religious differences led to riots, civil wars, and international conflicts in Europe during the sixteenth century. In the Holy Roman Empire fighting began in 1546. The empire was a confederation of hundreds of principalities, independent cities, duchies, and other polities loosely united under an elected emperor. The initial success of Emperor Charles V led to French intervention on the side of the Protestants, lest the emperor acquire even more power. In 1555 Charles agreed to the Peace of Augsburg, which officially recognized Lutheranism and ended religious war in Germany for many decades. Under this treaty, the political authority in each territory of the Holy Roman Empire was permitted to decide whether the territory would be Catholic or Lutheran. His hope of uniting his empire under a single church dashed, Charles V abdicated in 1556, transferring power over his Spanish and Dutch holdings to his son Philip II and his imperial power to his brother Ferdinand.

In France armed clashes between Catholic royalists and Calvinist antiroyalists occurred in many parts of the country. A savage Catholic attack on Calvinists in Paris on August 24, 1572—Saint Bartholomew's Day—occurred at the marriage of the king's sister Margaret of Valois to the Protestant Henry of Navarre. The Saint Bartholomew's Day massacre initiated a civil war that dragged on for fifteen years, destroying agriculture and commercial life in many areas.

In the Netherlands the movement for church reform developed into a struggle for Dutch independence. In the 1560s Spanish authorities attempted to suppress

Jesuits Members of the Society of Jesus, founded by Ignatius Loyola in 1540, whose goal was the spread of the Roman Catholic faith through schools and missionary activity.

Calvinist worship and raised taxes. Civil war broke out from 1568 to 1578 between Catholics and Protestants in the Netherlands and between the provinces of the Netherlands and Spain. Eventually the ten southern provinces came under the control of the Spanish Habsburg forces. The seven northern provinces, led by Holland, formed the Union of Utrecht (United Provinces of the Netherlands) and in 1581 declared their independence from Spain. The north was Protestant, and the south remained Catholic. Hostilities continued until 1609, when Spain agreed to a truce that recognized the independence of the northern provinces.

The era of religious wars was also the time of the most extensive witch persecutions in European history, with between 100,000 and 200,000 people officially tried for witchcraft in the sixteenth and seventeenth centuries. Both Protestants and Catholics persecuted accused witches, with church officials and secular authorities acting together. The heightened sense of God's power and divine wrath in the Reformation era was an important factor in the witch-hunts, as were new demonological ideas, legal procedures involving torture, and neighborhood tensions. Though the gender balance of the accused varied widely in different parts of Europe, between 75 and 85 percent of those tried and executed were women, whom some demonologists viewed as weaker and so more likely to give in to the Devil.

How did seventeenth-century European rulers overcome social and economic crisis to build strong states?

Seventeenth-Century Crisis and Rebuilding

Historians often refer to the seventeenth century as an "age of crisis" because Europe was challenged by population losses, economic decline, and social and political unrest. These difficulties were partially due to climate changes that reduced agricultural productivity. But they also resulted from military competition among European powers, the religious divides of the Reformations, increased taxation, and war. Peasants and the urban poor were especially hard hit by the economic problems, and they frequently rioted against high food prices.

The atmosphere of crisis encouraged governments to take emergency measures to restore order, measures that they successfully turned into long-term reforms that strengthened the power of the state. In the long run, European states proved increasingly able to impose their will on the populace.

The Social Order and Peasant Life

Peasants occupied the lower tiers of a society organized in hierarchical levels. In much of Europe, the monarch occupied the summit and was celebrated as a semidivine being chosen by God to embody the state. The clergy generally constituted the first order of society, due to its sacred role interceding with God on behalf of its flocks. Next came nobles, whose privileged status derived from their ancient bloodlines and leadership in battle. Many prosperous mercantile families had bought their way into the nobility through service to the monarchy in the fifteenth and sixteenth centuries, and they constituted a second tier of nobles. Those lower on the social scale, the peasants and artisans who formed the vast majority of the population, were expected to show deference to their betters. This was the "Great Chain of Being" that linked God to his creation in a series of ranked social groups.

In addition to being rigidly hierarchical, European societies were patriarchal. Religious and secular law commanded a man's wife, children, servants, and apprentices to respect and obey him. Fathers were entitled to use physical violence, imprisonment, and other forceful measures to impose their authority. These powers were balanced by expectations that a good father would care benevolently for his dependents.

In the seventeenth century the vast majority of Europeans lived in the countryside, as was the case in most parts of the world. In western Europe a small number of peasants owned enough land to feed themselves and possessed the livestock and plows necessary to work their land. Independent farmers were leaders of the peasant village. Below them were small landowners and tenant farmers who did not have enough land to be self-sufficient. At the bottom were villagers who worked as dependent laborers and servants. Private landowning among peasants was a distinguishing feature of western Europe. In central and eastern Europe the vast majority of peasants toiled as serfs for noble landowners, while in the Ottoman Empire all land belonged to the sultan.

Economic Crisis and Popular Revolts

In the seventeenth century a period of colder and more variable climate afflicted much of the globe. Dubbed the "little ice age" by historians, this period of cold weather accompanied by both too much rain and episodes of severe drought resulted in shorter growing seasons with lower yields. A bad harvest created food shortages; a series of bad harvests could lead to famine. Recurrent famines significantly diminished the population of Europe and Asia in this period, through reduced fertility, increased susceptibility to disease, and outright starvation.

Industry also suffered. In Europe the output of woolen textiles, the most important industrial sector, declined sharply. Food prices were high, wages stagnated, and unemployment soared. This economic crisis was not universal: it struck various regions at different times and to different degrees. In the middle decades of the century, for example, Spain, France, Germany, and the British Isles all experienced great economic difficulties, as did China, but these years were the golden age of the Netherlands (see "The Dutch Republic"). Japan also emerged relatively unscathed, as did South Asia and the Americas.

The urban poor and peasants were the hardest hit. When the price of bread rose beyond their capacity to pay, they frequently expressed their anger by rioting. Women often led these actions, since their role as mothers gave them some impunity in authorities'

The Young Beggar   The mid-seventeenth century was a harsh period for many Europeans, who faced meager harvests, unemployment, high taxation, and social unrest. (Louvre, Paris, France/Bridgeman Images)

moral economy The early modern European view that community needs predominated over competition and profit and that necessary goods should thus be sold at a fair price.

eyes. Historians have used the term **moral economy** for this vision of a world in which community needs predominate over competition and profit and in which necessary goods should thus be sold at a fair price.

During the middle years of the seventeenth century, harsh conditions transformed neighborhood bread riots into armed uprisings across much of Europe. Popular revolts were common in England, France, and throughout the Spanish Empire, particularly during the 1640s. At the same time that he struggled to put down an uprising in Catalonia, the economic center of the realm, Spanish king Philip IV faced revolt in Portugal, the northern provinces of the Netherlands, and Spanish-occupied Sicily. France suffered an uprising in the same period that won enthusiastic support from both nobles and peasants, while the English monarch was tried and executed by his subjects and Russia experienced an explosive rebellion. In China a series of popular revolts culminated in the fall of the Ming empire in 1644, demonstrating the global reach of the seventeenth-century crisis.

Municipal and royal authorities struggled to overcome popular revolt in the mid-seventeenth century. They feared that stern repressive measures, such as sending in troops to fire on crowds, would create martyrs and further inflame the situation, while full-scale occupation of a city would be very expensive and detract from military efforts elsewhere. The limitations of royal authority gave some leverage to rebels. To quell riots, royal edicts were sometimes suspended, prisoners released, and discussions initiated. By the beginning of the eighteenth century rulers had gained much greater control over their populations, as a result of the achievements in state-building discussed below (see "European Achievements in State-Building").

The Thirty Years' War

Thirty Years' War A large-scale conflict extending from 1618 to 1648 that pitted Protestants against Catholics in central Europe, but also involved dynastic interests, notably of Spain and France.

In addition to harsh economic conditions, popular unrest was greatly exacerbated by the impact of the decades-long conflict known as the **Thirty Years' War** (1618–1648), a war that drew in almost every European state. The background to the war was a shift in the balance between the population of Protestants and Catholics in the Holy Roman Empire that led to the deterioration of the Peace of Augsburg. Lutheran princes felt compelled to form the Protestant Union (1608), and Catholics retaliated with the Catholic League (1609). Dynastic interests were also involved; the Spanish Habsburgs strongly supported the goals of their Austrian relatives: the unity of the empire and the preservation of Catholicism within it.

The war began with a conflict in Bohemia (part of the present-day Czech Republic) between the Catholic League and the Protestant Union but soon spread through the Holy Roman Empire, drawing in combatants from across Europe. After a series of initial Catholic victories, the tide of the conflict turned due to the intervention of Sweden, under its king Gustavus Adolphus (r. 1594–1632), and then France, whose prime minister, Cardinal Richelieu (REESH-uh-lyuh), intervened on the side of the Protestants to undermine Habsburg power.

The 1648 Peace of Westphalia that ended the Thirty Years' War marked a turning point in European history. The treaties that established the peace not only ended conflicts fought over religious faith but also recognized the independent authority of more than three hundred German princes (Map 18.2), reconfirming the emperor's severely limited authority. The Augsburg agreement of 1555 became permanent, adding Calvinism to Catholicism and Lutheranism as legally permissible creeds. The

MAP 18.2 Europe After the Thirty Years' War Which country emerged from the Thirty Years' War as the strongest European power? What dynastic house was that country's major rival in the early modern period?

United Provinces of the Netherlands, known as the Dutch Republic, won official freedom from Spain.

The Thirty Years' War was probably the most destructive event in central Europe prior to the world wars of the twentieth century. Perhaps one-third of urban residents and two-fifths of the rural population died, and agriculture and industry withered. Across Europe, states increased taxes to meet the cost of war, further increasing the suffering of a traumatized population.

European Achievements in State-Building

In this context of warfare, economic crisis, popular revolt, and demographic decline, rulers took urgent measures to restore order and rebuild their states. In some states, absolutist models of government prevailed. In others, constitutionalist forces dominated. Despite their political differences, all these states sought to protect and expand their frontiers, raise taxes, consolidate central control, establish social welfare programs, and compete for colonies and trade in the New and Old Worlds. In so doing, they followed a broad pattern of state-building and consolidation of power found across Eurasia in this period.

Rulers who wished to increase their authority encountered formidable obstacles, including poor communications, entrenched local power structures, and ethnic and linguistic diversity. Nonetheless, over the course of the seventeenth century both absolutist and constitutional governments achieved new levels of power and national unity. They did so by transforming emergency measures of wartime into permanent structures of government and by subduing privileged groups through the combined use of force and economic and social incentives. Increased state authority may be seen in four areas in particular: a tremendous growth in the size and professionalism of armies; much higher taxes; larger and more efficient bureaucracies; and territorial expansion both within Europe and overseas. A fifth important area of European state growth—government sponsorship of scientific inquiry—will be discussed in Chapter 19.

Over time, centralized power added up to something close to **sovereignty**. A state may be termed sovereign when it possesses a monopoly over the instruments of justice and the use of force within clearly defined boundaries. In a sovereign state, no nongovernmental system of courts competes with state courts in the dispensation of justice. Also, private armies present no threat to central authority. While seventeenth-century states did not acquire full sovereignty, they made important strides toward that goal.

sovereignty Authority of states that possess a monopoly over the instruments of justice and the use of force within clearly defined boundaries and in which private armies present no threat to central control; seventeenth-century European states made important advances toward sovereignty.

Absolutist States in Western and Central Europe

What was absolutism, and how did it evolve in seventeenth-century Spain, France, and Austria?

Rulers in absolutist states asserted that, because they were chosen by God, they were responsible to God alone. Under the rule of **absolutism**, monarchs claimed exclusive power to make and enforce laws, denying any other institution or group the authority to check their power. This system was limited in practice by the need to maintain legitimacy and compromise with elites. Spain, France, and Austria provide three key examples of the development of the absolutist state.

absolutism A political system common to early modern Europe in which monarchs claimed exclusive power to make and enforce laws, without checks by other institutions; this system was limited in practice by the need to maintain legitimacy and compromise with elites.

Spain

The discovery of silver at Potosí in 1545 had produced momentous wealth for Spain, allowing it to dominate Europe militarily (see "Spanish Silver and Its Economic Effects" in Chapter 16). Yet Spain had inherent weaknesses that the wealth of empire had hidden. When Philip IV took the throne in 1621, he inherited a vast and overstretched empire, which combined different kingdoms with their own traditions and loyalties. Spanish silver had created great wealth but also dependency. While Creoles undertook new industries in the colonies and European nations targeted Spanish colonial trade, industry and finance in Spain itself remained undeveloped.

Spain's limitations became apparent during the first half of the seventeenth century. Between 1610 and 1650 Spanish trade with the colonies in the New World fell 60 percent due to competition from colonial industries and from Dutch and English

Diego Rodriguez de Silva y Velázquez, *Las Meninas*, 1656
The royal princess Margaret Theresa is shown here surrounded by her ladies-in-waiting. The painter Velázquez has portrayed himself working on a canvas, while her parents, the king and queen of Spain, are reflected in the mirror behind the princess. (Museo del Prado, Madrid, Spain/Bridgeman Images)

traders. To make matters worse, in 1609 the Crown expelled some three hundred thousand Moriscos, or former Muslims, significantly reducing the pool of skilled workers and merchants. At the same time, disease decimated the enslaved workers who toiled in South American silver mines. Moreover, the mines started to run dry, and the quantity of metal produced steadily declined after 1620 and Dutch privateers seized the entire silver fleet in 1628.

In Madrid the expenses of war and imperial rule constantly exceeded income. Despite the efforts of Philip's able chief minister, Gaspar de Guzmán, Count-Duke of Olivares, it proved impossible to force the kingdoms of the empire to shoulder the cost of its defense. To meet state debt, the Spanish crown repeatedly devalued the coinage and declared bankruptcy, which resulted in the collapse of national credit and steep inflation.

Spanish aristocrats, attempting to maintain an extravagant lifestyle they could no longer afford, increased the rents on their estates. High rents and heavy taxes drove the peasants from the land, leading to a decline in agricultural productivity. In cities wages and production stagnated. Spain also ignored new scientific methods that might have improved agricultural or manufacturing techniques because they came from the heretical nations of Holland and England.

Spain's situation worsened with internal rebellions and fresh military defeats during the Thirty Years' War and the remainder of the seventeenth century. The Treaty of Westphalia, which ended the Thirty Years' War, compelled Spain to recognize the independence of the Dutch Republic, and another treaty in 1659 granted extensive territories to France. Finally, in 1688 the Spanish crown reluctantly recognized the independence of Portugal. With these losses, the era of Spanish dominance in Europe ended.

The Foundations of French Absolutism

Although France was the largest and most populous state in western Europe, its position at the beginning of the seventeenth century appeared extremely weak. Struggling to recover from decades of religious civil war, France posed little threat to Spain's predominance in Europe. By the end of the century the countries' positions were reversed.

Henry IV (r. 1589–1610) inaugurated the Bourbon dynasty, defusing religious tensions and rebuilding France's economy. He issued the Edict of Nantes in 1598, allowing Huguenots (French Protestants) the right to worship in 150 traditionally Protestant towns throughout France. He invested in infrastructure and raised revenue by selling royal offices instead of charging high taxes. Despite his efforts at peace, Henry was murdered in 1610 by a Catholic zealot.

Cardinal Richelieu (1585–1642) became first minister of the French crown on behalf of Henry's young son Louis XIII (r. 1610–1643). Richelieu designed his domestic policies to strengthen royal control. He extended the use of intendants, commissioners for each of France's thirty-two districts who were appointed by and were responsible to the monarch. By using the intendants to gather information and ensure royal edicts were enforced, Richelieu reduced the power of provincial nobles. Richelieu also viewed France's Huguenots as potential rebels, and he laid seige to La Rochelle, a Protestant stronghold. Richelieu's main foreign policy goal was to destroy the Habsburgs' grip on territories that surrounded France. Consequently, Richelieu supported Habsburg enemies, including Protestants, during the Thirty Years' War (see "The Thirty Years' War").

Cardinal Jules Mazarin (1602–1661) succeeded Richelieu as chief minister for the next child-king, the four-year-old Louis XIV, who inherited the throne from his father in 1643. Mazarin's struggle to increase royal revenues to meet the costs of the Thirty Years' War led to the uprisings of 1648–1653 known as the Fronde. In Paris magistrates of the Parlement of Paris, the nation's most important law court, were outraged by the Crown's autocratic measures. These so-called robe nobles (named for the robes they wore in court) encouraged violent protest by the common people. As rebellion spread outside Paris and to the sword nobles (the traditional warrior nobility), civil order broke down completely, and young Louis XIV had to flee Paris.

Much of the rebellion faded, however, when Louis XIV was declared king in his own right in 1651, ending the regency of his mother, Anne of Austria. The French people were desperate for peace and stability after the disorders of the Fronde and were willing to accept a strong monarch who could restore order. Louis pledged to do just that, insisting that only his absolute authority stood between the French people and a renewed descent into chaos.

Louis XIV and Absolutism

divine right of kings
The belief propagated by absolutist monarchs in Europe that they derived their power from God and were answerable only to him.

During the long reign of Louis XIV (r. 1643–1715), known as the Sun King, the French monarchy overcame weakness and division to become the most powerful nation in western Europe. Louis based his authority on the **divine right of kings**: God had established kings as his rulers on earth, and they were answerable ultimately to him alone. However, Louis also recognized that kings could not simply do as they pleased. They had to obey God's laws and rule for the good of the people.

Like his counterpart, the Kangxi emperor of China, who inherited his realm only two decades after the Sun King did (see "Competent and Long-Lived Emperors" in Chapter 21), Louis XIV impressed his subjects with his discipline and hard work. (See "Global Viewpoints: Descriptions of Louis XIV of France and the Kangxi Emperor of China," page 532.) He ruled his realm through several councils of state and insisted on taking a personal role in many of the councils' decisions. Despite increasing financial problems, Louis never called a meeting of the Estates General, the traditional French representative assembly composed of the three estates of clergy, nobility, and commoners. The nobility, therefore, had no means of united expression or action. To further restrict their political power, he excluded them from his councils and chose instead capable men of modest origins.

Although personally tolerant, Louis hated division. He insisted that religious unity was essential to the security of the state. In 1685 Louis revoked the Edict of Nantes. Around two hundred thousand Protestants, including some of the kingdom's most highly skilled artisans, fled France. Louis's insistence on "one king, one law, one religion" contrasts sharply with the religious tolerance exhibited by Muslim empires in the Middle East and South Asia (see "Non-Muslims Under Muslim Rule" in Chapter 17).

Despite his claims to absolute authority, there were multiple constraints on Louis's power. As a representative of divine power, he was obliged to rule in a way that seemed consistent with virtue and paternal benevolence. He had to uphold the laws issued by his royal predecessors. Moreover, he also relied on the collaboration of nobles. Without their cooperation, it would have been impossible for Louis to extend his power throughout France or wage his many foreign wars.

The Wars of Louis XIV

Louis XIV kept France at war for thirty-three of the fifty-four years of his personal rule. Under the leadership of François le Tellier, marquis de Louvois, Louis's secretary of state for war, France acquired a huge professional army. The French army almost tripled in size. Uniforms and weapons were standardized, and a system of training and promotion was devised. As in so many other matters, Louis's model was emulated across Europe, resulting in a continent-wide transformation in military capability that scholars have referred to as a "military revolution."

During this long period of warfare, Louis's goal was to expand France to what he considered its natural borders and to win glory for the Bourbon dynasty. His results were mixed. During the 1660s and 1670s, French armies won a number of important victories. The wars of the 1680s and 1690s, however, brought no additional territories and placed unbearable strains on French resources.

Louis's last war, the War of the Spanish Succession (1701–1713), was endured by a French people suffering high taxes, crop failure, and widespread malnutrition and death. This war was the result of Louis's unwillingness to abide by a previous agreement to divide Spanish possessions between France and the Holy Roman emperor upon the death of the childless Spanish king Charles II (r. 1665–1700). In 1701 the English, Dutch, Austrians, and Prussians formed the Grand Alliance against Louis XIV. War dragged on until 1713, when it was ended by the Peace of Utrecht (Map 18.3).

Descriptions of Louis XIV of France and the Kangxi Emperor of China

King Louis XIV of France (1638–1715) and the Kangxi emperor of Qing China (1654–1722) lived remarkably parallel lives. They both inherited realms in childhood and learned to rule from powerful women, in Louis's case his mother, Queen Anne of Austria, and in Kangxi's case his grandmother, Grand Empress Dowager Xiaozhuang. Both rulers built magnificent palaces and demonstrated hard work, discipline, and a thirst for glory and power. Louis sent Jesuits to the Chinese court to spread European scientific knowledge and Catholicism. The emperor originally welcomed them and was fascinated by their learning and technology, but he eventually banned them and Christianity from his realm. The following descriptions of Louis XIV and the Kangxi emperor, written by a French courtier and a Jesuit missionary, respectively, underline the similar qualities observers noted in the two rulers.

The Duke of Saint-Simon, *Memoirs of Louis XIV, His Court, and the Regency, 1739–1749.*

■ [He was] the very figure of a hero, so impregnated with a natural but most imposing majesty that it appeared even in his most insignificant gestures and movements, without arrogance but with simple gravity. . . . He was as dignified and majestic in his dressing gown as when dressed in robes of state, or on horseback at the head of his troops.

He excelled in all sorts of exercise and liked to have every facility for it. No fatigue nor stress of weather made any impression on that heroic figure and bearing; drenched with rain or snow, pierced with cold, bathed in sweat or covered with dust, he was always the same. . . .

[He had] the ability to speak well and to listen with quick comprehension; much reserve of manner adjusted with exactness to the quality of different persons; a courtesy always grave, always dignified, always distinguished, and suited to the age, rank, and sex of each individual, and, for the ladies, always an air of natural gallantry. . . .

Nothing could be regulated with greater exactitude than were his days and hours. In spite of all his variety

---

The Peace of Utrecht marked the end of French expansion. Thirty-three years of war had given France the rights to all of Alsace and some commercial centers in the north. But at what price? At the time of Louis's death in 1715, an exhausted France hovered on the brink of bankruptcy.

The Economic Policy of Mercantilism

France's ability to build armies and fight wars depended on a strong economy. Fortunately for Louis, Jean-Baptiste Colbert (1619–1683) brilliantly occupied the position of controller general of finance from 1665 to 1683. Colbert's central principle was that the wealth and the economy of France should serve the state. To this end, Colbert rigorously applied mercantilist policies to France.

Mercantilism is a collection of governmental policies for the regulation of economic activities by and for the state, with the aim of increasing state power. It derives from the idea that a nation's international power is based on its wealth, specifically its supply of gold and silver. To accumulate wealth, a country always had to sell more goods abroad than it bought from foreign countries.

To increase exports, Colbert supported old industries and created new ones. He enacted new production regulations, created guilds to boost quality standards, and

mercantilism A system of economic regulations aimed at increasing the power of the state derived from the belief that a nation's international power was based on its wealth, specifically its supply of gold and silver.

of places, affairs, and amusements, with an almanac and a watch one might tell, three hundred leagues away, exactly what he was doing. . . . If he administered reproof, it was rarely, in few words, and never hastily. He did not lose control of himself ten times in his whole life, and then only with inferior persons, and not more than four or five times seriously.

Father Joachim Bouvet, *The History of Cang-Hy, the Present Emperour of China, 1699*

■ His whole Deportment is very Majestick, being well proportion'd in his Limbs, and pretty Tall, the Feature of his Face very exact, with a large and brisk Eye, beyond what is observable among others of that Nation; He is a little crooked Nosed, and pitted with the Small-pox, but not so as to be in the least disfigur'd by them.

But the rare Accomplishments of his Mind, surpass infinitely those of his Body. His Natural Genius is such as can be parallel'd but by few, being endow'd with a Quick and piercing Wit, a vast Memory, and Great Understanding; His Constancy is never to be shaken by any sinister Event, which makes him the fittest Person in the World, not only to undertake, but also to accomplish Great Designs.

To be short, his inclinations are so Noble, and in all respects so Answerable to the High Station of so Great a Prince, that his People stand in Admiration of his Person, being equally Charm'd with his Love and Justice, and the Tenderness he shews for his Subjects, and with his virtuous Inclinations; which as they are always guided by the Dictates of Reason, so, they render him an Absolute Master of his Passions.

QUESTIONS FOR ANALYSIS

1. What qualities did the Duke of Saint-Simon and Father Bouvet admire in Louis XIV and the Kangxi emperor? What similarities do you find among the qualities they describe?
2. Based on what you have read in this chapter, why was it important for an absolute ruler to possess the qualities the authors describe? What weaknesses do these excerpts suggest a would-be ruler should avoid, and why?

Sources: J. H. Robinson, ed., *Readings in European History*, vol. 2 (Boston: Ginn, 1906), pp. 285–286; Father Joachim Bouvet, *The History of Cang-Hy, the Present Emperour of China* (London: F. Coggan, 1699), p. 2.

encouraged foreign craftsmen to immigrate to France. To encourage the purchase of French goods, he abolished many domestic tariffs and raised tariffs on foreign products. In 1664 Colbert founded the Company of the East Indies with hopes of competing with the Dutch for Asian trade. Colbert also sought to increase France's control over and presence in New France (Canada) (see "Colonial Empires of England and France").

During Colbert's tenure as controller general, Louis was able to pursue his goals without massive tax increases and without creating a stream of new offices. The constant pressure of warfare after Colbert's death, however, undid many of his economic achievements.

The Austrian Habsburgs

Absolutism was also the dominant form of monarchical rule among the more than one thousand states that composed the Holy Roman Empire. Prussia, a minor power with scattered holdings, emerged in the seventeenth and eighteenth centuries under the Hohenzollern dynasty as a major rival to the Austrian Habsburg dynasty (see "Enlightened Absolutism and Its Limits" in Chapter 19). Like all of central Europe, the Austrian Habsburgs emerged from the Thirty Years' War impoverished and

MAPPING THE PAST

MAP 18.3 Europe After the Peace of Utrecht, 1715 The series of treaties commonly called the Peace of Utrecht ended the War of the Spanish Succession and redrew the map of Europe. A French Bourbon king succeeded to the Spanish throne. France surrendered the Spanish Netherlands (later Belgium), then in French hands, to Austria and recognized the Hohenzollern rulers of Prussia. Spain ceded Gibraltar to Great Britain, for which it has been a strategic naval station ever since. Spain also granted Britain the *asiento*, the contract for supplying African slaves to America.

ANALYZING THE MAP Identify the areas on the map that changed hands as a result of the Peace of Utrecht. How did these changes affect the balance of power in Europe?

CONNECTIONS How and why did so many European countries possess scattered or discontiguous territories? What does this suggest about European politics in this period? Does this map suggest potential for future conflict?

exhausted. Their efforts to destroy Protestantism in the German lands and to turn the weak Holy Roman Empire into a real state had failed. Defeat in central Europe encouraged the Austrian Habsburgs to turn away from a quest for imperial dominance and to focus inward and eastward in an attempt to unify their diverse holdings.

Habsburg victory over Bohemia during the Thirty Years' War was an important step in this direction. Ferdinand II (r. 1619–1637) drastically reduced the power of the Bohemian Estates, the largely Protestant representative assembly. He also confiscated the landholdings of Protestant nobles and gave them to his supporters. After 1650 a large portion of the Bohemian nobility was of recent origin and owed its success to the Habsburgs.

With the support of this new nobility, the Habsburgs established direct rule over Bohemia. Under their rule, the condition of the serfs worsened substantially. The Habsburgs also successfully eliminated Protestantism in Bohemia. These changes were important steps in creating absolutist rule.

Ferdinand III (r. 1637–1657) continued to build state power. He centralized the government in the empire's German-speaking provinces, which formed the core Habsburg holdings, and established a permanent standing army. The Habsburg monarchy then turned east toward Hungary, which had been divided between the Ottomans and the Habsburgs in the early sixteenth century. Between 1683 and 1699 the Habsburgs pushed the Ottomans from most of Hungary and Transylvania. The recovery of all of the former kingdom of Hungary was completed in 1718.

Despite its reduced strength, the Hungarian nobility effectively thwarted the full development of Habsburg absolutism. Throughout the seventeenth century Hungarian nobles periodically rose in revolt against the Habsburgs. In 1703, with the Habsburgs bogged down in the War of the Spanish Succession, the Hungarians rose in one last patriotic rebellion under Prince Francis Rákóczy (RAH-coht-see). Rákóczy and his forces were eventually defeated, but the Habsburgs agreed to restore many of the traditional privileges of the Hungarian aristocracy in return for the country's acceptance of Habsburg rule.

Elsewhere, the Habsburgs made significant achievements in state-building by forging consensus with the church and the nobility. A sense of common identity and loyalty to the monarchy grew among elites in Habsburg lands. German became the language of the state, and Vienna became the political and cultural center of the empire.

■ Austrian Habsburg territory in 1648
■ Lands taken from Ottomans by Austrian Habsburgs, to 1699

Austrian Expansion, to 1699

The Absolutist Palace

In 1682 Louis moved his court and government to the newly renovated palace at Versailles (vayr-SIGH), in the countryside southwest of Paris. The themes of the interior paintings and the sculptures in the gardens hailed Louis's power, with images of the Roman gods Apollo (the sun god) and Neptune (the sea god) making frequent appearances. The gardens' rational orderliness and symmetry showed that Louis's force extended even to nature, while their terraces and waterworks served as showcases for the latest techniques in military and civil engineering.

The palace quickly became the center of political, social, and cultural life, and all high-ranking nobles were required to spend at least part of the year in residence.

Louis established an elaborate set of etiquette rituals for courtiers that encompassed every moment of his day, from waking up and dressing in the morning to removing his clothing and retiring at night. These rituals were far from meaningless or trivial. The king controlled immense resources and privileges; access to him meant favored treatment for government offices, military and religious posts, state pensions, honorary titles, and a host of other benefits.

A system of patronage—in which a higher-ranked individual protected a lower-ranked one in return for loyalty and services—flowed from the court to the provinces. Through this mechanism Louis gained cooperation from powerful nobles. Although they were denied public offices and posts, women played a central role in the patronage system. At court the king's wife, mistresses, and other female relatives recommended individuals for honors, advocated policy decisions, and brokered alliances between noble factions.

With Versailles as the center of European politics, French culture grew in international prestige. French became the language of polite society and international diplomacy, and France inspired a cosmopolitan European culture in the late seventeenth century that looked to Versailles as its center. Moreover, Louis's rival European monarchs soon followed his example, and palace building became a Europe-wide phenomenon.

Constitutionalism and Empire in England and the Dutch Republic

Why and how did the constitutional state triumph in England and the Dutch Republic?

While most European nations emerged from the crises of the seventeenth century with absolutist forms of government, England and the Netherlands evolved toward **constitutionalism**, which is the limitation of government by law. Constitutionalism also implies a balance between the authority and power of the government, on the one hand, and the rights and liberties of the subjects, on the other.

After decades of civil war, the English briefly adopted **republicanism**, a form of government in which there is no monarch and power rests in the hands of the people as exercised through elected representatives. Finally, in 1688 the English settled on a lasting political solution, constitutional monarchy. Under this system of government, England retained a monarch as the titular head of government but vested sovereignty in an elected parliament. For their part, the Dutch rejected monarchical rule in 1648, when their independence from Spain was formally recognized. Instead they adopted a republican form of government in which elected Estates (assemblies) held supreme power. Neither the English nor the Dutch were democratic by any standard, but to other Europeans, they were shining examples of the restraint of arbitrary power and the rule of law.

Religious Divides and Civil War

In 1603 beloved Queen Elizabeth was succeeded by her Scottish cousin James Stuart, who ruled England as James I (r. 1603–1625). Like Louis XIV, James believed that a monarch had a divine right to his authority and was responsible only to God. James I and his son Charles I (r. 1625–1649) considered any legislative constraint on their power a threat to their divine-right prerogative. Consequently, at every meeting of

constitutionalism A form of government in which power is limited by law and balanced between the authority and power of the government, on the one hand, and the rights and liberties of the subject or citizen, on the other; it includes constitutional monarchies and republics.

republicanism A form of government in which there is no monarch and power rests in the hands of the people as exercised through elected representatives.

Puritan Occupations These twelve engravings depict typical Puritan occupations and show that the Puritans came primarily from the artisan and lower middle classes. The governing classes and peasants made up a much smaller percentage of Puritans, and most generally adhered to the traditions of the Church of England. (Visual Connection Archive)

Parliament between 1603 and 1640, bitter squabbles erupted between the Crown and the House of Commons.

Religious issues also embittered relations between the king and the House of Commons. In the early seventeenth century many English people felt dissatisfied with the Church of England. Calvinist **Puritans** wanted to take the Reformation further by "purifying" the Anglican Church of Roman Catholic elements, including crown-appointed bishops, elaborate ceremonials, and wedding rings. James I responded to such ideas by declaring, "No bishop, no king." His son and successor, Charles I, further antagonized subjects by marrying a French Catholic princess and supporting the high-handed policies of archbishop of Canterbury William Laud (1573–1645). Political and religious conflict in this period was exacerbated by economic distress caused by severe weather conditions and periodic bouts of plague.

Charles avoided direct confrontation with his subjects by refusing to call Parliament into session from 1629 to 1640, instead financing the realm through extraordinary stopgap levies considered illegal by most English people. However, when Scottish Calvinists revolted against his religious policies, Charles was forced to summon Parliament to obtain funding for an army to put down the revolt. Angry with the king's behavior and sympathetic with the Scots' religious beliefs, the House of Commons passed the Triennial Act in 1641, which compelled the king to call Parliament every three years. The Commons also impeached Archbishop Laud and then threatened to abolish bishops. King Charles, fearful of a Scottish invasion, reluctantly accepted these measures. The next act in the conflict was precipitated by the outbreak of rebellion in Ireland. In 1641 the Catholic gentry of Ireland led an uprising in response to a feared invasion by British anti-Catholic forces.

Without an army, Charles I could neither come to terms with the Scots nor respond to the Irish rebellion. After a failed attempt to arrest parliamentary leaders, Charles left London and began to raise an army. In response, Parliament formed its own army, the New Model Army.

The English civil war (1642–1649) pitted the power of the king against that of Parliament. After three years of fighting, Parliament's army defeated the king's forces at the Battles of Naseby and Langport in the summer of 1645. Charles refused to concede defeat, and both sides waited for a decisive event. This arrived in the form of the army under the leadership of Oliver Cromwell, a member of the House of

Puritans Members of a sixteenth- and seventeenth-century reform movement within the Church of England that advocated purifying it of Roman Catholic elements, such as bishops, elaborate ceremonials, and wedding rings.

The English Civil War, 1642–1649

Commons and a devout Puritan. In 1647 Cromwell's troops captured the king and dismissed members of the Parliament who opposed Cromwell's actions. In 1649 the remaining representatives, known as the Rump Parliament, put Charles on trial for high treason. Charles was found guilty and beheaded on January 30, 1649.

The Puritan Protectorate

With the execution of Charles, the monarchy was abolished and a commonwealth, or republican government, was proclaimed. Theoretically, legislative power rested in the surviving members of Parliament, and executive power was lodged in a council of state. In fact, the army that had defeated the king controlled the government, and Oliver Cromwell controlled the army. Though called the Protectorate, the rule of Cromwell (1653–1658) was a form of military dictatorship. Reflecting Puritan ideas of morality, Cromwell's state forbade sports, kept the theaters closed, and rigorously censored the press.

On the issue of religion, Cromwell favored some degree of tolerance, and all Christians except Roman Catholics had the right to practice their faiths. Cromwell had long associated Catholicism in Ireland with sedition and heresy, and he led an army there to reconquer the country in August 1649. Following Cromwell's reconquest, the English banned Catholicism in Ireland, executed priests, and confiscated land from Catholics for English and Scottish settlers.

The Protectorate collapsed when Cromwell died in 1658 and his ineffectual son succeeded him. Fed up with military rule, the English longed for a return to civilian government. By 1660 they were ready to restore the monarchy.

Constitutional Monarchy

The Restoration of 1660 brought to the throne Charles II (r. 1660–1685), the eldest son of Charles I. Both houses of Parliament were also restored, as was the Anglican Church. However, Charles was succeeded by his Catholic brother James II, arousing fears of a return of Catholicism. A group of eminent persons in Parliament and the Church of England wrote to James's Protestant daughter Mary and her Dutch husband, Prince William of Orange, inviting them to invade and take the throne of England. In November 1688 William arrived on the English coast with five hundred ships and over twenty thousand soldiers, causing James II, his queen, and their infant son to flee for France. Early in 1689 William and Mary were jointly crowned as king and queen of England.

The English called the events of 1688 and 1689 the Glorious Revolution because they believed it replaced one king with another with barely any bloodshed. In truth, William's arrival sparked riots and violence across the British Isles and in North American cities such as Boston and New York. Uprisings by supporters of James, known as Jacobites, occurred in 1689 in Scotland. In Ireland the two sides waged outright war from 1689 to 1691. William's victory at the Battle of the Boyne (1690) and the subsequent Treaty of Limerick (1691) sealed his accession to power.

In England the revolution represented the final destruction of the idea of divine-right monarchy. The men who brought about the revolution framed their opposition to Stuart-style absolutism in the **Bill of Rights of 1689**, which was passed by Parliament and formally accepted by William and Mary. Law was to be made in

Bill of Rights of 1689
A bill passed by Parliament and accepted by William and Mary that limited the powers of British monarchs and affirmed those of Parliament.

Parliament; once made, it could not be suspended by the Crown. Parliament had to be called at least once every three years. The Bill of Rights also established the independence of the judiciary and mandated that there be no standing army in peacetime. Protestants could possess arms, but the Catholic minority could not. Catholics could not inherit the throne. Additional legislation granted freedom of worship to Protestant dissenters but not to Catholics.

The Glorious Revolution and the concept of representative government found its best defense in political philosopher John Locke's *Second Treatise of Civil Government* (1690). Locke (1632–1704) maintained that a government that oversteps its proper function—protecting the natural rights of life, liberty, and property—becomes a tyranny. Under a tyrannical government, he argued, the people have the natural right to rebellion.

Although the events of 1688 and 1689 brought England closer to Locke's ideal, they did not constitute a democratic revolution. The Glorious Revolution placed sovereignty in Parliament, and Parliament represented the upper classes.

The Dutch Republic

In the late sixteenth century the seven northern provinces of the Netherlands fought for and won their independence from Spain. The independence of the Republic of the United Provinces of the Netherlands was recognized in 1648 in the treaty that ended the Thirty Years' War. In this period, often called the "golden age of the Netherlands," Dutch ideas and attitudes played a profound role in shaping a new and modern worldview. At the same time, the United Provinces developed its own distinctive model of a constitutional state.

Rejecting the rule of a monarch, the Dutch established a republic, a state in which power rested in the hands of the people and was exercised through elected representatives. Other examples of republics in early modern Europe included the Swiss Confederation and several autonomous city-states of Italy and the Holy Roman Empire. Among the Dutch, an oligarchy of wealthy businessmen called regents handled domestic affairs in each province's Estates, or assemblies. The provincial Estates held virtually all the power. A federal assembly, or States General, handled foreign affairs and war, but all issues had to be referred back to the local Estates for approval, and each of the seven provinces could veto any proposed legislation. Holland, the province with the largest navy and the most wealth, usually dominated the republic and the States General.

In each province, the Estates appointed an executive officer, known as the stadholder. Although in theory the stadholder was freely chosen by the Estates, in practice the reigning prince of Orange usually held the office of stadholder in several of the seven provinces of the republic. Tensions persisted between supporters of the House of Orange and those of the staunchly republican Estates, who suspected the princes of harboring monarchical ambitions.

Global trade and commerce brought the Dutch the highest standard of living in Europe, perhaps in the world. Salaries were high, and all classes of society ate well. Consequently, the Netherlands experienced very few of the riots and popular revolts that characterized the rest of Europe.[2] The moral and ethical bases of Dutch commercial wealth were thrift, frugality, and religious tolerance. Jews enjoyed a level of acceptance and assimilation in Dutch business and general culture unique in early modern Europe. (See "Individuals in Society: Glückel of Hameln," at right.) In the Dutch Republic tolerance not only seemed the right way but also contributed to profits by attracting a great deal of foreign capital and investment.

How did European nations compete for global trade and empire in the Americas and Asia?

Colonial Expansion and Empire

For much of the sixteenth century the Spanish and Portuguese dominated European overseas trade and colonization (see "Conquest and Settlement" in Chapter 16). In the early seventeenth century, however, England, France, and the Netherlands challenged Spain's monopoly. They eventually succeeded in creating overseas empires, consisting of settler colonies in North America, slave plantations in the Caribbean, and scattered trading posts in West Africa and Asia. Competition among them was encouraged by mercantilist economic doctrine, which dictated that foreign trade was a zero-sum game in which one country's gains necessarily entailed another's loss.

The Dutch Trading Empire

The so-called golden age of the Dutch Republic in the seventeenth century was built on its commercial prosperity and its highly original republican system of government. The Dutch came to dominate the European shipping business by putting profits from their original industry — herring fishing — into shipbuilding. They then took aim at Portugal's immensely lucrative Asian trade empire.

In 1599 a Dutch fleet returned to Amsterdam from a voyage to South East Asia carrying a huge cargo of spices. Those who had invested in the expedition received a 100 percent profit. The voyage led to the establishment in 1602 of the Dutch East India Company, founded with the stated intention of capturing the spice trade from the Portuguese.

In return for assisting Indonesian princes in local conflicts and disputes with the Portuguese, the Dutch won broad commercial concessions. Through agreements, seizures, and outright military aggression, they gained control of the western access to the Indonesian archipelago in the first half of the seventeenth century. Gradually, they acquired political domination over the archipelago itself. The Dutch were willing to use force more ruthlessly than the Portuguese were and had superior organizational efficiency. These factors allowed them to expel the Portuguese from Ceylon and other East Indian islands in the 1660s and henceforth dominate the production and trade of spices. The company also established the colony of Cape Town on the southern tip of Africa as a provisioning point for its Asian fleets.

The Dutch also aspired to a role in the Americas (Map 18.4). Founded in 1621, the Dutch West India Company aggressively sought to open trade with North and South America and capture Spanish territories there. The company captured or destroyed hundreds of Spanish ships, seized the Spanish silver fleet in 1628, and claimed portions of Brazil and the Caribbean. The Dutch also successfully interceded in the transatlantic slave trade, establishing a large number of trading stations on the west coast of Africa. Ironically, the nation that was known as a bastion of tolerance and freedom came to be one of the principal operators of the slave trade starting in the 1640s.

Glückel of Hameln

IN 1690 A JEWISH WIDOW IN THE SMALL GERMAN town of Hameln in Lower Saxony sat down to write her autobiography. She wanted to distract her mind from the terrible grief she felt over the death of her husband and to provide her twelve children with a record. She told them that she was writing her memoirs "so you will know from what sort of people you have sprung, lest today or tomorrow your beloved children or grandchildren came and know naught of their family." Out of her pain and heightened consciousness, Glückel (1646–1724) produced an invaluable source for scholars.

She was born in Hamburg two years before the end of the Thirty Years' War. In 1649 the merchants of Hamburg expelled the Jews, who moved to nearby Altona, then under Danish rule. When the Swedes overran Altona in 1657–1658, the Jews returned to Hamburg "purely at the mercy of the Town Council." Glückel's narrative unfolds against a background of the constant harassment to which Jews were subjected— special papers, permits, bribes—and in Hameln she wrote, "And so it has been to this day and, I fear, will continue in like fashion."

When Glückel was "barely twelve," her father betrothed her to Chayim Hameln, and they married when she was fourteen. She describes him as "the perfect pattern of the pious Jew," a man who stopped his work every day for study and prayer, fasted, and was scrupulously honest in his business dealings. Only a few years older than Glückel, Chayim earned his living dealing in precious metals and in making small loans on pledges (pawned goods). This work required constant travel to larger cities, markets, and fairs, often in bad weather, always over dangerous roads. Chayim consulted his wife about all his business dealings. As he lay dying, a friend asked if he had any last wishes. "None," he replied. "My wife knows everything. She shall do as she has always done." For thirty years Glückel had been his friend, full business partner, and wife. They had thirteen children, twelve of whom survived their father, eight then unmarried. As Chayim had foretold, Glückel succeeded in launching the boys in careers and in providing dowries for the girls.

Glückel's world was her family, the Jewish community of Hameln, and the Jewish communities into which her children married. Her social and business activities took her across Europe, from Amsterdam to Berlin, from Danzig to Vienna; thus her world was far from narrow or provincial. She took great pride that Prince Frederick of Cleves, later king of Prussia, danced at the wedding of her eldest daughter. The rising prosperity of Chayim's businesses allowed the couple to maintain up to six servants.

Glückel was deeply religious, and her culture was steeped in Jewish literature, legends, and mystical and secular works. Above all, she relied on the Bible. Her language, heavily sprinkled with scriptural references, testifies to a rare familiarity with the Scriptures.

Students who wish to learn about seventeenth-century business practices, the importance of the dowry in marriage, childbirth, Jewish life, birthrates, family celebrations, and even the meaning of life can gain a good deal from the memoirs of this extraordinary woman who was, in the words of one of her descendants, the poet Heinrich Heine, "the gift of a world to me."

Rembrandt, *The Jewish Bride.* (Rijksmuseum, Amsterdam, The Netherlands/Bridgeman Images)

QUESTIONS FOR ANALYSIS

1. Consider the ways in which Glückel of Hameln was both an ordinary and an extraordinary woman of her times. Would you call her a marginal or a central person in her society? Why?
2. How might Glückel's successes be attributed to the stabilizing force of absolutism in the seventeenth century?

Source: *The Memoirs of Glückel of Hameln* (New York: Schocken Books, 1977).

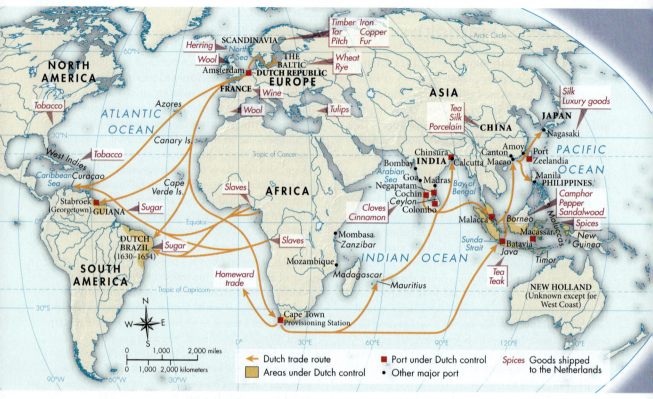

MAP 18.4 **Seventeenth-Century Dutch Commerce** Dutch wealth rested on commerce, and commerce depended on the huge Dutch merchant marine, manned by perhaps forty-eight thousand sailors. The fleet carried goods from all parts of the globe to the port of Amsterdam.

Colonial Empires of England and France

England and France followed the Dutch in challenging Iberian dominance overseas. Unlike the Iberian powers, whose royal governments financed exploration and directly ruled the colonies, England, France, and the Netherlands conducted the initial phase of colonization through chartered companies with monopolies over settlement and trade in a given area.

Just as the Spanish explorers had learned from the Reconquista, English expansion drew on long experience at home conquering and colonizing Ireland. After an unsuccessful first colony at Roanoke (in what is now North Carolina), the English colony of Virginia, founded at Jamestown in 1607, gained a steady hold by producing tobacco for a growing European market. Indentured servants obtained free passage to the colony in exchange for several years of work and the promise of greater opportunity than could be found in England. In the 1670s English colonists from the Caribbean island of Barbados settled Carolina, where conditions were suitable for large rice plantations. During the late seventeenth century enslaved Africans replaced indentured servants as laborers on tobacco and rice plantations, and a harsh racial divide was imposed.

For the first settlers on the coast of New England, the reasons for seeking a new life in the colonies were more religious than economic. Many of these colonists were radical Protestants escaping Anglican repression. The small and struggling Puritan outpost of Plymouth Colony (1620) was followed by Massachusetts Bay Colony (1630), which grew into a prosperous settlement. Religious disputes in Massachusetts led to the dispersion of settlers into the new communities of Providence, Connecticut, Rhode Island, and New Haven. Because New England lacked the conditions for plantation agriculture, slavery was always a minor factor there.

Whereas the Spanish established wholesale dominance over Mexico and Peru and its indigenous inhabitants, English settlements hugged the Atlantic coastline and expelled indigenous people from their lands, leading to attacks by displaced groups and wars of reprisal and extermination. In place of the unified rule exerted by the Spanish crown, English colonization was haphazard and decentralized in nature, leading to greater colonial autonomy and diversity. As the English crown grew more interested in colonial expansion, efforts were made to acquire the territory between New England in the north and Virginia in the south. The goal was to unify English holdings and minimize French and Dutch competition on the Atlantic seaboard. The results of these efforts were the mid-Atlantic colonies: the Catholic settlement of Maryland (1632); New York, captured from the Dutch in 1664; and the Quaker colony of Pennsylvania (1681).

The French represented yet another model of settlement and interaction, somewhat akin to the Portuguese in Asia and Africa. While the Spanish incorporated the large populations of pre-existing empires and the English expelled indigenous groups to provide agricultural land for their numerous colonists, the French focused on establishing trade and diplomatic relations with tribes that remained largely autonomous. In 1605 the French founded the settlement of Port-Royal on the Bay of Fundy in Acadia, as a base for fishing and the fur trade. In the following years, under the leadership of Samuel de Champlain the French moved west into the St. Lawrence River Valley, establishing the forts of Quebec (1608), Three Rivers (1634), and Montreal (1642). The French formed trade and military alliances with several tribes, including the Montagnais, Hurons, and Algonquins, which allowed them to acquire valuable furs throughout the Great Lakes region. Contact with French traders, settlers, and missionaries resulted in devastating epidemics for their indigenous allies as well as increased political instability and violent conflict.

In the 1660s Louis XIV's capable controller general, Jean-Baptiste Colbert, established direct royal control over New France (Canada) and tried to enlarge its population by sending colonists. Nevertheless, immigration to New Canada remained minuscule compared with the stream of settlers who came to British North America. The Jesuits, who were the most active missionary orders in New France, established a college in Quebec as early as 1635.

Following the waterways of the St. Lawrence River, the Great Lakes, and the Mississippi River, the French ventured into much of North America in the 1670s and 1680s. In 1673 the Jesuit Jacques Marquette and the merchant Louis Joliet sailed down the Mississippi as far as present-day Arkansas. In 1682 Robert de La Salle traveled the Mississippi to the Gulf of Mexico, opening the way for French occupation of Louisiana.

In the first decades of the seventeenth century, English and French captains also challenged Spain's hold over the Caribbean, seizing a number of islands. These islands

European Claims in North America, 1714

Navigation Acts Mid-seventeenth-century English mercantilist laws that greatly restricted other countries' rights to trade with England and its colonies.

acquired new importance after 1640, when the Portuguese brought sugar plantations to Brazil. Sugar and slaves quickly followed in the West Indies (see "Sugar and Early Transatlantic Slavery" in Chapter 16), making the Caribbean plantations the most lucrative of all colonial possessions.

The northern European powers also expanded in Africa and Asia. During the seventeenth century, France and England—along with Denmark and other northern European powers—established fortified trading posts, or factory-forts, in West Africa as bases for purchasing slaves and in India and the Indian Ocean for spices and other luxury goods. Thus, by the end of the seventeenth century, a handful of European powers possessed overseas empires that truly spanned the globe.

Mercantilism and Colonial Wars

Trade to and among European overseas possessions was governed by mercantilist economic policy (see "The Economic Policy of Mercantilism"). The acquisition of colonies was intended to increase the wealth and power of the mother country, and to that end, European states—starting with Spain in the sixteenth century—imposed trading monopolies on their overseas colonies and factories. The mercantilist notion of a "zero-sum game," in which any country's gain must come from another country's loss, led to hostile competition and outright warfare among European powers over their colonial possessions.

In England Oliver Cromwell established the first of a series of **Navigation Acts** in 1651, and the restored monarchy of Charles II extended them in 1660 and 1663. The acts required most goods imported into England and Scotland (Great Britain after 1707) to be carried on British-owned ships with British crews or on ships of the country producing the article. Moreover, these laws gave British merchants and shipowners a virtual monopoly on trade with British colonies. These economic regulations were intended to eliminate foreign competition and to encourage the development of a British shipping industry whose seamen could serve when necessary in the Royal Navy.

The Navigation Acts were a form of economic warfare against the Dutch, who were far ahead of the English in shipping and foreign trade in the mid-seventeenth century. In conjunction with three Anglo-Dutch wars between 1652 and 1674, the Navigation Acts seriously damaged Dutch shipping and commerce. By the late seventeenth century the Netherlands was falling behind England in shipping, trade, and settlement.

Thereafter France was England's most serious rival in the competition for overseas empire. France was continental Europe's leading military power. It was already building a powerful fleet and a worldwide system of rigidly monopolized colonial trade. But the War of the Spanish Succession, the last of Louis XIV's many wars (see "The Wars of Louis XIV") tilted the balance in favor of England. The 1713 Peace of Utrecht forced France to cede its North American holdings in Newfoundland, Nova Scotia, and the Hudson Bay territory to Britain. Spain was compelled to give Britain control of its West African slave trade and to let Britain send one ship of merchandise into the Spanish colonies annually. These acquisitions primed Britain to take a leading role in the growing Atlantic trade of the eighteenth century, including the transatlantic slave trade (see Chapter 19).

People Beyond Borders

As they seized new territories, European nations produced maps proudly outlining their possessions. The situation on the ground, however, was often much more complicated than the lines on those maps would suggest. Many groups of people lived in the contested frontiers between empires, habitually crisscrossed their borders, or carved out niches within empires where they carried out their own lives in defiance of the official rules.

Restricted from owning land and holding many occupations in Europe, Jews were eager participants in colonial trade and established closely linked mercantile communities scattered across many different empires. Similarly, a community of Christian Armenians in Isfahan in the Safavid Empire (modern-day Iran) formed the center of a trade network extending from London to Manila and Acapulco (see "Merchant Networks in the Islamic Empires" in Chapter 17). Family ties and trust within these minority groups were a tremendous advantage in generating the financial credit and cooperation necessary for international commerce. Yet Jews and Armenians were minorities where they settled and vulnerable to persecution.

The nomadic Cossacks and Tartars who inhabited the steppes of the Don River basin that bordered the Russian and Ottoman Empires are yet another example of "in-between" peoples. The Cossacks and the Tartars maintained considerable political and cultural autonomy through the seventeenth century and enjoyed a degree of peaceful interaction. By the eighteenth century, however, both Ottoman and Russian rulers had expanded state control in their frontiers and had reined in the raiding and migration of nomadic steppe peoples. As their example suggests, the assertion of state authority in the seventeenth and eighteenth centuries made it progressively harder for all of these groups to retain autonomy from the grip of empire.

The Russian Empire

Russia occupied a unique position among Eurasian states. With borders straddling eastern Europe and northwestern Asia, its development into a strong imperial state drew on elements from both continents. As in the Muslim empires in Central and South Asia and the Ming Dynasty in China, the expansion of Russia was a result of the weakening of the great Mongol and Timurid Empires. After declaring independence from the Mongols, the Russian tsars conquered a vast empire, extending through North Asia all the way to the Pacific Ocean. State-building and territorial expansion culminated during the reign of Peter the Great, who turned Russia toward the West by intervening in western European wars and politics and forcing his people to adopt elements of Western culture.

> **How did Russian rulers build a distinctive absolutist monarchy and expand into a vast and powerful empire?**

Mongol Rule in Russia and the Rise of Moscow

In the thirteenth century the Mongols had conquered Kievan Rus, the medieval Slavic state that included most of present-day Ukraine, Belarus, and part of northwest Russia. For two hundred years the Mongols forced the Slavic princes to submit to their rule. The princes of the Grand Duchy of Moscow, a principality within Kievan Rus, became particularly adept at serving the Mongols. Eventually the Muscovite princes were able to destroy the other princes who were their rivals for power.

Ivan III (r. 1462–1505), known as Ivan the Great, greatly expanded the principality of Moscow, claiming large territories in the north and east to the Siberian frontier.

By 1480 Ivan III was strong enough to declare the autonomy of Moscow. To legitimize his new position, Ivan and his successors borrowed elements of Mongol rule. They forced weaker Slavic principalities to render tribute and adopted Mongol institutions such as the tax system, postal routes, and census. Loyalty from the highest-ranking nobles, or boyars, helped the Muscovite princes consolidate their power.

Another source of legitimacy lay in Moscow's claim to the political and religious inheritance of the Byzantine Empire. After the empire's capital, Constantinople, fell to the Ottomans in 1453, the princes of Moscow saw themselves as heirs of the Byzantine caesars (emperors) and guardians of the Orthodox Christian Church.

Building the Russian Empire

Developments in Russia took a chaotic turn with the reign of Ivan IV (r. 1533–1584), the famous Ivan the Terrible, who ascended to the throne at age three. His mother died when he was eight, leaving Ivan to suffer insults and neglect from the boyars at court. At age sixteen he pushed aside his advisers and crowned himself tsar.

After the sudden death of his wife, however, Ivan began a campaign of persecution against those he suspected of opposing him. He executed members of leading boyar families, along with their families, friends, servants, and peasants. To replace them, Ivan created a new service nobility, whose loyalty was guaranteed by their dependence on the state for land and titles.

Cossacks Free groups and outlaw armies living on the borders of Russian territory from the fourteenth century onward. In the mid-sixteenth century they formed an alliance with the Russian state.

As landlords demanded more from the serfs who survived the persecutions, growing numbers of peasants fled toward recently conquered territories to the east and south. There they joined free groups and warrior bands, known as **Cossacks**, who had been living on the borders of Russian territory since the fourteenth century. Ivan responded by tying serfs ever more firmly to the land. Simultaneously, he ordered that urban dwellers be bound to their towns and jobs so that he could tax them more heavily. These restrictions checked the growth of the Russian middle classes and stood in sharp contrast to economic and social developments in western Europe.

Ivan's reign was successful in defeating the remnants of Mongol power, adding vast new territories to the realm, and laying the foundations for the huge multiethnic Russian Empire. In the 1550s, strengthened by an alliance with Cossack bands, Ivan conquered the Muslim khanates of Kazan and Astrakhan and brought the fertile steppe region around the Volga River under Russian control. In the 1580s Cossacks fighting for the Russian state crossed the Ural Mountains and began the long conquest of Siberia. Because of the size and distance of the new territories, the Russian state did not initially seek to impose the Orthodox religion and maintained local elites in positions of honor and leadership, buying their loyalty with grants of land. In relying on cooperation from local elites and ruthlessly exploiting the common people, the Russians followed the pattern of the Spanish and other early modern European imperial states.

Following Ivan's death, Russia entered a chaotic period known as the Time of Troubles (1598–1613). While Ivan's relatives struggled for power, the Cossacks and peasants rebelled against nobles and officials. This social explosion from below brought the nobles together. They crushed the Cossack rebellion and elected Ivan's grandnephew, Michael Romanov (r. 1613–1645), the new hereditary tsar.

Despite the turbulence of the period, the Romanov tsars, like their western European counterparts, made further achievements in territorial expansion and state-building. After a long war, Russia gained land to the west in Ukraine in 1667. By the end of the century it had completed the conquest of Siberia to the east. This vast territorial expansion brought Russian power to the Pacific Ocean and was only checked by the powerful Qing Dynasty. Like the French in Canada, the basis of Russian wealth in Siberia was furs, which the state collected by forced annual tribute payments from local peoples. Profits from furs and other natural resources, especially mining in the eighteenth century, funded expansion of the Russian bureaucracy and the army.

Russian Peasants An eighteenth-century French artist visiting Russia recorded his impressions of the daily life of the Russian people in this etching of a fish merchant pulling his wares on a sleigh through a snowy village. Two caviar vendors behind him make a sale to a young mother standing at her doorstep with her baby in her arms. (From Jean-Baptiste le Prince's second set of Russian etchings, 1765. Private Collection/ Gérard PIERSON/www.amis-paris-petersbourg.org)

The growth of state power did nothing to improve the lot of the common people. In 1649 a new law code extended serfdom to all peasants in the realm, giving lords unrestricted rights over their serfs and establishing penalties for harboring runaways. The new code also removed the privileges that non-Russian elites had enjoyed within the empire and required conversion to Russian orthodoxy. Henceforth, Moscow maintained strict control of trade and administration throughout the empire.

The peace imposed by harsh Russian rule was disrupted in 1670 by a failed rebellion led by the Cossack Stenka Razin, who attracted a great army of urban poor and peasants. The ease with which Moscow crushed the rebellion by the end of 1671 testifies to the success of the Russian state in unifying and consolidating its empire.

Peter the Great and Russia's Turn to the West

Heir to Romanov efforts at state-building, Peter the Great (r. 1682–1725) embarked on a tremendous campaign to accelerate and complete these processes. Peter built on the service obligations of Ivan the Terrible and his successors and continued their tradition of territorial expansion. Peter's ambitions hinged on gaining access to the sea by extending Russia's borders to the Black Sea (controlled by the Ottomans) and to the Baltic Sea (dominated by Sweden).

Peter embarked on his first territorial goal by conquering the Ottoman fort of Azov in 1696 and quickly built Russia's first navy base nearby. In 1697 the tsar went on an eighteen-month tour of western European capitals. Peter was fascinated by foreign technology, and he hoped to forge an anti-Ottoman alliance to strengthen his hold on the Black Sea. Peter failed to secure a military alliance, but he did learn his lessons from the growing power of the Dutch and the English. He also engaged more than a hundred foreign experts to return with him to Russia to help build the navy and improve Russian infrastructure. (See "Analyzing the Evidence: Peter the Great and Foreign Experts," page 550.)

To realize his second goal, Peter entered the Great Northern War (1700–1721) against Sweden. After a humiliating defeat at the Battle of Narva in 1700, Peter responded with measures designed to increase state power, strengthen his military, and gain victory. He required all nobles to serve in the army or in the civil administration—for life. Peter also created schools of navigation and mathematics, medicine, engineering, and finance to produce skilled technicians and experts. Furthermore, he established an interlocking military-civilian bureaucracy with fourteen ranks, and he decreed that everyone had to start at the bottom and work toward the top. He sought talented foreigners and placed them in his service. These measures gradually combined to make the army and government more powerful and efficient.

Peter also greatly increased the service requirements of commoners. He established a regular standing army of peasant-soldiers, drafted for life. In addition, he created special regiments of Cossacks and foreign mercenaries. To fund the army, taxes on peasants increased threefold during Peter's reign. Serfs were also arbitrarily assigned to work in the growing number of factories and mines that supplied the military.

In 1709 Peter's new war machine was able to crush Sweden's army in Ukraine at Poltava (Map 18.5). Russia's victory against Sweden was conclusive in 1721, and Estonia and present-day Latvia came under Russian rule for the first time. The cost was high: warfare consumed 80 to 85 percent of all revenues. But Russia became the dominant power in the Baltic and very much a great European power.

Peter the Great The compelling portrait above captures the strength and determination of the warrior-tsar in 1723, after more than three decades of personal rule. In his hand Peter holds the scepter, symbol of royal sovereignty, and across his breastplate is draped an ermine fur, a mark of honor. In the background are the battleships of Russia's new Baltic fleet and the famous St. Peter and St. Paul Fortress that Peter built in St. Petersburg. The image on the left portrays Peter dressed as a ship carpenter's apprentice during his incognito tour of western Europe. (tsar portrait: Hermitage, St. Petersburg, Russia/Bridgeman Images; carpenter's apprentice: Universal Images Group/UIG via Getty Images)

MAP 18.5 The Expansion of Russia, 1462–1689 In little more than two centuries, Russia expanded from the small principality of Muscovy to an enormous multiethnic empire, stretching from the borders of western Europe through northern Asia to the Pacific.

After his victory at Poltava, Peter channeled enormous resources into building a new Western-style capital on the Baltic. The city of St. Petersburg was designed to reflect modern urban planning with wide, straight avenues; buildings set in a uniform line; and large parks. Each summer, twenty-five thousand to forty thousand peasants were sent to provide construction labor in St. Petersburg without pay.

There were other important consequences of Peter's reign. For Peter, modernization meant westernization, and both Westerners and Western ideas flowed into Russia for the first time. He required nobles to shave their heavy beards and wear Western clothing. He also required them to attend parties where young men and women would mix together and freely choose their own spouses. From these efforts a new elite class of Western-oriented Russians began to emerge.

Peter's reforms were unpopular with many Russians. For nobles, one of Peter's most detested reforms was the imposition of unigeniture — inheritance of land by one son alone. For peasants, the reign of the tsar saw a significant increase in the bonds of serfdom. Nonetheless, Peter's modernizing and westernizing of Russia paved the way for it to move somewhat closer to the European mainstream in its thought and institutions during the Enlightenment, especially under Catherine the Great (see "Enlightened Absolutism and Its Limits" in Chapter 19).

Peter the Great and Foreign Experts

John Deane, an eminent English shipbuilder, was one of the many foreign artisans and experts brought to Russia by Peter the Great after his foreign tour of 1697. Several months after arriving in Russia, Deane sent a glowing account of the tsar's technical prowess to his patron in England, the marquess of Carmarthen, admiral of the English fleet.

■ I Have deferr'd writing, till I could be able to give Your Lordship a true Account (from my own Knowledge) of the *Czar* (our Master's) Navy, which being a New Thing in the World as yet, I believe is variously talk'd of in *England, &c.* First, at *Voronize* there is already in the Water and Rigg'd, 36, and to be Launch'd in the Spring 20 more stout Ships, from 30 to 60 Guns. Next, 18 very large Gallies (built after the *Venetian* manner by *Italian* Masters) are already compleated; and 100 smaller Gallies or Brigantines are equipt for the Sea; 7 Bomb-Ships are Launch'd and Rigg'd, and 4 Fireships are Building against the Spring, when they are all to go down to *Azoph.* The Ships are chiefly built by the *Dutch* and *Danes.*

The 25th of *August* last his Majesty came to *Moscow, incognito*; immediately he took in hand the rewarding of General *Gordon*'s Soldiers, that fought against the Rebels he defeated in *June* last, and next day gave Orders to fetch up all those of the Rebels who were dispersed by way of Banishment, which were in all then left about 2700. I suppose Your Lordship has been inform'd by Publick News, how they are hung round the Walls of this City, some hundreds beheaded, some broke upon the Wheel, *&c.* to the whole Number of them, which was in all 3000.

At my arrival in Moscow, I fell very ill of the Bloody-Flux, which made me be in Moscow when his Majesty came home: About the latter end of October I was somewhat recovered, his Majesty then carried me down to Voronize [site of the naval shipyard] with him. Voronize is about 400 English Miles South-East from Moscow. There the Czar immediately set up a ship of 60 guns, where he is both Foreman and Master-Builder; and not to flatter him, I'll assure your Lordship it will be the best ship among them, and 'tis all from his own Draught; How he fram'd her together and how he made the Mould, and in so short a time as he did is really wonderful: But he is able at this day to put his own notions into practice, and laugh at his Dutch and Italian builders for their ignorance. There are several pieces of workmanship, as in the keel, stem, and post, which are all purely his own invention, and sound good work, and would be approved of by all the shipwrights of England if they saw it he has a round Tuck, and a narrow Floor, a good tumbling Home, and Circular Side; none are to exceed 11 Dutch Foot Draught of Water. He has not run into any Extreme, But taken the Mediums of all good Sailing Properties, which seem best. One may, methinks, call her an Abstract of his own private Observations whilst Abroad, strengthened by Your Lordship's Improving Discourses to him on that Subject, and his own extraordinary Notion of Sailing. One thing as to her Keel is, That should it wholly be beat out, yet it is so ordered, that the Ship will be tight and safe, and may continue so at Sea afterwards.

Chapter Summary

Most parts of Europe experienced the first centuries of the early modern era as a time of crisis. Following the religious divides of the sixteenth-century Protestant and Catholic Reformations, Europeans in the seventeenth century suffered from economic stagnation, social upheaval, and renewed military conflict. Overcoming these obstacles, both absolutist and constitutional European states emerged from the seventeenth century with increased powers and more centralized control.

Monarchs in Spain, France, and Austria used divine right to claim they possessed absolute power and were not responsible to any representative institutions. Absolute monarchs overcame the resistance of the nobility both through military force and by

I likewise made a Suit of Moulds for a Ship of Sixty Guns, but after fell sick again; and at Christmas, when his Majesty came to Moscow, he brought me back again for recovery of my health, where I am at present; notwithstanding both our Ships go forward, having put things in such a posture, as that a *Grecian* (who has been in *England*) carries on the Business. Mr. *Ney* is Building of a 60 Gun Ship there too; besides, there are four of that Size (near built) upon the *Done*, two of 40 Guns already at *Azoph*, carried down some time since, and a great many Galleys, &c.

The Rivers *Vorona*, at *Voronitz*, when I was there, was hardly so broad as the Ships are long; but in the Spring about the latter End of *April*, or beginning of *May*, when the Snow melts, there is 16 Foot Water in that little River, and continues this height about 12 or 14 days, with a Rapid Torrent, with that force, that though it be 1000 Miles down to *Azoph* [Azov], yet the Ships will easily be there in 9 or 10 days. There is 30000 Soldiers at *Voronize*, to defend the Ships from the *Tartars*, who are very mischievous, and very swift in setting a place on Fire, and running away again. Those Ships that are Launcht lie fast in Ice about two Foot thick, so that the River is now as firm as Land, although this is reckoned a very mild Winter; for I remember in *January* one Afternoon with a *Southerly* Wind it thaw'd and rain'd for 3 or 4 hours, which is rare enough for an Almanack. The Ground is covered with Snow about a Yard deep, and 'tis mighty clear, piercing cold Weather, such as in *England* we can't imagine.

. . . His Majesty was at my Chamber two days of last Week, with Mr. *Styles* as Interpreter (who gives his humble duty to Your Lordship). You may guess what His Majesty came to be inform'd in whilst he was there;

I shew'd him a Model of a Machine to bring up the *Royal Transport* to the *Volga*, at 17 Inches Draught of Water; he was pleas'd to like it, but gave no Orders for putting it in Execution, so I believe she will lie where she is now, and perish. Here are Three Envoys, *viz.* the *Emperor's*, the *Danes*, and *Brandenburgs*, in this *Slabado*, (as it is call'd), which lies from *Moscow*, as *Lambeth* does from *London*. The whole place is inhabited by the Dutch; I believe there may be 400 families. Last Sunday and Monday the strangers were invited to the consecration of General La Fort's house, which is the noblest building in Russia, and finely furnisht. There were all the envoys, and as near as I could guess 200 gentlemen, English, French, and Dutch, and about as many ladies; each day were dancing and musick. All the envoys, and all the lords (but three in Moscow) are going to Voronize to see the fleet, I suppose. His majesty went last Sunday to Voronize with Prince Alexander and I am to go down (being something recovered) with the Vice-Admiral about six days hence.

QUESTIONS FOR ANALYSIS

1. According to Deane, what evidence did Peter the Great give of his skills in shipbuilding? Based on this document, how would you characterize the relationship between Peter and his foreign experts?
2. What evidence does Dean provide of the impact of foreigners on life in Russia?
3. What image of Peter as a ruler emerges from this document? How does Deane characterize the tsar and his rule?

Source: John Deane, "A Letter from Moscow to the Marquess of Carmarthen, Relating to the Czar of Muscovy's Forwardness in His Great Navy, &c. Since His Return Home," in Sir John Barrow, *A Memoir of the Life of Peter the Great* (New York: Harper & Brothers, 1834), pp. 110–113.

confirming existing economic and social privileges. England and the Netherlands defied the general trend toward absolute monarchy, adopting distinctive forms of constitutional rule.

As Spain's power weakened, other European nations bordering the Atlantic Ocean sought their own profits and glory from overseas empires, with England emerging in the early eighteenth century with a distinct advantage over its rivals. Henceforth, war among European powers would include conflicts over territories and trade in the colonies. European rulers' increased control over their own subjects thus went hand in glove with the expansion of European power in the world.

In Russia, Mongol conquest and rule set the stage for a harsh tsarist autocracy that was firmly in place by the time of the reign of Ivan the Terrible in the sixteenth

century. The reign of Ivan and his successors saw a great expansion of Russian territory, laying the foundations for a huge multiethnic empire. Peter the Great forcibly
turned Russia toward the West by adopting Western technology and culture.

NOTES

1. Theodore K. Rabb, *The Struggle for Stability in Early Modern Europe* (Oxford: Oxford University Press, 1975), p. 10.
2. Simon Schama, *The Embarrassment of Riches: An Interpretation of Dutch Culture in the Golden Age* (New York: Alfred A. Knopf, 1987), pp. 165–170.

CONNECTIONS

The seventeenth century represented a difficult passage between two centuries of dynamism and growth in Europe. On one side lay the sixteenth century's religious enthusiasm and strife, overseas discoveries, rising populations, and vigorous commerce. On the other side stretched the eighteenth century's renewed population growth, economic development, and cultural flourishing. The first half of the seventeenth century was marked by harsh climate conditions and violent conflict across Europe and much of the world. Recurring crop failure, famine, and epidemic disease contributed to a stagnant economy and population loss. In the middle decades of the seventeenth century, the very survival of the European monarchies established in the Renaissance appeared in doubt.

With the re-establishment of order in the second half of the century, maintaining stability was of paramount importance to European rulers. While a few nations placed their trust in constitutionally limited governments, many more were ruled by monarchs proclaiming their absolute and God-given authority. Despite their political differences, most European states emerged from the period of crisis with shared achievements in state power, territorial expansion, and long-distance trade. In these achievements, they resembled the Qing in China and the Mughals in India, who also saw the consolidation of imperial authority in this period; by contrast, the Ottoman Empire recovered more slowly from the crises of the seventeenth century.

The eighteenth century was to see these power politics thrown into question by new Enlightenment aspirations for human society, which themselves derived from the inquisitive and self-confident spirit of the Scientific Revolution. These movements are explored in the next chapter. By the end of the eighteenth century demands for real popular sovereignty, colonial self-rule, and slave emancipation challenged the very bases of order so painfully achieved in the seventeenth century. Chapter 22 recounts the revolutionary movements that swept the late-eighteenth-century Atlantic world, while Chapters 25, 26, and 27 follow the story of European imperialism and the resistance of colonized peoples in Africa, Asia, and the Americas into the nineteenth century.

CHAPTER 18 **Review and Explore**

Identify Key Terms

Identify and explain the significance of each item below.

Protestant Reformation (p. 520)

Jesuits (p. 523)

moral economy (p. 526)

Thirty Years' War (p. 526)

sovereignty (p. 528)

absolutism (p. 528)

divine right of kings (p. 530)

mercantilism (p. 532)

constitutionalism (p. 536)

republicanism (p. 536)

Puritans (p. 537)

Bill of Rights of 1689 (p. 538)

Navigation Acts (p. 544)

Cossacks (p. 546)

Review the Main Ideas

Answer the focus questions from each section of the chapter.

1. How did the Protestant and Catholic Reformations change power structures in Europe and shape European colonial expansion? (p. 520)

2. How did seventeenth-century European rulers overcome social and economic crisis to build strong states? (p. 524)

3. What was absolutism, and how did it evolve in seventeenth-century Spain, France, and Austria? (p. 528)

4. Why and how did the constitutional state triumph in England and the Dutch Republic? (p. 536)

5. How did European nations compete for global trade and empire in the Americas and Asia? (p. 540)

6. How did Russian rulers build a distinctive absolutist monarchy and expand into a vast and powerful empire? (p. 545)

Make Comparisons and Connections

Analyze the larger developments and continuities within and across chapters.

1. This chapter has argued that, despite their political differences, rulers in absolutist and constitutionalist nations faced similar obstacles in the mid-seventeenth century and achieved many of the same goals. Based on the evidence presented here, do you agree with this argument? Why or why not?

2. Proponents of absolutism in western Europe believed that their form of monarchical rule was fundamentally different from and superior to what they saw as the "despotism" of Russia and the Ottoman Empire (Chapter 17). What was the basis of this belief, and how accurate do you think it was?

3. What common features did the Muslim empires of the Middle East and India (Chapter 17) share with European empires? How would you characterize interaction among these Eurasian empires?

TIMELINE

Suggested Resources

BOOKS

Beik, William. *A Social and Cultural History of Early Modern France.* 2009. An overview of early modern French history, by one of the leading authorities on the period.

Elliott, John H. *Imperial Spain, 1469–1716,* 2d ed. 2002. An authoritative account of Spain's rise to imperial greatness and its slow decline.

Gaunt, Peter, ed. *The English Civil War: The Essential Readings.* 2000. A collection showcasing leading historians' interpretations of the civil war.

Goldgar, Anne. *Tulipmania: Money, Honor, and Knowledge in the Dutch Golden Age.* 2007. A fresh look at the speculative fever for tulip bulbs in the early-seventeenth-century Dutch Republic.

Hughes, Lindsey, ed. *Peter the Great and the West: New Perspectives.* 2001. Essays by leading scholars on the reign of Peter the Great and his opening of Russia to the West.

Ingrao, Charles W. *The Habsburg Monarchy, 1618–1815,* 2d ed. 2000. An excellent synthesis of the political and social development of the Habsburg empire in the early modern period.

Parker, Geoffrey. *Global Crisis: War, Climate Change and Catastrophe in the Seventeenth Century.* 2013. A sweeping account of the worldwide crisis of the seventeenth century, which the author argues was largely caused by climatic changes known as the "little ice age."

Rountree, Helen C. *Pocahontas, Powhatan, Opechancanough: Three Indian Lives Changed by Jamestown.* 2005. Biographies of three important Native Americans involved in the Jamestown settlement; a rich portrait of the life of the Powhatan people and their encounter with the English.

Wilson, Peter H. *The Thirty Years War: Europe's Tragedy.* 2011. An overview of the origins and outcomes of the Thirty Years' War, focusing on political and economic issues in addition to religious conflicts.

1660 Restoration of English monarchy under Charles II

1682–1725 Reign of Peter the Great in Russia

1642–1649 English civil war, ending with the execution of Charles I

1653–1658 Oliver Cromwell's military rule in England (the Protectorate)

1688–1689 Glorious Revolution in England

1643–1715 Reign of Louis XIV in France

1651 First of the Navigation Acts

1665–1683 Jean-Baptiste Colbert applies mercantilism to France

1670–1671 Cossack revolt led by Stenka Razin

1701–1713 War of the Spanish Succession

1683–1718 Habsburgs push the Ottoman Turks from Hungary

1603–1867 Tokugawa Shogunate in Japan **(Chs. 21, 26)**

1652 East India Company settles Cape Town **(Ch. 20)**

1625	1650	1675	1700

FEATURE FILMS AND TELEVISION DRAMAS

Alatriste (Agustín Díaz Yanes, 2006). Set in the declining years of Spain's imperial glory, this film follows the violent adventures of an army captain who takes the son of a fallen comrade under his care.

Black Robe (Bruce Beresford, 1991). A classic film about French Jesuit missionaries among Algonquin and Huron Indians in New France in the seventeenth century.

Charles II: The Power and the Passion (BBC, 2003). An award-winning television miniseries about the son of executed English king Charles I and the Restoration that brought him to the throne in 1660.

Cromwell (Ken Hughes, 1970). The English civil war from its origin to Oliver Cromwell's victory, with battle scenes as well as personal stories of Cromwell and other central figures.

Girl with a Pearl Earring (Peter Webber, 2003). The life and career of painter Johannes Vermeer told through the eyes of a young servant girl who becomes his assistant and model.

Molière (Laurent Tirard, 2007). A film about the French playwright Molière, a favorite of King Louis XIV, which fancifully incorporates characters and plotlines from some of the writer's most celebrated plays.

WEBSITES

Chateau de Versailles. The official website of the palace of Versailles, built by Louis XIV and inhabited by French royalty until the revolution of 1789. **en.chateauversailles.fr/homepage**

The Invitation to a Funeral Tour: A Free-Style Jaunt around Restoration London. A website offering information on the places, food, and people of Restoration London, inspired by the novel *Invitation to a Funeral* by Molly Brown (1999). **www.okima.com/**

The Plymouth Colony Archive Project. A site hosted by the University of Illinois with searchable primary and secondary sources relating to the Plymouth colony, including court records, laws, journals and memoirs, wills, maps, and biographies of colonists. **www.histarch.uiuc.edu/Plymouth/index.html**

19

New Worldviews and Ways of Life
1540–1790

From the mid-sixteenth century on, age-old patterns of knowledge and daily life were disrupted by a series of transformative developments. Just as European explorers and conquerors overturned ancient models of the globe, so scholars challenged, and eventually discarded, ancient frameworks for understanding the heavens. The resulting conception of the universe and its laws remained in force until Albert Einstein's discoveries in the first half of the twentieth century. Accompanied by new discoveries in botany, zoology, chemistry, and other domains, these developments constituted a fundamental shift in the basic framework for understanding the natural world and the methods for examining it known collectively as the "Scientific Revolution."

In the eighteenth century philosophers extended the use of reason from nature to human society. Self-proclaimed members of an "Enlightenment" movement, they wished to bring the same progress to human affairs that their predecessors had brought to the understanding of the natural world. The Enlightenment created concepts of human rights, equality, progress, and tolerance that still guide Western societies. At the same time, some Europeans used their new understanding of reason to explain their own superiority, thus rationalizing attitudes now regarded as racist and sexist. Despite these biases, European intellectual change drew on contact and exchange with non-European peoples, ideas, and natural organisms.

Changes in the material world encouraged the emergence of new ideas. With the growth of population, the revitalization of industry, and growing world trade, Europeans began to consume at a higher level. Feeding the growth of consumerism was the expansion of transatlantic trade and lower prices for colonial goods, often produced by slaves. During the eighteenth century ships crisscrossing the Atlantic circulated commodities, ideas, and people to all four continents bordering the ocean. As trade became more integrated and communication intensified, an Atlantic world of mixed identities and vivid debates emerged.

Free People of Color

A sizable mixed-race population emerged in many European colonies in the Americas, including descendants of unions between masters and enslaved African women. The wealthiest of the free people of color, as they were called, were plantation owners with slaves of their own.

Portrait of a Young Woman, by an unknown artist, previously attributed to Jean-Etienne Liotard (1702–1789) (pastel on paper)/Saint Louis Art Museum/Bridgeman Images

CHAPTER PREVIEW

THE SCIENTIFIC REVOLUTION
What revolutionary discoveries were made in the sixteenth and seventeenth centuries, and what was their global context?

IMPORTANT CHANGES IN SCIENTIFIC THINKING AND PRACTICE
What intellectual and social changes occurred as a result of the Scientific Revolution?

THE RISE AND SPREAD OF THE ENLIGHTENMENT
How did the Enlightenment emerge, and what were major currents of Enlightenment thought?

KEY ISSUES OF ENLIGHTENMENT DEBATE
How did Enlightenment thinkers address issues of cultural and social difference and political power?

ECONOMIC CHANGE AND THE ATLANTIC WORLD
How did economic and social change and the rise of Atlantic trade interact with Enlightenment ideas?

What revolutionary discoveries were made in the sixteenth and seventeenth centuries, and what was their global context?

The Scientific Revolution

Building on developments in the Middle Ages and the Renaissance, tremendous advances in Europeans' knowledge of the natural world and techniques for establishing such knowledge took place between 1500 and 1700. Collectively known as the "Scientific Revolution," these developments emerged because many more people studied the natural world, using new methods to answer fundamental questions about the universe and how it operated. The authority of ancient Greek texts was replaced by a conviction that knowledge should be acquired by observation and experimentation and that mathematics could be used to understand and represent the workings of the physical world. By 1700 precise laws governing physics and astronomy were known, and a new emphasis on the practical uses of knowledge had emerged.

Hailed today as pioneers of a modern worldview, the major figures of the Scientific Revolution were for the most part devout Christians who saw their work as heralding the glory of creation and who combined older traditions of magic, astrology, and alchemy with their pathbreaking experimentation. Their discoveries took place in a broader context of international trade, imperial expansion, and cultural exchange. Alongside developments in modern science and natural philosophy, the growth of natural history in this period is now recognized by historians as a major achievement of the Scientific Revolution.

Why Europe?

In 1500 scientific activity flourished in many parts of the world. With the expansion of Islam into the lands of the Byzantine Empire in the seventh and eighth centuries, Muslim scholars inherited ancient Greek learning, which itself was built on centuries of borrowing from older civilizations in Egypt, Babylonia, and India. The interaction of peoples and cultures across the vast Muslim world, facilitated by religious tolerance and the common scholarly language of Arabic, was highly favorable to advances in learning.

In a great period of cultural and intellectual flourishing from 1000 to 1500, Muslim scholars thrived in cultural centers such as Baghdad and Córdoba. They established the world's first universities. In this fertile atmosphere, scholars surpassed the texts they had inherited in areas such as mathematics, physics, astronomy, and medicine. Arab and Persian mathematicians, for example, invented algebra, the concept of the algorithm, and decimal point notation, while Arab astronomers improved on measurements recorded in ancient works.

China was also a vital center of scientific activity, which reached a peak in the mid-fourteenth century. Among its many achievements, papermaking, gunpowder, and the use of the compass in navigation would be the most influential for the West. In Mesoamerica, civilizations such as the Maya and the Aztecs devised complex calendar systems based on astronomical observations and developed mathematics and writing.

Given the multiple world sites of learning and scholarship, it was by no means inevitable that Europe would take the lead in scientific thought. In world history, periods of advancement produced by intense cultural interaction, such as those that occurred after the spread of Islam, are often followed by stagnation and decline during times of conflict and loss of authority. This is what happened in western Europe after the fall of the Western Roman Empire in the fifth century and in the Maya civilization after the collapse of its cultural and political centers around 900.

The re-establishment of stronger monarchies and the growth of trade in the High Middle Ages contributed to a renewal of learning in western Europe. As Europeans began to encroach on Islamic lands in Iberia, Sicily, and the eastern Mediterranean, they became aware of the rich heritage of Greek learning in these regions and the ways scholars had improved upon ancient knowledge. In the twelfth century many ancient Greek texts were translated into Latin, along with the commentaries of Arab scholars. A number of European cities created universities in which Aristotle's works dominated the curriculum.

As Europe recovered from the ravages of the Black Death in the late fourteenth and fifteenth centuries, the intellectual and cultural movement known as the Renaissance provided a crucial foundation for the Scientific Revolution. Scholars called humanists emphasized the value of acquiring knowledge for the practical purposes of life. The quest to restore the glories of the ancient past led to the rediscovery of a host of important classical texts. The fall of Constantinople to the Ottomans in 1453 resulted in a great influx of little-known Greek works, as Christian scholars fled to Italy with their precious texts.

In this period, western European universities established new professorships of mathematics, astronomy, and natural philosophy. The prestige of the new fields was low, especially mathematics, which was reserved for practical problems but not used as a tool to understand the functioning of the physical world itself. Nevertheless, these professorships eventually enabled the union of mathematics with natural philosophy that was to be a hallmark of the Scientific Revolution.

European overseas expansion in the fifteenth and sixteenth centuries provided another catalyst for new thought about the natural world. In particular, the navigational problems of long oceanic voyages in the age of expansion stimulated scientific research and invention. To help solve these problems, inventors developed many new scientific instruments, such as the telescope, barometer, thermometer, pendulum clock, microscope, and air pump. Better instruments, which permitted more accurate observations, often led to important new knowledge. Another crucial technology in this period was printing, which provided a faster and less expensive way to circulate knowledge.

Political and social conflicts were widespread in Eurasia in the sixteenth and early seventeenth centuries, but they had different results. The three large empires of the Muslim world (see "The Turkish Ruling Houses: The Ottomans, Safavids, and Mughals" in Chapter 17) that arose in the wake of the Mongol Empire sought to restore order and assert legitimacy in part by imposing Islamic orthodoxy. Their failure to adopt the printing press can be seen as part of a wider reaction against earlier traditions of innovation. Similarly, in China after the Manchu invasion of 1644, the new Qing Dynasty legitimized its authority through stricter adherence to Confucian tradition. By contrast, western Europe remained politically fragmented into smaller competitive nations, divisions that were augmented by the religious fracturing of the Protestant Reformation. These conditions made it impossible for authorities to impose one orthodox set of ideas and thus allowed individuals to question dominant patterns of thinking.

Scientific Thought to 1550

For medieval scholars, philosophy was the path to true knowledge about the world, and its proofs consisted of the authority of ancients (as interpreted by Christian theologians) and their techniques of logical argumentation. Questions about the physical nature of the universe and how it functioned belonged to a minor branch of philosophy called natural philosophy. Natural philosophy was based primarily on the ideas of Aristotle, the great Greek philosopher of the fourth century B.C.E. According to the Christianized version of Aristotle, a motionless earth stood at the center of the universe and was encompassed by ten separate concentric crystal spheres in which were embedded the moon, sun, planets, and stars. Beyond the spheres was Heaven with the throne of God and the souls of the saved.

Aristotle's views also dominated thinking about physics and motion on earth. Aristotle had distinguished between the world of the celestial spheres and that of the earth—the sublunar world. The sublunar realm was made up of four imperfect, changeable elements: air, fire, water, and earth. Aristotle and his followers also believed that a uniform force moved an object at a constant speed and that the object would stop as soon as that force was removed. The ancient Greek scholar Ptolemy amended Aristotle's physics by positing that the planets moved in small circles, called epicycles, each of which moved in turn along a larger circle, or deferent. This theory accounted for the apparent backward motion of the planets (which in fact occurs as planets closer to the sun overtake the earth on their orbits) and provided a surprisingly accurate model for predicting planetary motion.

Ptolemy's work also provided the basic foundation of knowledge about the earth. Rediscovered around 1410, his *Geography* presented crucial advances on medieval cartography by representing a round earth divided into 360 degrees with the major latitude marks. However, Ptolemy's map reflected the limits of ancient knowledge, showing only the continents of Europe, Africa, and Asia, with land covering three-quarters of the world.

Astronomy and Physics

The first great departure from the medieval understanding of cosmology was the work of the Polish cleric Nicolaus Copernicus (1473–1543). Copernicus came to believe that Ptolemy's cumbersome rules detracted from the majesty of a perfect creator. He preferred an idea espoused by some ancient Greek and Arab scholars: that the sun, rather than the earth, was at the center of the universe. Without questioning the Aristotelian belief in crystal spheres, Copernicus theorized that the stars and planets, including the earth, revolved around a fixed sun. Fearing the ridicule of other astronomers, Copernicus did not publish his *On the Revolutions of the Heavenly Spheres* until 1543, the year of his death.

One astronomer who agreed with the **Copernican hypothesis** was the Danish astronomer Tycho Brahe (TEE-koh BRAH-hee) (1546–1601). Brahe established himself as Europe's leading astronomer with his detailed observations of a new star that

Copernican hypothesis
The idea that the sun, not the earth, was the center of the universe.

appeared suddenly in 1572 and shone very brightly for almost two years. The new star, which was actually a distant exploding star, challenged the idea that the heavenly spheres were unchanging and therefore perfect. Aided by grants from the king of Denmark, Brahe built the most sophisticated observatory of his day. After falling out with the king, Brahe acquired a new patron in the Holy Roman emperor Rudolph II, who built him a new observatory in Prague. For twenty years Brahe and his assistants observed the stars and planets with the naked eye in order to create new and improved tables of planetary motions, dubbed the *Rudolphine Tables* in honor of his patron.

Brahe's assistant, Johannes Kepler (1571–1630), carefully re-examined his predecessor's notations and came to believe that they could not be explained by Ptolemy's astronomy. Abandoning the notion of epicycles and deferents, Kepler used Brahe's data to develop three revolutionary laws of planetary motion. First, he demonstrated that the orbits of the planets around the sun are elliptical rather than circular. Second, he demonstrated that the planets do not move at a uniform speed in their orbits. When a planet is close to the sun it accelerates, and it slows as it moves farther away from the sun. Finally, Kepler's third law stated that the time a planet takes to make its complete orbit is precisely related to its distance from the sun.

Kepler's contribution was monumental. Whereas Copernicus had speculated, Kepler used mathematics to prove the precise relations of a sun-centered (solar) system. He thus united for the first time the theoretical cosmology of natural philosophy with mathematics. His work demolished the old system of Aristotle and Ptolemy, and with his third law he came close to formulating the idea of universal gravitation. In 1627 he also completed Brahe's *Rudolphine Tables*, which were used by astronomers for many years.

While Kepler was unraveling planetary motion, a young Florentine named Galileo Galilei (1564–1642) was challenging Aristotelian ideas about motion on earth. He measured the movement of a rolling ball across a surface, repeating the action again and again to verify his results. In his famous acceleration experiment, he showed that a uniform force—in this case, gravity—produced a uniform acceleration. Through another experiment, he formulated the **law of inertia**. He found that rest was not the natural state of objects. Rather, an object continues in motion

law of inertia A law formulated by Galileo stating that motion, not rest, is the natural state of an object and that an object continues in motion forever unless stopped by some external force.

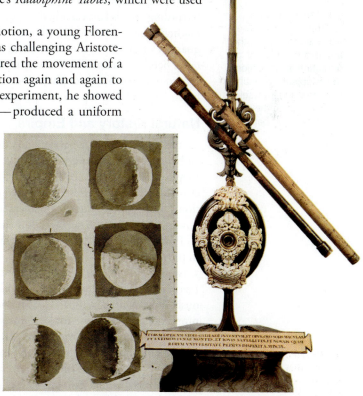

Galileo's Telescopic Observations of the Moon
Among the many mechanical devices Galileo invented was a telescope that could magnify objects twenty times (other contemporary telescopes could magnify objects only three times). Using this telescope, he obtained the empirical evidence that proved the Copernican system. He sketched many illustrations of his observations, including the six phases of the moon, two of which are shown here.
(moon: Biblioteca Nazionale, Florence, Italy/Rabatti-Domingi/akg-images; telescope: Museo delle Scienze, Florence, Italy/akg-images)

forever unless stopped by some external force. His discoveries proved Aristotelian physics wrong.

On hearing details about the invention of the telescope in Holland, Galileo made one for himself in 1609. He quickly discovered the first four moons of Jupiter, which clearly demonstrated that Jupiter could not possibly be embedded in an impenetrable crystal sphere as Aristotle and Ptolemy maintained. This discovery provided concrete evidence for the Copernican theory.

Newton's Synthesis

By about 1640 the work of Brahe, Kepler, and Galileo had been largely accepted by the scientific community despite opposition from religious leaders (see "Science and Religion"). But the new findings failed to explain what forces controlled the movement of the planets and objects on earth. That challenge was taken up by English scientist Isaac Newton (1642–1727).

Newton arrived at some of his most basic ideas about physics in 1666 at age twenty-four but was unable to prove them mathematically. In 1684, after years of studying optics, Newton returned to physics for eighteen intensive months. The result was his towering accomplishment, a single explanatory system that integrated the astronomy of Copernicus, as corrected by Kepler's laws, with the physics of Galileo and his predecessors. Newton did this through a set of mathematical laws that explain motion and mechanics. These laws were published in 1687 in Newton's *Mathematical Principles of Natural Philosophy* (also known as the *Principia*).

law of universal gravitation Newton's law that all objects are attracted to one another and that the force of attraction is proportional to the object's quantity of matter and inversely proportional to the square of the distance between them.

The key feature of the Newtonian synthesis was the **law of universal gravitation**. According to this law, each body in the universe attracts every other body in a precise mathematical relationship, whereby the force of attraction is proportional to the quantity of matter of the objects and inversely proportional to the square of the distance between them. The whole universe was unified in one majestic system. Matter moved on earth and throughout the heavens according to the same laws, which could be understood and expressed in mathematical terms.

Natural History and Empire

At the same time that they made advances in astronomy and physics, Europeans embarked on the pursuit of knowledge about unknown geographical regions. Because they were the first to acquire a large overseas empire, the Spanish pioneered these efforts. The Spanish crown sponsored many scientific expeditions to gather information and specimens, out of which emerged new discoveries that reshaped the fields of botany, zoology, cartography, and metallurgy, among others.

Plants were a particular source of interest because they offered tremendous profits in the form of spices, medicines, dyes, and cash crops. King Philip II of Spain sent his personal physician, Francisco Hernández, to New Spain for seven years in the 1560s. Hernández filled fifteen volumes with illustrations of three thousand plants previously unknown in Europe. He interviewed local healers about the plants' medicinal properties, thereby benefiting from centuries of Mesoamerican botanical knowledge.

Other countries followed the Spanish example as their global empires expanded, relying both on official expeditions and the private initiative of merchants, missionaries, and settlers. Over time, the stream of new information about plant and animal species overwhelmed existing intellectual frameworks. Carl Linnaeus (1707–1778) of Sweden sent his students on exploratory voyages around the world and, based on their observations and the specimens they collected, devised a system of naming and classifying living organisms still used today (with substantial revisions).

Magic and Alchemy

Recent historical research on the Scientific Revolution has focused on the contribution of ideas and practices that no longer belong to the realm of science, such as astrology and alchemy. Many of the most celebrated astronomers were also astrologers. Used as a diagnostic tool in medicine, astrology formed a regular part of the curriculum of medical schools.

Centuries-old practices of magic and alchemy also remained important traditions for natural philosophers. Early modern practitioners of magic strove to understand and control hidden connections they perceived among different elements of the natural world, such as that between a magnet and iron. The idea that objects possessed hidden or "occult" qualities that allowed them to affect other objects was a particularly important legacy of the magical tradition.

Johannes Kepler exemplifies the interaction among these different strands of interest in the natural world. His duties as court mathematician included casting horoscopes for the royal family, and he based his own life on astrological principles. He also wrote at length on cosmic harmonies and explained elliptical motion through ideas about the beautiful music created by the combined motion of the planets. Another example of the interweaving of ideas and beliefs is Sir Isaac Newton, who was both intensely religious and also fascinated by alchemy, whose practitioners believed (among other things) that base metals could be turned into gold.

Important Changes in Scientific Thinking and Practice

What intellectual and social changes occurred as a result of the Scientific Revolution?

The Scientific Revolution was not accomplished by a handful of brilliant individuals working alone. Advancements occurred in many fields as scholars developed new methods to seek answers to long-standing problems with the collaboration and assistance of skilled craftsmen who invented new instruments and helped conduct experiments. These results circulated in an international intellectual community from which women were usually excluded.

The Methods of Science

The English politician and writer Francis Bacon (1561–1626) was the greatest early propagandist for the experimental method. Rejecting the Aristotelian and medieval method of using speculative reasoning to build general theories, Bacon argued that new knowledge had to be pursued through empirical research. The researcher who wants to learn more about leaves or rocks, for example, should not speculate about the subject but should rather collect a multitude of specimens and then compare and analyze them to derive general principles. Bacon's contribution was to formalize the empirical method, which had already been used by Brahe and Galileo, into the general theory of inductive reasoning known as **empiricism**.

empiricism A theory of inductive reasoning that calls for acquiring evidence through observation and experimentation rather than reason and speculation.

On the continent more speculative methods retained support. In 1619 the French philosopher René Descartes (day-KAHRT) (1596–1650) experienced a life-changing intellectual vision. Descartes saw that there was a perfect correspondence between geometry and algebra and that geometrical spatial figures could be expressed as

MAJOR CONTRIBUTORS TO THE SCIENTIFIC REVOLUTION

Nicolaus Copernicus (1473–1543)	Published *On the Revolutions of the Heavenly Spheres* (1543); theorized that the sun, rather than the earth, was the center of the galaxy
Paracelsus (1493–1541)	Pioneered the use of chemicals and drugs to address perceived chemical imbalances
Andreas Vesalius (1514–1564)	Published *On the Structure of the Human Body* (1543)
Tycho Brahe (1546–1601)	Built observatories and compiled data for the *Rudolphine Tables*, improved tables of planetary motions
Francis Bacon (1561–1626)	Advocated experimental method, formalizing theory of inductive reasoning known as empiricism
Galileo Galilei (1564–1642)	Used telescopic observation to provide evidence for Copernican hypothesis; experimented to formulate laws of physics, such as inertia
Johannes Kepler (1571–1630)	Used Brahe's data to mathematically prove the Copernican hypothesis; his new laws of planetary motion united for the first time natural philosophy and mathematics; completed the *Rudolphine Tables* in 1627
William Harvey (1578–1657)	Discovered blood circulation (1628)
René Descartes (1596–1650)	Used deductive reasoning to formulate theory of Cartesian dualism
Robert Boyle (1627–1691)	Founded the modern science of chemistry; created the first vacuum; discovered Boyle's law on the properties of gases
Isaac Newton (1642–1727)	Introduced the law of universal gravitation, synthesizing the theories of Copernicus and Galileo

algebraic equations and vice versa. A major step forward in mathematics, Descartes's discovery of analytic geometry provided scientists with an important new tool.

Descartes used mathematics to elaborate a highly influential vision of the workings of the cosmos. Drawing on ancient Greek atomist philosophies, Descartes developed the idea that matter was made up of identical "corpuscules" (tiny particles) that collided together in an endless series of motions, akin to the working of a machine. All occurrences in nature could be analyzed as matter in motion, and, according to Descartes, the total "quantity of motion" in the universe was constant. Descartes's mechanistic philosophy of the universe depended on the idea that a vacuum was impossible, which meant that every action had an equal reaction, continuing in an eternal chain reaction.

Descartes's greatest achievement was to develop his initial vision into a whole philosophy of knowledge and science. When experiments proved that sensory impressions could be wrong, Descartes decided it was necessary to doubt them and everything that could reasonably be doubted, and then, as in geometry, to use deductive reasoning from self-evident truths, which he called "first principles," to ascertain scientific laws. Descartes's reasoning ultimately reduced all substances to "matter" and "mind"—that is, to the physical and the spiritual. His view of the world as consisting of two fundamental entities is known as Cartesian dualism.

Both Bacon's inductive experimentalism and Descartes's deductive mathematical reasoning had flaws. Bacon's inability to appreciate the importance of mathematics and his obsession with practical results illustrated the limitations of antitheoretical empiricism. Likewise, some of Descartes's positions demonstrated the inadequacy of rigid, dogmatic rationalism. He believed, for example, that it was possible to deduce the whole science of medicine from first principles. Although insufficient on their own, Bacon's and Descartes's extreme approaches are combined in the modern scientific method, which began to crystallize in the late seventeenth century.

Medicine, the Body, and Chemistry

The Scientific Revolution, which began with the study of the cosmos, soon transformed the understanding of the human body. For many centuries the ancient Greek physician Galen's explanation of the body carried the same authority as Aristotle's account of the universe. According to Galen, the body contained four humors: blood, phlegm, black bile, and yellow bile. Illness was believed to result from an imbalance of these humors.

Swiss physician and alchemist Paracelsus (1493–1541) was an early proponent of the experimental method in medicine and pioneered the use of chemicals and drugs to address what he saw as chemical, rather than humoral, imbalances. Another experimentalist, Flemish physician Andreas Vesalius (1514–1564), studied anatomy by dissecting human bodies. In 1543, the same year Copernicus published *On the Revolutions of the Heavenly Spheres*, Vesalius issued *On the Structure of the Human Body*. Its two hundred precise drawings revolutionized the understanding of human anatomy, disproving Galen. The experimental approach also led English royal physician William Harvey (1578–1657) to discover the circulation of blood through the veins and arteries in 1628.

The work of Irishman Robert Boyle (1627–1691) led to the development of modern chemistry. Following Paracelsus's lead, he undertook experiments to discover the basic elements of nature, which he believed was composed of infinitely small atoms. Boyle was the first to create a vacuum, thus disproving Descartes's belief that a vacuum could not exist in nature, and he discovered Boyle's law (1662), which states that the pressure of a gas varies inversely with volume.

Science and Religion

It is sometimes assumed that the relationship between science and religion is fundamentally hostile and that the pursuit of knowledge based on reason and proof is incompatible with faith. Yet during the Scientific Revolution most practitioners were devoutly religious and saw their work as contributing to the celebration of God's glory. However, the concept of heliocentrism, which displaced the earth from the center of the universe, threatened the understanding of the place of mankind in creation as stated in Genesis. All religions derived from the Old Testament thus faced difficulties accepting the Copernican system. The leaders of the Catholic Church were initially less hostile than Protestant and Jewish religious leaders, but in the first decades of the sixteenth century Catholic attitudes changed. In 1616 the Holy Office placed the works of Copernicus and his supporters, including Kepler, on a list of books Catholics were forbidden to read.

Out of caution Galileo Galilei silenced his views on heliocentrism for several years, until 1623 saw the ascension of Pope Urban VIII, a man sympathetic to the new science. However, Galileo's 1632 *Dialogue on the Two Chief Systems of the World* went too far. Published in Italian and widely read, it openly lampooned the Aristotelian

Frontispiece to *De Humani Corporis Fabrica* (*On the Structure of the Human Body*) The frontispiece to Vesalius's pioneering work, published in 1543, shows him dissecting a corpse before a crowd of students. This was a revolutionary new hands-on approach for physicians, who usually worked from a theoretical, rather than a practical, understanding of the body. Based on direct observation, Vesalius replaced ancient ideas drawn from Greek philosophy with a much more accurate account of the structure and function of the body. (© SSPL/Science Museum/The Image Works)

view and defended Copernicus. In 1633 Galileo was tried for heresy by the papal Inquisition. Imprisoned and threatened with torture, the aging Galileo recanted.

Science and Society

The rise of modern science had many consequences. First, it led to the rise of a new and expanding social group—the international scientific community. Members of this community were linked together by common interests and values as well as by journals and scientific societies. The personal success of scientists and scholars depended on making new discoveries, and as a result science became competitive. Second, as governments intervened to support and sometimes direct research, the new scientific community became closely tied to the state and its agendas. National academies of science were created under state sponsorship in London in 1662, Paris in 1666, Berlin in 1700, and later across Europe.

It was long believed that the Scientific Revolution was the work of exceptional geniuses. More recently, historians have emphasized the importance of skilled craftsmen in the rise of science, particularly in the development of the experimental method. Many artisans developed a strong interest in emerging scientific ideas, and, in turn, the practice of science in the seventeenth century relied heavily on artisans' expertise in making instruments and conducting precise experiments.

Some things did not change in the Scientific Revolution. For example, scholars willing to challenge received ideas about the natural universe did not question traditional inequalities between the sexes. Instead the emergence of professional science may have worsened the inequality in some ways. When Renaissance courts served as centers of learning, talented noblewomen could find niches in study and research. But the rise of a scientific community raised barriers for women because the universities and academies that furnished professional credentials refused them entry.

There were, however, a number of noteworthy exceptions. In Italy universities and academies did accept women. Across Europe women worked as makers of wax anatomical models and as botanical and zoological illustrators. They were also very much involved in informal scientific communities, attending salons (see "Women and the Enlightenment"), conducting experiments, and writing learned treatises.

How did the Enlightenment emerge, and what were major currents of Enlightenment thought?

Enlightenment
An intellectual and cultural movement in late-seventeenth- and eighteenth-century Europe and the wider world that used rational and critical thinking to debate issues such as political sovereignty, religious tolerance, gender roles, and racial difference.

The Rise and Spread of the Enlightenment

The political, intellectual, and religious developments of the early modern period that gave rise to the Scientific Revolution further contributed to a series of debates about key issues in late-seventeenth- and eighteenth-century Europe and the wider world that came to be known as the **Enlightenment**. By shattering the unity of Western Christendom, the conflicts of the Reformation brought old religious certainties into question; the strong states that emerged to quell the disorder soon inspired questions about political sovereignty and its limits. Increased movement of peoples, goods, and ideas within and among the states of Asia, Africa, Europe, and its colonies offered examples of shockingly different ways of life and values. Finally, the tremendous achievements of the Scientific Revolution inspired intellectuals to believe that answers to all the questions being asked could be found through the use of rational and critical thinking. Progress was possible in human society as well as science.

The Early Enlightenment

Loosely united by certain key questions and ideas, the European Enlightenment (ca. 1690–1789) was a broad intellectual and cultural movement that gained strength gradually and did not reach its maturity until about 1750. Its origins in the late seventeenth century lie in a combination of developments, including political opposition to absolutist rule, religious conflicts between Protestants and Catholics and within Protestantism, and the attempt to apply principles and practices from the Scientific Revolution to human society.

A key crucible for Enlightenment thought was the Dutch Republic, with its proud commitments to religious tolerance and republican rule. When Louis XIV demanded that all Protestants convert to Catholicism, many Huguenots fled the country and resettled in the Dutch Republic. From this haven of tolerance, French Huguenots and their supporters began to publish tracts denouncing religious intolerance and suggesting that only a despotic monarch would deny religious freedom. Their challenge to authority thus combined religious and political issues.

These dual concerns drove the career of one important early Enlightenment writer, Pierre Bayle (1647–1706), a Huguenot who took refuge from government persecution in the Dutch Republic. Bayle critically examined the religious beliefs and persecutions of the past in his *Historical and Critical Dictionary* (1697). Demonstrating that human beliefs had been extremely varied and very often mistaken, he concluded that nothing can ever be known beyond all doubt, a view known as skepticism.

The Dutch Jewish philosopher Baruch Spinoza (1632–1677) was a key figure in the transition from the Scientific Revolution to the Enlightenment. Deeply inspired by advances in the Scientific Revolution, Spinoza sought to apply natural philosophy to thinking about human society. He borrowed Descartes's emphasis on rationalism and his methods of deductive reasoning but rejected the French thinker's mind-body dualism. Instead Spinoza came to espouse monism, the idea that mind and body are united in one substance and that God and nature were merely two names for the same thing. He envisioned a deterministic universe in which good and evil were merely relative values, and human actions were shaped by outside circumstances, not free will. Spinoza was excommunicated by the relatively large Jewish community of Amsterdam for his controversial religious ideas, but he was heralded by his Enlightenment successors as a model of personal virtue and courageous intellectual autonomy.

German philosopher and mathematician Gottfried Wilhelm von Leibniz (1646–1716) refuted both Cartesian dualism and Spinoza's monism. Instead he adopted the idea of an infinite number of substances, or "monads," from which all matter is composed according to a harmonious divine plan. His *Theodicy* (1710) declared that ours must be "the best of all possible worlds" because it was created by an omnipotent and benevolent God.

Out of this period of intellectual turmoil came John Locke's *Essay Concerning Human Understanding* (1690), perhaps the most important text of the early Enlightenment. In this work Locke (1632–1704) set forth a new theory about how human beings learn and form their ideas. Whereas Descartes based his deductive logic on the conviction that certain first principles, or innate ideas, are imbued in humans by God, Locke insisted that all ideas are derived from experience. According to Locke, the human mind at birth is like a blank tablet, or tabula rasa, on which understanding and beliefs are inscribed by experience. Human development is therefore

sensationalism An idea, espoused by John Locke, that all human ideas and thoughts are produced as a result of sensory impressions.

philosophes A group of French intellectuals who proclaimed that they were bringing the light of knowledge to their fellow humans.

determined by external forces, like education and social institutions, not innate characteristics. Locke's essay contributed to the theory of **sensationalism**, the idea that all human ideas and thoughts are produced as a result of sensory impressions.

The Influence of the Philosophes

Divergences among the early thinkers of the Enlightenment show that, while they shared many of the same premises and questions, the answers they found differed widely. The spread of this spirit of inquiry and debate owed a great deal to the work of the **philosophes**, a group of influential French intellectuals who proclaimed that they were bringing the light of knowledge to their fellow humans.

To appeal to the public and get around the censors, the philosophes wrote novels and plays, histories and philosophies, and dictionaries and encyclopedias, all filled with satire and double meanings to spread their message. One of the greatest philosophes, the baron de Montesquieu (mahn-tuhs-KYOO) (1689–1755), pioneered this approach in *The Persian Letters* (1721). This work consists of letters supposedly written by two Persian travelers, Usbek and Rica, who as outsiders see European customs in unique ways and thereby allow Montesquieu a vantage point for criticizing existing practices and beliefs.

Disturbed by the growth in royal power under Louis XIV and inspired by the example of the physical sciences, Montesquieu set out to apply the critical method to the problem of government in *The Spirit of Laws* (1748). Arguing that forms of government were shaped by history, geography, and customs, Montesquieu identified three main types: monarchies, republics, and despotisms. A great admirer of the English parliamentary system, Montesquieu argued for a separation of powers, with political power divided among different classes and legal estates holding unequal rights and privileges. Decades later, his theory of separation of powers had a great impact on the constitutions of the United States in 1789 and of France in 1791.

The most famous philosophe was François-Marie Arouet, known by the pen name Voltaire (1694–1778). In his long career, Voltaire wrote more than seventy witty volumes, hobnobbed with royalty, and died a millionaire through shrewd speculations. His early career, however, was turbulent, and he was twice arrested for insulting noblemen. To avoid a prison term, Voltaire moved to England for three years, and there he came to share Montesquieu's enthusiasm for English liberties and institutions.

Returning to France, Voltaire met Gabrielle-Emilie Le Tonnelier de Breteuil, marquise du Châtelet (1706–1749), a gifted noblewoman. Madame du Châtelet invited Voltaire to live in her country house at Cirey in Lorraine. Passionate about science, she studied physics and mathematics and published the first French translation of Newton's *Principia*. Excluded from the Royal Academy of Sciences because she was a woman, Madame du Châtelet had no doubt that women's limited role in science was due to their unequal education.

While living at Cirey, Voltaire wrote works praising England and popularizing English scientific progress. Yet, like almost all the philosophes, Voltaire was a reformer, not a revolutionary. He pessimistically concluded that the best form of government was a good monarch, since human beings "are very rarely worthy to govern themselves." Nor did Voltaire believe in social and economic equality. The only realizable equality, Voltaire thought, was that "by which the citizen only depends on the laws which protect the freedom of the feeble against the ambitions of the strong."[1]

Voltaire's philosophical and religious positions were much more radical. Voltaire believed in God, but, like many Enlightenment thinkers, he rejected the established church in favor of **deism**, belief in a distant, noninterventionist deity. Above all, Voltaire and most of the philosophes hated religious intolerance, which they believed led to fanaticism and cruelty.

> **deism** Belief in a distant, noninterventionist deity, shared by many Enlightenment thinkers.

The strength of the philosophes lay in their number, dedication, and organization. Their greatest achievement was a group effort — the seventeen-volume *Encyclopedia: The Rational Dictionary of the Sciences, the Arts, and the Crafts*, edited by Denis Diderot (1713–1784) and Jean le Rond d'Alembert (1717–1783). Completed in 1765 despite opposition from the French state and the Catholic Church, the *Encyclopedia* contained hundreds of thousands of articles by leading scientists, writers, skilled workers, and progressive priests. Science and the industrial arts were exalted, religion and immortality questioned. Intolerance, legal injustice, and out-of-date social institutions were openly criticized.

After about 1770 a number of thinkers and writers began to attack the philosophes' faith in reason and progress. The most famous of these was the Swiss intellectual Jean-Jacques Rousseau (1712–1778). Like other Enlightenment thinkers, Rousseau was passionately committed to individual freedom. Unlike them, however, he attacked rationalism and civilization as destroying, rather than liberating, the individual. Warm, spontaneous feeling, Rousseau believed, had to complement and correct cold intellect. Rousseau's ideals greatly influenced the early Romantic movement, which rebelled against the culture of the Enlightenment in the late eighteenth century.

Rousseau's contribution to political theory in *The Social Contract* (1762) was based on two fundamental concepts: the general will and popular sovereignty. According to Rousseau, the **general will** is sacred and absolute, reflecting the common interests of all people, who have displaced the monarch as the holder of sovereign power. The general will is not necessarily the will of the majority, however. At times the general will may be the authentic, long-term needs of the people as correctly interpreted by a farseeing minority.

> **general will** A concept associated with Rousseau, referring to the common interests of all the people, who have displaced the monarch as the holder of sovereign power.

Enlightenment Movements Across Europe

The Enlightenment was a movement of international dimensions, with thinkers traversing borders in a constant exchange of visits, letters, and printed materials. The Republic of Letters, as this international group of scholars and writers was called, was a truly cosmopolitan set of networks stretching from western Europe to its colonies in the Americas, to Russia and eastern Europe, and along the routes of trade and empire to Africa and Asia.

Within this broad international conversation, scholars have identified regional and national particularities. Outside France, many strains of Enlightenment thought sought to reconcile reason with faith, rather than emphasizing the errors of religious fanaticism and intolerance. Some scholars point to a distinctive "Catholic Enlightenment" that aimed to renew and reform the church from within, looking to divine grace rather than human will as the source of social progress.

The Scottish Enlightenment, centered in Edinburgh, was marked by an emphasis on common sense and scientific reasoning. A central figure in Edinburgh was David Hume (1711–1776). Building on Locke's writings on learning, Hume argued that

MAJOR FIGURES OF THE ENLIGHTENMENT

Baruch Spinoza (1632–1677)	Early Enlightenment thinker excommunicated from the Jewish community for his concept of a deterministic universe
John Locke (1632–1704)	*Essay Concerning Human Understanding* (1690)
Gottfried Wilhelm von Leibniz (1646–1716)	Early German philosopher and mathematician
Pierre Bayle (1647–1706)	*Historical and Critical Dictionary* (1697)
Montesquieu (1689–1755)	*The Persian Letters* (1721); *The Spirit of Laws* (1748)
Voltaire (1694–1778)	Renowned French philosopher and author of more than seventy works
Gabrielle-Emilie Le Tonnelier de Breteuil, marquise du Châtelet (1706–1749)	French scholar and supporter of equal education for women
David Hume (1711–1776)	Central figure of the Scottish Enlightenment
Jean-Jacques Rousseau (1712–1778)	*The Social Contract* (1762)
Denis Diderot (1713–1784) and **Jean le Rond d'Alembert** (1717–1783)	Editors of *Encyclopedia: The Rational Dictionary of the Sciences, the Arts, and the Crafts* (1765)
Adam Smith (1723–1790)	*Theory of Moral Sentiments* (1759); *An Inquiry into the Nature and Causes of the Wealth of Nations* (1776)
Immanuel Kant (1724–1804)	*On the Different Races of Man* (1775); *What Is Enlightenment?* (1784)

the human mind is really nothing but a bundle of impressions. These impressions originate only in sensory experiences and our habits of joining these experiences together. Since our ideas ultimately reflect only our sensory experiences, our reason cannot tell us anything about questions that cannot be verified by sensory experience (in the form of controlled experiments or mathematics), such as the origin of the universe or the existence of God. Hume further argued, in opposition to Descartes, that reason alone could not supply moral principles and that they derived instead from emotions and desires, such as feelings of approval or shame. Hume's rationalistic inquiry thus ended up undermining the Enlightenment's faith in the power of reason by emphasizing the superiority of the passions over reason in driving human behavior.

Hume's ideas had a formative influence on another major figure of the Scottish Enlightenment, Adam Smith (1723–1790). In his *Theory of Moral Sentiments* (1759), Smith argued that social interaction produced feelings of mutual sympathy that led people to behave in ethical ways, despite inherent tendencies toward self-interest. Smith believed that the thriving commercial life of the eighteenth century was likely to produce civic virtue through the values of competition, fair play, and individual autonomy. In *An Inquiry into the Nature and Causes of the Wealth of Nations* (1776), Smith attacked the laws and regulations created by mercantilist governments that, he argued, prevented commerce from reaching its full capacity (see "Mercantilism and Colonial Wars" in Chapter 18). For Smith, ordinary people were capable of forming correct judgments based on their own experience and should therefore not be hampered by government regulations. Instead, the pursuit of individual self-interest in a competitive market would lead to rising prosperity and greater social equality. Smith's **economic liberalism** became the dominant form of economic thought in the early nineteenth century.

Inspired by philosophers of moral sentiments, like Hume and Smith, as well as by physiological studies of the role of the nervous system in human perception, the celebration of sensibility became an important element of eighteenth-century culture. Sensibility referred to an acute sensitivity of the nerves and brain to outside stimuli that produced strong emotional and physical reactions. Novels, plays, and other literary genres depicted moral and aesthetic sensibility as a particular characteristic of women and the upper classes. The proper relationship between reason and the emotions became a key question.

After 1760 Enlightenment ideas were hotly debated in the German-speaking states, often in dialogue with Christian theology. Immanuel Kant (1724–1804) was the greatest German philosopher of his day. Kant posed the question of the age when he published a pamphlet in 1784 titled *What Is Enlightenment?* He answered, "*Sapere Aude* (dare to know)! 'Have the courage to use your own understanding' is therefore the motto of enlightenment." He argued that if intellectuals were granted the freedom to exercise their reason publicly in print, enlightenment would surely follow. Kant was no revolutionary; he also insisted that in their private lives, individuals must obey all laws, no matter how unreasonable. Like other Enlightenment figures in central and east-central Europe, Kant thus tried to reconcile absolutism and religious faith with a critical public sphere.

Important developments in Enlightenment thought also took place in the Italian peninsula. After achieving independence from Habsburg rule (1734), the kingdom of Naples entered a period of intellectual flourishing. In northern Italy a central figure was Cesare Beccaria (1738–1794). His *On Crimes and Punishments* (1764) was a passionate plea for reform of the penal system that decried the use of torture, arbitrary imprisonment, and capital punishment and advocated the prevention of crime over its punishment.

economic liberalism
The theory, associated with Adam Smith, that the pursuit of individual self-interest in a competitive market would lead to rising prosperity and greater social equality, rendering government intervention unnecessary and undesirable.

Key Issues of Enlightenment Debate

How did Enlightenment thinkers address issues of cultural and social difference and political power?

The Scientific Revolution and the political and religious conflicts of the late seventeenth century were not the only developments that influenced European thinkers. Europeans' increased interactions with non-European peoples and cultures also helped produce the Enlightenment spirit. Enlightenment thinkers struggled to assess differences between Western and non-Western cultures, often adopting Eurocentric views, but sometimes expressing admiration for other societies. These same thinkers focused a great deal of attention on other forms of cultural and social difference, developing new ideas about race, gender, and political power. Although new "scientific" ways of thinking often served to justify inequality, the Enlightenment did see a rise in religious tolerance, a particularly crucial issue for Europe's persecuted Jewish population.

Shifting Views of the Non-Western World

In the wake of the great discoveries of the fifteenth and sixteenth centuries, the rapidly growing travel literature taught Europeans that the peoples of China, India, Africa, and the Americas had very different beliefs and customs. Educated Europeans began to look at truth and morality in relative, rather than absolute, terms.

Portrait of Mary Wortley Montagu in Turkish Attire Lady Mary Wortley Montagu accompanied her husband, the British ambassador to the Ottoman Empire, on his diplomatic mission from 1717 to 1719. Her letters to friends and relatives provide a rare glimpse of the sultan's court and an unusually sympathetic depiction of life in the Muslim empire, including a positive appreciation of the status of Ottoman women. Lady Montagu had several portraits painted of herself in Ottoman dress, reflecting her fascination with Ottoman culture. (NYPL/ Science Source/Getty Images)

The powerful and advanced nations of Asia were obvious sources of comparison with the West. Seventeenth-century Jesuit missionaries served as a conduit for transmission of knowledge to the West about Chinese history and culture. The philosopher and mathematician Leibniz corresponded with Jesuits stationed in China, coming to believe that Chinese ethics and political philosophy were superior but that Europeans had equaled China in science and technology; some scholars believe his concept of monads was influenced by Confucian teaching on the inherent harmony between the cosmic order and human society.[2]

During the eighteenth century Enlightenment opinion on China was divided. Voltaire and some other philosophes revered China—without ever visiting or seriously studying it—as an ancient culture replete with wisdom and learning, ruled by benevolent absolutist monarchs. They enthusiastically embraced Confucianism as a natural religion in which universal moral truths were uncovered by reason. By contrast, Montesquieu and Diderot criticized China as a despotic land ruled by fear.

Attitudes toward Islam and the Muslim world were similarly mixed. As the Ottoman military threat receded at the end of the seventeenth century, some Enlightenment thinkers assessed Islam favorably. Others, including Spinoza, saw Islamic culture as superstitious and favorable to despotism. In most cases, writing about Islam and Muslim cultures served primarily as a means to reflect on Western values and practices.

One writer with considerable personal experience in a Muslim country was Lady Mary Wortley Montagu, wife of the English ambassador to the Ottoman Empire. Her letters challenged prevailing ideas by depicting Turkish people as sympathetic and civilized. Montagu also disputed the notion that women were more oppressed in Ottoman society than at home in Europe.

Apart from debates about Asian and Muslim lands, the "discovery" of the New World and subsequent explorations in the Pacific Ocean also destabilized existing norms and values in Europe. One popular idea, among Rousseau and others, was that indigenous peoples of the Americas were living examples of "natural man," who embodied the essential goodness of humanity uncorrupted by decadent society.

New Definitions of Race

As scientists developed taxonomies of plant and animal species in response to discoveries in the Americas, they also began to classify humans into hierarchically ordered "races" and to speculate on the origins of perceived racial differences. The French naturalist Georges-Louis Leclerc, comte de Buffon (1707–1788), argued that humans originated with one species that then developed into distinct races due largely to climatic conditions.

Enlightenment thinkers such as David Hume and Immanuel Kant helped popularize these ideas. In *Of Natural Characters* (1748), Hume expressed his conviction that "negroes and in general all other species of men" were "naturally inferior to the whites."[3] In *On the Different Races of Man* (1775), Kant claimed that there were four human races, each of which derived from an original race. According to Kant, the closest descendants of the original race were the white inhabitants of northern Germany. (Scientists now know that humans originated in Africa.)

Using the word *race* to designate biologically distinct groups of humans was new in European thought. Previously, Europeans had grouped other peoples into "nations" based on their historical, political, and cultural affiliations, rather than on supposedly innate physical differences. While Europeans had long believed they were culturally superior to people from other nations, the new idea that racial difference was physical and innate rather than cultural taught them they were biologically superior as well. In turn, scientific racism helped legitimize and justify the tremendous growth of slavery that occurred during the eighteenth century.

Racist ideas did not go unchallenged. The abbé Raynal's *History of the Two Indies* (1770) fiercely attacked slavery and the abuses of European colonization. *Encyclopedia* editor Denis Diderot adopted Montesquieu's technique of criticizing European attitudes through the voice of outsiders in his dialogue between Tahitian villagers and their European visitors. Former slaves, like Olaudah Equiano and Ottobah Cugoano, published eloquent memoirs testifying to the horrors of slavery and the innate equality of all humans. These challenges to racism, however, were in the minority. More often, Enlightenment thinkers supported racial inequality.

Women and the Enlightenment

Dating back to the Renaissance debate about women, the question of women's proper role in society and the nature of gender differences fascinated Enlightenment thinkers. Some philosophes championed greater rights and expanded education for women, claiming that the position and treatment of women were the best indicators of a society's level of civilization and decency. In the 1780s the marquis de Condorcet, a celebrated mathematician and contributor to the *Encyclopedia*, went so far as to urge that women should share equal rights with men. This was a rare position; most philosophes espoused modest reforms and did not challenge male superiority over women.

From the first years of the Enlightenment, women writers made crucial contributions both to debates about women's rights and to the broader Enlightenment discussion. In 1694 Mary Astell published *A Serious Proposal to the Ladies*, which encouraged women to aspire to the life of the mind and proposed the creation of a women's college. Astell also harshly criticized the institution of marriage. Echoing arguments made against the absolute authority of kings during the Glorious Revolution (see "Constitutional Monarchy" in Chapter 18), she argued that husbands should not exercise absolute control over their wives in marriage. Yet Astell, like most female authors of the period, was careful to acknowledge women's God-given duties to be good wives and mothers.

The explosion of printed literature over the eighteenth century (see "Urban Life and the Public Sphere") brought significant numbers of women writers into print, but they remained a small proportion of published authors. In the second half of the eighteenth century, women produced some 15 percent of published novels, the genre in which they enjoyed the greatest success. They represented a much smaller percentage of nonfiction authors.[4]

If they remained marginal in the world of publishing, women played a much more active role in the informal dimensions of the Enlightenment: conversation,

Enlightenment Culture

Salons originated in seventeenth-century Paris and became social institutions during the cultural flourishing encouraged by French king Louis XIV.

They were gatherings hosted by wealthy women for discussion of the latest literary publications, theatrical performances, and scientific discoveries. During the eighteenth century salons became centers for the dissemination of the new ideas of the Enlightenment. The female hostesses of the salons, known as *salonnières*, opened their homes once or twice a week to carefully cultivated groups of guests that included aristocrats, rich financiers, high-ranking officials, and noteworthy foreigners. The *salonnières* guided the discussion and supervised the guests' social interaction. Madame du Deffand, a prominent *salonnière*, hosted such guests as Montesquieu, d'Alembert, and Benjamin Franklin, then serving as the first United States ambassador to France. Invitations to salons were highly coveted; introductions to the rich and powerful could make the career of an ambitious writer, and, in turn, the social elite found amusement and cultural prestige in their ties to up-and-coming artists and men of letters.

Salons did not keep formal records, but historians have learned about them from letters and memoirs written by *salonnières* and their guests. One of the few visual representations of the salons is this paint-ing, which depicts an actor performing the first reading of a new play by Voltaire at a 1755 meeting of the salon of Madame Geoffrin. The painter, Anicet Charles Gabriel Lemonnier, was a regular guest at Geoffrin's salon and benefited from her patronage. Virtually all the individuals he has depicted here are recognizable members of Parisian salon society, including Enlightenment writers Diderot, d'Alembert, and Rousseau. Lemonnier created the work in 1812 as a commission for the empress Josephine; thus it must be seen as an imaginative reconstruction of the salon, created several decades after it took place.

QUESTIONS FOR ANALYSIS

1. Which of these people do you think is the hostess, Madame Geoffrin, and why? What can we learn about Geoffrin from this painting of the salon hosted in her home?
2. Given that the salon was a central institution of the Enlightenment, what does this painting tell you about who belonged to the Enlightenment movement? How would you describe attendees in terms of social status, gender, and age?
3. Why would government ministers and wealthy nobles wish to socialize on a regular basis with philosophes, who were critical of French politics and society? How does this image help you understand the way that Enlightenment ideas were perceived by the elite of society?

---

salons Regular social gatherings held by talented and rich Parisian women in their homes, where philosophes and their followers met to discuss literature, science, and philosophy.

letter writing, travel, and patronage of artists and writers. A key element of their informal participation was as salon hostesses, or *salonnières* (sah-lahn-ee-EHRZ). **Salons,** which began in the early seventeenth century and reached their peak from 1740 to 1789, were weekly meetings held in wealthy households. They brought together writers, aristocrats, financiers, and noteworthy foreigners for meals and witty discussions of the latest trends in literature, science, and philosophy. (See "Analyzing the Evidence: Enlightenment Culture," above.)

Women's prominent role as society hostesses and patrons of the arts and letters outraged some Enlightenment thinkers. According to Rousseau, women and men were radically different beings and should play diametrically opposed roles in life. Destined by nature to assume the active role in sexual relations, men were naturally suited for the rough-and-tumble worlds of politics and public life. Women's role was to attract male sexual desire in order to marry and have children. For Rousseau, women's love for displaying themselves in public, attending salons, and pulling the strings of power was unnatural and had a corrupting effect on both politics and society.

(*The First Reading at Madame Geoffrin's of Voltaire's Tragedy "L'Orphelin de la Chine,"* 1755, by Gabriel Lemonnier [1743–1824] [oil on canvas]/ Musée National du Château de Malmaison, France/DEA/Gianni Dagli Orti/Getty Images)

Rousseau's emphasis on the natural laws governing women echoed a wider shift in ideas about gender during this period, as doctors, scientists, and philosophers increasingly agreed that women's essential characteristics were determined by their sexual organs and reproductive functions. This turn to nature, rather than tradition or scripture, as a means to understand human society had parallels in contemporary views on racial difference.

Enlightened Absolutism and Its Limits

Enlightenment thinkers' insistence on questioning long-standing traditions and norms inevitably led to issues of power and politics. Most philosophes were political moderates, who distrusted the uneducated masses and hoped for reform, not revolution. As Enlightenment ideas reached from Parisian salons to the centers of government, some absolutist rulers, without renouncing their own absolute authority, took up the call to reform their governments in accordance with the rational and humane principles of the Enlightenment. The result was what historians have called the **enlightened absolutism** of the later eighteenth century. This concept was reflected

enlightened absolutism
Term coined by historians to describe the rule of eighteenth-century monarchs who, without renouncing their own absolute authority, took up the call to reform their governments in accordance with the rational and humane principles of the Enlightenment.

575

in programs of reform in Prussia, Russia, and Austria. (Similar programs in France and Spain will be discussed in Chapter 22.)

Frederick II (r. 1740–1786) of Prussia, known as Frederick the Great, promoted religious tolerance and free speech and improved the educational system. Under his reign, Prussia's laws were simplified, torture of prisoners was abolished, and judges decided cases quickly and impartially. However, Frederick did not free the serfs of Prussia; instead he extended the privileges of the nobility over them.

Frederick's reputation as an enlightened prince was rivaled by that of Catherine the Great of Russia (r. 1762–1796). Catherine pursued three major goals. First, she worked hard to continue Peter the Great's efforts to bring the culture of western Europe to Russia (see "Peter the Great and Russia's Turn to the West" in Chapter 18). Catherine's second goal was domestic reform. Like Frederick, she restricted the practice of torture, allowed limited religious tolerance, and tried to improve education and local government. The philosophes applauded these measures and hoped more would follow.

These hopes were dashed by a massive uprising of serfs in 1733 under the leadership of a Cossack soldier named Emelian Pugachev. Although Pugachev was ultimately captured and executed, his rebellion shocked Russian rulers. After 1775 Catherine gave nobles absolute control of their serfs and extended serfdom into new areas. In 1785 she formally freed nobles from taxes and state service. Under Catherine the Russian nobility thus attained its most exalted position, and serfdom entered its most oppressive phase.

Catherine's third goal was territorial expansion. Her armies subjugated the last descendants of the Mongols and the Crimean Tartars and began the conquest of the Caucasus on the border between Europe and Asia. Her greatest coup was the partition of Poland, which took place in stages from 1772 to 1795 (Map 19.1).

Joseph II (r. 1780–1790), the Austrian Habsburg emperor, was perhaps the most sincere proponent of enlightened absolutism. Joseph abolished serfdom in 1781, and in 1789 he decreed that peasants could pay landlords in cash rather than through compulsory labor. When Joseph died at forty-nine, the Habsburg empire was in turmoil. His brother Leopold II (r. 1790–1792) canceled Joseph's radical edicts in order to re-establish order.

Perhaps the best example of the limitations of enlightened absolutism is the debates surrounding the possible emancipation of the Jews. For the most part, Jews in Europe were confined to tiny, overcrowded ghettos; were excluded by law from most occupations; and could be ordered out of a kingdom at a moment's notice.

In the eighteenth century an Enlightenment movement known as the **Haskalah** emerged from within the European Jewish community, led by the Prussian philosopher Moses Mendelssohn (1729–1786). Christian and Jewish Enlightenment philosophers, including Mendelssohn, began to advocate for freedom and civil rights for European Jews.

Arguments for tolerance won some ground, especially under Joseph II of Austria. Most monarchs, however, refused to entertain the idea of emancipation. In 1791 Catherine the Great established the Pale of Settlement, a territory encompassing modern-day Belarus, Lithuania, Latvia, Moldova, Ukraine, and parts of Poland, in which most Jews were required to live until the Russian Revolution of 1917.

Haskalah A Jewish Enlightenment movement led by Prussian philosopher Moses Mendelssohn.

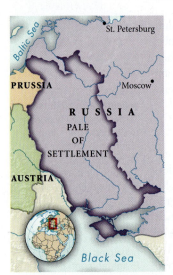

The Pale of Settlement, 1791

MAPPING THE PAST

MAP 19.1 The Partition of Poland, 1772–1795 In 1772 the threat of war between Russia and Austria arose over Russian gains from the Ottoman Empire. To satisfy desires for expansion without fighting, Prussia's Frederick the Great proposed dividing parts of Poland among Austria, Prussia, and Russia. In 1793 and 1795 the three powers partitioned the remainder, and Poland ceased to exist as an independent nation.

ANALYZING THE MAP Of the three powers that divided the kingdom of Poland, which benefited the most? How did the partition affect the geographical boundaries of each state, and what was the significance of these geographical boundaries? What border with the former Poland remained unchanged? Why do you think this was the case?

CONNECTIONS Why was Poland vulnerable to partition in the later half of the eighteenth century? What does the fact that a country could simply cease to exist on the map say about European politics at the time? Could such an event happen today? Why or why not?

Economic Change and the Atlantic World

> How did economic and social change and the rise of Atlantic trade interact with Enlightenment ideas?

Enlightenment debates took place within a rapidly evolving material world. Agricultural reforms contributed to a rise in population that in turned fueled substantial economic growth in eighteenth-century Europe. A new public sphere emerged in the growing cities of Europe and its colonies in which people exchanged opinions in cafés, bookstores, and other spaces. A consumer revolution brought fashion and imported foods into the reach of common people for the first time.

These economic and social changes were fed by an increasingly integrated Atlantic economy that circulated finished European products, raw materials from the colonies, and enslaved people from Africa. Over time, the people, goods, and ideas that crisscrossed the ocean created distinctive Atlantic communities and identities.

Economic and Demographic Change

The seventeenth century saw important gains in agricultural productivity in northwestern Europe that slowly spread throughout the continent. Using new scientific techniques of observation and experimentation, a group of scientists, government officials, and a few big landowners devised agricultural practices and tools that raised crop yields dramatically, especially in England and the Netherlands. These included new forms of crop rotation, better equipment, and selective breeding of livestock. The controversial process of **enclosure**, fencing off common land to create privately owned fields, allowed a break with traditional methods but at the cost of reducing poor farmers' access to land.

Colonial plants also provided new sources of calories and nutrition. Introduced into Europe from the Americas—along with corn, squash, tomatoes, and many other useful plants—the potato provided an excellent new food source and offset the lack of fresh vegetables and fruits in common people's winter diet. The potato had become an important dietary supplement in much of Europe by the end of the eighteenth century.

Increases in agricultural productivity and better nutrition, combined with the disappearance of bubonic plague after 1720 and improvements in sewage and water supply, contributed to the tremendous growth of the European population in the eighteenth century. The explosion of population was a major phenomenon in all European countries, leading to a doubling of the number of Europeans between 1700 and 1835.

Population growth increased the number of rural workers with little or no land, and this in turn contributed to the development of industry in rural areas. The poor in the countryside increasingly needed to supplement their agricultural earnings with other types of work. **Cottage industry**, which consisted of manufacturing with hand tools in peasant cottages and work sheds, grew markedly in the eighteenth century, particularly in England and the Low Countries.

Despite the rise in rural industry, life in the countryside was insufficient to support the rapidly growing population. Many people thus

enclosure The controversial process of fencing off common land to create privately owned fields that increased agricultural production at the cost of reducing poor farmers' access to land.

cottage industry Manufacturing with hand tools in peasant cottages and work sheds, a form of economic activity that became important in eighteenth-century Europe.

Cottage Industry Many steps went into making textiles. This 1791 illustration of the different tasks involved in spinning yarn is based on the artist's observations of linen manufacture in the north of Ireland. The yarn was spun on the wheel and then wound on the clock reel to measure it into "hanks" of set length. After being boiled in a pot over the fire and dried, the yarn was ready for weaving. (The British Library, London, UK/© British Library Board. All Rights Reserved/Bridgeman Images)

left their small villages to join the tide of migration to the cities, especially after 1750. London and Paris swelled to over five hundred thousand people, while Naples and Amsterdam had populations of more than one hundred thousand. It was in the bustling public life of these cities that the Enlightenment emerged and took root.

The Atlantic Economy

European economic growth in the eighteenth century was spurred by the expansion of trade across the Atlantic Ocean. Commercial exchange in the Atlantic is often referred to as the triangle trade, designating a three-way transport of goods: European commodities to Africa; enslaved Africans to the colonies; and colonial goods back to Europe. This model highlights some of the most important flows of trade but significantly oversimplifies the picture. For example, a brisk intercolonial trade existed, with the Caribbean slave colonies importing food from other American colonies in exchange for sugar and slaves (Map 19.2).

Moreover, the Atlantic economy was inextricably linked to trade with the Indian and Pacific Oceans. The rising economic and political power of Europeans in the eighteenth century thus drew on the connections they established between the long-standing Asian and Atlantic trade worlds.

Over the course of the eighteenth century the economies of European nations bordering the Atlantic Ocean relied more and more on colonial exports. In England sales to the mainland colonies of North America and the West Indian sugar islands soared from £500,000 to £4 million (Figure 19.1). Exports to England's colonies in Ireland and India also rose substantially from 1700 to 1800.

At the core of this Atlantic world was the misery and profit of the Atlantic slave trade (see "The African Slave Trade" in Chapter 20). The brutal practice intensified dramatically after 1700 and especially after 1750 with the growth of trade and the increase in demand for slave-produced goods. English dominance of the slave trade provided another source of large profits to the home country. (See "Global Viewpoints: Malachy Postlethwayt and Olaudah Equiano on the Abolition of Slavery," page 581.)

The French also profited enormously from colonial trade in the eighteenth century, even after losing their vast North American territories to England in 1763. The Caribbean colonies of Saint-Domingue (modern-day Haiti), Martinique, and Guadeloupe provided immense fortunes from slave-based plantation agriculture. The wealth generated from colonial trade fostered the confidence of the merchant classes in Nantes, Bordeaux, and other large cities, and merchants soon joined other elite groups clamoring for more political power.

The third major player in the Atlantic economy, Spain, also saw its colonial fortunes improve during the eighteenth century. Its mercantilist goals were boosted by a recovery in silver production. Spanish territory in North America expanded significantly in the second half of the eighteenth century. At the close of the Seven Years' War (1756–1763)

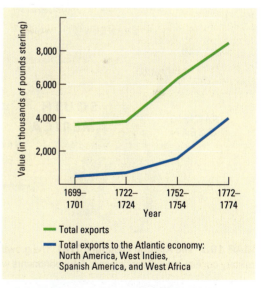

FIGURE 19.1 Exports of English Manufactured Goods, 1700–1774 While trade between England and Europe stagnated after 1700, English exports to Africa and the Americas boomed and greatly stimulated English economic development.

(Source: Data from R. Davis, "English Foreign Trade, 1700–1774," *Economic History Review*, 2nd ser., 15 [1962]: 302–303.)

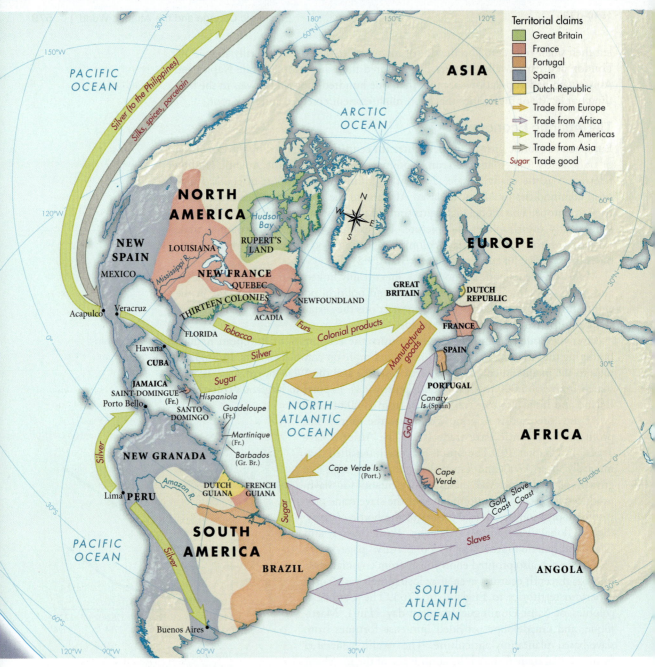

MAP 19.2 The Atlantic Economy, 1701 The growth of trade encouraged both economic development and military conflict in the Atlantic basin. Four continents were linked together by the exchange of goods and slaves.

(see "The Seven Years' War" in Chapter 22), Spain gained Louisiana from the French, and its influence extended westward all the way to northern California through the efforts of Spanish missionaries and ranchers.

Conflict among European powers in the late seventeenth century led to the rise of privateers in the Caribbean and elsewhere in the Atlantic world; these were ships sanctioned by their home government to attack and pillage those of enemy powers.

Malachy Postlethwayt and Olaudah Equiano on the Abolition of Slavery

As Britain came to dominate transatlantic commerce during the eighteenth century, debate arose over the morality of the slave trade and the country's involvement in it. Malachy Postlethwayt, an economist, rejected criticism of slavery by arguing that African nations treated their subjects much worse than slave traders did and that the benefits of Christianity by far outstripped any disadvantages slaves might endure. In his famous autobiography, former slave Olaudah Equiano (oh-lah-OO-dah ay-kwee-AH-noh) emphasized the cruelties of slavery. He argued, against authors like Postlethwayt, that trade with free peoples in Africa promised much more economic benefit to Britain than did slavery.

Malachy Postlethwayt, *The National and Private Advantages of the African Trade Considered*

■ Many are prepossessed against this trade, thinking it a barbarous, inhuman and unlawful traffic for a Christian country to trade in Blacks; to which I would beg leave to observe; that though the odious appellation of slaves is annexed to this trade, it being called by some the slave-trade, yet it does not appear from the best enquiry I have been able to make, that the state of those people is changed for the worse, by being servants to our British planters in America; they are certainly treated with great lenity and humanity: and as the improvement of the planter's estates depends upon due care being taken of their healths and lives, I cannot but think their condition is much bettered to what it was in their own country.

Besides, the negro princes in Africa, 'tis well known, are in perpetual war with each other, and since before they had this method of disposing of their prisoners of war to Christian merchants, they were wont not only to be applied to inhuman sacrifices, but to extreme torture and barbarity, their transportation must certainly be a melioration [improvement] of their condition; provided living in a civilized Christian country, is better than living among savages; Nay, if life be preferable to torment and cruel death, their state cannot, with any color or reason, be presumed to be worsened.

Olaudah Equiano, Appeal for the Abolition of Slavery

■ Tortures, murder, and every other imaginable barbarity and iniquity, are practiced upon the poor slaves with impunity. I hope the great slave trade will be abolished. I pray it may be an event at hand. The great body of manufacturers, uniting in the cause, will considerably facilitate and expedite it; and as I have already stated, it is most substantially their interest and advantage, and as such the nation's at large (except those persons concerned in the manufacturing neck yokes, collars, chains, handcuffs, leg bolts, drags, thumb screws, iron muzzles, and coffins; cats, scourges, and other instruments of torture used in the slave trade). In a short time one sentiment will alone prevail, from motives of interest as well as justice and humanity. . . . If the blacks were permitted to remain in their own country, they would double themselves every fifteen years. In proportion to such increase will be the demand for manufactures. Cotton and indigo grow spontaneously in most parts of Africa; a consideration this of no small consequence to the manufacturing towns of Great Britain. It opens a most immense, glorious and happy prospect—the clothing, &c. of a continent ten thousand miles in circumference, and immensely rich in productions of every denomination in return for manufactures.

QUESTIONS FOR ANALYSIS

1. What contrast does Postlethwayt draw between the treatment of African people under slavery and in their home countries? What conclusion does he draw from this contrast?
2. To whom does Equiano address his appeal for abolition of the slave trade? What economic reasons does he provide for trading goods rather than slaves with Africa?

Sources: Malachy Postlethwayt, *The National and Private Advantages of the African Trade Considered* (London: Jon and Paul Knapton, 1746), pp. 4–5; Olaudah Equiano, *The Interesting Narrative of the Life of Olaudah Equiano*, 2d ed., ed. Robert J. Allison (Boston: Bedford/St. Martin's, 2007), pp. 194–195.

Privateers operated with some semblance of legality, whereas the many pirates active in the Caribbean were outlaws subject to brutal punishment. The late seventeenth and early eighteenth centuries constituted the "golden age" of piracy, drawing poor European sailors and escaped slaves into the dangerous but lucrative activity.

Urban Life and the Public Sphere

Urban life in the Atlantic world gave rise to new institutions and practices that encouraged the spread of Enlightenment thought. From about 1700 to 1789 the production and consumption of books grew significantly. Lending libraries, bookshops, cafés, salons, and Masonic lodges provided spaces in which urban people debated new ideas. Together these spaces and institutions helped create a new **public sphere** that celebrated open debate informed by critical reason.

public sphere An idealized intellectual space that emerged in Europe during the Enlightenment. Here, the public came together to discuss important social, economic, and political issues.

The public sphere was an idealized space where members of society came together to discuss the social, economic, and political issues of the day. Although Enlightenment thinkers addressed their ideas to educated and prosperous readers, even poor and illiterate people learned about such issues as they were debated at the marketplace or tavern.

Economic growth in the second half of the eighteenth century also enabled a significant rise in the consumption of finished goods and new foodstuffs that historians have labeled a "consumer revolution." A boom in textile production and cheap reproductions of luxury items meant that the common people could afford to follow fashion for the first time. Colonial trade made previously expensive and rare foodstuffs, such as sugar, tea, coffee, chocolate, and tobacco, widely available.

Culture and Community in the Atlantic World

As contacts among the Atlantic coasts of the Americas, Africa, and Europe became more frequent, and as European settlements grew into well-established colonies, new identities and communities emerged. The term *Creole* referred to people of Spanish or other European ancestry born in the Americas. Wealthy Creoles throughout the Atlantic colonies prided themselves on following European ways of life.

The Consumer Revolution From the mid-eighteenth century on, the cities of western Europe witnessed a new proliferation of consumer goods. Items once limited to the wealthy few — such as fans, watches, snuffboxes, umbrellas, ornamental containers, and teapots — were now reproduced in cheaper versions for middling and ordinary people. The fashion for wide hoopskirts was so popular that the armrests of the chairs of the day, known as Louis XV chairs (left), were specially designed to accommodate them. Enlightenment fascination with Chinese culture was reflected in the tremendous popularity of *chinoiserie*, objects (such as the plate shown here) decorated in imitation of Chinese motifs and techniques. (chair: Louvre, Paris, France/© RMN–Grand Palais/Art Resource, NY; plate: Musée des Beaux-Arts, Moulins, France/Bridgeman Images)

Over time, however, the colonial elite came to feel that their circumstances gave them different interests and characteristics from people of their home countries. Creoles adopted native foods, like chocolate, chili peppers, and squash, and sought relief from tropical disease in native remedies. Also, they began to turn against restrictions from their home countries: Creole traders and planters, along with their counterparts in English colonies, increasingly resented the regulations and taxes imposed by colonial bureaucrats, and such resentment would eventually lead to revolutions against colonial powers (see Chapter 22).

Not all Europeans in the colonies were wealthy or well educated. Numerous poor and lower-middle-class whites worked as clerks, shopkeepers, craftsmen, and laborers. With the exception of the English colonies of North America, white Europeans made up a minority of the population, outnumbered by indigenous peoples in Spanish America and, in the Caribbean, by the growing numbers of enslaved people of African descent. Since most European migrants were men, much of the colonial population of the Atlantic world descended from unions—forced or through consent—of European men and indigenous or African women. Colonial attempts to identify and control racial categories greatly influenced developing Enlightenment thought on racial differences.

In the Spanish and French Caribbean, as in Brazil, many slave masters acknowledged and freed their mixed-race children, leading to sizable populations of free people of color. In the second half of the eighteenth century the prosperity of some free people of color brought a backlash from the white population of Saint-Domingue in the form of new race laws prohibiting nonwhites from marrying whites and forcing them to adopt distinctive attire. In the British colonies of the Caribbean and the southern mainland, by contrast, masters tended to leave their mixed-race progeny in slavery, maintaining a stark discrepancy between free whites and enslaved people of color.[5]

The identities inspired by the Atlantic world were equally complex. In some ways, the colonial encounter helped create new and more fixed forms of identity. Inhabitants of distinct regions of European nations came to see themselves as "Spanish" or "English" when they crossed the Atlantic; similarly, their colonial governments imposed the identity of "Indian" and "African" on peoples with vastly different linguistic, cultural, and political origins. The result was the creation of new Creole communities that melded cultural and social elements of various groups of origin with the new European cultures.

Mixed-race people represented complex mixtures of indigenous, African, and European ancestry, so their status was ambiguous. Spanish administrators applied purity of blood (*limpieza de sangre*) laws—originally used to exclude Jews and Muslims during the reconquista—to indigenous and African peoples. Some mixed-race people sought to enter Creole society and obtain its many official and unofficial privileges by passing as white. Over time, where they existed in any number, mestizos and free people of color established their own communities and social hierarchies based on wealth, family connections, occupation, and skin color. (See "Individuals in Society: Rebecca Protten," page 584.)

Restricted from owning land and holding many occupations in Europe, Jews were eager participants in the new Atlantic economy and established a network of mercantile communities along its trade routes. As in the Old World, Jews in European colonies faced discrimination. Jews were considered to be white Europeans and thus

Rebecca Protten

IN THE MID-1720s A YOUNG GIRL WHO CAME to be known as Rebecca traveled from Antigua to the small Danish sugar colony of St. Thomas, today part of the U.S. Virgin Islands. Eighty-five percent of St. Thomas's four thousand inhabitants were of African descent, almost all enslaved.

Surviving documents refer to Rebecca as a "mulatto," indicating a mixed European and African ancestry. A wealthy Dutch-speaking planter named van Beverhout purchased the girl as a servant, sparing her work in the grueling and deadly sugar fields. Rebecca won the family's favor, and they taught her to read, write, and speak Dutch. They also shared with her their Protestant faith and took the unusual step of freeing her.

As a free woman, she continued to work for the van Beverhouts and to study the Bible and spread its message of spiritual freedom. In 1736 she met missionaries for the Moravian Church, a German-Protestant sect that emphasized emotion and community in worship and devoted its mission work to the enslaved peoples of the Caribbean. The missionaries were struck by Rebecca's piety and her potential to assist their work. As one wrote: "She researches diligently in the Scriptures, loves the Savior, and does much good for other Negro women because she does not simply walk alone with her good ways but instructs them in the Scriptures as well." A letter Rebecca sent to Moravian women in Germany declared: "Oh! Help me to praise him, who has pulled me out of the darkness. I will take up his cross with all my heart and follow the example of his poor life."*

Rebecca soon took charge of the Moravians' female missionary work. Every Sunday and every evening after work, she would walk for miles to lead meetings with enslaved and free black women. The meetings consisted of reading and writing lessons, prayers, hymns, a sermon, and individual discussions in which she encouraged her new sisters in their spiritual growth.

In 1738 Rebecca married a German Moravian missionary, Matthaus Freundlich, a rare but not illegal case of mixed marriage. The same year, her husband bought a plantation, with slaves, to serve as the headquarters of their mission work. The Moravians—and presumably Rebecca herself—wished to spread Christian faith among slaves and improve their treatment, but did not oppose the institution of slavery itself.

A portrait of Rebecca Protten with her second husband and their daughter, Anna-Maria.

(Courtesy of Jon F. Sensbach. Used by permission of the Moravian Archives [Unity Archives, Herrnhut, Germany], GS-393.)

Authorities nonetheless feared that baptized and literate slaves would agitate for freedom, and they imprisoned Rebecca and Matthaus. Only the unexpected arrival of German aristocrat and Moravian leader Count Zinzendorf saved the couple. Exhausted, they left for Germany in 1741, but Matthaus and the couple's young daughter died soon after their arrival.

In Marienborn, a German center of the Moravian faith, Rebecca encountered other black Moravians, who lived in equality alongside their European brethren. In 1746 she married another missionary, Christian Jacob Protten, son of a Danish sailor and, on his mother's side, grandson of a West African king. She and another female missionary from St. Thomas were ordained as deaconesses, probably making them the first women of color to be ordained in the Western Christian Church.

In 1763 Rebecca and her husband set out for her husband's birthplace, the Danish slave fort at Christiansborg (in what is now Accra, Ghana) to establish a school for mixed-race children. Her husband died in 1769, leaving Rebecca a widow once more. She died in obscurity near Christiansborg in 1780.

QUESTIONS FOR ANALYSIS

1. Why did Moravian missionaries assign such an important leadership role to Rebecca? What particular attributes did she offer?
2. Why did Moravians, including Rebecca, accept the institution of slavery instead of fighting to end it?
3. What does Rebecca's story teach us about the Atlantic world of the mid-eighteenth century? What might a philosophe have to say about her life story and its relationship to the ideals of the Enlightenment?

*Quotations from Jon F. Sensbach, *Rebecca's Revival: Creating Black Christianity in the Atlantic World* (Cambridge, Mass.: Harvard University Press, 2006), pp. 61, 63.

ineligible to be slaves, but they did not enjoy equal status with Christians. The status of Jews adds one more element to the complexity of Atlantic identities.

The Atlantic Enlightenment

The colonies of British North America were deeply influenced by the Scottish Enlightenment, with its emphasis on pragmatic approaches to the problems of life. Following the Scottish model, leaders in the colonies adopted a moderate, "commonsense" version of the Enlightenment that emphasized self-improvement and ethical conduct. In most cases, this version of the Enlightenment was perfectly compatible with religion and was chiefly spread through the growing colleges and universities of the colonies.

Northern Enlightenment thinkers often depicted Spain and its American colonies as the epitome of the superstition and barbarity they contested. Nonetheless, the dynasty that took power in Spain in the early eighteenth century followed its own course of enlightened absolutism, just like its counterparts in the rest of Europe. Under King Carlos III (r. 1759–1788) and his son Carlos IV (r. 1788–1808), Spanish administrators attempted to strengthen colonial rule and improve government efficiency. Enlightened administrators debated the status of indigenous peoples and whether it would be better for these peoples if they maintained their distinct legal status or were integrated into Spanish society.

Educated Creoles were well aware of the new currents of thought, and the universities, newspapers, and salons of Spanish America produced their own reform ideas. As in other European colonies, one effect of Enlightenment thought was to encourage Creoles to criticize the policies of the mother country and aspire toward greater autonomy.

Chapter Summary

Decisive breakthroughs in astronomy and physics in the seventeenth century demolished the medieval synthesis of Aristotelian philosophy and Christian theology. The impact of these scientific breakthroughs on intellectual life was enormous, nurturing a new critical attitude in many disciplines. In addition, an international scientific community arose, and state-sponsored academies, which were typically closed to women, advanced scientific research.

Believing that all aspects of life were open to debate and skepticism, Enlightenment thinkers asked challenging questions about religious tolerance, political power, and racial and sexual difference. Enlightenment thinkers drew inspiration from the new peoples and cultures encountered by Europeans and devised new ideas about race as a scientific and biological category. The ideas of the Enlightenment inspired absolutist rulers in central and eastern Europe, but real reforms were limited.

In the second half of the eighteenth century agricultural reforms helped produce tremendous population growth. Economic growth and urbanization favored the spread of Enlightenment thought by producing a public sphere in which ideas could be debated. The expansion of transatlantic trade made economic growth possible, as did the lowering of prices on colonial goods due to the growth of slave labor. Atlantic trade involved the exchange of commodities among Europe, Africa, and the Americas, but it was also linked with trade in the Indian and Pacific Oceans. The movement of people and ideas across the Atlantic helped shape the identities of colonial inhabitants.

NOTES

1. Quoted in G. L. Mosse et al., eds., *Europe in Review* (Chicago: Rand McNally, 1964), p. 156.
2. D. E. Mungello, *The Great Encounter of China and the West, 1500–1800*, 2d ed. (Lanham, Md.: Rowman & Littlefield, 2005), p. 98.
3. Quoted in Emmanuel Chukwudi Eze, ed., *Race and the Enlightenment: A Reader* (Oxford: Blackwell, 1997), p. 33.
4. Aurora Wolfgang, *Gender and Voice in the French Novel, 1730–1782* (Aldershot, U.K.: Ashgate, 2004), p. 8.
5. Orlando Patterson, *Slavery and Social Death* (Cambridge, Mass.: Harvard University Press, 1982), p. 255.

CONNECTIONS

Hailed as the origin of modern thought, the Scientific Revolution must also be seen as a product of its past. With curriculum drawn from Islamic cultural achievements, medieval universities gave rise to important new scholarship in mathematics and natural philosophy. In turn, the ambition and wealth of Renaissance patrons nurtured intellectual curiosity and encouraged scholarly research and foreign exploration. Natural philosophers pioneered new methods of explaining and observing nature while drawing on centuries-old traditions of astrology, alchemy, and magic. A desire to control and profit from empire led the Spanish, followed by their European rivals, to explore and catalogue the flora and fauna of their American colonies. These efforts resulted in new frameworks in natural history.

Enlightenment ideas of the eighteenth century were a similar blend of past and present, progressive and traditional, inward-looking and cosmopolitan. Enlightenment thinkers advocated universal rights and liberties but also preached the biological inferiority of non-Europeans and women. Their principles often served as much to bolster absolutist regimes as to inspire revolutionaries to fight for human rights.

New notions of progress and social improvement would drive Europeans to embark on world-changing revolutions in politics and industry (see Chapters 22 and 23) at the end of the eighteenth century. These revolutions provided the basis for modern democracy and unprecedented scientific advancement. Yet some critics have seen a darker side. For them, the mastery over nature enabled by the Scientific Revolution now threatens to overwhelm the earth's fragile equilibrium, and the Enlightenment belief in the universal application of reason can lead to intolerance of other people's spiritual, cultural, and political values.

As the era of European exploration and conquest gave way to empire building, the eighteenth century witnessed increased consolidation of global markets and bitter competition among Europeans. The eighteenth-century Atlantic world thus tied the shores of Europe, the Americas, and Africa in a web of commercial and human exchange, including the tragedy of slavery, discussed in Chapter 20. The Atlantic world maintained strong ties with trade in the Pacific and the Indian Ocean.

CHAPTER 19 Review and Explore

Identify Key Terms

Identify and explain the significance of each item below.

Copernican hypothesis (p. 560)

law of inertia (p. 561)

law of universal gravitation (p. 562)

empiricism (p. 563)

Enlightenment (p. 566)

sensationalism (p. 568)

philosophes (p. 568)

deism (p. 569)

general will (p. 569)

economic liberalism (p. 571)

salons (p. 574)

enlightened absolutism (p. 575)

Haskalah (p. 576)

enclosure (p. 578)

cottage industry (p. 578)

public sphere (p. 582)

Review the Main Ideas

Answer the focus questions from each section of the chapter.

1. What revolutionary discoveries were made in the sixteenth and seventeenth centuries, and what was their global context? (p. 558)

2. What intellectual and social changes occurred as a result of the Scientific Revolution? (p. 563)

3. How did the Enlightenment emerge, and what were major currents of Enlightenment thought? (p. 566)

4. How did Enlightenment thinkers address issues of cultural and social difference and political power? (p. 571)

5. How did economic and social change and the rise of Atlantic trade interact with Enlightenment ideas? (p. 577)

Make Comparisons and Connections

Analyze the larger developments and continuities within and across chapters.

1. How did medieval and Renaissance developments contribute to the Scientific Revolution? Should the Scientific Revolution be seen as a sharp break with the past or as the culmination of long-term, gradual change?

2. The eighteenth century was the period of the European Enlightenment, which celebrated tolerance and human liberty. Paradoxically, it was also the era of a tremendous increase in slavery, which brought suffering and death to millions. How can you explain this paradox?

3. How did developments in population, global trade, and intellectual life affect each other in the eighteenth century? How and why did developments in one region affect other regions?

TIMELINE

EUROPE

← **ca. 1500–1700** Scientific Revolution

ca. 1600–1789 French salons led by elite women

MIDDLE EAST

← **1453** Ottoman conquest of Constantinople **(Ch. 17)**

← **1501–1722** Safavid Empire in Persia **(Ch. 17)**

EAST ASIA

1582–1610 Jesuit Matteo Ricci in China **(Ch. 21)**

1644–1911 Manchus establish Qing Dynasty in China **(Ch. 21)**

AFRICA

AMERICAS

AUSTRALIA

| 1600 | 1650 | 1700 |

Suggested Resources

BOOKS

Allen, Robert, et al., eds. *Living Standards in the Past: New Perspectives on Well-Being in Asia and Europe.* 2004. Offers rich comparative perspectives on population growth and living standards among common people.

Cañizares-Esguerra, Jorge. *Nature, Empire, and Nation: Explorations of the History of Science in the Iberian World.* 2006. Explores the role of Spain and Spanish America in the development of science in the early modern period.

Curran, Andrew S. *The Anatomy of Blackness: Science and Slavery in an Age of Enlightenment.* 2011. Examines how Enlightenment thinkers transformed traditional thinking about people of African descent into ideas about biological racial difference.

Ellis, Markman. *The Coffee House: A Cultural History.* 2004. An engaging study of the rise of the coffeehouse and its impact on European cultural and social life.

Manning, Susan, and Francis D. Cogliano. *The Atlantic Enlightenment.* 2008. A series of essays examining the exchange of Enlightenment ideas, authors, and texts across the Atlantic Ocean.

Massie, Robert K. *Catherine the Great: Portrait of a Woman.* 2011. Recounts the life story of Catherine, from obscure German princess to enlightened ruler of Russia.

Messbarger, Rebecca. *The Lady Anatomist: The Life and Work of Anna Morandi Manzolini.* 2010. The biography of an Italian woman artist and scientist whose life reflected the opportunities and constraints for eighteenth-century women.

Robertson, John. *The Case for the Enlightenment: Scotland and Naples, 1680–1760.* 2005. A comparative study of Enlightenment movements in Scotland and Naples, emphasizing commonalities between these two small kingdoms on the edges of Europe.

Shapin, Steven. *The Scientific Revolution.* 1996. A concise and well-informed general introduction to the Scientific Revolution.

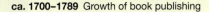

ca. 1700–1789 Growth of book publishing

◆ 1791 Establishment of the Pale of Settlement

ca. 1690–1789 Enlightenment

1780–1790 Reign of Joseph II of Austria

1740–1786 Reign of Frederick the Great of Prussia

1762–1796 Reign of Catherine the Great of Russia

◆ 1765 Philosophes publish *Encyclopedia: The Rational Dictionary of the Sciences, the Arts, and the Crafts*

1789–1807 Ottoman ruler Selim III introduces reforms **(Ch. 25)**

1738–1756 Major famine in West Africa **(Ch. 20)**

1780–1820 Peak of transatlantic slave trade **(Ch. 20)**

1756–1763 Seven Years' War **(Ch. 22)**

◆ 1770 Cook claims land in Australia for Britain **(Ch. 26)**

| 1750 | 1800 | 1850 |

Sorkin, David. *Moses Mendelssohn and the Religious Enlightenment.* 1996. A brilliant study of the Jewish philosopher and of the role of religion in the Enlightenment.

DOCUMENTARIES

Blackbeard: Terror at Sea (National Geographic, 2006). A documentary recounting the exploits of the most famous eighteenth-century pirate.

Newton's Dark Secrets (PBS, 2005). Explores Isaac Newton's fundamental scientific discoveries alongside his religious faith and practice of alchemy.

FEATURE FILMS AND TELEVISION DRAMAS

Amazing Grace (Michael Apted, 2006). An idealistic Briton's struggle to end his country's involvement in the slave trade alongside allies Olaudah Equiano and a repentant former slave-ship captain.

Catherine the Great (A&E, 1995). A made-for-television movie starring Catherine Zeta-Jones as the German princess who becomes Catherine the Great.

Ridicule (Patrice Leconte, 1996). When a provincial nobleman travels to the French court in the 1780s to present a project to drain a malarial swamp in his district, his naïve Enlightenment ideals incur the ridicule of decadent courtiers.

WEBSITES

The Encyclopedia of Diderot & d'Alembert Collaborative Translation Project. A collaborative project to translate the *Encyclopedia* edited by Denis Diderot and Jean le Rond d'Alembert into English, with searchable entries submitted by students and scholars and vetted by experts. **quod.lib.umich.edu/d/did/**

Mapping the Republic of Letters. A site hosted by Stanford University showcasing projects using mapping software to create spatial visualizations based on correspondence and travel of members of the eighteenth-century Republic of Letters. **republicofletters.stanford.edu/**

20

Africa and the World
1400–1800

African states and societies of the early modern period — from the fifteenth through the eighteenth centuries — included a wide variety of languages, cultures, political systems, and levels of economic development. Kingdoms and stateless societies coexisted throughout Africa, from small Senegambian villages to the Songhai (song-GAH-ee) kingdom and its renowned city of Timbuktu in West Africa, and from the Christian state of Ethiopia to the independent Swahili city-states along the East Africa coast. By the fifteenth century Africans had developed a steady rhythm of contact and exchange. Across the vast Sahara, trade goods and knowledge passed back and forth from West Africa to North Africa, and beyond to Europe and the Middle East. The same was true in East Africa, where Indian Ocean traders touched up and down the African coast to deliver goods from Arabia, India, and Asia and to pick up the ivory, gold, spices, and other products representing Africa's rich natural wealth. In the interior as well, extensive trading networks linked African societies across the vast continent.

Modern European intrusion into Africa beginning in the fifteenth century profoundly affected these diverse societies and ancient trading networks. The intrusion led to the transatlantic slave trade, one of the greatest forced migrations in world history, through which Africa made a substantial, though involuntary, contribution to the building of the West's industrial civilization. In the seventeenth century an increasing desire for sugar in Europe resulted in an increasing demand for slave labor in South America and the West Indies, where sugar was produced. In the eighteenth century Western technological changes created a demand for cotton and other crops that required extensive human labor, thus intensifying the West's "need" for African slaves.

Waist Pendant of Benin Worn by Royalty

European intrusion in Africa during the early modern period deeply affected the diverse societies of Africa. The facial features, the beard, and the ruffled collar on this Edo peoples' artifact dating from the sixteenth to the nineteenth centuries are clearly Portuguese, but the braided hair is distinctly African, probably signifying royalty.

Hip Ornament: Portuguese Face, 16th–19th century. Brass, iron. Gift of Mr. and Mrs. Klaus G. Perls, 1991 (1991.162.9)/The Metropolitan Museum of Art, New York/Image copyright © The Metropolitan Museum of Art/Image source: Art Resource, NY

CHAPTER PREVIEW

WEST AFRICA IN THE FIFTEENTH AND SIXTEENTH CENTURIES
What types of economic, social, and political structures were found in the kingdoms and states along the west coast and in the Sudan?

CROSS-CULTURAL ENCOUNTERS ALONG THE EAST AFRICAN COAST
How did the arrival of Europeans and other foreign cultures affect the East African coast, and how did Ethiopia and the Swahili city-states respond to these incursions?

THE AFRICAN SLAVE TRADE
What role did slavery play in African societies before the transatlantic slave trade began, and what was the effect of European involvement?

What types of economic, social, and political structures were found in the kingdoms and states along the west coast and in the Sudan?

West Africa in the Fifteenth and Sixteenth Centuries

In mid-fifteenth-century Africa, Benin (buh-NEEN) and a number of other kingdoms flourished along the two-thousand-mile west coast between Senegambia and the northeastern shore of the Gulf of Guinea. Further inland, in the region of the Sudan (soo-DAN), the kingdoms of Songhai, Kanem-Bornu (KAH-nuhm BOR-noo), and Hausaland benefited from the trans-Saharan caravan trade, which along with goods brought Islamic culture to the region. Stateless societies such as those in the region of Senegambia (modern-day Senegal and the Gambia) existed alongside these more centralized states. Despite their political differences and whether they were agricultural, pastoral, or a mixture of both, West African cultures all faced the challenges presented by famine, disease, and the slave trade.

The West Coast: Senegambia and Benin

The Senegambian states possessed a homogeneous culture and a common history. For centuries Senegambia — named for the Senegal and Gambia Rivers — served as an important entrepôt for desert caravan contact with North African and Middle Eastern Islamic civilizations (Map 20.1). Through the transatlantic slave trade, Senegambia came into contact with Europe and the Americas. Thus Senegambia felt the impact of Islamic culture to the north and of European influences from the maritime West.

The Senegambian peoples spoke Wolof, Serer, and Pulaar, which all belong to the West African language group. Both the Wolof-speakers and the Serer-speakers had clearly defined social classes: royalty, nobility, warriors, peasants, low-caste artisans such as blacksmiths and leatherworkers, and enslaved persons. The enslaved class consisted of individuals who were pawned for debt, house servants who could not be sold, and people who were acquired through war or purchase. Senegambian slavery varied from society to society. In some places slaves were considered chattel property and were treated as harshly as they would be later in the Western Hemisphere.

The word **chattel** originally comes from a Latin word meaning "head," as in "so many head of cattle." It reflects the notion that enslaved people are not human, but subhuman, like beasts of burden or other animals. Thus they can be treated like animals. But in Senegambia and elsewhere in Africa, many enslaved people were not considered chattel

chattel An item of personal property; a term used in reference to enslaved people that conveys the idea that they are subhuman, like animals, and therefore may be treated like animals.

The Oba of Benin The oba's palace walls were decorated with bronze plaques that date from about the sixteenth to eighteenth centuries. This plaque vividly conveys the oba's power, majesty, and authority. The two attendants holding his arms also imply that the oba needs the support of his people. The oba's legs are mudfish, which represent fertility, peace, well-being, and prosperity, but their elongation, suggesting electric eels, relates the oba's terrifying and awesome power to the eel's jolting shock. (National Museum, Lagos, Nigeria/photo: André Held/akg-images)

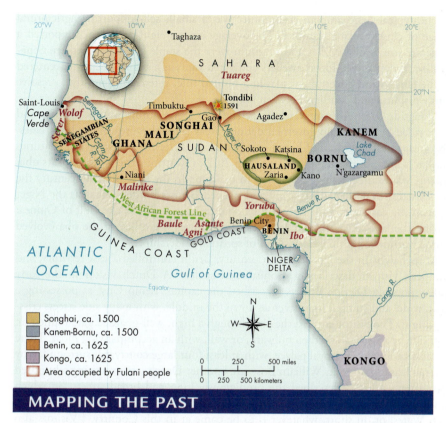

MAP 20.1 West African Societies, ca. 1500–1800 The coastal region of West Africa witnessed the rise of a number of kingdoms in the sixteenth century.

ANALYZING THE MAP What geographical features defined each of the kingdoms shown here? Consider rivers, lakes, oceans, deserts, and forests. How might they have affected the size and shape of these kingdoms?

CONNECTIONS Compare this map to the small map on page 608 called "The Slave Coast of West Africa." Consider the role that rivers and other geographical factors played in the development of the West African slave trade. Why were Luanda and Benguela the logical Portuguese sources for slaves?

property and could not be bought and sold. Some even served as royal advisers and enjoyed great power and prestige.[1] Unlike in the Americas, where slave status passed forever from one generation to the next, in Africa the enslaved person's descendants were sometimes considered free.

Senegambia was composed of stateless societies, culturally homogeneous ethnic populations living in small groups of villages without a central capital. Among these stateless societies, **age-grade systems** evolved. Age-grades were groups of teenage males and females whom the society initiated into adulthood at the same time. Age-grades cut across family ties, created community-wide loyalties, and provided a means of local law enforcement, because each age-grade was responsible for the behavior of all its members.

age-grade systems
Among the societies of Senegambia, groups of teenage males and females whom the society initiated into adulthood at the same time.

The typical Senegambian community was a small, self-supporting agricultural village of closely related families. The average six- to eight-acre farm supported a moderate-size family. Millet and sorghum were the staple grains in northern Senegambia; farther south, forest dwellers cultivated yams as a staple. Social life centered on the family, and government played a limited role, interceding mostly to resolve family disputes and conflicts between families.

Alongside West African stateless societies like Senegambia were kingdoms and states ruled by kings who governed defined areas through bureaucratic hierarchies. The great forest kingdom of Benin emerged in the fifteenth and sixteenth centuries in what is now southern Nigeria (see Map 20.1). Over time, the position of its **oba**, or king, was exalted, bringing stability to the state. In the later fifteenth century the oba Ewuare strengthened his army and pushed Benin's borders as far as the Niger River in the east, westward into Yoruba country, and south to the Gulf of Guinea. During the late sixteenth and seventeenth centuries the office of the oba evolved from a warrior-kingship to a position of spiritual leadership.

At its height in the late sixteenth century, Benin controlled a vast territory, and European visitors described a sophisticated society. A Dutch visitor in the early 1600s, possibly Dierick Ruiters, described the capital, Benin City, as possessing a great, wide, and straight main avenue down the middle, with many side streets crisscrossing it. The visitor entered the city through a high, well-guarded gate framed on each side by a very tall earthen bulwark, or wall, with an accompanying moat. There was also an impressive royal palace, with at least four large courtyards surrounded by galleries leading up to it. William Bosman, another Dutch visitor writing a hundred years later, in 1702, described the prodigiously long and broad streets "in which continual Markets are kept, either of Kine [cattle], Cotton, Elephants Teeth, European Wares; or, in short, whatever is to be come at in this Country."[2] Visitors also noted that Benin City was kept scrupulously clean and had no beggars and that public security was so effective that theft was unknown. The period also witnessed remarkable artistic creativity in ironwork, carved ivory, and especially bronze portrait busts. Over nine hundred brass plaques survive, providing important information about Benin court life, military triumphs, and cosmological ideas.

In 1485 Portuguese and other Europeans began to appear in Benin in pursuit of trade, and over the next couple of centuries Benin grew rich from the profits made through the slave trade and the export of tropical products, particularly pepper and ivory. Its main European trading partners along this stretch of the so-called slave coast were the Dutch and Portuguese. In the early eighteenth century tributary states and stronger neighbors nibbled at Benin's frontiers, challenging its power. Benin, however, survived as an independent entity until the British conquered and burned Benin City in 1898 as part of the European imperialist seizure of Africa (see "The Scramble for Africa, 1880–1914" in Chapter 25).

The Sudan: Songhai, Kanem-Bornu, and Hausaland

The Songhai kingdom, a successor state of the kingdoms of Ghana (ca. 900–1100) and Mali (ca. 1200–1450), dominated the whole Niger region of the western and central Sudan (see Map 20.1). The imperial expansion of Songhai began during the reign of the Songhai king Sonni Ali (r. ca. 1464–1492) and continued under his

oba The title of the king of Benin.

eventual successor, Muhammad Toure (TOO-ray) (r. 1493–1528). From his capital at Gao, Toure extended his rule as far north as the salt-mining center at **Taghaza** (tah-GAHZ-ah) in the western Sahara and as far east as Agadez (AH-gah-dez) and Kano (KA-no). A convert to Islam, Toure returned from a pilgrimage to Mecca impressed by what he had seen there. He tried to bring about greater centralization in his own territories by building a strong army, improving taxation procedures, and replacing local Songhai officials with more efficient Arabs in an effort to substitute royal institutions for ancient kinship ties.

We know little about daily life in Songhai society because of the paucity of written records and surviving artifacts. Some information is provided by Leo Africanus (ca. 1493–1554), a Moroccan who published an account in 1526 of his many travels, which included a stay in the Songhai kingdom.

As a scholar, Africanus was naturally impressed by Timbuktu, the second-largest city of the empire, which he visited in 1513. "Here [is] a great store of doctors, judges, priests, and other learned men, that are bountifully maintained at the King's court," he reported.[3] Many of these Islamic scholars had studied in Cairo and other Muslim learning centers. They gave Timbuktu a reputation for intellectual sophistication, religious piety, and moral justice. (See "Global Viewpoints: European Descriptions of Timbuktu and Jenne," page 596.)

Songhai under Muhammad Toure seems to have enjoyed economic prosperity. Leo Africanus noted the abundant food supply, which was produced in the southern savanna and carried to Timbuktu by a large fleet of canoes. The elite had immense wealth, and expensive North African and European luxuries—clothes, copperware, glass and stone beads, perfumes, and horses—were much in demand. The existence of many shops and markets implies the development of an urban culture. In Timbuktu merchants, scholars, judges, and artisans constituted a distinctive bourgeoisie, or middle class. The presence of many foreign merchants, including Jews and Italians, gave the city a cosmopolitan atmosphere.

Slavery played an important role in Songhai's economy. On the royal farms scattered throughout the kingdom, enslaved people produced rice for the royal granaries. Slaves could possess their own slaves, land, and cattle, but they could not bequeath any of this property; the king inherited all of it. Muhammad Toure greatly increased the number of royal slaves. He bestowed slaves on favorite Muslim scholars, who thus gained a steady source of income. Slaves were also sold at the large market at Gao, where traders from North Africa bought them to resell later in Cairo, Constantinople, Lisbon, Naples, Genoa, and Venice.

Despite its considerable economic and cultural strengths, Songhai had serious internal problems. Islam never took root in the countryside, and Muslim officials alienated the king from his people. Muhammad Toure's reforms were a failure. He governed diverse peoples—Tuareg, Mandinka, and Fulani as well as Songhai—who were often hostile to one another, and no cohesive element united them. Finally, the Songhai never developed an effective method of transferring power. Revolts, conspiracies, and palace intrigues followed the death of every king, and only three of the nine rulers in the dynasty begun by Muhammad Toure died natural deaths. Muhammad Toure himself was murdered by one of his sons. His death began a period of political instability that led to the kingdom's slow disintegration. The empire came to

Taghaza A settlement in the western Sahara, the site of the main salt-mining center.

European Descriptions of Timbuktu and Jenne

Timbuktu and Jenne were important cities in the West African empires of Ghana, Mali, and Songhai. The writings of al-Hassan Ibn Muhammad al-Wezaz al-Fasi, also known as Leo Africanus (ca. 1493–1554), provide the most authoritative accounts of West Africa between the writings of Ibn Battuta in the fourteenth century and the writings of European travelers in the nineteenth century. The *Tarikh al-Sudan* (*History of the Sudan*), written by Abd al-Rahman al-Sadi (1594–after 1656), is one of the most important histories of the Mali and Songhai Empires in the fifteenth, sixteenth, and seventeenth centuries.

Leo Africanus on Timbuktu

■ [Timbuktu] is situated within twelve miles of a certaine branch of Niger [River], all the houses whereof are now changed into cottages built of chalke, and covered with thatch. There is a most stately temple to be seene, the wals thereof are made of stone and lime; and a princely palace . . . built by a most excellent workeman of Granada. Here are many shops of artificers, and merchants, and especially of such as weave linen and cotton cloth. And hither do the Barbarie-merchants bring cloth of Europe. All the women of this region except maid-servants go with their faces covered. . . .

The inhabitants, & especially strangers there residing, are exceeding rich, insomuch, that the king that now is, married both his daughters unto two rich merchants. Here are many wels, containing most sweete water; and so often as the river Niger overfloweth, they conveigh the water thereof by certaine sluces into the towne.

Corne, cattle, milke, and butter this region yeeldeth in great abundance: but salt is verie scarce here; for it is brought hither by land from Tegaza, which is five hundred miles distant. When I myself was here, I saw one camels loade of salt sold for 80 ducates. The rich king of Tombuto hath many plates and scepters of gold, some whereof weigh 1300 pounds: and he keeps a magnificent and well furnished court. . . .

Here are great store of doctors, judges, priests, and other learned men, that are bountifully maintained at the kings cost and charges. And hither are brought divers manuscripts or written books out of Barbarie, which are sold for more money than any other merchandize.

an end in 1591 when a Moroccan army of three thousand soldiers — many of whom were slaves of European origin equipped with European muskets — crossed the Sahara and inflicted a crushing defeat on the Songhai at Tondibi.

East of Songhai lay the kingdoms of Kanem-Bornu and Hausaland (see Map 20.1). Under the dynamic military leader Idris Alooma (IH-dris ah-LOW-mah) (r. 1571–1603), Kanem-Bornu subdued weaker peoples and gained jurisdiction over an extensive area. Well drilled and equipped with firearms, his standing army and camel-mounted cavalry decimated warriors fighting with spears and arrows. Idris Alooma perpetuated a form of feudalism by granting land to able fighters in return for loyalty and the promise of future military assistance. Kanem-Bornu also shared in the trans-Saharan trade, shipping eunuchs and young girls to North Africa in return for horses and firearms.

A devout Muslim, Idris Alooma elicited high praise from ibn-Fartura, who wrote a history of his reign called *The Kanem Wars*:

Among the most surprising of his acts was the stand he took against obscenity and adultery, so that no such thing took place openly in his time. Formerly the people had been indifferent to such offences. . . . In fact he was a power among his people and from him came their strength.

The Sultan was intent on the clear path laid down by the Qur'an . . . in all his affairs and actions.[4]

Al-Sadi on Jenne

■ Jenne is a large . . . city, characterized by prosperity, good fortune and compassion. . . . It is the nature of Jenne's inhabitants to be kind and charitable, and solicitous for one another. . . .

Jenne is one of the great markets of the Muslims. Those who deal in salt from the mine of Taghaza meet there with those who deal in gold from the mine of Bitu. These two blessed mines have no equal in the entire world. . . . Jenne is the reason why caravans come to Timbuktu from all quarters—north, south, east and west. Jenne is situated to the south and west of Timbuktu beyond the two rivers. . . .

Jenne was founded as a pagan town in the middle of the second century of the *hijira* of the Prophet [150 anno hegirae (A.H.), the Islamic calendar, or 767–768 C.E.]. . . . Its people became Muslims at the end of the sixth century [A.H., or eleventh to twelfth century C.E.]. First, Sultan Kunburu became a Muslim, then people followed his example. When he made up his mind to embrace Islam he ordered that all the Muslim scholars within the city should be assembled. They totaled 4,200, and he made a profession of Islam before them, and told them to call upon God Most High to grant

the city three things: firstly, that anyone who fled there from his homeland in poverty and distress should have this translated by God into luxury and ease, so that he may forget his homeland; secondly, that more strangers than local folk should settle there; and thirdly, that those who came to trade there should lose patience and grow weary over selling their goods, and so dispose of them cheaply, allowing the people of Jenne to make a profit.

QUESTIONS FOR ANALYSIS

1. During the colonial era, and even to the present day, Africa and its inhabitants were described in the most denigrating terms, such as *pagan*, *savage*, *illiterate*, *poor*, and *uncivilized*. How do the descriptions of these two African market and learning centers conform to those characterizations?

2. How important was Islam to the success of these two cities? In what ways?

Sources: Al-Hassan ibn-Mohammad al-Wezaz al-Fasi, *The History and Description of Africa.* Done into English in 1600 by John Pory. Robert Brown, ed. (London: Hakluyt Society, 1896), vol. 3, pp. 824–825; John O. Hunwick, *Timbuktu and the Songhay Empire: Al-Sadi's Tarikh al-Sudan Down to 1613 and Other Contemporary Documents.* Reproduced by permission of BRILL ACADEMIC PUBLISHERS in the format Republish in a book via Copyright Clearance Center.

Idris Alooma built mosques at his capital city of N'gazargamu and substituted Muslim courts and Islamic law for African tribunals and ancient customary law. His eighteenth-century successors lacked his vitality and military skills, however, and the empire declined.

Between Songhai and Kanem-Bornu were the lands of the Hausa (HOUSE-uh). Hausa merchants carried on a sizable trade in slaves and kola nuts with North African communities across the Sahara. Obscure trading posts evolved into important Hausa city-states like Kano and Katsina (kat-SIN-ah), through which Islamic influences entered the region. Kano and Katsina became Muslim intellectual centers and in the fifteenth century attracted scholars from Timbuktu. The Muslim chronicler of the reign of King Muhammad Rimfa (RIMP-fah) (r. 1463–1499) of Kano records that the king introduced the Muslim practices of purdah (PUR-dah), or seclusion of women; Eid al-Fitr (eed-al-FITR), the festival after the fast of Ramadan; and the assignment of eunuchs to high state offices.[5] As in Songhai and Kanem-Bornu, however, Islam made no strong imprint on the Hausa masses until the nineteenth century.

The Lives of the People of West Africa

Wives and children were highly desired in African societies because they could clear and cultivate the land and because they brought prestige, social support, and security in old age. The results were intense competition for women, inequality of access to them, an emphasis on male virility and female fertility, and serious tension between male generations. Polygyny was almost universal.

Men acquired wives in two ways. In some cases, couples simply eloped and began their union. More commonly, a man's family gave bride wealth to the bride's family as compensation for losing the fruits of her productive and reproductive abilities. She was expected to produce children, to produce food through her labor, and to pass on the culture in the raising of her children. Because it took time for a young man to acquire the bride wealth, all but the richest men delayed marriage until about age thirty. Women married at about the onset of puberty.

The easy availability of land in Africa reduced the kinds of generational conflict that occurred in western Europe, where land was scarce. Competition for wives between male generations, however, was fierce. On the one hand, myth and folklore stressed respect for the elderly, and the older men in a community imposed their authority over the younger ones. On the other hand, young men possessed the powerful asset of their labor, which could easily be turned into independence where so much land was available.

"Without children you are naked" goes a Yoruba (YORE-uh-bah) proverb, and children were the primary goal of marriage. Just as a man's virility determined his honor, so barrenness damaged a woman's status. A wife's infidelity was considered a less serious problem than her infertility. A woman might have six widely spaced pregnancies in her fertile years; the universal practice of breast-feeding infants for two, three, or even four years may have inhibited conception. Long intervals between births due to food shortages also may have limited pregnancies and checked population growth. Harsh climate, poor nutrition, and infectious diseases also contributed to a high infant mortality rate.

Both nuclear and extended families were common in West Africa. Nuclear families averaged only five or six members, but the household of a Big Man (a local man of power) included his wives, married and unmarried sons, unmarried daughters, poor relations, dependents, and scores of children. Extended families were common among the Hausa and Mandinka peoples. On the Gold Coast in the seventeenth century, a well-to-do man's household might number 150 people; in the Kongo region in west-central Africa, several hundred.

In agriculture men did the heavy work of felling trees and clearing the land; women then planted, weeded, and harvested. Between 1000 and 1400, cassava (manioc), bananas, and plantains came to West Africa from Asia. In the sixteenth century the Portuguese introduced maize (corn), sweet potatoes, and new varieties of yams from the Americas. Fish supplemented the diets of people living near bodies of water. According to former slave Olaudah Equiano, the Ibo people in the mid-eighteenth century ate plantains, yams, beans, and Indian corn, along with stewed poultry, goat, or bullock (castrated steer) seasoned with peppers.[6] However, such a protein-rich diet was probably exceptional.

Disease posed perhaps the biggest obstacle to population growth. Malaria, spread by mosquitoes and rampant in West Africa, was the greatest killer, especially of infants. West Africans developed a relatively high degree of immunity to malaria and other parasitic diseases. Acute strains of smallpox introduced by Europeans certainly did not help population growth, nor did venereal syphilis, which possibly originated in Latin America. As in Chinese and European communities in the early modern period, the sick depended on folk medicine. African medical specialists administered a variety of treatments. Still, disease was common where the diet was poor and lacked adequate vitamins.

The devastating effects of famine represented another major check on population growth. Drought, excessive rain, swarms of locusts, and rural wars that prevented land cultivation all meant later food shortages. In the 1680s famine extended from the Senegambian coast to the Upper Nile, and many people sold themselves into slavery for food. In the eighteenth century "slave exports" reached their peak in times of famine, and ships could fill their cargo holds simply by offering food. The worst disaster occurred from 1738 to 1756, when, according to one chronicler, the poor were reduced literally to cannibalism, also considered a metaphor for the complete collapse of civilization.[7]

Because the Americas had been isolated from the Eurasian-African landmass for thousands of years, parasitic diseases common in Europe, Africa, and Asia were unknown in the Americas before the Europeans' arrival. Enslaved Africans taken to the Americas brought with them the diseases common to tropical West Africa, such as yellow fever, dengue fever, malaria, and hookworm. Thus the hot, humid disease environment in the American tropics, where the majority of enslaved Africans lived and worked, became more "African." On the other hand, cold-weather European diseases, such as chicken pox, mumps, measles, and influenza, prevailed in the northern temperate zone in North America and the southern temperate zone in South America. This difference in disease environment partially explains why Africans made up the majority of the unskilled labor force in the tropical areas of the Americas, and Europeans made up the majority of the unskilled labor force in the Western Hemisphere temperate zones, such as the northern United States and Canada.

Trade and Industry

As in all premodern societies, West African economies rested on agriculture. There was some trade and industry, but population shortages encouraged local self-sufficiency, slowed transportation, and hindered exchange. There were very few large markets, and their relative isolation from the outside world and failure to attract large numbers of foreign merchants limited technological innovation.

For centuries black Africans had exchanged goods with North African merchants in centers such as Gao and Timbuktu. This long-distance trans-Saharan trade was conducted and controlled by Muslim-Berber merchants using camels. The two primary goods exchanged were salt, which came from salt mines in North Africa, and gold, which came mainly from gold mines in modern-day Mali, and later, modern Ghana.

As elsewhere around the world, water was the cheapest method of transportation, and many small dugout canoes and larger trading canoes plied the Niger and its delta region (see Map 20.1). On land West African peoples used pack animals (camels or donkeys) rather than wheeled vehicles; only a narrow belt of land in the Sudan was suitable for animal-drawn carts. When traders reached an area infested with tsetse flies, they transferred each animal's load to human porters. Such difficulties in transport severely restricted long-distance trade, so most people relied on the regional exchange of local specialties.

West African communities had a well-organized market system. At informal markets on riverbanks, fishermen bartered fish for local specialties. More formal markets existed within towns and villages or on neutral ground between them.

West African Trade Routes

→ Trade route

Salt Making in the Central Sahara For centuries camel caravans transported salt south across the Sahara to the great West African kingdoms, where it was exchanged for gold. Here at Tegguida-n-Tessum, Niger, in the central Sahara, salt is still collected by pouring spring water into small pools dug out of the saline soil. The water leaches out the salt before evaporating in the desert sun, leaving deposits of pure salt behind, which are then shaped into blocks for transport. (Visual Connection Archive)

Markets also rotated among neighboring villages on certain days. Local sellers were usually women; traders from afar were men.

Salt had long been one of Africa's most critical trade items. Salt is essential to human health; the Hausa language has more than fifty words for it. The salt trade dominated the West African economies in the fifteenth, sixteenth, and seventeenth centuries. The main salt-mining center was at Taghaza (see Map 20.1) in the western Sahara. In the most wretched conditions, slaves dug the salt from desiccated lakes and loaded heavy blocks onto camels' backs. Nomadic **Tuareg** (Berber) peoples and later Moors (peoples of Berber and Arab descent) traded their salt south for gold, grain, slaves, and kola nuts. **Cowrie** (COW-ree) **shells**, imported from the Maldives in the Indian Ocean and North Africa, served as the medium of exchange. Gold continued to be mined and shipped from Mali until South American bullion flooded Europe in the sixteenth century. Thereafter, gold production in Mali steadily declined until the late twentieth and early twenty-first centuries, when it revived.

West African peoples engaged in many crafts, but the textile industry had the greatest level of specialization. The earliest fabric in West Africa was made of vegetable fiber. Muslim traders introduced cotton and its weaving in the ninth century. By the fifteenth century the Wolof and Mandinka regions had professional weavers producing beautiful cloth, but this cloth was too expensive to compete in the Atlantic and Indian Ocean markets after 1500. Although the relatively small quantities of cloth produced on very narrow looms (one to two inches wide) could not compete in a world market, they are the source of the famous multicolored African kente cloth made from threads of cotton, or cotton and silk, by the Akan people of Ghana and the Ivory Coast. The area around Kano, in northern Nigeria, is famous for the deeply dyed blue cloth produced on the narrowest looms in the world and favored by the Tuareg Berber peoples of North Africa.

Tuareg Major branch of the nomadic Berber peoples who controlled the north-south trans-Saharan trade in salt.

cowrie shells Imported from the Maldives, they served as the medium of exchange in West Africa.

How did the arrival of Europeans and other foreign cultures affect the East African coast, and how did Ethiopia and the Swahili city-states respond to these incursions?

Cross-Cultural Encounters Along the East African Coast

East Africa in the early modern period faced repeated incursions from foreign powers. At the beginning of the sixteenth century Ethiopia faced challenges from the Muslim state of Adal, and then from Europeans. Jesuit attempts to substitute Roman Catholic liturgical forms for the Coptic Christian liturgies (see below) met with fierce resistance and ushered in a centuries-long period of hostility to foreigners. The wealthy Swahili city-states along the southeastern African coast also resisted European intrusions in the sixteenth century, with even more disastrous results. Cities such as Mogadishu, Kilwa, and Sofala used Arabic as the language of communication, and their commercial economies had long been tied to the Indian Ocean trade. The arrival of the Portuguese in 1498 proved catastrophic for those cities, and the Swahili coast suffered economic decline as a result.

Muslim and European Incursions in Ethiopia, ca. 1500–1630

At the beginning of the sixteenth century the powerful East African kingdom of Ethiopia extended from Massawa in the north to several tributary states in the south (Map 20.2), but the ruling Solomonic dynasty in Ethiopia, in power since the thirteenth century, faced serious external threats. Alone among the states in northeast and eastern Africa, Ethiopia was a Christian kingdom that practiced **Coptic Christianity**, an orthodox form of the Christian faith that originated in Egypt in about 42–45. By the early 1500s Ethiopia was an island of Christianity surrounded by a sea of Muslim states.

Coptic Christianity
Orthodox form of Christianity from Egypt practiced in Ethiopia.

Adal, a Muslim state along the southern base of the Red Sea, began incursions into Ethiopia, and in 1529 the Adal general Ahmad ibn-Ghazi inflicted a disastrous defeat on the Ethiopian emperor Lebna Dengel (r. 1508–1540). Ibn-Ghazi followed up his victory with systematic devastation of the land; destruction of many Ethiopian artistic and literary works, churches, and monasteries; and the forced conversion of thousands to Islam. Lebna Dengel fled to the mountains and appealed to Portugal for assistance. The Portuguese came to his aid, but Dengel was killed in battle before the Portuguese arrived. The Muslim occupation of Christian Ethiopia, which began around 1531, ended in 1543, after a joint Ethiopian and Portuguese force defeated a larger Muslim army at the Battle of Wayna Daga.

In the late twelfth century tales of Prester John, rumored to be a powerful Christian monarch ruling a vast and wealthy African empire, reached western Europe. The search for Prester John, as well as for gold and spices, spurred the Portuguese to undertake a series of trans-African expeditions that reached Timbuktu and Mali in the 1480s and the Ethiopian court by 1508. Although Prester John was a mythical figure, Portuguese emissaries triumphantly but mistakenly identified the Ethiopian emperor as Prester John.[8] It was their desire to convert Ethiopians from Coptic Christianity to Roman Catholicism that motivated the Portuguese to aid the Ethiopians in defeating Adal's Muslim forces in 1543.

Saint George in Ethiopian Art This wall painting of Saint George slaying a dragon resides in the stone-carved Church of Saint George in Lalibela, Ethiopia, and attests to the powerful and pervasive Christian influence on Ethiopian culture. (Galen R. Frysinger)

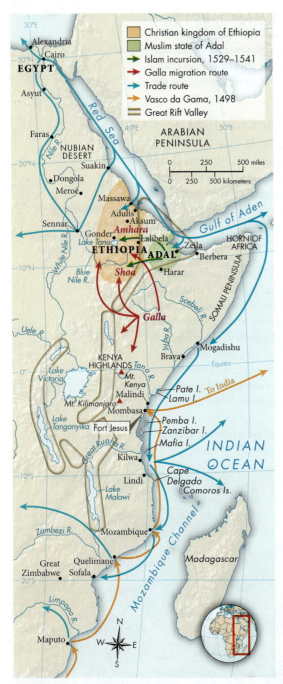

MAP 20.2 East Africa in the Sixteenth Century In early modern times, the Christian kingdom of Ethiopia, first isolated and then subjected to Muslim and European pressures, played an insignificant role in world affairs. But the East African city-states, which stretched from Sofala in the south to Mogadishu in the north, had powerfully important commercial relations with Mughal India, China, the Ottoman world, and southern Europe.

No sooner had the Muslim threat ended than Ethiopia encountered three more dangers. The Galla, now known as the Oromo, moved northward in great numbers in the 1530s, occupying portions of Harar, Shoa, and Amhara. The Ethiopians could not defeat them militarily, and the Galla were not interested in assimilation. For the next two centuries the two peoples lived together in an uneasy truce. Simultaneously, the Ottoman Turks seized Massawa and other coastal cities. Then the Jesuits arrived and attempted to force Roman Catholicism on a proud people whose Coptic form of Christianity long antedated the European version. Since Ethiopian national sentiment was closely tied to Coptic Christianity, violent rebellion and anarchy ensued.

In 1633 the Jesuit missionaries were expelled. For the next two centuries hostility to foreigners, weak political leadership, and regionalism characterized Ethiopia. Civil conflicts between Galla and Ethiopians erupted continually. The Coptic Church, though lacking strong authority, survived as the cornerstone of Ethiopian national identity.

The Swahili City-States and the Arrival of the Portuguese, ca. 1500–1600

The word **Swahili** means "People of the Coast" and refers to the people living along the East African coast and on the nearby islands. Although predominantly a Bantu-speaking people, the Swahili have incorporated significant aspects of Arab culture. The Arabic alphabet was used for the first written works in Swahili (although the Latin alphabet is now standard), and roughly 35 percent of Swahili words come from Arabic. Surviving texts in Swahili—from the earliest known Swahili documents dating from 1711—provide historians with a glimpse of early Swahili history that is not possible when studying early nonliterate African societies. By the eleventh century the Swahili had accepted Islam, which provided a common identity and unifying factor for all the peoples along coastal East Africa. Living on the Indian Ocean coast, the Swahili also felt the influences of Indians, Indonesians, Persians, and even the Chinese.

Swahili Meaning "People of the Coast," the term used for the people living along the East African coast and on nearby islands.

Swahili civilization was overwhelmingly maritime. A fertile, well-watered, and intensely cultivated stretch of land extending down the coast yielded valuable crops.

The region's considerable prosperity, however, rested on trade and commerce. The Swahili acted as middlemen in an Indian Ocean–East African economy that might be described as early capitalism. They exchanged cloves, ivory, rhinoceros horn, tortoise shells, inlaid ebony chairs, copra (dried coconut meat that yields coconut oil), and inland slaves for Arabian and Persian perfumes, toilet articles, ink, and paper; for Indian textiles, beads, and iron tools; and for Chinese porcelains and silks. In the fifteenth century the cosmopolitan city-states of Mogadishu, Pate, Lamu, Mombasa, and especially Kilwa enjoyed a worldwide reputation for commercial prosperity and high living standards.[9]

The arrival of the Portuguese explorer Vasco da Gama (VAS-ko dah GAH-ma) (see Map 16.2) in 1498 spelled the end of the Swahili cities' independence. Lured by the spice trade, da Gama wanted to build a Portuguese maritime empire in the Indian Ocean. Some Swahili rulers, such as the sultan of Malindi (ma-LIN-dee), quickly agreed to a trading alliance with the Portuguese. Others, such as the sultan of Mombasa (mahm-BAHS-uh), were tricked into commercial agreements. Swahili rulers who rejected Portuguese overtures saw their cities bombarded and attacked. To secure alliances made between 1502 and 1507, the Portuguese erected forts at the southern port cities of Kilwa, Zanzibar (ZAN-zuh-bahr), and Sofala. These fortified markets and trading posts served as the foundation of Portuguese commercial power on the Swahili coast. (See "Analyzing the Evidence: Duarte Barbosa on the Swahili City-States," page 604.) The better-fortified northern cities, such as Mogadishu, survived as important entrepôts for goods to India.

The Portuguese presence in the south did not yield the expected commercial fortunes. Rather than accept Portuguese commercial restrictions, the residents deserted the towns, and the town economies crumbled. Large numbers of Kilwa's people, for example, immigrated to northern cities. The gold flow from inland mines to Sofala (so-FALL-ah) slowed to a trickle. Swahili noncooperation successfully prevented the Portuguese from gaining control of the local coastal trade.

In the late seventeenth century pressures from the northern European maritime powers—the Dutch, French, and English, aided greatly by Omani Arabs—combined with local African rebellions to bring about the collapse of Portuguese influence in Africa. A Portuguese presence remained only at Mozambique in the far south and Angola (ahng-GO-luh) on the west coast.

The African Slave Trade

The exchange of peoples captured in local and ethnic wars within sub-Saharan Africa, the trans-Saharan slave trade with the Mediterranean Islamic world beginning in the seventh century, and the slave traffic across the Indian Ocean all testify to the long tradition and continental dimensions of the African slave trade before European intrusion. The enslavement of human beings was practiced in some form or another all over Africa—indeed, all over the world. Sanctioned by law and custom, enslaved people served critical and well-defined roles in the social, political, and economic organization of many African societies. Domestically these roles ranged from concubines and servants to royal guards and advisers. As was the case later in the Americas, some enslaved people were common laborers. In terms of economics, slaves were commodities for trade, no more or less important than other trade items, such as gold and ivory.

> **What role did slavery play in African societies before the transatlantic slave trade began, and what was the effect of European involvement?**

Duarte Barbosa on the Swahili City-States

The Portuguese writer, government agent, and traveler Duarte Barbosa made two voyages to India. Arriving first in 1500, he acted for five years as an interpreter and translator in Cochin and Cannanore in Kerala (in southwestern India on the Malabar coast), returning to Lisbon in 1506. On his second trip to India in 1511, he served the Portuguese government as chief scribe in the factory of Cannanore (a factory was a warehouse for the storage of goods, not a manufacturing center) and as the liaison with the local Indian rajah (prince). Barbosa returned to Portugal around 1516. In September 1519 he began his greatest adventure, setting off with Ferdinand Magellan to circumnavigate the globe. After Magellan was killed in a battle with native forces in the Philippines, Barbosa took joint command of the expedition, but was himself killed in the Philippines less than a week after Magellan, on May 1, 1521.

On the basis of his trips around the Indian Ocean in 1518, Barbosa completed his *Libro de Duarte Barbosa* (*The Book of Duarte Barbosa*), a geographical and ethnographic survey of peoples, lands, and commerce from the Cape of Good Hope to China. It was based largely on his personal observations. First published in Italian, the book won wide acclaim in Europe, and modern scholars consider its geographical information very accurate. The excerpts below describe some of the Swahili city-states along the East African coast.

Sofala

■ And the manner of their traffic was this: they came in small vessels named *zambucos* from the kingdoms of Kilwa, Mombasa, and Malindi, bringing many cotton cloths, some spotted and others white and blue, also some of silk, and many small beads, grey, red, and yellow, which things come to the said kingdoms from the great kingdom of Cambaya [in northwest India] in other greater ships. And these wares the said Moors who came from Malindi and Mombasa paid for in gold at such a price that those merchants departed well pleased; which gold they gave by weight.

The Moors of Sofala kept these wares and sold them afterwards to the Heathen of the Kingdom of Benametapa, who came thither laden with gold which they gave in exchange for the said cloths without weighing it. These Moors collect also great store of ivory which they find hard by Sofala, and this also they sell in the Kingdom of Cambaya at five or six cruzados the quintal. They also sell some ambergris, which is brought to them from the Hucicas, and is exceeding good. These Moors are black, and some of them tawny; some of them speak Arabic, but the more part use the language of the country. They clothe themselves from the waist down with cotton and silk cloths, and other cloths they wear over their shoulders like capes, and turbans on their heads. Some of them wear small caps dyed in grain in chequers and other woollen clothes in many tints, also camlets and other silks.

Their food is millet, rice, flesh and fish. In this river as far as the sea are many sea horses, which come out on the land to graze, which horses always move in the sea like fishes; they have tusks like those of small elephants in size, and the ivory is better than that of elephants, being whiter and harder, and it never loses colour. In the country near Sofala are many wild elephants, exceeding great (which the country-folk know not how to tame) lions, ounces [African lynx], deer and many other wild beasts. It is a land of plains and hills with many streams of sweet water.

Over time, the trans-Saharan slave trade became less important than the trans-atlantic trade, which witnessed an explosive growth during the seventeenth and eighteenth centuries. The millions of enslaved Africans forcibly exported to the Americas had a lasting impact on African society and led ultimately to a wider use of slaves within Africa itself.

The Institution of Slavery in Africa

Islamic practices strongly influenced African slavery. African rulers justified enslavement with the Muslim argument that prisoners of war could be sold and that cap-

Kilwa

◼ Going along the coast from this town of Mozambique, there is an island hard by the mainland which is called Kilwa, in which is a Moorish town with many fair houses of stone and mortar, with many windows after our fashion, very well arranged in streets, with many flat roofs. The doors are of wood, well carved, with excellent joinery. Around it are streams and orchards and fruit-gardens with many channels of sweet water. It has a Moorish king over it. From this place they trade with Sofala, whence they bring back gold, and from here they spread all over . . . the seacoast [which] is well-peopled with villages and abodes of Moors.

Before the King our Lord sent out his expedition to discover India the Moors of Sofala, Cuama, Angoya and Mozambique were all subject to the King of Kilwa, who was the most mighty king among them. And in this town was great plenty of gold, as no ships passed towards Sofala without first coming to this island. . . .

This town was taken by force from its king by the Portuguese, as, moved by arrogance, he refused to obey the King our Lord. There they took many prisoners and the king fled from the island, and His Highness ordered that a fort should be built there, and kept it under his rule and governance. Afterwards he ordered that it should be pulled down, as its maintenance was of no value nor profit to him, and it was destroyed by Antonio de Saldanha.

Malindi

◼ Journeying along the coast towards India, there is a fair town on the mainland lying along a strand, which is named Malindi. It pertains to the Moors and has a Moorish king over it; the which place has many fair stone and mortar houses of many storeys, with great plenty of windows and flat roofs, after our fashion. The place is well laid out in streets. The folk are both black and white; they go naked, covering only their private parts with cotton and silk cloths. Others of them wear cloths folded like cloaks and waist-bands, and turbans of many rich stuffs on their heads.

They are great barterers, and deal in cloth, gold, ivory, and divers other wares with the Moors and Heathen of the great kingdom of Cambaya; and to their haven come every year many ships with cargoes of merchandize, from which they get great store of gold, ivory and wax. In this traffic the Cambay merchants make great profits, and thus, on one side and the other, they earn much money. There is great plenty of food in this city (rice, millet, and some wheat which they bring from Cambaya), and divers sorts of fruit, inasmuch as there is here abundance of fruit-gardens and orchards. Here too are plenty of round-tailed sheep, cows and other cattle and great store of oranges, also of hens.

The king and people of this place ever were and are friends of the King of Portugal, and the Portuguese always find in them great comfort and friendship and perfect peace, and there the ships, when they chance to pass that way, obtain supplies in plenty.

QUESTIONS FOR ANALYSIS

1. What seems to have impressed Barbosa? What was his attitude toward the various peoples he saw? What Portuguese or Western prejudices do you discern?
2. What was the Portuguese relationship to the Swahili city-states at the time Barbosa saw them?
3. What was the source of Sofala's gold? Of Sofala's and Malindi's ivory? What did the Indian kingdom of Cambaya use ivory for?

Source: Mansel Longworth Dames, trans., *The Book of Duarte Barbosa*, vol. 1 (London: Bedford Press, 1918).

---

tured people were considered chattel, or personal possessions, to be used any way the owner saw fit. Between 650 and 1600 Muslims transported perhaps as many as 4.82 million black slaves across the trans-Saharan trade route.[10] In the fourteenth and fifteenth centuries the rulers and elites of Mali and Benin imported thousands of white Slavic slave women, symbols of wealth and status, who had been seized in slave raids from the Balkans and Caucasus regions of the eastern Mediterranean by Turks, Mongols, and others.[11] In 1444, when Portuguese caravels landed 235 slaves at Algarve in southern Portugal, a contemporary observed that they seemed "a marvelous (extraordinary) sight, for, amongst them, were some white enough, fair enough,

KITCHIN STUFF.

Below Stairs The prints and cartoons of Thomas Rowlandson (1756–1827) testify to the sizable numbers of blacks in eighteenth-century London, where they worked in naval and military service as well as domestic service. Here the household cook, maid, and footman relax before the kitchen fire. Interracial marriages were not uncommon. (© The Trustees of The British Museum/Art Resource, NY)

Cape Colony, ca. 1750

and well-proportioned; others were less white, like mulattoes; others again were black as Ethiops."[12]

Meanwhile, the flow of black people to Europe, begun during the Renaissance, continued. In the seventeenth and eighteenth centuries as many as two hundred thousand Africans entered European societies. Some arrived as slaves, others as servants; the legal distinction was not always clear. Eighteenth-century London, for example, had more than ten thousand blacks, most of whom arrived as sailors on Atlantic crossings or as personal servants brought from the West Indies. In England most were free, not slaves. Initially, a handsome black person was a fashionable accessory, a rare status symbol. Later, English aristocrats considered black servants too ordinary. The duchess of Devonshire offered her mother an eleven-year-old boy, explaining that the duke did not want a Negro servant because "it was more original to have a Chinese page than to have a black one; everybody had a black one."[13]

London's black population constituted a well-organized, self-conscious subculture, with black pubs, black churches, and black social groups assisting the black poor and unemployed. Some black people attained wealth and position, the most famous being Francis Barber, manservant of the sixteenth-century British literary giant Samuel Johnson and heir to Johnson's papers and to most of his sizable fortune.

In 1658 the Dutch East India Company began to allow the importation of slaves into the Cape Colony, which the company had founded on the southern tip of Africa at the Cape of Good Hope in 1652. Over the next century and a half about 75 percent of the slaves brought into the colony came from Dutch East India Company colonies in India and Southeast Asia or from Madagascar; the remaining 25 percent came from Africa. Most worked long and hard as field hands and at any other menial or manual forms of labor needed by their European masters. The Dutch East India Company was the single largest slave owner in the Cape Colony, employing its slaves on public works and company farms, but by 1780 half of all white men at the Cape had at least one slave. Slave ownership fostered a strong sense of racial and economic solidarity in the white master class.

Although in the seventeenth and eighteenth centuries Holland enjoyed a Europe-wide reputation for religious tolerance and intellectual freedom, in the Cape Colony the Dutch used a strict racial hierarchy and heavy-handed paternalism to maintain control over enslaved native and foreign-born peoples. In Muslim society the offspring of a free man and an enslaved woman were free, but in southern Africa such children remained enslaved. Because enslaved males greatly outnumbered enslaved females in the Cape Colony, marriage and family life were almost nonexistent for slaves. Because there were few occupations requiring special skills, those enslaved in the colony lacked opportunities to earn manumission, or freedom. And in contrast with North and South America and with Muslim societies, in the Cape Colony only a very small number of those enslaved won manumission; most of these were women.[14]

The slave trade expanded greatly in East Africa's savanna and Horn regions in the late eighteenth century and the first half of the nineteenth century. Why this increased demand? Merchants and planters wanted slaves to work the sugar plantations on the Mascarene Islands, located east of Madagascar; the clove plantations on Zanzibar and Pemba; and the food plantations along the Kenyan coast. The eastern coast also exported enslaved people to the Americas, particularly to Brazil. In the late eighteenth and early nineteenth centuries, precisely when the slave trade to North America and the Caribbean declined, the Arabian and Asian markets expanded.

The Transatlantic Slave Trade

Although the trade in African people was a worldwide phenomenon, the transatlantic slave trade involved the largest number of enslaved Africans. This forced migration of millions of human beings, extending from the early sixteenth to the late nineteenth centuries, represents one of the most inhumane, unjust, and shameful tragedies in human history. It also immediately provokes a troubling question: why, in the seventeenth and eighteenth centuries, did enslavement in the Americas become almost exclusively African?

European settlers first enslaved indigenous peoples, the Amerindians, to work on the sugar plantations in the New World (see "Sugar and Early Transatlantic Slavery" in Chapter 16). When they proved ill suited to the harsh rigors of sugar production, the Spaniards brought in Africans.

One scholar has argued that a pan-European insider-outsider ideology prevailed across Europe. This cultural attitude permitted the enslavement of outsiders but made the enslavement of white Europeans taboo. Europeans could not bear the sight of other Europeans doing plantation slave labor. According to this theory, a similar pan-African ideology did not exist, as Africans had no problem with selling Africans to Europeans.[15] Several facts argue against the validity of this theory. English landlords exploited their Irish peasants with merciless severity, French aristocrats often looked on their peasantry with cold contempt, and Russian boyars treated their serfs with casual indifference and harsh brutality. These and other possible examples contradict the existence of a pan-European ideology or culture that opposed the enslavement of white Europeans. Moreover, the flow of white enslaved Slavic peoples from the Balkans into the eastern Mediterranean continued unabated during the same period.

Another theory holds that in the Muslim and Arab worlds by the tenth century, an association had developed between blackness and menial slavery. The Arab word *abd*, or "black," had become synonymous with *slave*. Although the great majority of enslaved persons in the Islamic world were white, a racial element existed in Muslim perceptions: not all slaves were black, but blacks were identified with slavery. In Europe, after the arrival of tens of thousands of sub-Saharan Africans in the Iberian Peninsula during the fifteenth century, Christian Europeans also began to make a strong association between slavery and black Africans. Therefore, Africans seemed the "logical" solution to the labor shortage in the Americas.[16]

Another important question relating to the African slave trade is this: why were African peoples enslaved in a period when serfdom was declining in western Europe, and when land was so widely available and much of the African continent had a labor shortage? The answer seems to lie in a technical problem related to African agriculture. Partly because of the tsetse fly, which causes sleeping sickness and other diseases,

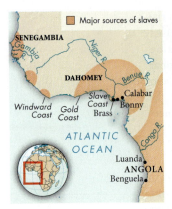

The Slave Coast of West Africa

and partly because of easily leached lateritic soils (containing high concentrations of oxides), farmers had great difficulty using draft animals. Tropical soils responded poorly to plowing, and most work had to be done with the hoe. Productivity, therefore, was low. Thus, in precolonial Africa the individual's agricultural productivity was low, so his or her economic value to society was less than the economic value of a European peasant in Europe. Enslaved persons in the Americas were more productive than free producers in Africa. And European slave dealers were very willing to pay a price higher than the value of an African's productivity in Africa.

The incidence of disease in the Americas also helps explain African enslavement. Smallpox took a terrible toll on Native Americans, and between 30 and 50 percent of Europeans exposed to malaria succumbed to that sickness. Africans had developed some immunity to both diseases, and in the Americas they experienced the lowest mortality rate of any people, making them, ironically, the most suitable workers for the environment.

Portuguese colonization of Brazil began in the early 1530s, and in 1551 the Portuguese founded a sugar colony at Bahia. Between 1551 and 1575, before the North American slave traffic began, the Portuguese delivered more African slaves to Brazil than ever reached British North America (Figure 20.1). Portugal essentially monopolized the slave trade until 1600 and continued to play a significant role in the seventeenth century, though the trade was increasingly taken over by the Dutch, French, and English. From 1690 until the British House of Commons abolished the slave trade in 1807, England was the leading carrier of African slaves.

Population density and supply conditions along the West African coast and the sailing time to New World markets determined the sources of slaves. As the demand for slaves rose, slavers moved down the West African coast from Senegambia to the more densely populated hinterlands of the Bight of Benin and the Bight of Biafra. The abundant supply of Africans to enslave in Angola, the region south of the Congo River, and the quick passage from Angola to Brazil and the Caribbean established that region as the major coast for Portuguese slavers.

Transatlantic wind patterns partly determined exchange routes. Shippers naturally preferred the swiftest crossing—that is, from the African port nearest the latitude of the intended American destination. Thus Portuguese shippers carried their cargoes from Angola to Brazil, and British merchants sailed from the Bight of Benin to the Caribbean. The great majority of enslaved Africans were intended for the sugar and coffee plantations extending from the Caribbean islands to Brazil. Angola produced 26 percent of all African slaves and 70 percent of all Portuguese slaves. Trading networks extending deep into the interior culminated at two major ports on the Angolan coast, Luanda (loo-AHN-da) and Benguela. The Portuguese acquired a

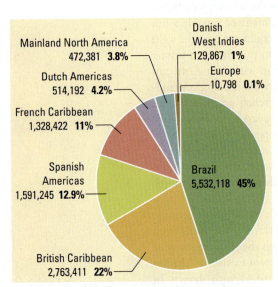

FIGURE 20.1 Estimated Slave Imports by Destination, 1501–1866 Brazil was the single largest importer of African slaves from 1501 to 1866. But when taken cumulatively, the British, French, Dutch, and Danish colonies of the Caribbean rivaled the much larger colony of Brazil for numbers of slaves imported from Africa.

(Source: Data from Emory University. "Assessing the Slave Trade: Estimates," in *Voyages: The Trans-Atlantic Slave Trade Database.* 2009. http://www.slavevoyages.org.)

few slaves through warfare but secured the vast majority through trade with African dealers. Whites did not participate in the inland markets, which were run solely by Africans.

Almost all Portuguese shipments went to satisfy the virtually insatiable Brazilian demand for slaves. The so-called **Middle Passage** was the horrific voyage under appalling and often deadly conditions of enslaved Africans across the Atlantic to the Americas.

Olaudah Equiano (see "Individuals in Society: Olaudah Equiano," page 610) describes the experience of his voyage as a captured slave from Benin to Barbados in the Caribbean:

> The stench of the hold while we were on the coast was so intolerably loathsome that it was dangerous to remain there for any time, and some of us had been permitted to stay on the deck for the fresh air; but now that the whole ship's cargo were confined together it became absolutely pestilential. The closeness of the place and the heat of the climate, added to the number in the ship, which was so crowded that each had scarcely room to turn himself, almost suffocated us. This produced copious perspirations, so that the air soon became unfit for respiration from a variety of loathsome smells, and brought on a sickness among the slaves, of which many died. . . . This wretched situation was again aggravated by the galling of the chains, now become insupportable, and the filth of the necessary tubs [of human waste], into which the children often fell and were almost suffocated. The shrieks of the women and the groans of the dying rendered the whole a scene of horror almost inconceivable.[17]

Although the demand was great, Portuguese merchants in Angola and Brazil sought to maintain only a steady trickle of slaves from the African interior to Luanda and across the ocean to Bahia and Rio de Janeiro: a flood of slaves would have depressed the American market. Planters and mine operators from the provinces traveled to Rio to buy slaves. Between 1795 and 1808 approximately 10,000 Angolans per year stood in the Rio slave market. In 1810 the figure rose to 18,000; in 1828 it reached 32,000.[18]

Middle Passage Enslaved Africans' horrific voyage across the Atlantic to the Americas, under appalling and often deadly conditions.

Peddlers in Rio de Janeiro

A British army officer sketched this early-nineteenth-century scene of everyday life in Rio de Janeiro, Brazil. The ability to balance large burdens on the head meant that the person's hands were free for other use. Note the player (on the left) of a musical instrument originating in the Congo. On the right a woman gives alms to the man with the holy image in return for being allowed to kiss the image as an act of devotion. We do not know whether the peddlers were free and self-employed or were selling for their owners. (From *Drawings Taken by Lieutenant Henry Chamberlain, During the Years 1819 and 1820* [London: Columbian Press, 1822]/Visual Connection Archive)

Olaudah Equiano

MOST OF THE LIVES OF PEOPLE TRAFFICKED in the transatlantic slave trade remain hidden to us. Olaudah Equiano (1745–1797) is probably the best-known African slave. His autobiography, *The Interesting Narrative of the Life of Olaudah Equiano* (1789), represents a rare window into the slaves' obscurity.

In his autobiography, Equiano says that he was born in Benin (modern Nigeria) of Ibo ethnicity.* In his village all people shared in the cultivation of family lands. One day, when the adults were in the fields, strangers broke into the family compound and kidnapped the eleven-year-old Olaudah and his sister. As it took six months to walk to the coast, Olaudah's home must have been far inland. The sea, the slave ship, and the strange appearance of the white crew terrified the boy. Equiano's first master took him to Jamaica, to Virginia, and then to England, where he placed him in the custody of a kind family. They gave him the rudiments of an education, and he was baptized a Christian.

Equiano eventually went to sea as a captain's boy (servant), serving in the Royal Navy. Back on shore in Portsmouth, England, Equiano's master urged him to read, study, and learn basic mathematics. He later sold Equiano to a Philadelphia Quaker, Robert King, who was a rum and sugar merchant. King paid Equiano to work as a clerk in King's warehouse, as a longshoreman loading and unloading cargo ships, and at sea where he developed good navigational skills. Equiano became an entrepreneur himself, buying and selling small goods in the islands and mainland ports. Equiano had amassed enough money by 1766 to buy his freedom, and King signed the deed of manumission. Equiano was twenty-one years old; he had been a slave for ten years.

In this 1789 portrait, Olaudah Equiano holds his Bible, open to the book of Acts.

(British Library, London, UK/© British Library Board. All Rights Reserved./The Bridgeman Art Library)

Equiano's *Narrative* reveals a complex and sophisticated man. He had a strong constitution and an equally strong character. His Christian faith undoubtedly sustained him. On his book's title page, he cited a verse from Isaiah (12:2): "The Lord Jehovah is my strength and my song."

Equiano loathed the brutal slavery he saw in the West Indies and the vicious racism he experienced in the North American colonies. He respected Robert King's fairness, admired British navigational and industrial technologies, and had many close white friends. He once described himself as "almost an Englishman." He was also involved in the black communities in the West Indies and in London.

Olaudah Equiano's *Narrative*, with its horrific descriptions of slavery, proved influential, and after its publication Equiano became active in the abolition movement. He spoke to large crowds in the industrial cities of Manchester and Birmingham in England, arguing that it was in the business interests of manufacturers to support abolition, as Africa was a huge, virtually untapped market for English cloth. Though he died in 1797, ten years before its passage, Equiano significantly advanced the abolitionist cause that led to the Slave Trade Act of 1807.

QUESTIONS FOR ANALYSIS

1. How typical was Olaudah Equiano's life as a slave? How atypical?
2. Describe Equiano's culture and his sense of himself.

Source: *Equiano's Travels: The Interesting Narrative of the Life of Olaudah Equiano*, ed. Paul Edwards (Portsmouth, N.H.: Heinemann, 1996).

*Recent scholarship has re-examined Equiano's life and raised some questions about his African origins and his experience of the Middle Passage. To explore the debate over Equiano's authorship of the African and Middle Passage portions of his autobiography, see Vincent Carretta, *Equiano, the African: Biography of a Self-Made Man* (New York: Penguin, 2007).

The English ports of London, Bristol, and particularly Liverpool dominated the British slave trade. In the eighteenth century Liverpool was the world's greatest slave-trading port. In all three cities, small and cohesive merchant classes exercised great public influence. The cities also had huge stores of industrial products for export, growing shipping industries, and large amounts of ready cash for investment abroad.

Slaving ships from Bristol plied back and forth along the Gold Coast, the Bight of Benin, Bonny, and Calabar looking for African traders who were willing to supply them with slaves. Liverpool's ships drew enslaved people from Gambia, the Windward Coast, and the Gold Coast. British ships carried textiles, gunpowder and flint, beer and spirits, British and Irish linens, and woolen cloth to Africa. A collection of goods was grouped together into what was called the **sorting**. An English sorting might include bolts of cloth, firearms, alcohol, tobacco, and hardware; this batch of goods was traded for an enslaved individual or a quantity of gold, ivory, or dyewood.[19]

> **sorting** A collection or batch of British goods that would be traded for a slave or for a quantity of gold, ivory, or dyewood.

European traders had two systems for exchange. First, especially on the Gold Coast, they established factory-forts. (For more on factory-forts, see "European Rivalry for Trade in the Indian Ocean" in Chapter 17.) These fortified trading posts were expensive to maintain but proved useful for fending off European rivals. Second, they used **shore trading**, in which European ships sent boats ashore or invited African dealers to bring traders and enslaved Africans out to the ships.

> **shore trading** A process for trading goods in which European ships sent boats ashore or invited African dealers to bring traders and slaves out to the ships.

The shore method of buying slaves allowed the ship to move easily from market to market. The final prices of those enslaved depended on their ethnic origin, their availability when the shipper arrived, and their physical health when offered for sale in the West Indies or the North or South American colonies.

The supply of slaves for the foreign market was controlled by a small, wealthy African merchant class or by a state monopoly. By contemporary standards, slave raiding was a costly operation, and only black African entrepreneurs with sizable capital and labor could afford to finance and direct raiding drives.

The transatlantic slave trade that the British, as well as the Dutch, Portuguese, French, Americans, and others, participated in was part of a much larger trading network that is known as the triangle trade. European merchants sailed to Africa on the first leg of the voyage to trade European manufactured goods for enslaved Africans. When they had filled their ships' holds with enslaved people, they headed across the Atlantic on the second leg of the voyage, the Middle Passage. When they reached the Americas, the merchants unloaded and sold their human cargoes and used the profits to purchase raw materials—such as cotton, sugar, and indigo—that they then transported back to Europe, completing the third leg of the commercial triangle.

Enslaved African people had an enormous impact on the economies and cultures of the Portuguese and Spanish colonies of South America and the Dutch, French, and British colonies of the Caribbean and North America. For example, on the sugar plantations of Mexico and the Caribbean; on the North American cotton, rice, and tobacco plantations; and in Peruvian and Mexican silver and gold mines, enslaved Africans not only worked in the mines and fields but also filled skilled, supervisory,

The African Slave Trade A European slave trader discusses the exchange of goods for slaves brought to him by the African on the right at Gorée Island off the coast of Senegal. (The British Library, London, UK/akg-images)

and administrative positions and performed domestic service. In the United States enslaved Africans and their descendants influenced many facets of American culture, such as language, music (ragtime and jazz), dance, and diet. Even the U.S. White House and Capitol building, where Congress meets, were built partly by slave labor.[20] But the importance of the slave trade extended beyond the Atlantic world. Both the expansion of capitalism and the industrialization of Western societies; Egypt; and the nations of West, Central, and South Africa were related in one way or another to the traffic in African people.

Impact on African Societies

What economic impact did European trade have on African societies? Africans possessed technology well suited to their environment. Over the centuries they had cultivated a wide variety of plant foods; developed plant and animal husbandry techniques; and mined, smelted, and otherwise worked a great variety of metals. Apart from a handful of items, most notably firearms, American tobacco and rum, and Portuguese brandy, European goods presented no novelty to Africans, but were desirable because of their low prices. Africans exchanged slaves, ivory, gold, pepper, and animal skins for those goods. African states eager to expand or to control commerce bought European firearms, although the difficulty of maintaining guns often gave gun owners only marginal superiority over skilled bowmen.[21]

The African merchants who controlled the production of exports gained the most from foreign trade. The king of Dahomey (duh-HO-mee) (modern-day Benin in West Africa), for example, had a gross income in 1750 of £250,000 (almost U.S. $33 million today) from the overseas export of his fellow Africans. A portion of his profit was spent on goods that improved his people's living standard. Slave-trading entrepôts, which provided opportunities for traders and for farmers who supplied foodstuffs to towns, caravans, and slave ships, prospered. But such economic returns did not spread very far.[22] International trade did not lead to Africa's economic development. Africa experienced neither technological growth nor the gradual spread of economic benefits in early modern times.

As in the Islamic world, women in sub-Saharan Africa also engaged in the slave trade. In Guinea these women slave merchants and traders were known as *nhara*. They acquired considerable riches, often by marrying the Portuguese merchants and serving as go-betweens for these outsiders who were not familiar with the customs and languages of the African coast. One of them, Mae Aurélia Correia (1810?–1875?), led a life famous in the upper Guinea coastal region for its wealth and elegance. Between the 1820s and 1840s she operated her own trading vessels and is said to have owned several hundred slaves. Some of them she hired out as skilled artisans and sailors. She and her sister (or aunt) Julia amassed a fortune in gold, silver jewelry, and expensive cloth while living in European-style homes. Julia and her husband, a trader from the Cape Verde Islands, also owned their own slave estates where they produced peanuts.

The intermarriage of French traders and Wolof women in Senegambia created a métis, or mulatto, class. In the emerging urban centers at Saint-Louis, members of this small class adopted the French language, the Roman Catholic faith, and a French manner of life, and they exercised considerable political and economic power. However, European cultural influences did not penetrate West African society beyond the seacoast.

The political consequences of the slave trade varied from place to place. The trade enhanced the power and wealth of some kings and warlords in the short run but promoted conditions of instability and collapse over the long run. In the Kongo kingdom the perpetual Portuguese search for Africans to enslave undermined the monarchy, destroyed political unity, and led to constant disorder and warfare; power passed to the village chiefs. Likewise in Angola, the slave trade decimated and scattered the population and destroyed the local economy. By contrast, the military kingdom of Dahomey, which entered into the slave trade in the eighteenth century and made it a royal monopoly, prospered enormously. Dahomey's economic strength rested on the slave trade. The royal army raided deep into the interior, and in the late eighteenth century Dahomey became one of the major West African sources of slaves. When slaving expeditions failed to yield sizable catches and when European demand declined, the resulting depression in the Dahomean economy caused serious political unrest. Iboland, inland from the Niger Delta, from whose great port cities of Bonny and Brass the British drained tens of thousands of enslaved Africans, experienced minimal political effects. A high birthrate kept pace with the incursions of the slave trade, and Ibo societies remained demographically and economically strong.

What demographic impact did the slave trade have on Africa? Between approximately 1501 and 1866 more than 12 million Africans were forcibly exported to the Americas, 6 million were traded to Asia, and 8 million were retained as slaves within Africa. Figure 20.2 shows the estimated number of slaves shipped to the Americas in the transatlantic slave trade. Export figures do not include the approximately 10 to 15 percent who died during procurement or in transit.

The early modern slave trade involved a worldwide network of relationships among markets in the Middle East, Africa, Asia, Europe, and the Americas. But Africa was the crucible of the trade. There is no small irony in the fact that Africa, which of all the continents was most desperately in need of population because of its near total dependence on labor-intensive agriculture and pastoralism, lost so many millions to the trade. Although the British Parliament abolished the slave trade in 1807 and

Queen Nzinga of Ndongo and Matamba
Queen Ana Nzinga (ca. 1583–1663) ruled the Ndongo and Matamba kingdoms of the Mbundu people in modern-day Angola. Here she meets with the Portuguese governor at his offices in Luanda in 1622. Tradition says that the governor offered her only a floor mat to sit on, which would have placed her in a subordinate position to him, so she ordered one of her servants down onto the floor so she could sit on his back. She is recognized as a brilliant military strategist who personally led her troops into battle against the Portuguese.
(Private Collection/Bridgeman Images)

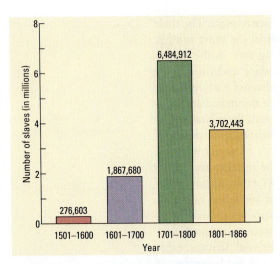

FIGURE 20.2 The Transatlantic Slave Trade, 1501–1866 The volume of slaves involved in the transatlantic slave trade peaked during the eighteenth century. These numbers show the slaves who embarked from Africa and do not reflect the 10 to 15 percent of enslaved Africans who died in transit.

(Source: Data from Emory University. "Assessing the Slave Trade: Estimates," in *Voyages: The Trans-Atlantic Slave Trade Database*. 2009. http://www.slavevoyages.org.)

traffic in Africans to Brazil and Cuba gradually declined, within Africa the trade continued at the levels of the peak years of the transatlantic trade, 1780–1820. In the later nineteenth century developing African industries, using slave labor, produced a variety of products for domestic consumption and export. Again, there is irony in the fact that in the eighteenth century European demand for slaves expanded the trade (and wars) within Africa, yet in the nineteenth century European imperialists defended territorial aggrandizement by arguing that they were "civilizing" Africans by abolishing slavery. But after 1880 European businessmen (and African governments) did not push abolition; they wanted cheap labor.

Markets in the Americas generally wanted young male slaves. Asian and African markets preferred young females. Women were sought for their reproductive value, as sex objects, and because their economic productivity was not threatened by the possibility of physical rebellion, as might be the case with young men. Consequently, two-thirds of those exported to the Americas were male, one-third female. As a result, the population on Africa's western coast became predominantly female; the population in the East African savanna and Horn regions was predominantly male. The slave trade therefore had significant consequences for the institutions of marriage, the local trade in enslaved people (as these local populations became skewed with too many males or too many females), and the sexual division of labor. Although Africa's overall population may have shown modest growth from roughly 1650 to 1900, that growth was offset by declines in the Horn and on the eastern and western coasts. While Europe and Asia experienced considerable demographic and economic expansion in the eighteenth century, Africa suffered a decline.[23]

The political and economic consequences of the African slave trade are easier to measure than the human toll taken on individuals and societies. While we have personal accounts from many slaves, ships' captains and crews, slave masters, and others of the horrors of the slave-trading ports along Africa's coasts, the brutality of the Middle Passage, and the inhuman cruelty enslaved Africans endured once they reached the Americas, we know much less about the beginning of the slave's journey in Africa. Africans themselves carried out much of the "man stealing," the term used by Africans to describe capturing enslaved men, women, and children and marching them to the coast, where they were traded to Arabs, Europeans, or others. Therefore, we have few written firsthand accounts of the pain and suffering these violent raids inflicted, either on the person being enslaved or on the families and societies they left behind.

Chapter Summary

In the early modern world, West African kingdoms and stateless societies existed side by side. Both had predominantly agricultural economies. Stateless societies revolved around a single village or group of villages without a central capital or ruler. Kings ruled over defined areas through bureaucratic hierarchies. The Sudanic empires controlled the north-south trans-Saharan trade in gold, salt, and other items. Led by predominantly Muslim rulers, these kingdoms belonged to a wider Islamic world, allowing them access to vast trade networks and some of the most advanced scholarship in the world. Still, Muslim culture affected primarily the royal and elite classes, seldom reaching the masses.

Europeans believed a wealthy (mythical) Christian monarch named Prester John ruled the Christian kingdom of Ethiopia. This fable attracted Europeans to Ethiopia, and partly explains why the Portuguese helped the Ethiopians fight off Muslim incursions. Jesuit missionaries tried to convert Ethiopians to Roman Catholicism but were fiercely resisted and expelled in 1633.

Swahili city-states on Africa's southeastern coast possessed a Muslim and mercantile culture. The Swahili acted as middlemen in the East African–Indian Ocean trade network, which in the late fifteenth and early sixteenth centuries Portugal sought to conquer and control. Swahili rulers who refused to form trading alliances with the Portuguese were attacked. The Portuguese presence caused the economic decline and death of many Swahili cities.

Slavery existed across Africa before Europeans arrived. Enslaved people were treated relatively benignly in some societies but elsewhere as chattel possessions, suffering harsh and brutal treatment. European involvement in the slave trade began around 1550, when the Portuguese purchased Africans to work in Brazil. The Dutch East India Company used enslaved Africans and southeast Asians in their Cape Colony. African entrepreneurs and merchants partnered in the trade, capturing people in the interior and exchanging them for firearms, liquor, and other goods with European slave ships. Though some kingdoms experienced a temporary rise of wealth and power, over time the slave trade was largely destabilizing. The individual suffering and social disruption in Africa caused by the enslavement of millions of Africans is impossible to estimate.

NOTES

1. P. D. Curtin, *Economic Change in Precolonial Africa: Senegambia in the Era of the Slave Trade* (Madison: University of Wisconsin Press, 1975), pp. 34–35; J. A. Rawley, *The Transatlantic Slave Trade: A History* (Lincoln: University of Nebraska Press, 2005).

2. Pieter de Marees, *Description of the Gold Kingdom of Guinea*, trans. and ed. Albert van Dantzig and Adam Jones (1602; repr., Oxford: Oxford University Press, 1987), pp. 226–228; William Bosman, *A New Description of the Coast of Guinea*, ed. John Ralph Willis (London: Frank Cass, 1967), p. 461.

3. Quoted in R. Hallett, *Africa to 1875* (Ann Arbor: University of Michigan Press, 1970), p. 151.

4. A. ibn-Fartura, "The Kanem Wars," in *Nigerian Perspectives*, ed. T. Hodgkin (London: Oxford University Press, 1966), pp. 111–115.

5. "The Kano Chronicle," quoted in *Nigerian Perspectives*, ed. T. Hodgkin (London: Oxford University Press, 1966), pp. 89–90.

6. *Equiano's Travels: The Interesting Narrative of the Life of Olaudah Equiano*, ed. P. Edwards (Portsmouth, N.H.: Heinemann, 1996), p. 4.

7. J. Iliffe, *Africans: The History of a Continent* (Cambridge: Cambridge University Press, 2007), p. 68.

8. See A. J. R. Russell-Wood, *The Portuguese Empire: A World on the Move* (Baltimore: Johns Hopkins University Press, 1998), pp. 11–13.

9. Ibid., pp. 35–38.

10. P. E. Lovejoy, *Transformations in Slavery: A History of Slavery in Africa* (Cambridge: Cambridge University Press, 1992), p. 25, Table 2.1, "Trans-Saharan Slave Trade, 650–1600."

11. Iliffe, *Africans*, p. 77.

12. Quoted in H. Thomas, *The Slave Trade* (New York: Simon and Schuster, 1997), p. 21.

13. G. Gerzina, *Black London: Life Before Emancipation* (New Brunswick, N.J.: Rutgers University Press, 1995), pp. 29–66 passim; quotation from p. 53.

14. R. Shell, *Children of Bondage: A Social History of the Slave Society at the Cape of Good Hope, 1652–1838* (Hanover, N.H.: University Press of New England, 1994), pp. 285–289.

15. See D. Eltis, *The Rise of African Slavery in the Americas* (Cambridge: Cambridge University Press, 2000), chap. 3; and the review/commentary by J. E. Inikori, *American Historical Review* 106.5 (December 2001): 1751–1753.

16. R. Blackburn, *The Making of New World Slavery: From the Baroque to the Modern, 1492–1800* (New York: Verso, 1998), pp. 79–80.

17. *Equiano's Travels*, pp. 23–26.

18. Rawley, *The Transatlantic Slave Trade*, pp. 45–47.

19. Robert W. July, *A History of the African People* (Prospect Heights, Ill.: Waveland Press, 1998), p. 171.

20. J. Thornton, *Africa and Africans in the Making of the Atlantic World* (New York: Cambridge University Press, 1992), pp. 138–142.

21. Robert W. July, *Precolonial Africa: An Economic and Social History* (New York: Scribner's, 1975), pp. 269–270.

22. A. G. Hopkins, *An Economic History of West Africa* (New York: Columbia University Press, 1973), p. 119.

23. P. Manning, *Slavery and African Life: Occidental, Oriental, and African Slave Trades* (New York: Cambridge University Press, 1990), pp. 22–23 and chap. 3, pp. 38–59.

CONNECTIONS

During the period from 1400 to 1800 many parts of Africa experienced a profound transition with the arrival of Europeans all along Africa's coasts. Ancient trade routes, such as those across the Sahara Desert or up and down the East African coast, were disrupted. In West Africa trade routes that had been purely internal now connected with global trade networks at European coastal trading posts. Along Africa's east coast the Portuguese attacked Swahili city-states in their effort to take control of the Indian Ocean trade nexus.

The most momentous consequence of the European presence along Africa's coast, however, was the introduction of the transatlantic slave trade. For more than three centuries Europeans, with the aid of African slave traders, enslaved millions of African men and women. Although many parts of Africa were untouched by the transatlantic slave trade, at least directly, areas where Africans were enslaved experienced serious declines in agricultural production, little progress in technological development, and significant increases in violence.

As we saw in Chapter 17 and will see in Chapter 21, early European commercial contacts with the empires of the Middle East and of South and East Asia were similar in many ways to those with Africa. Initially, the Portuguese, and then the English, Dutch, and French, did little more than establish trading posts at port cities and had to depend on the local people to bring them trade goods from the interior. Tropical diseases, particularly in India and Southeast Asia, took heavy death tolls on the Europeans, as they did in tropical Africa. What is more, while it was possible for the Portuguese to attack and conquer the individual Swahili city-states, Middle Eastern and Asian empires — such as the Ottomans in Turkey, the Safavids in Persia, the Mughals in India, and the

Ming and Qing Dynasties in China — were, like the West African kingdoms, economically and militarily powerful enough to dictate terms of trade with the Europeans.

Resistance to enslavement took many forms on both sides of the Atlantic. In Haiti, as discussed in Chapter 22, resistance led to revolution and independence, marking the first successful uprising of non-Europeans against a colonial power. At the end of the nineteenth century, as described in Chapter 25, Europeans used the ongoing Arab-Swahili slave raids from Africa's eastern coast far into the interior as an excuse to invade and eventually colonize much of central and eastern Africa. The racial discrimination that accompanied colonial rule in Africa set the stage for a struggle for equality that led to eventual independence after World War II.

CHAPTER 20 Review and Explore

Identify Key Terms

Identify and explain the significance of each item below.

chattel (p. 592)

age-grade systems (p. 593)

oba (p. 594)

Taghaza (p. 595)

Tuareg (p. 600)

cowrie shells (p. 600)

Coptic Christianity (p. 601)

Swahili (p. 602)

Middle Passage (p. 609)

sorting (p. 611)

shore trading (p. 611)

Review the Main Ideas

Answer the focus questions from each section of the chapter.

1. What types of economic, social, and political structures were found in the kingdoms and states along the west coast and in the Sudan? (p. 592)

2. How did the arrival of Europeans and other foreign cultures affect the East African coast, and how did Ethiopia and the Swahili city-states respond to these incursions? (p. 600)

3. What role did slavery play in African societies before the transatlantic slave trade began, and what was the effect of European involvement? (p. 603)

Make Comparisons and Connections

Analyze the larger developments and continuities within and across chapters.

1. In what ways did Islam enrich the Sudanic empires of West Africa?

2. Discuss the ways in which Africa came into greater contact with a larger world during the period discussed in this chapter.

3. How did the transatlantic slave trade affect West African society?

TIMELINE

AFRICA	← **1400–1600s** Salt trade dominates West African economy
	← **ca. 1464–1591** Songhai kingdom dominates the western Sudan

1493–1528 Muhammad Toure governs and expands kingdom of Songhai

1571–1603 Idris Alooma governs kingdom of Kanem-Bornu

◆ **1485** Portuguese and other Europeans first appear in Benin

◆ **1591** Moroccan army defeats Songhai

◆ **1498** Portuguese explorer Vasco da Gama sails around Africa

1502–1507 Portuguese erect forts at Kilwa, Zanzibar, and Sofala on Swahili coast

◆ **1529** Adal defeats Ethiopian emperor; begins systematic devastation of Ethiopia

◆ **1543** Joint Ethiopian and Portuguese force defeats Muslims in Ethiopia

MIDDLE EAST ← **1299–1922** Ottoman Empire **(Chs. 17, 25, 28)**

EUROPE ← **1350–1520** European Renaissance **(Ch. 15)**

EAST ASIA ← **1368–1644** Ming Dynasty in China **(Ch. 21)**

AMERICAS ◆ **1521** ◆ **1533** Spanish conquest of Aztecs, then Incas **(Ch. 16)**

SOUTH ASIA **1526–1761** Era of Mughal India **(Ch. 17)**

1500	1550	1600

Suggested Resources

BOOKS

Berger, Iris, E. Frances White, and Cathy Skidmore-Heiss. *Women in Sub-Saharan Africa: Restoring Women to History.* 1999. Necessary reading for a complete understanding of African history.

Cooper, Frederick. *Plantation Slavery on the East Coast of Africa.* 1997. Useful study of slavery in Africa.

Klein, Martin, and Claire C. Robertson. *Women and Slavery in Africa.* 1997. Written from the perspective that most slaves in Africa were women.

Law, Robin. *Oyo Empire, c. 1600–c. 1836: A West African Imperialism in the Era of the Atlantic Slave Trade.* 1977. Remains the definitive study of the powerful Oyo Empire in what is today Nigeria.

Lovejoy, Paul E. *Transformations in Slavery: A History of Slavery in Africa,* 3d ed. 2012. Essential for an understanding of slavery in an African context.

Middleton, John. *The World of the Swahili: An African Mercantile Civilization.* 1992. Introduction to East Africa and the Horn region.

Oliver, Roland, and Anthony Atmore. *Medieval Africa, 1250–1800.* 2001. A history of premodern Africa by two renowned historians of the continent.

Pearson, Michael N. *Port Cities and Intruders: The Swahili Coast, India, and Portugal in the Early Modern Era.* 2002. Comprehensive introduction to the Swahili coast and the Indian Ocean trade network.

Powell, Eve Troutt, and John O. Hunwick. *The African Diaspora in the Mediterranean Lands of Islam.* 2002. Important study of Islam and the African slave trade.

Robinson, David. *Muslim Societies in African History.* 2004. Valuable introduction to Islam in Africa by a renowned Africanist.

Shell, Robert C.-H. *Children of Bondage: A Social History of the Slave Society at the Cape of Good Hope, 1652–1838.* 1994. A massive study of Cape slave society filled with much valuable statistical data.

1652 Dutch East India Company establishes colony at Cape of Good Hope

1658 Dutch East India Company allows importation of slaves into Cape Colony

1789 Olaudah Equiano publishes autobiography

1680s Famine from Senegambian coast to Upper Nile

1738–1756 Major famine in West Africa

1688–1689 English Glorious Revolution **(Ch. 18)**

1644–1911 Qing Dynasty in China **(Chs. 21, 26)**

1603–1867 Tokugawa Shogunate in Japan **(Ch. 21)**

1650 | **1700** | **1750**

Shillington, Kevin. *History of Africa*, 3d ed. 2012. A soundly researched, highly readable, and well-illustrated survey.

Thornton, John. *Africa and Africans in the Making of the Atlantic World, 1400–1680*, 2d ed. 1998. Places African developments in an Atlantic context.

DOCUMENTARY

Africa: A Voyage of Discovery with Basil Davidson (Home Vision, 1984). An eight-part series about African history and society. See particularly episode 2, "Mastering the Continent"; episode 3, "Caravans of Gold"; and episode 4, "Kings and Cities."

FEATURE FILMS

Amistad (Steven Spielberg, 1997). The true story of a successful slave rebellion aboard *La Amistad*, a slave ship that was seized by the United States, and the legal battle over the status of the enslaved Africans that reached the U.S. Supreme Court.

12 Years a Slave (Steve McQueen, 2013). Academy Award–winning film adaptation of an 1853 slave narrative by Solomon Northup, a freeborn African American who was kidnapped and sold into slavery.

WEBSITES

Internet African History Sourcebook. A valuable reference site for historical sources on African history. **sourcebooks.fordham.edu/halsall/africa /africasbook.asp**

Voyages: The Trans-Atlantic Slave Trade Database. The premier database site for information about the transatlantic slave trade, including information and maps about nearly 36,000 slaving voyages, estimates of the number of enslaved Africans, and the identity of 91,491 Africans found in the slave records. **www.slavevoyages.org**

21

Continuity and Change in East Asia
1400–1800

The four centuries from 1400 to 1800 were a time of growth and dynamic change throughout East Asia. Although both China and Japan suffered periods of war, each ended up with expanded territories. The age of exploration brought New World crops to the region, leading to increased agricultural output and population growth. It also brought new opportunities for foreign trade and new religions. Another link between these countries was the series of massive Japanese invasions of Korea in the late sixteenth century, which led to war between China and Japan.

In China the native Ming Dynasty (1368–1644) brought an end to Mongol rule. Under the Ming, China saw agricultural reconstruction, commercial expansion, and the rise of a vibrant urban culture. In the early seventeenth century, after the Ming Dynasty fell into disorder, the non-Chinese Manchus founded the Qing Dynasty (1644–1911) and added Taiwan, Mongolia, Tibet, and Xinjiang to their realm. The Qing Empire thus was comparable to the other multiethnic empires of the early modern world, such as the Ottoman, Russian, and Habsburg Empires. In China itself the eighteenth century was a time of peace and prosperity.

In the Japanese islands the fifteenth century saw the start of civil war that lasted a century. At the end of the sixteenth century the world seemed to have turned upside down when a commoner, Hideyoshi, became the supreme ruler. He did not succeed in passing on his power to an heir, however. Power was seized by Tokugawa Ieyasu. Under the Tokugawa Shogunate (1603–1867), Japan restricted contact with the outside world and social mobility among its own people. Yet Japan thrived, as agricultural productivity increased and a lively urban culture developed.

The Manchu Imperial Bodyguard Zhanyinbao

Commissioned by the Qianlong emperor (r. 1736–1796), this portrait of imperial bodyguard Zhanyinbao was part of a large set that hung in the hall where the emperor received foreign emissaries.

Detail, *Portrait of the Imperial Bodyguard Zhanyinbao*, China, 18th century, Qing Dynasty (1644–1911). Hanging scroll; ink and color on silk. Purchase, The Dillon Fund Gift, 1986 (1986.206)/The Metropolitan Museum of Art, New York/Image copyright © The Metropolitan Museum of Art/Image source Art Resource, NY

CHAPTER PREVIEW

MING CHINA, 1368–1644
What sort of state and society developed in China after the Mongols were ousted?

THE MANCHUS AND QING CHINA, TO 1800
Did the return of alien rule with the Manchus have any positive consequences for China?

JAPAN'S MIDDLE AGES, CA. 1400–1600
How did Japan change during this period of political instability?

THE TOKUGAWA SHOGUNATE, TO 1800
What was life like in Japan during the Tokugawa peace?

MARITIME TRADE, PIRACY, AND THE ENTRY OF EUROPE INTO THE ASIAN MARITIME SPHERE
How did the sea link the countries of East Asia, and what happened when Europeans entered this maritime sphere?

What sort of state and society developed in China after the Mongols were ousted?

Ming China, 1368–1644

The founding of the Ming Dynasty ushered in an era of peace and prosperity. By the beginning of the seventeenth century, however, the Ming government was beset by fiscal, military, and political problems.

The Rise of Zhu Yuanzhang and the Founding of the Ming Dynasty

Ming Dynasty The Chinese dynasty in power from 1368 to 1644; it marked a period of vibrant urban culture.

The founder of the **Ming Dynasty**, Zhu Yuanzhang (JOO yoowan-JAHNG) (1328–1398), began life in poverty during the last decades of the Mongol Yuan Dynasty. His home region was hit by drought and then plague in the 1340s, and when he was only sixteen years old, his father, oldest brother, and that brother's wife all died, leaving two penniless boys with three bodies to bury. With no relatives to turn to, Zhu Yuanzhang asked a monastery to accept him as a novice. The monastery itself was short of funds, and the monks soon sent Zhu out to beg for food. For three or four years he wandered through central China. Only after he returned to the monastery did he learn to read.

A few years later, in 1351, members of a religious sect known as the Red Turbans rose in rebellion against the government. Red Turban teachings drew on Manichaean ideas about the incompatibility of the forces of good and evil as well as on the cult of the Maitreya Buddha, who according to believers would in the future bring his paradise to earth to relieve human suffering. When the temple where Zhu Yuanzhang was living was burned down in the fighting, Zhu joined the rebels and rose rapidly.

Zhu and his followers developed into brilliant generals, and gradually they defeated one rival after another. In 1356 Zhu took the city of Nanjing and made it his base. In 1368 his armies took Beijing, which the Mongol emperor and his closest followers had vacated just days before. Then forty years old, Zhu Yuanzhang declared himself emperor of the Ming (Bright) Dynasty. As emperor, he is known as Taizu (TIGH-dzoo) or the Hongwu emperor.

Taizu started his reign wanting to help the poor. To lighten the weight of government taxes and compulsory labor, he ordered a full-scale registration of cultivated land and population so that these burdens could be assessed more fairly. He also tried persuasion. He issued instructions to be read aloud to villagers, telling them to be obedient to their parents, live in harmony with their neighbors, work contentedly at their occupations, and refrain from evil.

Although in many ways anti-Mongol, Taizu retained some Yuan practices. One was setting up provinces as the administrative layer between the central government and the prefectures (local governments a step above counties). Another was the hereditary service obligation for both artisan and military households.

Garrisons were concentrated along the northern border and near the capital at Nanjing. Each garrison was allocated a tract of land that the soldiers took turns cultivating to supply their own food. Although in theory this system should have provided the Ming with a large but inexpensive army, the reality was less satisfactory. Garrisons were rarely self-sufficient. Furthermore, men compelled to become soldiers did not necessarily make good fighting men, and desertion was difficult to prevent.

Ming China, ca. 1600

Consequently, like earlier dynasties, the Ming turned to non-Chinese northerners for much of its armed forces.

Taizu had deeply ambivalent feelings about men of education and sometimes brutally humiliated them in open court. His behavior was so erratic that it is most likely that he suffered from some form of mental illness. When literary men began to avoid official life, Taizu made it illegal to turn down appointments or to resign from office. He began falling into rages that only the empress could stop, and after her death in 1382 no one could calm him. In 1376 Taizu had thousands of officials killed because they were found to have taken shortcuts in their handling of paperwork for the grain tax. In 1380 Taizu concluded that his chancellor was plotting to assassinate him, and thousands only remotely connected to the chancellor were executed. From then on, Taizu acted as his own chancellor, dealing directly with the heads of departments and ministries.

The next important emperor, called Chengzu or the Yongle emperor (r. 1403–1425), was also a military man. One of Taizu's younger sons, he took the throne by force from his nephew and often led troops into battle against the Mongols. Like his father, Chengzu was willing to use terror to keep government officials in line.

Early in his reign, Chengzu decided to move the capital from Nanjing to Beijing, which had been his own base as a prince and the capital during Mongol times. Constructed between 1407 and 1420, Beijing was a planned city. Like Chang'an in Sui and Tang times (581–907), it was arranged like a set of boxes within boxes and built on a north-south axis. The main outer walls were forty feet high and nearly fifteen miles around. Inside was the Imperial City, with government offices, and within that the palace itself, called the Forbidden City, with close to ten thousand rooms.

The areas surrounding Beijing were not nearly as agriculturally productive as those around Nanjing. To supply Beijing with grain, the Yuan Grand Canal connecting the city to the rice basket of the Yangzi River regions was broadened, deepened, and supplied with more locks and dams. The 15,000 boats and the 160,000 soldiers of the transport army who pulled loaded barges from the towpaths along the canal became the lifeline of the capital.

Problems with the Imperial Institution

Taizu had decreed that succession should go to the eldest son of the empress or to the son's eldest son if the son predeceased his father, the system generally followed by earlier dynasties. In Ming times, the flaws in this system became apparent as one mediocre, obtuse, or erratic emperor followed another.

Because Taizu had abolished the position of chancellor, emperors turned to secretaries and eunuchs to manage the paperwork. Eunuchs were essentially slaves who had been captured as boys and castrated. Society considered eunuchs the basest of servants, and Confucian scholars heaped scorn on them. Yet Ming emperors, like rulers in earlier dynasties, often preferred the always-compliant eunuchs to high-minded, moralizing civil service officials.

In Ming times, the eunuch establishment became huge. By the late fifteenth century the eunuch bureaucracy had grown as large as the civil service, with each having roughly twelve thousand positions. After 1500 the eunuch bureaucracy grew even more rapidly, and by the mid-sixteenth century seventy thousand eunuchs were in service throughout the country, with ten thousand in the capital. Tension between the two bureaucracies was high. In 1420 Chengzu set up a eunuch-run secret service to investigate cases of suspected corruption and sedition in the regular bureaucracy. Eunuch control over vital government processes became a severe problem.

In hope of persuading emperors to make reforms, many Ming officials risked their careers and lives by speaking out. To give an example, in 1519, when an emperor announced plans to make a tour of the southern provinces, over a hundred officials staged a protest by kneeling in front of the palace. The emperor ordered the officials to remain kneeling for three days, then had them flogged; eleven died. Rarely, however, did such acts move an emperor to change his mind.

Although the educated public complained about the performance of emperors, no one proposed or even imagined alternatives to imperial rule. High officials were forced to find ways to work around uncooperative emperors, but they were not able to put in place institutions that would limit the damage an emperor could do.

The Mongols and the Great Wall

The early Ming emperors held Mongol fighting men in awe and feared they might form another great military machine of the sort Chinggis Khan (ca. 1162–1227) had put together two centuries earlier. Although in Ming times the Mongols were never united in a pan-Mongol federation, groups of Mongols could and did raid. Twice they threatened the dynasty: in 1449 the khan of the western Mongols captured the Chinese emperor, and in 1550 Beijing was surrounded by the forces of the khan of the Mongols in Inner Mongolia. Fearful of anything that might strengthen the Mongols, Ming officials were reluctant to grant any privileges to Mongol leaders, such as trading posts along the borders. Instead they wanted the different groups of Mongols to trade only through the formal tribute system. When trade was finally liberalized in 1570, friction was reduced.

Two important developments shaped Ming-Mongol relations: the construction of the Great Wall and closer relations between Mongolia and Tibet. The Great Wall, much of which survives today, was built as a compromise when Ming officials could agree on no other way to manage the Mongol threat. The wall extends about 1,500 miles from northeast of Beijing into Gansu province. In the eastern 500 miles, the wall averages about 35 feet high and 20 feet across, with lookout towers every half mile.

Whether the wall did much to protect Ming China from the Mongols is still debated. Perhaps of more significance was the spread of Tibetan Buddhism among the Mongols. Tibet in this period was dominated by the major Buddhist monasteries, which would turn to competing Mongol leaders when they needed help. In 1577 the third Dalai Lama accepted the invitation of Altan Khan to visit Mongolia, and the khan declared Tibetan Buddhism to be the official religion of all the Mongols. The Dalai Lama gave the khan the title "King of Religion," and the khan swore that the Mongols would renounce blood sacrifice. When the third Dalai Lama's reincarnation was found to be the great-grandson of Altan Khan, the ties between Tibet and Mongolia, not surprisingly, became even stronger. From the perspective of Ming China, the growing influence of Buddhism among the Mongols seemed a positive development, as Buddhist emphasis on nonviolence was expected to counter the Mongols' love of war (though in fact the development of firearms was probably more crucial in the Mongols' loss of military advantage over their neighbors).

The Examination Life

In sharp contrast to Europe in this era, Ming China had few social barriers. It had no hereditary aristocracy that could have limited the emperor's absolute power. Although China had no titled aristocracy, it did have an elite whose status was based above all on government office acquired through education. Unlike in many European countries of the era, China's merchants did not become a politically articulate class of the well-to-do. Instead the politically active class was that of the scholars who Confucianism taught should aid the ruler in running the state. Merchants tried to marry into the scholar class in order to rise in the world.

Thus, despite the harsh and arbitrary ways in which the Ming emperors treated their civil servants, educated men were eager to enter the government. Reversing the policies of the Mongol Yuan Dynasty, the Ming government recruited almost all its officials through **civil service examinations**. Candidates had to study the Confucian classics and the interpretations of them by the twelfth-century Neo-Confucian scholar Zhu Xi (joo shee) (1130–1200), whose teachings were declared orthodox. To become officials, candidates had to pass examinations at the prefectural, the provincial, and the capital levels. To keep the wealthiest areas from dominating the exams, quotas were established for the number of candidates that each province could send on to the capital.

civil service examinations
A highly competitive series of written tests held at the prefecture, province, and capital levels in China to select men to become officials.

Of course, boys from well-to-do families had a significant advantage because their families could start their education with tutors at age four or five, though less costly schools were becoming increasingly available as well. Families that for generations had pursued other careers — for example, as merchants or physicians — had more opportunities than ever for their sons to become officials through the exams. (See "Individuals in Society: Tan Yunxian, Woman Doctor," page 626.) Clans sometimes operated schools for their members. Most of those who attended school stayed only a few years, but students who seemed most promising moved on to advanced schools where they practiced essay writing and studied the essays of men who had succeeded in the exams.

The examinations at the prefecture level lasted a day and drew hundreds if not thousands of candidates. The government compound would be taken over to give all candidates places to sit and write. The provincial and capital examinations were given in three sessions spread out over a week. In the first session, candidates wrote essays on passages from the classics. In the second and third sessions,

Portrait of a Scholar-Official The official Jiang Shunfu arranged to have his portrait painted wearing an official robe and hat and followed by two boy attendants, one holding a lute wrapped in cloth. During Ming and Qing times, the rank of an official was made visible by the badges he wore on his robes. The pair of cranes on Jiang's badge shows he held a first-rank post in the civil service hierarchy. (Visual Connection Archive)

Tan Yunxian, Woman Doctor

THE GRANDMOTHER OF TAN YUNXIAN (1461–1554) was the daughter of a physician, and her husband had married into her home to learn medicine himself. At least two of their sons—including Yunxian's father—passed the civil service examination and became officials, raising the social standing of the family considerably. The grandparents wanted to pass their medical knowledge down to someone, and because they found Yunxian very bright, they decided to teach it to her.

Tan Yunxian married and raised four children but also practiced medicine, confining her practice to women. At age fifty she wrote an autobiographical account, *Sayings of a Female Doctor*. In the preface she described how, under her grandmother's tutelage, she had first memorized the *Canon of Problems* and the *Canon of the Pulse*. Then when her grandmother had time, she asked her granddaughter to explain particular passages in these classic medical treatises.

Tan Yunxian began the practice of medicine by treating her own children, asking her grandmother to check her diagnoses. When her grandmother was old and ill, she gave Yunxian her notebook of prescriptions and her equipment for making medicines, telling her to study them carefully. Later, Yunxian herself became seriously ill and dreamed of her grandmother telling her on what page of which book to find the prescription that would cure her. When she recovered, she began her medical career in earnest.

Tan Yunxian's book records the cases of thirty-one patients she treated, most of them women with chronic complaints rather than critical illnesses. Many of the women had what the Chinese classed as women's complaints, such as menstrual irregularities, repeated miscarriages, barrenness, and postpartum fatigue. Some had ailments that men too could suffer, such as coughs, nausea, insomnia, diarrhea, rashes, and swellings. Like other literati physicians, Yunxian regularly prescribed herbal medications. She also practiced moxibustion, the technique of burning moxa (dried artemisia) at specified points on the body with the goal of stimulating the circulation of qi (life energy). Because the physician applying the moxa had to touch the patient, male physicians could not perform moxibustion on women.

Tan Yunxian would have consulted traditional herbals, like this one, with sketches of plants of medicinal value and descriptions of their uses. (Wellcome Library, London, UK)

Yunxian's patients included working women, and Yunxian seems to have thought that their problems often sprang from overwork. One woman came to her because she had had vaginal bleeding for three years. When questioned, the woman told Yunxian that she worked all day with her husband at their kiln making bricks and tiles. Yunxian's diagnosis was overwork, and she gave the woman pills to replenish her yin energies. A boatman's wife came to her complaining of numbness in her hands. When the woman told Yunxian that she worked in the wind and rain handling the boat, the doctor advised some time off. In another case Yunxian explained to a servant girl that she had gone back to work too soon after suffering a wind damage fever.

By contrast, when patients came from upper-class families, Tan Yunxian believed negative emotions were the source of their problems, particularly if a woman reported that her mother-in-law had scolded her or that her husband had recently brought a concubine home. Yunxian told two upper-class women who had miscarried that they lost their babies because they had hidden their anger, causing fire to turn inward and destabilize the fetus.

Tan Yunxian herself lived a long life, dying at age ninety-three.

QUESTIONS FOR ANALYSIS

1. Why do you think Tan Yunxian treated only women? Why might she have been more effective with women patients than a male physician would have been?
2. What do you think of Yunxian's diagnoses? Do you think she was able to help many of her patients?

Source: Based on Charlotte Furth, *A Flourishing Yin: Gender in China's Medical History, 960–1665* (Berkeley: University of California Press, 1999), pp. 285–295.

candidates had to write essays on practical policy issues and on a passage from the *Classic of Filial Piety* (a brief text celebrating devotion to parents and other superiors). In addition, they had to show that they could draft state papers such as edicts, decrees, and judicial rulings. Reading the dynastic histories was a good way to prepare for policy questions and state paper exercises.

The provincial examinations were major local events. From five thousand to ten thousand candidates descended on the city and filled up its hostels. To prevent cheating, no written material could be taken into the cells, and candidates were searched before being admitted. Anyone caught wearing a cheat-sheet (an inner gown covered with the classics in minuscule script) was thrown out of the exam and banned from the next session as well. During the sessions candidates had time to write rough drafts of their essays, correct them, and then copy neat final versions. Throughout this time, tension was high.

After the papers were handed in, clerks recopied them and assigned them numbers to preserve anonymity. Proofreaders checked the copying before handing the papers to the assembled examiners, who divided them up to grade, which generally took about twenty days. Those 2 to 10 percent who passed could not spend long celebrating, however, because they had to begin preparing for the capital exams, less than a year away.

Everyday Life in Ming China

For civil servants and almost everyone else, everyday life in Ming China followed patterns established in earlier periods. The family remained central to most people's lives, and almost everyone married. Beyond the family, people's lives were shaped by the type of work they did and where they lived.

Large towns and cities proliferated in Ming times and became islands of sophistication in the vast sea of rural villages. In these urban areas small businesses manufactured textiles, paper, and luxury goods such as silks and porcelains. The southeast became a center for the production of cotton and silks; other areas specialized in the grain and salt trades and in silver.

Printing reached the urban middle classes by the late Ming period, when publishing houses were putting out large numbers of books aimed at general audiences. To make their books attractive in the marketplace, entrepreneurial book publishers commissioned artists to illustrate them. By the sixteenth century more and more books were being published in the vernacular language (the language people spoke), especially short stories, novels, and plays. Ming vernacular short stories depicted a world much like that of their readers, full of shop clerks and merchants, monks and prostitutes, students and matchmakers. (See "Global Viewpoints: Chinese and European Commentators on Urban Amusements," page 628.)

The full-length novel made its first appearance during the Ming period. The plots of the early novels were heavily indebted to story cycles developed by oral storytellers over the course of several centuries. Competing publishers brought out their own editions of these novels, sometimes adding new illustrations or commentaries.

The Chinese found recreation and relaxation in many ways besides reading. The affluent indulged in an alcoholic drink made from fermented and distilled rice, and once tobacco was introduced from the Americas, both men and women took up pipes. Plays were also very popular. Owners of troupes would purchase young

Chinese and European Commentators on Urban Amusements

Zhang Dai (1597–1684?) lived the life of a well-to-do urban aesthete in Nanjing in the last decades of the Ming Dynasty, and then saw that life destroyed by the Manchu invasion. In later years, in much reduced circumstances, he wrote with nostalgia about the pleasures of his youth. His account of a popular storyteller can be compared to a Swiss visitor's account of the London theater scene in 1599.

Zhang Dai on a Nanjing Storyteller

■ Pockmarked Liu of Nanjing . . . is an excellent storyteller.

He tells one episode a day, and his fee is one ounce of silver. To engage him you have to make your booking, and forward his retainer, ten days in advance, and even then you may be out of luck. . . . I heard him tell the story of Wu Song killing the tiger on Jingyang Ridge. His version diverged greatly from the original text. He will describe things in the minutest particular, but his choice of what to put in and leave out is nice and neat, and he is never wordy. His bellow is like the boom of a mighty bell, and when he gets to some high point in the action he will let loose such a peal of thunder that the building will shake on its foundations. I remember that when Wu Song goes into the inn to get a drink and finds no one there to serve him, he suddenly gave such a roar as to set all the empty vessels humming and vibrating. To make dull patches come to life like this is typical of his passion for detail.

When he goes to perform in someone's house, he will not loosen his tongue until his hosts sit quietly, hold their breath, and give him their undivided attention. If he spots the servants whispering, or if his listeners yawn or show any signs of fatigue, he will come to an abrupt halt, and be impervious to persuasion to continue. He will often talk till past midnight, still keeping up an unhurried flow, while the servants wipe the tables, trim the lamp, and silently serve tea in cups of tasteful porcelain. His pacing and his inflexions, his articulation and his cadences, are exactly suited to the situation, and lay bare the very body and fibre of the matter. If one plucked all the other storytellers alive by the ear and made them listen to him, I do not doubt but they would be struck dumb with wonder and give up the ghost on the spot.

Thomas Platter on London Theater

■ On September 21st after lunch, about two o'clock, I and my party crossed the water, and there in the house with the thatched roof witnessed an excellent performance of the tragedy of the first Emperor Julius Caesar with a cast of some fifteen people; when the play was over, they danced very marvelously and gracefully together as is their wont, two dressed as men and two as women. . . . Thus daily at two in the afternoon, London has two, sometimes three plays running in different places, competing with each other, and those which play best obtain most spectators. The playhouses are so constructed that they play on a raised platform, so that everyone has a good view. There are different galleries and places, however, where the seating is better and more comfortable and therefore more expensive. For whoever cares to stand below only pays one English penny, but if he wishes to sit he enters by another door and pays another penny, while if he desires to sit in the most comfortable seats, which are cushioned, where he not only sees everything well, but can also be seen, then he pays yet another English penny at another door. And during the performance food and drink are carried round the audience, so that for what one cares to pay one may also have refreshment.

QUESTIONS FOR ANALYSIS

1. What similarities do you see in the way the performers in these descriptions entertained their audiences? What differences do you see?
2. What makes foreign visitors' accounts useful? What advantage do local observers have?

Sources: David Pollard, trans. and ed., *The Chinese Essay* (New York: Columbia University Press, 2000), pp. 89–90. Reproduced with permission of C. HURST & CO. LTD. in the format Book via Copyright Clearance Center; Clare Williams, trans., *Thomas Platter's Travels in England, 1599* (London: J. Cape, 1937), pp. 166–167.

Popular Romance Literature Women were among the most avid readers of the scripts for plays, especially romantic ones like *The Western Chamber*, a story of a young scholar who falls in love with a well-educated girl he encounters by chance. In this scene, the young woman looks up at the moon as her maid looks at its reflection in the pond. Meanwhile, her young lover scales the wall. This multicolor woodblock print, made in 1640, was one of twenty-one created to illustrate the play. (Pictures from History/CPA Media)

children and train them to sing and perform. Jesuit missionary Matteo Ricci, who lived in China from 1582 to 1610, thought too many people were addicted to these performances:

> These groups of actors are employed at all imposing banquets, and when they are called they come prepared to enact any of the ordinary plays. The host at the banquet is usually presented with a volume of plays and he selects the one or several he may like. The guests, between eating and drinking, follow the plays with so much satisfaction that the banquet at times may last for ten hours.[1]

Rice supplied most of the calories of the population in central and south China. (In north China, wheat, made into steamed or baked bread or into noodles, served as the dietary staple.) Farmers began to stock the rice paddies with fish, which continuously fertilized the rice fields, destroyed malaria-bearing mosquitoes, and enriched the diet. Farmers also grew cotton, sugarcane, and indigo as commercial crops. New methods of crop rotation allowed for continuous cultivation and for more than one harvest per year from a single field.

The Ming rulers promoted the repopulation and colonization of war-devastated regions through reclamation of land and massive transfers of people. Immigrants to these areas received large plots and exemption from taxation for many years. Reforestation played a dramatic role in the agricultural revolution. In 1391 the Ming government ordered 50 million trees planted in the Nanjing area to produce lumber for the construction of a maritime fleet. In 1392 each family holding a land grant in Anhui province had to plant two hundred mulberry, jujube, and persimmon trees. In 1396 peasants in the present-day provinces of Hunan and Hubei in central China planted 84 million fruit trees. Historians have estimated that 1 billion trees were planted during Taizu's reign.

Increased food production led to steady population growth and the multiplication of markets, towns, and small cities. Larger towns had permanent shops; smaller towns had periodic markets convening every five or ten days. They sold essential goods — such as pins, matches, oil for lamps, candles, paper, incense, and tobacco — to country people from the surrounding hamlets. Markets usually offered essential goods such as lamp oil and matches as well as the services of moneylenders, pawnbrokers, and craftsmen such as carpenters, barbers, joiners, and locksmiths.

Ming Decline

Beginning in the 1590s the Ming government was beset by fiscal, military, and political problems. The government went nearly bankrupt helping defend Korea against a Japanese invasion (see "Piracy and Japan's Overseas Adventures"). Then came a series of natural disasters: floods, droughts, locusts, and epidemics ravaged one region after another. At the same time, a "little ice age" brought a drop in average temperatures that shortened the growing season and reduced harvests. In areas of serious food shortages, gangs of army deserters and laid-off soldiers began scouring the countryside in search of food. Once the gangs had stolen all their grain, hard-pressed farmers joined them just to survive. The Ming government had little choice but to try to increase taxes to deal with these threats, but the last thing people needed was heavier taxes.

Adding to the hardship was a sudden drop in the supply of silver. In place of the paper money that had circulated in Song and Yuan times, silver ingots came into general use as money in Ming times. Much of this silver originated in either Japan or the New World and entered China as payment for the silk and porcelains exported from China. When events in Japan and the Philippines led to disruption of trade, silver imports dropped. This led to deflation in China, which caused real rents to rise. Soon there were riots among urban workers and tenant farmers. In 1642 a group of rebels cut the dikes on the Yellow River, causing massive flooding. A smallpox epidemic soon added to the death toll. In 1644 the last Ming emperor, in despair, took his own life when rebels entered Beijing, opening the way for the start of a new dynasty.

Did the return of alien rule with the Manchus have any positive consequences for China?

The Manchus and Qing China, to 1800

The next dynasty, the **Qing Dynasty** (1644–1911), was founded by the Manchus, a non-Chinese people who were descended from the Jurchens. In the late sixteenth century the Manchus began expanding their territories, and in 1644 they founded the Qing (CHING) Dynasty, which brought peace and in time prosperity. Successful Qing military campaigns extended the borders into Mongol, Tibetan, and Uighur regions, creating a multiethnic empire that was larger than any earlier Chinese dynasty.

Qing Dynasty The dynasty founded by the Manchus that ruled China from 1644 to 1911.

MAP 21.1 The Qing Empire, ca. 1800 The sheer size of the Qing Empire in China almost inevitably led to its profound cultural influence on the rest of Asia.

ANALYZING THE MAP How many different cultural groups are depicted? Which occupied the largest territories? Where was crop agriculture most prevalent?

CONNECTIONS What geographical and political factors limited the expansion of the Qing Empire?

The Rise of the Manchus

In the Ming period, the Manchus lived in dispersed communities in what is loosely called Manchuria (the northeast of modern-day China). In the more densely populated southern part of Manchuria, the Manchus lived in close contact with Mongols, Koreans, and Chinese (Map 21.1). They were not nomads but rather hunters, fishers, and farmers. Like the Mongols, they also were excellent horsemen and archers and had a strongly hierarchical social structure, with elites and slaves. Slaves, often Korean or Chinese, were generally acquired through capture. Manchu villages were often at odds with each other over resources, and men did not leave their villages without arming themselves with bows and arrows or swords. Interspersed among these Manchu settlements were groups of nomadic Mongols who lived in tents.

The Manchus credited their own rise to Nurhaci (1559–1626). Over several decades, he united the Manchus and expanded their territories. Like Chinggis Khan, who had reorganized the Mongol armies to reduce the importance of tribal affiliations, Nurhaci created a new social basis for his armies in units called **banners**. Each banner was made up of a set of military companies and included the families and slaves of the soldiers. Each company had a hereditary captain, often from Nurhaci's own lineage. When new groups were defeated, their members were distributed among several banners to lessen their potential for subversion.

The Manchus entered China by invitation of the distinguished Ming general Wu Sangui, who was near the eastern end of the Great Wall when he heard that the rebels had captured Beijing. The Manchus proposed to Wu that they join forces and liberate Beijing. Wu opened the gates of the Great Wall to let the Manchus in, and within a couple of weeks they occupied Beijing. When the Manchus made clear that they intended to conquer the rest of the country and take the throne themselves, Wu and many other Chinese generals joined forces with them. Before long, China was again under alien rule.

In the summer of 1645 the Manchus ordered all Chinese men to shave the front of their heads and braid the rest in the Manchu fashion, an order many refused to comply with. Their resistance led Manchu commanders to order the slaughter of defiant cities. After quelling resistance, the Qing put in place policies and institutions that gave China a respite from war and disorder. Most of the political institutions of the Ming Dynasty were taken over relatively unchanged, including the examination system.

After peace was achieved, population growth took off. Between 1700 and 1800 the Chinese population seems to have nearly doubled, from about 150 million to over 300 million. Population growth during the eighteenth century has been attributed to many factors: global warming that extended the growing season, expanded use of New World crops, slowing of the spread of new diseases that had accompanied the sixteenth-century expansion of global traffic, and the efficiency of the Qing government in providing relief in times of famine.

Some scholars have recently argued that China's overall standard of living in the mid-eighteenth century was comparable to Europe's and that the standards of China's most developed regions, such as the lower Yangzi region, compared favorably to those of the most developed regions of Europe at the time, such as England and the Netherlands. Life expectancy, food consumption, and even facilities for transportation were at similar levels.

Competent and Long-Lived Emperors

For more than a century, China was ruled by only three rulers, each of them hardworking, talented, and committed to making the Qing Dynasty a success. Two, the Kangxi and Qianlong emperors, had exceptionally long reigns.

Kangxi (KAHNG-shee) (r. 1661–1722) proved adept at meeting the expectations of both the Chinese and the Manchu elites. Kangxi could speak, read, and write Chinese and made efforts to persuade educated Chinese that the Manchus had a legitimate claim to rule, even trying to attract Ming loyalists who had been unwilling

banners Units of the Manchu army, composed of soldiers, their families, and slaves.

Presenting a Horse to the Emperor This detail from a 1757 hand scroll shows the Qianlong emperor, seated, receiving envoys from the Kazakhs. Note how the envoy, presenting a pure white horse, is kneeling to the ground performing the kowtow, which involved lowering his head to the ground as an act of reverence. The artist was Giuseppe Castiglione, an Italian who worked as a painter in Qianlong's court. (Musée des Arts Asiatiques-Guimet, Paris, France/© RMN–Grand Palais/Art Resource, NY)

to serve the Qing. He undertook a series of tours of the south, where Ming loyalty had been strongest, and he held a special exam to select men to compile the official history of the Ming Dynasty.

Qianlong (chyan-luhng) (r. 1736–1796) understood that the Qing's capacity to hold the multiethnic empire together rested on their ability to appeal to all those they ruled. Besides speaking Manchu and Chinese, Qianlong learned to converse in Mongolian, Uighur, Tibetan, and Tangut, and he addressed envoys in their own languages. He became as much a patron of Tibetan Buddhism as of Chinese Confucianism. He initiated a massive project to translate the Tibetan Buddhist canon into Mongolian and Manchu and had huge multilingual dictionaries compiled.

To demonstrate to the Chinese scholar-official elite that he was a sage emperor, Qianlong worked on affairs of state from dawn until early afternoon and then turned to reading, painting, and calligraphy. He was ostentatious in his devotion to his mother, visiting her daily and tending to her comfort with all the devotion of the most filial Chinese son. He took several tours down the Grand Canal to the southeast, in part to emulate his grandfather, in part to entertain his mother, who accompanied him on these tours.

Despite these displays of Chinese virtues, the Qianlong emperor was alert to any signs of anti-Manchu thoughts or actions. He ordered full searches for books with disparaging references to the Manchus or to previous alien conquerors like the Jurchens and Mongols. Sometimes passages were deleted or rewritten, but when an entire book was offensive, it was destroyed.

Throughout Qianlong's reign, China remained an enormous producer of manufactured goods and led the way in assembly-line production. The government operated huge textile factories, but some private firms were even larger. Hangzhou had a textile firm that gave work to 4,000 weavers, 20,000 spinners, and 10,000 dyers and finishers. The porcelain kilns at Jingdezhen employed the division of labor on a large scale and were able to supply porcelain to much of the world. The growth of the economy benefited the Qing state, and the treasury became so full that the Qianlong emperor was able to cancel taxes on several occasions.

Imperial Expansion

The Qing Dynasty put together a multiethnic empire that was larger than that of any earlier Chinese dynasty. Taiwan was acquired in 1683. In 1696 Kangxi led an army of eighty thousand men into Mongolia, and within a few years Manchu supremacy was accepted there. Cannon and muskets gave Qing forces military superiority over the Mongols, who were armed only with bows and arrows. Thus the Qing could dominate the steppe cheaply, effectively ending two thousand years of Inner Asian military advantage.

In the 1720s the Qing established a permanent garrison of banner soldiers in Tibet. By this time, the expanding Qing and Russian Empires were nearing each other. In 1689 the Manchu and the Russian rulers approved a treaty—written in Russian, Manchu, Chinese, and Latin—defining their borders in Manchuria and regulating trade. Another treaty in 1727 allowed a Russian ecclesiastical mission to reside in Beijing and a trade caravan to make a trip from Russia to Beijing once every three years.

The last region to be annexed was Chinese Turkestan (the modern province of Xinjiang). Both the Han and the Tang Dynasties had stationed troops in the region, exercising loose overlordship, but neither the Song nor the Ming had tried to control the area. The Qing won the region in the 1750s through a series of campaigns against Uighur and Dzungar Mongol forces.

How did Japan change during this period of political instability?

Japan's Middle Ages, ca. 1400–1600

In the twelfth century Japan entered an age dominated by military men, an age that can be compared to Europe's feudal age. The Kamakura Shogunate (1185–1333) had its capital in the east, at Kamakura. It was succeeded by the Ashikaga Shogunate (1338–1573), which returned the government to Kyoto (KYOH-toh) and helped launch, during the fifteenth century, the great age of Zen-influenced Muromachi culture. The sixteenth century brought civil war over succession to the shogunate, leading to the building of massive castles and the emergence of rulers of obscure origins who eventually unified the realm.

Muromachi Culture

The headquarters of the Ashikaga shoguns were on Muromachi Street in Kyoto, and the refined and elegant style that they promoted is often called Muromachi culture. The shoguns patronized Zen Buddhism, the school of Buddhism associated with meditation and mind-to-mind transmission of truth.

Zen ideas of simplicity permeated the arts. The Silver Pavilion built by the shogun Yoshimasa (r. 1449–1473) epitomizes Zen austerity. Yoshimasa was also influential in the development of the tea ceremony, which celebrated the beauty of imperfect objects, such as plain or misshapen cups or pots. Spare monochrome paintings fit into this aesthetic, as did simple asymmetrical flower arrangements.

The shoguns were also patrons of the **Nō theater**. Nō drama originated in popular forms of entertainment, including comical skits and dances directed to the gods. It was transformed into high art by Zeami (1363–1443), an actor and playwright. Nō was performed on a bare stage with a pine tree painted across the backdrop. One or two actors wearing brilliant brocade robes performed, using stylized gestures and stances, one wearing a mask. The actors were accompanied by a chorus and a couple of musicians playing drums and flute. Many of the stories concerned ghosts consumed by jealous passions or the desire for revenge. The performers conveyed emotions and ideas as much through gestures, stances, and dress as through words. Zeami argued that the most meaningful moments came during silence, when the actor's spiritual presence allowed the audience to catch a glimpse of the mysterious and inexpressible.

Nō theater A type of Japanese theater performed on a bare stage by one or two actors wearing brilliant brocade robes, one actor wearing a mask. The performers conveyed emotions and ideas as much through gestures, stances, and dress as through words.

Civil War

Civil war began in Kyoto in 1467 as a struggle over succession to the shogunate. Rival claimants and their followers used arson as their chief weapon and burned down temples and mansions, destroying much of the city and its treasures. Once Kyoto was laid waste, war spread to outlying areas. When the shogun could no longer protect cities, merchants banded together to hire mercenaries. In the political vacuum, the Lotus League, a commoner-led religious sect united by faith in the saving power of the Lotus Sutra, set up a commoner-run government that collected taxes and settled disputes. In 1536, during eight days of fighting, the powerful Buddhist monastery Enryakuji attacked the League and its temples, burned much of the city, and killed men, women, and children who were thought to be believers.

In these confused and violent circumstances, power devolved to the local level, where warlords, from the **daimyo** (DIGH-myoh) class of regional lords, built their power bases. Many of the most successful daimyo were self-made men who rose from obscurity.

daimyo Regional lords in Japan, many of whom were self-made men.

The violence of the period encouraged castle building. The castles were built not on mountaintops but on level plains, and they were surrounded by moats and walls made from huge stones. Inside a castle was an elegantly decorated many-storied keep. Though relatively safe from incendiary missiles, the keeps were vulnerable to Western-style cannon, introduced in the 1570s.

The Victors: Nobunaga and Hideyoshi

The first daimyo to gain a predominance of power was Oda Nobunaga (1534–1582). A samurai of the lesser daimyo class, he recruited followers from masterless samurai who had been living by robbery and extortion. After he won control of his native province in 1559, he immediately set out to extend his power through central Japan. A key step was destroying the military power of the great monasteries. To increase revenues, he minted coins, the first government-issued money in Japan since 958. He also eliminated customs barriers and opened the little fishing village of Nagasaki to foreign commerce; it soon became Japan's largest port.

In 1582, in an attempted coup, Nobunaga was forced by one of his vassals to commit suicide. His general and staunchest adherent, Toyotomi Hideyoshi (1537–

Hideyoshi's Campaigns in Japan and Korea, 1592–1598

1598), avenged him and continued the drive toward unification of the daimyo-held lands, finally completed in 1590.

Like the Ming founder, Hideyoshi (HEE-deh-YOH-shee) was a peasant's son who rose to power through military talent. A series of campaigns brought all of Japan under Hideyoshi's control. Hideyoshi soothed the vanquished daimyo as Nobunaga had done—with lands and military positions—but he also required them to swear allegiance and to obey him down to the smallest particular. For the first time in over two centuries, Japan had a single ruler.

Hideyoshi did his best to ensure that future peasants' sons would not be able to rise as he had. His great sword hunt of 1588 collected weapons from farmers, who were no longer allowed to wear swords. Restrictions were also placed on samurai; they were prohibited from leaving their lord's service or switching occupations. To improve tax collection, Hideyoshi ordered a survey of the entire country that tied each peasant household to the land. With the country pacified, Hideyoshi embarked on an ill-fated attempt to conquer Korea and China that ended only with his death, discussed later in this chapter.

What was life like in Japan during the Tokugawa peace?

The Tokugawa Shogunate, to 1800

On his deathbed, Hideyoshi set up a council of regents to govern during the minority of his infant son. The strongest regent was Hideyoshi's long-time supporter Tokugawa Ieyasu (toh-koo-GAH-wuh ee-eh-YAH-soo) (1543–1616). In 1600 at Sekigahara, Ieyasu smashed a coalition of daimyo defenders of the heir and began building his own government—thus ending the long period of civil war. In 1603 he took the title "shogun." The **Tokugawa Shogunate** that Ieyasu fashioned lasted until 1867. This era is also called the Edo (AY-doh) period after the location of the shogunate in the city of Edo (now called Tokyo), starting Tokyo's history as Japan's most important city (Map 21.2).

Tokugawa Shogunate The Japanese government in Edo founded by Tokugawa Ieyasu. It lasted from 1603 to 1867.

Tokugawa Government

Over the course of the seventeenth century the Tokugawa shoguns worked to consolidate relations with the daimyo. In a scheme resembling the later residency requirements imposed by Louis XIV in France (see "The Absolutist Palace" in Chapter 18), Ieyasu set up the **alternate residence system**, which compelled the lords to live in Edo every other year and to leave their wives and sons there—essentially as hostages.

alternate residence system Arrangement in which Japanese lords were required to live in Edo every other year and left their wives and sons there as hostages to the Tokugawa Shogunate.

The peace imposed by the Tokugawa Shogunate brought a steady rise in population to about 30 million people by 1800. To maintain stability, the early Tokugawa shoguns froze social status. Daimyo were prohibited from moving troops outside their frontiers, making alliances, and coining money. Samurai and peasants were kept strictly apart. Samurai were defined as those permitted to carry swords. Prohibited from owning land, they had to live in castles (which evolved into castle-towns), and they depended on stipends from their lords, the daimyo. Likewise, merchants and artisans had to live in towns and could not own land.

After 1639 Japan limited its contacts with the outside world because of concerns both about the loyalty of subjects converted to Christianity by European missionaries and about the imperialist ambitions of European powers (discussed below). However, China remained an important trading partner and source of ideas. The Edo

Daimyo Procession The system of alternate residence meant that some daimyo were always on the road. The constant travel of daimyo with their attendants between their domains and Edo, the shogun's residence, stimulated construction of roads, inns, and castle-towns.

(*Daimyo's Processions Passing Along the Tokaido*, by Utagawa Sadahide [1807–1873]/triptych of polychrome woodblock prints; ink and color on paper, Edo period [1615–1868]. Bequest of William S. Lieberman, 2005, accession 2007.49.290a–c/Metropolitan Museum of Art, New York/Image copyright © The Metropolitan Museum of Art/Image source: Art Resource, NY)

period also saw the development of a school of native learning that rejected Buddhism and Confucianism as alien and tried to identify a distinctly Japanese sensibility.

Commercialization and the Growth of Towns

During the civil war period, warfare seems to have promoted social and economic change, much as it had in China during the Warring States Period (403–221 B.C.E.). Trade grew, and greater use was made of coins imported from Ming China. Markets began appearing at river crossings, at the entrances to temples and shrines, and at other places where people congregated. Towns and cities sprang up all around the country, some of them around the new castles. Traders and artisans dealing in a specific product began forming guilds. Foreign trade also flourished, despite chronic problems with pirates who raided the Japanese, Korean, and Chinese coasts (see "Piracy and Japan's Overseas Adventures").

In most cities, merchant families with special privileges from the government controlled the urban economy. Frequently, a particular family dominated the trade in a particular product and then branched out into other businesses. Japanese merchant families also devised distinct patterns and procedures for their business operations.

In the seventeenth century underemployed farmers and samurai, not to mention the ambitious and adventurous, thronged to the cities. As a result, Japan's cities grew tremendously. Kyoto became the center for the manufacture of luxury goods like lacquer, brocade, and fine porcelain. Osaka was the chief market, especially for rice. Edo was a center of consumption by the daimyo, their vassals, and government bureaucrats. Both Osaka and Edo reached about a million residents.

Two hundred fifty towns came into being in this period. Most ranged in size from 3,000 to 20,000 people, but a few, such as Hiroshima, Kagoshima, and Nagoya, had

MAP 21.2 Tokugawa Japan, 1603–1867 The lands that the shogunate directly controlled were concentrated near its capital at Edo. The daimyo of distant places, such as the island of Kyushu, were required to make long journeys to and from Edo every year.

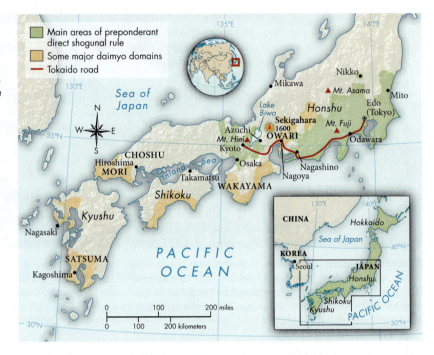

populations of between 65,000 and 100,000. In addition, perhaps two hundred towns along the main road to Edo emerged to meet the needs of men traveling on the alternate residence system. In the eighteenth century perhaps 4 million people, 15 percent of the Japanese population, resided in cities or towns.

The Life of the People in the Edo Period

The Tokugawa shoguns brought an end to civil war by controlling the military. Stripped of power and required to spend alternate years at Edo, many of the daimyo and samurai passed their lives in idle pursuit of pleasure. They spent extravagantly on paintings, concubines, boys, the theater, and the redecoration of their castles. These temptations, as well as more sophisticated pleasures and the heavy costs of maintaining alternate residences at Edo, gradually bankrupted the warrior class.

All major cities contained places of amusement for men—teahouses, theaters, restaurants, and houses of prostitution. Desperately poor parents sometimes sold their daughters to entertainment houses (as they did in China and medieval Europe), and the most attractive or talented girls, trained in singing, dancing, and conversational arts, became courtesans, later called geishas (GAY-shahz), "accomplished persons."

Cities were also the center for commercial publishing. The art of color woodblock printing also was perfected during this period. As in contemporary China, the reading public eagerly purchased fiction and the scripts for plays. Ihara Saikaku (1642–1693) wrote stories of the foibles of townspeople in such books as *Five Women Who Loved Love* and *The Life of an Amorous Man*. One of the puppet plays of Chikamatsu Monzaemon (1653–1724) tells the story of the son of a business owner who, caught between duty to his family and love of a prostitute, decides to resolve the situation by double suicide. Similar stories were also performed in Kabuki theater, where plays could go on all day, actors wore elaborate makeup, and men trained to impersonate women performed female roles. (See "Analyzing the Evidence: Interior View of a Kabuki Theater," page 640.)

Almost as entertaining as attending the theater was watching the long processions of daimyo, their retainers, and their luggage as they passed back and forth to and from Edo every year. The shogunate prohibited most travel by commoners, but they could get passports to take pilgrimages, visit relatives, or seek the soothing waters of medicinal hot springs. Setting out on foot, groups of villagers would travel to such shrines as Ise, often taking large detours to visit Osaka or Edo to sightsee or attend the theater.

During the seventeenth and eighteenth centuries daimyo and upper-level samurai paid for their extravagant lifestyles by raising taxes on their subordinate peasants from 30 or 40 percent of the rice crop to 50 percent. Not surprisingly, this angered peasants, and peasant protests became chronic during the eighteenth century. Natural disasters also added to the peasants' misery. In 1783 Mount Asama erupted, spewing volcanic ash that darkened the skies all summer; the resulting crop failures led to famine. When famine recurred again in 1787, commoners rioted for five days in Edo, smashing merchants' stores and pouring sake and rice into the muddy streets. The shogunate responded by trying to control the floating population of day laborers without families in the city. At one point they were rounded up and transported to work the gold mines in an island off the north coast, where most of them died within two or three years.

This picture of peasant hardship tells only part of the story. Agricultural productivity increased substantially during the Tokugawa period. Peasants who improved their lands and increased their yields continued to pay the same assessed tax and could pocket the surplus as profit. They could also take on other work. At Hirano near Osaka, for example, 61.7 percent of all arable land was sown in cotton. The peasants ginned the cotton locally before transporting it to wholesalers in Osaka. In many rural places, as many peasants worked in the manufacture of silk, cotton, or vegetable oil as in the production of rice.

In comparison to farmers, merchants had a much easier life, even if they had no political power. In 1705 the shogunate confiscated the property of a merchant in Osaka "for conduct unbecoming a member of the commercial class" (but more likely because too many samurai owed him money). The government seized 50 pairs of gold screens, 360 carpets, several mansions, 48 granaries and warehouses scattered around the country, and hundreds of thousands of gold pieces. Few merchants possessed such fabulous wealth, but many lived very comfortably.

Within a village, some families would be relatively well-off, others barely able to get by. The village headman generally came from the

Edo Craftsman at Work
Less than 3 inches tall, this ivory figure shows a parasol maker seated on the floor (the typical Japanese practice) eating his lunch, his tools by his side. (Private Collection/Photo © Boltin Picture Library/Bridgeman Images)

Interior View of a Kabuki Theater

In the Edo period, kabuki theater was one of the most popular forms of entertainment in Japanese cities, where it was patronized by merchants, samurai, and other townspeople. It originated in crude, bawdy skits dealing with love and romance and performed by women. Because actresses were thought to corrupt public morals, the Tokugawa government banned them from the stage in 1629. From that time on, men played all the parts. Male actors in female dress and makeup performed as seductively as possible to entice the men who thronged the theaters. Some moralists complained from time to time about the licentiousness of kabuki, but the Tokugawa government decided to accept both kabuki and prostitution as necessary evils.

Kabuki performances generally took all day and consisted of several short plays or one long five-act play. Historical plays were very popular but were always set far enough in the past so that the government would not see them as a form of political protest. The main characters of historical plays were usually samurai. Ordinary townsmen or farmers could be the main characters in dramas and love stories, which were also popular. Some of these revolved around lovers who cannot overcome the obstacles to life together, leading them to decide to be together in death through double suicide.

The makeup worn by kabuki actors allowed the audience to see from a distance the sort of person being portrayed. Black generally suggested villainy, red passion or heroism, and green the supernatural. Actors became quite famous, and their stage names tied them to lineages of actors known for certain roles or acting styles.

Kabuki theaters had not only a central stage but also a walkway that projected out into the audience and was used for dramatic entrances and exits and other important scenes. Movable scenery and lighting effects made possible the staging of storms, fires, and hurricanes. The theater was not darkened, so the audience also got to see who else was attending the theater and what they were wearing.

Kabuki had a close connection to the art of the colored woodblock print, both of which flourished in the eighteenth century. Artists created not only prints like this one, showing the inside of a theater, but also single-sheet portraits of actors, which increased the performers' fame.

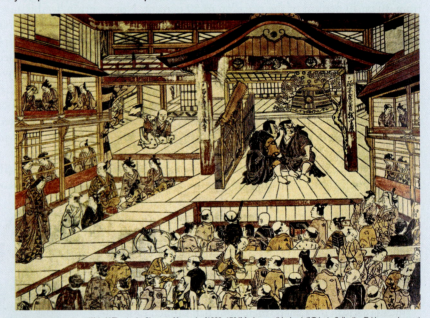

(*Kabuki* Theatre by Okumara Masanobu [1686–1764] [color woodblock print]/Private Collection/Bridgeman Images)

QUESTIONS FOR ANALYSIS

1. How many people are performing in this scene? What are they doing?
2. Are there more men or women in the audience? How do you distinguish them? Are any of the men samurai? How can you tell?
3. What is going on in the audience? Is everyone looking at the actors?

richest family, but he consulted a council of elders on important matters. Women in better-off families were much more likely to learn to read than women in poor families. Daughters of wealthy peasants studied penmanship, the Chinese classics, poetry, and the proper forms of correspondence, and they rounded out their education with travel. By contrast, girls from middle-level peasant families might have had from two to five years of formal schooling, focused on moral instruction.

By the fifteenth and sixteenth centuries Japan's family and marriage systems had evolved in the direction of a patrilocal, patriarchal system more like China's, and Japanese women had lost the prominent role in high society that they had occupied during the Heian period. It became standard for women to move into their husbands' homes, where they occupied positions subordinate to both their husbands and their mothers-in-law. In addition, elite families stopped dividing their property among all their children; instead they retained it for the sons alone or increasingly for a single son who would continue the family line. Wedding rituals involved both the exchange of betrothal gifts and the movement of the bride from her parents' home to her husband's home. She brought with her a trousseau that provided her with clothes and other items she would need for daily life, but not with land, which would have given her economic autonomy. On the other hand, her position within her new family was more secure, for it became more difficult for a husband to divorce his wife. If her husband fathered children with concubines, she was their legal mother.

A peasant wife shared responsibility for the family's economic well-being with her husband. If of poor or middling status, she worked alongside her husband in the fields, doing the routine work while he did the heavy work. If they were farm hands and worked for wages, the wife invariably earned a third or a half less than her husband. Wives of prosperous farmers never worked in the fields, but they reeled silk, wove cloth, helped in any family business, and supervised the maids. When cotton growing spread to Japan in the sixteenth century, women took on the jobs of spinning and weaving it. Families were growing smaller in this period in response to the spread of single-heir inheritance. Japanese families restricted the number of children they had by practicing abortion and infanticide, turning to adoption when no heir survived.

Widows and divorcées of the samurai elite—where female chastity was the core of fidelity—were not expected to remarry. Among the peasant classes, by contrast, divorce seems to have been fairly common—the divorce rate was at least 15 percent in the villages near Osaka in the eighteenth century. A poor woman wanting a divorce could simply leave her husband's home. Sometimes Buddhist temple priests served as divorce brokers: they went to the village headman and had him force the husband to agree to a divorce. News of the coming of temple officials was usually enough to produce a letter of separation.

Maritime Trade, Piracy, and the Entry of Europe into the Asian Maritime Sphere

How did the sea link the countries of East Asia, and what happened when Europeans entered this maritime sphere?

In the period 1400–1800 maritime trade and piracy connected China and Japan to each other and also to Korea, Southeast Asia, and Europe. Both Korea and Japan relied on Chinese coinage, and China relied on silver from Japan. During the fifteenth century China launched overseas expeditions. Japan was a major base for pirates. In the sixteenth century European traders appeared, eager for Chinese porcelains and silks. Christian missionaries followed. Political changes in Europe changed the international makeup of the European traders in East Asia, with the dominant groups first the Portuguese, next the Dutch, and then the British.

Zheng He's Voyages

Early in the Ming period, the Chinese government tried to revive the tribute system of the Han (206 B.C.E.–220 C.E.) and Tang (618–907) Dynasties, when China had dominated East Asia and envoys had arrived from dozens of distant lands. To invite more countries to send missions, the third Ming emperor (Chengzu, or Yongle) authorized an extraordinary series of voyages to the Indian Ocean under the command of the Muslim eunuch Zheng He (juhng huh) (1371–1433).

Zheng He's father had made the trip to Mecca, and the seven voyages that Zheng led between 1405 and 1433 followed old Arab trade routes. The first of the seven was made by a fleet of 317 ships, of which 62 were huge, 440 feet long. Each expedition involved from twenty thousand to thirty-two thousand men. Their itineraries included stops in Vietnam, Malaysia, Indonesia, Sri Lanka, India, and, in the later voyages, Hormuz (on the coast of Persia) and East Africa (see Map 16.1). At each stop Zheng He went ashore to visit rulers, transmit messages of China's peaceful intentions, and bestow lavish gifts. Rulers were invited to come to China or send envoys and were offered accommodation on the return voyages. Near the Straits of Malacca, Zheng's fleet battled Chinese pirates, bringing them under control. Zheng He made other shows of force as well, deposing rulers deemed unacceptable in Java, Sumatra, and Sri Lanka.

On the return of these expeditions, the Ming emperor was delighted by the exotic things the fleet brought back, such as giraffes and lions from Africa, fine cotton cloth from India, and gems and spices from Southeast Asia. Ma Huan, an interpreter who accompanied Zheng He, collected data on the plants, animals, peoples, and geography that they encountered and wrote a book titled *The Overall Survey of the Ocean's Shores*. Still, these expeditions were not voyages of discovery; they followed established routes and pursued diplomatic rather than commercial goals.

Why were these voyages abandoned? Officials complained about their cost and modest returns. As a consequence, after 1474 all the remaining ships with three or more masts were broken up and used for lumber. Chinese did not pull back from trade in the South China Sea and Indian Ocean, but the government no longer promoted trade, leaving the initiative to private merchants and migrants.

Piracy and Japan's Overseas Adventures

One goal of Zheng He's expeditions was to suppress piracy, which had become a problem all along the China coast. Already in the thirteenth century social disorder and banditry in Japan had expanded into seaborne banditry, which occurred within the Japanese islands around the Inland Sea (Map 21.3), in the straits between Korea and Japan, and along the Korean and Chinese coasts. Pirates not only looted settlements but often captured people and held them for ransom. As maritime trade throughout East Asia grew more lively, sea bandits also took to attacking ships to steal their cargo. Although the pirates were called the "Japanese pirates" by both the Koreans and the Chinese, pirate gangs in fact recruited from all countries. The Ryūkyū (ryoo-kyoo) Islands and Taiwan became major bases.

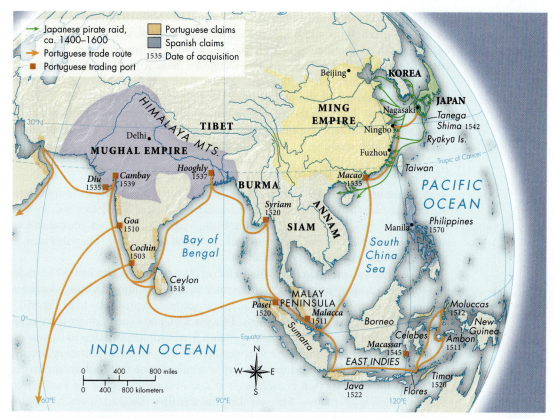

MAP 21.3 East Asia, ca. 1600 Pirates and traders often plied the same waters as seaborne trade grew in the sixteenth century. The Portuguese were especially active in setting up trading ports.

Possibly encouraged by the exploits of these bandits, Hideyoshi, after his victories in unifying Japan, decided to extend his territory across the seas. In 1590, after receiving congratulations from Korea on his victories, Hideyoshi sent a letter asking the Koreans to allow his armies to pass through their country, declaring that his real target was China. He also sent demands for submission to countries of Southeast Asia and to the Spanish governor of the Philippines.

In 1592 Hideyoshi mobilized 158,000 soldiers and 9,200 sailors for his invasion and equipped them with muskets and cannon, which had recently been introduced into Japan. His forces overwhelmed Korean defenders and reached Seoul within three weeks and Pyongyang in two months. A few months later, in the middle of winter, Chinese armies arrived to help defend Korea, and Japanese forces were pushed back from Pyongyang. A stalemate remained in place until 1597, when Hideyoshi sent out new Japanese troops. This time the Ming army and the Korean navy were more successful in resisting the Japanese. In 1598, after Hideyoshi's death, the Japanese army withdrew from Korea, but Korea was left devastated.

After recovering from the setbacks of these invasions, Korea began to advance socially and economically. During the Chosŏn (joe-sun) Dynasty (1392–1910), the Korean elite (the yangban) turned away from Buddhism and toward strict Neo-Confucian orthodoxy. As agricultural productivity improved, the population grew from about 4.4 million in 1400 to about 8 million in 1600, 10 million in 1700, and 14 million in 1810 (or about half the size of Japan's population and one-twentieth of China's). With economic advances, slavery declined. When slaves ran away, land-owners found that it was less expensive to replace them with sharecroppers than to recapture them. Between 1750 and 1790 the slave population dropped from 30 percent to 5 percent of the population. The hold of the yangban elite, however, remained strong. Through the eighteenth century about two dozen yangban families dominated the civil service examinations, leaving relatively few slots for commoners to rise to through study.

Europeans Enter the Scene

In the sixteenth century Portuguese, Spanish, and Dutch merchants and adventurers began to participate in the East Asian maritime world (see "The European Voyages of Discovery" in Chapter 16). The trade among Japan, China, and Southeast Asia was very profitable, and the European traders wanted a share of it. They also wanted to develop trade between Asia and Europe.

The Portuguese and Dutch were not reluctant to use force to gain control of trade, and they seized many outposts along the trade routes, including Taiwan. Moreover, they made little distinction between trade, smuggling, and piracy. In 1521 the Ming tried to ban the Portuguese from China. Two years later an expeditionary force commissioned by the Portuguese king to negotiate a friendship treaty defeated its mission by firing on Chinese warships near Guangzhou. In 1557, without informing Beijing, local Chinese officials decided that the way to regulate trade was to allow the Portuguese to build a trading post on uninhabited land near the mouth of the Pearl River. The city they built there—Macao—became the first destination for Europeans going to China until the nineteenth century, and it remained a Portuguese possession until 1999.

European products were not in demand in China, but silver was. Japan had supplied much of China's silver, but with the development of silver mines in the New World, European traders began supplying large quantities of silver to China, allowing the expansion of China's economy.

Chinese were quick to take advantage of the new trading ports set up by European powers. Manila, under Spanish control, and Taiwan and Batavia, both under Dutch control, all attracted thousands of Chinese colonists. In Batavia harbor (now Jakarta, Indonesia) Chinese ships outnumbered those from any other country by two or three to one. Local people felt the intrusion of Chinese more than of Europeans, and riots against Chinese led to massacres on several occasions.

A side benefit of the appearance of European traders was New World crops. Sweet potatoes, maize, peanuts, tomatoes, chili peppers, tobacco, and other crops were quickly adopted in East Asia. Sweet potatoes and maize in particular facilitated population growth because they could be grown on land previously thought too sandy or too steep to cultivate. Sweet potatoes became a common poor people's food.

Christian Missionaries

The Spanish and Portuguese kings supported missionary activity, and merchant vessels soon brought Catholic missionaries to East Asia. The Jesuit priest Francis Xavier had worked in India and the Indies before China and Japan attracted his attention.

The Jesuit Presence in China
This French engraving shows three generations of European Jesuits active at the Chinese court, Matteo Ricci (1552–1610) and two mathematicians and astronomers, Johann Adam Schall von Bell (1592–1666) and Ferdinand Verbiest (1623–1688). Below them are two prominent Chinese converts, the official Xu Guangqi and his granddaughter. (Private Collection/Bridgeman Images)

In 1549 he was the first Christian missionary to arrive in Japan, landing on Kyushu, Japan's southernmost island (see Map 21.2). After he was expelled by the local lord, he traveled throughout western Japan as far as Kyoto, proselytizing wherever warlords allowed. He soon made many converts among the poor and even some among the daimyo. Xavier then set his sights on China but died on an uninhabited island off the China coast in 1552.

Other missionaries carried on his work, and by 1600 there were three hundred thousand baptized Christians in Japan. Most of them lived on Kyushu, where the shogun's power was weakest and the loyalty of the daimyo most doubtful. In 1615 bands of Christian samurai supported Tokugawa Ieyasu's enemies at the fierce Battle of Osaka. A couple of decades later, thirty thousand peasants in the heavily Catholic area of northern Kyushu revolted. The Tokugawa Shogunate thus came to associate Christianity with domestic disorder and insurrection and in 1639 stepped up its repression of Christianity. Foreign priests were expelled and thousands of Japanese Christians crucified.

Meanwhile, in China the Jesuits concentrated on gaining the linguistic and scholarly knowledge they would need to convert the educated class. The Jesuit Matteo Ricci studied for years in Macao before setting himself up in Nanjing and trying to win over members of the educated class. In 1601 he was given permission to reside in Beijing, where he made several high-placed conversions. He also interested educated Chinese men in Western geography, astronomy, and Euclidean mathematics.

Ricci and his Jesuit successors believed that Confucianism was compatible with Christianity. The Jesuits thought that both faiths shared similar concerns for morality and virtue, and they viewed the Confucian practice of making food offerings to ancestors as an expression of filial reverence rather than as a form of worship. The Franciscan and Dominican friars, who had taken a vow of poverty, disagreed with the Jesuit position. In 1715 religious and political quarrels in Europe led the pope to decide that the Jesuits' accommodating approach was heretical. Angry at this insult, the Kangxi emperor forbade all Christian missionary work in China.

Learning from the West

Although both China and Japan ended up prohibiting Christian missionary work, other aspects of Western culture were seen as impressive and worth learning. The closed-country policy that Japan instituted in 1639 restricted Japanese from leaving the country and kept European merchants in small enclaves. Still, Japanese interest in Europe did not disappear. Through the Dutch enclave of Deshima on a tiny island in Nagasaki harbor, a stream of Western ideas, arts, and inventions trickled into Japan in the eighteenth century.

In China, too, both scholars and rulers showed an interest in Western learning. The Kangxi emperor frequently discussed scientific and philosophical questions with the Jesuits at court. When he got malaria, he accepted the Jesuits' offer of the medicine quinine. The court was impressed with the Jesuits' skill in astronomy and quickly appointed them to the Board of Astronomy. In 1674 the emperor asked them to re-equip the observatory with European instruments. In the visual arts the emperor and his successors employed Italian painters to make imperial portraits. Firearms and mechanical clocks were also widely admired. The court established its own clock and watch factory, and in 1673 the emperor insisted that the Jesuits manufacture cannon for him and supervise gunnery practice.

Dutch in Japan The Japanese were curious about the appearance, dress, and habits of the Dutch who came to the enclave of Deshima to trade. In this detail from a long hand scroll, Dutch traders are shown interacting with a Japanese samurai in a room with Japanese tatami mats on the floor. Note also the Western musical instrument. (Private Collection/ Bridgeman Images)

Admiration was not one-sided. In the early eighteenth century China enjoyed a positive reputation in Europe. The French philosopher Voltaire wrote of the rationalism of Confucianism and saw advantages to the Chinese political system because the rulers did not put up with parasitical aristocrats or hypocritical priests. Chinese medical practice also drew European interest. One Chinese practice that Europeans adopted was "variolation," an early form of smallpox inoculation.

The Shifting International Environment in the Eighteenth Century

The East Asian maritime world underwent many changes from the sixteenth to the eighteenth centuries. As already noted, the Japanese pulled back their own traders and limited opportunities for Europeans to trade in Japan. In China the Qing government limited trading contacts with Europe to Guangzhou in the far south in an attempt to curb piracy. Portugal lost many of its bases to the Dutch, and by the eighteenth century the British had become as active as the Dutch. In the seventeenth century the British and Dutch sought primarily porcelains and silk, but in the eighteenth century tea became the commodity in most demand.

By the late eighteenth century Britain had become a great power and did not see why China should be able to dictate the terms of trade. Wanting to renegotiate relations, King George III sent Lord George Macartney to China in 1793 with six hundred cases of British goods, ranging from clocks and telescopes to Wedgwood pottery and landscape paintings. The Qianlong emperor was, however, not impressed. As he pointed out in his formal reply, the Qing Empire "possesses all things in prolific abundance and lacks no product within its own borders"; thus trading with Europe was a kindness, not a necessity.[2]

Chapter Summary

After the fall of the Mongols, China was ruled by the native Ming Dynasty for nearly three centuries. The dynasty's founder ruled for thirty years, becoming more paranoid and despotic over time. Very few of his successors were particularly good rulers, yet China thrived in many ways. Population grew as food production increased. Educational levels were high as more and more men prepared for the civil service examinations. Urban culture was lively, and publishing houses put out novels, short stories, and plays in the vernacular language for large audiences.

In 1644 the Ming Dynasty fell to the non-Chinese Manchus. The Manchu rulers proved more competent than the Ming emperors and were able to both maintain peace and expand the empire to incorporate Mongolia, Tibet, and Central Asia. Population grew steadily under Manchu rule.

During the fifteenth and sixteenth centuries Japan was fragmented by civil war. As daimyo attacked and defeated each other, power was gradually consolidated, until Hideyoshi gained control of most of the country. Japan also saw many cultural developments during this period, including the increasing influence of Zen ideas on the arts and the rise of Nō theater.

After Hideyoshi's death, power was seized by Tokugawa Ieyasu, the founder of the Tokugawa Shogunate. During the seventeenth and eighteenth centuries Japan reaped the rewards of peace. The early rulers tried to create stability by freezing the social structure and limiting foreign contact to the city of Nagasaki. As the wealth of the business classes grew, the samurai, now dependent on fixed stipends, became progressively poorer. Samurai and others in search of work and pleasure streamed into the cities.

Between 1400 and 1800 maritime trade connected the countries of Asia, but piracy was a perpetual problem. Early in this period China sent out naval expeditions looking to promote diplomatic contacts, reaching as far as Africa. In the sixteenth century European traders arrived in China and Japan and soon developed profitable trading relationships. The Chinese economy became so dependent on huge imports of silver acquired through this trade that a cutoff in supplies caused severe hardship. Trade with Europe also brought New World crops and new ideas. The Catholic missionaries who began to arrive in Asia introduced Western science and learning as well as Christianity, until they were banned in both Japan and China. Although the shogunate severely restricted trade, some Western scientific ideas and technology entered Japan through the port of Nagasaki. Chinese, too, took an interest in Western painting, astronomy, and firearms. Because Europeans saw much to admire in East Asia in this period, ideas also flowed from East to West.

NOTES

1. L. J. Gallagher, trans., *China in the Sixteenth Century: The Journals of Matthew Ricci, 1583–1610* (New York: Random House, 1953), p. 23.
2. Pei-kai Cheng and M. Lestz, with J. Spence, eds., *The Search for Modern China: A Documentary History* (New York: W. W. Norton, 1999), p. 106.

CONNECTIONS

During the four centuries from 1400 to 1800, the countries of East Asia became increasingly connected. On the oceans trade and piracy linked them, and for the first time a war involved China, Korea, and Japan. At the same time, their cultures and social structures were in no sense converging. The elites of China and Japan were very different: in Japan elite status was hereditary, while in China the key route to status and power involved doing well on a written examination. In Japan the samurai elite were expected to be skilled warriors, but in China the highest prestige went to men of letters. The Japanese woodblock prints that capture many features of the entertainment quarters in Japanese cities show a world distinct from anything in China.

By the end of this period, East Asian countries found themselves in a rapidly changing international environment, mostly because of revolutions occurring far from their shores. The next two chapters take up the story of these revolutions, first the political ones in America, France, and Haiti, and then the Industrial Revolution that began in Britain. In time, these revolutions would profoundly alter East Asia as well.

CHAPTER 21 **Review and Explore**

Identify Key Terms

Identify and explain the significance of each item below.

Ming Dynasty (p. 622)   **Nō theater** (p. 635)

civil service examinations (p. 625)   **daimyo** (p. 635)

Qing Dynasty (p. 630)   **Tokugawa Shogunate** (p. 636)

banners (p. 632)   **alternate residence system** (p. 636)

Review the Main Ideas

Answer the focus questions from each section of the chapter.

1. What sort of state and society developed in China after the Mongols were ousted? (p. 622)

2. Did the return of alien rule with the Manchus have any positive consequences for China? (p. 630)

3. How did Japan change during this period of political instability? (p. 634)

4. What was life like in Japan during the Tokugawa peace? (p. 636)

5. How did the sea link the countries of East Asia, and what happened when Europeans entered this maritime sphere? (p. 641)

Make Comparisons and Connections

Analyze the larger developments and continuities within and across chapters.

1. How does the Qing Dynasty compare as an empire to other Eurasian empires of its day (Chapters 17 and 18)?

2. How were the attractions of city life in China and Japan of this period similar to those in other parts of Eurasia (Chapters 17 and 18)?

3. Can you think of any other cases in world history in which a farmer's son rose to the top of the power structure the way that Zhu Yuanzhang and Hideyoshi did? Why was this uncommon?

TIMELINE

EAST ASIA

1405–1433 Zheng He's naval expeditions

1368–1644 Ming Dynasty in China

1549 First Jesuit missionaries land in Japan

1407–1420 Construction of Beijing as Chinese capital

1467–1600 Period of civil war in Japan

1557 Portuguese set up trading base at Macao

EUROPE

1517 Luther's Ninety-five Theses **(Ch. 15)**

← **ca. 1350–1520** Italian Renaissance **(Ch. 15)**

SOUTH ASIA

AMERICAS

1492 Columbus reaches America **(Ch. 16)**

| 1400 | 1500 | 1600 |

Suggested Resources

BOOKS

Berry, Mary Elizabeth. *The Culture of Civil War in Kyoto*. 1994. Uses diaries and other records to examine how people made sense of violence and social change.

Crossley, Pamela. *The Manchus*. 2002. A lively account that lets one think about Qing history from the rulers' point of view.

Dardess, John W. *Ming China, 1368–1644*. 2012. A short but informative look at Ming China from its emperors at the top to its outlaws at the bottom.

Elliott, Mark C. *Emperor Qianlong: Son of Heaven, Man of the World*. 2009. Examines the Qing Dynasty at its height from the perspective of a remarkable emperor.

Elvin, Mark. *The Pattern of the Chinese Past*. 1973. Offers an explanation of China's failure to maintain its technological superiority in terms of a "high-level equilibrium trap."

Hanley, Susan B. *Everyday Things in Premodern Japan*. 1999. Shows that the standard of living during the Edo period was comparable to that in the West at the same time.

Hegel, Robert E., ed. and trans. *True Crimes in Eighteenth-Century China: Twenty Case Histories*. 2009. Describes various crimes (including neighborhood feuds, murder, and sedition) and how the Chinese government dealt with them at several levels.

Keene, Donald. *Yoshimasa and the Silver Pavilion: The Creation of the Soul of Japan*. 2003. A lively introduction to the aesthetic style associated with Zen and its connection to shogunate patrons.

Mann, Susan. *Precious Records: Women in China's Long Eighteenth Century*. 1997. A well-written analysis of women's lives in the educated class.

McDermott, Joseph. *A Social History of the Chinese Book: Books and Literati Culture in Late Imperial China*. 2006. Places Chinese printing in a comparative perspective.

Mungello, David. *The Great Encounter of China and the West, 1500–1800*. 1999. A short but stimulating examination of the various dimensions of the first phase of Chinese-European relations.

Pomeranz, Kenneth. *The Great Divergence: China, Europe, and the Making of the Modern World Economy*. 2000. Argues that the most advanced areas of China were on a par with the most advanced regions of Europe through the eighteenth century.

1644–1911 Manchus' Qing Dynasty in China

◆ **1639** Japan restricts contact with the outside world and intensifies suppression of Christianity

◆ **1793** Lord Macartney's diplomatic visit to China

1603–1867 Tokugawa Shogunate in Japan

ca. 1690–1789 The Enlightenment in Europe **(Ch. 19)**

1631–1648 Construction of Taj Mahal under Shah Jahan in India **(Ch. 17)**

◆ **1763** Treaty of Paris recognizes British control over much of India **(Ch. 17)**

| 1700 | 1800 | 1900 |

Rowe, William T. *China's Last Empire: The Great Qing*. 2009. An up-to-date and thoughtful narrative of the Manchu rulers and the empire over which they presided.

Stanley, Amy. *Selling Women: Prostitution, Markets, and the Household in Early Modern Japan*. 2012. Connects the state, the family, and the market.

Totman, Conrad. *A History of Japan*. 2000. An excellent, well-balanced survey.

Vaporis, Constantine Komitos. *Breaking Barriers: Travel and the State in Early Modern Japan*. 1994. An examination of recreational and religious travel.

Waldron, Arthur. *The Great Wall of China: From History to Myth*. 1990. Places the construction of the current Great Wall in the context of Ming-Mongol relations.

DOCUMENTARY

Presenting River Elegy. (Deep Dish TV, 1990). A condensed version of a controversial Chinese documentary contrasting Chinese civilization, tied to the Yellow River, to other civilizations connecting more to the ocean.

FEATURE FILMS

Rikyu (Hiroshi Teshigahara, 1989). An award-winning movie that brings together the famous tea master Sen no Rikyu and Toyotomi Hideyoshi, the warlord who united Japan in the late sixteenth century.

Silence (Martin Scorsese, 2016). A dramatization of the experience of Jesuit missionaries in Japan after the government began persecuting Christians.

The Sino-Dutch War 1661 (Ziniu Wu, 2000). A dramatization of the conflict between the Ming loyalists in Taiwan and the Dutch, in which some see reflections of the conflicts between the Nationalists in Taiwan and the Communists in the twentieth century.

WEBSITES

Asian Topics: Tokugawa Japan. Videos of scholars discussing many issues concerning the Tokugawa period; part of Columbia University's Asian Topics website. **afe.easia.columbia.edu/at/tokugawa/tj01 .html**

Golden Ornaments Decorate Tomb of Ming Dynasty Duchess. History Channel site on a recent archaeological find of a Ming tomb. **www.history.com /news/golden-ornaments-decorate-tomb-of-ming -dynasty-duchess**

22

Revolutions in the Atlantic World

1775–1825

A great wave of revolution rocked the Atlantic world from 1775 to 1825. As trade goods, individuals, and ideas circulated in ever-greater numbers across the Atlantic Ocean, debates and events in one locale soon influenced those in another. With changing social realities challenging the old order of life and the emergence of Enlightenment ideals of freedom and equality, reformers in many places demanded fundamental changes in politics and government. At the same time, wars fought for dominance of the Atlantic economy burdened European governments with crushing debts, making them vulnerable to calls for reform.

The revolutionary era began in 1775 in North America, where the United States of America won freedom from Britain in 1783. Then in 1789 France became the leading revolutionary nation. It established first a constitutional monarchy, then a radical republic, and finally a new empire under Napoleon that would last until 1815. Inspired both by the ideals of the revolution on the continent and by internal colonial conditions, the slaves in the French colony of Saint-Domingue rose up in 1791, followed by colonial settlers, indigenous people, and slaves in Latin America. Their rebellion would eventually lead to the creation of independent nations in the Caribbean, Mexico, and South America. In Europe and its colonies abroad, the world of modern politics was born.

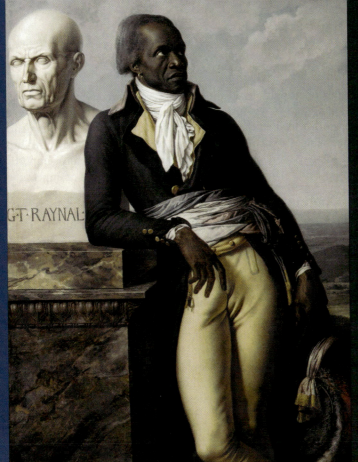

Jean-Baptiste Belley

Born in Senegal and enslaved in the colony of Saint-Domingue, Jean-Baptiste Belley fought in the American War of Independence and was elected as a deputy to the French National Convention. His career epitomizes the transnational connections of the era of Atlantic revolutions.

Jean-Baptiste Belley (1747–1805), Deputy of Santo Domingo at the French Convention, 1797, by Anne-Louis Girodet de Roussy-Trioson (1767–1824) (oil on canvas). Inv. MV4616. Photo: Gerard Blot/Château de Versailles, France/ © RMN–Grand Palais/Art Resource, NY

CHAPTER PREVIEW

BACKGROUND TO REVOLUTION   What were the factors behind the age of revolution in the Atlantic world?

THE AMERICAN REVOLUTIONARY ERA, 1775–1789   Why and how did American colonists forge a new, independent nation?

REVOLUTION IN FRANCE, 1789–1799   Why and how did revolutionaries in France transform the nation first into a constitutional monarchy and then into a republic that entered war with European powers?

NAPOLEON'S EUROPE, 1799–1815   How did Napoleon Bonaparte assume control of France and much of Europe, and what factors led to his downfall?

THE HAITIAN REVOLUTION, 1791–1804
How did a slave revolt on colonial Saint-Domingue lead to the creation of the independent nation of Haiti in 1804?

REVOLUTIONS IN LATIN AMERICA   Why and how did the Spanish and Portuguese colonies of North and South America shake off European domination and develop into national states?

What were the factors behind the age of revolution in the Atlantic world?

Background to Revolution

The origins of revolutions in the Atlantic world were complex. No one cause lay behind them, nor was revolution inevitable or certain of success. However, a series of shared factors helped set the stage for reform. They included fundamental social and economic changes and political crises that eroded state authority; the impact of political ideas derived from the Enlightenment; and, perhaps most important, imperial competition and financial crises generated by the expenses of imperial warfare.

Social Change

Eighteenth-century European society was legally divided into groups with special privileges, such as the nobility and the clergy, and groups with special burdens, such as the peasantry. Nobles were the largest landowners. They enjoyed exemption from many taxes and exclusive rights such as hunting and bearing swords. In most countries, various middle-class groups—professionals, merchants, and guild masters—enjoyed privileges that allowed them to monopolize all sorts of economic activity.

Traditional prerogatives persisted in societies undergoing dramatic change. Due to increased agricultural production, Europe's population rose rapidly after 1750, and its cities and towns swelled in size. Inflation kept pace with demography, making it increasingly difficult for urban people to find affordable food and living space. One way they kept up, and even managed to participate in the new consumer revolution (see "Urban Life and the Public Sphere" in Chapter 19), was by working harder and for longer hours. More positive developments were increased schooling and a rise in literacy rates, particularly among urban men.

Economic growth created new inequalities between rich and poor. While the poor struggled with rising prices, investors grew rich from the spread of rural manufacture and overseas trade. Old distinctions between the landed aristocracy and city merchants began to fade as enterprising nobles put money into trade and rising middle-class bureaucrats and merchants bought landed estates and noble titles. Marriages between nobles and wealthy, educated commoners (called the *bourgeoisie* [boorzh-wah-ZEE] in France) served both groups' interests, and a mixed-caste elite began to take shape.

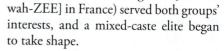

The Awakening of the Third Estate

French inhabitants were legally divided into three orders, or estates: the clergy, the nobility, and everyone else. This cartoon from July 1789 represents the third estate as a common man throwing off his chains and rising up against his oppression during the French Revolution, as the first estate (the clergy) and the second estate (the nobility) look on in fear. (Musée de la Ville de Paris, Musée Carnavalet, Paris, France/Bridgeman Images)

Another social change involved the racial regimes established in European colonies. By the late eighteenth century European law accepted that only Africans and people of African descent were subject to slavery. Even free people of color—a term for nonslaves of African or mixed African-European descent—were subject to significant restrictions on their legal rights. Racial privilege conferred a new dimension of entitlement on European settlers in the colonies, and they used extremely brutal methods to enforce it.

In Spanish America and Brazil, people of European and African descent intermingled with the very large indigenous population. Demographers estimate that indigenous people accounted for 60 to 75 percent of the population of Latin America at the end of the colonial period, in spite of tremendous population losses in the sixteenth and seventeenth centuries. The colonies that became Peru and Bolivia had indigenous majorities; the regions that became Argentina and Chile had European majorities. Until the reforms of Charles III, indigenous people and Spaniards were required by law to live in separate communities, although many of the former secretly fled to Spanish cities and haciendas to escape forced labor obligations. Mestizos (meh-STEE-zohz), people of mixed European and indigenous descent, held a higher social status than other nonwhites, but a lower status than Europeans who could prove the "purity" of their blood.

Demands for Liberty and Equality

In addition to destabilizing social changes, the ideals of liberty and equality helped fuel revolutions in the Atlantic world. The call for liberty was first of all a call for individual human rights. Supporters of the cause of individual liberty (who became known as "liberals" in the early nineteenth century) demanded freedom to worship according to the dictates of their consciences, an end to censorship, and freedom from arbitrary laws and from judges who simply obeyed orders from the government.

The call for liberty was also a call for a new kind of government. Reformers believed that the people had sovereignty—that is, that the people alone had the authority to make laws limiting an individual's freedom of action. In practice, this system of government meant choosing legislators who represented the people and were accountable to them. Monarchs might retain their thrones, but their rule should be constrained by the will of the people.

Equality was a more ambiguous idea. Eighteenth-century liberals argued that, in theory, all citizens should have identical rights and liberties. However, they accepted a number of distinctions. First, most male eighteenth-century liberals believed that equality between men and women was neither practical nor desirable. Women played an important informal role in the Atlantic revolutions, but in each case male legislators limited formal political rights—the right to vote, to run for office, to participate in government—to men. Second, few questioned the superiority of people of European descent over those of indigenous or African origin. Even those who believed that the slave trade was unjust and should be abolished, such as Thomas Jefferson, usually felt that emancipation was so socially and economically dangerous that it must be undertaken slowly and gradually, if at all.

Finally, liberals never believed that everyone should be equal economically. Great differences in wealth and income between rich and poor were perfectly acceptable, so long as every free white male had a legally equal chance at economic gain. However limited they appear to modern eyes, these demands for liberty and equality were revolutionary, given that a privileged elite had long existed with little opposition.

The two most important Enlightenment influences for late-eighteenth-century liberals were John Locke and the baron de Montesquieu. Locke maintained that England's long political tradition rested on "the rights of Englishmen" and on representative government through Parliament. He argued that if a government oversteps its proper function of protecting the natural rights of life, liberty, and private property, it becomes a tyranny. Montesquieu was also an admirer of England's Parliament. He believed that powerful "intermediary groups"—such as the judicial nobility of which he was a proud member—offered the best defense of liberty against despotism.

The Atlantic revolutions began with aspirations for equality and liberty among the social elite. Soon, however, dissenting voices emerged as some revolutionaries became frustrated with the limitations of liberal notions of equality and liberty and clamored for a fuller realization of these concepts. Depending on location, their demands included political rights for women and free people of color, the emancipation of slaves, better treatment of indigenous people, and government regulations to reduce economic inequality. The age of revolution was thus characterized by bitter conflicts over how far reform should go and to whom it should apply.

The Seven Years' War

The roots of revolutionary ideology could be found in Enlightenment texts, but it was by no means inevitable that such ideas would result in revolution. Instead events—political, economic, and military—created crises that opened the door for radical action. One of the most important was the global conflict known as the Seven Years' War (1756–1763).

The war's battlefields stretched from central Europe to India to North America, pitting a new alliance of England and Prussia against the French, Austrians, and, later, Spanish. Its origins were in conflicts left unresolved at the end of the War of the Austrian Succession in 1748, during which Prussia had seized the Austrian territory of Silesia. In central Europe, Austria's monarch Maria Theresa vowed to win back Silesia and to crush Prussia. By the end of the Seven Years' War, Maria Theresa had almost succeeded, but Prussia survived with its boundaries intact.

In North America the encroachment of English settlers into territory claimed by the French in the Ohio Valley resulted in skirmishes that soon became war. Although the inhabitants of New France were greatly outnumbered by British colonists, their forces achieved major victories until 1758. Both sides relied on the participation of Native American tribes with whom they had long-standing trade contacts and actively sought new indigenous allies during the conflict. The tide of the conflict turned when the British diverted resources from the war in Europe, using superior sea power to destroy the French fleet and choke French commerce around the world.

Treaty of Paris The 1763 peace treaty that ended the Seven Years' War, according vast French territories in North America and India to Britain and Louisiana to Spain.

British victory on all colonial fronts was ratified in the 1763 **Treaty of Paris**. Canada and all French territory east of the Mississippi River passed to Britain, and France ceded Louisiana to Spain as compensation for Spain's loss of Florida to Britain. France also gave up most of its holdings in India, opening the way to British dominance on the subcontinent (Map 22.1).

The war was costly for all participants, and in its aftermath British, French, and Spanish governments had to increase taxes to repay loans, raising a storm of protest and demands for political reform. Since the Caribbean colony of Saint-Domingue

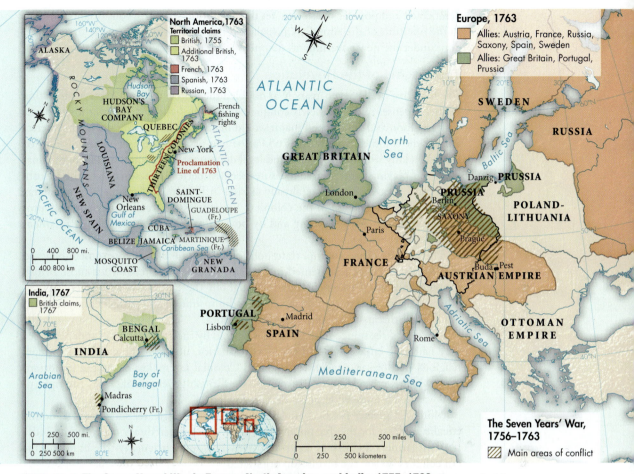

MAP 22.1 The Seven Years' War in Europe, North America, and India, 1755–1763 As a result of the war, France lost its vast territories in North America and India. In an effort to avoid costly conflicts with Native Americans living in the newly conquered territory, the British government in 1763 prohibited colonists from settling west of the Appalachian Mountains. One of the few remaining French colonies in the Americas, Saint-Domingue (on the island of Hispaniola) was the most profitable plantation in the New World.

(san-doh-MANGH) remained French, revolutionary turmoil in the mother country would directly affect its population. The seeds of revolutionary conflict in the Atlantic world were thus sown.

The American Revolutionary Era, 1775–1789

> Why and how did American colonists forge a new, independent nation?

Increased taxes and government control sparked colonial protests in the New World, where the era of liberal political revolution began. After revolting against their home country, the thirteen mainland colonies of British North America succeeded in establishing a new unified government. Participants in the revolution believed they were demanding only the traditional rights of English men and women. But those traditional rights were liberal rights, and in the American context they had strong democratic and popular overtones. Yet the revolution was a grievous disappointment to the one-fifth of the American population living in slavery who were denied freedom under the new government, despite its liberal principles.

The Origins of the Revolution

The high cost of the Seven Years' War doubled the British national debt. Anticipating further expenses to defend newly conquered territories, the British government broke with tradition and announced that it would maintain a large army in North America and tax the colonies directly. In 1765 Parliament passed the Stamp Act, which levied taxes on a long list of commercial and legal documents, diplomas, newspapers, almanacs, and playing cards. These measures seemed perfectly reasonable to the British, for a much heavier stamp tax already existed in Britain, and proceeds from the tax were to fund the defense of the colonies. Nonetheless, the colonists vigorously protested the Stamp Act by rioting and by boycotting British goods. Thus Parliament reluctantly repealed it.

This dispute raised an important political issue. The British government believed that Americans were represented in Parliament, albeit indirectly (like most British people), and that Parliament ruled throughout the empire. Many Americans felt otherwise, and came to see British colonial administration and parliamentary supremacy as grave threats to existing American liberties.

Americans' resistance to these threats was fed by the great degree of independence they had long enjoyed. In British North America, unlike in England and Europe, religious freedom was taken for granted. Colonial assemblies made the important laws, which were seldom overturned by the British government. Also, the right to vote was much more widespread than in England.

Moreover, greater political equality was matched by greater social and economic equality, at least for the free population. There was no hereditary nobility, and independent farmers dominated colonial society. This was particularly true in the northern colonies, where the revolution originated.

In 1773 disputes over taxes and representation flared up again. Under the Tea Act of that year, the East India Company secured a profitable monopoly on the tea trade, and colonial merchants were excluded. The price on tea was actually lowered for colonists, but the act generated a great deal of opposition because of its impact on local merchants.

In protest, Boston men disguised as Native Americans held a rowdy Tea Party in which they boarded East India Company ships and threw tea from them into the harbor. In response, the so-called Coercive Acts of 1774 instated a series of harsh measures. County conventions in Massachusetts urged that the acts be "rejected as the attempts of a wicked administration to enslave America." Other colonial assemblies joined in the denunciations. In September 1774 the First Continental Congress met in Philadelphia. The more radical members of this assembly argued successfully against concessions to the English crown. The British Parliament also rejected compromise, and in April 1775 fighting between colonial and British troops began at Lexington and Concord.

Independence from Britain

As fighting spread, the colonists moved slowly toward open calls for independence. The uncompromising attitude of the British government and its use of German

The Signing of the Declaration of Independence, July 4, 1776 John Trumbull's famous painting shows the dignity and determination of America's revolutionary leaders. An extraordinarily talented group, they succeeded in rallying popular support without losing power to more radical forces in the process. (U.S. Capitol Collection/Photo © Boltin Picture Library/Bridgeman Images)

mercenaries did much to dissolve loyalties to the home country and to unite the separate colonies. *Common Sense* (1775), a brilliant attack by the recently arrived English radical Thomas Paine (1737–1809), also mobilized public opinion in favor of independence.

On July 4, 1776, the Second Continental Congress adopted the **Declaration of Independence**. Written by Thomas Jefferson and others, this document boldly listed the tyrannical acts committed by George III (r. 1760–1820) and proclaimed the natural rights of mankind and the sovereignty of the American states. The Declaration of Independence in effect universalized the traditional rights of English people and made them the rights of all mankind.

After the Declaration of Independence, the conflict often took the form of a civil war pitting patriots against Loyalists, those who maintained an allegiance to the Crown. The Loyalists, who numbered up to 20 percent of the total white population, tended to be wealthy and politically moderate. They were few in number in New England and Virginia, but more common in the Deep South and on the western frontier. British commanders also recruited Loyalists from enslaved people by promising freedom to any slave who left his master to fight for the mother country.

On the international scene, the French wanted revenge against the British for the humiliating defeats of the Seven Years' War. Thus they sympathized with the rebels and supplied guns and gunpowder from the beginning of the conflict. In 1778 the French government offered the Americans a formal alliance, and in 1779 and 1780 the Spanish and Dutch declared war on Britain. Catherine the Great of Russia helped organize the League of Armed Neutrality to protect neutral shipping rights and succeeded in hampering Britain's naval power.

Thus by 1780 Britain was engaged in an imperial war against most of Europe as well as the thirteen colonies. In these circumstances, and in the face of severe reverses in India, in the West Indies, and at Yorktown in Virginia, a new British government decided to cut its losses and end the war. Under the Treaty of Paris of 1783, Britain recognized the independence of the thirteen colonies and ceded all its territory between the Allegheny Mountains and the Mississippi River to the Americans.

Declaration of Independence The 1776 document in which the American colonies declared independence from Great Britain and recast traditional English rights as universal human rights.

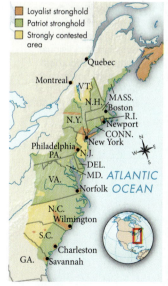

Loyalist Strength in the Colonies, ca. 1774–1776

KEY EVENTS OF THE AMERICAN REVOLUTION

1765	Britain passes the Stamp Act
1773	Britain passes the Tea Act
1774	Britain passes the Coercive Acts in response to the Tea Party in the colonies; the First Continental Congress refuses concessions to the English crown
April 1775	Fighting begins between colonial and British troops
July 4, 1776	The Second Continental Congress adopts the Declaration of Independence
1778–1780	The French, Spanish, and Dutch side with the colonists against Britain
1783	The Treaty of Paris recognizes the independence of the American colonies
1787	The U.S. Constitution is signed
1791	The first ten amendments to the Constitution are ratified (the Bill of Rights)

Antifederalists Opponents of the American Constitution who felt it diminished individual rights and accorded too much power to the federal government at the expense of the states.

Framing the Constitution

The liberal program of the American Revolution was consolidated by the federal Constitution, the Bill of Rights, and the creation of a national republic. Assembling in Philadelphia in the summer of 1787, the delegates to the Constitutional Convention were determined to end the period of economic depression, social uncertainty, and leadership under a weak central government that had followed independence. The delegates thus decided to grant the federal, or central, government important powers: regulation of domestic and foreign trade, the right to tax, and the means to enforce its laws.

The central government would operate in Montesquieu's framework of checks and balances, under which authority was distributed across three different branches—the executive, legislative, and judicial branches—which would prevent one interest from gaining too much power. The power of the federal government would in turn be checked by that of the individual states.

When the results of the Constitutional Convention were presented to the states for ratification, a great public debate began. The opponents of the proposed Constitution—the **Antifederalists**—charged that the framers of the new document had taken too much power from the individual states and made the federal government too strong. Moreover, many Antifederalists feared for the individual freedoms for which they had fought. To overcome these objections, the Federalists promised to spell out these basic freedoms as soon as the new Constitution was adopted. The result was the first ten amendments to the Constitution, which the first Congress passed shortly after it met in New York in March 1789. These amendments, ratified in 1791, formed an effective Bill of Rights to safeguard the individual.

Limitations of Liberty and Equality

The American Constitution and the Bill of Rights exemplified the strengths and the limits of what came to be called classical liberalism. Liberty meant individual freedoms and political safeguards. Liberty also meant representative government, but it did not mean democracy, with its principle of one person, one vote. Equality meant equality before the law, not equality of political participation or wealth. It did not mean equal rights for slaves, Native Americans, or women.

A vigorous abolitionist movement during the 1780s led to the passage of emancipation laws in all northern states, but slavery remained prevalent in the South, and discord between pro- and antislavery delegates roiled the Constitutional Convention of 1787. The result was a set of compromises that ensured that slavery would endure in the United States for the foreseeable future.

The new republic also failed to protect the Native American tribes whose lands fell within or alongside the territory ceded by Britain at the Treaty of Paris. The 1787 Constitution promised protection to Native Americans and guaranteed that their land would not be taken without consent. Nonetheless, the rights and interests of Native Americans were generally ignored as a growing colonial population pushed westward.

Women played a vital role in the American Revolution. They were essential participants in boycotts of British goods, which squeezed profits from British merchants and fostered the revolutionary spirit. After the outbreak of war, women raised funds for the Continental Army and took care of homesteads, workshops, and other businesses when their men went off to fight. Women did not, however, receive the right to vote in the new Constitution, an omission confirmed by a clause added in 1844.

Revolution in France, 1789–1799

Although inspired in part by events in North America, the French Revolution did not mirror the American example. It was more radical and more complex, more influential and more controversial. For Europeans and most of the rest of the world, it was the great revolution of the eighteenth century, the revolution that opened the modern era in politics.

Why and how did revolutionaries in France transform the nation first into a constitutional monarchy and then into a republic that entered war with European powers?

Breakdown of the Old Order

As did the American Revolution, the French Revolution had its immediate origins in the financial difficulties of the government. The efforts of the ministers of King Louis XV (r. 1715–1774) to raise taxes to meet the expenses of the War of the Austrian Succession and the Seven Years' War were thwarted by the high courts, known as the parlements. The noble judges of the parlements resented this threat to their exemption from taxation and decried the government's actions as a form of royal despotism.

When renewed efforts to reform the tax system similarly failed in 1776, the government was forced to finance its enormous expenditures during the American war with borrowed money. As a result, the national debt soared. In 1786 the finance minister informed King Louis XVI (r. 1774–1792) that the nation was on the verge of bankruptcy.

Louis XVI's minister of finance convinced the king to call an assembly of notables in 1787 to gain support for major fiscal reforms. The assembled notables declared that sweeping tax changes required the approval of the **Estates General**, the representative body of all three estates. Louis XVI's efforts to reject their demands failed, and in July 1788 he reluctantly called the Estates General into session.

Estates General Traditional representative body of the three estates of France that met in 1789 in response to imminent state bankruptcy.

The National Assembly

The Estates General was a legislative body with representatives from the three orders of society: the clergy, nobility, and commoners. On May 5, 1789, the twelve hundred newly elected delegates of the three estates gathered in Versailles for the opening session of the Estates General. They met in an atmosphere of deepening economic crisis, triggered by a poor grain harvest in 1788.

The Estates General was almost immediately deadlocked by arguments about voting procedures. The government insisted that each estate should meet and vote

Abbé Sieyès, *What Is the Third Estate?*

In the flood of pamphlets that appeared after Louis XVI's call for a meeting of the Estates General, the most influential was written in 1789 by a Catholic priest named Emmanuel Joseph Sieyès. In *What Is the Third Estate?* the abbé Sieyès vigorously condemned the system of privilege that lay at the heart of French society. The term *privilege* combined the Latin words for "private" and "law." In Old Regime France, no one set of laws applied to all; over time, the monarchy had issued a series of particular laws, or privileges, that enshrined special rights and entitlements for select individuals and groups. Noble privileges were among the weightiest.

Sieyès rejected this entire system of legal and social inequality. Deriding the nobility as a foreign parasite, he argued that the common people of the third estate, who did most of the work and paid most of the taxes, constituted the true nation. His pamphlet galvanized public opinion and played an important role in convincing representatives of the third estate to proclaim themselves a "National Assembly" in June 1789. Sieyès later helped bring Napoleon Bonaparte to power, abandoning the radicalism of 1789 for an authoritarian regime.

■ 1. What is the Third Estate? Everything.
2. What has it been until now in the political order? Nothing.
3. What does it want? To become something.

. . . What is a Nation? A body of associates living under a *common* law and represented by the same *legislature*.

Is it not more than certain that the noble order has privileges, exemptions, and even rights that are distinct from the rights of the great body of citizens? Because of this, it [the noble order] does not belong to the common order, it is not covered by the law common to the rest. Thus its civil rights already make it a people apart inside the great Nation. It is truly *imperium in imperio* [a law unto itself].

As for its *political* rights, the nobility also exercises them separately. It has its own representatives who have no mandate from the people. Its deputies sit separately, and even when they assemble in the same room with the deputies of the ordinary citizens, the nobility's representation still remains essentially distinct and separate: it is foreign to the Nation by its very principle, for its mission does not emanate from the people, and by its purpose, since it consists in defending, not the general interest, but the private interests of the nobility.

The Third Estate therefore contains everything that pertains to the Nation and nobody outside of the Third Estate can claim to be part of the Nation. What is the Third Estate? EVERYTHING. . . .

By Third Estate is meant the collectivity of citizens who belong to the common order. Anybody who holds a legal privilege of any kind leaves that common order, stands as an exception to the common law, and in consequence does not belong to the Third Estate. . . . It is certain that the moment a citizen acquires privileges contrary to common law, he no longer belongs to the common order. His new interest is opposed to the general interest; he has no right to vote in the name of the people. . . .

In vain can anyone's eyes be closed to the revolution that time and the force of things have brought to pass; it is none the less real. Once upon a time the Third Estate

separately. Critics had demanded instead a single assembly dominated by the third estate. In his famous pamphlet *What Is the Third Estate?* the abbé Emmanuel Joseph Sieyès argued that the nobility was a tiny, overprivileged minority and that commoners constituted the true strength of the French nation. (See "Analyzing the Evidence: Abbé Sieyès, *What Is the Third Estate?*" above.) The issue came to a crisis in June 1789 when delegates of the third estate refused to meet until the king ordered the clergy and nobility to sit with them in a single body. A few parish priests began to go over to the third estate, which on June 17 voted to call itself the **National Assembly**. On June 20 the delegates of the third estate, excluded from their hall because of

National Assembly French representative assembly formed in 1789 by the delegates of the third estate and some members of the clergy, the second estate.

was in bondage and the noble order was everything that mattered. Today the Third is everything and nobility but a word. Yet under the cover of this word a new and intolerable aristocracy has slipped in, and the people has every reason to no longer want aristocrats. . . .

What is the will of a Nation? It is the result of individual wills, just as the Nation is the aggregate of the individuals who compose it. It is impossible to conceive of a legitimate association that does not have for its goal the common security, the common liberty, in short, the public good. No doubt each individual also has his own personal aims. He says to himself, "protected by the common security, I will be able to peacefully pursue my own personal projects, I will seek my happiness where I will, assured of encountering only those legal obstacles that society will prescribe for the common interest, in which I have a part, and with which my own personal interest is so usefully allied." . . .

Advantages which differentiate citizens from one another lie outside the purview of citizenship. Inequalities of wealth or ability are like the inequalities of age, sex, size, etc. In no way do they detract from the *equality* of citizenship. These individual advantages no doubt benefit from the protection of the law; but it is not the legislator's task to create them, to give privileges to some and refuse them to others. The law grants nothing; it protects what already exists until such time that what exists begins to harm the common interest. These are the only limits on individual freedom. I imagine the law as being at the center of a large globe; we the citizens without exception, stand equidistant from it on the surface and occupy equal places; all are equally dependent on the law, all present it with their liberty and their property to be protected; and this is what I call the *common rights* of citizens, by which they are all alike.

All these individuals communicate with each other, enter into contracts, negotiate, always under the common guarantee of the law. If in this general activity somebody wishes to get control over the person of his neighbor or usurp his property, the common law goes into action to repress this criminal attempt and puts everyone back in their place at the same distance from the law. . . .

It is impossible to say what place the two privileged orders [the clergy and the nobility] ought to occupy in the social order: this is the equivalent of asking what place one wishes to assign to a malignant tumor that torments and undermines the strength of the body of a sick person. It must be *neutralized*. We must re-establish the health and working of all organs so thoroughly that they are no longer susceptible to these fatal schemes that are capable of sapping the most essential principles of vitality.

QUESTIONS FOR ANALYSIS

1. What criticism of noble privileges does Sieyès offer? Why does he believe nobles are "foreign" to the nation?
2. How does Sieyès define the nation, and why does he believe that the third estate constitutes the nation?
3. What relationship between citizens and the law does Sieyès envision? What limitations on the law does he propose?

Source: Excerpt from pp. 65–70 in *The French Revolution and Human Rights: A Brief Documentary History*, edited, translated, and with an introduction by Lynn Hunt. Copyright © 1996 by Bedford Books of St. Martin's Press. Used by permission of the publisher.

"repairs," moved to a large indoor tennis court where they swore the famous Oath of the Tennis Court, pledging not to disband until they had been recognized as a National Assembly and had written a new constitution.

The king's response was disastrously ambivalent. Although he made a conciliatory speech accepting the deputies' demands, he called a large army toward the capital to bring the Assembly under control, and on July 11 he dismissed his finance minister and other liberal ministers. On July 14, 1789, several hundred common people, angered by the king's actions, stormed the Bastille (ba-STEEL), a royal prison. Ill-judged severity on the part of the Crown thus led to the first episodes of popular violence.

Uprisings also rocked the countryside. In July and August 1789 peasants through-out France began to rise in insurrection against their lords. Fear of marauders and vagabonds hired by vengeful landlords—called the Great Fear by contemporaries—seized the rural poor and fanned the flames of rebellion.

The National Assembly responded to the swell of popular anger with a surprise maneuver on the night of August 4, 1789. By a decree of the Assembly, all the old noble privileges—peasant serfdom where it still existed, exclusive hunting rights, the right to collect fees for having legal cases judged in the lord's court, the right to make peasants work on the roads, and a host of other entitlements—were abolished along with tithes paid to the church. On August 27, 1789, the Assembly further issued the Declaration of the Rights of Man and of the Citizen. This clarion call of the liberal revolutionary ideal guaranteed equality before the law, representative government for a sovereign people, and individual freedom. It was quickly disseminated throughout France, the rest of Europe, and around the world.

The National Assembly's declaration had little practical effect for the poor and hungry people of Paris. The economic crisis worsened after the fall of the Bastille, as aristocrats fled the country and the luxury market collapsed. Foreign markets also shrank, and unemployment among the urban working class grew.

Constitutional Monarchy

The next two years, until September 1791, saw the consolidation of the liberal revo-lution. In June 1790 the National Assembly abolished the nobility, and in July the king swore to uphold the as-yet-unwritten constitution. The king remained the head of state, but all lawmaking power now resided in the National Assembly, elected by the wealthiest half of French males. The constitution finally passed in September 1791 was the first in French history. It legalized divorce and broadened women's rights to inherit property and to obtain financial support for illegitimate children from fathers, but excluded women from political office and voting.

In addition to ruling on women's rights, the National Assembly replaced the patchwork of historic provinces with eighty-three departments of approximately equal size. The deputies prohibited monopolies, guilds, and workers' associations and abolished barriers to trade within France. Thus the National Assembly applied the spirit of the Enlightenment in a thorough reform of France's laws and institutions.

The National Assembly also imposed a radical reorganization on religious life. It granted religious freedom to the small minority of French Jews and Protestants. Fur-thermore, in November 1789 it nationalized the property of the Catholic Church and abolished monasteries.

In July 1790 the Civil Constitution of the Clergy established a national church with priests chosen by voters. The National Assembly then forced the Catholic clergy to take an oath of loyalty to the new government. The pope formally condemned this measure, and only half the priests of France swore the oath. Many sincere Christians, especially those in the countryside, were also upset by these changes in the religious order. The attempt to remake the Catholic Church, like the abolition of guilds and workers' associations, sharpened the conflict between the educated classes and the common people that had been emerging in the eighteenth century.

The National Convention

The outbreak and progress of revolution in France produced great excitement and a sharp division of opinion in Europe and the United States. Liberals and radicals saw a triumph of liberty over despotism, while conservative leaders were deeply troubled by the aroused spirit of reform. In 1790 Edmund Burke published *Reflections on the Revolution in France*, one of the great expressions of European conservatism. He derided abstract principles of "liberty" and "rights" and insisted on the importance of inherited traditions and privileges as a bastion of social stability.

The kings and nobles of continental Europe, who had at first welcomed the revolution in France as weakening a competing power, now feared its impact. In June 1791 the royal family was arrested and returned to Paris after a failed attempt to escape France. To the monarchs of Austria and Prussia, the arrest of a crowned monarch was unacceptable. Two months later they issued the Declaration of Pillnitz, proclaiming their willingness to intervene in France to restore Louis XVI's rule, if necessary.

The new French representative body, called the Legislative Assembly, was dominated by members of the **Jacobin club**, one of the many political clubs that had formed to debate the issues of the day. The Jacobins and other deputies reacted with patriotic fury to the Declaration of Pillnitz, and in April 1792 France declared war on Francis II of Austria, the Habsburg monarch.

France's crusade against tyranny went poorly at first. Prussian forces joined Austria against the French, who broke and fled at their first military encounter with this First Coalition of antirevolutionary foreign powers. The Legislative Assembly declared the country in danger, and volunteers rallied to the capital. In August the Assembly suspended the king from all his functions and imprisoned him.

The fall of the monarchy marked a rapid radicalization of the Revolution. In late September 1792 a new assembly, called the National Convention, was elected by universal manhood suffrage. The Convention proclaimed France a republic, a nation in which the people, instead of a monarch, held sovereign power. Under the leadership of the **Mountain**, the radical faction of the Jacobin club led by Maximilien Robespierre (ROHBZ-pyayr) and Georges Jacques Danton, the Convention tried and convicted the king for treason. On January 21, 1793, Louis was executed. His wife, Marie Antoinette, suffered the same fate later that year.

In February 1793 the National Convention declared war on Britain, the Dutch Republic, and Spain. Republican France was now at war with almost all of Europe, and it faced mounting internal opposition. Peasants in western France revolted against being drafted into the army, with the Vendée region of Brittany emerging as the epicenter of revolt. Devout Catholics, royalists, and foreign agents encouraged their rebellion.

By March 1793 the National Convention was locked in struggle between two factions of the Jacobin club, the radical Mountain and the more moderate **Girondists** (juh-RON-dist). With the middle-class delegates so bitterly divided, the laboring poor of Paris once again emerged as the decisive political factor. The laboring poor and the petty traders were often known as the **sans-culottes** (san-koo-LAHT) ("without breeches") because their men wore trousers instead of the knee breeches of the wealthy. They demanded radical political action to guarantee them their daily bread. The Mountain, sensing an opportunity to

Jacobin club A political club during the French Revolution to which many of the deputies of the Legislative Assembly belonged.

Mountain Led by Robespierre, the French National Convention's radical faction, which led the Convention in 1793.

Girondists A moderate group that fought for control of the French National Convention in 1793.

sans-culottes The laboring poor of Paris, so called because the men wore trousers instead of the knee breeches of the wealthy; the term came to refer to the militant radicals of the city.

Areas of French Insurrection, 1793

KEY EVENTS OF THE FRENCH REVOLUTION

May 5, 1789	Estates General meets at Versailles
June 20, 1789	Oath of the Tennis Court
July 14, 1789	Storming of the Bastille
July–August 1789	Great Fear
August 4, 1789	National Assembly abolishes noble privileges
August 27, 1789	National Assembly issues Declaration of the Rights of Man and of the Citizen
July 1790	Civil Constitution of the Clergy establishes a national church; Louis XVI agrees to a constitutional monarchy
June 1791	Royal family is arrested while attempting to flee France
August 1791	Austria and Prussia issue the Declaration of Pillnitz
April 1792	France declares war on Austria
August 1792	Legislative Assembly takes Louis XVI prisoner and suspends him from functions
September 1792	National Convention declares France a republic and abolishes monarchy
January 21, 1793	Louis XVI is executed
February 1793	France declares war on Britain, the Dutch Republic, and Spain; revolts in some provinces
March 1793	Struggle between Girondists and the Mountain
June 1793	Sans-culottes invade the National Convention; Girondist leaders are arrested
September 1793	Price controls are instituted to aid the poor
1793–1794	Reign of Terror
Spring 1794	French armies are victorious on all fronts
July 1794	Robespierre is executed; Thermidorian reaction begins
1795	Economic controls are abolished, and suppression of the sans-culottes begins
1795–1799	Directory rules
1798–1799	Austria, Britain, and Russia form the Second Coalition against France
1799	Napoleon Bonaparte overthrows the Directory and seizes power

outmaneuver the Girondists, joined with sans-culotte activists to engineer a popular uprising. On June 2, 1793, armed sans-culottes invaded the Convention and forced its deputies to arrest twenty-nine Girondist deputies for treason. All power passed to the Mountain.

This military and political crisis led to the most radical period of the Revolution, which lasted from spring 1793 until summer 1794. To deal with threats from within and outside France, the Convention formed the Committee of Public Safety in April 1793. Led by Robespierre, the Committee advanced on several fronts in 1793 and 1794. First, in September 1793 Robespierre and his colleagues established a planned economy. Rather than let supply and demand determine prices, the government set maximum allowable prices for key products. Though the state was too weak to enforce all its price regulations, it did fix the price of bread in Paris at levels the poor could afford.

The government also put the people to work producing arms, munitions, and uniforms for the war effort. The government told craftsmen what to produce, nationalized many small workshops, and requisitioned raw materials and grain. These economic reforms amounted to an emergency form of socialism, which thoroughly frightened Europe's propertied classes and greatly influenced the subsequent development of socialist ideology.

Second, the **Reign of Terror** (1793–1794) enforced compliance with republican beliefs and practices. Special revolutionary courts tried "enemies of the nation" for political crimes. As a result, some forty thousand French men and women were executed or died in prison. Presented as a necessary measure to save the republic, the Terror was a weapon directed against all suspected of opposing the revolutionary government.

In their efforts to impose unity, the Jacobins also took actions to suppress women's participation in political debate, which they perceived as disorderly and a distraction from women's proper place in the home. On October 30, 1793, the National Convention declared, "The clubs and popular societies of women, under whatever denomination are prohibited."

The third element of the Committee's program was to bring about a cultural revolution that would transform former royal subjects into republican citizens. The government sponsored revolutionary art and songs as well as secular holidays and open-air festivals to celebrate republican virtues. It also attempted to rationalize daily life by adopting the decimal system for weights and measures and a new calendar based on ten-day weeks. A campaign of de-Christianization aimed to eliminate Catholic symbols and beliefs. Fearful of the hostility aroused in rural France, however, Robespierre called for a halt to de-Christianization measures in mid-1794.

The final element in the program of the Committee of Public Safety was its appeal to a new sense of national identity and patriotism. With a common language and a common tradition reinforced by the revolutionary ideals of popular sovereignty and democracy, many French people developed an intense emotional attachment to the nation. This was the birth of modern nationalism, the strong identification with one's nation, which would have a profound effect on subsequent European history.

To defend the nation, a decree of August 1793 imposed a draft on all unmarried young men. By January 1794 French armed forces outnumbered those of their enemies almost four to one. By spring 1794 French armies were victorious on all fronts and domestic revolt was largely suppressed. The republic was saved.

Reign of Terror The period from 1793 to 1794, during which Robespierre's Committee of Public Safety tried and executed thousands suspected of political crimes and a new revolutionary culture was imposed.

The Directory

The success of French armies led the Committee of Public Safety to relax emergency economic controls, but they extended the political Reign of Terror. The revolutionary tribunals sent many critics to the guillotine, including long-standing collaborators whom Robespierre believed had turned against him. A group of radicals and moderates in the Convention, knowing that they might be next, organized a conspiracy. They howled down Robespierre when he tried to speak to the National Convention on July 27, 1794—a date known as 9 Thermidor according to France's newly adopted republican calendar. The next day it was Robespierre's turn to be guillotined.

The respectable middle-class lawyers and professionals who had led the liberal Revolution of 1789 then reasserted their authority. This period of **Thermidorian reaction**, as it was called, harkened back to the moderate beginnings of the Revolution. In 1795 the National Convention abolished many economic controls and severely restricted local political organizations. In addition, the middle-class members of the National Convention wrote a new constitution restricting eligibility to serve as a deputy to men of substantial means. To prevent a new Robespierre from monopolizing power, the new Assembly granted executive power to a five-man body, called the Directory.

The Directory continued to support military expansion abroad, but war was no longer so much a crusade as a response to economic problems. Large, victorious armies reduced unemployment at home. However, the French people quickly grew weary of the corruption and ineffectiveness that characterized the Directory. This general dissatisfaction revealed itself clearly in the national elections of 1797, which returned a large number of conservative and even monarchist deputies. Fearing for its survival, the Directory used the army to nullify the elections and began to govern dictatorially. Two years later Napoleon Bonaparte ended the Directory in a coup

Thermidorian reaction
A reaction in 1794 to the violence of the Reign of Terror, resulting in the execution of Robespierre and the loosening of economic controls.

The Execution of Robespierre

Completely wooden except for the heavy iron blade, the guillotine was devised by a French revolutionary doctor named Guillotin as a humane method of execution. The guillotine was painted red for Robespierre's execution. Large crowds witnessed the execution in a majestic public square in central Paris, then known as the Place de la Revolution and now called the Place de la Concorde (Harmony Square).

(Robespierre: National Library, Madrid, Spain/Photo © Tarker/Bridgeman Images; guillotine: Musée de la Ville de Paris, Musée Carnavalet, Paris, France/Bridgeman Images)

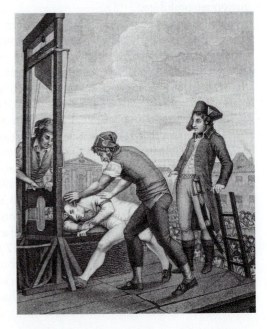

d'état (koo day-TAH) and substituted a strong dictatorship for a weak one. While claiming to uphold revolutionary values, Napoleon would install authoritarian rule.

Napoleon's Europe, 1799–1815

For almost fifteen years, from 1799 to 1814, France was in the hands of a keen-minded military dictator of exceptional ability. Napoleon Bonaparte (1769–1821) realized the need to put an end to civil strife in France in order to create unity and consolidate his rule. And he did. But Napoleon saw himself as a man of destiny, and the glory of war and the dream of universal empire proved irresistible.

Napoleon's Rule of France

Born on the Mediterranean island of Corsica into an impoverished noble family, Napoleon left home and became a lieutenant in the French artillery in 1785. Rising rapidly in the new army, Napoleon was placed in command of French forces in Italy and won brilliant victories there in 1796 and 1797. His next campaign, in Egypt, was a failure, but Napoleon returned to France before the fiasco was generally known. French aggression in Egypt and elsewhere provoked the British to organize a new alliance in 1798, the Second Coalition, which included Austria and Russia.

Napoleon soon learned that some prominent members of the legislature were plotting against the Directory. The dissatisfaction of these plotters stemmed not so much from the fact that the Directory was a dictatorship as from the fact that it was a weak dictatorship.

The young Napoleon, nationally revered for his heroism, was an ideal figure of authority. On November 9, 1799, Napoleon and his conspirators ousted the Directors, and the following day soldiers disbanded the legislature. Napoleon was named first consul of the republic, and a new constitution consolidating his position was overwhelmingly approved in a plebiscite in December 1799. Republican appearances were maintained, but Napoleon became the real ruler of France.

Napoleon worked to maintain order and end civil strife by appeasing powerful groups in France, offering them favors in return for loyal service. Napoleon's bargain with the middle class was codified in the Civil Code of March 1804, also known as the **Napoleonic Code**, which reasserted two of the fundamental principles of the Revolution of 1789: equality of all male citizens before the law and absolute security of wealth and private property. Napoleon and the leading bankers of Paris established the privately owned Bank of France in 1800, which served the interests of both the state and the financial oligarchy. Napoleon won over peasants by defending the gains in land and status they had won during the Revolution.

At the same time, Napoleon consolidated his rule by recruiting disillusioned revolutionaries for the network of government officials. Nor were members of the old nobility slighted. In 1800 and again in 1802 Napoleon granted amnesty to noble émigrés on the condition that they return to France and take a loyalty oath. Members of this returning elite soon occupied high posts in the expanding centralized state. Napoleon also created a new imperial nobility to reward his most talented generals and officials.

Furthermore, Napoleon sought to restore the Catholic Church in France so that it could serve as a bulwark of social stability. Napoleon and Pope Pius VII (pontificate 1800–1823) signed the Concordat of 1801. Under this agreement the pope gained

---

How did Napoleon Bonaparte assume control of France and much of Europe, and what factors led to his downfall?

Napoleonic Code French civil code promulgated in 1804 that reasserted the 1789 principles of the equality of all male citizens before the law and the absolute security of wealth and private property.

the right for French Catholics to practice their religion freely, but Napoleon's government now nominated bishops, paid the clergy, and exerted great influence over the church in France.

Order and unity had a price: authoritarian rule. Women lost many of the gains they had made in the 1790s. Under the Napoleonic Code, women were dependents of either their fathers or their husbands, and they could not make contracts or have bank accounts in their own names. Napoleon also curtailed free speech and freedom of the press and manipulated voting in the occasional elections. After 1810 political suspects were held in state prisons, as they had been during the Terror.

Napoleon's Expansion in Europe

After coming to power in 1799, Napoleon sent peace feelers to Austria and Britain, the dominant powers of the Second Coalition. When these overtures were rejected, French armies led by Napoleon decisively defeated the Austrians. Subsequent treaties with Austria in 1801 and Britain in 1802 consolidated France's hold on the territories its armies had won up to that point.

In 1802 Napoleon was secure but still driven to expand his power. Aggressively redrawing the map of German-speaking lands so as to weaken Austria and encourage the secondary states of southwestern Germany to side with France, Napoleon tried to restrict British trade with all of Europe. He then plotted to attack Britain, but his Mediterranean fleet was destroyed by Lord Nelson at the Battle of Trafalgar on October 21, 1805.

Austria, Russia, and Sweden joined with Britain to form the Third Coalition against France shortly before the Battle of Trafalgar. Yet the Austrians and the Russians were no match for Napoleon, who scored a brilliant victory over them at the Battle of Austerlitz in December 1805. Russia decided to pull back, and Austria accepted large territorial losses in return for peace as the Third Coalition collapsed.

Napoleon then reorganized the German states to his liking. In 1806 he abolished many tiny German states as well as the Holy Roman Empire and established by decree the German Confederation of the Rhine, a union of fifteen German states minus Austria, Prussia, and Saxony.

Jacques-Louis David, *Napoleon Bonaparte, First Consul, Crossing the Alps at Great St. Bernard Pass, 20 May 1800* Napoleon Bonaparte commissioned this portrait by the great painter David to immortalize his crossing of the Alps with the French army on the way to conquer Italy. Napoleon was a master at the use of visual imagery as a form of propaganda to disseminate the legend of his military prowess and extraordinary charisma. (Château de Versailles, France/Bridgeman Images)

Napoleon's intervention in German affairs alarmed the Prussians, who mobilized their armies. In October 1806 Napoleon attacked them and won two more victories at Jena and Auerstädt. The war with Prussia, now joined by Russia, continued into the following spring. After Napoleon won another victory, Alexander I of Russia was ready to negotiate for peace. In the treaties of Tilsit in 1807, Prussia lost half its population through land concessions, while Russia accepted Napoleon's reorganization of western and central Europe and promised to enforce Napoleon's economic blockade against British goods.

The Grand Empire and Its End

Napoleon's so-called **Grand Empire** encompassed virtually all of Europe except Great Britain. It consisted of three parts. The core, or first part, was an ever-expanding France (Map 22.2). The second part consisted of a number of dependent satellite kingdoms. The third part comprised the independent but allied states of Austria, Prussia, and Russia. After 1806 both satellites and allies were expected to support Napoleon's **Continental System**, a blockade in which no ship coming from Britain or her colonies was permitted to dock at any port that was controlled by the French. The blockade was intended to destroy the British economy and, thereby, its ability to wage war.

In the areas incorporated into France and in the satellites, French rule sparked patriotic upheavals and encouraged the growth of reactive nationalism. The first great revolt occurred in Spain. In 1808 Napoleon deposed Spanish king Ferdinand VII and placed his own brother Joseph on the throne. A coalition of Catholics, monarchists, and patriots rebelled against this attempt to turn Spain into a satellite of France. French armies occupied Madrid, but the foes of Napoleon fled to the hills and waged guerrilla warfare. Events in Spain sent a clear warning: resistance to French imperialism was growing.

German Confederation of the Rhine, 1806

Grand Empire The empire over which Napoleon and his allies ruled, encompassing virtually all of Europe except Great Britain.

Continental System A blockade imposed by Napoleon in which no ship coming from Britain or its colonies was permitted to dock at any port controlled by the French.

Francisco Goya, *The Third of May 1808* Spanish master Francisco Goya created a passionate and moving indictment of the bruality of war in this painting from 1814, which depicts the close-range execution of Spanish rebels by Napoleon's forces in May 1808. Goya's painting evoked the bitterness and despair of many Europeans who suffered through Napoleon's invasions. It forms a devastating counterpoint to the glorious portrait of Napoleon by David earlier in the chapter. (Museo del Prado, Madrid, Spain/Bridgeman Images)

MAPPING THE PAST

MAP 22.2 Napoleonic Europe in 1812 At the height of the Grand Empire in 1810, Napoleon had conquered or allied with every major European power except Britain. But in 1812, angered by Russian repudiation of his ban on trade with Britain, Napoleon invaded Russia with disastrous results. Compare this map with Map 18.3, which shows the division of Europe in 1715.

ANALYZING THE MAP How had the balance of power shifted in Europe from 1715 to 1812? What changed, and what remained the same? What was the impact of Napoleon's wars on Germany, the Italian peninsula, and Russia?

CONNECTIONS Why did Napoleon achieve vast territorial gains where Louis XIV did not?

Yet Napoleon pushed on. In 1810, when the Grand Empire was at its height, Britain still remained at war with France, helping the guerrillas in Spain and Portugal. The Continental System was a failure. Instead of harming Britain, the system provoked the British to set up a counter-blockade, which created hard times for French consumers. Perhaps looking for a scapegoat, Napoleon turned on Alexander I of Russia, who in 1811 openly repudiated Napoleon's prohibitions against British goods.

Napoleon's invasion of Russia began in June 1812 with a force that eventually numbered 600,000. Originally planning to winter in the Russian city of Smolensk, Napoleon recklessly pressed on toward Moscow (see Map 22.2). The Battle of Borodino that followed was a draw. Alexander ordered the evacuation of Moscow, which the Russians then burned in part, and he refused to negotiate. Finally, after five weeks in the scorched city, Napoleon ordered a disastrous retreat. When the frozen remnants of Napoleon's army staggered into Poland and Prussia in December, 370,000 men had died and another 200,000 had been taken prisoner.[1]

Leaving his troops to their fate, Napoleon raced to Paris to raise another army. Meanwhile, Austria and Prussia deserted Napoleon and joined Russia and Britain in the Treaty of Chaumont in March 1814, by which the four powers formed the Quadruple Alliance to defeat the French emperor. Less than a month later, on April 4, 1814, a defeated Napoleon abdicated his throne. The victorious allies then exiled Napoleon to the island of Elba off the coast of Italy.

In February 1815 Napoleon staged a daring escape from Elba. Landing in France, he issued appeals for support and marched on Paris. But Napoleon's gamble was a desperate long shot, for the allies were united against him. At the end of a frantic period known as the Hundred Days, they crushed his forces at Waterloo on June 18, 1815, and imprisoned him on the island of St. Helena, off the western coast of Africa. The restored Bourbon dynasty took power under Louis XVIII, a younger brother of Louis XVI.

The Haitian Revolution, 1791–1804

The events that led to the creation of the independent nation of Haiti constitute the third, and perhaps most extraordinary, chapter of the revolutionary era in the Atlantic world. The French colony that was to become Haiti reaped huge profits through a ruthless system of slave-based plantation agriculture. News of revolution in France lit a powder keg of contradictory aspirations among white planters, free people of color, and slaves. Free people of color and, later, the enslaved rose up to claim their freedom. They succeeded, despite invasion by the British and Spanish and Napoleon Bonaparte's bid to reimpose French control. In 1804 Haiti became the only nation in history to claim its freedom through slave revolt.

> How did a slave revolt on colonial Saint-Domingue lead to the creation of the independent nation of Haiti in 1804?

Revolutionary Aspirations in Saint-Domingue

On the eve of the French Revolution, Saint-Domingue was inhabited by a variety of social groups who resented and mistrusted one another. The European population included French colonial officials, wealthy plantation owners and merchants, and poor artisans and clerks. Individuals of European descent born in the colonies were called **Creoles**, and over time they had developed their own interests, distinct from those of metropolitan France. Vastly outnumbering the white population were the colony's five hundred thousand enslaved people, along with a sizable population of some forty thousand free people of African and mixed African and European descent. Members of this last group referred to themselves as "free people of color."

Creoles People of European descent born in the Americas.

Most of the island's enslaved population performed grueling toil in the island's sugar plantations. The highly outnumbered planters used extremely harsh methods, such as beating, maiming, and executing slaves, to maintain their control. The 1685 Code Noir (Black Code) that legally regulated slavery was intended to provide minimal

KEY EVENTS OF THE HAITIAN REVOLUTION

1760s	Colonial administrators begin rescinding the rights of free people of color
July 1790	Vincent Ogé leads a failed rebellion to gain rights for free people of color
August 1791	Slave revolts begin
April 4, 1792	National Assembly enfranchises all free men of African descent
September 1793	British troops invade Saint-Domingue
February 4, 1794	National Convention ratifies the abolition of slavery and extends it to all French territories
May 1796	Toussaint L'Ouverture is named lieutenant governor of Saint-Domingue
1800	After invading the south of Saint-Domingue, L'Ouverture gains control of the entire colony
1802	French general Charles-Victor-Emmanuel Leclerc arrests L'Ouverture and deports him to France
1803	L'Ouverture dies
1804	After defeating French forces, Jean Jacques Dessalines declares the independence of Saint-Domingue and the creation of the sovereign nation of Haiti

standards of humane treatment, but its tenets were rarely enforced. Masters calculated that they could earn more by working slaves ruthlessly and purchasing new ones when they died than by providing the food, rest, and medical care needed to allow the enslaved population to reproduce naturally. This meant that a constant inflow of newly enslaved people from Africa was necessary to work the plantations.

Despite their brutality, slaveholders on Saint-Domingue freed a certain number of their slaves, mostly their own mixed-race children, thereby producing one of the largest populations of free people of color in any slaveholding colony. The Code Noir had originally granted free people of color the same legal status as whites. From the 1760s on, however, colonial administrators began rescinding these rights, and by the time of the French Revolution free people of color were subject to many discriminatory laws.

The political and intellectual turmoil of the 1780s, with its growing rhetoric of liberty, equality, and fraternity, raised new challenges and possibilities for each of Saint-Domingue's social groups. For enslaved people, news of abolitionist movements in France led to hopes that the mother country might grant them freedom. Free people of color looked to reforms in Paris as a means of gaining political enfranchisement and reasserting equal status with whites. The white Creole elite, however, was determined to protect its way of life, including slaveholding. They hoped to gain control of their own affairs, as had the American colonists before them.

The National Assembly frustrated the hopes of all these groups. Cowed by colonial representatives who claimed that support for free people of color would result in slave insurrection, the Assembly refused to extend French constitutional safeguards to the colonies. At the same time, however, the Assembly also reaffirmed French monopolies over colonial trade, thereby angering planters as well.

In July 1790 Vincent Ogé (aw-ZHAY) (ca. 1750–1791), a free man of color, returned to Saint-Domingue from Paris determined to win rights for his people. He raised an army and sent letters to the new Provincial Assembly of Saint-Domingue demanding political rights for all free citizens. When Ogé's demands were refused, he and his followers turned to armed insurrection. After initial victories, his army was defeated, and Ogé was executed by colonial officials. Revolutionary leaders in Paris were more sympathetic to Ogé's cause. In May 1791 the National Assembly granted political rights to free people of color born to two free parents who possessed sufficient property. When news of this legislation arrived in Saint-Domingue, the colonial governor refused to enact it. Violence then erupted between groups of whites and free people of color in parts of the colony.

The Outbreak of Revolt

Just as the sans-culottes helped push forward more radical reforms in France, the second stage of revolution in Saint-Domingue also resulted from decisive action from below. In August 1791 slaves took events into their own hands. Groups of slaves held a series of nighttime meetings to plan a mass insurrection. In doing so, they drew on their own considerable military experience; the majority of slaves had been born in Africa, and many had served in the civil wars of the kingdom of Kongo and other conflicts before being taken into slavery.[2] They also drew on a long tradition of slave resistance prior to 1791, which had ranged from work slowdowns, to running away, to taking part in African-derived religious rituals and dances known as *vodou* (or voodoo). According to some sources, the August 1791 pact to take up arms was sealed by such a voodoo ritual.

Revolts began on a few plantations on the night of August 22. As the uprising spread, rebels joined together in an ever-growing slave army. During the next month enslaved combatants attacked and destroyed hundreds of sugar and coffee plantations.

On April 4, 1792, as war loomed with the European states, the National Assembly issued a decree extending full citizenship rights to free men of African descent. The Assembly hoped this measure would win their political loyalty and their aid in defeating the slave rebellion.

Warfare in Europe soon spread to Saint-Domingue (Map 22.3). Since the beginning of the slave insurrection, the Spanish colony of Santo Domingo, on the eastern side of the island of Hispaniola, had supported rebel slaves. In early 1793 the Spanish began to bring slave leaders and their soldiers into the Spanish army. Toussaint

French Forces Under Napoleon Attack Saint-Domingue In 1802 an expedition of French forces sent by Napoleon Bonaparte arrived in Saint-Domingue. Its mission was to regain French control of the colony and re-establish slavery (which had been abolished in 1794 by the National Convention). French soldiers — including the leader of the expedition — succumbed to yellow fever and to the strong resistance of armies composed of former slaves and free people of color. In 1804 France recognized the independence of Haiti. (Bibliothèque Nationale, Paris, France/Bridgeman Images)

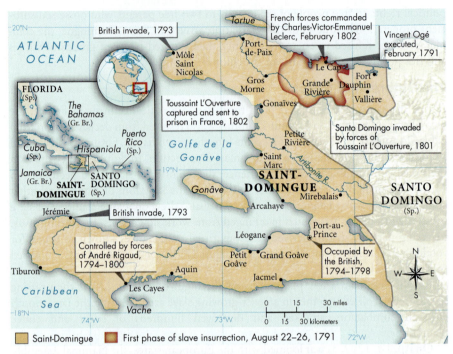

MAP 22.3 The War of Haitian Independence, 1791–1804 Neighbored by the Spanish colony of Santo Domingo, Saint-Domingue was the most profitable European colony in the Caribbean. In 1791 slave revolts erupted in the north near Le Cap, which had once been the capital. In 1770 the French had transferred the capital to Port-au-Prince, which in 1804 became the capital of the newly independent Haiti.

L'Ouverture (TOO-sahn LOO-vair-toor) (1743–1803), a freed slave who had joined the revolt, was named a Spanish officer. In September the British navy blockaded the colony, and invading British troops captured French territory on the island. For the Spanish and British, revolutionary chaos provided a tempting opportunity to capture a profitable colony.

Desperate for forces to oppose France's enemies, commissioners sent by the newly elected National Convention promised freedom to slaves who fought for France. By October 1793 the commissioners had abolished slavery throughout the colony. On February 4, 1794, the Convention ratified the abolition of slavery and extended it to all French territories.

The tide of battle began to turn when Toussaint L'Ouverture switched sides. By 1796 the French had regained control of the colony, and L'Ouverture had emerged as a key military leader. (See "Individuals in Society: Toussaint L'Ouverture," at right.) In March 1796, after he rescued the French colonial governor from hostile forces, L'Ouverture was named lieutenant governor of Saint-Domingue.

The War of Haitian Independence

With Toussaint L'Ouverture acting increasingly as an independent ruler of the western province of Saint-Domingue, another general, André Rigaud (ree-GO)

Toussaint L'Ouverture

LITTLE IS KNOWN OF THE EARLY LIFE OF SAINT-Domingue's brilliant military and political leader Toussaint L'Ouverture. He was born in 1743 on a plantation outside Le Cap owned by the Count de Bréda. According to tradition, L'Ouverture was the eldest son of a captured African prince from modern-day Benin. Toussaint Bréda, as he was then called, occupied a privileged position among slaves. Instead of performing backbreaking labor in the fields, he served his master as a coachman and livestock keeper. He also learned to read and write French and some Latin, but he was always more comfortable with the Creole dialect.

During the 1770s the plantation manager emancipated L'Ouverture, who subsequently leased his own small coffee plantation, worked by slaves. He married Suzanne Simone, who already had one son, and the couple had another son during their marriage. In 1791 he joined the slave uprisings that swept Saint-Domingue, and he took on the *nom de guerre* (war name) L'Ouverture, meaning "the opening." L'Ouverture rose to prominence among rebel slaves allied with Spain and by early 1794 controlled his own army. A devout Catholic who led a frugal and ascetic life, L'Ouverture impressed others with his enormous physical energy, intellectual acumen, and air of mystery. In 1794 he defected to the French side and led his troops to a series of victories against the Spanish. In 1795 the National Convention promoted L'Ouverture to brigadier general.

Over the next three years L'Ouverture successively eliminated rivals for authority on the island. First he freed himself of the French commissioners sent to govern the colony. With a firm grip on power in the northern province, L'Ouverture defeated General André Rigaud in 1800 to gain control in the south. His army then marched on the capital of Spanish Santo Domingo on the eastern half of the island, meeting little resistance. The entire island of Hispaniola was now under his command.

With control in his hands, L'Ouverture was confronted with the challenge of building a post-emancipation society, the first of its kind. The task was made even more difficult by the chaos wreaked by war, the destruction of plantations, and bitter social and racial tensions. For L'Ouverture the most pressing concern was to re-establish the plantation economy. With-

Equestrian portrait of Toussaint L'Ouverture.
(Bibliothèque Nationale, Paris, France/Archives Charmet/Bridgeman Images)

out revenue to pay his army, the gains of the rebellion could be lost. He therefore encouraged white planters to return and reclaim their property. He also adopted harsh policies toward former slaves, forcing them back to their plantations and restricting their ability to acquire land. When they resisted, he sent troops across the island to enforce submission. L'Ouverture's 1801 constitution reaffirmed his draconian labor policies and named L'Ouverture governor for life, leaving Saint-Domingue as a colony in name alone. In June 1802 French forces arrested L'Ouverture and jailed him at Fort de Joux in France's Jura Mountains near the Swiss border. He died of pneumonia on April 7, 1803, leaving his lieutenant, Jean Jacques Dessalines, to win independence for the new Haitian nation.

QUESTIONS FOR ANALYSIS

1. Toussaint L'Ouverture was both slave and slave owner. How did each experience shape his life and actions?
2. What did L'Ouverture and Napoleon Bonaparte have in common? How did they differ?

677

(1761–1811), set up his own government in the southern peninsula. Tensions mounted between L'Ouverture and Rigaud. While L'Ouverture was a freed slave of African descent, Rigaud belonged to the elite group of free people of color. This elite resented the growing power of former slaves like L'Ouverture, who in turn accused the elite of adopting the prejudices of white settlers. Civil war broke out between the two sides in 1799, when L'Ouverture's forces, led by his lieutenant, Jean Jacques Dessalines (1758–1806), invaded the south. Victory over Rigaud in 1800 gave L'Ouverture control of the entire colony.

This victory was soon challenged by Napoleon, who had his own plans for using the profits from a re-established system of plantation slavery as a basis for expanding the French empire. In 1802 French forces under the command of Napoleon's brother-in-law, General Charles-Victor-Emmanuel Leclerc, arrested L'Ouverture and deported him to France, where the revolutionary leader died in 1803.

It was left to L'Ouverture's lieutenant, Jean Jacques Dessalines (duh-sah-LEEN), to unite the resistance, and he led it to a crushing victory over French forces. On January 1, 1804, Dessalines formally declared the independence of Saint-Domingue and the creation of the new sovereign nation of Haiti, the name used by the pre-Columbian inhabitants of the island.

Haiti, the second independent state in the Americas and the first in Latin America, was born from the only successful large-scale slave revolt in history. This event spread shock and fear through slaveholding societies in the Caribbean and the United States, bringing to life their worst nightmares of the utter reversal of power and privilege. Fearing the spread of slave rebellion to the United States, President Thomas Jefferson refused to recognize Haiti. The liberal proponents of the American Revolution thus chose to protect slavery at the expense of revolutionary ideals of universal human rights. Yet Haitian independence had fundamental repercussions for world history, helping spread the idea that liberty, equality, and fraternity must apply to all people. The next phase of Atlantic revolution soon opened in the Spanish-American colonies.

Why and how did the Spanish and Portuguese colonies of North and South America shake off European domination and develop into national states?

Revolutions in Latin America

In 1800 the Spanish Empire in the Americas stretched from the headwaters of the Mississippi River in present-day Minnesota to the tip of Cape Horn in the Antarctic (Map 22.4). Portugal controlled the vast territory of Brazil. Spain and Portugal believed that the great wealth of the Americas existed for the benefit of the Iberian powers, a stance that fostered bitterness and a thirst for independence in the colonies. Between 1806 and 1825 the colonies in Latin America were convulsed by upheavals that ultimately resulted in their independence. For Latin American republicans, their struggles were a continuation of the transatlantic wave of democratic revolution.

The Origins of the Revolutions Against Colonial Powers

Spain's humiliating defeat in the War of the Spanish Succession (1701–1713) (see "The Wars of Louis XIV" in Chapter 18) prompted demands for sweeping reform of all of Spain's institutions, including its colonial policies and practices. The new Bourbon dynasty initiated a decades-long effort known as the Bourbon reforms, which aimed to improve administrative efficiency and increase central control. Under Charles III (r. 1759–1788), Spanish administrators drew on Enlightenment ideals of rationalism

Before Independence

Spanish colonies
- Viceroyalty of New Spain
- Viceroyalty of New Granada
- Viceroyalty of Peru and Audiencia of Chile
- Viceroyalty of Rio de la Plata

Portuguese colonies
- Viceroyalty of Brazil

✗ Silver mine

In 1830

1811 Year independence gained

Colony

MAP 22.4 Latin America, ca. 1780 and 1830 By 1830 almost all of Central America, South America, and the Caribbean islands had won independence. Note that the many nations that now make up Central America were unified when they first won independence from Mexico. Similarly, modern Venezuela, Colombia, and Ecuador were still joined in Gran Colombia.

and progress to strengthen colonial rule and thereby increase the fortunes and power of the Spanish state. They created a permanent standing army and enlarged colonial militias, sought to bring the church under tighter control, and dispatched intendants (government commissioners) with extensive new powers to oversee the colonies.

Additionally, Spain ended its policy of insisting that all colonial trade pass through its own ports and instead permitted free trade within the Spanish Empire. This was intended to favor Spain's competition with Great Britain and Holland by stimulating trade and thereby increasing the imperial government's tax revenues. In Latin America these actions stimulated the production and export of agricultural commodities that were in demand in Europe. Colonial manufacturing, however, which had been growing steadily, suffered a heavy blow under free trade. Colonial textiles and china, for example, could not compete with cheap Spanish products.

Madrid's tax reforms also aggravated discontent. Like Great Britain, Spain believed its colonies should bear some of the costs of their own defense. Accordingly, Madrid raised the prices of its monopoly products—tobacco and liquor—and increased sales taxes on many items. War with revolutionary France in the 1790s led to additional taxes and forced loans, all of which were widely resented. Moreover, high prices and heavier taxes imposed a great burden on indigenous communities, which bore the brunt of all forms of taxation and suffered from the corruption and brutality of tax collectors.

Political conflicts beyond the colonies also helped drive aspirations for independence. The French Revolution and the Napoleonic Wars, which involved France's occupation of Spain and Britain's domination of the seas, isolated Spain and weakened its control over its Latin American colonies.

Racial and ethnic divisions further fueled discontent. At this time, Creoles numbered approximately 3 million of a population of roughly 14 million. They resented the economic and political dominance of the roughly 200,000 **peninsulares** (puh-nihn-suh-LUHR-ayz), as the colonial officials and other natives of Spain or Portugal were called. The Creoles wanted to free themselves from Spain and Portugal and to rule the colonies themselves. They had little interest in improving the lot of the Indians, who constituted by far the largest population group, or that of the mestizos of mixed Spanish and Indian background and the mulattos of mixed Spanish and African heritage.

Slavery was practiced throughout Latin America, but unevenly. The Andes, Mexico, and Central America had relatively small enslaved populations. By contrast, regions dominated by plantation agriculture—especially the Caribbean islands and Brazil—relied on massive numbers of enslaved laborers. Sizable populations of free people of color existed throughout colonial Latin America, greatly outnumbering slaves in many cities. Despite prejudicial laws, they played an important role in urban public life, serving in large numbers in the militia units of cities such as Havana, Mexico City, Lima, and Buenos Aires. As in Saint-Domingue, white Creoles spurred a backlash against the rising social prominence of free people of color in the last decades of the eighteenth century.

A final factor contributing to rebellion was cultural and intellectual ideas. One set of such ideas was Enlightenment thought, which had been trickling into Latin America for decades (see "The Atlantic Enlightenment" in Chapter 19). By 1800 the Creole elite throughout Latin America was familiar with Enlightenment political thought and its role in inspiring colonial demands for independence. Another

peninsulares A term for natives of Spain and Portugal.

important set of ideas consisted of indigenous traditions of justice and reciprocity, which often looked back to an idealized precolonial past. Local people thus perceived Spanish impositions as an assault on the traditional moral communities that bound them to each other and to the Crown. Creoles took advantage of indigenous symbols as a source of legitimacy, but this did not mean they were prepared to view Indians and mestizos as equals.

Resistance, Rebellion, and Independence

The mid-eighteenth century witnessed frequent Andean Indian rebellions against increased taxation and the Bourbon crown's other impositions. In 1780, under the leadership of a descendant of the Inca rulers who took the name Tupac Amaru II, a massive insurrection exploded in the Cuzco region (see Map 22.4). Indian chieftains from the region gathered a powerful force of Indians and people of mixed race. Rebellion swept across highland Peru, where many Spanish officials were executed. Creoles joined forces with Spaniards and Indian nobles to crush the rebellion, shocked by the radical social and economic reforms promised by its leaders. The government was obliged to concede to some of the rebels' demands by abolishing the repartimiento system, which required Indians to buy goods solely from tax collectors, and establishing assemblies of local representatives in Cuzco.

As news of the rebellion of Tupac Amaru II trickled northward, it helped stimulate the 1781 Comuneros Revolt in the New Granada viceroyalty (see Map 22.4). In this uprising, an Indian and mestizo peasant army commanded by Creole captains marched on Bogotá to protest high taxation, loss of communal lands, and state monopolies on liquor and tobacco. Dispersed by the ruling Spanish, who made promises they did not intend to keep, the revolt in the end did little to improve the Indians' lives.

Authorities were shaken by these revolts and the many smaller uprisings that broke out through the eighteenth century, including slave rebellions in Venezuela in the 1790s. But the uprisings did not give rise directly to the independence movements that followed. Led from below, they did not question monarchical rule or the colonial relationship between Spain and Spanish America.

Two events outside of Spanish America did much to shape the ensuing struggle for independence. First, the revolution on Saint-Domingue and the subsequent independence of the nation of Haiti in 1804 convinced Creole elites, many of whom were slaveholders, of the dangers of slave revolt and racial warfare (see Map 22.3). Their plans and strategies would henceforth be shaped by their determination to avoid a similar outcome in Spanish America.

Second, in 1808 Napoleon Bonaparte deposed Spanish king Ferdinand VII and placed his own brother on the Spanish throne (see "The Grand Empire and Its End"). Spanish leaders meeting in exile defiantly began work on the nation's first constitution. Completed in 1812, the Constitution of Cadiz enshrined universal manhood suffrage, freedom of the press, limited monarchy, and other liberal principles. Colonial deputies obtained the right to representation in future assemblies, but not proportional to their population. Many future founding fathers of Latin American republics participated actively in the constitutional congress, which thus greatly influenced the spread of liberal ideas.

In the colonies, the political crisis engendered by Napoleon's coup encouraged movements for self-governance. In cities like Buenos Aires and Caracas, town councils, known as cabildos, took power into their own hands, ostensibly on behalf of the

Declarations of Independence: The United States and Venezuela

Within fifty years of the drafting of the Declaration of Independence by Thomas Jefferson and others in 1776, some twenty other independence movements in Europe and the Americas had issued similar proclamations. The rapid spread of this new type of political declaration testifies to the close connections among transatlantic revolutionary movements in this period. Many of the later declarations of independence modeled themselves self-consciously on the language and arguments of the 1776 text, excerpted below, but they also reflected the unique circumstances in which they were created, as demonstrated by the Venezuelan declaration, also excerpted below.

A Declaration by the Representatives of the United States of America, July 4, 1776

■ We hold these Truths to be self-evident, that all Men are created equal, that they are endowed by their Creator with certain unalienable Rights, that among these are Life, Liberty, and the Pursuit of Happiness—That to secure these Rights, Governments are instituted among Men, deriving their just Powers from the Consent of the Governed, that whenever any Form of Government becomes destructive of these Ends, it is the Right of the People to alter or to abolish it, and to institute new Government, laying its Foundation on such Principles, and organizing its Powers in such Form, as to them shall seem most likely to effect their Safety and Happiness. Prudence, indeed, will dictate that Governments long established should not be changed for light and transient Causes; and accordingly all Experience hath shewn, that Mankind are more disposed to suffer, while Evils are sufferable, than to right themselves by abolishing the Forms to which they are accustomed. But when a long Train of Abuses and Usurpations, pursuing invariably the same Object, evinces a Design to reduce them under absolute Despotism, it is their Right, it is their Duty, to throw off such Government, and to provide new Guards for their future Security. . . . The History of the present King of Great-Britain is a History of repeated Injuries and Usurpations, all having in direct Object the Establishment of an Absolute Tyranny over these States.

deposed king, Ferdinand. In July 1811 a regional congress in Caracas declared the independence of the United States of Venezuela and drafted a liberal constitution guaranteeing basic freedoms and abolishing the slave trade but restricting political participation to property owners. (See "Global Viewpoints: Declarations of Independence: The United States and Venezuela," above.) The republic failed after only one year, but patriots continued to fight royalist forces for the next eight years under the leadership of Simón Bolívar (1783–1830), who belonged to a wealthy land- and slave-owning family.

Bolívar and other Creole elites fighting for independence were forced to acknowledge that victory against Spain would require support from the nonwhites they had previously despised and who had often supported sympathetic royalist leaders against slave-owning Creoles. In return for promising to abolish slavery after independence, Bolívar received military and financial aid from the new Haitian nation. He granted immediate emancipation to slaves who joined the revolutionary struggle and named former slaves and free people of color to positions of authority in the army.

His victories over Spanish armies won Bolívar the presidency of the new republic of Gran Colombia (formerly the New Granada viceroyalty) in 1819. The republic passed laws for the gradual emancipation of slavery and issued a liberal constitution,

Venezuelan Declaration of Independence, July 5, 1811

■ In the Name of the All-powerful God, We, the Representatives of the united Provinces . . . , forming the American Confederation of Venezuela, in the South Continent, in Congress assembled, considering the full and absolute possession of our Rights, which we recovered justly and legally from the 19th of April, 1810, in consequence of the occurrences in Bayona,* and the occupation of the Spanish Throne by conquest, and the succession of a new Dynasty, constituted without our consent, . . . calling on the SUPREME BEING to witness the justice of our proceedings and the rectitude of our intentions, do implore his divine and celestial help; and ratifying, at the moment in which we are born to the dignity which his Providence restores to us, the desire we have of living and dying free, and of believing and defending the holy Catholic and Apostolic Religion of Jesus Christ. We, therefore, in the name and by the will and authority which we hold from the virtuous People of Venezuela, DO declare solemnly to the world, that its united Provinces are, and ought to be, from this day, by act and right, Free, Sovereign, and Independent States; and that they are absolved from every submission and dependence on the Throne of Spain . . . and that a free and independent State, thus constituted, has full power to take that form of Government which may be conformable to the general will of the People, to declare war, make peace, form alliances, regulate treaties of commerce, limits, and navigation; and to do and transact every act, in like manner as other free and independent States.

QUESTIONS FOR ANALYSIS

1. What justification does the first declaration offer for the independence of the United States of America from Great Britain? What influences from Enlightenment thought are evident in this text?
2. What similarities and differences do you find between the declaration of the United States of America and that of Venezuela?

Sources: The Declaration of Independence (1776); *Interesting Official Documents Relating to the United Provinces of Venezuela* (London: Longman and Co., 1812), pp. 3, 18–19.

*The forced abdication of Spanish king Ferdinand VII in favor of Joseph Bonaparte.

---

similar to that of 1811. Bolívar and other military leaders continued attacks against the Spanish, eventually freeing or helping to liberate the future nations of Colombia, Ecuador, Peru, Chile, and Bolivia (named after the great liberator). Bolívar encouraged the new states to begin the process of manumission, a suggestion that met with great success in the Republic of Chile, which abolished slavery in 1823, but elsewhere encountered resistance from Creole slaveholders.

Dreaming of a continental political union, Bolívar summoned a conference of the new American republics in 1826 in Panama City. The meeting achieved little, however. The territories of Gran Colombia soon splintered (see Map 22.4), and a sadly disillusioned Bolívar went into exile.

Events in Mexico followed a different course. Under Spain, Mexico had been united with Central America as the Viceroyalty of New Spain. In 1808, after Napoleon's coup, the Spanish viceroy assumed control of the government of New Spain from its capital in Mexico City. Meanwhile, groups of rebels plotted to overthrow royalist power. Under the leadership of Miguel Hidalgo, a Jesuit priest who espoused racial and social equality, poor Creoles and indigenous and mestizo peasants rose up against the Spanish in 1810. Although Hidalgo was quickly caught and executed by the combined forces of Spain and Creole elites, popular revolts spread across Mexico.

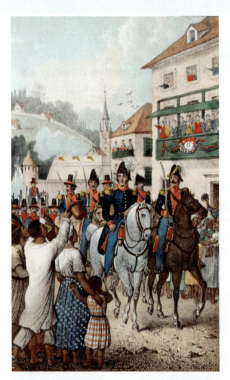

Triumph of Bolívar Bolívar was treated as a hero everywhere he went in South America. (Sammlung Archiv für Kunst und Geschichte, Berlin, Germany/akg-images)

By 1820 the desire for autonomy from Spain had spread among Creole elites. They joined forces with rebellious armies to make common cause against Spain and succeeded in winning over many royalist troops. In 1821 they issued a declaration of Mexican independence. Originally established as a constitutional monarchy, the new state became a republic in 1823. Gradual steps toward the abolition of slavery culminated in the freeing of all slaves by the end of the 1820s and the election of a president of African descent in 1829.

Portuguese Brazil followed a less turbulent path to independence than the Spanish-American republics. When Napoleon's troops entered Portugal, the royal family fled to Brazil and made Rio de Janeiro the capital of the Portuguese Empire. The king returned to Portugal in 1821, leaving his son Pedro in Brazil as regent. Under popular pressure, Pedro proclaimed Brazil's independence in 1822, issued a constitution, and even led resistance against Portuguese troops. He accepted the title Emperor Pedro I (r. 1822–1831). Although Brazil remained a monarchy, Creole elites dominated society in Brazil, as they did elsewhere in Latin America. Because they had gained independence without military struggle, Brazil's Creole elites avoided making common cause with poor whites and people of color, and they refused to consider ending slavery once independence arrived.

The Aftermath of Revolution in the Atlantic World

The Atlantic revolutions shared many common traits. They had common origins in imperial competition, war debt, social conflict, and Enlightenment ideals. Over the course of revolution, armed struggle often took the form of civil war, in which the participation of ordinary people—sans-culottes, slaves, free people of color, mestizos, and Indians—played a decisive role. Perhaps their most important similarity was in the democratic limitations of the regimes these revolutions created and the frustrated aspirations they bequeathed to subsequent generations of marginalized citizens.

For the most part, the elite liberals who led the revolutions were not democrats and had no intention of creating regimes of full economic or social equality. The constitutions they wrote generally restricted political rights to landowners and middle-class men. Indigenous people may have gained formal equality as citizens, yet they found that the actual result was the removal of the privileged status they had negotiated with their original conquerors. Thus they suffered the loss of rights over their land and other resources. Moreover, none of the postrevolutionary constitutions gave women a role in political life.

The issue of slavery, by contrast, divided the revolutions. The American Revolution was led in part by slaveholding landowners, who were determined to retain slavery in its aftermath, while the more radical French republic abolished it throughout the French empire (a measure soon reversed by Napoleon). The independent nation of Haiti was built on the only successful slave revolt in history, but the need for revenue from plantation agriculture soon led to the return of coercive labor requirements, if not outright slavery. In Latin America independence speeded the abolition of slavery, bringing an immediate ban on the slave trade and gradual emancipation from the 1820s to the 1850s. Still, Cuba and Brazil, which had enormous slave populations, did not end slavery until 1886 and 1888, respectively.

The aftermath of the Atlantic revolutions brought extremely different fortunes to the new nations that emerged from them. France returned to royal rule with the restoration of the Bourbon monarchy in 1815. A series of revolutionary crises ensued in the nineteenth century as succeeding generations struggled over the legacies of monarchicism, republicanism, and Bonapartism. It was not until 1871 that republicanism finally prevailed (see "Republican France" in Chapter 24). The transition to an independent republic was permanent and relatively smooth in the United States. Nevertheless, the unresolved conflict over slavery would lead to catastrophic civil war in 1860. Haiti faced crushing demands for financial reparations from France and the hostility of the United States and other powers.

The newly independent nations of Latin America had difficulty achieving economic and political stability when the wars of independence ended. In the 1830s regional separatism caused New Spain to break up into five separate countries. The failure of political union in New Spain and Gran Colombia isolated individual countries, prevented collective action, and later paved the way for the political and economic intrusion of the United States and other powers. Spain's Caribbean colonies of Puerto Rico and Cuba remained loyal, in large part due to fears that slave revolt would spread from neighboring Haiti.

The Creole leaders of the revolutions had little experience in government, and the wars left a legacy of military, not civilian, leadership. Despite these disappointments, liberal ideals of political and social equality born of the revolutionary era left a crucial legacy for future generations in Latin America (see Chapter 27).

KEY EVENTS IN EARLY LATIN AMERICAN REVOLUTIONS

1759–1788	Reign of Charles III, who instituted administrative and economic reforms
July 1811	Regional congress in Caracas declares independence of the United States of Venezuela
1822	Proclamation of Brazil's independence from Portugal
1826	Call by Simón Bolívar for Panama conference on Latin American union
1830s	New Spain breaks up into five separate countries
1888	Emancipation of slaves in Brazil

Chapter Summary

From 1775 to 1825 a wave of revolution swept through the Atlantic world. Its origins included long-term social and economic changes, Enlightenment ideals of liberty and equality, and the costs of colonial warfare. British efforts to raise taxes after the Seven Years' War aroused violent protest in the American colonies. In 1776 the Second Continental Congress issued the Declaration of Independence, and by 1783 Britain had recognized the independence of the thirteen colonies.

In 1789 delegates to the Estates General defied royal authority to declare themselves a National Assembly, which promulgated France's first constitution in 1791. Led by the Jacobin club, the Assembly waged war on Austria and Prussia and proclaimed France a republic. From the end of 1793, under the Reign of Terror, the Revolution pursued internal and external enemies ruthlessly and instituted economic controls to aid the poor. The weakness of the Directory government after the fall of Robespierre enabled Napoleon Bonaparte to claim control of France. Napoleon's relentless military ambitions allowed him to spread French power through much of Europe but ultimately led to his downfall.

After a failed uprising by free men of color, slaves rose in revolt in the French colony of Saint-Domingue in August 1791. Their revolt, combined with the outbreak of war and the radicalization of the French Revolution, led to a sequence of conflicts and rebellions that culminated in independence for the new Haitian nation in 1804.

Latin American independence movements drew strength from Spain's unpopular policies and the political crisis engendered by Napoleon's invasion of Portugal and Spain. Under the leadership of Simón Bolívar, the United States of Venezuela claimed independence in 1811. Led by Creole officers but reliant on nonwhite soldiers, rebel armies successfully fought Spanish forces over the next decade. Despite Bolívar's efforts to build a unified state, in the 1830s New Spain split into five separate countries. In Brazil the royal regent proclaimed independence in 1822 and reigned as emperor of the new state.

NOTES

1. Donald Sutherland, *France, 1789–1815: Revolution and Counterrevolution* (New York: Oxford University Press, 1986), p. 420.
2. John K. Thornton, "'I Am the Subject of the King of Congo': African Political Ideology and the Haitian Revolution," *Journal of World History* 4.2 (Fall 1993): 181–214.

CONNECTIONS

The Atlantic world was the essential context for a great revolutionary wave in the late eighteenth and early nineteenth centuries. The movement of peoples, commodities, and ideas across the Atlantic Ocean in the eighteenth century created a world of common debates, conflicts, and aspirations. Moreover, the high stakes of colonial empire heightened competition among European states, leading to a series of wars that generated crushing costs for overburdened treasuries. For the British and Spanish in their American colonies and the French at home, the desperate need for new taxes weakened government authority and opened the door to rebellion. In turn, the ideals of the French Revolution inspired slaves and free people of African descent in Saint-Domingue and Latin America to rise up and claim the promise of liberty, equality, and fraternity for people of all races.

The chain reaction did not end with the liberation movements in Latin America that followed the Haitian Revolution. Throughout the nineteenth and early twentieth centuries periodic convulsions occurred in Europe, the Americas, and elsewhere as successive generations struggled over political rights first proclaimed by late-eighteenth-century revolutionaries (see Chapters 24 and 27). Meanwhile, as dramatic political events unfolded, a parallel economic revolution was gathering steam. This was the Industrial Revolution, the topic of the next chapter, which originated around 1780 and accelerated through the end of the eighteenth century. After 1815 the twin forces of industrialization and democratization would combine to transform Europe and the world.

CHAPTER 22 **Review and Explore**

Identify Key Terms

Identify and explain the significance of each item below.

Treaty of Paris (p. 656)

Declaration of Independence (p. 659)

Antifederalists (p. 660)

Estates General (p. 661)

National Assembly (p. 662)

Jacobin club (p. 665)

Mountain (p. 665)

Girondists (p. 665)

sans-culottes (p. 665)

Reign of Terror (p. 667)

Thermidorian reaction (p. 668)

Napoleonic Code (p. 669)

Grand Empire (p. 671)

Continental System (p. 671)

Creoles (p. 673)

peninsulares (p. 680)

Review the Main Ideas

Answer the focus questions from each section of the chapter.

1. What were the factors behind the age of revolution in the Atlantic world? (p. 654)

2. Why and how did American colonists forge a new, independent nation? (p. 657)

3. Why and how did revolutionaries in France transform the nation first into a constitutional monarchy and then into a republic that entered war with European powers? (p. 661)

4. How did Napoleon Bonaparte assume control of France and much of Europe, and what factors led to his downfall? (p. 669)

5. How did a slave revolt on colonial Saint-Domingue lead to the creation of the independent nation of Haiti in 1804? (p. 673)

6. Why and how did the Spanish and Portuguese colonies of North and South America shake off European domination and develop into national states? (p. 678)

Make Comparisons and Connections

Analyze the larger developments and continuities within and across chapters.

1. What was revolutionary about the age of revolution? How did the states that emerged out of the eighteenth-century revolutions differ from the states that predominated in previous centuries?

2. To what extent would you characterize the revolutions discussed in this chapter as Enlightenment movements? (See "The Atlantic Enlightenment" in Chapter 19.) How did the increased circulation of goods, people, and ideas across the Atlantic in the eighteenth century contribute to the outbreak of revolution on both sides of the ocean?

3. In what sense did the age of revolution mark the beginning of modern politics in Europe and the Americas?

TIMELINE

EUROPE	

← **1715–1774** Reign of Louis XV

◆ **1763** Treaty of Paris

1756–1763 Seven Years' War

AMERICAS	

1743–1803 Life of Toussaint L'Ouverture

ASIA	
MIDDLE EAST	
AFRICA	

1725 | 1750

Suggested Resources

BOOKS

Armitage, David, and Sanjay Subrahmanyam, eds. *The Age of Revolutions in Global Context, c. 1760–1840.* 2009. Presents the international causes and consequences of the age of revolutions.

Bell, David A. *The First Total War: Napoleon's Europe and the Birth of Warfare as We Know It.* 2007. Argues that the French Revolution created a new form of "total" war that prefigured the world wars of the twentieth century.

Calloway, Colin G. *The Scratch of a Pen: 1763 and the Transformation of North America.* 2006. A study of the dramatic impact of the Seven Years' War on the British and French colonies of North America.

Desan, Suzanne. *The Family on Trial in Revolutionary France.* 2004. Studies the effects of revolutionary law on the family, including the legalization of divorce.

Dubois, Laurent. *Avengers of the New World: The Story of the Haitian Revolution.* 2004. An excellent and highly readable account of the revolution that transformed the French colony of Saint-Domingue into the independent state of Haiti.

Gould, Eliga H., and Peter S. Onuf, eds. *Empire and Nation: The American Revolution in the Atlantic World.* 2005. A collection of essays placing the American Revolution in its wider Atlantic context, including studies of its impact on daily life in the new republic and the remaining British Empire.

Klooster, Wim. *Revolutions in the Atlantic World: A Comparative History.* 2009. An accessible and engaging comparison of the revolutions in North America, France, Haiti, and Spanish America.

McPhee, Peter, ed. *A Companion to the French Revolution.* 2013. A wide-ranging collection of essays on the French Revolution, written by experts.

Schechter, Ronald. *Obstinate Hebrews: Representations of Jews in France, 1715–1815.* 2003. An illuminating study of Jews and attitudes toward them in France, from the Enlightenment to emancipation.

Van Young, Eric. *The Other Rebellion: Popular Violence, Ideology, and the Mexican Struggle for Independence, 1810–1821.* 2001. Authoritative study of why ordinary Mexicans joined the fight for independence from Spain.

Wood, Gordon S. *The American Revolution: A History.* 2003. A concise introduction to the American Revolution by a Pulitzer Prize–winning historian.

DOCUMENTARIES

Égalité for All: Toussaint Louverture and the Haitian Revolution (PBS, 2009). Uses music, interviews, voodoo rituals, and dramatic re-enactments to explore the Haitian Revolution and its fascinating leader, Toussaint L'Ouverture.

Liberty! The American Revolution (PBS, 1997). A dramatic documentary about the American Revolution, consisting of six hour-long episodes that cover events from 1763 to 1788.

The War That Made America (PBS, 2006). This miniseries about the Seven Years' War (known as the French and Indian War in North America) focuses on alliances between Native Americans and the French and British; it also examines George Washington's role in the conflict as a young officer.

FEATURE FILMS

Farewell, My Queen (Benoît Jacquot, 2012). A fictional view of the final days of the French monarchy, from the perspective of a female servant whose job is to read to Queen Marie Antoinette.

The Liberator (Alberto Arvelo, 2014). The first Venezuelan film to be nominated for an Oscar presents an epic survey of the life and battles of Simón Bolívar, hero of the Spanish-American wars of independence.

Master and Commander: The Far Side of the World (Peter Weir, 2003). A British navy captain pursues a French vessel along the coast of South America during the Napoleonic Wars.

WEBSITES

Haiti Digital Library. A guide to online primary sources, articles, and websites related to Haitian history, from the revolution to modern times; sponsored by the Haiti Laboratory at Duke University. **sites.duke.edu/haitilab/english/**

Liberty, Equality, Fraternity: Exploring the French Revolution. Features a large image and document collection from the era of the French Revolution, as well as songs, maps, and thematic essays written by scholars in the field. **chnm.gmu.edu/revolution/**

The Papers of George Washington. A site with online versions of many documents pertaining to and written by George Washington, accompanied by articles on themes related to Washington's life and views. **gwpapers.virginia.edu**

23

The Revolution in Energy and Industry
1760–1850

While the revolutions of the Atlantic world were opening a new political era, another revolution was beginning to transform economic and social life. The Industrial Revolution began in Great Britain around 1780 and soon began to influence continental Europe and the United States. Quite possibly only the development of agriculture during Neolithic times had a comparable impact and significance in world history. Non-Western nations began to industrialize after 1860.

Industrialization profoundly modified human experience. It changed patterns of work, transformed the social structure, and eventually altered the international balance of political power in favor of the most rapidly industrialized nations, especially Great Britain. What was revolutionary about the Industrial Revolution was not its pace or that it represented a sharp break with the previous period. On the contrary, the Industrial Revolution built on earlier developments, and the rate of progress was slow. What was remarkable about the Industrial Revolution was that it inaugurated a period of sustained economic and demographic growth that has continued to the present. Although it took time, the Industrial Revolution eventually helped ordinary people in the West gain a higher standard of living.

Young Factory Worker

Children composed a substantial element of the workforce in early factories, where they toiled long hours in dangerous and unsanitary conditions. Until a mechanized process was invented at the end of the nineteenth century, boys working in glass-bottle factories, like the youth pictured here, stoked blazing furnaces with coal and learned to blow glass.

(*Interior of a Furnace*, 1865 [oil on canvas] [detail] by Charles Housez [1822–1888]/BOURNE GALLERY ARCHIVE/ © Bourne Gallery, Reigate, Surrey, UK/ Bridgeman Images)

CHAPTER PREVIEW

THE INDUSTRIAL REVOLUTION IN BRITAIN
Why did the Industrial Revolution begin in Britain, and how did it develop between 1780 and 1850?

INDUSTRIALIZATION IN EUROPE AND THE WORLD
How did countries in Europe and around the world respond to the challenge of industrialization after 1815?

NEW PATTERNS OF WORKING AND LIVING
How did work evolve during the Industrial Revolution, and how did daily life change for working people?

RELATIONS BETWEEN CAPITAL AND LABOR
How did the changes brought about by the Industrial Revolution lead to new social classes, and how did people respond to the new structure?

Why did the Industrial Revolution begin in Britain, and how did it develop between 1780 and 1850?

The Industrial Revolution in Britain

The Industrial Revolution began in Great Britain, the nation created by the formal union of Scotland, Wales, and England in 1707. The transformation in industry was something new in history, and it was unplanned. It originated from a unique combination of possibilities and constraints in late-eighteenth-century Britain. With no models to copy and no idea of what to expect, Britain pioneered not only in industrial technology but also in social relations and urban living.

Why Britain?

Perhaps the most important debate in economic history focuses on why the Industrial Revolution originated in western Europe, and Britain in particular, rather than in other parts of the world, such as Asia. Historians continue to debate this issue, but the best answer seems to be that Britain possessed a unique set of possibilities and constraints—abundant coal, high wages, a relatively peaceful and centralized government, well-developed financial systems, innovative culture, highly skilled craftsmen, and a strong position in empire and global trade, including slavery—that spurred its people to adopt a capital-intensive, machine-powered system of production.

Thus a number of factors came together over the long term to give rise to the Industrial Revolution in Britain. The Scientific Revolution and the Enlightenment fostered a new worldview that embraced progress and the role of research and experimentation in understanding and mastering the natural world. Moreover, Britain's intellectual culture emphasized the public sharing of knowledge, including that of scientists and technicians from other countries.

In the economic realm, the seventeenth-century expansion of rural industry produced a surplus of English woolen cloth. Exported throughout Europe, English cloth brought commercial profits and high wages. By the eighteenth century the expanding Atlantic economy and trade with India and China were also serving Britain well. The mercantilist colonial empire Britain aggressively built, augmented by a strong position in Latin America and in the transatlantic slave trade, provided raw materials like cotton and a growing market for British manufactured goods (see "The Atlantic Economy" in Chapter 19). Strong demand for British manufacturing meant that British workers earned high wages compared to the rest of the world's laborers.

Agriculture also played an important role in bringing about the Industrial Revolution. English farmers were second only to the Dutch in productivity in 1700, and they were continually adopting new methods of farming. Because of increasing efficiency, landowners were able to produce more food with a smaller workforce. The enclosure movement had deprived many small landowners of their land, leaving the landless poor to work as hired agricultural laborers or in rural industry. These groups created a pool of potential laborers for the new factories.

Abundant food and high wages in turn meant that the ordinary English family no longer had to spend almost everything it earned just to buy bread. Thus the family could spend more on manufactured goods. They could also pay to send their children to school. Britain's populace enjoyed high levels of education compared to that of the rest of Europe. Moreover, in the eighteenth century the members of the average British family—including women and girls—were redirecting their labor away from unpaid work for household consumption and toward work for wages that they could spend on goods.

Britain also benefited from rich natural resources and a well-developed infrastructure. In an age when it was much cheaper to ship goods by water than by land, no part of England was more than fifty miles from navigable water. Beginning in the 1770s a canal-building boom enhanced this advantage. Rivers and canals facilitated easy movement of England and Wales's enormous deposits of iron and coal. The abundance of coal combined with high wages in manufacturing placed Britain in a unique position among the nations of the world: its manufacturers had extremely strong incentives to develop technologies to draw on the power of coal to increase workmen's productivity. In regions with lower wages, such as India and China, the costs of mechanization outweighed potential gains in productivity.

A final factor favoring British industrialization was the heavy hand of the British state and its policies. Britain's parliamentary system taxed its population aggressively and spent the money on a navy to protect imperial commerce and on an army that could be used to quell uprisings by disgruntled workers. Starting with the Navigation Acts under Oliver Cromwell (see "Mercantilism and Colonial Wars" in Chapter 18), the British state also adopted aggressive tariffs, or duties, on imported goods to protect its industries.

All these factors combined to initiate the **Industrial Revolution**, a term first coined to describe the burst of major inventions and technical changes that took place in certain industries. This technical revolution went hand in hand with an impressive quickening in the annual rate of industrial growth in Britain. Whereas industry had grown at only 0.7 percent between 1700 and 1760 (before the Industrial Revolution), it grew at the much higher rate of 3 percent between 1801 and 1831, when industrial transformation was in full swing.[1]

Technological Innovations and Early Factories

The pressure to produce more goods for a growing market and to reduce the labor costs of manufacturing was directly related to the first decisive breakthrough of the Industrial Revolution: the creation of the world's first machine-powered factories in the British cotton textile industry. Technological innovations in the manufacture of cotton cloth led to a new system of production and social relationships.

The putting-out system that developed in the seventeenth-century textile industry involved a merchant who loaned, or "put out," raw materials to cottage workers who processed the raw materials in their own homes and returned the finished products to the merchant. There was always a serious imbalance in textile production based on cottage industry: the work of four or five spinners was needed to keep one weaver steadily employed. During the eighteenth century the putting-out system grew across Europe, but most extensively in Britain. The growth of demand only increased pressures on the supply of thread.

Many a tinkering worker knew that devising a better spinning wheel promised rich rewards. It proved hard to spin the traditional raw materials—wool and flax— with improved machines, but cotton was different. Cotton textiles had first been imported into Britain from India by the East India Company as a rare and delicate luxury for the upper classes. In the eighteenth century a lively market for cotton cloth emerged in West Africa, where the English and other Europeans traded it for enslaved people. By 1760 a tiny domestic cotton industry had emerged in northern England based on imported raw materials, but it could not compete with cloth produced

Industrial areas · **Coal deposit** · **Metal goods** · **Woolen cloth** · **Canals, 1800** · **Navigable rivers**

SCOTLAND
Newcastle
North Sea
Manchester
Sheffield
Birmingham
WALES
Iron
ENGLAND
London
Iron
Bath
Exeter
Iron
English Channel

Cottage Industry and Transportation in Great Britain in the 1700s

Industrial Revolution
A term first coined in the 1830s to describe the burst of major inventions and economic expansion that took place in certain industries, such as cotton textiles and iron, between 1780 and 1850.

Samuel Crompton

SAMUEL CROMPTON'S LIFE STORY ILLUSTRATES the remarkable ingenuity and determination of the first generation of inventors in the Industrial Revolution as well as the struggles they faced in controlling and profiting from their inventions. Crompton was born in 1753 in Bolton-in-the Moors, a Lancashire village active in the domestic production of cotton thread and cloth. Crompton descended from small landowners and weavers, but his grandfather had lost the family land and his father died shortly after his birth.

Crompton's mother was a pious and energetic woman who supported the family by tenant farming and spinning and weaving cotton. Crompton spent years spinning in childhood until he was old enough to begin weaving. His mother ensured that he was well educated at the local school, and as a teenager he attended night classes, studying algebra, mathematics, and trigonometry.

This was the period when John Kay's invention of the flying shuttle doubled the speed of handloom weaving, leading to a drastic rise in the demand for thread. Crompton's family acquired one of the new spinning jennies—invented by James Hargreaves—and he saw for himself how they increased productivity. He was also acquainted with Richard Arkwright, inventor of the water frame, who then operated a barbershop in Bolton.

In 1774 Crompton began work on the spinning machine that would consume what little free time, and spare money, he possessed over the next five years. Solitary by nature and fearful of competition, Crompton worked alone and in secret. He earned a little extra money playing violin in the Bolton theater orchestra, and he possessed a set of tools left over from his father's own mechanical experiments.

The result of all this effort was the spinning mule, so called because it combined the rollers of Arkwright's water frame with the moving carriage of Hargreaves's spinning jenny. With the mule, spinners could produce very fine and strong thread in large quantities, something no previous machine had permitted. The mule effectively ended England's reliance on India for the finest muslin cloth.

In 1780, possessed of a spectacular technological breakthrough and a beloved bride, Crompton seemed poised for a prosperous and happy life. Demand surged for the products of his machine, and manufacturers were desperate to learn its secrets. Too poor and naïve to purchase a patent for his invention, Crompton shared it with manufacturers through a subscription agreement. Unfortunately, he received little of the promised money in return.

Once exposed to the public, the spinning mule quickly spread across Great Britain. Crompton continued to make high-quality yarn, but had to compete with all the other workshops using his machine.

---

by workers in India and other parts of Asia. International competition thus drove English entrepreneurs to invent new technologies to bring down labor costs.

After many experiments over a generation, a carpenter and jack-of-all-trades, James Hargreaves, invented his cotton-spinning jenny about 1765. At almost the same moment, a barber-turned-manufacturer named Richard Arkwright invented (or possibly pirated) another kind of spinning machine, the water frame. These breakthroughs produced an explosion in the infant cotton textile industry in the 1780s and made some inventors, like Richard Arkwright, extremely wealthy. By 1790 the new machines were producing ten times as much cotton yarn as had been made in 1770.

Hargreaves's **spinning jenny** was simple, inexpensive, and powered by hand. In early models from six to twenty-four spindles were mounted on a sliding carriage, and each spindle spun a fine, slender thread. The machines were usually worked by women, who moved the carriage back and forth with one hand and turned a wheel

spinning jenny A simple, inexpensive, hand-powered spinning machine created by James Hargreaves about 1765.

Moreover, he could not keep skilled workers, since they were constantly lured away by his competitors' higher wages.

As others earned great wealth with the mule, Crompton grew frustrated by his relative poverty. In 1811 he toured Great Britain to document his invention's impact. He estimated that 4,600,000 mules were then in operation that directly employed 70,000 people. Crompton's supporters took these figures to Parliament, which granted him a modest reward of £5,000. However, this boost did little to improve his fortunes, and his subsequent business ventures failed. In 1824 local benefactors took up a small subscription to provide for his needs, but he died in poverty in 1827 at the age of seventy-four.

Samuel Crompton, inventor of the spinning mule. (Photo by SSPL/Getty Images)

Replica of the spinning mule, a hybrid machine that combined features from Hargreaves's spinning jenny and Arkwright's water frame. (Photo by SSPL/Getty Images)

QUESTIONS FOR ANALYSIS

1. What factors in Crompton's life enabled him to succeed as an inventor?
2. Why did Crompton fail to profit from his inventions?
3. What does the contrast between Richard Arkwright's financial success and Crompton's relative failure tell us about innovation and commercial enterprise in the Industrial Revolution?

Source: Gilbert James France, *The Life and Times of Samuel Crompton, Inventor of the Spinning Machine Called the Mule* (London: Simpkin Marshall, 1859).

to supply power with the other. Now it was the male weaver who could not keep up with the vastly more efficient female spinner.

Arkwright's **water frame** employed a different principle. It quickly acquired a capacity of several hundred spindles and demanded much more power than a single operator could provide. A solution was found in waterpower. The water frame required large specialized mills located beside rivers, factories that employed as many as one thousand workers. The major drawback of the water frame was that it could spin only a coarse, strong thread. Around 1780 a hybrid machine invented by Samuel Crompton proved capable of spinning very fine and strong thread in large quantities. (See "Individuals in Society: Samuel Crompton," above.) Gradually, all cotton spinning was concentrated in large-scale factories.

These revolutionary developments in the textile industry allowed British manufacturers to compete successfully in international markets in both fine and coarse cotton thread. At first, the machines were too expensive to build and did not provide

water frame A spinning machine created by Richard Arkwright that had a capacity of several hundred spindles and used waterpower; it therefore required a larger and more specialized mill — a factory.

Woman Working a Spinning Jenny The loose cotton strands on the slanted bobbins shown in this illustration of Hargreaves's spinning jenny passed up to the sliding carriage and then on to the spindles (inset) in back for fine spinning. The worker, almost always a woman, regulated the sliding carriage with one hand, and with the other she turned the crank on the wheel to supply power. By 1783 one woman could spin a hundred threads at a time. (spinning jenny: © Mary Evans Picture Library/The Image Works; spindle: Picture Research Consultants & Archives)

enough savings in labor to be adopted in continental Europe or elsewhere. Where wages were low and investment capital was scarce, there was little point in adopting mechanized production until the machines' productivity increased significantly and the cost of manufacturing the machines dropped, both of which occurred in the first decades of the nineteenth century.[2]

Families using cotton in cottage industry were freed from their constant search for adequate yarn from scattered part-time spinners, because all the thread needed could be spun in the cottage on the jenny or obtained from a nearby factory. The income of weavers, now hard-pressed to keep up with the spinners, rose markedly until about 1792. In response, mechanics and capitalists sought to invent a power loom to save on labor costs. This Edmund Cartwright achieved in 1785. But the power looms of the factories worked poorly at first and did not fully replace handlooms until the 1820s.

Working conditions in the early cotton factories were so poor that adult workers were reluctant to work in them. Factory owners often turned to orphans and abandoned children instead. By placing them in "apprenticeship" with factory owners, parish officers charged with caring for such children saved money. The owners gained workers over whom they exercised almost the authority of slave owners. Housed, fed, and locked up nightly in factory dormitories, the young workers labored thirteen or fourteen hours a day, six days a week, for little or no pay.

The Steam Engine Breakthrough

Well into the eighteenth century, Europe, like other areas of the world, relied mainly on wood for energy, and human beings and animals performed most work. This dependence meant that Europe and the rest of the world remained poor in energy and power.

By the eighteenth century wood was in ever-shorter supply in Britain. Processed wood (charcoal) was mixed with iron ore in blast furnaces to produce pig iron that could be processed into steel, cast iron, or wrought iron. The iron industry's appetite for wood was enormous, and by 1740 the British iron industry was stagnating. As wood became ever more scarce, the British looked to coal as an alternative. They had first used coal in the late Middle Ages as a source of heat. By 1640 most homes in London were heated with coal, and it was also used in industry to provide heat for making beer, glass, soap, and other products. The breakthrough came when industrialists began to use coal to produce mechanical energy and to power machinery.

To produce more coal, mines had to be dug deeper and deeper and were constantly filling with water. Mechanical pumps, usually powered by animals walking in circles at the surface, had to be installed. Animal power was expensive and bothersome. In an attempt to overcome these disadvantages, Thomas Savery in 1698 and Thomas Newcomen in 1705 invented the first primitive **steam engines**. Both engines burned coal to produce steam that drove the water pumps.

In 1763 a gifted young Scot named James Watt (1736–1819) was drawn to a critical study of the steam engine. Watt worked at the University of Glasgow as a skilled craftsman making scientific instruments. In 1763 Watt was called on to repair a Newcomen engine being used in a physics course. Watt discovered that the Newcomen engine could be significantly improved by adding a separate condenser. This invention, patented in 1769, greatly increased the efficiency of the steam engine.

To make his invention a practical success, Watt needed skilled workers, precision parts, and capital, and the relatively advanced nature of the British economy proved essential. A partnership in 1775 with Matthew Boulton, a wealthy English industrialist, provided Watt with adequate capital and exceptional skills in salesmanship. Among Britain's highly skilled locksmiths, tinsmiths, and millwrights, Watt found mechanics who could install, regulate, and repair his sophisticated engines. From ingenious manufacturers, Watt was gradually able to purchase precision parts. By the late 1780s the firm of Boulton and Watt had made the steam engine a practical and commercial success in Britain.

The coal-burning steam engine of Watt and his followers was the Industrial Revolution's most fundamental advance in technology. For the first time in history, humanity had, at least for a few generations, almost unlimited power at its disposal.

steam engines
A breakthrough invention by Thomas Savery in 1698 and Thomas Newcomen in 1705 that burned coal to produce steam, which was then used to operate a pump; the early models were superseded by James Watt's more efficient steam engine, patented in 1769.

James Nasmyth's Mighty Steam Hammer Nasmyth's invention was the forerunner of the modern pile driver, and its successful introduction in 1832 epitomized the rapid development of steam-power technology in Britain. In this painting by the inventor himself, workers manipulate a massive iron shaft being hammered into shape at Nasmyth's foundry near Manchester. (Ann Ronan Pictures/Print Collector/Getty Images)

For the first time, inventors and engineers could devise and implement all kinds of power equipment to aid people in their work. Steam power began to replace waterpower in cotton-spinning mills during the 1780s, contributing greatly to that industry's phenomenal rise. Steam also took the place of waterpower in flour mills, in the malt mills used in breweries, in the flint mills supplying the pottery industry, and in the mills exported by Britain to the West Indies to crush sugarcane.

The British iron industry was also radically transformed. After 1770 the adoption of steam-driven bellows in blast furnaces allowed for great increases in the quantity of pig iron produced by British ironmakers. In the 1780s Henry Cort developed the puddling furnace, which allowed pig iron to be refined with coke, a smokeless and hot-burning fuel produced by heating coal to rid it of impurities.

Cort also developed steam-powered rolling mills, which were capable of spewing out finished iron in every shape and form. The economic consequence of these technical innovations was a great boom in the British iron industry. In 1740 annual British iron production was only 17,000 tons. With the spread of coke smelting and the impact of Cort's inventions, production had reached 260,000 tons by 1806. In 1844 Britain produced 3 million tons of iron. Once expensive, iron became the cheap, basic, indispensable building block of the British economy.

Steam-Powered Transportation

Rocket The name given to George Stephenson's effective locomotive that was first tested in 1829 on the Liverpool and Manchester Railway and reached a maximum speed of 35 miles per hour.

The first steam locomotive was built by Richard Trevithick after much experimentation. George Stephenson's locomotive named **Rocket** sped down the track of the just-completed Liverpool and Manchester Railway at a maximum speed of 35 miles per hour in 1829. The line from Liverpool to Manchester was the first modern railroad, using steam-powered locomotives to carry customers to the new industrial cities. It was a financial as well as a technical success, and many private companies were organized to build more rail lines. Within twenty years they had completed the main trunk lines of Great Britain (Map 23.1). Other countries were quick to follow, with the first steam-powered trains operating in the United States in the 1830s and in Brazil, Chile, Argentina, and the British colonies of Canada, Australia, and India in the 1850s (Figure 23.1).

FIGURE 23.1 Railroad Track Mileage, 1890 Steam railroads were first used by the general public for shipping in England in the 1820s, and they quickly spread to other countries. The United States was an early adopter of railroads and by 1890 had surpassed all other countries in miles of track, as shown in this figure.

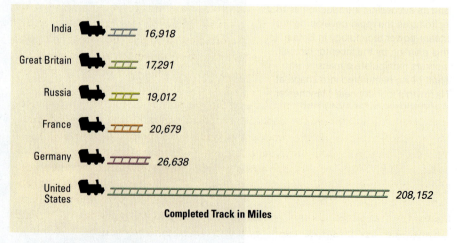

The arrival of the railroad had many significant consequences. It dramatically reduced the cost and uncertainty of shipping freight over land. Previously, markets had tended to be small and local; as the barrier of high transportation costs was lowered, markets became larger and even nationwide. Larger markets encouraged manufacturers to build larger factories with more sophisticated machinery in a growing number of industries. Such factories could make goods more cheaply and gradually subjected most cottage workers and many urban artisans to severe competitive pressures. In all countries, the construction of railroads created a strong demand for unskilled labor and contributed to the growth of a class of urban workers.

The railroad also had a tremendous impact on cultural values and attitudes. The last and culminating invention of the Industrial Revolution, the railroad dramatically revealed the power and increased the speed of the new age. (See "Analyzing the Evidence: *Rain, Steam, and Speed—the Great Western Railway,*" page 700.)

The steam engine also transformed water travel. French engineers completed the first steamships in the 1770s, and the first commercial steamships came into use in North America several decades later. The *Clermont*, designed by Robert Fulton, began to travel the Hudson River in New York State in 1807, shortly followed by ships belonging to brewer John Molson on the St. Lawrence River. The steamship brought the advantages of the railroad—speed, reliability, efficiency—to water travel.

MAP 23.1 The Industrial Revolution in Great Britain, ca. 1850 Industry concentrated in the rapidly growing cities of the north and the center of England, where rich coal and iron deposits were close to one another.

Industry and Population

In 1851 London hosted an industrial fair called the Great Exhibition in the newly built **Crystal Palace**. More than 6 million visitors from all over Europe marveled at the gigantic new exhibition hall set in the middle of a large, centrally located park. The building was made entirely of glass and iron, both of which were now cheap and abundant. Sponsored by the British royal family, the exhibition celebrated the new era of industrial technology and the kingdom's role as world economic leader.

Britain's claim to be the "workshop of the world" was no idle boast, for it produced two-thirds of the world's coal and more than half of its iron and cotton cloth. More generally, in 1860 Britain produced a remarkable 20 percent of the entire world's output of industrial goods, whereas it had produced only about 2 percent of the world total in 1750.[3] As the British economy significantly increased its production of manufactured goods, the gross national product (GNP) rose roughly fourfold at constant prices between 1780 and 1851. At the same time, the population of Britain boomed, growing from about 9 million in 1780 to almost 21 million in 1851. Thus growing numbers consumed much of the increase in total production.

Crystal Palace The location of the Great Exhibition in 1851 in London, an architectural masterpiece made entirely of glass and iron.

Rain, Steam, and Speed — the Great Western Railway

The last and culminating invention of the Industrial Revolution, the railroad dramatically revealed the power and increased the speed of the new age. Until the coming of the railroad, travel was largely measured by the distance that a human or a horse could cover before becoming exhausted. Steam power created a revolution in human transportation, allowing a constant, rapid rate of travel with no limits on its duration. Time and space suddenly and drastically contracted, as faraway places could be reached in one-third the time or less. As the poet Heinrich Heine proclaimed in 1843, "What changes must now occur, in our way of looking at things, in our notions! . . . I feel as if the mountains and forests of all countries were advancing on Paris. Even now, I can smell the German linden trees; the North Sea's breakers are rolling against my door."*

Racing down the track at speeds that reached 50 miles per hour by 1850 was an overwhelming experience. Some great artists succeeded in expressing this sense of power and awe. An outstanding example of this is depicted here in the painting by Joseph M. W. Turner (1775–1851): *Rain, Steam, and Speed — the Great Western Railway*. Contemporary novelists also recorded their impressions of early train travel, as in this striking passage by Charles Dickens: "Through the hollow, on the height, by the heath, by the orchard, by the park, by the garden, over the canal, across the river, where the sheep are feeding, where the mill is going, where the barge is floating, where the dead are lying, where the factory is smoking, where the stream is running, where the village clusters . . . away with a strike and a roar and a rattle, and no trace to leave behind but dust and vapour."†
The increase in speed also led doctors to worry

about the effects of the constant noise and vibration on passengers and crew.

Despite these concerns, the railroad quickly became a central institution of society. So did the massive new train stations, the cathedrals of the industrial age. Leading railway engineers such as Isambard Kingdom Brunel and Thomas Brassey, whose tunnels pierced mountains and whose bridges spanned valleys, became public idols — the astronauts of their day.

(National Gallery, London, UK/Bridgeman Images)

QUESTIONS FOR ANALYSIS

1. What impression of train travel does this painting convey to the viewer? What techniques did Turner employ to create this impression? Would you describe Turner's painting as a negative or a positive depiction?

2. How would you compare this representation of travel by train to images you have seen in current media of travel by automobile or airplane? How would you account for any similarities or differences in nineteenth-century and contemporary depictions of travel?

*Quoted in Wolfgang Schivelbusch, *The Railway Journey: The Industrialization of Time and Space in the Nineteenth Century* (Berkeley: University of California Press, 1986), p. 37.

†Charles Dickens, *Dombey and Son* (Ware, U.K.: Wordsworth Editions, 1999), p. 262.

Interior View of the Crystal Palace Built for the Great Exhibition of 1851, the Crystal Palace was a spectacular achievement in engineering, prefabricated from three hundred thousand sheets of glass. With almost fifteen thousand exhibitors, the event constituted the first international industrial exhibition, showcasing manufactured products from Britain, its empire, and the rest of the world. Later, the building was disassembled and moved to another site in London, where it stood until destroyed by fire in 1936. (London Metropolitan Archives, City of London, UK/Bridgeman Images)

Rapid population growth in Great Britain was key to industrial development. More people meant a more mobile labor force, with a wealth of young workers in need of employment and ready to go where the jobs were. Sustaining the dramatic increase in population, in turn, was possible only through advances in agriculture and industry. Many contemporaries feared that the rapid growth in population would inevitably lead to disaster. In his *Essay on the Principle of Population* (1798), Thomas Malthus (1766–1834) argued that population would always tend to grow faster than the food supply. Malthus concluded that the only hope of warding off such "positive checks" to population growth as war, famine, and disease was "prudential restraint."[4] That is, young men and women had to limit the growth of population by marrying late in life. But Malthus was not optimistic about this possibility. The powerful attraction of the sexes would cause most people to marry early and have many children.

Economist David Ricardo (1772–1823) spelled out the pessimistic implications of Malthus's thought. Ricardo's depressing **iron law of wages** posited that, because of the pressure of population growth, wages would always sink to subsistence level. That is, wages would be just high enough to keep workers from starving.

Malthus, Ricardo, and their followers were proved wrong in the long run. However, until the 1820s, or even the 1850s, contemporary observers might reasonably have concluded that the economy and the total population were racing neck and neck, with the outcome very much in doubt. There was another problem as well. Perhaps workers, farmers, and ordinary people did not get their rightful share of the new wealth. Perhaps only the rich got richer, while the poor got poorer or made no progress. We will turn to this great issue after situating the process of industrialization in its European and global context.

iron law of wages Theory proposed by English economist David Ricardo suggesting that the pressure of population growth prevents wages from rising above the subsistence level.

How did countries in Europe and around the world respond to the challenge of industrialization after 1815?

Industrialization in Europe and the World

As new technologies and a new organization of labor began to revolutionize production in Britain, other countries took notice and began to emulate its example. With the end of the Napoleonic Wars, the nations of the European continent quickly adopted British inventions and achieved their own pattern of technological innovation and economic growth. By the last decades of the nineteenth century, western European countries as well as the United States and Japan had industrialized their economies to a considerable, albeit varying, degree.

Industrialization in other parts of the world proceeded more gradually, with uneven jerks and national and regional variations. Scholars are still struggling to explain these variations as well as the dramatic advantage in economic production that Western nations gained for the first time in history over non-Western ones. These questions are especially important because they may offer valuable lessons for poor countries that today are seeking to improve their material condition through industrialization and economic development. The latest findings on the nineteenth-century experience are encouraging. They suggest that there were alternative paths to the industrial world and that there was and is no need to follow a rigid, predetermined British model.

National and International Variations

Comparative data on industrial production in different countries over time help give us an overview of what happened. One set of data, the work of a Swiss scholar, compares the level of industrialization on a per capita basis in several countries from 1750 to 1913. These data are far from perfect, but they reflect basic trends and are presented in Table 23.1 for closer study.

Table 23.1 presents a comparison of how much industrial product was produced, on average, for each person in a given country in a given year. All the numbers are expressed in terms of a single index number of 100, which equals the per capita level of industrial goods in Great Britain and Ireland in 1900. Every number in the table is thus a percentage of the 1900 level in Britain and is directly comparable with other numbers. The countries are listed in roughly the order that they began to use large-scale, power-driven technology.

What does this overview tell us? First, one sees in the first column that in 1750 all countries were fairly close together, including non-Western areas such as China and India. However, the column headed 1800 shows that Britain had opened up a noticeable lead over all countries by 1800, and that gap progressively widened as the British Industrial Revolution accelerated through 1830 and reached full maturity by 1860.

Second, the table shows that Western countries began to emulate the British model successfully over the nineteenth century, with significant variations in the timing and in the extent of industrialization. Belgium led in adopting Britain's new technology, and it experienced a truly revolutionary surge between 1830 and 1860. France developed factory production more gradually and did not experience "revolutionary" growth in industrial output. Slow but steady economic growth in France was overshadowed by the spectacular rise of Germany and the United States after 1860 in what has been termed the "Second Industrial Revolution." In general, eastern and southern Europe began the process of industrialization later than north-

TABLE 23.1 Per Capita Levels of Industrialization, 1750–1913

	1750	1800	1830	1860	1880	1900	1913
Great Britain	10	16	25	64	87	100	115
Belgium	9	10	14	28	43	56	88
United States	4	9	14	21	38	69	126
France	9	9	12	20	28	39	59
Germany	8	8	9	15	25	52	85
Austria-Hungary	7	7	8	11	15	23	32
Italy	8	8	8	10	12	17	26
Russia	6	6	7	8	10	15	20
China	8	6	6	4	4	3	3
India	7	6	6	3	2	1	2

Note: All entries are based on an index value of 100, equal to the per capita level of industrialization in Great Britain in 1900. Data for Great Britain include Ireland, England, Wales, and Scotland.

Source: Data from P. Bairoch, "International Industrialization Levels from 1750 to 1980," *Journal of European Economic History* 11 (Spring 1982): 294, U.S. Journals at Cambridge University Press.

western and central Europe. Nevertheless, these regions made real progress in the late nineteenth century, as growth after 1880 in Austria-Hungary, Italy, and Russia suggests. This meant that all European states as well as the United States managed to raise per capita industrial levels in the nineteenth century.

These increases stood in stark contrast to the decreases that occurred at the same time in many non-Western countries, most notably in China and India, as Table 23.1 shows. European countries industrialized to a greater or lesser extent even as most of the non-Western world stagnated. Japan, which is not included in this table, stands out as an exceptional area of non-Western industrial growth in the second half of the nineteenth century. After the forced opening of the country to the West in the 1850s, Japanese entrepreneurs began to adopt Western technology and manufacturing methods, resulting in a production boom by the late nineteenth century (see "Industrialization" in Chapter 26). Differential rates of wealth- and power-creating industrial development, which heightened disparities within Europe, also greatly magnified existing inequalities between Europe and the rest of the world (see "The Rise of Global Inequality" in Chapter 25).

Industrialization in Continental Europe

Throughout Europe the eighteenth century was an era of agricultural improvement, population increase, expanding foreign trade, and growing cottage industry. Thus, when the pace of British industry began to accelerate in the 1780s, continental businesses began to adopt the new methods as they proved their profitability. During the period of the revolutionary and Napoleonic Wars, from 1793 to 1815, however, western Europe experienced tremendous political and social upheaval that temporarily halted economic development. With the return of peace in 1815, however, western European countries again began to play catch-up.

They faced significant challenges. In the newly mechanized industries, British goods were being produced very economically, and these goods had come to dominate world markets. In addition, British technology had become so advanced that very few engineers or skilled technicians outside England understood it. Moreover, the technology of steam power involved large investments in the iron and coal industries and, after 1830, required the existence of railroads. Continental business people had great difficulty amassing the large sums of money the new methods demanded, and laborers bitterly resisted the move to working in factories. All these factors slowed the spread of mechanization (Map 23.2).

Nevertheless, western European nations possessed a number of advantages that helped them respond to these challenges. First, most had rich traditions of putting-out enterprise, merchant capitalism, and skilled urban trades. These assets gave their firms the ability to adapt and survive in the face of new market conditions. Second, continental capitalists did not need to develop their own advanced technology. Instead they could "borrow" the new methods developed in Great Britain, as well as the engineers and some of the financial resources they lacked. Finally, European countries had strong, independent governments that were willing to use the power of the state to promote industry and catch up with Britain.

Agents of Industrialization

Western European success in adopting British methods took place despite the best efforts of the British to prevent it. The British realized the great value of their technical discoveries and tried to keep their secrets to themselves. Until 1825 it was illegal for artisans and skilled mechanics to leave Britain; until 1843 the export of textile machinery and other equipment was forbidden. Many talented, ambitious workers, however, slipped out of the country illegally and introduced the new methods abroad.

Thus British technicians and skilled workers were a powerful force in the spread of early industrialization. A second agent of industrialization consisted of talented European entrepreneurs such as Fritz Harkort (1793–1880). Serving in England as a Prussian army officer during the Napoleonic Wars, Harkort was impressed with what he saw. Harkort set up shop building steam engines in the Ruhr Valley, on the western border with France. In spite of problems obtaining skilled workers and machinery, Harkort succeeded in building and selling engines. However, his ambitious efforts failed to turn a profit. His career illustrates both the great efforts of a few important business leaders to duplicate the British achievement and the difficulty of the task.

tariff protection
A government's way of supporting and aiding its own economy by laying high taxes on imported goods from other countries, as when the French responded to the flood of cheaper British goods in their country by imposing high tariffs on some imported products.

National governments played an even more important role in supporting industrialization in continental Europe than in Britain. **Tariff protection** was one such support. The French, for example, responded to a flood of cheap British goods in 1815, after the Napoleonic Wars, by laying high taxes on imported goods. Customs agreements emerged among some German states starting in 1818, and in 1834 a

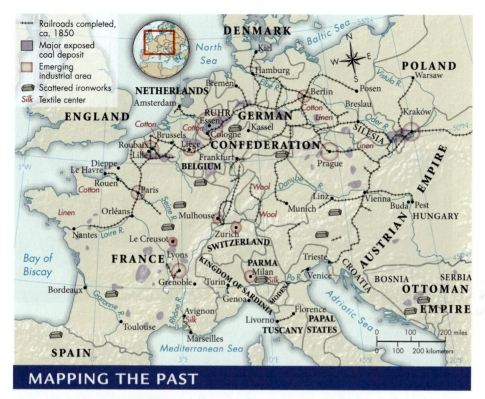

MAPPING THE PAST

MAP 23.2 Continental Industrialization, ca. 1850 Although continental countries were beginning to make progress by 1850, they still lagged far behind Britain. For example, continental railroad building was still in an early stage, whereas the British rail system was essentially complete (see Map 23.1). Coal played a critical role in nineteenth-century industrialization, both as a power source for steam engines and as a raw material for making iron and steel.

ANALYZING THE MAP Locate the major exposed (that is, known) coal deposits in 1850. Which countries and areas appear rich in coal resources, and which appear poor? Is there a difference between northern and southern Europe?

CONNECTIONS What is the relationship between known coal deposits and emerging industrial areas in continental Europe? In England?

number of states signed a treaty creating a customs union, or *Zollverein*. The treaty allowed goods to move between member states without tariffs, while erecting a single uniform tariff against other nations.

After 1815 continental governments also bore the cost of building roads, canals, and railroads to improve transportation. Belgium led the way in the 1830s and 1840s, building a state-owned railroad network that stimulated the development of heavy industry and made the country an early industrial leader. In France the state shouldered all the expense of acquiring and laying roadbed, including bridges and tunnels.

Finally, banks, like governments, also played a larger and more creative role on the continent than in Britain. Previously, almost all banks in Europe had been private.

The Circle of the Rue Royale, Paris, 1868 The Circle of the Rue Royale was an exclusive club of aristocrats, bankers, railway owners, and other members of Parisian high society. This group portrait projects the wealth and elegance of the club's members, who are gathered on the balcony of a hotel. (Fine Art Images/Heritage Images/Getty Images)

Because of the possibility of unlimited financial loss, the partners of private banks generally avoided industrial investment as being too risky.

In the 1830s two important Belgian banks pioneered in a new direction. They received permission from the growth-oriented government to establish themselves as corporations enjoying limited liability. That is, if the bank went bankrupt, stockholders would lose only their original investments in the bank's common stock, and they could not be forced to pay for additional losses out of other property they owned. Limited liability helped these banks attract investors. They mobilized impressive resources for investment in big companies, became industrial banks, and successfully promoted industrial development. Similar corporate banks became important in France and Germany in the 1850s and 1860s.

The combined efforts of skilled workers, entrepreneurs, governments, and industrial banks meshed successfully between 1850 and the financial crash of 1873. In Belgium, France, and the German states key indicators of modern industrial development increased at average annual rates of 5 to 10 percent. As a result, rail networks were completed in western Europe and much of central Europe, and the leading continental countries mastered the industrial technologies that had first been developed in Great Britain. In the early 1870s Britain was still Europe's most industrial nation, but a select handful of countries were closing the gap.

The Global Picture

The Industrial Revolution did not have a transformative impact beyond Europe prior to the 1860s, with the exception of the United States and Japan. In many countries, national governments and pioneering entrepreneurs promoted industrialization, but fell short of transitioning to an industrial economy. For example, in Russia the imperial government brought steamships to the Volga River and a railroad to the capital, St. Petersburg, in the first decades of the nineteenth century. By midcentury ambitious entrepreneurs had established steam-powered cotton factories using imported British machines. However, these advances did not lead to overall industrialization of the country. Instead Russia confirmed its role as provider of raw materials, especially timber and grain, to the hungry West.

Egypt, a territory of the Ottoman Empire, similarly began an ambitious program of modernization after a reform-minded viceroy took power in 1805. This program included the use of imported British technology and experts in textile manufacture and other industries (see "Egypt: From Reform to British Occupation" in Chapter 25). These industries, however, could not compete with lower-priced European imports. Like Russia, Egypt fell back on agricultural exports, such as sugar and cotton, to European markets.

Such examples of faltering efforts at industrialization could be found in many other places in the Middle East, Asia, and Latin America. Where European governments maintained direct or indirect control, they acted to maintain colonial markets as sources of raw materials and consumers for their own products, rather than encouraging the spread of industrialization. In India millions of poor textile workers lost their livelihood because they could not compete with industrially produced

Press for Packing Indian Cotton, 1864 British industrialization destroyed a thriving Indian cotton textile industry, whose weavers could not compete with cheap British imports. India continued to supply raw cotton to British manufacturers.

Indian Cotton Manufacturers

The mechanization of spinning and weaving in Britain led to tremendous increases in productivity, which in turn allowed British manufacturers to produce large volumes of cloth at low prices. The East India Company sold this cloth in India at prices lower than those for locally produced cotton, but imposed a stiff tariff on Indian cloth imported to Britain. This unequal situation and its destructive impact on Indian cloth manufacturers — who had previously led the world in cotton cloth production — quickly became apparent. Despite appeals from the manufacturers themselves, defenders of this policy claimed that it would be better for Indians to focus on producing raw cotton, which could then be brought to Britain to be finished. The two documents excerpted below exemplify the two sides of the dispute.

Petition of Natives of Bengal to the British Privy Council for Trade, 1831

■ The humble Petition of the undersigned Manufacturers and Dealers in Cotton and Silk Piece-Goods, the fabrics of Bengal;

Sheweth,

That of late years your Petitioners have found their business nearly superseded by the introduction of the fabrics of Great Britain into Bengal, the importation of which augments every year, to the great prejudice of the native manufactures.

That the fabrics of Great Britain are consumed in Bengal without any duties being levied thereon to protect the native fabrics.

That the fabrics of Bengal are charged with the following duties when they are used in Great Britain:

On manufactured cottons, 10 per cent
On manufactured silks, 24 per cent . . .

They therefore pray to be admitted to the privilege of British subjects, and humbly entreat your Lordships to allow the cotton and silk fabrics of Bengal to be used in Great Britain "free of duty," or at the same rate which may be charged on British fabrics consumed in Bengal.

Your Lordships must be aware of the immense advantages the British manufacturers derive from their skill in constructing and using machinery, which enables them to undersell the unscientific manufacturers of Bengal in their own country; . . . such an instance of justice to the natives of India would not fail to endear the British Government to them.

Robert Rickards, Testimony to the Select Committee of the House of Lords, 1821

■ I think it very likely that the further introduction of our cheap cotton manufactures into India may supersede, as they have done already to a certain degree, the use and consumption of many of the cotton manufactures of the country; but I am not aware of any injury to the population of India that is likely to result from this state of things; probably, the most beneficial trade that can be carried on between India and this country will be found to consist in the exchange of the raw produce of the East for the manufactured goods of Britain. I believe the native Indians have it in their power, from the cheapness of labour and food in that country, and the great fertility of the soil, to produce raw articles calculated for the manufactures of Britain, at a cheaper rate than perhaps any other country in the world; and if their industry should be directed to this point, instead of to local manufactures, it will interfere the less with their present occupations and employments; inasmuch as the weavers generally throughout India are cultivators of the soil also, and are occupied to the full as much in their fields as at their looms.

QUESTIONS FOR ANALYSIS

1. Why did Robert Rickards believe that Indians would not be harmed if their cloth manufacturing industry was destroyed by cheap British imports?
2. What response might the Bengal cotton and silk manufacturers have made to Rickards?

Sources: Appendix to the Report from the Select Committee of the House of Commons on the Affairs of the East-India Company, 16th August 1832 (London: J. L. Cox and Son, 1833), pp. 774–775; Third Report from the Select Committee Appointed to Consider the Means of Improving and Maintaining the Foreign Trade of the Country, East Indies, and China, 1821 (746), VI.340.

British cotton. The British charged stiff import duties on Indian cottons entering the kingdom, but prohibited the Indians from doing the same to British imports. (See "Global Viewpoints: Indian Cotton Manufacturers," at left.) The arrival of railroads in India in the mid-nineteenth century served the purpose of agricultural rather than industrial development.

Latin American economies were disrupted by the early-nineteenth-century wars of independence (see "The Aftermath of Revolution in the Atlantic World" in Chapter 22). As these countries' economies recovered in the mid-nineteenth century, they increasingly adopted steam power for sugar and coffee processing and for transportation. Like elsewhere, this technology first supported increased agricultural production for export and only later drove domestic industrial production.

The rise of industrialization in Britain, western Europe, and the United States thus caused other regions of the world to become increasingly economically dependent. Instead of industrializing, many territories underwent a process of deindustrialization or delayed industrialization. In turn, relative economic weakness made them vulnerable to the new wave of imperialism undertaken by industrialized nations in the second half of the nineteenth century (see "The New Imperialism, 1880–1914" in Chapter 25).

As for China, it did not adopt mechanized production until the end of the nineteenth century, but continued as a market-based, commercial society with a massive rural sector and industrial production based on traditional methods. In the 1860s and 1870s, when Japan was successfully adopting industrial methods, the Chinese government showed similar interest in Western technology and science. However, in the mid-nineteenth century China faced widespread uprisings, which drained attention and resources to the military; moreover, after the Boxer Uprising of 1900 (see "Republican Revolution" in Chapter 26), Western powers forced China to pay massive indemnities, further reducing its capacity to promote industrialization.

New Patterns of Working and Living

> How did work evolve during the Industrial Revolution, and how did daily life change for working people?

Having first emerged in the British countryside in the late eighteenth century, factories and industrial labor began migrating to cities by the early nineteenth century. For some people, the Industrial Revolution brought improvements, but living and working conditions for the poor stagnated or even deteriorated until around 1850, especially in overcrowded industrial cities.

Work in Early Factories

The first factories of the Industrial Revolution were cotton mills, which began functioning in the 1770s along fast-running rivers and streams and were often located in sparsely populated areas. Cottage workers, accustomed to the putting-out system, were reluctant to work in the new factories even when they received relatively good wages. In a factory, workers had to keep up with the machine and follow its relentless tempo. Moreover, they had to show up every day, on time, and work long, monotonous hours under the constant supervision of demanding overseers.

Cottage workers were not used to that way of life. All members of the family worked hard and long, but in spurts, setting their own pace. Women and children could break up their long hours of spinning with other tasks. On Saturday afternoon the head of the family delivered the week's work to the merchant manufacturer and got paid. Saturday night was a time of relaxation and drinking, especially for men.

Also, early factories resembled English poorhouses, where totally destitute people went to live at public expense. The similarity between large brick factories and large stone poorhouses increased the cottage workers' fear of factories and their hatred of factory discipline. It was cottage workers' reluctance to work in factories that prompted early cotton mill owners to turn to pauper children.

Working Families and Children

By the 1790s the early labor pattern was rapidly changing. The use of pauper apprentices was in decline, and in 1802 it was forbidden by Parliament. Many more textile factories were being built, mainly in urban areas, where they could use steam power rather than waterpower and attract a workforce more easily than in the countryside. People came from near and far to work in the cities. Collectively, these wage laborers came to be known as the "working class," a term first used in the late 1830s.

In some cases, workers accommodated to the system by carrying over familiar working traditions. Some came to the mills and the mines as family units, as they had worked on farms and in the putting-out system. The mill or mine owner bargained with the head of the family and paid him or her for the work of the whole family.

Workers at a U.S. Mill Female workers at a U.S. cotton mill in 1890 take a break from operating belt-driven weaving machines to pose for this photograph, accompanied by their male supervisor. The first textile mills, established in the 1820s in Massachusetts, employed local farm girls. As competition intensified, conditions deteriorated and the mills increasingly relied on immigrant women who had few alternatives to the long hours, noise, and dangers of factory work. By 1900 more than 1 million women worked in factories in the United States. (Courtesy of George Eastman Museum, accession number 1966:0039:0013)

Ties of kinship were particularly important for newcomers, who often traveled great distances to find work. Many urban workers in Great Britain were from Ireland. They were forced out of rural Ireland by population growth and deteriorating economic conditions from 1817. Their numbers increased dramatically during the desperate years of the potato famine, from 1845 to 1851. Like many other immigrant groups held together by ethnic and religious ties, the Irish worked together, formed their own neighborhoods, and maintained their cultural traditions.

In the early decades of the nineteenth century, however, technical changes made it less and less likely that workers could continue to labor in family groups. As control and discipline passed into the hands of impersonal managers and overseers, adult workers began to protest against inhuman conditions on behalf of their children. Some enlightened employers and social reformers in Parliament agreed that more humane standards were necessary, and they used widely circulated parliamentary reports to influence public opinion. For example, Robert Owen (1771–1858), a successful textile manufacturer, testified in 1816 before an investigating committee on the basis of his experience. He argued that employing children under ten years of age as factory workers was "injurious to the children, and not beneficial to the proprietors."[5] Workers also provided graphic testimony at such hearings as the reformers pressed Parliament to pass corrective laws.

These efforts resulted in a series of British Factory Acts from 1802 to 1833 that progressively limited the workday of child laborers and set minimum hygiene and safety requirements. The **Factory Act of 1833** stated that children between ages nine and thirteen could work a maximum of eight hours per day, not including two hours for education. Teenagers aged fourteen to eighteen could work up to twelve hours, while those under nine were banned from employment. The act also installed a system of full-time professional inspectors to enforce labor regulations. The Factory Acts constituted significant progress in preventing the exploitation of children. One unintended drawback of restrictions on child labor, however, was that they broke the pattern of whole families working together in the factory, because efficiency required standardized shifts for all workers. After 1833 the number of children employed in industry declined rapidly.

Factory Act of 1833
English law that led to a sharp decline in the employment of children by limiting the hours that children over age nine could work and banning employment of children younger than nine.

The Sexual Division of Labor

With the restriction of child labor and the collapse of the family work pattern in the 1830s came a new sexual division of labor. By 1850 the man was emerging as the family's primary wage earner, while the married woman found only limited job opportunities. Generally denied good jobs at high wages in the growing urban economy, wives were expected to concentrate on their duties at home. Evolving gradually, but largely in place by 1850, this new pattern of **separate spheres** in Britain constituted a major development in the history of women and of the family.

Several factors combined to create this new sexual division of labor. First, the new and unfamiliar discipline of the clock and the machine was especially hard on married women of the laboring classes. Factory discipline conflicted with child care in a way that labor on the farm or in the cottage had not.

Second, running a household in conditions of urban poverty was an extremely demanding job in its own right. There were no supermarkets or public transportation.

separate spheres
A gender division of labor with the wife at home as mother and homemaker and the husband as wage earner.

Shopping and feeding the family constituted a never-ending challenge. Taking on a brutal job outside the house had limited appeal for the average married woman from the working class. Thus many women might well have accepted the emerging division of labor as the best available strategy for family survival in the industrializing society.

Third, to a large degree the young, generally unmarried women who did work for wages outside the home were segregated from men and confined to certain "women's jobs" because the new sexual division of labor replicated long-standing patterns of gender segregation and inequality. In the preindustrial economy, a small sector of the labor market had always been defined as "women's work," especially tasks involving needlework, spinning, food preparation, child care, and nursing. This traditional sexual division of labor took on new overtones, however, in response to the factory system. The growth of factories and mines brought unheard-of opportunities for girls and boys to mix on the job, free of familial supervision. Such opportunities led to more unplanned pregnancies and fueled the illegitimacy explosion that had begun in the late eighteenth century and that gathered force until at least 1850. Thus segregation of jobs by gender was partly an effort by older people to help control the sexuality of working-class youths.

Investigations into the British coal industry before 1842 provide a graphic example of this concern. The middle-class men leading the inquiry professed horror at the sight of girls and women working without shirts, which was a common practice because of the heat, and they quickly assumed the prevalence of licentious sex with the male miners. In fact, most girls and married women worked for related males in a family unit that provided considerable protection and restraint. Yet many witnesses from the working class also believed that the mines were inappropriate and dangerous places for women and girls. Some miners stressed particularly the danger of sexual aggression for girls working past puberty. As one explained, "I consider it a scandal for girls to work in the pits. Till they are 12 or 14 they may work very well but after that it's an abomination. . . . The work of the pit does not hurt them, it is the effect on their morals that I complain of."[6] The **Mines Act of 1842** prohibited underground work for all women and girls as well as for boys under ten.

Mines Act of 1842
English law prohibiting underground work for all women and girls as well as for boys under ten.

A final factor encouraging working-class women to withdraw from paid labor was the domestic ideals emanating from middle-class women, who had largely embraced the "separate spheres" ideology. Middle-class reformers published tracts and formed societies to urge poor women to devote more care and attention to their homes and families.

Living Standards for the Working Class

Although the evidence is complex and sometimes contradictory, most historians now agree that overall living standards for the working class did not rise substantially until 1850. Factory wages began to rise after 1815, but these gains were modest and were offset by a decline in married women's and children's participation in the labor force, meaning that many households had less total income than before. Moreover, many people still worked outside the factories as cottage workers or rural laborers, and in those sectors wages declined. Thus the increase in the productivity of industry did not lead to an increase in the purchasing power of the British working classes. Only after 1830, and especially after 1840, did real wages rise substantially, so that the

Working-Class Housing in Glasgow, 1868 Like other British cities, Glasgow experienced a population boom in the nineteenth century. Migrant workers from Ireland and the Highlands were housed in cramped, damp, and dark tenements without running water and were thus vulnerable to infectious disease. This photograph was taken as part of a campaign to expose the dismal living conditions of industrial workers. (Private Collection/The Stapleton Collection/Bridgeman Images)

average worker earned roughly 30 percent more in real terms in 1850 than in 1770.

Up to that point, the harshness of labor in the new industries probably outweighed their benefits as far as working people were concerned. With industrialization, workers toiled longer and harder at jobs that were often more grueling and more dangerous. In England nonagricultural workers labored about 250 days per year in 1760 as compared to 300 days per year in 1830, while the normal workday remained an exhausting eleven hours throughout the entire period.[7]

As the factories moved to urban areas, workers followed them in large numbers, leading to an explosion in the size of cities, especially in the north of England. By the end of the nineteenth century England had become by far the most urbanized country in Europe. Life in the new industrial cities, such as Manchester and Liverpool, was grim. Given extremely high rates of infant mortality, average life expectancy was around only twenty-five to twenty-seven years, some fifteen years less than the national average.[8] Migrants to the booming cities found expensive, hastily constructed, overcrowded apartments and inadequate sanitary systems.

Another way to consider the workers' standard of living is to look at the goods they purchased, which also suggest stagnant or declining living standards until the middle of the nineteenth century. One important area of improvement was in the consumption of cotton goods, which became much cheaper and could be enjoyed by all classes. However, in other areas, food in particular, the modest growth in factory wages was not enough to compensate for rising prices.

From the 1850s onward, matters improved considerably as wages made substantial gains and the prices of many goods dropped. A greater variety of foods became available, including the first canned goods. Some of the most important advances were in medicine. Smallpox vaccination became routine, and surgeons began to use anesthesia in the late 1840s. By 1850 trains and steamships had revolutionized transportation for the masses, while the telegraph made instant communication possible for the first time in human history. Gaslights greatly expanded the possibilities of nighttime activity.

In addition to the technical innovations that resulted from industrialization, other, less tangible changes were also taking place. As young men and women migrated away from their villages to seek employment in urban factories, many close-knit rural communities were destroyed. The loss of skills and work autonomy, along with the loss of community, must be included in the assessment of the Industrial Revolution's impact on the living conditions of the poor.

How did the changes brought about by the Industrial Revolution lead to new social classes, and how did people respond to the new structure?

Relations Between Capital and Labor

In Great Britain industrial development led to the creation of new social groups and intensified long-standing problems between capital and labor. A new class of factory owners and industrial capitalists arose. The demands of modern industry regularly brought the interests of the middle-class industrialists into conflict with those of the people who worked for them—the working class. As observers took note of these changes, they raised new questions about how industrialization affected social relationships. Meanwhile, enslaved laborers in European colonies contributed to the industrialization process in multiple ways.

The New Class of Factory Owners

Early industrialists operated in a highly competitive economic system. There were countless production problems, and success and large profits were by no means certain. Manufacturers therefore waged a constant battle to cut their production costs and stay afloat. Much of the profit had to go back into the business for new and better machinery.

Most early industrialists drew upon their families and friends for labor and capital, but they came from a variety of backgrounds. Many were from well-established merchant families with rich networks of contacts and support. Others were of modest means, especially in the early days. Artisans and skilled workers of exceptional ability had unparalleled opportunities. Members of ethnic and religious groups who had been discriminated against in the traditional occupations controlled by the landed aristocracy jumped at the new chances and often helped each other.

As factories and firms grew larger, and opportunities declined, it became harder for a gifted but poor young mechanic to start a small enterprise and end up as a wealthy manufacturer. Expensive, formal education became more important for young men as a means of success and advancement. In Britain by 1830 and in France and Germany by 1860, leading industrialists were more likely to have inherited their well-established enterprises, and they were financially much more secure than their struggling parents had been.

Just like working-class women, the wives and daughters of successful businessmen also found fewer opportunities for active participation in Europe's business world. Rather than contributing as vital partners in a family-owned enterprise, as so many middle-class women had done before, these women were increasingly valued for their ladylike gentility.

Responses to Industrialization

From the beginning, the British Industrial Revolution had its critics. Among the first were the Romantic poets, including William Blake (1757–1827) and William

Wordsworth (1770–1850). Some handicraft workers—notably the **Luddites**, who attacked factories in northern England in 1811 and later—smashed the new machines, which they believed were putting them out of work. Doctors and reformers wrote of problems in the factories and new towns, while Malthus and Ricardo concluded that workers would earn only enough to stay alive.

Luddites Group of handicraft workers who attacked factories in northern England in 1811 and after, smashing the new machines that they believed were putting them out of work.

This pessimistic view was accepted and reinforced by Friedrich Engels (1820–1895), the future revolutionary and colleague of Karl Marx (see "The Birth of Socialism" in Chapter 24). After studying conditions in northern England, this young son of a wealthy Prussian cotton manufacturer published in 1844 *The Condition of the Working Class in England*, a blistering indictment of the capitalist classes. Engels's extremely influential account of capitalist exploitation and increasing worker poverty was embellished by Marx and later socialists.

Analysis of industrial capitalism, often combined with reflections on the French Revolution, led to the development of a new overarching interpretation—a new paradigm—regarding social relationships. Briefly, this paradigm argued that individuals were members of separate classes based on their relationship to the means of production, that is, the machines and factories that dominated the new economy. As owners of expensive industrial machinery and as dependent laborers in their factories, the two main groups of society had separate and conflicting interests. Accordingly, the comfortable, well-educated "public" of the eighteenth century came increasingly to be defined as the middle class, and the "people" gradually began to perceive themselves as composing a modern working class. And while the new class interpretation was open to criticism, it appealed to many because it seemed to explain what was happening. Therefore, conflicting classes existed, in part, because many individuals came to believe they existed and developed an awareness that they belonged to a particular social class—this awareness is what Karl Marx called **class-consciousness**.

class-consciousness An individual's sense of class differentiation, a term introduced by Karl Marx.

Meanwhile, other observers believed that conditions were improving for the working people. In his 1835 study of the cotton industry, Andrew Ure (yoo-RAY) wrote that conditions in most factories were not harsh and were even quite good. Edwin Chadwick, a government official well acquainted with the problems of the working population, concluded that the "whole mass of the laboring community" was increasingly able "to buy more of the necessities and minor luxuries of life."[9] Nevertheless, those who thought, correctly, that conditions were stagnating or getting worse for working people were probably in the majority.

The Early Labor Movement in Britain

Not everyone worked in large factories and coal mines during the Industrial Revolution. In 1850 more British people still worked on farms than in any other single occupation. The second-largest occupation was domestic service, with more than 1 million household servants, 90 percent of whom were women.

Within industry itself, the pattern of artisans working with hand tools in small shops remained unchanged in many trades, even as others were revolutionized by technological change. For example, the British iron industry was completely dominated by large-scale capitalist firms by 1850. Yet the firms that fashioned iron into small metal goods employed on average fewer than ten wage workers who used handicraft skills.

Working-class solidarity and class-consciousness developed in small workshops as well as in large factories. In the northern factory districts, anticapitalist sentiments were frequent by the 1820s. Commenting in 1825 on a strike in the woolen center of Bradford and the support it had gathered from other regions, one newspaper claimed with pride that "it is all the workers of England against a few masters of Bradford."[10]

Such sentiments ran contrary to the liberal tenets of economic freedom. Liberal economic principles were embraced by statesmen and middle-class business owners in the late eighteenth century and continued to gather strength in the early nineteenth century. In 1799 Parliament passed the **Combination Acts**, which outlawed unions and strikes. In 1813 and 1814 Parliament repealed an old law regulating the wages of artisans and the conditions of apprenticeship. As a result of these and other measures, certain skilled artisan workers found aggressive capitalists ignoring traditional work rules and trying to flood their trades with unorganized women workers and children to beat down wages.

Combination Acts English laws passed in 1799 that outlawed unions and strikes, favoring capitalist business owners over skilled artisans. Bitterly resented and widely disregarded by many craft guilds, the acts were repealed by Parliament in 1824.

The capitalist attack on artisan guilds and work rules was bitterly resented by many craftworkers, who subsequently played an important part in Great Britain and in other countries in gradually building a modern labor movement. The Combination Acts were widely disregarded by workers. Craftsmen continued to take collective action, and societies of skilled factory workers also organized unions. Unions sought to control the number of skilled workers, to limit apprenticeship to members' own children, and to bargain with owners over wages. In the face of widespread union activity, Parliament repealed the Combination Acts in 1824, and unions were tolerated, though not fully accepted, after 1825.

The next stage in the development of the British trade-union movement was the attempt to create a single large national union. This effort was led not so much by working people as by social reformers such as Robert Owen. Owen, a self-made cotton manufacturer, had pioneered in industrial relations by combining firm discipline with concern for the health, safety, and hours of his workers. After 1815 he experimented with cooperative and socialist communities. Then in 1834 Owen organized one of the largest and most visionary of the early national unions, the Grand National Consolidated Trades Union.

When Owen's and other grandiose schemes collapsed, the British labor movement moved once again after 1851 in the direction of craft unions. These unions won real benefits for members by fairly conservative means and thus became an accepted part of the industrial scene.

British workers also engaged in direct political activity in defense of their interests. After the collapse of Owen's national trade union, many working people went into the Chartist movement, which fought for universal manhood suffrage. Workers were also active in campaigns to limit the workday in factories to ten hours and to permit duty-free importation of wheat into Great Britain to secure cheap bread. Thus working people developed a sense of their own identity and played an active role in shaping the new industrial system. They were neither helpless victims nor passive beneficiaries.

The Impact of Slavery

Another mass labor force of the Industrial Revolution was composed of the millions of enslaved men, women, and children who toiled in European colonies in the Caribbean and in the nations of North and South America. Historians have long debated the extent to which revenue from slavery contributed to Britain's achievements in the Industrial Revolution.

Most now agree that profits from colonial plantations and slave trading were a small portion of British national income in the eighteenth century. Nevertheless, the impact of slavery on Britain's economy was much broader than direct profits alone. In the mid-eighteenth century the need for items to exchange for colonial cotton, sugar, tobacco, and slaves stimulated demand for British manufactured goods in the Caribbean, North America, and West Africa. Britain's dominance in the slave trade also led to the development of finance and credit institutions that would help early industrialists obtain capital for their businesses.

The British Parliament abolished the slave trade in 1807 and freed all slaves in British territories in 1833, but by 1850 most of the cotton processed by British mills was supplied by the coerced labor of slaves in the southern United States. Thus the Industrial Revolution was integrally connected to the Atlantic world and the misery of slavery.

Chapter Summary

As markets for manufactured goods increased both domestically and overseas, Britain was able to respond with increased production, largely because of its stable government, abundant natural resources, and flexible labor force. The first factories arose as a result of innovations in the textile industry. The demand for improvements in energy led to innovations and improvements in the steam engine, which transformed the iron industry, among others. In the early nineteenth century transportation of goods was greatly enhanced with the adoption of steam-powered trains and ships.

After 1815 continental European countries gradually built on England's technical breakthroughs. Entrepreneurs set up their own factories and hired skilled local artisans along with English immigrants experienced in the new technologies. Newly established corporate banks worked in conjunction with government interventions in finance and tariff controls to promote railroads and other industries. Beginning around 1850 Japan and the United States also began to rapidly industrialize, but generally the Industrial Revolution spread more slowly outside Europe, as many countries were confined to producing agricultural goods and other raw materials to serve European markets.

The rise of modern industry had a profound impact on society, beginning in Britain in the late eighteenth century. Industrialization led to the growing size and wealth of the middle class and the rise of a modern industrial working class. Rigid rules, stern discipline, and long hours weighed heavily on factory workers, and improvements in the standard of living came slowly, but they were substantial by 1850. Married women withdrew increasingly from wage work and concentrated on child care and household responsibilities. The era of industrialization also fostered new attitudes toward child labor, encouraged protective factory legislation, and called forth a new sense of class feeling and an assertive labor movement. Slave labor in European colonies contributed to the rise of the Industrial Revolution by increasing markets for European goods, supplying raw materials, and encouraging the development of financial systems.

NOTES

1. N. F. R. Crafts, *British Economic Growth During the Industrial Revolution* (Oxford: Oxford University Press, 1985), p. 32.
2. John Allen, *The British Industrial Revolution* (Cambridge: Cambridge University Press, 2009), pp. 1–2.
3. P. Bairoch, "International Industrialization Levels from 1750 to 1980," *Journal of European Economic History* 11 (Spring 1982): 269–333.
4. Quoted in J. Bowditch and C. Ramsland, eds., *Voices of the Industrial Revolution* (Ann Arbor: University of Michigan Press, 1961), p. 55, from Thomas Malthus, *Essay on the Principle of Population*, 4th ed. (1807).
5. Quoted in E. R. Pike, *"Hard Times": Human Documents of the Industrial Revolution* (New York: Praeger, 1966), p. 109.
6. Quoted in J. Humphries, ". . . 'The Most Free from Objection' . . . : The Sexual Division of Labor and Women's Work in Nineteenth-Century England," *Journal of Economic History* 47 (December 1987): 941.
7. H.-J. Voth, *Time and Work in England, 1750–1830* (Oxford: Oxford University Press, 2000), pp. 268–270; also pp. 118–133.
8. Joel Mokyr, *The Enlightened Economy: An Economic History of Britain, 1700–1850* (New Haven: Yale University Press, 2009), p. 455.
9. Quoted in W. A. Hayek, ed., *Capitalism and the Historians* (Chicago: University of Chicago Press, 1954), p. 126.
10. Quoted in D. Geary, ed., *Labour and Socialist Movements in Europe Before 1914* (Oxford: Berg, 1989), p. 29.
11. Kenneth Pomeranz, *The Great Divergence: China, Europe, and the Making of the Modern World Economy* (Princeton, N.J.: Princeton University Press, 2000).

CONNECTIONS

For much of its history, Europe lagged behind older and more sophisticated civilizations in China and the Middle East. And yet by 1800 Europe had broken ahead of the other regions of the world in terms of wealth and power, a process historians have termed "the Great Divergence."[11]

One prerequisite for the rise of Europe was its growing control over world trade, first in the Indian Ocean in the sixteenth and seventeenth centuries and then in the eighteenth-century Atlantic world. A second crucial factor behind the Great Divergence was the Industrial Revolution, which dramatically increased the pace of production and distribution while reducing their cost, thereby allowing Europeans to control other countries first economically and then politically. By the middle of the nineteenth century the gap between Western industrial production and standards of living and those of the non-West had grown dramatically, bringing with it the economic dependence of non-Western nations, meager wages for their largely impoverished populations, and increasingly aggressive Western imperial ambitions (see "The World Market" in Chapter 25). In the late nineteenth century non-Western countries began to experience their own processes of industrialization. Today's world is witnessing a surge in productivity in China, India, and other non-Western nations, with uncertain consequences for the global balance of power.

Identify Key Terms

Identify and explain the significance of each item below.

Industrial Revolution (p. 693)

spinning jenny (p. 694)

water frame (p. 695)

steam engines (p. 697)

Rocket (p. 698)

Crystal Palace (p. 699)

iron law of wages (p. 701)

tariff protection (p. 704)

Factory Act of 1833 (p. 711)

separate spheres (p. 711)

Mines Act of 1842 (p. 712)

Luddites (p. 715)

class-consciousness (p. 715)

Combination Acts (p. 716)

Review the Main Ideas

Answer the focus questions from each section of the chapter.

1. Why did the Industrial Revolution begin in Britain, and how did it develop between 1780 and 1850? (p. 692)

2. How did countries in Europe and around the world respond to the challenge of industrialization after 1815? (p. 702)

3. How did work evolve during the Industrial Revolution, and how did daily life change for working people? (p. 709)

4. How did the changes brought about by the Industrial Revolution lead to new social classes, and how did people respond to the new structure? (p. 714)

Make Comparisons and Connections

Analyze the larger developments and continuities within and across chapters.

1. Why did Great Britain take the lead in industrialization, and when did other countries begin to adopt the new techniques and organization of production?

2. How did historical developments between 1600 and 1800 contribute to the rise of Europe to world dominance in the nineteenth century? Argue for or against the following proposition: "Given contemporary trends, the dominance of the West in the nineteenth and twentieth centuries should be seen as a temporary aberration, rather than as a fundamental and permanent shift in the global balance of power."

3. How would you compare the legacy of the political revolutions of the late eighteenth century (Chapter 22) with that of the Industrial Revolution? Which seems to you to have created the most important changes, and why?

TIMELINE

Suggested Resources

BOOKS

Allen, Robert C. *The British Industrial Revolution in Global Perspective.* 2009. Explains the origins of the Industrial Revolution and why it took place in Britain and not elsewhere.

Davidoff, Leonore, and Catherine Hall. *Family Fortunes: Men and Women of the English Middle Class, 1750–1850,* rev. ed. 2003. Examines both economic activities and cultural beliefs with great skill.

Griffin, Emma. *A Short History of the British Industrial Revolution.* 2010. An accessible and lively introduction to the subject.

Horn, Jeff, Leonard N. Rosenband, and Merritt Roe Smith. *Reconceptualizing the Industrial Revolution.* 2010. A collection of essays by leading scholars that re-examines the most contentious debates in the field.

Humphries, Jane. *Childhood and Child Labour in the British Industrial Revolution.* 2010. A moving account of the experience of children during the Industrial Revolution, based on numerous autobiographies.

James, Harold. *Family Capitalism.* 2006. A study of the entrepreneurial dynasties of the British Industrial Revolution.

Mokyr, Joel. *The Enlightened Economy: An Economic History of Britain, 1700–1850.* 2009. A masterful explanation of industrialization and economic growth in Britain that emphasizes the impact of Enlightenment openness and curiosity.

Morris, Charles R. *The Dawn of Innovation: The First American Industrial Revolution.* 2012. Tells the story of the individuals, inventions, and trade networks that transformed the United States from a rural economy to a global industrial power.

Prados de la Escosura, Leandro, ed. *Exceptionalism and Industrialisation: Britain and Its European Rivals, 1688–1815.* 2004. Compares the path toward economic development in Britain and the rest of Europe.

Rosenthal, Jean-Laurent, and R. Bin Wong, *Before and Beyond Divergence: The Politics of Economic Change in China and Europe.* 2011. A study of the similarities and differences between Europe and China that led to the origins and growth of industrialization in Europe.

Stearns, Peter N. *The Industrial Revolution in World History*, 4th ed. 2012. A useful brief survey.

DOCUMENTARIES

The Children Who Built Victorian Britain (BBC, 2011). An account of the role of child labor in the Industrial Revolution, based on written testimonies from children of that era.

The Men Who Built America (History Channel, 2013). A miniseries on the bankers and industrialists who created modern America from the Civil War to the Great Depression.

Mill Times (PBS, 2006). A combination of documentary video and animated re-enactments that tells the story of the mechanization of the cotton industry in Britain and the United States.

FEATURE FILMS AND TELEVISION DRAMAS

Germinal (Claude Berri, 1993). In a European coal-mining town during the Industrial Revolution, exploited workers go on strike and encounter brutal repression from the authorities.

Hard Times (Granada TV, 1977). A four-hour mini-series adaptation of Charles Dickens's famous novel about the bitter life of mill workers in England during the Industrial Revolution.

Oliver Twist (Roman Polanski, 2005). A film based on a novel by Charles Dickens depicting the harsh conditions of life for orphans and poor children in nineteenth-century London.

WEBSITES

Images of the Industrial Revolution in Britain. Annotated images from the eighteenth and nineteenth centuries covering various aspects of the Industrial Revolution. **www.netnicholls.com/neh2001/index.html**

Spinning the Web. A website offering comprehensive information on the people, places, industrial processes, and products involved in the mechanization of the British cotton industry. **www.spinningtheweb.org.uk/industry**

Women Working, 1800–1930. A digital collection of the Harvard University Library, with sources and links related to women's labor in the nineteenth and early twentieth centuries. **ocp.hul.harvard.edu/ww**

24

Ideologies of Change in Europe
1815–1914

The momentous transformations wrought by the political and economic revolutions of the late eighteenth and early nineteenth centuries left a legacy of unfinished hopes and dreams for many Europeans: for democracy, liberty, and equality and for higher living standards for all. These aspirations would play out with unpredictable and tumultuous consequences over the course of the nineteenth century. After 1815 the powers that defeated Napoleon united under a revived conservatism to stamp out the spread of liberal and democratic reforms. But the political and social innovations made possible by the unfinished revolutions proved difficult to contain.

In politics, powerful ideologies — liberalism, nationalism, and socialism — emerged to oppose conservatism. All played critical roles in the political and social battles of the era and the great popular upheaval that eventually swept across Europe in the revolutions of 1848. These revolutions failed, however, and gave way to more sober — and more successful — nation building in the 1860s. European political leaders and middle-class nationalists also began to deal effectively with the challenges of the emerging urban society. One way they did so was through nationalism — mass identification with a nation-state that was increasingly responsive to the needs of its people. At the same time, the triumph of nationalism promoted bitter rivalries between states and peoples, spurred a second great wave of imperialism, and in the twentieth century brought an era of tragic global conflict.

Christabel Pankhurst, Militant Suffragette

Christabel Pankhurst led the British Women's Social and Political Union, whose motto was "deeds, not words." This photo was taken in 1912 in Paris, where Pankhurst was living to avoid arrest for her increasingly violent actions to obtain the vote for women, including bombing the home of the future prime minister. Women in Britain and many other countries gained the right to vote in the years immediately after World War I.

© Maurice Branger/Roger-Viollet/The Image Works

CHAPTER PREVIEW

A CONSERVATIVE PEACE GIVES WAY TO RADICAL IDEAS
How did the allies fashion a peace settlement in 1815, and what radical ideas emerged between 1815 and 1848?

REFORMS AND REVOLUTIONS, 1815–1850
Why did revolutions triumph briefly throughout most of Europe in 1848, and why did they fail?

NATION BUILDING IN ITALY, GERMANY, AND RUSSIA
How did strong leaders and nation building transform Italy, Germany, and Russia?

URBAN LIFE IN THE AGE OF IDEOLOGIES
What was the impact of urban growth on cities, social classes, families, and ideas?

NATIONALISM AND SOCIALISM, 1871–1914
How did nationalism and socialism shape European politics in the decades before the Great War?

How did the allies fashion a peace settlement in 1815, and what radical ideas emerged between 1815 and 1848?

Congress of Vienna
A meeting of the Quadruple Alliance (Russia, Prussia, Austria, Great Britain) and France held in 1814–1815 to fashion a general peace settlement after the defeat of Napoleonic France.

conservatism A political philosophy that stressed retaining traditional values and institutions, including hereditary monarchy and a strong landowning aristocracy.

A Conservative Peace Gives Way to Radical Ideas

After finally defeating Napoleon, the conservative aristocratic monarchies of Russia, Prussia, Austria, and Great Britain—known as the Quadruple Alliance (see "The Grand Empire and Its End" in Chapter 22)—reaffirmed their determination to hold France in line and to defeat the intertwined dangers of war and revolution. At the **Congress of Vienna** (1814–1815), they fashioned a lasting peace settlement that helped produce fifty years without major warfare in Europe. On the domestic front, they sought to restore order and limit the spread of revolutionary ideas.

Despite the congress's success on the diplomatic front, many observers at the time were frustrated by the high-handed dictates of the Great Powers and their refusal to adopt social reforms. After 1815 such critics sought to harness the radical ideas of the revolutionary age to new political movements. Many rejected **conservatism**, a political philosophy that stressed retaining traditional values and institutions, including hereditary monarchy and a strong landowning aristocracy. Radical thinkers developed alternative ideologies and tried to convince society to act on them.

The Political and Social Situation After 1815

When the Quadruple Alliance, along with representatives of minor powers, met together at the Congress of Vienna they combined leniency toward France with strong defensive measures. The Low Countries—Belgium and Holland—were united under an enlarged Dutch monarchy capable of opposing France more effectively. Prussia received considerably more territory along France's eastern border to stand as a "sentinel on the Rhine" against renewed French aggression. The congress recognized the neutrality of certain territories—for example, the cantons of Switzerland—as a means of creating buffer zones between potentially hostile states. The first Peace of Paris returned France to the boundaries it possessed in 1792, which were larger than those of 1789. Even after Napoleon's brief return to power tested the allies' patience, France did not have to give up much additional territory and had to pay only modest reparations.

In their moderation toward France, the allies were motivated by self-interest and traditional ideas about the balance of power. To the peacemakers, especially to Klemens von Metternich (1773–1859), Austria's foreign minister, the balance of power meant an international equilibrium of political and military forces that would discourage aggression by any state or combination of states. This required, among other measures, ensuring the internal stability of France. The Quadruple Alliance members also agreed to meet periodically to discuss their common interests and to consider appropriate measures to maintain peace in Europe. This agreement represented a transformation of European diplomacy; the "congress system" it inaugurated lasted long into the nineteenth century.

The leaders of the congress reached their decisions with little recognition of the interests of smaller states and subject peoples within multiethnic states. They also left aside the question of the European territories of the Ottoman Empire, which Napoleon had schemed to divide between France and Russia. With the rise of nationalism, these neglected issues would pose serious threats to the post-1815 order. On a more positive note, the leading powers of the congress, led by Britain,

The Congress of Vienna A French political cartoon shows the rulers of Europe dividing the map of Europe among themselves at the Congress of Vienna. Meanwhile, Napoleon (who had escaped from Elba at the time) removes the section with France on it, and the English representative holds a set of scales loaded with gold coins, a reference to the English role in financing the allies. (Musée de la Ville de Paris, Musée Carnavalet, Paris, France/Archives Charmet/Bridgeman Images)

issued a declaration condemning the slave trade and calling on European states to begin the process of abolition.

Conservatism After 1815

In 1815, under Metternich's leadership, Austria, Prussia, and Russia formed the Holy Alliance, dedicated to crushing the ideas and politics of the revolutionary era. Metternich's policies dominated the entire German Confederation of thirty-eight independent German states (Map 24.1). It was through the German Confederation that Metternich had the repressive Karlsbad Decrees issued in 1819. These decrees required the member states to root out radical ideas in their universities and newspapers, and a permanent committee was established to investigate and punish any liberal or radical organizations.

Adhering to a conservative political philosophy, Metternich believed that strong governments were needed to protect society from its worst instincts. Like many European conservatives of his time, Metternich believed that liberalism (see the next section), as embodied in revolutionary America and France, had been responsible for a generation of war with untold bloodshed and suffering. He blamed liberal revolutionaries for stirring up the lower classes, which he believed desired nothing more than peace and quiet.

Another belief that Metternich opposed, which was often allied with liberalism, was nationalism, the idea that each national group had a right to establish its own independent government. The Habsburg's Austrian Empire was a dynastic state dominated by Germans but containing many other national groups. This multinational state was both strong and weak. It was strong because of its large population and vast territories, but weak because of its many and potentially dissatisfied nationalities. In these circumstances, Metternich opposed both liberalism and nationalism, for Austria could not accommodate those ideologies and remain a powerful empire. Metternich's antinationalist efforts were supported by the two great multinational empires on Austria's borders, Russia and the Ottoman Empire.

Liberalism and the Middle Class

liberalism A philosophy whose principal ideas were equality and liberty; liberals demanded representative government and equality before the law as well as such individual freedoms as freedom of the press, freedom of speech, freedom of assembly, and freedom from arbitrary arrest.

The principal ideas of **liberalism** — liberty and equality — were by no means defeated in 1815. First realized in the American Revolution and then achieved in part in the French and Latin American Revolutions, liberalism demanded representative government and equality before the law. The idea of liberty also meant specific individual freedoms: freedom of the press, freedom of speech, freedom of assembly, and freedom from arbitrary arrest. In Europe only France, with Louis XVIII's Constitutional Charter, and Great Britain, with its Parliament and historic liberties of English men and women, had realized much of the liberal program in 1815. Even in those countries, liberalism had only begun to succeed

Liberalism faced more radical ideological competitors in the early nineteenth century. Opponents of liberalism especially criticized its economic principles, which called for unrestricted private enterprise and no government interference in the economy. This philosophy was popularly known as the doctrine of **laissez faire** (lay-say FEHR). In early-nineteenth-century Britain economic liberalism was embraced most enthusiastically by business groups and thus became a doctrine associated with corporate interests.

laissez faire A doctrine of economic liberalism advocating unrestricted private enterprise and no government interference in the economy.

In the early nineteenth century liberal political ideals also became more closely associated with narrow class interests. Early-nineteenth-century liberals favored representative government, but they generally wanted property qualifications attached to the right to vote and to serve in Parliament.

As liberalism became increasingly identified with the middle class after 1815, some intellectuals and foes of conservatism felt that liberalism did not go nearly far enough. They called for replacing monarchical rule with republics, for democracy through universal male suffrage, and for greater economic and social equality. These democrats and republicans were more radical than the liberals, and they were more willing to endorse violence to achieve goals. As a result, liberals and radical republicans could join forces against conservatives only up to a point.

The Growing Appeal of Nationalism

nationalism The idea that each people had its own spirit and its own cultural unity, which manifested itself especially in a common language and history and could serve as the basis for an independent political state.

Nationalism was a radical new ideology that emerged in the years after 1815 — an idea destined to have an enormous influence in the modern world. Early advocates of the "national idea" argued that the members of what we would call today an ethnic group had their own spirit and their own cultural unity, which were manifested especially in a common language, history, and territory. In fact, such cultural unity was more a dream than a reality as local dialects abounded, historical memory divided the inhabitants of the different states as much as it unified them, and a variety of ethnic groups shared the territory of most states.

Nevertheless, many European nationalists sought to make the territory of each people coincide with well-defined boundaries in an independent nation-state. It was this political goal that made nationalism so explosive in central and eastern Europe after 1815, when there were either too few states (Austria, Russia, and the Ottoman Empire) or too many (the Italian peninsula and the German Confederation), and when different peoples overlapped and intermingled.

Between 1815 and 1850 most people who believed in nationalism also believed in either liberalism or radical democratic republicanism. A common faith in the cre-

MAPPING THE PAST

MAP 24.1 Europe in 1815 In 1815 Europe contained many different states, but after the defeat of Napoleon international politics was dominated by the five Great Powers: Russia, Prussia, Austria, Great Britain, and France. (The number rises to six if one includes the Ottoman Empire.)

ANALYZING THE MAP Trace the political boundaries of each Great Power, and compare their geographical strengths and weaknesses. What territories did Prussia and Austria gain as a result of the war with Napoleon?

CONNECTIONS How did Prussia's and Austria's territorial gains contribute to the balance of power established at the Congress of Vienna? What other factors enabled the Great Powers to achieve such a long-lasting peace?

ativity and nobility of the people was perhaps the single most important reason for the linking of these two concepts. Liberals and especially democrats saw the people as the ultimate source of all good government. They agreed that the benefits of self-government would be possible only if the people were united by common traditions that transcended class and local interests. Thus individual liberty and love of a free nation overlapped greatly.

Popular Image of the National Anthem of Germany In the late nineteenth and early twentieth centuries, patriotic nationalism swept European populations. This attitude was encouraged by printed images such as this trading card (distributed in packets of beef bouillon cubes) that showed the words and music for the new German national anthem, flanked by a female embodiment of the new nation and a pair of happy peasants in folkloric dress. (Private Collection/© Look and Learn/Bridgeman Images)

Yet early nationalists also stressed the differences among peoples, and they developed a strong sense of "we" and "they." Thus, while European nationalism's main thrust was liberal and democratic, below the surface lurked ideas of national superiority and national mission.

The Birth of Socialism

socialism A radical political doctrine that opposed individualism and that advocated cooperation and a sense of community; key ideas were economic planning, greater economic equality, and state regulation of property.

Socialism, a second radical doctrine after 1815, began in France. Early French socialists shared a sense of disappointment in the outcome of the French Revolution. They were also alarmed by the rise of laissez faire and the emergence of modern industry, which they saw as fostering inequality and selfish individualism. There was, they believed, an urgent need for a further reorganization of society to establish cooperation and a new sense of community.

Early French socialists felt an intense desire to help the poor, whose conditions had not been improved by industrial advances, and they preached greater economic equality between the rich and the poor. Inspired by the economic planning implemented in revolutionary France (see "The National Convention" in Chapter 22), they argued that the government should rationally organize the economy to control prices and prevent unemployment. Socialists also believed that government should regulate private property or that private property should be abolished and replaced by state or community ownership.

Up to the 1840s France was the center of socialism, as it had been the center of revolution in Europe, but in the following decades the German intellectual Karl Marx (1818–1883) would weave the diffuse strands of social thought into a distinctly modern ideology. Marx had studied philosophy at the University of Berlin before turning to journalism and economics. In 1848 the thirty-year-old Karl Marx and the twenty-eight-year-old Friedrich Engels published *The Communist Manifesto*, which became the guiding text of socialism.

Marx argued that middle-class interests and those of the industrial working class were inevitably opposed to each other. According to the *Manifesto*, the "history of all previously existing society is the history of class struggles." In Marx's view, one class had always exploited the other, and, with the advent of modern industry, society was split more clearly than ever before: between the well-educated and prosperous middle class — the **bourgeoisie** — and the modern working class — the **proletariat**.

Just as the bourgeoisie had triumphed over the feudal aristocracy in the French Revolution, Marx predicted that the proletariat would conquer the bourgeoisie in a new revolution. While a tiny majority owned the means of production and grew richer, the ever-poorer proletariat was constantly growing in size and in class-consciousness. Marx believed that the critical moment when class conflict would result in revolution was very near, as the last lines of *The Communist Manifesto* make clear:

> Germany . . . is on the eve of a bourgeois revolution, that is bound to be . . . the prelude to an immediately following proletarian revolution. . . .
>
> Let the ruling classes tremble at a Communist revolution. The proletarians have nothing to lose but their chains. They have a world to win. WORKING MEN OF ALL COUNTRIES, UNITE!

Marx drew on the arguments of Adam Smith and David Ricardo, who taught that labor was the source of all value. He went on to argue that profits were really wages stolen from the workers. Moreover, Marx incorporated Friedrich Engels's account of the terrible oppression of the new class of factory workers in England. Thus Marx pulled together powerful ideas and insights to create one of the great secular religions out of the intellectual ferment of the early nineteenth century.

bourgeoisie The well-educated, prosperous, middle-class groups.

proletariat The Marxist term for the working class of modern industrialized society.

Reforms and Revolutions, 1815–1850

As liberal, nationalist, and socialist forces battered the conservatism of 1815, social and economic conditions continued to deteriorate for many Europeans, adding to the mounting pressures. In some countries, such as Great Britain, change occurred gradually and largely peacefully, but in 1848 radical political and social ideologies combined with economic crisis to produce revolutionary movements that demanded an end to repressive government. Between 1815 and 1848 many European countries, including France, Austria, and Prussia, experienced variations on this basic theme.

> **Why did revolutions triumph briefly throughout most of Europe in 1848, and why did they fail?**

Social and Economic Conflict

The slow and uneven spread of industrialization in Europe after 1815 meant that the benefits of higher productivity were not felt by many. In Great Britain, the earliest adopter of industrial methods, living standards only began to rise after 1850, and this trend took longer to spread to the continent. Indeed, for many people in the cities and countryside, the first half of the nineteenth century brought a decline in the conditions of daily life. In Europe's rapidly growing cities, migrants encountered overcrowding, shoddy housing, and poor sanitation, ideal conditions for the spread of infectious disease.

Despite booming urbanization, much of the continent remained agricultural, and the traditional social hierarchy, dominated by a landowning aristocracy, persisted. Serfdom still existed in the Hungarian provinces of the Austrian Empire, Prussian Silesia, and Russia. In the early nineteenth century, however, the pressures of a rapidly growing population, the adoption of new forms of agriculture, and the spread of exploitative rural industry destabilized these existing patterns. Many peasants lost access to collective land due to enclosure and the adoption of more efficient farming techniques. Meanwhile, the growing number of cottage workers resisted exploitation by merchant capitalists, and journeymen battled masters in urban industries.

Social malaise was exacerbated by the fact that the retracing of borders at the Congress of Vienna had placed many populations in new and unfamiliar states. Lack of loyalty to the central government only worsened popular anger over rising tax rates and other burdens. These simmering tensions broke to the surface in the 1840s, as widespread crop failure in 1845–1846 led to economic crisis.

In spring 1848 many people's grievances about enclosure and taxation resembled those of the eighteenth century. What transformed these conflicts was the political ideologies born from the struggles and unfulfilled hopes of the French Revolution—liberalism, nationalism, and socialism—as well as the newly invigorated conservatism that stood against them. These ideologies helped turn economic and social conflicts into the revolutions of 1848.

Liberal Reform in Great Britain

The English parliamentary system guaranteed basic civil rights, but only about 8 percent of the population could vote for representatives to Parliament. By the 1780s there was growing interest in reform, but the French Revolution threw the British aristocracy into a panic. After 1815 the British government put down popular protests over unemployment and the high cost of grain caused by the Napoleonic Wars with repressive legislation and military force.

By the early 1830s the social and economic changes created by industrialization began to be felt in politics. In 1832 continuous pressure from the liberal middle classes and popular unrest convinced the king and the House of Lords that they needed to act. The Reform Bill of 1832 moved British politics in a more democratic direction by giving new industrial areas increased representation in the House of Commons and by increasing the number of voters by about 50 percent. For the first time, comfortable middle-class urban groups, the main beneficiaries of industrialization, as well as some substantial farmers, received the vote. Two years later, the New Poor Law called for unemployed and indigent families to be placed in harsh workhouses rather than receiving aid from local parishes to remain in their own homes. With this act, Britain's rulers sought to relieve middle-class taxpayers of the burden of poor relief and to encourage unemployed rural workers to migrate to cities and take up industrial work.

Thus limited democratic reform was counterbalanced by harsh measures against the poor, both linked to the new social and economic circumstances of the Industrial Revolution. Many working people protested their exclusion from voting and the terms of the New Poor Law. Between 1838 and 1848 they joined the Chartist movement (see "The Early Labor Movement in Britain" in Chapter 23), which demanded universal male suffrage. In 1847 the ruling conservative party, known as the Tories, sought to appease working people with the Ten Hours Act, which limited the workday for women and young people in factories to ten hours. Tory aristocrats championed such legislation in order to compete with the middle class for working-class support.

This competition meant that the Parliamentary state relied on eliciting support from its people and thereby succeeded in managing unrest without the outbreak of revolution. Another factor favoring Great Britain's largely peaceful evolution in the nineteenth century was the fact that living standards had begun to rise significantly by the late 1840s, as the benefits of industrialization finally began to be felt. Thus England avoided the violence and turmoil of the revolutions of 1848 that shook continental Europe.

The people of Ireland did not benefit from these circumstances. Long ruled as a conquered people, the population was mostly composed of Irish Catholic peasants who rented their land from a tiny minority of Protestant landowners, many of whom resided in England. Ruthlessly exploited and growing rapidly in numbers, the rural population around 1800 lived under abominable conditions.

In spite of terrible conditions, Ireland's population doubled from 4 million to 8 million between 1780 and 1840, fueled in large part by the calories and nutritive qualities of the potato. However, the potato crop failed in 1845, 1846, 1848, and 1851 in Ireland and throughout much of Europe. Many suffered in Europe, but in Ireland, where dependency on the potato was much more widespread, the result was starvation and death. The British government, committed to laissez-faire economic policies, reacted slowly and utterly inadequately. One and a half million people died, while another million fled between 1845 and 1851, primarily to the United States and Great Britain. The Great Famine, as this tragedy came to be known, intensified anti-British feeling and promoted Irish nationalism.

Revolutions in France

Louis XVIII's Constitutional Charter of 1814 was essentially a liberal constitution. It protected economic and social gains made by the middle class and the peasantry in the French Revolution, recognized intellectual and artistic freedom, and created a parliament with upper and lower houses. The charter was anything but democratic, however. Only a tiny minority of males had the right to vote for the legislative deputies who, with the king and his ministers, made the nation's laws.

Louis's conservative successor, Charles X (r. 1824–1830), wanted to re-establish the old order in France. To rally French nationalism and gain popular support, he exploited a long-standing dispute with Muslim Algeria, a vassal state of the Ottoman Empire. In June 1830 a French force crossed the Mediterranean and took the capital of Algiers. The French continued to wage war against Algerian resistance until 1847, when they finally subdued the country. Bringing French and other European settlers to Algeria and expropriating large amounts of Muslim-owned land, the conquest of Algeria marked the rebirth of French colonial expansion.

Buoyed by this success, Charles overplayed his hand and repudiated the Constitutional Charter. After three days of uprisings in Paris, which sparked a series of revolts by frustrated liberals and democrats across Europe, Charles fled. His cousin Louis Philippe (r. 1830–1848) accepted the Constitutional Charter of 1814 and assumed the title of the "king of the French people." Still, the situation in France remained fundamentally unchanged. Political and social reformers and the poor of Paris were bitterly disappointed.

During the 1840s this sense of disappointment was worsened by bad harvests and the slow development of industrialization, which meant that living conditions for the majority of the working classes were deteriorating rather than improving. Similar conditions prevailed across continental Europe, which was soon rocked by insurrections. In February full-scale revolution broke out in France, and its shock waves rippled across the continent.

Louis Philippe had refused to approve social legislation or consider electoral reform. Frustrated desires for change, high-level financial scandals, and crop failures in 1845 and 1846 united diverse groups of the king's opponents, including merchants, intellectuals, shopkeepers, and workers. In February 1848, as popular revolt broke out, barricades went up and Louis Philippe abdicated.

The revolutionaries quickly drafted a democratic, republican constitution for France's Second Republic, granting the right to vote to every adult male. Slaves in the French colonies were freed, the death penalty was abolished, and national workshops were established for unemployed Parisian workers.

Yet there were profound differences within the revolutionary coalition in Paris. The socialism promoted by radical republicans frightened not only the liberal middle and upper classes but also the peasants, many of whom owned land. When the French masses voted for delegates to the new Constituent Assembly in late April 1848, the monarchists won a clear majority. When the new government dissolved the national workshops in Paris, workers rose in a spontaneous insurrection. After three terrible "June Days" and the death or injury of more than ten thousand people, the republican army stood triumphant in a sea of working-class blood and hatred.

The revolution in France thus ended in failure. The middle and working classes had turned against each other. In place of a generous democratic republic, the Constituent Assembly completed a constitution featuring a strong executive. This allowed Louis Napoleon, nephew of Napoleon Bonaparte, to win a landslide victory in the December 1848 election based on promises to lead a strong government in favor of popular interests.

President Louis Napoleon at first shared power with a conservative National Assembly. But in 1851 Louis Napoleon dismissed the Assembly and seized power in a coup d'état. A year later he called on the French to make him hereditary emperor, and 97 percent voted to do so in a national plebiscite. Louis Napoleon then ruled France's Second Empire as Napoleon III, initiating policies favoring economic growth and urban development to appease the populace.

The Revolutions of 1848 in Central Europe

Throughout central Europe, social conflicts were exacerbated by the economic crises of 1845 to 1846. News of the upheaval in France in 1848 provoked the outbreak of revolution. Liberals demanded written constitutions, representative government, and greater civil liberties from authoritarian regimes. When governments hesitated, popular revolts followed. Urban workers and students allied with middle-class liberals and peasants. In the face of these coalitions, monarchs made hasty concessions. Soon, however, popular revolutionary fronts broke down as they had in France.

Compared with the situation in France, where political participation by working people reached its peak, revolts in central Europe tended to be dominated by social elites. They were also more sharply divided between moderate constitutionalists and radical republicans. The revolution in the Austrian Empire began in 1848 in Hungary, when nationalistic Hungarians demanded national autonomy, full civil liberties, and universal suffrage. When Viennese students and workers also took to the streets and peasant disorders broke out, the Habsburg emperor Ferdinand I (r. 1835–1848) capitulated and promised reforms and a liberal constitution. The coalition of revolutionaries was not stable, however. When the monarchy abolished serfdom, the newly free peasants lost interest in the political and social questions agitating the cities.

The revolutionary coalition was also weakened and ultimately destroyed by conflicting national aspirations. In March the Hungarian revolutionary leaders pushed through an extremely liberal constitution, but they also sought to create a unified Hungarian nation. The minority groups, including Romanians, Serbs, and Croats, that formed half the population objected that such unification would hinder their own political autonomy and cultural independence. Likewise, Czech (CHEK) nationalists based in Bohemia and the city of Prague came into conflict with German nationalists. Thus nationalism within the Austrian Empire enabled the monarchy to play off one ethnic group against the other.

The monarchy's first breakthrough came in June when the army crushed a working-class revolt in Prague. In October the predominantly peasant troops of the regular Austrian army attacked the student and working-class radicals in Vienna and retook the city. When Ferdinand I abdicated in favor of his young nephew, Franz Joseph (see "Great Britain and the Austro-Hungarian Empire"), only Hungary had yet to be brought under control. Fearing the spread of liberal ideas to his realm, Nicholas I of Russia (r. 1825–1855) obligingly lent his support. In June 1849, 130,000 Russian troops poured into Hungary and subdued the country. For a number of years the Habsburgs ruled Hungary as a conquered territory.

After Austria, Prussia was the largest and most influential kingdom in the German Confederation. Prior to 1848 middle-class Prussian liberals had sought to reshape Prussia into a liberal constitutional monarchy, which would lead the confederation's thirty-eight states into a unified nation. When artisans and factory workers in Berlin exploded in revolt in March 1848 and joined with middle-class liberals against the monarchy, Prussian king Frederick William IV (r. 1840–1861) caved in. On March 21 he promised to grant Prussia a liberal constitution and to merge Prussia into a new national German state.

Elections were held across the German Confederation for a national parliament, which convened to write a federal constitution for a unified German state. Members of the new parliament completed drafting a liberal constitution in March 1849 and elected King Frederick William of Prussia emperor of the new German national state. By early 1849, however, Frederick William had reasserted his royal authority, contemptuously refusing to accept the "crown from the gutter." When Frederick William tried to get the small monarchs of Germany to elect him emperor on his own terms, with authoritarian power, Austria balked. Supported by Russia, Austria forced Prussia to renounce all its unification schemes in late 1850.

Thus, across Europe, the uprisings of 1848, which had been inspired by the legacy of the late-eighteenth-century revolutionary era, were unsuccessful. Reform movements splintered into competing factions, while the forces of order proved better organized and more united, on both a domestic and international level.

German and Italian Views on Nationalism

German philosopher Johann Gottfried von Herder's *Ideas for the Philosophy of History of Humanity* (1784–1791) described the long evolution of human communities. According to Herder, this process had produced distinct national communities in Europe, each united by a common language and shared traditions. Herder respected these cultural traditions but did not believe they should lead to distinct nation-states. Instead he celebrated the common spirit that existed among Europeans based on their centuries-old history of interaction. By contrast, Giuseppe Mazzini, the leading prophet of Italian nationalism before 1848, believed fervently that nations should exist as sovereign states. He founded a secret society to fight for the unification of the Italian states in a democratic republic. The excerpt below was written in 1858 and addressed to Italian workingmen.

Johann Gottfried von Herder, *Ideas for the Philosophy of History of Humanity*

■ This is more or less a picture of the peoples of Europe. What a multicolored and composite picture! . . . Sea voyages and long migrations of people finally produced on the small continent of Europe the conditions for a great league of nations. Unwittingly the Romans had prepared it by their conquests. Such a league of nations was unthinkable outside of Europe. Nowhere else have people intermingled so much, nowhere else have they changed so often and so much their habitats and thereby their customs and ways of life. In many European countries it would be difficult today for the inhabitants, especially for single families and individuals, to say, from which people they descend, whether from Goths, Moors, Jews, Carthaginians or Romans, whether from Gauls, Burgundians, Franks, Normans, Saxons, Slavs, Finns or Illyrians, or how in the long line of their ancestors their blood had been mixed. Hundreds of causes have tempered and changed the old tribal composition of the European nations in the course of the centuries; without such an intermingling the common spirit of Europe could hardly have been awakened.

Giuseppe Mazzini, "Duties Towards Your Country"

■ God gave you the means of multiplying your forces and your powers of action indefinitely when he gave you a Country, when, like a wise overseer of labor, who distributes the different parts of the work according to the capacity of the workmen, he divided Humanity into distinct groups upon the face of our globe, and thus planted the seeds of nations. Evil governments have disfigured the design of God, which you may see clearly

---

How did strong leaders and nation building transform Italy, Germany, and Russia?

Nation Building in Italy, Germany, and Russia

Louis Napoleon's triumph in 1848 and his authoritarian rule in the 1850s provided Europe's victorious forces of order with a new political model. To what extent might the expanding urban middle classes and even portions of the working classes rally to a strong and essentially conservative national state that also promised change? This was one of the great political questions in the 1850s and 1860s. In central Europe a resounding answer came with the national unification of Germany and Italy. (See "Global Viewpoints: German and Italian Views on Nationalism," above.)

modernization The changes that enable a country to compete effectively with the leading countries at a given time.

The Russian Empire also experienced profound political crises in this period, but they were unlike those in Germany or Italy because Russia was already a vast multinational state. It became clear to Russian leaders that they had to embrace the process of **modernization**, defined narrowly as the changes that enable a country to compete effectively with the leading countries at a given time.

marked out, as far, at least, as regards Europe, by the courses of the great rivers, by the lines of the lofty mountains, and by other geographical conditions; they have disfigured it by conquest, by greed, by jealousy of the just sovereignty of others; disfigured it so much that today there is perhaps no nation except England and France whose confines correspond to this design.

[These evil governments] did not, and they do not, recognize any country except their own families and dynasties, the egoism of caste. But the divine design will infallibly be fulfilled. Natural divisions, the innate spontaneous tendencies of the peoples will replace the arbitrary divisions sanctioned by evil governments. The map of Europe will be remade. The Countries of the People will rise, defined by the voice of the free, upon the ruins of the Countries of Kings and privileged castes. . . .

Without Country you have neither name, voice, nor rights, no admissions as brothers into the fellowships of the Peoples. You are the bastards of Humanity. Soldiers without a banner, . . . you will find neither faith nor protection. . . . Do not beguile yourselves with the hope of emancipation from unjust social conditions if you do not first conquer a Country for yourselves; where there is no Country there is no common agreement to which you can appeal; . . . and he who has the upper hand keeps it, since there is no common safeguard for the interests of all.

QUESTIONS FOR ANALYSIS

1. How does Herder describe the "common spirit" of Europe, and what is his explanation for how it came into being?
2. How does Mazzini explain and justify the existence of individual countries (or nations)? According to Mazzini, why have Italians been prevented from having their own nation, and why is it so important that they obtain one?
3. How would you compare the views of Herder and Mazzini?

Sources: Hans Kohn, *Nationalism: Its Idea and History* (Princeton, N.J.: D. Van Nostrand Company, 1955), pp. 108–110; G. Mazzini, *The Duties of Man and Other Essays* (London: M. M. Dent and Sons, 1907), pp. 51–54.

Cavour, Garibaldi, and the Unification of Italy

Italy had never been a united nation prior to 1850. A battleground for the Great Powers after 1494, Italy was reorganized in 1815 at the Congress of Vienna. Austria received the rich northern provinces of Lombardy and Venetia (vih-NEE-shuh). Sardinia and Piedmont fell under the rule of an Italian monarch, and Tuscany shared north-central Italy with several smaller states. The papacy ruled over central Italy and Rome, while a branch of the Bourbons ruled Naples and Sicily (Map 24.2).

After 1815 the goal of a unified Italian nation captivated many Italians, but there was no agreement on how it could be achieved. In 1848 the efforts of idealistic nationalist Giuseppe Mazzini (joo-ZEP-pay maht-SEE-nee) to form a democratic Italian republic were crushed by Austrian forces. Temporarily driven from Rome during the upheavals of 1848, a frightened Pope Pius IX (pontificate 1846–1878) turned against most modern trends, including national unification. At the same time, Victor Emmanuel, king of independent Sardinia, retained the moderate liberal constitution

MAP 24.2 The Unification of Italy, 1859–1870 The leadership of Sardinia-Piedmont, nationalist fervor, and Garibaldi's attack on the Kingdom of the Two Sicilies were decisive factors in the unification of Italy.

Legend:
- Kingdom of Sardinia-Piedmont before 1859
- To Kingdom of Sardinia-Piedmont, 1859
- To Kingdom of Sardinia-Piedmont, 1860
- To Kingdom of Italy, 1866, 1870
- Major battle
- Northern boundary of Kingdom of Italy after unification

granted under duress in March 1848. To the Italian middle classes, Sardinia (see Map 24.2) appeared to be a liberal, progressive state ideally suited to drive Austria out of northern Italy and achieve the goal of national unification.

Sardinia had the good fortune of being led by Count Camillo Benso di Cavour. Cavour's national goals were limited and realistic. Cavour came from a noble family and embraced the economic doctrines and business activities associated with the prosperous middle class. Until 1859 he sought unity only for the states of northern and perhaps central Italy in a greatly expanded kingdom of Sardinia.

In the 1850s Cavour worked to consolidate Sardinia as a liberal constitutional state capable of leading northern Italy. He entered a secret alliance with Napoleon III, and in July 1858 he goaded Austria into attacking Sardinia. The combined Franco-Sardinian forces were victorious, but Napoleon III decided on a compromise peace with the Austrians in July 1859 to avoid offending French Catholics by supporting an enemy of the pope. Sardinia would receive only Lombardy, the area around Milan. Cavour resigned in protest.

Popular revolts and Italian nationalism salvaged Cavour's plans. While the war against Austria raged in the north, dedicated nationalists in central Italy had risen and driven out their rulers. Cavour returned to power in early 1860, and the people of central Italy voted overwhelmingly to join a greatly enlarged kingdom of Sardinia. Cavour had achieved his original goal of a north Italian state (see Map 24.2).

For superpatriots such as Giuseppe Garibaldi (1807–1882), the job of unification was still only half done. A poor sailor's son, Garibaldi personified the romantic revolutionary nationalism of 1848. Having led a unit of volunteers to several victories over Austrian troops in 1859, Garibaldi emerged in 1860 as an independent force in Italian politics. (See "Individuals in Society: Giuseppe Garibaldi," page 738.)

Secretly supported by Cavour, Garibaldi landed on the shores of Sicily in May 1860. His guerrilla band captured the imagination of the Sicilian peasantry, which rose in rebellion. Garibaldi captured Palermo and crossed to the mainland. When Garibaldi and Victor Emmanuel rode through Naples to cheering crowds, they symbolically sealed the union of north and south, of monarch and people.

The new kingdom of Italy, which did not include Venice until 1866 or Rome until 1870, was a parliamentary monarchy under Victor Emmanuel, neither radical nor democratic. Only a small minority of Italian males could vote. Despite political unity, the propertied classes and the common people were divided. A great social and cultural gap separated the industrializing north from the agrarian south.

Bismarck and German Unification

In the aftermath of 1848 the German states, particularly Austria and Prussia, were locked in a political stalemate, each seeking to block the power of the other within the German Confederation. At the same time, powerful economic forces were undermining the political status quo. Modern industry was growing rapidly within the German customs union, or *Zollverein*. By 1853 all the German states except Austria had joined the customs union, and a new Germany excluding Austria was becoming an economic reality. Rising prosperity from the rapid growth of industrialization after 1850 gave new impetus to middle-class liberals.

By 1859 liberals had assumed control of the parliament that emerged from the upheavals of 1848 in Prussia. The national uprising in Italy in 1859, however, convinced Prussia's tough-minded Wilhelm I (r. 1861–1888) that political change and even war with Austria or France was possible. Wilhelm I pushed to raise taxes and increase the defense budget to double the army's size. The Prussian parliament, reflecting the middle class's desire for a less militaristic society, rejected the military budget in 1862, and the liberals triumphed in new elections. King Wilhelm then called on Count Otto von Bismarck (1815–1898) to head a new ministry and defy the parliament.

Born into the Prussian landowning aristocracy, Bismarck (BIZ-mark) loved power, but he was also extraordinarily flexible and pragmatic in pursuing his goals. When Bismarck took office as chief minister in 1862, he declared that government would rule without parliamentary consent. Bismarck had the Prussian bureaucracy continue to collect taxes even though the parliament refused to approve the budget, and he reorganized the army. For their part, the voters of Prussia continued to express their opposition to Bismarck's policies by sending large liberal majorities to the parliament from 1862 to 1866.

Giuseppe Garibaldi

Giuseppe Garibaldi, the charismatic leader, shown in a portrait painted in 1850.

(*Giuseppe Garibaldi*, 1850, by Auguste Etienne [1794–1865] [oil on panel]/Musée de l'Armée, Paris, France/akg-images)

WHEN GIUSEPPE GARIBALDI VISITED ENGLAND in 1864, he received the most triumphant welcome ever given to any foreigner. Honored and fêted by politicians and high society, he also captivated the masses. An unprecedented crowd of a half million people cheered his carriage through the streets of London. These ovations were no fluke. In his time, Garibaldi was probably the most famous and most beloved figure in the world.* How could this be?

A rare combination of wild adventure and extraordinary achievement partly accounted for his demigod status. Born in Nice, Garibaldi went to sea at fifteen and sailed the Mediterranean for twelve years. At seventeen his travels took him to Rome, and he was converted in an almost religious experience to the "New Italy, the Italy of all the Italians." As he later wrote in his bestselling *Autobiography*, "The Rome that I beheld with the eyes of youthful imagination was the Rome of the future—the dominant thought of my whole life."

Sentenced to death in 1834 for his part in a revolutionary uprising in Genoa, Garibaldi barely escaped to South America. For twelve years he led a guerrilla band in Uruguay's struggle for independence from Argentina. "Shipwrecked, ambushed, shot through the neck," he found in a tough young woman, Anna da Silva, a mate and companion in arms. Their first children nearly starved in the jungle while Garibaldi, clad in his long red shirt, fashioned a legend as a fearless freedom fighter.

After he returned to Italy in 1848, the campaigns of his patriotic volunteers against the Austrians in 1848 and 1859 mobilized democratic nationalists. The stage was set for his volunteer army to liberate Sicily against enormous odds, astonishing the world and creating a large Italian state. Garibaldi's achievement matched his legend.

A brilliant fighter, the handsome and inspiring leader was an uncompromising idealist of absolute integrity. He never drew personal profit from his exploits, continuing to milk his goats and rarely possessing more than one change of clothing. When Victor Emmanuel offered him lands and titles after his great victory in 1860, even as the left-leaning volunteers were disbanded and humiliated, Garibaldi declined, saying he could not be bought off. Returning to his farm on a tiny rocky island, he denounced the government without hesitation when he concluded that it was betraying the dream of unification with its ruthless rule in the south. Yet even after a duplicitous Italian government caused two later attacks on Rome to fail, his faith in the generative power of national unity never wavered. Garibaldi showed that ideas and ideals count in history.

Above all, millions of ordinary men and women identified with Garibaldi because they believed that he was fighting for them. They recognized him as one of their own and saw that he remained true to them in spite of his triumphs, thereby ennobling their own lives and aspirations. Welcoming runaway slaves as equals in Latin America, advocating the emancipation of women, introducing social reforms in the south, and pressing for free education and a broader suffrage in the new Italy, Garibaldi the national hero fought for freedom and human dignity. The common people understood and loved him for it.

QUESTIONS FOR ANALYSIS

1. Why was Garibaldi so famous and popular?
2. Nationalism evolved and developed in the nineteenth century. How did Garibaldi fit into this evolution? What kind of a nationalist was he?

*Denis Mack Smith, *Garibaldi: A Great Life in Brief* (New York: Alfred A. Knopf, 1956), pp. 136–147; Denis Mack Smith, "Giuseppe Garibaldi," *History Today*, August 1991, pp. 20–26.

MAP 24.3 The Unification of Germany, 1866–1871

This map shows how Prussia expanded and a new German Empire was created through two wars, the Austro-Prussian War of 1866 and the Franco-Prussian War of 1870–1871.

In 1866 Bismarck launched the Austro-Prussian War with the intent of expelling Austria from German politics. The war lasted only seven weeks, as the reorganized Prussian army defeated Austria decisively. Bismarck forced Austria to withdraw from German affairs and dissolved the existing German Confederation. The mainly Protestant states north of the Main River were grouped in the new North German Confederation, led by an expanded Prussia (Map 24.3). Each state retained its own local government, but the federal government—Wilhelm I and Bismarck—controlled the army and foreign affairs.

To make peace with the liberal middle class and the nationalist movement, Bismarck asked the Prussian parliament to approve after the fact all the government's "illegal" spending between 1862 and 1866. Overawed by Bismarck's achievements, middle-class liberals now jumped at the chance to cooperate, opting for national unity and military glory over the battle for truly liberal institutions. Bismarck also followed Napoleon III's example by creating a legislature with members of the lower house elected by universal male suffrage, allowing him to bypass the middle class and appeal directly to the people if necessary. The constitutional struggle in Prussia was over, and the German middle class was respectfully accepting the monarchical authority and aristocratic superiority that Bismarck represented.

The final act in the drama of German unification followed quickly with a patriotic war against France. The apparent issue—whether a distant relative of Prussia's Wilhelm I might become king of Spain—was only a diplomatic pretext. By 1870, alarmed by Prussia's growing power, French leaders had decided on a war to teach Prussia a lesson.

As soon as war against France began in 1870, Bismarck had the wholehearted support of the south German states. The Germans quickly defeated Louis Napoleon's armies at Sedan on September 1, 1870. Three days later French patriots in Paris proclaimed yet another French republic and vowed to continue fighting. But after five months, in January 1871, a starving Paris surrendered, and France accepted Bismarck's harsh peace terms. By this time the south German states had agreed to join a new German Empire.

The Franco-Prussian War released an enormous surge of patriotic feeling in Germany. The new German Empire had become Europe's most powerful state, and most Germans were enormously proud. Semi-authoritarian nationalism and a "new conservatism," which was based on an alliance of the propertied classes and sought the active support of the working classes, had triumphed in Germany.

The Modernization of Russia

In the 1850s Russia was a poor agrarian society with a rapidly growing population. Almost 90 percent of the population lived off the land, and serfdom was still the basic social institution. Then the Crimean War of 1853 to 1856 arose from the breakdown of the balance of power established at the Congress of Vienna, European competition over influence in the Middle East, and Russian desires to expand into European territories held by the Ottoman Empire. France and Great Britain, aided by Sardinia and the Ottoman Empire, inflicted a humiliating defeat on Russia.

Russia's military defeat showed that it had fallen behind the industrializing nations of western Europe. Moreover, the war had caused hardship and raised the specter of massive peasant rebellion. Military disaster thus forced the new tsar, Alexander II (r. 1855–1881), and his ministers along the path of rapid social change and general modernization.

The first and greatest of the reforms was the freeing of the serfs in 1861. The emancipated peasants received, on average, about half of the land, which was to be collectively owned by peasant villages. The prices for the land were high, and collective ownership limited the possibilities of agricultural improvement and migration to urban areas. Thus the effects of the reform were limited. More successful was reform of the legal system, which established independent courts and equality before the law. The government also relaxed censorship and partially liberalized policies toward Russian Jews.

The Crimean War, 1853–1856

Russia's greatest strides toward modernization were economic rather than political. Rapid, government-subsidized railroad construction to 1880 enabled agricultural Russia to export grain and thus earn money for further industrialization. Industrial suburbs grew up around Moscow and St. Petersburg, and a class of modern factory workers began to take shape. Russia began seizing territory in far eastern Siberia, on the border with China; in Central Asia, north of Afghanistan; and in the Islamic lands of the Caucasus.

In 1881 an anarchist assassinated Alexander II, and the reform era came to an abrupt end. Political modernization remained frozen until 1905, but economic modernization sped forward in the massive industrial surge of the 1890s. The key leader was Sergei Witte (suhr-GAY VIH-tuh), the energetic minister of finance. Under Witte's leadership, the government doubled Russia's railroad network by the end of the century and promoted Russian industry with high protective tariffs.

By 1900 Russia was catching up with western Europe and expanding its empire in Asia. By 1903 Russia had established a sphere of influence in Chinese Manchuria and was eyeing northern Korea. When the protests of equally imperialistic Japan were ignored, the Japanese launched a surprise attack on Russian forces in Manchuria in February 1904. After Japan scored repeated victories, Russia was forced in September 1905 to accept a humiliating defeat.

Military disaster in East Asia brought political upheaval at home. On January 22, 1905, workers peacefully protesting for improved working conditions and higher wages were attacked by the tsar's troops outside the Winter Palace. This event, known as Bloody Sunday, set off a wave of strikes, peasant uprisings, and troop mutinies across Russia. The revolutionary surge culminated in October 1905 in a paralyzing general strike, which forced the government to capitulate. The tsar, Nicholas II (r. 1894–1917), issued the **October Manifesto**, which granted full civil rights and promised a popularly elected Duma (DOO-muh) (parliament) with real legislative power.

October Manifesto The result of a great general strike in Russia in October 1905, it granted full civil rights and promised a popularly elected Duma (parliament) with real legislative power.

The Russian Revolution of 1905

Bloody Sunday, Russia, 1905
On January 22, 1905, Russian troops fired on striking workers who had peacefully assembled in front of the Winter Palace in St. Petersburg, hoping to present their grievances to the tsar. Over a hundred demonstrators died and many hundreds more were injured in the ensuing massacre. The event, known as Bloody Sunday, helped rouse resistance to the imperial government. (Laski Diffusion/Newsmakers/Getty Images)

Under the new constitution, Nicholas II retained great powers and the Duma had only limited authority. The middle-class liberals, the largest group in the newly elected Duma, were badly disappointed, and efforts to cooperate with the tsar's ministers soon broke down. In 1907 Nicholas II and his reactionary advisers rewrote the electoral law so as to greatly increase the weight of the propertied classes. On the eve of World War I, Russia was a partially modernized nation, a conservative constitutional monarchy with an agrarian but industrializing economy.

What was the impact of urban growth on cities, social classes, families, and ideas?

Urban Life in the Age of Ideologies

By 1900 western Europe was urban and industrial as surely as it had been rural and agrarian in 1800. Rapid urban growth in the nineteenth century worsened long-standing overcrowding and unhealthy living conditions, lending support to voices calling for revolutionary change. In response, government leaders, city planners, reformers, and scientists urgently sought solutions to these challenges. Over the long term, success in improving the urban environment and the introduction of social welfare measures encouraged people to put their faith in a responsive national state.

Urban Development

Since the Middle Ages, European cities had been centers of government, culture, and large-scale commerce. They had also been congested, dirty, and unhealthy. Industrialization greatly worsened these conditions. The steam engine freed industrialists from dependence on the energy of streams and rivers so that by 1800 there was every incentive to build new factories in cities, which had better shipping facilities and a large and ready workforce. Therefore, as industry grew, overcrowded and unhealthy cities expanded rapidly.

In the 1820s and 1830s people in Britain and France began to worry about the condition of their cities. Parks and open areas were almost nonexistent, and narrow houses were built wall to wall in long rows. Highly concentrated urban populations lived in extremely unsanitary conditions, with open drains and sewers flowing alongside or down the middle of unpaved streets. Infected water contributed to a European cholera epidemic in 1831–1832, killing hundreds of thousands and contributing to social unrest.

The urban challenge — and the pressure of radical ideas including those of the revolutions of 1848 — eventually brought an energetic response from a generation of reformers. The most famous early reformer was Edwin Chadwick, a British official. Collecting detailed reports from local officials and publishing his findings in 1842, Chadwick concluded that the stinking excrement of communal outhouses could be carried off by water through sewers at less than one-twentieth the cost of removing it by hand. In 1848 Chadwick's report became the basis of Great Britain's first public health law, which created a national health board and gave cities broad authority to build modern sanitary systems. Such sanitary movements won dedicated supporters in the United States, France, and Germany from the 1840s on.

Early sanitary reformers were handicapped by the prevailing miasmatic theory of disease — the belief that people contract disease when they breathe foul odors. In the 1840s and 1850s keen observation by doctors and public health officials suggested that contagion spread through physical contact with filth and not by its odors, thus weakening the miasmatic idea. An understanding of how this occurred came out of the work of Louis Pasteur (1822–1895), who developed the **germ theory** of disease. By 1870 the work of Pasteur and others had demonstrated that specific living organisms caused specific diseases and that those organisms could be controlled. These discoveries led to the development of a number of effective vaccines. Surgeons also applied the germ theory in hospitals, sterilizing not only the wound but everything else that entered the operating room.

germ theory The idea that disease is caused by the spread of living organisms that can be controlled.

The achievements of the bacterial revolution coupled with the public health movement saved millions of lives, particularly after about 1890. In England, France, and Germany death rates declined dramatically, and diphtheria, typhoid, typhus, cholera, and yellow fever became vanishing diseases in the industrializing nations.

More effective urban planning after 1850 also improved the quality of urban life. France took the lead during the rule of Napoleon III (r. 1848–1870), who believed that rebuilding Paris would provide employment, improve living conditions, and glorify and strengthen his empire. Baron Georges Haussmann (HOWSS-mun) (1809–1884), whom Napoleon III placed in charge of Paris, destroyed the old medieval core of Paris to create broad tree-lined boulevards, long open vistas, monumental buildings, middle-class housing, parks, and improved sewers and aqueducts. In addition to easing traffic and providing impressive vistas, the broad boulevards were intended to prevent a recurrence of the easy construction and defense of barricades by revolutionary crowds that had occurred in 1848. The rebuilding of Paris stimulated urban development throughout Europe, particularly after 1870.

Mass public transportation was also of great importance in the improvement of urban living conditions. In the 1890s countries in North America and Europe adopted an American transit innovation, the electric streetcar. Millions of riders hopped on

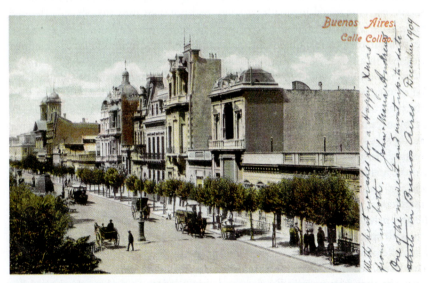

Buenos Aires Postcard, ca. 1908 Between 1880 and 1910 the modern city of Buenos Aires, the capital of Argentina, emerged. City planners adopted the wide boulevards, monuments, and long vistas that Baron Haussmann had brought to Paris in the mid-nineteenth century. (© Mary Evans Picture Library/Grenville Collins Postcard Collection/The Image Works)

board during the workweek. On weekends and holidays streetcars carried city people on outings to parks and the countryside, racetracks, and music halls.[1] Electric streetcars also gave people of modest means access to improved housing, as the still-crowded city was able to expand and become less congested.

Industrialization and the growth of global trade led to urbanization outside of Europe. The tremendous appetite of industrializing nations for raw materials, food, and other goods caused the rapid growth of port cities and mining centers across the world. These included Alexandria in Egypt, the major port for transporting Egyptian cotton, and mining cities like San Francisco in California and Johannesburg in South Africa. Many of these new cities consciously emulated European urban planning. For example, from 1880 to 1910 the Argentine capital of Buenos Aires modernized rapidly. The development of Buenos Aires was greatly stimulated by the arrival of many Italian and Spanish immigrants, part of a much larger wave of European migration in this period (see "Immigration" in Chapter 27).

Social Inequality and Class

By 1850 at the latest, the wages and living conditions of the working classes were finally improving. Greater economic rewards, however, did not significantly narrow the gap between rich and poor. In fact, economic inequality worsened in Europe over the course of the nineteenth century and reached its height on the eve of World War I. In every industrialized country around 1900, the richest 20 percent of households received anywhere from 50 to 60 percent of all national income, whereas the bottom 30 percent of households received 10 percent or less of all income. Despite the promises of the political and economic revolutions of the late eighteenth century, the gap between rich and poor in the early twentieth century was thus as great as or even wider than it had been in the eighteenth-century age of agriculture and aristocracy.

Despite extreme social inequality, society had not split into two sharply defined opposing classes, as Marx had predicted. Instead economic specialization created an almost unlimited range of jobs, skills, and earnings; one group or subclass blended into another in a complex, confusing hierarchy.

Between the tiny elite of the very rich and the sizable mass of the dreadfully poor existed a range of subclasses, each filled with individuals struggling to rise or at least to hold their own in the social order. A confederation of middle classes was loosely linked by occupations requiring mental, rather than physical, skill. As the upper middle class, composed mainly of successful business families, gained in income and progressively lost all traces of radicalism after the trauma of 1848, they were drawn toward the aristocratic lifestyle.

One step below was a much larger group of moderately successful industrialists and merchants, professionals in law and medicine, and midlevel managers of large public and private institutions. The expansion of industry and technology called for experts with specialized knowledge, and the most valuable of the specialties became solid middle-class professions. Next came independent shopkeepers, small traders, and tiny manufacturers—the lower middle class. Industrialization and urbanization also diversified the lower middle class and expanded the number of white-collar employees. White-collar employees were propertyless, but generally they were fiercely committed to the middle class and to the ideal of moving up in society.

The Happiness of the Drawing Room depends upon *the Comfort of the Kitchen.*

HUDSON'S SOAP

Hudson's Soap Advertising Postcard, ca. 1903
Early-twentieth-century advertisements, such as this one for Hudson's Soap, reflected the strict class divisions of society. (Collection/REX/Shutterstock)

Food, housing, clothes, and behavior all expressed middle-class values. Employment of at least one full-time maid was the clearest sign that a family had crossed the divide from the working classes into the middle classes. Freed from domestic labor, the middle-class wife directed her servants, supervised her children's education, and used her own appearance and that of her home to display the family's status. The middle classes shared a code of expected behavior and morality, which stressed hard work, self-discipline, and personal achievement.

At the beginning of the twentieth century about four out of five Europeans belonged to the working classes—that is, people whose livelihoods depended primarily on physical labor. Many of them were small landowning peasants and hired farm hands, especially in eastern Europe. The urban working classes were even less unified than the middle classes. Economic development and increased specialization during the nineteenth century expanded the traditional range of working-class skills, earnings, and experiences. Skilled, semiskilled, and unskilled workers accordingly developed widely divergent lifestyles and cultural values, and their differences contributed to a keen sense of social status and hierarchy within the working classes.

Highly skilled workers, who made up about 15 percent of the working classes, became known as the labor aristocracy. They were led by construction bosses and factory foremen. The labor aristocracy also included members of the traditional highly skilled handicraft trades that had not transitioned to mechanized production, as well as new kinds of skilled workers such as shipbuilders and railway locomotive engineers.

Below the labor aristocracy stood the complex world of semiskilled and unskilled urban workers. A large number of the semiskilled were factory workers who earned good wages and whose relative importance in the labor force was increasing. Below the semiskilled workers was a larger group of unskilled workers that included day laborers and domestic servants.

To make ends meet, many working-class wives had to join the ranks of working women in the "sweated industries." These industries resembled the old putting-out and cottage industries of earlier times, and they were similar to what we call sweatshops today. The women normally worked at home and were paid by the piece, often making clothing after the advent of the sewing machine in the 1850s.

Despite their harsh lives, the urban working classes found outlets for fun and recreation. Across Europe drinking remained a favorite working-class leisure-time activity along with sports and music halls. Religion continued to provide working people with solace and meaning, although church attendance among the urban working classes declined in the late nineteenth century, especially among men.

The Changing Family

Industrialization and the growth of modern cities also brought great changes to the lives of women and families. As economic conditions improved, only women in poor families tended to work outside the home. The ideal became separate spheres, the strict division of labor by sex. This rigid division meant that married women faced great obstacles if they needed or wanted to move into the world of paid employment outside the home. Well-paying jobs were off-limits to women, and a woman's wage was almost always less than a man's, even for the same work.

Because they needed to be able to support their wives, middle-class men did not marry until they were well established in their careers. The system encouraged marriages between older men and younger women with little experience with adult life. Men were encouraged to see themselves as the protectors of their fragile and vulnerable wives.

As the ideology and practice of rigidly separate spheres narrowed women's horizons, their control and influence in the home became increasingly strong throughout Europe in the late nineteenth century. The comfortable home run by the middle-class wife was idealized as a warm shelter in a hard and impersonal urban world. By 1900 working-class families had adopted many middle-class values, but they did not have the means to fully realize the ideals of domestic comfort or separate spheres. Nevertheless, the working-class wife generally determined how the family's money was spent and took charge of all major domestic decisions. The woman's guidance of the household went hand in hand with the increased emotional importance of home and family for all social groups.

Ideas about sexuality within marriage varied. Many French marriage manuals of the late nineteenth century stressed that women had legitimate sexual needs. In the more puritanical United States, however, sex manuals recommended sexual abstinence for unmarried men and limited sexual activity for married men. Respectable women were thought to experience no sexual pleasure at all from sexual activity, and anything vaguely sexual was to be removed from their surroundings; even the legs of pianos were to be covered. (See "Analyzing the Evidence: Stefan Zweig on Middle-Class Youth and Sexuality," page 748.)

Medical doctors in both Europe and the United States began to study sexual desires and behavior more closely, and to determine what was considered "normal" and "abnormal." Same-sex attraction, labeled "homosexuality" for the first time, was identified as a "perversion." Governments increasingly regulated prostitution, the treatment of venereal disease, and access to birth control in ways that were shaped by class and gender hierarchies. Medical science also turned its attention to mother-hood, and a wave of books instructed middle-class women on how to be better mothers.

Ideas about sexuality and motherhood were inextricably tied up with ideas about race. As European nations embarked on imperialist expansion in the second half of the nineteenth century, the need to maintain the racial superiority that justified empire led to increased concerns about the possible dilution or weakening of the European races. Maintaining healthy bodies, restricting sexuality, preventing inter-racial marriages, and ensuring that women properly raised their children were all components of racial strength, in the eyes of many European thinkers.

Women in industrializing countries also began to limit the number of children they bore. This revolutionary reduction in family size, in which the comfortable and well-educated classes took the lead, was founded on parents' desire to improve their economic and social position and that of their children. By having fewer youngsters, parents could give those they had advantages, from music lessons to expensive uni-versity educations.

The ideal of separate spheres and the rigid gender division of labor meant that middle-class women lacked legal rights and faced discrimination in education and employment. Organizations founded by middle-class feminists campaigned for legal equality as well as for access to higher education and professional employment. In the late nineteenth century middle-class women scored some significant victories, such as the 1882 law giving British married women full property rights. Rather than con-testing existing notions of women as morally superior guardians of the home, femi-nists drew on these ideas for legitimacy in speaking out about social issues.

Socialist women leaders usually took a different path. They argued that the liber-ation of working-class women would come only with the liberation of the entire working class. In the meantime, they championed the cause of working women and won some practical improvements. In a general way, these different approaches to women's issues reflected the diversity of classes and political views in urban society.

Science for the Masses

Breakthroughs in industrial technology stimulated basic scientific inquiry as research-ers sought to explain how such things as steam engines and blast furnaces actually worked. The result from the 1830s onward was an explosive growth of fundamental scientific discoveries that were increasingly transformed into material improvements for the general population.

A perfect example of the translation of better scientific knowledge into practical human benefits was the development of the branch of physics known as thermo-dynamics, the study of the relationship between heat and mechanical energy. By midcentury physicists had formulated the fundamental laws of thermodynamics, which were then applied to mechanical engineering, chemical processes, and many other fields. Electricity was transformed from a curiosity in 1800 to a commercial form of energy. By 1890 the internal combustion engine fueled by petroleum was an emerging competitor to steam and electricity.

Everyday experience and innumerable articles in newspapers and magazines impressed the importance of science on the popular mind. The methods of science acquired unrivaled prestige after 1850. Many educated people came to believe that

Stefan Zweig on Middle-Class Youth and Sexuality

Growing up in Vienna in a prosperous Jewish family, Stefan Zweig (1881–1942) became an influential voice calling for humanitarian values and international culture in early-twentieth-century Europe. Passionately opposed to the First World War, Zweig wrote poetry, plays, and novels. But he was most famous for his biographies: shrewd psychological portraits of historical figures such as Magellan and Marie Antoinette. After Hitler came to power in 1933, Zweig lived in exile until his death in 1942. Zweig's last work was *The World of Yesterday* (1943), one of the truly fascinating autobiographies of the twentieth century. In the following passage, Zweig recalls the romantic experiences and sexual separation of middle-class youth before the First World War.

■ During the eight years of our higher schooling [beyond grade school], something had occurred which was of great importance to each one of us: we ten-year-olds had grown into virile young men of sixteen, seventeen, and eighteen, and Nature began to assert its rights. . . . It did not take us long to discover that those authorities in whom we had previously confided—school, family, and public morals—manifested an astonishing insincerity in this matter of sex. But what is more, they also demanded secrecy and reserve from us in this connection. . . .

This "social morality," which on the one hand privately presupposed the existence of sexuality and its natural course, but on the other would not recognize it openly at any price, was doubly deceitful. While it winked one eye at a young man and even encouraged him with the other "to sow his wild oats," as the kindly language of the home put it, in the case of a woman it studiously shut both eyes and acted as if it were blind. That a man could experience desires, and was permitted to experience them, was silently admitted by custom. But to admit frankly that a woman could be subject to similar desires, or that creation for its eternal purposes also required a female polarity, would have transgressed the conception of the "sanctity of womanhood." In the pre-Freudian era, therefore, the axiom was agreed upon that a female person could have no physical desires as long as they had not been awakened by man, and that, obviously, was officially permitted only in marriage. But even in those moral times, in Vienna in particular, the air was full of dangerous erotic infection, and a girl of good family had to live in a completely sterilized atmosphere, from the day of her birth until the day when she left the altar on her husband's arm. In order to protect young girls, they were not left alone for a single moment. . . . Every book which they read was inspected, and above all else, young girls were constantly kept busy to divert their attention from any possible dangerous thoughts. They had to practise the piano, learn singing and drawing, foreign languages, and the history of literature and art. They were educated and overeducated. But while the aim was to make them as educated and as socially correct as possible, at the same time society anxiously took great pains that they should remain innocent of all natural things to a degree unthinkable today. A young girl of good family was not allowed to have any idea of how the male body was formed, or to know how children came into the world, for the angel was to enter into matrimony not only physically untouched, but completely "pure" spiritually as well. "Good breeding," for a young girl of that time, was identical with ignorance of life; and this ignorance ofttimes lasted for the rest of their lives. . . .

the union of careful experiment and abstract theory was the only reliable route to truth and objective reality. The Enlightenment idea that natural processes were determined by rigid laws, leaving little room for either divine intervention or human will, won broad acceptance.

Living in an era of rapid change, nineteenth-century thinkers in Europe were fascinated with the idea of evolution and dynamic development. The most influential of all nineteenth-century evolutionary thinkers was Charles Darwin (1809–1882). Darwin believed that all life had gradually evolved from a common ancestral

What possibilities actually existed for a young man of the middle-class world? In all the others, in the so-called lower classes, the problem was no problem at all. . . . In most of our Alpine villages the number of natural children greatly exceeded the legitimate ones. Among the proletariat, the worker, before he could get married, lived with another worker in free love. . . . It was only in our middle-class society that such a remedy as an early marriage was scorned. . . . And so there was an artificial interval of six, eight, or ten years between actual manhood and manhood as society accepted it; and in this interval the young man had to take care of his own "affairs" or adventures.

Those days did not give him too many opportunities. Only a very few particularly rich young men could afford the luxury of keeping a mistress, that is, taking an apartment and paying her expenses. And only a very few fortunate young men achieved the literary ideal of love of the times — the only one which it was permitted to describe in novels — an affair with a married woman. The others helped themselves for the most part with shopgirls and waitresses, and this offered little inner satisfaction. . . . But, generally speaking, prostitution was still the foundation of the erotic life outside of marriage; in a certain sense it constituted a dark underground vault over which rose the gorgeous structure of middle-class society with its faultless, radiant façade.

The present generation has hardly any idea of the gigantic extent of prostitution in Europe before the [First] World War. Whereas today it is as rare to meet a prostitute on the streets of a big city as it is to meet a wagon in the road, then the sidewalks were so sprinkled with women for sale that it was more difficult to avoid than to find them. To this was added the countless number of "closed houses," the night clubs, the cabarets, the dance parlours with their dancers and singers, and the bars with their "come-on" girls. At that time female wares were offered for sale at every hour and at every price. . . . And this was the same city, the same society, the same morality, that was indignant when young girls rode bicycles, and declared it a disgrace to the dignity of science when Freud in his calm, clear, and penetrating manner established truths that they did not wish to be true. The same world that so pathetically defended the purity of womanhood allowed this cruel sale of women, organized it, and even profited thereby.

We should not permit ourselves to be misled by sentimental novels or stories of that epoch. It was a bad time for youth. The young girls were hermetically locked up under the control of the family, hindered in their free bodily as well as intellectual development. The young men were forced to secrecy and reticence by a morality which fundamentally no one believed or obeyed. Unhampered, honest relationships — in other words, all that could have made youth happy and joyous according to the laws of Nature — were permitted only to the very few.

QUESTIONS FOR ANALYSIS

1. According to Zweig, how did the sex lives of young middle-class women and young middle-class men differ? What accounted for these differences?
2. What were the differences between the sex lives of the middle class and those of the so-called lower classes? What was Zweig's opinion of these differences?
3. Zweig ends with a value judgment: "It was a bad time for youth." Do you agree or disagree? Why?

Source: Excerpts from *World of Yesterday* by Stefan Zweig, translated by Helmut Ripperger and B. W. Huebsch, translation copyright 1943, renewed © 1971 by the Viking Press, Inc. Used by permission of Viking Books, an imprint of Penguin Publishing Group, a division of Penguin Random House LLC. All rights reserved. Any third party use of this material, outside of this publication, is prohibited. Interested parties must apply directly to Penguin Random House LLC for permission.

origin in an unending "struggle for survival." Darwin's theory of **evolution** is summarized in the title of his work *On the Origin of Species by the Means of Natural Selection* (1859). He argued that small variations within individuals in one species enabled them to acquire more food and better living conditions and made them more successful in reproducing, thus allowing them to pass their genetic material to the next generation. When a number of individuals within a species became distinct enough that they could no longer interbreed successfully with others, they became a new species.

evolution The idea, developed by Charles Darwin, that all life had gradually evolved from a common origin through a process of natural selection.

Madrid in 1900 This wistful painting of a Spanish square on a rainy day, by Enrique Martínez Cubells y Ruiz (1874–1917), includes a revealing commentary on how scientific discoveries transformed urban life. Coachmen wait atop their expensive hackney cabs for a wealthy clientele, while modern electric streetcars that carry the masses converge on the square from all directions. In this way the development of electricity brought improved urban transportation and enabled the city to expand to the suburbs. (Museo Municipal, Madrid, Spain/Bridgeman Images)

Darwin's theory of natural selection provoked resistance, particularly because he extended the theory to humans. His findings reinforced the teachings of secularists such as Marx, who scornfully dismissed religious belief in favor of agnostic or atheistic materialism. Many writers also applied the theory of biological evolution to human affairs. Herbert Spencer (1820–1903), an English philosopher, saw the human race as driven forward to ever-greater specialization and progress by a brutal economic struggle that determines the "survival of the fittest." The idea that human society also evolves, and that the stronger will become powerful and prosperous while the weaker will be conquered or remain poor, became known as **Social Darwinism**. Powerful nations used this ideology to justify nationalism and expansion, and colonizers to justify imperialism.

Social Darwinism The application of the theory of biological evolution to human affairs, it sees the human race as driven to ever-greater specialization and progress by an unending economic struggle that determines the survival of the fittest.

Not only did science shape society, but society also shaped science. As nations asserted their differences from one another, they sought "scientific" proof for those differences, which generally meant proof of their own superiority. European and American scientists, anthropologists, and physicians sought to prove that Europeans and those of European descent were more intelligent than other races, and that northern Europeans were more advanced than southern Europeans. Africans were described and depicted as "missing links" between chimpanzees and Europeans. This scientific racism extended to Jews, who were increasingly described as a separate and inferior race, not a religious group.

Cultural Shifts

The French Revolution kindled the belief that radical reconstructions of politics and society were also possible in cultural and artistic life. The most significant expression of this belief in the early nineteenth century was the Romantic movement. In part a revolt against what was perceived as the cold rationality of the Enlightenment,

Romanticism was characterized by a belief in emotional exuberance, unrestrained imagination, and spontaneity in both art and personal life. Preoccupied with emotional excess, Romantic works explored the awesome power of love and desire and of hatred, guilt, and despair. Where Enlightenment thinkers embraced secularization and civic life, Romantics delved into religious ecstasy and the hidden recesses of the self. The Romantics were passionately moved by nature and decried the growth of modern industry and industrial cities.

The French Romantic painter Eugène Delacroix (oo-ZHEHN deh-luh-KWAH) (1798–1863) depicted dramatic, colorful scenes that stirred the emotions. He frequently painted non-European places and people, whether lion hunts in Morocco or women in a sultan's harem. Like other Romantic works, Delacroix's art reveals the undercurrents of desire and fascination within Europe's imperial ambitions in "exotic" and "savage" places in the nineteenth century.

It was in music that Romanticism realized most fully and permanently its goals of free expression and emotional intensity. Abandoning well-defined structures, the great Romantic composers used a wide range of forms to create musical landscapes and evoke powerful emotion. The first great Romantic composer is among the most revered today, Ludwig van Beethoven (1770–1827).

Romanticism also found a distinctive voice in poetry. In 1798 William Wordsworth (1770–1850) and his fellow Romantic poet Samuel Taylor Coleridge (1772–1834) published their *Lyrical Ballads*, which abandoned flowery classical conventions for the language of ordinary speech. Wordsworth described his conception of poetry as the "spontaneous overflow of powerful feeling recollected in tranquility."

Victor Hugo's (1802–1885) powerful novels exemplified the Romantic fascination with fantastic characters, strange settings, and human emotions. The hero of Hugo's famous *Hunchback of Notre Dame* (1831) is the great cathedral's deformed bell-ringer, a "human gargoyle" overlooking the teeming life of fifteenth-century Paris.

The study of history became a Romantic passion. History was the key to a universe that was now perceived to be organic and dynamic, not mechanical and static as the Enlightenment thinkers had believed. Historical studies supported the development of national aspirations and encouraged entire peoples to seek in the past their special destinies.

In central and eastern Europe, in particular, literary Romanticism and early nationalism reinforced each other. Romantics turned their attention to peasant life and transcribed the folk songs, tales, and proverbs that the cosmopolitan Enlightenment had disdained. The brothers Jacob and Wilhelm Grimm were particularly successful at rescuing German fairy tales from oblivion. In the Slavic lands Romantics played a decisive role in converting spoken peasant languages into modern written languages.

Beginning in the 1840s Romanticism gave way to a new artistic genre, Realism. Influenced by the growing prestige of science in this period, Realist writers believed that literature should depict life exactly as it is. Forsaking poetry for prose and replacing the personal, emotional viewpoint of the Romantics with strict scientific objectivity, the Realists simply observed and recorded.

Realist writers focused on creating fiction based on contemporary everyday life. Beginning with a dissection of the middle classes, from which most of them sprang, many Realists eventually focused on the working classes, especially the urban working classes, which had been neglected in literature before this time. The Realists put

Romanticism A movement in art, literature, and music characterized by a belief in emotional exuberance, unrestrained imagination, and spontaneity in both art and personal life.

a microscope to unexplored and taboo topics—sex, strikes, violence, alcoholism— shocking middle-class critics.

The Realists' claims of objectivity did not prevent the elaboration of a definite worldview. Realists such as the famous French novelist Émile Zola (1840–1902) and English novelist Thomas Hardy (1840–1928) were determinists. They believed that human beings, like atoms, are components of the physical world and that all human actions are caused by unalterable natural laws: heredity and environment determine human behavior; good and evil are merely social conventions. They were also critical of the failures of industrial society; by depicting the plight of poor workers, they hoped to bring about positive social change.

Nationalism and Socialism, 1871–1914

How did nationalism and socialism shape European politics in the decades before the Great War?

After 1871 Europe's heartland was organized into strong national states. Only on Europe's borders—in Ireland and Russia, in Austria-Hungary and the Balkans—did people still strive for national unity and independence. Nationalism served, for better or worse, as a new unifying political principle. At the same time, socialist parties grew rapidly. Governing elites manipulated national feeling to create a sense of unity to divert attention from underlying class conflicts, and increasingly channeled national sentiment in an antiliberal and militaristic direction, tolerating anti-Semitism and waging wars in non-Western lands. This policy helped manage domestic conflicts, but only at the expense of increasing the international tensions that erupted in World War I.

Trends in Suffrage

There were good reasons why ordinary people felt increasing loyalty to their governments in central and western Europe by the turn of the twentieth century. Ordinary men felt they were becoming "part of the system," quite simply, because more of them could vote. By 1914 universal male suffrage had become the rule rather than the exception.

Women also began to demand the right to vote. The first important successes occurred in Scandinavia and Australia. In Sweden taxpaying single women and widows could vote in municipal elections after 1862. Australia and Finland gave women the right to vote in national elections and stand for parliament in 1902 and 1906, respectively (although restrictions on Aboriginal women's voting rights in Australia continued until the 1960s). In the western United States, women could vote in twelve states by 1913. One example among the thousands of courageous "suffragettes" was French socialist Hubertine Auclert (ew-ber-TEEN o-CLAIR), who in 1880–1881 led demonstrations, organized women in a property-tax boycott, and created the first suffragist newspaper in France.[2] Auclert and her counterparts elsewhere in Europe had little success before 1914, but they prepared the way for the female vote in many countries immediately after World War I.

As the right to vote spread, politicians and parties in national parliaments usually represented the people more responsively. The multiparty system prevailing in most countries meant that parliamentary majorities were built on shifting coalitions, which gave political parties leverage to obtain benefits for their supporters. Governments also passed laws to alleviate general problems, thereby acquiring greater legitimacy and appearing more worthy of support.

The German Empire

The new German Empire was a federal union of Prussia and twenty-four smaller states. The separate states conducted much of the everyday business of government. Unifying the whole was a strong national government with a chancellor—Bismarck until 1890—and a popularly elected parliament called the Reichstag (RIGHKS-tahg). Although Bismarck repeatedly ignored the wishes of the parliamentary majority, he nonetheless preferred to win the support of the Reichstag to lend legitimacy to his policy goals.

Bismarck was a fierce opponent of socialism. In 1878 he pushed through a law outlawing the German Social Democratic Party, but he was unable to force socialism out of existence. Bismarck then urged the Reichstag to enact new social welfare measures to gain the allegiance of the working classes. In 1883 the Reichstag created national health insurance, followed in 1884 by accident insurance and in 1889 by old-age pensions and retirement benefits. Together, these laws created a national social security system that was the first of its kind anywhere, funded by contributions from wage earners, employers, and the state.

Under Kaiser Wilhelm I (r. 1861–1888), Bismarck had managed the domestic and foreign policies of the state. In 1890 the new emperor, Wilhelm II (r. 1888–1918), eager to rule in his own right and to earn the workers' support, forced Bismarck to resign. Following Bismarck's departure, the Reichstag passed new laws to aid workers and to legalize socialist political activity.

Although Wilhelm II was no more successful than Bismarck in getting workers to renounce socialism, in the years before World War I the Social Democratic Party broadened its base and adopted a more patriotic tone. German socialists identified increasingly with the German state and concentrated on gradual social and political reform.

Republican France

Although Napoleon III's reign made some progress in reducing antagonisms between classes, the Franco-Prussian War undid these efforts, and in 1871 France seemed hopelessly divided once again. The republicans who proclaimed the Third Republic in Paris refused to admit defeat by the Germans. They defended Paris with great heroism for weeks, until they were starved into submission by German armies in January 1871. When national elections then sent a large majority of conservatives and monarchists to the National Assembly, France's leaders decided they had no choice but to achieve peace by surrendering Alsace and Lorraine to Germany. Parisians exploded in patriotic frustration and proclaimed the Paris Commune in March 1871.

Commune leaders wanted to govern Paris without interference from the conservative French countryside. The National Assembly, led by conservative politician Adolphe Thiers, ordered the French army into Paris and brutally crushed the Commune. Twenty thousand people died in the fighting. As in June 1848, it was Paris against the provinces, French against French. Out of this tragedy France slowly formed a new national unity, achieving considerable stability before 1914.

The moderate republicans who governed France sought to preserve their creation by winning the loyalty of the next generation. Trade unions were fully legalized, and France acquired a colonial empire (see "The Scramble for Africa" in Chapter 25 and "Mainland Southeast Asia" in Chapter 26). A series of laws between 1879 and 1886 established free compulsory elementary education for both girls and boys, thereby greatly reducing the role of parochial Catholic schools, which had long been hostile to republicanism. In France and throughout the world, the general expansion of public education served as a critical nation- and nationalism-building tool in the late nineteenth century.

Although the educational reforms of the 1880s disturbed French Catholics, many of them rallied to the republic in the 1890s, and tensions between church and state eased. Unfortunately, the **Dreyfus affair** changed all that. In 1894 Alfred Dreyfus (DRY-fuss), a Jewish captain in the French army, was falsely accused and convicted of treason. In 1898 and 1899 the case split France apart. On one side was the army, which had manufactured evidence against Dreyfus, joined by anti-Semites and most of the Catholic establishment. On the other side stood the civil libertarians and most of the more radical republicans.

This battle, which eventually led to Dreyfus's being declared innocent, revived militant republican feeling against the church. Between 1901 and 1905 the government severed all ties between the state and the Catholic Church after centuries of close relations.

Dreyfus affair A divisive case in which Alfred Dreyfus, a Jewish captain in the French army, was falsely accused and convicted of treason. The Catholic Church sided with the anti-Semites against Dreyfus; after Dreyfus was declared innocent, the French government severed all ties between the state and the church.

Great Britain and the Austro-Hungarian Empire

The development of Great Britain and Austria-Hungary, two leading but quite different powers, throws a powerful light on the dynamics of nationalism in Europe before 1914. At home Britain made more of its citizens feel a part of the nation by passing consecutive voting rights bills that culminated with the establishment of universal male suffrage in 1884. Moreover, overdue social welfare measures were passed in a spectacular rush between 1906 and 1914. The ruling Liberal Party substantially raised taxes on the rich to pay for national health insurance, unemployment benefits, old-age pensions, and a host of other social measures. The state was integrating the urban masses socially as well as politically.

On the eve of World War I, however, the unanswered question of Ireland brought Great Britain to the brink of civil war. The terrible Irish famine of the 1840s and early 1850s had fueled an Irish revolutionary movement. The English slowly granted concessions, and in 1913 the British Parliament passed a bill granting Ireland self-government, or home rule.

The Irish Catholic majority in the southern counties ardently desired home rule. Irish Protestants in the northern counties of Ulster, however, vowed to resist home rule, fearing they would fall under the control of the majority Catholics. Unable to resolve the conflict as World War I started in August 1914, the British government postponed indefinitely the whole question of Irish home rule.

The Irish dilemma helps one appreciate how desperate the situation in the Austro-Hungarian Empire had become by the early twentieth century. Reacting to the upheaval of 1848, Austrian emperor Franz Joseph (r. 1848–1916) and his bureaucracy ruled Hungary as a conquered territory. This was part of broader efforts to centralize Austria and Germanize the language and culture of the different nationalities.

After its defeat by Prussia in 1866, however, a weakened Austria was forced to establish the so-called dual monarchy. The empire was divided in two, and the nationalistic Magyars gained virtual independence for Hungary. The two states were joined only by a shared monarch and common ministries for finance, defense, and foreign affairs. Still, the disintegrating force of competing nationalisms continued unabated, and the Austro-Hungarian Empire was progressively weakened and eventually destroyed by the conflicting national aspirations of its different ethnic groups. It was these ethnic conflicts in the Balkans that touched off the Great War in 1914 (see "The Outbreak of War" in Chapter 28).

Jewish Emancipation and Modern Anti-Semitism

Revolutionary changes in political principles and the triumph of the nation-state brought equally revolutionary changes in Jewish life in western and central Europe. Beginning in France in 1791, Jews gradually gained civil rights. In the 1850s and 1860s liberals in Austria, Italy, and Prussia pressed successfully for legal equality for all regardless of religion. In 1871 the constitution of the new German Empire abolished restrictions on Jewish marriage, choice of occupation, place of residence, and property ownership.

By 1871 a majority of Jews in western and central Europe had improved their economic situations and entered the middle classes. Most Jews identified strongly

"The Expulsion of the Jews from Russia" So reads this postcard, correctly suggesting that Russian government officials often encouraged popular anti-Semitism and helped drive many Jews out of Russia in the late nineteenth century. The road signs indicate that these poor Jews are crossing into Germany, where they will find a grudging welcome and a meager meal at the Jolly Onion Inn. Other Jews from eastern Europe settled in France and Britain, thereby creating small but significant Jewish populations in both countries for the first time since they had expelled most of their Jews in the Middle Ages. (Alliance Israélite Universelle, Paris, France/Archives Charmet/Bridgeman Images)

with their respective nation-states and considered themselves patriotic citizens. Exclusion from government employment and discrimination in social relations continued, however, in central Europe.

Vicious anti-Semitism reappeared after the stock market crash of 1873, beginning in central Europe. Drawing on long traditions of religious intolerance, this hostility also drew on modern, supposedly scientific ideas about Jews as a separate race (see "Science for the Masses" in Chapter 24). Anti-Semitic beliefs were particularly popular among conservatives, extremist nationalists, and people who felt threatened by Jewish competition.

Anti-Semites also created modern political parties. In Austrian Vienna in the early 1890s, Karl Lueger (LOO-guhr), the popular mayor of Vienna from 1897 to 1910, combined fierce anti-Semitic rhetoric with his support of municipal ownership of basic services. In response to spreading anti-Semitism, a Jewish journalist named Theodor Herzl (1860–1904) turned from German nationalism to advocate Jewish political nationalism, or **Zionism**, and the creation of a Jewish state.

Zionism The movement toward Jewish political nationhood started by Theodor Herzl.

Before 1914 anti-Semitism was most oppressive in eastern Europe, where Jews also suffered from terrible poverty. In the Russian Empire, where there was no Jewish emancipation and 4 million of Europe's 7 million Jewish people lived in 1880, officials used anti-Semitism to channel popular discontent away from the government. In 1881–1882 a wave of violent pogroms commenced in southern Russia. The police and the army stood aside for days while peasants assaulted Jews and looted and destroyed their property. Official harassment continued in the following decades, and many Russian Jews emigrated to western Europe and the United States.

The Socialist Movement

Socialism appealed to large numbers of working men and women in the late nineteenth century, and the growth of socialist parties after 1871 was phenomenal. By 1912 the German Social Democratic Party, which espoused Marxist principles, had millions of followers and was the Reichstag's largest party. Socialist parties also grew in other countries, and Marxist socialist parties were linked together in an international organization.

As socialist parties grew and attracted large numbers of members, they looked more and more toward gradual change and steady improvement for the working class and less and less toward revolution. Workers themselves were progressively less inclined to follow radical programs for several reasons. As workers gained the right to vote and won real benefits, their attention focused more on elections than on revolutions. Workers were also not immune to nationalistic patriotism. Nor were workers a unified social group. Perhaps most important of all, workers' standard of living rose steadily after 1850, and the quality of life improved substantially in urban areas.

The growth of labor unions reinforced this trend toward moderation. In Great Britain new unions that formed for skilled workers after 1850 avoided radical politics and concentrated on winning better wages and hours for their members through collective bargaining and compromise. After 1890 unions for unskilled workers developed in Britain.

German unions were not granted important rights until 1869, and until the Anti-Socialist Laws were repealed in 1890 the government frequently harassed them as socialist fronts. But after most legal harassment was eliminated, union member-ship skyrocketed.

The German trade unions and their leaders were thoroughgoing revisionists. **Revisionism** was an effort by various socialists to update Marxist doctrines to reflect the realities of the time. The socialist Eduard Bernstein (1850–1932) argued in his *Evolutionary Socialism* in 1899 that Marx's predictions of ever-greater poverty for work-ers had been proved false. Therefore, Bernstein suggested, socialists should reform their doctrines and win gradual evolutionary gains for workers through legislation, unions, and further economic development.

revisionism An effort by various socialists to update Marxist doctrines to reflect the realities of the time.

Socialist parties in other countries had clear-cut national characteristics. Russians and socialists in the Austro-Hungarian Empire tended to be the most radical. In Great Britain the socialist but non-Marxist Labour Party formally committed to gradual reform. In Spain and Italy anarchism, seeking to smash the state rather than the bourgeoisie, dominated radical thought and action.

In short, socialist policies and doctrines varied from country to country. Socialism itself was to a large extent "nationalized." This helps explain why almost all socialist leaders supported their governments when war came in 1914.

Chapter Summary

In 1814 the victorious allied powers sought to restore peace and stability in Europe. The conservative powers used intervention and repression as they sought to prevent the spread of subversive ideas and radical changes in politics. After 1815 ideologies of liberalism, nationalism, and socialism all developed to challenge the new order. The growth of these forces culminated in the liberal and nationalistic revolutions of 1848, revolutions that were crushed by resurgent conservative forces. In the second half of the nineteenth century Italy and Germany became unified nation-states, while Russia undertook a modernization program and struggled with popular discontent.

Living conditions in rapidly growing industrial cities declined until the mid-nineteenth century, when governments undertook major urban development, includ-ing new systems of sewerage, water supply, and public transportation. Major changes in the class structure and family life occurred, as the separate spheres ideology strength-ened, and the class structure became more complex and diversified. The prestige of science grew tremendously, and scientific discoveries, such as Darwin's theory of nat-ural selection, challenged the traditional religious understanding of the world. In the realm of literature and the arts, the Romantic movement reinforced the spirit of change. Romanticism gave way to Realism in the 1840s.

Western society became increasingly nationalistic as well as urban and industrial in the late nineteenth century. Nation-states became more responsive to the needs of their people, and they enlisted widespread support as political participation expanded, educational opportunities increased, and social security systems took shape. Even socialism became increasingly national in orientation, gathering strength as a cham-pion of working-class interests in domestic politics. Yet even though nationalism served to unite peoples, it also drove them apart and contributed to the tragic con-flicts of the twentieth century.

NOTES

1. J. McKay, *Tramways and Trolleys: The Rise of Urban Mass Transport in Europe* (Princeton, N.J.: Princeton University Press, 1976), p. 81.
2. "*La Citoyenne* in the World: Hubertine Auclert and Feminist Imperialism," *French Historical Studies* 31.1 (Winter 2009): 63–84.

CONNECTIONS

Much of world history in the past two centuries can be seen as a struggle over the unfinished legacies of the late-eighteenth-century revolutions in politics and economics. Although defeated in 1848, the new political ideologies associated with the French Revolution re-emerged decisively after 1850. Nationalism, with its commitment to the nation-state, became the most dominant of the new ideologies. National movements brought about the creation of unified nation-states in two of the most fractured regions in Europe, Germany and Italy.

After 1870 nationalism and militarism, its frequent companion, touched off increased competition between the major European powers for raw materials and markets for manufactured goods. As discussed in the next two chapters, during the last decades of the nineteenth century Europe colonized nearly all of Africa and large areas in Asia. In Europe itself nationalism promoted bitter competition between states, threatening the very progress and unity it had helped to build. In 1914 the power of unified nation-states turned on itself, unleashing an unprecedented conflict among Europe's Great Powers. Chapter 28 tells the story of this First World War.

Nationalism also sparked worldwide challenges to European dominance by African and Asian leaders who fought to liberate themselves from colonialism, and it became a rallying cry in nominally independent countries like China and Japan, whose leaders sought freedom from European and American influence and a rightful place among the world's leading nations. Chapters 25, 26, and 33 explore these developments. Likewise, Chapter 33 discusses how the problems of rapid urbanization and the huge gaps between rich and poor caused by economic transformations in America and Europe in the nineteenth century are now the concern of policymakers in Africa, Asia, and Latin America.

Another important ideology of change, socialism, remains popular in Europe, which has seen socialist parties democratically elected to office in many countries. Marxist revolutions that took absolute control of entire countries, as in Russia, China, and Cuba, occurred in the twentieth century.

CHAPTER 24 **Review and Explore**

Identify Key Terms

Identify and explain the significance of each item below.

Congress of Vienna (p. 724)

conservatism (p. 724)

liberalism (p. 726)

laissez faire (p. 726)

nationalism (p. 726)

socialism (p. 728)

bourgeoisie (p. 729)

proletariat (p. 729)

modernization (p. 734)

October Manifesto (p. 741)

germ theory (p. 743)

evolution (p. 749)

Social Darwinism (p. 750)

Romanticism (p. 751)

Dreyfus affair (p. 754)

Zionism (p. 756)

revisionism (p. 757)

Review the Main Ideas

Answer the focus questions from each section of the chapter.

1. How did the allies fashion a peace settlement in 1815, and what radical ideas emerged between 1815 and 1848? (p. 724)

2. Why did revolutions triumph briefly throughout most of Europe in 1848, and why did they fail? (p. 729)

3. How did strong leaders and nation building transform Italy, Germany, and Russia? (p. 734)

4. What was the impact of urban growth on cities, social classes, families, and ideas? (p. 742)

5. How did nationalism and socialism shape European politics in the decades before the Great War? (p. 752)

Make Comparisons and Connections

Analyze the larger developments and continuities within and across chapters.

1. How did the spread of radical ideas and the movements for reform and revolution explored in this chapter draw on the "unfinished" political and industrial revolutions of the late eighteenth century (Chapters 22, 23)?

2. How and why did the relationship between the state and its citizens change in the last decades of the nineteenth century?

3. How did the emergence of a society divided into working and middle classes affect the workplace, homemaking, and family values and gender roles?

TIMELINE

EUROPE

← ca. 1790s–1840s Romantic movement in literature and the arts

1814–1815 Congress of Vienna   ◆ 1832 Reform Bill in Britain

1845–1851
Great Famine in Ireland

1848 ◆
Revolutions in France, Austria, and Prussia

ASIA

AMERICAS

1846–1848
Mexican-American War **(Ch. 27)**

AFRICA

1800   1825   1850

Suggested Resources

BOOKS

Barnes, David S. *The Great Stink of Paris and the Nineteenth-Century Struggle Against Filth and Germs.* 2006. An outstanding introduction to sanitary developments and attitudes toward public health.

Baycroft, Timothy, and Mark Hewitson, eds. *What Is a Nation? Europe 1789–1914.* 2009. A sweeping study of nationalism in all its forms and all the processes that affected its evolution.

Berger, Stefan, ed. *A Companion to Nineteenth-Century Europe, 1789–1914.* 2006. A useful study with an up-to-date bibliography.

Coontz, Stephanie. *Marriage, A History: From Obedience to Intimacy, or How Love Conquered Marriage.* 2005. A lively inquiry into the historical background to current practice.

Fuchs, Rachel. *Gender and Poverty in Nineteenth-Century Europe.* 2005. A history of the transformation of poor women's daily lives in the nineteenth century, dealing with sexuality, death, work, and family.

Gildea, Robert. *Barricades and Borders: Europe, 1800–1914,* 2d ed. 1996. A recommended general study.

Koven, Seth. *Slumming: Sexual and Social Politics in Victorian London.* 2006. A provocative, in-depth account of middle-class encounters with the London working class in the late nineteenth century.

Malia, Martin, and Terrence Emmons. *History's Locomotives: Revolutions and the Making of the Modern World.* 2006. An ambitious comparative work of high quality.

Merriman, John. *Massacre: The Life and Death of the Paris Commune.* 2014. A gripping account of a revolutionary uprising in nineteenth-century Paris.

Otis, Laura. *Literature and Science in the Nineteenth Century: An Anthology.* 2009. A fascinating selection of writings from a time when humanities and science were not considered separate disciplines.

Sperber, Jonathan. *Karl Marx: A Nineteenth-Century Life.* 2013. An even-handed, cradle-to-grave biography of the famous revolutionary theorist.

Winks, Robin W., and Joan Neuberger. *Europe and the Making of Modernity: 1815–1914.* 2005. A grand narrative of the forces that shaped modern Europe from the Congress of Vienna to the Great War.

ca. 1840s–1890s Realism dominates Western literature

1853–1856 Crimean War

1859–1870 Unification of Italy

1866–1871 Unification of Germany

◆ 1859 Darwin, *On the Origin of Species by the Means of Natural Selection*

◆ 1861 Russian serfs freed

1851–1864 Taiping Rebellion **(Ch. 26)**

◆ 1857 Great Mutiny / Great Revolt in India **(Ch. 26)**

1861–1865 U.S. Civil War **(Ch. 27)**

◆ 1905 Revolution in Russia

1906–1914 Social reform in Britain

1904–1905 Russo-Japanese War

◆ 1898 Spanish-American War **(Ch. 27)**

1880–1914 European "scramble for Africa" **(Ch. 25)**

DOCUMENTARIES

English Poetry Anthology: The Romantic Poets (Kultur Video, 2006). Documents the Romantic poetry movement in England, featuring Wordsworth, Byron, and Keats.

Landmarks of Western Art: Romanticism (Kultur Video, 2003). Documents the Romantic movement in painting, highlighting artists such as Turner, Constable, Goya, and Géricault.

The Rise, from *Heaven on Earth: The Rise and Fall of Socialism* (PBS, 2005). The first of a three-part series, this documentary follows the rise of the socialist movement.

FEATURE FILMS

Bright Star (Jane Campion, 2009). A drama about the British Romantic poet John Keats and his relationship with Fanny Brawne, which was cut short by Keats's early death.

Frankenstein (James Whale, 1931). Based on the classic Romantic novel by Mary Shelley, the film tells the story of an obsessed scientist who creates a living being in a bizarre science experiment.

Les Misérables (Tom Hooper, 2012). Adapted from Victor Hugo's epic novel, the film portrays ex-convict Jean Valjean's pursuit of redemption. The film is also a commentary on social unrest in early-nineteenth-century France and depicts the student uprising in Paris in 1832.

WEBSITES

Heilbrunn Timeline of Art History: Romanticism. The Metropolitan Museum of Art's overview of the Romantic movement within art, along with a slide show of eighteen pieces of artwork from the period. **www.metmuseum.org/toah/hd/roma/hd_roma.htm**

Marxists Internet Archive. This archive offers a vast amount of material and sources related to Karl Marx, communism, and Communist revolutions. **marxists.org/index.htm**

25

Africa, the Ottoman Empire, and the New Imperialism
1800–1914

While industrialization and nationalism were transforming society in Europe and the neo-European countries (the United States, Canada, Australia, New Zealand, and, to an extent, South Africa), Western society itself was reshaping the world. European commercial interests went in search of new sources of raw materials and markets for their manufactured goods. At the same time, millions of Europeans and Asians emigrated abroad. What began as a relatively peaceful exchange of products with Africa and Asia in the early nineteenth century had transformed by century's end into a frenzy of imperialist occupation and domination that had a profound impact on both colonizer and colonized.

The political annexation of territory in the 1880s — the "New Imperialism," as it is often called by historians — was the capstone of Western society's underlying economic and technological transformation. More directly, Western imperialism rested on a formidable combination of superior military might and strong authoritarian rule, and it posed a brutal challenge to African and Asian peoples. Indigenous societies met this Western challenge in different ways and with changing tactics. By 1914 local elites in many lands were rallying their peoples and leading an anti-imperialist struggle for dignity and genuine independence that would triumph after 1945.

Sengbe Pieh

Enslaved in 1839, Pieh (later known as Joseph Cinqué) led a famous revolt on the slave ship *Amistad*. He and his fellow slaves were charged with mutiny and murder, but in March 1840 the U.S. Supreme Court found them innocent because they had been illegally captured and sold. They returned to their native Sierra Leone as free men.

Portrait, 1839, by Nathaniel Jocelyn (1796–1881) (oil on canvas)/Granger, NY—All rights reserved

CHAPTER PREVIEW

AFRICA: FROM THE SLAVE TRADE TO EUROPEAN COLONIAL RULE
What were the most significant changes in Africa during the nineteenth century, and why did they occur?

THE NEW IMPERIALISM, 1880–1914
What were the causes and consequences of European empire building after 1880?

THE ISLAMIC HEARTLAND UNDER PRESSURE
How did the Ottoman Empire and Egypt try to modernize themselves, and what were the most important results?

THE EXPANDING WORLD ECONOMY
What were the global consequences of European industrialization between 1800 and 1914?

THE GREAT GLOBAL MIGRATION
What fueled migration, and what was the general pattern of this unprecedented movement of people?

763

What were the most significant changes in Africa during the nineteenth century, and why did they occur?

Africa: From the Slave Trade to European Colonial Rule

In the nineteenth and early twentieth centuries the different regions of Africa experienced gradual but monumental change. The transatlantic slave trade declined and practically disappeared by the late 1860s. In the early nineteenth century Islam expanded its influence south of the Sahara Desert, and Africa still generally remained free of European political control. After about 1880 further Islamic expansion to the south stopped, but the pace of change accelerated as France and Britain led European nations in the "scramble for Africa," dividing and largely conquering the continent. By 1900 the foreigners were consolidating their authoritarian empires.

Trade and Social Change

palm oil A West African tropical product often used to make soap; the British encouraged its cultivation as an alternative to the slave trade.

The most important development in West Africa before the European conquest was the decline of the Atlantic slave trade and the simultaneous rise in exports of **palm oil** and other commodities. This shift in African foreign trade marked the beginning of modern economic development in sub-Saharan Africa.

Although the trade in enslaved Africans was a global phenomenon, the transatlantic slave trade between Africa and the Americas became the most extensive and significant portion of it (see "The Transatlantic Slave Trade" in Chapter 20). Until 1700, and perhaps even 1750, most Europeans considered the African slave trade a legitimate business activity. After 1775 a broad campaign to abolish slavery developed in Britain and grew into one of the first peaceful mass political movements based on the mobilization of public opinion in British history. British women played a critical role in this movement, denouncing the immorality of human bondage and stressing the cruel treatment of female slaves and slave families. Abolitionists also argued for a transition to legitimate (nonslave) trade to end both the transatlantic slave trade and the internal African slave systems. In 1807 Parliament declared the slave trade illegal. Britain then began using its navy to seize slave runners' ships, liberate the captives, and settle them in the British port of Freetown, in Sierra Leone, as well as in Liberia (see Map 25.1, page 767). Freed American slaves had established the colony of Liberia in 1821–1822.

British action had a limited impact at first. Britain's navy intercepted fewer than 10 percent of all slave ships, and the demand for slaves remained high on the sugar and coffee plantations of Cuba and Brazil until the 1850s and 1860s. The United States banned slave importation from January 1, 1808. From that time on, natural increase (slaves having children) mainly accounted for the subsequent growth of the African American slave population before the Civil War. Strong financial incentives remained, however, for Portuguese and other European slave traders and for those African rulers who relied on profits from the trade for power and influence.

As more nations joined Britain in outlawing the slave trade, shipments of human cargo slackened along the West African coast (see Map 25.1). At the same time the ancient but limited shipment of slaves across the Sahara and from the East African coast into the Indian Ocean and through the Red Sea expanded dramatically. Only in the 1860s did this trade begin to decline rapidly. As a result, total slave exports from all regions of sub-Saharan Africa declined only marginally, from 7.4 million in the eighteenth century to 6.1 million in the nineteenth century.[1] Abolitionists failed to achieve their vision that "legitimate trade" in tropical products would quickly replace illegal slave exports.

Nevertheless, beginning in West Africa, a legitimate trade did make steady progress for several reasons. First, with Britain encouraging palm tree cultivation as an alternative to the slave trade, palm oil sales from West Africa to Britain surged, from only one thousand tons in 1810 to more than forty thousand tons in 1855. Second, the sale of palm oil admirably served the self-interest of industrializing Europe. Manufacturers used palm oil to lubricate their giant machines and to make cheap soap and other cosmetics. Third, peanut production for export also grew rapidly, in part because both small, independent African family farmers and large-scale enterprises could produce peanuts for the substantial American and European markets.

Finally, powerful West African rulers and warlords who had benefited from the Atlantic slave trade redirected some of their slaves' labor into the production of legitimate goods for world markets. This was possible because local warfare and slave raiding continued to enslave large numbers of people in sub-Saharan Africa, so slavery and slave markets remained strong. Although some enslaved captives might still be sold abroad, now women were often kept as wives, concubines, or servants, while men were used to transport goods, mine gold, grow crops, and serve in slave armies. Thus the transatlantic slave trade's slow decline coincided with the most intensive use of slaves within Africa.

All the while, a new group of African merchants was emerging to handle legitimate trade, and some grew rich. Women were among the most successful of these merchants. There is a long tradition of West African women's active involvement in trade, but the arrival of Europeans provided new opportunities. The African wife of a European trader served as her husband's interpreter and learned all aspects of his business. When the husband died, as European men invariably did in the hot, humid, and mosquito-infested conditions of tropical West Africa, the African wife inherited his commercial interests, including his inventory and his European connections. Many such widows used their considerable business acumen to make small fortunes.

By the 1850s and 1860s legitimate African traders, flanked by Western-educated African lawyers, teachers, and journalists, had formed an emerging middle class in the West African coastal towns. Unfortunately for West Africans, in the 1880s and 1890s African business leadership gave way to imperial subordination.

Islamic Revival and Expansion in Africa

The Sudanic savanna is that vast belt of flat grasslands stretching across Africa below the Sahara's southern fringe (the Sahel). By the early eighteenth century Islam had been practiced throughout this region for five hundred to one thousand years, depending on the area. City dwellers, political rulers, and merchants in many small states were Muslim. Yet the rural peasant farmers and migratory cattle raisers—the vast majority of the population—generally held on to traditional animist practices, worshipping ancestors, praying at local shrines, and invoking protective spirits. Since many Muslim rulers shared some of these beliefs, they did not try to convert their subjects in the countryside or enforce Islamic law.

A powerful Islamic revival began in the eighteenth century and gathered strength in the early nineteenth century. In essence, Muslim scholars and fervent religious leaders arose to wage successful **jihads** (JEE-hahds), or religious wars, against both animist rulers and Islamic states they deemed corrupt. The new reformist rulers

jihad Religious war waged by Muslim scholars and religious leaders against both animist rulers and Islamic states that they deemed corrupt.

believed African cults and religious practice could no longer be tolerated, and they often effected mass conversions of animists to Islam.

Sokoto caliphate Founded in 1809 by Uthman dan Fodio, this African state was based on Islamic history and law.

The most important of these revivalist states, the **Sokoto caliphate** (SOH-kuh-toh KAL-uh-fate), illustrates the pattern of Islamic revival in Africa. It was founded by Uthman dan Fodio (AHTH-mun dahn FOH-dee-oh) (1754–1817), a Muslim teacher who first won followers among both the Fulani herders and in the Muslim state of Gobir in the northern Sudan. After his religious community was attacked by Gobir's rulers, Uthman launched the jihad of 1804, one of the most important events in nineteenth-century West Africa. Uthman claimed the Hausa rulers of Muslim Gobir "worshipped many places of idols, and trees, and rocks, and sacrificed to them," killing and plundering their subjects without any regard for Islamic law.[2] He recruited young religious students and discontented Fulani cattle raisers to form the backbone of his jihadi fighters and succeeded in overthrowing the Hausa rulers and expanding Islam into the Sudan. In 1809 Uthman established the new Sokoto caliphate (see Map 20.1).

The triumph of the Sokoto caliphate had profound consequences for Africa and the Sudan. First, the caliphate was governed by a sophisticated written constitution based on Islamic history and law. This government of laws, rather than men, provided stability and made Sokoto one of the most prosperous regions in tropical Africa. Second, because of Sokoto and other revivalist states, Islam became much more widely and deeply rooted in sub-Saharan Africa than ever before. Finally, as one historian explained, Islam had always approved of slavery for non-Muslims and Muslim heretics, and "the *jihads* created a new slaving frontier on the basis of rejuvenated Islam."[3] In 1900 the Sokoto caliphate had at least 1 million and perhaps as many as 2.5 million slaves.

Islam also expanded in East Africa. From the 1820s on, Arab merchants and adventurers pressed far into the interior in search of slaves and ivory, converting and intermarrying with local Nyamwezi (nyahm-WAY-zee) elites and establishing small Muslim states. The Arab immigrants brought literacy, administrative skills, and increased trade and international contact, as well as the intensification of slavery, to East Africa. In 1837 Sayyid Said (sa-EED sa-EED) (r. 1804–1856), the sultan of Oman, conquered Mombasa, the great port city in modern Kenya. After moving his capital from southern Arabia to the island of Zanzibar in 1840, Said gained control of most of the Swahili-speaking East African coast. He then routed all slave shipments from the coast to the Ottoman Empire and Arabia through Zanzibar. He also successfully encouraged Indian merchants to develop slave-based clove plantations in his territories. In 1870, before Christian missionaries and Western armies began to arrive in force and halt Islam's spread, it appeared that most of the East and Central African populations would accept Islam within a generation.[4]

The Scramble for Africa, 1880–1914

Between 1880 and 1914 Britain, France, Germany, Belgium, Spain, and Italy, worried that they would not get "a piece of that magnificent African cake" (in Belgian king Leopold II's graphic words), scrambled for African possessions as if their national livelihoods were at stake. In 1880 Europeans controlled barely 20 percent of the African continent, mainly along the coast; by 1914 they controlled over 90 percent. Only Ethiopia in northeast Africa and Liberia on the West African coast remained independent (Map 25.1).

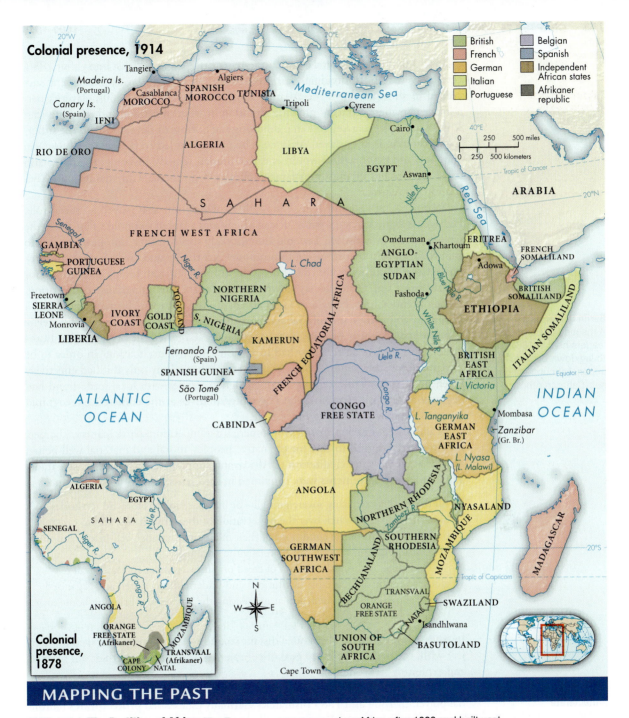

Colonial presence, 1914

Legend:
- British
- French
- German
- Italian
- Portuguese
- Belgian
- Spanish
- Independent African states
- Afrikaner republic

Madeira Is. (Portugal)
Tangier
Canary Is. (Spain)
IFNI
RIO DE ORO
Casablanca
MOROCCO
SPANISH MOROCCO
Algiers
TUNISIA
Tripoli
Cyrene
Cairo
Aswan
ARABIA
ALGERIA
LIBYA
EGYPT
Mediterranean Sea
S A H A R A
FRENCH WEST AFRICA
GAMBIA
PORTUGUESE GUINEA
Senegal R.
Niger R.
L. Chad
Omdurman
Khartoum
ERITREA
Adowa
FRENCH SOMALILAND
ANGLO-EGYPTIAN SUDAN
Fashoda
BRITISH SOMALILAND
Freetown
SIERRA LEONE
Monrovia
LIBERIA
IVORY COAST
GOLD COAST
TOGOLAND
NORTHERN NIGERIA
S. NIGERIA
KAMERUN
FRENCH EQUATORIAL AFRICA
Blue Nile R.
White Nile R.
Nile R.
ETHIOPIA
ITALIAN SOMALILAND
Fernando Pó (Spain)
SPANISH GUINEA
São Tomé (Portugal)
CABINDA
Uele R.
CONGO FREE STATE
Congo R.
BRITISH EAST AFRICA
L. Victoria
Mombasa
Zanzibar (Gr. Br.)
GERMAN EAST AFRICA
L. Tanganyika
L. Nyasa (L. Malawi)
ATLANTIC OCEAN
INDIAN OCEAN
ANGOLA
NORTHERN RHODESIA
NYASALAND
Zambezi R.
MADAGASCAR
GERMAN SOUTHWEST AFRICA
BECHUANALAND
SOUTHERN RHODESIA
MOZAMBIQUE
TRANSVAAL
SWAZILAND
ORANGE FREE STATE
NATAL
Isandhlwana
BASUTOLAND
UNION OF SOUTH AFRICA
Cape Town

Tropic of Cancer
40°E
20°N
Equator — 0°
20°S
Tropic of Capricorn
20°W
0°
20°E

0   250   500 miles
0   250   500 kilometers

Colonial presence, 1878

ALGERIA
EGYPT
SAHARA
SENEGAL
Nile R.
Niger R.
Congo R.
ANGOLA
ORANGE FREE STATE (Afrikaner)
MOZAMBIQUE
TRANSVAAL (Afrikaner)
CAPE COLONY
NATAL

MAPPING THE PAST

MAP 25.1 The Partition of Africa The European powers carved up Africa after 1880 and built vast political empires.

ANALYZING THE MAP What European countries were leading imperialist states in Africa, and what lands did they hold? What countries maintained political independence?

CONNECTIONS The late nineteenth century was the high point of European imperialism. What were the motives behind the rush for land and empire in Africa?

767

In addition to the general causes underlying Europe's imperialist burst after 1880, certain events and individuals stand out. First, as the antislavery movement succeeded in shutting down the Atlantic slave trade by the late 1860s, slavery's persistence elsewhere attracted growing attention in western Europe and the Americas. Missionaries played a key role in publicizing the horrors of slave raids and the suffering of thousands of enslaved Africans. The public was led to believe that European conquest and colonization would end this human tragedy by bringing, in Scottish missionary David Livingstone's famous phrase, "Commerce, Christianity, and Civilization" to Africa.

Second, King Leopold II (r. 1865–1909) of Belgium also played a crucial role. His agents signed treaties with African chiefs and planted Leopold's flag along the Congo River. In addition, Leopold intentionally misled other European leaders to gain their support by promising to promote Christianity and civilization in his proposed Congo Free State. By 1883 Europe had caught "African fever," and the race for territory was on. Third, to lay down some rules for this imperialist competition, French premier Jules Ferry and German chancellor Otto von Bismarck arranged a European conference on sub-Saharan Africa in Berlin in 1884–1885. The **Berlin Conference**, to which Africans were not invited, established the principle that European claims to African territory had to rest on "effective occupation" in order to be recognized by other states. A nation could establish a colony only if it had effectively taken possession of the territory through signed treaties with local leaders and had begun to develop it economically. The representatives at the conference recognized Leopold's rule over the Congo Free State.

In addition to developing rules for imperialist competition, participants at the Berlin Conference agreed to care for the native peoples' moral and material well-being, bring Christianity and civilization to Africa, and suppress slavery and the slave trade. These rules and agreements were contained in the General Act of the conference:

> All the Powers exercising sovereign rights or influence in the aforesaid territories bind themselves to watch over the preservation of the native tribes, and to care for the improvement of the conditions of their moral and material well-being, and to help in suppressing slavery, and especially the slave trade.
>
> They shall, without distinction of creed or nation, protect and favour all religious, scientific or charitable institutions and undertakings created and organized for the above ends, or which aim at instructing the natives and bringing home to them the blessings of civilization.[5]

In truth, however, these ideals ran a distant second to, and were not allowed to interfere with, the nations' primary goal of commerce — holding on to their old markets and exploiting new ones.

Fourth, the Berlin Conference coincided with Germany's emergence as an imperial power. In 1884 and 1885 Bismarck's Germany established **protectorates** (autonomous states or territories partly controlled and protected by a stronger outside power) over a number of small African kingdoms and societies (see Map 25.1). In acquiring colonies, Bismarck cooperated with France's Jules Ferry against the British. The French expanded into West Africa and also formed a protectorate on the Congo River. Meanwhile, the British began enlarging their West African enclaves and pushed northward from the Cape Colony and westward from the East African coast.

Berlin Conference
A meeting of European leaders held in 1884–1885 to lay down basic rules for imperialist competition in sub-Saharan Africa.

protectorate
An autonomous state or territory partly controlled and protected by a stronger outside power.

Brutality in the Congo No Africans suffered more violent and brutal treatment under colonial rule than those living in Belgian king Leopold II's Congo Free State. When not having their hands, feet, or heads cut off as punishment, Africans were whipped with *chicottes*, whips made of dried hippopotamus hide. Some Congolese were literally whipped to death. (© TopFoto/The Image Works)

The British also moved southward from Egypt, which they had seized in 1882 (see "Egypt: From Reform to British Occupation"), but were blocked in the eastern Sudan by fiercely independent Muslims. In 1881 a pious Sudanese leader, Muhammad Ahmad (AH-mad) (1844–1885), proclaimed himself the "Mahdi" (MAH-dee) (a messianic redeemer of Islam) and led a revolt against foreign control of Egypt. In 1885 his army massacred a British force and took the city of Khartoum (khar-TOUM), forcing the British to retreat to Cairo. Ten years later a British force returned, building a railroad to supply arms and reinforcements as it went. In 1898 these troops, under the command of Field Marshal Horatio Hubert Kitchener, met their foe at Omdurman (AHM-dur-man), where Sudanese Muslims armed with spears were cut down by the recently invented machine gun. In the end eleven thousand Muslim fighters lay dead, while only twenty-eight Britons had been killed. Their commander received the title of "Lord Kitchener of Khartoum."

All European nations resorted to some violence in their colonies to retain control, subdue the population, appropriate land, and force African laborers to work long hours at physically demanding, and often dangerous, jobs. In no colony, however, was the violence and brutality worse than in Leopold II's Congo Free State. Rather than promoting Leopold's promised Christianity and civilization, the European companies operating in the Congo Free State introduced slavery, unimaginable savagery, and terror. Missionaries and others were not even allowed into the colony, to prevent them from reporting the horrors they would witness there.

Profits in the Congo Free State came first from the ivory trade, but in the 1890s, after many of the Congo's elephant herds had been decimated, a new cash crop arose to take ivory's place. In the mid-1880s Scottish-born John Dunlop developed a process to make inflatable rubber tires. A worldwide boom in the demand for raw rubber soon followed, as new uses for rubber were found. By the mid-1890s rubber had surpassed ivory as the Congo Free State's major income producer, as more than half the colony possessed wild rubber vines growing thickly in the equatorial rain forest. The companies Leopold allowed to make profits in the Congo soon could not get enough rubber. Violence and brutality increased exponentially as Europeans and their well-armed mercenaries terrorized entire regions, cutting off hands, feet, and heads, and wiping out whole villages to send the message that Africans must either work for the Europeans or die. The shed African blood is recalled in the colony's frightening nickname—the "red rubber colony." In the first years of the nineteenth century, human rights activists such as Edmund Morel (moh-REHL) exposed the truth about the horrific conditions in the Congo Free State. In 1908 Leopold was forced to turn over his private territory to Belgium as a colony, the Belgian Congo. (See "Global Viewpoints: The Congo Free State," at right.)

Southern Africa in the Nineteenth Century

The development of southern Africa diverged from that of the rest of sub-Saharan Africa in important ways. Whites settled in large numbers, modern capitalist industry took off, and British imperialists had to wage all-out war.

When the British took possession of the Dutch Cape Colony during the Napoleonic Wars, there were about twenty thousand free Dutch citizens and twenty-five thousand African slaves, with substantial mixed-race communities on the northern frontier of white settlement. After 1815 powerful African chiefdoms; the Boers, or **Afrikaners** (descendants of the original Dutch settlers); and British colonial forces waged a complicated three-cornered battle to build strong states in southern Africa.

While the British consolidated their rule in the Cape Colony, the talented Zulu king Shaka (SHAHK-ah) (r. 1818–1828) was creating the largest and most powerful kingdom in southern Africa in the nineteenth century. Shaka's warriors, drafted by age groups and placed in highly disciplined regiments, perfected the use of a short stabbing spear in deadly hand-to-hand combat. The Zulu armies often destroyed their African enemies completely, sowing chaos and sending refugees fleeing in all directions. Shaka's wars led to the creation of Zulu, Tswana (TSWAH-nah), Swazi (SWAH-zee), Ndebele (n-deh-BELL-ee), and Sotho (SOO-too, not SOH-thoh) states in southern Africa. By 1890 these states were largely subdued by Dutch and British invaders, but only after many hard-fought frontier wars.

Between 1834 and 1838 the British abolished slavery in the Cape Colony and introduced racial equality before the law to protect African labor. In 1836 about ten thousand Afrikaner cattle ranchers and farmers, resentful of equal treatment of blacks by British colonial officials and missionaries after the abolition of slavery, began to make their so-called Great Trek northward into the interior. In 1845 another group of Afrikaners joined them north of the Orange River. Over the next thirty years Afrikaner and British settlers reached a mutually advantageous division of southern Africa. The British ruled the strategically valuable colonies of Cape Colony and Natal (nuh-TAHL) on the coast, and the Afrikaners controlled the ranch-land republics of Orange Free State and the Transvaal (TRANS-vahl) in the interior. The Zulu, Xhosa, Sotho, Ndebele, and other African peoples lost much of their land but remained the majority—albeit an exploited majority.

The discovery of incredibly rich deposits of diamonds in 1867 near Kimberley, and of gold in 1886 in the Afrikaners' Transvaal Republic around modern Johannesburg, revolutionized the southern African economy, making possible large-scale industrial capitalism and transforming the lives of all its peoples. The extraction of these minerals, particularly the deep-level gold deposits, required big foreign investment, European engineering expertise, and an enormous labor force. Thus small-scale miners soon gave way to powerful financiers, particularly Cecil Rhodes (1853–1902). Rhodes came from a large middle-class British family and at seventeen went to southern Africa to seek his fortune. By 1888 Rhodes's firm, the De Beers mining

Afrikaners Descendants of the Dutch settlers in the Cape Colony in southern Africa.

The Congo Free State

One historian estimates that between 1890 and 1910 the African population of the Congo Free State declined by nearly 10 million souls.* The public learned of the brutal conditions in the Congo through the efforts of reformers and journalists. George Washington Williams (1849–1891), an African American Baptist minister, lawyer, and historian, was dazzled, as were many others, by the noble humanitarian goals that Leopold II claimed to have for the Congo, but when Williams visited the Congo in 1890 he was sickened by what he saw. His public letter to King Leopold, excerpted below, offers one of the earliest firsthand accounts of the horrors of the Congo. Edmund Morel (1873–1924), a British clerk, was similarly galvanized to undertake a campaign against Leopold after noticing that nearly 80 percent of the goods that his shipping firm sent to the Congo were weapons, shackles, and ammunition, while arriving ships were filled with cargoes of rubber, ivory, and other high-value goods.

George Washington Williams, "An Open Letter to His Serene Majesty Leopold II," 1890

■ Your Majesty's Government has been, and is now, guilty of waging unjust and cruel wars against natives, with the hope of securing slaves and women, to minister to the behests of the officers of your Government. . . . I have no adequate terms with which to depict to your Majesty the brutal acts of your soldiers upon such raids as these. The soldiers who open the combat are usually the bloodthirsty cannibalistic Bangalas, who give no quarter to the aged grandmother or nursing child at the breast of its mother. There are instances in which they have brought the heads of their victims to their white officers on the expeditionary steamers, and afterwards eaten the bodies of slain children. In one war two Belgian Army officers saw, from the deck of their steamer, a native in a canoe some distance away. He was not a combatant and was ignorant of the conflict . . . upon the shore, some distance away. The officers made a wager of £5 that they could hit the native with their rifles. Three shots were fired and the native fell dead, pierced through the head, and the trade canoe was transformed into a funeral barge and floated silently down the river.

Edmund Morel, from *King Leopold's Rule in Africa*, 1904

■ One of the most atrocious features of the persistent warfare of which year in year out the Congo territories are the scene, is the mutilation both of the dead and of the living which goes on under it. . . . The first intimation that Congo State troops were in the habit of cutting off the hands of men, women, and children in connection with the rubber traffic reached Europe through the Rev. J. B. Murphy, of the American Baptist Missionary Union, in 1895. He described how the State soldiers had shot some people on Lake Mantumba . . . , "cut off their hands and took them to the Commissaire." The survivors of the slaughter reported the matter to a missionary at Irebu, who went down to see if it were true, and was quickly convinced by ocular demonstration. Among the mutilated victims was a little girl, not quite dead, who subsequently recovered. In a statement which appeared in the [London] *Times*, Mr. Murphy said, "These hands—the hands of men, women, and children—were placed in rows before the Commissary, who counted them to see that the soldiers had not wasted cartridges."

QUESTIONS FOR ANALYSIS

1. What factors might have allowed such horrible atrocities to be committed without greater public awareness and outcry?
2. How do these two readings exemplify the theory that the colonial experience brutalized both colonized and colonizer?

Sources: George Washington Williams, "An Open Letter to Leopold II, King of the Belgians and Sovereign of the Independent State of Congo, July 18, 1890," in John Hope Franklin, *George Washington Williams: A Biography* (Chicago: University of Chicago Press, 1985), pp. 245–246, 250–251; Edmund D. Morel, *King Leopold's Rule in Africa* (New York: Funk and Wagnalls, 1905), pp. 110–111.

*Adam Hochschild, *King Leopold's Ghost* (Boston: Houghton Mifflin, 1999), pp. 225–234.

company, monopolized the world's diamond industry and earned him fabulous profits. The "color bar" system of the diamond fields gave whites the well-paid skilled positions and put black Africans in the dangerous, low-wage jobs far below the earth's surface. Southern Africa became one of the world's leading diamond and gold producers, pulling in black migratory workers from all over the region (as it does to this day).

The mining bonanza whetted the appetite of British imperialists led by the powerful Rhodes, who was considered the ultimate British imperialist. He once famously observed that the British "happen to be the best people in the world, with the highest ideals of decency and justice and liberty and peace, and the more of the world we inhabit, the better for humanity."[6] Between 1888 and 1893 Rhodes used missionaries and his British South Africa Company, chartered by the British government, to force African chiefs to accept British protectorates, and he managed to add Southern and Northern Rhodesia (modern-day Zimbabwe and Zambia) to the British Empire.

Southern Rhodesia is one of the most egregious examples of a region where Europeans misled African rulers to take their land. In 1888 the Ndebele (or Matabele) king, Lobengula (loh-ben-GUL-ah) (1845–1894), ruler over much of modern southwestern Zimbabwe, met with three of Rhodes's men, led by Charles Rudd, and signed the Rudd Concession. Lobengula believed he was simply allowing a handful of British fortune hunters a few years of gold prospecting in Matabeleland. Lobengula had been misled, however, by the resident London Missionary Society missionary (and Lobengula's supposed friend), the Reverend Charles Helm, as to the document's true meaning and Rhodes's hand behind it. Even though Lobengula soon repudiated the agreement, he opened the way for Rhodes's seizure of the territory.

In 1889 Rhodes's British South Africa Company received a royal charter from Queen Victoria to occupy Matabeleland on behalf of the British government. Though Lobengula died in early 1894, his warriors bravely fought Rhodes's private army in the First and Second Matabele Wars (1893–1894, 1896–1897), but were decimated by British Maxim guns. By 1897 Matabeleland had ceased to exist; it had been replaced by the British-ruled settler colony of Southern Rhodesia. Before his death,

Republic Gold Mining Company, South Africa, ca. 1888 This early photo, taken only a couple of years after the discovery of gold and the beginning of the Witwatersrand gold rush, shows both black and white miners at a gold mine. By this time, twenty-one years after the discovery of diamonds at Kimberley, labor segregation had become a regular feature of mine work. White workers claimed the supervisory jobs, while blacks were limited to dangerous low-wage labor. (Bettmann Collection/Getty Images)

Lobengula asked Reverend Helm, "Did you ever see a chameleon catch a fly? The chameleon gets behind the fly and remains motionless for some time, then he advances very slowly and gently, first putting forward one leg and then the other. At last, when well within reach, he darts his tongue and the fly disappears. England is the chameleon and I am that fly."[7]

The Transvaal gold fields still remained in Afrikaner hands, however, so Rhodes and the imperialist clique initiated a series of events that sparked the South African War of 1899–1902 (also known as the Anglo-Boer War). The British needed 450,000 troops to crush the Afrikaners, who never had more than 30,000 men in the field. Often considered the first "total war," this conflict witnessed the British use of a scorched-earth strategy to destroy Afrikaner property, and concentration camps to detain Afrikaner families and their servants, thousands of whom died of illness. Africans were sometimes forced and sometimes volunteered to work for one side or the other; estimates of their number range from 15,000 to 40,000 for each side. They did everything from scouting and guard duty to heavy manual labor, driving wagons, and guarding the livestock.

The long and bitter war divided whites in South Africa, but South Africa's blacks were the biggest losers. The British had promised the Afrikaners representative government in return for surrender in 1902, and they made good on their pledge. In 1910 the Cape Colony, Natal, the Orange Free State, and the Transvaal formed a new self-governing Union of South Africa. After the peace settlement, because the white minority held almost all political power in the new union, and because Afrikaners outnumbered English-speakers, the Afrikaners began to regain what they had lost on the battlefield. South Africa, under a joint British-Afrikaner government within the British Empire, began the creation of a modern segregated society that culminated in an even harsher system of racial separation, or apartheid (uh-PAHRT-ayte), after World War II.

The South African War, 1899–1902

Colonialism's Impact After 1900

By 1900 much of Africa had been conquered and a system of colonial administration was taking shape. In general, this system weakened or shattered the traditional social order.

The self-proclaimed political goal of the French and the British — the principal colonial powers — was to provide good government for their African subjects, especially after World War I. "Good government" meant, above all, law and order. It meant a strong, authoritarian government, which maintained a small army, built up an African police force, and included a modern bureaucracy capable of taxing and governing the population. Many African leaders and their peoples had chosen not to resist the invaders' superior force, and others stopped fighting and turned to other, less violent means of resisting colonial rule. Thus the goal of law and order was widely achieved.

Colonial governments demonstrated much less interest in providing basic social services. Education, public health, hospital, and other social service expenditures increased after the Great War but still remained limited. Europeans feared the political implications of mass education and typically relied instead on the modest efforts of state-subsidized mission schools. Moreover, they tried to make even their poorest colonies pay for themselves through taxation.

Missionary School, South Africa, 1910
In this photo, African students are taught by a Roman Catholic nun. In the early days of a mission station, before a school building had been erected, nuns and priests held classes outside. Sometimes they also traveled to surrounding African villages and held classes outside there. The students were generally given a mixture of academic subject matter and religious instruction.
(© Sz Photo/Scherl/The Image Works)

Economically, the colonial goal was to draw the African interior into the world economy on terms favorable to the dominant Europeans. Railroads linking coastal trading centers to interior outposts facilitated easy shipment of raw materials out and manufactured goods in. Railroads had two other important outcomes: they allowed quick troop movements to put down local unrest, and they allowed many African peasants to earn wages for the first time.

The focus on economic development and low-cost rule explains why colonial governments were reluctant to move decisively against slavery within Africa. Officials feared that an abrupt abolition of slavery where it existed would disrupt production and lead to costly revolts by powerful slaveholding elites, especially in Muslim areas. Thus colonial regimes settled for halfway measures designed to satisfy humanitarian groups in Europe and also make all Africans, free or enslaved, participate in a market economy and work for wages. Even this cautious policy emboldened many slaves to run away, thereby facilitating a rapid decline of slavery within Africa.

Colonial governments also often imposed taxes. Payable only in labor or European currency, these taxes compelled Africans to work for their white overlords. Africans despised no aspect of colonialism more than forced labor, widespread until about 1920. In some regions, particularly in West Africa, African peasants continued to respond freely to the new economic opportunities by voluntarily shifting to export crops on their own farms. Overall, the result of these developments was an increase in wage work and production geared to the world market and a decline in nomadic herding and traditional self-sufficient farming of sustainable crops. In sum, the imposition of bureaucratic Western rule and the gradual growth of a world-oriented cash economy after 1900 had a revolutionary impact on large parts of Africa.

What were the causes and consequences of European empire building after 1880?

The New Imperialism, 1880–1914

Western expansion into Africa and Asia reached its apex between about 1880 and 1914. In those years the leading European nations sent streams of money and manufactured goods to both continents and also rushed to create or enlarge vast overseas political empires. This frantic activity differed sharply from the limited economic penetration of non-Western territories between 1816 and 1880, which had left a China or a Japan "opened" but politically independent. By contrast, late-nineteenth-century empires recalled the old European colonial empires of the seventeenth and eighteenth centuries and led contemporaries to speak of the **New Imperialism**.

Characterized by a frenzied rush to plant the flag over as many people and as much territory as possible, the most spectacular manifestation of the New Imperialism was the seizure of almost all of Africa. Less striking but equally important was Europe's extension of political control in Asia, the subject of Chapter 26.

New Imperialism The late-nineteenth-century drive by European countries to create vast political empires abroad.

Causes of the New Imperialism

Many factors contributed to the West's late-nineteenth-century rush for territory in Africa and Asia, and controversies continue to rage over interpretation of the New Imperialism. Despite complexity and controversy, however, basic causes are clearly identifiable.

Economic motives played an important role in the extension of political empires, especially of the British Empire. By the 1870s France, Germany, and the United States were rapidly industrializing. For a century Great Britain had been the "work-shop of the world," the dominant modern industrial power. Now it was losing its industrial leadership, as its share of global manufacturing output dropped from 33 percent to just 14 percent between 1870 and 1914, and facing increasingly tough competition in foreign markets. In this changing environment of widening economic internationalism, the world experienced one of the worst economic depressions in history, the Long Depression of 1873 to 1879 (originally called the Great Depression until the Great Depression of the 1930s supplanted it). To protect home industries, America and Europe (except for Britain and the Netherlands) raised tariff barriers, abandoning the century-long practice of free trade and laissez-faire capitalism. Unable to export their goods and faced with excess production, market saturation, and high unemployment, Britain, the other European powers, and the United States turned to imperial expansion, seeking African and Asian colonies to sell their products and acquire cheap raw materials. The Long Depression was arguably the single most important spark touching off the age of New Imperialism.

Economic gains from the New Imperialism proved limited, however, before 1914. The new colonies were too poor to buy much, and they offered few immediately profitable investments. Nonetheless, colonies became important for political and diplomatic reasons. Each leading European country considered them crucial to national security, military power, and international prestige.

Colonial rivalries reflected the increasing aggressiveness of Social Darwinian theories of brutal competition among races. As one prominent English economist argued in 1873, the "strongest nation has always been conquering the weaker . . . and the strongest tend to be best."[8] Thus European nations, considered as racially distinct parts of the dominant white race, had to seize colonies to prove their strength and virility. Moreover, since racial struggle was nature's inescapable law, the conquest of "inferior" peoples was just. Social Darwinism and harsh racial doctrines fostered imperialist expansion.

So, too, did the industrial world's unprecedented technological and military superiority. Three developments were crucial. First, the rapidly firing machine gun was

quinine An agent that proved effective in controlling attacks of malaria, which had previously decimated Europeans in the tropics.

an ultimate weapon in many unequal battles. Second, newly discovered **quinine** (KWIGH-nighn) effectively controlled malaria attacks, which had previously decimated Europeans in the tropics. Third, the introduction of steam power strengthened the Western powers in two ways. Militarily, they could swiftly transport their armies by sea or rail where they were most needed. Economically, steamships with ever-larger cargoes now made round-trip journeys to far-flung colonies much more quickly and economically. Small steamboats could travel back and forth along the coast and also carry goods up and down Africa's great rivers, as portrayed in the classic American film *The African Queen* (1951). Likewise, freight cars pulled by powerful steam engines—immune to disease, unlike animals and humans—replaced the thousands of African porters hitherto responsible for carrying raw materials from the interior to the coast. Never before—and never again after 1914—would the technological gap between the West and the non-Western regions of the world be so great.

Domestic political and class conflicts also contributed to overseas expansion. Conservative political leaders often manipulated colonial issues in order to divert popular attention from domestic problems and to create a false sense of national unity. Imperial propagandists relentlessly stressed that colonies benefited workers as well as capitalists, and they encouraged the masses to savor foreign triumphs and imperial glory.

Finally, special-interest groups in each country were powerful agents of expansion. Shipping companies wanted lucrative subsidies. White settlers wanted more land. Missionaries and humanitarians wanted to spread religion and stop the slave trade.

Tools for Empire Building
Western technological advances aided imperialist ambitions in Africa. The Maxim gun was highly mobile and could lay down a continuous barrage that decimated charging enemies, as in the slaughter of Muslim tribesmen at the Battle of Omdurman in Sudan. Quinine, first taken around 1850 to prevent the contraction of malaria, enabled Europeans to move safely into the African interior and overwhelm native peoples. And the development of the electromagnetic telegraph in the 1840s permitted rapid long-distance communications for the first time in history.

(quinine bottle: Science Museum, London, UK/Wellcome Images; gun: Private Collection/Peter Newark Military Pictures/Bridgeman Images; telegraph: John D. Jenkins, The Spark Museum of Electrical Invention, www.sparkmuseum.com)

Military men and colonial officials foresaw rapid advancement and high-paid positions in growing empires. The actions of such groups pushed the course of empire forward.

A "Civilizing Mission"

To rationalize their aggressive and racist actions, Europeans and Americans argued they could and should "civilize" supposedly primitive non-Western peoples. According to this view, Africans and Asians would benefit from Western educations, modern economies, cities, advanced medicine, and higher living standards and eventually might be ready for self-government and Western democracy.

European imperialists also argued that imperial government protected colonized peoples from ethnic warfare, the slave trade within Africa, and other forms of exploitation by white settlers and business people. Thus the French spoke of their sacred "civilizing mission." In 1899 Rudyard Kipling (1865–1936), perhaps the most influential British writer of the 1890s, exhorted Westerners to unselfish service in distant lands (while warning of the high costs involved) in his poem "The White Man's Burden."

> Take up the White Man's Burden—
> Send forth the best ye breed—
> Go bind your sons to exile
> To serve your captives' need,
> To wait in heavy harness,
> On fluttered folk and wild—
> Your new-caught, sullen peoples
> Half-devil and half-child.[9]

Kipling's poem, written in response to America's seizure of the Philippines after the Spanish-American War, and his concept of a **white man's burden** won wide acceptance among American imperialists. This principle was an important factor in the decision to rule, rather than liberate, the Philippines after the Spanish-American War (see "The Philippines" in Chapter 26). Like their European counterparts, these Americans believed their civilization had reached unprecedented heights, enabling them to bestow unique benefits on all "less advanced" peoples. (See "Analyzing the Evidence: Pears' Soap Advertisement," page 778.)

Imperialists also claimed that peace and stability under European or American dominion permitted the spread of Christianity. In Africa Catholic and Protestant missionaries competed with Islam south of the Sahara, seeking converts and building schools. Many Africans' first real contact with Europeans and Americans was in mission schools. Some peoples, such as the Ibo in Nigeria, became highly Christianized. Such successes in black Africa contrasted with the general failure of missionary efforts in the Islamic world and in much of Asia.

white man's burden The idea that Europeans could and should civilize more primitive nonwhite peoples and that imperialism would eventually provide nonwhites with modern achievements and higher standards of living.

Critics of Imperialism

Imperial expansion aroused sharp, even bitter, critics. One forceful attack was delivered in 1902, after the unpopular South African War, by radical English economist J. A. Hobson (1858–1940) in his *Imperialism*. Hobson contended that the rush to acquire colonies resulted from the economic needs of unregulated (by governments)

Pears' Soap Advertisement

Andrew Pears began making his transparent soap in London in 1789. Starting in the late nineteenth century, it was marketed worldwide as a product symbolizing progress in advancing Europe's "civilizing mission." Massive quantities of palm oil were shipped from Africa to Europe, where palm oil replaced whale oil as the preferred oil for oiling machinery and producing cosmetics. In 1910 the Lever brothers, William and James, bought Pears's company and sold Pears' Soap along with their own brands, including Sunlight, Lifebuoy, and Lux, under the name Lever Brothers (now Unilever). These soaps were made with palm oil from Lever plantations in the Congo and the Solomon Islands. Pears' Soap is still made today in India. Refined petroleum eventually supplanted palm oil, but contemporary brand names like Palmolive and Lever are vestiges of the days when palm oil was king.

Interestingly, the idea of cleanliness through using soap and taking baths was a relatively new "civilized" phenomenon in England. The soapmaking industry had its beginnings in the late eighteenth century. Only with the rise of the urbanized middle class in the mid-nineteenth century did cleanliness join with other Victorian values like morality, elitism, industrialism, mental and physical improvement, and Christianity. Thus using soap and taking frequent baths were practices still relatively new in England when manufacturers started advertising soap throughout the empire.

The first step towards lightening

The White Man's Burden

is through teaching the virtues of cleanliness.

Pears' Soap

is a potent factor in brightening the dark corners of the earth as civilization advances, while amongst the cultured of all nations it holds the highest place—it is the ideal toilet soap.

(© North Wind Picture Archives/Alamy Stock Photo)

QUESTIONS FOR ANALYSIS

1. Which elements or words in this advertisement suggest the Western ideal of "civilization"? Which elements or words are used to describe non-Europeans?
2. How does this advertisement relate to Europe's "civilizing mission" and the English maxim "Cleanliness is next to godliness"?
3. How can Pears' Soap lighten "the white man's burden" and brighten "the dark corners of the earth"? To whom does the phrase "the cultured of all nations" refer?

capitalism. Moreover, Hobson argued, the quest for empire diverted popular attention away from domestic reform and the need to reduce the great gap between rich and poor at home. These and similar arguments had limited appeal because most people fervently believed imperialism was economically profitable for the homeland. Both Hobson and public opinion were wrong, however. Most British and European investors put the bulk of their money in the United States, Canada, Russia, and other industrializing countries. Sub-Saharan Africa accounted for less than 5 percent of

British exports in 1890, and British investments in Africa flowed predominantly to the mines in southern African. Thus, while some sectors of the British economy did profit from imperial conquests, and trade with these conquests was greater just before the Great War than in 1870, overall profits from imperialism were marginal at best.

Hobson and many Western critics struck home, however, with their moral condemnation of whites' imperiously ruling nonwhites. Kipling and his kind were lampooned as racist bullies whose rule rested on brutality, racial contempt, and the Maxim machine gun. Polish-born novelist Joseph Conrad (1857–1924), in *Heart of Darkness* (1902), castigated the "pure selfishness" of Europeans in "civilizing" Africa.

Critics charged Europeans with applying a degrading double standard and failing to live up to their own noble ideals. At home Europeans had won or were winning representative government, individual liberties, and a certain equality of opportunity. In their empires Europeans imposed military dictatorships on Africans and Asians, forced them to work involuntarily, and discriminated against them shamelessly.

African and Asian Resistance

To African and Asian peoples, Western expansion represented a profoundly disruptive assault, which threatened traditional ruling classes, economies, and ways of life. Christian missionaries and European secular ideologies challenged established beliefs and values. African and Asian societies experienced crises of identity, although the details of each people's story varied substantially.

Initially African and Asian rulers often responded to imperialist incursions by trying to drive the unwelcome foreigners away, as in China and Japan (see "The Opium War" and "The 'Opening' of Japan" in Chapter 26). Violent antiforeign reactions exploded elsewhere again and again, but the industrialized West's superior military technology almost invariably prevailed. In addition, Europeans sought to divide and conquer by giving special powers and privileges to some individuals and groups from among the local population, including traditional leaders such as chiefs, landowners, and religious figures; and Western-educated professionals and civil servants, including police officers and military officers. These local elites recognized the imperial power realities in which they were enmeshed and manipulated them to maintain or gain authority over the masses. Some concluded that the West was superior in certain ways and that they needed to reform and modernize their societies by copying some European achievements. By ruling indirectly through a local elite (backed by the implied threat of force), relatively small numbers of Europeans could maintain control over much larger populations without constant rebellion and protest. European empires were won by force, but they were maintained by cultural as well as military and political means.

Nevertheless, imperial rule was in many ways an imposing edifice built on sand. Acceptance of European rule was shallow and weak among the colonized masses. They were often quick to follow determined charismatic personalities who came to oppose the Europeans. Such leaders always arose, both when Europeans ruled directly, or indirectly through native governments, for at least two basic reasons.

First, the nonconformists—the eventual anti-imperialist leaders—developed a burning desire for human dignity. They felt such dignity was incompatible with, and impossible under, foreign rule. Second, potential leaders found in the Western world the necessary ideologies and justification for their protest, such as liberalism, with its credo of civil liberty and political self-determination. Above all, they found themselves attracted to the nineteenth-century Western ideology of nationalism, which asserted that every people had the right to control their own destiny. After 1917 anti-imperialist revolt found another weapon in Lenin's version of Marxist socialism.

The Islamic Heartland Under Pressure

How did the Ottoman Empire and Egypt try to modernize themselves, and what were the most important results?

Stretching from West Africa into southeastern Europe and across Southwest Asia to the East Indies, Islamic civilization competed successfully with western Europe for centuries. Beginning in the late seventeenth century, however, the rising absolutist states of Austria and Russia began to challenge the Ottoman Empire and gradually to reverse Ottoman rule in southeastern Europe. In the nineteenth century European industrialization and nation building further altered the long-standing balance of power, and Western expansion eventually posed a serious challenge to Muslims everywhere.

Decline and Reform in the Ottoman Empire

Although the Ottoman Empire began a slow decline after Suleiman (SOO-lay-man) the Magnificent in the sixteenth century, the relationship between the Ottomans and the Europeans in about 1750 was still one of roughly equal strength. This parity began to change quickly and radically, however, in the later eighteenth century, as the Ottomans fell behind western Europe in science, industrial skill, and military technology.

A transformation of the army was absolutely necessary to battle the Europeans more effectively and enhance the sultanate's authority within the empire. There were two primary obstacles to change, however. First, Ottoman military weakness reflected the decline of the sultan's "slave army," the janissary corps. With time, the janissaries—boys and other slaves raised in Turkey as Muslims, then trained to serve in the Ottoman infantry's elite corps—became a corrupt and privileged hereditary caste, absolutely opposed to any military innovations that might undermine their high status. Second, the empire was no longer a centralized military state. Instead local governors were becoming increasingly independent, pursuing their own interests and even seeking to establish their own governments and hereditary dynasties.

Sultan Selim III (r. 1789–1807) understood these realities, but when he tried to reorganize the army, the janissaries refused to use any "Christian" equipment. In 1807 they revolted and executed Selim in a palace revolution, one of many that plagued the Ottoman state. Selim's successor, the reform-minded Mahmud II (r. 1808–1839), proceeded cautiously, picking loyal officers and building his dependable artillery corps. In 1826 his council ordered the janissaries to drill in the European manner. As expected, the janissaries revolted and charged the palace, where they were mowed down by the waiting artillery.

The destruction and abolition of the janissaries cleared the way for building a new army, but it came too late to stop the rise of Muhammad Ali, the Ottoman governor in Egypt. In 1831 his French-trained forces occupied the Ottoman province of Syria and appeared ready to depose Mahmud II. The Ottoman sultan survived, but only with help from Britain, Russia, and Austria. The Ottomans were saved again in 1839, after their forces were routed trying to drive Muhammad Ali from Syria. In the last months of 1840 Russian diplomatic efforts, British and Austrian naval blockades, and threatened military action convinced Muhammad Ali to return Syria to the Ottomans. European powers preferred a weak and dependent Ottoman state to a strong and revitalized Muslim entity under a leader such as Muhammad Ali.

In 1839, realizing their precarious position, liberal Ottoman statesmen launched an era of radical reforms, which lasted until 1876 and culminated in a constitution and a short-lived parliament. Known as the **Tanzimat** (TAHN-zee-maht) (literally, "regulations" or "orders"), these reforms were designed to remake the empire on a western European model. The new decrees called for Muslim, Christian, and Jewish equality before the law and in business, security of life and property, and a modernized administration and military. New commercial laws allowed free importation of foreign goods, as British advisers demanded, and permitted foreign merchants to operate freely throughout an economically dependent empire. Under British pressure, slavery in the empire was drastically curtailed, though not abolished completely. Of great significance, growing numbers among the elite and the upwardly mobile embraced Western education, adopted Western manners and artistic styles, and accepted secular values to some extent.

Intended to bring revolutionary modernization such as that experienced by Russia under Peter the Great (see "Peter the Great and Russia's Turn to the West" in Chapter 18) and by Japan in the Meiji era (see "The Meiji Restoration" in Chapter 26), the Tanzimat achieved only partial success. The Ottoman state and society failed to regain its earlier power and authority for several reasons. First, implementation of the reforms required a new generation of well-trained and trustworthy officials, and that generation did not exist. Second, the liberal reforms failed to halt the growth of nationalism among Christian subjects in the Balkans (discussed below), which resulted in crises and defeats that undermined all reform efforts. Third, the Ottoman initiatives did not curtail the appetite of Western imperialism, and European bankers gained a

Tanzimat A set of radical reforms designed to remake the Ottoman Empire on a western European model.

Pasha Halim Receiving Archduke Maximilian of Austria As this painting suggests, Ottoman leaders became well versed in European languages and culture. They also mastered the game of power politics, playing one European state against another and securing the Ottoman Empire's survival. The black servants on the right may be slaves from the Sudan. (Miramare Palace, Trieste, Italy/De Agostini Picture Library/Gianni Dagli Orti/Bridgeman Images)

stranglehold on Ottoman finances. In 1875 the Ottoman state had to declare partial bankruptcy and place its finances in the hands of European creditors.

Finally, the elaboration—at least on paper—of equal rights for citizens and religious communities failed to create greater unity within the state. Religious disputes increased, worsened by the Great Powers' relentless interference. This development embittered relations between religious communities, distracted the government from its reform mission, and split Muslims into secularists and religious conservatives. Islamic conservatives became the most dependable supporters of Sultan Abdülhamid II (ahb-DUHL-ah-mid) (r. 1876–1909), who abandoned the model of European liberalism in his long and repressive reign.

Meanwhile, the Ottoman Empire gradually lost control of its vast territories. Serbian nationalists rebelled and forced the Ottomans to grant Serbia local autonomy in 1816. The Greeks revolted against Ottoman rule in 1821 and won their national independence in 1830. As the Ottomans dealt with these uprisings by their Christian subjects in Europe, they failed to defend their Islamic provinces in North Africa. In 1830 French armies began their conquest of the Arabic-speaking province of Algeria.

Finally, during the Russo-Turkish War (1877–1878), absolutist Russia and a coalition of Balkan countries pushed southward into Ottoman lands and won a decisive victory. At the Congress of Berlin in 1878, the European Great Powers and the Ottoman Empire met to formally recognize Bulgarian, Romanian, Serbian, and Montenegrin independence. The Ottomans also lost territory to the Russians in the Caucasus, Austria-Hungary occupied the Ottoman provinces of Bosnia-Herzegovina (BAHZ-nee-uh HERT-suh-go-vee-nuh) and Novi Pazar (NOH-vi PAH-zar), and Great Britain took over Cyprus (SIGH-pruhs). The Ottoman Empire, now labeled the "sick man of Europe" in the European press, left the meeting significantly weakened and humiliated.

The combination of declining international power and conservative tyranny eventually led to a powerful resurgence of the modernizing impulse among idealistic Turkish exiles in Europe and young army officers in Istanbul. These fervent patriots, the so-called **Young Turks**, seized power in the 1908 revolution, overthrowing Sultan Abdülhamid II. They made his brother Mehmed V (r. 1909–1918) the figurehead sultan and forced him to implement reforms. The Young Turks helped prepare the way for the birth of modern secular Turkey after the defeat and collapse of the Ottoman Empire in World War I.

Egypt: From Reform to British Occupation

The ancient land of the pharaohs had been ruled by a succession of foreigners from 525 B.C.E. to the Ottoman conquest in the early sixteenth century. In 1798, as France and Britain prepared for war in Europe, Napoleon Bonaparte invaded Egypt, thereby threatening British access to India, and occupied the territory for three years. Into the power vacuum left by the French withdrawal stepped an extraordinary Albanian-born Turkish general, Muhammad Ali (1769–1849).

Appointed Egypt's governor by Sultan Selim III in 1805, Muhammad Ali set out to build his own state on the strength of a large, powerful army organized along European lines. He also reformed the government and promoted modern industry. (See "Individuals in Society: Muhammad Ali," at right.) For a time Muhammad Ali's

Ottoman Decline in the Balkans, 1818–1830

Young Turks Fervent patriots who seized power in the revolution of 1908, forcing the conservative sultan to implement reforms; they helped pave the way for the birth of modern secular Turkey.

Muhammad Ali

Muhammad Ali, the Albanian-born ruler of Egypt, in 1839.
(Mary Evans Picture Library/The Image Works)

THE DYNAMIC LEADER MUHAMMAD ALI STANDS across the history of modern Egypt like a colossus. Yet the essence of the man remains a mystery, and historians vary greatly in their interpretations of him. Sent by the Ottomans, with Albanian troops, to oppose the French occupation of Egypt in 1799, Muhammad Ali maneuvered skillfully after the French withdrawal in 1802. In 1805 he was named pasha, or Ottoman governor, of Egypt. Only the Mamluks remained as rivals. Originally an elite corps of Turkish slave soldiers, the Mamluks had become a semifeudal military ruling class living off the Egyptian peasantry. In 1811 Muhammad Ali offered to make peace, and he invited the Mamluk chiefs and their retainers to a banquet in Cairo's Citadel. As the unsuspecting guests processed through a narrow passage, his troops opened fire, slaughtering all the Mamluk leaders.

After eliminating his foes, Muhammad Ali embarked on a program of radical reforms. He reorganized agriculture and commerce, reclaiming most of the cultivated land for the state domain, which he controlled. He also established state agencies to monopolize, for his own profit, the sale of agricultural goods. Commercial agriculture geared to exports to Europe developed rapidly, especially after the successful introduction of high-quality cotton in 1821. Canals and irrigation systems along the Nile were rebuilt and expanded.

Muhammad Ali used his growing revenues to recast his army along European lines. He recruited French officers to train the soldiers. As the military grew, so did the need for hospitals, schools of medicine and languages, and secular education. Young Turks and some Egyptians were sent to Europe for advanced study. The ruler boldly financed factories to produce uniforms and weapons, and he prohibited the importation of European goods so as to protect Egypt's infant industries. In the 1830s state factories were making one-fourth of Egypt's cotton into cloth. Above all, Muhammad Ali drafted Egyptian peasants into the military for the first time, thereby expanding his army to one hundred thousand men. It was this force that conquered the Ottoman province of Syria, threatened the sultan in Istanbul, and triggered European intervention. Grudgingly recognized by his Ottoman overlord as Egypt's hereditary ruler in 1841, Muhammad Ali nevertheless had to accept European and Ottoman demands to give up Syria and abolish his monopolies and protective tariffs. The old ruler then lost heart; his reforms languished, and his factories disappeared.

In the attempt to understand Muhammad Ali and his significance, many historians have concluded that he was a national hero, the "founder of modern Egypt." His ambitious state-building projects—hospitals, schools, factories, and the army—were the basis for an Egyptian reawakening and eventual independence from the Ottomans' oppressive foreign rule. Similarly, state-sponsored industrialization promised an escape from poverty and Western domination, which was foiled only by European intervention and British insistence on free trade.

A growing minority of historians question these views. They see Muhammad Ali primarily as an Ottoman adventurer. In their view, he did not aim for national independence for Egypt, but rather "intended to carve out a small empire for himself and for his children after him."* Paradoxically, his success, which depended on heavy taxes and brutal army service, led to Egyptian nationalism among the Arabic-speaking masses, but that new nationalism was directed against Muhammad Ali and his Turkish-speaking entourage. Continuing research into this leader's life will help resolve these conflicting interpretations.

QUESTIONS FOR ANALYSIS

1. Which of Muhammad Ali's actions support the interpretation that he was the founder of modern Egypt? Which actions support the opposing view?
2. After you have studied Chapter 26, compare Muhammad Ali and the Meiji reformers in Japan. What accounts for the similarities and differences?

*K. Fahmy, *All the Pasha's Men: Mehmed Ali, His Army, and the Making of Modern Egypt* (Cambridge: Cambridge University Press, 1997), p. 310.

ambitious strategy seemed to work, but it eventually foundered when his armies occupied Syria and he threatened the Ottoman sultan, Mahmud II. In the face of European military might and diplomatic entreaties, Muhammad Ali agreed to peace with his Ottoman overlords and withdrew. In return he was given unprecedented hereditary rule over Egypt and Sudan. By his death in 1849, Muhammad Ali had established a strong and virtually independent Egyptian state within the Ottoman Empire.

To pay for a modern army and industrialization, Muhammad Ali encouraged the development of commercial agriculture geared to the European market, which had profound social implications. Egyptian peasants had been largely self-sufficient, growing food on state-owned land allotted to them by tradition. High-ranking officials and members of Muhammad Ali's family began carving private landholdings out of the state domain, and they forced the peasants to grow cash crops for European markets.

Muhammad Ali's modernization policies attracted growing numbers of Europeans to the banks of the Nile. Europeans served as army officers, engineers, doctors, government officials, and police officers. Others worked in trade, finance, and shipping. Above all, Europeans living in Egypt combined with landlords and officials to continue steering commercial agriculture toward exports. As throughout the Ottoman Empire, Europeans enjoyed important commercial and legal privileges and formed an economic elite.

The Suez Canal, 1869

In 1863 Muhammad Ali's grandson Ismail began his sixteen-year rule (r. 1863–1879) as Egypt's khedive (kuh-DEEV), or prince. He was a westernizing autocrat who received his education at France's leading military academy and dreamed of European technology and capital to modernize Egypt and build a vast empire in northwestern Africa. He promoted cotton production, and exports to Europe soared. Ismail also borrowed large sums, and with his support the Suez Canal was completed by a French company in 1869, shortening the voyage from Europe to Asia by thousands of miles. Cairo acquired modern boulevards and Western hotels. As Ismail proudly declared, "My country is no longer in Africa, we now form part of Europe."[10]

Major cultural and intellectual changes accompanied the political and economic ones. The Arabic of the masses, rather than the conqueror's Turkish, became the official language, and young, European-educated Egyptians helped spread new skills and ideas in the bureaucracy. A host of writers, intellectuals, and religious thinkers responded to the novel conditions with innovative ideas that had a powerful impact in Egypt and other Muslim societies.

Three influential figures who represented broad families of thought were especially significant. The teacher and writer Jamal al-Din al-Afghani (jah-MAL al-DIN al-af-GHAN-ee) (1838/39–1897) argued for the purification of Islamic religious belief, Muslim unity, and a revolutionary overthrow of corrupt Muslim rulers and foreign exploiters. The more moderate Muhammad Abduh (AHB-duh) (1849–1905) launched the modern Islamic reform movement. Abduh concluded that Muslims should adopt a flexible, reasoned approach to change, modernity, science, social questions, and foreign ideas and not reject these out of hand.

Finally, the writer Qasim Amin (KAH-zim ah-MEEN) (1863–1908) represented those who found inspiration in the West in the late nineteenth century. In his influential book *The Liberation of Women* (1899), Amin argued forcefully that superior

Egyptian Travel Guide Ismail's efforts to transform Cairo were fairly successful. As a result, European tourists could more easily visit the country that their governments dominated. Ordinary Europeans were lured to exotic lands by travel books like this colorful "Official Guide" to an exhibition on Cairo held in Berlin. (Private Collection/Archives Charmet/Bridgeman Images)

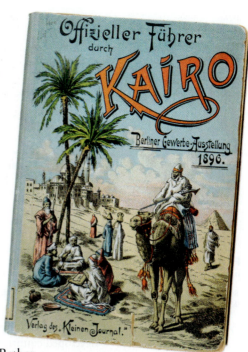

education for European women had contributed greatly to the Islamic world's falling far behind the West. In his view, the rejuvenation of Muslim societies required greater equality for women:

> History confirms and demonstrates that the status of women is inseparably tied to the status of a nation. Where the status of a nation is low, reflecting an uncivilized condition for that nation, the status of women is also low, and when the status of a nation is elevated, reflecting the progress and civilization of that nation, the status of women in that country is also elevated.[11]

Egypt changed rapidly during Ismail's rule, but his projects were reckless and enormously expensive. By 1876 the Egyptian government could not pay the interest on its colossal debt. Rather than let Egypt go bankrupt and repudiate its loans, France and Great Britain intervened, forcing Ismail to appoint French and British commissioners to oversee Egyptian finances. This meant that Europeans would determine the state budget and in effect rule Egypt.

Foreign financial control evoked a violent nationalistic reaction. Continuing diplomatic pressure, which forced Ismail to abdicate in favor of his weak son, Tewfiq (teh-FEEK) (r. 1879–1892), resulted in bloody anti-European riots in Alexandria in 1882. In response, the British fleet bombarded Alexandria, and a British expeditionary force occupied all of Egypt. British armies remained in Egypt until 1956.

Initially the British maintained the fiction that Egypt was an autonomous province of the Ottoman Empire, but the khedive was a mere puppet. In reality, the British consul, General Evelyn Baring, later Lord Cromer, ruled the country after 1883. Baring was a paternalistic reformer. He initiated tax reforms and made some improvements to conditions for peasants. Foreign bondholders received their interest payments, while Egyptian nationalists chafed under foreign rule.

The Expanding World Economy

Over the course of the nineteenth century the Industrial Revolution expanded and transformed economic relations across the face of the earth. As a result, the world's total income grew as never before, and international trade boomed. Western nations used their superior military power to force non-Western nations to open their doors to Western economic interests. Consequently, the largest share of the ever-increasing gains from trade flowed to the West, resulting in a stark division between rich and poor countries.

What were the global consequences of European industrialization between 1800 and 1914?

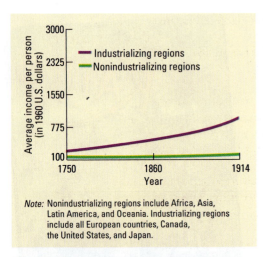

Note: Nonindustrializing regions include Africa, Asia, Latin America, and Oceania. Industrializing regions include all European countries, Canada, the United States, and Japan.

FIGURE 25.1 The Growth of Average Income per Person Worldwide, 1750–1914

(Source of data: P. Bairoch and M. Lévy-Leboyer, eds., *Disparities in Economic Development Since the Industrial Revolution* [New York: Macmillan, 1980].)

The Rise of Global Inequality

From a global perspective, the ultimate significance of the Industrial Revolution was that it allowed those world regions that industrialized in the nineteenth century to increase their wealth and power enormously in comparison with those that did not. A gap between the industrializing regions (Europe, North America, Japan) and the nonindustrializing regions (mainly Africa, Asia, and Latin America) opened and grew steadily throughout the nineteenth century (Figure 25.1). Moreover, this pattern of uneven global development became institutionalized, built into the structure of the world economy. Thus evolved a world of economic haves and have-nots, with the have-not peoples and nations far outnumbering the haves.

In 1750 the average living standard was no higher in Europe as a whole than in the rest of the world. By 1914 the average person in the wealthiest countries had an income four or five times as great (and in Great Britain nine or ten times as great) as an average person's income in the poorest countries of Africa and Asia. The rise in average income and well-being reflected the rising level of industrialization in Great Britain and then in the other developed countries before World War I.

The reasons for these enormous income disparities have generated a great deal of debate. One school of interpretation stresses that the West used science, technology, capitalist organization, and even its critical worldview to create its wealth and greater physical well-being. An opposing school argues that the West used its political, economic, and military power to steal much of its riches through its rapacious colonialism in the nineteenth and twentieth centuries.

These issues are complex, and there are few simple answers. As noted in Chapter 23, the wealth-creating potential of technological improvement and more intensive capitalist organization was great. At the same time, the initial breakthroughs in the late eighteenth century rested in part on Great Britain's having already used political force to dominate a substantial part of the world economy. In the nineteenth century other industrializing countries joined with Britain to extend Western dominion over the entire world economy. Unprecedented wealth was created, but the lion's share of that new wealth flowed to the West and its propertied classes and to a tiny indigenous elite of cooperative rulers, landowners, and merchants.

The World Market

World trade was a powerful stimulus to economic development in the nineteenth century. In 1913 the value of world trade was about twenty-five times what it had been in 1800, even though prices of manufactured goods and raw materials were lower in 1913 than in 1800. In a general way, this enormous increase in international commerce summed up the growth of an interlocking world economy centered in Europe.

Great Britain played a key role in using trade to tie the world together economically. In 1815 Britain already possessed a colonial empire, including India, Canada, and Australia. The technological breakthroughs of the Industrial Revolution encouraged British manufacturers to seek export markets around the world. After Parliament repealed laws restricting grain importation in 1846, Britain also became the world's leading importer of foreign goods. Free access to Britain's market stimulated the development of mines and plantations in Africa and Asia.

The conquest of distance facilitated the growth of trade. Wherever railroads were built, they drastically reduced transportation costs, opened new economic opportunities, and called forth new skills and attitudes.

Much of the railroad construction undertaken in Africa, Asia, and Latin America connected seaports with inland cities and regions, as opposed to linking and developing cities and regions within a country. Thus railroads dovetailed with Western economic interests, facilitating the inflow and sale of Western manufactured goods and the export and development of local raw materials.

Steam power also revolutionized transportation by sea. Steam power was first used to supplant sails on the world's oceans in the late 1860s. Passenger and freight rates tumbled, and the shipment of low-priced raw materials from one continent to another became feasible.

The revolution in land and sea transportation helped European settlers seize vast, thinly populated territories and produce agricultural products and raw materials for sale in Europe. Improved transportation enabled Asia, Africa, and Latin America to export not only the traditional tropical products — spices, dyes, tea, sugar, coffee — but also new raw materials for industry, such as jute, rubber, cotton, and peanut and coconut oil. Intercontinental trade was enormously facilitated by the Suez Canal in Egypt and the Panama Canal in Central America. Of great importance, too, was large and continual investment in modern port facilities, which made loading and unloading cheaper, faster, and more dependable. Finally, transoceanic telegraph cables inaugurated rapid communications among the world's financial centers and linked world commodity prices in a global network.

The growth of trade and the conquest of distance encouraged Europeans to make massive foreign investments beginning about 1840, but not to European colonies or protectorates in Asia and Africa. About three-quarters of total European investment went to other European countries, the United States and Canada, Australia and New Zealand, and Latin America. Here booming, industrializing economies offered the most profitable investment opportunities. Much of this investment was peaceful and mutually beneficial for lenders and borrowers. The victims were Native Americans, Australian Aborigines (AB-or-ij-uh-nees), New Zealand Maoris (MAO-reez), and other native peoples who were displaced and decimated by the diseases, liquor, and weapons of an aggressively expanding Western society.

The Great Global Migration

A poignant human drama was interwoven with this worldwide economic expansion: millions of people left their ancestral lands in one of history's greatest migrations, the so-called **great migration**. In the early eighteenth century the world's population entered a period of rapid growth that continued unabated through the nineteenth and twentieth centuries. Europe's population (including Asiatic Russia) more than doubled during the nineteenth century, from approximately 188 million in 1800 to roughly 432 million in 1900. Since African and Asian populations increased more slowly than those in Europe, Europeans and peoples of predominantly European origin jumped from about 22 percent of the world's total in 1850 to a high of about 38 percent in 1930.

What fueled migration, and what was the general pattern of this unprecedented movement of people?

great migration The mass movement of people from Europe in the nineteenth century; one reason that the West's impact on the world was so powerful and complex.

Rapid population growth led to relative overpopulation in area after area in Europe and was a driving force behind emigration and Western expansion. Millions of country folk moved to nearby cities, and the more adventuresome went abroad, in search of work and economic opportunity. Some governments encouraged their excess populations to emigrate, even paying part of their expenses. Wars, famine, poverty, and, particularly in the case of Russian and eastern European Jews, bigotry and discrimination were also leading causes for emigrants to leave their ancestral homelands. More than 60 million people left Europe over the course of the nineteenth century, primarily for the rapidly growing "areas of European settlement" — North and South America, Australia, New Zealand, and Siberia. European emigration crested in the first decade of the twentieth century, when more than five times as many men and women departed as in the 1850s.

The European migrant was most often a small peasant landowner or a village craftsman whose traditional way of life was threatened by too little land, estate agriculture, and cheap factory-made goods. Determined to maintain or improve their precarious status, the vast majority of migrants were young and often unmarried. Many European migrants eventually returned home after some time abroad. Moreover, when the economic situation improved at home or when people began to win basic political and social reforms, migration slowed.

Ties of family and friendship played a crucial role in the movement of peoples. Over several years a given province or village might lose significant numbers of its inhabitants to migration. These people then settled together in rural enclaves or tightly knit urban neighborhoods in foreign lands thousands of miles away. Very often a strong individual — a businessman, a religious leader — blazed the way, and others followed, forming a **migration chain**.

migration chain The movement of peoples in which one strong individual blazes the way and others follow.

A substantial number of Asians — especially Chinese, Japanese, Indians, and Filipinos — also responded to population pressure and rural hardship with temporary or permanent migration. At least 3 million Asians moved abroad before 1920. Most went as indentured laborers to work on the plantations or in the gold mines of Latin America, southern Asia, Africa, California, Hawaii, and Australia. White estate owners often used Asians to replace or supplement black Africans after the suppression of the Atlantic slave trade.

Asian migration would undoubtedly have been much greater if planters and mine owners desiring cheap labor had had their way. But usually they did not. Asians fled the plantations and gold mines as soon as possible, seeking greater opportunities in trade and towns. Here, however, they came into conflict with white settlers, who demanded a halt to Asian immigration. By the 1880s Americans and Australians were building **great white walls** — discriminatory laws designed to keep Asians out.

great white walls Discriminatory laws passed by Americans and Australians to keep Asians from settling in their countries in the 1880s.

The general policy of "whites only" in the lands of large-scale European settlement meant that Europeans and people of European ancestry reaped the main benefits of the great migration. By 1913 people in Australia, Canada, and the United States all had higher average incomes than did people in Great Britain, still Europe's wealthiest nation. This, too, contributed to Western dominance in the increasingly lopsided world.

Within Asia and Africa the situation was different. Migrants from south China frequently settled in Dutch, British, and French colonies of Southeast Asia, where they established themselves as peddlers and small shopkeepers. These "overseas Chinese" gradually emerged as a new class of entrepreneurs and office workers. Traders from India and modern-day Lebanon performed the same function in much of sub-

Mulberry Street, New York, ca. 1900
This photo captures the vibrancy and energy of Manhattan's Lower East Side at the height of new immigration to America from around the 1880s to the early 1920s. Mulberry Street, and many others such as Delancey, Bowery, Orchard, and Hester, were home to millions of newly arrived immigrants from all over the world. Leaving their small, crowded tenement rooms, they would fill the streets with a cacophony of languages, dress, music, and the smell of exotic foods. (Image Asset Management/IAM/akg-images)

Saharan Africa after European colonization in the late nineteenth century. Thus in some parts of Asia and Africa the business class was both Asian and foreign, protected and tolerated by Western imperialists who found these business people useful.

Chapter Summary

Following Europe's Industrial Revolution in the late eighteenth and early nineteenth centuries, European demands for raw materials and new markets reoriented Africa's economy. The transatlantic slave trade declined dramatically as Africans began producing commodities for export. This legitimate trade in African goods proved profitable and led to the emergence of a small black middle class. Islam revived and expanded until about 1870.

After 1880 a handful of Western nations seized most of Africa and parts of Asia and rushed to build authoritarian empires. The reasons for this empire building included trade rivalries, competitive nationalism in Europe, and self-justifying claims of a civilizing mission. European nations' unprecedented military superiority enabled them to crush resistance and impose their will.

The Ottoman Empire and Egypt prepared to become modern nation-states in the twentieth century by introducing reforms to improve the military, provide technical and secular education, and expand personal liberties. They failed, however, to defend themselves from Western imperialism. The Ottoman Empire lost territory but survived in a weakened condition. Egypt's Muhammad Ali reformed the government and promoted modern industry, but Egypt went bankrupt and was conquered and ruled by Britain. Western domination was particularly bitter for most Muslims because they saw it as profaning Islam and taking away their political independence.

Population pressures at home and economic opportunities abroad caused millions of European emigrants to resettle in the sparsely populated areas of European settlement in North and South America, Australia, and Asiatic Russia. Migration from Asia was much more limited, mainly because European settlers raised high barriers to prevent the settlement of Asian immigrants.

NOTES

1. P. Lovejoy, *Transformations in Slavery: A History of Slavery in Africa*, 2d ed. (Cambridge: Cambridge University Press, 2000), p. 142.
2. Quoted in J. Iliffe, *Africans: The History of a Continent* (Cambridge: Cambridge University Press, 1995), p. 169.
3. Lovejoy, *Transformations in Slavery*, p. 15.
4. R. Oliver, *The African Experience* (New York: Icon Editions, 1991), pp. 164–166.
5. Quoted in H. Wheaton, *Elements of International Law* (London: Stevens & Sons, 1889), p. 804.
6. Quoted in Bernard Porter, *The Lion's Share: A Short History of British Imperialism, 1850–1970* (London: Longman, 1975), p. 134.
7. Quoted in Anthony Thomas, *Rhodes* (New York: St. Martin's Press, 1996), p. 194.
8. Walter Bagehot, *Physics and Politics, or Thoughts on the Application of the Principle of "Natural Selection" and "Inheritance" to Political Society* (New York: D. Appleton, 1873), pp. 43, 49.
9. Rudyard Kipling, *The Five Nations* (London, 1903).
10. Quoted in Earl of Cromer, *Modern Egypt* (London, 1911), p. 48.
11. Qasim Amin, *The Liberation of Women and The New Woman* (The American University of Cairo Press, 2000), p. 6.

CONNECTIONS

By the end of the nineteenth century broader industrialization across Europe increased the need for raw materials and markets, and with it came a rush to create or enlarge vast political empires abroad. The New Imperialism was aimed primarily at Africa and Asia, and in the years before 1914 the leading European nations not only created empires abroad, but also continued to send massive streams of migrants, money, and manufactured goods around the world. (The impact of this unprecedented migration is taken up in the next two chapters.) This political empire building contrasted sharply with the economic penetration of non-Western territories between 1816 and 1880, which had allowed Africa to develop a "legitimate trade" and end the transatlantic slave trade, and which left China and Japan "opened" but politically independent, as Chapter 26 will show.

European influence also grew in the Middle East. Threatened by European military might, modernization, and Christianity, Turks and Arabs tried to implement reforms that would assure their survival and independence but also endeavored to retain key aspects of their cultures, particularly Islam. Although they made important advances in the modernization of their economies and societies, their efforts were not enough to overcome Western imperialism. With the end of World War I and the collapse of the Ottoman Empire, England and France divided much of the Middle East into colonies and established loyal surrogates as rulers in other, nominally independent, countries. Chapter 29 will take up the story of these developments.

Easy imperialist victories over weak states and poorly armed non-Western peoples encouraged excessive pride and led Europeans to underestimate the fragility of their accomplishments. Imperialism also made nationalism more aggressive and militaristic. As European imperialism was dividing the world after the 1880s, the leading European states were also dividing themselves into two opposing military alliances. As Chapter 28 will show, when the two armed camps stumbled into war in 1914, the results were disastrous. World War I set the stage for a new anti-imperialist struggle in Africa and Asia for equality and genuine independence, the topic of Chapters 31 and 32.

CHAPTER 25 Review and Explore

Identify Key Terms

Identify and explain the significance of each item below.

palm oil (p. 764)

jihad (p. 765)

Sokoto caliphate (p. 766)

Berlin Conference (p. 768)

protectorate (p. 768)

Afrikaners (p. 770)

New Imperialism (p. 775)

quinine (p. 776)

white man's burden (p. 777)

Tanzimat (p. 781)

Young Turks (p. 782)

great migration (p. 787)

migration chain (p. 788)

great white walls (p. 788)

Review the Main Ideas

Answer the focus questions from each section of the chapter.

1. What were the most significant changes in Africa during the nineteenth century, and why did they occur? (p. 764)

2. What were the causes and consequences of European empire building after 1880? (p. 774)

3. How did the Ottoman Empire and Egypt try to modernize themselves, and what were the most important results? (p. 780)

4. What were the global consequences of European industrialization between 1800 and 1914? (p. 785)

5. What fueled migration, and what was the general pattern of this unprecedented movement of people? (p. 787)

Make Comparisons and Connections

Analyze the larger developments and continuities within and across chapters.

1. Explain the transitions in Africa from the slave trade to legitimate trade to colonialism in the late eighteenth and nineteenth centuries. How was Europe's Industrial Revolution (Chapter 23) related to these transitions?

2. Europeans had been visiting Africa's coasts for four hundred years before colonizing the entire continent in thirty years in the second half of the nineteenth century. Why hadn't they colonized Africa earlier, and what factors allowed them to do it then?

3. What were the causes of the great migration in the late nineteenth and early twentieth centuries?

TIMELINE

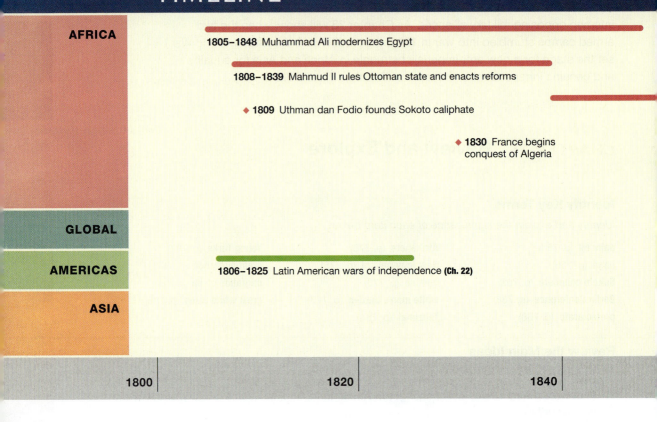

AFRICA

1805–1848 Muhammad Ali modernizes Egypt

1808–1839 Mahmud II rules Ottoman state and enacts reforms

◆ 1809 Uthman dan Fodio founds Sokoto caliphate

◆ 1830 France begins conquest of Algeria

GLOBAL

AMERICAS

1806–1825 Latin American wars of independence **(Ch. 22)**

ASIA

| 1800 | 1820 | 1840 |

Suggested Resources

BOOKS

Bagachi, Amiya Kumar. *Perilous Passage: Mankind and the Ascendancy of Capital*. 2005. A spirited radical critique of Western imperialism.

Conklin, Alice. *A Mission to Civilize: The French Republican Ideal and West Africa, 1895–1930*. 1997. An outstanding examination of French imperialism.

Cook, Scott B. *Colonial Encounters in the Age of High Imperialism*. 1996. A stimulating and very readable overview.

Coquery-Vidrovitch, Catherine. *Africa and the Africans in the Nineteenth Century: A Turbulent History*. 2009. English translation of a highly regarded history by a premier African scholar.

Findley, C. *The Turks in World History*. 2005. An exciting reconsideration of the Turks in long-term perspective.

Harper, Marjory, and Stephen Constantine. *Migration and Empire*. 2010. A comparative study of migration throughout the British Empire.

Headrick, Daniel R. *Tools of Empire*. 1991. Stresses technological superiority in Western expansion.

Hochschild, Adam. *King Leopold's Ghost: A Story of Greed, Terror, and Heroism in Colonial Africa*. 1999. The definitive account of King Leopold II's Congo and the human rights crusaders who exposed its horrors.

Hourani, Albert. *A History of the Arab Peoples*, 2d ed. 2010. Offers brilliant insights on developments in the nineteenth century.

Law, Robin, ed. *From Slave Trade to "Legitimate" Commerce: The Commercial Transition in Nineteenth-Century West Africa*. 2002. Leading scholars describe the transition to legitimate trade from an African perspective.

Lovejoy, P. *Transformations in Slavery: A History of Slavery in Africa*, 3d ed. 2012. A fine synthesis of current knowledge.

Medard, Henri, and Shane Doyle. *Slavery in the Great Lakes Region of East Africa*. 2007. A significant contribution to the understudied story of slavery in East Africa, mainly in the nineteenth and early twentieth centuries.

1884–1885 Berlin Conference   **1899–1902** South African War

1880–1914 Most of Africa falls under European rule; height of New Imperialism in Asia and Africa

1839–1876 Western-style reforms (Tanzimat) in Ottoman Empire

◆ **1899** Kipling, "The White Man's Burden"; Amin, *The Liberation of Women*

◆ **1869** Completion of Suez Canal

1902 ◆ Conrad, *Heart of Darkness*; Hobson, *Imperialism*

1908 ◆ Young Turks seize power in Ottoman Empire

1870s–1914 Second Industrial Revolution **(Ch. 23)**

1861–1865 U.S. Civil War **(Ch. 27)**

◆ **1898** Spanish-American War **(Ch. 27)**

1859–1885 French conquest of Vietnam **(Ch. 26)**

◆ **1858** Completion of British rule over India **(Ch. 26)**

◆ **1867** Meiji Restoration in Japan **(Ch. 26)**

1911 ◆ Chinese revolution **(Ch. 26)**

1860   1880   1900

Meredith, Martin. *Diamonds, Gold, and War: The British, the Boers, and the Making of South Africa.* 2007. An excellent account of the British scramble for South Africa from 1806 to the South African War (1899–1902).

Nugent, Walter. *Crossings: The Great Transatlantic Migrations, 1870–1914.* 1992. A classic study of migration history.

Wright, John. *The Trans-Saharan Slave Trade.* 2007. A well-researched study of slavery in a long-neglected region of Africa.

DOCUMENTARIES

Africa: A Voyage of Discovery with Basil Davidson (Home Vision, 1984). An eight-part series about African history and society. See particularly episode 5, "The Bible and the Gun"; and episode 6, "The Magnificent African Cake."

King Leopold's Ghost (Pippa Scott and Oreet Rees, 2006). Based on Adam Hochschild's bestselling book by the same title, this documentary recounts the history of King Leopold II's Congo in all its brutality and horror.

The Ottomans: Europe's Muslim Emperors (BBC, 2013). A three-part BBC documentary that tells the history of the Ottoman Empire from its founding in the late thirteenth century to its downfall in the Great War.

FEATURE FILM

Mountains of the Moon (Bob Rafelson, 1990). A beautifully filmed telling of the efforts by two English explorers, Sir Richard Burton and John Speke, to find the source of the Nile River in the late 1850s and early 1860s.

WEBSITE

"Imperialism" in the *Internet Modern History Sourcebook.* A valuable reference site for historical sources on New Imperialism, from a global perspective, including primary sources, analyses, and links to other related websites. **sourcebooks.fordham.edu /halsall/mod/modsbook34.asp**

26

Asia and the Pacific in the Era of Imperialism
1800–1914

During the nineteenth century the societies of Asia underwent enormous changes as a result of population growth, social unrest, and the looming presence of Western imperialist powers. At the beginning of the century Spain, the Netherlands, and Britain had colonies in the Philippines, modern Indonesia, and India, respectively. By the end of the century much more land — most of the southern tier of Asia, from India to the Philippines — had been made colonies of Western powers. Most of these colonies became tied to the industrializing world as exporters of agricultural products or raw materials, including timber, rubber, tin, sugar, tea, cotton, and jute. The Western presence brought benefits, especially to educated residents of major cities, where the colonizers often introduced modern public health, communications, and educational systems. Still, cultural barriers between the colonizers and the colonized were huge, and the Western presence rankled.

Not all the countries in Asia were reduced to colonies. Although Western powers put enormous pressures on China and exacted many concessions from it, China remained politically independent. Much more impressively, Japan became the first non-Western nation to meet the many-sided challenge of Western expansion. Japan emerged from the nineteenth-century crisis stronger than any other Asian nation, becoming the first non-Western country to industrialize successfully. By the end of this period Japan had become an imperialist power itself.

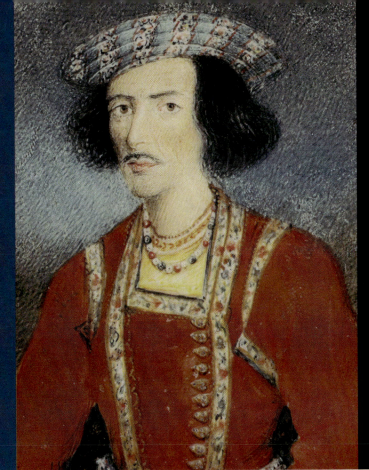

Rammohun Roy

The expansion of British power in India posed intellectual and cultural challenges to the native elite. Among those who rose to this challenge was writer and reformer Rammohun Roy, depicted here.

Victoria and Albert Museum, London, UK/V&A Images/Art Resource, NY

CHAPTER PREVIEW

INDIA AND THE BRITISH EMPIRE IN ASIA
In what ways did India change as a consequence of British rule?

COMPETITION FOR SOUTHEAST ASIA
Why were most but not all Southeast Asian societies reduced to colonies?

CHINA UNDER PRESSURE   Was China's decline in the nineteenth century due more to internal problems or to Western imperialism?

JAPAN'S RAPID TRANSFORMATION
How was Japan able to quickly master the challenges posed by the West?

THE PACIFIC REGION AND THE MOVEMENT OF PEOPLE
What were the causes and consequences of the vast movement of people in the Pacific region?

THE COUNTRIES OF ASIA IN COMPARATIVE PERSPECTIVE
What explains the similarities and differences in the experiences of Asian countries in this era?

In what ways did India change as a consequence of British rule?

India and the British Empire in Asia

Arriving in India on the heels of the Portuguese in the seventeenth century, the British East India Company outmaneuvered French and Dutch rivals and was there to pick up the pieces as the Mughal Empire decayed during the eighteenth century (see "From the British East India Company to the British Empire in India" in Chapter 17). By 1757 the company had gained control over much of India. During the nineteenth century the British government replaced the company, progressively unified the subcontinent, and harnessed its economy to British interests.

Travel and communication between Britain and India became much faster, safer, and more predictable in this period. The time it took to travel to India from Britain dropped from six months to three weeks, due both to the development of steamships and the 1869 opening of the Suez Canal. Whereas at the beginning of the nineteenth century someone in England had to wait a year or more to get an answer to a letter sent to India, by 1870 it took only a couple of months—or, if the matter was urgent, only a few hours by telegraph.

The Evolution of British Rule

In India the British ruled with the cooperation of local princely allies, whom they could not afford to offend. To assert their authority, the British disbanded and disarmed local armies, introduced simpler private property laws, and enhanced the powers of local princes and religious leaders, both Hindu and Muslim. The British administrators were on the whole competent and concerned about the welfare of the Indian peasants. Slavery was outlawed and banditry suppressed, and new laws designed to improve women's position in society were introduced. Sati (widow suicide) was outlawed in 1829, legal protection of widow remarriage was extended in 1856, and infanticide (disproportionately of female newborns) was banned in 1870.

Great Mutiny / Great Revolt The terms used by the British and the Indians, respectively, to describe the last armed resistance to British rule in India, which occurred in 1857.

The last armed resistance to British rule occurred in 1857. By that date the British military presence in India had grown to include two hundred thousand Indian sepoy troops and thirty-eight thousand British officers. In 1857 groups of sepoys, especially around Delhi, revolted in what the British called the **Great Mutiny** and the Indians called the **Great Revolt**. The sepoys' grievances were many, ranging from the use of fat from cows (sacred to Hindus) and pigs (regarded as filthy by Muslims) to grease rifle cartridges to high tax rates and the incorporation of low-caste soldiers into the army. The insurrection spread rapidly throughout northern and central India before it was finally crushed, primarily by native troops from other parts of India loyal to the British. Thereafter, although princely states were allowed to continue, Britain ruled India much more tightly. Moreover, the British in India acted more like an occupying power and mixed less with the Indian elite.

After 1858 India was ruled by the British Parliament in London and administered by a civil service in India, the upper echelons of which were all white. In 1900 this elite consisted of fewer than 3,500 top officials for a population of 300 million.

The Great Mutiny / Great Revolt, 1857

The Socioeconomic Effects of British Rule

The impact of British rule on the Indian economy was multifaceted. In the early stages, the British East India Company expanded agricultural production, creating

Breakfast at Home In India the families of British civil servants could live more comfortably than they could back home. The artist Augustus Jules Bouvier captured their lifestyle in this 1842 engraving. (Private Collection/The Stapleton Collection/Bridgeman Images)

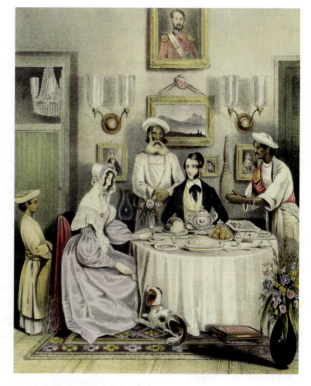

large plantations. Early crops were opium to export to China (see "The Opium War") and tea to substitute for imports from China. India gradually replaced China as the leading exporter of tea to Europe. Clearing land for tea and coffee plantations, along with massive commercial logging operations, led to extensive deforestation.

To aid the transport of goods, people, and information, the colonial administration invested heavily in India's infrastructure. By 1855 India's major cities had all been linked by telegraph and railroads, and postal service was being extended to local villages. By 1900 the rail network extended 25,000 miles, serving 188 million passengers. By then over 370,000 Indians worked for the railroads. Irrigation also received attention, and by 1900 India had the world's most extensive irrigation system.

At the same time, Indian production of textiles suffered a huge blow. Britain imported India's raw cotton but exported machine-spun yarn and machine-woven cloth, displacing millions of Indian hand-spinners and hand-weavers. By 1900 India was buying 40 percent of Britain's cotton exports. Not until 1900 were small steps taken toward industrializing India. By 1914 about a million Indians worked in factories.

Although the economy expanded, the poor did not see much improvement in their standard of living. Tenant farming and landlessness increased with the growth in plantation agriculture. Increases in production were eaten up by increases in population, which, as noted, had reached approximately 300 million by 1900. There was also a negative side to improved transportation. As Indians traveled more widely on the convenient trains, disease spread, especially cholera, which is transmitted by exposure to contaminated water. Pilgrims customarily bathed in and drank from sacred pools and rivers, worsening this problem. Despite improvements made to sanitation, in 1900 four out of every one thousand residents of British India still died of cholera each year.

The British and the Indian Educated Elite

The Indian middle class probably gained more than the poor from British rule, because they were the ones to benefit from the English-language educational system Britain established in India. Missionaries also established schools with Western curricula, and 790,000 Indians were attending some 24,000 schools by 1870. High-caste Hindus came to form a new elite profoundly influenced by Western thought and culture.

By creating a well-educated, English-speaking Indian elite and a bureaucracy aided by a modern communication system, the British laid the groundwork for a unified, powerful state. Britain placed under the same general system of law and administration the various Hindu and Muslim peoples of the subcontinent who had resisted one another for centuries. University graduates tended to look on themselves as Indians more than as residents of separate states and kingdoms, a necessary step for the development of Indian nationalism.

Some Indian intellectuals sought to reconcile the values of the modern West and their own traditions. Rammohun Roy (1772–1833), who had risen to the top of the native ranks in the British East India Company, founded a college that offered instruction in Western languages and subjects. He also founded a society to reform traditional customs, especially child marriage, the caste system, and restrictions on widows. He espoused a modern Hinduism founded on the *Upanishads* (oo-PAH-nih-shadz), the ancient sacred texts of Hinduism.

The more that Western-style education was developed in India, the more the inequalities of the system became apparent to educated Indians. Indians were eligible to take the examinations for entry into the elite **Indian Civil Service**, the bureaucracy that administered the Indian government, but the exams were given in England. Since few Indians could travel such a long distance to take the test, in 1870 only 1 of the 916 members of the service was Indian. In other words, no matter how Anglicized educated Indians became, they could never become the white rulers' equals. The top jobs, the best clubs, the modern hotels, and even certain railroad compartments were sealed off to brown-skinned men and women. Most of the British elite considered the jumble of Indian peoples and castes to be racially inferior. For example, when the British Parliament in 1883 was considering a bill to allow Indian judges to try white Europeans in India, the British community rose in protest and defeated the measure. As Lord Kitchener, one of the most distinguished British military commanders in India, stated:

> It is this consciousness of the inherent superiority of the European which has won for us India. However well educated and clever a native may be, and however brave he may prove himself, I believe that no rank we can bestow on him would cause him to be considered an equal of the British officer.[1]

The peasant masses might accept such inequality as the latest version of age-old class and caste hierarchies, but the well-educated, English-speaking elite eventually could not. They had studied not only Milton and Shakespeare but also English traditions of democracy, liberty, and national pride.

In the late nineteenth century the colonial ports of Calcutta, Bombay, and Madras, now all linked by railroads, became centers of intellectual ferment. In these and other cities, newspapers in English and in regional languages gained influence. Lawyers trained in English law began agitating for Indian independence. By 1885, when a group of educated Indians came together to found the **Indian National Congress**, demands were increasing for the equality and self-government that Britain had already granted white-settler colonies such as Canada and Australia. The Congress Party called for more opportunities for Indians in the Indian Civil Service and reallocation of the government budget from military expenditures to the alleviation of poverty. The party advocated unity across religious and caste lines, but most members were upper-caste, Western-educated Hindus.

Indian Civil Service
The bureaucracy that administered the government of India. Entry into its elite ranks was through examinations that Indians were eligible to take, but these tests were offered only in England.

Indian National Congress
A political association formed in 1885 that worked for Indian self-government.

Wooden Model of a Colonial Courtroom The presiding judge, an officer with the British East India Company, is seated on a chair with his top hat on the table. The Indian assistants are seated on the floor, and the plaintiffs and defendants in the case are standing. Notice the attention the Indian craftsman paid to the details of the dress and hats of each of the figures in this 20-inch-long wooden model. (Victoria and Albert Museum, London, UK/V&A Images/Art Resource, NY)

Defending British possessions in India became a key element of Britain's foreign policy during the nineteenth century and led to steady expansion of the territory Britain controlled in Asia. By 1852 the British had annexed Burma (now Myanmar), administering it as a province of India (Map 26.1). The establishment of a British base in Singapore was followed by expansion into Malaya (now Malaysia) in the 1870s and 1880s. In both Burma and Malaya, Britain tried to foster economic development, building railroads and promoting trade. Burma became a major exporter of timber and rice, Malaya of tin and rubber. So many laborers were brought into Malaya for the expanding mines and plantations that its population came to be approximately one-third Malay, one-third Chinese, and one-third Indian.

Competition for Southeast Asia

At the beginning of the nineteenth century only a small part of Southeast Asia was under direct European control. By the end of the century most of the region would be in foreign hands.

> Why were most but not all Southeast Asian societies reduced to colonies?

The Dutch East Indies

Although Dutch forts and trading posts in the East Indies dated back to the seventeenth century, in 1816 the Dutch ruled little more than the island of Java. Thereafter they gradually brought almost all of the 3,000-mile-long archipelago under their political authority. In extending their rule, the Dutch, like the British in India, brought diverse peoples with different languages and distinct cultural traditions into a single political entity (see Map 26.1).

Taking over the Dutch East India Company in 1799, the Dutch government modified the company's loose control of Java and gradually built a modern bureaucratic state. Javanese resistance to Dutch rule led to the bloody **Java War** (1825–1830). In 1830, after the war, the Dutch abolished the combination of tribute from rulers and forced labor from peasants that they had used to obtain spices, and they established instead a particularly exploitive policy called the Culture System. Under this system, Indonesian peasants were forced to plant a fifth of their land in export crops, especially coffee and sugar, to turn over to the Dutch as tax.

At the end of the nineteenth century the Dutch began to encourage Western education in the East Indies. The children of local rulers and privileged elites, much like

> **Java War** The 1825–1830 war between the Dutch government and the Javanese, fought over the extension of Dutch control of the island.

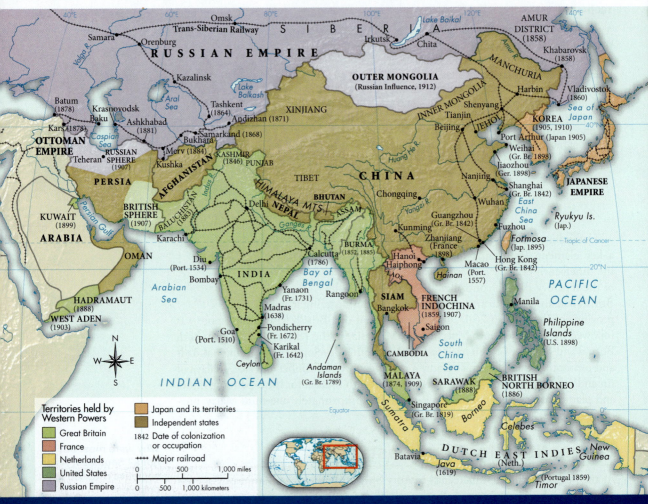

MAP 26.1 Asia in 1914

MAP 26.1 Asia in 1914 India remained under British rule, while China precariously preserved its political independence. The Dutch Empire in modern-day Indonesia was old, but French control of Indochina was a product of the New Imperialism.

ANALYZING THE MAP Consider the colonies of the different powers on this map. What European countries were leading imperialist states, and what lands did they hold? Can you see places where colonial powers were likely to come into conflict with each other?

CONNECTIONS Do the sizes of the various colonial territories as seen on this map adequately reflect their importance to the countries that possessed them? If not, what else should be taken into account in thinking about the value of these sorts of colonial possessions?

their counterparts in India, encountered new ideas in Dutch-language schools. They began to question the long-standing cooperation of local elites with Dutch colonialism, and they searched for a new national identity. Thus anticolonial nationalism began to take shape in the East Indies in the early twentieth century, and it would blossom after World War I.

Mainland Southeast Asia

Unlike India and Java, mainland Southeast Asia had escaped European rule during the eighteenth century. In 1802 the **Nguyen Dynasty** (1802–1945) came to power in Vietnam, putting an end to thirty years of peasant rebellion and civil war. For the first time in the country's history, a single Vietnamese monarchy ruled the entire country. Working through a centralizing scholar bureaucracy fashioned on the Chinese model, the Nguyen (GWIHN) Dynasty energetically built irrigation canals, roads and bridges, and impressive palaces in Hue (HWAY), the new capital city. Construction placed a heavy burden on the peasants drafted to do the work, and this hardship contributed to a resurgence of peasant unrest.

Roman Catholic missionaries from France posed a second, more dangerous threat to Vietnam's Confucian ruling elite. The king and his advisers believed that Christianity would undermine Confucian moral values and the unity of the Vietnamese state. In 1825 King Minh Mang (r. 1820–1841) outlawed the teaching of Christianity, and soon his government began executing Catholic missionaries and Vietnamese converts. As many as thirty thousand Vietnamese Christians were executed in the 1850s. In response, in 1859–1860 a French naval force seized Saigon and three surrounding provinces in southern Vietnam, making that part of Vietnam a French colony. In 1884–1885 France launched a second war against Vietnam and conquered the rest of the country. Laos and Cambodia were added to form French Indochina in 1887. In all three countries the local rulers were left on their thrones, but France dominated and tried to promote French culture.

After the French conquest, Vietnamese patriots continued to resist the colonial occupiers. After Japan's victory over Russia in 1905 (see "Japan as an Imperial Power"), a new generation of nationalists saw Japan as a model for Vietnamese revitalization and freedom. They went to Japan to study and planned for anticolonial revolution in Vietnam.

In all of Southeast Asia, only Siam (today Thailand) succeeded in preserving its independence. Siam was sandwiched between the British in Burma and the French in Indochina. Siam's very able king, Chulalongkorn (r. 1868–1910), took advantage of this situation to balance the two competitors against each other. Chulalongkorn had studied Greek and Latin and Western science and kept up with Western news by reading British newspapers from Hong Kong and Singapore. He outlawed slavery and implemented modernizing reforms that centralized the government so that it could more effectively control outlying provinces coveted by the imperialists.

Nguyen Dynasty The last Vietnamese ruling house, which lasted from 1802 to 1945.

The French Governor General and the Vietnamese Emperor
The twelfth emperor of the Nguyen Dynasty, Khai Dinh (1885–1925), had to find ways to get along with the French governor general (in this picture, Albert Sarraut) if he wished to preserve his dynasty. Seen here in 1917 or 1918, he had adopted Western leather shoes but otherwise tried to keep a distinct Vietnamese identity in his dress. (Maurice-Louis Branger/Roger-Viollet/Getty Images)

Independent Siam gradually developed a modern centralizing state similar to those constructed by Western imperialists in their Asian possessions.

The Philippines

The United States became one of the imperialist powers in Asia when it took the Philippines from Spain in 1898. When the Spanish established rule in the Philippines in the sixteenth century, the islands had no central government or literate culture; order was maintained by village units dominated by local chiefs. Under the Spanish, Roman Catholic churches were established, and Spanish priests able to speak the local languages became the most common intermediaries between local populations, who rarely could speak Spanish, and the new rulers. The government of Spain encouraged Spaniards to colonize the Philippines through the encomienda system (see "Indigenous Population Loss and Economic Exploitation" in Chapter 16); Spaniards who had served the Crown were rewarded with grants giving them the exclusive right to control public affairs and collect taxes in a specific locality of the Philippines. A local Filipino elite also developed, aided by the Spanish introduction of private ownership of land. Manila developed into an important entrepôt in the galleon trade between Mexico and China, and this trade also attracted a large Chinese community, which handled much of the trade within the Philippines.

In the late nineteenth century wealthy Filipinos began to send their sons to study abroad, and a movement to press Spain for reforms emerged among those who had been abroad. When the Spanish cracked down on critics, a rebellion erupted in 1896. (See "Individuals in Society: José Rizal," at right.)

In 1898 war between Spain and the United States broke out in Cuba (see "The Spanish-American War" in Chapter 27), and in May the American naval commodore George Dewey sailed into Manila Bay and sank the Spanish fleet anchored there. Dewey called on the Filipino rebels to help defeat the Spanish forces, but when the rebels declared independence, the U.S. government refused to recognize them. U.S. forces fought the Filipino rebels, and by the end of the insurrection in 1902 the war had cost the lives of five thousand Americans and about two hundred thousand Filipinos. In the following years the United States introduced a form of colonial rule that included public works and economic development projects, improved education and medicine, and, in 1907, an elected legislative assembly.

Was China's decline in the nineteenth century due more to internal problems or to Western imperialism?

China Under Pressure

In 1800 most Chinese had no reason to question the concept of China as the central kingdom. A century later China's world standing had sunk precipitously. In 1900 foreign troops marched into China's capital to protect foreign nationals, and more and more Chinese had come to think that their government, society, and cultural values needed to be radically changed.

The Opium War

Seeing little to gain from trade with European countries, the Qing (Manchu) emperors, who had been ruling China since 1644 (see "The Rise of the Manchus" in Chapter 21), permitted Europeans to trade only at the port of Guangzhou (Canton) and only through licensed Chinese merchants. Initially, the balance of trade was in

José Rizal

IN THE MID-SEVENTEENTH CENTURY A CHINESE merchant immigrated to the Philippines and married a woman who was half Chinese, half Filipino. Because of anti-Chinese animosity, he changed his name to Mercado, Spanish for "merchant."

Mercado's direct patrilineal descendant José Rizal (1861–1896) was born into a well-to-do family that leased a plantation from Dominican friars. Both of his parents were educated, and he was a brilliant student himself. In 1882, after completing his studies at the Jesuit-run college in Manila, he went to Madrid to study medicine. During his ten years in Europe he not only earned a medical degree in Spain and a Ph.D. in Germany but also found time to learn several European languages and make friends with scientists, writers, and political radicals.

While in Europe, Rizal became involved with Filipino revolutionaries and contributed numerous articles to their newspaper, *La Solidaridad*, published in Barcelona. Rizal advocated making the Philippines a province of Spain, giving it representation in the Spanish parliament, replacing Spanish friars with Filipino priests, and making Filipinos and Spaniards equal before the law. He spent a year at the British Museum doing research on the early phase of the Spanish colonization of the Philippines. He also wrote two novels.

The first novel, written in Spanish, was fired by the passions of nationalism. In satirical fashion, it depicts a young Filipino of mixed blood who studies for several years in Europe before returning to the Philippines to start a modern secular school in his hometown and to marry his childhood sweetheart. The church stands in the way of his efforts, and the colonial administration proves incompetent. The novel ends with the hero

José Rizal. (The Library of Congress, Prints and Photographs Division, LC-USZ62-43453)

being gunned down after the friars falsely implicate him in a revolutionary conspiracy. Rizal's own life ended up following this narrative surprisingly closely.

In 1892 Rizal left Europe, stopped briefly in Hong Kong, and then returned to Manila to help his family with a lawsuit. Though he secured his relatives' release from jail, he ran into trouble himself. Because his writings were critical of the power of the church, he made many enemies, some of whom had him arrested. He was sent into exile to a Jesuit mission town on the relatively primitive island of Mindanao. There he founded a school and a hospital, and the Jesuits tried to win him back to the church. He kept busy during his four years in exile, not only teaching English, science, and self-defense, but also maintaining his correspondence with scientists in Europe. When a nationalist secret society rose in revolt in 1896, Rizal, in an effort to distance himself, volunteered to go to Cuba to help in an outbreak of yellow fever. Although he had no connections with the secret society and was on his way across the ocean, Rizal was arrested and shipped back to Manila.

Tried for sedition by the military, Rizal was found guilty. When handed his death certificate, Rizal struck out the words "Chinese half-breed" and wrote "pure native." He was publicly executed by a firing squad in Manila at age thirty-five, making him a martyr of the nationalist cause.

QUESTIONS FOR ANALYSIS

1. How did Rizal's comfortable family background contribute to his becoming a revolutionary?
2. How would Rizal's European contemporaries have reacted to his opposition to the Catholic Church?

China's favor. Great Britain and the other Western nations used silver to pay for tea, since they had not been able to find anything the Chinese wanted to buy. By the 1820s, however, the British had found something the Chinese would buy: opium. Grown legally in British-occupied India, opium was smuggled into China, where its use and sale were illegal. Huge profits and the cravings of addicts led to rapid increases in sales, from 4,500 chests a year in 1810 to 10,000 in 1830 and 40,000 in 1838. At this point it was China that suffered a drain of silver, since it was importing more than it was exporting.

To deal with this crisis, the Chinese government dispatched Lin Zexu to Guangzhou in 1839. He dealt harshly with Chinese who purchased opium and seized the opium stores of British merchants. Lin even wrote to Queen Victoria: "Suppose there were people from another country who carried opium for sale to England and seduced your people into buying and smoking it; certainly your honorable ruler would deeply hate it and be bitterly aroused."[2] Although for years the little community of foreign merchants had accepted Chinese rules, by 1839 the British, the dominant group, were ready to flex their muscles. British merchants wanted to create a market for their goods in China and get tea more cheaply by trading closer to its source in central China. They also wanted a European-style diplomatic relationship with China, with envoys and ambassadors, commercial treaties, and published tariffs. With the encouragement of their merchants in China, the British sent an expeditionary force from India with forty-two warships.

With its control of the seas, the British easily shut down key Chinese ports and forced the Chinese to negotiate. Dissatisfied with the resulting agreement, the British sent a second, larger force, which took even more coastal cities, including Shanghai. This **Opium War** was settled at gunpoint in 1842. The Treaty of Nanjing and subsequent agreements opened five ports to international trade, fixed the tariff on imported goods at 5 percent, imposed an indemnity of 21 million ounces of silver on China to cover Britain's war expenses, and ceded the island of Hong Kong to Britain. Through the clause on **extraterritoriality** (the legal principle that exempts individuals from local law), British subjects in China became answerable only to British law, even in disputes with Chinese. The treaties also had a "most-favored nation" clause, which meant that whenever one nation extracted a new privilege from China, it was extended automatically to Britain.

The treaties satisfied neither side. China continued to refuse to accept foreign diplomats at its capital in Beijing, and the expansion of trade fell far short of Western expectations. Between 1856 and 1860 Britain and France renewed hostilities with China. British and French troops occupied Beijing and set the emperor's summer palace on fire. Another round of harsh treaties gave European merchants and missionaries greater privileges and forced the Chinese to open several more cities to foreign trade.

Internal Problems

China's problems in the nineteenth century were not all of foreign origin. By 1850 China, for centuries the world's most populous country, had more than 400 million people. As the population grew, farm size shrank, forests were put to the plow, surplus labor suppressed wages, and conflicts over rights to water and tenancy increased. Hard times also led to increased female infanticide, as families felt that they could

Opium War The 1839–1842 war between the British and the Chinese over limitations on trade and the importation of opium into China.

extraterritoriality The legal principle that exempts individuals from local law, applicable in China because of the agreements reached after China's loss in the Opium War.

not afford to raise more than two or three children and saw sons as necessities. (See "Global Viewpoints: Chinese and British Efforts to Reduce Infant Deaths," page 806.)

These economic and demographic circumstances led to some of the most destructive rebellions in China's history. The worst was the **Taiping Rebellion** (1851–1864), in which some 20 million people lost their lives, making it one of the bloodiest wars in world history.

The Taiping (TIGH-ping) Rebellion was initiated by Hong Xiuquan (hong shoh-chwan) (1814–1864). After reading a Christian tract given to him by a missionary, Hong interpreted visions he had had to mean he was Jesus's younger brother and had a mission to wipe out evil in China. He soon gathered followers, whom he instructed to destroy idols and ancestral temples, give up opium and alcohol, and renounce foot binding and prostitution. In 1851 he declared himself king of the Heavenly Kingdom of Great Peace (Taiping), an act of open insurrection.

By 1853 the Taiping rebels, as Hong's followers were known, had moved north and established their capital at the major city of Nanjing, which they held on to for a decade. From this base they set about creating a utopian society based on the equalization of landholdings and the equality of men and women. To suppress the Taipings, the Manchus had to turn to Chinese scholar-officials, who raised armies on their own, revealing the Manchus' military weakness.

The Self-Strengthening Movement

After the various rebellions were suppressed, forward-looking reformers began addressing the Western threat. Under the slogan "self-strengthening," they set about modernizing the military along Western lines. Some of the most progressive reformers also initiated new industries, which in the 1870s and 1880s included railway lines, steam navigation companies, coal mines, telegraph lines, and cotton spinning and weaving factories.

Chinese Rebellions, 1851–1911

Taiping Rebellion
A massive rebellion by believers in the religious teachings of Hong Xiuquan, begun in 1851 and not suppressed until 1864.

Hong Kong Tailors In 1872 the newspaper *Shenbao* was founded in Shanghai, and in 1884 it added an eight-page weekly pictorial supplement. Influenced by the pictorial press then popular in Europe, it depicted both news and human interest stories, both Chinese and foreign, helping readers understand all of the social and cultural changes then taking place. This scene shows a tailor shop in Hong Kong where Chinese tailors use sewing machines and make women's clothes in current Western styles. To Chinese readers, men making women's clothes and placing them on bamboo forms would have seemed as peculiar as the style of the dresses. (From *Dianshizhai huabao*, a Shanghai picture magazine, 1885 or later/Visual Connection Archive)

Chinese and British Efforts to Reduce Infant Deaths

In the premodern world, infant survival was precarious. Chinese scholars knew that one reason was infanticide among the poor. In the first document, from the 1840s, the Chinese scholar You Zhi describes setting up a private charity to provide small payments to poverty-stricken parents so that they would not kill a newborn child. This charitable practice can be compared to the foundling hospitals put in place in England in the 1760s. Jonas Hanway, the English author of the second document, does not accuse parents of deliberately killing babies but observes that abandoned children die in high numbers.

You Zhi, "The Society to Save Babies"

■ When poor families have too many children, their difficult circumstances often compel them to drown newborn babies, a practice which has already become so widespread that no one considers it strange. Not only are baby girls drowned, at times even baby boys are; not only do the poor drown their children, even the well-to-do do it. . . .

Those making the effort to accumulate good deeds will buy live animals just to release them! Aren't human lives even more precious? . . .

We have formed a society named "The Society to Save Babies." Every time a baby is born to a truly poor family unable to raise it, our society will as a rule grant them money and rice to cover six months. Only when it is absolutely impossible for them to keep the child at home will the society send the child to an orphanage as a way to save its life. The parents may at first keep the baby for the subsidy, but they will come to love it more every day and so eventually will keep it out of love. . . .

In the area we serve, any family too destitute to keep a newborn should report to the Society, accompanied by neighbors who are willing to serve as witnesses. The Society's inspector will then go personally to the home to assess the situation, and if it is as reported, will give the parents one peck of white rice and two hundred coins. For the next five months they can claim the same amount each month, identifying themselves with a ticket. . . . After five months, if they definitely cannot afford to keep the child, the Society will arrange for it to be taken to an orphanage. . . .

These measures drew resistance from conservatives, who thought copying Western practices was compounding defeat. A highly placed Manchu official objected that "from ancient down to modern times" there had never been "anyone who could use mathematics to raise a nation from a state of decline or to strengthen it in times of weakness."[3] Yet knowledge of the West gradually improved with more translations and travel in both directions. Newspapers covering world affairs began publication in Shanghai and Hong Kong. By 1880 China had embassies in London, Paris, Berlin, Madrid, Washington, Tokyo, and St. Petersburg.

Despite the enormous effort put into trying to catch up, China was humiliated yet again at the end of the nineteenth century. First came the discovery that Japan had so successfully modernized that it posed a threat to China. Then in 1894 Japanese efforts to separate Korea from Chinese influence led to the brief Sino-Japanese War, in which China was decisively defeated the next year. China's helplessness in the face of aggression led to a scramble among the European powers for concessions and protectorates in China. At the high point of this rush in 1898, it appeared that the European powers might actually divide China among themselves, the way they had recently divided Africa.

With the passage of time, people will find ways to cheat. Once a payment system is started, there inevitably will be people who could support their children but pretend to be poor to obtain the money and rice. . . .

As to babies born from illicit relations, making it difficult for the mother to keep them, we should tell midwives that they will receive four hundred to five hundred cash as a reward if they secretly bring such babies to the Society. In this way we will be able to save quite a few additional lives.

Jonas Hanway, *An Earnest Appeal for Mercy to the Children of the Poor*

■ One of our most important inquietudes, especially in time of war, is that we want people, and yet many lives are lost by the grossest negligence in our police. . . .

Many children instead of being nourished with care, by the fostering hand or breast of a wholesome country nurse, are thrust into the impure air of a workhouse, into the hands of some careless, worthless young female, or decrepit old woman, and inevitably lost for want of such means as the God of nature, their father as well as ours, has appointed for their preservation. . . .

[W]e ought no more to suffer a child to die for want of the common necessaries of life, though he is born to labor, than one who is the heir to a dukedom. The extinction of those who labor would be more fatal to the community than if the number of the highest ranks of the people were reduced. . . .

Never shall I forget the evidence given at Guild-Hall, upon occasion of a master of a workhouse of a large parish, who was challenged for forcing a child from the breast of the mother, and sending it to the Foundling Hospital. He alleged this in his defense, "We send all our children to the Foundling Hospital; we have not saved one alive for fourteen years. We have no place fit to preserve them in; the air is too confined."

QUESTIONS FOR ANALYSIS

1. How similar are the two authors' goals? How do their religious values shape their goals?
2. How do the two authors view the poor?
3. What differences between their countries might account for the differences in the authors' strategies?

Sources: *Deyi lu*, 2. 32, 40, 41, 55, http://ctext.org/wiki.pl?if=gb&chapter=276413, trans. Patricia Ebrey; Jonas Hanway, *An Earnest Appeal for Mercy to the Children of the Poor* (London: Dodsley, 1766), pp. 1–9.

Republican Revolution

China's humiliating defeat in the Sino-Japanese War in 1895 led to a renewed drive for reform. In 1898 a group of educated young reformers gained access to the twenty-seven-year-old Qing emperor. They warned him of the fate of Poland (divided by the European powers in the eighteenth century; see "Enlightened Absolutism and Its Limits" in Chapter 19) and regaled him with the triumphs of the Meiji reformers in Japan. They proposed redesigning China as a constitutional monarchy with modern financial and educational systems. For three months the emperor issued a series of reform decrees. But the Manchu establishment and the empress dowager felt threatened and not only suppressed the reform movement but imprisoned the emperor as well. Hope for reform from the top was dashed.

A period of violent reaction swept the country, reaching its peak in 1900 with the uprising of a secret society that foreigners dubbed the **Boxers**. The Boxers blamed China's ills on foreigners, especially Christian missionaries. After the Boxers laid siege to the foreign legation quarter in Beijing, a dozen nations, including Japan, sent twenty thousand troops to lift the siege. In the negotiations that followed, China had to agree to cancel civil service examinations and pay a staggering indemnity.

Boxers A Chinese secret society that blamed the country's ills on foreigners, especially missionaries, and rose in rebellion in 1900.

Foreign Soldiers in Shanghai In this photo taken in 1900, British, French, German, and Japanese officers pose for a portrait. The foreign armies that suppressed the Boxer Uprising stayed for months in China. (Private Collection/Bridgeman Images)

After this defeat, gradual reform lost its appeal. More and more Chinese were studying abroad and learning about Western political ideas, including democracy and revolution. The most famous was Sun Yatsen (1866–1925). Sent by his peasant family to Hawaii, he learned English and then continued his education in Hong Kong. From 1894 on, he spent his time abroad organizing revolutionary societies. He joined forces with Chinese student revolutionaries studying in Japan, and together they sparked the **1911 Revolution**, which brought China's long history of monarchy to an end, to be replaced by a Western-style republic. China had escaped direct foreign rule but would never be the same.

1911 Revolution The uprising that brought China's monarchy to an end.

Japan's Rapid Transformation

How was Japan able to quickly master the challenges posed by the West?

During the eighteenth century Japan (much more effectively than China) kept foreign merchants and missionaries at bay. It limited trade to a single port (Nagasaki), where only the Dutch were allowed, and forbade Japanese to travel abroad. Because Japan's land and population were so much smaller than China's, the Western powers never expected much from Japan as a trading partner and did not press it as urgently. Still, the European threat was part of what propelled Japan to modernize.

The "Opening" of Japan

Wanting to play a greater role in the Pacific, the United States decided to force the Japanese to open to trade. In 1853 Commodore Matthew Perry steamed into Edo (now Tokyo) Bay and demanded diplomatic negotiations with the emperor. Under threat of **gunboat diplomacy**, and after consulting with the daimyo (major lords), the officials signed a treaty with the United States that opened two ports and permitted trade.

gunboat diplomacy The imposition of treaties and agreements under threat of military violence, such as the opening of Japan to trade after Commodore Perry's demands.

Japan at this time was a complex society. The emperor in Kyoto had no effective powers. For more than two hundred years real power had been in the hands of the

Tokugawa shogun in Edo (AY-doh) (see "Tokugawa Government" in Chapter 21). The country was divided into numerous domains, each under a daimyo (DIGH-myoh). Each daimyo had under him samurai, warriors who had hereditary stipends and privileges, such as the right to wear a sword. Peasants and merchants were also legally distinct classes, and in theory social mobility from peasant to merchant or merchant to samurai was impossible. After two centuries of peace, there were many more samurai than were needed to administer or defend the country, and many lived very modestly. They were proud, however, and felt humiliated by the sudden American intrusion and the unequal treaties that the Western countries imposed. Some began agitating against the shogunate under the slogan "Revere the emperor and expel the barbarians."

When foreign diplomats and merchants began to settle in Yokohama after 1858, radical samurai reacted with a wave of antiforeign terrorism and antigovernment assassinations. The response from Western powers was swift and unambiguous. They sent an allied fleet of American, British, Dutch, and French warships to demolish key Japanese forts, further weakening the power and prestige of the shogun's government.

The Meiji Restoration

In 1867 a coalition of reform-minded daimyo led a coup that ousted the Tokugawa Shogunate. The samurai who led this coup declared a return to direct rule by the emperor, which had not been practiced in Japan for more than six hundred years. This emperor was called the Meiji (MAY-jee) emperor and this event the **Meiji Restoration**, a great turning point in Japanese history.

The domain leaders who organized the coup, called the Meiji Oligarchs, moved the boy emperor to Tokyo castle. They used the young sovereign to win over both the lords and the commoners. Real power remained in the hands of the oligarchs.

The battle cry of the Meiji reformers had been "strong army, rich nation." How were these goals to be accomplished? Convinced that they could not beat the West until they had mastered the secrets of its military and industrial might, they initiated a series of measures to reform Japan along modern Western lines. Within four years a delegation was traveling the world to learn what made the Western powers strong. Its members examined everything from the U.S. Constitution to the factories, shipyards, and railroads that made the European landscape so different from Japan's.

Japan under the shoguns had been decentralized, with most of the power over the population in the hands of the many daimyo. By elevating the emperor, the oligarchs were able to centralize the government. In 1871 they abolished the domains and merged the domain armies. Following the example of the French Revolution, they dismantled the four-class legal system and declared everyone equal. This amounted to stripping the samurai (7 to 8 percent of the population) of their privileges. Even their monopoly on the use of force was eliminated: the new army recruited commoners along with samurai. Not surprisingly, some samurai rose up against their loss of privileges. None of these uncoordinated uprisings made any difference.

Several leaders of the Meiji Restoration, in France on a fact-finding mission during the Franco-Prussian War of 1870–1871, were impressed by the active participation of French citizens in the defense of Paris. For Japan to survive in the hostile international environment, they concluded, ordinary people had to be trained to fight.

Meiji Restoration
The 1867 ousting of the Tokugawa Shogunate that "restored" the power of the Japanese emperors.

Consequently, a conscription law, modeled on the French law, was issued in 1872. To improve the training of soldiers, the new War College was organized along German lines, and German instructors were recruited to teach there. Young samurai were trained to form the new professional officer corps.

Many of the new institutions established in the Meiji period reached down to the local level. Schools open to all were rapidly introduced beginning in 1872. Teachers were trained in newly established teachers' colleges, where they learned to inculcate discipline, patriotism, and morality. Another modern institution that reached the local level was a national police force. In 1884 police training schools were established in every prefecture, and within a few years one- or two-man police stations were set up throughout the country. These policemen came to act as local agents of the central government. They not only dealt with crime but also enforced public health rules, conscription laws, and codes of behavior.

In 1889 Japan became the first non-Western country to adopt the constitutional form of government. A commission sent abroad to study European constitutional governments had come to the conclusion that the German constitutional monarchy would provide the best model for Japan, rather than the more democratic governments of the British, French, and Americans. Japan's new government had a two-house parliament, called the Diet. The upper house of lords was drawn largely from former daimyo and nobles, and the lower house was elected by a limited electorate (about 5 percent of the adult male population in 1890). Although Japan now had a government based on laws, it was authoritarian rather than democratic. The emperor was declared "sacred and inviolable." He had the right to appoint the prime minister and cabinet. He did not have to ask the Diet for funds because wealth assigned to the imperial house was entrusted to the Imperial Household Ministry, which was outside the government's control.

Ito Hirobumi and His Family The statesman Ito Hirobumi posed for this picture with his wife, son, and two grandsons at his country residence in 1908. Although as an official he promoted rapid political and economic change, at home he kept to many traditional practices, such as wearing traditional dress. (Popperfoto/Getty Images)

Cultural change during the Meiji period was as profound as political change. For more than a thousand years China had been the major source of ideas and technologies introduced into Japan. But in the late nineteenth century China, beset by Western pressure, had become an object lesson on the dangers of stagnation. The influential author Fukuzawa Yukichi began urging Japan to pursue "civilization and enlightenment," by which he meant Western civilization. (See "Analyzing the Evidence: Fukuzawa Yukichi, 'Escape from Asia,'" page 812.) Soon Japanese were being told to conform to Western taste, eat meat, wear Western-style clothes, and drop customs that Westerners found odd, such as married women's blackening their teeth.

Industrialization

The leaders of the Meiji Restoration, wanting to strengthen Japan's military capacity, promoted industrialization. The government paid large salaries to attract foreign experts to help with industrialization, and Japanese were encouraged to go abroad to study science and engineering.

The government played an active role in getting railroads, mines, and factories started. Early on, the Japanese government decided to compete with China in the export of tea and silk to the West. Introducing the mechanical reeling of silk gave Japan a strong price advantage in the sale of silk, and Japan's total foreign trade increased tenfold from 1877 to 1900. The next stage was to develop heavy industry. A huge indemnity exacted from China in 1895, as part of the peace agreement, was used to establish the Yawata Iron and Steel Works. The third stage of Japan's industrialization would today be called import substitution. Factories such as cotton mills were set up to help cut the importation of Western consumer goods.

Most of the great Japanese industrial conglomerates known as *zaibatsu* (zigh-BAHT-dzoo), such as Mitsubishi, got their start in this period, often founded by men with government connections. Sometimes the government set up plants that it then sold to private investors at bargain prices. Successful entrepreneurs were treated as patriotic heroes.

As in Europe, the early stages of industrialization brought hardship to the countryside. Farmers often rioted as their incomes failed to keep up with prices or as their tax burdens grew. Workers in modern industries were no happier, and in 1898 railroad workers went on strike for better working conditions and overtime pay. Still, rice production increased, death rates dropped as public health was improved, and the population grew from about 33 million in 1868 to about 45 million in 1900.

Japan as an Imperial Power

During the course of the Meiji period, Japan became an imperial power, making Taiwan and Korea into its colonies. The conflicts that led to Japanese acquisition of both of them revolved around Korea.

The Chosŏn Dynasty had been on the throne in Korea since 1392. In the second half of the nineteenth century Korea found itself caught between China, Japan, and Russia, each trying to protect or extend its sphere of influence. Westerners also began demanding that Korea be "opened." Korea's first response was to insist that its foreign relations be handled through Beijing. Matters were complicated by the rise in the 1860s of a religious cult, the Tonghak movement,

Japanese Expansion, 1875–1914

Fukuzawa Yukichi, "Escape from Asia"

Fukuzawa Yukichi was one of the most prominent intellectuals and promoters of westernization in Meiji Japan. His views on domestic policy were decidedly liberal, but he took a hard-line approach to foreign affairs. His ruthless criticism of Korea and China published on March 16, 1885, can be read as inviting colonialism. In 1895, ten years after writing this call to action, he rejoiced at Japan's victory over China in the conflict over Korea.

■ Civilization is like an epidemic of measles. The current measles in Tokyo, which has advanced eastwards from Nagasaki in western Japan, seems to have begun to claim more victims with the arrival of springtime. Will we be able now to find a means of checking this epidemic? It is obvious that we have no way to do so. We cannot put up effective resistance, even against an epidemic that carries with it only harm; much less against civilization, which is always accompanied by both harm and good, but by more good than harm.

Though our land of Japan is situated on the Eastern edge of Asia, the spirit of its people has already shaken off the backwardness of Asia to accept the civilization of the West. Unfortunately, however, we have two neighboring countries, one being called China, the other called Korea. The people of these two countries are no different from us Japanese people in having been brought up since olden times in the Asian culture and customs, and yet, whether because they are of another racial origin, or because, while similar in culture and customs, differ from us in the main lines of their traditional education, a comparison of the three countries, Japan, China, and Korea, reveals that the latter two resemble each other more closely than they do Japan. The people of those two countries do not know how to go about reforming and making progress, whether individually or as a country. It is not that they have not seen or heard of civilized things in the present world of facile communication; yet what their eyes and ears perceive have failed to stimulate their minds, and their emotional attachment to ancient manners and customs has changed little for the past hundreds and thousands of years. In this lively theater of civilization, where things change daily, they still speak of education in terms of Confucianism, cite humanity, justice, civility, and wisdom as their principles of school education, are completely obsessed only with outward appearance, are in reality not only ignorant of truths and principles but so extreme in their cruelty and shamelessness that for them morality is completely nonexistent, and yet are as arrogant as if they never gave a thought to self-examination.

In our view, these countries have no likelihood of maintaining their independence in the current tide of civilization's eastward advance. Let there not be the slightest doubt that, unless they are fortunate enough to have motivated men appear in their lands who, as a first step to improve the condition of their countries will

that had strong xenophobic elements. Although the government executed the cult founder in 1864, this cult continued to gain support, especially among impoverished peasants. Thus, like the Chinese government in the same period, the Korean government faced simultaneous internal and external threats.

In 1871 the U.S. minister to China took five warships to try to open Korea, but left after exchanges of fire resulted in 250 Koreans dead without any progress in getting the Korean government to make concessions. Japan tried next and in 1876 forced the Korean government to sign an unequal treaty and open three ports to Japanese trade. On China's urging, Korea also signed treaties with the European powers in an effort to counterbalance Japan.

Over the next couple of decades reformers in China and Japan tried to encourage Korea to adopt its own self-strengthening movement, but Korean conservatives did

plan such a great enterprise of overall reform of their governments as our Restoration was, and succeed in altering their people's minds through political reforms, those countries will meet their doom in but a few years, with their territories divided among the civilized countries of the world. The reason is that China and Korea, confronted by an epidemic of civilization comparable to measles, are impossibly trying to ward it off, despite its inevitability, by shutting themselves up in a room, with the result being that they are cutting off their supply of fresh air and asphyxiating themselves. Though mutual help between neighboring countries has been likened to the relationship between the lips and the teeth, China and Korea of today cannot be of any assistance at all to our country of Japan.

Civilized western man is not without a tendency to regard all three countries as identical because of their geographic proximity and to apply his evaluation of China and Korea to Japan also. For example, when he finds that the governments of China and Korea are old-fashioned autocracies without abiding laws, the western man will suppose Japan too to be a lawless country. When he finds that the gentlemen of China and Korea are too deeply infatuated to know what science is, the western scholar will think that Japan too is a land of Yin-Yang and the Five Elements. When the Chinese display their servility and shamelessness, they obscure the chivalrous spirit of the Japanese. When the Koreans employ cruel means of physical punishment, the Japanese too are surmised to be just as inhuman. Such examples are too numerous to count. This may

be compared to the case in which most of those in a string of houses within a village or town are foolish, lawless, cruel, and inhuman; an occasional family that heeds what is just and right will be eclipsed by the other's evil and its virtue will never be noticed. It is indeed not infrequent that something similar happens in our foreign relations and indirectly interferes with them. This should be regarded a great misfortune for our country of Japan.

To plan our course now, therefore, our country cannot afford to wait for the enlightenment of our neighbors and to cooperate in building Asia up. Rather, we should leave their ranks to join the camp of the civilized countries of the West. Even when dealing with China and Korea, we need not have special scruples simply because they are our neighbors, but should behave toward them as the westerners do. One who befriends an evil person cannot avoid being involved in his notoriety. In spirit, then, we break with our evil friends of Eastern Asia.

QUESTIONS FOR ANALYSIS

1. What does Fukuzawa mean by "civilization"?
2. How does Fukuzawa's justification of colonialism compare to Europeans' justification of it during the same period?

Source: Centre for East Asian Cultural Studies, comp., *Meiji Japan Through Contemporary Sources*. Vol. 3: *1869–1894* (Tokyo: Centre for East Asian Cultural Studies, 1972), pp. 129–133, modified. Used by permission of the Center for East Asian Cultural Studies.

their best to undo reform efforts. In 1894, when the religious cult rose in a massive revolt, both China and Japan sent military forces, claiming to come to the Korean government's aid. They ended up fighting each other instead in what is known as the Sino-Japanese War (see "The Self-Strengthening Movement"). With its decisive victory, Japan gained Taiwan from China and was able to make Korea a protectorate. In 1910 Korea was formally annexed as a province of Japan.

Japan also competed aggressively with the leading European powers for influence and territory in China, particularly in the northeast (Manchuria). There Japanese and Russian imperialism met and collided. In 1904 Japan attacked Russian forces and, after its 1905 victory in the bloody **Russo-Japanese War**, emerged with a valuable foothold in China—Russia's former protectorate over Port Arthur (see Map 26.1).

Russo-Japanese War The 1904–1905 war between Russia and Japan fought over imperial influence and territory in northeast China (Manchuria).

Japan's victories over China and Russia changed the way European nations looked at Japan. Through negotiations Japan was able to eliminate extraterritoriality in 1899 and gain control of its own tariffs in 1911. Within Japan, the success of the military in raising Japan's international reputation added greatly to its political influence.

What were the causes and consequences of the vast movement of people in the Pacific region?

The Pacific Region and the Movement of People

The nineteenth century was marked by extensive movement of people into, across, and out of Asia and the broad Pacific region. Many of these migrants moved from one Asian country to another, but there was also a growing presence of Europeans in Asia, a consequence of the increasing integration of the world economy (see "The Expanding World Economy" in Chapter 25).

Settler Colonies in the Pacific: Australia and New Zealand

The largest share of the Europeans who moved to the Pacific region in the nineteenth century went to the settler colonies in Australia and New Zealand (Map 26.2). In 1770 the English explorer James Cook visited New Zealand, Australia, and Hawaii. All three of these places in time became destinations for migrants.

Between 200 and 1300 C.E. Polynesians settled numerous islands of the Pacific, from New Zealand in the south to Hawaii in the north and Easter Island in the east. Thus most of the lands that explorers like Cook encountered were occupied by societies with chiefs, crop agriculture, domestic animals such as chickens and pigs, excellent sailing technology, and often considerable experience in warfare. Australia had been settled millennia earlier by a different population. When Cook arrived in Australia, it was occupied by about three hundred thousand Aborigines who lived entirely by food gathering, fishing, and hunting. Like the Indians of Central and South America, the people in all these lands fell victim to Eurasian diseases and died in large numbers.

Australia was first developed by Britain as a penal colony. Between 1787 and 1869, when the penal colony system was abolished, a total of 161,000 convicts were transported to Australia. After the end of the Napoleonic Wars in 1815, a steady stream of nonconvicts chose to relocate to Australia. Raising sheep proved suitable to Australia's climate, and wool exports steadily increased, from 75,400 pounds in 1821 to 24 million pounds in 1845. To encourage migration, the government offered free passage and free land to immigrants. By 1850 Australia had five hundred thousand inhabitants. The discovery of gold in Victoria in 1851 quadrupled that number in a few years. The gold rush also provided the financial means for cultural development. Public libraries, museums, art galleries, and universities opened in the thirty years after 1851. These institutions dispensed a distinctly British culture.

Not everyone in Australia was of British origin, however. Chinese and Japanese built the railroads and ran the shops in the towns and the market gardens nearby. Filipinos and Pacific Islanders did the hard work in the sugarcane fields. Afghans and their camels controlled the carrying trade in some areas. But fear that Asian labor would lower living standards and undermine Australia's distinctly British culture led to efforts to keep Australia white.

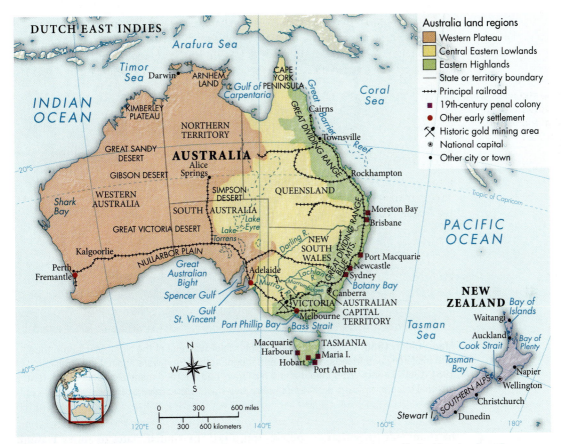

MAP 26.2 Australia Because of the vast deserts in western Australia, cities and industries developed mainly in the east. Australia's early geographical and cultural isolation bred a sense of inferiority. Air travel, the communications revolution, and the massive importation of Japanese products and American popular culture have changed that.

Australia gained independence in stages. In 1850 the British Parliament passed the Australian Colonies Government Act, which allowed the four most populous colonies — New South Wales, Tasmania, Victoria, and South Australia — to establish colonial legislatures, determine the franchise, and frame their own constitutions. In 1902 Australia became one of the first countries in the world to give women the vote.

By 1900 New Zealand's population had reached 750,000, only a fifth of Australia's. One major reason more people had not settled these fertile islands was the resistance of the native Maori people. They quickly mastered the use of muskets and tried for decades to keep the British from taking their lands.

Foreign settlement in Hawaii began gradually. Initially, whalers stopped there for supplies, as they did at other Pacific Islands. Missionaries and businessmen came next, and soon other settlers followed, both whites and Asians. A plantation economy developed centered on sugarcane. In the 1890s leading settler families overthrew the

Maori Chief, 1885 This photograph depicts Chief Wahanui of the Ngati Maniapoto tribe with his family and friends. The chief had fought in the Maori wars against the British in 1864–1865. Twenty years later, he and his family had adopted many elements of Western material culture. (By Alfred Burton [1834–1914] [albumen print]/Private Collection/© Michael Graham-Stewart/Bridgeman Images)

native monarchy, set up a republic, and urged the United States to annex Hawaii, which it did in 1898.

Asian Emigration

Like Europeans, Asians left their native countries in unprecedented numbers in the nineteenth century (Map 26.3). As in Europe, both push and pull factors prompted people to leave home. Between 1750 and 1900 world population grew rapidly, in many places tripling. China and India were extremely densely populated countries—China with more than 400 million people in the mid-nineteenth century, India with more than 200 million. Not surprisingly, these two giants were the leading exporters of people in search of work or land. On the pull side were the new opportunities created by the flow of development capital into previously underdeveloped areas. In many of the European colonies in Asia the business class came to consist of both Asian and European migrants. Asian diasporas formed in many parts of the world, with the majority in Asia itself, especially Southeast Asia.

By the nineteenth century Chinese formed key components of mercantile communities throughout Southeast Asia. Chinese often assimilated in Siam and Vietnam, but they rarely did so in Muslim areas such as Java, Catholic areas such as the Philippines, and primitive tribal areas such as northern Borneo. In these places distinct Chinese communities emerged, usually dominated by speakers of a single Chinese dialect.

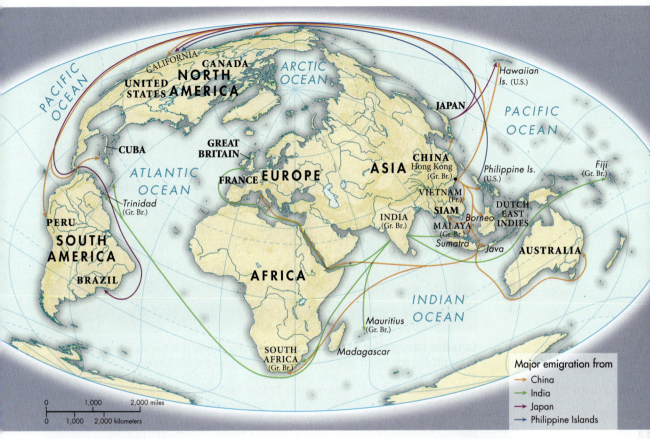

MAP 26.3 Emigration Out of Asia, 1820–1914 As steamships made crossing oceans quicker and more reliable, many people in Asia left their home countries to find new opportunities elsewhere. European imperialism contributed to this flow, especially by recruiting workers for newly established plantations or mines. Many emigrants simply wanted to work a few years to build their savings and planned to return home. Often, however, they ended up staying in their new countries and forming families there.

With the growth in trade that accompanied the European imperial expansion, Chinese began to settle in the islands of Southeast Asia in larger numbers. After Singapore was founded by the British in 1819, Chinese rapidly poured in, soon becoming the dominant ethnic group. In British-controlled Malaya, some Chinese built great fortunes in the tin business, while others worked in the mines. Chinese also settled in the Spanish-controlled Philippines and in Dutch-controlled Indonesia.

Discovery of gold in California in 1848, Australia in 1851, and Canada in 1858 encouraged Chinese to book passage to those places. In California few arrived soon enough to strike gold, but they quickly found work building railroads, and others took up mining in Wyoming and Idaho.

Indian entrepreneurs were similarly attracted by the burgeoning commerce of the growing British Empire. The bulk of Indian emigrants were **indentured laborers,**

indentured laborers
Laborers who agreed to a term of employment, specified in a contract.

Canadian Immigration Certificate This certificate proved that the eleven-year-old boy in the photograph had a legal right to be in Canada, as the $500 head tax required for immigration of Chinese had been paid. The head tax on Chinese immigrants introduced in 1885 started at $50, but it was raised to $100 in 1900 and to $500 in 1903. Equal to about what a laborer could earn in two years, the tax succeeded in its goal of slowing the rate of Asian immigration to Canada.

(Head tax certificate for Jung Bak Hun, issued January 3, 1919/© Government of Canada. Reproduced with the permission of the Minister of Public Works and Government Services Canada [2016]. Source: Library and Archives Canada/Department of Employment and Immigration fonds/Vol. 712, C.I.5 certificate 88103)

recruited under contract. The rise of indentured labor from Asia was a direct result of the outlawing of the African slave trade in the early nineteenth century by Britain and the United States. Sugar plantations in the Caribbean and elsewhere needed new sources of workers, and planters in the British colonies discovered that they could recruit Indian laborers to replace blacks. After the French abolished slavery in 1848, they recruited workers from India as well. Later in the century many Indians emigrated to British colonies in Africa, the largest numbers to South Africa.

Indentured laborers secured as substitutes for slaves were often treated little better than slaves. In response to such abuse, the Indian colonial government established regulations stipulating a maximum indenture period of five years, after which the migrant would be entitled to passage home. Even though government "protectors" were appointed at the ports of embarkation, exploitation of indentured workers continued largely unchecked.

In areas outside the British Empire, China offered the largest supply of ready labor. Starting in the 1840s contractors arrived at Chinese ports to recruit labor for plantations and mines in Cuba, Peru, Hawaii, Sumatra, South Africa, and elsewhere.

Chinese laborers did not have the British government to protect them and seem to have suffered even more than Indian workers.

India and China sent more people abroad than any other Asian countries during this period, but they were not alone. As Japan started to industrialize, its cities could not absorb all those forced off the farms, and people began emigrating in significant numbers, many to Hawaii and later to South America. Emigration from the Philippines also was substantial, especially after it became a U.S. territory in 1898.

Asian migration to the United States, Canada, and Australia—the primary destinations of European emigrants—would undoubtedly have been greater if it had not been so vigorously resisted by the white settlers in those regions. In 1882 Chinese were barred from becoming American citizens, and the immigration of Chinese laborers was suspended. Australia also put a stop to Asian immigration with the Commonwealth Immigration Restriction Act of 1901, which established the "white Australia policy" that remained on the books until the 1970s.

Most of the Asian migrants discussed so far were illiterate peasants or business people, not members of traditional educated elites. By the beginning of the twentieth century, however, another group of Asians was going abroad in significant numbers: students. Most of these students traveled abroad to learn about Western science, law, and government in the hope of strengthening their own countries. On their return they contributed enormously to the intellectual life of their societies, increasing understanding of the modern Western world and also becoming the most vocal advocates of overthrowing the old order and driving out the colonial masters.

Among the most notable of these foreign-educated radicals were Mohandas Gandhi (1869–1948) (see "Gandhi's Resistance Campaign in India" in Chapter 29) and Sun Yatsen. Sun developed his ideas about the republican form of government while studying in Hawaii and Hong Kong. Gandhi, after studying law in Britain, took a job in South Africa, where he became involved in trying to defend the interests of the Indians who lived and worked there. It was there that he gradually elaborated his idea of passive resistance.

The Countries of Asia in Comparative Perspective

What explains the similarities and differences in the experiences of Asian countries in this era?

At the start of the nineteenth century the societies of Asia varied much more than those of any other part of the world. In the temperate zones of East Asia, the old established monarchies of China, Japan, and Korea were all densely populated and boasted long literary traditions and traditions of unified governments. They had ties to each other that dated back many centuries and shared many elements of their cultures. South of them, in the tropical and subtropical regions, cultures were more diverse. India was just as densely populated as China, Japan, and Korea, but politically and culturally less unified, with several major languages and dozens of independent rulers reigning in kingdoms large and small, not to mention the growing British presence. In both India and Southeast Asia, Islam was much more important than it was in East Asia. All the countries with long written histories and literate elites were at a great remove from the thinly populated and relatively primitive areas without literate cultures and sometimes even without agriculture, such as Australia and some of the islands of the Philippines and Indonesia.

The nineteenth century gave the societies of Asia more in common in that all of them in one way or another had come into contact with the expanding West. Still, the Western powers did not treat all the countries the same way. Western powers initially wanted manufactured goods from the more developed Asian societies, especially Indian cotton textiles and Chinese porcelains. At the beginning of the nineteenth century Britain had already gained political control over large parts of India and was intent on forcing China to trade on terms more to its benefit. It paid virtually no attention to Korea and Japan, not seeing in them the same potential for profit. The less developed parts of Asia also attracted increasing Western interest, not because they could provide manufactured goods, but because they offered opportunities for Western development, much as the Americas had earlier.

The West that the societies of Asia faced during the nineteenth century was itself rapidly changing, and the steps taken by Western nations to gain power in Asia naturally also changed over time. Western science and technology were making rapid advances, which gave European armies progressively greater advantages in weaponry. The Industrial Revolution made it possible for countries that industrialized early, such as Britain, to produce huge surpluses of goods for which they had to find markets; this development shifted their interest in Asia from a place to buy goods to a place to sell goods. Britain had been able to profit from its colonization of India, and this profit both encouraged it to consolidate its rule and invited its European rivals to look for their own colonies. For instance, rivalry with Britain led France to seek colonies in Southeast Asia not only for its own sake but also as a way to keep Britain from extending its sphere of influence any farther.

There were some commonalities in the ways Asian countries responded to pressure from outside. In the countries with long literary traditions, often the initial response of the established elite was to try to drive the unwelcome foreigners away. This was the case in China, Japan, and Korea in particular. Violent antiforeign reactions exploded again and again, but the superior military technology of the industrialized West almost invariably prevailed. Some Asian leaders insisted on the need to preserve their cultural traditions at all costs. Others came to the opposite conclusion that the West was indeed superior in some ways and that they would have to adopt European ideas or techniques for their own purposes. This can be seen both among Indians who acquired education in English and in many of the Meiji reformers in Japan. The struggles between the traditionalists and the westernizers were often intense. As nationalism took hold in the West, it found a receptive audience among the educated elites in Asia. How could the assertion that every people had the right to control its own destiny not appeal to the colonized?

Whether they were colonized or not, most countries in Asia witnessed the spread of new technologies between 1800 and 1914. Railroads, telegraphs, modern sanitation, and a wider supply of inexpensive manufactured goods brought fundamental changes in everyday life not only to lands under colonial rule, such as India and Vietnam, but also, if less rapidly, to places that managed to remain independent, such as China and Japan. In fact, the transformation of Japan between 1860 and 1900 was extraordinary. By 1914 Japan had urban conveniences and educational levels comparable to those in Europe.

Chapter Summary

In the nineteenth century the countries of Asia faced new challenges. In India Britain extended its rule to the whole subcontinent, though often the British ruled indirectly through local princes. Britain brought many modern advances to India, such as railroads and schools. Slavery was outlawed, as was widow suicide and infanticide. Resistance to British rule took several forms. In 1857 Indian soldiers in the employ of the British rose in a huge revolt, and after Britain put down this rebellion it ruled India much more tightly. Indians who received English education turned English ideas of liberty and representative rule against the British and founded the Indian National Congress, which called for Indian independence.

In Southeast Asia by the end of the nineteenth century most countries, from Burma to the Philippines, had been made colonies of Western powers, which developed them as exporters of agricultural products or raw materials, including rubber, tin, sugar, tea, cotton, and jute. The principal exception was Siam (Thailand), whose king was able to play the English and French off against each other and institute centralizing reforms. In the Philippines more than three centuries of Spanish rule ended in 1898, but Spain was replaced by another colonial power: the United States.

In the nineteenth century China's world standing declined as a result of both foreign intervention and internal unrest. The government's efforts to suppress opium imports from Britain led to military confrontation with the British and to numerous concessions that opened China to trade on Britain's terms. Within its borders, China faced unprecedented population pressure and worsening economic conditions that resulted in uprisings in several parts of the country. Further humiliations by the Western powers led to concerted efforts to modernize, but China never quite caught up. Inspired by Western ideas of republican government, revolutionaries tried to topple the dynasty, finally succeeding in 1911–1912.

Japan was the one Asian country to quickly transform itself when confronted by the military strength of the West. It did this by overhauling its power structure. The Meiji centralized and strengthened Japan's power by depriving the samurai of their privileges, writing a constitution, instituting universal education, and creating a modern army. At the same time they guided Japan toward rapid industrialization. By the early twentieth century Japan had become an imperialist power with colonies in Korea and Taiwan.

The nineteenth century was also a great age of migration. Citizens of Great Britain came east in large numbers, many to join the Indian civil service or army, others to settle in Australia or New Zealand. Subjects of Asian countries also went abroad, often leaving one Asian country for another. Asian students traveled to Europe, Japan, or the United States to continue their educations. Millions more left in search of work. With the end of the African slave trade, recruiters from the Americas and elsewhere went to India and China to secure indentured laborers. Asian diasporas formed in many parts of the world.

By the turn of the twentieth century the countries in the Asia and Pacific region varied greatly in wealth and power. There are several reasons for this. The countries did not start with equivalent circumstances. Some had long traditions of unified rule;

others did not. Some had manufactured goods that Western powers wanted; others offered raw materials or cheap labor. The timing of the arrival of Western powers also made a difference, especially because Western military superiority increased over time. European Great Power rivalry had a major impact, especially after 1860. Similarities in the experiences of Asian countries are also notable and include many of the benefits (and costs) of industrialization seen elsewhere in the world, such as modernizations in communication and transportation, extension of schooling, and the emergence of radical ideologies.

NOTES

1. Quoted in K. M. Panikkar, *Asia and Western Dominance: A Survey of the Vasco da Gama Epoch of Asian History* (London: George Allen & Unwin, 1959), p. 116.
2. Ssu-yu Teng and J. K. Fairbank, *China's Response to the West: A Documentary Survey* (New York: Atheneum, 1971), p. 26.
3. Ibid., p. 76, modified.

CONNECTIONS

The nineteenth century brought Asia change on a much greater scale than did any earlier century. Much of the change was political — old political orders were ousted or reduced to tokens by new masters, often European colonial powers. Old elites found themselves at a loss when confronted by the European powers with their modern weaponry and modern armies. Cultural change was no less dramatic as the old elites pondered the differences between their traditional values and the ideas that seemed to underlie the power of the European states. In several places ordinary people rose in rebellion, probably in part because they felt threatened by the speed of cultural change. Material culture underwent major changes as elites experimented with Western dress and architecture and ordinary people had opportunities to travel on newly built railroads. Steamships, too, made long-distance travel easier, facilitating the out-migration of people seeking economic opportunities far from their countries of birth.

In the Americas, too, the nineteenth century was an era of unprecedented change and movement of people. Colonial empires were being overturned there, not imposed as they were in Asia in the same period. The Americas were on the receiving end of the huge migrations taking place, while Asia, like Europe, was much more an exporter of people. The Industrial Revolution brought change to all these areas, both by making available inexpensive machine-made products and by destroying some old ways of making a living. Intellectually, in both Asia and the Americas the ideas of nationalism and nation building shaped how people, especially the more educated, thought about the changes they were experiencing.

CHAPTER 26   **Review and Explore**

Identify Key Terms

Identify and explain the significance of each item below.

Great Mutiny / Great Revolt (p. 796)   **Taiping Rebellion** (p. 805)

Indian Civil Service (p. 798)   **Boxers** (p. 807)

Indian National Congress (p. 798)   **1911 Revolution** (p. 808)

Java War (p. 799)   **gunboat diplomacy** (p. 808)

Nguyen Dynasty (p. 801)   **Meiji Restoration** (p. 809)

Opium War (p. 804)   **Russo-Japanese War** (p. 813)

extraterritoriality (p. 804)   **indentured laborers** (p. 817)

Review the Main Ideas

Answer the focus questions from each section of the chapter.

1. In what ways did India change as a consequence of British rule? (p. 796)

2. Why were most but not all Southeast Asian societies reduced to colonies? (p. 799)

3. Was China's decline in the nineteenth century due more to internal problems or to Western imperialism? (p. 802)

4. How was Japan able to quickly master the challenges posed by the West? (p. 808)

5. What were the causes and consequences of the vast movement of people in the Pacific region? (p. 814)

6. What explains the similarities and differences in the experiences of Asian countries in this era? (p. 819)

Make Comparisons and Connections

Analyze the larger developments and continuities within and across chapters.

1. How quickly was Asia affected by the Industrial Revolution in Europe (Chapter 23)? Explain your answer.

2. How do the experiences of European colonies in Asia compare to those in Africa (Chapter 25)?

3. How does China's response to the challenge of European pressure compare to that of the Ottoman Empire (Chapter 25) during the same period?

TIMELINE

ASIA AND THE PACIFIC

1839–1842 Opium War

1851 ◆
Gold found in Australia, leads to increased immigration

1853 ◆
Commodore Perry opens Japanese ports to foreign trade

AMERICAS

1806–1825 Latin American wars of independence **(Ch. 22)**

EUROPE

◆ **1807** Slave trade abolished in British Empire **(Ch. 25)**

1848 ◆
Revolutions in France, Austria, and Prussia **(Ch. 24)**

1820 | 1840

Suggested Resources

BOOKS

Bayly, C. A. *Indian Society and the Making of the British Empire*. 1990. A synthesis of recent research that provides a complex portrait of the interaction of Indian society and British colonial administration.

Bose, Sugata, and Ayesha Jalal. *Modern South Asia: History, Culture, Political Economy*. 1998. Incorporates recent scholarship with postcolonial perspective in a wide-ranging study.

Duus, Peter. *The Abacus and the Sword: The Japanese Penetration of Korea, 1895–1910*. 1995. Analyzes the interplay of business interests (the abacus) and military interests (the sword) in Japan's push for colonial possessions.

Fairbank, John King, and Merle Goldman. *China: A New History*, 2d ed. 2006. A treatment of China's experiences in the nineteenth century that is rich in interesting detail.

Hane, Mikiso. *Peasants, Rebels, Women, and Outcastes: The Underside of Modern Japan*, 2d ed. 2003. Draws on wide-ranging sources to provide a fuller picture of Japanese history.

Hopper, Helen. *Fukuzawa Yukichi: From Samurai to Capitalist*. 2005. A brief account of the life of a key westernizing intellectual.

Irokawa, Daikichi. *The Culture of the Meiji Period*. 1988. Makes excellent use of letters, diaries, and songs to probe changes in the ways ordinary people thought during a crucial period of political change.

Kuhn, Philip A. *Chinese Among Others: Emigration in Modern Times*. 2008. A history of Chinese emigration that is global in scope and vividly written.

Metcalf, Barbara D., and Thomas Metcalf. *A Concise History of Modern India*. 2012. A well-crafted overview.

Pruitt, Ida. *A Daughter of Han: The Autobiography of a Chinese Working Woman*. 1967. A highly revealing glimpse of Chinese society fashioned by journalist Ida Pruitt in the 1930s based on what a Chinese woman born in 1867 told Pruitt of her life.

Rowe, William T. *China's Last Empire: The Great Qing*. 2009. An overview of the Qing Empire by a major historian.

Spence, Jonathan. *God's Chinese Son*. 1997. Tells the story of the Taipings as much as possible from their own perspective.

Steinberg, David Joel, ed. *In Search of Southeast Asia: A Modern History*, rev. ed. 1987. An impressive work on Southeast Asia by seven specialists.

Walthall, Anne. *Japan: A Cultural, Social, and Political History*. 2006. A concise overview with good coverage of local society and popular culture.

Yeh, Catherine. *Shanghai Love: Courtesans, Intellectuals, and Entertainment Culture: 1850–1910.* 2006. An engaging account of the culture that developed in the treaty ports of China.

DOCUMENTARIES

The Meiji Revolution (PBS, 1992). Part of the award-winning *Pacific Century* series. Makes extensive use of photographs and woodblock prints as well as feature films.

The Two Coasts of China: Asia and the Challenge of the West (PBS, 1992). Part of the award-winning *Pacific Century* series. Focuses mostly on the elite response to the shift in foreign threat from the north to the seacoast.

FEATURE FILMS

Burning of the Imperial Palace (Han Hsiang Li, 1983). This joint Hong Kong–Chinese film dramatizes the events that culminated in the looting and destruction of the imperial Old Summer Palace by invading English and French troops in 1860.

Mangal Pandey: The Rising (Ketan Mehta, 2005). A fictional story of friendship and betrayal during the time of the 1857 uprising in India.

The Man Who Would Be King (John Huston, 1975). In this popular film based on a Rudyard Kipling story, two rogue ex-noncommissioned officers of the Indian army set off from late-nineteenth-century British India in search of adventure. The actors include Sean Connery, Michael Caine, and Christopher Plummer.

The Opium War (Jin Xie, 1997). The Chinese view of the Opium War, dramatized.

WEBSITES

British India and the "Great Rebellion." A good overview of the 1857 conflict in India. **www.bbc.co.uk/history/british/victorians /indian_rebellion_01.shtml**

Early Photography of Japan. A well-organized, easy-to-use portal to more than two thousand early photos of Japan in Harvard collections. **hcl.harvard.edu/collections/epj/index.cfm**

27

The Americas in the Age of Liberalism
1810–1917

Independence brought striking change and stubborn continuities to the Americas. With the exception of Haiti's revolution, American nations gained independence with their colonial social orders mostly intact. Slavery endured in the United States, Cuba, and Brazil until the second half of the nineteenth century. In Spanish America land remained concentrated in the hands of colonial elites. Territorial expansion displaced most of the indigenous communities that had withstood colonialism. By 1900 millions of immigrants from Europe, the Middle East, and Asia had settled in the Americas.

Though new political systems and governing institutions emerged, political rivals struggled to share power. Liberal republicanism became the most common form of government. But there were exceptions, such as the monarchy that ruled Brazil until 1889 and the parliamentary system tied to Britain that developed in Canada, which retained a symbolic role for the British monarch. Economically, the United States nurtured expanding internal markets and assumed an influential place in Atlantic and Pacific trade. Across Latin America, new nations with weak internal markets and often poorly consolidated political systems struggled to accumulate capital or industrialize.

Yaqui Woman

Indians across the Americas found their world under assault during the nineteenth century as new nation-states completed the process of territorial consolidation begun in the colonial era. Yaqui people like the woman depicted here faced the dual pressures of the United States' westward expansion and Mexico's integration of northern borderlands.

Edward S. Curtis Collection/Library of Congress, Prints and Photographs Division, Washington, D.C./LC-USZ62-1044492

CHAPTER PREVIEW

NEW NATIONS
How and why did the process of nation-state consolidation vary across the Americas?

SLAVERY AND ABOLITION
Why did slavery last longer in the United States, Brazil, and Cuba than in the other republics of the Americas? How did resistance by slaves shape abolition?

EXPORT-LED GROWTH AND SOCIAL UNREST
As Latin America became more integrated into the world economy, how did patterns of economic growth shape political culture and social reactions?

IMMIGRATION
What factors shaped patterns of immigration to the Americas? How did immigrants shape — and how were they shaped by — their new settings?

A NEW AMERICAN EMPIRE
In what ways did U.S. policies in the Caribbean and Central America resemble European imperialism? How did U.S. foreign policy depart from European imperialism?

How and why did the process of nation-state consolidation vary across the Americas?

New Nations

After American nations gained their independence between 1783 and 1825, each began a long and often-violent process of state-building and consolidating its eventual national territory. In countries such as Mexico and Argentina new governments failed to establish the trust needed for political stability. In the United States long-standing tensions culminated in the Civil War, while in Cuba nationalists fought a long struggle for independence from Spain.

Liberalism and Caudillos in Spanish America

To establish political and economic frameworks, American nations reached for ideologies that circulated in the Atlantic in the age of revolution (see "Demands for Liberty and Equality" in Chapter 22). The dominant ideology of the era was liberalism. Liberals sought to create representative republics with strong central governments framed by constitutions that defined and protected individual rights, in particular the right to freely own and buy and sell private property. Beginning with the United States, colonies that became independent nations in the Americas all adopted liberal constitutions.

The U.S. Constitution, in its earliest form, is an example of classic liberalism: it defined individual rights, but those individual rights were subordinated to property rights. Slaves were considered property rather than individuals with constitutional rights. Only property owners could vote, only men could own property, and the new government did not recognize the property of Indians. Liberalism mainly served and protected **oligarchs**—the small number of individuals and families who had monopolized political power and economic resources since the colonial era. Liberalism preserved slavery, created tools that allowed the wealthy and powerful to continue to concentrate landownership in the countryside, gave industrialists a free hand over their workers, and concentrated political power in the hands of those who held economic power.

By the end of the nineteenth century liberalism commingled with other ideologies such as Social Darwinism and scientific racism (see "Science for the Masses" in Chapter 24). This combination also inspired the imperial ambitions of the United States toward Mexico and the **Circum-Caribbean**, the region that includes the Antilles as well as the lands that bound the Caribbean Sea in Central America and northern South America.

The implementation of liberalism took different shapes. The United States deferred questions about centralized federal power over local state authority, as well as the legality of slavery, until its Civil War (1861–1865). After the North prevailed, liberal economic growth gave rise to business and industrial empires and stimulated the immigration of millions of people to provide cheap labor for the booming economy. In Spanish America wars of independence left behind a weak consensus about government, which led to long cycles of civil war across many countries.

The lack of a shared political culture among powerful groups in Spanish America created a crisis of confidence. Large landowners held great local power that they refused to yield to politicians in a distant capital. Political factions feared that if a rival faction won power, it would not abide by the rules and limits framed by the constitution, or that a rival would use its governing authority to crush its opponents.

oligarchs In Latin America, the small number of individuals and families that had monopolized political power and economic resources since the colonial era.

Circum-Caribbean The region encompassing the Antilles as well as the lands that bound the Caribbean Sea in Central America and northern South America.

The power vacuum that resulted was often filled by caudillos, strong leaders who came to power and governed through their charisma and leadership abilities. This form of leadership is known as **caudillismo** (COW-deeh-is-moh).

The rule of a caudillo often provided temporary stability amid the struggles between liberals and conservatives, but caudillos cultivated their own prestige at the expense of building stable political institutions.

caudillismo Government by figures who rule through personal charisma and the support of armed followers in Latin America.

Mexico and the United States

The rumblings of independence first stirred Mexico in 1810. A century later, in 1910, the country was engulfed in the first great social upheaval of the twentieth century, the Mexican Revolution. In the century between these events, Mexico declined politically and economically from its status as the most prosperous and important colony of the Spanish Empire. It lost most of its national territory as Central American provinces broke away and became independent republics and as the United States expanded westward and captured or purchased Mexico's northern lands.

Mexicans experienced political stabilization and economic growth again in the second half of the nineteenth century when liberal leaders, especially the dictator Porfirio Díaz (r. 1876–1911), imposed order and attracted foreign investment. But as Díaz himself is said to have remarked, "Poor Mexico, so far from God, so close to the United States."[1] The United States pursued territorial expansion under the doctrine of **manifest destiny**, by which the United States would absorb all the territory spanning from its original Atlantic states to the Pacific Ocean. To do so, the United States took lands from Indian nations and Mexico (Map 27.1).

Mexico's woes after independence resulted mainly from the inability of its political leaders to establish a consensus about how to govern the new nation. The general

manifest destiny The doctrine that the United States should absorb the territory spanning from the original Atlantic states to the Pacific Ocean.

Caudillo Juan Manuel de Rosas of Argentina Frees a Group of Enslaved Women, 1841
One of the best-known caudillos, Rosas ruled Argentina from 1829 to 1852. To maintain his power, Rosas relied on the loyalty of his armed followers and his ability to cultivate a popular following through measures like the gradual abolition of slavery. (Pictures from History/CPA Media)

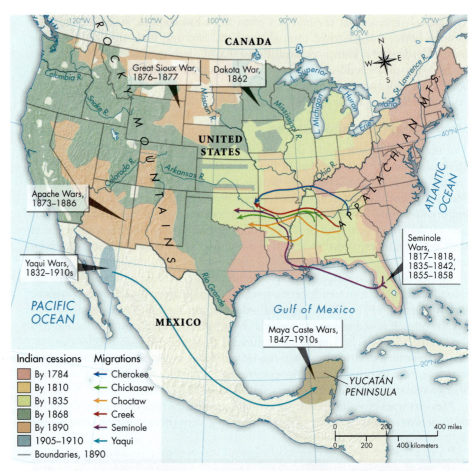

MAP 27.1 Displacement of Indigenous Peoples, 1780s–1910s The United States and Mexico waged repeated wars to claim the lands of Native American nations. This was the last stage of the process of conquest and dispossession that began with the arrival of Europeans in the Americas three centuries earlier. As national armies seized native lands, displaced native peoples were forcibly removed, leading to the deaths of thousands and the destruction of cultures.

who led the war against Spain, Agustín de Iturbide, proclaimed himself emperor in 1822. When he was deposed a year later, the country's southern provinces broke away, becoming Guatemala, Honduras, Nicaragua, El Salvador, and Costa Rica. Power in Mexico rested in the hands of regional caudillos and local bosses. The presidency changed hands frequently as rival factions competed against each other. Antonio López de Santa Anna, the most powerful of Mexico's caudillos, held the presidency ten times between 1833 and 1854—three separate times in 1833 alone.

By contrast, the United States established a clearer vision of government embodied in the 1789 Constitution. Deep disagreements remained over questions such as the power of the federal government relative to state governments, which played out in debates about the future of slavery and westward expansion. These tensions lasted well into the nineteenth century and culminated in the Civil War (1861–1865).

Economically, the United States remained integrated into the expanding and industrializing British Empire, so U.S. merchants retained access to Atlantic markets and credit. But the United States faced deepening regional differences: in the first half of the nineteenth century the North grew fastest, becoming the center of immigration, banking, and industrialization. In the South slavery and tenant farming kept much of the population at the economic margins and weakened internal markets. Slavery also inhibited immigration, since immigrants avoided settling in areas where they had to compete with unfree labor.

The dichotomy between the economies of the U.S. North and South repeated itself in the difference between the economies of the United States and Latin America. Latin American economies were organized around the export of agricultural and mineral commodities like sugar and silver, not around internal markets as in the United States, and these export economies were disrupted by the independence process.

The fate of the major silver mine in Mexico illustrates the challenges presented by independence. La Valenciana in central Mexico was the most productive silver mine in the world. It was one of the first places where the steam engine was used to pump water out of shafts, allowing the mine to reach below the water table. The machinery was destroyed during Mexico's war of independence (1810–1821), and the flooded mine ceased operation. Neither private investors nor the new government had the capital necessary to reactivate the mine after independence.

Mexico entered a vicious cycle: without capital and economic activity, tax revenues evaporated, public administration disintegrated, and the national government became unmanageable. The lack of political stability, in turn, drove investors away. The consequences are striking: in 1800 Mexico produced half the goods and services that the United States did; by 1845 production had dropped to only 8 percent. Per capita income fell by half.[2]

Politically and economically weakened after independence, Mexico was vulnerable to expansionist pressure from the United States. At independence, Mexico's northern territories included much of what is today the U.S. Southwest and West. These territories attracted the interest of U.S. politicians, settlers, and land speculators. In the 1820s settlers from the U.S. South petitioned the Mexican government for land grants in the province of Texas, in return for which they would adopt Mexican citizenship. The U.S. government encouraged these settlers to declare the independence of Texas in 1836.

After Texas and Florida became U.S. states in 1845, President James Polk expanded the nation's border westward, precipitating the Mexican-American War (1846–1848). (See "Global Viewpoints: Perspectives on the Mexican-American War," page 832.) In the **Treaty of Guadalupe Hidalgo** (1848), Mexico ceded half its territory to the United States. With the U.S. acquisition of Florida from Spain in 1819 and the conquest of Mexican territory, many Latinos—U.S. citizens or residents of Latin American origin or descent—became U.S. citizens not because they moved to the United States but because the United States moved to them.

Treaty of Guadalupe Hidalgo The 1848 treaty between the United States and Mexico in which Mexico ceded large tracts of land to the United States.

Liberal Reform in Mexico

In 1853 Mexican president Santa Anna unintentionally ushered in a new era of liberal consolidation and economic reform by triggering a backlash against his sale of

Perspectives on the Mexican-American War

The Mexican-American War (1846–1848) was fought over U.S. control of northern Mexico, which became the Southwest and West of the United States. But the war was not fought only on the border: the U.S. Army and Navy fought far less armed and prepared Mexican forces from the Pacific to the borderlands and the Caribbean, going so far as to capture Mexico City.

José Joaquín de Herrera, President of Mexico, on the Loss of Texas, December 1845

■ In order to start a war, politicians agree that three questions must be examined: 1st, that of justice, 2nd, that of availability of resources, 3rd, that of convenience. . . . If, for launching war, one would only have to consider our justice, any hesitation in this matter would be either a crime or a lack of common sense. But next come the questions of feasibility and convenience for starting and maintaining hostilities with firmness and honor and all the consequences of a war of this nature.

A foreign war against a powerful and advanced nation that possesses an impressive navy and a . . . population that increases every day because of immigrants attracted to its great . . . prosperity, would imply immense sacrifices of men and money—not to assure victory, but simply to avoid defeat. Are such sacrifices possible for the Mexican Republic in her present state of exhaustion, after so many years of error and misadventure?

Manuel Crescencio Rejón, Minister of the Interior and Foreign Affairs Under Two Mexican Presidents, Arguing Against Ratification of the Treaty of Guadalupe Hidalgo, 1848

■ The social advantages which would accrue to us by accepting a peace now have been exaggerated, as well as the ease with which we would be able to maintain our remaining territories. It would be necessary, in order to sustain such illusions, to underestimate the spirit of enterprise of the North American people in industrial and commercial pursuits, to misunderstand their history and their tendencies, and also to presuppose in our own spirit less resistance than we have already shown toward the sincere friends of progress. Only through such illusions might one maintain that the treaty would bring a change that would be advantageous to us—as has been claimed.

Walt Whitman, Editorial in Favor of the War in the *Brooklyn Daily Eagle*, May 11, 1846

■ We are justified in the face of the world, in having treated Mexico with more forbearance than we have ever yet treated an enemy—for Mexico, though contemptible in many respects, is an enemy deserving a vigorous "lesson." . . . Let our arms now be carried with a spirit which shall teach the world that, while we are not forward for a quarrel, America knows how to crush, as well as how to expand!

Ulysses S. Grant, Looking Back on His Participation in the War, 1885

■ I was bitterly opposed to the measure, and to this day regard the war, which resulted, as one of the most unjust ever waged by a stronger against a weaker nation. It was an instance of a republic following the bad example of European monarchies, in not considering justice in their desire to acquire additional territory. . . . The occupation, separation and annexation [of Mexico] were, from the inception of the movement to its final consummation, a conspiracy to acquire territory out of which slave states might be formed for the American Union.

QUESTIONS FOR ANALYSIS

1. What issues do the Mexican politicians raise? What are their areas of disagreement?
2. How does the knowledge that Whitman's piece was a newspaper editorial shape your reading of it?
3. What might the implications have been for the U.S. forces if many officers had disapproved of the war the way Grant did?

Sources: Carol and Thomas Christensen, *The U.S. Mexican War* (San Francisco: Bay Books, 1998), p. 50; Ernesto Chávez, *The U.S. War with Mexico: A Brief History with Documents* (Boston: Bedford/St. Martin's, 2008), pp. 127, 83; Ulysses S. Grant, *Memoirs*, chap. 3, accessed through Project Gutenberg, http://www.gutenberg.org/files/5860/5860-h/5860-h.htm.

Mexican territory along the northern border to the United States in a deal known as the Gadsden Purchase. Many Mexicans thought Santa Anna betrayed the nation and threw their support behind a new generation of liberal leaders. Beginning with the presidency of Ignacio Comonfort (pres. 1855–1858), these liberals carried out sweeping legal and economic changes called *La Reforma*, or "the reform."

Liberal reformers sought to make all individuals equal under the law and established property ownership as a basic right and national goal. The first major step in La Reforma was the Juárez Law (1855), which abolished old legal privileges for military officers and members of the clergy. The law was written by Minister of Justice Benito Juárez (hoo-AH-rehs), an Indian from Oaxaca (whah-HAH-kah) whose first language was Zapotec. Juárez began life as a farmer but earned a law degree and became the most important force in consolidating Mexico's political system in the decades after independence. An even more consequential measure, the **Lerdo Law** (1856), banished another legacy of colonialism: "corporate lands," meaning lands owned by groups or institutions, such as the Catholic Church, a major landowner, rather than by individual property owners. Liberals saw those landholdings as backward and inefficient and wanted to replace them with small rural farm owners.

Lerdo Law An 1856 Mexican law that barred corporate landholdings.

These reforms triggered a backlash from conservative landowners and the church. When liberals ratified a new constitution in 1857, the Catholic Church threatened to excommunicate anyone who swore allegiance to it. Conservatives revolted, triggering a civil war called the Wars of Reform (1857–1861). Liberal forces led by Benito Juárez defeated the conservatives, who then conspired with French emperor Napoleon III to invite a French invasion of Mexico. Napoleon III saw an opportunity to re-establish France's American empire. His propaganda gave currency to the term "Latin America," used to assert that France had a natural role to play in Mexico because of a common "Latin" origin.

The French army invaded Mexico in 1862. Its main resistance was the defense mounted by a young officer named Porfirio Díaz, who blocked the invaders' advance through the city of Puebla on their way to Mexico City. The day of the Battle of Puebla, May 5, became a national holiday (known in the United States as "Cinco de Mayo"). Mexican conservatives and Napoleon III installed his Austrian cousin Maximilian of Habsburg as emperor of Mexico.

The deposed Juárez led a guerrilla war against the French troops backing Maximilian. When the U.S. Civil War ended in 1865, the U.S. government sought to root out France's influence on its border. The United States threw its support behind Juárez and pressured France to remove its troops. Bolstered by surplus Civil War armaments that flooded across the border into Mexico, Juárez's nationalists prevailed and executed Maximilian. Conservatives had been completely discredited: they had conspired with another country to install a foreign leader through a military invasion.

We can compare Benito Juárez, who governed the restored republic until 1876, with Abraham Lincoln. Both rose from humble rural origins to become able liberal lawyers. They became agile political and military leaders who prevailed in civil wars. The decade between the Wars of Reform and Juárez's restoration of the republic in 1867 can also be compared to the U.S. Civil War: both were watersheds in which questions that had lingered since independence were violently resolved and liberalism emerged as the dominant political philosophy.

Brazil: A New World Monarchy

Brazil gained independence in 1822 as a monarchy ruled by Emperor Pedro I, the son and heir of the Portuguese emperor. The creation of a Brazilian monarchy marked the culmination of a process that began in 1808, when Napoleon's armies crossed the Pyrenees from France to invade the Iberian Peninsula. Napoleon toppled the Spanish crown, but the Portuguese royal family, many of the government's bureaucrats, and most of the aristocracy fled aboard British warships to Portugal's colony of Brazil. This would be the first and only time a European empire would be ruled from one of its colonies.

Before the seat of Portuguese power relocated to Brazil, colonial policies had restricted many activities in Brazil in order to keep the colony dependent and subordinate to Portugal. It was only with the arrival of the imperial court that Brazil gained its first printing press, library, and military and naval academies, as well as schools for engineering, medicine, law, and the arts.

With the flight of the emperor to Brazil in 1808 and the declaration of independence by his son in 1822, Brazil achieved something that had eluded Spanish-American nations: it retained territorial unity under relative political stability. A liberal constitution adopted in 1824 lasted until a republican military coup in 1889. It established a two-chamber parliamentary system and a role for the emperor as a guide and intermediary in political affairs. Pedro I was not adept in this role and abdicated in 1831, leaving behind a regency governing in the name of his young son, Pedro II. In 1840, at the age of fourteen, Pedro II declared himself an adult and assumed the throne, ruling Brazil for the next forty-nine years.

Independent Brazil had many continuities with its colonial past. It remained the society with the largest number of African slaves in the Americas. It also continued to be economically and militarily dependent on Britain, as its mother-country, Portugal, had been in the eighteenth century. Britain negotiated with Brazil a "Friendship Treaty" that allowed British industrial goods to enter the country with very low

A Government Functionary Leaving Home with His Family and Servants, 1839 This lithograph is a depiction of Brazilian patriarchal and slave society social hierarchies that are shown through differences of gender, race, and age. The male patriarch is followed by members of the household ordered by their diminishing rank. (Bibliothèque Nationale, Paris, France/Archives Charmet/Bridgeman Images)

tariffs. The flood of cheap British imports inhibited Brazilian industrialization. British economic and political influence, as well as special privileges enjoyed by British citizens in Brazil, were examples of **neocolonialism**, the influence that European powers and the United States exerted over politically and economically weaker countries after independence.

> **neocolonialism** The establishment of political and economic influence over regions after they have ceased to be formal colonies.

Slavery and Abolition

In former Spanish-American colonies, the abolition of slavery quickly followed independence. In British colonies, slavery ended in 1834, and the British navy suppressed the Atlantic slave trade. But in the United States, Cuba, and Brazil slavery endured well into the nineteenth century. In each of these countries the question of abolition became entwined with the disputes over the nature of government and authority—federal unionism versus states' rights in the United States, independence for Cuba, and monarchy versus republicanism in Brazil.

> **Why did slavery last longer in the United States, Brazil, and Cuba than in the other republics of the Americas? How did resistance by slaves shape abolition?**

Slave Societies in the Americas

Africans and their descendants were enslaved in every country of the Americas. The experiences in slavery and freedom of Africans and African Americans, defined here as the descendants of slaves brought from Africa anywhere in the New World, varied considerably. Several factors shaped their experiences: the nature of slave regimes in different economic regions, patterns of manumission (individual slaves' gaining their freedom), the nature of abolition (the ending of the institution of slavery), and the proportion of the local population they represented.

The settlement of Africans as slaves was the most intense in areas that relied on plantation agriculture. (See "Analyzing the Evidence: Slaves Sold South from Richmond, 1853," page 836.) Plantations cultivated a single crop—especially sugar, coffee, tobacco, and cotton—on a vast scale that supplied distant global markets. Cotton from Alabama was spun by looms in New England or Britain; sugar and coffee from Brazil were consumed in European salons. Enslaved Africans played many other roles as well. From Buenos Aires to Boston, slavery was widespread in port cities, where it was fed by easy access to the slave trade and the demand for street laborers such as porters. And across the Americas, enslaved women were forced into domestic service, a role that conferred social prestige on their masters, but which also added sexual abuse to the miseries that enslaved people endured.

Independence and Abolition

Slavery and abolition became intertwined with the process of political independence. The different relationships between independence and abolition in the United States and Haiti shaped perceptions across the rest of the continent. In Haiti independence was achieved in a revolution in which slaves turned against their oppressors. By contrast, the United States gained its independence in a war that did not result in widespread slave revolt, and it created a liberal political regime that preserved the institution of slavery. When elites in other American colonies contemplated independence, they weighed whether the U.S. or the Haitian experience awaited them. As a result, in colonies where the subordinated population was the largest, independence movements proceeded the slowest. News of the Haitian Revolution spread briskly through slave communities. Slaves far from the Caribbean wore

Slaves Sold South from Richmond, 1853

This scene was painted by a British artist, based on events he witnessed in the U.S. South twenty years after slavery was abolished in the British Empire. Being "sold south," as this image depicts, was a terrifying fate. In addition to having their families ripped apart, those who were sold were sent to plantations where the labor regimes were famously harsh. Note the ways in which the artist depicts not only the slave families but also the white, mixed, and free black traders.

The experience of being "sold south" in the United States had its equivalents in other slave societies. In Cuba the dreaded destination was the easternmost province of Oriente, with the fearsome intensity of its sugar plantation regime. In Brazil slaves faced the threat of being sent across the Atlantic to Portuguese colonies in west and central Africa. The threat of being sent to a more grueling and often-lethal region was a terrible power masters wielded over slaves, but so too was the power to destroy a family by selling away husbands or wives, or separating parents from young children. Slave regimes in the Americas endured in part because of the terror that masters wielded over slaves, and these threats were powerful tools in maintaining slave owners' domination over enslaved people.

(*After the Sale: Slaves Going South from Richmond*, 1853, by Eyre Crowe [1824–1910] [oil on canvas]/© Chicago History Museum, Illinois, USA/Bridgeman Images)

QUESTIONS FOR ANALYSIS

1. How does the artist try to provoke a reaction against slavery?
2. How are whites and free blacks represented in the image?
3. Can you think of other examples of art with social or political messages? How would this painting compare in its effectiveness?

pendants with images of Haitian revolutionary leader Toussaint L'Ouverture. (See "Individuals in Society: Toussaint L'Ouverture" in Chapter 22.)

British efforts to keep their North American colonies, as well as a combination of moral and economic appeals for the abolition of slavery in British territories, hastened the end of the slave trade to the Americas. When British forces fought to prevent the independence of the United States, they offered freedom to slaves who joined them. Many slaves did so, and after the British defeat and withdrawal, they dispersed to Spanish Florida, the Caribbean, and West Africa.

In 1807 British abolitionists pressured the British Parliament to end the Atlantic slave trade to British colonies, and in 1833 Parliament voted to abolish slavery the following year in Canada and Britain's Caribbean colonies. To reduce economic competition, the British government pressured other nations to follow suit. A British naval squadron patrolled the Atlantic to suppress the slave trade. The squadron captured slave ships, freed the slaves they carried, and resettled them in a colony the British government established in Sierra Leone in 1787 to settle former slaves who had sided with Britain in the American Revolution.

In Spanish America independence forces enlisted the participation of slaves and offered freedom in return. Thousands gained manumission by siding with rebel forces, and new national governments enacted gradual abolition. The first step toward abolition was often through **free womb laws** that freed children born to slave women. These laws, passed across independent Spanish America between 1811 and 1825, created gradual abolition but did not impose an immediate financial loss on slaveholders: to the contrary, the free children of slaves remained apprenticed to their masters until they reached adulthood. Similar laws hastened the abolition of slavery in the Northern states of the United States.

The combination of free womb laws and manumission as a reward for military service meant that unlike in the United States, by the time slavery was abolished in Latin American countries, most peoples of African descent had already gained their freedom (Map 27.2).

In the United States the questions of nation building and slavery remained connected. The determination of Southern states to protect the slave regime was enshrined in the Constitution, which granted individual states autonomy in matters such as slavery. As slavery was abolished in Northern states, westward expansion tested the political compromise between the North and South, culminating in the Civil War. In 1854, even as slavery was abolished in the last Spanish-American republics, armed confrontations erupted in Kansas over whether that territory would be incorporated as a state permitting slavery. Tensions between the North and the South reached a breaking point when Abraham Lincoln, opposed to the spread of slavery, was elected president in 1860. Southern political leaders, fearing that Lincoln might abolish slavery, seceded and formed a new nation, the Confederate States of America. Lincoln declared the secession illegal and waged war to preserve the territorial integrity of the United States. The ensuing civil war resulted in the deaths of over 750,000 combatants and civilians.

In 1862 Lincoln sought to pressure the Confederate states to rejoin the Union by issuing the Emancipation Proclamation. The proclamation, which became effective January 1, 1863, abolished slavery in all states that remained opposed to the Union. It was intended as leverage to bring the rebel states back, not to abolish slavery altogether; consequently it freed slaves only in states that had seceded. Nevertheless, the proclamation hastened the demise of slavery. In 1865 Southern rebel states surrendered after Northern armies decimated their industrial, agricultural, and military capacity. Months later, the Thirteenth Amendment to the Constitution fully abolished slavery. Subsequent amendments recognized the citizenship and rights of people formerly enslaved.

free womb laws Laws passed across the nineteenth-century Americas that instituted a gradual form of abolition through which children born to slaves gained their freedom.

MAPPING THE PAST

MAP 27.2 Abolition in the Americas

The process of abolition in the Americas was gradual and varied across regions. In some areas, such as Mexico and parts of New England, slavery was abolished soon after independence, while in the U.S. South it lasted until the end of the Civil War. In Texas slavery was abolished by the Mexican government, but when Texas became part of the United States, slavery was legally reinstated. In British territories slavery was abolished in 1834. Across Latin America the abolition of slavery was hastened by civil wars that mobilized slaves as combatants. The last country to abolish slavery, Brazil, did so only in 1888.

ANALYZING THE MAP How did the United States resemble Latin America in its patterns of abolition?

CONNECTIONS Why did some countries abolish slavery earlier, and why did others do so much later?

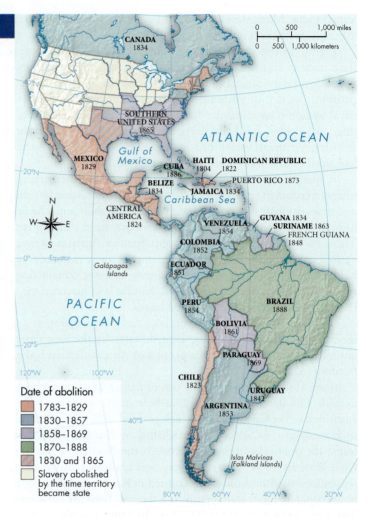

Date of abolition
- 1783–1829
- 1830–1857
- 1858–1869
- 1870–1888
- 1830 and 1865
- Slavery abolished by the time territory became state

Two aspects made slavery in the United States different from slavery in Latin America: gradual abolition in the North made it a regional rather than a national institution; and the Civil War, followed by military occupation of the South (1865–1877), created a lasting regional backlash that codified racial segregation. This did not make the South entirely racist and the North entirely antiracist: segregation is a form of racism but hardly the only one. Instead race relations in the northern and western states of the United States resembled those of Latin America, where racial prejudice and the marginalization of African Americans were perpetuated through largely informal practices, such as discrimination in employment, housing, and lending. Meanwhile, the U.S. South erected a distinct legal edifice preserving white privilege that best resembled the oppressive white-minority regimes of South Africa and Rhodesia (see "Resistance to White Rule in Southern Africa" in Chapter 32).

Abolition in Cuba and Brazil

Cuba and Brazil followed long paths to abolition. In Cuba nationalist rebels fought for independence from Spain in the Ten Years' War (1868–1878). Many slaves and free blacks joined the failed anticolonial struggle, and rebel leaders expressed support for abolition. Spanish authorities sought to defuse the tensions feeding that struggle by granting freedom to slaves who fought on the Spanish side in the war, to the children of slaves born since 1868, and to slaves over age sixty. By 1878 Spanish forces had defeated the nationalists, but the conflict had set in motion an irreversible process of abolition.

In Brazil an 1871 law granted freedom to children born to slaves, and an 1885 law granted freedom to slaves over age sixty. At best, these laws were half measures, aimed at placating abolitionists without disrupting the economic reliance on slave labor. At worst, they mocked the meaning of abolition: children freed under the free womb laws remained apprenticed to their mother's master until they reached adulthood. These laws preserved masters' access to the labor of the children of slaves, while freeing masters from their obligations to care for elderly slaves. Slavery was finally abolished in Cuba in 1886 and in Brazil in 1888, making them the last regions of the Americas to end slavery. Abolition did not come about solely through laws from the top down. Pressure exerted by slaves contributed to abolition. Slave resistance, in its many forms, intensified in the later years of the nineteenth century. Slaves escaped in growing numbers. In many cases, they settled in communities of runaway slaves, particularly in Brazil, where the vast interior offered opportunities to resettle out of the reach of slave society. In the years preceding abolition, in some regions of Brazil slave flight became so widespread that slaves might simply leave their plantation and hire themselves out to a nearby planter whose own slaves had also run away. In the end, the costs of slavery had become unsustainable.

Export-Led Growth and Social Unrest

Beginning in the 1850s and accelerating through conflicts like Mexico's Wars of Reform, the U.S. Civil War, and the Paraguay War in South America, the consolidation of liberalism in the Americas created conditions for a return of foreign investment that brought economic growth. But liberal reforms created new economic pressures against rural workers and indigenous communities who led reform and resistance movements such as those unleashed by the Mexican Revolution.

> As Latin America became more integrated into the world economy, how did patterns of economic growth shape political culture and social reactions?

Latin America Re-enters the World Economy

The wars of independence in Spanish America disrupted the trade networks that had sustained the region's economies, while civil war and rule by caudillos delayed the consolidation of liberal regimes. In the first decades of independence, Latin America's economic integration with the world decreased. For rural peasants and indigenous communities, this was a benefit in disguise: the decline of trade made lands less valuable. The rents landowners could charge tenant farmers decreased, making it easier for peasants to gain access to land.

By the second half of the nineteenth century Latin American elites reached a compromise that combined liberal political ideas about the way national government should be structured with liberal economic policies that favored large landowners. Political stability and economic growth returned. Foreign investment intensified. By the turn of the twentieth century Latin American countries were firmly tied to the world economy. Indigenous and rural communities paid a high price for this return to economic growth: as the value of agricultural exports increased, so did the value of

Barranquilla, Colombia, ca. 1910
Like port cities across Latin America, Barranquilla in Colombia began as a center of trade, and by the early twentieth century it was a bustling center of immigration and industrialization. (© Mary Evans Picture Library/Grenville Collins Postcard Collection/The Image Works)

land. Governments, foreign investors, and large landowners seized indigenous lands through war, legal action, or coercion at a dizzying rate.

For example, in the late 1880s the Argentine government sold off lands it took from indigenous communities. The land was inexpensive, but because it was sold in such large parcels, the few who could purchase it did so by mortgaging existing land-holdings. Though reformers had imagined the creation of a class of small farmers, the result was the opposite: more than 20 million acres were sold to just 381 landowners who created vast estates known as **latifundios**.[3]

latifundios Vast landed estates in Latin America.

Liberal economic policies and the intensification of foreign trade concentrated land in the hands of wealthy exporters. Governments represented the interests of large landowners by promoting commodity exports and industrial imports, following the liberal economic principle of comparative advantage (that countries should export what they could produce the most efficiently and import what other countries could produce more cheaply and efficiently). Brazil became the world's largest exporter of coffee and experienced a brief but intense boom in rubber production. Argentina became one of the most efficient and profitable exporters of grains and beef. Chile and Peru served the international market for fertilizers by exporting nitrates and bat guano.

These export booms depended on imported capital and technology. In the Circum-Caribbean this came mostly from investors in the United States, while in South America it often came from Britain. (See "Individuals in Society: Henry Meiggs, Promoter and Speculator," at right.)

British capital and technology built Argentina's network of railroads and refrigerated meatpacking plants. Chile's nitrate-mining industry was expanded through the War of the Pacific (1879–1883), a conflict in which Chile seized territory in bordering Peru and Bolivia. As a result, Bolivia lost its access to the Pacific and became a landlocked nation. The war and its outcomes revealed British influence as well: to finance the war, the Chilean government issued bonds bought by British investors. The bonds were repaid through the sale of concessions for mining the nitrate-rich lands that Chile conquered from Bolivia. In 1878 British companies controlled 13 percent of nitrate mining. By 1890 they controlled 90 percent.

Henry Meiggs, Promoter and Speculator

ALL THROUGHOUT THE AMERICAS IN THE NINE-
teenth century, opportunities beckoned. Henry Meiggs, born in upstate New York in 1811, responded to several of them, building and losing fortunes in Brooklyn, San Francisco, Chile, and Peru.

Meiggs, with only an elementary school education, began work at his father's shipyard. He soon started his own lumber business and did well until he lost everything in the financial panic of 1837. He rebuilt his business, and when gold was discovered in California in 1848, he filled a ship with lumber and sailed around Cape Horn to San Francisco, where he sold his cargo for $50,000, twenty times what he had paid for it. He then entered the lumber business, organizing crews of five hundred men to fell huge California redwoods and bring them to his steam sawmills. As his business flourished, he began speculating in real estate, which led to huge debts when the financial crisis of 1854 hit. In an attempt to save himself and his friends, Meiggs forged warrants for more than $900,000; when discovery of the fraud seemed imminent, he sailed with his wife and children for South America.

Although at one point Meiggs was so strapped for cash that he sold his watch, within three years of arriving in Chile, he had secured his first railway contract, and by 1867 he had built about 200 miles of rail lines in that country. In 1868 he went to Peru, which had less than 60 miles of track at the time. In the next nine years he would add 700 more.

Meiggs was not an engineer, but he was a good manager. He recruited experienced engineers from abroad and arranged the purchase of foreign rolling stock, rails, and ties, acting as a promoter and developer. Much of the funding came from international investors in Peruvian bonds.

The most spectacular of the rail lines Meiggs built was Peru's Callao-Lima-Oroya line, which crosses the Andes at about seventeen thousand feet above sea level, making it the highest standard-gauge railway in the world. Because water was scarce in many areas along the construction site, it had to be transported up to workers, who were mostly local people. Dozens of bridges and tunnels had to be built, and casualties were high. Eight hundred people were invited to the banquet that marked the beginning of work on the Oroya Railway. Meiggs drummed up enthusiasm at the event by calling the locomotive the "irresistible battering ram of modern civilization."

In Peru Meiggs became known for his extravagance and generosity, and some charged that he bribed Peruvian officials on a large scale to get his projects approved. He was a good speaker and loved to entertain lavishly. In one example of his generosity, he distributed thousands of pesos and soles to the victims of the earthquake of 1868. He also contributed to the beautification of Lima by tearing down an old wall and putting a seven-mile-long park in its place.

The challenges in building the Callao-Lima-Oroya railroad across the Andes can be imagined from this picture of one of its many bridges. (Michael Maslan/Corbis/VCG via Getty Images)

Always the speculator, Meiggs died poor in 1877, with his debts exceeding his assets. He was beloved, however, and more than twenty thousand Peruvians, many of whom had labored on his projects, attended his funeral at a Catholic church in Lima.

QUESTIONS FOR ANALYSIS

1. What accounts for the changes in fortune that Meiggs experienced?
2. Were the Latin American governments that awarded contracts to Meiggs making reasonable decisions?
3. Should it matter whether Meiggs had to bribe officials to get the railroads built? Why or why not?

Liberal Consolidation in South America

As in the United States and Mexico, the process of liberal nation-state consolidation in South America took place through military conflict. The War of the Triple Alliance, or Paraguay War (1865–1870), in which Paraguay fought Brazil, Argentina, and Uruguay, played a similar role to Mexico's Wars of Reform and the U.S. Civil War in consolidating liberalism. In 1865 Paraguayan leader Francisco Solano López declared war against the three neighboring countries after political competition between Argentina and Brazil threatened Paraguay's use of Uruguay's port of Montevideo. Landlocked Paraguay depended on Montevideo as a shipping point for its imports and exports.

The war was devastating for Paraguay, which lost more than half its national population, including most adult men. But victory, too, was traumatic for Argentina and Brazil: why had it taken five years to defeat a much smaller neighbor? The war prompted debates about the need for economic modernization and the reform of national governments.

In Brazil, where Emperor Pedro II's calls for volunteers to enlist in the army fell on deaf ears, the army enlisted slaves who, if they served honorably and survived, would be granted freedom. What did it mean that the free citizens of a nation would not mobilize to defend it, and that the nation prevailed only through the sacrifices borne by its slaves? For many, especially officers who were veterans of the conflict, the lesson was that being a monarchy that relied on slavery made Brazil a weak and backward nation. Veteran officers and liberal opponents of the war formed a movement to create a liberal republic and abolish slavery. These republicans overthrew monarchy in 1889 and created a liberal republic.

In Argentina, after the war with Paraguay, liberal leaders beginning with Domingo Sarmiento (pres. 1868–1874) pressed modernizing reforms. These included a military campaign called the Conquest of the Desert (1878–1885), in which Argentine troops took control of the lands of Mapuche Indians in the southern region of Patagonia and opened new lands for sale to ranchers. The wars were accompanied by ambitious railroad construction that linked inland areas to the coast to transport goods, which brought the introduction of barbed wire fencing that intensified ranching capabilities and the development of new strains of cattle and wheat that increased production.

The Porfiriato and Liberal Stability in Mexico

When Porfirio Díaz became president of Mexico in 1876, the hero of the Battle of Puebla inherited a country in which much had been achieved: President Juárez had established national unity against the French invasion. His generation of liberal leaders had also created a legal and political framework based on the 1857 constitution. But it was a country that faced enormous challenges: per capita income was less than it had been at independence in 1821. The country had barely four hundred miles of railroads, compared to more than seventy thousand miles in the United States. Díaz's first challenge was to attract foreign investment.

Porfirio Díaz built a regime — the **Porfiriato** — with unprecedented stability and ruled, with a single term out of power, from 1876 to 1911. He ruled by the mantra "*pan o palo*," bread or the stick, rewarding supporters and ruthlessly punishing opponents. The political stability he created made Mexico a haven for foreign investment,

Porfiriato The regime of Porfirio Díaz, who presided in Mexico from 1876 to 1880 and again from 1884 to 1911.

The Growth of Industry in Mexico Workers at a textile mill in Mexico around 1900. (© akg-images/ The Image Works)

particularly from the United States. Foreign trade increased tenfold, and the country became the third-largest oil producer in the world. Railroads rapidly expanded, reaching fifteen thousand miles of track by 1910, much of it connecting Mexico to the United States. Railroads also connected regions long isolated from each other and sustained national markets for the first time since the colonial era.

The Porfiriato was a modernizing regime. The government swelled with techno-crats called *científicos* (see-en-TEE-fee-kohs), to whom Díaz granted great autonomy and lavish rewards. By contrast, the Porfiriato considered indigenous peoples racially inferior and suppressed them. This was the case of the Yaqui Indians of Sonora, at the border with Arizona (see Map 27.1). Díaz's army vanquished Yaqui communities, seized their land, and dispatched survivors to the Yucatán, where they worked as slaves on plantations cultivating *henequén* (hen-eh-KEN), a plant whose fibers were used in the hay-baling machines increasingly used by U.S. farmers. The Porfiriato used the mission of modernization and economic development to justify a range of abuses.

Economic progress enriched Díaz and his allies but proved perilous to rural com-munities. As the rise in foreign investment and economic activity made land valu-able, small landholders became vulnerable. Large landowners and speculative inves-tors used the Lerdo Law to usurp the lands of peasants across the countryside. In addition, the 1883 Law of Barren Lands allowed real estate companies to identify land that was not being cultivated (often land that communities allowed to lie fallow as they rotated crops) so it could be surveyed and auctioned off. The abuse of these laws by land speculators had devastating consequences: by 1910, 80 percent of rural peasants had no land.

The Porfiriato and its liberal ideology favored the needs of foreign investors over its own citizens. Most of Mexico's 1910 population of 12 million remained tied to the land. The expansion of railroads into that land made it valuable, and liberal reforms provided the tools to transfer that value from peasants to capitalists. Given Mexico's proximity to the United States, that process was swifter and more intense than it was elsewhere in Latin America, and it led to the first great social upheaval of the twentieth century.

The Mexican Revolution

Porfirio Díaz declared himself the unanimous winner of Mexico's 1910 elections. His defeated challenger, wealthy landowner and liberal lawyer Francisco Madero, issued a manifesto calling the election illegitimate and pronouncing himself the provisional president of Mexico. Madero's call to arms was the spark that ignited a powder keg of grievances from peasants whose lands had been taken or threatened, and from exploited urban workers.

Peasants and workers across the country rose up, drove out Díaz, and annointed Madero provisional president. Madero proved to be a weak reformer, and armed peasant groups rose up again, this time against him. The U.S. ambassador, who considered Madero to be inadequate in his defense of U.S. business interests, conspired with the commander of Madero's army to assassinate him in 1912. Mexico's revolution now deepened, as factions around the country joined the fighting.

The ideological leadership of the Mexican Revolution came from Emiliano Zapata and his supporters, who hailed from rural communities south of Mexico City whose lands were threatened. The Zapatistas made their demands in a document called the **Plan de Ayala** (ai-YAH-lah) that called for the return of all land, forests, and waters taken from rural communities. Their pledge to fight until these demands were met was taken up by many armed groups across Mexico, particularly the army commanded by the charismatic Pancho Villa (pahn-choh VEE-yah). They found allies as well in the Red Brigades of anarchist and socialist workers who controlled the capital, Mexico City, during much of the war.

Supporters of the Plan de Ayala were gradually beaten back by the faction that would eventually prevail, a group called the Constitutionalists, led by politician

Plan de Ayala Document written by Zapatistas during the Mexican Revolution that demanded the government return all land, forests, and waters taken from rural communities.

Emiliano Zapata and Pancho Villa in Mexico's Presidential Palace, 1914 Villa sits in the presidential chair topped with the golden eagle, and Zapata appears next to him on the right, holding a sombrero. Two small children peer over their shoulders as each leader insists he will not claim the presidency since his goal was reform and not power. (Universal History Archive/UIG/Bridgeman Images)

Venustiano Carranza and Álvaro Obregón, a skilled general who emulated tactics and strategies employed in Europe in the First World War. But to consolidate political control and to convince rebels like those supporting Zapata and Villa to put down their arms, their constitution included key demands from the Plan de Ayala and from urban workers.

In meeting the demands of peasants and workers, Mexico's 1917 constitution imposed the most significant limits to liberalism yet attempted in the Americas. It broke the fundamental liberal embrace of private property by asserting that all land, water, and subsoil resources belong to the nation, which allows their use for the public good. This clause allowed the government to expropriate lands from large estates to make grants of collective land called *ejidos* (eh-HEE-dohz) to rural communities. Over 80 million acres of farmland and forests would be redistributed as ejidos. The constitution included the most advanced labor code in the world at the time, guaranteeing workers the right to unionize and strike, an eight-hour workday, a minimum wage, and protections for women workers, including maternity leave.

By agreeing to these social demands, the Constitutionalist faction was able to consolidate control over a new political order that would enjoy remarkable stability: the political party that emerged from the Constitutionalists would hold presidential power for almost all of the next one hundred years.

Immigration

During the late nineteenth and early twentieth centuries unprecedented numbers of people from Europe, Asia, and the Middle East settled across North and South America. The largest wave of immigrants—some 28 million between 1860 and 1914—settled in the United States. Another 8 million had settled in Argentina and Brazil by 1930. This cycle of immigration was a product of liberal political and economic reforms that abolished slavery, established stable political systems, and created a framework for integrating immigrants as factory and farm laborers.

What factors shaped patterns of immigration to the Americas? How did immigrants shape — and how were they shaped by — their new settings?

Immigration to Latin America

In 1852 the Argentine political philosopher Juan Bautista Alberdi published *Bases and Points of Departure for Argentine Political Organization*, in which he argued that the development of his country depended on immigration. Drawing on the Social Darwinist theory that whites were racially more advanced than Indians and blacks, Alberdi maintained that black and indigenous Argentines lacked basic skills, and it would take too long to train them. Thus he pressed for massive immigration from northern Europe and the United States:

> Each European who comes to our shores brings more civilization in his habits, which will later be passed on to our inhabitants, than many books of philosophy. . . . Do we want to sow and cultivate in America English liberty, French culture, and the diligence of men from Europe and from the United States? Let us bring living pieces of these qualities.[4]

Alberdi's ideas, guided by the aphorism "to govern is to populate," won immediate acceptance and were even incorporated into the Argentine constitution, which declared, "The Federal government will encourage European immigration." Other countries of the Americas, also influenced by Social Darwinism, adopted similar immigration policies.

Coffee barons in Brazil, *latifundiarios* (owners of vast estates) in Argentina, or investors in nitrate and copper mining in Chile made enormous profits that they reinvested in new factories. Latin America had been tied to the Industrial Revolution in Britain and northern Europe from the outset as a provider of raw materials and as a consumer of industrial goods. In the major exporting countries of Argentina, Brazil, and Mexico, domestic industrialization now began to take hold in the form of textile mills, food-processing plants, and mechanized transportation such as modern ports and railroads.

By the turn of the twentieth century an industrial working class had begun to emerge. In Brazil and Argentina these workers, who were mainly European immigrants, proved unexpectedly contentious: they brought with them radical ideologies that challenged liberalism, particularly anarchism and **anarcho-syndicalism**, a version of anarchism that advocated placing power in the hands of workers' unions. These workers clashed with bosses and political leaders who rejected the idea that workers had rights. The authorities suppressed worker organizations such as unions, and they resisted implementing labor laws such as a minimum wage, restrictions on child labor, the right to strike, or factory safety regulations.

Radicalized workers mounted labor actions that at times grew into general strikes with over one hundred thousand workers picketing. But outside of Mexico, the movements of urban workers did not merge with rural unrest in the formula that produced revolution.

Although Europe was a significant source of immigrants to Latin America, so were Asia and the Middle East. In the late nineteenth and early twentieth centuries large numbers of Japanese arrived in Brazil,

anarcho-syndicalism
A version of anarchism that advocated placing power in the hands of workers' unions.

Immigrants in the Americas
Indian immigrants at a Jamaican banana plantation (above) and German immigrants in Brazil (right) at the turn of the twentieth century. Immigrants brought new cultures and worldviews to the Americas. (Jamaica: © The Print Collector/Heritage/The Image Works; Brazil: © SZ Photo/Sherl/The Image Works)

most settling in São Paulo state, creating the largest Japanese community in the world outside of Japan. From the Middle East, Lebanese, Turks, and Syrians also entered Brazil. South Asian laborers went to Trinidad, Jamaica, Guyana, and other British territories in the Caribbean, mostly as indentured servants under five-year contracts. Perhaps one-third returned to India, but the rest stayed, saved money, and bought small businesses or land. After slavery was abolished in Cuba in 1886, some work in the cane fields was done by Chinese indentured laborers. Likewise, the abolition of slavery in Mexico led to the arrival of thousands of Chinese bonded servants.

Thanks to the influx of new arrivals, Buenos Aires, São Paulo, Mexico City, Montevideo, Santiago, and Havana experienced spectacular growth. By 1914 Buenos Aires had emerged as one of the most cosmopolitan cities in the world, with a population of 3.6 million. As Argentina's political capital, the city housed its government bureaucracies and agencies. The meatpacking, food-processing, flour-milling, and wool industries were concentrated there as well. Half of all overseas tonnage passed through the city, which was also the heart of the nation's railroad network. Elegant shops near the Plaza de Mayo catered to the expensive tastes of the elite upper classes that constituted about 5 percent of the population. By contrast, the thousands of immigrants who toiled twelve hours a day, six days a week, on docks and construction sites and in meatpacking plants were crowded into the city's one-room tenements.

Immigrants brought wide-ranging skills that helped develop industry and commerce. In Argentina, Italian and Spanish settlers stimulated the expansion of cattle ranching, meat processing, wheat farming, and the shoe industry. In Brazil, Italians gained a leading role in the coffee industry, and Japanese farmers made the country self-sufficient in rice production. Chinese laborers built Peruvian railroads, and in sections of large cities such as Lima, the Chinese dominated the ownership of shops and restaurants.

Immigration to the United States

After the Civil War ended in 1865, the United States underwent an industrial boom powered by exploitation of the country's natural resources. The federal government turned over vast amounts of land and mineral resources to private industrialists for development. In particular, railroad companies—the foundation of industrial expansion—received 130 million acres. By 1900 the U.S. railroad system was 193,000 miles long, connected every part of the nation, and represented 40 percent of the railroad mileage in the world, and it was all built by immigrant labor.

Between 1860 and 1914, 28 million immigrants came to the United States. Though many became rural homesteaders, industrial America developed through the labor of immigrants. Chinese, Scandinavian, and Irish immigrants laid railroad tracks. At the Carnegie Steel Corporation, Slavs and Italians produced one-third of the world's total steel supply in 1900. As in South America, immigration fed the growth of cities. In 1790 only 5.1 percent of Americans were living in centers of twenty-five hundred or more people. By 1860 this figure had risen to 19.9 percent, and by 1900 almost 40 percent of the population lived in cities. Also by 1900, three of the largest cities in the world were in the United States—New York City with 3.4 million people, Chicago with 1.7 million, and Philadelphia with 1.4 million.

Working conditions for new immigrants were often deplorable. Industrialization had created a vast class of workers who depended entirely on wage labor. Employers

"The Chinese Must Go!" Anti-immigrant sentiment intensified as immigration to the United States accelerated in the late nineteenth and early twentieth centuries. This 1880 campaign advertisement presented Chinese immigrants as a threat to native-born workers. (Sarin Images/Granger, NY — All rights reserved.)

paid women and children much less than men. Some women textile workers earned as little as $1.56 for seventy hours of work, while men received from $7 to $9 for the same work. Because business owners resisted government efforts to install costly safety devices, working conditions in mines and mills were frightful. In 1913 alone, even after some safety measures had been instituted, twenty-five thousand people died in industrial accidents. Between 1900 and 1917 seventy-two thousand railroad workers died on the job. Workers responded to these conditions with strikes, violence, and, gradually, unionization.

Immigrants faced more than economic exploitation: they were also subjected to harsh ethnic stereotypes and faced pressure to culturally assimilate. An economic depression in the 1890s increased resentment toward immigrants. Powerful owners of mines, mills, and factories fought the organization of labor unions, fired thousands of workers, slashed wages, and ruthlessly exploited their workers. Workers in turn feared that immigrant labor would drive salaries lower. Some of this antagonism sprang from racism, some from old Protestant prejudice against Catholicism, the faith of many of the new arrivals. Anti-Semitism against Jewish immigrants from eastern Europe intensified, while increasingly violent agitation against Asians led to race riots in California and finally culminated in the Chinese Exclusion Act of 1882, which denied Chinese laborers entrance to the country. Japanese immigration to the United States was restricted in 1907, so later Japanese immigrants settled in South America.

Immigrants were received very differently in Latin America, where oligarchs encouraged immigration from Europe, the Middle East, and Japan because they believed these "whiter" workers were superior to black or indigenous workers. By contrast, in the United States the descendants of northern European Protestants developed prejudices and built social barriers out of their belief that Catholic Irish, southern and eastern European, or Jewish immigrants were not white enough.

Immigration to Canada

Canada was sparsely populated in the nineteenth century relative to other areas of the Americas. Provinces of the British colony gained governing autonomy after 1840 and organized a national government, the Dominion of Canada, in 1867 (Map 27.3).

British authorities agreed to grant the provinces political independence in order to avoid the disruption and loss of influence that followed U.S. independence, and in return the Dominion retained a symbolic role for the British monarchy. By 1900 Canada still had only a little over 5 million people (as compared to 13.6 million in Mexico and 76 million in the United States). As in the United States and Latin America, native peoples were pushed aside by Canada's development plans, and their population dropped by half or more during the century, many succumbing to the newcomers' diseases. By 1900 there were only about 127,000 indigenous people left in Canada. French Canadians were the largest minority in the population, and they remained different in language, law, and religion.

Immigration to Canada increased in the 1890s. Between 1897 and 1912, 961,000 people entered Canada from the British Isles, 594,000 from Europe, and 784,000 from the United States. Some immigrants went to work in the urban factories of Hamilton, Toronto, and Montreal. However, most immigrants from continental Europe—Poles, Germans, Scandinavians, and Russians—flooded the midwestern plains and soon transformed the prairies into one of the world's greatest grain-growing regions. Between 1891 and 1914 wheat production soared from 2 million

MAP 27.3 The Dominion of Canada, 1871 Shortly after the Dominion of Canada came into being as a self-governing nation within the British Empire in 1867, new provinces were added. Vast areas of Canada were too sparsely populated to achieve provincial status. Alberta and Saskatchewan did not become part of the Dominion until 1905; Newfoundland was added only in 1949.

bushels per year to 150 million bushels. Mining expanded, and British Columbia, Ontario, and Quebec produced large quantities of wood pulp, much of it sold to the United States. Canada's great rivers were harnessed to supply hydroelectric power for industrial and domestic use. But Canada remained a predominantly agricultural country, with less than 10 percent of its population engaged in manufacturing.

A New American Empire

In what ways did U.S. policies in the Caribbean and Central America resemble European imperialism? How did U.S. foreign policy depart from European imperialism?

By 1890 the United States had claimed the contiguous territories it acquired through purchase, war, and displacement. Its frontier was closed. The United States redirected its expansionist pressures outward, beginning with the remnants of the Spanish Empire: Cuba and Puerto Rico in the Caribbean, and the Philippine Islands and Guam in the Pacific.

The United States emulated the imperialism of European nations like Britain and France by claiming control of land and people that served its economic interests and justifying its domination by arguing that it was advancing civilization.

U.S. Intervention in Latin America

Between 1898 and 1932 the U.S. government intervened militarily thirty-four times in ten nations in the Caribbean and Central America to extend and protect its economic interests. U.S. influence in the Circum-Caribbean was not new, however, and stretched back to the early nineteenth century. In 1823 President James Monroe proclaimed in the **Monroe Doctrine** that the United States would keep European influence out of Latin America. This doctrine asserted that Latin America was part of the U.S. sphere of influence. U.S. intervention in Latin America was also a byproduct of the manifest destiny ideal of consolidating national territory from the Atlantic to the Pacific. Often the easiest way to connect the two sides of the continent was through Latin America.

Monroe Doctrine An 1823 proclamation that established a U.S. sphere of influence over the Americas by opposing European imperialism on the continent.

The California gold rush of the 1840s created pressure to move people and goods quickly and inexpensively between the eastern and western parts of the United States decades before its transcontinental railroad was completed in 1869. It was cheaper, faster, and safer to travel to the east or west coast of Mexico and Central America, traverse the continent where it was narrower, and continue the voyage by sea. The Panama Railway, the first railroad constructed in Central America, served exactly this purpose and was built with U.S. investment in 1855.

Facing pressure from abolitionists against expanding the slave regime westward, planters and politicians in the U.S. South responded by seeking opportunities to annex new lands in Latin America and the Caribbean. They eyed Cuba, the Dominican Republic, El Salvador, and Nicaragua. In Nicaragua, Tennessean William Walker employed a mercenary army to depose the government and install himself as president (1856–1857). One of his first acts was to reinstate slavery. He was overthrown by armies sent from Costa Rica, El Salvador, and Honduras.

By the end of the nineteenth century U.S. involvement in Latin America had intensified, first through private investment and then through military force. In 1893 a group of U.S. investors formed the Santo Domingo Improvement Company, which bought the foreign debt of the Dominican Republic and took control of its customs houses in order to repay investors and creditors. After the government propped up by the U.S. company fell, President Theodore Roosevelt introduced what would be known as the **Roosevelt Corollary** to the Monroe Doctrine, which stated that the United States, as a civilized nation, would correct the "chronic wrong-doing" of its neighbors, such as failure to protect U.S. investments.

To this end, in 1903 and 1904 Roosevelt deployed Marines to the Dominican Republic to protect the investments of U.S. firms. Marines occupied and governed the Dominican Republic again from 1916 to 1924. The violent and corrupt dictator Rafael Trujillo (troo-HEE-yo) ruled from 1930 to 1961 with the support of the United States. When he eventually defied the United States, he was assassinated by rivals acting with the encouragement of the Central Intelligence Agency.

Versions of the Dominican Republic's experience played out across the Circum-Caribbean. U.S. Marines occupied Haiti from 1915 to 1934 and Nicaragua from 1912 to 1934. These military occupations followed a similar pattern of using military force to protect private U.S. companies' investments in banana and sugar plantations, railroads, mining, ports, and utilities. And as U.S. forces departed, they left power in the hands of dictators who served U.S. interests. These dictators governed not through popular consent but through force, corruption, and the support of the United States.

> **Roosevelt Corollary**
> A corollary to the Monroe Doctrine stating that the United States would correct what it saw as "chronic wrongdoing" in neighboring countries.

The Spanish-American War

In Cuba a second war of independence erupted in 1895 after it had failed to gain freedom from Spain in the Ten Years' War (1868–1878). A brutal war of attrition ensued, and by 1898 the countryside was in ruins and Spanish colonial control was restricted to a handful of cities. Cuban nationalists were on the verge of defeating the Spanish forces and gaining independence. But before they could realize this goal, the United States intervened, resulting in the Spanish-American War (1898).

The U.S. intervention began with a provocative act: sailing the battleship *Maine* into Havana harbor. This was an aggressive act because the battleship was capable of bombarding the entire city. But soon after it laid anchor, the *Maine* exploded and sank, killing hundreds of sailors. The U.S. government accused Spain of sinking the warship, a charge Spain denied, and demanded that the Spanish government provide restitution. Later investigations determined that a kitchen fire spread to the main munitions storage and blew up the ship. The sinking of the *Maine* led to war between Spain and the United States over control of Cuba and the Philippines. The U.S. Navy and Marines fought and defeated Spanish forces in the Pacific and the Caribbean. With its victory, the United States acquired Guam and Puerto Rico and launched a military occupation of Cuba and the Philippines.

Puerto Rico and Guam became colonies directly ruled by U.S. administrators, and residents of both island territories did not gain the right to elect their own leaders until after the Second World War. They remained commonwealths (territories that are not states) of the United States. The U.S. government also established direct rule in the Philippines, brushing aside the government established by Filipino nationalists who had fought for freedom from Spain. Nationalists then fought against the United States in the Philippine-American War (1899–1902) in an unsuccessful effort to establish an independent government.

Cuba alone gained independence, but U.S. pressure limited that independence. The Platt Amendment, which the United States imposed as a condition of Cuban independence, gave the U.S. Senate the power to cancel laws passed by the Cuban congress, withheld the Cuban government's right to establish foreign treaties, and granted the United States control over Guantanamo Bay, where it established a permanent naval base. In addition to imposing legal limits on Cuban independence, the United States militarily occupied Cuba in 1899–1902, 1906–1908, and 1912. Between 1917 and 1922 U.S. administrator Enoch Crowder governed the island from his staterooms on the battleship *Minnesota*.

The constraints that the U.S. government imposed on Cuban politics, along with its willingness to deploy troops and periodically establish military rule, created a safe and fertile environment for U.S. investment. As the first U.S. commander of Cuba, General Leonard Wood equated good government with investor confidence: "When people ask me what I mean by stable government, I tell them 'money at six percent.'"[5] Cuban farmers had been bankrupted by the war of independence that had raged since 1895. One hundred thousand farms and three thousand ranches were destroyed. U.S. investors flooded in. By 1919 half of the island's sugar mills were owned by U.S. businesses. Small farms were consolidated into estates as twenty-two companies took hold of 20 percent of Cuba's national territory. U.S. companies like Coca-Cola and Hershey were among the new landowners that took control of their most important ingredient: sugar.

The United States exported its prevailing racial prejudices to its new Caribbean territories. In Cuba, U.S. authorities encouraged political parties to exclude black Cubans. Black war veterans established the Independent Party of Color in 1908 in order to press for political inclusion. Party leaders Evaristo Estenoz and Pedro Ivonet sought to use the party's potential electoral weight to incorporate black Cubans into government and education. The party was banned in 1910, and in 1912 its leaders organized a revolt that led to a violent backlash by the army and police, supported by U.S. Marines. The campaign against members of the party was followed by a wave of lynchings of black Cubans across the island.

In Puerto Rico the influence of U.S. racism was more direct. In 1913, as the U.S. Congress debated granting Puerto Ricans U.S. citizenship, the federal judge for Puerto Rico appointed by President Woodrow Wilson objected and wrote to the president that Puerto Ricans "have the Latin American excitability and I think Americans should go slowly in granting them anything like autonomy. Their civilization is not at all like ours yet." Later the judge declared, "The mixture of black and white in Porto Rico threatens to create a race of mongrels of no use to anyone, a race of Spanish American talkers. A governor of the South, or with knowledge of southern remedies for that trouble could, if a wise man, do much."[6]

The United States instituted the "remedies" to which the judge alluded, such as the sterilization of thousands of Puerto Rican women as part of a policy aimed at addressing what the government saw as overpopulation on the island. In addition, Puerto Rican men drafted into U.S. military service were organized into segregated units, as African Americans were.

The Panama Canal

U.S. imperialism in the Caribbean extended beyond Cuba and Puerto Rico to the prize the United States had pursued for decades: a canal to connect the Atlantic and Pacific Oceans. The canal would transport cargo between the east and west of the

United States much less expensively than rail. In the mid-nineteenth century the U.S. railroad tycoon Cornelius Vanderbilt tried but failed to build a canal through Nicaragua. Later in the century, a consortium of French investors pursued the construction of a canal in the Colombian province of Panama, encouraged by the success of the Suez Canal that connected the Mediterranean to the Red Sea and the Indian Ocean, completed in 1869. Engineers and laborers completed some excavation before the French company went bankrupt.

After the Spanish-American War gave the U.S. more direct control of the Caribbean, U.S. authorities negotiated with the Colombian government for the right to continue the project started by the French company. When the Colombian congress balked at the U.S. government's demand that it should have territorial control of the canal, the U.S. government encouraged an insurrection in Panama City and recognized the rebels as leaders of the new country of Panama. The new Panamanian government gave the United States permanent control over the canal in 1904 and the land upon which it was built, which became known as the Canal Zone. The Canal Zone became an unincorporated U.S. territory, similar in status to Puerto Rico and Guam. It housed canal workers as well as U.S. military installations.

Tens of thousands of migrant workers from around the Caribbean provided labor for construction of the canal, which opened in 1914. U.S. authorities instituted the same segregationist policies applied in their other Caribbean territories. Workers were divided into a "gold roll" of highly paid white U.S. workers and a "silver role" of mostly black workers, who came from Barbados, Panama, Nicaragua, Colombia, and other parts of the Caribbean. They were paid lower wages, faced much higher rates of death and injury, and lived in less healthy conditions. The Canal Zone itself functioned as a segregated enclave: U.S. residents could move freely between it and Panamanian territory, but it was closed to Panamanians except those who entered through labor contracts.

Chapter Summary

In the century after independence, political consolidation and economic integration varied across the Americas. The North of the United States became the continent's main engine of capital accumulation, immigration, and industrialization. In the U.S. South and Brazil reliance on slavery weakened internal markets, inhibited immigration, and slowed industrialization. In Spanish America the lack of a governing consensus until the second half of the nineteenth century resulted in "lost decades" after independence, in which new countries fell behind not only relative to other regions of the world, but even relative to their past colonial experiences.

The cycle of war that began in the 1850s and continued for the next two decades reshaped the Americas politically and economically, consolidating a liberal order that placed great wealth in few hands while dealing misery and dislocation to many others. Liberalism had a modernizing influence on trade and industry, but it further concentrated wealth. Just as the United States waged wars against the Indians and pushed its frontier westward, so Brazil, Venezuela, Ecuador, Peru, and Bolivia expanded into the Amazonian frontier at the expense of indigenous peoples. Likewise, Mexico, Chile, and Argentina had their own "Indian wars" and frontier expansion. Racial prejudice kept most African Americans at the social and economic margins.

By the beginning of the twentieth century, the economies of American nations were tightly integrated into the world economy, and powerful currents of immigration further deepened ties between continents. Industrialization that began in the northeast of the United States developed elsewhere in the continent, but the lead in industrialization held by the United States allowed it to increasingly impose its will over other nations. The economic and social dislocations produced by the liberal model of export-oriented economic growth also awoke growing social demands by the rural and urban poor. These boiled over the most dramatically in Mexico's 1910 revolution, but in cities to the south such as Buenos Aires, Argentina, and Santiago, Chile, workers' demands for the right to organize for better wages and for political representation also became too insistent to ignore.

NOTES

1. Jürgen Buchenau, *Mexican Mosaic: A Brief History of Mexico* (Wheeling, Ill.: Harlan-Davidson, 2008), p. 2.
2. Jaime E. Rodriguez O., *Down from Colonialism: Mexico's Nineteenth Century Crisis* (Los Angeles: Chicano Studies Center Research Publications, UCLA, 1983), p. 15.
3. David Rock, *Argentina, 1516–1987: From Spanish Colonization to Alfonsín* (Berkeley: University of California Press, 1987), p. 154.
4. Quoted in Nicolas Shumway, *The Invention of Argentina* (Berkeley: University of California Press, 1991), p. 147.
5. Quoted in Luis A. Pérez, *The War of 1898: The United States and Cuba in History and Historiography* (Chapel Hill: University of North Carolina Press, 1998), p. 32.
6. Quoted in Arturo Morales Carrión, *Puerto Rico: A Political and Cultural History* (New York: W. W. Norton, 1983), pp. 187–188.

CONNECTIONS

In the Americas the century or so between independence and World War I was a time of nation building. Colonial governments were overthrown, new constitutions were written, settlement was extended, slavery was ended, and immigrants from around the world settled across the continent. Although wealth was very unevenly distributed, in most of these countries it was not hard to find signs of progress: growing cities, expanding opportunities for education, modern conveniences. This progress came with harsh costs for indigenous communities, rural peasants, and the growing ranks of urban industrial workers. The great upheaval of the Mexican Revolution was a reaction against these costs, and resulted in a society that curbed some of the excesses facilitated by liberalism.

World War I, the topic of the next chapter, affected these countries in a variety of ways. Canada followed Britain into the war in 1914 and sent six hundred thousand men to fight, losing many in some of the bloodiest battles of the war. The United States did not join the war until 1917, but quickly mobilized several million men and in 1918 began sending soldiers and materials in huge numbers. Even countries that maintained neutrality, as all the Latin American countries other than Brazil did, felt the economic impact of the war deeply, especially the increased demand for food and manufactured goods. For the working class the global demand for exported foods drove up the cost of living, but the profits that oligarchs accumulated fueled the process of industrialization.

CHAPTER 27 **Review and Explore**

Identify Key Terms

Identify and explain the significance of each item below.

oligarchs (p. 828)

Circum-Caribbean (p. 828)

caudillismo (p. 829)

manifest destiny (p. 829)

Treaty of Guadalupe Hidalgo (p. 831)

Lerdo Law (p. 833)

neocolonialism (p. 835)

free womb laws (p. 837)

latifundios (p. 840)

Porfiriato (p. 842)

Plan de Ayala (p. 844)

anarcho-syndicalism (p. 846)

Monroe Doctrine (p. 850)

Roosevelt Corollary (p. 851)

Review the Main Ideas

Answer the focus questions from each section of the chapter.

1. How and why did the process of nation-state consolidation vary across the Americas? (p. 828)

2. Why did slavery last longer in the United States, Brazil, and Cuba than in the other republics of the Americas? How did resistance by slaves shape abolition? (p. 835)

3. As Latin America became more integrated into the world economy, how did patterns of economic growth shape political culture and social reactions? (p. 839)

4. What factors shaped patterns of immigration to the Americas? How did immigrants shape — and how were they shaped by — their new settings? (p. 845)

5. In what ways did U.S. policies in the Caribbean and Central America resemble European imperialism? How did U.S. foreign policy depart from European imperialism? (p. 850)

Make Comparisons and Connections

Analyze the larger developments and continuities within and across chapters.

1. How did the embrace of liberalism in Latin America resemble or differ from its expression in other parts of the world?

2. How did factors that influenced the Mexican Revolution express themselves in other parts of the Americas?

3. In what ways did the United States come to resemble European powers in building overseas empires (Chapters 25, 26)? How did U.S. expansionism and the colonialism practiced by Britain and France differ?

4. How did neocolonialism make Latin America after independence resemble regions of Asia and Africa (Chapters 25, 26) that were subjected to direct colonial rule?

TIMELINE

Suggested Resources

BOOKS

Baptist, Edward E. *The Half Has Never Been Told: Slavery and the Making of American Capitalism.* 2014. Examines how the development of the United States shaped the experiences of slaves.

Bayly, C. A. *The Birth of the Modern World, 1780–1914.* 2003. Useful for viewing the countries of the Americas in the context of global developments.

Beckert, Sven. *Empire of Cotton: A Global History.* 2014. A history of the commodity that shows the global connections forged around a plantation slave regime.

Beezley, William. *Judas at the Jockey Club and Other Episodes of Porfirian Mexico*, 2d ed. 2004. A provocative study of Mexico under the Porfiriato.

Bender, Thomas. *A Nation Among Nations: America's Place in World History.* 2006. Shows that key events in American history are best seen in global context.

Da Costa, Emilia Viotti. *The Brazilian Empire: Myths and Histories.* 2000. Examines nation building, liberalism, and abolition in the largest slave society of the Americas.

Fernandez-Armesto, Felipe. *The Americas: A Hemispheric History.* 2003. Provocative and engagingly written.

Goldfield, David. *Still Fighting the Civil War: The American South and Southern History*, updated ed. 2013. Examines the Civil War and its enduring legacies for the U.S. South.

Helg, Aline. *Our Rightful Share: The Afro-Cuban Struggle for Equality, 1886–1912.* 1995. An insightful reading of race relations amid Cuban independence and the abolition of slavery.

Knight, Alan. *The Mexican Revolution: A Very Short Introduction.* 2016. A concise interpretation of the Mexican Revolution by one of its leading scholars.

Lesser, Jeffrey. *Immigration, Ethnicity, and National Identity in Brazil, 1808 to the Present.* 2013. A broad-ranging social history.

Morton, Desmond. *A Short History of Canada*, 6th ed. 2006. A well-written popular history.

DOCUMENTARIES

The Civil War (PBS, 1990). A documentary by Ken
Burns offering a gripping account of the conflict.

The Storm That Swept Mexico (Raymond Telles, 2011).
A PBS documentary that explores the Mexican
Revolution.

FEATURE FILMS

Lincoln (Steven Spielberg, 2012) and *Django
Unchained* (Quentin Tarantino, 2012). As a pair,
these films reflect stylized visions of ending slavery
from above and from below.

El Otro Francisco (Sergio Giral, 1975). Re-examines
the Cuban abolitionist novel *Francisco*, by Anselmo
Suárez y Romero, from a Marxist viewpoint on
slavery and resistance.

WEBSITES

A Guide to the Mexican War. This Library of Congress
site compiles documents, maps, and music related to
the war. **www.loc.gov/rr/program/bib/mexicanwar/**

Topics in Chronicling America. This Library of Congress project has a wealth of material on the Spanish-
American War and the creation of the Panama
Canal. **www.loc.gov/rr/news/topics/spanishAmWar
.htmlwww.loc.gov/rr/news/topics/panama.html**

28

World War and Revolution
1914–1929

In summer 1914 the nations of Europe went willingly to war. They believed they had no other choice, but everyone confidently expected a short war leading to a decisive victory. Such a war, they believed, would "clear the air." Then European society could continue as before. They were wrong. The First World War was long, global, indecisive, and tremendously destructive. It quickly degenerated into a senseless military stalemate lasting four years. To the shell-shocked generation of survivors, it became simply the Great War.

In March 1917, as Russia suffered horrendous losses on the eastern front, its war-weary people rebelled against their tsar, Nicholas II, forcing him to abdicate. Moderate reformists established a provisional government but made the fatal decision to continue the war against Germany. In November Vladimir Lenin and his Communist Bolshevik Party staged a second revolution, this time promising an end to the war. The Germans forced a harsh peace on the Russians, but Lenin believed this a small price to pay for the establishment of history's first Communist state. Few then could have realized how profoundly this event would shape the course of the twentieth century.

When the Great War's victorious Allies, led by Great Britain, France, and the United States, gathered in Paris in 1919 to write the peace, they were well aware of the importance of their decisions. Some came to Paris seeking revenge, some came looking for the spoils of war, and some promoted nationalist causes, while a few sought an idealistic end to war. The process was massive and complex, but in the end few left Paris satisfied with the results. The peace and prosperity the delegates had so earnestly sought lasted barely a decade.

Senegalese Soldier

A *tirailleur* (literally, "skirmisher") from French West Africa who fought in Europe during the Great War. Across the bottom of this postcard image from the era, the soldier proclaimed his loyalty with the phrase "Glory to the Greater France," meaning France and its colonies. Note the two German *pickelhaube* (spike helmets) he wears on his head.

Private Collection/Archives Charmet/Bridgeman Images

CHAPTER PREVIEW

THE FIRST WORLD WAR, 1914–1918
What were the long-term and immediate causes of World War I, and how did the conflict become a global war?

THE HOME FRONT   How did total war affect the home fronts of the major combatants?

THE RUSSIAN REVOLUTION   What factors led to the Russian Revolution, and what was its outcome?

THE WAR'S CONSEQUENCES   What were the global consequences of the First World War?

THE SEARCH FOR PEACE AND POLITICAL STABILITY, 1919–1929
How did leaders deal with the political dimensions of uncertainty and try to re-establish peace and prosperity in the interwar years?

THE AGE OF ANXIETY
In what ways were the anxieties of the postwar world expressed or heightened by revolutionary ideas in modern thought, art, and science and in new forms of communication?

What were the long-term and immediate causes of World War I, and how did the conflict become a global war?

The First World War, 1914–1918

The First World War clearly marked a major break in the course of world history. The maps of Europe and southwest Asia were redrawn, nationalist movements took root and spread across Asia (the subject of the next chapter), America consolidated its position as a global power, and the world experienced, for the first time, industrialized, total war. Europe's Great Powers started the war and suffered the most—in casualties, in costs, in destruction, and in societal and political upheaval. Imperialism also brought the conflict to the Middle East, Africa, and Asia, making this a global war of unprecedented scope. The young soldiers who went to war believed in the pre-1914 world of order, progress, and patriotism. Then, in the words of German soldier and writer Erich Remarque (rih-MAHRK), the "first bombardment showed us our mistake, and under it the world as they had taught it to us broke in pieces."[1]

Origins and Causes of the Great War

Scholars began arguing over the Great War's origins soon after it began, and the debate continues a century after its end. The victorious Allied powers expressed their opinion—that Germany caused the war—in the Versailles treaty. But history seldom offers such simple answers, particularly to questions so complex. The war's origins lie in the nineteenth century, and its immediate causes lie in the few years and months before the war, especially one particular morning in June 1914.

Any study of the Great War's origins must begin with nationalism (see "The Growing Appeal of Nationalism" in Chapter 24), one of the major ideologies of the nineteenth century, and its armed companion, **militarism**, the glorification of the military as the supreme ideal of the state with all other interests subordinate to it. European concerns over national security, economies, welfare, identities, and overseas empires set nation against nation, alliance against alliance, and army against army until they all went to war at once.

Competition between nations intensified greatly when Germany became a unified nation-state and the most powerful country in Europe in 1871. A new era in international relations began, as Chancellor Bismarck declared Germany a "satisfied" power, having no territorial ambitions within Europe and desiring only peace.

But how to preserve the peace? Bismarck's first concern was to keep rival France diplomatically isolated and without military allies. His second concern was to prevent Germany from being dragged into a war between the two rival empires, Austria-Hungary and Russia, as they sought to fill the power vacuum created in the Balkans by the Ottoman Empire's decline (see "Decline and Reform in the Ottoman Empire" in Chapter 25). To these ends, Bismarck brokered a series of treaties and alliances, all meant to ensure the balance of power in Europe and to prevent the outbreak of war.

In 1890 Germany's new emperor, Wilhelm II, forced Bismarck to resign and then abandoned many of Bismarck's efforts to ensure German security through promoting European peace and stability. Wilhelm refused to renew a nonaggression pact Bismarck had signed with Russia in 1887, for example, which prompted France to court the tsar, offering loans and arms, and sign a Franco-Russian Alliance in 1892. With France and Russia now allied against Germany, Austria, and Italy, Great Britain's foreign policy became increasingly crucial. Many Germans and some Britons felt that

militarism The glorification of the military as the supreme ideal of the state with all other interests subordinate to it.

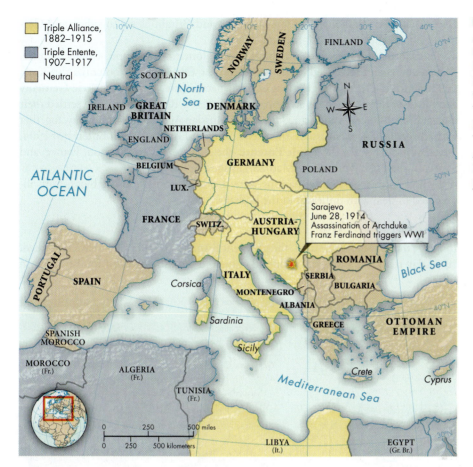

MAP 28.1 **European Alliances at the Outbreak of World War I, 1914** By the time war broke out, Europe was divided into two opposing alliances: the Triple Entente of Britain, France, and Russia and the Triple Alliance of Germany, Austria-Hungary, and Italy. Italy switched sides and joined the Entente in 1915.

the ethnically related Germanic and Anglo-Saxon peoples were natural allies. However, the good relations that had prevailed between Prussia and Great Britain since the mid-eighteenth century gave way after 1890 to a bitter Anglo-German rivalry.

There were several reasons for this development. Germany and Great Britain's commercial rivalry in world markets and Kaiser Wilhelm's publicly expressed intention to create a global German empire unsettled the British. German nationalist militarists saw a large navy as the legitimate mark of a great world power, and their decision in 1900 to add a fleet of big-gun battleships to their already expanding navy heightened tensions. British leaders considered this expansion a military challenge to their long-standing naval supremacy.

Thus British leaders set about shoring up their exposed position with their own alliances and agreements. Britain improved its relations with the United States, concluded an alliance with Japan in 1902, and in the Anglo-French Entente (ahn-TAHNT) of 1904 settled all outstanding colonial disputes with France. Frustrated by Britain's closer relationship with France, Germany's leaders decided to test the entente's strength by demanding an international conference to challenge French control over Morocco. At the Algeciras (al-jih-SIR-uhs) (Spain) Conference in 1906,

Germany's crude bullying only forced France and Britain closer together, and Germany left the meeting empty-handed.

The Moroccan crisis was something of a diplomatic revolution. Britain, France, Russia, and even the United States began to view Germany as a potential threat. At the same time, German leaders began to suspect sinister plots to encircle Germany and block its development as a world power. In 1907 Russia and Britain settled their outstanding differences and signed the Anglo-Russian Agreement. This treaty, together with the earlier Franco-Russian Alliance of 1892 and Anglo-French Entente of 1904, served as a catalyst for the **Triple Entente**, the alliance of Great Britain, France, and Russia in the First World War (Map 28.1, page 861).

By 1909 Europe's leading nations were divided into two hostile blocs, both ill-prepared to deal with upheaval in the Balkans.

Triple Entente The alliance of Great Britain, France, and Russia in the First World War.

The Outbreak of War

In 1897, the year before he died, the prescient Bismarck is reported to have remarked, "One day the great European War will come out of some damned foolish thing in

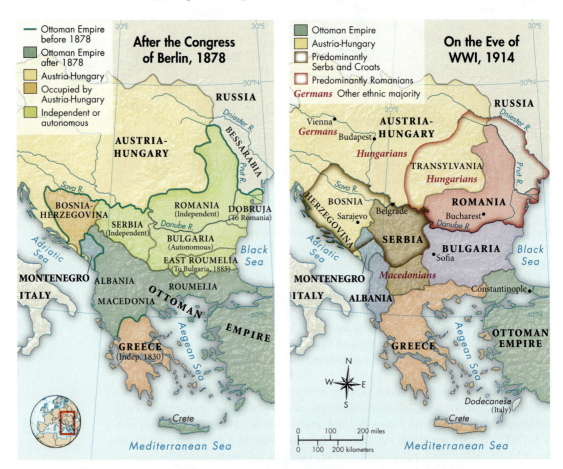

MAP 28.2 The Balkans, 1878–1914 The Ottoman Empire suffered large territorial losses after the Congress of Berlin in 1878 but remained a power in the Balkans. By 1914 ethnic boundaries that did not follow political boundaries had formed, and Serbian national aspirations threatened Austria-Hungary.

the Balkans."[2] By the early twentieth century a Balkans war seemed inevitable. The reason was simple: nationalism was destroying the Ottoman Empire in Europe and threatening to break up the Austro-Hungarian Empire.

Serbia led the way, becoming openly hostile to both Austria-Hungary and the Ottoman Empire. The Slavic Serbs looked to Slavic Russia for support of their national aspirations. In 1908, to block Serbian expansion, Austria formally annexed Bosnia and Herzegovina, with their large Serbian, Croatian (kroh-AY-shuhn), and Muslim populations. Serbia erupted in rage but could do nothing without Russia's support.

Then two nationalist wars, the first and second Balkan wars in 1912 and 1913, finally destroyed the centuries-long Ottoman presence in Europe (Map 28.2). This sudden but long-expected event elated Balkan nationalists but dismayed Austria-Hungary's leaders, who feared that Austria-Hungary might next be broken apart.

Within this tense context, Serbian nationalist Gavrilo Princip (gah-VRIH-loh prin-SIP) assassinated Archduke Franz Ferdinand, heir to the Austro-Hungarian throne, and his wife, Sophie, on June 28, 1914, during a state visit to the Bosnian capital of Sarajevo (sar-uh-YAY-voh). Austria-Hungary's leaders held Serbia responsible and on July 23 presented Serbia with an unconditional ultimatum that included demands amounting to Austrian control of the Serbian state. When Serbia replied moderately but evasively, Austria declared war on Serbia on July 28.

Of prime importance in Austria-Hungary's fateful decision was Germany's unconditional support. Kaiser Wilhelm II and his chancellor, Theobald von Bethmann-Hollweg (THEE-uh-bawld von BAYT-mahn-hawl-vayk), realized that war between Austria and Russia was likely, for Russia could not stand by and watch the Serbs be crushed. Yet Bethmann-Hollweg hoped that while Russia (and its ally France) might go to war, Great Britain would remain neutral.

Anticipating a possible conflict, Europe's military leaders had been drawing up war plans and timetables for years, and now these, rather than diplomacy, began to dictate policy. On July 28, as Austrian armies bombarded Belgrade, Tsar Nicholas II ordered a partial mobilization against Austria-Hungary but almost immediately found this was impossible. Russia had assumed a war with both Austria and Germany, and it could not mobilize against one without mobilizing against the other. Therefore, on July 29 Russia ordered full mobilization and in effect declared general war. The German general staff had also prepared for a two-front war. Its Schlieffen (SHLEE-fuhn) plan, first drafted in 1905, called for first knocking out France with a lightning attack through neutral Belgium to capture Paris before turning on a slower-to-mobilize Russia. On August 3 German armies invaded Belgium. Great Britain declared war on Germany the following day. In each country the great majority of the population rallied to defend its nation and enthusiastically embraced war in August 1914.

The Schlieffen Plan

◀- - Planned German offensive

◀— Actual German offensive

▢ Neutral nations

Stalemate and Slaughter

When the Germans invaded Belgium in August 1914, the Belgian army defended its homeland and then fell back to join a rapidly landed British army corps near the Franco-Belgian border. Instead of quickly capturing Paris in a vast encircling movement, German soldiers were advancing slowly along an enormous front. On September 6 the French attacked the German line at the Battle of the Marne (MAHRN). For three days France threw everything into the attack, forcing the Germans to fall back (Map 28.3).

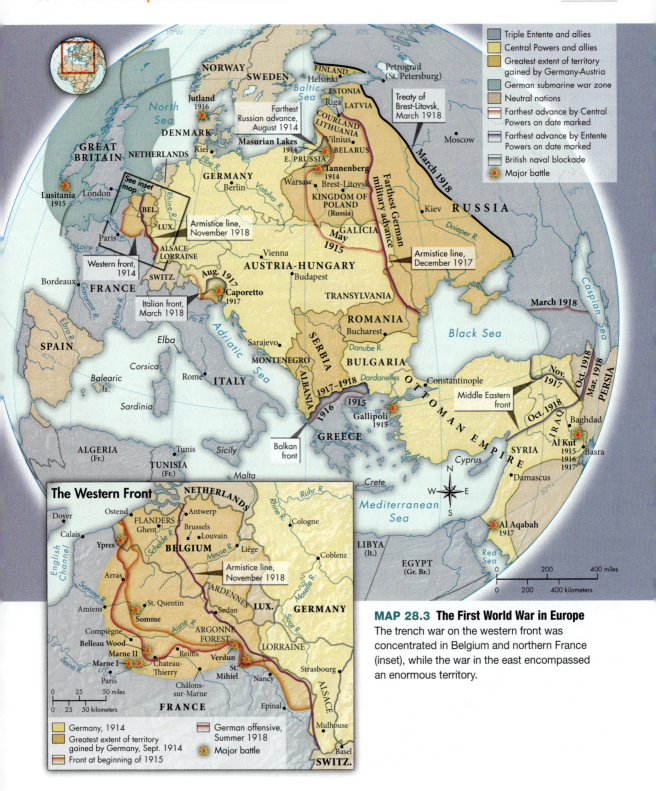

MAP 28.3 The First World War in Europe
The trench war on the western front was concentrated in Belgium and northern France (inset), while the war in the east encompassed an enormous territory.

The two stalled armies then dug in behind rows of trenches, mines, and barbed wire. A "no-man's land" of one hundred to three hundred yards lay between the two combatants. Eventually an unbroken line of parallel zigzag trenches stretched over four hundred miles from the Belgian coast to the Swiss frontier. By November 1914 the slaughter on the western front had begun in earnest. For four years battles followed the same plan: after ceaseless heavy artillery shelling to "soften up" the enemy, young soldiers went "over the top" of the trenches in frontal attacks on the enemy's line.

German writer Erich Remarque described a typical attack in his celebrated novel *All Quiet on the Western Front* (1929):

> We see men living with their skulls blown open; we see soldiers run with their two feet cut off. . . . Still the little piece of convulsed earth in which we lie is held. We have yielded no more than a few hundred yards of it as a prize to the enemy. But on every yard there lies a dead man.[3]

The human cost of **trench warfare** was staggering, while territorial gains were minuscule. In the Battle of the Somme (SAWM) in summer 1916, the British and French gained an insignificant 125 square miles at a cost of 600,000 dead or wounded. The Germans lost 500,000 men. That same year the unsuccessful German attack on Verdun (vehr-DUHN) cost 700,000 lives on both sides. The slaughter was made even greater by new weapons of war—including chemical gases, tanks, airplanes, flamethrowers, and the machine gun. British poet Siegfried Sassoon (1886–1967) wrote of the Somme offensive, "I am staring at a sunlit picture of Hell."[4] (See "Global Viewpoints: British and Canadian Poetry of the Great War," page 866.) The year 1917 was equally terrible.

On the eastern front, the Russians moved into eastern Germany but suffered appalling losses against the Germans at the Battles of Tannenberg and the Masurian Lakes in August and September 1914 (see Map 28.3). German and Austrian forces

trench warfare Fighting behind rows of trenches, mines, and barbed wire; used in World War I with a staggering cost in lives and minimal gains in territory.

John Nash, *Over the Top* John Nash was an English artist who served as a soldier with the First Battalion Artists' Rifles from 1916 to 1918 and then served as an official war artist in 1918. This painting depicts the Artists' Rifles leaving their trench to attack at Welsh Ridge in France on December 30, 1917. In a unit of eighty men, Nash was one of only twelve soldiers not wounded or killed by German shelling and gunfire; many of the casualties occurred during the first few minutes of the advance.

(*Over the Top, 1st Artists' Rifles at Marcoing, 30th December 1917*, 1918, by John Nash [1893–1977] [oil on canvas]/ Imperial War Museum, London, UK/© IWM [Art.IWM.ART 1656]/ Bridgeman Images)

British and Canadian Poetry of the Great War

Some of the finest and most memorable literature and poetry of the twentieth century came from the generation who experienced the Great War. These are three of the most famous poems of the Great War, all written by soldiers during the war. Rupert Brooks's "The Soldier" is the most famous of a series of sonnets he wrote in 1914. Brooks died on April 23, 1915, at the age of twenty-seven while traveling with the British Mediterranean Expeditionary Force to Gallipoli. John McCrae, a Canadian doctor, published "In Flanders Fields" in December 1915. He died of pneumonia while serving at a Canadian field hospital in northern France on January 28, 1918. British poet Wilfred Owen wrote "Dulce et Decorum Est" in 1917. He was killed in battle a week before the armistice on November 4, 1918.

Rupert Brooks, "The Soldier," 1914

If I should die, think only this of me:
    That there's some corner of a foreign field
That is for ever England. There shall be
    In that rich earth a richer dust concealed;

A dust whom England bore, shaped, made aware,
    Gave, once, her flowers to love, her ways to roam,
A body of England's, breathing English air,
    Washed by the rivers, blest by suns of home.

And think this heart, all evil shed away,
    A pulse in the eternal mind, no less
        Gives somewhere back the thoughts by England given;
Her sights and sounds; dreams happy as her day;
    And laughter, learnt of friends; and gentleness,
        In hearts at peace, under an English heaven.

John McCrae, "In Flanders Fields," 1915

In Flanders fields the poppies blow
    Between the crosses, row on row,
  That mark our place; and in the sky
  The larks, still bravely singing, fly
Scarce heard amid the guns below.

We are the Dead. Short days ago
We lived, felt dawn, saw sunset glow,
    Loved and were loved, and now we lie
    In Flanders fields.

then reversed the Russian advances of 1914 and forced the Russians to retreat deep into their own territory in the 1915 eastern campaign. A staggering 2.5 million Russians were killed, wounded, or taken prisoner.

These changing tides of victory and hopes of territorial gains brought neutral countries into the war. Italy, a member of the Triple Alliance since 1882, declared its neutrality in 1914. Then, in May 1915, Italy joined the Triple Entente of Great Britain, France, and Russia in return for promises of Austrian territory. In September Bulgaria joined the Triple Alliance in order to settle old scores with Serbia.

The War Becomes Global

In October 1914 the Ottoman Empire joined with Austria and Germany, by then known as the Central Powers. A German alliance permitted the Turks to renounce the limitations on Ottoman sovereignty imposed by Europeans in the nineteenth century and also to settle old grievances with Russia, the Turks' historic enemy.

The entry of the Ottoman Turks pulled the entire Middle East into the war and made it truly a global conflict. While Russia attacked the Ottomans in the Caucasus, the British protected their rule in Egypt. In 1915, at the Battle of Gallipoli (guh-LIP-uh-lee), British forces tried to take the Dardanelles (dahr-duh-NELZ) and Constan-

Take up our quarrel with the foe:
To you from falling hands we throw
   The torch; be yours to hold it high.
   If ye break faith, with us who die
We shall not sleep, though poppies grow
      In Flanders fields.

Wilfred Owen, "Dulce et Decorum Est," 1917

Bent double, like old beggars under sacks,
Knock-kneed, coughing like hags, we cursed through
   sludge,
Till on the haunting flares we turned our backs
And towards our distant rest began to trudge.
Men marched asleep. Many had lost their boots
But limped on, blood-shod. All went lame; all blind;
Drunk with fatigue, deaf even to the hoots
Of gas shells dropping softly behind.

Gas! Gas! Quick, boys!—An ecstasy of fumbling,
Fitting the clumsy helmets just in time;
But someone still was yelling out and stumbling,
And floundering like a man in fire or lime . . .
Dim, through the misty panes and thick green light,
As under a green sea, I saw him drowning.

In all my dreams, before my helpless sight,
He plunges at me, guttering, choking, drowning.

If in some smothering dreams you too could pace
Behind the wagon that we flung him in,
And watch the white eyes writhing in his face,
His hanging face, like a devil's sick of sin;
If you could hear, at every jolt, the blood
Come gargling from the froth-corrupted lungs,
Obscene as cancer, bitter as the cud
Of vile, incurable sores on innocent tongues —
My friend, you would not tell with such high zest
To children ardent for some desperate glory,
The old Lie: *Dulce et decorum est* [It is sweet and fitting]
Pro patria mori. [To die for one's country.]

QUESTIONS FOR ANALYSIS

1. Which of these poems would you describe as the most idealistic and patriotic? Why?
2. What do you think explains the obvious antiwar nature of Owen's poem compared to the poems of Brooks and McCrae?

Source: Jon Silkin, ed., *The Penguin Book of First World War Poetry*, 2d ed. rev. (New York: Penguin Putnam, 1996), pp. 81–82, 85, 192–193.

tinople from the Ottoman Turks but were badly defeated. Casualties were high on both sides and included thousands of Australians and New Zealanders. Deeply loyal to the mother country, Australia sent 329,000 men and vast economic aid to Britain during the war. Over 100,000 New Zealanders also served in the war, almost a tenth of New Zealand's entire population, and they suffered a 58 percent casualty rate— one of the highest of any country. Nearly 4,000 native New Zealand Maori soldiers also fought at Gallipoli and on the western front. Ormond Burton, a New Zealand infantryman, later observed that "somewhere between the landing at Anzac [a cove on the Gallipolian peninsula] and the end of the battle of the Somme, New Zealand very definitely became a nation."[5] The British had more success inciting Arabs to revolt against their Turkish overlords. The foremost Arab leader was Hussein ibn-Ali (1856–1931), who governed much of the Ottoman Empire's territory along the Red Sea (see Map 29.1, page 901). In 1915 Hussein won vague British commitments for an independent Arab kingdom, with himself as king of the Arabs. In return, he joined forces with the British under T. E. Lawrence, who in 1917 led Arab tribesmen and Indian soldiers in a successful guerrilla war against the Turks on the Arabian peninsula. In the Ottoman province of Iraq, Britain occupied Basra (BAHS-rah) in 1914 and captured Baghdad in 1917. In 1918 British armies, aided by imperial forces from Egypt, India, Australia, and New Zealand, smashed the old Ottoman state. Thus war brought revolutionary change to the Middle East.

Japan, allied with the British since 1902, joined the Triple Entente on August 23, 1914, and began attacking German-controlled colonies and territories in the Pacific. Later that year Japan seized Germany's holdings on the Shandong (shan-dawng) Peninsula in China.

War also spread to colonies in Africa and East Asia. Colonized peoples provided critical supplies and fought in Europe, Africa, and the Ottoman Empire. More than a million Africans and Asians served in the various armies of the warring powers, with more than double that number serving as porters to carry equipment. Drawn primarily from Senegal, French West Africa, and British South Africa, over 140,000 Africans fought on the western front, and 31,000 of them died there.

Many of these men joined up to get clothes (uniforms), food, and money for enlisting. Others did so because colonial recruiters promised them better lives when they returned home. Most were illiterate and had no idea of why they were going or what they would experience. One West African infantryman, Kande Kamara, later wrote:

> We black African soldiers were very sorrowful about the white man's war. . . . I didn't really care who was right—whether it was the French or the Germans—I went to fight with the French army and that was all I knew. The reason for war was never disclosed to any soldier. . . . We just fought and fought until we got exhausted and died.[6]

The war had a profound impact on these colonial troops. Fighting against and killing Europeans destroyed the impression that the Europeans were superhuman. New concepts like nationalism and individual freedoms—ideals for which the Europeans were supposedly fighting—were carried home to become rallying cries for future liberation struggles.

A crucial turning point in the expanding conflict came in April 1917 when the United States declared war on Germany. American interven-

Indian Soldiers Convalescing in England Over 130,000 Indian soldiers served on the western front during the Great War, mostly during the first year of battle before being transferred to the Middle East to fight at Gallipoli and in the Mesopotamian campaign. Wounded Indian troops convalesced at the Royal Pavilion at Brighton, a former royal residence built in a faux-Oriental style that drew on several elements of Indian and Islamic architecture. In this posed piece, one of a series of photos of the Indian "martial races" distributed as postcards and used for slide-show lectures, some men sit playing cards, while others watch. Such photos reassured British and Indians alike that Britain took good care of its loyal imperial soldiers. (© Mary Evans Picture Library/The Image Works)

tion grew out of the war at sea and sympathy for the Triple Entente. At the beginning of the war Britain and France established a naval blockade to strangle the Central Powers. In early 1915 Germany launched a counter-blockade using the new and deadly effective submarine. In May a German submarine sank the British passenger liner *Lusitania* (loo-sih-TAY-nee-uh) (which, besides regular passengers, was secretly and illegally carrying war materials to Britain). More than a thousand people died, including 139 U.S. citizens. President Woodrow Wilson protested vigorously. Germany was forced to restrict its submarine warfare for almost two years or face almost certain war with the United States.

Early in 1917 the German military command—confident that improved submarines could starve Britain into submission before the United States could come to its rescue—resumed unrestricted submarine warfare. This was a reckless gamble. The United States declared war on Germany and eventually tipped the balance in favor of the Triple Entente.

The Home Front

The war's impact on civilians was no less massive than on the men crouched in trenches. Total war mobilized entire populations, led to increased state power, and promoted social equality. It also led to dissent and a growing antiwar movement.

How did total war affect the home fronts of the major combatants?

Mobilizing for Total War

Within months of the outbreak of the First World War, national unity governments began to plan and control economic and social life in order to wage **total war**. Governments imposed rationing, price and wage controls, and even restrictions on workers' freedom of movement. These total-war economies blurred the old distinction between soldiers on battlefields and civilians at home. (See "Analyzing the Evidence: The Experience of War," page 870.) The ability of central governments to manage and control highly complicated economies increased and strengthened their powers, often along socialist lines.

total war Practiced by countries fighting in World War I, a war in which the government plans and controls all aspects of economic and social life in order to make the greatest possible military effort.

Germany went furthest in developing a planned economy to wage total war. Soon after war began, the Jewish industrialist Walter Rathenau (RAHT-uh-now) convinced the German government to set up the War Raw Materials Board to ration and distribute raw materials. Food was also rationed, and the board successfully produced substitutes, such as synthetic rubber and synthetic nitrates, for scarce war supplies. Following the terrible Battles of Verdun and the Somme in 1916, military leaders forced the Reichstag (RIGHKS-tahg) to accept the Auxiliary Service Law, which required all males between seventeen and sixty to work only at jobs considered critical to the war effort. Women also worked in war factories, mines, and steel mills.

As mature liberal democracies, France and Great Britain mobilized economically for total war less rapidly and less completely than autocratic Germany, aided by the fact that they could import materials from their colonies and from the United States. When it became apparent that the war was not going to end quickly, however, the Western Allies all passed laws giving their governments sweeping powers over all areas of the nation's daily life—including industrial and agricultural production, censorship, education, health and welfare, the curtailment of civil liberties, labor, and foreign aliens.

The Experience of War

World War I was a total war: it enlisted the efforts of male and female adults and children, both at home and on the battlefield. It was a terrifying and painful experience for all those involved, not the romantic endeavor it was purported to be. The documents below offer two different wartime experiences. The first is from a letter written by a German soldier fighting in the trenches. The second is from the diary of a Viennese woman. As you read both passages, think about the different ways war and its consequences were made real for these two people.

A German Soldier Writes from the Trenches, March 1915

■ *Souchez, March 11th, 1915*

"So fare you well, for we must now be parting," so run the first lines of a soldier-song which we often sang through the streets of the capital. These words are truer than ever now, and these lines are to bid farewell to you, to all my nearest and dearest, to all who wish me well or ill, and to all that I value and prize.

Our regiment has been transferred to this dangerous spot, Souchez. No end of blood has already flowed down this hill. A week ago the 142nd attacked and took four trenches from the French. It is to hold these trenches that we have been brought here. There is something uncanny about this hill-position. Already, times without number, other battalions of our regiment have been ordered here in support, and each time the company came back with a loss of twenty, thirty or more men. In the days when we had to stick it out here before, we had 22 killed and 27 wounded. Shells roar, bullets whistle; no dugouts, or very bad ones; mud, clay, filth, shell-holes so deep that one could bathe in them.

This letter has been interrupted no end of times. Shells began to pitch close to us — great English 12-inch ones — and we had to take refuge in a cellar. One such shell struck the next house and buried four men, who were got out from the ruins horribly mutilated. I saw them and it was ghastly!

Everybody must be prepared now for death in some form or other. Two cemeteries have been made up here, the losses have been so great. I ought not to write that to you, but I do so all the same, because the newspapers have probably given you quite a different impression. They tell only of our gains and say nothing about the blood that has been shed, of the cries of agony that never cease. The newspaper doesn't give any description either of *how* the "heroes" are laid to rest, though it talks about "heroes' graves" and writes poems and such-like about them. Certainly in Lens I have attended funeral-parades where a number of dead were buried in one large grave with pomp and circumstance. But up here it is pitiful the way one throws the dead bodies out of the trench and lets them lie there, or scatters dirt over the remains of those which have been torn to pieces by shells.

I look upon death and call upon life. I have not accomplished much in my short life, which has been chiefly occupied with study. I have commended my soul to the Lord God. It bears His seal and is altogether His. Now I am free to dare anything. My future life belongs to God, my present one to the Fatherland, and I myself still possess happiness and strength.

A Viennese Woman Remembers Home-Front Life

■ Ten dekagrammes [3½ ounces] of horse-flesh per head are to be given out to-day for the week. The cavalry horses held in reserve by the military authorities are being slaughtered for lack of fodder, and the people of Vienna are for a change to get a few mouthfuls of meat of which they have so long been deprived. Horse-flesh! I should like to know whether my instinctive repugnance to horse-flesh as food is personal, or whether my dislike is shared by many other housewives. My loathing of it is based, I believe, not on a physical but on a psychological prejudice.

I overcame my repugnance, rebuked myself for being sentimental, and left the house. A soft, steady rain was falling, from which I tried to protect myself with galoshes, waterproof, and umbrella. As I left the house before seven o'clock and the meat distribution did not begin until nine o'clock, I hoped to get well to the front of the queue.

No sooner had I reached the neighbourhood of the big market hall than I was instructed by the police to take a certain direction. I estimated the crowd waiting here for a meagre midday meal at two thousand at least. Hundreds of women had spent the night here in order to be among the first and make sure of getting their bit of meat. Many had brought with them improvised seats—a little box or a bucket turned upside down. No one seemed to mind the rain, although many were already wet through. They passed the time chattering, and the theme was the familiar one: What have you had to eat? What are you going to eat? One could scent an atmosphere of mistrust in these conversations: they were all careful not to say too much or to betray anything that might get them into trouble.

At length the sale began. Slowly, infinitely slowly, we moved forward. The most determined, who had spent the night outside the gates of the hall, displayed their booty to the waiting crowd: a ragged, quite freshly slaughtered piece of meat with the characteristic yellow fat. [Others] alarmed those standing at the back by telling them that there was only a very small supply of meat and that not half the people waiting would get a share of it. The crowd became very uneasy and impatient, and before the police on guard could prevent it, those standing in front organized an attack on the hall which the salesmen inside were powerless to repel. Everyone seized whatever he could lay his hands on, and in a few moments all the eatables had vanished. In the confusion stands were overturned, and the police forced back the aggressors and closed the gates. The crowds waiting outside, many of whom had been there all night and were soaked through, angrily demanded their due, whereupon the mounted police made a little charge, provoking a wild panic and much screaming and cursing. At length I reached home, depressed and disgusted, with a broken umbrella and only one galosh.

We housewives have during the last four years grown accustomed to standing in queues; we have also grown accustomed to being obliged to go home with empty hands and still emptier stomachs. Only very rarely do those who are sent away disappointed give cause for police intervention. On the other hand, it happens more and more frequently that one of the pale, tired women who have been waiting for hours collapses from exhaustion. The turbulent scenes which occurred to-day inside and outside the large market hall seemed to me perfectly natural. In my dejected mood the patient apathy with which we housewives endure seemed to me blameworthy and incomprehensible.

QUESTIONS FOR ANALYSIS

1. What is the soldier's view of the war? Would you characterize the letter as optimistic or pessimistic? Why?

2. What similarities and differences do you see in the experiences of the soldier and the Viennese woman?

3. Why does the Viennese woman describe the housewives as "blameworthy" and "incomprehensible"?

Sources: Alfons Ankenbrand, in *German Students' War Letters*, ed. A. F. Wedd (London: Methuen, 1929), pp. 72–73; *Blockade: The Diary of an Austrian Middle-Class Woman, 1914–1924*, trans. Winifred Ray (New York: Ray Long & Richard Smith, 1932), pp. 63–68.

Women Working at a Munitions Factory These women, working at the Woolwich munitions factory in southeast London, are shoveling thousands of cartridge shells into wooden boxes to be shipped to the front in France. Women worked in munitions factories in all the warring nations, handling highly explosive materials and toxic chemicals and operating dangerous machines. Women's war efforts were rewarded in some countries after the war when they received the right to vote. (© TopFoto/The Image Works)

The Social Impact of War

The social impact of total war was no less profound than the economic impact, though again there were important national variations. The military's insatiable needs—nearly every belligerent power resorted to conscription to put soldiers in the field—created a tremendous demand for workers at home. This situation brought about momentous changes.

One such change was increased power and prestige for labor unions. Unions cooperated with war governments in return for real participation in important decisions. This entry of labor leaders into policymaking councils paralleled the entry of socialist leaders into the war governments.

Women's roles also changed dramatically. In every belligerent country, large numbers of women went to work in industry, transportation, and offices. A former parlor maid reportedly told her boyfriend as he prepared to leave for France:

> While you are at the front firing shells, I am going into a munitions factory to make shells. The job will not be as well paid as domestic service, it will not be as comfortable as domestic service; it will be much harder work, but it will be my bit, and every time you fire your gun you can remember I am helping to make the shells.[7]

Moreover, women became highly visible—not only as munitions workers but as bank tellers, mail carriers, and even police officers. Women also served as nurses and doctors at the front. (See "Individuals in Society: Vera Brittain," at right.) In general, the war greatly expanded the range of women's activities and changed attitudes toward women. Although at war's end most women were quickly let go and their jobs were given back to the returning soldiers, their many-sided war effort caused Britain, Germany, the United States, and Austria to grant them the right to vote after the war.

Recent scholarship has shown, however, that traditional views of gender—of male roles and female roles—remained remarkably resilient and that there was a significant conservative backlash in the postwar years. Even as the war progressed, many

Vera Brittain

Vera Brittain was marked forever by her wartime experiences.
(Hulton Archive/Getty Images)

ALTHOUGH THE GREAT WAR UPENDED MILLIONS of lives, it struck Europe's young people with the greatest force. For Vera Brittain (1893–1970), as for so many in her generation, the war became life's defining experience, which she captured forever in her famous autobiography, *Testament of Youth* (1933).

Raised in a wealthy business family in northern England, Brittain bristled at small-town conventions and discrimination against women. She read voraciously and dreamed of being a successful writer. After finishing boarding school and against her father's objections, Brittain passed Oxford's rigorous entry exams and won a scholarship to its women's college. She also fell in love with Roland Leighton, an equally brilliant student from a literary family and the best friend of her younger brother, Edward. All three, along with two more close friends, Victor Richardson and Geoffrey Thurlow, confidently prepared to enter Oxford in late 1914.

But war intervened and Brittain shared with millions of Europeans a thrilling surge of patriotic support for her government. She wrote in her diary that her "great fear" was that England would declare its neutrality and commit the "grossest treachery" toward France.* She supported Roland's decision to enlist, agreeing with her sweetheart's romantic view of war as "very ennobling and very beautiful." Later, exchanging anxious letters with Roland in France in 1915, Brittain began to see the conflict in more personal, human terms, and wondered if any victory or defeat could be worth Roland's life.

Struggling to quell her doubts, Brittain redoubled her commitment to England's cause and volunteered as an army nurse. For the next three years she served with distinction in military hospitals in London, Malta, and northern France, repeatedly torn between the vision of noble sacrifice and the reality of human tragedy. She lost her sexual inhibitions caring for mangled male bodies, and she longed to consummate her love with Roland. Awaiting his return on leave on Christmas Day, 1915, she was greeted instead with a telegram: Roland had been killed two days before.

Roland's death was the first of several devastating blows that eventually overwhelmed Brittain's idealistic patriotism. In 1917 first Geoffrey and then Victor died from gruesome wounds. In early 1918, as the last great German offensive filled her war-zone hospital with maimed and dying German prisoners, the bone-weary

Vera felt a common humanity and saw only more victims. Weeks later, her brother Edward died in action. When the war ended, she was, she said, a "complete automaton," with her "deepest emotions paralyzed if not dead."

Returning to Oxford and finishing her studies, Brittain gradually recovered. She formed a deep, restorative friendship with another talented woman writer, Winifred Holtby; published novels and articles; and became a leader in the feminist campaign for gender equality. She also married and had children. But her wartime memories remained. Finally, Brittain succeeded in coming to grips with them in *Testament of Youth*, her powerful antiwar autobiography. The unflinching narrative spoke to the experiences of an entire generation and became a runaway bestseller. Above all, perhaps, Brittain captured the ambivalent, contradictory character of the war, in which millions of young people found excitement, courage, and common purpose but succeeded only in destroying their lives with their superhuman efforts and futile sacrifices. Becoming ever more committed to pacifism, Brittain opposed England's entry into World War II.

QUESTIONS FOR ANALYSIS

1. What were Brittain's initial feelings toward the war? How and why did they change as the conflict continued?
2. Why did Brittain volunteer as a nurse, as many women did? How might wartime nursing have influenced women of her generation?
3. In portraying the ambivalent, contradictory character of World War I for Europe's youth, was Brittain describing the contradictory character of all modern warfare? Explain your answer.

*Quoted in the excellent study by P. Berry and M. Bostridge, *Vera Brittain: A Life* (London: Virago Press, 2001), p. 59; additional quotations are from pp. 80 and 136.

men, particularly soldiers, grew increasingly hostile toward women. Some were angry at mothers, wives, and girlfriends for urging them to enlist and fight in the horrible war. Soldiers with wives and girlfriends back home grew increasingly convinced that they were cheating on them. Others worried that factory or farm jobs had been taken by women and there would be no work when they returned home. Men were also concerned that if women received the vote at war's end, they would vote themselves into power. These concerns, as well as the fear that women would lose their femininity, are reflected in a letter from Private G. F. Wilby, serving in East Africa, to his fiancée in London, Ethel Baxter, in August 1918:

> Whatever you do, don't go in Munitions or anything in that line — just fill a Woman's position and remain a woman. . . . I want to return and find the same loveable little woman that I left behind — not a coarse thing more of a man than a woman.[8]

War also promoted social equality, blurring class distinctions and lessening the gap between rich and poor. Greater equality was reflected in full employment, rationing according to physical needs, and a sharing of hardships. Society became more uniform and more egalitarian.

Growing Political Tensions

During the war's first two years, belief in a just cause and patriotic nationalism united soldiers and civilians behind their various national leaders. Each government employed censorship and propaganda to maintain popular support.

By spring 1916, however, cracks were appearing under the strain of total war. In April Irish nationalists in Dublin unsuccessfully rose up against British rule in the Easter Rebellion. Strikes and protest marches over inadequate food flared up on every home front. In April 1917 nearly half the French infantry divisions mutinied for two months after suffering enormous losses in the Second Battle of the Aisne. Later that year there was a massive mutiny of Russian soldiers supporting the revolution.

The Central Powers experienced the most strain. In October 1916 a young socialist assassinated Austria's chief minister. By 1917 German political unity was also collapsing, and prewar social conflicts were re-emerging. A coalition of Socialists and Catholics in the Reichstag called for a compromise "peace without annexations or reparations." Thus Germany, like its ally Austria-Hungary and its enemy France, began to crack in 1917. But it was Russia that collapsed first and saved the Central Powers — for a time.

What factors led to the Russian Revolution, and what was its outcome?

The Russian Revolution

The 1917 Russian Revolution, directly related to the Great War, opened a new era with a radically new prototype of state and society that changed the course of the twentieth century.

The Fall of Imperial Russia

Imperial Russia in 1914 was still predominantly a rural and nonurbanized society. Industrialization came late to Russia and, although rapidly expanding, was still in its early stages. Peasants still made up perhaps 80 percent of the population. Besides the royal family and the nobility, the rest of Russian society consisted of the bourgeoisie (the elite, educated upper and middle classes, such as liberal politicians, propertied and professional classes, military officer corps, and landowners) and the proletariat (the urban working class, which remained small, and rank-and-file soldiers and sailors). These two factions contended for power when the tsar abdicated in 1917.

Like their allies and their enemies, Russians embraced war with patriotic enthusiasm in 1914. For a moment Russia was united, but soon the war began to take its toll. Russia quickly exhausted its supplies of shells and ammunition, and better-equipped German armies inflicted terrible losses—1.5 million casualties and nearly 1 million captured in 1915 alone. Russian soldiers were sent to the front without rifles; they were told to find their arms among the dead. The Duma (DOO-muh), Russia's lower house of parliament, and *zemstvos* (ZEMST-vohs), local governments, led the effort toward full mobilization on the home front. These efforts improved the military situation, but overall Russia mobilized less effectively for total war than did the other warring nations.

Although limited industrial capacity was a serious handicap in a war against highly industrialized Germany, Russia's real problem was leadership. A kindly, slightly dull-witted man, Tsar Nicholas II (r. 1894–1917) distrusted the moderate Duma and rejected any democratic sharing of power. As a result, the Duma, whose members came from the elite classes, and the popular masses became increasingly critical of the tsar's leadership and the appalling direction of the war. In response, Nicholas (who had no military background) traveled to the front in September 1915 to lead Russia's armies—and thereafter received all the blame for Russian losses.

His departure was a fatal turning point. His German-born wife, Tsarina Alexandra, took control of the government and the home front. She tried to rule absolutely in her husband's absence with an uneducated Siberian preacher, Rasputin (ra-SPOO-tin), as her most trusted adviser. In a desperate attempt to right the situation, three members of the high aristocracy murdered Rasputin in December 1916. In this convulsive atmosphere, the government slid steadily toward revolution.

Large-scale strikes, demonstrations, and protest marches were now commonplace, as were bread shortages. On March 8, 1917, a women's bread march in Petrograd (formerly St. Petersburg) started riots, which spread throughout the city. While his ministers fled the city, the tsar ordered that peace be restored, but discipline broke down, and the soldiers and police joined the revolutionary crowd. The Duma declared a provisional government on March 12, 1917. Three days later, Nicholas abdicated.

KEY EVENTS OF THE RUSSIAN REVOLUTION

1914	Russia enters World War I
1916–1917	Tsarist government in crisis
March 1917	March Revolution; Duma declares a provisional government; tsar abdicates; Petrograd Soviet issues Army Order No. 1
April 1917	Lenin returns from exile
October 1917	Bolsheviks gain a majority in the Petrograd Soviet
November 7, 1917	Bolsheviks seize power; Lenin named head of new Bolshevik government
1917–1922	Civil war
March 1918	Treaty of Brest-Litovsk; Trotsky becomes head of the Red Army
1922	Civil war ends; Lenin and the Bolshevik Communists take control of Russia

The Provisional Government

March Revolution The first phase of the Russian Revolution of 1917, in which unplanned uprisings led to the abdication of the tsar and the establishment of a provisional democratic government that was then overthrown in November by Lenin and the Bolsheviks.

The **March Revolution** was joyfully accepted throughout the country. A new government formed in May 1917, with the understanding that an elected democratic government, ruling under a new constitution drafted by a future Constituent Assembly, would replace it when circumstances permitted. The provisional government established equality before the law; freedom of religion, speech, and assembly; the right of unions to organize and strike; and other classic liberal measures.

The provisional government soon made two fatal decisions, however, that turned the people against it. First, it refused to confiscate large landholdings and give them to peasants, fearing that such drastic action in the countryside would only complete the disintegration of Russia's peasant army. Second, the government decided that the continuation of war was still the all-important national duty and that international alliances had to be honored. Neither decision was popular. The peasants believed that when the tsar's autocratic rule ended, so too did the nobles' title to the land, which was now theirs for the taking. The army believed that the March Revolution meant the end of the war.

Petrograd Soviet A counter-government to the 1917 Russian provisional government, this organization was a huge, fluctuating mass meeting of two to three thousand workers, soldiers, and socialist intellectuals.

From its first day, the provisional government had to share power (dual power) with a formidable rival that represented the popular masses—the **Petrograd Soviet** (or council) of Workers' and Soldiers' Deputies, a huge, fluctuating mass organization composed of two to three thousand workers, soldiers, and socialist intellectuals. This counter-government, or half government, issued its own radical orders, further weakening the provisional government. Most famous of these was Army Order No. 1, issued in March 1917, which stripped officers of their authority and gave power to elected committees of common soldiers.

Order No. 1 led to a total collapse of army discipline. Peasant soldiers began "voting with their feet," to use Lenin's graphic phrase, returning to their villages to get a share of the land that peasants were seizing from landowners, either through peasant soviets (councils) or by force, in a great agrarian upheaval. Through the summer of 1917, the provisional government, led from July by the socialist Alexander Kerensky, became increasingly more conservative and authoritarian as it tried to maintain law and order and protect property (such as nobles' land and factories). The government was being threatened from one side by an advancing German army and from the other by proletarian forces, urban and rural alike, shouting "All power to the soviets!" and calling for an even more radical revolution.

Lenin and the Bolshevik Revolution

According to most traditional twentieth-century accounts of the two Russian revolutions in 1917 written by both anti-Soviet Russian and Western scholars, in March Russia successfully overthrew the tsar's autocratic rule and replaced it with a liberal, Western-style democracy. Then in November a small group of hard-core radicals, led by Vladimir Lenin, somehow staged a second revolution and installed an atheistic Communist government. More recently, however, and especially since the Soviet archives were opened in the 1990s following the dissolution of the Soviet Union, a different picture has emerged. Scholars are recognizing that the second revolution had widespread popular support and that Lenin was often following events as much as leading them.

Born into the middle class, Vladimir Ilyich Lenin (1870–1924) became an enemy of imperial Russia when his older brother was executed for plotting to kill the tsar in 1887. As a law student Lenin studied Marxist doctrines with religious ferocity. Exiled to Siberia for three years because of socialist agitation, Lenin lived in western Europe after his release for seventeen years and developed his own revolutionary interpretations of Marxist thought (see "The Birth of Socialism" in Chapter 24).

Three interrelated ideas were central for Lenin. First, he stressed that only violent revolution could destroy capitalism. Second, Lenin believed that a socialist revolution was possible even in an agrarian country like Russia. According to classical Marxist theory, a society must reach the capitalist, industrial stage of development before its urban workers, the proletariat, can rise up and create a Communist society. Lenin thought that although Russia's industrial working class was small, the peasants, who made up the bulk of the army and navy, were also potential revolutionaries. Third, Lenin believed that at a given moment revolution was determined more by human leadership than by vast historical laws. He called for a highly disciplined workers' party, strictly controlled by a dedicated elite of intellectuals and full-time revolutionaries like him. This "vanguard of the proletariat" would not stop until revolution brought it to power.

Lenin's ideas did not go unchallenged by other Russian Marxists. At a Social Democratic Labor Party congress in London in 1903, Lenin demanded a small, disciplined, elitist party; his opponents wanted a more democratic party with mass membership. The Russian Marxists split into two rival factions. Because his side won one crucial vote at the congress, Lenin's camp became known as **Bolsheviks**, or "majority group"; his opponents were Mensheviks, or "minority group."

Bolsheviks The "majority group"; this was Lenin's camp of the Russian party of Marxist socialism.

In March 1917 Lenin and nearly all the other leading Bolsheviks were living in exile abroad or in Russia's remotest corners. After the March Revolution, the German government provided safe passage for Lenin from his exile in Switzerland across Germany and back into Russia, hoping he would undermine Russia's sagging war effort. They were not disappointed. Arriving in Petrograd on April 16, Lenin attacked at once, issuing his famous April Theses. To the Petrograd Bolsheviks' great astonishment, he rejected all cooperation with what he called the "bourgeois" provisional government and instead called for exactly what the

Lenin and Stalin at Lenin's Country House at Gorki This controversial photo, supposedly taken by Lenin's sister in 1922, two years before Lenin's death, has stirred much scholarly debate. Some argue that Stalin had himself airbrushed into the photo later to support his claim as Lenin's legitimate successor. Even if the photo is authentic, it appears to have been retouched later, on Stalin's orders, to clear his severely pockmarked face; to make his shorter and stiffer left arm, injured in a childhood accident, appear normal; and to make him taller (he was only 5 feet 4 inches tall) and larger than the smaller and more passive-looking Lenin. (Gorki Haynes Archive/Popperfoto/Getty Images)

popular masses themselves were demanding: "All power to the soviets!" and "Peace, Land, Bread!" Bolshevik support increased through the summer, culminating in mass demonstrations in Petrograd on July 16–20 by soldiers, sailors, and workers. Lenin and the Bolshevik Central Committee had not planned these demonstrations and were completely unprepared to support them. Nonetheless, the provisional government labeled Lenin and other leading Bolsheviks traitors and ordered them arrested. Lenin had to flee to Finland.

Meanwhile, however, the provisional government itself was collapsing. The coalition between liberals and socialists was breaking apart as their respective power bases—bourgeoisie and proletariat—demanded they move further to the right or left. Prime Minister Kerensky's unwavering support for the war lost him all credit with the army, the only force that might have saved him and democratic government in Russia. In early September an attempted right-wing military coup failed as Petrograd workers organized themselves as Red Guards to defend the city and then convinced the coup's soldiers to join them. Lenin, from his exile in Finland, now called for an armed Bolshevik insurrection before the Second All-Russian Congress of Soviets met in early November.

In October the Bolsheviks gained a fragile majority in the Petrograd Soviet. Lenin did not return to Russia until mid-October and even then remained in hiding. It was Lenin's supporter Leon Trotsky (1879–1940) who brilliantly executed the Bolshevik seizure of power. On November 6 militant Trotsky followers joined with trusted Bolshevik soldiers to seize government buildings and arrest provisional government members. That evening Lenin came out of hiding and took control of the revolution. The following day revolutionary forces seized the Winter Palace, and Kerensky capitulated. At the Congress of Soviets, a Bolshevik majority declared that all power had passed to the soviets and named Lenin head of the new government.

The Bolsheviks came to power for three key reasons. First, by late 1917 democracy had given way to anarchy as the popular masses no longer supported the provisional government. Second, in Lenin and Trotsky the Bolsheviks had truly superior leaders who were utterly determined to provoke a Marxist revolution. Third, the Bolsheviks appealed to soldiers, urban workers, and peasants who were exhausted by war and eager for socialism.

Dictatorship and Civil War

The Bolsheviks' true accomplishment was not taking power but keeping it and conquering the chaos they had helped create. Once again, Lenin was able to profit from developments over which he and the Bolsheviks had no control. Since summer 1917 an unstoppable peasant revolution had swept across Russia, as peasants divided among themselves the estates of the landlords and the church. Thus Lenin's first law, which supposedly gave land to the peasants, actually merely approved what peasants were already doing. Lenin then met urban workers' greatest demand with a decree giving local workers' committees direct control of individual factories.

The Bolsheviks proclaimed their regime a "provisional workers' and peasants' government," promising that a freely elected Constituent Assembly would draw up a new constitution. However, when Bolshevik delegates won fewer than one-fourth of the seats in free elections in November, the Constituent Assembly was permanently disbanded by Bolshevik soldiers acting under Lenin's orders.

Lenin then moved to make peace with Germany, at any price. That price was very high. Germany demanded the Soviet government surrender all its western territories in the Treaty of Brest-Litovsk (BREHST lih-TAWFSK) in March 1918. With Germany's defeat eight months later, the treaty was nullified, but it allowed Lenin time to escape the disaster of continued war and pursue his goal of absolute political power for the Bolsheviks—now renamed Communists—within Russia.

The war's end and the demise of the democratically elected Constituent Assembly revealed Bolshevik rule as a dictatorship. "Long live the [democratic] soviets; down with the Bolsheviks" became a popular slogan. Officers of the old army organized so-called White opposition to the Bolsheviks in southern Russia, Ukraine, Siberia, and west of Petrograd and plunged the country into civil war from November 1917 to October 1922. The Whites came from many political factions and were united only by their hatred of the Bolsheviks—the Reds. In almost five years of fighting, 125,000 Reds and 175,000 Whites and Poles were killed before the Red Army, formed in March 1918 under Trotsky's command, claimed final victory.

The Bolsheviks' Red Army won for several reasons. Strategically, they controlled the center, while the disunited Whites attacked from the fringes. Moreover, the Whites' poorly defined political program failed to unite all of the Bolsheviks' foes under a progressive democratic banner. Most important, the Communists developed a better army, against which the divided Whites were no match.

The Bolsheviks also mobilized the home front. Establishing **War Communism**—the application of the total-war concept to a civil conflict—they seized grain from peasants, introduced rationing, nationalized all banks and industry, and required everyone to work. Although these measures contributed to a breakdown of normal economic activity, they also served to maintain labor discipline and to keep the Red Army supplied.

Revolutionary terror also contributed to the Communist victory. The old tsarist secret police was re-established as the Cheka (CHEHK-kah), which hunted down and executed thousands of real or supposed foes, including the tsar and his family. During the so-called Red Terror of 1918–1920, the Cheka sowed fear, silenced opposition, and executed an estimated 250,000 "class enemies."

Finally, foreign military intervention in the civil war ended up helping the Communists. The Allies sent troops to prevent war materiel that they had sent to the provisional government from being captured by the Germans. After the Soviet government nationalized all foreign-owned factories without compensation and refused to pay foreign debts, Western governments began to support White armies. While these efforts did little to help the Whites' cause, they did permit the Communists to appeal to the ethnic Russians' patriotic nationalism.

Ceded after Treaty of Brest-Litovsk, 1918

Bolshevik territory, 1919

Occupied by Allies, 1919

White Army forces

Boundary of U.S.S.R., 1921

The Russian Civil War, 1917–1922

War Communism
The application of the total-war concept to a civil conflict; the Bolsheviks seized grain from peasants, introduced rationing, nationalized all banks and industry, and required everyone to work.

The War's Consequences

What were the global consequences of the First World War?

In spring 1918 the Germans launched their last major attack against France and failed. A defeated Germany finally aeed to an armistice on November 11, following ones already signed by the Austrian-Hungarian (November 3) and Ottoman (October

30) leaders. All three monarchies fell and their empires broke apart. In January 1919 the victorious Western Allies came together in Paris hoping to establish a lasting peace.

Laboring intensively, the Allies soon worked out peace terms with Germany, created the peacekeeping League of Nations, and reorganized eastern Europe and southwest Asia. The 1919 peace settlement, however, failed to establish a lasting peace or to resolve the issues that had brought the world to war. World War I and the treaties that ended it shaped the course of the twentieth century, often in horrible ways. Surely this was the ultimate tragedy of the Great War that cost $332 billion and left 10 million people dead and another 20 million wounded.

The End of the War

Peace and an end to the war did not come easily. Victory over revolutionary Russia had temporarily boosted sagging German morale, and in spring 1918 the German army attacked France once more. The German offensive was turned back in July at the Second Battle of the Marne, where 140,000 fresh American soldiers saw action. Adding 2 million men in arms to the war effort by August, the late but massive American intervention decisively tipped the scales in favor of Allied victory.

By September British, French, and American armies were advancing steadily on all fronts. On October 4 the German emperor formed a new, more liberal German government to sue for peace. As negotiations over an armistice dragged on, the frustrated German people rose up. On November 3 sailors in Kiel (KEEL) mutinied, and throughout northern Germany soldiers and workers established revolutionary councils on the Russian soviet model. With army discipline collapsing, Kaiser Wilhelm abdicated and fled to Holland. Socialist leaders in Berlin proclaimed a German republic on November 9 and agreed to tough Allied terms of surrender. The armistice went into effect at 11 o'clock on November 11, 1918.

The Paris Peace Treaties

Seventy delegates from twenty-seven nations attended the opening of the Paris Peace Conference at the Versailles (vayr-SIGH) Palace on January 18, 1919. By August 1920 five major treaties with the defeated powers had been agreed upon. The most well-known, the Treaty of Versailles, laid out peace terms with Germany and also included the Covenant of the League of Nations and an article establishing the International Labour Organization. The conference also yielded a number of minor treaties, unilateral declarations, bilateral treaties, and League of Nations mandates (Map 28.4). The delegates had met with great expectations. A young British diplomat later wrote that the victors "were journeying to Paris . . . to found a new order in Europe. We were preparing not Peace only, but Eternal Peace."⁹

This idealism was strengthened by President Wilson's January 1918 peace proposal, his Fourteen Points. Wilson stressed national self-determination and the rights of small countries and called for the creation of a **League of Nations**, a permanent international organization designed to protect member states from aggression and avert future wars.

The real powers at the conference were the "Big Three": the United States, Great Britain, and France. Germany and Russia were excluded, and Italy's role was limited. President Wilson wanted to immediately deal with the establishment of a League of

League of Nations
A permanent international organization established during the 1919 Paris Peace Conference to protect member states from aggression and avert future wars.

FINLAND
NORWAY
Oslo • Helsinki •
• Stockholm Petrograd (St. Petersburg) •
SWEDEN Tallinn
North ESTONIA
Sea LATVIA
Riga
Moscow •
DENMARK LITHUANIA
IRELAND • Copenhagen • Vilnius
GREAT Danzig EAST SOVIET
BRITAIN POLISH PRUSSIA UNION
London • Amsterdam CORRIDOR
GERMANY • Warsaw
RHINELAND • Berlin POLAND
ATLANTIC Brussels • Cologne Kiev •
OCEAN BELGIUM • Weimar
• Paris • Frankfurt
Versailles • LUX. SAAR • Prague GALICIA
LORRAINE • Strasbourg CZECHOSLOVAKIA BESSARABIA
ALSACE
FRANCE Vienna •
Geneva • SWITZ. AUSTRIA • Budapest
Locarno • TYROL HUNGARY ROMANIA
Milan • Zagreb •
Venice • Trieste CROATIA Bucharest •
Genoa • Rapallo Belgrade • Black
Elba YUGOSLAVIA Danube R. Sea
SPAIN Sarajevo •
Corsica ITALY SERBIA BULGARIA
Rome • MONTENEGRO • Sofia
PORTUGAL Sardinia (To Yugoslavia 1921) Constantinople •
Naples • ALBANIA
GREECE TURKEY
0 100 200 miles Izmir •
0 100 200 kilometers Sicily Athens •
Mediterranean Sea Crete

— Boundaries of German, Russian, and Austro-Hungarian Empires in 1914
🟩 New and reconstituted nations
🟪 Demilitarized or Allied occupation zone

MAPPING THE PAST

MAP 28.4 Territorial Changes in Europe After World War I The Great War brought tremendous changes to eastern Europe. Empires were shattered, new nations were established, and a dangerous power vacuum was created by the relatively weak states established between Germany and Soviet Russia.

ANALYZING THE MAP What territory did Germany lose, and to whom? What new independent states were formed from the old Russian Empire?

CONNECTIONS How were the principles of national self-determination applied to the redrawing of Europe after the war? Did this theory work out?

Nations, while Prime Ministers Lloyd George of Great Britain and, especially, Georges Clemenceau (klem-uhn-soh) of France were primarily concerned with punishing Germany.

Although personally inclined to make a somewhat moderate peace with Germany, Lloyd George felt pressured for a victory worthy of the sacrifices of total war. As Rudyard Kipling summed up the general British feeling at war's end, the Germans were "a people with the heart of beasts."[10] For his part, Clemenceau wanted revenge and lasting security for France, which, he believed, required the creation of a buffer state between France and Germany, Germany's permanent demilitarization, and vast German reparations. Wilson, supported by Lloyd George, would hear none of this. In the end, Clemenceau agreed to a compromise, abandoning the French demand for a Rhineland buffer state in return for a formal defensive alliance with the United States and Great Britain.

On June 28, 1919, in the great Hall of Mirrors at Versailles (where Germany had forced France to sign the armistice ending the Franco-Prussian War), German representatives of the ruling moderate Social Democrats and the Catholic Party reluctantly signed the treaty.

Germany's African colonies were mandated to Great Britain, France, South Africa, and Belgium. Germany's hold over the Shandong Peninsula in China passed to Japan, provoking an eruption of outrage among Chinese nationalists (see "The Rise of Nationalist China" in Chapter 29). Germany's territorial losses within Europe were minor: Alsace-Lorraine was returned to France, and parts of Germany were ceded to the new Polish state (see Map 28.4). The treaty limited Germany's army to one hundred thousand men and allowed no new military fortifications in the Rhineland.

More harshly, the Allies demanded that Germany (with Austria) accept responsibility for the war and pay reparations equal to all civilian damages caused by the war, although the Allies left the actual reparations figure to be set at a later date when tempers had cooled. These much-criticized "war-guilt" and "reparations" clauses reflected British and French popular demands for revenge, but were bitterly resented by the German people.

Treaty of Versailles The 1919 peace settlement that ended World War I; it declared Germany responsible for the war, limited Germany's army to one hundred thousand men, and forced Germany to pay huge reparations.

The **Treaty of Versailles** and the other agreements reached in Paris were seen as the first steps toward re-establishing international order, albeit ones that favored the victorious Allies, and they would have far-reaching consequences for the remainder of the twentieth century and beyond.

In eastern Europe, Poland regained its independence (see Map 19.1), and the independent states of Austria, Hungary, Czechoslovakia, and a larger Romania were created out of the Austro-Hungarian Empire (see Map 28.4). A greatly expanded Serbian monarchy united Slavs in the western Balkans and took the name Yugoslavia.

Promises of independence made to Arab leaders were largely brushed aside, and Britain and France extended their power in the Middle East, taking advantage of the breakup of the Ottoman Empire. As League of Nations mandates, the French received Lebanon and Syria, and Britain took Iraq and Palestine. Palestine was to include a Jewish national homeland first promised by Britain in 1917 in the Balfour Declaration (see "Nationalist Movements in the Middle East" in Chapter 29). Only Hussein's Arab kingdom of Hejaz (hee-JAZ) received independence. These Allied acquisitions, although officially League of Nations mandates, were simply colonialism under another name. They left colonized peoples in the Middle East, Asia (see Chapter 29), and Africa bitterly disappointed and demonstrated that the age of Western and Eastern imperialism lived on.

American Rejection of the Versailles Treaty

The 1919 peace settlement was not perfect, but for war-shattered Europe it was an acceptable beginning. Moreover, Allied leaders wanted a quick settlement for another reason: they detested Lenin and feared his Bolshevik Revolution might spread. The remaining problems could be worked out in the future.

Such hopes were dashed, however, when the United States quickly reverted to its prewar preferences for isolationism and the U.S. Senate, led by Republican Henry Cabot Lodge, rejected the Versailles treaty on November 19, 1919. Wilson obstinately rejected all attempts at compromise on the treaty, ensuring that it would never be ratified in any form and that the United States would never join the League of Nations. Moreover, the Senate refused to ratify Wilson's defensive alliance with France and Great Britain. Using U.S. action as an excuse, Great Britain also refused to ratify its defensive alliance with France. Betrayed by its allies, France stood alone, and the great hopes of early 1919 had turned to ashes by year's end.

The Search for Peace and Political Stability, 1919–1929

> **How did leaders deal with the political dimensions of uncertainty and try to re-establish peace and prosperity in the interwar years?**

The pursuit of real and lasting peace in the first half of the interwar years proved difficult for many reasons. Germany hated the Treaty of Versailles. France was fearful and isolated. Britain was undependable, and the United States had turned its back on Europe's problems. Eastern Europe was in ferment, and no one could predict Communist Russia's future. Moreover, the international economic situation was poor and was greatly complicated by war debts and disrupted patterns of trade. Yet for a time, from 1925 to late 1929, it appeared that peace and stability were within reach.

Germany and the Western Powers

Nearly all Germans and many other observers immediately and for decades after believed the Versailles treaty represented a harsh dictated peace and should be revised or repudiated as soon as possible. Many right-wing Germans, including Adolf Hitler, believed there had been no defeat; instead they believed German soldiers had been betrayed (*Dolchstoss*—"stabbed in the back") by liberals, Marxists, Jews, and other "November criminals" who had surrendered in order to seize power.

Historians have recently begun to reassess the treaty's terms, however, and many scholars currently view them as relatively reasonable. They argue that much of the German anger toward the Allies was based more on perception than reality. With the collapse of Austria-Hungary, the dissolution of the Ottoman Empire, and the revolution in Russia, Germany emerged from the war an even stronger power in eastern Europe than before, and an economically stronger and more populated nation than France or Great Britain. Moreover, when contrasted with the extremely harsh Treaty of Brest-Litovsk that Germany had forced on Lenin's Russia, and the peace terms Germany had intended to impose on the Allies if it won the war, the Versailles treaty was far from being a vindictive and crippling peace. Had it been, Germany could hardly have become the economic and military juggernaut that it was only twenty years later.

This is not to say, however, that France did not seek some degree of revenge on Germany for both the Franco-Prussian War (see "Bismarck and German Unification" and Map 24.3 in Chapter 24) and the Great War. Most of the war on the western front had been fought on French soil. The expected reconstruction costs and the amount of war debts France owed to the United States were staggering. Thus the French believed that heavy German reparations were an economic necessity that could hold Germany down indefinitely and would enable France to realize its goal of security.

The British felt differently. Prewar Germany had been Great Britain's second-best market, and after the war a healthy, prosperous Germany appeared to be essential to the British economy. In addition, the British were suspicious of France's army—the largest in Europe—and the British and French were at odds over their League of Nations mandates in the Middle East.

While France and Britain drifted in different directions, the Allied reparations commission completed its work and announced in April 1921 that Germany had to pay the enormous sum of 132 billion gold marks ($33 billion) in annual installments of 2.5 billion gold marks. The young German republic—known as the Weimar Republic—made its first reparations payment in that year. Then in 1922, wracked by rapid inflation and political assassinations, and motivated by hostility and arrogance as well, the Weimar Republic announced its inability to pay more and proposed a reparations moratorium for three years.

French Occupation of the Ruhr, 1923–1925

The British were willing to accept a moratorium, but the French were not. Led by their prime minister, Raymond Poincaré (pwan-kah-RAY) (1860–1934), the French decided they had to either call Germany's bluff or see the entire peace settlement dissolve to their great disadvantage. In January 1923 French and Belgian armies occupied the Ruhr (ROO-uhr) district, industrial Germany's heartland, creating the most serious international crisis of the 1920s.

Strengthened by a wave of patriotism, the German government ordered the people of the Ruhr to stop working and to resist French occupation nonviolently. The French responded by sealing off not only the Ruhr but also the entire Rhineland from the rest of Germany, letting in only enough food to prevent starvation.

By summer 1923 France and Germany were engaged in a great test of wills. French armies could not collect reparations from striking workers at gunpoint. But French occupation was paralyzing Germany and its economy, and the German government was soon forced to print money to pay its bills. Prices soared, and German money rapidly lost all value. In 1919 one American dollar equaled nine German marks; by November 1923 it took over 4.2 trillion German marks to purchase one American dollar. As retired and middle-class people saw their savings wiped out, many Germans felt betrayed. They hated and blamed for their misfortune the Western governments, their own government, big business, the Jews, the workers, and the Communists. The crisis left them psychologically prepared to follow radical right-wing leaders.

In August 1923, as the mark's value fell and political unrest grew throughout Germany, Gustav Stresemann (GOOS-tahf SHTRAY-zuh-mahn) (1878–1929) became German chancellor. Stresemann adopted a compromising attitude. He called off the peaceful resistance campaign in the Ruhr and in October agreed in principle to pay reparations but asked first for a re-examination of Germany's ability to pay. Poincaré accepted. Thus, after five years of hostility and tension, Germany and France, with British and American help, decided to try compromise and cooperation.

Hope in Foreign Affairs

In 1924 an international committee of financial experts headed by American banker Charles G. Dawes met to re-examine reparations. Under the terms of the resulting **Dawes Plan** (1924), Germany's yearly reparations were reduced and linked to the

Dawes Plan The product of the 1924 World War I reparations commission, accepted by Germany, France, and Britain, that reduced Germany's yearly reparations, made payment dependent on German economic prosperity, and granted Germany large loans from the United States to promote recovery.

level of German economic prosperity. Germany would also receive large loans from the United States to promote German recovery, as well as to pay reparations to France and Britain, thus enabling those countries to repay the large sums they owed the United States. This circular flow of international payments was complicated and risky, but it worked for a while, facilitating a worldwide economic recovery in the late 1920s.

This economic settlement was matched by a political settlement. In 1925 European leaders met in Locarno, Switzerland. Germany and France solemnly pledged to accept their common border, and both Britain and Italy agreed to fight either France or Germany if one invaded the other. Stresemann also agreed to settle boundary disputes with Poland and Czechoslovakia by peaceful means, and France promised those countries military aid if Germany attacked them. Other developments also strengthened hopes for international peace. In 1926 Germany joined the League of Nations, and in 1928 fifteen countries signed the Kellogg-Briand Pact. The signing nations "condemned and renounced war as an instrument of national policy."

The pact fostered the cautious optimism of the late 1920s and also encouraged the hope that the United States would accept its international responsibilities.

Hope in Democratic Government

European domestic politics also offered reason for hope. During the Ruhr occupation and the great inflation, Germany's republican government appeared ready to collapse. But the moderate businessmen who tended to dominate the various German coalition governments believed that economic prosperity demanded good relations with the Western powers, and they supported parliamentary government at home. Elections were held regularly, and as the economy boomed in the aftermath of the Dawes Plan, republican democracy appeared to have growing support among a majority of Germans.

There were, however, sharp political divisions in the country. Many unrepentant nationalists and monarchists populated the right and the army. In November 1923 an obscure politician named Adolf Hitler, who had become leader of an obscure workers party, the National Socialist German Workers Party, in July 1921, proclaimed a "national socialist revolution" in a Munich beer hall. Hitler's plot to seize government control was poorly organized and easily crushed. Hitler was sentenced to prison, where he outlined his theories and program in his book ***Mein Kampf*** (*My Struggle*, 1925). Members of Germany's Communist Party received directions from Moscow, and they accused the Social Democrats of betraying the revolution. The working classes were divided politically, but a majority supported the socialist, but nonrevolutionary, Social Democrats.

Mein Kampf Adolf Hitler's autobiography, published in 1925, which also contains Hitler's political ideology.

France's situation was similar to Germany's. Communists and socialists battled for the workers' support. After 1924 the democratically elected government rested mainly in the hands of moderate coalitions, and business interests were well represented. France's great accomplishment was the rapid rebuilding of its war-torn northern region, and good times prevailed until 1930.

Britain, too, faced challenges after 1920. The great problem was unemployment, which hovered around 12 percent throughout the 1920s. The state provided unemployment benefits and a range of additional social services. These and other measures kept living standards from seriously declining, defused class tensions, and pointed the way to the welfare state Britain established after World War II.

The wartime trend toward greater social equality also continued, helping to maintain social harmony. Relative social harmony was accompanied by the rise of the Labour Party, which, under Prime Minister Ramsay MacDonald (1866–1937), governed the country in 1924 and 1929–1935. The Labour Party sought a gradual and democratic move toward socialism, so that the middle classes were not overly frightened as the working classes won new benefits.

The British Conservatives under Stanley Baldwin (1867–1947) showed the same compromising spirit on social issues, and Britain experienced only limited social unrest in the 1920s and 1930s. In 1922 Britain granted southern, Catholic Ireland full autonomy after a bitter guerrilla war, thereby removing another source of prewar friction. Thus developments in both international relations and domestic politics gave the leading democracies cause for cautious optimism in the late 1920s.

In what ways were the anxieties of the postwar world expressed or heightened by revolutionary ideas in modern thought, art, and science and in new forms of communication?

The Age of Anxiety

Many people hoped that happier times would return after the war, along with the familiar prewar ideals of peace, prosperity, and progress. The war had caused such social, economic, and psychological upheaval, however, that great numbers of men and women felt themselves increasingly adrift in an age of anxiety and continual crisis.

Uncertainty in Philosophy and Religion

Before 1914 most people in the West still believed in Enlightenment philosophies of progress, reason, and individual rights. As the century began, progress was a daily reality, apparent in the rising living standard, the taming of the city, the spread of political rights to women and workers, and the growth of state-supported social programs. Just as there were laws of science, many thinkers felt, there were laws of society that rational human beings could discover and wisely act on. Even before the war, however, some philosophers, such as the German Friedrich Nietzsche (NEE-chuh) (1844–1900), called such faith in reason into question. The First World War accelerated the revolt against established philosophical certainties. Logical positivism, often associated with Austrian philosopher Ludwig Wittgenstein (VIHT-guhn-shtighn) (1889–1951), rejected most concerns of traditional philosophy—from God's existence to the meaning of happiness—as nonsense and argued that life must be based on facts and observation. Others looked to **existentialism** for answers. Highly diverse and even contradictory, existential thinkers were loosely united in a search for moral values in a terrifying and uncertain world. They did not believe that a supreme being had established humanity's fundamental nature and given life its meaning. In the words of the French existentialist Jean-Paul Sartre (1905–1980), "Man's existence precedes his essence. . . . To begin with he is nothing. He will not be anything until later, and then he will be what he makes of himself."[11]

existentialism The name given to a highly diverse and even contradictory philosophy that stresses the meaninglessness of existence and the search for moral values in a world of terror and uncertainty.

In contrast, the loss of faith in human reason and in continual progress led to a renewed interest in Christianity. After World War I several thinkers and theologians began to revitalize Christian fundamentals, and intellectuals increasingly turned to religion between about 1920 and 1950. Sometimes described as Christian existentialists because they shared the loneliness and despair of atheistic existentialists, these believers felt that religion was one meaningful answer to terror and anxiety. In the words of a famous Roman Catholic convert, English novelist Graham Greene, "One began to believe in heaven because one believed in hell."[12]

The New Physics

For people no longer committed to traditional religious beliefs, a belief in unchanging natural laws offered some comfort. These laws seemed to determine physical processes and permit useful solutions to more and more problems. A series of discoveries beginning around the turn of the century, however, challenged the established certainties of Newtonian physics (see "Newton's Synthesis" in Chapter 19).

An important first step toward the new physics was the British physicist J. J. Thomson's 1897 discovery of subatomic particles, which proved that atoms were not stable and unbreakable. The following year Polish-born physicist Marie Curie (1867–1934) and her French husband, Pierre (1859–1906), discovered radium and demonstrated that it constantly emits subatomic particles and thus does not have a constant atomic weight. Building on this, German physicist Max Planck (1858–1947) showed in 1900 that subatomic energy is emitted in uneven little spurts, which he called "quanta," and not in a steady stream, as previously believed.

In 1905 the German-Jewish genius Albert Einstein (1879–1955) further undermined Newtonian physics. His theory of special relativity postulated that time and space are relative to the observer's viewpoint and that only the speed of light is constant for all frames of reference in the universe. In addition, Einstein's theory that matter and energy are interchangeable and that even a particle of matter contains enormous levels of potential energy, would later become the scientific basis for the atomic bomb.

The 1920s opened the "heroic age of physics," in the apt words of one of its leading pioneers, Ernest Rutherford (1871–1937). In 1919 Rutherford first split the atom. Breakthrough followed breakthrough, but some discoveries raised new doubts about reality. In 1927 German physicist Werner Heisenberg (VEHR-nuhr HIGH-zuhn-burg) theorized his "uncertainty principle," whereby any act of measurement in quantum physics is affected by, and blurred by, the experimenter. Thus, if experiments in an exact science like physics can be distorted by human observation, what other areas of human knowledge are similarly affected? Is ultimate truth unknowable?

The implications of the new theories and discoveries were disturbing to millions of people in the 1920s and 1930s. The new universe was strange and troubling, and, moreover, science appeared distant from human experience and human problems.

En amerikansk tecknares bekymmer för framtiden.

Då professorn äntligen efter årslånga experiment lyckades sönderdela en atom.

Unlocking the Power of the Atom Many of the fanciful visions of science fiction came true in the twentieth century, although not exactly as first imagined. This 1927 cartoon satirizes a professor who has split the atom and has unwittingly destroyed his building and neighborhood in the process. In the Second World War scientists harnessed the atom in bombs and decimated faraway cities and their inhabitants. (© Mary Evans Picture Library/The Image Works)

Freudian Psychology

With physics presenting an uncertain universe so unrelated to ordinary human experience, questions about the power and potential of the human mind assumed special significance. The findings and speculations of psychologist Sigmund Freud (1856–1939) were particularly disturbing.

Before Freud, most psychologists assumed that human behavior resulted from rational thinking by the conscious mind. By analyzing dreams and hysteria, Freud developed a very different view of the human psyche. Freud concluded that human behavior was governed by three parts of the self: the **id**, **ego**, and **superego**. The primitive, irrational unconscious, which he called the id, was driven by sexual, aggressive, and pleasure-seeking desires and was locked in constant battle with the mind's two other parts: the rationalizing conscious—the ego—which mediates what a person can do, and ingrained moral values—the superego—which specify what a person should do. Thus, for Freud, human behavior was a product of a fragile compromise between instinctual drives and the controls of rational thinking and moral values.

id, ego, superego Freudian terms for the primitive, irrational unconscious (id), the rationalizing conscious that mediates what a person can do (ego), and the ingrained moral values that specify what a person should do (superego).

Twentieth-Century Literature

Western literature was also influenced by the general intellectual climate of pessimism, relativism, and alienation. In the twentieth century many writers adopted the limited, often confused viewpoint of a single individual. Like Freud, these novelists focused on the complexity and irrationality of the human mind.

Some novelists used the stream-of-consciousness technique with its reliance on internal monologues to explore the psyche. The most famous stream-of-consciousness novel is *Ulysses*, published by Irish novelist James Joyce (1882–1941) in 1922. Abandoning conventional grammar and blending foreign words, puns, bits of knowledge, and scraps of memory together in bewildering confusion, the language of *Ulysses* was intended to mirror modern life itself.

Creative writers rejected the idea of progress; some even described "anti-utopias," nightmare visions of things to come. In 1918 Oswald Spengler (1880–1936) published *The Decline of the West*, in which he argued that Western civilization was in its old age and would soon be conquered by East Asia. Likewise, T. S. Eliot (1888–1965) depicted a world of growing desolation in his famous poem *The Waste Land* (1922). Franz Kafka's (1883–1924) novels *The Trial* (1925) and *The Castle* (1926) portrayed helpless individuals crushed by inexplicably hostile forces.

Modern Architecture, Art, and Music

Like scientists and intellectuals, creative artists rebelled against traditional forms and conventions at the end of the nineteenth century and beginning of the twentieth. This **modernism** in architecture, art, and music, which grew more influential after the war, meant constant experimentation and a search for new kinds of expression.

The United States pioneered in the new architecture. In the 1890s the Chicago School of architects, led by Louis H. Sullivan (1856–1924), used cheap steel, reinforced concrete, and electric elevators to build skyscrapers and office buildings lacking almost any exterior ornamentation. The buildings of Frank Lloyd Wright (1867–1959) were renowned for their sometimes-radical design, their creative use of wide varieties of materials, and their appearance of being part of the landscape.

modernism A variety of cultural movements at the end of the nineteenth century and beginning of the twentieth that rebelled against traditional forms and conventions of the past.

Eiffel Tower, 1926 The works of the French artist Robert Delaunay (1885–1941) represent most of the major art styles of the early twentieth century, including modernism, abstraction, Futurism, Fauvism, Cubism, and Orphism. His early renderings of the Eiffel Tower (1909–1912), the iconic symbol of urbanization, the machine age, and, as a radio tower, limitless communication, possess features drawn from several of these styles. His later paintings of the Eiffel Tower, such as the one shown here, draw on a much wider palette of brilliant colors, reflecting aspects of a style known as Orphism, with which he is most closely identified. (Private Collection/Photo © Christie's Images/Bridgeman Images)

In Europe architectural leadership centered in German-speaking countries. In 1919 Walter Gropius (1883–1969) merged the schools of fine and applied arts at Weimar into a single interdisciplinary school, the Bauhaus. Throughout the 1920s the Bauhaus movement stressed good design for everyday life and **functionalism**—that is, a building should serve the purpose for which it is designed. The movement attracted enthusiastic students from all over the world.

Art increasingly took on a nonrepresentational, abstract character. In 1907 in Paris the famous Spanish painter Pablo Picasso (1881–1973), along with Georges Braque (BRAHK), Marcel Duchamp, and other artists, established Cubism—an artistic approach concentrated on a complex geometry of zigzagging lines and sharply angled overlapping planes. Since the Renaissance, artists had represented objects from a single viewpoint and had created unified human forms. In his first great Cubist work, *Les Demoiselles d'Avignon* (lay dehm-wuh-ZEHL da-vee-NYAWN) (1907), Picasso's figures present a radical new view of reality with a strikingly non-Western depiction of the human form. Their faces resemble carved African masks, reflecting the growing importance of non-Western artistic traditions in Europe in the early twentieth century.

The ultimate stage in the development of abstract, nonrepresentational art occurred around 1910. Artists such as the Russian-born Wassily Kandinsky (1866–1944) turned away from nature completely. "The observer," said Kandinsky, "must learn to look at [my] pictures . . . as form and color combinations . . . as a representation of mood and not as a representation of *objects*."[13]

Radicalization accelerated after World War I. The most notable new developments were New Objectivity (*Sachlichkeit* [SAHK-leech-kight] in German), Dadaism (DAH-dah-ihz-uhm), and Surrealism. New Objectivity emerged from German artists' experiences in the Great War and the Weimar Republic. Paintings by artists like George Grosz (GRAWSH) and Otto Dix were provocative, emotionally disturbing, and harshly satirical. Dadaism attacked all accepted standards of art and behavior, delighting in outrageous conduct. After 1924 many Dadaists were attracted to

functionalism The principle that buildings, like industrial products, should serve the purpose for which they were made as well as possible.

Surrealism. Surrealists, such as Salvador Dalí (1904–1989), painted fantastic worlds of wild dreams and complex symbols.

Developments in modern music were strikingly parallel to those in painting. Attracted by the emotional intensity of expressionism, composers depicted unseen inner worlds of emotion and imagination. Just as abstract painters arranged lines and color but did not draw identifiable objects, so modern composers arranged sounds atonally without creating recognizable harmonies. Led by composers such as the Austrian Arnold Schönberg (SHUHN-buhrg) (1874–1951) and the Russian Igor Stravinsky (1882–1971), modern composers turned their backs on long-established musical conventions. The pulsating, dissonant rhythms and the dancers' earthy representation of lovemaking in Stravinsky's ballet *The Rite of Spring* nearly caused a riot when first performed in Paris in 1913.

Movies and Radio

In the decades following the First World War, motion pictures became the main entertainment of the masses worldwide. During the First World War the United States became the dominant force in the rapidly expanding silent-film industry, and Charlie Chaplin (1889–1978), an Englishman working in Hollywood, demonstrated that in the hands of a genius the new medium could combine mass entertainment and artistic accomplishment.

Motion pictures also became powerful tools of indoctrination, especially in countries with dictatorial regimes. Lenin encouraged the development of Soviet film making, and Sergei Eisenstein (1898–1948), the most famous of his film makers, and others dramatized the Communist view of Russian history. In Germany Hitler, who rose to power in 1933, turned to a talented woman film maker, Leni Riefenstahl

The International Appeal of Cinema A movie house in Havana, Cuba, in 1933 showing two American films made in 1932: *El Rey de la Plata* (*Silver Dollar*), starring Edward G. Robinson, and *6 horas de Vida* (*Six Hours to Live*), featuring Warner Baxter. The partially visible poster in the upper right is advertising *El último varon sobre la Tierra* (*The Last Man on Earth*), an American-produced Spanish-language movie starring Raul Roulien, first released in Spain in January 1933.

(Walker Evans [1903–1975]/*Cinema*, 1933, printed ca. 1970. Gelatin silver print, The Metropolitan Museum of Art. Gift of Arnold H. Crane, 1971 [1971.646.12]/© Walker Evans Archive, The Metropolitan Museum of Art, New York/Image copyright © The Metropolitan Museum of Art/Image source: Art Resource, NY)

(REE-fuhn-shtahl) (1902–2003), for a masterpiece of documentary propaganda, *Triumph of the Will*, based on the 1934 Nazi Party rally at Nuremberg. Her film was a brilliant and all-too-powerful depiction of Germany's rebirth as a great power under Nazi leadership.

Whether foreign or domestic, motion pictures became the main entertainment of the masses worldwide until after the Second World War. Motion pictures offered ordinary people a temporary escape from the hard realities of international tensions, uncertainty, unemployment, and personal frustrations.

Radio also dominated popular culture after the war. In 1920 the first major public broadcasts were made in Great Britain and the United States. Every major country quickly established national broadcasting networks. LOR, Radio Argentina, became the first formal radio station in the world when it made its first broadcast in August 1920. Radios were revolutionary in that they were capable of reaching all of a nation's citizens at once, offering them a single perspective on current events and teaching them a single national language and pronunciation.

Chapter Summary

Nationalism, militarism, imperialism, and the alliance system increased political tensions across Europe at the end of the nineteenth century. Franz Ferdinand's assassination in 1914 sparked a regional war that soon became global. Four years of stalemate and slaughter followed. Entire societies mobilized for total war, and government powers greatly increased. Women earned greater social equality, and labor unions grew. Many European countries adopted socialism as a realistic economic blueprint.

Horrible losses on the eastern front led to Russian tsar Nicholas II's abdication in March 1917. A provisional government controlled by moderate social democrats replaced him but refused to withdraw Russia from the war. A second Russian revolution followed in November 1917, led by Lenin and his Bolshevik Party. The Bolsheviks established a radical Communist regime, smashed existing capitalist institutions, and posed an ongoing challenge to Europe and its colonial empires.

The "war to end all wars" brought only a fragile truce. The Versailles treaty took away Germany's colonies, limited its military, and demanded admittance of war guilt and exorbitant war reparations. Separate treaties redrew the maps of Europe and the Middle East. Allied wartime solidarity faded, and Germany remained unrepentant, setting the stage for World War II. Globally, the European powers refused to extend self-determination to their colonies, instead creating a mandate system that sowed further discontent among colonized peoples.

In the 1920s moderate political leaders sought to create an enduring peace and rebuild prewar prosperity through compromise. By decade's end they seemed to have succeeded: Germany experienced an economic recovery, France rebuilt its war-torn regions, and Britain's Labour Party expanded social services. Ultimately, however, these measures were short-lived.

The war's horrors, particularly the industrialization of war that slaughtered millions, shattered Enlightenment ideals and caused widespread anxiety. In the interwar years philosophers, artists, and writers portrayed these anxieties in their work. Movies and the radio initially offered escape but soon became powerful tools of indoctrination and propaganda.

NOTES

1. Erich Maria Remarque, *All Quiet on the Western Front*, trans. A. W. Wheen (New York: Fawcett, 1996), p. 13.
2. Winston Churchill, *The World Crisis, 1911–1918* (New York: Free Press, 2005), p. 96.
3. Remarque, *All Quiet*, pp. 134–135.
4. Siegfried Sassoon, *The Memoirs of George Sherston: Memoirs of an Infantry Officer* (New York: Literary Guild of America, 1937), p. 74.
5. Quoted in Keith Sinclair, *The Growth of New Zealand Identity, 1890–1980* (Auckland, N.Z.: Longman Paul, 1987), p. 24.
6. Svetlana Palmer and Sarah Wallis, eds., *Intimate Voices from the First World War* (New York: William Morrow, 2003), p. 221.
7. Ethel Alec-Tweedie, *Women and Soldiers*, 2d ed. (London: John Lane, 1918), p. 29.
8. Janet S. K. Watson, "Khaki Girls, VADS, and Tommy's Sisters: Gender and Class in First World War Britain," *The International History Review* 19 (1997): 49.
9. Quoted in H. Nicolson, *Peacemaking 1919* (New York: Grosset & Dunlap Universal Library, 1965), pp. 8, 31–32.
10. Quoted ibid., p. 24.
11. Quoted in John Macquarrie, *Existentialism* (New York: Penguin Books, 1972), p. 15.
12. G. Greene, *Another Mexico* (New York: Viking Press, 1939), p. 3.
13. Quoted in A. H. Barr, Jr., *What Is Modern Painting?* 9th ed. (New York: Museum of Modern Art, 1966), p. 25.

CONNECTIONS

The Great War continues to influence global politics and societies, nearly a century after the guns went silent in November 1918. To understand the origins of many modern world conflicts, one must study first the intrigues and treaties and the revolutions and upheavals that were associated with this first truly world war.

In Chapter 30 we will see how the conflict contributed to a worldwide depression, the rise of totalitarian dictatorships, and a Second World War more global and destructive than the first. In the Middle East the Ottoman Empire came to an end, allowing France and England to carve out mandated territories — including modern Iraq, Palestine/Israel, and Lebanon — that remain flash points for violence and political instability in the twenty-first century. Nationalism, the nineteenth-century European ideology of change, took root in Asia, partly driven by Wilson's promise of self-determination. In Chapter 29 the efforts of various nationalist leaders — Atatürk in Turkey, Gandhi in India, Mao Zedong in China, Ho Chi Minh in Vietnam, and others — to throw off colonial domination will be examined, as well as the rise of ultranationalism in Japan, which led it into World War II and to ultimate defeat.

America's entry into the Great War placed it on the world stage, a place it has not relinquished as a superpower in the twentieth and twenty-first centuries. Russia, too, eventually became a superpower, but this outcome was not so clear in 1919 as its leaders fought for survival in a vicious civil war. By the outbreak of World War II Joseph Stalin had solidified Communist power, and the Soviet Union and the United States would play leading roles in defeating totalitarianism in Germany and Japan. But at war's end, as explained in Chapter 31, the two superpowers found themselves opponents in a Cold War that lasted for much of the rest of the twentieth century.

CHAPTER 28   **Review and Explore**

Identify Key Terms

Identify and explain the significance of each item below.

militarism (p. 860)   League of Nations (p. 880)

Triple Entente (p. 862)   Treaty of Versailles (p. 882)

trench warfare (p. 865)   Dawes Plan (p. 884)

total war (p. 869)   *Mein Kampf* (p. 885)

March Revolution (p. 876)   existentialism (p. 886)

Petrograd Soviet (p. 876)   id, ego, superego (p. 888)

Bolsheviks (p. 877)   modernism (p. 888)

War Communism (p. 879)   functionalism (p. 889)

Review the Main Ideas

Answer the focus questions from each section of the chapter.

1. What were the long-term and immediate causes of World War I, and how did the conflict become a global war? (p. 860)

2. How did total war affect the home fronts of the major combatants? (p. 869)

3. What factors led to the Russian Revolution, and what was its outcome? (p. 874)

4. What were the global consequences of the First World War? (p. 879)

5. How did leaders deal with the political dimensions of uncertainty and try to re-establish peace and prosperity in the interwar years? (p. 883)

6. In what ways were the anxieties of the postwar world expressed or heightened by revolutionary ideas in modern thought, art, and science and in new forms of communication? (p. 886)

Make Comparisons and Connections

Analyze the larger developments and continuities within and across chapters.

1. The war between Austria and Serbia should have been a small regional conflict in one corner of Europe. How did nationalism, militarism, and the New Imperialism contribute to its expansion into a global conflict?

2. In what ways would someone transported in time from 1900 to 1925 have been shocked and surprised at the changes that had occurred in that short time?

3. How did the mandate system established by the League of Nations reflect the Social Darwinian ideas of the late nineteenth century (Chapter 24)?

TIMELINE

Suggested Resources

BOOKS

Andelman, David A. *A Shattered Peace: Versailles 1919 and the Price We Pay Today.* 2007. A clearly written study of the Paris Peace Conference and how it has shaped world history to the present day.

Camus, Albert. *The Stranger* and *The Plague.* 1942 and 1947. The greatest existential novelist at his unforgettable best.

Eksteins, Modris. *Rites of Spring: The Great War and the Birth of the Modern Age.* 1989. An imaginative cultural investigation that has won critical acclaim.

Figes, Orlando. *A People's Tragedy: The Russian Revolution, 1891–1924.* 1996. Massive but accessible, this masterful synthesis traces the revolution from its origins to Lenin's death in 1924.

Fitzpatrick, Sheila. *The Russian Revolution*, 3d ed. 2008. A concise history that incorporates previously inaccessible Russian archives and the latest research. Fitzpatrick argues that the revolution ended only with the Stalinist purges in the late 1930s.

Fromkin, David. *Europe's Last Summer: Who Started the Great War?* 2004. A well-argued, compulsively readable discussion of responsibility for the war by a master historian.

Fromkin, David. *A Peace to End All Peace: The Fall of the Ottoman Empire and the Creation of the Modern Middle East*, 2d ed. 2009. A brilliant account of the Middle East in the critical years between 1914 and 1922.

Gay, Peter. *Modernism: The Lure of Heresy.* 2007. A personal perspective on twentieth-century high culture by a leading intellectual and cultural historian.

Gilbert, Martin. *The First World War: A Complete History.* 1994. A comprehensive study in one volume by a major military historian.

Macmillan, Margaret. *Paris, 1919: Six Months That Changed the World.* 2001. A masterful account of the negotiations and issues at the Paris Peace Conference.

Reed, John. *Ten Days That Shook the World.* 1919. The classic eyewitness account of the Russian Revolution by a young, pro-Bolshevik American.

Young, Louise. *Japan's Total Empire: Manchuria and the Culture of Wartime Imperialism.* 1998. A fascinating pioneering work on Japanese imperialism.

DOCUMENTARY

The First World War (Channel Four, 2003). Based on the book by the distinguished Great War historian Hew Strachan, this ten-episode series is a powerful and comprehensive account of all aspects of the Great War.

The Great War and the Shaping of the 20th Century. (BBC, PBS, 1996) A well-organized and comprehensive introduction to the Great War. An eight-part series on each stage of the war, how the war shaped the twentieth century, and historians' views of the war, as well as a timeline and maps.

FEATURE FILMS

All Quiet on the Western Front (Lewis Milestone, 1930). Based on the famous novel by Erich Maria Remarque, this cinematic masterpiece portraying the horrors of World War I trench warfare is one of the most powerful war, and antiwar, films of all time.

Paths of Glory (Stanley Kubrick, 1957). Considered one of the best war movies of all time, this story of the trial of three French soldiers accused of cowardice on the battlefield is based on a real-life event during the Great War.

Suffragette (Sarah Gavron, 2015). Set in the years just before the Great War, this film is a powerful portrayal of the efforts by militant suffragettes in England to gain the vote for women.

WEBSITES

"Russian Revolution" in the *Internet Modern History Sourcebook.* An excellent reference site for the Russian Revolution, with many primary documents and several links to other related websites. **sourcebooks.fordham.edu/halsall/mod/modsbook39.asp**

Spartacus Educational: Causes and Events of WW I. A comprehensive introduction to the Great War, including a glossary, statistics, and a bibliography. **spartacus-educational.com/FWW.htm**

29

Nationalism in Asia
1914–1939

From Asia's perspective, the First World War was largely a European civil war that shattered Western imperialism's united front, underscored the West's moral bankruptcy, and convulsed prewar relationships throughout Asia. Most crucially, the war sped the development of modern Asian nationalism. Before 1914 the nationalist gospel of anti-imperialist political freedom and racial equality had already won converts among Asia's westernized, educated elites. In the 1920s and 1930s it increasingly won the allegiance of the masses. Nationalism in Asia between 1914 and 1939 became a mass movement with potentially awesome power.

The modern nationalism movement was never monolithic. In Asia especially, where the new and often narrow ideology of nationalism was grafted onto old, rich, and complex civilizations, the shape and eventual outcome of nationalist movements varied enormously. Between the outbreaks of the First and Second World Wars, each Asian country developed a distinctive national movement rooted in its own unique culture and history. Each nation's people created their own national reawakening, which reinvigorated thought and culture as well as politics and economics. Nationalist movements gave rise in Asia to conflict both within large, multiethnic states and between independent states.

The Asian nationalist movement witnessed the emergence of two of the true giants of the twentieth century. Mohandas Gandhi in India and Mao Zedong in China both drew their support from the peasant masses in the world's two most populous countries. Gandhi successfully used campaigns of peaceful nonviolent resistance to British colonial rule to gain Indian independence. Mao, on the other hand, used weapons of war and socialist promises of equality to defeat his westernized nationalist opponents and establish a modern Communist state.

Kasturba Gandhi

Wife of Indian political leader Mohandas Gandhi, Kasturba was barely fourteen years old and he thirteen when their marriage took place. Kasturba (1869–1944) supported Gandhi through decades of struggle for Indian independence. Here she spins cotton on a *charkha*, or spinning wheel, part of Gandhi's campaign for Indians to become self-sufficient by making their own cloth and freeing themselves from imported British goods.

© Dinodia Photo Library/The Image Works

CHAPTER PREVIEW

THE FIRST WORLD WAR'S IMPACT ON NATIONALIST TRENDS
Why did modern nationalism develop in Asia between the First and Second World Wars, and what was its appeal?

NATIONALIST MOVEMENTS IN THE MIDDLE EAST
How did the Ottoman Empire's collapse in World War I shape nationalist movements in the Middle East?

TOWARD SELF-RULE IN INDIA
What role did Gandhi and his campaign of militant nonviolence play in leading India to independence from the British?

NATIONALIST STRUGGLES IN EAST AND SOUTHEAST ASIA
How did nationalism shape political developments in East and Southeast Asia?

Why did modern nationalism develop in Asia between the First and Second World Wars, and what was its appeal?

The First World War's Impact on Nationalist Trends

In the late nineteenth and early twentieth centuries the peoples of Asia adapted the European ideology of nationalism to their own situations. The First World War profoundly affected Asian nationalist aspirations by altering relations between Asia and Europe. For four years Asians watched Kipling's haughty bearers of "the white man's burden" (see "A 'Civilizing Mission'" in Chapter 25) vilify and destroy each other. Japan's defeat of imperial Russia in 1905 (see "Japan as an Imperial Power" in Chapter 26) had shown that an Asian power could beat a European Great Power; Asians now saw the entire West as divided and vulnerable.

Asian Reaction to the War in Europe

The Great War was a global conflict, but some peoples were affected more significantly than others. The Japanese and Ottoman Turks were directly involved, fighting with the Allies and Central Powers, respectively. The Chinese, who overthrew their emperor in 1911, were more concerned with internal events and the threat from Japan than with the war in Europe. In British India and French Indochina the war's impact was unavoidably greater. Total war required the British and the French to draft their colonial subjects into the conflict. An Indian or Vietnamese soldier who fought in France and came in contact there with democratic and republican ideas, however, was less likely to accept foreign rule when he returned home. The British and the French therefore had to make rash promises to gain the support of these colonial peoples and other allies during the war. After the war the nationalist genie the colonial powers had called on refused to slip meekly back into the bottle.

U.S. president Wilson's war aims also raised the hopes of peoples under imperial rule. In January 1918 Wilson proposed his Fourteen Points (see "The Paris Peace Treaties" in Chapter 28), whose key idea was national self-determination for the peoples of Europe and the Ottoman Empire. Wilson recommended in Point 5 that in all colonial questions "the interests of native populations be given equal weight with the desires of European governments," and he seemed to call for national self-rule. This message had enormous appeal for educated Asians, fueling their hopes of freedom.

The Mandates System

After winning the war, the Allies tried to re-establish or increase their political and economic domination of their Asian and African colonies. Although fatally weakened, Western imperialism remained very much alive in 1918, partly because President Wilson was no revolutionary. At the Paris Peace Conference Wilson compromised on colonial questions in order to achieve some of his European goals and create the League of Nations.

The compromise at the Paris Peace Conference between Wilson's vague, moralistic idealism and the European determination to maintain control over colonial empires was a system of League of Nations mandates over Germany's former colonies and the old Ottoman Empire. Article 22 of the League of Nations Covenant, which was part of the Treaty of Versailles, assigned territories "inhabited by peoples incapable of governing themselves" to various "developed nations." "The well-being and development of such peoples" was declared "a sacred trust of civilization." The **Permanent Mandates Commission**, whose members came from European countries with colonies, was created to oversee the developed nations' fulfillment of their international responsibility. Thus the League elaborated a new principle—development toward the eventual goal of self-government—but left its implementation to the colonial powers themselves. Industrialized Japan was the only Asian state to obtain mandates.

The mandates system demonstrated that Europe was determined to maintain its imperial power and influence. Bitterly disappointed patriots throughout Asia saw the system as an expansion of the imperial order. Yet they did not give up. They preached national self-determination and struggled to build mass movements capable of achieving freedom and independence.

In this struggle Asian nationalists were encouraged by Soviet communism. After seizing power in 1917, Lenin declared that the Asian inhabitants of the new Soviet Union were complete equals of the Russians with a right to their own development. The Communists also denounced European and American imperialism and pledged to support revolutionary movements in colonial countries. The example, ideology, and support of Soviet communism exerted a powerful influence in the 1920s and 1930s, particularly in China and French Indochina (see "China's Intellectual Revolution" and "Striving for Independence in Southeast Asia").

Nationalism's Appeal

There were at least three reasons for the upsurge of nationalism in Asia. First and foremost, nationalism provided the most effective means of organizing anti-imperialist resistance both to direct foreign rule and to indirect Western domination. Second, nationalism called for fundamental changes and challenged old political and social practices and beliefs. As in Russia after the Crimean War, in Turkey after the Ottoman Empire's collapse, and in Japan after the Meiji Restoration, the nationalist creed after World War I went hand in hand with acceptance of modernization by the educated elites, who used modernization to contest the influence and power of conservative traditionalists. Third, nationalism offered a vision of a free and prosperous future and provided an ideology to ennoble the sacrifices the struggle would require.

Nationalism also had a dark side. As in Europe (see "The Growing Appeal of Nationalism" in Chapter 24), Asian nationalists developed a strong sense of "we" and "they." "They" were often the enemy. European imperialists were just such a "they," and nationalist feelings generated the will to challenge European domination. But, as in Europe, Asian nationalism also stimulated bitter conflicts and wars between peoples, in three different ways.

First, as when the ideology of nationalism first developed in Europe in the early 1800s, Asian (and African) elites were often forced to create a national identity in colonies that Europeans had artificially created, or in multiethnic countries held together by authoritarian leaders but without national identities based on shared ethnicities or histories. Second, nationalism stimulated conflicts between relatively homogeneous peoples in large states, rallying, for example, Chinese against Japanese and vice versa. Third, nationalism often heightened tensions between ethnic or religious groups within states. In nearly all countries there were ancient ethnic and religious differences and rivalries. Imperial rulers of colonial powers (like the British and French) and local authoritarian rulers (like the Chinese emperor) exploited these

Permanent Mandates Commission A commission created by the League of Nations to oversee the developed nations' fulfillment of their international responsibility toward their mandates.

ethnic and religious differences to "divide and conquer" the peoples in their empires. When the rigid imperial rule ended, the different national, religious, or even ideological (communists versus capitalists) factions turned against each other, each seeking to either seize control of or divide the existing state, and to dominate the enemy "they" within its borders. This habit of thinking in terms of "we" versus "they" was, and still is, a difficult frame of mind to abandon, and these divisions made it difficult for nationalist leaders to unite people under a common national identity.

Nationalism's appeal in Asia was not confined to territories under direct European rule. Europe and the United States had forced even the most solid Asian states, China and Japan, to accept humiliating limitations on their sovereignty. Thus the nationalist promise of genuine economic independence and true political equality with the West appealed as powerfully in old but weak states like China as in colonial territories like British India.

Nationalist Movements in the Middle East

How did the Ottoman Empire's collapse in World War I shape nationalist movements in the Middle East?

The most flagrant attempt to expand Western imperialism occurred in southwest Asia (Map 29.1). There the British and the French successfully encouraged an Arab revolt in 1916 and destroyed the Ottoman Empire. Europeans then sought to replace Turks as principal rulers throughout the region. Turkish, Arab, and Persian nationalists, as well as Jewish nationalists arriving from Europe, reacted violently. They struggled to win nationhood, and as the Europeans were forced to make concessions, they sometimes came into sharp conflict with each other, most notably in Palestine.

The Arab Revolt

Long subject to European pressure, the Ottoman Empire failed to reform and modernize in the late nineteenth century (see "The Islamic Heartland Under Pressure" in Chapter 25). Declining international stature and domestic tyranny led idealistic exiles to engage in revolutionary activity and motivated army officers to seize power and save the Ottoman state. These patriots, the so-called Young Turks, succeeded in the 1908 revolution, and subsequently they were determined to hold together the remnants of the vast multiethnic empire. Defeated in the Balkan war of 1912 and stripped of practically all territory in Europe, the Young Turks redoubled their efforts in southwest Asia. The most important of their possessions were Syria—consisting of modern-day Lebanon, Syria, Israel, the West Bank, the Gaza Strip, and Jordan—and Iraq. The Ottoman Turks also claimed the Arabian peninsula but exercised only loose control there.

For centuries the largely Arab populations of Syria and Iraq had been tied to their Ottoman rulers by their common faith in Islam (though there were Christian Arabs as well). Yet beneath the surface, ethnic and linguistic tensions simmered between Turks and Arabs.

Young Turk actions after 1908 made the embryonic "Arab movement" a reality. The majority of Young Turks promoted a narrow Turkish nationalism. They further centralized the Ottoman Empire and extended the sway of Turkish language and culture. In 1909 the Turkish government brutally slaughtered thousands of Armenian Christians, a prelude to the wholesale massacre of more than a million Armenians during the First World War. Meanwhile, Arab discontent grew.

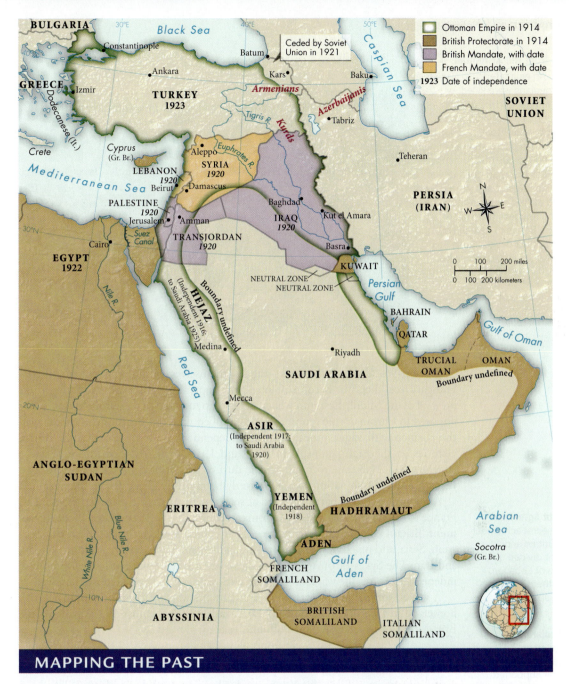

MAPPING THE PAST

MAP 29.1 The Partition of the Ottoman Empire, 1914–1923 By 1914 the Ottoman Turks had been pushed out of the Balkans, and their Arab provinces were on the edge of revolt. That revolt erupted in the First World War and contributed greatly to the Ottomans' defeat. When the Allies then attempted to implement their plans, including independence for the Armenian people, Mustafa Kemal arose to forge in battle the modern Turkish state.

ANALYZING THE MAP What new countries were established as a result of the partition of the Ottoman Empire? Where were mandates established? What might you conclude about European views of the Middle East based on how Europe divided up the region?

CONNECTIONS How might the collapse of the Ottoman Empire in World War I have contributed to the current situation in the Middle East?

901

Refugees from the Armenian Genocide An estimated 1.5 million Armenians were killed, or died from hunger and exhaustion, during forced deportation marches carried out by the Ottoman Turks in 1915–1917. This photo shows some of the 100,000 to 200,000 Armenians who survived. They had been driven into the Syrian Desert and were later discovered at As-Salt in northern Jordan. The refugees were later taken by the British to Jerusalem, and some of their descendants still live in the Armenian Quarter there. (Pictures from History/Bridgeman Images)

During World War I the Turks aligned themselves with Germany and Austria-Hungary (see "The War Becomes Global" in Chapter 28). As a result, the Young Turks drew all of the Middle East into what had been up to that point a European war. Arabs opposed to Ottoman rule found themselves allied with the British, who encouraged the alliance with vague promises of an independent Arab kingdom. After British victories on the Arab peninsula in 1917 and 1918, many Arab patriots expected a large, unified Arab state to rise from the dust of the Ottoman collapse. Within two years, however, Arab nationalists felt bitterly betrayed by Great Britain and its allies.

Arab bitterness was partly directed at secret wartime treaties between Britain and France to divide and rule the old Ottoman Empire. In the 1916 **Sykes-Picot Agreement**, Britain and France secretly agreed that France would receive modern-day Lebanon, Syria, and much of southern Turkey, and Britain would receive Palestine, Jordan, and Iraq. The Sykes-Picot Agreement contradicted British promises concerning Arab independence after the war and left Arab nationalists feeling cheated and betrayed.

A related source of Arab frustration was Britain's wartime commitment to a Jewish homeland in Palestine. The **Balfour Declaration** of November 1917, made by the British foreign secretary Arthur Balfour, declared:

> His Majesty's Government views with favour the establishment in Palestine of a national home for the Jewish People, and will use their best endeavors to facilitate the achievement of this object, it being clearly understood that nothing shall be done which may prejudice the civil and religious rights of existing non-Jewish communities in Palestine.[1]

As a careful reading reveals, the Balfour Declaration made contradictory promises to European Jews and Middle Eastern Arabs.

Some British Cabinet members believed the Balfour Declaration would appeal to German, Austrian, and American Jews and thus help the British war effort. Others sincerely supported the Zionist vision of a Jewish homeland (see "Jewish Emancipa-

Sykes-Picot Agreement
The 1916 secret agreement between Britain and France that divided up the Arab lands of Lebanon, Syria, southern Turkey, Palestine, Jordan, and Iraq.

Balfour Declaration
A 1917 statement by British foreign secretary Arthur Balfour that supported the idea of a Jewish homeland in Palestine.

tion and Modern Anti-Semitism" in Chapter 24), but also believed that Jews living in this homeland would be grateful to Britain and thus help maintain British control of the Suez Canal.

In 1914 Jews made up about 11 percent of the predominantly Arab population in the Ottoman territory that became, under British control, Palestine. The "national home for the Jewish People" mentioned in the Balfour Declaration implied to the Arabs—and to the Zionist Jews as well—some kind of Jewish state that would be incompatible with majority rule.

After Faisal bin Hussein's failed efforts at the Paris Peace Conference to secure Arab independence, Arab nationalists met in Damascus at the General Syrian Congress in 1919 and unsuccessfully called again for political independence. Ignoring Arab opposition, the British mandate in Palestine formally incorporated the Balfour Declaration and its commitment to a Jewish national home. In March 1920 the Syrian National Congress proclaimed Syria independent, with Faisal bin Hussein as king. A similar congress declared Iraq an independent kingdom.

Western reaction to events in Syria and Iraq was swift and decisive. A French army stationed in Lebanon attacked Syria, taking Damascus in July 1920. Faisal fled, and the French took over. Meanwhile, the British put down an uprising in Iraq and established effective control there. Western imperialism appeared to have replaced Turkish rule in the Middle East (see Map 29.1).

The Turkish Revolution

Days after the end of the First World War, French and then British troops entered Constantinople to begin a five-year occupation of the Ottoman capital. A young English official wrote that he found the Ottoman Empire "utterly smashed." The Turks were "worn out" from the war, and without bitterness they awaited the construction of a "new system."[2] The Allies' new system was blatant imperialism, which proved harsher for the defeated Turks than for the Arabs now free from Turkish rule. A treaty forced on the helpless sultan dismembered Turkey and reduced it to a puppet state. Great Britain and France occupied parts of Turkey, and Italy and Greece claimed shares as well. There was a sizable Greek minority in western Turkey, and Greek nationalists cherished the "Great Idea" of a modern Greek empire modeled on long-dead Christian Byzantium. In 1919 Greek armies carried by British ships landed on the Turkish coast at Smyrna and advanced into the interior. Turkey seemed finished.

But Turkey produced a great leader and revived to become an inspiration to the entire Middle East. Mustafa Kemal (moo-STAH-fah kuh-MAHL) (1881–1938), considered the father of modern Turkey, was a military man sympathetic to the Young Turk movement. After the armistice, he watched with anguish the Allies' aggression and the sultan's cowardice. In early 1919 he began working to unify Turkish resistance.

The sultan, bowing to Allied pressure, initially denounced Kemal, but the cause of national liberation proved more powerful. The catalyst was the Greek invasion and attempted annexation of much of western Turkey. A young Turkish woman described feelings she shared with countless others:

> After I learned about the details of the Smyrna occupation by Greek armies, I hardly opened my mouth on any subject except when it concerned the sacred struggle. . . .
> I suddenly ceased to exist as an individual. I worked, wrote and lived as a unit of that magnificent national madness.[3]

Mustafa Kemal Surnamed Atatürk, meaning "father of the Turks," Mustafa Kemal and his supporters imposed revolutionary changes aimed at modernizing and westernizing Turkish society and the new Turkish government. Dancing here with his adopted daughter at her high-society wedding, Atatürk often appeared in public in elegant European dress — a vivid symbol for the Turkish people of his radical break with traditional Islamic teaching and custom. (Hulton Archive/Getty Images)

Treaty of Lausanne The 1923 treaty that ended the Turkish war and recognized the territorial integrity of a truly independent Turkey.

Refusing to acknowledge the Allied dismemberment of their country, the Turks battled on through 1920 despite staggering defeats. The next year the Greeks advanced almost to Ankara, the nationalist stronghold in central Turkey. There Mustafa Kemal's forces took the offensive and won a great victory. The Greeks and their British allies sued for peace. The resulting **Treaty of Lausanne** (1923) recognized a truly independent Turkey, and Turkey lost only its former Arab provinces (see Map 29.1).

Mustafa Kemal believed Turkey should modernize and secularize along Western lines. His first moves, beginning in 1923, were political. Kemal called on the National Assembly to depose the sultan and establish a republic, and he had himself elected president. Kemal savagely crushed the demands for independence of ethnic minorities within Turkey like the Armenians and the Kurds, but he realistically abandoned all thought of winning back lost Arab territories. He then created a one-party system in order to work his will.

Kemal's most radical changes pertained to religion and culture. For centuries most believers' intellectual and social activities had been regulated by Islamic religious authorities. Profoundly influenced by the example of western Europe, Mustafa Kemal set out, like the philosophes of the Enlightenment, to limit religious influence in daily affairs, but, like Russia's Peter the Great, he employed dictatorial measures rather than reason and democracy to reach his goal. Kemal decreed a revolutionary separation of church and state. Secular law codes inspired by European models replaced religious courts. State schools replaced religious schools and taught such secular subjects as science, mathematics, and social sciences.

Mustafa Kemal also struck down many entrenched patterns of behavior. Women, traditionally secluded and inferior to males in Islamic society, received the right to vote. Civil law on a European model, rather than the Islamic code, now governed marriage. Women could seek divorces, and no man could have more than one wife at a time. Men were forbidden to wear the tall red fez of the Ottoman era as headgear; government employees were ordered to wear business suits and felt hats, erasing the visible differences between Muslims and "infidel" Europeans. The old Arabic script was replaced with a new Turkish alphabet based on Roman letters, which facilitated massive government efforts to spread literacy after 1928. Finally, in 1935, surnames on the European model were introduced. The National Assembly granted Mustafa Kemal the surname Atatürk, which means "father of the Turks."

By his death in 1938, Atatürk and his supporters had consolidated their revolution. Government-sponsored industrialization was fostering urban growth and new attitudes, encouraging Turks to embrace business and science. Poverty persisted in rural areas, as did some religious discontent among devout Muslims. But like the Japanese after the Meiji Restoration, the Turkish people had rallied around the nationalist banner to repulse European imperialism and were building a modern secular nation-state.

Modernization Efforts in Persia and Afghanistan

In Persia (renamed Iran in 1935) strong-arm efforts to build a unified modern nation ultimately proved less successful than in Turkey. In the late nineteenth century Persia had also been subject to extreme foreign pressure, which stimulated efforts to reform the government as a means of reviving Islamic civilization. In 1906 a nationalistic coalition of merchants, religious leaders, and intellectuals revolted. The despotic shah was forced to grant a constitution and establish a national assembly, the **Majlis** (MAHJ-lis).

Yet the 1906 Persian revolution was doomed to failure, largely because of European imperialism. Without consulting Iran, in 1907 Britain and Russia divided the country into spheres of influence. Britain's sphere ran along the Persian Gulf; the Russian sphere encompassed the whole northern half of Persia (see Map 29.1). Thereafter Russia intervened constantly. It blocked reforms, occupied cities, and completely dominated the country by 1912. When Russian power collapsed in the Bolshevik Revolution, British armies rushed into the power vacuum. By bribing corrupt Persians, Great Britain in 1919 negotiated a treaty allowing the installation of British "advisers" in every government department.

The Majlis refused to ratify the treaty, and the blatant attempt to make Persia a British satellite aroused the national spirit. In 1921 reaction against the British brought to power a military dictator, Reza Shah Pahlavi (PAH-luh-vee) (1877–1944), who proclaimed himself shah in 1925 and ruled until 1941.

Inspired by Turkey's Mustafa Kemal, Reza Shah had three basic goals: to build a modern nation, to free Persia from foreign domination, and to rule with an iron fist. The challenge was enormous. Persia was a vast, undeveloped country. The rural population was mostly poor and illiterate, and among the Persian majority were sizable ethnic minorities with their own aspirations. Furthermore, Iran's powerful religious leaders hated Western (Christian) domination but were equally opposed to a more secular, less Islamic society.

To realize his vision of a strong Persia, the shah created a modern army, built railroads, and encouraged commerce. He won control over ethnic minorities such as the Kurds in the north and Arab tribesmen on the Iraqi border. He reduced the privileges granted to foreigners and raised taxes on the powerful Anglo-Persian Oil Company, which had been founded in 1909 to exploit the first great oil strike in the Middle East. Yet Reza Shah was less successful than Atatürk.

Because the European-educated elite in Persia was smaller than the comparable group in Turkey, the idea of re-creating Persian greatness on the basis of a secularized society attracted relatively few determined supporters. Many powerful religious leaders turned against Reza Shah, and he became increasingly brutal, greedy, and tyrannical.

Afghanistan, meanwhile, was nominally independent in the nineteenth century, but the British imposed political restrictions and constantly meddled in the country's affairs. In 1919 emir Amanullah Khan (1892–1960) declared war on the British government in India and won complete independence for the first time. Amanullah (ah-man-UL-lah) then decreed revolutionary modernizing reforms designed to hurl his primitive country into the twentieth century. He established modern, secular schools for both boys and girls, and adult education classes for the predominantly illiterate population. He did away with seclusion

Majlis The national assembly established by the despotic shah of Iran in 1906.

Afghanistan Under Amanullah Khan

and centuries-old dress codes for women, abolished slavery, created the country's first constitution in 1923, restructured and reorganized the economy, and established a legislative assembly and secular (rather than Islamic) court system. The result was tribal and religious revolt, civil war, and retreat from reform. Islam remained both religion and law. A powerful but primitive patriotism enabled Afghanistan to win political independence from the West, but not to build a modern society.

Gradual Independence in the Arab States

French and British mandates forced Arab nationalists to seek independence by gradual means after 1920. Arab nationalists were indirectly aided by Western taxpayers who wanted cheap — that is, peaceful — empires. As a result, Arabs won considerable control over local affairs in the mandated states, except Palestine, though the mandates remained European satellites in international and economic affairs.

In Iraq the British chose Faisal bin Hussein, whom the French had deposed in Syria, as king. Faisal obligingly gave British advisers broad behind-the-scenes control. The king also accepted British ownership of Iraq's oil fields, consequently giving the West a stranglehold on the Iraqi economy. Given the severe limitations imposed on him, Faisal (r. 1921–1933) proved to be an able ruler, gaining his peoples' support and encouraging moderate reforms. In 1932 he secured Iraqi independence at the price of a restrictive long-term military alliance with Great Britain.

Egypt had been occupied by Great Britain since 1882 (see "Egypt: From Reform to British Occupation" in Chapter 25) and had been a British protectorate since 1914. Following intense nationalist agitation after the Great War, Great Britain in 1922 proclaimed Egypt formally independent but continued to occupy the country militarily and control its politics. In 1936 the British agreed to restrict their troops to their bases in the Suez Canal Zone.

The French compromised less in their handling of their mandated Middle East territories. Following the Ottoman Empire's collapse after World War I, the French designated Lebanon as one of several ethnic enclaves within a larger area that became part of the French mandate of Syria. They practiced a policy of divide and rule and generally played off ethnic and religious minorities against each other. In 1926 Lebanon became a separate republic but remained under the control of the French mandate. Arab nationalists in Syria finally won promises of Syrian independence in 1936 in return for a friendship treaty with France.

In short, the Arab states gradually freed themselves from Western political mandates but not from Western military threats or from pervasive Western influence. Since large Arab landowners and urban merchants increased their wealth and political power after 1918, they often supported the Western hegemony. Radical nationalists, on the other hand, recognized that Western control of the newly discovered Arab oil fields was proof that economic independence and genuine freedom had not yet been achieved.

Arab-Jewish Tensions in Palestine

Relations between the Arabs and the West were complicated by the tense situation in the British mandate of Palestine, and that situation deteriorated in the interwar years. Both Arabs and Jews denounced the British, who tried unsuccessfully to compromise with both sides. Arab nationalist anger, however, was aimed primarily at Jewish settlers. The key issue was Jewish migration from Europe to Palestine.

Jewish nationalism, known as Zionism, took shape in Europe in the late nineteenth century under Theodor Herzl's leadership (see "Jewish Emancipation and Modern Anti-Semitism" in Chapter 24). Herzl believed only a Jewish state could guarantee Jews dignity and security. The Zionist movement encouraged some of the world's Jews to settle in Palestine, but until 1921 the great majority of Jewish emigrants preferred the United States.

After 1921 the situation changed radically. An isolationist United States drastically limited immigration from eastern Europe, where war and revolution had kindled anti-Semitism. Moreover, the British began honoring the Balfour Declaration despite Arab protests. Thus Jewish immigration to Palestine from turbulent Europe in the interwar years grew rapidly, particularly after Adolf Hitler became German chancellor in 1933. By 1939 Palestine's Jewish population had increased almost fivefold since 1914 and accounted for about 30 percent of all inhabitants.

Jewish settlers in Palestine faced formidable difficulties. Although much of the land purchased by the Jewish National Fund was productive, the sellers of such land were often wealthy absentee Arab landowners who cared little for their Arab tenants' welfare. When the Jewish settlers replaced those long-time Arab tenants, Arab farmers and intellectuals burned with a sense of injustice. Moreover, most Jewish immigrants came from urban backgrounds and preferred to establish new cities like Tel Aviv or to live in existing towns, where they competed with the Arabs. The land issue combined with economic and cultural friction to harden Arab protest into hatred.

The British gradually responded to Arab pressure and tried to slow Jewish immigration. This effort satisfied neither Jews nor Arabs, and between 1936 and 1939 the three communities (Arab, Jewish, and British) were engaged in an undeclared civil war. On the eve of the Second World War, the frustrated British proposed an

Kibbutz Children Picking Grapes Many of the early kibbutzim, such as this one at Kfar Blum in Israel's northern Galilee, were agricultural settlements that produced cotton and fruits such as grapes, oranges, and apples, which were then packed and shipped around the world. They also produced most of the food eaten by the members. On the kibbutz, as these children illustrate, all did their share of the work. Collection boxes for the Zionist cause (above) date back to 1884, but donations became more standardized after the founding of the Jewish National Fund in 1901. The first Blue Box appeared in 1904, with the suggestion that a box be placed in every Jewish home around the world and contributed to as often as possible. Still collected today, Blue Box donations fund projects such as planting forests, establishing parks, and building roads and water reservoirs in the Israeli state. (kibbutz: Courtesy, Kibbutz Kfar Blum Archives; box: Courtesy National Jewish Fund)

independent Palestine with the number of Jews permanently limited to only about one-third of the total population. Zionists felt themselves in grave danger of losing their dream of an independent Jewish state.

Nevertheless, in the face of adversity Jewish settlers gradually succeeded in forging a cohesive community in Palestine. Hebrew, for centuries used only in religious worship, was revived as a living language in the 1920s–1930s to bind the Jews in Palestine together. Despite its slow beginnings, rural development achieved often remarkable results. The key unit of agricultural organization was the **kibbutz**, a collective farm on which each member shared equally in the work, rewards, and defense. An egalitarian socialist ideology also characterized industry, which grew rapidly. By 1939 a new but old nation was emerging in the Middle East.

> **kibbutz** A Jewish collective farm, first established by Zionists in Palestine, on which each member shared equally in the work, rewards, and defense.

Toward Self-Rule in India

> **What role did Gandhi and his campaign of militant nonviolence play in leading India to independence from the British?**

The nationalist movement in British India grew out of two interconnected cultures, Hindu and Muslim. While the two joined together to challenge British rule, they also came to see themselves as fundamentally different. Nowhere has modern nationalism's power both to unify and to divide been more strikingly demonstrated than in India.

British Promises and Repression

Indian nationalism had emerged in the late nineteenth century (see "The British and the Indian Educated Elite" in Chapter 26), and when the First World War began, the British feared an Indian revolt. Instead Indians supported the war effort. About 1.2 million Indian soldiers and laborers voluntarily served in Europe, Africa, and the Middle East. The British government in India and the native Indian princes sent large supplies of food, money, and ammunition. In return, the British opened more good government jobs to Indians and made other minor concessions.

As the war in distant Europe ground on, however, inflation, high taxes, food shortages, and a terrible influenza epidemic created widespread suffering and discontent. The prewar nationalist movement revived, becoming stronger than ever, and moderates and radicals in the Indian National Congress Party joined forces. Moreover, in 1916 Hindu leaders in the Congress Party hammered out an alliance — the **Lucknow Pact** — with India's Muslim League. The Lucknow (LUHK-noh) Pact forged a powerful united front of Hindus and Muslims and called for putting India on an equal footing with self-governing British dominions like Canada, Australia, and New Zealand.

> **Lucknow Pact** A 1916 alliance between the Hindus leading the Indian National Congress Party and the Muslim League.

The British response to the Lucknow Pact was mixed. In August 1917 the British called for the "gradual development of self-governing institutions with a view to the progressive realization of responsible government in India."[4] But the proposed self-government was much more limited than that granted the British dominions. In late 1919 the British established a dual administration: part Indian and elected, part British and authoritarian. Such uncontroversial activities as agriculture and health were transferred from British to Indian officials, but sensitive matters like taxes, police, and the courts remained solely in British hands.

Old-fashioned authoritarian rule also seriously undermined whatever positive impact this reform might have had. The 1919 Rowlatt Acts indefinitely extended wartime "emergency measures" designed to curb unrest and root out "conspiracy." The result was a wave of rioting across India.

Under these tense conditions a crowd of some ten thousand gathered to celebrate a Sikh religious festival in an enclosed square in the Sikh (SEEK) holy city of Amritsar (ahm-RIHT-suhr) in the northern Punjab province. Unknown to the crowd, the local English commander, General Reginald Dyer, had banned all public meetings that very day. Dyer marched his troops into the square and, without warning, ordered them to fire into the crowd until the ammunition ran out. Official British records of the Amritsar Massacre list 379 killed and 1,137 wounded, but these figures remain hotly contested as being too low. Tensions flared, and India stood on the verge of more violence and repression. That India took a different path to national liberation was due largely to Mohandas K. Gandhi (1869–1948), the most influential Indian leader of modern times.

The Roots of Militant Nonviolence

Gandhi grew up in a well-to-do family, and after his father's death he went to study law in England, where he passed the English bar. Upon returning to India, he decided in 1893 to try a case for some wealthy Indian merchants in the British colony of Natal (part of modern South Africa). It was a momentous decision.

In Natal Gandhi took up the plight of the expatriate Indian community. White plantation owners had been importing thousands of poor Indians as indentured laborers since the 1860s. Some of these Indians, after completing their period of indenture, remained in Natal as free persons and economic competitors. In response, the Afrikaner (of Dutch descent) and British settlers passed brutally discriminatory laws. Poor Indians had to work on plantations or return to India. Rich Indians, who had previously had the vote in Natal, lost that right in 1896. Gandhi undertook his countrymen's legal defense.

Meanwhile, Gandhi was searching for a spiritual theory of social action. He studied Hindu and Christian teachings and gradually developed a weapon for the poor and oppressed that he called **satyagraha** (suh-TYAH-gruh-huh). Gandhi conceived of satyagraha, loosely translated as "soul force," as a means of striving for truth and social justice through love and a willingness to suffer the oppressor's blows, while trying to convert him or her to one's views of what is true and just. Its tactic was active nonviolent resistance.

When South Africa's white government severely restricted Asian immigration and internal freedom of movement, Gandhi put his philosophy into action and organized a nonviolent mass resistance campaign. Thousands of Indian men and women marched in peaceful protest and withstood beatings, arrest, and imprisonment.

In 1914 South Africa's exasperated whites agreed to many of the Indians' demands. They passed a law abolishing discriminatory taxes on Indian traders, recognized the legality of non-Christian marriages, and permitted the continued immigration of free Indians.

Gandhi's Resistance Campaign in India

In 1915 Gandhi returned to India a hero. The masses hailed him as a mahatma, or "great soul"—a Hindu title of veneration for a man of great knowledge and humanity. In 1920 Gandhi launched a national campaign of nonviolent resistance to British rule. He urged his countrymen to boycott British goods, jobs, and honors and told peasants not to pay taxes.

satyagraha Loosely translated as "soul force," which Gandhi believed was the means of striving for truth and social justice through love, suffering, and conversion of the oppressor.

The nationalist movement had previously touched only the tiny, prosperous, Western-educated elite. Now both the illiterate masses of village India and the educated classes heard Gandhi's call for militant nonviolent resistance. It particularly appealed to the masses of Hindus who were not members of the warrior caste or the so-called military races and who were traditionally passive and nonviolent. The British had regarded ordinary Hindus as cowards. Gandhi told them that they could be courageous and even morally superior:

> What do you think? Wherein is courage required—in blowing others to pieces from behind a cannon, or with a smiling face to approach a cannon and be blown to pieces? Who is the true warrior—he who keeps death always as a bosom-friend, or he who controls the death of others? Believe me that a man devoid of courage and manhood can never be a passive resister.[5]

Gandhi made the Indian National Congress into a mass political party, welcoming members from every ethnic group and cooperating closely with the Muslim minority.

In 1922 some Indian resisters turned to violence, murdering twenty-two policemen. Savage riots broke out, and Gandhi abruptly called off his campaign, observing that he had "committed a Himalayan blunder in placing civil disobedience before those who had never learnt the art of civil disobedience."[6] Arrested for fomenting rebellion, Gandhi served two years in prison. Upon his release Gandhi set up a commune, established a national newspaper, and set out to reform Indian society and improve the lot of the poor. For Gandhi moral improvement, social progress, and the national movement went hand in hand. Above all, Gandhi nurtured national identity and self-respect. He also tried to instill in India's people the courage to overcome their fear of their colonial rulers and to fight these rulers with nonviolence. (See "Global Viewpoints: Gandhi and Mao on Revolutionary Means," at right.)

During Gandhi's time in prison (1922–1924) the Indian National Congress had splintered into various factions, and Gandhi spent the years after his release quietly trying to reunite the organization. In 1929 the radical nationalists, led by Jawaharlal Nehru (juh-WAH-hur-lahl NAY-roo) (1889–1964), pushed through the National Congress a resolution calling for virtual independence within a year. The British stiffened in their resolve against Indian independence, and Indian radicals talked of a bloody showdown.

Into this tense situation Gandhi masterfully reasserted his leadership, taking a hard line toward the British but insisting on nonviolent methods. He organized a massive resistance campaign against the tax on salt, which gave the British a veritable monopoly on the salt that was absolutely necessary for survival in India's heat and humidity and affected every Indian family. From March 12 to April 6, 1930, Gandhi led tens of thousands of people in a spectacular march to the sea, where he made salt in defiance of the law. A later demonstration at the British-run Dharasana (dahr-AH-sahn-nah) salt works resulted in many of the 2,500 nonviolent marchers being beaten senseless by policemen in a brutal and well-publicized encounter. Over the next months the British arrested Gandhi and sixty thousand

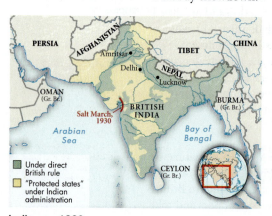

India, ca. 1930

Gandhi and Mao on Revolutionary Means

India's Mohandas Gandhi and China's Mao Zedong successfully led two of the largest and most populous nations to independence in the late 1940s. Although both drew much of their support from the peasant masses, their political philosophies were exact oppposites.

Gandhi believed active nonviolent disobedience to British rule was the only way Indians could break free of British rule and gain independence. Mao, in his *Little Red Book*, argues that "power flows from the barrel of a gun," and that only through the use of violence can the Chinese masses rid themselves of corrupt warlords, cruel landowners, imperialist occupiers, and ruling elites.

Mohandas Gandhi

■ Complete civil disobedience is rebellion without the element of violence in it. An out-and-out resister simply ignores the authority of the State. He becomes an outlaw claiming to disregard every unmoral State law. Thus, for instance, he may refuse to pay taxes, he may refuse to recognize the authority in his daily intercourse. . . . In doing all this he never uses force and never resists force when it is used against him. In fact, he invites imprisonment and other uses of force against himself. This he does because and when he finds the bodily freedom he seemingly enjoys to be an intolerable burden. He argues to himself that a State allows personal freedom only in so far as the citizen submits to its regulations. Submission to the State law is the price a citizen pays for his personal liberty. Submission, therefore, to a State wholly or largely unjust is an immoral barter for liberty. . . .

A body of civil resisters is, therefore, like an army subject to all the discipline of a soldier. . . . And as a civil resistance army is or ought to be free from passion because free from the spirit of retaliation, it requires the fewest number of soldiers. Indeed, one *perfect* civil resister is enough to win the battle of Right against Wrong. [1921]

You might of course say that there can be no nonviolent rebellion and there has been none known to history. Well, it is my ambition to provide an instance, and it is my dream that my country may win its freedom through nonviolence. And, I would like to repeat to the world times without number, that I will not purchase my country's freedom at the cost of nonviolence. My marriage to nonviolence is such an absolute thing that I would rather commit suicide than be deflected from my position. I have not mentioned truth in this connection, simply because truth cannot be expressed except by nonviolence. [1931]

Mao Zedong

■ *War* is the highest form of struggle for resolving contradictions, when they have developed to a certain state, between classes, nations, states, or political groups, and it has existed ever since the emergence of private property and of classes.

The seizure of power by armed force, the settlement of the issue by war, is the central task and the highest form of revolution. This Marxist-Leninist principle of revolution holds good universally, for China and for all other countries.

According to the Marxist theory of the state, . . . whoever wants to seize and retain state power must have a strong army. Some people ridicule us as advocates of the "omnipotence of war." Yes, we are advocates of the omnipotence of revolutionary war; that is good, not bad, it is Marxist. Experience in the class struggle in the era of imperialism teaches us that it is only by the power of the gun that the working class and the laboring masses can defeat the armed bourgeoisie and landlords; in this sense we may say that only with guns can the whole world be transformed.

QUESTIONS FOR ANALYSIS

1. According to Gandhi, when should people resort to nonviolent disobedience in opposing their rulers?
2. According to Mao, what is the highest form of revolution? What theory does he draw on for this conclusion?

Sources: Mahatma Gandhi, "Young India, November 10, 1921" and "Young India, November 12, 1931," in *All Men Are Brothers: Autobiographical Reflections*, ed. Krishna Kripalani (New York: Continuum, 1997), pp. 81, 135–136. Reprinted by permission of the Navajivan Trust; Mao Tsetung, *Quotations from Chairman Mao Tsetung* (Peking: Foreign Languages Press, 1972), pp. 58, 61–63.

Gandhi on the Salt March, March 1930 A small, frail man, Gandhi possessed enormous courage and determination. His campaign of nonviolent resistance to British rule inspired the Indian masses and mobilized a nation. Here he is shown walking on his famous march to the sea to protest the English-Indian government's monopoly on salt production. (© SZ Photo/Scherl/Bridgeman Images)

other protesters for making and distributing salt. But the protests continued, and in 1931 the frustrated and unnerved British released Gandhi from jail and sat down to negotiate with him over Indian self-rule. Negotiations resulted in a new constitution, the Government of India Act, in 1935, which greatly strengthened India's parliamentary representative institutions and gave Indians some voice in the administration of British India.

Despite his best efforts, Gandhi failed to heal a widening split between Hindus and Muslims. Indian nationalism, based largely on Hindu symbols and customs, increasingly disturbed the Muslim minority, represented by the Muslim League led by the Western-educated Bombay lawyer Muhammad Ali Jinnah (jee-NAH) (1876–1948). Tempers mounted, and both sides committed atrocities. By the late 1930s Muslim League leaders were calling for the creation of a Muslim nation in British India, a "Pakistan," or "land of the pure." As in Palestine, the rise of conflicting nationalisms in India based on religion would lead to tragedy (see "Independence in India, Pakistan, and Bangladesh" in Chapter 31).

How did nationalism shape political developments in East and Southeast Asia?

Nationalist Struggles in East and Southeast Asia

Because of the efforts of the Meiji reformers, nationalism and modernization were well developed in Japan by 1914. Japan competed politically and economically with the world's leading nations, building its own empire and proclaiming its special mission in Asia. Initially China lagged behind, but after 1912 the pace of nationalist development began to quicken.

By promoting extensive modernization in the 1920s, the Chinese nationalist movement managed to reduce the power and influence both of the warlords who controlled large territories in the interior and of the imperialist West. This achievement was soon undermined, however, by an internal civil war followed by war with an expanding Japan. Nationalism also flourished elsewhere in Asia, scoring a major victory in the Philippines.

The Rise of Nationalist China

The 1911 Revolution led by Sun Yatsen (1866–1925) overthrew the Qing (CHING) Dynasty, and after four thousand years of monarchy the last Chinese emperor, Puyi (1906–1967), abdicated in February 1912 (see "Republican Revolution" in Chapter 26). Sun Yatsen (soon yaht-SEHN) proclaimed China a republic and thereby opened an era of unprecedented change for Chinese society. In 1912 Sun Yatsen turned over leadership of the republican government to the other central figure in the revolution, Yuan Shigai (yoo-AHN shee-KIGH). Originally called out of retirement to save the Qing Dynasty, Yuan (1859–1916) betrayed its Manchu leaders and convinced the revolutionaries that he could unite the country peacefully and prevent foreign intervention. Once elected president of the republic, however, Yuan concentrated on building his own power. In 1913 he used military force to dissolve China's parliament and ruled as a dictator. China's first modern revolution had failed.

The extent of the failure became apparent only after Yuan's death in 1916, when the central government in Beijing almost disintegrated. For more than a decade thereafter, power resided in a multitude of local military leaders, the so-called warlords. Their wars, taxes, and corruption created terrible suffering.

Foreign imperialism intensified the agony of warlordism. Japan's expansion into Shandong and southern Manchuria during World War I angered China's growing middle class and enraged China's young patriots (see Map 29.2, page 920). On May 4, 1919, five thousand students in Beijing exploded against the decision of the Paris Peace Conference to leave the Shandong Peninsula in Japanese hands. This famous incident launched the **May Fourth Movement**, which opposed both foreign domination and warlord government.

The May Fourth Movement, which was both strongly pro-Marxist and passionately anti-imperialist, looked to the October 1917 Bolshevik Revolution in Russia as a model for its own nationalist revolution. In 1923 Sun Yatsen decided to ally his Nationalist Party, or Guomindang (gwoh-mihn-dang), with Lenin's Communist Third International and the newly formed Chinese Communist Party. The result was the first of many so-called national liberation fronts.

Sun, however, was no Communist. In his *Three Principles of the People*, elaborating on the official Nationalist Party ideology—nationalism, democracy, and people's livelihood—nationalism remained of prime importance:

> Compared to the other peoples of the world we have the greatest population and our civilization is four thousand years old; we should be advancing in the front rank with the nations of Europe and America. But the Chinese people . . . do not have national spirit. . . . If we do not earnestly espouse nationalism and weld together our four hundred million people into a strong nation, there is a danger of China's being lost and our people being destroyed. If we wish to avert this catastrophe, we must . . . bring this national spirit to the salvation of the country.[7]

Democracy, in contrast, had a less exalted meaning. Sun equated it with firm rule by the Nationalists, who would improve people's lives through land reform and welfare measures.

May Fourth Movement
A Chinese nationalist movement against foreign imperialists and warlord rule; it began as a 1919 student protest against the decision of the Paris Peace Conference to leave the Shandong Peninsula in the hands of Japan.

Sun planned to use the Nationalist Party's revolutionary army to crush the war-lords and reunite China under a strong central government. When Sun unexpectedly died in 1925, Jiang Jieshi (known in the West as Chiang Kai-shek) (1887–1975) took his place. In 1926 and 1927 Jiang Jieshi (jee-ang jee-shee) led Nationalist armies in a successful attack on warlord governments in central and northern China. In 1928 the Nationalists established a new capital at Nanjing. Foreign states recognized the Nanjing government, and superficial observers believed China to be truly reunified.

In fact, national unification was only skin-deep. China remained a vast agricul-tural country plagued by foreign concessions, regional differences, and a lack of mod-ern communications. Moreover, the uneasy alliance between the Nationalist Party and the Chinese Communist Party had turned into a bitter, deadly rivalry. Fearful of Communist subversion of the Nationalist government, Jiang decided in April 1927 to liquidate his left-wing "allies" in a bloody purge. Chinese Communists went into hiding and vowed revenge.

China's Intellectual Revolution

New Culture Movement
An intellectual revolution beginning in 1916 that attacked traditional Chinese, particularly Confucian, culture and promoted Western ideas of science, democracy, and individualism.

Nationalism was the most powerful idea in China between 1911 and 1929, but it was only one aspect of a complex intellectual revolution, generally known as the **New Culture Movement**, that hammered at traditional Chinese thought and custom, advocated cultural renaissance, and pushed China into the modern world. The New Culture Movement was founded around 1916 by young Western-oriented intellec-tuals in Beijing. These intellectuals attacked Confucian ethics, which subordinated subjects to rulers, sons to fathers, and wives to husbands. As modernists, they advo-cated new and anti-Confucian virtues: individualism, democratic equality, and the critical scientific method. They also promoted the use of simple, understandable written language as a means to clear thinking and mass education. China, they said, needed a whole new culture, a radically different worldview.

Many intellectuals thought the radical worldview China needed was Marxist socialism. It, too, was Western in origin, "scientific" in approach, and materialist in its denial of religious belief and Confucian family ethics. But while liberalism and individualism reflected the bewildering range of Western thought since the Enlight-enment, Marxist socialism offered the certainty of a single all-encompassing creed. As one young Communist intellectual exclaimed, "I am now able to impose order on all the ideas which I could not reconcile; I have found the key to all the problems which appeared to me self-contradictory and insoluble."[8]

Marxism provided a means of criticizing Western dominance, thereby salving Chi-nese pride. Chinese Communists could blame China's pitiful weakness on rapacious foreign capitalistic imperialism. Thus Marxism, as modified by Lenin and applied by the Bolsheviks in the Soviet Union, appeared as a means of catching up with the hated but envied West. For Chinese believers, it promised salvation soon. (See "Ana-lyzing the Evidence: The Fate of a Chinese Patriot," at right.)

Chinese Communists could and did interpret Marxism-Leninism to appeal to the masses — the peasants. Mao Zedong (sometimes spelled Mao Tse-tung) in particular quickly recognized the impoverished Chinese peasantry's enormous revolutionary potential. (See "Global Viewpoints: Gandhi and Mao on Revolutionary Means," page 911.) A member of a prosperous, hard-working peasant family, Mao Zedong (maow-dzuh-dahng) (1893–1976) converted to Marxist socialism in 1918. He began

The Fate of a Chinese Patriot

On May 30, 1925, British municipal police in Shanghai opened fire on a group of Chinese demonstrators who were protesting unfair labor practices and wages and the foreign imperialist presence in their country. The police killed thirteen people and wounded many others, touching off nationwide and international protests and attacks on foreign offices and businesses. Merchants and workers across the country organized strikes and boycotts against Japanese and British goods and factories. The Chinese Communist Party in particular benefited significantly from the anti-imperialist sentiment stirred up by this incident, with party membership swelling from only a few hundred members to over twenty thousand. The unrest lasted for three months, until the British fired the policemen involved and paid a cash indemnity to the families of the wounded and dead.

This political cartoon shows the fate of the Chinese patriots at the hands of warlords and foreign imperialists. The Chinese characters on the plume of the soldier's hat say "Warlords," referring to the large private armies that many landowners employed to maintain control over the territory they had seized. The label on the chest of the fat, obviously Western man says, "Foreign Imperialism." The waistband on the patriot being choked reads, "Patriotic compatriot." In the upper left-hand corner the characters read, "Warlords and Imperialists' oppression of the Chinese people, before and after May 30, 1925." The "map" that the figures stand on represents "The Republic of China." Each place where there is a pile of skulls and blood is labeled with the name of a city where massacres occurred: Qingdao, Nanjing, Shanghai, Jiujiang, Guangzhou, Hankou, and Chongqing. The Chinese characters on the map in the lower left corner read, "The massacres of the entire country." The name of the organization producing the cartoon is written across the bottom: "Membership Drive of the Chinese Salvation Association."

(Library of Congress, Prints and Photographs Division, Washington, D.C./LC-USZ62-99451)

QUESTIONS FOR ANALYSIS

1. Which figures represent Chinese warlords, foreign imperialists, and Chinese patriots?
2. What does the cartoon suggest about the fate of the Chinese demonstrators?
3. What emotions are these images trying to evoke in the person viewing the cartoon?

his revolutionary career as an urban labor organizer. In 1925 protest strikes by Chinese textile workers against their Japanese employers unexpectedly spread from the big coastal cities to rural China, prompting Mao (like Lenin in Russia) to reconsider the peasants (see "Lenin and the Bolshevik Revolution" in Chapter 28). Investigating the rapid growth of radical peasant associations in Hunan province, Mao argued passionately in a 1927 report:

> The force of the peasantry is like that of the raging winds and driving rain. It is rapidly increasing in violence. No force can stand in its way. The peasantry will tear apart all nets which bind it and hasten along the road to liberation. They will bury beneath them all forces of imperialism, militarism, corrupt officialdom, village bosses and evil gentry.[9]

Mao's first experiment in peasant revolt — the Autumn Harvest Uprising of September 1927 — was not successful, but Mao learned quickly. He advocated equal distribution of land and broke up his forces into small guerrilla groups. After 1928 he and his supporters built up a self-governing Communist soviet, centered at Jiangxi (jee-AHNG-shee) in southeastern China, and dug in against Nationalist attacks.

China's intellectual revolution also stimulated profound changes in popular culture and family life. (See "Individuals in Society: Ning Lao, a Chinese Working Woman," at right.) After the 1911 Revolution Chinese women enjoyed increasingly greater freedom and equality, and gradually gained unprecedented educational and economic opportunities. Thus rising nationalism and the intellectual revolution interacted with monumental changes in Chinese family life.

From Liberalism to Ultranationalism in Japan

The nearly total homogeneity of the Japanese population (98.5 percent ethnic Japanese) was a major factor in the Meiji reformers' efforts to build a powerful, nationalistic, modern state and resist Western imperialism. Their spectacular success deeply impressed Japan's fellow Asians. The Japanese, alone among Asia's peoples, had mastered modern industrial technology by 1910 and had fought victorious wars against both China and Russia. The First World War brought more triumphs. In 1915 Japan seized Germany's Asian holdings and retained most of them as League of Nations mandates. The Japanese economy expanded enormously. Profits soared as Japan won new markets that wartime Europe could no longer supply.

In the early 1920s Japan made further progress on all fronts. In 1922 Japan signed a naval arms limitation treaty with the Western powers and returned some of its control over the Shandong Peninsula to China. These conciliatory moves reduced tensions in East Asia. At home Japan seemed headed toward genuine democracy. The electorate expanded twelvefold between 1918 and 1925 as all males over twenty-five won the vote. Two-party competition was intense. Japanese living standards were the highest in Asia. Literacy was universal.

Japan's remarkable rise was accompanied by serious problems. Japan had a rapidly growing population but scarce natural resources. As early as the 1920s Japan was exporting manufactured goods in order to pay for imports of food and essential raw materials. Deeply enmeshed in world trade, Japan was vulnerable to every boom and bust. These economic realities broadened support for Japan's colonial empire. Before World War I Japanese leaders saw colonial expansion primarily in terms of international prestige and national defense. They believed that control of Taiwan,

Ning Lao, a Chinese Working Woman

The tough and resilient Ning Lao (right) with Ida Pruitt. (Reproduced with permission of Eileen Hsu-Balzer)

THE VOICE OF THE POOR AND UNEDUCATED IS often muffled in history. Thus *A Daughter of Han*, a rare autobiography of an illiterate working woman as told to an American friend, Ida Pruitt, offers unforgettable insights into the evolution of ordinary Chinese life and family relations.

Ning Lao was born in 1867 to poor parents in the northern city of Penglai on the Shandong Peninsula. Her foot binding was delayed to age nine, since she "loved so much to run and play." She described the pain when the bandages were finally drawn tight: "My feet hurt so much that for two years I had to crawl on my knees."* Her arranged marriage at age fourteen was a disaster. She found that her husband was a drug addict ("in those days everyone took opium to some extent") who sold everything to pay for his habit. Yet "there was no freedom then for women," and "it was no light thing for a woman to leave her house" and husband. Thus Ning Lao endured her situation until her husband sold their four-year-old daughter to buy opium. Taking her remaining baby daughter, she fled.

Taking off her foot bandages, Ning Lao became a beggar. Her feet began to spread, quite improperly, but she walked without pain. And the beggar's life was "not the hardest one," she thought, for a beggar woman could go where she pleased. To better care for her child, Ning Lao became a servant and a cook in prosperous households. Some of her mistresses were concubines (secondary wives taken by rich men in middle age), and she concluded that concubinage resulted in nothing but quarrels and heartache. Hot tempered and quick to take offense and leave an employer, the hard-working woman always found a new job quickly. In time she became a peddler of luxury goods to wealthy women confined to their homes.

The two unshakable values that buoyed Ning Lao were a tough, fatalistic acceptance of life—"Only fortune that comes of itself will come. There is no use to seek for it"—and devotion to her family. She eventually returned to her husband, who had mellowed, seldom took opium, and was "good" in those years. She reflected, "But I did not miss him when he died. I had my newborn son and I was happy. My house was established. . . . Truly all my life I spent thinking of my family." Her lifelong devotion was reciprocated by her son and granddaughter, who cared for her well in her old age.

Ning Lao's remarkable life story encompasses both old and new Chinese attitudes toward family life. Her son moved to the capital city of Beijing, worked in an office, and had only one wife. Her granddaughter, Su Teh, studied in missionary schools and became a college teacher and a determined foe of arranged marriages. She personified the trend toward greater freedom for Chinese women.

Generational differences also highlighted changing political attitudes. When the Japanese invaded China and occupied Beijing in 1937, Ning Lao thought that "perhaps the Mandate of Heaven had passed to the Japanese . . . and we should listen to them as our new masters." Her nationalistic granddaughter disagreed. She urged resistance and the creation of a new China, where the people governed themselves. Leaving to join the guerrillas in 1938, Su Teh gave her savings to her family and promised to continue to help them. One must be good to one's family, she said, but one must also work for the country.

QUESTIONS FOR ANALYSIS

1. Compare the lives of Ning Lao and her granddaughter. In what ways were they different and similar?
2. In a broader historical perspective, what do you find most significant about Ning Lao's account of her life? Why?

*Ida Pruitt, *A Daughter of Han: The Autobiography of a Chinese Working Woman* (New Haven, Conn.: Yale University Press, 1945), p. 22. Other quotations are from pages 83, 62, 71, 182, 166, 235, and 246.

Japanese Suffragists In the 1920s Japanese women pressed for political emancipation in demonstrations like this one, but they did not receive the right to vote until 1946. Like these suffragists, some young Japanese women adopted Western fashions. Most workers in modern Japanese textile factories were women. (Mansell/ The LIFE Picture Collection/Getty Images)

Korea, and Manchuria provided an essential "outer ring of defense" to protect the home islands from Russian attack and Anglo-American imperialism. Now, in the 1920s, Japan's colonies also seemed essential for markets, raw materials, and economic growth.

Japan's rapid industrial development also created an imbalanced "dualistic" economy. The modern sector consisted of a handful of giant conglomerate firms, the **zaibatsu** (zigh-BAHT-dzoo), or "financial combines." Zaibatsu firms wielded enormous economic power and dominated the other sector of the economy, an unorganized multitude of peasant farmers and craftsmen. The result was financial oligarchy, corruption of government officials, and a weak middle class.

zaibatsu Giant conglomerate firms established in Japan beginning in the Meiji period and lasting until the end of World War II.

Behind the façade of party politics, Japanese elites—the emperor, high government officials, big business and military leaders—jockeyed savagely for power. Cohesive leadership, which had played such an important role in Japan's modernization by the Meiji reformers, had ceased to exist. By far the most serious challenge to peaceful progress was fanatical nationalism. As in Europe, ultranationalism first emerged in Japan in the late nineteenth century but did not flower fully until the First World War and the 1930s.

Though their views were often vague, Japan's ultranationalists shared several fundamental beliefs. They were violently anti-Western, rejecting democracy, big business, and Marxist socialism. Reviving old myths, they stressed the emperor's godlike qualities and the samurai warrior's code of honor, obedience, and responsibility. Despising party politics, they assassinated moderate leaders and plotted armed uprisings to achieve their goals. Above all else, the ultranationalists preached foreign expansion. Like Western imperialists shouldering "the white man's burden," Japanese ultranationalists thought their mission was a noble one. "Asia for the Asians" was their anti-Western rallying cry. As the famous ultranationalist Kita Ikki wrote in 1923, "Our seven hundred million brothers in China and India have no other path to independence than that offered by our guidance and protection."[10]

The ultranationalists were noisy and violent in the 1920s, but it took the Great Depression of the 1930s to tip the scales decisively in their favor. The worldwide depression (see "Worldwide Effects" in Chapter 30) hit Japan like a tidal wave in 1930. Exports and wages collapsed; unemployment and raw suffering soared. The ultranationalists blamed the system, and people listened.

Japan Against China

Among those who listened with particular care were young Japanese army officers in Manchuria, the underpopulated, resource-rich province of northeastern China controlled by the Japanese army since its victory over Russia in 1905. The rise of Chinese nationalism embodied in the Guomindang unification of China challenged Japanese control over Manchuria. In response, junior Japanese officers in Manchuria, in cooperation with top generals in Tokyo, secretly manufactured an excuse for aggression in late 1931. They blew up some Japanese-owned railroad tracks near the city of Shenyang (Mukden) and then, with reinforcements rushed in from Korea, quickly occupied all of Manchuria in "self-defense."

In 1932 Japan proclaimed Manchuria an independent state, renaming it Manchukuo, and in 1934 installed Puyi, the last Qing emperor, as puppet emperor over the puppet state. When the League of Nations condemned Japanese aggression in Manchuria, Japan resigned in protest. Japanese aggression in Manchuria proved that the army, though reporting directly to the Japanese emperor, was an independent force subject to no outside control.

For China the Japanese conquest of Manchuria was disastrous. Japanese aggression in Manchuria drew attention away from modernizing efforts. The Nationalist government promoted a massive boycott of Japanese goods but lost interest in social reform. Above all, the Nationalist government after 1931 completely neglected land reform and the Chinese peasants' grinding poverty. A contemporaneous Chinese economist spelled out the revolutionary implications: "It seems clear that the land problem in China today is as acute as that of eighteenth-century France or nineteenth-century Russia."[11] Mao Zedong agreed.

Having abandoned land reform, partly because they themselves were often landowners, the Nationalists under Jiang Jieshi devoted their energies between 1930 and 1934 to great campaigns of encirclement and extermination of the Communists' rural power base in southeastern China. In 1934 they closed in for the kill, but, in one of the most incredible sagas of modern times, the main Communist army broke out, beat off attacks, and retreated 6,000 miles in twelve months to a remote region on the northwestern border (Map 29.2). Of the estimated 100,000 men and women who began the **Long March**, only 8,000 to 10,000 reached the final destination in Yan'an (YEH-nahn).

There Mao built up his forces once again, established a new territorial base, and won local peasant support in five unprecedented ways. First, Mao's forces did not pillage and rape across the countryside as imperialist and warlord armies had always done. Second, Mao set up schools, albeit for Marxist education, so the nearly universally illiterate peasants could learn to read and write. Third, Mao established health clinics to provide the peasants with basic medical care. Fourth, Mao's armies, rather than stealing the peasants' produce, put down their weapons and helped the peasants plant and harvest their crops. Fifth, Communist courts tried the warlords and landlords for crimes against the peasants, who for the first time in Chinese history received economic and social justice.

Long March The 6,000-mile retreat of the Chinese Communist army in 1934 to a remote region on the northwestern border of China, during which tens of thousands lost their lives.

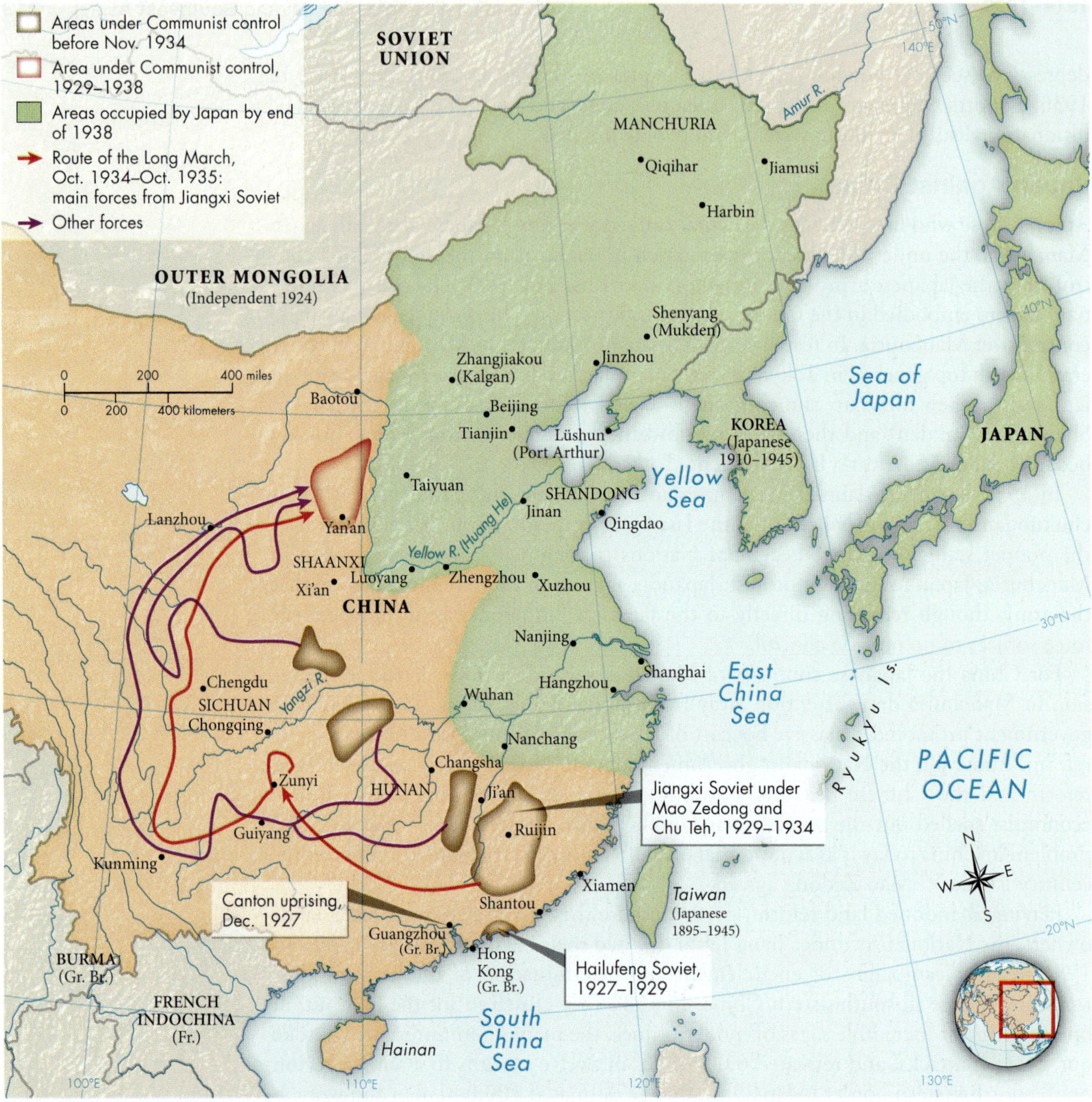

Areas under Communist control before Nov. 1934
Area under Communist control, 1929–1938
Areas occupied by Japan by end of 1938
Route of the Long March, Oct. 1934–Oct. 1935: main forces from Jiangxi Soviet
Other forces
SOVIET UNION
OUTER MONGOLIA
(Independent 1924)
MANCHURIA
Amur R.
Qiqihar
Jiamusi
Harbin
Shenyang (Mukden)
Jinzhou
Zhangjiakou (Kalgan)
Baotou
Beijing
Tianjin
Lüshun (Port Arthur)
KOREA (Japanese 1910–1945)
Sea of Japan
JAPAN
Taiyuan
SHANDONG
Jinan
Qingdao
Yellow Sea
Lanzhou
Yan'an
Yellow R. (Huang He)
SHAANXI
Xi'an
Luoyang
Zhengzhou
Xuzhou
CHINA
Nanjing
Shanghai
Hangzhou
East China Sea
Chengdu
SICHUAN
Yangzi R.
Chongqing
Wuhan
Nanchang
Changsha
Ryukyu Is.
PACIFIC OCEAN
Zunyi
HUNAN
Ji'an
Jiangxi Soviet under Mao Zedong and Chu Teh, 1929–1934
Ruijin
Guiyang
Kunming
Xiamen
Taiwan (Japanese 1895–1945)
Canton uprising, Dec. 1927
Shantou
Guangzhou (Gr. Br.)
Hong Kong (Gr. Br.)
Hailufeng Soviet, 1927–1929
BURMA (Gr. Br.)
FRENCH INDOCHINA (Fr.)
Hainan
South China Sea
0 200 400 miles
0 200 400 kilometers

MAP 29.2 The Chinese Communist Movement and the War with Japan, 1927–1938 After urban uprisings ordered by Stalin failed in 1927, Mao Zedong succeeded in forming a self-governing Communist soviet in mountainous southern China. Relentless Nationalist attacks between 1930 and 1934 finally forced the Long March to Yan'an, where the Communists were well positioned for guerrilla war against the Japanese.

In Japan politics became increasingly chaotic. In 1937 the Japanese military and the ultranationalists were in command. Unable to force China to cede more territory in northern China, they used a minor incident near Beijing as a pretext for a general attack. This marked the beginning of what became World War II in Asia, although Japan issued no declaration of war. The Nationalist government, which had just formed a united front with the Communists, fought hard, but Japanese troops

Mao Zedong and the Chinese Long March Mao's Communist forces were welcomed by the peasants during the Long March and at the army's final destination at Yan'an because the soldiers treated them with respect. In Yan'an they set up schools and health clinics, helped the farmers with their crops, and tried and punished the warlords and landlords. Here Mao talks with some peasants while on the Long March. (akg-images)

quickly took Beijing and northern China. After taking the port of Shanghai, the Japanese launched an immediate attack up the Yangzi River.

Foretelling the horrors of World War II, the Japanese air force bombed Chinese cities and civilian populations with unrelenting fury. Nanjing, the capital, fell in December 1937. Entering the city, Japanese soldiers went berserk and committed dreadful atrocities over seven weeks. They brutally murdered an estimated 200,000 to 300,000 Chinese civilians and unarmed soldiers, and raped 20,000 to 80,000 Chinese women. The "Rape of Nanjing" combined with other Japanese atrocities to outrage world opinion. The Western powers denounced Japanese aggression but, with tensions rising in Europe, took no action.

By late 1938 Japanese armies occupied sizable portions of coastal China (see Map 29.2). But the Nationalists and the Communists had retreated to the interior, and both refused to accept defeat. In 1939, as Europe edged toward another great war, China and Japan were bogged down in a savage stalemate. This undeclared war — called by historians the Second Sino-Japanese War (1937–1945) — provided a spectacular example of conflicting nationalisms.

Striving for Independence in Southeast Asia

The tide of nationalism was also rising in Southeast Asia. Nationalists in French Indochina and the Philippines urgently wanted genuine political independence and freedom from foreign rule. In French Indochina they ran up against an imperialist stone wall. The obstacle to Filipino independence came from America and Japan.

The French in Indochina, as in all their colonies, refused to export the liberal policies contained in the stirring words of their own Declaration of the Rights of Man and of the Citizen: liberty, equality, and fraternity (see "The National Assembly" in Chapter 22). This uncompromising attitude stimulated the growth of an equally stubborn Communist opposition under Ho Chi Minh (hoh chee mihn) (1890–

The Spanish-American War in the Philippines, 1898

1969), which despite ruthless repression emerged as the dominant anti-French force in Indochina.

In the Philippines, however, a well-established nationalist movement achieved greater success. As in colonial Latin America, the Spanish in the Philippines had been indefatigable missionaries. By the late nineteenth century the Filipino population was 80 percent Catholic. Filipinos shared a common cultural heritage and a common racial origin. Education, especially for girls, was advanced for Southeast Asia, and already in 1843 a higher percentage of people could read in the Philippines than in Spain itself. Economic development helped to create a westernized elite, which turned first to reform and then to revolution in the 1890s.

Filipino nationalists were bitterly disillusioned when the United States, having taken the Philippines from Spain in the Spanish-American War of 1898, ruthlessly beat down a patriotic revolt and denied the universal Filipino desire for independence. The Americans claimed the Philippines was not ready for self-rule and might be seized by Germany or Britain if it could not establish a stable, secure government. As the imperialist power in the Philippines, the United States encouraged education and promoted capitalistic economic development. And as in British India, an elected legislature was given some real powers.

As in India and French Indochina, demands for independence grew. One important contributing factor was American racial attitudes. Americans treated Filipinos as inferiors and introduced segregationist practices borrowed from the American South. American racism made passionate nationalists of many Filipinos. However, it was the Great Depression that had the most radical impact on the Philippines.

As the United States collapsed economically in the 1930s, the Philippines suddenly appeared to be a liability rather than an asset. American farm groups lobbied for protection from cheap Filipino sugar. To protect American jobs, labor unions demanded an end to Filipino immigra-

Uncle Sam as Schoolmaster In this cartoon that first appeared on the cover of *Harper's Weekly* in August 1898, unruly students from Spain's former colonies in Cuba and the Philippines, now living under American rule, are identified as a "Cuban Ex-patriot" and a "Guerilla." They are being disciplined with a switch by a stern Uncle Sam as he tries to teach them self-government. The gentleman to the left reading a book is José Miguel Gómez, one of Cuba's revolutionary heroes, while the Filipino insurrectionist Emilio Aguinaldo is made to wear a dunce cap and stand in the corner. The two well-behaved girls to the right represent Hawaii and Puerto Rico. (Sarin Images/Granger, NYC—All rights reserved.)

tion. Responding to public pressure, in 1934 Congress made the Philippines a self-governing commonwealth and scheduled independence for 1944. Sugar imports were reduced, and immigration was limited to only fifty Filipinos per year.

Some Filipino nationalists denounced the continued U.S. presence, but others were less certain that it was the immediate problem. Japan was fighting in China and expanding economically into the Philippines and throughout Southeast Asia. By 1939 a new threat to Filipino independence would come from Japan itself.

Chapter Summary

The Ottoman Empire's collapse in World War I left a power vacuum that both Western imperialists and Asian nationalists sought to fill. Strong leaders, such as Turkey's Mustafa Kemal, led successful nationalist movements in Turkey, Persia, and Afghanistan. British and French influence over the League of Nations–mandated Arab states declined in the 1920s and 1930s as Arab nationalists pushed for complete independence. The situation in Palestine, where the British had promised both Palestinians and Jewish Zionists independent homelands, deteriorated in the interwar years as increasingly larger numbers of European Jews migrated there.

Britain's centuries-long colonial rule over the Indian subcontinent met increasing resistance from Indian nationalists, particularly from Indian National Congress leaders, in the first decades of the twentieth century. Gandhi's active, nonviolent resistance campaign, which he called satyagraha, was principally responsible for convincing the British that their colonial hegemony in India was doomed. China's 1911 Revolution successfully ended the ancient dynastic system before the Great War, while the 1919 May Fourth Movement renewed nationalist hopes after it. Jiang Jieshi's Nationalist Party and Mao Zedong's Communists, however, would violently contest who would rule over a unified China. Japan, unlike China, industrialized early and by the 1920s seemed headed toward genuine democracy, but militarists and ultranationalists then launched an aggressive campaign of foreign expansion based on "Asia for Asians," which contributed to the buildup to World War II. As the Great Depression took hold, Filipino nationalists achieved independence from the United States. The diversity of these nationalist movements, arising out of separate historical experiences and distinct cultures, helps explain why Asian nationalists, like European nationalists, developed a strong sense of "we" and "they." In Asia "they" included other Asians as well as Europeans.

NOTES

1. Howard M. Sachar, *A History of Israel: From the Rise of Zionism to Our Time* (New York: Alfred A. Knopf, 1985), p. 109.
2. H. Armstrong, *Turkey in Travail: The Birth of a New Nation* (London: John Lane, 1925), p. 75.
3. Quoted in Lord Kinross, *Atatürk: A Biography of Mustafa Kemal, Father of Modern Turkey* (New York: Morrow, 1965), p. 181.
4. Lawrence James, *Raj: The Making and Unmaking of British India* (New York: St. Martin's Press, 1998), p. 458.
5. Quoted in E. Erikson, *Gandhi's Truth: On the Origins of Militant Nonviolence* (New York: W. W. Norton, 1969), p. 225.
6. M. K. Gandhi, *Non-Violent Resistance (Satyagraha)* (New York: Schocken Books, 1961), p. 365.
7. Quoted in W. T. de Bary, W. Chan, and B. Watson, *Sources of Chinese Tradition* (New York: Columbia University Press, 1964), pp. 768–769.

8. Quoted in J. F. Fairbank, E. O. Reischauer, and A. M. Craig, *East Asia: Tradition and Transformation* (Boston: Houghton Mifflin, 1973), p. 774.

9. Quoted in B. I. Schwartz, *Chinese Communism and the Rise of Mao* (Cambridge, Mass.: Harvard University Press, 1951), p. 74.

10. Quoted in W. T. de Bary, R. Tsunoda, and D. Keene, *Sources of Japanese Tradition*, vol. 2 (New York: Columbia University Press, 1958), p. 269.

11. Institute of Pacific Relations, *Agrarian China: Selected Source Material from Chinese Authors* (Chicago: University of Chicago Press, 1938), p. 1.

CONNECTIONS

Just as nationalism drove politics and state-building in Europe in the nineteenth century, so it took root across Asia in the late nineteenth and early twentieth centuries. While nationalism in Europe developed out of a desire to turn cultural unity into political reality and create imagined communities out of millions of strangers, in Asia nationalist sentiments drew their greatest energy from opposition to European imperialism and domination. Asian modernizers, aware of momentous advances in science and technology and of politics and social practices in the West, also pressed the nationalist cause by demanding an end to outdated conservative traditions that they argued only held back the development of modern, independent nations capable of throwing off Western domination and existing as equals with the West.

The nationalist cause in Asia took many forms and produced some of the twentieth century's most remarkable leaders. In Chapter 32 we will discuss how nationalist leaders across Asia shaped the freedom struggle and the resulting independence according to their own ideological and personal visions. China's Mao Zedong is the giant among the nationalist leaders who emerged in Asia, but he replaced imperialist rule with one-party Communist rule. Gandhi's dream of a unified India collapsed with the partition of British India into Hindu India and Muslim Pakistan and Bangladesh. India and Pakistan remain bitter, and nuclear-armed, enemies today, as we will see in Chapter 33. Egypt assumed a prominent position in the Arab world after World War II under Gamal Nasser's leadership and, after a series of wars with Israel, began to play a significant role in efforts to find a peaceful resolution to the Israeli-Palestinian conflict. That conflict, however, continues unabated as nationalist and religious sentiments inflame feelings on both sides. Ho Chi Minh eventually forced the French colonizers out of Vietnam, only to face another Western power, the United States, in a long and deadly war. As described in Chapter 31, a unified Vietnam finally gained its independence in 1975, but, like China, the country was under one-party Communist control.

Japan remained an exception to much of what happened in the rest of Asia. After a long period of isolation, the Japanese implemented an unprecedented program of modernization and westernization in the late nineteenth century. Japan continued to model itself after the West when it took control of former

German colonies as mandated territories after the Great War and occupied territory in China, Korea, Vietnam, Taiwan, and elsewhere. In the next chapter we will see how ultranationalism drove national policy in the 1930s, ultimately leading to Japan's defeat in World War II.

CHAPTER 29 Review and Explore

Identify Key Terms

Identify and explain the significance of each item below.

Permanent Mandates Commission (p. 899)

Sykes-Picot Agreement (p. 902)

Balfour Declaration (p. 902)

Treaty of Lausanne (p. 904)

Majlis (p. 905)

kibbutz (p. 908)

Lucknow Pact (p. 908)

satyagraha (p. 909)

May Fourth Movement (p. 913)

New Culture Movement (p. 914)

zaibatsu (p. 918)

Long March (p. 919)

Review the Main Ideas

Answer the focus questions from each section of the chapter.

1. Why did modern nationalism develop in Asia between the First and Second World Wars, and what was its appeal? (p. 898)

2. How did the Ottoman Empire's collapse in World War I shape nationalist movements in the Middle East? (p. 900)

3. What role did Gandhi and his campaign of militant nonviolence play in leading India to independence from the British? (p. 908)

4. How did nationalism shape political developments in East and Southeast Asia? (p. 912)

Make Comparisons and Connections

Analyze the larger developments and continuities within and across chapters.

1. Asian leaders adopted several of the ideologies of change that evolved in nineteenth-century Europe (Chapter 24) to unite their peoples against European imperialism in the twentieth century. Give examples of some of these ideologies and where they were adopted.

2. How were Indian, Chinese, and Turkish responses to European imperialism in the twentieth century affected by the different individual histories of these nations (Chapters 25, 26)?

3. Compare and contrast Japan's actions as a modern, imperial power in the late nineteenth century and the first three decades of the twentieth century with those of the European imperial powers at the same time (Chapters 25, 26).

TIMELINE

Suggested Resources

BOOKS

Fenby, Jonathan, *The Penguin History of Modern China: The Fall and Rise of a Great Power, 1850 to the Present*, 2d ed. 2013. An up-to-date comprehensive account of China's fall and rise.

Fromkin, David. *A Peace to End All Peace: The Fall of the Ottoman Empire and the Creation of the Modern Middle East*, 20th anniversary ed. 2009. A thorough but readable introduction to the Middle East in the early twentieth century.

Gandhi, Rajmohan. *Gandhi: The Man, His People, and the Empire.* 2008. Monumental scholarly biography written by a university professor who is also Gandhi's grandson.

Hane, Mikiso, and Louis G. Perez. *Modern Japan: A Historical Survey*, 5th ed. 2012. Highly readable and comprehensive study of modern Japan.

Hourani, Albert. *A History of the Arab Peoples*, rev. ed. 2010. One of the best single-volume histories of the Arab peoples.

Kawamura, Noriko, *Emperor Hirohito and the Pacific War.* 2015. A new biography of the controversial emperor that draws on new and reappraised sources.

Mango, Andrew. *Atatürk.* 2000. Rich, well-researched biography of this complex Turkish leader.

Osborne, Milton. *Southeast Asia: An Introductory History*, 11th ed. 2013. Remains the classic introduction to the region's history.

Sachar, Howard M. *A History of Israel: From the Rise of Zionism to Our Time*, 3d ed. 2007. A detailed history of Zionism and the Jewish state.

Spence, Jonathan. *The Search for Modern China*, 3d ed. 2012. Important study of modern China by a leading Chinese scholar.

Wolpert, Stanley. *A New History of India*, 8th ed. 2008. An excellent introduction to India's history.

Young, Louise. *Japan's Total Empire: Manchuria and the Culture of Wartime Imperialism.* 1998. A fascinating pioneering work on Japanese imperialism.

◆ **1927** Jiang Jieshi, leader of Chinese Nationalist Party, purges Communist allies

◆ **1937** Japanese militarists launch attack on China

◆ **1930** Gandhi's march to the sea to protest the British salt tax

◆ **1932** Iraq gains independence in return for military alliance with Great Britain

◆ **1934** Mao Zedong leads Chinese Communists on Long March

◆ **1931** Japan occupies Manchuria

◆ **1934** Philippines gains self-governing commonwealth status from U.S.

◆ **1933** Hitler and Nazi Party take power in Germany **(Ch. 30)**

1929–1939 Great Depression **(Ch. 30)**

| 1930 | 1935 | 1940 |

DOCUMENTARIES

Mahatma Gandhi: Pilgrim of Peace (A&E, 2000). A brief examination of Gandhi's life; part of A&E's *Biography* series.

Mao Tse Tung: China's Peasant Emperor (A&E, 1998). An introduction to Mao Zedong's life as a revolutionary and as the leader of Communist China; part of A&E's *Biography* series.

FEATURE FILMS

Gandhi (Richard Attenborough, 1982). Nominated for eleven Academy Awards, and winner of Best Picture, Best Director (Richard Attenborough), and Best Actor (Ben Kingsley), this film received broadly positive critical acclaim, both in India and internationally.

The Last Emperor (Bernardo Bertolucci, 1987). Winner of nine Academy Awards, including Best Picture, this is a beautifully filmed epic biographical movie about the last Chinese emperor, Puyi, who ascended to the throne when he was two in 1908 and was then forced to abdicate in 1912. The Japanese made him puppet emperor of the puppet Manchukuo Empire from 1934 to 1945.

WEBSITES

East Asian History Sourcebook. Includes primary and secondary sources and links to other websites, for most of East Asia, including China, Japan, and Korea. **sourcebooks.fordham.edu/Halsall/eastasia /eastasiasbook.asp**

Internet Indian History Sourcebook. A good starting point for sources on India's history, including links to other sites. **sourcebooks.fordham.edu/Halsall /india/indiasbook.asp**

30

The Great Depression and World War II
1929–1945

The years of anxiety and political maneuvering in Europe after World War I were made much worse when a massive economic depression spread around the world following the American stock market crash of October 1929. An increasingly interconnected global economy now collapsed. Free-market capitalism appeared to have run its course. People everywhere looked for relief to new leaders, some democratically elected, many not. In Europe, on the eve of the Second World War, few liberal democratic governments survived. Worldwide, in countries such as Brazil, Japan, the Soviet Union, and others, as well as in Europe, dictatorships seemed the wave of the future.

The mid-twentieth-century era of dictatorship is a deeply disturbing chapter in the history of civilization. The key development was not only the resurgence of authoritarian rule, but also the rise of a particularly ruthless brand of totalitarianism that reached its fullest realization in the Soviet Union, Nazi Germany, and Japan in the 1930s. Stalin, Hitler, and Japan's military leaders intervened radically in society and ruled with unprecedented severity. Hitler's sudden attack on Poland in 1939 started World War II in Europe. His successes encouraged the Japanese to expand their stalemated Chinese campaign into a vast Pacific war. By war's end, millions had died on the battlefields and in the bombed-out cities. Millions more died in the Holocaust, in Stalin's Soviet Union from purges and forced imposition of communism, and during Japan's quest to create an "Asia for Asians."

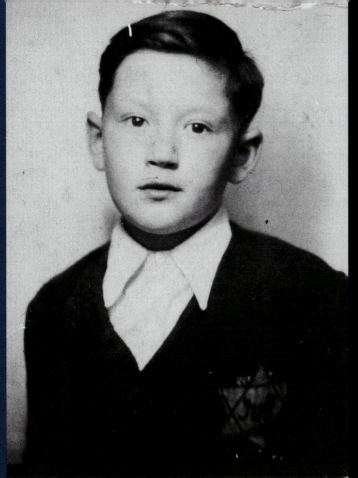

Jewish Boy in Nazi-Controlled France

Israel Lichtenstein, wearing a Jewish star, was born in Paris in 1932. His father was one of an estimated 1 million Jews who died in the Auschwitz concentration camp. Israel and his mother were also sent to a concentration camp, but they escaped and survived the Holocaust by going into hiding until the end of the war. Israel later immigrated to the nation of Israel.

United States Holocaust Memorial Museum, courtesy of Israel Lichtenstein

CHAPTER PREVIEW

THE GREAT DEPRESSION, 1929–1939
What caused the Great Depression, and what were its consequences?

AUTHORITARIAN STATES
What was the nature of the new totalitarian dictatorships, and how did they differ from conservative authoritarian states and from each other?

STALIN'S SOVIET UNION
How did Stalin and the Communist Party build a totalitarian order in the Soviet Union?

MUSSOLINI AND FASCISM IN ITALY   How did Italian fascism develop?

HITLER AND NAZISM IN GERMANY
Why were Hitler and his Nazi regime initially so popular, and how did their actions lead to World War II?

THE SECOND WORLD WAR, 1939–1945
How did Germany and Japan build empires in Europe and Asia, and how did the Allies defeat them?

What caused the Great Depression, and what were its consequences?

The Great Depression, 1929–1939

Like the Great War, the Great Depression must be spelled with capital letters. Beginning in 1929 an exceptionally long and severe economic depression struck the entire world with ever-greater intensity, and recovery was uneven and slow. Only the Second World War brought it to an end.

The Economic Crisis

Though economic activity was already declining moderately in many countries by early 1929, the U.S. stock market crash in October of that year really started the Great Depression. The American stock market boom was built on borrowed money. Two factors explain why. First, the wealth gap (or income inequality) between America's rich and poor reached its greatest extent in the twentieth century in 1928–1929. One percent of Americans then held 70 percent of all America's wealth. Eventually, with not enough money to go around, the remaining 99 percent of Americans had to borrow to make even basic purchases—as a result, the cost of farm credit, installment loans, and home mortgages skyrocketed. Then a point was reached where the 99 percent could borrow no more, so they stopped buying.

Second, wealthy investors and speculators took increasingly greater investment risks. One such popular risk was to buy stocks by paying only a small fraction of the total purchase price and borrowing the remainder from their stockbrokers or from banks. Such buying "on margin" was extremely dangerous. When prices started falling, the hard-pressed margin buyers started selling to pay their debts. The result was a financial panic. Countless investors and speculators were wiped out in a matter of days or weeks, and the New York stock market's crash started a domino effect that hit most of the world's major stock exchanges.

The financial panic in the United States triggered a worldwide financial crisis. Throughout the 1920s American bankers and investors had lent large sums to many countries, and as panic spread, New York bankers began recalling their short-term loans. Frightened citizens around the world began to withdraw their bank savings, leading to general financial chaos. The recall of American loans also accelerated the collapse in world prices, as business people dumped goods in a frantic attempt to get cash to pay what they owed.

The financial chaos led to a drastic decline in production in country after country. Between 1929 and 1933 world output of goods fell by an estimated 38 percent. Countries now turned inward and tried to go it alone. Many followed the American example, in which protective tariffs were raised to their highest levels ever in 1930 to seal off shrinking national markets for American producers only.

Although historians' opinions differ, two factors probably best explain the relentless slide to the bottom from 1929 to early 1933. First, the international economy lacked leadership able to maintain stability when the crisis came. Neither the seriously weakened Britain nor the United States—the world's economic leaders—stabilized the international economic system in 1929. Instead Britain and the United States cut back international lending and erected high tariffs.

Second, in almost every country, governments cut their budgets and reduced spending instead of running large deficits to try to stimulate their economies. That is, governments needed to put large sums of money into the economy to stimulate job growth and spending. After World War II such a "counter-cyclical policy," advocated by the British economist John Maynard Keynes (1883–1946), became a well-established weapon against depression. But in the 1930s orthodox economists generally regarded Keynes's prescription with horror.

Mass Unemployment

The need for large-scale government spending was tied to mass unemployment. The 99 percent's halt in buying contributed to the financial crisis, which led to production cuts, which in turn caused workers to lose their jobs and have even less money to buy goods. This led to still more production cuts, and unemployment soared. In Britain unemployment had averaged 12 percent in the 1920s; between 1930 and 1935 it averaged more than 18 percent. Germany and Austria had some of the highest unemployment rates, 30–32 percent in 1932. The worst unemployment was in the United States. In the 1920s unemployment there had averaged only 5 percent; in 1933 it soared to about 33 percent of the entire labor force: 14 million people were out of work. This was the only time in American history when more people left America than immigrated in—including thousands of Mexican Americans who suffered increasing hostility, accused of stealing jobs from those who considered themselves to be "real Americans," and perhaps a hundred thousand Americans who migrated to the Soviet Union, attracted by communism's promises of jobs and a new life.

Mass unemployment created great social problems. Poverty increased dramatically, although in most industrialized countries unemployed workers generally received some meager unemployment benefits or public aid that prevented starvation. Millions of unemployed people lost their spirit, and homes and ways of life were disrupted in countless personal tragedies. In 1932 workers in Manchester, England, appealed to their city officials—a typical appeal echoed throughout the Western world:

> We tell you that thousands of people . . . are in desperate straits. We tell you that men, women, and children are going hungry. . . . We tell you that great numbers are being rendered distraught through the stress and worry of trying to exist without work. . . .

Louisville Flood Victims, 1937

During the Great Depression, Louisville, Kentucky, was hit by the worst flood in its history. The famous documentary photographer Margaret Bourke-White captured this image of African American flood victims lining up for food. Not only does the billboard message mock the Depression-era conditions, but the smiling white family appears to be driving its car through the line of people, drawing attention to America's race and class differences. (Margaret Bourke-White/Time & Life Pictures/Getty Images)

If you do not provide useful work for the unemployed—what, we ask, is your alternative? Do not imagine that this colossal tragedy of unemployment is going on endlessly without some fateful catastrophe. Hungry men are angry men.[1]

The New Deal in the United States

The Great Depression and the response to it marked a major turning point in American history. Herbert Hoover (U.S. pres. 1929–1933) and his administration initially reacted with limited action. When the financial crisis struck Europe with full force in summer 1931 and boomeranged back to the United States, banks failed and unemployment soared. In 1932 industrial production fell to about 50 percent of its 1929 level.

New Deal Franklin Delano Roosevelt's plan to reform capitalism in the United States through forceful government intervention in the economy.

In these desperate circumstances Franklin Delano Roosevelt (U.S. pres. 1933–1945) won a landslide presidential victory in 1932 with promises of a "**New Deal** for the forgotten man." Roosevelt's basic goal was to preserve capitalism by reforming it. Rejecting socialism and government ownership of industry, Roosevelt advocated forceful federal government intervention in the economy. His commitment to national relief programs marked a profound shift from the traditional stress on family support and local community responsibility.

Roosevelt attacked mass unemployment by creating new federal agencies that launched a vast range of public works projects so the federal government could directly employ as many people as financially possible. The Works Progress Administration (WPA), set up in 1935, employed one-fifth of the entire U.S. labor force at some point in the 1930s, and these workers constructed public buildings, bridges, and highways.

In 1935 the U.S. government established a national social security system with old-age pensions and unemployment benefits. The 1935 National Labor Relations Act declared collective bargaining to be U.S. policy, and union membership more than doubled. In general, between 1935 and 1938 government rulings and social reforms chipped away at the privileges of the wealthy and tried to help ordinary people.

Despite undeniable accomplishments in social reform, the New Deal was only partly successful as a response to the Great Depression. Unemployment was still a staggering 10 million when war broke out in Europe in 1939. The New Deal brought fundamental reform, but it never did pull the United States out of the depression; only the Second World War did that.

The European Response to the Depression

The American stock market's collapse in October 1929 set off a chain of economic downturns that hit Europe, particularly Germany and Great Britain, the hardest. Postwar Europe had emerged from the Great War deeply in debt and in desperate need of investment capital to rebuild. The United States became the primary creditor and financier. Germany borrowed, for example, to pay Britain war reparations, and then Britain took that money and repaid its war debts and investment loans to America. When the American economy crashed, the whole circular system crashed with it.

Of all the Western democracies, the Scandinavian countries under socialist leadership responded most successfully to the challenge of the Great Depression. When the economic crisis struck in 1929, Sweden's socialist government pioneered the use of large-scale deficits to finance public works projects and thereby maintain production and employment. Scandinavian governments also increased social welfare benefits. All this spending required a large bureaucracy and high taxes. Yet both private and cooperative enterprise thrived, as did democracy. Some observers considered Scandinavia's welfare socialism an appealing middle way between what they considered to be sick capitalism and cruel communism or fascism.

In Britain, Ramsay MacDonald's Labour government (1929–1931) and, after 1931, the Conservative-dominated coalition government followed orthodox economic theory. The budget was balanced, but unemployed workers received barely enough welfare support to live. Nevertheless, the economy recovered considerably after 1932, reflecting the gradual reorientation of the British economy. Britain concentrated increasingly on the national, rather than the international, market. Old export industries, such as textiles and coal, continued to decline, but new industries, such as automobiles and electrical appliances, grew. These developments encouraged British isolationism and often had devastating economic consequences for Britain's far-flung colonies and dominions, which depended heavily upon reciprocal trade with Great Britain and the United States.

The Great Depression came late to France as it was relatively less industrialized and more isolated from the world economy. But once the depression hit, it stayed. Economic stagnation both reflected and heightened an ongoing political crisis, as liberals, democratic socialists, and Communists fought for control of the French government with conservatives and the far right. The latter groups agitated against parliamentary democracy and turned to Mussolini's Italy and Hitler's Germany for inspiration. At the same time, the Communist Party and many workers looked to Stalin's Russia for guidance.

Frightened by the growing popularity of Hitler- and Mussolini-style right-wing dictatorships at home and abroad, the Communist, Socialist, and Radical Parties in France formed an alliance—the **Popular Front**—for the May 1936 national elections. Following its clear victory, the Popular Front government launched a far-reaching New Deal–inspired program of social and economic reform. Popular with workers (because it supported unions) and the lower middle class, these measures were quickly sabotaged by rapid inflation, rising wages, a decline in overseas exports, and cries of socialist revolution from frightened conservatives. Politically, the Popular Front lost many left-wing supporters when it failed to back the republican cause in the Spanish Civil War while Hitler and Mussolini openly armed and supported Franco's nationalists. In June 1937, with the country hopelessly divided, the Popular Front collapsed.

Popular Front A party formed in 1936 in France that encouraged unions and launched a far-reaching New Deal–inspired program of social reform.

Worldwide Effects

The Great Depression's magnitude was unprecedented, and its effect rippled well beyond Europe and the United States. Because many countries and colonies in Africa, Asia, and Latin America were nearly totally dependent on one or two commodities—such as coffee beans or cocoa—for income, the implementation of protectionist trade policies by the leading industrial nations had devastating effects.

The Great Depression hit the vulnerable commodity economies of Latin America especially hard. With foreign sales plummeting, Latin American countries could not buy the industrial goods they needed from abroad. The global depression provoked a profound shift toward economic nationalism after 1930, as popularly based governments worked to reduce foreign influence and gain control of their own economies and natural resources. These efforts were fairly successful. By the late 1940s factories in Argentina, Brazil, and Chile could generally satisfy domestic consumer demand for the products of light industry. But as in Hitler's Germany, the deteriorating economic conditions in Latin America also gave rise to dictatorships, some of them modeled along European Fascist lines.

The Great Depression marked a decisive turning point in the development of African nationalism. For the first time, educated Africans faced widespread unemployment. African peasants and small business people who had been drawn into world trade, and who sometimes profited from booms, also felt the economic pain, as did urban workers. In some areas the result was unprecedented mass protest.

While Asians were somewhat affected by the Great Depression, the consequences varied greatly by country or colony and were not as serious generally as they were elsewhere. That being said, where the depression did hit, it was often severe. The price of rice fell by two-thirds between 1929 and 1932. Also crippling to the region's economies was Asia's heavy dependence on raw material exports. With debts to local moneylenders fixed in value and taxes to colonial governments hardly ever reduced, many Asian peasants in the 1930s struggled under crushing debt and suffered terribly. (See "Global Viewpoints: Socialism and the Working Class," at right.)

When the Great Depression reached China in the early 1930s, it hit the rural economy the hardest. China's economy depended heavily on cash-crop exports and these declined dramatically, while cheap foreign agricultural goods—such as rice and wheat—were dumped in China. While Chinese industrial production dropped off after 1931, it quickly recovered. Much of this growth was in the military sector, as China tried to catch up with the West and also prepare for war with Japan.

In Japan the terrible suffering caused by the Great Depression caused ultranationalists and militarists to call for less dependence on global markets and the expansion of a self-sufficient empire. Such expansion began in 1931 when Japan invaded Chinese Manchuria, which became a major source of the raw materials needed to feed Japanese industrial growth (see "Japan Against China" in Chapter 29). Japan recovered more quickly from the Great Depression than did any other major industrial power because of prompt action by the civilian democratic government, but the government and large corporations continued to be blamed for the economic downturn. By the mid-1930s this lack of confidence, combined with the collapsing international economic order, Europe's and America's increasingly isolationist and protectionist policies, and a growing admiration for Nazi Germany and its authoritarian, militaristic model of government, had led the Japanese military to topple the civilian authorities and dictate Japan's future.

What was the nature of the new totalitarian dictatorships, and how did they differ from conservative authoritarian states and from each other?

Authoritarian States

Both conservative and radical totalitarian dictatorships arose in Europe in the 1920s and the 1930s. Although they sometimes overlapped in character and practice, they were profoundly different in essence.

Conservative Authoritarianism

The traditional form of antidemocratic government in world history was conservative authoritarianism. Like Russia's tsars and China's emperors, the leaders of such

Socialism and the Working Class

James Keir Hardie (1856–1915) was the first Socialist member of the British Parliament and a founder of the British Labour Party. His *From Serfdom to Socialism* (1907) was intended to make a "brief unadorned statement of the case for Socialism, easily understandable by plain folks."

In 1936–1937 George Orwell (1903–1950), famous for his novels *1984* and *Animal Farm*, lived in Wigan, a mill town in a coal-mining district near Manchester in the north of England. In *The Road to Wigan Pier*, he tried to explain why socialism did not have more support among the workers.

James Keir Hardie, *From Serfdom to Socialism*

■ But it is to the working-class itself that we must look for changing the system of production and making it a means of providing for the healthy human need of all the people. This is so not only because of their numbers but also because unless they consciously set themselves to win Socialism it can never be won. It is, in the fullest sense of a very much abused phrase, a People's Cause. When it has been won it will be their fight which has won it; should it never be won, and should our Western civilisation totter on until it falls into the depths of a merciful oblivion, that too will be their doing, and be due entirely to their not having had the courage and the intelligence to put up a fight strong enough to save it and themselves.

Somewhat dimly at present, but with growing clearness of vision, the worker begins to see that he will remain a menial, outcast and forlorn, until he has made himself master of the machine he tends and the soil he tills. Hence the growth of Socialism.

George Orwell, *The Road to Wigan Pier*

■ Socialism . . . is a theory confined entirely to the middle class. The typical Socialist is not, as tremulous old ladies imagine, a ferocious-looking workingman with greasy overalls and a raucous voice. He is either a youthful snob-Bolshevik who in five years' time will

quite probably have made a wealthy marriage and been converted to Roman Catholicism; or, still more typically, a prim little man with a white-collar job, usually a secret teetotaler . . . often with vegetarian leanings . . . and, above all, with a social position which he has no intention of forfeiting. . . . In addition to this there is the horrible . . . prevalence of cranks. . . . The mere words "Socialism" and "Communism" draw towards them . . . every fruit-juice drinker, nudist, sandal-wearer, sex-maniac, Quaker, "Nature Cure" quack, pacifist, and feminist in England. . . .

A working man, so long as he remains a genuine working man, is seldom or never a Socialist. . . . Very likely he votes Labour, or even Communist if he gets the chance, but his conception of Socialism is quite different from that of the book-trained Socialist. . . . To [him] . . . Socialism does not mean much more than better wages and shorter hours and nobody bossing you about. . . . Often . . . he is a truer Socialist than the orthodox Marxist, because he does remember, what the other so often forgets, that Socialism means justice and common decency. . . . His vision of the Socialist future is a vision of present society with the worst abuses left out, and with . . . the same things as at present — family life, the pub, football, and local politics. As for the philosophic side of Marxism, . . . I have yet to meet a *working* miner, steel-worker, cotton-weaver, docker, navvy, or whatnot who was "ideologically" sound.

QUESTIONS FOR ANALYSIS

1. Both Hardie and Orwell were writing about socialism in Great Britain, one in 1907 and the other in the 1930s. What aspects of Hardie's analysis of potential socialists would Orwell agree with, and what aspects would he disagree with?
2. What events occurred between 1907 and the 1930s that might have affected the socialist movement in Great Britain? Explain your answer.
3. Is one of these authors more pessimistic about the spread of socialism than the other is? Which one? Why?

governments relied on obedient bureaucracies, vigilant police departments, and trustworthy armies to control society. They forbade or limited popular participation in government and often jailed or exiled political opponents. Yet they had neither the ability nor the desire to control many aspects of their subjects' lives. As long as the people did not try to change the system, they often enjoyed considerable personal independence.

After the First World War, conservative authoritarianism revived, especially in Latin America. Conservative dictators also seized power in Spain and Portugal, and in the less-developed eastern part of Europe. There were several reasons for this development. These lands lacked strong traditions of self-government, and many new states, such as Yugoslavia, were torn by ethnic conflicts. Dictatorship appealed to nationalists and military leaders as a way to repress such tensions and preserve national unity. Large landowners and the church were still powerful forces in these predominantly agrarian areas and often looked to dictators to protect them from progressive land reform or Communist agrarian upheaval. Conservative dictatorships were concerned more with maintaining the status quo than with mobilizing the masses or forcing society into rapid change or war.

Radical Totalitarian Dictatorships

By the mid-1930s a new kind of radical dictatorship—termed totalitarian—had emerged in the Soviet Union, Germany, and, to a lesser extent, Italy. Scholars disagree over the definition of totalitarianism, its origins, and to what countries and leaders the term should apply. Moreover, when the Cold War began in the late 1940s (see "The World Remade" in Chapter 31), conservatives, particularly in the United States, commandeered the term as shorthand for the "evil" Communist regimes in the Soviet Union and its satellites. Liberals, especially in the 1960s, used the term more loosely to refer to every system they felt inhibited freedom—from local police to the U.S. Pentagon. Thus by the 1980s many scholars questioned the term's usefulness. More recently, with these caveats, scholars have returned to the term to explain and understand fascism, Nazism, and communism in the 1920s, 1930s, and 1940s.

totalitarianism A radical dictatorship that exercises complete political power and control over all aspects of society and seeks to mobilize the masses for action.

It can be argued that **totalitarianism** began with the total war effort of 1914–1918 (see "Mobilizing for Total War" in Chapter 28), as governments acquired total control over all areas of society in order to achieve one supreme objective: victory. This provided a model for future totalitarian states. As the French thinker Élie Halévy (AY-lee ah-LAY-vee) observed in 1936, the varieties of modern totalitarian tyranny—fascism, Nazism, and communism—could be thought of as "feuding brothers" with a common father: the nature of modern war.[2]

The consequences of the Versailles treaty (1919) and the severe economic and political problems that Germany and Italy faced in the 1920s left both those countries ripe for new leadership, but not necessarily totalitarian dictators. It was the Great Depression that must be viewed as the immediate cause of the modern totalitarian state.

In 1956 American historians Carl Friedrich and Zbigniew Brzezinski (z-BIG-nyef bzheh-ZIN-skee) identified at least six key features of modern totalitarian states: (1) an official ideology; (2) a single ruling party; (3) complete control of "all weapons of armed combat"; (4) complete monopoly of all means of mass communication;

The Spread of Fascism in Spain, 1937
In the 1920s and 1930s most European countries had Fascist sympathizers. Between 1936 and 1939 Fascist nationalist forces led by General Francisco Franco, pictured here, fought a brutal war against the government of Spain's left-leaning, democratic Second Spanish Republic. Socialist and liberal volunteers from around the world came to Spain to fight against Franco's army, as recounted in Ernest Hemingway's novel *For Whom the Bell Tolls*. Pablo Picasso portrayed the destruction to one town caused by German Nazi and Italian Fascist warplanes, supporting Franco, in his famous painting *Guernica*. Following the nationalist victory, Franco ruled Spain as a dictator for thirty-six years.
(© Imagno/Austrian Archives/The Image Works)

(5) a system of terror, physical and psychic, enforced by the party and the secret police; and (6) central control and direction of the entire economy.[3]

While all these features were present in Stalin's Communist Soviet Union and Hitler's Nazi Germany, there were some major differences. Most notably, Soviet communism seized private property for the state and sought to level society by crushing the middle classes. Nazi Germany also criticized big landowners and industrialists but, unlike the Communists, did not try to nationalize private property, so the middle classes survived. This difference in property and class relations led some scholars to speak of "totalitarianism of the left" — Stalinist Russia — and "totalitarianism of the right" — Nazi Germany.

Moreover, Soviet Communists ultimately had international aims: they sought to unite the workers of the world. Mussolini and Hitler claimed they were interested in changing state and society on a national level only, although Hitler envisioned a greatly expanded "living space," or *lebensraum* (LAY-buhns-rowm), for Germans in eastern Europe and Russia. Both Mussolini and Hitler used the term **fascism** (FASH-iz-uhm) to describe their movements' supposedly "total" and revolutionary character. Orthodox Marxist Communists argued that the Fascists were powerful capitalists seeking to destroy the revolutionary working class and thus protect their enormous profits. So while Communists and Fascists both sought the overthrow of existing society, their ideologies clashed, and they were enemies.

European Fascist movements shared many characteristics, including extreme, often expanionist, nationalism; anti-socialism aimed at destroying working-class movements; a dynamic and violent leader; a crushing of human individualism; alliances with powerful capitalists and landowners; and glorification of war and the military. Fascists, especially in Germany, also embraced racial homogeneity. Indeed, while class was the driving force in communist ideology, race and racial purity were profoundly important to Nazi ideology.

fascism A movement characterized by extreme, often expansionist nationalism, anti-socialism, a dynamic and violent leader, and glorification of war and the military.

Although 1930s Japan has sometimes been called a Fascist society, most recent scholars disagree with this label. Japanese political philosophers were attracted by some European Fascist ideas, such as Hitler's desire for eastward expansion, which would be duplicated by Japan's expansion to the Asian mainland. Other appealing concepts included nationalism, militarism, the corporatist economic model, and a single, all-powerful political party. The idea of a Japanese dictator, however, clashed with the emperor's divine status. There were also various ideologically unique forces at work in Japan, including ultranationalism, militarism (building on the historic role of samurai warriors in Japanese society), reverence for traditional ways, emperor worship, and the profound changes to Japanese society beginning with the Meiji Restoration in 1867 (see "The Meiji Restoration" in Chapter 26). These also contributed to the rise of a totalitarian, but not Fascist, state before the Second World War.

In summary, the concept of totalitarianism remains a valuable tool for historical understanding. It correctly highlights that in the 1930s Germany, the Soviet Union, and Japan made an unprecedented "total claim" on the beliefs and behaviors of their respective citizens.[4] However, none of these nations were successful in completely dominating their citizens. Thus totalitarianism is an idea never fully achieved.

How did Stalin and the Communist Party build a totalitarian order in the Soviet Union?

Stalin's Soviet Union

Joseph Stalin (1879–1953) consolidated his power following Lenin's death in 1924 and by 1927 was the de facto leader of the Soviet Union. In 1928 he launched the first **five-year plan**—a "revolution from above,"[5] as he so aptly termed it, to transform Soviet society along socialist lines, and to generate a Communist society with new attitudes, new loyalties, and a new socialist humanity. Stalin and the Communist Party used constant propaganda, enormous sacrifice, and unlimited violence and state control to establish a dynamic, modern totalitarian state in the 1930s.

From Lenin to Stalin

By spring 1921 Lenin and the Bolsheviks had won the civil war, but they ruled a shattered and devastated land. Facing economic disintegration, the worst famine in generations, riots by peasants and workers, and an open rebellion by previously pro-Bolshevik sailors at Kronstadt (kruhn-SHTAHT), Lenin changed course. In March 1921 he announced the **New Economic Policy (NEP)**, which re-established limited economic freedom in an attempt to rebuild agriculture and industry. Peasant producers could sell their surpluses in free markets, as could private traders and small handicraft manufacturers. Heavy industry, railroads, and banks, however, remained wholly nationalized.

The NEP was successful both politically and economically. Politically, it was a necessary but temporary compromise with the Soviet Union's overwhelming peasant majority. Economically, the NEP brought rapid recovery. In 1926 industrial output surpassed prewar levels, and peasants were producing almost as much grain as before the war.

As the economy recovered, an intense power struggle began in the Communist Party's inner circles, for Lenin left no chosen successor when he died in 1924. The principal contenders were Stalin and Leon Trotsky. While Trotsky appeared to be the stronger of the two, in the end Stalin won because he gained the support of the party, the only genuine source of power in the one-party state.

five-year plan Launched by Stalin in 1928 and termed the "revolution from above," its goal was to modernize the Soviet Union and generate a Communist society with new attitudes, new loyalties, and a new socialist humanity.

New Economic Policy (NEP) Lenin's 1921 policy re-establishing limited economic freedom in the Soviet Union in an attempt to rebuild agriculture and industry in the face of economic disintegration.

Stalin gradually achieved absolute power between 1922 and 1927. He used the moderates to crush Trotsky and then turned against the moderates and destroyed them as well. Stalin's final triumph came at the party congress of December 1927, which condemned all deviation from the general party line as formulated by Stalin.

The Five-Year Plans

The 1927 party congress marked the end of the NEP and the beginning of socialist five-year plans. The first five-year plan had staggering economic objectives. In just five years, total industrial output was to increase by 250 percent and agricultural production by 150 percent. By 1930 economic and social change was sweeping the country in a frenzied effort to modernize and industrialize, much like in Britain in the nineteenth century (see "The Industrial Revolution in Britain" in Chapter 23), and dramatically changing the lives of ordinary people, sometimes at great personal cost. One worker complained, "The workers . . . made every effort to fulfill the industrial and financial plan and fulfilled it by more than 100 percent, but how are they supplied? The ration is received only by the worker, except for rye flour, his wife and small children receive nothing. Workers and their families wear worn-out clothes, the kids are in rags, their naked bellies sticking out."[6]

Stalin unleashed his "second revolution" because, like Lenin, he was deeply committed to socialism. Stalin was also driven to catch up with the advanced and presumably hostile Western capitalist nations. In February 1931 Stalin famously declared:

> It is sometimes asked whether it is not possible to slow down the tempo a bit. . . . No, comrades, it is not possible! The tempo must not be reduced! . . . To slacken the tempo would mean falling behind. And those who fall behind get beaten. No, we refuse to be beaten! . . . We are fifty or a hundred years behind the advanced countries. We must make good this distance in ten years. Either we do it, or we shall be crushed.[7]

Domestically, there was the peasant problem. For centuries peasants had wanted to own the land, and finally they had it. Sooner or later, the Communists reasoned, the peasants would become conservative capitalists and threaten the regime. Stalin therefore launched a preventive war against the peasantry to bring it under the state's absolute control.

That war was **collectivization** — the forcible consolidation of individual peasant farms into large, state-controlled enterprises. Beginning in 1929 peasants were ordered to give up their land and animals and become members of collective farms. As for the kulaks, the better-off peasants, Stalin instructed party workers to "break their resistance, to eliminate them as a class."[8] Stripped of land and livestock, many starved or were deported to forced-labor camps for "re-education."

collectivization Stalin's forcible consolidation, beginning in 1929, of individual peasant farms in the Soviet Union into large, state-controlled enterprises.

Because almost all peasants were poor, the term *kulak* soon meant any peasant who opposed the new system. Whole villages were often attacked. One conscience-stricken colonel in the secret police confessed to a foreign journalist:

> I am an old Bolshevik. I worked in the underground against the Tsar and then I fought in the Civil War. Did I do all that in order that I should now surround villages with machine guns and order my men to fire indiscriminately into crowds of peasants? Oh, no, no![9]

Forced collectivization led to disaster. Many peasants slaughtered their animals and burned their crops in protest. Nor were the state-controlled collective farms more productive. Grain output barely increased, and collectivized agriculture made no substantial financial contribution to Soviet industrial development during the first five-year plan.

In Ukraine Stalin instituted a policy of all-out collectivization with two goals: to destroy all expressions of Ukrainian nationalism, and to break the Ukrainian peasants' will so they would accept collectivization and Soviet rule. Stalin began by purging Ukraine of its intellectuals and political elite. He then set impossibly high grain quotas for the collectivized farms. This grain quota had to be turned over to the government before any peasant could receive a share. Many scholars and dozens of governments and international organizations have declared Stalin's and the Soviet government's policies a deliberate act of genocide. As one historian observed:

> Grain supplies were sufficient to sustain everyone if properly distributed. People died mostly of terror-starvation (excess grain exports, seizure of edibles from the starving, state refusal to provide emergency relief, bans on outmigration, and forced deportation to food-deficit locales), not poor harvests and routine administrative bungling.[10]

The result was a terrible man-made famine, called in Ukrainian the *Holodomor* (HAU-lau-dau-mohr) (Hunger extermination), in Ukraine in 1932 and 1933, which probably claimed 3 to 5 million lives.

Collectivization was a cruel but real victory for Communist ideologues who were looking to institute their brand of communism and to crush opposition as much as improve production. By 1938, 93 percent of peasant families had been herded onto collective farms at a horrendous cost in both human lives and resources. Regimented as state employees and dependent on the state-owned tractor stations, the collectivized peasants were no longer a political threat.

The industrial side of the five-year plans was more successful. Soviet industry produced about four times as much in 1937 as in 1928. No other major country had ever achieved such rapid industrial growth. Heavy industry led the way, and urban development accelerated: more than 25 million people migrated to cities to become industrial workers during the 1930s.

The sudden creation of dozens of new factories demanded tremendous resources. Funds for industrial expansion were collected from the people through heavy hidden sales taxes. Firm labor discipline also contributed to rapid industrialization. Trade unions lost most of their power, and individuals could not move without police permission. When factory managers needed more hands, they were sent "unneeded" peasants from collective farms.

Foreign engineers were hired to plan and construct many of the new factories. Highly skilled American engineers, hungry for work in the depression years, were particularly important until newly trained Soviet experts began to replace them after 1932. Thus Stalin's planners harnessed the skill and technology of capitalist countries to promote the surge of socialist industry.

Life and Culture in Soviet Society

Daily life was hard in Stalin's Soviet Union. Despite these hardships, many Communists saw themselves as heroically building the world's first socialist society while capitalism crumbled and fascism rose in the West.

The Soviet Forced-Labor Camp at Arkhangelsk From 1929 to 1953 millions of Soviet citizens were sent to forced-labor prison camps such as this one, and over 1.5 million died. Ten to 20 percent of these prisoners were women, many of them found guilty of nothing more than being married to men considered enemies of the state. Here male and female prisoners work in a lumberyard in a cold and snowy climate near the Arctic Circle. (© SZ Photo/Bridgeman Images)

Offsetting the hardships were the important social benefits Soviet workers received, such as old-age pensions, free medical services and education, and day-care centers for children. Unemployment was almost unknown. Moreover, there was the possibility of personal advancement. Rapid industrialization required massive numbers of trained experts. Thus the Stalinist state broke with the egalitarian policies of the 1920s and provided tremendous incentives to those who acquired specialized skills. A growing technical and managerial elite joined the political and artistic elites in a new upper class, whose members were rich and powerful.

Soviet society's radical transformation profoundly affected women's lives. The Russian Bolshevik Revolution immediately proclaimed complete equality of rights for women. In the 1920s divorce and abortion were made easily available, and women were urged to work outside the home. After Stalin came to power, however, he encouraged a return to traditional family values.

The most lasting changes for women involved work and education. Peasant women continued to work on farms, and millions of women now toiled in factories and heavy construction. The more determined women entered the ranks of the better-paid specialists in industry and science. By 1950, 75 percent of all doctors in the Soviet Union were women.

Culture was thoroughly politicized through constant propaganda and indoctrination. Party activists lectured workers in factories and peasants on collective farms, while newspapers, films, and radio broadcasts recounted socialist achievements and warned of capitalist plots.

Stalinist Terror and the Great Purges

In the mid-1930s the push to build socialism and a new society culminated in ruthless police terror and a massive purging of the Communist Party. In August 1936 sixteen prominent "Old Bolsheviks" — party members before the 1917 revolution — confessed to all manner of plots against Stalin in spectacular public show trials in Moscow. Then in 1937 the secret police arrested a mass of lesser party officials and newer members, torturing them and extracting confessions for more show trials. In addition to the party faithful, union officials, managers, intellectuals, army officers, and countless ordinary citizens were struck down. One Stalin functionary admitted, "Innocent people were arrested: naturally—otherwise no one would be frightened. If people were arrested only for specific misdemeanors, all the others would feel safe and so become ripe for treason."[11] In all, at least 8 million people were arrested, and millions of these were executed. Those not immediately executed were sent to gulags (GOO-lagz)—labor camps from which few escaped. Many were simply worked to death as they provided convict labor for Stalin's industrialization drive in areas of low population.

Stalin recruited 1.5 million new members to replace those purged. Thus more than half of all Communist Party members in 1941 had joined since the purges. This new generation of Stalin-formed Communists served the leader effectively until his death in 1953 and then governed the Soviet Union until the early 1980s. Stalin's mass purges remain baffling, for most historians believe those purged posed no threat and confessed to crimes they had not committed. Some historians have challenged the long-standing interpretation that blames the great purges on Stalin's cruelty or madness. They argue that Stalin's fears were exaggerated but genuine and were shared by many in the party and in the general population. Investigations and trials snowballed into a mass hysteria, a new witch-hunt.[12] Historians who have accessed recently opened Soviet archives, however, continue to hold that Stalin was intimately involved with the purges and personally directed them, abetted by amenable informers, judges, and executioners. Oleg Khlevniuk, a Ukrainian historian familiar with these archives, writes, "Theories about the elemental, spontaneous nature of the terror, about a loss of central control over the course of mass repression, and about the role of regional leaders in initiating the terror are simply not supported by the historical record."[13] In short, a ruthless and paranoid Stalin found large numbers of willing collaborators for crime as well as for achievement.

How did Italian fascism develop?

Mussolini and Fascism in Italy

Benito Mussolini's Fascist movement and his seizure of power in 1922 were important steps in the rise of dictatorships between the two world wars. Mussolini and his supporters were the first to call themselves "Fascists." His dictatorship was brutal and theatrical, and it contained elements of both conservative authoritarianism and modern totalitarianism.

The Seizure of Power

In the early twentieth century Italy was a liberal state with civil rights and a constitutional monarchy. On the eve of the First World War, the parliamentary regime granted universal male suffrage. But there were serious problems. Poverty was widespread, and many peasants were more attached to their villages and local interests than to the national state. Church-state relations were often tense. Class differences were also extreme, and by 1912 the Socialist Party's radical wing led the powerful revolutionary socialist movement.[14]

World War I worsened the political situation. Having fought on the Allied side almost exclusively for purposes of territorial expansion, Italian nationalists were disappointed with Italy's modest gains at the Paris Peace Conference. Workers and peasants also felt cheated: to win their support during the war, the government had promised social and land reform, which it failed to deliver after the war.

The Russian Revolution inspired and energized Italy's revolutionary socialist movement, and radical workers and peasants began occupying factories and seizing land in 1920. These actions scared and mobilized the property-owning classes. Thus by 1921 revolutionary socialists, antiliberal conservatives, and frightened property owners were all opposed — though for different reasons — to the liberal parliamentary government.

Into these crosscurrents of unrest and fear stepped Benito Mussolini (1883–1945). Mussolini began his political career as a Socialist Party leader and radical newspaper editor before World War I. Expelled from the Italian Socialist Party for supporting the war, and wounded on the Italian front in 1917, Mussolini returned home and began organizing bitter war veterans into a band of Fascists — Italian for "a union of forces."

At first Mussolini's program was a radical combination of nationalist and socialist demands. As such, it competed directly with the well-organized Socialist Party and failed to attract followers. When Mussolini realized his violent verbal assaults on rival Socialists won him growing support from conservatives and the frightened middle classes, he began to shift gears and to exalt nation over class. By 1921 he was ridiculing and dismissing the Marxist interpretation of history:

> We deny the existence of two classes, because there are many more than two classes. We deny that human history can be explained in terms of economics. We deny your internationalism. That is a luxury article, which only the elevated can practice, because peoples are passionately bound to their native soil.[15]

Mussolini and his private army of **Black Shirts** also turned to physical violence. Few people were killed, but Socialist newspapers, union halls, and local Socialist Party headquarters were destroyed, eventually pushing Socialists out of the city governments of northern Italy. A skillful politician, Mussolini convinced his followers they were opposing the "Reds," while also promoting a real revolution of the little people against the established interests.

Black Shirts A private army under Mussolini in Italy that destroyed Socialist newspapers, union halls, and local Socialist Party headquarters, eventually pushing Socialists out of the city governments of northern Italy.

Mussolini Leading a Parade in Rome Benito Mussolini was a master showman who drew on Rome's ancient heritage to promote Italian fascism. He wanted a grand avenue to stage triumphal marches with thousands of troops, so he had the Way of the Imperial Forums built through the old city. Here Mussolini rides at the head of a grand parade in 1932 to inaugurate the new road, passing the Roman Coliseum, one of the focal points along the route. (Stefano Bianchetti/Corbis via Getty Images)

With the government breaking down in 1922, Mussolini stepped forward as the savior of order and property. In October 1922 thirty thousand Fascists marched on Rome, threatening the king and demanding he appoint Mussolini prime minister. Victor Emmanuel III (r. 1900–1946), forced to choose between Fascists or Socialists, asked Mussolini to form a new cabinet. Thus, after widespread violence and a threat of armed uprising, Mussolini seized power "legally."

The Regime in Action

In 1924 Mussolini declared his desire to "make the nation Fascist"[16] and imposed a series of repressive measures. Press freedom was abolished, elections were fixed, and the government ruled by decree. Mussolini arrested his political opponents, disbanded all independent labor unions, and put dedicated Fascists in control of Italy's schools. He created a Fascist youth movement, Fascist labor unions, and many other Fascist organizations. He trumpeted his goal in a famous slogan of 1926: "Everything in the state, nothing outside the state, nothing against the state."[17] By year's end Italy was a one-party dictatorship under Mussolini's unquestioned leadership.

Mussolini was only primarily interested, however, in personal power. Rather than destroy the old power structure, he remained content to compromise with the conservative classes that controlled the army, the economy, and the state. He controlled labor but left big business to regulate itself, profitably and securely. There was no land reform.

Mussolini also drew increasing support from the Catholic Church. In the **Lateran Agreement** of 1929, he recognized the Vatican as a tiny independent state and agreed to give the church heavy financial support. The pope in return urged Italians to support Mussolini's government.

Like Stalin and Hitler, Mussolini favored a return of traditional roles for women. He abolished divorce and told women to stay at home and produce children. In 1938 women were limited by law to a maximum of 10 percent of the better-paying jobs in industry and government.

Mussolini's government passed no racial laws until 1938 and did not persecute Jews savagely until late in the Second World War, when Italy was under Nazi control. Nor did Mussolini establish a truly ruthless police state. Only twenty-three political prisoners were condemned to death between 1926 and 1944. Mussolini's Fascist Italy, though repressive and undemocratic, was never really totalitarian.

Lateran Agreement
A 1929 agreement in which Mussolini in Italy recognized the Vatican as an independent state and agreed to give the church heavy financial support in return for the pope's public support.

Hitler and Nazism in Germany

The most frightening dictatorship developed in Nazi Germany. Here Nazism asserted an unlimited claim over German society and proclaimed the ultimate power of its leader, Adolf Hitler. Nazism's aspirations were truly totalitarian.

The Roots of Nazism

Nazism grew out of many complex concepts, of which the most influential were extreme nationalism and racism. These ideas captured the mind of the young Adolf Hitler (1889–1945) and evolved into Nazism.

The son of an Austrian customs official, Hitler did poorly in high school and dropped out at age sixteen. He then headed to Vienna, where he was exposed to

Why were Hitler and his Nazi regime initially so popular, and how did their actions lead to World War II?

Nazism A movement born of extreme nationalism and racism and dominated by Adolf Hitler from 1933 until the end of World War II in 1945.

extreme Austro-German nationalists who believed Germans to be a superior people and central Europe's natural rulers. They advocated union with Germany and violent expulsion of "inferior" peoples from the Austro-Hungarian Empire.

From these extremists Hitler eagerly absorbed virulent anti-Semitism, racism, and hatred of Slavs. He developed an unshakable belief in the crudest distortions of Social Darwinism (see "Science for the Masses" in Chapter 24), the superiority of Germanic races, and the inevitability of racial conflict. The Jews, he claimed, directed an international conspiracy of finance capitalism and Marxist socialism against German culture, German unity, and the German race. Anti-Semitism and racism became Hitler's most passionate convictions.

Hitler greeted the Great War's outbreak as a salvation. The struggle and discipline of serving as a soldier in the war gave his life meaning, and when Germany suddenly surrendered in 1918, Hitler's world was shattered. Convinced that Jews and Marxists had "stabbed Germany in the back," he vowed to fight on.

In late 1919 Hitler joined a tiny extremist group in Munich called the German Workers' Party. By 1921 Hitler had gained absolute control of this small but growing party, now renamed the National Socialist German Worker's Party, or Nazi Party. A master of mass propaganda and political showmanship, Hitler worked his audiences into a frenzy with wild attacks on the Versailles treaty, the Jews, war profiteers, and Germany's Weimar Republic.

In late 1923 Germany under the Weimar Republic was experiencing unparalleled hyperinflation and seemed on the verge of collapse (see "Germany and the Western Powers" in Chapter 28). Hitler, inspired by Mussolini's recent victory, attempted an armed uprising in Munich. Despite the failure of the poorly organized plot and Hitler's arrest, Nazism had been born.

Hitler's Road to Power

At his trial Hitler violently denounced the Weimar Republic and attracted enormous publicity. During his brief prison term in 1924 he dictated *Mein Kampf* (*My Struggle*), in which he expounded on his basic ideas on race and anti-Semitism, the notion of territorial expansion based on "living space" for Germans, and the role of the leader-dictator, called the *Führer* (FYOOR-uhr).

The Nazis remained a small splinter group until the 1929 Great Depression shattered the economic prosperity and stability of the late 1920s. By the end of 1932, 32 percent or more of Germany's labor force was unemployed. Industrial production fell by one-half between 1929 and 1932. No factor contributed more to Hitler's success than this economic crisis.

Hitler rejected free-market capitalism and advocated government programs to promote recovery. He pitched his speeches to middle- and lower-middle-class groups and to skilled workers. As the economy collapsed, great numbers of these people "voted their pocketbooks"[18] and deserted the conservative and moderate parties for the Nazis. In the July 1932 election the Nazis won 14.5 million votes — 38 percent of the total — and became the largest party in the Reichstag.

Hitler and the Nazis appealed strongly to German youth; Hitler himself was only forty in 1929. In 1931 almost 40 percent of Nazi Party members were under thirty, compared with 20 percent of Social Democrats. "National Socialism is the organized will of the youth,"[19] proclaimed the official Nazi slogan. National recovery, exciting

Young People in Hitler's Germany This photo from 1930 shows Hitler admiring a young boy dressed in the uniform of Hitler's storm troopers, a paramilitary organization of the Nazi Party that supported Hitler's rise to power in the 1920s and early 1930s. Only a year after the founding of the storm troopers in 1921, Hitler began to organize Germany's young people into similar paramilitary groups in an effort to militarize all of German society. The young paramilitaries became the Hitler Youth, who eventually numbered in the millions. (Popperfoto/Getty Images)

and rapid change, and personal advancement made Nazism appealing to millions of German youths.

Hitler also came to power because of the breakdown of democratic government. Germany's economic collapse in the Great Depression convinced many voters that the country's republican leaders were incompetent and corrupt. Disunity on the left was another nail in the republic's coffin. The Communists refused to cooperate with the Social Democrats, even though the two parties together outnumbered the Nazis in the Reichstag.

Finally, Hitler excelled in backroom politics. In 1932 he succeeded in gaining support from key people in the army, big business, and politics, who thought they could manipulate and use him to their own advantage. Thus in January 1933 President Paul von Hindenburg (1847–1934) legally appointed Hitler, leader of Germany's largest party, as German chancellor.

The Nazi State and Society

Hitler quickly established an unshakable dictatorship. When the Reichstag building was partly destroyed by fire in February 1933, Hitler blamed the Communist Party. He convinced President von Hindenburg to sign dictatorial emergency acts that abolished freedom of speech and assembly and most personal liberties. He also called for new elections in an effort to solidify his political power.

When the Nazis won only 44 percent of the votes, Hitler outlawed the Communist Party and arrested its parliamentary representatives. Then on March 23, 1933, the Nazis forced through the Reichstag the so-called **Enabling Act**, which gave Hitler absolute dictatorial power for four years.

Enabling Act An act pushed through the Reichstag by the Nazis in 1933 that gave Hitler absolute dictatorial power for four years.

Hitler and the Nazis took over the government bureaucracy, installing many Nazis in top positions. Hitler next outlawed strikes and abolished independent labor unions, which were replaced by the Nazi Labor Front. Professional people—doctors and lawyers, teachers and engineers—also saw their independent organizations swallowed up in Nazi associations. Publishing houses and universities were put under Nazi control, and students and professors publicly burned forbidden books. Modern art and architecture were ruthlessly prohibited. Life became violently anti-intellectual. As the cynical Joseph Goebbels, later Nazi minister of propaganda, put it, "When I hear the word 'culture' I reach for my gun."[20] By 1934 a brutal dictatorship characterized by frightening dynamism and total obedience to Hitler was already largely in place.

In 1934 Hitler also ordered that all civil servants and members of the German armed forces swear a binding oath of "unquestioning obedience" to Adolf Hitler. The

SS—Hitler's elite personal guard—grew rapidly. Under Heinrich Himmler (1900–1945), the SS took over the political police (the Gestapo) and expanded its network of concentration camps.

From the beginning, German Jews were a special object of Nazi persecution. By late 1934 most Jewish lawyers, doctors, professors, civil servants, and musicians had been banned from their professions. In 1935 the infamous Nuremberg Laws classified as Jewish anyone having three or more Jewish grandparents and deprived Jews of all rights of citizenship. By 1938 roughly one-quarter of Germany's half million Jews had emigrated, sacrificing almost all their property in order to leave Germany.

In late 1938 the attack on the Jews accelerated and grew more violent. On November 9 and 10, 1938, the Nazis initiated a series of well-organized attacks against Jews throughout Nazi Germany and some parts of Austria. This infamous event is known as Kristallnacht (krees-TAHL-nahkht), or Night of Broken Glass, after the broken glass that littered the streets following the frenzied destruction of Jewish homes, shops, synagogues, and neighborhoods by German civilians and uniformed storm troopers. U.S. consul David Buffum reported of the Nazis in Leipzig:

> The most hideous phase of the so-called "spontaneous" action, has been the whole-sale arrest and transportation to concentration camps of male German Jews between the ages of sixteen and sixty. . . . Having demolished dwellings and hurled most of the effects to the streets, the insatiably sadistic perpetrators threw many of the trembling inmates into a small stream that flows through the Zoological Park, commanding horrified spectators to spit at them, defile them with mud and jeer at their plight.[21]

Many historians consider this night the beginning of Hitler's Final Solution against the Jews, and after this event it became very difficult for Jews to leave Germany.

Some Germans privately opposed these outrages, but most went along or looked the other way. Although this lack of response reflected the individual's helplessness in a totalitarian state, it also reflected the strong popular support Hitler's government enjoyed.

Hitler's Popularity

Hitler had promised the masses economic recovery—"work and bread"—and he delivered. The Nazi Party launched a large public works program to pull Germany out of the depression. In 1935 Germany turned decisively toward rearmament. Unemployment dropped steadily, and by 1938 the Nazis boasted of nearly full employment. For millions of Germans economic recovery was tangible evidence that Nazi promises were more than show and propaganda.

For ordinary German citizens, in contrast to those deemed "undesirable" (Jews, Slavs, Gypsies, Jehovah's Witnesses, Communists, and homosexuals), Hitler's government offered greater equality and more opportunities. In 1933 class barriers in Germany were generally high. Hitler's rule introduced changes that lowered these barriers. The new Nazi elite included many young and poorly educated dropouts, rootless lower-middle-class people like Hitler who rose to the top with breathtaking speed. More generally, however, the Nazis tolerated privilege and wealth only as long as they served party needs.

EVENTS LEADING TO WORLD WAR II

1919	Treaty of Versailles is signed
1921	Hitler heads National Socialist German Worker's Party (Nazis)
1922	Mussolini seizes power in Italy
1927	Stalin takes control of the Soviet Union
1929–1939	Great Depression
1931	Japan invades Manchuria
January 1933	Hitler is appointed chancellor of Germany
March 1933	Reichstag passes the Enabling Act, granting Hitler absolute dictatorial power
October 1933	Germany withdraws from the League of Nations
1935	Nuremberg Laws deprive Jews of all rights of citizenship
March 1935	Hitler announces German rearmament
October 1935	Mussolini invades Ethiopia and receives Hitler's support
March 1936	German armies move unopposed into the demilitarized Rhineland
1936–1939	Spanish Civil War
October 1936	Rome-Berlin Axis created
1937	Japan invades China
March 1938	Germany annexes Austria
September 1938	Munich Conference: Britain and France agree to German seizure of the Sudetenland from Czechoslovakia
March 1939	Germany occupies the rest of Czechoslovakia; appeasement ends in Britain
August 1939	Nazi-Soviet nonaggression pact is signed
September 1, 1939	Germany invades Poland
September 3, 1939	Britain and France declare war on Germany

Yet Hitler and the Nazis failed to bring about a real social revolution. The well-educated classes held on to most of their advantages, and only a modest social leveling occurred in the Nazi years. Significantly, the Nazis shared with the Italian Fascists the stereotypical view of women as housewives and mothers. Only when facing labor shortages during the war did they reluctantly mobilize large numbers of German women for office and factory work.[22]

Not all Germans supported Hitler, and a number of German groups actively resisted him after 1933. Tens of thousands of political enemies were imprisoned, and thousands were executed. In the first years of Hitler's rule, the principal resisters were trade-union Communists and Socialists. Catholic and Protestant churches produced a second group of opponents. Their efforts were directed primarily at preserving genuine religious life, however, not at overthrowing Hitler. Finally, in 1938 and again during the war, some high-ranking army officers, who feared the consequences of Hitler's reckless aggression, plotted, unsuccessfully, against him.

Aggression and Appeasement, 1933–1939

After Germany's economic recovery and Hitler's success in establishing Nazi control of society, Hitler turned to the next item on his agenda: aggressive territorial expansion. Germany's withdrawal from the League of Nations in October 1933 indicated its determination to rearm. When in March 1935 Hitler established a general military draft and declared the "unequal" Versailles treaty disarmament clauses null and void, leaders in Britain, France, and Italy issued a rather tepid joint protest and warned him against future aggressive actions.

But the emerging united front against Hitler quickly collapsed. Britain adopted a policy of appeasement, granting Hitler everything he could reasonably want (and more) in order to avoid war. British appeasement, which practically dictated French policy, had the support of many powerful British conservatives who, as in Germany, underestimated Hitler. The British people, still horrified by the memory, the costs, and the losses of the First World War, generally supported pacifism rather than war.

Some British leaders at the time, however, such as Winston Churchill, bitterly condemned appeasement as peace at any price. After the war, British appeasement came to be viewed as "the granting from fear or cowardice of unwarranted concessions in order to buy temporary peace at someone else's expense."[23] Beginning in the 1990s some historians have argued that British leaders had no real choice but to appease Hitler in the 1930s, because neither Great Britain nor France was prepared psychologically or militarily to fight another war.[24]

In March 1936 Hitler marched his armies without notice into the demilitarized Rhineland, violating the Treaties of Versailles and Locarno. France would not move without British support, and Britain refused to act. As Britain and France opted for appeasement, Hitler found powerful allies, particularly Mussolini, who in October 1935 had attacked the independent African kingdom of Ethiopia. Western powers had condemned the Italian aggression, but Hitler supported Italy energetically. In October 1936 Italy and Germany established the so-called Rome-Berlin Axis. Japan, which wanted support for its occupation of Manchuria, joined the Axis alliance in 1940 (see "Japan Against China" in Chapter 29).

➔ Italian campaigns, 1935–1936

Italy's Ethiopian Campaign, 1935–1936

At the same time, Germany and Italy intervened in the Spanish Civil War (1936–1939), where their support helped General Francisco Franco's Fascist movement defeat republican Spain. Republican Spain's only official aid in the fight against Franco came from the Soviet Union.

In late 1937 Hitler moved forward with his plans to crush Austria and Czechoslovakia as the first step in his long-contemplated drive to the east for living space. On March 12, 1938, German armies moved into Austria unopposed, and Austria became two provinces of Greater Germany (Map 30.1).

Simultaneously, Hitler demanded that the pro-Nazi, German-speaking territory of western Czechoslovakia — the Sudetenland — be turned over to Germany. Democratic Czechoslovakia was prepared to defend itself, but appeasement triumphed again. In September 1938 British prime minister Arthur Neville Chamberlain (1869–1940) and French negotiators met with Hitler in Munich and agreed with him that the Sudetenland should be ceded to Germany immediately. Returning to London from the Munich Conference, Chamberlain told cheering crowds that he had secured "peace with honour . . . peace for our time."[25] Sold out by the Western powers, Czechoslovakia gave in.

Hitler's armies occupied the remainder of Czechoslovakia, however, in March 1939. This time, there was no possible rationale of self-determination for Nazi aggression. When Hitler used the question of German minorities in Danzig as a pretext to confront Poland, Chamberlain declared that Britain and France would fight if Hitler attacked his eastern neighbor. Hitler did not take these warnings seriously and pressed on.

Through the 1930s Hitler had constantly referred to ethnic Slavs in the Soviet Union and other countries as *Untermenschen* (OON-ter-men-schen) (inferior people), and relations between the two countries had grown increasingly tense. War between Germany and the Soviet Union seemed inevitable, and, indeed, Stalin believed that Great Britain and France secretly hoped the Nazis and Bolsheviks would destroy each

Hitler Playing with All the Statesmen This satirical cartoon from 1938 shows Hitler playing with all the statesmen attending the Four Power (Italy, Germany, England, France) Peace Conference that year in Munich. The Munich Agreement that came out of this meeting permitted Germany to annex the Sudetenland in Czechoslovakia, although representatives of that country were not invited to the conference. British prime minister Neville Chamberlain is portrayed in the lower right corner, under Hitler's boot. (Kelen Collection/Snark Archives © Photo12/The Image Works)

MAP 30.1 The Growth of Nazi Germany, 1933–1939 Until March 1939 Hitler brought ethnic Germans into the Nazi state; then he turned on the Slavic peoples, whom he had always hated. He stripped Czechoslovakia of its independence and prepared for an attack on Poland in September 1939.

other. Then, in an about-face that stunned the world, sworn enemies Hitler and Stalin signed a nonaggression pact in August 1939. Each dictator promised to remain neutral if the other became involved in war. An attached secret protocol divided eastern Europe into German and Soviet zones "in the event of a political and territorial reorganization."[26] Stalin agreed to the pact for three reasons: he distrusted Western intentions, he needed more time to build up Soviet industry and military reserves, and Hitler offered territorial gain.

For Hitler, everything was now set. He told his generals on the day of the nonaggression pact, "My only fear is that at the last moment some dirty dog will come up with a mediation plan."[27] On September 1, 1939, the Germans attacked Poland from three sides. Two days later, Britain and France, finally true to their word, declared war on Germany. The Second World War in Europe had begun.

How did Germany and Japan build empires in Europe and Asia, and how did the Allies defeat them?

The Second World War, 1939–1945

World war broke out because Hitler's and Japan's ambitions were essentially unlimited. Nazi soldiers scored enormous successes in Europe until late 1942, establishing a vast empire of death and destruction. Japan attacked the United States in December 1941 and then moved to expand its empire throughout Asia and the Pacific Ocean. Eventually, the mighty Grand Alliance of Britain, the United States, and the Soviet Union overwhelmed the aggressors in manpower and military strength. Thus the Nazi and Japanese empires proved short-lived.

Hitler's Empire in Europe, 1939–1942

blitzkrieg "Lightning war" using planes, tanks, and trucks, first used by Hitler to crush Poland in four weeks.

Using planes, tanks, and trucks in the first example of a **blitzkrieg** (BLITZ-kreeg), or "lightning war," Hitler's armies crushed Poland in four weeks. The Soviet Union quickly took its share agreed to in the secret protocol—the eastern half of Poland and the Baltic states of Lithuania, Estonia, and Latvia. In spring 1940 the Nazi lightning war struck again. After occupying Denmark, Norway, and Holland, German motorized columns broke through southern Belgium and into France.

As Hitler's armies poured into France, aging marshal Henri-Philippe Pétain, a national hero of the Great War, formed a new French government—the so-called Vichy (VIH-shee) government—and accepted defeat. By July 1940 Hitler ruled practically all of western continental Europe; Italy was an ally, the Soviet Union a friendly neutral (Map 30.2). Only Britain, led by Winston Churchill (1874–1965), remained unconquered.

To prepare for an invasion of Britain, Germany first needed to gain control of the air. In the Battle of Britain, which began in July 1940, German planes attacked British airfields and key factories, dueling with British defenders high in the skies. In September Hitler began indiscriminately bombing British cities to break British morale. British aircraft factories increased production, and Londoners defiantly dug in. By September Britain was winning the air war, and Hitler abandoned his plans for an immediate German invasion of Britain.

Hitler now allowed his lifetime obsession of creating a vast eastern European empire for the "master race" to dictate policy. In June 1941 Germany broke the Nazi-Soviet nonaggression pact and attacked the Soviet Union. By October Leningrad was practically surrounded, Moscow was besieged, and most of Ukraine had been conquered. But the Soviets did not collapse, and when a severe winter struck German armies outfitted in summer uniforms, the invaders were stopped.

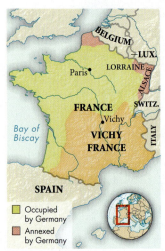

Vichy France, 1940

New Order Hitler's program, based on the guiding principle of racial imperialism, which gave preferential treatment to the Nordic peoples above "inferior" Latin peoples and, at the bottom, "subhuman" Slavs and Jews.

Although stalled in Russia, Hitler ruled an enormous European empire. He now began building a **New Order** based on the guiding principle of Nazi totalitarianism: racial imperialism. Within the New Order, the Dutch, Norwegians, Swedes, and Danes received preferential treatment, for the Germans believed they were racially related to the German "Aryan" master race. The French, an "inferior" Latin people, occupied the middle position. At the bottom of the New Order were the harshly treated "subhumans," Jews and Slavs.

Hitler envisioned a vast eastern colonial empire where enslaved Poles, Ukrainians, and Russians would die or be killed off while Germanic peasants would resettle the abandoned lands. Himmler and the elite SS corps implemented a program of destruction in the occupied territories to create a "mass settlement space" for Germans.

MAP 30.2 World War II in Europe and Africa, 1939–1945 The map shows the extent of Hitler's empire at its height, before the Battle of Stalingrad in late 1942 and the subsequent advances of the Allies until Germany surrendered on May 7, 1945.

The Holocaust

Finally, the Nazi state condemned all European Jews to extermination in the **Holocaust**. After Warsaw fell in 1939, the Nazis forced Jews in the occupied territories to move to urban ghettos, while German Jews were sent to occupied Poland. After Germany attacked Russia in June 1941, forced expulsion spiraled into extermination. In late 1941 Hitler and the Nazi leadership ordered the SS to speed up planning

Holocaust The attempted systematic extermination of all European Jews and other "undesirables" by the Nazi state during World War II.

953

Axis powers and their allies
Occupied by Germany and its allies
■ Extermination camp
● Major concentration camp
♦ Site of mass killing
✹ Ghetto

The Holocaust, 1941–1945

Prelude to Murder This photo captures the terrible inhumanity of Nazi racism. Frightened and bewildered families from the soon-to-be-destroyed Warsaw Ghetto are being forced out of their homes by German soldiers for deportation to concentration camps. There they faced murder in the gas chambers. (Keystone/Getty Images)

for "the final solution of the Jewish question."[28] Throughout the Nazi empire Jews were systematically arrested, packed like cattle onto freight trains, and dispatched to extermination camps.

Arriving at their destination, small numbers of Jews were sent to nearby slave labor camps, where they were starved and systematically worked to death. (See "Individuals in Society: Primo Levi," at right.) Most victims were taken to "shower rooms," which were actually gas chambers. By 1945 about 6 million Jews had been murdered.

Who was responsible for this terrible crime? After the war, historians laid the guilt on Hitler and the Nazi leadership, arguing that ordinary Germans had little knowledge of the extermination camps, or that those who cooperated had no alternative given the brutality of Nazi terror and totalitarian control. Beginning in the 1990s studies appeared revealing a much broader participation of German people in the Holocaust and popular indifference (or worse) to the Jews' fate.[29] In most occupied countries local non-German officials also cooperated in the arrest and deportation of Jews.

Japan's Asian Empire

By late 1938, 1.5 million Japanese troops were bogged down in China, holding a great swath of territory but unable to defeat the Nationalists and the Communists (see "Japan Against China" in Chapter 29). In 1939, as war broke out in Europe, the Japanese redoubled their ruthless efforts in China. Implementing a savage policy of "kill all, burn all, destroy all," Japanese troops committed shocking atrocities, including the so-called Rape of Nanjing. During Japan's war in China — the second Sino-Japanese War (1937–1945) — the Japanese are estimated to have killed 4 million Chinese people.

Primo Levi

Primo Levi, who never stopped thinking, writing, and speaking about the Holocaust.
(Bernard Gotfryd/Getty Images)

MOST JEWS DEPORTED TO AUSCHWITZ WERE murdered as soon as they arrived, but the Nazis made some prisoners into slave laborers, and a few of these survived. Primo Levi (1919–1987), an Italian Jew, became one of the most influential witnesses to the Holocaust and its death camps.

Like many in Italy's small Jewish community, Levi's family belonged to the urban professional classes. The young Primo Levi graduated in 1941 from the University of Turin with highest honors in chemistry. Since 1938, when Italy introduced racial laws, he had faced growing discrimination, and two years after graduation he joined the antifascist resistance movement. Quickly captured, he was deported to Auschwitz with 650 Italian Jews in February 1944. Stone-faced SS men picked only ninety-six men and twenty-nine women to work in their respective labor camps. Levi was one of them.

Nothing had prepared Levi for what he encountered. The Jewish prisoners were kicked, punched, stripped, branded with tattoos, crammed into huts, and worked unmercifully. Hoping for some sign of prisoner solidarity in this terrible environment, Levi found only a desperate struggle of each against all and enormous status differences among prisoners. Many stunned and bewildered newcomers, beaten and demoralized by their bosses—the most privileged prisoners—collapsed and died. Others struggled to secure their own privileges, however small, because food rations and working conditions were so abominable that ordinary Jewish prisoners perished in two to three months.

Sensitive and noncombative, Levi found himself sinking into oblivion. But instead of joining the mass of the "drowned," he became one of the "saved"—a complicated surprise with moral implications that he would ponder all his life. As Levi explained in *Survival in Auschwitz* (1947), the usual road to salvation in the camps was some kind of collaboration with German power.* Savage German criminals were released from prison to become brutal camp guards; non-Jewish political prisoners competed for jobs entitling them to better conditions; and, especially troubling for Levi, a small number of Jewish men plotted and struggled for the power of life and death over other Jewish prisoners. Though not one of these Jewish bosses, Levi believed that he himself, like almost all survivors, had entered the "gray zone" of moral compromise. Only a very few superior individuals, "the stuff of saints and martyrs,"

survived the death camps without shifting their moral stance.

For Levi, compromise and salvation came from his profession. Interviewed by a German technocrat for the camp's synthetic rubber program, Levi performed brilliantly in scientific German and savored his triumph as a Jew over Nazi racism. Work in the warm camp laboratory offered Levi opportunities to pilfer equipment that could then be traded to other prisoners for food and necessities. Levi also gained critical support from three saintly prisoners who refused to do wicked and hateful acts. And he counted "luck" as essential for his survival: in the camp infirmary with scarlet fever in February 1945 as advancing Russian armies prepared to liberate the camp, Levi was not evacuated by the Nazis and shot to death like most Jewish prisoners.

After the war Primo Levi was forever haunted by the nightmare that the Holocaust would be ignored or forgotten. Always ashamed that so many people whom he considered better than himself had perished, he wrote and lectured tirelessly to preserve the memory of Jewish victims and guilty Nazis. Wanting the world to understand the Jewish genocide in all its complexity so that never again would people tolerate such atrocities, he grappled tirelessly with his vision of individual choice and moral compromise in a hell designed to make the victims collaborate and persecute each other.

QUESTIONS FOR ANALYSIS

1. Describe Levi's experience at Auschwitz. How did camp prisoners treat each other? Why?
2. What does Levi mean by the "gray zone"? How is this concept central to his thinking?
3. Will a vivid historical memory of the Holocaust help prevent future genocide? Why or why not?

*Primo Levi, *Survival in Auschwitz: The Nazi Assault on Humanity*, rev. ed. 1958 (London: Collier Books, 1961), pp. 79–84, and *The Drowned and the Saved* (New York: Summit Books, 1988). These powerful testimonies are highly recommended.

Ultranationalist Pamphlet for Japanese Students

In August 1941, only four months before Japan's coordinated attacks on Pearl Harbor and colonial empires in Southeast Asia, Japan's Ministry of Education issued "The Way of Subjects." Required reading for high school and university students, this twenty-page pamphlet summed up the basic tenets of Japanese ultranationalism, which had become dominant in the 1930s.

As this selection suggests, ultranationalism in Japan combined a sense of mission with intense group solidarity and unquestioning devotion to a semidivine emperor. Thus Japanese expansion into Manchuria and the war in China were part of Japan's sacred calling to protect the throne and to free Asia from Western exploitation and misrule. Of course, an unknown percentage of students (and adults) did not believe that the myths of Japan's state religion were literally true. Nevertheless, they were profoundly influenced by extremist nationalism: Japanese soldiers' determination to fight to the death was a prime indicator of that influence.

■ The way of the subjects of the Emperor issues from the polity of the Emperor, and is to guard and maintain the Imperial Throne coexistent with the Heavens and the Earth. This is not the sphere of the abstract, but a way of daily practice based on history. The life and activities of the nation are all attuned to the task of giving great firmness to the foundation of the Empire. . . .

Modern history, in a nutshell, has been marked by the formation of unified nations in Europe and their contests for supremacy in the acquisition of colonies. Early in the modern period of history, the American continent was discovered and, stimulated by this,

Europeans vigorously found their way to India and China by sounding the furrows of the oceans. Their march into all parts of the world paved the way for their subsequent world domination politically, economically, and culturally and led them to act freely as they pleased, and to believe that they alone were justified in their outrageous behavior. . . .

The industrial development propelled by invention of machines demanded a considerably large amount of materials and the consequent overseas markets for the disposal of manufactured goods. The result was that a severe contest for colonial acquisition and trade competition ensued naturally and that wars of the strong preying on the weak were repeated. The history of wars waged among Spain, Portugal, Holland, Britain, France, and other countries in the modern age, and the rise and fall of their influence, have close connections with their overseas aggression. . . .

The self-destruction in the shape of the World War finally followed. It was only natural that cries were raised even among men of those countries after the war that the Occidental [Western] civilization was crumbling. A vigorous movement was started by Britain, France, and the United States to maintain the status quo by all means. Simultaneously, a movement aiming at social revolution through class conflict on the basis of thoroughgoing materialism like communism also was developed with unremitting vigor. On the other hand, Nazism and Fascism arose with great force. The basic theories of these new racial principles and the totalitarianism in Germany and Italy are to remove and improve the evils of individualism and liberalism.

That these [totalitarian] principles show great concern for Oriental [Eastern] culture and spirit is a noteworthy fact that suggests the future of the Occidental civilization and the creation of a new culture. Thus the orientation of world history has made the collapse of the world of the old order an assured conclusion.

In August 1940 the Japanese announced the formation of a self-sufficient Asian economic zone. Although they spoke of liberating Asia from Western imperialism and of "Asia for the Asians," their true intentions were to eventually rule over a vast Japanese empire. Ultranationalists moved to convince Japan's youth that Japan had a sacred liberating mission in Asia. (See "Analyzing the Evidence: Ultranationalist Pamphlet for Japanese Students," above.)

Japan has hereby opened the start for the construction of a new world order based on moral principles.

The Manchurian Affair was a violent outburst of Japanese national life long suppressed. Taking advantage of this, Japan in the glare of all the Powers stepped out for the creation of a world based on moral principles and the construction of a new order. This was a manifestation of the spirit, profound and lofty, embodied in the Empire-founding, and an unavoidable action for its national life and world mission. . . .

Japan has a political mission to help various regions in the Greater East Asia Co-prosperity Sphere [the Japanese term for Japan's Asian empire], which are reduced to a state of quasi colony by Europe and America, so as to rescue them from their control. Economically, this country will have to eradicate the evils of their exploitation and then set up an economic structure for coexistence and co-prosperity. Culturally, Japan must strive to fashion East Asiatic nations to change their following of European and American culture and to develop Oriental culture for the purpose of contributing to the creation of a right world. The Orient has been left to destruction for the past several hundred years. Its rehabilitation is not an easy task. It is natural that unusual difficulties attend the establishment of a new order and the creation of a new culture. The conquest of these difficulties alone will do much to help in establishing a morally controlled world, in which all nations can cooperate and all people can secure their proper position. . . .

Japan, since the founding of the Empire, has been basking under a benign rule of a line of Emperors unbroken for ages eternal, and has been growing and developing in an atmosphere of great harmony as a nation, consisting of one large family. However diverse the Empire's structures in politics, economy, culture, military affairs, and others may be, all finally are unified under the Emperor, the center. The country has lived under the Imperial rule and glory.

The ideals of Japan are to manifest to the entire world the spirit of her Empire-founding represented by the principle that "the benevolent rule of the Emperor may be extended so as to embrace the whole world." There is virtually no country in the world other than Japan having such a superb and lofty mission bearing world significance. So it can be said that the construction of a new structure and a defense state is all in order that Japan may revive her proper national structure and come back to her original status of national strength and leaving no stone unturned in displaying her total power to the fullest extent. . . .

The Imperial Family is the fountain source of the Japanese nation, and national and private lives issue from this. . . .

The way of the subjects is to be loyal to the Emperor in disregard of self, thereby supporting the Imperial Throne coexistence with the Heaven and with the Earth. . . .

The great duty of the Japanese people to guard and maintain the Imperial Throne has lasted to the present since the Empire founding and will last forever and ever. To serve the Emperor is its key point. Our lives will become sincere and true when they are offered to the Emperor and the state. Our own private life is fulfillment of the way of the subjects; in other words, it is not private, but public, insofar as it is held by the subjects supporting the Throne.

QUESTIONS FOR ANALYSIS

1. How does "The Way of Subjects" interpret modern history? In what ways do Western thought and action threaten Japan?
2. What is Japan's mission in Asia?
3. What is the basis of Japanese sovereignty? What is the individual's proper role in society?

Source: "The Way of Subjects," in *Japan Times Advertiser*, August 1941. Reprinted in David J. Lu, *Japan: A Documentary History* (Armonk: N.Y.: M. E. Sharpe, 1997), pp. 435–440.

For the moment, however, Japan needed allies. In September 1940 Japan signed a formal alliance (the Axis alliance) with Germany and Italy, and Vichy France granted the Japanese dominion over northern French Indochina. The United States, upset with Japan's occupation of Indochina and fearing embattled Britain would collapse if it lost its Asian colonies, froze scrap iron sales to Japan and applied further economic sanctions in October.

As 1941 opened, Japan's leaders faced a critical decision. At the time, the United States was the world's largest oil producer and supplied over 90 percent of Japan's oil needs. Japan had only a year and a half's worth of military and economic oil reserves, which the war in China and the Japanese military and merchant navies were quickly drawing down. The Netherlands' colonial possessions in Indonesia (Netherlands East Indies) could supply all of Japan's oil, rubber, and tin needs, but the Japanese feared an attack there would bring American reprisal. On July 26, 1941, President Roosevelt embargoed all oil exports to Japan and froze its assets in the United States. Japan now had to either recall its forces from China or go to war before running out of oil. It chose war.

On December 7, 1941, Japan launched a surprise attack on the U.S. fleet in Pearl Harbor in the Hawaiian Islands. Japan hoped to cripple its Pacific rival, gain time to build a defensible Asian empire, and eventually win an ill-defined compromise peace.

The Japanese attack was a limited success. The Japanese sank or crippled every American battleship, but by chance all the American aircraft carriers were at sea and escaped unharmed. Hours later the Japanese destroyed half of the American Far East Air Force stationed at Clark Air Base in the Philippines. Americans were humiliated by these unexpected defeats, which soon overwhelmed American isolationism and brought the United States into the war.

Hitler immediately declared war on the United States. Simultaneously, Japanese armies successfully attacked European and American colonies in Southeast Asia. Small but well-trained Japanese armies defeated larger Dutch and British armies to seize the Netherlands East Indies and the British colonies of Hong Kong, Malaya, and Singapore. After American forces surrendered the Philippines in May 1942, Japan held a vast empire in Southeast Asia and the western Pacific (Map 30.3).

The Japanese claimed they were freeing Asians from Western imperialism, and they called their empire the Greater East Asian Co-Prosperity Sphere. Most local populations were glad to see the Western powers go, but Asian faith in "co-prosperity" and support for Japan steadily declined as the war progressed. Although the Japanese set up anticolonial governments and promised genuine independence, real power always rested with Japanese military commanders and their superiors in Tokyo. Moreover, the Japanese never treated local populations as equals, and the occupiers exploited local peoples for Japan's wartime needs.

The Japanese often exhibited great cruelty toward prisoners of war and civilians. Dutch, Indonesian, and perhaps as many as two hundred thousand Korean women were forced to provide sex for Japanese soldiers as "comfort women." Recurring cruel behavior aroused local populations against the invaders.

The Grand Alliance

While the Nazis and the Japanese built their empires, Great Britain (the greatest colonial power), the United States (the greatest capitalist power), and the Soviet Union (the greatest Communist power) joined together in an unlikely military pact called the Grand Alliance. The vagaries of war, rather than choice, brought them together. Stalin had been cooperating with Hitler before Germany attacked Russia in June 1941, and the United States entered the war only after the Japanese attack on Pearl Harbor in December.

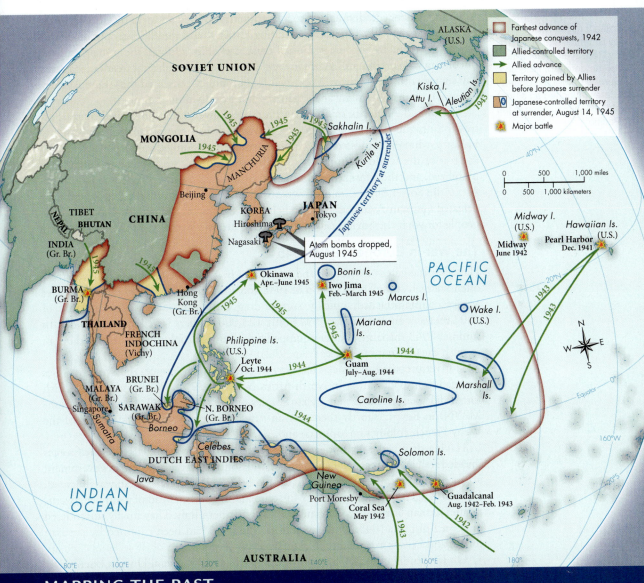

MAPPING THE PAST

MAP 30.3 World War II in the Pacific In 1942 Japanese forces overran an enormous amount of territory, which the Allies slowly recaptured in a long, bitter struggle.

ANALYZING THE MAP Locate the extent of the Japanese empire in 1942, and compare it to the Japanese-controlled territory at surrender in 1945. Where was the fighting in the Pacific concentrated?

CONNECTIONS How was the course of the war's end in Europe different from that of Asia, and what does this suggest about the difficulties that the Allies faced in fighting the Japanese?

Europe first policy The military strategy, set forth by Churchill and adopted by Roosevelt, that called for the defeat of Hitler in Europe before the United States launched an all-out strike against Japan in the Pacific.

Grand Alliance leaders agreed to a **Europe first policy** set forth by Churchill and adopted by Roosevelt. Only after defeating Hitler would the Allies mount an all-out attack on Japan. To encourage mutual trust, the Allies adopted the principle of the unconditional surrender of Germany and Japan, and no unilateral treaties (as Russia had signed with Germany in World War I). This policy cemented the Grand Alliance because it denied Germany and Japan any hope of dividing their foes.

The Grand Alliance's military resources were awesome. The United States possessed a unique capacity to wage global war with its large population and mighty industry, which it harnessed in 1943 to outproduce not only the Axis powers but also the rest of the world combined.[30] The British economy was totally and effectively mobilized, and the country became an important staging area for the war in Europe. As for the Soviet Union, so great was its economic strength that it might well have defeated Germany without Western help. Stalin drew on the massive support of the people for what the Soviets called the "Great Patriotic War of the Fatherland."

The War in Europe, 1942–1945

Halted at the gates of Moscow and Leningrad in 1941, the Germans renewed their offensive against the Soviet Union in 1942 and attacked Stalingrad in July. The Soviet armies counterattacked, quickly surrounding the entire German Sixth Army of 300,000 men. By late January 1943 only 123,000 soldiers were left to surrender. In summer 1943 the larger, better-equipped Soviet armies took the offensive and began to push the Germans back (see Map 30.2).

Not yet prepared to attack Germany directly through France, the Western Allies engaged in heavy fighting in North Africa (see Map 30.2). In autumn 1942 British forces defeated German and Italian armies at the Battle of El Alamein (el a-luh-MAYN) in Egypt. Shortly thereafter an Anglo-American force took control of the Vichy French colonies of Morocco and Algeria.

Having driven the Axis powers from North Africa by spring 1943, Allied forces invaded Italy. War-weary Italians deposed Mussolini, and the new Italian government accepted unconditional surrender in September 1943. Italy, it seemed, was liberated. But German commandos rescued Mussolini and made him head of a puppet government. German armies seized Rome and all of northern Italy. They finally surrendered only on April 29, 1945. Two days earlier Mussolini had been captured by partisan forces, and he was executed the next day.

On June 6, 1944, American and British forces under General Dwight Eisenhower landed on the beaches of Normandy, France, in history's greatest naval invasion. More than 2 million men and almost 0.5 million vehicles pushed inland and broke through the German lines.

In early February 1945 a sick and feeble Franklin Roosevelt met with Stalin and Churchill at Yalta in the Russian Crimea to negotiate plans for the remainder of the war in Europe, Russia's participation in the war in Asia, and the postwar world. Roosevelt was later severely criticized by some for supposedly "handing over" eastern Europe and northeast Asia (North Korea in particular) to the Soviet Union. Other scholars have noted, however, that Stalin made substantial concessions as well.

In March 1945 American troops crossed the Rhine and entered Germany. The Soviets had been advancing steadily since July 1943, and on April 26, 1945, the Red Army met American forces on the Elbe River in Germany. As Soviet forces fought

Roosevelt, Churchill, and Stalin at Yalta
In February 1945, three months before his death, President Roosevelt met with the other two leaders of the Grand Alliance, Churchill and Stalin, at the Crimean resort town of Yalta. With victory against Germany clearly in sight, they met to discuss the reconstruction of war-torn Europe, the treatment and occupation of Germany and eastern Europe after the war, and the Soviet Union's entry into the war in the Pacific. Although Stalin made some important concessions, many historians argue that Roosevelt was already too ill to join Churchill in demanding stronger guarantees from Stalin regarding self-determination for eastern Europe. (Franklin D. Roosevelt Presidential Library and Museum/ National Archives and Records Administration/U.S. National Archives/ photo CT53-70:5)

their way into Berlin, Hitler committed suicide in his bunker on April 30. On May 7 the remaining German commanders capitulated.

The War in the Pacific, 1942–1945

While gigantic armies clashed on land in Europe, the greatest naval battles in history decided the fate of the war in Asia. In April 1942 the Japanese devised a plan to take Port Moresby in New Guinea and also destroy U.S. aircraft carriers in an attack on Midway Island (see Map 30.3). Having broken the secret Japanese code, the Americans skillfully won a series of decisive naval victories. First, in the Battle of the Coral Sea in May 1942, an American carrier force halted the Japanese advance on Port Moresby. Then, in the Battle of Midway in June 1942, American pilots sank all four of the attacking Japanese aircraft carriers and established overall naval equality with Japan in the Pacific.

The United States gradually won control of the sea and air as it geared up its war industry. By 1943 the United States was producing one hundred thousand aircraft a year, almost twice as many as Japan produced in the entire war. In July 1943 the Americans and their Australian allies opened an "island-hopping" campaign toward Japan. By 1944 hundreds of American submarines were hunting in "wolf packs," decimating shipping and destroying economic links in Japan's far-flung, overextended empire.

The Pacific war was brutal—a "war without mercy"—and atrocities were committed on both sides.[31] Aware of Japanese atrocities in China and the Philippines, the U.S. forces seldom took Japanese prisoners after the Battle of Guadalcanal in August 1942, killing even those rare Japanese soldiers who offered to surrender. American forces moving across the central and western Pacific in 1943 and 1944 faced unyielding resistance, and this resistance hardened soldiers as American casualties kept rising. A product of spiraling violence, mutual hatred, and dehumanizing

A Hiroshima Survivor Remembers Yasuko Yamagata was seventeen when she saw the brilliant blue-white "lightning flash" that became a fiery orange ball consuming everything that would burn. Thirty years later Yamagata painted this scene, her most unforgettable memory of the atomic attack. An incinerated woman, poised as if running with her baby clutched to her breast, lies near a water tank piled high with charred corpses. (GE15-05 drawn by Yasuko Yamagata, Hiroshima Peace Memorial Museum)

racial stereotypes, the war without mercy intensified as it moved toward Japan.

In June 1944 U.S. bombers began a relentless bombing campaign of the Japanese home islands. In October 1944 American forces under General Douglas MacArthur landed on Leyte Island in the Philippines. In the ensuing Battle of Leyte Gulf, the Japanese lost 13 large warships, including 4 aircraft carriers, while the Americans lost only 3 small ships. The Japanese navy was practically finished.

In spite of massive defeats, Japanese troops continued to fight on. Indeed, the bloodiest battles of the Pacific war took place on Iwo Jima in February 1945 and on Okinawa in June 1945. American commanders believed that an invasion of Japan might cost 1 million American casualties and possibly 10 to 20 million Japanese lives. In fact, Japan was almost helpless, its industry and cities largely destroyed by intense American bombing. As the war in Europe ended in April 1945, Japanese leaders were divided. Hardliners argued that surrender was unthinkable; Japan had never been invaded or lost a war. A peace faction sought a negotiated end to the war.

On July 26 Truman, Churchill, and Stalin issued the Potsdam Declaration, which demanded unconditional surrender. The declaration left unclear whether the Japanese emperor would be treated as a war criminal. The Japanese, who considered Emperor Hirohito a god, sought clarification and amnesty for him. The Allies remained adamant that the surrender be unconditional. The Japanese felt compelled to fight on.

On August 6 and 9, 1945, the United States dropped atomic bombs on Hiroshima and Nagasaki in Japan. Also on August 9, Soviet troops launched an invasion of the Japanese puppet state of Manchukuo (Manchuria, China). To avoid a Soviet invasion and further atomic bombing, the Japanese announced their surrender on August 14, 1945. The Second World War, which had claimed the lives of more than 50 million soldiers and civilians, was over.

Chapter Summary

The 1929 American stock market crash triggered a global Great Depression. Western democracies expanded their powers and responded with relief programs. Authoritarian and Fascist regimes arose to replace some capitalist democracies. Only World War II ended the depression.

The radical totalitarian dictatorships of the 1920s and 1930s were repressive, profoundly antiliberal, and exceedingly violent. Mussolini set up the first Fascist government, a one-party dictatorship, but it was never truly a totalitarian state on the order of Hitler's Germany or Stalin's Soviet Union. In the Soviet Union Stalin launched a socialist "revolution from above" to modernize and industrialize the U.S.S.R. Mass purges of the Communist Party in the 1930s led to the imprisonment and deaths of millions.

Hitler and the Nazi elite rallied support by recalling the humiliation of World War I and the terms of the Versailles treaty, condemning Germany's leaders, building on racist prejudices against "inferior" peoples, and warning of a vast Jewish conspiracy to harm Germany and the German race. The Great Depression caused German voters to turn to Hitler for relief. After he declared the Versailles treaty disarmament clause null and void, British and French leaders tried appeasement. On September 1, 1939, his unprovoked attack on Poland forced the Allies to declare war, starting World War II.

Nazi armies first seized Poland and Germany's western neighbors and then turned east. Here Hitler planned to build a New Order based on racial imperialism. In the Holocaust that followed, millions of Jews and other "undesirables" were systematically exterminated. In Asia the Japanese created the Greater East Asian Co-Prosperity Sphere. This was a sham, as "Asia for the Asians" meant nothing but Japanese domination and control. After Japan attacked Pearl Harbor, the United States entered the war. In 1945 the Grand Alliance of the United States, Britain, and the Soviet Union defeated, outproduced, and outmanned Germany and Japan.

NOTES

1. Quoted in S. B. Clough et al., eds., *Economic History of Europe: Twentieth Century* (New York: Harper & Row, 1968), pp. 243–245.
2. E. Halévy, *The Era of Tyrannies* (Garden City, N.Y.: Doubleday, 1965), pp. 265–316, esp. p. 300.
3. Carl J. Friedrich and Zbigniew K. Brzezinski, *Totalitarian Dictatorship and Autocracy*, 2d ed. (Cambridge, Mass.: Harvard University Press, 1965), pp. 21–23.
4. I. Kershaw, *The Nazi Dictatorship: Problems and Perspectives of Interpretation*, 2d ed. (London: Edward Arnold, 1989), p. 34.
5. See Robert C. Tucker, *Stalin in Power: The Revolution from Above, 1928–1941* (New York: W. W. Norton, 1992).
6. Lewis Siegelbaum and Andrei Sokolov, *Stalinism as a Way of Life: A Narrative in Documents* (New Haven, Conn.: Yale University Press, 2000), pp. 38–39.
7. Joseph Stalin, "Speech to First All-Congress Conference of Managers of Socialist Industry, February 4, 1931," in Joseph Stalin, *Leninism* (London: George Allen & Unwin, 1940), pp. 365–366.
8. Robert Service, *Stalin: A Biography* (Cambridge, Mass.: Harvard University Press, 2005), p. 266.
9. Quoted in I. Deutscher, *Stalin: A Political Biography*, 2d ed. (New York: Oxford University Press, 1967), p. 325, fn. 1.
10. Steven Rosefielde, *Red Holocaust* (New York: Routledge, 2010), p. 259, fn. 12.
11. Malcolm Muggeridge, *Chronicles of Wasted Time. Chronicle 1: The Green Stick* (New York: William Morrow, 1973), pp. 234–235.
12. M. Malia, *The Soviet Tragedy: A History of Socialism in Russia, 1917–1991* (New York: Free Press, 1995), pp. 227–270; see also the controversial work by historian John Archibald Getty, *Origins of the Great Purges: The Soviet Communist Party Reconsidered, 1933–1938* (New York: Cambridge University Press, 1985).
13. Oleg V. Khlevniuk, *Master of the House: Stalin and His Inner Circle* (New Haven, Conn.: Yale University Press, 2009), p. xix.
14. R. Vivarelli, "Interpretations on the Origins of Fascism," *Journal of Modern History* 63 (March 1991): 41.
15. Ion Smeaton Munro, *Through Fascism to World Power: A History of the Revolution in Italy* (London: Alexander Maclehose, 1933), p. 120.

16. Christopher Seton-Watson, *Italy from Liberalism to Fascism, 1870–1925* (London: Methuen, 1967), p. 661.

17. Ibid.

18. W. Brustein, *The Logic of Evil: The Social Origins of the Nazi Party, 1925–1933* (New Haven, Conn.: Yale University Press, 1996), pp. 52, 182.

19. Karl Dietrich Bracher, *The German Dictatorship: The Origins, Structure, and Effects of National Socialism*, trans. Jean Steinberg (New York: Praeger, 1970), p. 146.

20. Quoted in R. Stromberg, *An Intellectual History of Modern Europe* (New York: Appleton-Century-Crofts, 1966), p. 393.

21. Quoted in R. Moeller, *The Nazi State and German Society: A Brief History with Documents* (Boston: Bedford/St. Martin's, 2010), p. 108.

22. See Claudia Koonz, *Mothers in the Fatherland: Women, the Family, and Nazi Politics* (New York: St. Martin's Press, 1987).

23. D. N. Dilks, "Appeasement Revisited," *University of Leeds Review* 15 (1972): 28–56.

24. See Frank McDonough, *Neville Chamberlain, Appeasement, and the British Road to War* (Manchester: Manchester University Press, 1998).

25. Winston Churchill, *The Second World War: The Gathering Storm* (Boston: Houghton Mifflin, 1948), p. 318.

26. Izidors Vizulis, *The Molotov-Ribbentrop Pact of 1939: The Baltic Case* (New York: Praeger, 1990), p. 16.

27. Anthony Read, *The Devil's Disciples: Hitler's Inner Circle* (New York: W. W. Norton, 2004), pp. 571–572.

28. Jeremy Noakes and Geoffrey Pridham, eds., "Message from Hermann Göring to Reinhard Heydrich, 31 July, 1941," in *Documents on Nazism, 1919–1945* (New York: Viking Press, 1974), p. 486.

29. See, for example, Christopher Browning, *Ordinary Men: Reserve Police Battalion 101 and the Final Solution in Poland* (New York: HarperCollins, 1992); Robert Gellately, *Backing Hitler: Consent and Coercion in Nazi Germany* (Oxford: Oxford University Press, 2001); Ian Kershaw, *Hitler, the Germans, and the Final Solution* (New Haven, Conn.: Yale University Press, 2008).

30. H. Willmott, *The Great Crusade: A New Complete History of the Second World War* (New York: Free Press, 1989), p. 255.

31. J. Dower, *War Without Mercy: Race and Power in the Pacific War* (New York: Pantheon, 1986).

CONNECTIONS

If anyone still doubted the interconnectedness of all the world's inhabitants following the Great War, those doubts faded as events on a truly global scale touched everyone as never before. First a Great Depression shook the financial foundations of the wealthiest capitalist economies and the poorest producers of raw materials and minerals. Another world war followed, bringing global death and destruction. At war's end, as we shall see in Chapter 31, the world's leaders revived Woodrow Wilson's idea of a League of Nations and formed the United Nations in 1946 to prevent such tragedies from ever reoccurring.

Although the United Nations was an attempt to bring nations together, the postwar world became more divided than ever. Chapter 31 will describe how two new superpowers — the United States and the Soviet Union — emerged from World War II to engage one another in the Cold War for nearly the rest of the century. Then in Chapters 32 and 33 we will see how less developed nations in Asia, Africa, and Latin America emerged after the war. Many of them did so by turning the nineteenth-century European ideology of nationalism against its creators, breaking the bonds of colonialism.

CHAPTER 30   ## Review and Explore

Identify Key Terms

Identify and explain the significance of each item below.

New Deal (p. 932)

Popular Front (p. 933)

totalitarianism (p. 936)

fascism (p. 937)

five-year plan (p. 938)

New Economic Policy (NEP) (p. 938)

collectivization (p. 939)

Black Shirts (p. 943)

Lateran Agreement (p. 944)

Nazism (p. 944)

Enabling Act (p. 946)

blitzkrieg (p. 952)

New Order (p. 952)

Holocaust (p. 953)

Europe first policy (p. 960)

Review the Main Ideas

Answer the focus questions from each section of the chapter.

1. What caused the Great Depression, and what were its consequences? (p. 930)

2. What was the nature of the new totalitarian dictatorships, and how did they differ from conservative authoritarian states and from each other? (p. 934)

3. How did Stalin and the Communist Party build a totalitarian order in the Soviet Union? (p. 938)

4. How did Italian fascism develop? (p. 942)

5. Why were Hitler and his Nazi regime initially so popular, and how did their actions lead to World War II? (p. 944)

6. How did Germany and Japan build empires in Europe and Asia, and how did the Allies defeat them? (p. 952)

Make Comparisons and Connections

Analyze the larger developments and continuities within and across chapters.

1. Compare the effects of the Great Depression on the peoples and economies of Europe, Latin America, and East Asia. How did governments in these regions and their citizens respond to this economic cataclysm?

2. Which ideologies of change from nineteenth-century Europe (Chapter 24) contributed to the outbreak of World War II? What new ideologies arose at this time that led the world to war?

3. Is it possible to compare the death and destruction of the Great War with that of World War II? Why or why not? Did the horrors of total war in World War I somehow make the greater scale of mass killing and devastation more acceptable in World War II? Explain.

TIMELINE

GLOBAL

1929–1939 Great Depression

EUROPE

◆ **1922** Mussolini seizes power in Italy

1924–1929 Buildup of Nazi Party in Germany

◆ **1927** Stalin is de facto ruler
of the Soviet Union

◆ **1929** Start of collectivization
in Soviet Union

MIDDLE EAST

ASIA

1931 ◆
Japan invades Manchuria

AMERICAS

1925

1930

Suggested Resources

BOOKS

Brendon, Piers. *The Dark Valley: A Panorama of the 1930s*. 2002. Masterful, sweeping account of this tumultuous decade.

Brooker, Paul. *Twentieth-Century Dictatorships: The Ideological One-Party State*. 1995. A comparative analysis.

Crowe, David M. *The Holocaust: Roots, History, and Aftermath*. 2008. Analyzes the origins and ghastly implementation of Nazi racial politics.

Geyer, Michael, and Sheila Fitzpatrick. *Beyond Totalitarianism: Stalinism and Nazism Compared*. 2009. Comparative studies of the two dictatorships based on archival sources that have only recently become available to historians.

Gilbert, Martin. *The Second World War: A Complete History*, rev. ed. 2004. Massively detailed global survey.

Glantz, David M., and Jonathan M. House. *When Titans Clashed: How the Red Army Stopped Hitler*, rev. ed. 2015. Authoritative account of the eastern front in World War II.

Hasegawa, Tsuyoshi. *Racing the Enemy: Stalin, Truman, and the Surrender of Japan*. 2005. Masterful diplomatic history with a controversial new account of the end of the war.

Kindleberger, Charles P. *The World in Depression, 1929–1939*, 40th anniversary ed. 2013. Perhaps the best analytical account of the global origins, events, and aftermath of the Great Depression.

Parker, Selwyn. *The Great Crash: How the Stock Market Crash of 1929 Plunged the World into Depression*. 2008. A lively and readable account of the global consequences of the Great Depression.

Spector, Ronald H. *Eagle Against the Sun: The American War with Japan*. 1985. Although this book focuses primarily on the war from the Japanese and American perspectives, many consider it the best single-volume history of the war in the Pacific.

Weinberg, Gerhard. *A World at Arms: A Global History of World War II*, 2d ed. 2005. Global survey with a political-diplomatic emphasis.

Wright, Gordon. *The Ordeal of Total War*, rev. ed. 1997. Explores the scientific, psychological, and economic dimensions of the war.

DOCUMENTARIES

Triumph of the Will (Leni Riefenstahl, 1935). The classic documentary/propaganda film directed by Hitler's cinema propagandist Leni Riefenstahl. It celebrates the birth of the thousand-year Reich through its portrayal of the 1934 Nuremberg Nazi rally.

The World at War (Thames Television, 1973–1974). Often called the definitive documentary on World War II, this twenty-six-episode chronicle of the war was produced in Britain and is narrated by Laurence Olivier.

FEATURE FILMS

Letters from Iwo Jima (Clint Eastwood, 2006). A joint Japanese-American production that tells the story of the Battle of Iwo Jima from the Japanese soldiers' perspective. Directed by American film director Clint Eastwood, the movie is in Japanese (with English subtitles) and has an all-Japanese cast. A companion film, *Flags of Our Fathers*, portrays the same battle from the American perspective.

Saving Private Ryan (Steven Spielberg, 1998). Generally recognized as one of the best war films of all time, this movie about the invasion of Normany is noted for its realistic portrayal of war, particularly the Allied assault on Omaha Beach on June 6, 1944.

Schindler's List (Steven Spielberg, 1993). Based on the true story of Oskar Schindler, a German businessman who rescued more than a thousand mainly Polish-Jewish refugees during the Holocaust.

WEBSITES

Spartacus Educational: The Second World War. One of the websites of the Spartacus Educational project, this site contains a large collection of entries about all aspects of World War II. **spartacus-educational.com/2WW.htm**

The World at War, History of WW 1939–1945. This well-organized and comprehensive website covers all aspects of World War II, includes a discussion forum and message board, and allows users to search the site by keyword. **www.euronet.nl/users/wilfried/ww2/ww2.htm**

31

Decolonization, Revolution, and the Cold War
1945–1968

After the Second World War, the world faced deep and swift currents of change that swept from the decolonization of Asia and Africa to social revolutions such as those in China and Cuba. These transformations were the outcome of movements that began well before the Second World War and were accelerated by the war's upheaval. The transformations took place in the international context of the Cold War, a rivalry between the United States and the Soviet Union.

As people in Asia and Africa pushed back against centuries of Western expansion and demanded national self-determination and racial equality, new nations emerged and nearly every colonial territory gained formal independence between 1945 and the early 1960s. A revolution in China consolidated Communist rule and initially followed the Soviet model, but then veered in new directions. Rather than form an allied Communist front, China and the Soviet Union became economic and political rivals.

The Cold War that emerged between the U.S. and U.S.S.R. following the world war did not involve armed conflict between the two nations. But it became a global experience in which each country backed rival factions in conflicts around the world. The Cold War also imposed a division between western European countries allied to the United States, and eastern European nations that the Soviet Union brought into its zone of influence.

China Charts a New Revolutionary Path

A member of the Red Guards, part of the mass mobilization known as the Proletarian Cultural Revolution, which was directed by Chinese leader Mao Zedong between 1966 and 1976.

Pictures from History/Bridgeman Images

CHAPTER PREVIEW

THE WORLD REMADE   How did the Cold War and decolonization shape the postwar world?

NATIONALISM IN SOUTH ASIA AND THE MIDDLE EAST
How did religion and the legacies of colonialism affect the formation of new nations in South Asia and the Middle East after World War II?

REVOLUTION AND RESURGENCE IN EAST AND SOUTHEAST ASIA
How did the Cold War shape reconstruction, revolution, and decolonization in East and Southeast Asia?

DECOLONIZATION IN AFRICA   What factors influenced decolonization in Africa after World War II?

POPULIST AND REVOLUTIONARY PATHWAYS IN LATIN AMERICA
Why did populism emerge as such a powerful political force in Latin America?

THE LIMITS OF POSTWAR PROSPERITY
Why did the world face growing social unrest in the 1960s?

How did the Cold War and decolonization shape the postwar world?

Cold War The post–World War II conflict between the United States and the Soviet Union.

The World Remade

The rivalry between the United States and the Soviet Union divided postwar Europe and became a long, tense standoff, the **Cold War**. As the Cold War took shape, three events separated by barely two years foreshadowed the changes that would take place in the world following the Second World War: the independence of India and Pakistan in 1947; the establishment of the state of Israel in 1948; and the Communist revolution in China in 1949. All had their roots in the decades preceding the Second World War—and even predating the First World War. Yet each was shaped by the war and its outcomes.

The Cold War

The Cold War originated in disputes over the political outcome of the war. Soviet leader Joseph Stalin insisted that his country needed control of eastern Europe to guarantee military security from Germany. While U.S. president Franklin Roosevelt had been inclined to accommodate these demands, his successor, Harry Truman, demanded free elections throughout eastern Europe. Stalin refused.

The United States' status as the only country that possessed atomic weapons at the end of the war bolstered Truman's tough stance. Just as the U.S. sense of security came from having a monopoly on the atomic bomb, Stalin pursued security by militarily occupying eastern Europe and imposing compliant governments that would provide a buffer against the threat of western European aggression. These countries were considered Soviet satellites—nations whose politics and economics were modeled on and dictated by the Soviet Union.

President Truman misread these occupations as a campaign for world domination. Communist movements in Greece and China, beyond Stalin's occupation zone,

Berlin Airlift Residents of Berlin watch a U.S. Air Force cargo plane land with supplies to support West Berliners during the Soviet blockade (1948–1949). (Courtesy CSU Archives/The Everett Collection)

fed these fears. In October 1945 Truman issued the **Truman Doctrine**, aimed at "containing" communism to areas already occupied by the Soviet army by providing military and economic support to governments threatened by Communist control. (His reference to regimes imposed by force applied only to Europe and countries threatened by communism, not to European colonial domination of Asia and Africa.)

Truman asked Congress for military aid for Greece and Turkey to prevent the spread of communism. Soon after, Secretary of State George C. Marshall proposed a broader package of economic and food aid — the **Marshall Plan** — to help Europe rebuild. Stalin refused Marshall Plan assistance for eastern Europe. The Soviet Union's support for the overthrow of the democratically elected Czechoslovakian government in 1948 and its replacement by a Communist government shocked the U.S. Congress into approving the Marshall Plan in April 1948.

A lasting pattern of escalating reactions to real and perceived provocations was established between the U.S. and Soviet Union. Stalin retaliated by blocking road traffic through the Soviet zone of Germany to Berlin, prompting the U.S. and its allies to airlift millions of tons of provisions to the West Berliners. After 324 days the Soviets backed down: containment seemed to work. In 1949 the United States formed an anti-Soviet military alliance of Western governments: the North Atlantic Treaty Organization (**NATO**). Stalin countered by tightening his hold on his satellites, united in 1955 under the Warsaw Pact. Europe was divided into two hostile blocs. British prime minister Winston Churchill warned that an "iron curtain has descended across the Continent."

The Soviet Union, with its massive army arrayed across eastern Europe, and the United States, with its industrial strength and atomic weapons, emerged as superpowers whose might dwarfed that of other countries. Superpower status reached an awkward balance after the Soviet Union developed its own atomic weapons in 1949. Both nations pitched themselves into a military and geopolitical confrontation that stopped short of outright war: the Cold War (Map 31.1).

An ideological divide defined the rivalry between the United States and the Soviet Union. The United States saw itself as the defender of a "free world" governed by liberal principles such as free markets, private property, and individual rights protected by democratic constitutions. The Soviet Union defined itself as the defender of the rights of workers and peasants against their exploiters, the rights of colonial peoples against their colonizers, and economic development based on planning and equitable distribution. The Cold War sharpened the distinctions between these models, creating opposing paths that the superpowers pressured other countries to follow.

The United Nations

In 1945 representatives of fifty nations met in San Francisco to draft a charter for a new intergovernmental organization called the United Nations. Like that of its predecessor, the League of Nations (see "The Paris Peace Treaties" in Chapter 28), the immediate goal of the United Nations was to mediate international conflicts in order to preserve peace. But in 1945 the founders of the United Nations foresaw a more ambitious role than the League of Nations had played: the UN would also support decolonization; promote economic development; and expand access to health care, worker protections, environmental conservation, and gender equity.

Truman Doctrine The 1945 American policy of preventing the spread of Communist rule.

Marshall Plan A 1948 American plan for providing economic aid to Europe to help it rebuild after World War II.

NATO The North Atlantic Treaty Organization, an anti-Soviet military alliance of Western nations, formed in 1949.

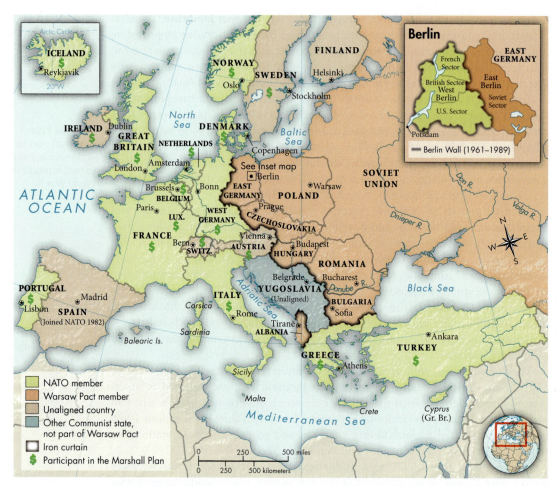

MAP 31.1 Cold War Europe in the 1950s Europe was divided by an "iron curtain" during the Cold War. None of the Communist countries of eastern Europe were participants in the Marshall Plan.

The United Nations was divided into two bodies: a General Assembly that met annually and included all nations that signed the UN Charter; and a Security Council made up of five regional powers, each of which held veto power over the council's decisions, making it a body that in effect functioned only through unanimous consent. Roosevelt intended the Security Council to include the United States, the Soviet Union, Great Britain, China, and Brazil. Because of U.S. influence over Latin America, British and Soviet leaders feared the Brazilian seat would simply be a second vote for the United States, so they insisted that France instead be the fifth member of the Security Council. After the Chinese Revolution in 1949, the government of Taiwan held China's seat until the United Nations transferred it to the People's Republic of China in 1971.

The UN gave critical support to decolonization efforts. Its charter defended the right of self-determination, and it served as a forum for liberation movements to make claims or negotiate the terms of independence. The UN also provided a platform for opponents of colonialism to condemn those colonial powers that resisted their calls for self-determination. In addition, UN member nations volunteered military forces to serve around the world as peacekeepers, who have provided a buffer to ease violent disputes and served as observers to ensure that agreements were being met or that abuses were not being committed in conflict areas.

In its early years, the United Nations mediated Indonesia's demand for independence from the Netherlands, which fought a four-year war to reoccupy the former colony. The UN deployed peacekeepers in the newly created border between India and Pakistan, and it helped determine the terms under which Britain relinquished control of Palestine and Jordan, as well as the terms for the creation of Israel in 1948. The agenda of the United Nations evolved as new member states joined. In 1960 alone, eighteen African nations were seated at the UN, forming part of an "Afro-Asian bloc" committed to rapidly completing the decolonization process and advancing postcolonial economic development.

The Politics of Liberation

The term *Third World* emerged in the 1950s among obervers who viewed Africa, Asia, and Latin America as a single entity, different from both the capitalist, industrialized "First World" and the Communist, industrialized "Second World." The idea of a Third World had particular appeal amid the Cold War rivalry, because it allowed advocates to try to stake out an autonomous space outside of Cold War pressures. Despite deep differences between them, most so-called Third World countries in Africa, Asia, and Latin America were poor and economically underdeveloped — meaning less industrialized — and were thus also referred to as "nonindustrial" or "industrializing" nations.

Many areas of the Third World were still colonies of European countries at the end of the Second World War, though this status was challenged by nationalist liberation movements. The roots of many liberation movements often reached back to the nineteenth century. Colonial powers repressed these movements, but after the Second World War those colonial powers were weaker and nationalist movements grew more insistent. The quest for liberation took many forms. Economically, nations emerging from colonialism sought industrialization and development to end dependence on former colonizers. Politically, they sought alliances with other industrializing nations to avoid the neocolonial influences of more powerful nations. Intellectually, they reacted against Western assumptions of white supremacy.

The former colonies faced intense pressure to align themselves ideologically and economically with either the United States or the Soviet Union, and few could resist the pressure or the incentives those powers brought to bear. Nonetheless, to varying degrees, they tried to operate independently from the two superpowers in a number of ways. In 1955 leaders of twenty-nine recently independent nations in Asia and Africa met in Bandung, Indonesia, to create a framework for political and economic cooperation so they could emerge from colonialism without having to resubordinate their nations either to their former colonizers or to pressures from the Cold War superpowers. The participants outlined principles for rejecting pressure from the superpowers and supporting decolonization. In 1961 nations participating in the Bandung Conference met in Yugoslavia, where Marxists who had come to power in the struggle against Nazi Germany zealously guarded their independence from the Soviet Union, to form a Non-Aligned Nations Movement.

U.S. and Latin American Views on Development

Is economic development something all nations share democratically as it spreads from Great Powers to the industrializing world? By outlining a linear progression of economic growth, the American economist Walt Whitman Rostow used modernization theory to create a road map for countries to follow as they evolved from "traditional" to "mature" states. Brazilian dependency theorist Celso Furtado disagreed. For Furtado, economic development in the United States and Europe made the rest of the world dependent upon those regions and inhibited the spread of development. A key difference in these economists' interpretations concerns countries' relationships to the international economy.

Walt Whitman Rostow, 1960

■ It is possible to identify all societies, in their economic dimensions, as lying within one of five categories: the traditional society, the preconditions for take-off, the take-off, the drive to maturity, and the age of high mass-consumption. . . .

First, the traditional society. A traditional society is one whose structure is developed within limited production functions, based on pre-Newtonian science and technology, and on pre-Newtonian attitudes towards the physical world. Newton is here used as a symbol for that watershed in history when men came widely to believe that the external world was subject to a few knowable laws. . . .

The second stage of growth embraces societies in the process of transition; . . . it takes time to transform a traditional society in the ways necessary for it to exploit the fruits of modern science, to fend off diminishing returns, and thus to enjoy the blessings and choices opened up by the march of compound interest. . . .

We now come to the great watershed in the life of modern societies: . . . the take-off. . . . The forces making for economic progress, which yielded limited bursts and enclaves of modern activity, expand and come to dominate the society. . . .

After take-off there follows a long interval of sustained if fluctuating progress, as the now regularly growing economy drives to extend modern technology over the whole front of its economic activity. . . . The economy finds its place in the international economy: goods formerly imported are produced at home; new import requirements develop, and new export commodities to match them. . . .

We now come to the age of high mass-consumption, where, in time, the leading sectors shift towards durable

Dependency and Development Theories

In 1948 the United Nations established the Economic Commission for Latin America (ECLA) in Santiago, Chile, to study economic development. Under the direction of Argentine economist Raúl Prebisch, ECLA produced Latin America's main intellectual contributions to the twentieth century: a diagnosis of reasons why less industrialized regions of the world lagged economically and technologically behind Europe and the United States. These ideas were known as **dependency theory**.

According to dependency theory, the first regions to industrialize in the nineteenth century—western Europe and the United States—locked in a lasting economic advantage magnified by colonialism and neocolonialism. This advantage trapped countries in Latin America, Africa, and Asia in roles as exporters of agricultural and mineral commodities and importers of capital and technology. According to this analysis, the prosperity of Europe and the United States was built on the impoverishment of other regions, an inequality that increased over time as the value of commodities decreased relative to the value of manufactured and technological goods.

dependency theory
The belief, formulated in Latin America in the mid-twentieth century, that development in some areas of the world locks other nations into underdevelopment.

consumers' goods and services: a phase from which Americans are beginning to emerge; whose not unequivocal joys Western Europe and Japan are beginning energetically to probe; and with which Soviet society is engaged in an uneasy flirtation. . . .

When technological maturity is reached, and the nation has at its command a modernized and differentiated industrial machine, to what ends should it be put, and in what proportions: to increase social security, through the welfare state; to expand mass-consumption into the range of durable consumers' goods and services; to increase the nation's stature and power on the world scene; or to increase leisure?

Celso Furtado, 1970

■ As a consequence of the rapid spread of new production methods from a small number of centers radiating technological innovations, there has come into existence a process tending to create a world-wide economic system. It is thus that underdevelopment is considered a creature of development, or rather, as a consequence of the impact of the technical processes and the international division of labor commanded by the small number of societies that espoused the Industrial Revolution of the nineteenth century. The resulting relations between these societies and the underdeveloped areas involve forms of dependence that can hardly be over-

come. . . . [D]ependence [is] maintained by controlling the assimilation of new technological processes through the installation of productive activities within the dependent economies, all under the control of groups integrated into the dominant economies.

On the assumption of the foregoing, we infer that underdevelopment cannot be studied as a "phase" of the development process since such a "phase" would be overcome if certain factors came into play simultaneously. And, since the underdeveloped economies are contemporaries of—and in one way or another, dependent on—their developed counterparts, the former cannot retrace the experiences of the latter. Therefore, development and underdevelopment should be considered as two aspects of the same historical process involving the creation and the spread of modern technology.

QUESTIONS FOR ANALYSIS

1. Which model of economic development better explains the historical experiences of developing countries as described in this chapter, and why?
2. What alternative interpretations might better explain the histories of underdeveloped countries?

Sources: W. W. Rostow, *The Stages of Economic Growth* (Cambridge: Cambridge University Press, 1960), pp. 4–10, 16. © Cambridge University Press, 1960. Reprinted with permission of Cambridge University Press; Celso Furtado, *Obstacles to Development in Latin America*, trans. Charles Ekker (Garden City, N.Y.: Anchor Books, 1970), p. xvi.

How could this pattern be broken? Could a country that grew coffee become a country that manufactured cars? This question would be asked many times around the world in the second half of the twentieth century, and it would be answered in many ways.

One approach was **modernization theory**, which suggested that societies passed through phases of development from primitive to modern, and that adopting the political, economic, or cultural practices of places like the United States was the best remedy for poverty. (See "Global Viewpoints: U.S. and Latin American Views on Development," above.) This theory shaped U.S. foreign aid programs, which deployed armies of experts offering advice in areas ranging from revising legal codes to digging wells. These experts often did not understand local conditions, believing that the American way was always best. Regardless of their intentions, these projects were often riddled with unintended negative consequences, which led to mistrust of U.S. aid.

For peoples emerging from colonialism, dependency theory was more appealing. Newly independent nations faced enormous pressures: rural poverty pushed millions

modernization theory
The belief, held in countries such as the United States in the mid-twentieth century, that all countries evolved in a linear progression from traditional to mature.

into cities where good jobs were scarce. Cities and the countryside alike had insufficient schools and health care. Dependency theorists favored state planning to both induce industrialization and distribute resources more equitably. A common tool to do this was **import substitution industrialization (ISI)**. Under ISI policies, countries imposed trade barriers to keep certain foreign products out and provided subsidies for domestic industries to make the same goods. Dependency suggested that even ISI was not enough, and that deep social reforms were needed, such as the redistribution of large farming estates to rural workers, as well as state control of major industries and banks.

import substitution industrialization (ISI)
The use of trade barriers to keep certain foreign products out of one's country so that domestic industry can emerge and produce the same goods.

The governments that attempted land redistribution or the nationalization of foreign firms faced a backlash by landowners, foreign corporations, and political conservatives. In many cases, reformist governments were deposed in military coups supported by the United States. One example was Guatemala, where a democratically elected government pursued the redistribution of land held by large U.S. companies. The government was overthrown in 1954 in a coup organized by the U.S. government.

liberation theology
A movement within the Catholic Church to support the poor in situations of exploitation that emerged with particular force in Latin America in the 1960s.

The experience in Guatemala hardened Cold War views. The events led the United States to expand its containment doctrine to Latin America, where it stepped in to block governments whose reforms it interpreted as Communist. For Latin American reformers, the events in Guatemala suggested that peaceful, gradual change would be blocked by the U.S. and that more radical paths were needed. One person drawing this lesson was an Argentine medical student volunteering in Guatemala at the time of the coup. Ernesto "Che" Guevara (CHAY goo-eh-vahrah) (1928–1967) developed an approach to revolution using tactics he outlined in a manual called *Guerilla Warfare*. Guevara believed that private property and wage labor were forms of exploitation that could be overthrown by free workers volunteering their labor to help liberate others.

Within Catholicism, ideas of social reform and liberation crystallized into a movement called **liberation theology**. The movement emerged in Latin America amid reforms of the Catholic Church by Pope John XXIII (pontificate 1958–1963), who called on clergy to engage with the contemporary world—a world characterized by poverty and exclusion. In 1968 the Latin American Council of Bishops gathered in Medellín, Colombia, and invoked dependency theory as it called on clergy to exercise a "preferential option for the poor" by working toward "social justice," including

Liberation Theology Participants at a meeting of ecclesiastical base communities in Brazil gather under a banner reading "Altar of Martyrs: Your Blood Nourishes Our Base Communities." This 1986 meeting, eighteen years after the Medellín Conference, shows the lasting impact of liberation theology in Latin America. (Bernard Bisson/Sygma via Getty Images)

land redistribution, the recognition of peasants' and labor unions, and condemnation of economic dependency and neocolonialism.

Drawing on dependency theory and sometimes verging on revolutionary Marxism, priests attracted to liberation theology challenged governments, fought against landowners and business owners they saw as oppressors, and formed community organizations, or ecclesiastical base communities, where the residents of poor neighborhoods could gather to discuss their problems and devise solutions. After the 1970s Popes John Paul II (pontificate 1978–2005) and Benedict XVI (pontificate 2005–2013) suppressed liberation theology and silenced its most outspoken thinkers. Advocates of liberation theology greeted the naming of a pope from Latin America, Francis, in 2013 as a return to the focus on fighting poverty and social exclusion within the Catholic Church.

Interpreting the Postcolonial Experience

Many intellectuals who came of age during and after the struggle for political emancipation embraced a vision of solidarity among peoples oppressed by colonialism and racism. Some argued that genuine freedom required a total rejection of Western values in addition to an economic and political break with the former colonial powers. Frantz Fanon (1925–1961) expressed these views in his powerful study of colonial peoples, *The Wretched of the Earth* (1961).

According to Fanon, a French-trained black psychiatrist from the Caribbean island of Martinique, decolonization is always a violent process whereby colonizers are replaced by an absolutely different species—the colonized, those he called "the wretched of the earth." During decolonization the colonized masses mock colonial values, "insult them, and vomit them up" in a psychic purge. Fanon believed that throughout Africa and Asia the former imperialists and their local collaborators— the "white men with black faces"—remained the enemy:

> During the colonial period the people are called upon to fight against oppression; after national liberation, they are called upon to fight against poverty, illiteracy, and underdevelopment. The struggle, they say, goes on. . . . We are not blinded by the moral reparation of national independence; nor are we fed by it. The wealth of the imperial countries is our wealth too. . . . Europe is literally the creation of the Third World. The wealth which smothers her is that which was stolen from the underdeveloped peoples.[1]

Fanon gave voice to radicals attacking imperialism and struggling for liberation.

As countries gained independence, some writers looked beyond wholesale rejection of the industrialized powers. They, too, were anti-imperialist, but they were often also activists and cultural nationalists who celebrated the histories and cultures of their peoples. Many did not hesitate to criticize their own leaders or fight oppression and corruption.

The Nigerian writer Chinua Achebe (chee-NOO-ah ah-CHAY-beh) (1930–2013) sought to restore his people's self-confidence by reinterpreting the past. For Achebe, the "writer in a new nation" had first to embrace the "fundamental theme" that Africans had their own culture before the Europeans came and that it was the duty of writers to help Africans reclaim their past. In his 1958 novel *Things Fall Apart*, Achebe brings to life the men and women of an Ibo village at the beginning of the twentieth century, with all their virtues and frailties. Woven into the story are the proverbs and wisdom of a sophisticated people and the beauty of a vanishing world:

> [The white man] says that our customs are bad; and our own brothers who have taken up his religion also say that our customs are bad. How do you think we can fight when our own brothers have turned against us? The white man is very clever. He came quietly and peaceably with his religion. We were amused at his foolishness and allowed him to stay. Now he has won our brothers, and our clan can no longer act like one. He has put a knife on the things that held us together and we have fallen apart.[2]

In later novels Achebe portrayed the postindependence disillusionment of many writers and intellectuals, which reflected trends in many developing nations in the 1960s and 1970s. He developed a sharp critique of rulers who seemed increasingly estranged from national realities and corrupted by Western luxury.

Novelist V. S. Naipaul, born in Trinidad in 1932 of Indian parents, also castigated governments in the developing countries for corruption, ineptitude, and self-deception. Another of Naipaul's recurring themes is the poignant loneliness and homelessness of people uprooted by colonialism and Western expansion.

For peoples emerging from colonial domination, or confronting the poverty and social exclusion that was commonplace outside of industrialized nations, the postwar challenge of liberation was not simply political and economic, but also cultural and spiritual. The middle decades of the twentieth century saw a broad awakening of voices among peoples who had been rendered voiceless by their marginalization.

How did religion and the legacies of colonialism affect the formation of new nations in South Asia and the Middle East after World War II?

Nationalism in South Asia and the Middle East

The three South Asian countries created through independence from Britain and subsequent partition, India, Pakistan, and Bangladesh, reflected the dominant themes of cultural and economic nationalism that characterized the end of colonialism, but ethnic and religious rivalries greatly complicated their renewal and development.

Throughout the vast *umma* (world of Islam), nationalism became a powerful force after 1945, stressing modernization and the end of subordination to Western nations. The nationalists who guided the formation of modern states in the Arab world struggled to balance Cold War pressures from the United States and the Soviet Union, as well as the tension between secular modernization and Islam. At the heart of this world, Jewish nationalists founded the state of Israel following the Second World War. The Zionist claim to a homeland came into sharp, and often violent, conflict with the rights and claims of the Palestinian people displaced by the creation of Israel.

Independence in India, Pakistan, and Bangladesh

World War II accelerated the drive toward Indian independence begun by Mohandas Gandhi (see "Gandhi's Resistance Campaign in India" in Chapter 29). In 1942 Gandhi called on the British to "quit India" and threatened another civil disobedience campaign. He and the other Indian National Congress Party leaders were soon after arrested and were jailed for much of the war. Thus India's wartime support for

Britain was substantial but not always enthusiastic. Meanwhile, the Congress Party's prime rival skillfully seized the opportunity to increase its influence.

The Congress Party's rival was the **Muslim League**, led by lawyer Muhammad Ali Jinnah (1876–1948). Jinnah feared that India's Hindu majority would dominate national power at the expense of Muslims. He proposed the creation of two separate countries divided along religious lines:

> The Hindus and Muslims have two different religions, philosophies, social customs, literatures. They neither inter-marry, nor dine together, and indeed, they belong to two different civilizations which are based mainly on conflicting ideas and conceptions. . . . To yoke together two such nations under a single State, one as a numerical minority and the other as majority, must lead to growing discontent and final destruction of any fabric that may be so built up for the government of such a State.[3]

Muslim League Political party founded in 1906 in colonial India that advocated for a separate Muslim homeland after independence.

Gandhi disagreed with Jinnah's two-nation theory, which he believed would lead to ethnic sectarianism rather than collaboration.

Britain agreed to speedy independence for India after 1945, but conflicts between Hindu and Muslim nationalists led to murderous clashes in 1946. When it became clear that Jinnah and the Muslim League would accept nothing less than an independent state of Pakistan, the British government mediated a partition that created a predominantly Hindu nation and a predominantly Muslim nation. In 1947 India and Pakistan gained political independence from Britain as two separate nations (Map 31.2).

Violence and mass expulsions followed independence. Perhaps a hundred thousand Hindus and Muslims were slaughtered, and an estimated 5 million became refugees. "What is there to celebrate?" exclaimed Gandhi in reference to independence, "I see nothing but rivers of blood."[4] Gandhi labored to ease tensions between Hindus and Muslims, but in the aftermath of riots in January 1948, he was killed by a Hindu gunman who resented what he saw as Gandhi's appeasement of Muslims.

After the ordeal of independence, relations between India and Pakistan remained tense. Fighting over the disputed area of Kashmir, a strategically important northwestern border state with a Muslim majority annexed by India, lasted until 1949 and broke out again in 1965–1966, 1971, and 1999 as tensions continued.

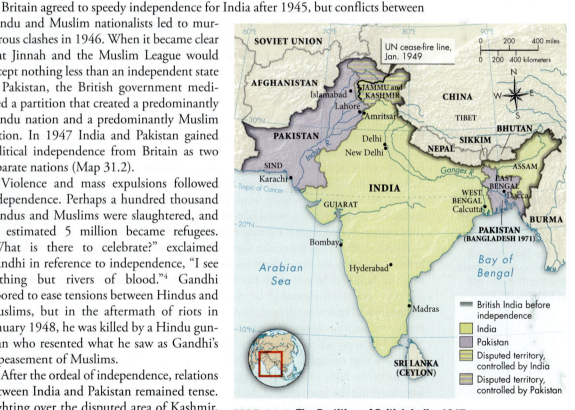

MAP 31.2 The Partition of British India, 1947 Violence and fighting were most intense where there were large Hindu and Muslim minorities — in Kashmir, the Punjab, and Bengal. The tragic result of partition, which occurred repeatedly throughout the world in the twentieth century, was a forced exchange of populations and greater homogeneity on both sides of the border.

In India, Jawaharlal Nehru (1889–1964) and the Indian National Congress Party ruled for a generation and introduced major social reforms. Hindu women gained legal equality, including the right to vote, to seek divorce, and to marry outside their castes. The constitution abolished the untouchable caste. In practice, less discriminatory attitudes toward women and untouchables evolved slowly—especially in rural villages, where 85 percent of the people lived.

The Congress Party pursued state-driven economic development, but population growth of about 2.4 percent per year consumed much of the increased output of economic expansion. The relocation of millions during the partition of India and Pakistan exacerbated poverty. The Congress Party maintained neutrality in the Cold War, distancing itself from both the United States and the Soviet Union. Instead India became one of the leading voices in the Non-Aligned Nations Movement.

At independence, Pakistan was divided between eastern and western provinces separated by more than a thousand miles of Indian territory, as well as by language, ethnic background, and social custom. The Bengalis of East Pakistan constituted a majority of Pakistan's population as a whole, but were neglected by the central government, which remained in the hands of West Pakistan's elite after Jinnah's death. In 1971 the Bengalis revolted and won their independence as the new nation of Bangladesh after a violent civil war. Bangladesh, a secular parliamentary democracy, struggled to find political and economic stability amid famines that resulted from monsoon floods, tornadoes, and cyclones in the vast, low-lying, and intensely farmed Ganges Delta.

Arab Socialism in the Middle East

In the postwar period, new Arab states in the Middle East emerged from colonial rule. For centuries the region had been dominated by the Ottoman Empire. After the First World War, France and Britain claimed protectorates in the former Ottoman territories. Britain already claimed Egypt as a protectorate and France controlled Algeria. New nations emerging from colonial rule in the Middle East embraced **Arab socialism**, a modernizing, secular, and nationalist project of nation building aimed at economic development, a strong military, and Pan-Arab unity.

Arab socialism
A modernizing, secular, and nationalist project of nation building in the Middle East aimed at economic development and the development of a strong military.

Arab socialism held particular significance for women in Middle Eastern societies. It cast aside religious restrictions on women's education, occupations, public activities, and fashions. In countries like Egypt and Iraq, the openness of education and access to professions enjoyed by urban, typically affluent women symbolized an embrace of Western modernity, although senior posts in government, the professions, and business were still dominated by men.

In 1952 army officers overthrew Egypt's monarchy and expelled the British military force that occupied the country. The movement's leader, Gamal Abdel Nasser (1918–1970), built a nationalist regime aimed at eradicating the vestiges of colonialism. Applying the principles of Arab socialism, Nasser pursued the secularization of Egyptian society, created an extensive social welfare network, redistributed rural lands, and promoted industrialization.

Nasser's National Charter called for the nationalization of transportation, mining, dams, banks, utilities, insurance, and heavy industry. In the countryside the size of landholdings was limited and estates were broken up. As Nasser declared, "When we started this revolution, we wanted to put an end to exploitation. Hence our struggle to put capital at the service of man, and to put land at the service of man, instead of leaving man at the service of the feudalist who owns the land."[5]

In 1956 Nasser took a symbolic and strategic step toward national sovereignty when he ordered the army to take control of the Suez Canal, still held by Britain and France. A coalition of British, French, and Israeli forces invaded to retake the canal. The Soviet Union offered support to Egypt. To prevent Soviet intervention and a Soviet-Egyptian alliance, the United States negotiated a cease-fire that granted Egypt control of the canal. Alongside control of the canal, Nasser's other main economic accomplishment was the Aswan Dam on the Nile River, which generated electricity for industrialization in northern Egypt while allowing southern Egypt to control flooding and increase agricultural production. Nasser negotiated the funding and technical expertise for the dam with both the United States and the Soviet Union, eventually settling on Soviet aid. The Suez crisis and the Aswan Dam were examples in which a nationalist leader like Nasser successfully played the superpowers against each other.

Military officers in other Arab countries emulated Nasser's nationalism and social-ist developmentalism. In Syria and Iraq these nationalists formed the Pan-Arab socialist Ba'ath Party. For members of national Ba'ath parties, Egypt was a model for developing a single-party state that implemented nationalist and development aspi-rations. Syria briefly merged with Egypt from 1958 until 1961, forming the United Arab Republic. Officers who resented Nasser's control of Syria revolted against Egypt and established a separate Syrian government dominated by the Ba'ath Party. In Iraq the Ba'ath Party helped overthrow the British-backed monarchy in 1958, leading to Ba'ath Party rule that ended when a U.S. military invasion toppled Saddam Hussein in 2003.

The Arab-Israeli Conflict

Before the Second World War, Arab nationalists were loosely united in their oppo-sition to the colonial powers and to Jewish migration to Palestine. In the aftermath of the Second World War, Palestinians and new Arab states emerging from British and French domination strenuously opposed Jewish settlement in Palestine (see "Arab-Jewish Tensions in Palestine" in Chapter 29). In 1947 the British government announced its intention to withdraw from Palestine in 1948. The difficult problem of a Jewish homeland was placed in the hands of the United Nations, which passed a plan to partition Palestine into two separate states—one Arab and one Jewish (Map 31.3). The Jews accepted, and the Arabs rejected, the partition of Palestine.

By early 1948 an undeclared civil war raged in Palestine. When the British man-date ended on May 14, 1948, the Jews proclaimed the state of Israel. Arab countries immediately attacked the new state, but Israeli forces drove off the invaders and conquered more territory. Roughly nine hundred thousand Palestinian refugees fled or were expelled from old Palestine. The war left an enormous legacy of Arab bit-terness toward Israel and its political allies, Great Britain and the United States. In 1964 a loose union of Palestinian refugee groups opposed to Israel and seeking a Palestinian state joined together, under the leadership of Yasir Arafat (1929–2004), to form the **Palestine Liberation Organization (PLO)**.

Nationalist leaders in neighboring Syria and Egypt cultivated political support at home through opposition to Israel and threats to crush it militarily. This tension repeatedly erupted into war. On June 1, 1967, when Syrian and Egyptian armies

Palestine Liberation Organization (PLO)
Created in 1964, a loose union of Palestinian refugee groups opposed to Israel and united in the goal of establishing a Palestinian state.

MAP 31.3 The Middle East After 1947 The partition of Palestine by the United Nations resulted in the creation in 1948 of Israel, which faced repeated conflicts with rival Arab states.

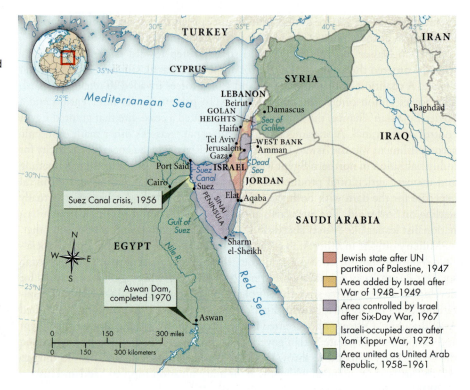

Legend:
- Jewish state after UN partition of Palestine, 1947
- Area added by Israel after War of 1948–1949
- Area controlled by Israel after Six-Day War, 1967
- Israeli-occupied area after Yom Kippur War, 1973
- Area united as United Arab Republic, 1958–1961

massed on Israel's borders, the Israeli government went to war, launching air strikes that destroyed most of the Egyptian, Syrian, and Jordanian air forces. Over the next five days Israeli armies defeated Egyptian, Syrian, Jordanian, and Palestinian forces and took control of the Sinai Peninsula and the Gaza Strip from Egypt, the West Bank and East Jerusalem from Jordan, and the Golan Heights from Syria. In the Six-Day War (also known as the 1967 Arab-Israeli War), Israel proved itself to be the pre-eminent military force in the region, and it expanded the territory under its control threefold.

After the war Israel began to build large Jewish settlements in the Gaza Strip and the West Bank, home to millions of Palestinians. On November 22, 1967, the UN Security Council adopted Resolution 242, which contained a "land for peace" formula by which Israel was called upon to withdraw from the occupied territories, and in return the Arab states were to withdraw all claims to Israeli territory, cease hostilities, and recognize the sovereignty of the Israeli state. The tension between rival territorial claims persisted.

How did the Cold War shape reconstruction, revolution, and decolonization in East and Southeast Asia?

Revolution and Resurgence in East and Southeast Asia

In Asia Japan's defeat ended the Second World War, but other conflicts continued: nationalists in European colonies intensified their struggle for independence, and in China Nationalist and Communist armies that had cooperated against the Japanese invaders now confronted each other in a renewed civil war. In 1949 Communist forces under Mao Zedong triumphed and established the People's Republic of China. The Communist victory in China shaped the nature of Japan's reconstruction, as its U.S. occupiers determined that an industrially and economically strong Japan would serve as a counterweight to Mao. U.S. fear of the spread of communism drew the country into conflicts in Korea and Vietnam, intensifying the stakes in the decolonization struggle across East and Southeast Asia.

The Communist Victory in China

When Japan surrendered to the Allies in August 1945, Communists and Nationalists both rushed to seize evacuated territory. Communists and Nationalists had fought each other before the Second World War, but had put aside their struggle to resist Japanese invasion. With the war over, the Nationalists and Communists resumed their conflict. By 1948 the Nationalist forces had disintegrated before the better-led, more determined Communists. The following year Nationalist leader Jiang Jieshi and 2 million mainland Chinese fled to Taiwan, and in October 1949 Mao Zedong proclaimed the People's Republic of China (Map 31.4).

Communism triumphed in China for many reasons. Mao Zedong and the Communists had avoided pitched battles and concentrated on winning peasant support and forming a broad anti-Japanese coalition. By reducing rents and promising land redistribution, they emerged in peasant eyes as China's true patriots. (See "Analyzing the Evidence: Poster Art in Communist China," page 984.)

Between 1949 and 1954 the Communists consolidated their rule. They seized the vast landholdings of a minority of landlords and rich peasants and redistributed the land to 300 million poor peasants. Meanwhile, as Mao admitted in 1957, mass arrests led to the summary execution of eight hundred thousand "class enemies"; the true figure is probably much higher. Millions more were deported to forced-labor camps.

Mao and the party looked to the Soviet Union for inspiration in the early 1950s. China adopted collective agriculture and Soviet-style five-year plans to promote industrialization. The Soviet Union provided considerable economic aid, and Soviet technicians built factories. In the cultural and intellectual realms, too, the Chinese followed the Soviet example. Basic civil and political rights were abolished. Temples and churches were closed. The Chinese enthusiastically promoted Soviet Marxist ideas concerning women and the

MAP 31.4 Decolonization in Asia After the Second World War, countries colonized by Britain, France, the Netherlands, Japan, Australia, and the United States gained their independence. In cases such as Vietnam and Indonesia, independence came through armed struggles against colonizers who were reluctant to leave.

Poster Art in Communist China

One of the most popular art forms in Communist China was poster art, millions of copies of which were printed to adorn the walls of homes, offices, factories, and businesses. This uniquely Chinese form did not contain abstract, modern, or bourgeois elements and did not reflect classical Chinese art styles. Instead, such posters glorified the state, its leaders, and the heroes of the revolution. The two young women in this poster wear uniforms and caps bearing the Communist red star, the five points of which represent the five components of Communist society: the youth, the army, the peasants, the workers, and the intellectuals.

This poster, called "Lei Feng Is Everywhere," was part of an early 1960s campaign by China's People's Liberation Army. The campaign featured an ordinary soldier, Lei Feng, and celebrated his virtues of selflessness, modesty, and dedication to the Communist Party. Lei Feng appears in the small poster behind the woman on the telephone. By emphasizing the virtues of ordinary people, the campaign modeled behaviors for the public to follow. In this poster of a family, the presence of a poster about Lei Feng was meant to show how these messages are brought into the family's home. The main poster also shows us images of order and prosperity in family life under the Communist Party.

(© Pictures from History/The Image Works)

QUESTIONS FOR ANALYSIS

1. Who is depicted, and what are they doing? Describe the space the four figures are in and what appears in the space. What message do you think the artist seeks to convey with this image?

2. What social function or application might posters such as this one have?

3. Consider the people who are represented in the poster. What is the choice of figures intended to show? What roles do women play, based on their dress? And what do you infer from the different ages represented?

family. Full equality, work outside the home, and state-supported child care became primary goals.

In 1958 China broke from the Marxist-Leninist course of development and began to go its own way. Mao proclaimed a **Great Leap Forward** in which industrial growth would be based on small-scale backyard workshops and steel mills run by peasants living in gigantic self-contained communes. The plan led to economic disaster, as land in the countryside went untilled when peasants turned to industrial production. As many as 30 million people died in famines that swept the country in 1960–1961. When Soviet premier Nikita Khrushchev criticized Chinese policy in 1960, Mao condemned him and his Soviet colleagues as detestable "modern revisionists." Khrushchev cut off aid, splitting the Communist world apart.

Mao lost influence in the party after the Great Leap Forward fiasco and the Sino-Soviet split, but in 1965 he staged a dramatic comeback, launching the **Great Proletarian Cultural Revolution**. He sought to purge the party and to recapture the revolutionary fervor of the guerrilla struggle. The army and the nation's young people responded enthusiastically, organizing themselves into radical cadres called Red Guards. Students denounced their teachers and practiced rebellion in the name of revolution. Mao's thoughts, through his speeches and writings, were collected in the *Little Red Book*, which became scripture to the Red Guards. Here the young Red Guards learned the underlying maxim of Mao's revolution: "Every communist must grasp the truth, 'Political power grows out of the barrel of a gun.'"[6]

The Red Guards sought to erase all traces of "feudal" and "bourgeois" culture and thought. Ancient monuments and countless works of art, antiques, and books were destroyed. Party officials, professors, and intellectuals were exiled to remote villages to purify themselves with heavy labor. Universities were shut down for years. Thousands of people died, many of them executed, and millions more were sent to rural forced-labor camps. The Red Guards attracted enormous worldwide attention and served as an extreme model for the student rebellions in the West in the late 1960s.

Conflict in Korea

As Japanese forces were withdrawn after 1945, Korea was divided into Soviet and American zones of occupation, which in 1948 became Communist North Korea and anticommunist South Korea. When the Communists triumphed in China in late 1949, many fearful Americans saw new evidence of a powerful worldwide Communist conspiracy. When the Russian-backed Communist forces of North Korea invaded South Korea in 1950, President Truman sent U.S. troops to lead a UN coalition force to stop what he interpreted as a coordinated Communist effort to dominate Asia.

The Korean War (1950–1953) ended in a stalemate with little more than symbolic gains for either side. North Korea conquered most of the peninsula, but the South Korean, American, and UN troops repelled their foes north to the Chinese border. At that point China intervened and pushed the South Koreans and Americans back south. In 1953 a fragile truce was negotiated, and the fighting stopped. The United States had extended its policy of containing communism to Asia, but drew back from invading Communist China and possibly provoking nuclear war.

Great Leap Forward Mao Zedong's acceleration of Chinese development in which industrial growth was to be based on small-scale backyard workshops run by peasants living in gigantic self-contained communes.

Great Proletarian Cultural Revolution A movement launched in 1965 by Mao Zedong that attempted to recapture the revolutionary fervor of his guerrilla struggle.

The Korean War

Baseball in Japan Though baseball arrived in Japan in the late nineteenth century, it increased in popularity during U.S. occupation. This photo from 1950 shows children in their baseball uniforms, with a U.S. Jeep in the background. (Courtesy CSU Archives/The Everett Collection)

Japan's American Reconstruction

When American occupation forces landed in the Tokyo-Yokohama area after Japan's surrender in August 1945, they found only smokestacks and large steel safes standing amid miles of rubble in what had been the heart of industrial Japan. Japan, like Germany, was formally occupied by all the Allies, but real power resided in American hands. U.S. general Douglas MacArthur exercised almost absolute authority. MacArthur and the Americans had a revolutionary plan for defeated Japan, introducing reforms designed to make Japan a free, democratic society along American lines.

Japan's sweeping American revolution began with demilitarization and a systematic purge of convicted war criminals and wartime collaborators. The American-dictated constitution of 1946 allowed the emperor to remain the "symbol of the State." Real power resided in the Japanese Diet, whose members were popularly elected. A bill of rights granted basic civil liberties and freed all political prisoners, including Communists. Article 9 of the new constitution abolished the Japanese armed forces and renounced war. The American occupation left Japan's powerful bureaucracy largely intact and used it to implement fundamental social and economic reforms. The occupation promoted the Japanese labor movement, introduced American-style antitrust laws, and "emancipated" Japanese women, granting them equality before the law. The occupation also imposed land reform that strengthened the small independent farmers, who became staunch defenders of postwar democracy.

America's efforts to remake Japan in its own image were powerful but short-lived. As Mao's forces prevailed in China, American leaders began to see Japan as a potential ally, not as an object of social reform. The American command began purging leftists and rehabilitating prewar nationalists. The Japanese prime minister during much of the occupation and early post-occupation period was Shigeru Yoshida. A former diplomat with a facility for negotiating with Western nations, Yoshida was the ideal leader in Western eyes for postwar Japan. He channeled all available resources to the rebuilding of Japan's industrial infrastructure, while he left the military defense of the country to the American occupying forces.

The occupation ended in 1952 with a treaty that restored Japan's independence and a role for Japan as the chief Asian ally of the United States in its efforts to contain the spread of communism. Japan's industry provided matériel used by the U.S. armed forces in Korea and Vietnam, and a Security Treaty provided territory for U.S. military installations, particularly the island of Okinawa.

The Vietnam War

French Indochina experienced the bitterest struggle for independence in Southeast Asia. With financial backing from the United States, France tried to reimpose imperial rule there after the Communist and nationalist guerrilla leader Ho Chi Minh (1890–1969) declared an independent republic in 1945. French forces were decisively defeated in the 1954 Battle of Dien Bien Phu. At an international peace conference later that year, French Indochina gained independence. Laos and Cambodia became separate states, and Vietnam was temporarily divided into separately governed northern and southern regions pending elections to select a single unified government within two years. The South Vietnamese government refused to hold the elections, and civil war between it and the Communist Democratic Republic of Vietnam, or North Vietnam, broke out in 1959.

Cold War fears and U.S. commitment to the ideology of containment drove the United States to get involved in Vietnam. The administration of President Dwight D. Eisenhower (elected in 1952) refused to sign the Geneva Accords that temporarily divided the country, and provided military aid to help the south resist North Vietnam. Eisenhower's successor, John F. Kennedy, increased the number of American "military advisers."

In 1964 U.S. president Lyndon Johnson greatly expanded America's role in the Vietnam conflict, seeking to "escalate" the war sufficiently to break the will of the North Vietnamese and their southern allies without resorting to "overkill," which might risk war with the entire Communist bloc. South Vietnam received massive U.S. military aid, and large numbers of American forces joined in combat. The United States bombed North Vietnam with ever-greater intensity, but it did not invade North Vietnam or launch a naval blockade of its ports.

Most Americans first saw the war as a legitimate defense against communism, but the combined effect of watching the results of the violent conflict on the nightly television news and experiencing the widening military draft spurred a growing antiwar movement on U.S. college campuses. By the late 1960s growing numbers of critics in the U.S. and around the world denounced American involvement in the conflict. The north's Tet Offensive in January 1968, a major attack on South Vietnamese cities, shook Americans' confidence in their government's ability to manage the conflict. Within months President Johnson announced he would not stand for re-election, and he called for negotiations with North Vietnam.

Elected in 1968, President Richard Nixon sought to disengage America from Vietnam. He intensified the bombardment of the enemy while simultaneously pursuing peace talks with the North Vietnamese. He also began a slow process of withdrawal from Vietnam in a process called "Vietnamization," which transferred the burden of the war to the South Vietnamese army, cutting American forces from 550,000 to 24,000 in four years. Nixon finally reached a peace agreement with North Vietnam in 1973 that allowed the remaining American forces to withdraw by 1975.

Despite U.S. efforts, the Communists proved victorious in 1975 and created a unified Marxist Vietnam. After more than thirty-five years of battle, the Communists turned to a nation-building process that had been delayed by decades of war against colonial rule and the U.S. effort to force a political and economic model on the country as part of its doctrine of containment of communism. Millions of Vietnamese civilians faced reprisals for aligning with the United States, including Hmong (ha-MUHNG) and Degar peoples, such as the Mnong (MUH-nong), and other ethnic minorities. They first fled to refugee camps elsewhere in Southeast Asia and later settled as refugees in the United States. (See "Individuals in Society: Sieng, a Mnong Refugee in an American High School" in Chapter 33.)

The Vietnam War

→ U.S. and South Vietnamese forces

→ Major North Vietnamese supply route into South Vietnam

✸ Important battle or action

What factors influenced decolonization in Africa after World War II?

Decolonization in Africa

By 1964 most of Africa had gained independence (Map 31.5). Only Portugal's colonies and southern Africa remained under white minority rule, gaining their independence after long armed struggles that ended in 1975. Many national leaders saw socialism as the best way to sever colonial ties and erase exploitation within their new borders. But institutional barriers left over from the colonial era hampered these efforts: new nations inherited inefficient colonial bureaucracies, economic systems that privileged the export of commodities, and colonial educational systems intended to build servants of empire. The range of actions available to new leaders was narrowed by former colonizers' efforts to retain their economic influence and by the political and ideological divisions of the Cold War.

The Growth of African Nationalism

African nationalism resembled similar movements in Asia and the Middle East in its reaction against colonialism, but there were important differences. First, because the imperial system and Western education did not solidify in Africa until after 1900 (see "Colonialism's Impact After 1900" in Chapter 25), national movements came of age in the 1920s and reached maturity after 1945. Second, Africa's multiplicity of ethnic groups, coupled with colonial boundaries that often bore no resemblance to existing ethnic geography, greatly complicated the development of political — as distinct from cultural — nationalism. Was a modern national state based on ethnic or clan loyalties? Was it to be a continent-wide union? Would the multiethnic territories carved out by European empires become the new African nations? Such questions were not fully addressed until after 1945.

The first nationalist impetus came from the United States and the Caribbean. The most renowned participant in this "black nationalism" was W. E. B. Du Bois (1868–1963). Du Bois (doo-BOISS) was a cofounder of the National Association for the Advancement of Colored People (NAACP) in the United States and organized Pan-African congresses in Paris during the Paris Peace Conference in 1919 and in Brussels in 1921. **Pan-Africanists** sought black solidarity and a self-governing union of all African peoples. Jamaican-born Marcus Garvey (1887–1940) was the most influential Pan-Africanist, rallying young, educated Africans to his call of "Africa for the Africans."

In the 1920s a surge of anticolonial nationalism swept educated Africans in French and British colonies. African intellectuals in Europe formulated and articulated *négritude*, or blackness: pride, self-confidence, and joy in black creativity and the black spirit. This westernized African elite pressed for better access to government jobs, steps toward self-government, and an end to discrimination. They claimed the right to speak for ordinary Africans and denounced government-supported chiefs for subordinating themselves to white colonial leaders.

The mass protests that accompanied the deprivations of the Great Depression, in particular the **cocoa holdups** of 1930–1931 and 1937–1938, fueled the new nationalism. Cocoa dominated the British colonial economy in the Gold Coast (which became Ghana). As prices plummeted after 1929, cocoa farmers refused to sell their beans to the British firms that fixed prices and monopolized exports. Farmers organized cooperatives to cut back production and sell their crops directly to European

Pan-Africanists People who, through a movement beginning in 1919, sought black solidarity and envisioned a vast self-governing union of all African peoples.

cocoa holdups Mass protests in Africa's Gold Coast in the 1930s by producers of cocoa who refused to sell their beans to British firms and instead sold them directly to European and American chocolate manufacturers.

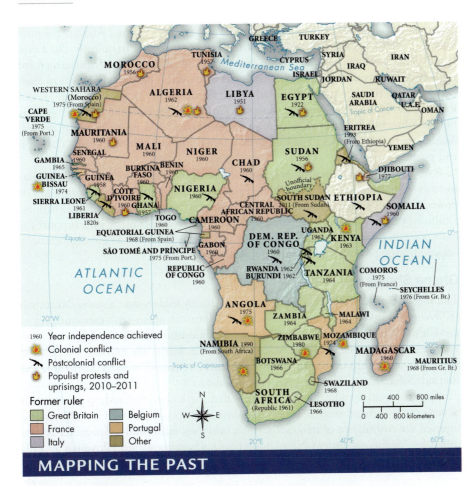

MAPPING THE PAST

MAP 31.5 Decolonization in Africa, 1947 to the Present Most African territories achieved statehood by the mid-1960s, as European empires passed away, unlamented.

ANALYZING THE MAP How many African states achieved independence after 1945? How many experienced some sort of postcolonial conflict?

CONNECTIONS How did the imperialist legacy serve to complicate the transition to stable, independent nations in Africa, Asia, and Latin America?

and American chocolate manufacturers. The cocoa holdups mobilized the population against the foreign companies and demonstrated the power of mass organization and protest.

The repercussions of the Second World War in Africa greatly accelerated the changes begun in the 1930s. Many African soldiers who served in India had been powerfully impressed by Indian nationalism. As African mines and plantations strained to meet wartime demands, towns mushroomed into cities, which became centers of discontent and hardship.

Western imperialism also changed. The principle of self-government was written into the United Nations charter and was supported by Great Britain's postwar Labour government. Thus the key question for Great Britain's various African colonies became the terms of self-government. Briitian and France were in no rush. But a new type of African leader was emerging. Impatient and insistent, these spokesmen for modern African nationalism were remarkably successful. These postwar African leaders formed an elite by virtue of their advanced European or American education, and they were influenced by Western thought. But compared with the interwar generation of educated Africans, they were more radical and had humbler social origins. Among them were former schoolteachers, union leaders, government clerks, lawyers, and poets.

Postwar African nationalists pragmatically accepted prevailing colonial boundaries to avoid border disputes and achieve freedom as soon as possible. Sensing a loss of power, traditional rulers sometimes became the new leaders' worst political enemies. Skillfully, the new leaders channeled postwar hope and discontent into support for mass political organizations that offset this traditional authority. These organizations staged gigantic protests and became political parties.

Ghana Shows the Way

The most charismatic of this generation of African leaders was Kwame Nkrumah (KWA-may ihn-CROO-mah) (1909–1972). Nkrumah spent ten years studying in the United States, where he was influenced by European socialists and Marcus Garvey. He returned to the Gold Coast after the Second World War and entered politics. Under his leadership the Gold Coast—which he renamed "Ghana"—became the first sub-Saharan state to emerge from colonialism.

Nkrumah built a radical party that appealed particularly to modern groups such as veterans, merchant women, union members, and cocoa farmers. He and his party injected the enthusiasm of religious revivals into their rallies and propaganda as they called for "Self-Government Now." Rejecting halfway measures, Nkrumah and his Convention People's Party staged strikes and riots.

Kwame Nkrumah Visits China

Ghana's first prime minister, Kwame Nkrumah, faced challenges similar to those confronted by other leaders of newly independent African nations, which included building new nation-states, emerging from the structures of colonialism, and navigating the pressures of the Cold War. The experiences of other societies that underwent revolution or liberation offered a guide. Nkrumah, accompanied here by Chinese premier Zhou Enlai, visited China in 1961 to study its economic system. (Keystone-France/Gamma-Rapho via Getty Images)

After he was arrested in 1950, the "Deliverer of Ghana" campaigned from jail and saw his party win a smashing victory in the 1951 national elections. He was released from prison to head the transitional government. By 1957 now Prime Minister Nkrumah had achieved worldwide fame and influence as Ghana became independent. After Ghana's breakthrough, independence for other African colonies followed. The main problem in some colonies was the permanent white settlers, not the colonial officials: wherever white settlers were numerous, as in Algeria, Kenya, and Rhodesia, they fought to preserve their privileged position.

French-Speaking Regions

Decolonization took a different course in French-speaking Africa. The events in the French North African colony of Algeria in the 1950s and early 1960s help clarify France's attitude toward its sub-Saharan African colonies.

France attempted to retain Algeria, home to a large, mostly Catholic, European settler population, known as the pieds-noirs (black feet) because its members wore black shoes instead of sandals. In 1954 Algeria's anticolonial movement, the **National Liberation Front** (FLN), began a war for independence, which the French colonial police and armed forces bitterly contested, leaving over 500,000 Algerians dead and millions more displaced. After the FLN won and created an independent Algerian state in 1962, an estimated 900,000 of the 1.25 million Europeans and indigenous Jews fled.

National Liberation Front
The anticolonial movement in Algeria, which began a war against the French in 1954 and won independence in 1962.

The war in Algeria and Indochina's military victory divided France and undermined its political stability. As a result, it was difficult for France to respond to nationalists in its other African colonies until Charles de Gaulle returned to power in 1958. Seeking to maximize France's influence over the future independent nations, de Gaulle devised a divide-and-rule strategy. He divided the French West Africa and French Equatorial Africa federations into thirteen separate governments, thus creating a "French commonwealth." Plebiscites were called in each territory to ratify the new arrangement. An affirmative vote meant continued ties with France; a negative vote signified immediate independence and a complete break with France.

De Gaulle's gamble was shrewd. The educated black elite—as personified by the influential poet-politician Léopold Sédar Senghor (LAY-o-pold SAY-dar SEHN-gohr) (1906–2001), who led Senegal's government—identified with France and dreaded an abrupt separation. They also wanted French aid to continue. France, in keeping with its ideology of assimilation, had given the vote to the educated colonial elite after the Second World War, and about forty Africans held French parliamentary seats after 1946. These factors moderated French African leaders' pursuit of independence.

In Guinea, however, a young nationalist named Sékou Touré (SAY-koo too-RAY) (1922–1984) led his people to overwhelmingly reject the new constitution in 1958. Inspired by Ghana's Nkrumah, Touré laid it out to de Gaulle face-to-face: "We have one prime and essential need: our dignity. But there is no dignity without freedom. . . . We prefer freedom in poverty to opulence in slavery."[7]

Weaker European nations such as Belgium and Portugal responded to decolonization in ways that were more destabilizing. Portugal's dictatorship fought to keep its colonies, such as Angola and Mozambique. To ensure this, the Portuguese regime intensified white settlement and repression of nationalist groups. Belgium, which had discouraged the development of an educated elite in the Congo, abruptly granted independence in 1959, leaving in place a weak government. Independence resulted in violent ethnic conflict and foreign intervention. The United States backed a dictatorship by Mobutu Sese Seko (Muh-BOO-too SEH-seh SEH-koh), who renamed the country Zaire. Poverty deepened as the tremendous wealth generated from mining went into the hands of foreign companies and Mobutu's family and cronies.

Why did populism emerge as such a powerful political force in Latin America?

Populist and Revolutionary Pathways in Latin America

In the decades after the Second World War, Latin American nations struggled to find a political balance that integrated long-excluded groups such as women, workers, and peasants. Populist politicians built a base of support among the urban and rural poor. They often combined charisma with promises of social change, particularly through national economic development that would create more and better job opportunities. In many cases, the conservative reaction against populists led the armed forces to seize power. Revolutionary leader Fidel Castro carved an alternative path in Cuba. Castro went beyond the reforms advocated by populists and sought an outright revolutionary transformation of Cuban society.

Economic Nationalism in Mexico

In the decades following the Mexican Revolution, a durable political and economic formula emerged under the Institutional Revolutionary Party (PRI), which dominated public life while adhering to the social goals demanded by the movements that had fought in the revolution, especially the redistribution of land. By the end of the Second World War, Mexico had embraced economic nationalism—the effort to promote economic development through substitution of imports with domestic manufacturing and through state control of key industries like the oil sector.

As before the revolution, Mexicans faced a curtailed democracy, though in this case the government was controlled by a single party rather than a single individual. The PRI came to control elected office at every level, as well as networks of patronage. The party was also an omnipresent intermediary between business and labor. Mexico's economy also grew consistently through the 1970s, in what was termed an "economic miracle." This was a time of rapid urbanization, with people leaving rural areas for jobs in factories or for lower-paying service jobs, such as maids and janitors. The embrace of economic nationalism softened some of the edges of economic change that Mexicans had experienced in the liberal era, but social inequities remained. The upper and middle classes reaped the lion's share of the benefits of this economic growth.

A housing and civic complex in the Tlatelolco (tlah-tehl-OL-koh) district of Mexico City symbolized both the promise of the Mexican economic miracle and also the limits to democracy in Mexico. In the 1960s the Mexican government built dozens of modernist apartment buildings and government ministries. Their centerpiece was the Plaza of the Three Cultures, which contained ruins from the Aztec Empire, a colonial Spanish church, and the contemporary nation reflected in modernist architecture. It was in Tlatelolco where government forces silenced political dissent in advance of the 1968 Olympics by opening fire on a student march.

Populism in Argentina and Brazil

Argentina and Brazil's postwar economic development was shaped by populist politicians who championed economic nationalism. These politicians sought support from millions of people who gained the right to vote for the first time as universal suffrage spread through Latin America. Universal male suffrage was achieved in Argentina in 1912 and in Mexico in 1917. Women gained the right to vote across Latin America in the decades that followed, beginning with Ecuador in 1929 and Brazil in 1932. In most cases voters still needed to be literate to vote. To appeal to these millions of new voters, populist candidates promised schools and hospitals, higher wages, and nationalist projects that would create more industrial jobs.

At the turn of the century Argentina's economy prospered through its liberal export boom (see "Latin America Re-enters the World Economy" in Chapter 27), but industrialization followed only haltingly and the economy faltered. Populist Juan Perón, an army colonel, was elected president in 1946 with the support of Argentina's unions. Juan Perón was charismatic, but his wife, Eva, known as Evita, was even more so, and played a vital role in promoting Perón. Once in power, Perón embarked on an ambitious scheme to transform Argentina's economy: The government would purchase all the country's agricultural exports in order to negotiate their sale abroad at a higher price. Perón would then reinvest the profits in industry and raise worker wages to stimulate demand.

Perón's scheme worked in the immediate postwar period, when European agricultural production had not yet recovered from the war. But as commodity prices declined, Perón reduced government payments to farmers, who ceased to bring their harvests to market. In the coming decades Argentina never returned to the high rates of economic growth it had enjoyed at the beginning of the century. Many blamed Perón for distorting the economy for his own political gain. Others saw Perón's efforts as halting a worse decline: Argentina's economy had long been dependent on Britain, and as Britain's capacity to import declined, so did Argentina's fortunes.

Despite these economic setbacks, Perón initially remained highly popular, buoyed by the public appeals made by Evita. (See "Individuals in Society: Eva Perón," page 994.) After Evita died of cancer in 1952, much of the magic slipped away. Amid the stagnating economy even Perón's union supporters faltered, and he responded harshly to press criticism. In 1955 the armed forces deposed and exiled Perón. The military ruled Argentina for the next three years, conducting a process of "de-Perónization." It banned Perón's party and even forbade mention of his name. But Perón remained the most popular politician in the country. Presidential candidates could not win without discreetly winning the exiled Perón's endorsement, and this veiled support for Perón by civilian leaders prompted repeated military interventions in politics.

In Brazil, reacting against the economic and political liberalism through which coffee planters dominated the country, the armed forces installed Getúlio Vargas as president in 1930. Vargas initiated democratic reforms but veered into a nationalist dictatorship known as the "New State" (1937–1945), inspired by European fascism. Despite his harsh treatment of opponents, he was popular with workers and was elected in 1950 to a new term as president, now reinvented as a populist who promised nationalist economic reforms. The armed forces and conservatives mistrusted

Eva Perón

OFTEN CALLED EVITA (THE SPANISH DIMINU-
tive of Eva), Eva Duarte de Perón (1919–1952)
was one of five children born outside of marriage
to Juan Duarte and Juana Ibarguren, near Buenos
Aires. Duarte returned to his legitimate wife and children when Eva was a year old,
leaving Juana and her children
destitute and dependent on Juana's sewing for their existence.
As they grew older, all the children had to work.

At fifteen Eva Duarte moved
to the cosmopolitan city of Buenos Aires. Although she had little
formal education and no connections, she possessed beauty and
charisma, and soon she joined a
professional theater group. She
also modeled, appeared in a few
movies, and acted in a radio
series. By 1943, although only
twenty-three years old, she was
one of the highest-paid actresses
in the country.

**Eva Perón waves to supporters from the balcony
of the presidential palace, Casa Rosada, in
Buenos Aires, on October 17, 1951.** (Archivo Clarin/AP
Photo/AP Images)

In 1943 Eva met widowed Colonel Juan Perón, then
secretary of labor and social welfare in the military government that had seized power that year. Juan Perón
had grand ambitions, intending to run for president.
Eva Duarte became his partner and confidante, and she
won him support among the Argentine masses. In 1945
Juan Perón and Eva Duarte married.

A year later Perón won the presidency. Eva had campaigned for her husband and had organized support
from *los descamisados* (the shirtless ones), her name for
Argentina's poor. When Perón assumed the presidency,
Eva, though not officially appointed, became the secretary of labor. Having come from a childhood of poverty
herself, she now worked tirelessly for the poor, for the
working classes, and with organized labor. She instituted
a number of social welfare measures and promoted a
new Ministry of Health, which resulted in the creation
of new hospitals and disease-treatment programs. In

1948 she established the Eva Perón Welfare Foundation, which grew into an immense semiofficial welfare
agency, helping the poor throughout Argentina.

From early on, Eva Perón had supported women's
suffrage, and in September 1947 Argentine women won
the right to vote. Eva then formed the Female Perónist
Party, which by 1951 had five hundred thousand members. In 1951 she seemed ready
to run for vice president beside
her husband. Her declining
health, however, forced her to
turn down the nomination.
Juan Perón won the election
by over 30 percent, but when
Eva died the following year,
his authoritarian rule and bad
economic policies lost him
support, and a military junta
forced him into exile.

Eva Perón's life story is an
amazing one, but what happened following her death is
just as extraordinary. Before the
massive monument intended to
hold her embalmed body could
be built, the military seized
power and her body disappeared. Seventeen years later
the generals finally revealed that it was in a tomb in
Milan, Italy. Juan Perón, living in Spain with his third
wife, had the body exhumed and brought to Spain,
where he kept it in his house. Perón returned to Argentina in 1973 and won the presidential election, but died
the following year. His wife, Isabelita Perón, succeeded
him as president. Juan and Eva's bodies were briefly displayed together at his funeral and then, finally, buried.

QUESTIONS FOR ANALYSIS

1. Why do you think Eva Perón was adored by many
   Argentines when she died?
2. What were some of the welfare and government
   programs that Eva Perón promoted?

Source: Nicholas Fraser and Marysa Navarro, *Evita: The Real Life of Eva Perón* (New York:
Norton, 1976).

Vargas's appeals to workers and organized to depose him in 1954. Before they could act, Vargas killed himself.

The Vargas era saw rapid industrialization, the legalization of labor unions, and the creation of a minimum wage. Juscelino Kubitschek, elected in 1955, continued to build upon Vargas's populism and nationalism. Between 1956 and 1960 Kubitschek's government borrowed heavily from abroad to promote industry and build the futuristic new capital of Brasília in the midst of a wilderness. Kubitschek's slogan was "Fifty Years' Progress in Five."

In 1961 leftist populist João Goulart became Brazil's president. Goulart sought deeper reforms, including the redistribution of land and limits on the profits multinational corporations could take out of the country. In 1964 the armed forces, backed by the United States, deposed Goulart and held on to power for the next twenty-one years.

Building a Modern Capital Architect Oscar Niemeyer at the site of the construction of the futuristic National Congress building in Brazil's new planned capital, Brasília, in 1960. (© Rene Burri/Magnum Photos)

Communist Revolution in Cuba

Cuba remained practically an American colony until the 1930s, when a series of rulers with socialist and Communist leanings seized and lost power. Cuba's political institutions were weak and its politicians corrupt. In March 1952 Fulgencio Batista (1901–1973) staged a coup with American support and instituted an authoritarian regime that favored wealthy Cubans and U.S. businesses.

The Cuban Revolution (1953–1959) brought Fidel Castro (1927–2016) to power through an armed insurgency that used guerrilla tactics crafted by Argentine revolutionary Ernesto "Che" Guevara. Castro pursued deep economic reforms such as land redistribution and rent caps to help the urban poor. Because Castro's nationalization of utilities and industries as well as land reform came at the expense of U.S. businesses, U.S. president John F. Kennedy staged an invasion of Cuba to topple Castro. When the invasion force, composed of Cuban exiles, landed at the Bay of Pigs, the Cuban revolutionary army, commanded by Castro, repelled it in an embarrassment to the United States.

Castro had not come to power as a Communist: his main aim had been to regain control of Cuba's economy and politics from the United States. But U.S. efforts to overthrow him and to starve the Cuban economy drove him to form an alliance with the Soviet Union, which agreed to place nuclear missiles in Cuba to protect against another U.S. invasion. When Kennedy demanded the missiles be removed, the military and diplomatic brinksmanship of the 1962 Cuban missile crisis ensued. In 1963 the United States placed a complete commercial embargo on Cuba that remains in place although diplomatic relations were restored in 2015.

Cuba

Revolutionaries in Cuba Che Guevara (left) and Fidel Castro (right), whose successful revolution in Cuba inspired armed movements across Latin America. (© United Archives/Topfoto/The Image Works)

Castro now declared himself a Marxist-Leninist and relied on Soviet military and economic support, though Cuba retained a revolutionary mind-set that differed from the rest of the Soviet bloc. Castro was committed to spreading revolution to the rest of Latin America, and Guevara participated in armed struggles in the Congo and Bolivia before being assassinated by U.S.-trained Bolivian forces in 1967. Within Cuba activists swept into the countryside and taught people who were illiterate. Medical attention and education became free and widely accessible. The Cuban Revolution inspired young radicals across Latin America to believe in the possibility of swift revolution and brisk reforms to combat historic inequalities. But these reforms were achieved at great cost and through the suppression of political dissent. Castro declared in 1961, "Inside of the revolution anything, outside the revolution, nothing."[8] Political opponents were jailed or exiled.

Why did the world face growing social unrest in the 1960s?

The Limits of Postwar Prosperity

In the 1950s and 1960s the United States and the Soviet Union, as well as both western and eastern Europe, rebounded economically from the combined strains of the Great Depression and the Second World War. The postwar return of prosperity increased living standards but did not resolve underlying tensions and conflicts.

The Soviet Union Struggles to Move Beyond Stalin

The Cold War provided Stalin with the opportunity to revive many of the harshest aspects of the repression citizens of the Soviet Union had experienced in the 1930s, such as purges of soldiers and civilian officials and the revival of forced-labor camps. Stalin reasserted control of the government and society by reintroducing five-year plans to cope with the enormous task of reconstruction. He exported this system to eastern Europe. Rigid indoctrination, attacks on religion, and a lack of civil liberties became facts of life in the region's one-party states. Only Yugoslavia's Josip Tito (1892–1980), the popular resistance leader and Communist Party chief, could resist Soviet domination successfully because there was no Russian army in Yugoslavia.

After Stalin died in 1953, his successor Nikita Khrushchev (CROO-shehv) (1894–1971) realized that reforms were necessary because of widespread fear and hatred of Stalin's political terrorism. Khrushchev and the reformers in his administration curbed the secret police and gradually closed many forced-labor camps. Change was also necessary for economic reasons. Agriculture struggled, and shortages of consumer goods discouraged hard work. Moreover, Stalin's foreign policy had provoked a strong Western alliance, isolating the Soviet Union.

Khrushchev denounced Stalin and his crimes in a "secret speech" delivered to a closed session of the Twentieth Party Congress in 1956:

> It is clear that . . . Stalin showed in a whole series of cases his intolerance, his brutality, and his abuse of power. Instead of proving his political correctness and mobilizing the masses, he often chose the path of repression and physical annihilation, not only against actual enemies, but also against individuals who had not committed any crimes against the party and the Soviet Government.[9]

The liberalization of the Soviet Union—labeled de-Stalinization in the West—was genuine. Khrushchev declared that "peaceful coexistence" with capitalism was possible. The government shifted some economic resources to production of consumer goods, improving standards of living throughout the booming 1960s. De-Stalinization opened new space for creative work and for expressing dissent. The writer Aleksandr Solzhenitsyn (1918–2008) created a sensation when his *One Day in the Life of Ivan Denisovich* was published in the Soviet Union in 1962. Solzhenitsyn's novel portrayed life in a Stalinist concentration camp in grim detail and was a damning indictment of the Stalinist past.

De-Stalinization stimulated rebelliousness in the eastern European satellites. Poland won greater autonomy in 1956 after extensive protests forced the Soviets to allow a new Communist government. Led by students and workers, the people of Budapest, Hungary, installed a liberal Communist reformer as their new chief in October 1956. The rebellion was short-lived. After the government promised open elections and renounced Hungary's military alliance with Moscow, the Soviet army invaded and crushed the revolution, killing thousands. When the United States did not come to Hungary's aid, many eastern European reformers concluded that their best hope was to strive for incremental gains rather than broad change.

In August 1961 the East German government began construction of a twenty-seven-mile wall between East and West Berlin. It also built a ninety-mile-long barrier between the three allied sectors of West Berlin and East Germany, thereby completely cutting off West Berlin. Officially the wall was called the "Anti-Fascist Protection Wall." In reality the Berlin Wall prevented East Germans from "voting with their feet" by defecting to the West.

By late 1962 opponents had come to see Khrushchev's policies as a dangerous threat to party authority. Moreover, Khrushchev did not succeed in alleviating tensions with the West. In 1962 Khrushchev ordered missiles with nuclear warheads installed in Cuba to shield it from U.S. invasion, triggering the Cuban missile crisis. The hard line taken by the U.S. over the placement of the missiles put the superpowers on the brink of war until Khrushchev backed down and removed the missiles. Two years later, Communist Party leaders removed him. After Leonid Brezhnev (1906–1982) and his supporters took over in 1964, they stopped further liberalization and launched an arms buildup, determined not to repeat Khrushchev's humiliation by the United States.

Postwar Challenges in Western Europe and the United States

In 1945 much of western Europe was devastated by the war, and it faced mass unemployment, shortages of food and fuel, and the dislocation of millions of people. But in the decades that followed, western Europe experienced a dramatic recovery. Democratic governments thrived in an atmosphere of broadening civil liberties. Progressive Catholics and their Christian Democratic political parties were particularly influential. Socialists and Communists active in the resistance against Hitler returned with renewed prestige. In the immediate postwar years welfare measures such as family stipends, health insurance, and expanded public housing were enacted throughout much of Europe.

An immediate result of the Cold War was the partition between a Soviet-controlled German Democratic Republic (East Germany) and a Federal Republic of Germany (West Germany) that had been occupied by the United States, Britain, and France. With the support of the United States, which wanted to turn an economically resurgent West Germany into a bulwark against Soviet expansion, Chancellor Konrad Adenauer (1881–1967), brought Germany firmly into the Western capitalist camp. He forged close ties with the United States, Great Britain, and France. He also initiated dialogues with leaders of Europe's Jewish community and with Israel to encourage a reconciliation following the Holocaust. As Germany recovered from the war, it became Europe's leading economic power, a member of NATO, and an architect of efforts at European unity.

Amid the destruction and uncertainty brought by two world wars caused by Europeans and fought in Europe, many Europeans believed that only unity could forestall future European conflicts. The first steps toward economic unity were taken through close cooperation over Marshall Plan aid. These were followed by the creation in 1952 of a Coal and Steel Community, made up of France, West Germany, Italy,

Guest Workers in Europe

In the 1950s and 1960s thousands of workers from Spain, Portugal, Italy, Greece, and Turkey immigrated into parts of Europe where the postwar growth in industrial production had created a scarcity of labor. Workers like this Italian seamstress and supervisor in a German factory fled a weak economy and high unemployment in their country of origin, seeking work in countries like Germany and France. (Max Scheler/Suddeutsche Zeitung Photo/Alamy Stock Photo)

Belgium, the Netherlands, and Luxembourg. In 1957 these nations signed the Treaty of Rome, creating the European Economic Community, popularly known as the **Common Market**. The treaty's primary goal was to eliminate trade barriers between them and create a single market almost as large as that of the United States.

Migrant laborers, mainly from southern Italy, North Africa, Turkey, Greece, and Yugoslavia, also shaped western European societies and drove their economic recovery. Tens of millions of migrant workers made it possible for western European economies to continue to grow beyond their postwar labor capacity. This was especially important in Germany, where they filled gaps left by the wartime loss of a large proportion of the adult male population. Governments at first labeled the migrants as "guest workers" to signal their temporary status, though in practice many would remain in their new homes. As their communities became more settled, migrants faced a backlash from majority populations and came to resent and resist their treatment as second-class citizens.

In the United States the postwar era was also shaped by economic recovery and social pressures. The Second World War ended the Great Depression in the United States, bringing about an economic boom that increased living standards dramatically. By the end of the war, the United States had the strongest economy and held an advantage over its past commercial rivals: its industry and infrastructure had not been damaged by war. After the war, U.S. manufactured goods saturated markets around the world that had previously been dominated by Britain, France, and Germany.

Postwar America experienced a social revolution as well: after a long struggle African Americans began to experience major victories against the deeply entrenched system of segregation and discrimination. This civil rights movement advanced on several fronts, none more prominent than legal victories that ended the statutory segregation of schools. African American civil rights activists challenged inequality by using Gandhian methods of nonviolent resistance: as civil rights leader Martin Luther King, Jr. (1929–1968), said, "Christ furnished the spirit and motivation, while Gandhi furnished the method." He told the white power structure, "We will not hate you, but we will not obey your evil laws."[10]

Common Market The European Economic Community created in 1957.

The World in 1968

In 1968 pressures for social change boiled over into protests worldwide. The preceding two decades offered the world an example of how much people could change as decolonization swept much of the world. Revolutionary struggles stretched from Cuba to the remaining colonies in Africa and the war in Southeast Asia. The architecture of white supremacism and racial segregation was being dismantled in the United States. Young protesters drew upon recent history to appreciate how much could be achieved and looked at their world to see how much more was needed. Around the world, streets and squares filled with protesters.

In Czechoslovakia the "Prague Spring"—a brief period of liberal reform and loosening of political controls—unfolded as reformers in the Czechoslovakian Communist Party gained a majority and replaced a long-time Stalinist leader with Alexander Dubček (DOOB-chehk), whose new government launched dramatic reforms. Dubček and his allies called for "socialism with a human face," which meant rolling

The Soviet Invasion of Prague, 1968 Czech demonstrators throw torches and wave flags in an attempt to stop a tank as the Soviet army crushes the protests of the Prague Spring in 1968. (Libo Hajsky/AFP/Getty Images)

back many of the strictures imposed by Stalin. He restored freedom of speech and freedom of the press. Communist leaders in the Soviet Union and other eastern European states feared that they would face similar demands for reform from their own citizens. Protests against the excesses of Communist rule erupted in Poland and Yugoslavia.

In France students went on strike over poor university conditions. When government responded with harsh punishments, larger and more radical student protests erupted. Labor unions called a general strike. The strikes captured the anxieties of the generation that had been raised in postwar Europe. For many of them, their governments' postwar socialist reforms were incomplete and the time was now ripe for more far-ranging change—if not outright revolution. Similar student movements erupted across western Europe.

In Latin America students rose in protest as well. In Argentina students in the industrial city of Córdoba went on strike against the military dictatorship that had been in place since 1966. Joined by factory workers, the protesters took control of the city in an event known as the Cordobazo. In Brazil a national student strike challenged the military dictatorship that had been in power since 1964. In Mexico City, where the 1968 Olympic games would be held, students used the international visibility of the event to protest the heavy-handed ruling PRI Party. The Latin American students challenging their regimes were motivated by the example offered by revolutionary Cuba, which they saw as a model of swift social transformation.

The ongoing U.S. military intervention in Vietnam met with growing opposition worldwide. In Japan protesters denounced what they saw as the complicity of their government and businesses in the U.S. military intervention in Vietnam, and challenged the Security Treaty that bound Japan and the United States. As the continuation of the war depended increasingly on military drafts, protests against the Vietnam War and against the draft erupted on college campuses across the United States and in its ally in the conflict, Australia.

In the United States the antiwar movement marked an increase in popular mobilization: civil rights marches in the South now extended to protests against discrimination and police violence in cities like Boston and Chicago. Protesters around the world were aware of each other and felt empowered by the sense that they were participating in a worldwide movement against the abuses of the established order. Their actions echoed Che Guevara's call for "two, three or many Vietnams" of resistance against imperialism.

In 1968 it seemed that social movements worldwide were on the verge of opening the floodgates to a wave of radical change, but the opposite was more true. Protesters and reformers faced violent reactions from the powerful political and economic groups they challenged. Conservatives reacted against more than the protests of 1968: they sought to slow or sometimes reverse the dramatic changes that had taken place in the postwar era.

Around the world, protests were followed by violent crackdowns such as the Soviet deployment of tanks in Czechoslovakia in October 1968, which crushed the Prague Spring, unseated Dubček, and led to harsh persecutions of the Prague Spring's supporters. In Mexico, Argentina, and Brazil, military and paramilitary groups launched violent campaigns against protesting students and workers, such as the Mexican government's shooting of protesters in Tlatelolco before the Olympics. In the United States assassins killed Martin Luther King, Jr., and other civil rights leaders. In 1967 Che Guevara was executed by Bolivian troops trained and led by the U.S. government. Around the world, revolutionary violence was met with increasingly violent repression.

Chapter Summary

The decades after the Second World War were an era of rebuilding, a term that had different meanings for different peoples. In Europe, the Soviet Union, and Japan, rebuilding literally meant clearing the rubble from wartime devastation and restoring what had been destroyed. In Germany and Japan in particular, rebuilding meant charting political and economic paths different from the ones that nationalist fervor had forged.

For the United States and the Soviet Union, rebuilding meant developing a military and ideological complex with which to confront each other in the Cold War. In each country individually, rebuilding took other forms: in the Soviet Union it meant finding ways to reform the system of political terror and coercion through which Stalin had ruled; in the United States it meant struggling to overcome the structures of white supremacy and other forms of racial discrimination.

The idea of rebuilding took on its deepest meaning in Asia, Africa, and the Middle East, where rebuilding meant dismantling European colonialism to establish independent states. This required replacing not just colonial institutions but colonial mentalities, patterns of production, and forms of education, and developing ways of relating that were not based on terms dictated by colonizers. Intellectuals and artists strove to decolonize the mind as politicians worked to decolonize the state in a process that proved slow and difficult. In Latin America rebuilding meant finding the means to overcome patterns of social exclusion that were legacies of colonialism and neocolonialism. It also meant finding the means to industrialize, overcoming the patterns of dependency and underdevelopment diagnosed by Latin American intellectuals and social scientists.

The decades after 1945 showed how much was possible through mass movements, advancing industrialization, and political self-determination. But the balance of these years also showed how much more work remained to overcome poverty, underdevelopment, and neocolonialism.

NOTES

1. Frantz Fanon, *The Wretched of the Earth*, trans. Constance Farrington (New York: Grove Press, 1968), pp. 43, 93–94, 97, 102.
2. Chinua Achebe, *Things Fall Apart* (London: Heinemann, 2000), pp. 124–125.
3. Syed Sharifuddin Pirzada, ed., *Foundations of Pakistan: All-India Muslim League Documents*. Vol. 2: *1924–1947* (Karachi: National Publishing House, 1970), p. 338.
4. Quoted in K. Bhata, *The Ordeal of Nationhood: A Social Study of India Since Independence, 1947–1970* (New York: Atheneum, 1971), p. 9.
5. Cited in Sami Hanna and George Gardner, *Arab Socialism: A Documentary Survey* (Leiden: Brill, 1969), p. 106.
6. Mao Zedong, *Quotations from Chairman Mao Tsetung* (Peking: Foreign Language Press, 1972), p. 61.
7. Quoted in R. Hallett, *Africa Since 1875: A Modern History* (Ann Arbor: University of Michigan Press, 1974), pp. 378–379.
8. Quoted in Samuel Farber, *Cuba Since the Revolution of 1959: A Critical Assessment* (Chicago: Haymarket Books, 2011), p. 22.
9. *Congressional Record: Proceedings and Debates of the 84th Congress, 2nd Session* (May 22, 1956–June 11, 1956), C11, Part 7 (June 4, 1956), pp. 9389–9403.
10. Regarding Gandhi's methods: see M. L. King, Jr., *Stride Toward Freedom: The Montgomery Story* (New York: Perennial Library, 1964), p. 67. Regarding evil laws: quoted in S. E. Morison et al., *A Concise History of the American Republic* (New York: Oxford University Press), p. 697.

CONNECTIONS

The great transformations experienced by peoples around the world following the Second World War can best be compared to the age of revolution in the late eighteenth and early nineteenth centuries (see Chapter 22). In both eras peoples rose up to undertake the political, economic, social, and cultural transformation of their societies. In both eras, history seemed to accelerate, driven by events that had impacts across the globe. As in the age of revolution, which saw the independence of the United States and most of Spanish America as well as the Haitian and French Revolutions, people swept aside old notions of authority tied to kings and empires. In Asia the Chinese Revolution and the independence of India and Pakistan marked the accelerating pace of liberation movements that dismantled European colonialism and ushered in new political ideologies and economic systems.

Liberation movements spanning the globe sought not only to end imperial domination and remove social boundaries imposed by white racism, but also to make deeper changes in how peoples perceived themselves and their societies. As radical and new as these ideas were, they nonetheless owed much to the Enlightenment ideals about liberal individual rights that were promoted by the ideologues of the French and American Revolutions.

Though the social revolutions in countries like China and Cuba and the independence movements across Africa, Asia, and the Middle East brought unprecedented deep and fast changes, they were only the first steps in remaking societies that had been created by centuries of colonialism. Uprooting the legacies of colonialism — in the form of poverty, continued domination of economies by foreign powers, limited industrialization, and weak states — remained a daunting challenge that societies continued to face in the future.

CHAPTER 31 **Review and Explore**

Identify Key Terms

Identify and explain the significance of each item below.

Cold War (p. 970)

Truman Doctrine (p. 971)

Marshall Plan (p. 971)

NATO (p. 971)

dependency theory (p. 974)

modernization theory (p. 975)

import substitution industrialization (ISI) (p. 976)

liberation theology (p. 976)

Muslim League (p. 979)

Arab socialism (p. 980)

Palestine Liberation Organization (PLO) (p. 981)

Great Leap Forward (p. 985)

Great Proletarian Cultural Revolution (p. 985)

Pan-Africanists (p. 988)

cocoa holdups (p. 988)

National Liberation Front (p. 991)

Common Market (p. 999)

Review the Main Ideas

Answer the focus questions from each section of the chapter.

1. How did the Cold War and decolonization shape the postwar world? (p. 970)

2. How did religion and the legacies of colonialism affect the formation of new nations in South Asia and the Middle East after World War II? (p. 978)

3. How did the Cold War shape reconstruction, revolution, and decolonization in East and Southeast Asia? (p. 982)

4. What factors influenced decolonization in Africa after World War II? (p. 988)

5. Why did populism emerge as such a powerful political force in Latin America? (p. 992)

6. Why did the world face growing social unrest in the 1960s? (p. 996)

Make Comparisons and Connections

Analyze the larger developments and continuities within and across chapters.

1. What changes in the postwar world had their roots in developments that predated the war? How did the Second World War (Chapter 30) itself accelerate or spur changes in the postwar era?

2. What effect did the Cold War have on the process of decolonization?

3. How might the postwar era be compared to the age of revolution (Chapter 22)?

TIMELINE

GLOBAL	◆ **1945** United Nations established	
	1947–1975 Decolonization in Africa, Asia, and Middle East	
ASIA		**1950–1953** Korean War
	◆ **1947** Independence of India	
	◆ **1949** Chinese Revolution	
EUROPE	◆ **1948** Marshall Plan enacted	
	◆ **1949** Formation of NATO	
MIDDLE EAST	◆ **1948** Creation of Israel	
AMERICAS	**1946–1955** Populist Juan Perón leads Argentina	
AFRICA	← **1920s** Anticolonial nationalism sweeps Western-educated Africans in French and British colonies	
	← **1930–1931; 1937–1938** Cocoa holdups in the Gold Coast	

1945	1950	1955

Suggested Resources

BOOKS

Borstelmann, Thomas. *The Cold War and the Color Line: American Race Relations in the Global Arena.* 2003. An incisive discussion of the connections between racial thought and policy.

Cleveland, William L., and Martin Bunton. *A History of the Modern Middle East,* 6th ed. 2016. Well-crafted survey introduction to the modern history and politics of the Middle East.

Collins, Robert O., and James M. Burns. *A History of Sub-Saharan Africa.* 2007. Clearly written introduction to the continent's history.

Gaddis, John Lewis. *The Cold War: A New History.* 2005. A concise, authoritative, and accessible account of the Cold War by one of its leading historians.

Guha, Ramachandra. *India After Gandhi: The History of the World's Largest Democracy.* 2007. In-depth study of the last sixty years of Indian history and development.

Halberstam, David. *The Coldest Winter: America and the Korean War.* 2007. The last, and perhaps best, history written by one of America's finest journalist-historians.

Kamrava, Mehran. *The Modern Middle East: A Political History Since the First World War,* 3d ed. 2013. A concise overview of modern Middle East history, economics, and politics.

Keddie, Nikki R. *Modern Iran: Roots and Results of Revolution.* 2006. A classic survey of Iranian history and politics by a leading scholar of modern Iran.

Meade, Teresa A. *A History of Modern Latin America, 1800 to the Present.* 2009. A comprehensive history and analysis of the continent and its peoples.

Meredith, Martin. *The Fate of Africa: A History of Fifty Years of Independence.* 2006. A very accessible study of modern independent Africa that spans the entire continent.

Moaddel, Mansoor. *Islamic Modernism, Nationalism, and Fundamentalism.* 2005. A scholarly historical introduction to the society and politics of the Middle East.

1959–1975 War in Vietnam

1965 Great Proletarian Cultural Revolution in China

1956 Soviet invasion of Hungary

1961 East German government builds Berlin Wall

1957 Formation of Common Market

1953–1964 Khrushchev implements de-Stalinization in the Soviet Union

1956 Nasser nationalizes Suez Canal

1967 Six-Day War in Israel

1962 Cuban missile crisis

1953–1959 Cuban Revolution

1957 Ghana gains independence from colonial rule, marking the beginning of a rapid wave of decolonization in Africa

1960

1965

Osborne, Milton. *Southeast Asia: An Introductory History*, 12th ed. 2016. Classic introduction to the region.

DOCUMENTARIES

China: A Century of Revolution (Sue Williams, 1997). This six-episode documentary explores the roots and course of China's Communist revolution.

The Cold War (CNN, 1998). A twenty-four-episode series that takes a detailed look at the Cold War's European origins, global reach, and resolution.

The 50 Years War: Israel and the Arabs (PBS/BBC, 1998). Examines the Arab-Israeli conflict beginning with the 1947 UN partition of Palestine.

FEATURE FILMS

The Battle of Algiers (Gillo Pontecorvo, 1966). Chronicling the Algerian war for independence from France, this film is a rich reflection on the practices of guerrilla warfare and the anticolonial struggle.

Fail Safe (Sidney Lumet, 1964). A thriller centered on the phone conversations between the U.S. president

and Soviet premier as they seek to defuse a nuclear crisis.

Z and *State of Siege* (Costa-Gavras, 1969 and 1972). Two powerful films that explore Greece's descent into dictatorship in the 1960s and U.S. support for torture and repression in Latin America.

WEBSITES

Africana Age: African & African Diasporan Transformations in the 20th Century. The Schomburg Center for Research in Black Culture at the New York Public Library offers essays and research materials on topics such as "Négritude," "Black Power," and "African Decolonization." **exhibitions.nypl.org/africanaage /essay-landing.html**

The United Nations and Decolonization. Documents on the founding of the United Nations and the question of decolonization. **www.un.org/en/decolonization/**

Universal Newsreels. The Internet Archive contains many newsreels on subjects in this chapter. **archive.org detailsuniversal_newsreels?&sort =-downloads&page=2**

32

Liberalization
1968–2000s

In the 1970s two currents ran against each other in much of the world. The radicalism of liberation in decolonization, revolutions, and mass social movements continued. Women's movements achieved important successes in pressing for reproductive rights and equity in education, employment, and compensation, both in the West and in nationalist regimes around the world. The most dramatic phase of decolonization in Africa and black civil rights mobilization in the United States had succeeded, but the hard work of making new nations function, or of achieving racial equality, continued.

But alongside this current ran a different one whose influence was not easily apparent in the early 1970s but was undeniable by the 1990s: liberalization. Liberal political and economic ideology experienced a resurgence. After the Second World War, the United States had championed liberal economic policies and global free trade, but this objective ran against the desires of other countries to protect and promote their own industrialization and economic development. But in the last decades of the century, the U.S. drive for global liberalization of trade experienced greater success, while reform movements in the Eastern bloc and in Latin America pursued human rights and political liberalization.

Sandinista Soldier in Nicaragua

Street art in Jinotega, Nicaragua, shows an armed female soldier of the Sandinista National Liberation Front picking coffee beans in her military camouflage. The Sandinistas overthrew the U.S.-backed dictator Anastasio Somoza in 1979. After their victory, the socialist Sandinistas ruled Nicaragua until 1990 and then returned to power in 2006.

Thalia Watmough/aliki image library/Alamy Stock Photo

CHAPTER PREVIEW

What were the short-term and long-term consequences of the OPEC oil embargo?

Oil Shocks and Liberalization

In 1973 war erupted again between Israel and its neighbors Egypt and Syria. The conflict became known both as the Yom Kippur War because it coincided with the Jewish religious holiday of atonement, and as the Ramadan War because it occurred during the Muslim month of fasting. Armed with advanced weapons from the Soviet Union, Egyptian and Syrian armies came close to defeating Israel before the U.S. government airlifted sophisticated arms to Israel. Israel counterattacked, reaching the outskirts of both Cairo and Damascus before the fighting ended.

Arab oil-exporting countries retaliated against U.S. support for Israel by imposing an embargo on oil sales to countries that had aided Israel during the war. Amid the oil embargo, the war in Vietnam, and political conflict within the United States, U.S. political and economic influence as a global superpower seemed to decline.

The OPEC Oil Embargo

Organization of the Petroleum Exporting Countries (OPEC) A cartel formed in 1960 by oil-exporting countries designed to coordinate oil production and raise prices, giving those countries greater capacity for economic development and greater leverage in world affairs.

In 1960 oil-exporting countries formed a cartel called the **Organization of the Petroleum Exporting Countries (OPEC)** to coordinate production and raise prices. They aimed to increase national revenue to support economic development. Until the early 1970s OPEC had failed to control the market for oil. But in 1973 OPEC countries agreed to an embargo, withholding oil sales to the United States and western Europe in response to their support for Israel in the Yom Kippur War.

Since oil is a commodity that is traded globally, it remained available in Europe and the United States despite the embargo. But the embargo disrupted the market and caused panic. The price of oil increased almost overnight from $3 to $12 per barrel, quadrupling energy costs. OPEC's ability to disrupt the world economy, and the U.S. government's powerlessness to reverse the disruption, suggested a new world order. Brazil's military leaders, for example, distanced themselves from their traditional alliance with the United States and built relations with OPEC countries. Fearing reprisal from Arab countries, Brazil quietly halted exports to Israel, while promoting arms sales and engineering services to Libya and Iraq. Brazil's foreign minister told U.S. secretary of state Henry Kissinger, "If you could supply us with a million barrels of oil a day, perhaps this shift would not be so abrupt."[1]

Oil prices remained high and peaked again in the second oil shock of 1979, which resulted from the Iranian revolution that ousted the secular government and brought religious leaders to power. In the United States energy costs sapped economic growth and triggered inflation, a combination dubbed stagflation. Europe and Japan, heavily dependent on oil imports, resorted to bicycles and mass transit to reduce their energy needs, as well as intense development of nuclear energy.

petrodollars The global recirculation by international banks of profits from the higher price of oil following the 1973 OPEC oil embargo.

In the decade after the first oil shock, OPEC countries such as Saudi Arabia deposited their profits in international banks, particularly in the United States, which in turn reinvested these deposits as loans that governments around the world used to finance development. This money was known as **petrodollars**. In this economic cycle, consumers around the world paid higher prices for fuel, which generated profits for oil exporters, who invested the profits in large banks. In turn, these banks loaned this capital out to foreign governments. Many industrializing countries faced both high energy costs and heavy debts amassed through petrodollar loans.

In the United States, as stagflation and the 1979 second oil shock fueled inflation, the Federal Reserve Bank raised interest rates. Increased interest rates in the United States made it more expensive to borrow money, which slowed economic activity and led to an economic recession. The recession diminished consumer demand for goods, which reduced inflation. But the United States was not the only country to experience this recession: countries that exported to the United States faced reduced demand for their goods, and countries that borrowed from U.S. banks found that the interest on their debts increased as well. In industrializing nations the rapid increase in interest on their heavy debts became a crippling burden, triggering a global crisis. Countries facing soaring debts and interest rates became dependent on U.S. assistance to restructure unsustainable loans, allowing the U.S. government to dictate terms that imposed neoliberal free-market reforms.

Beginning in the 1980s neoliberal policies increasingly shaped the world economy. **Neoliberalism** promoted free-market policies and the free circulation of capital across national borders. Debtor countries needed to continue to borrow in order to pay the interest on the debts they held, and their ability to secure loans now depended on their adherence to a set of liberal principles known as the **Washington Consensus**: policies that restricted public spending, lowered import barriers, privatized state enterprises, and deregulated markets.

The forces unleashed by the Yom Kippur War and the OPEC oil embargo of 1973 at first tipped the scale in favor of less industrialized nations, but by the 1980s the scale had swung back as debt and liberalization returned power to the most economically powerful countries, in particular the United States. The experiences of Mexico and Nigeria reflect the effects of the boom-and-bust cycle ignited by the oil embargo. In both cases, the oil boom of the 1970s fueled long-standing projects for development and industrialization. But as boom turned to bust, both countries were left with enduring challenges: ethnic and religious divisions continued to undermine Nigeria, while Mexico's one-party state struggled to retain power as it yielded to liberalizing pressure from the United States.

neoliberalism A return beginning in the 1980s to policies intended to promote free markets and the free circulation of capital across national borders.

Washington Consensus Policies restricting public spending, lowering import barriers, privatizing state enterprises, and deregulating markets in response to the 1980s debt crisis in Latin America.

Mexico Under the PRI

By the 1970s Mexico's Institutional Revolutionary Party (PRI) had been in power since the revolution. PRI candidates held nearly every public office. The PRI controlled both labor unions and federations of businessmen. More than a party, it was a vast system of patronage. It was also the party of land reform, universal public education, industrialization, and state ownership of the country's oil reserves. Mexico's road from economic nationalism to the liberal reforms of the 1970s and 1980s is also the story of the PRI.

In the aftermath of the 1968 Tlatelolco massacre, the PRI chose and elected as president populist Luis Echeverría, who sought to reclaim the mantle of revolutionary reform by nationalizing utilities and increasing social spending. He and his successor, José López Portillo, embarked on development projects financed through projected future earnings of the state oil monopoly PEMEX. Amid the decline of oil prices during the global recession, in 1982 the Mexican government stopped payments on its foreign debt, nationalized the banks, and steeply devalued the peso.

The PRI was further undermined by its inept and corrupt response to a devastating earthquake that struck Mexico City in 1986. Two years later the PRI faced

The Power of the PRI A lottery board game with the Mexican Institutional Revolutionary Party (PRI) logo in the top left corner indicates its widespread presence in everyday Mexican life. (Courtesy, MODO, Museo del Objeto del Objeto, Mexico City)

its first real presidential election challenge. Cuauhtémoc (kwow-TAY-mokh) Cárdenas, who was the son of populist Lázaro Cárdenas and was named after the last Aztec ruler, ran against PRI candidate Carlos Salinas de Gortari. On election night, as the vote counting favored Cárdenas, the government declared that the computers tabulating the votes had crashed and declared Salinas the winner. The PRI-controlled congress ordered the ballots burned afterward.

As Mexican leaders found themselves hemmed in by the debt crisis, they were compelled to embrace the Washington Consensus, which meant restricted spending, opening trade borders, and privatization. They abandoned the economic nationalism that had driven development, and negotiated a free-trade agreement with the United States and Canada, the North American Free Trade Agreement (NAFTA), which went into effect in 1994.

Nigeria, Africa's Giant

Nigeria's boom-and-bust oil economy aggravated the challenges of nation building after independence. The British imposed the name "Nigeria" on a region of many ancient kingdoms and hundreds of ethnic groups (see Map 31.5, page 989). After the country gained independence from Britain in 1960, Nigeria's key constitutional question was the relationship between the central government and its ethnically distinct regions. Under the federal system created after independence, each region had a dominant ethnic group and a corresponding political party. After independence Nigeria's ethnic rivalries intensified, and in 1967 they erupted in the Biafran war in which the Igbo ethnic group in southeastern Nigeria fought unsuccessfully to form a separate nation. The war lasted three years and resulted in famine that left millions dead.

The wealth generated by oil exports in the 1970s had contradictory effects on Nigerian society. On one hand, a succession of military leaders who held power after a 1966 coup grew increasingly corrupt throughout the 1970s. When the dictator General Murtala Muhammad (1938–1976) sought to eradicate corruption, fellow officers assassinated him. On the other hand, oil wealth allowed the country to rebuild after the Biafran war. By the mid-1970s Nigeria had the largest middle and professional classes on the continent outside of South Africa. Nigeria's oil boom in the 1970s resembled Mexico's experience: the expectation of future riches led to growing indebtedness, and when global demand and oil prices collapsed amid the global recession of the early 1980s, Nigeria faced a debt crisis.

Oil in Nigeria Nigeria's oil has brought great profits to some, but poorer Nigerians have been excluded from the profits and have borne the costs of oil production. This fisherman displays his nets, which have been fouled by spilled oil. (George Ojodi/Bloomberg via Getty Images)

Oil wealth allowed Nigeria to develop one innovative solution to its ethnic divisions: the construction of a modernist new capital, Abuja, modeled on Brazil's project in Brasília (see "Populism in Argentina and Brazil" in Chapter 31). Located in the center of the country at the confluence of major regional and ethnic boundaries, Abuja symbolized equal representation in government. Urban planning reflected both the reality of ethnic divisions and the objective of integration: residential areas were divided by ethnicity, but shopping and services were located between them to encourage commingling.

Except for an early period of civilian rule, Muslim army officers ruled Nigeria until 1998, when the dictator General Sani Abacha suddenly died. Nigerians adopted a new constitution in 1999, and that same year they voted in free elections and re-established civilian rule. Subsequent elections in 2007 marked the first civilian-to-civilian transfer of power. Ethnic tensions remained. Since 2000 ethnic riots and violence by the fundamentalist Islamic group Boko Haram have left thousands dead in the predominantly Muslim northern Nigerian states. Much of the violence can be attributed to conflicts between Muslims and non-Muslim groups that resented the introduction of shari'a (Islamic law) in the state of Zamfara in 1999. Since then, another eleven northern Nigerian states have adopted shari'a, spurring resentment from the non-Muslim populations in these states.

War and Revolution in the Middle East

How did war and revolution reshape the Middle East?

The 1973 Yom Kippur War had a lasting effect across the Middle East. Egypt and Syria had again been defeated, but Israelis also felt more vulnerable after the war. The oil embargo empowered oil-exporting nations like Saudi Arabia, Libya, and Iraq. The Middle East faced deepening divisions, which added to the conflict between Israel and its neighbors. The region was reshaped by the increasing wealth of oil producers relative to other Arab states. Rising Islamic militancy led to revolution in Iran, as well as religious challenges to the rule of secular, modernizing dictatorships in countries like Egypt.

The Palestinian-Israeli Conflict

After the 1973 war, the United States intensified efforts to mediate a resolution to conflicts in the Middle East. Peacemaking efforts by U.S. president Jimmy Carter led to the 1978 Camp David Accords, which normalized relations between Israel and its neighbors Egypt and Jordan. With the prospect of border wars between Israel and its neighbors diminished, political attention turned to the conflict between Israel and Palestinian nationalist organizations. Tensions between Syria and Israel shifted from their border into Lebanon, where Syria backed the militia Hezbollah, or Party of God. Hezbollah condemned the 1978 and 1982 Israeli invasions of Lebanon aimed at eradicating the Palestine Liberation Organization's control of southern Lebanon, and had as one of its stated objectives the complete destruction of the state of Israel.

intifada Beginning in 1987, a prolonged campaign of civil disobedience by Palestinian youth against Israeli soldiers; the Arabic word *intifada* means "shaking off."

In 1987 young Palestinians in the occupied territories of the Gaza Strip and the West Bank began the **intifada**, a prolonged campaign of civil disobedience against Israeli soldiers. Inspired increasingly by Islamic fundamentalists, the Palestinian uprising eventually posed a serious challenge not only to Israel but also to the secular Palestine Liberation Organization (PLO), long led from abroad by Yasir Arafat. The result was an unexpected and mutually beneficial agreement in 1993 between Israel and the PLO. Israel agreed to recognize Arafat's organization and start a peace process that granted Palestinian self-rule in Gaza and called for self-rule throughout the West Bank in five years. In return, Arafat renounced violence and abandoned the demand that Israel must withdraw from all land occupied in the 1967 war.

The peace process increasingly divided Israel. In 1995 a right-wing Jewish extremist assassinated Prime Minister Yitzhak Rabin. In 1996 a coalition of opposition parties won a slender majority, charging the Palestinian leadership with condoning anti-Jewish violence. The new Israeli government limited Palestinian self-rule and expanded Jewish settlements in the West Bank. On the Palestinian side, dissatisfaction with the peace process grew. Between 1993 and 2000 the number of Jewish settlers in the West Bank doubled to two hundred thousand, and Palestinian per capita income declined by 20 to 25 percent.

Israel's Wall of Separation This wall, shown under construction in 2006, blocks off a Palestinian refugee camp in Arab East Jerusalem, limiting the camp inhabitants' access to the city they call home. (AWAD/Getty Images)

Failed negotiations between Arafat and Israel in 2000 unleashed an explosion of violence between Israelis and Palestinians known as the Second Intifada. In 2003 the Israeli government began to build a barrier around the West Bank, which met with opposition from Israelis and Palestinians alike.

The death of Yasir Arafat, the PLO's long-time leader, in November 2004 marked a turning point in the Israeli-Palestinian conflict. Mahmoud Abbas, Arafat's pragmatic successor, found little room for negotiation. In January 2006 Hamas, a Sunni Muslim political party, won 72 of the 136 seats in the Palestinian legislature, seizing control from Abbas and the PLO. Considered by Israel to be a terrorist organization, Hamas had gained widespread support from many Palestinians for the welfare programs it established in the West Bank and Gaza Strip.

Immediately after the Hamas victory, Israel, the United States, and the European Union suspended aid to the Palestinian Authority, the governing body of the West Bank and Gaza Strip established by the 1994 peace agreement. Since then, economic and humanitarian conditions for Palestinians living in the Gaza Strip have deteriorated. In 2007 Hamas, a political organization committed to building an Islamic state in the area now composed of Israel, Gaza, and the West Bank, assumed control of the Gaza Strip, deepening political divisions in Palestinian territory. In 2010, 63 percent of the 1.5 million citizens of Gaza lived below the United Nations–defined poverty line.

Egypt: Arab World Leader

From the time of Gamal Nasser's seizure of power in 1956 to the mid-1970s, Egypt, due to its large military, its anti-imperialist rhetoric, and its support for Arab unity, was recognized as the leader of the Arab world. In 1978 Egypt's president, Anwar Sadat (1918–1981), negotiated a peace settlement with Israel known as the Camp David Accords. Though Egypt gained the return of the Sinai Peninsula from Israel, some Arab leaders denounced Sadat's initiative as treason.

After Sadat was assassinated by religious radicals in 1981, Egyptian relations with Israel deteriorated, but Egypt and Israel maintained their fragile peace as Sadat's successor, Hosni Mubarak, took office. Mubarak remained a consistent supporter of Israel and a mediator between Israel and the Arab world. In return for helping to stabilize the region, the United States gave Egypt billions of dollars in development, humanitarian, and military aid. Domestically, this aid failed to yield economic development, and Mubarak ruled with an increasingly dictatorial hand. Many of the government's critics charged that massive fraud and corruption funneled Egypt's wealth to a privileged few. Over 40 percent of Egyptians lived in poverty.

Under Mubarak's thirty-year regime, an emergency law that had been in place since 1967 legalized censorship, suspended limited freedom of expression and assembly, allowed for the establishment of a special security court, and gave the government the right to arrest people without charge and detain prisoners indefinitely. Mubarak used the emergency law to create a wholly separate justice system in order to silence opposition and repress anyone perceived as a threat to his rule. Demonstrations, political organizations, and even financial donations that were not approved by the government were banned under the law. Thousands of people were arrested.

In December 2010 demonstrations broke out in Tunisia against the twenty-three-year authoritarian rule of President Zine Ben Ali, leading to his downfall in January

2011. This populist revolt soon spread across North Africa and the Middle East, including to the streets of Cairo and other cities in Egypt as Egyptians of all ages united in revolt against Mubarak's dictatorial rule. After three weeks of growing demonstrations, coordinated through Facebook, Twitter, and other communications networks, Mubarak stepped down as president in 2011 and was arrested soon after. Libya, located between Tunisia and Egypt, also witnessed an uprising against its dictatorial leader of forty-two years, Muammar Gaddafi. Gaddafi struggled violently to remain in power, but was deposed and killed amid European and U.S. air strikes. That same year, a lengthy and intense civil war erupted in Syria, pitting opponents of ruler Bashar al-Assad against an army equipped and trained to oppose Israel.

The "Arab Spring" uprisings that swept the Middle East shook a political order that had rested in the hands of the armed forces and pursued secular, nationalist objectives. The deposed leaders were the ideological descendants of Nasser, though their regimes had come to rely more on force than on modernizing social reform. The reaction against these regimes was often religious and culturally conservative. The political transitions resulting from this upheaval tended to pit secular and religious factions against each other amid debates over the nature of government and social change. Among the countries where regimes were brought down by Arab Spring protesters, Egypt alone reversed course, returning to rule by the secular armed forces under the leadership of General Abdel Fattah el-Sisi.

Revolution and War in Iran and Iraq

In oil-rich Iran foreign powers competed for political influence in the decades after the Second World War, and the influence of the United States in particular helped trigger a revolutionary backlash. In 1953 Iran's prime minister, Muhammad Mossa-degh (MOH-sah-dehk) (1882–1967), tried to nationalize the British-owned Anglo-Iranian Oil Company, forcing the pro-Western shah Muhammad Reza Pahlavi (r. 1941–1979) to flee to Europe. Mossadegh's victory was short-lived. Loyal army officers, with the help of the American CIA, quickly restored the shah to his throne.

Pahlavi set out to build a powerful modern nation to ensure his rule, and Iran's gigantic oil revenues provided the necessary cash. The shah pursued land reform, secular education, and increased power for the central government. Modernization was accompanied by corruption and dictatorship. The result was a violent reaction against secular values: an Islamic revolution in 1979 aimed at infusing Islamic principles into all aspects of personal and public life. Led by the cleric Ayatollah Ruholla Khomeini, the fundamentalists deposed the shah and tried to build their vision of a true Islamic state.

Iran's revolution frightened its neighbors. Iraq, especially, feared that Iran—a nation of Shi'ite (SHEE-ight) Muslims—would succeed in getting Iraq's Shi'ite majority to revolt against its Sunni leaders (Map 32.1). In September 1980 Iraq's ruler, Ba'ath Party leader Saddam Hussein (1937–2006), launched a surprise attack against Iran. With their enormous oil revenues and powerful armed forces, Iran and Iraq—Persians and Arabs, Islamists and nationalists—clashed in an eight-year conflict that killed hundreds of thousands of soldiers on both sides before ending in a modest victory for Iran in 1988.

In 1990, saddled with the costs of war, Hussein commanded an invasion of oil-rich Kuwait and proclaimed its annexation to Iraq. To Hussein's surprise, his troops

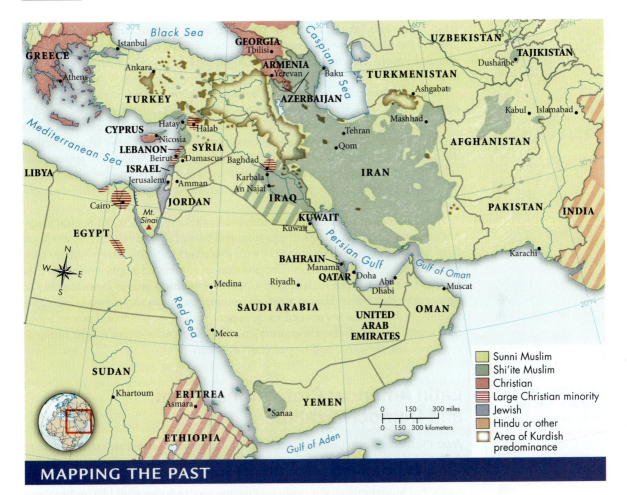

MAPPING THE PAST

MAP 32.1 Abrahamic Religions in the Middle East and Surrounding Regions Islam, Judaism, and Christianity, which all trace their origins back to the patriarch Abraham, have significant populations in the Middle East. Since the 1979 Iranian revolution, Shi'ites throughout the region have become more vocal in their demands for equality and power. One of the largest stateless ethnic groups, the Kurds, who follow various religions, has become a major player in the politics of the region, especially in Iraq and Turkey, where the group seeks Kurdish independence.

ANALYZING THE MAP Which religion dominates? Where are the largest concentrations of Jews and Christians in the Middle East located?

CONNECTIONS How have divisions between Shi'ite and Sunni Muslims contributed to war in the region?

were driven out of Kuwait by an American-led, United Nations–sanctioned military coalition, which included Arab forces from Egypt, Syria, and Saudi Arabia. The United Nations Security Council imposed economic sanctions on Iraq as soon as it invaded Kuwait, and these sanctions continued after the 1990–1991 Persian Gulf War, to force Iraq to destroy its stockpiles of chemical and biological weapons under United Nations supervision. Alleging that Iraq still had such weapons, the United

States led an invasion of Iraq in 2003 that overthrew Saddam Hussein's regime. The invasion led to the Second Persian Gulf War, which involved a lengthy U.S. occupation and a violent insurgency against U.S. military forces, which remained in Iraq until 2011.

As secular Iraq staggered, Iran's revolutionary regime seemed to moderate. Executive power in Iran was divided between a Supreme Leader and twelve-member Guardian Council selected by high Islamic clerics, and a popularly elected president and parliament. After reformist leaders pressed for relaxation of strict Islamic decrees, the Supreme Leader, controlling the army and the courts, vetoed the reforms and jailed some of the religious leadership's most vocal opponents, creating a context for the election of conservative populist Mahmoud Ahmadinejad (ahh-MAH-deen-eh-jahd) (b. 1956).

Ahmadinejad engaged in brinksmanship over the development of a nuclear weapons program, called for Israel's destruction, and backed the Hamas Party in the Gaza Strip and Hezbollah in Lebanon. He won re-election in 2009 after a bitterly contested challenge from moderates. The government suppressed a "green revolution" of protests that echoed the Arab Spring. In 2013 opposition groups came together to support the election of Hassan Rouhani, a centrist cleric who promised civil rights reforms. In 2015 Rouhani reached an agreement with a group of world powers led by the United States to freeze the country's nuclear program in return for the lifting of economic sanctions that had sapped Iran's economy.

What effect did the Cold War and debt crisis have on Latin America?

Latin America: Dictatorship, Debt, and Democratization

After the Cuban Revolution in 1959, the United States financed and armed military dictatorships to suppress any dissent that might lead to communism and to secure U.S. influence in the region. Many elected governments were toppled in military coups that brought right-wing military dictatorships to power with U.S. military and financial support.

Civil Wars in Central America

Central America experienced the greatest violence in Latin America during the Cold War. In the second half of the twentieth century reformers in Central America sought economic development that was less dependent on the United States and U.S. corporations, and groups of peasants and urban workers began to press for political rights and improved living standards. Through the lens of the Cold War, Central American conservatives and the U.S. government saw these nationalists, peasants, and workers as Communists who should be suppressed. In turn, many workers and peasants radicalized and formed Marxist revolutionary movements. The result of this conflict, and of U.S. support for right-wing governments, officers, and paramilitary groups, was hundreds of thousands of deaths.

In Guatemala, after reformist president Jacobo Arbenz was deposed in 1954 by a military coup organized by the CIA, subsequent Guatemalan leaders, backed by the U.S. government, violently suppressed peasant movements, killing over two hundred thousand mostly indigenous people. In 2013 former dictator José Efraín Ríos Montt

Genocide in Guatemala's Civil War The United Nations declared the systematic killing of indigenous Guatemalans during the country's civil war an act of genocide. In recent years investigators have worked to identify victims of the government's violence, such as six people who disappeared in 1982, whose remains have been returned to their community for burial. (Reuters/Newscom)

was convicted of genocide against Maya communities, though the Guatemalan Constitutional Court annulled the conviction.

El Salvador and Nicaragua, too, faced civil wars. In 1979 the Sandinista movement overthrew dictator Anastasio Somoza Debayle in Nicaragua. The Sandinistas, who conducted a revolutionary transformation of Nicaragua inspired by Communist rule in Cuba, were undermined by war with a U.S.-trained and U.S.-financed insurgent army called the Contras. In El Salvador a right-wing death squad killed Archbishop Oscar Romero in 1980 for speaking out against their violence.

U.S. policies that encouraged one faction to fight against the other deepened political instability and repression and intensified these civil wars. Acting against U.S. wishes, Costa Rican president Oscar Arias mediated peace talks in 1986 among the warring factions in Nicaragua, El Salvador, and Guatemala, which ended the wars and initiated open elections in each country, with former armed rivals competing instead at the ballot box. Peace did not bring prosperity, and in the decades following the end of the civil wars both poverty and violence have remained intense, prompting many Central Americans to seek opportunity in Mexico and the United States.

Boom and Bust in Chile

In the 1960s Chilean voters pushed for greater social reforms, culminating in the election of the Marxist candidate Salvador Allende (ah-YEHN-day) as president in 1970. Allende redistributed land and nationalized foreign businesses, including the country's vast copper mines, drawing fiery opposition from conservative Chileans, foreign businesses, and the U.S. government. Allende used mining revenue to pay for housing, education, health care, and other social welfare projects. U.S. president Richard Nixon created a clandestine task force to organize an "invisible blockade" to disrupt the Chilean economy by withholding economic aid and quietly instructing U.S. companies not to trade with or invest in Chile. Nixon instructed his task force to "make [Chile's] economy scream."[2]

junta A government headed by a council of commanders of the branches of the armed forces.

In 1973 Chile's armed forces deposed Allende, who killed himself when the military stormed the presidential palace. A **junta**, or council of commanders of the branches of the armed forces, took power. Its leader, General Augusto Pinochet (peen-oh-CHEHT) (1915–2006), instituted radical economic reforms, giving neoliberal economists a free hand to conduct what they called "shock treatment" to remake Chile as a free-market economy. Schools, health care, pensions, and public services were turned over to private companies. Regulatory protections for industry were slashed, and land was concentrated into the hands of large agricultural corporations. The U.S. government lavished Pinochet with economic aid.

The reforms created a boom-and-bust cycle in which Chile became especially vulnerable to global economic changes. At its peak, Chile's economy grew at 8 percent per year. The costs of the reforms were just as intense. Income inequality soared: a handful of Chileans tied to big business conglomerates and banks made fortunes, while workers faced job loss and an increasing cost of living. In 1975 the implementation of reforms that cut social programs and caused mass unemployment left half of the country's children malnourished. The 1982 recession in Chile put one-third of Chileans out of work.

Under Pinochet, thousands of Chileans disappeared, and tens of thousands were tortured. These abuses brought international condemnation and resistance within Chile. Women who had lost relatives gathered under the protection of the Catholic Church and embroidered quilts known as *arpilleras*, rendering images of their missing relatives or experiences with repression. Catholic leaders used the church's privileged position to investigate human rights abuses, uncovering mass graves that served as proof of the dictatorship's violence.

Amid the excesses of Pinochet's dictatorship, opponents and even many allies looked for ways to curb his power and find the path for redemocratization. After the 1982 economic crisis, businessmen joined opposition groups such as the Catholic Church to press for liberalization. These groups formed a coalition called Concertación, which proposed a return to democracy that maintained the major elements of free-market reforms. Concertación called on Chileans to vote "NO" in a 1988 plebiscite on whether Pinochet would remain in power. The "NO" vote won, and Chile held its first democratic elections in two decades.

The opposition alliance in Chile resembled many other alliances around the world that sought transitions from authoritarian rule: political opponents who advocated for human rights joined forces with business groups that sought markets in order to produce a postdictatorship democracy founded on free-market principles and support for human rights.

The Dirty War in Argentina

The Argentine military intervened repeatedly in politics for decades after it deposed populist Juan Perón in 1955 (see "Populism in Argentina and Brazil" in Chapter 31). By 1973 the armed forces conceded that their efforts to erase Perón's legacy—to "de-Perónize" the country—had failed. They allowed Perón to return, and he was again elected president, with his wife Isabelita, a political novice, as vice president. Soon after the election, Juan Perón died. Isabelita Perón, the first woman to become president in Latin America, faced daunting circumstances: Marxist groups such as the Montoneros waged a guerrilla war against the regime, while the armed forces and death squads waged war on them.

In March 1976 a military junta took power and announced a Process of National Reorganization. Influenced by French military theorists who had been stung by their defeats in guerrilla wars in Vietnam and Algeria, the generals waged a "dirty war," seeking to kill and "disappear" people whom they considered a destructive "cancer" on the nation. Between fourteen and thirty thousand Argentines perished at the hands of the armed forces during the dirty war.

A handful of mothers whose children had disappeared began appearing in the Plaza de Mayo in front of the presidential palace holding pictures of their missing children and carrying signs reading "Where are they?" A growing organization of the Mothers of the Plaza de Mayo was soon joined by the Grandmothers, who demanded the whereabouts of children born to women who were detained and disappeared while pregnant. These mothers were only kept alive until they gave birth. Their children were placed with adoptive families tied to the police or armed forces. Unlike in Chile and Brazil, in Argentina senior Catholic clergy did not advocate for human rights or the protection of dissidents. Instead Argentine bishops praised the coup and defended the military regime until it ended in 1983.

In 1982, emboldened by its success in eradicating its opposition, the Argentine junta occupied a set of islands off its southern coast that were claimed by Britain. Known in Britain as the Falklands and in Argentina as the Malvinas, the islands were home to a small British settlement. Britain resisted the invasion, and the Falklands/Malvinas War resulted in a humiliating defeat for the Argentine junta. After the war the junta abruptly called for elections, and a civilian president took office in 1983.

The new president, Raúl Alfonsín, faced a debt crisis similar to Mexico's. He also struggled to find justice for the crimes committed by the junta. Prosecution and conviction of the junta leaders created a backlash in the armed forces: mid-ranking officers revolted out of fear that they, too, would be prosecuted, and they forced the government to halt prosecutions. Trapped by the economic and political crises, Alfonsín left office early. His successor, Carlos Menem, tried a different approach. Menem pardoned the junta members and embarked on free-market reforms, privatizing businesses and utilities and reducing trade barriers. Investment flooded in, and Argentina seemingly put the past to rest.

As the capacity to attract foreign investment through privatization ran out by the end of the century, Argentina faced economic crisis again. In 2001, amid a run on banks and a collapse of the Argentine peso, the country had five different presidents in a single month. Eventually, the economy stabilized during the presidency of Néstor Kirchner, succeeded by his wife, Cristina Fernández de Kirchner. Néstor Kirchner, who died in 2010 while Cristina Fernández de Kirchner was president, prosecuted those responsible for violence during the dirty war again, achieving convictions of not just the junta leaders but members of the armed forces and police who perpetrated human rights violations.

Development and Dictatorship in Brazil

Brazil's military dictatorship, in power since 1964, began with liberal reforms but moved to a nationalist project of industrialization and infrastructure development that resembled some of the prescriptions of dependency theorists: increased state control of industry, restrictions on imports, and heavy investments in infrastructure. They initially achieved annual growth rates averaging 11 percent between 1968 and 1973. This growth depended on cheap imported oil and harsh political repression. When the oil embargo threatened growth, the generals borrowed heavily from abroad to subsidize fuel costs and conducted costly alternative energy projects to substitute oil with hydroelectric dams and ethanol made from sugarcane.

The Brazilian cycle of borrowing petrodollars to subsidize oil imports and development projects was ruinous for the country. By the end of the 1970s Brazil had the largest foreign debt in the developing world. When the second oil shock hit in 1979 and the U.S. government raised interest rates, making Brazil's dollar-dominated debt more expensive to manage, the country entered what became known as a "lost decade" of recession and inflation. Many workers earned less in 1989 than they had in 1980.

The economic crisis set the tone for a transition to democracy: as the generals made painful cuts to public services and as Brazilians faced soaring inflation and recession, the public overwhelmingly turned against military rule and supported redemocratization. When the first civilian president took office in 1985, inflation stood at 235 percent per year and the foreign debt at $95 billion (compared to $3.2 billion when the military took power). Inflation peaked at 3,375 percent per year before being tamed by the introduction of a new currency linked to the U.S. dollar, coupled with high interest rates.

As in Chile, Brazil's transition to democracy was shaped by liberalization. Business groups, which had grown uneasy with the dictatorship's borrowing and central planning, joined forces with human rights advocates to return the "rule of law," rather than arbitrary rule by generals. The debt left behind by Brazil's military leaders drove liberal economic reforms. To sustain its debt payments, the Brazilian government accepted the Washington Consensus, reducing public spending and opening the economy to imports and foreign investment. Neoliberal reforms included privatizing state enterprises, reducing protections for domestic industry against foreign competition, and keeping interest rates high to control inflation. Inflation remained low, but Brazilians faced a high cost of living, and high interest rates reduced lending to businesses and suppressed economic growth.

How did white-minority rule end in southern Africa?

Resistance to White Rule in Southern Africa

The racially segregated system of apartheid in South Africa was part of a region of white-minority rule that included Portuguese Angola and Mozambique, the government of Ian Smith in Rhodesia, and South African control of the former German colony of Namibia. Wars of independence in Angola and Mozambique eroded the buffer of neighboring white-minority governments around South Africa, and domestic and foreign pressure brought a political transition to majority rule in Namibia and South Africa in the 1990s.

Portuguese Decolonization and Rhodesia

At the end of World War II Portugal was the poorest country in western Europe and was ruled by a dictatorship, but it still claimed an immense overseas empire that included Angola, Mozambique, Guinea-Bissau, and Cape Verde. Since the 1920s Portuguese dictator António Salazar (1889–1970) had relied on forced labor in Angola's diamond mines to finance his regime. To alleviate poverty in Portugal, Salazar also promoted colonial settlement in Angola and Mozambique, where the white population rose from seventy thousand in 1940 to over five hundred thousand in 1970.

Salazar was determined to resist decolonization, insisting that Portuguese territories were "overseas provinces," whose status he compared to Alaska and Hawaii's relationship to the United States. Without the ability to negotiate decolonization, nationalists in the colonies resorted to armed insurrections. By the early 1970s independence movements in Cape Verde, Guinea-Bissau, and Mozambique fought guerrilla wars against the Portuguese army and colonial militias. The human toll was immense. To stop the wars Portuguese officers returning from the colonies overthrew Portugal's government in 1974. Guinea-Bissau and Cape Verde became independent that same year, Angola and Mozambique a year later. The nationalist movements that took power were all Marxist. Their radicalism was a product of their long struggle against oppression, inequality, and lack of access to their countries' resources.

The end of colonialism in Angola and Mozambique shifted the political landscape of southern Africa. Mozambique helped rebels fighting white-minority rule in Rhodesia, while the South African government saw independent Angola as a threat to apartheid and to its control over Namibia. The bloc of white-minority rule had been shattered. But after more than a decade of war for independence, neither Angola nor Mozambique would soon find peace.

The new government of Mozambique faced a guerrilla movement financed by Rhodesia. As Angola became independent, it faced immediate invasions from Zaire (encouraged by the United States) and South Africa. The new president of Angola, Agostinho Neto (nay-TOH) (1922–1978), requested military aid from Cuba, which airlifted troops that repelled both invasions and kept the regime in place. Until the late 1980s tens of thousands of Cuban troops faced off with the South African Defense Force and mercenary armies to defend the government of Angola.

In the British colony of Rhodesia white settlers, a small minority of the population, declared independence on their own to avoid sharing power with the black majority. In 1965 they established a white-minority government under farmer and politician Ian Smith. The new Rhodesian state faced international condemnation for its treatment of black citizens, including the first economic sanctions imposed by the United Nations. The Rhodesian army and police dealt violently with black political activists who challenged white rule.

The Zimbabwe African People's Union (ZAPU) fought a guerrilla war against Rhodesia's white regime. Rebuffed by the United States and Britain, ZAPU turned to China and the Soviet Union for support. When Mozambique gained independence in 1974, its government allowed ZAPU and other guerrilla groups to use neighboring Mozambican territory as a staging ground to launch attacks on Rhodesia, making it impossible for Ian Smith's government to endure. Open elections were negotiated, and these were easily won in 1979 by ZAPU leader Robert Mugabe. The following year, the Mugabe government renamed the newly independent country Zimbabwe after an ancient city-state that predated colonial rule.

South Africa Under Apartheid

apartheid The system of racial segregation and discrimination that was supported by the Afrikaner government in South Africa.

In 1948 the ruling South African National Party created a racist and segregationist system of discrimination known as **apartheid**, meaning "apartness" or "separation." The population was legally divided into racial groups: whites, blacks, Asians, and racially mixed "coloureds." Good jobs in the cities were reserved for whites, who lived in luxurious modern central neighborhoods. Blacks were restricted to precarious outlying townships plagued by poverty, crime, and mistreatment from white policemen.

In the 1950s black South Africans and their allies mounted peaceful protests. A turning point came in 1960, when police in the township of Sharpeville fired at demonstrators and killed sixty-nine black protesters. The main black political orga-

African National Congress (ANC) The main black nationalist organization in South Africa, led by Nelson Mandela.

nization—the **African National Congress (ANC)**—was outlawed but continued in exile. Other ANC members, led by a young lawyer, Nelson Mandela (1918–2013), stayed in South Africa to mount armed resistance. In 1962 Mandela was captured, tried for treason, and sentenced to life imprisonment.

In the 1970s the South African government fell into the hands of "securocrats," military and intelligence officers who adopted a policy known as the "total strategy," directing the state's resources into policing apartheid and dominating South Africa's neighbors by force. At the United Nations, African leaders denounced the South African government, and activists in countries around the world pressured their governments to impose economic sanctions against the South African regime. South Africa's white leaders responded with cosmetic reforms in 1984 to improve their international standing. The 3 million coloureds and the 1 million South Africans of Asian descent gained limited parliamentary representation, but no provision was made for any representation of the country's 22 million blacks.

The reforms provoked a backlash. In the segregated townships young black militants took to the streets, clashing with white security forces; these protests left five thousand dead and fifty thousand jailed without charges between 1985 and 1989.

The Sharpeville Massacre In March 1960, South Africans flee the area around the Sharpeville police station, where police opened fire on protesters demonstrating against the apartheid policy of requiring blacks to carry pass books to restrict their movements. (World History Archive/Ann Ronan Collection/age-fotostock)

Across the Angolan border, South African troops fought escalating conflicts with Angolan, ANC, and Cuban forces. Mounting casualties and defeat in major battles shook white South Africans' confidence.

Isolated politically, besieged by economic sanctions, and defeated on the battlefield, South African president Frederik W. de Klerk opened a dialogue with ANC leaders in 1989. He lifted the state of emergency imposed in 1985, legalized the ANC, and freed Mandela in February 1990. Mandela suspended the ANC's armed struggle and negotiated a 1991 agreement with de Klerk calling for universal suffrage and an end to apartheid legislation, which meant black-majority rule.

In May 1994 Mandela was elected president of South Africa by an overwhelming majority. Heading the new "government of national unity," which included de Klerk as vice president, Mandela along with the South African people set about building a multiracial democracy. The government established a Truth and Reconciliation Commission modeled on the commission impaneled in Chile to investigate abuses under Pinochet. The commission let black victims speak out, and it offered white perpetrators amnesty in return for fully confessing their crimes. Seeking to avoid white flight and to sustain the economy built through South Africa's industrialization, Mandela repudiated his Marxist beliefs and reassured domestic and foreign investors of his commitment to liberalization.

Political Change in Africa Since 1990

Democracy's rise in South Africa was part of a trend toward elected civilian rule that swept through sub-Saharan Africa after 1990. The end of the Cold War that followed the breakup of the Soviet Union in 1990 transformed Africa's relations with Russia and the United States. Both superpowers had treated Africa as a Cold War battleground, and both had given large-scale military and financial aid to their allies to undermine rivals. Communism's collapse in Europe brought an abrupt end to Communist aid to Russia's African clients. Since the world was no longer divided between allies of the United States and of the Soviet Union, U.S. support for pro-Western dictators, no matter how corrupt or repressive, declined as well. But the decrease in support for dictators left a power vacuum in which ethnic conflicts intensified, with often-disastrous results. For instance, in the early 1990s the United States cut off decades of support for the anticommunist General Mobutu Sese Seko (1930–1997), who seized power in 1965 in Zaire (the former Belgian Congo, renamed the Democratic Republic of the Congo in 1997) and looted the country. Opposition groups toppled the dying tyrant in 1997. The Second Congo War, a civil war that began in 1998 and continues, left more than 5 million dead over the next decade. Hundreds of thousands more have died in the years since, making it the world's deadliest conflict since World War II.

The agreement by national independence leaders across the continent to respect colonial borders prevented one kind of violence, but resulted in another. In countries whose national boundaries had been created by colonial powers irrespective of historic divisions, political parties were often based on ethnicity and kinship. The armed forces, too, were often dominated by a single ethnic group.

At times, ethnic strife boiled over into deep violence, such as the genocides of ethnic Hutus by Tutsis in Burundi in 1972 and by Tutsis of Hutus in 1993 and 1994 in Rwanda, which left hundreds of thousands dead. In Kenya disputes about the

Medical Students in Kenya

Medical students make rounds at Moi University Hospital in Eldoret, Kenya. They are part of the growing professional classes in many African nations.

legitimacy of the 2007 re-election of Mwai Kibaki left hundreds dead before the National Accord and Reconciliation Act in 2008 ended the violence. A test of the alternative to preserving national boundaries came amid efforts to ease tensions that had created famine and hardship in Sudan. In 2011, 98 percent of the electorate in southern Sudan voted to break away and form a new country, South Sudan. The early promise of peace after separation was challenged by increased ethnic and political violence in South Sudan.

Amid these conflicts, political and economic reform occurred in other African nations where years of mismanagement and repression had delegitimized one-party rule. Above all, the strength of the democratic opposition rested on a growing class of educated urban Africans. Postindependence governments expanded opportunities in education, especially higher education. In Cameroon, for example, the number of students graduating from the national university jumped from 213 in 1961 to 10,000 in 1982 and 41,000 in 1992.[3] The growing middle class of educated professionals chafed at the ostentatious privilege of tiny closed elites and pressed for political reforms that would democratize social and economic opportunities. Thus after 1990 sub-Saharan Africa accompanied the global trend toward liberalization and human rights.

How have East and South Asian nations pursued economic development, and how have political regimes shaped those efforts?

Growth and Development in Asia

China, Japan, and the countries that became known as the "Asian Tigers" (South Korea, Taiwan, Hong Kong, and Singapore) experienced fantastic economic growth in the last decades of the twentieth century. The Chinese Communist Party managed a transition in which it maintained tight political control amid liberalization and economic growth. Japan's economy stagnated in the 1990s and struggled to recover amid growing competition from its neighbors. In South Asia tensions between India and Pakistan persisted.

Japan's Economic Miracle and the Emergence of the "Asian Tigers"

Japan's postwar economic recovery, like Germany's, proceeded slowly at first. But during the Korean War, the Japanese economy took off and grew with spectacular speed. Between 1950 and 1970 Japan's economic growth averaged a breathtaking 10 percent a year. By 1978 Japan had the second-largest economy in the world. In 1986 Japan's average per capita income exceeded that of the United States for the first time.

Japan's emergence as an economic superpower fascinated outsiders. Many Asians and Africans looked to Japan for the secrets of successful modernization, but some of Japan's Asian neighbors again feared Japanese exploitation. In the 1970s and 1980s some Americans and Europeans bitterly accused **"Japan, Inc."** of an unfair alliance between government and business and urged their own governments to retaliate.

"Japan, Inc." A nickname from the 1970s and 1980s used to describe what some considered the unfair relationship between Japan's business world and government.

In Japan's system of managed capitalism, the government protected its industry from foreign competition, decided which industries were important, and then made loans and encouraged mergers to create powerful firms in those industries. The government rewarded large corporations and encouraged them to develop extensive industrial and financial activities. Workers were hired for life, and employees' social lives revolved around the company. (Discrimination against women remained severe: their wages and job security were strikingly inferior to men's.) In the 1990s Japan's economy stagnated amid the bursting of a speculative bubble that crippled banks and led to record postwar unemployment as the country faced competition from industrializing neighbors in Asia. In the twenty-first century the return to growth remained elusive as Japan faced a decades-long crisis of deflation (a reduction of the value of goods and services that saps profits and increases debt burdens).

Japan's competition in Asia was intensified by the "Asian Tigers"—South Korea, Taiwan, Hong Kong, and Singapore—so named for their rapid economic development. In the early postwar years, South Korea and Taiwan were underdeveloped agrarian countries. They also had suffered from Japanese imperialism and from destructive civil wars with Communist foes.

Asian "Economic Tigers"

They pursued development through a similar series of reforms. First, land reform allowed small farmers to become competitive producers as well as consumers. Second, governments stimulated business through lending, import barriers, and control of labor. Third, nationalist leaders (Park Chung Hee in South Korea and Jiang Jieshi in Taiwan) maintained stability at the expense of democracy. When Park was assassinated in 1979, South Korea faced an even more authoritarian regime until democracy was established at the end of the 1980s. By the late 1990s South Korea had one of the largest economies in the world, leading in shipbuilding and electronics.

In Singapore, Lee Kwan Yew (1923–2015), the prime minister who shepherded the island's independence from Britain in 1965 and held power until 1990, also pursued a modernization project that came at the cost of political dissent. This project made Singapore into an affluent banking and trade center linking markets in East Asia, the Middle East, Europe, and the United States.

In 1949, after Jiang Jieshi had fled to Taiwan with his Nationalist troops and around 2 million refugees, he re-established the Republic of China (ROC) in exile.

Over the next fifty years Taiwan created one of the world's most industrialized economies, becoming a leader in electronic manufacturing and design. Mainland China continued to claim Taiwan, considering it part of "One China." Hong Kong, which was returned to Chinese control by Britain in 1997, became a Special Administrative Region (SAR), as did the former Portuguese colony Macau, under a "one country, two systems" formula of partial autonomy.

China's Economic Resurgence

Amid the Cultural Revolution of 1965–1969, Chairman Mao and the Red Guards mobilized the masses, shook up the Communist Party, and created greater social equality (see "The Communist Victory in China" in Chapter 31). But the Cultural Revolution also created chaos and a general crisis of confidence, especially in the cities. Intellectuals, technicians, and purged party officials launched a counterattack on the radicals and regained much of their influence by 1969. This shift opened the door to a limited but lasting reconciliation between China and the United States in 1972.

In the years following Mao's death in 1976, Chinese leader Deng Xiaoping (shee-ow-ping) (1904–1997) and his supporters initiated the "Four Modernizations": agriculture, industry, science and technology, and national defense. China's 800 million peasants experienced the greatest change from what Deng called China's "second revolution." Rigid collectivization had failed to provide the country with adequate food. Deng allowed peasants to farm in small family units rather than in large collectives and to "dare to be rich" by producing crops of their choice. Peasants responded enthusiastically, increasing food production by more than 50 percent by 1984.

The successful use of free markets in agriculture encouraged further experimentation. Foreign capitalists were allowed to open factories in southern China and to export their products around the world. Private enterprise was permitted in cities, where snack shops and other small businesses sprang up. China's Communist Party also drew on the business talent of "overseas" Chinese in Hong Kong and Taiwan who understood world markets and sought cheap labor. The Chinese economy grew rapidly between 1978 and 1987, and per capita income doubled in those years. Most large-scale industry remained state owned, however, and cultural change proceeded slowly.

Economic change was not accompanied by greater political openness. Pressures for democratization grew as Mao's health declined. After Mao's death, the People's Congress ratified a new constitution in 1978 that granted "Four Big Rights," which protected freedom of speech and political debate. This opening gave rise to popular political mobilization and debate, particularly in the form of the Democracy Wall Movement, in which citizens, first in Beijing and later in other cities, put up posters calling for political reforms. (See "Analyzing the Evidence: A Member of China's Red Guards on Democratic Reform," page 1028.) The movement was suppressed in 1980. A new constitution enacted in 1982 removed references to the Four Big Rights, emphasizing economic development and reinforcing the political primacy of the Communist Party.

As the worldwide movement for political liberalization gained momentum, the government of China maintained restrictions on demonstrations and slowed economic reform. Inflation soared to more than 30 percent a year. The economic reversal, the continued lack of political freedom, and the conviction that Chinese society was becoming more corrupt led idealistic university students to spearhead demonstrations in 1989.

More than a million people streamed into Beijing's central **Tiananmen Square** in support of the students' demands. The government declared martial law and ordered the army to clear the students. Masses of courageous citizens blocked the soldiers' entry into the city for two weeks, but in the early hours of June 4, 1989, tanks rolled into Tiananmen Square. At least seven hundred students died as a wave of repression, arrests, and executions descended on China. As communism fell in eastern Europe and the Soviet Union broke apart, China's rulers felt vindicated. They believed their action had preserved Communist power, prevented chaos, and demonstrated the limits of reform. People in China were not alone in pressing for democratization — popular protest met with repression in other Communist or military regimes, such as in Burma. (See "Global Viewpoints: Dissidents in Burma and China," page 1030.)

China became politically Communist and economically capitalist. In 2001 China joined the World Trade Organization, completing its immersion in the liberal global economy. From 1978, when Deng Xiaoping began economic reforms, through 2012, the Chinese economy grew at an average annual rate of over 9 percent, and foreign trade at an average of 16 percent. Average per capita income in China doubled every ten years, and in March 2011 China replaced Japan as the world's second-largest economy, surpassed only by the United States. After 2012 China's economic growth slowed to near 7 percent — a high rate, but one that has strained the capacity of the government to pursue economic development and diminished Chinese imports. As China's economy became one of the world's leading economic engines, its growth fueled global trade of commodities imported to China and manufactured goods exported around the world. In turn, the cooling of China's economy reduced demand for commodities, slowing growth from Asia to Africa and Latin America.

Tiananmen Square The site of a Chinese student revolt in 1989 at which Communists imposed martial law and arrested, injured, or killed hundreds of students.

Development Versus Democracy in India and Pakistan

Jawaharlal Nehru's daughter, Indira Gandhi (no relation to Mohandas Gandhi) (1917–1984), became prime minister of India in 1966. She dominated Indian political life for a generation. In 1975 she subverted parliamentary democracy and proclaimed a state of emergency. Gandhi applied her expanded powers across a broad range of areas, including combating corruption, quelling labor unrest, and jailing political opponents. She also initiated a mass sterilization campaign to reduce population growth. More than 7 million men were forcibly sterilized in 1976. Many believed that Gandhi's emergency measures marked the end of liberal democracy, but in 1977 Gandhi called for free elections. She suffered a spectacular electoral defeat. Her successors fell to fighting among themselves, and in 1980 she returned to power in an equally stunning electoral victory.

Separatist ethnic nationalism plagued Indira Gandhi's last years in office. India remained a patchwork of religions, languages, and peoples, always threatening to further divide the country along ethnic or religious lines. Most notable were the 15 million Sikhs of the Punjab in northern India (see Map 31.2), with their own religion, distinctive culture, and aspirations for greater autonomy for the Punjab. By 1984 some Sikh radicals were fighting for independence. Gandhi cracked down and was assassinated by Sikhs in retaliation. Violence followed as Hindu mobs slaughtered over a thousand Sikhs throughout India.

One of Indira Gandhi's sons, Rajiv Gandhi, was elected prime minister in 1984. Rajiv Gandhi departed from his mother's and the Congress Party's socialism and

A Member of China's Red Guards on Democratic Reform

In the decades following the Cultural Revolution, China experienced repeated pressures for democratization such as the 1989 Tiananmen Square protests. The 1979 Democracy Wall Movement was one such effort that capitalized on a moment of Communist Party reform to push for political change. This account of the movement is by Fan Shen, who grew up in a military family during the Cultural Revolution and joined the Red Guards. He was sent to live in a peasant village at age fourteen and later worked in an aircraft factory, experiences that made him uneasy about the revolution. The Democracy Wall Movement began while he was a student at Lanzhou University in northwest China. After the movement was suppressed, Fan was posted to a teaching appointment in an industrial town, where, as everyone around him became ill from toxins in the water, he waited to become eligible for a passport to study in the United States.

■ The Democracy Wall Movement, which [the secret police] wanted me to spy on, started quietly in Beijing in 1979, like a hungry mosquito landing noiselessly on a content, unsuspecting pig. In January, to commemorate the late premier Zhou Enlai, . . . some people put out posters and wreaths on a stretch of wall in Xidan, a busy commercial district in Beijing. The brick wall, barely the length of a basketball court, attracted thousands of passers-by every day. The commemorative posters, however, had a political undertone from the beginning. The mourners, mostly young students and factory workers, cleverly played off of and expanded on the Communist Party's latest official policy—the "Four Modernizations"—to modernize industry, agriculture, the military, and science. The posters suggested that China need[ed] modernization in a fifth area, democracy. The posters struck a chord in people's hearts. Within a few weeks the Democracy Wall became a nationwide movement. People began demanding free speech and free elections for student unions and trade unions.

Being fifteen hundred miles from the capital, Lanzhou University was slow to catch on to the democracy movement. But when it arrived, it exploded with a violent energy. To me, the spring of 1980 was almost a carbon copy of the spring of 1966 when the Cultural Revolution began. Hundreds of big letter posters appeared overnight on building walls, parades were held daily, and like the Red Guards, people soon separated into two opposing camps: the Official Election Committee headed by the Secretary of the Communist Party, and the Independent Student Election Committee headed by a lanky economics student, Song Pingtai. The latter's campaign headquarters was in a dormitory room, next to mine. Revolutions have a way of picking unlikely heroes. Few could have imagined that Song, a quiet and shy man, would be the hero who dared to run against a candidate picked by the Party.

When the Party consented to the demands of the Independent Student Committee to hold a debate before the election on campus—the first that anyone had experienced—the Democracy Movement became a euphoric festival. Perhaps because of my recent dealings with the secret police, I had a strong desire for political reform and I eagerly participated in Song's campaign. My roommates . . . also got involved. We wrote posters, printed handbills, and collected donations. The day before the debate, I spent the whole night writing a speech for Song. The next day, at the debate, our hero trounced the Party candidate. Song won the election

prepared the way for Finance Minister Manmohan Singh to introduce market reforms, capitalist development, and Western technology and investment from 1991 onward. These reforms were successful, and since the 1990s India's economy has experienced rapid growth.

Though the Congress Party held power in India almost continuously after 1947, in the 1990s Hindu nationalists increasingly challenged the party's grip on power. These nationalists argued that India was based, above all, on Hindu culture and religion and that these values had been undermined by the Western secularism of the

by a landslide, capturing seventy-eight percent of the student vote and becoming the first freely elected president of the Student Union.

A month later, he ran for the District People's Congress against another Party candidate, who was none other than [the university's party secretary]. The Party mobilized its members and campaigned hard. . . . But Song . . . again won handily. We were ecstatic. In May, we saw Song walk into the auditorium of the District People's Congress, and we could feel tremendous excitement and tension in the hall. All the gray heads of the Party delegates turned toward the door silently, as our man sauntered down the aisle in jeans and a blue jacket. "He is *The One*," we heard the gray heads say, and we knew what they meant. Song was the one who upset the tradition, the one not appointed by the Party, the one who was not one of them. There was anger among the roomful of tenured Party appointees. It was plain that to them the Democracy Movement had gone too far.

For five weeks, it was a wonderful spring. At the height of the euphoria, however, I had a nagging fear at the back of my mind that the Party would step in sooner or later and extinguish the flame of the free election because I knew how closely the secret police had been monitoring the democracy movement. But still I never expected the Party to put an end to the Democracy Movement so quickly and so brutally. Just three days after Song's triumphant march into the People's Congress, the police tore down all the democracy posters in the university and declared that the Independent Student Union was illegal and was banned. In Beijing and other cities, we soon heard, the police had arrested many activists of the movement.

"Another victory for the Democratic Dictatorship!" declared the headline of an editorial in the *People's Daily* a few days later. "The so-called Democracy Movement is actually an 'anti-revolutionary movement' aimed at undermining the socialist dictatorship, and it has been mercilessly crushed." In just a few days, as all signs of the democracy movement disappeared, [the party secretary at the university] . . . resurfaced victoriously on campus and ordered a special two-week workshop for all students, to clear our minds of any thoughts of democracy.

"No one should doubt the Party's resolve," he said firmly to us on the first day of the workshop. "You young people often forget who brought liberation and freedom to China. You must remember that our freedom is socialist freedom, our democracy is socialist democracy, and they must be under the guidance of the Party. You must never forget that on top of democracy there is the Party. The Party hears the people and decides what's best for them. This is what the Great Leader [Mao] called democratic dictatorship. The Party will forgive most of you for what you have done as long as you confess your mistakes. But those who led the charge against the Party will be remembered and dealt with."

. . . All the leaders of the democracy movement were punished upon graduation two years later and were sent to the most remote regions. Song himself was sent to the Xinjiang Uighur Autonomous Region (China's Siberia), and none of us heard anything from him again.

QUESTIONS FOR ANALYSIS

1. What spaces did people take advantage of to challenge the Communist Party during the Democracy Wall Movement?
2. Why did Fan Shen see the protest movement as important despite the fact that it was suppressed?

Source: Fan Shen, *Gang of One: Memoirs of a Red Guard* (Lincoln: University of Nebraska Press, 2004), pp. 199–201. Reprinted by permission of the University of Nebraska Press. Copyright © 2004 by Fan Shen.

Congress Party and the influence of India's Muslims. The Hindu nationalist party, known as the BJP, gained power in 1998. The new government immediately tested nuclear devices, asserting its vision of a militant Hindu nationalism. Promising to accelerate economic growth, BJP candidate Narendra Modi became prime minister after a sweeping electoral victory in 2014.

When Pakistan announced that it had developed nuclear weapons in 1998, relations between Pakistan and India worsened. In 2001 the two nuclear powers seemed poised for conflict until intense diplomatic pressure brought them back from the

Dissidents in Burma and China

Aung San Suu Kyi spent a total of fifteen years under house arrest between 1989 and 2010 for her opposition to the military junta that ruled Burma. Suu Kyi was arrested while campaigning for a peaceful transition to a democratic civilian government. In the first excerpt, from her 1991 acceptance speech for the Sakharov Prize for Freedom of Thought awarded by the European Parliament, she discusses resistance to the Burmese dictatorship. Liu Xiaobo was a professor of literature lecturing at Columbia University in New York when students began protesting in Beijing's Tiananmen Square in 1989. He returned to China to join the demonstrations and became a vocal critic of China's human rights policies, for which he faced repeated arrests. In 2009 he was sentenced to prison, where he remained until his death in 2017. Both dissidents received the Nobel Peace Prize for their efforts, but the Chinese government did not allow Liu to accept his award in 2010. Liu sent a letter that was read at the ceremony, from which the second excerpt is drawn.

Aung San Suu Kyi, "Freedom from Fear"

■ Fearlessness may be a gift but perhaps more precious is the courage acquired through endeavour, courage that comes from cultivating the habit of refusing to let fear dictate one's actions, courage that could be described as "grace under pressure"—grace which is renewed repeatedly in the face of harsh, unremitting pressure.

Within a system which denies the existence of basic human rights, fear tends to be the order of the day. Fear of imprisonment, fear of torture, fear of death, fear of losing friends, family, property or means of livelihood, fear of poverty, fear of isolation, fear of failure. . . . It is not easy for a people conditioned by fear under the iron rule of the principle that might is right to free themselves from the enervating miasma of fear. Yet even under the most crushing state machinery courage rises up again and again, for fear is not the natural state of civilized man.

The wellspring of courage and endurance in the face of unbridled power is generally a firm belief in the sanctity of ethical principles combined with a historical sense that despite all setbacks the condition of man is set on an ultimate course for both spiritual and material advancement. . . . Concepts such as truth, justice and compassion cannot be dismissed as trite when these are often the only bulwarks which stand against ruthless power.

Liu Xiaobo, "Final Statement"

■ I still want to tell the regime that deprives me of my freedom, I stand by the belief I expressed twenty years ago in my "June Second Hunger Strike Declaration"— I have no enemies, and no hatred. None of the police who have monitored, arrested and interrogated me, the prosecutors who prosecuted me, or the judges who sentence me, are my enemies. While I'm unable to accept your surveillance, arrest, prosecution or sentencing, I respect your professions and personalities. . . .

I firmly believe that China's political progress will never stop, and I'm full of optimistic expectations of freedom coming to China in the future, because no force can block the human desire for freedom. China will eventually become a country of the rule of law in which human rights are supreme. I'm also looking forward to such progress being reflected in the trial of this case, and look forward to the full court's just verdict—one that can stand the test of history. . . .

I look forward to my country being a land of free expression, where all citizens' speeches are treated the same; here, different values, ideas, beliefs, political views . . . both compete with each other and coexist peacefully; here, . . . political views different from those in power will be fully respected and protected; . . . I hope to be the last victim of China's endless literary inquisition, and that after this no one else will ever be jailed for their speech.

Freedom of expression is the basis of human rights, the source of humanity and the mother of truth. To block freedom of speech is to trample on human rights, to strangle humanity and to suppress the truth.

QUESTIONS FOR ANALYSIS

1. How do Suu Kyi and Liu frame their appeals as just?
2. What does freedom mean to Suu Kyi? To Liu?

Sources: Aung San Suu Kyi, *Freedom from Fear and Other Writings*, ed. Michael Aris (New York: Penguin, 2010), pp. 180–185; "Text of Chinese Dissident's 'Final Statement,'" *The Lede* (blog), *New York Times*, December 10, 2010, http://thelede.blogs.nytimes.com/2010/12/10 /text-of-chinese-dissidents-final-statement/. Used by permission of David Kelly.

brink of nuclear war. In 2005 both countries agreed to open business and trade relations and to try to negotiate a peaceful solution to the Kashmir dispute (see "Independence in India, Pakistan, and Bangladesh" in Chapter 31). Tensions again increased in 2008 when a Pakistan-based terrorist organization carried out a widely televised shooting and bombing attack across Mumbai, India's largest city, killing 164 and wounding over 300.

In the decades following the separation of Bangladesh, Pakistan alternated between civilian and military rule. General Muhammad Zia-ul-Haq, who ruled from 1977 to 1988, drew Pakistan into a close alliance with the United States that netted military and economic assistance. Relations with the United States chilled as Pakistan pursued its nuclear weapons program. In Afghanistan, west of Pakistan, Soviet military occupation lasted from 1979 to 1989. Civil war followed the Soviet withdrawal, and in 1996 a fundamentalist Muslim group, the Taliban, seized power. The Taliban's leadership allowed the terrorist organization al-Qaeda to base its operations in Afghanistan. It was from Afghanistan that al-Qaeda conducted acts of terrorism like the attack on the U.S. World Trade Center and the Pentagon in 2001. Following that attack, the United States invaded Afghanistan, driving the Taliban from power.

When the United States invaded Afghanistan in 2001, Pakistani dictator General Pervez Musharraf (b. 1943) renewed the alliance with the United States, and Pakistan received billions of dollars in U.S. military aid. But U.S. combat against the Taliban and al-Qaeda drove militants into regions of northwest Pakistan, where they undermined the government's already tenuous control. Cooperation between Pakistan and the United States in the war was strained when U.S. Special Forces killed al-Qaeda leader Osama bin Laden on May 1, 2011. He had been hiding for years in a compound several hundred yards away from a major Pakistani military academy outside of the capital, Islamabad.

In 2007 Musharraf attempted to reshape the country's Supreme Court by replacing the chief justice with one of his close allies, bringing about calls for his impeachment. Benazir Bhutto (1953–2007), who became the first female elected head of a Muslim state when she was elected prime minister in 1988, returned from exile to challenge Musharraf's increasingly repressive military rule. She was assassinated while campaigning. After being defeated at the polls in 2008, Musharraf resigned and went into exile in London.

The End of the Cold War

How did decolonization and the end of the Cold War change Europe?

In the late 1960s and early 1970s the United States and the Soviet Union pursued a relaxation of Cold War tensions that became known as **détente** (day-TAHNT). But détente stalled when Brezhnev's Soviet Union invaded Afghanistan to save an unpopular Marxist regime.

The United States reacted with alarm to the spread of Soviet influence. Ronald Reagan (U.S. pres. 1981–1989) sought to halt the spread of Soviet influence, much like predecessors John F. Kennedy and Harry Truman had. But as Reagan and conservative allies in Europe rekindled the Cold War, the Soviet Union began reforms that culminated in the release of control over eastern Europe and the dismantling of the Soviet Union and its Communist state.

détente The progressive relaxation of Cold War tensions between the United States and the Soviet Union in the late 1960s and early 1970s.

The Limits of Reform in the Soviet Union and Eastern Europe

After their 1968 intervention in Czechoslovakia, Soviet leaders worked to restore order and stability. Free expression and open protest disappeared throughout their satellite nations.

A rising standard of living helped ensure stability as well. Beneath this appearance of stability, however, the Soviet Union underwent a social revolution. The urban population expanded rapidly. The number of highly trained professionals increased fourfold between 1960 and 1985. The education that created expertise helped foster the growth of Soviet public opinion about questions ranging from pollution to urban transportation.

When Mikhail Gorbachev (b. 1931) became premier in 1985, he set out to reform the Soviet system with policies he called democratic socialism. The first set of reforms was intended to transform and restructure the economy. **Perestroika** permitted freer prices, more autonomy for state enterprises, and the establishment of some profit-seeking private cooperatives. A more far-reaching campaign of openness, or **glasnost**, introduced in 1985, allowed significant new space for public debate by increasing transparency and allowing a more open media.

Democratization under Gorbachev led to the first free elections in the Soviet Union since 1917. Gorbachev and the party remained in control, but an independent minority was elected in 1989 to a revitalized Congress of People's Deputies. Democratization encouraged demands for greater autonomy from non-Russian minorities, especially in the Baltic region and in the Caucasus.

Finally, Gorbachev brought "new political thinking" to foreign affairs. He withdrew Soviet troops from Afghanistan in 1989 and sought to reduce Cold War tensions. Gorbachev pledged to respect the political choices of eastern Europe's peoples. Soon after, a wave of peaceful revolutions swept across eastern Europe, overturning Communist regimes.

Poland led the way. In August 1980 strikes grew into a working-class revolt. Led by Lech Wałęsa (lehk vah-LEHN-suh) (b. 1943), workers organized the independent trade union **Solidarity**. Communist leaders responded by imposing martial law in December 1981 and arresting Solidarity's leaders. By 1988 labor unrest and inflation had brought Poland to the brink of economic collapse, pressuring Poland's Communist Party leaders into legalizing Solidarity and allowing free elections in 1989 for some seats in the Polish parliament. Solidarity won every contested seat. A month later Solidarity member Tadeusz Mazowiecki (mah-zoh-VYEHT-skee) (1927–2013) was sworn in as the first noncommunist prime minister in eastern Europe in a generation.

Czechoslovakia and Romania reflected different paths to reform: Czechoslovakia's Velvet Revolution led to the peaceful ouster of Communist leaders amid massive street protests led by students and intellectuals. (See "Individuals in Society: Václav Havel," at right.)

But in Romania the revolution was violent. Communist dictator Nicolae Ceaușescu (chow-SHEHS-koo) (1918–1989) unleashed his security forces on protesters, sparking an armed uprising. After Ceaușescu's forces were defeated, he and his wife were captured and executed by a military court.

Amid the transformation of eastern Europe, Germany reunified. Reunification began with the millions of East Germans who flooded across their country's borders to reach West Germany (see Map 31.1). As neighboring countries liberalized, East Germany's leaders gave in to public pressure and opened the Berlin Wall in

perestroika Economic restructuring and reform implemented by Soviet premier Mikhail Gorbachev that permitted an easing of government price controls on some goods, more independence for state enterprises, and the establishment of profit-seeking private cooperatives.

glasnost Soviet premier Mikhail Gorbachev's popular campaign for government transparency and more open media.

Solidarity Led by Lech Wałęsa, an independent Polish trade union organized in 1980 that worked for the rights of workers and political reform.

Václav Havel

ON THE NIGHT OF NOVEMBER 24, 1989, the revolution in Czechoslovakia reached its climax. Three hundred thousand people had poured into Prague's historic Wenceslas Square to continue the massive protests that had erupted a week earlier after the police savagely beat student demonstrators. Now all eyes were focused on a high balcony. There an elderly man with a gentle smile and a middle-aged intellectual wearing jeans and a sports jacket stood arm in arm and acknowledged the cheers of the crowd. "Dubček-Havel," the people roared. "Dubček-Havel!" Alexander Dubček, who represented the failed promise of reform communism in the 1960s (see "The World in 1968" in Chapter 31), was symbolically passing the torch to Václav Havel, who embodied the uncompromising opposition to communism that was sweeping the country. That very evening, the hard-line Communist government resigned, and soon Havel was the unanimous choice to head a new democratic Czechoslovakia. Who was this man to whom the nation turned in 1989?

Born in 1936 into a prosperous, cultured, upper-middle-class family, the young Havel was denied admission to the university because of his class origins. Loving literature and philosophy, he gravitated to the theater, became a stagehand, and emerged in the 1960s as a leading playwright. His plays were set in vague settings, developed existential themes, and poked fun at the absurdities of life and the pretensions of communism. In his private life, Havel thrived on good talk, Prague's lively bar scene, and officially forbidden rock 'n' roll.

In 1968 the Soviets rolled into Czechoslovakia, and Havel watched in horror as a tank commander opened fire on a crowd of peaceful protesters in a small town. "That week," he recorded, "was an experience I shall never forget."[*] The free-spirited artist threw himself into the intellectual opposition to communism and became its leading figure for the next twenty years. The costs of defiance were enormous. Purged and blacklisted, Havel lifted barrels in a brewery and wrote bitter

Václav Havel, playwright, dissident leader, and the first postcommunist president of the Czech Republic.
(Pascal George/AFP/Getty Images)

satires that could not be staged. In 1977 he and a few other dissidents publicly protested Czechoslovakian violations of human rights, and in 1989 this Charter '77 group became the inspiration for Civic Forum, the democratic coalition that toppled communism. Havel spent five years in prison and was constantly harassed by the police.

Havel's thoughts and actions focused on truth, decency, and moral regeneration. In 1975, in a famous open letter to Czechoslovakia's Communist boss, Havel wrote that the people were indeed quiet, but only because they were "driven by fear. . . . Everyone has something to lose and so everyone has reason to be afraid." Havel saw lies, hypocrisy, and apathy undermining and poisoning all human relations in his country: "Order has been established—at the price of a paralysis of the spirit, a deadening of the heart, and a spiritual and moral crisis in society."[†]

Yet Havel saw a way out of the Communist quagmire. He argued that a profound but peaceful revolution in human values was possible. Such a revolution could lead to the moral reconstruction of Czech and Slovak society, where, in his words, "values like trust, openness, responsibility, solidarity and love" might again flourish and nurture the human spirit. Havel was a voice of hope and humanity who inspired his compatriots with a lofty vision of a moral postcommunist society. As president of his country from 1989 to 2003, Havel continued to speak eloquently on the great questions of our time.

QUESTIONS FOR ANALYSIS

1. Why did Havel oppose Communist rule? How did his goals differ from those of Dubc̆ek and other advocates of reform communism?
2. Havel has been called a "moralist in politics." Is this a good description of him? Why or why not?

[*]Quoted in M. Simmons, *The Reluctant President: A Political Life of Václav Havel* (London: Methuen, 1991), p. 91.

[†]Quoted ibid., p. 110.

Fall of the Berlin Wall A man stands atop the partially destroyed Berlin Wall flashing the *V* for victory sign as he and thousands of other Berliners celebrate the opening of the Berlin Wall in November 1989. Within a year the wall was torn down, communism collapsed, and the Cold War ended. (Lionel Cironneau/AP Photo/AP Images)

November 1989, before being swept aside. An "Alliance for Germany" won general elections and negotiated an economic union with West Germany.

West German chancellor Helmut Kohl reassured American, Soviet, and European leaders that a reunified Germany would have peaceful intentions. Within the year, East and West Germany merged into a single nation under West Germany's constitution and laws.

Many people in eastern Europe faced unexpected hardships in the process of liberalization as economies underwent difficult transformations and the state infrastructure of social welfare crumbled. But the greatest postcommunist tragedy was in Yugoslavia, whose federation of republics and regions had been held together under Josip Tito's Communist rule. After Tito's death in 1980, rising territorial and ethnic tensions were intensified by economic decline.

The revolutions of 1989 accelerated the breakup of Yugoslavia. Serbian president Slobodan Milošević (SLOH-buh-dayn muh-LOH-suh-vihch) (1941–2006) attempted to grab land from other republics to create a "greater Serbia." His ambitions led to civil wars that between 1991 and 2001 engulfed Kosovo, Slovenia, Croatia, and Bosnia-Herzegovina (Map 32.2). In 1999 Serbian aggression prompted NATO air strikes, led by the United States, against the Serbian capital of Belgrade as well as against Serbian military forces until Milošević relented. Milošević was voted out of office in 2000. The new Serbian government extradited him to a United Nations war crimes tribunal in the Netherlands to stand trial for crimes against humanity as peace was restored to the former Yugoslav republics.

Recasting Russia Without Communism

In February 1990 the Soviet Communist Party was defeated in local elections throughout the country, eroding Gorbachev's power and strengthening his rival, Boris Yeltsin (1931–2007), the former mayor of Moscow. In May 1990, as leader of the Russian parliament, Yeltsin announced that Russia would declare its independence from the Soviet Union. In August 1991 Gorbachev faced an attempted coup by Communist hardliners who wanted to preserve a Communist Soviet Union. Instead their coup attempt hastened the end of the Soviet Union. Yeltsin emerged as a popular hero for his dramatic resistance: at one point, he climbed atop a tank deployed by the conspirators to deliver a rousing speech calling for a general strike in resistance to the coup.

In the aftermath of the attempted takeover, an anticommunist revolution swept the Russian Federation. The Communist Party was outlawed and its property confiscated. Yeltsin and his liberal allies declared Russia independent and withdrew from the Soviet Union. All the other Soviet republics followed suit. Gorbachev agreed to their independence, and the Soviet Union ceased to exist on December 25, 1991 (Map 32.3). The newly independent post-Soviet republics faced challenges, includ-

MAP 32.2 The Breakup of Yugoslavia Yugoslavia had the most ethnically diverse population in eastern Europe. The Republic of Croatia had substantial Serbian and Muslim minorities, and Bosnia-Herzegovina had large Muslim, Serbian, and Croatian populations, none of which had a majority. In June 1991 Serbia's brutal effort to seize territory and unite all Serbs in a single state brought a tragic civil war to the region.

ing the need to quickly build new political systems and the urgency of economic reforms meant to open socialist economies to free-market principles. Liberal reforms doomed much of Russia's industry, and its economy depended increasingly on oil and natural gas exports. Despite its weakened economy, Russia retained the world's second-largest nuclear arsenal, as well as a powerful vote (and veto) in the United Nations Security Council.

As Yeltsin presided over newly independent Russia, he opted for breakneck liberalization. This shock therapy, which followed methods similar to radical free-market policies in Chile and other parts of Latin America, freed prices on most goods and launched a rapid privatization of industry. Prices soared and production collapsed. State industrial monopolies became private monopolies that cut production and raised prices in order to maximize profits. The quality of public services and health care declined to the point that the average male life expectancy dropped from sixty-nine years in 1991 to fifty-nine years in 2007. In 2003 Russia's per capita income was lower than at any time since 1978.

MAP 32.3 Russia and the Successor States After the attempt in August 1991 to depose Gorbachev failed, an anticommunist revolution swept the Soviet Union. Led by Russia and Boris Yeltsin, the republics that formed the Soviet Union declared their sovereignty and independence. Eleven of the fifteen republics then formed a loose confederation called the Commonwealth of Independent States, but the integrated economy of the Soviet Union dissolved into separate national economies, each with its own goals and policies.

The election of Yeltsin's handpicked successor, President Vladimir Putin (b. 1952), in 2000 ushered in a new era of "managed democracy." Putin's stress on public order and economic reform was popular, even as he became progressively more authoritarian. Significant restrictions were placed on media freedoms, regional elections were abolished, and the distinction between judicial and executive authority collapsed. Putin consolidated the power and authority of the state around himself and his closest advisers, closing off the development of democratic pluralism and an independent legal system in Russia.

Putin's illiberal tendencies were also evident in his brutal military campaign against Chechnya (CHEHCH-nyuh), a tiny republic of 1 million Muslims in southern Russia (see Map 32.3, inset) that in 1991 declared its independence. Up to two hundred thousand Chechen civilians are estimated to have been killed between 1994 and 2011. Many more became refugees. Chechen resistance to Russian domination continued, often in the form of attacks such as a suicide bombing at Moscow's airport in 2011 that killed scores of travelers.

In the aftermath of the dissolution of the Soviet Union, political and ethnic divisions threatened peace and stability among the post-Soviet republics. In Ukraine, in 2014 pro-Western protesters toppled a president who refused to sign agreements with the European Union. In the aftermath of the uprising, Russian forces occupied the Ukrainian province of Crimea along the Black Sea and backed secessionist movements in ethnically Russian regions of Ukraine. Russia's seizure of Crimea undermined the terms under which the Soviet Union had dissolved into separate republics, provoking unease among other new states such as the Baltic republics.

Integration and Reform in Europe

Germany and France continued to lead the push for European unity, building on integration efforts in the 1940s and 1950s established through NATO and the Common Market (see "Postwar Challenges in Western Europe and the United States" in Chapter 31). French president François Mitterrand (1916–1996) and German chancellor Helmut Kohl (b. 1930) pursued the economic integration of European Community members, and in 1993 the European Community rechristened itself the **European Union (EU)**. The European Union, a political and economic body, allowed for the free movement of people and goods among twelve member countries; created a common currency, the euro, introduced in 2002; and formed a European Parliament that established regulations and pooled infrastructure and education investments.

The creation of the European Union resolved diverse challenges for different parts of Europe. It created a logic for a unified Germany integrated with Europe. For eastern Europe it provided a blueprint for reforming economies and institutions in countries transitioning away from Soviet models. For western Europe it created an alternative path after the loss of colonies in Africa and Asia. For five centuries overseas empires had not only provided the engine for economic development at home but also shaped international relations as well as intellectual currents ranging from abolitionism to scientific racism and even Marxism. Empires had provided raw materials and markets that produced industrialization. For different reasons but for the first time since before the French Revolution, almost all of Europe now followed the same general political model.

European leaders embraced a neoliberal, free-market vision of capitalism. The most radical economic changes had been implemented in the 1980s by Margaret Thatcher (1925–2013) in Britain, who drew inspiration from Pinochet's Chile. Other governments also introduced austerity measures to slow the growth of public spending and the welfare state. Many individuals suffered under the impact of these reductions in public spending and social welfare. Harder times meant that more women entered or remained in the workforce after they married.

European Union (EU)
An economic and political alliance of twelve European nations formed in 1993 that has since grown to include twenty-eight European nations.

MAP 32.4 The European Union, 2017 No longer divided by ideological competition and the Cold War, much of today's Europe banded together in a European Union that has become strained by economic and migration pressures.

The success of the euro encouraged the EU to accelerate plans for an ambitious enlargement to the east. On May 1, 2004, the EU started admitting eastern European countries and by 2009 had adopted a common constitution. In 2017 the European Union had twenty-eight member states, including most of eastern Europe, and a population of nearly 500 million. As it grew, the EU faced questions about the limits of its expansion and the meaning of European unity and identity. If the EU expanded to include eastern Europe and some former Soviet republics, how could

Turkey, a secular nation with a Muslim majority, be denied its long-standing request for membership? Turkey had been a member of NATO since 1952 and had labored to meet membership requirements (Map 32.4).

This debate deepened as the economic crisis that began in 2008 tested and frayed the European Union. Countries that had adopted the euro currency had to meet stringent fiscal standards and imposed deep budget cuts. The resulting reductions in health care and social benefits hit ordinary citizens hard. National governments could no longer expand their own monetary supplies to promote recovery, and governments were forced to slash budgets to meet debt obligations. At the same time, the EU struggled to find a unified response to the growing numbers of refugees crossing the Mediterranean from North Africa and the Middle East as they fled conflict zones and poverty. In western Europe, tensions also emerged over the movement of peoples from poorer eastern European member nations to wealthier countries like France and the United Kingdom.

Austerity brought ruinous economic conditions that crippled Greece, prompting its near-departure from the Eurozone in 2015, while the economies of Portugal, Spain, and Italy struggled. The consequences of liberalization in Europe resembled the consequences elsewhere: economic growth was greater, but economic hardship and dislocation were deeper. The costs of liberalization to European unity were felt again as voters in the United Kingdom chose in 2016 to leave the European Union after a campaign fueled by anxieties about immigration. The British voters' decision, popularly called Brexit, was the first vote of its kind and, together with the Greek economic crisis, cast doubts about the stability and future of the European Union.

Chapter Summary

In 1976 most of the world was governed by undemocratic regimes. These regimes came in many different types: some were controlled by Communist parties and others by right-wing military officers loyal to the United States. There were dictatorships ruled by nationalist leaders, by strongmen who unseated independence leaders, and by members of families that owned much of a nation's resources. Some of these dictators created an illusion of governing democratically, but they restricted opposition or required one-party rule.

Some dictatorships created the space to engage in utopian projects to remake nations. Even when such dictatorships succeeded in their goals, they did so at enormous costs, measured in debt and inflation, famine and malnutrition, the tattering of public institutions, and the reliance on repression to maintain order.

By the mid-1980s dictatorships around the world had begun to fall, and democratic transitions followed. During the 1980s most of Latin America returned to democracy, and in 1989 the fall of the Berlin Wall culminated a wave of political and economic change in the Soviet Union and eastern Europe. The end of the Cold War division of Europe accelerated a process of integration and unification that had its roots in reconstruction after the Second World War and the process of decolonization that dismantled European empires. Alongside political transitions, a wave of economic liberalization, often promoted by the United States, swept the world. Liberalization resulted in increased trade and economic activity, but it also created growing gaps between rich and poor.

Amid these changes, East Asia came to play a growing role in the world economy. The rapid economic growth of Japan and the industrialization of South Korea were accompanied by an economic liberalization without political liberalization in China. In the 1970s Japan became the second-largest national economy by GDP in the world after the United States. By 2010 China had surpassed Japan amid projections that it would soon emerge as the world's largest national economy.

NOTES

1. *Jornal do Brasil*, March 14, 1976, quoted in Roberto Jorge Ramalho Cavalcanti, "O presidente Ernesto Geisel e o estabelecimento do retorno à democracia ao Brasil pós Regime Militar de 1964," *Governo e Política*, November 7, 2010, http://www.webartigos.com/artigos/artigo-o-presidente-ernesto-geisel-e-o-estabelecimento-do-retorno-a-democracia-ao-brasil-pos-regime-militar-de-1964/51497/.
2. CIA Director Richard Helms, notes on Nixon's plan for Chile, September 15, 1970, accessed October 14, 2012, http://www2.gwu.edu/~nsarchiv/NSAEBB/NSAEBB8/docs/doc26.pdf.
3. D. Birmingham and P. Martin, eds., *History of Central Africa: The Contemporary Years Since 1960* (London: Routledge, 1998), p. 59.

CONNECTIONS

The experiences of people living under authoritarian regimes varied greatly. Many supported the regimes from which they drew privileges or found a reassuring sense of order. Others avoided political questions and stayed out of trouble. But even they were affected by authoritarianism: censorship and propaganda meant that official pronouncements lacked credibility, so rumors, some true and others wild, became their basic currency of exchange.

Many, however, resisted the regimes. For some, a closed political system meant the only tools available were armed resistance. Guerrilla movements against authoritarian regimes were common, though the imbalance in their resources meant they mostly met with violent ends at the hands of security forces. Another form of resistance proved more effective: nonviolent, and ostensibly nonpolitical, resistance was harder for regimes to repress. Mothers asking for the whereabouts of missing children or quilting the scenes of their grief in Argentina and Chile, or workers organizing an independent union in Poland, found ways to challenge their regimes.

The most successful resistance was often opposition that was not explicitly ideological, such as the defense of human rights, or the establishment of the rule of law that would restrict a regime's arbitrary power. These pressures had a similar effect when applied to right-wing or socialist dictatorships alike: they were liberalizing. As dictatorships in Latin America, East Asia, and eastern Europe moved toward multiparty democracy, and as the Soviet bloc disintegrated, those countries shared a historical moment in which liberal economic and political reforms swept the world.

CHAPTER 32 **Review and Explore**

Identify Key Terms

Identify and explain the significance of each item below.

Organization of the Petroleum Exporting
  Countries (OPEC) (p. 1008)

petrodollars (p. 1008)

neoliberalism (p. 1009)

Washington Consensus (p. 1009)

intifada (p. 1012)

junta (p. 1018)

apartheid (p. 1022)

African National Congress (ANC) (p. 1022)

"Japan, Inc." (p. 1025)

Tiananmen Square (p. 1027)

détente (p. 1031)

perestroika (p. 1032)

glasnost (p. 1032)

Solidarity (p. 1032)

European Union (EU) (p. 1037)

Review the Main Ideas

Answer the focus questions from each section of the chapter.

1. What were the short-term and long-term consequences of the OPEC oil embargo?
(p. 1008)

2. How did war and revolution reshape the Middle East? (p. 1011)

3. What effect did the Cold War and debt crisis have on Latin America? (p. 1016)

4. How did white-minority rule end in southern Africa? (p. 1020)

5. How have East and South Asian nations pursued economic development, and
how have political regimes shaped those efforts? (p. 1024)

6. How did decolonization and the end of the Cold War change Europe? (p. 1031)

Make Comparisons and Connections

Analyze the larger developments and continuities within and across chapters.

1. How did transitions to democracy and free markets around the world draw on
earlier ideologies (Chapters 22, 24, 29)?

2. How did the impact of oil shocks resemble previous economic crises?

3. What similarities do you see among social movements that advocated for
democracy and for majority rule around the world?

4. What historical factors shaped the formation of the European Union? How have
recent events challenged European unity?

TIMELINE

GLOBAL		**1983–1991** Transitions to democracy in the Soviet Union, eastern Europe, Latin America, South America
AFRICA	◆ **1975** Independence from Portugal of Angola and Mozambique ends European colonial rule in Africa	◆ **1980** Segregationist white-minority government in Rhodesia replaced by majority rule; country renamed Zimbabwe
MIDDLE EAST	← **1973** Yom Kippur War/Ramadan War triggers OPEC oil embargo	**1980–1988** Iran-Iraq War ◆ **1987** Palestinian intifada
	◆ **1979** Islamic revolution in Iran leads to second oil shock	
ASIA	◆ **1978** Deng Xiaoping initiates economic reforms in China	**1989** ◆ Tiananmen Square protests in China
AMERICAS	◆ **1982** Falklands (or Malvinas) War leads to collapse of Argentina's military junta	
	◆ **1982** Mexico defaults on loan payments, triggering debt crisis	
	1988 ◆ The "NO" vote wins the Chilean plebiscite ousting dictator Pinochet	
EUROPE	◆ **1985** Glasnost leads to greater freedom of speech and expression in the Soviet Union	

1975	1985

Suggested Resources

BOOKS

Beck, Roger B. *The History of South Africa.* 2nd ed. 2013. Introduction to South African history with emphasis on the twentieth century.

Buchenau, Jurgen. *Mexican Mosaic: A Brief History of Mexico.* 2012. A concise but rich look at modern Mexico.

Dávila, Jerry. *Dictatorship in South America.* 2013. Examines the experiences with dictatorship, development, and democracy in Argentina, Brazil, and Chile.

Guha, Ramachandra. *India After Gandhi: The History of the World's Largest Democracy.* 2007. In-depth study of the last sixty years of Indian history and development.

Judt, Tony. *Postwar: A History of Europe Since 1945.* 2006. A broad and insightful reading of reconstruction, the Cold War, and unification.

Kapuscinski, Ryszard. *Another Day of Life.* 2001. A renowned Polish journalist on the South African invasion of Angola and the Cuban intervention.

Kingston, Jeffrey. *Japan's Quiet Transformation.* 2004. A leading scholar considers Japan's economic problems in the 1990s and their effects on Japanese politics and society.

Lampe, J. *Yugoslavia as History: Twice There Was a Country*, 2d ed. 2000. Judiciously and insightfully considers the history and violent collapse of Yugoslavia.

Mahbubani, Kishore. *The New Asian Hemisphere: The Irresistible Shift of Global Power to the East.* 2008. A history and analysis of the rise of Asia in world politics and economics by one of Asia's leading intellectuals.

McCann, Bryan. *The Throes of Democracy: Brazil Since 1989.* 2008. A rich overview of the Brazilian experience of redemocratization.

Nepstad, Sharon Erickson. *Nonviolent Revolutions: Civil Resistance in the Late 20th Century.* 2011. A comparative study of nonviolent political movements and their effect on political transitions.

Wapshott, Nicholas. *Ronald Reagan and Margaret Thatcher: A Political Marriage.* 2007. Particularly good analysis of Reagan and Thatcher's policies of economic conservatism and anticommunism in the 1980s.

◆ **1997** First civilian-to-civilian transfer of political power in Nigeria

1990–1991 Persian Gulf War

2003–2011 Second Persian Gulf War

2007 →
Hamas seizes control of Gaza Strip from Palestinian Authority

2009–2014 →
Popular uprisings and protests across the Middle East

◆ **1991** Congress Party in India embraces Western capitalist reforms

1991–2001 Civil war in Yugoslavia

◆ **1993** Formation of the European Union

1995

2005

DOCUMENTARIES

The Tank Man (PBS, 2006). A *Frontline* episode that examines the 1989 Tiananmen Square protest and the Chinese government's suppression of it, with a focus on the man alone facing down a tank.

Tokyo Olympiad (Kon Ichikawa, 1965). This documentary about the 1964 Toyko Olympics reflects Japan's re-emergence in the decades following the Second World War, occupation, and reconstruction.

When We Were Kings (Leon Gast, 1996). Covers the 1974 "Rumble in the Jungle" boxing match in Zaire between Muhammad Ali and George Foreman, focusing on the dynamics of dictator Mobutu Sese Seko's rule and expressions of Pan-African connections.

FEATURE FILMS

The Official Story (Luis Puenzo, 1985). A film about children taken as infants by the Argentine military dictatorship that "disappeared" their parents.

24 City (Jia Zhang-Ke, 2008). A Chinese docudrama about the economic and social transitions that occur as a state aircraft factory is converted into luxury apartments. The film depicts interviews of generations of migrants drawn to work at the factory.

WEBSITES

Forward to Freedom: The History of the British Anti-Apartheid Movement, 1959–1994. The British Anti-Apartheid Movement organization maintains a retrospective website that includes interviews with participants in the movement, as well as documents and images. **www.aamarchives.org**

The National Security Archive. The National Security Archive at George Washington University has an incomparable online collection of declassified U.S. national security and foreign policy documents, including records that show secret U.S. support for dictatorships and their human rights violations in Latin America. **nsarchive.gwu.edu**

33

The Contemporary World in Historical Perspective

The approaches to the history of world societies in the preceding chapters give us critical thinking skills to help interpret the contemporary world. Through this lens, we can understand contemporary events and debates as rooted in history and also see those events as subjects of study that we can analyze using the same tools we employ for interpreting the past.

Since the end of the Cold War, many nations around the world have undergone transitions from dictatorship to democracy, and a growing number of nations have pursued free trade. These new experiences have been shaped by past struggles, and they have intensified global connections, aided by revolutions in communications and information technology. Amid these changes, stubborn regional and political conflicts remain in many parts of the world, and the experiences of poverty and marginalization continue to be widespread. But this is also a world in which, as in the past, humans have had the ability to shape, adapt, and transform the problems they confront.

The Digital Revolution

People throughout the world have embraced the ease and convenience of mobile phone technology, which has increased dramatically since the introduction of the first cellular phones in 1985.

Masterfile/Royalty-Free

CHAPTER PREVIEW

THE END OF HISTORY?
Does the contemporary world reflect the "end of history"?

GLOBAL CIRCULATION AND EXCHANGE
How have migration and the circulation of capital and technology continued to shape the world?

SOCIAL MOVEMENTS
What challenges did social reformers address at the turn of the twenty-first century?

SCIENCE AND TECHNOLOGY: CHANGES AND CHALLENGES
How have science and technology kept pace with population change?

Does the contemporary world reflect the "end of history"?

The End of History?

In 1989, as the Berlin Wall fell and the Soviet system disintegrated, a historian wrote a provocative article called "The End of History?" in which he argued that the collapse of the Soviet system meant the triumph of liberalism as a political and economic philosophy. Amid the transitions to democracy from Russia and eastern Europe to Latin America, political leaders embraced liberalism as the ideology of government and of economics. This was the "triumph of the West, of the Western *idea* . . . in the total exhaustion of viable systematic alternatives to Western liberalism."[1] Was liberalism the ultimate stage of human political and economic development?

By the beginning of the twenty-first century, liberalism had certainly emerged as the world's dominant political and economic philosophy. But there have been limits to liberalism's reach and effectiveness. For instance, economic liberalism has tended to increase social inequality and the disparity of wealth between nations and regions. As a result, liberalism has been met by a growing range of social activism aimed at reducing social inequality; gender, ethnic, and racial marginalization; and the environmental costs of economic development.

The tension between liberalism and activism is one example of the kinds of contradictory and competing pressures that shape the contemporary world. For instance, the earth's growing population has increased demands for food production, prompting a revolution in agricultural sciences. Although new technologies have helped meet the world's demand for food, the diversion of water resources and the expansion of farming at the expense of forests remind us that new technologies often bring unintended costs. Similarly, the end of the Cold War has been met not with peace but with regional conflicts around the world. And the intensification of communications, increase in travel, and spread of technology have been met with conservative, often religious reactions in different regions of the world. Some of the most intense reactions have come from movements in the Middle East and Africa whose actions have a global impact.

Complexity and Violence in a Multipolar World

The end of the Cold War led to the emergence of new regional relationships. Increasingly assertive **middle powers**, countries with significant economic influence either in relation to their neighbors or in broader trade networks, competed for regional leadership. Mexico, both highly industrialized and economically integrated with the United States, emerged as the leader of the Spanish-speaking Americas. Brazil, a rapidly industrializing country with 200 million people and vast territory and resources, emerged as the dominant nation-state in South America. France and Germany re-emerged as central economic powers in Europe. Nigeria and South Africa became the leading powers in sub-Saharan Africa. Turkey, Egypt, and Israel were also regional powers in the Middle East, and Iran increasingly projected its influence over neighbors like Iraq. China, India, and Japan all became leading regional powers, and several other Asian countries—notably South Korea, Indonesia, and Pakistan—were determined to join them.

While the end of the Cold War reduced superpower pressures that intensified regional conflicts, other factors continued to feed conflicts that killed over a million people and dispersed hundreds of thousands of refugees. Since 2000, new conflicts have caused millions more deaths and new currents of refugees, particularly in Syria,

middle powers Countries with significant economic influence that became increasingly assertive regional leaders after the Cold War.

Sierra Leone, Liberia, the Democratic Republic of the Congo, Mali, Afghanistan, and Iraq. Rivalries between ethnic groups often lie at the heart of these wars.

An Expanding Atomic Age

After the bombing of Hiroshima and Nagasaki in 1945 (see "The War in the Pacific" in Chapter 30), the United States briefly held a monopoly on atomic weapons. Since then, a growing number of nations have developed nuclear arms.

The Cold War arms race resulted in intense competition for the development of increasingly powerful atomic weapons, and it also meant massive spending in the United States, the Soviet Union, and Europe on other military technologies. While the superpowers and their closest allies sought to restrict access to nuclear weapons, they also sold huge numbers of conventional arms to other nations.

Amid the Cold War arms race, atomic tests brought fear that radiation would enter the food chain and cause leukemia, bone cancer, and genetic damage. Concerned scientists called for a ban on atomic bomb testing. In 1963 the United States, Great Britain, and the Soviet Union reached an agreement, eventually joined by more than 150 countries, to ban nuclear tests in the atmosphere. In 1970 more than sixty countries signed the Treaty on the Non-Proliferation of Nuclear Weapons. The treaty slowed but did not stop the spread of nuclear weapons.

The nuclear arms race between the Soviet Union and the United States was so intense that after the 1960s both sides sought ways of slowing it and negotiated shared limits to their nuclear arsenals. But other nations pursued nuclear weapons to bolster their defense and their regional influence. French and Chinese leaders disregarded the test ban and by 1968 had developed their own nuclear weapons, although they later signed the nonproliferation treaty. India developed its atomic capability partly out of fear of China, but India's nuclear test in 1974 in turn frightened Pakistan, which pursued its own nuclear weapons. In 1998 both India and Pakistan tested nuclear devices within weeks of each other. Other nations discreetly pursued nuclear arms without publicly stating that they possessed them.

In the 1950s Israel began developing nuclear weapons, and it is generally believed to have had an arsenal of nuclear weapons since the 1970s, though Israel has never publicly confirmed this. Israel's apparent nuclear superiority was threatening to Arab states that for decades had tried to vanquish Israel. When Iraq attempted, with help from France, to develop nuclear capability in the 1980s, Israel responded by attacking and destroying the Iraqi nuclear reactor in 1981.

Limiting Iran's Nuclear Energy Program
Following sanctions from the United States, France, Germany, Great Britain, and Russia, Iran agreed to freeze its nuclear energy program. Here International Atomic Energy Agency inspectors and Iranian technicians gather to cut connections in uranium enrichment equipment in Iran's Natanz nuclear facility in 2014. (Kazem Ghane/IRNA/AP Photo/AP Images)

The risks associated with the proliferation of nuclear weapons helped mobilize the international community and contributed to positive developments through the 1980s and 1990s. Between 1983 and 2003 Argentina, Romania, Brazil, South Africa, and Libya all agreed to abandon their nuclear weapons programs. Several of the former Soviet republics that possessed nuclear arsenals, including Ukraine, Belarus (bay-luh-ROOS), and Kazakhstan (KA-zak-stan), returned their nuclear weapons to Russia. International agencies monitored exports of nuclear material, technology, and missiles that could carry atomic bombs. These measures encouraged confidence in global cooperation and in the nonproliferation treaty, eventually signed by 190 countries.

Despite these efforts, nuclear proliferation has continued. In 2003 the United States accused Iran of seeking to build nuclear weapons, and for many years diplomatic efforts, sanctions, and other punitive measures by France, Germany, Britain, China, the United States, and Russia failed to induce Iran to limit its nuclear program. However, the sanctions isolated Iran and undermined its economy, and in 2015 Iran signed an agreement freezing development of its nuclear program. There is also the threat that enriched nuclear materials will fall into the hands of terrorist organizations or that countries possessing nuclear weapons technology will share it with other nations.

In the new century long-standing tensions between North Korea and the United States, which had never signed a peace treaty to end the 1950–1953 Korean War, intensified over North Korea's pursuit of nuclear weapons and ballistic missile technology that would allow it to launch atomic weapons at South Korea and Japan. As each side accused the other of failing to live up to its agreements, North Korea tested its first nuclear device in 2006. After 2009, North Korean authorities pursued the development of long-range ballistic missiles capable of delivering a bomb, engaging in nuclear brinksmanship not seen since the Cold War.

Al-Qaeda and Afghanistan

In the Middle East and Central Asia, conflicts that had involved the superpowers continued beyond the Cold War. The 1979 Soviet invasion of Afghanistan, as well as the Iranian revolution, which was followed by the Iran-Iraq War, led to enduring political upheaval that continued to draw the United States into violent conflicts in the twenty-first century.

In Afghanistan rebel groups supported by the United States fought the Soviet armed forces occupying the country and forced a humiliating Soviet withdrawal in 1989. In 1996, after years of civil war, a puritanical Islamic movement called the Taliban filled the military and political vacuum left by the Soviet Union. The Taliban pursued a radical religious transformation of Afghan society, in particular by imposing harsh restrictions on women. The Taliban government provided safe haven in Afghanistan for a terrorist organization called al-Qaeda (al-KIGH-duh), which included militants who had fought in Afghanistan against the Soviet occupation. In the 1990s, led by Osama bin Laden (1957–2011), al-Qaeda attacked U.S. diplomatic and military targets in Africa and the Middle East.

On September 11, 2001, al-Qaeda militants hijacked four passenger planes in the United States. They flew two of them into the World Trade Center buildings in New York City and a third into the Pentagon in Washington, D.C. A fourth, believed to be targeting the White House or the U.S. Capitol, crashed into a field in rural

Pennsylvania. These terrorist attacks killed almost three thousand people. Though the U.S. government had repeatedly attacked al-Qaeda in the 1990s, it had failed to destroy it. Now the U.S. government demanded that the Taliban government in Afghanistan surrender the al-Qaeda leadership it hosted. When the Taliban refused, the United States formed a military coalition including NATO members as well as Russia, Pakistan, and rebel groups in Afghanistan. The coalition mounted an invasion, deposed the Taliban, and pursued al-Qaeda.

After the U.S.-led coalition deposed the Taliban in 2001 and installed a new government in Afghanistan, it faced a protracted guerrilla war against Taliban forces that controlled rural areas. The Taliban drew upon Afghanistan's long experience in resisting foreign military incursions such as the Soviet and earlier British invasions. The conflict in Afghanistan spread to Pakistan, where some members of al-Qaeda found refuge, and acts of terrorism increased around the world in the years following the invasion of Afghanistan.

Through years of war, the United States and allied governments devastated al-Qaeda's leadership, but local groups acting in conflicts in the Middle East and Africa continued to act under al-Qaeda's name. These actions included bombings in 2004 and 2005 that killed 191 in Madrid and 56 in London, as well as wounding thousands. A suicide bomber who may have had links to al-Qaeda has also been blamed for the 2007 assassination of Pakistani presidential candidate Benazir Bhutto. In 2011 U.S.

New York, September 11, 2001 Pedestrians race for safety as the World Trade Center towers collapse after being hit by jet airliners. (Amy Sanetta/AP Photo/AP Images)

intelligence services identified bin Laden's hideout in Pakistan in a compound located near the country's main military academy in Abbottabad. In a night raid, U.S. forces killed bin Laden.

In the decade following the conclusion of the Persian Gulf War (1990–1991), Iraq faced international economic sanctions along with constant political and military pressure from the United States to surrender its chemical and biological weapons stockpiles. After 2001, amid the U.S. invasion of Afghanistan, U.S. president George W. Bush accused Iraq of rebuilding its nuclear, chemical, and biological weapons programs. To build domestic support for an invasion, the U.S. government also falsely implied that there were connections between Iraq and al-Qaeda. In 2002 UN inspectors determined that Iraq's chemical and biological weapons had been destroyed. France, Russia, China, Germany, and a majority of the smaller states argued for continued weapons monitoring, and France threatened to veto any resolution authorizing an invasion of Iraq. Rather than risk this veto, the United States and Britain claimed that earlier Security Council resolutions provided sufficient authorization and invaded Iraq in 2003.

A coalition of U.S.-led forces defeated the Iraqi military, and in the power vacuum that ensued, armed groups representing all three main factions in Iraq—Sunni Muslims, Shi'ite Muslims, and Kurds—carried out daily attacks on Iraqi military and police, government officials, religious leaders, and civilians. Estimates of Iraqi deaths since the beginning of the war in 2003 and the U.S. withdrawal in 2011 ranged from 100,000 to over 1 million. Though the

Iraq, ca. 2010

U.S. military occupation ended in 2011, the violence continued. Ironically, though the connection between al-Qaeda and the government of Saddam Hussein implied by President Bush did not exist, the violent environment of postwar Iraq became a place where militant groups that identified with al-Qaeda proliferated.

The most powerful of these groups called itself the Islamic State (commonly known as ISIS). ISIS took advantage of the political vacuum created by the U.S. invasion of Iraq and the Syrian civil war to establish a radical Islamic regime that spanned regions of the two countries and controlled several major cities. ISIS emerged as an ideological and militant heir to al-Qaeda. It used a sophisticated Internet footprint to recruit disaffected youth around the world to join its ranks, prompting terrorist attacks in 2015 and 2016 by individuals claiming to act in ISIS's name in the United States, France, Turkey, and Bangladesh.

How have migration and the circulation of capital and technology continued to shape the world?

Global Circulation and Exchange

Much of the history in this textbook is driven by the circulation of peoples over great distances. Migration continues to be one of the great engines of history, though its experience exposes one of the major contradictions in the way liberalization has been conducted: governments have pressed for the free circulation of goods and capital, but have sought to limit the movement of people across borders.

Migration

National immigration policies vary considerably. In Europe the process of integration has meant that European Union member countries permit the free movement of citizens from other EU nations. But in many other cases, restrictions on migration have increased even as barriers to trade and investment have fallen.

The border between the United States and Mexico reflects many of the challenges of contemporary migrations. Since long before a border existed between the United States and Mexico, migrants have circulated throughout North America, but as the United States conquered land that had belonged to Mexico in the nineteenth century (see "Mexico and the United States" in Chapter 27), it restricted the movement of migrants northward across the border. At the beginning of the twenty-first century the U.S. government began building a wall at its border with Mexico, further restricting the circulation of people even as the United States and Mexico implemented a free-trade agreement that made it easier for goods and capital to cross the border.

In the 2016 U.S. presidential election, the border between the United States and Mexico became a symbolic flash point of anxieties over two basic elements of globalization and liberalization: the movement of peoples and the free circulation of goods and capital. Real estate developer Donald Trump rode resentments over trade and migration into the presidency in a U.S. expression of the nationalist sentiments that provoked the British vote to exit the European Union and the rise of nationalist parties in continental Europe. The patterns of migration and the votes against migration that resulted in Brexit and Trump's election reflected the unevenness in wealth distribution both globally and within nations.

Behind the politics of immigration lies a more complex reality: circuits of migration—the patterns by which peoples move between one region of the world and another—are shaped by many forces. Historical connections, such as the spaces shared by indigenous and Latino peoples on both sides of the U.S.-Mexico border, are one such force. A second is the intensification of trade, which reshapes national economies and the connections between them. A third is the history of U.S. military intervention: countries that are the sites of conflict spurred by or involving the United States are reshaped in ways that often create migrant and refugee circuits connected to the United States. The experience of immigration following U.S. military intervention in Central America, the Caribbean, and Southeast Asia forms a pattern into which future immigration from the Middle East may well fit.

Since the 1960s millions of people, first from South Korea and then Vietnam, Cambodia, and Laos, countries that had experienced great upheavals in conflicts involving the United States, found legal refuge in the United States. (See "Individuals in Society: Sieng, a Mnong Refugee in an American High School," page 1052.) Immigrants to the United States most commonly come from regions transformed by U.S. foreign policy or economic activity; new immigrants frequently encounter discrimination, and efforts are made to restrict the entry of future immigrants.

In many cases, restrictions on immigration have increased in countries where national economic growth has slowed. For instance, as Japanese industry boomed in the 1980s, the country welcomed descendants of Japanese emigrants who had settled in South America in the first half of the century. Because these migrants were culturally and linguistically different from natives, Japanese citizens considered them *dekasegi*, or "temporary guest workers," who had no right to citizenship despite their ancestry.

As manufacturing and economic growth stagnated in the 1990s, this circuit of migration to Japan dwindled. Though pursuit of economic opportunity and flight from persecution are the major factors that drive international migration, other factors shape the creation of migratory circuits. A migratory circuit is a deep connection created between two regions through an initial experience of migration that results in a greater circulation of people. Migrants usually become ethnic, religious, or linguistic minorities in the countries where they settle, and they commonly face discrimination. Sometimes this discrimination is expressed in violence and oppression, such as that experienced by contemporary Zimbabwean workers in South Africa.

In 2015 the European Union became the setting of a new migration crisis as over 1 million refugees fled armed conflicts and poverty in Africa and the Middle East.[2] The largest contingent was refugees from Syria's civil war. The refugees faced a succession of challenges ranging from perilous crossings of the Mediterranean, in which thousands perished, to the hostility of peoples and governments, particularly in eastern Europe, where countries like Hungary had once welcomed East Germans fleeing communism but now blocked the

Brazilians in Japan Over two hundred thousand descendants of Japanese migrants to Brazil and Peru now live in Japan as temporary workers, particularly in auto parts manufacturing. Here Brazilians of Japanese descent attend a church service in the Japanese city of Tsu. (Sean Sprague/Alamy Stock Photo)

Sieng, a Mnong Refugee in an American High School

Mnong students and their teaching assistant at a high school in Wisconsin recite the Pledge of Allegiance. (Morry Gash/AP Photo/AP Images)

IN 2008, AT A LARGE URBAN HIGH SCHOOL IN THE U.S. South, Sieng, a seventeen-year-old Mnong refugee, recited the Pledge of Allegiance in his JROTC class. His aspiration to join the U.S. Marine Corps was an act of belonging that bridged both his life in the United States and his sense of his family and its history.

The Mnong are among a diverse group of ethnic minorities, known broadly as Montagnards, whose communities stretch across the central highlands of Vietnam. They are also a religious minority in Vietnam — many had converted to Christianity. During the Vietnam War, many Mnong provided military service alongside the United States, particularly with the U.S. Army Special Forces. After the war ended in 1975, the Mnong faced persecution, and over time many fled the country, joining the current of refugees who resettled in camps in Thailand, Malaysia, the Philippines, and later Cambodia. Sieng's family left Vietnam when he was a child in the late 1990s. He recalled his journey:

> We had a hard time in Vietnam, so we had to leave. We didn't have no choice because we had no food, and no land. And [the Vietnamese government] wanted my dad and took my grandpa. So we left in the night and went through the jungle. We walked and walked and got lost. So me and my dad tried to find the way and we found a house. Some people let us sleep there and also gave us food. Then we got to a [refugee] camp in Cambodia and stayed there for a year. I didn't have school in Vietnam, and I didn't have school at the camp. Then we came here.

Arriving in the United States at the age of sixteen, Sieng was not literate in Mnong, Vietnamese, or English, the language of his new school. Sieng aspired to become a Marine so he could help other refugees and his family. He explained, "A man needs to take care of the family too, and that's what I want to do. The Marines will help me take care of my family."

For Sieng, being a refugee instilled a sense of pride, a sense of what he and his family had overcome in coming to the United States, and a sense of what he desired for the future. As the oldest male child, Sieng was, in his words, "second in command" in the home while his father worked the third shift at a shipping facility. In the United States Sieng was an ethnic minority and a refugee with limited English skills. He was misunderstood. A classmate in a world history class asked him where he was from in Mexico, and the question made him indignant:

> I am a *refugee*, not an immigrant! I am *Mnong*, not Vietnamese! But people call me Spanish. Some kids once asked me to say something in Spanish. . . . And Mexican students think I'm Chinese. They say, *"Hey Chino! Hey Chino!"* I get mad when they do this because I am more like American. My grandpa worked with Americans [in the war].

In a diverse school, amid other immigrants and ethnic minorities, Sieng found comfort in his identity as a refugee, reflecting on his family's past, its connection to the United States, and his role facilitating its journey, as he confronted a new environment, struggling to be understood.

QUESTIONS FOR ANALYSIS

1. What aspects of Sieng's experience reflect broader patterns of migration?
2. How does Sieng's experience as a refugee shape his identity?
3. What role does JROTC play in Sieng's sense of belonging?

Source: Liv T. Dávila, "Performing Allegiance: An Adolescent Refugee's Construction of Patriotism in JROTC," *Educational Studies* 39.5 (2014). Reprinted by permission of Taylor & Francis LLC (http://www.tandfonline.com).

transit of refugees. Countries began erecting fences and border controls to limit the flow of refugees, and British voters elected to exit the EU, threatening the principle of free movement that had been a pillar of the EU.

Urbanization

Cities in Africa, Asia, and Latin America expanded at an astonishing pace after 1945. Many doubled or even tripled in size in a single decade (Table 33.1). In 1950 there were only eight **megacities** (5 million or more inhabitants), and only two were in developing countries. Of the fifty-nine megacities anticipated to exist by 2017 forty-eight will be outside North America and Europe.

megacities Cities with populations of 5 million people or more.

What caused this urban explosion? First, the overall population growth in the developing nations was critical. Urban residents gained substantially from a medical revolution that provided improved health care but only gradually began to reduce the size of their families. Second, more than half of all urban growth came from rural migration. Manufacturing jobs in the developing nations were concentrated in cities. In 1980 half of all the industrial jobs in Mexico were located in Mexico City. Even when industrial jobs have been scarce, migrants have streamed to cities, seeking any type of employment. As large landowners found it more profitable to produce export crops, their increasingly mechanized operations reduced the need for agricultural laborers. Ethnic or political unrest in the countryside can also send migrants into cities.

Most of the growing numbers of urban poor earned precarious livings in a **bazaar economy** made up of petty traders and unskilled labor. In the bazaar economy, which echoed early preindustrial markets, regular salaried jobs were rare and highly prized, and a complex world of tiny, unregulated businesses and service occupations predominated. Peddlers and pushcart operators hawked their wares, and sweatshops and home-based workers manufactured cheap goods for popular consumption. These workers typically lacked job security, unemployment insurance, and pensions.

bazaar economy An economy with few salaried jobs and an abundance of tiny, unregulated businesses such as peddlers and pushcart operators.

TABLE 33.1 Urban Population as a Percentage of Total Population in the World and in Eight Major Areas, 1925–2025

AREA	1925	1950	1975	2000	2025 (EST.)
World Total	21%	28%	39%	50%	63%
North America	54	64	77	86	93
Europe	48	55	67	79	88
Soviet Union	18	39	61	76	87
East Asia	10	15	30	46	63
Latin America	25	41	60	74	85
Africa	8	13	24	37	54

Note: Little more than one-fifth of the world's population was urban in 1925. In 2000 the total urban proportion in the world was about 50 percent. According to United Nations experts, the proportion should reach two-thirds by about 2025. The most rapid urban growth will occur in Africa and Asia, where the move to cities is still in its early stages.

After 1945 large-scale urban migration profoundly affected traditional family patterns in developing countries, just as it had during the Industrial Revolution. Particularly in Africa and Asia, the great majority of migrants to cities were young men seeking temporary or seasonal work. For rural women, the consequences of male out-migration to cities were mixed. Asian and African women found themselves heads of households, faced with added burdens in managing the farm and sustaining families. African and Asian village women became unprecedentedly self-reliant and began to assert greater rights.

In Latin America migration patterns differed: whole families generally migrated, often to squatter settlements. These families frequently belonged to the class of landless laborers, which was generally larger in Latin America than in Africa and Asia. Migration was also more likely to be permanent. Another difference was that single women were as likely as single men to move to the cities, in part because women were in high demand as domestic servants. Some women also left to escape male-dominated villages where they faced narrow social and economic opportunities.

In cities the concentration of wealth in few hands has resulted in unequal consumption, education, and employment. The gap between rich and poor around the world can be measured both between the city and the countryside, and within cities (Map 33.1). Wealthy city dwellers in developing countries often had more in common with each other than with the poorer urban and rural people in their own country. As a result, the elites have often favored globalization that connects them with wealthier nations.

multinational corporations
Business firms that operate in a number of different countries and tend to adopt a global rather than a national perspective.

Multinational Corporations

A striking feature of global interdependence beginning in the early 1950s was the rapid emergence of **multinational corporations**, or multinationals, which are business firms that operate in a number of different countries and tend to adopt a global rather than a national perspective. Their rise was partly due to the revival of capitalism after the Second World War, increasingly free international economic relations, and the worldwide drive for rapid industrialization. Multinationals treated the world as one big market, coordinating complex activities across political boundaries and escaping political controls and national policies.

The impact of multinational corporations, especially on less industrialized countries, has been mixed. The presence of multinationals helped spread the products and values of consumer society to elites in the developing world. Critics considered this part of the process of neo-

Multinational Companies in China Shoppers at a Sam's Club in the outskirts of Beijing reflect the globalization of consumption. Global commodity chains, multinational corporations, and converging consumer tastes, particularly among the middle class, create increasingly similar experiences across the world. (David G. McIntyre/EPA/Newscom)

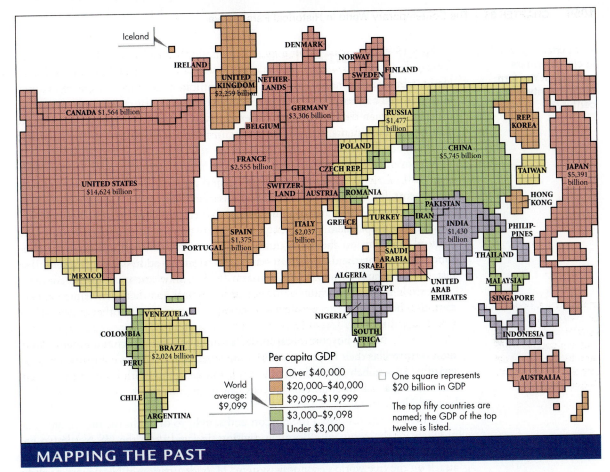

MAP 33.1 The Global Distribution of Wealth, ca. 2010 This size-comparison map, arranged according to global wealth distribution, vividly illustrates the gap in wealth between the Northern and Southern Hemispheres. The two small island nations of Japan and the United Kingdom have more wealth than all the nations of the Southern Hemisphere combined, although wealth creation in India and Brazil has advanced significantly. The wealthiest countries are also the most highly urbanized. As market capitalism expands in China, Vietnam, and other Asian countries and in Latin America and Africa, the relative-size ratios on the map will continue to change and evolve. Tiny Iceland, whose GDP is less than $20 billion, nevertheless has one of the highest per capita GDPs in the world.

ANALYZING THE MAP Which three countries are the wealthiest? Where are the poorest countries concentrated?

CONNECTIONS How were the two small nations of Japan and the United Kingdom able to acquire such enormous wealth?

colonialism, whereby local elites abandoned their nation's interests and contributed to continued foreign domination.

Multinational corporations are among the main beneficiaries of economic liberalism: growing openness of national markets and growing economic integration allow corporations to move goods, capital, and technology more fluidly and more intensely. But the growing interconnectedness of world markets comes with costs. In particular, it has meant increased economic volatility, as exemplified by the banking crisis that swept the United States and Europe in 2008 and plunged countries into deep and long recessions.

What challenges did social reformers address at the turn of the twenty-first century?

Social Movements

Just as nineteenth-century social reformers embraced the cause of ending slavery, modern social reformers have sought to end global inequality, racism, and sexism and to expand human rights. Social movements played a critical role in the victory of the democratic movements in Latin America and Europe and the end of the apartheid system in South Africa.

As movements for human rights and social reform gained ground in the 1960s and 1970s, activists increasingly looked beyond national borders to form alliances. Movements for women's rights, nuclear disarmament, environmental protection, and addressing climate change all became both local and global efforts. For example, the global anti-apartheid movement kept pressure on nations to apply economic and political sanctions on the white-minority regime in South Africa. But at the same time, the anti-apartheid movement served as a means to address local problems. For instance, in Brazil anti-apartheid activism helped draw attention to the country's own racial inequalities, while in the United States anti-apartheid activism on college campuses helped students organize movements concerned with other issues such as gender equality.

The 1977 Nestlé boycott exemplified the kinds of success such movements could achieve as well as their limitations. Critics charged that the Swiss company's marketing of powdered baby formula in poor countries or regions with little access to clean water posed a risk to children. Activists called on consumers around the world to boycott Nestlé products.

At first, Nestlé dismissed the boycott and sought to discredit the movement. The president of the company's Brazilian division declared that "the US Nestlé Co has advised me that their research indicates that this [boycott] is actually an indirect attack on the free world's economic system."[3] Condemnation of Nestlé mounted. In a 1978 hearing, U.S. senator Ted Kennedy asked a Nestlé executive: "Can a product which requires clean water, good sanitation, adequate family income and a literate parent to follow printed instructions be properly and safely used in areas where water is contaminated, sewage runs in the streets, poverty is severe and illiteracy is high?"[4]

In 1981 the UN World Health Organization responded to the campaign by developing a set of voluntary standards regulating the marketing of infant formula in countries where access to clean water was precarious. Nestlé agreed to follow the standards. The movement succeeded, but its success raised questions: multinational corporations operated beyond the reach of single governments and often operated in regions with weak regulatory or investigatory structures. As a result, it was hard to hold them accountable when their conduct was unethical. At the same time, social movements and nongovernmental organizations also acted outside the realm of public accountability.

Environmentalism

The modern environmental movement began with concerns about chemical waste, rapid consumption of energy and food supplies, global deforestation, and threats to wildlife. By the 1970s citizens had begun joining together in nongovernmental organizations to pursue preservation or restoration of the natural environment.

The environmental movement is actually several different movements, each with its own agenda. (See "Analyzing the Evidence: Protest Against Genetically Modified

Foods," page 1058.) American biologist and writer Rachel Carson was an early proponent of the environmental health movement. In *Silent Spring* (1962), she warned of the dangers of pesticides and pollution:

> Along with the possibility of the extinction of mankind by nuclear war, the central problem of our age has therefore become the contamination of man's total environment with such substances of incredible potential for harm—substances that accumulate in the tissues of plants and animals and even penetrate the germ cells to shatter or alter the very material of heredity upon which the shape of the future depends.[5]

Carson and others were concerned about the harmful effects of chemicals, radiation, pollution, waste, and urban development on the environment and on human health. Environmentalists like Carson acted out of concern that all living things were connected and that damage to one part of an ecological system could have consequences across that ecosystem.

Environmentalists today are especially concerned about **global warming**, the increase of global temperatures over time caused by the buildup of carbon in the atmosphere that captures heat. As a result of global warming, average temperatures have increased worldwide in recent decades, a trend that most scientists expect will intensify without curbs on carbon emissions. The decade from 2000 to 2010 was the warmest in recorded history, and the decade beginning in 2010 is projected to be even warmer. Scientists believe that man-made climate change began with the Industrial Revolution in the eighteenth century. The subsequent release of hydrocarbons produced through the burning of fossil fuels—coal, oil, natural gas—has caused a greenhouse effect that traps these gases and heats up the earth's atmosphere. Paradoxically, industrialization and increased consumption in the developing world meant diminished global inequalities but intensified global carbon emissions.

Scientists predict that the effects of global warming over the next century will include a catastrophic rise in sea levels that threatens to put many coastal cities and islands underwater; ecosystem changes that may threaten many species; destruction of the earth's ozone layer, which shields the planet from harmful solar radiation; and a decline in agricultural production.

International concerns over global warming resulted in a 1997 agreement, the Kyoto Protocol, which amended the United Nations Framework Convention on Climate Change. Countries that ratify the Kyoto Protocol agree to reduce their emissions of carbon dioxide and five other greenhouse gases. As

global warming The consensus view of an overwhelming majority of the world's scientists that hydrocarbons produced through the burning of fossil fuels have caused a greenhouse effect that has increased global temperatures over time.

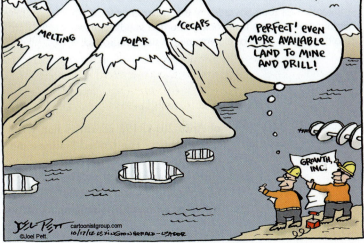

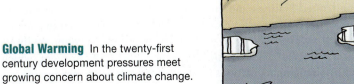

Global Warming In the twenty-first century development pressures meet growing concern about climate change.

(Joel Pett Editorial Cartoon used with the permission of Joel Pett and the Cartoonist Group)

Protest Against Genetically Modified Foods

The Chilean demonstrators in this photo are protesting the introduction of genetically modified crops. The banner reads, "I do not want transgenic crops in Chile: Movement for Food Sovereignty." Worldwide, people oppose genetically modified (GMO) crops for a variety of reasons. Some opponents fear that GMO foods present unforeseen health risks. Other opponents believe that the proliferation of genetically modified crops could damage biodiversity by reducing the variety of strains that are planted; they are also concerned that gene transfer from GMOs, particularly through pollination, could be damaging to other plant species, as well as to other organisms such as bees. Some opponents also note that GMOs can undermine small farmers who cannot afford the patented seeds of multinational companies such as Monsanto, placing them at a disadvantage relative to large landowners and threatening their land tenure.

The protesters in this image are members of a movement for food sovereignty that advocates for the production of crops from locally sourced seeds. Some are dressed as bees or clowns, and in the foreground

(Eliseo Fernandez/Reuters/Newscom)

a marcher dressed as the grim reaper bears a sign that reads, "Mon$anto patents your life."

QUESTIONS FOR ANALYSIS

1. What do the costumes suggest about the protesters' views about the effects of genetically modified foods?

2. Examine the concerns of these protesters in the context of the promises of the green revolution. What are some of the advantages and disadvantages of the scientific engineering of food crops?

of April 2014, 191 countries had ratified it. The most notable exception was the United States. The United Nations and environmental activists have continued to pursue an international environmental accord that can bring all nations into a shared effort to combat climate change. The U.S. government agreed to the voluntary limits on greenhouse gas emissions called for in the 2015 Paris Climate Agreement, which would be achieved by changing regulations in areas such as electicity production.

Lesbian, Gay, and Transgender Rights

In the United States and western Europe the growing focus on liberal individual freedoms since the 1960s has opened social space for same-sex unions and affinities, which had long been suppressed by religious and cultural strictures. By the early 1970s a global gay rights movement championed the human rights of people who are lesbian, gay, or transgender. The movement intensified in the 1980s as it became clear that governments neglected medical research and treatment for people sick with AIDS, which they dismissed as a "gay disease." The organization ACT UP's advocacy campaign for AIDS research created a powerful symbol using the words "Silence = Death" beneath a pink triangle to represent the AIDS crisis. A journalist who wrote about AIDS in the 1980s described his reaction to the ACT UP symbol:

> When I first saw the [ACT UP] poster, I didn't really know what it was. . . . I recognized the triangle as the symbol of homosexual victimization by the Nazis, but this triangle pointed up. Did it suggest supremacy? And the phrase itself, with its diabolical math, lodged in my imagination. Did it suggest conspiracy? Because of the word "death" I supposed it was about AIDS; had I noticed the tiny type at the bottom, which for a time included the instruction "Turn anger, fear, grief into action," perhaps I would have been sure.[6]

By the 1990s gay rights activists had broadened their efforts to challenge discrimination in employment, education, and public life. In 1995 Canada became the first country to allow same-sex marriage. In the ensuing years many European countries followed suit. But the legalization of same-sex marriage was not only a Western achievement: by 2013 Argentina, South Africa, Ecuador, and Uruguay had legalized same-sex marriage, while many other nations provided legal protections for families that stopped shy of marriage. Argentina led the way in legal support for transgender people and made sexual reassignment surgery a legal right in 2012. In 2014 the U.S. Supreme Court invalidated state laws and constitutional amendments barring same-sex marriage.

The movement toward recognition of same-sex marriage reflects the connection between liberalization and human rights: beyond dignifying discriminated groups, marriage rights give same-sex families legal equality to manage property rights and financial activities, such as the ability to inherit a home or jointly purchase insurance. Human rights successes in Latin America or Europe have widened the disparity in the experiences of people who are lesbian, gay, or transgender in many other regions of the world, where religious strictures against same-sex relationships can include imprisonment or death.

Equal Marriage in Argentina José Maria Di Bella, right, and his partner, Alex Freyre, celebrate Latin America's first same-sex marriage, which occurred in Tierra del Fuego, Argentina, in 2009. (Roger Bacon/Reuters/Alamy Stock Photo)

Women Activists in Chiapas, Mexico

In 1994 peasants and activists in the southern Mexican state of Chiapas staged a revolt against landowners, government authorities, and paramilitary groups who were taking their land. They called their movement the Zapatista Army for National Liberation, named after Emiliano Zapata, leader of a peasant army in the Mexican Revolution. Though the activists armed themselves for defense, they did not wage war. Instead they employed tools such as early Internet activism to demonstrate to the world the abuses their communities faced. These Zapatista women relate the struggles through which they built their political awareness.

María

■ Life on the plantation was very hard because there was never any rest from work. There was a man who was the overseer, who forced people to work all the time. . . . We had to give a third of all the firewood we cut to the plantation owner. Another service was to clean the patio. All these "services" were not paid, of course. We had to provide them in exchange for the little piece of land where we planted our corn. . . .

As a child my life was learning to make tortillas, cook the cornmeal and wash clothes. My mother liked to work in the fields with my father, so she would leave very early to go to the fields. When I was about 13 years old, I was in charge of the household. My siblings were boys, so I had to do everything—wash everybody's clothes, prepare the food and clean the house.

. . . We continued renting land at the plantation. My father grew potatoes, corn and beans on that land. . . . But after a few years, we were asked to plant grass [for the owner's cattle], and the owner put cattle on the grassland. We couldn't work the land after that. . . . We lost it. We lost our corn there.

Guadalupe

■ I'm about 50 years old, I think. My husband is about 80. He's much older than I am. I married when I was 14 years old. I had no father and my mother didn't want me to be alone, so she married me to this man. He was already very old. He doesn't work any more. I work. I built my own house. I work in the fields. . . . In my house I do everything. I carry the corn. I carry the wood for the fire. . . . I built my own house. It's my own. I owe it to my work, not to the government. . . .

Now, in my community . . . we can't go out to work. We can't go to our cornfields. Paz y Justicia [paramilitary]

Women's Right to Equality

The 1995 United Nations Fourth World Conference on Women, held in Beijing, China, called on the world community to take action in twelve areas of critical concern to women: poverty, access to education and training, access to health care, violence against women, women and war, economic inequality with men, political inequality with men, creation of institutions for women's advancement, lack of respect for women's rights, stereotyping of women, gender inequalities and the environment, and violation of girl children's rights.[7] These are concerns that all women share, although degrees of inequality vary greatly from one country to another.

feminization of poverty
The issue that those living in extreme poverty are disproportionately women.

The **feminization of poverty**, the disproportionate number of women living in extreme poverty, applies to even the wealthiest countries, where two out of every three poor adults are women. There are many causes for this phenomenon. Because women are primarily responsible for child care in many cultures, they have less time and opportunity for work. Male labor migration increases the number of households headed by women and thus the number of families living in poverty. Job restrictions, discrimination, and limited access to education reduce women's employment options, except in the "informal economy" of domestic service, prostitution, and street vend-

men are looking for people out on the roads. They have weapons and they kill people. . . . They killed all the cows my son had, and they ate the meat. They took my horses, too. I had seven good horses to carry wood and to carry the corn. They killed all my pigs. They even killed my dog with a machete.

Now the government says they don't have money to pay us back for our horses and for our cows. Why did they allow Paz y Justicia to do this to us in the first place? . . .

I'm really angry now! We've been at this sit-in for two months waiting in front of the government building.

Isabel

■ I went to work as a maid. I was only nine years old. I cleaned the house and took care of the children, and I lived in their house. There was a school nearby, so I asked my employers if I could go there to study, and they said yes. . . .

I was very lucky that I worked with these people. Many indigenous women who come from the countryside don't have it so good. A lot of them are mistreated. . . . There's a lot of racism and discrimination here in San Cristóbal, and the indigenous women are constantly humiliated. . . .

In 1992, [we] . . . formed an indigenous women's street theater group, and we began performing in village plazas, in the streets, in schools and in auditoriums. . . . [W]e started preparing our first play, *La mujer desesperada* (The Desperate Woman). This is a tragedy about domestic violence and violence in general. We performed this play in San Cristóbal on March 8, 1993, on International Women's Day.

QUESTIONS FOR ANALYSIS

1. What are the sources of insecurity in these women's lives?
2. How do these women respond to the pressures they face?
3. How do these accounts reflect themes of poverty, migration, and women's inequalities in the contemporary world?

Source: Teresa Ortiz, *Never Again a World Without Us: Voices of Mayan Women in Chiapas, Mexico* (Washington, D.C.: EPICA, 2001), pp. 38–40, 82–85, 153–154. Used by permission of the author.

ing. Birthrates are higher among poor women, particularly among adolescents, who make up many of the estimated 585,000 women who die every year during pregnancy and childbirth. The poorest women usually suffer most from government policies, usually legislated by men, that restrict their access to reproductive health care and family planning.

Women have made gains in the workplace, making up 38 percent of the non-farm-sector global workforce in the early 2000s, as compared to 35 percent in 1990. But segregated labor markets remain the rule, with higher-paying jobs reserved for men. In the farm sector, women produce more than half of all the food and up to 80 percent of subsistence crops grown in Africa. Because this is informal labor and often unpaid, these women laborers are denied access to loans, and many cannot own the land they farm. (See "Global Viewpoints: Women Activists in Chiapas, Mexico," above.)

Beyond the labor market, women also began in the 1960s to experience more control over pregnancy and childbirth decisions, particularly following the introduction of the birth control pill in the early 1960s. In the early twenty-first century more than half of the world's couples practiced some form of birth control, up from one in

United Nations Fourth World Conference on Women International Women's Day, March 8, and the UN Conferences on Women have served as platforms for framing the rights of women as a basic component of human rights. Here Hillary Rodham Clinton addresses the Fourth World Conference on Women in Beijing in 1995.

eight just forty years earlier. Birth control and abortion were most accepted in North America, Protestant regions in Europe, the Soviet Union, and East Asia.

Social class continues to be a major divider of women's opportunities. Over the course of the twentieth century women from more affluent backgrounds experienced far greater gains in access to education, employment, and political representation than women in poverty did. In the aftermath of decolonization and state formation, women emerged as heads of state in Bangladesh, India, Israel, and Pakistan. A wave of democratic political transitions in the 1980s yielded women heads of state in the Philippines and Nicaragua. In the years following democratic transitions, the same occurred in Panama, Chile, Argentina, Brazil, Indonesia, and Liberia.

Children: The Right to Childhood

In 1989 the United Nations General Assembly adopted the Convention on the Rights of the Child, which spelled out a number of rights that are due every child. These include civil and human rights and economic, social, and cultural rights. The convention addresses the reality that globally a billion children live in poverty—one in every two children in the world—and that children make up half the world's refugees. It also focuses on the problems of child labor and exploitation, sexual violence and sex trafficking, police abuse of street children, HIV/AIDS orphans, lack of access to education, and lack of access to adequate health care. The convention has been ratified by more countries than any other human rights treaty—196 countries as of 2017. The only United Nations member nation that has not ratified it is the United States.

As the twenty-first century began, nearly a billion people—mostly women denied equitable access to education—were illiterate. Increasing economic globalization has put pressure on all governments to improve literacy rates and educational opportunities; the result has been reduced gender inequalities in education. While the percentage of illiterate adults in 2010 who were women was 64 percent, the percentage of girls among illiterate children was 60 percent, with the greatest gains in literacy occurring in South Asia and the Middle East.

In the 1990s Mexico pioneered a new approach to combating poverty that has been implemented in a growing number of countries. Conditional cash transfer, or CCT, provides a stipend to families who meet certain goals, such as keeping their children in school. This approach addresses poverty directly, while enlisting families to work toward its long-term solution by increasing education levels, which will broaden opportunities for new generations. Mexico's Oportunidades (Opportunities) CCT was followed by Brazil's Bolsa Família (Family Scholarship) and by similar projects in many other countries in Latin America. Versions of the program have been introduced across Asia and the Middle East, including in Bangladesh, where a CCT program promotes the education of girls.

Science and Technology: Changes and Challenges

How have science and technology kept pace with population change?

Since 1950 the world's population has increased from 2.5 billion people to over 7 billion. This population growth has been matched by increasing demand for food and has placed growing strains on natural resources. Advances in agriculture and medicine have helped offset this challenge, while technological innovations in areas such as transportation and communications have increased the complexity of interactions among the world's growing population.

Intensified Agriculture and the Green Revolution

As the world's population grew in the second half of the twentieth century, food production strained to keep pace, prompting a greater emphasis on rural development and agricultural sciences. Before 1939 the countries of Asia, Africa, and Latin America had collectively produced more grain than they consumed. After 1945, as their populations soared, they began importing food from countries like the United States. Although crops might fail in poor countries, starvation seemed a thing of the past.

Then, in 1966 and 1967, a devastating famine struck India. That close brush with mass starvation created widespread alarm that population growth was outpacing food production. The American scientist Paul Ehrlich envisioned a grim future in his 1968 bestseller *The Population Bomb*, which warned of a population crisis:

> The battle to feed all of humanity is over. In the 1970s the world will undergo famines—hundreds of millions of people are going to starve to death in spite of any crash programs embarked upon now.[8]

Ehrlich was not the first scientist to make such dire predictions, and like Thomas Malthus before him (see "Industry and Population" in Chapter 23), he failed to understand the adaptability of farmers and the ability of agricultural technology to keep pace with population growth.

Plant scientists continued to develop new genetically engineered and hybridized seeds to suit particular growing conditions. The first breakthrough came in Mexico in the 1950s when an American-led team developed new strains of wheat that enabled farmers to double their yields, though the plants required greater amounts of fertilizer and water for irrigation. Mexican wheat production soared. A similar innovation in Asia introduced a new "miracle rice" that allowed farmers to plant two to four crops a year rather than one. Thus began the transformation of agriculture in some poor countries—the so-called **green revolution**.

green revolution
Beginning in the 1950s, the increase in food production stemming from the introduction of high-yielding wheat, hybrid seeds, and other advancements.

As they applied green revolution technologies, many Asian countries experienced rapid increases in grain production. Farmers in India increased production more than 60 percent in fifteen years. China followed with its own highly successful version of the green revolution.

The green revolution offered new hope to industrializing nations, though its benefits often flowed to large landowners and export farms that could afford the necessary investments in irrigation and fertilizer. Experiences in China and other Asian countries showed, however, that even peasant families with tiny farms could gain substantially. Indeed, the green revolution's greatest successes occurred in Asian countries with broad-based peasant ownership of land. However, few of the poorest villagers benefited from the technological revolution in equipment because they rarely owned land or had enough capital to invest in new agricultural technology to increase their yields. This helps explain why in Latin America, where 3 to 4 percent of the rural population owned 60 to 80 percent of the land, the green revolution spread slowly beyond Mexico, where land had been redistributed after the 1910 revolution.

The Medical Revolution

The medical revolution began in the late nineteenth century with the development of the germ theory of disease (see "Urban Development" in Chapter 24) and continued rapidly after World War II. Scientists discovered vaccines for many of the most deadly diseases. The Salk polio vaccine, developed in 1952, was followed by the first oral polio vaccine (1962) and vaccines for measles (1964), mumps (1967), rubella (1970), chicken pox (1974), hepatitis B (1981), and human papilloma virus (2006). According to the UN World Health Organization, medical advances reduced deaths from smallpox, cholera, and plague by more than 95 percent worldwide between 1951 and 1966.

Following independence, Asian and African countries increased the small numbers of hospitals, doctors, and nurses they had inherited from colonial regimes. In addition, local people were successfully trained as paramedics to staff rural outpatient clinics that offered medical treatment, health education, and prenatal and postnatal care. Many paramedics were women, who traditionally addressed health problems that involved childbirth and infancy.

Medical advances significantly lowered death rates and lengthened life expectancies worldwide. Children became increasingly likely to survive their early years, although infant and juvenile mortality remained far higher in poor countries than in rich ones. By 1980 the average inhabitant of the developing countries could expect to live about fifty-four years, although life expectancy at birth varied from forty to sixty-four years depending on the country. In industrialized countries, life expectancy at birth averaged seventy-one years.

The medical benefits of scientific advances have been limited by unequal access to health care, which is more readily available to the wealthy than to the poor. Between 1980 and 2000 the number of children under the age of five dying annually of diarrhea dropped by 60 percent through the global distribution of a cheap sugar-salt solution mixed in water. Still, over 1.5 million children worldwide continue to die each year from diarrhea, primarily in poorer nations. Deaths worldwide from HIV/AIDS, malaria, and tuberculosis are concentrated in the world's poorest regions, while tuberculosis remains the leading killer of women worldwide.

Tuberculosis (TB) claims millions of lives every year, even though it is a curable disease. Malaria kills a million people a year worldwide, 90 percent of them in Africa. In 2007 the Population Division of the United Nations calculated that 36 million persons globally were infected with HIV, the virus that causes AIDS, and that AIDS was the world's fourth-leading cause of death. About 90 percent of all persons who die from AIDS and 86 percent of those currently infected with HIV live in sub-Saharan Africa (Map 33.2). In Africa HIV/AIDS is most commonly spread through heterosexual sex. Widespread disease and poverty are also significant factors in that Africans already suffering from other illnesses such as malaria or tuberculosis are less resistant to HIV and have less access to health care for treatment.

Another factor contributing to the spread of AIDS in Africa is political instability—particularly in the corridor running from Uganda to South Africa. This region

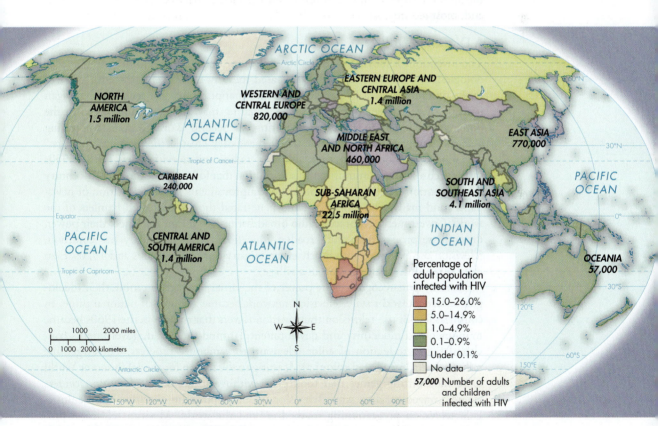

MAP 33.2 People Living with HIV/AIDS Worldwide, ca. 2010 As this map illustrates, Africa has been hit the hardest by the HIV/AIDS epidemic. It currently has 70 percent of the world's cases of HIV infection. AIDS researchers expect that in the coming decade, however, Russia and South and East Asia will overtake and then far surpass Africa in the number of infected people. (Source: Data from World Health Organization.)

was the scene of conflicts that resulted in massive numbers of refugees and a break-down in health-care services. The people living in this area in the countries of Uganda, Rwanda, Burundi, Zaire/Congo, Angola, Zimbabwe, Mozambique, and South Africa have been decimated by HIV/AIDS. South Africa has the largest number of HIV/AIDS cases in the world. In 2010 around 10 percent of the South African population, about 5.6 million people, was living with HIV/AIDS. Since 2001 relatively inexpensive HIV/AIDS drugs that are widely available in the West have been dispensed freely to many of those infected in Africa and Asia, but the availability of these drugs has generally failed to keep up with the need.

Climate change has emerged as a growing factor in the spread of disease as the habitats for organisms that carry diseases—such as mosquitoes—expand. Changes in rainfall also play a role because areas that experience increasing rain have more standing water where mosquito larvae can incubate. Paradoxically, areas beset by drought also experience an intensification of mosquito-borne disease because in dry periods people tend to store water, which then becomes a breeding ground for mosquitoes. In Africa, Asia, the Pacific, and the Americas, these factors have accelerated the intensification of mosquito-borne diseases such as malaria, dengue, chikungunya, and, most recently, Zika.

A Digital Revolution

The invention of moving pictures, the telephone, and other communications technologies between 1875 and 1900 prepared the way for a twentieth-century era of mass communications. In parallel, new information-processing technologies began with the development of adding and calculating machines and culminated in the development of the first computers during the Second World War. As computing and communications technologies converged, they created the "information age." The global availability and affordability of radios and television sets in the 1950s introduced a second communications revolution that followed the nineteenth-century first revolution (telegraph, telephone, and improvements in the circulation of newspapers and mail). The transistor radio penetrated the most isolated hamlets of the world. Governments embraced radio broadcasting as a means to project their power, disseminate propaganda, and broaden education. Though initially less common, television use expanded into nearly every country during the 1960s and 1970s, even if there was only one television in a village.

Governments recognized the power of the visual image to promote their ideologies or leaders, and a state television network became a source of national pride. In countries like Brazil, television transmission towers that rose up in the 1960s became monuments to modernity and development. Around the world, governments controlled the introduction of color television to symbolize progress. The Argentine military junta introduced color broadcasting to the nation for the 1978 soccer World Cup, transmitting games that took place within earshot of the detention centers where it waged its "dirty war." Television became a powerful disseminator of culture: U.S. television programming reached around the world. Mexican television programs dominated Spanish-speaking regions. Brazilian soap operas gained loyal followers from the Soviet Union to Angola.

The third, and perhaps greatest, communications revolution began with the first personal computers in 1976, followed by the introduction of cell phones in

1985. The rapid diffusion of computing and cellular technology has allowed nations in the developing world to bypass traditional telephone lines, installation, and other obstacles. Smartphones have become the most common instruments for connecting to the Internet, allowing people in poorer and rural regions of the world to communicate and access information digitally without a computer or physical network.

Broader Internet access has made global access to information and communications seemingly infinite. Meanwhile, authoritarian governments have realized that the Internet and social media platforms like Facebook and Twitter pose a threat to their power and control. The governments of China and North Korea, for example, restrict information that travels in and out of their countries over the Internet, while the governments of the United States and other nations have invested heavily in monitoring that information. Even as expanding means of communication through cell phones, computers, and their networks have made censorship more difficult to enforce, they have made it even harder to keep information or communications private.

The intensity of innovation in communications and information technology created new multinational giants. The success of these technology companies and the proliferation of computer, smartphone, and Internet use are remarkable changes, but they also deepen socioeconomic inequalities between countries and within countries. For instance, when Windows XP was released in 2001, a Nigerian cocoa laborer would have had to save his or her entire year's earnings to buy the Home Edition.[9] The unevenness of both the production and consumption of computer technology has resulted in a **digital divide**, meaning the gap in access to Internet, computer, and telecommunications resources. This gap is the greatest between nations like the United States, western European countries, and Japan and nations in Africa and South and Southeast Asia. The digital divide also exists between the wealthy and poor, as well as between urban and rural areas within countries. As the Internet becomes more integral to business, education, and government, communities with no or limited access face growing disadvantages.

Smartphones Expand Access to Information
The rapid spread of cellular communication networks has made smartphone use the leading way in which people around the world access information and communicate. In this 2015 photo, a migrant mother uses her cell phone to map her route at the border between Serbia and Hungary. (© Balint Porneczi/Signatures/Redux)

digital divide The gap between levels of access to computing, Internet, and telecommunications between rich and poor regions and populations.

Chapter Summary

The end of the Cold War confrontation between superpowers has resulted in a world in which regional tensions endure and sometimes become international conflicts. Consequently, in a way similar to its actions in the Cold War era, the United States after 1990 continued to be involved in military conflicts far from home in regions ranging from the Balkans to Libya, Iraq, and Afghanistan. These conflicts have also spurred arms races that have led to the emergence of new nuclear powers in South Asia and East Asia.

The transitions to economic and political liberalism in the former Soviet bloc and in Latin America were particularly dramatic expressions of the rise of liberalism worldwide, which included the economic and political integration of Europe and the emergence of China as an economic superpower. Growing interconnectedness of world markets has meant increased economic volatility, such as the global financial market crisis of 2008. Cycles of economic growth and crisis, as well as contradictory experiences of integration and regional conflict, are tensions of the modern world rooted in historical experiences.

NOTES

1. Francis Fukuyama, "The End of History?" *The National Interest*, Summer 1989, p. 3.
2. United Nations High Commisssioner for Human Rights (UN Refugee Agency), "Europe Situation," updated January 24, 2017, http://www.unhcr.org/europe-emergency.html.
3. Quoted in Judith Richter, *Holding Corporations Accountable: Corporate Conduct, International Codes, and Citizen Action* (London: Zed Books, 2002), p. 55.
4. Quoted in Simon Robinson, "Nestlé Baby Milk Substitute and International Marketing: A Case History," in *Case Histories in Business Ethics*, ed. Chris Megone and Simon Robinson (New York: Routledge, 2002), p. 141.
5. Rachel Carson, *Silent Spring* (1962; repr., New York: Houghton Mifflin, 1994), pp. 1–3, 7–8.
6. Jesse Green, "When Political Art Mattered," *New York Times*, December 7, 2003, http://www.nytimes .com/learning/teachers/featured_articles/20031208monday.html.
7. United Nations, "Critical Areas of Concern," *Report of the Fourth World Conference on Women* (New York: United Nations Department for Policy Coordination and Sustainable Development, 1995), ch. 1, annex II, ch. 3, pp. 41–44, http://www.un.org/esa/gopher-data/conf/fwcw/off/a--20.en. See also Population Reference Bureau, *Women of Our World 2005* (Washington, D.C.: Population Reference Bureau, 2005) for the latest data and ten-year follow-up to the Beijing meeting.
8. Paul Ehrlich, *The Population Bomb* (New York: Ballantine, 1968), p. 11.
9. James Gockowski and S. Oduwole, *Labor Practices in the Cocoa Sector of Southwest Nigeria with a Focus on the Role of Children* (Ibadan, Nigeria: International Institute of Tropical Agriculture, 2003), p. 23.

CONNECTIONS

The present shapes the ways we ask questions about the past. Understanding of the past also shapes our questions about the present and the future. Our history of world societies shows that the forces that shape the world we live in have deep roots: Globalization reaches back for centuries. Current armed conflicts are based on historic tensions often rooted in ethnic differences or legacies of colonialism. The gaps between rich and poor countries, and between the rich and poor within countries, have sometimes been diminished by advances in science and technology or by reforms in social policy. But science, technology, and public policy also deepen those inequalities, as uneven industrialization and the digital divide reflect.

Our relationship with the past is one of continuity and change. The study of history allows us to frame questions about complex, competing, and often-contradictory experiences. Asking these questions sharpens our focus on not only the past but also the present. We are shaped by history. But we also make it.

CHAPTER 33 **Review and Explore**

Identify Key Terms

Identify and explain the significance of each item below.

middle powers (p. 1046)

megacities (p. 1053)

bazaar economy (p. 1053)

multinational corporations (p. 1054)

global warming (p. 1057)

feminization of poverty (p. 1060)

green revolution (p. 1064)

digital divide (p. 1067)

Review the Main Ideas

Answer the focus questions from each section of the chapter.

1. Does the contemporary world reflect the "end of history"? (p. 1046)

2. How have migration and the circulation of capital and technology continued to shape the world? (p. 1050)

3. What challenges did social reformers address at the turn of the twenty-first century? (p. 1056)

4. How have science and technology kept pace with population change? (p. 1063)

Make Comparisons and Connections

Analyze the larger developments and continuities within and across chapters.

1. Why hasn't the end of the Cold War been followed by an easing of regional conflicts?

2. How do socioeconomic inequalities in the twenty-first-century world resemble the gaps between rich and poor in earlier eras?

3. How do contemporary technological and scientific developments reflect historical change and continuity?

TIMELINE

GLOBAL	**1950s** Beginning of green revolution ◆ **1970** Treaty on the Non-Proliferation of Nuclear Weapons
AFRICA	**1957–1975** Decolonization **(Chs. 31, 32)**
AMERICAS	◆ **1962** Cuban missile crisis **(Ch. 31)**
ASIA	**1959–1975** Vietnam War **(Ch. 31)** **1978** ◆ Deng Xiaoping initiates economic reforms in China **(Ch. 32)** ◆ **1965** Great Proletarian Cultural Revolution in China **(Ch. 31)**
EUROPE	
MIDDLE EAST	◆ **1967** Six-Day War between Israel, Egypt, Syria, and Jordan **(Ch. 31)**

1960	1970	1980

Suggested Resources

BOOKS

Abrahamson, Mark. *Global Cities.* 2004. Explores the global historical patterns of urbanization.

Gareis, Sven Bernhard, and Johannes Varwick. *The United Nations: An Introduction.* 2005. An overview of the United Nations.

Gore, Al. *An Inconvenient Truth: The Planetary Emergency of Global Warming and What We Can Do About It.* 2006. Reasoned discussion of the greatest threat to the planet in the twenty-first century, for which Gore won the Nobel Peace Prize.

Hawkesworth, Mary. *Political Worlds of Women: Activism, Advocacy, and Governance in the Twenty-First Century.* 2012. A survey of global women's social movements amid persistent challenges of political exclusion and economic inequality.

Jones, Geoffrey. *Multinationals and Global Capitalism: From the Nineteenth to the Twenty-First Century.* 2005. A historical overview of the development of multinational corporations and a global capitalist economy.

Law, Randall D. *Terrorism: A History*, 2d ed. 2016. Explores the history of violent political actions, with a focus on ethnic, nationalist, and religious violence.

O'Neill, Bard E. *Insurgency and Terrorism: From Revolution to Apocalypse*, 2d ed. 2005. An excellent introduction to the nature of modern war.

O'Neill, John Terence, and Nicholas Rees. *United Nations Peacekeeping in the Post–Cold War Era.* 2005. Discusses the problems associated with United Nations peacekeeping efforts.

Pécoud, Antoine, and Paul de Guchteneire, eds. *Migration Without Borders: Essays on the Free Movement of People.* 2007. Regional perspectives on contemporary migration.

Piketty, Thomas. *Capital in the Twenty-First Century.* 2014. A fresh look at the history of social inequality and the accumulation of wealth.

Sasson, Tehila. "Milking the Third World? Humanitarianism, Capitalism, and the Moral Economy of the Nestlé Boycott." *American Historical Review* 121.4 (October 2016). Explores the role of human rights activism in relation to multinational corporations.

2000–2010 Warmest decade in recorded history

◆ **1997** Kyoto Protocol on global warming

◆ **1994** Nelson Mandela elected president of South Africa **(Ch. 32)**

◆ **1994** North American Free Trade Agreement **(Ch. 32)**

◆ **1994** Zapatista Army for National Liberation insurrection in Chiapas, Mexico

◆ **2001** Al-Qaeda attacks on World Trade Center and U.S. Pentagon

◆ **1993** Formation of the European Union **(Ch. 32)**

2016 ➔ British "Brexit" vote to leave European Union

1989–1991 Fall of communism in the Soviet Union and eastern Europe **(Ch. 32)**

2003–2011 Second Persian Gulf War **(Ch. 32)**

◆ **1987** Palestinian intifada **(Ch. 32)**

◆ **2001** U.S. invasion and occupation of Afghanistan

2011 ◆ Civil war in Syria begins **(Ch. 32)**

| 1990 | 2000 | 2010 |

Seel, Peter B. *Digital Universe: The Global Telecommunication Revolution.* 2012. Discusses the historical trajectory of information and communications technology.

Shah, Sonia. *Pandemic: Tracking Contagions, from Cholera to Ebola and Beyond.* 2016. Examines patterns of global epidemics, both old and new.

DOCUMENTARIES

Children of Syria (PBS, 2016). A PBS *Frontline* documentary tracing the story of four refugee children from Syria who found a new home in Germany.

Last Train Home (Lixin Fan, 2009). Explores the experience of China's more than 100 million migrant workers, focusing on the tensions between rural agrarian and urban industrial settings.

The Salt of the Earth (Juliano Ribeiro Salgado and Wim Wenders, 2014). Unpacks the work of Brazilian photographer Sebastião Salgado, whose images capture peoples in motion, often fleeing the hardships of war. The documentary explores the question of healing amid conflict.

FEATURE FILMS

Dheepan (Jacques Audiard, 2015). Focuses on the experience of Sri Lankan refugees in a housing project in Paris's suburbs. Fleeing war, they find new conflicts fueled by the drug trade.

Sin Nombre (Cary Joji Fukunaga, 2009). Depicts the journey of two young Hondurans traveling through Mexico to reach the United States.

WEBSITES

Country Resources. Maintained by the Migration Policy Institute, this site presents country-by-country information on currents of international migration. **www.migrationpolicy.org/programs/migration -information-source/country-resources**

Europe's Migration Crisis. Resources maintained by the U.S. Council on Foreign Relations that offer a broad view on migration policy and pressures in Europe. **www.cfr.org/refugees-and-the-displaced /europes-migration-crisis/p32874**

absolutism A political system common to early modern Europe in which monarchs claimed exclusive power to make and enforce laws, without checks by other institutions; this system was limited in practice by the need to maintain legitimacy and compromise with elites. (Ch. 18)

African National Congress (ANC) The main black nationalist organization in South Africa, led by Nelson Mandela. (Ch. 32)

Afrikaners Descendants of the Dutch settlers in the Cape Colony in southern Africa. (Ch. 25)

age-grade systems Among the societies of Senegambia, groups of teenage males and females whom the society initiated into adulthood at the same time. (Ch. 20)

Age of Division The period after the fall of the Han Dynasty, when China was politically divided. (Ch. 7)

Agricultural Revolution Dramatic transformation in human history resulting from the change from foraging to raising crops and animals. (Ch. 1)

Aksum A kingdom in northwestern Ethiopia that was a sizable trading state and the center of Christian culture. (Ch. 10)

alternate residence system Arrangement in which Japanese lords were required to live in Edo every other year and left their wives and sons there as hostages to the Tokugawa Shogunate. (Ch. 21)

anarcho-syndicalism A version of anarchism that advocated placing power in the hands of workers' unions. (Ch. 27)

animism Idea that people, animals, plants, natural occurrences, and other parts of the physical world have spirits. (Ch. 1)

Antifederalists Opponents of the American Constitution who felt it diminished individual rights and accorded too much power to the federal government at the expense of the states. (Ch. 22)

Anyang One of the Shang Dynasty capitals from which the Shang kings ruled for more than two centuries. (Ch. 4)

apartheid The system of racial segregation and discrimination that was supported by the Afrikaner government in South Africa. (Ch. 32)

Arab socialism A modernizing, secular, and nationalist project of nation building in the Middle East aimed at economic development and the development of a strong military. (Ch. 31)

Aryans The dominant people in north India after the decline of the Indus Valley civilization; they spoke an early form of Sanskrit. (Ch. 3)

Aztec Empire An alliance between the Mexica people and their conquered allies, with its capital in Tenochtitlan (now Mexico City), that rose in size and power in the fifteenth century and possessed a sophisticated society and culture, with advanced mathematics, astronomy, and engineering. (Ch. 16)

Balfour Declaration A 1917 statement by British foreign secretary Arthur Balfour that supported the idea of a Jewish homeland in Palestine. (Ch. 29)

banners Units of the Manchu army, composed of soldiers, their families, and slaves. (Ch. 21)

Bantu Speakers of a Bantu language living south and east of the Congo River. (Ch. 10)

bazaar economy An economy with few salaried jobs and an abundance of tiny, unregulated businesses such as peddlers and pushcart operators. (Ch. 33)

Berbers North African peoples who controlled the caravan trade between the Mediterranean and the Sudan. (Ch. 10)

Berlin Conference A meeting of European leaders held in 1884–1885 to lay down basic rules for imperialist competition in sub-Saharan Africa. (Ch. 25)

Bill of Rights of 1689 A bill passed by Parliament and accepted by William and Mary that limited the powers of British monarchs and affirmed those of Parliament. (Ch. 18)

bishop A Christian Church official with jurisdiction over a certain area and the power to determine the correct interpretation of Christian teachings. (Ch. 6)

Black Death The plague that first struck Europe in 1347, killing perhaps one-third of the population. (Ch. 14)

Black Legend The notion that the Spanish were uniquely brutal and cruel in their conquest and settlement of the Americas, an idea propagated by rival European powers. (Ch. 16)

Black Shirts A private army under Mussolini in Italy that destroyed Socialist newspapers, union halls, and local Socialist Party headquarters, eventually pushing Socialists out of the city governments of northern Italy. (Ch. 30)

blitzkrieg "Lightning war" using planes, tanks, and trucks, first used by Hitler to crush Poland in four weeks. (Ch. 30)

bodhisattvas Buddhas-to-be who stayed in the world after enlightenment to help others on the path to salvation. (Ch. 3)

Bolsheviks The "majority group"; this was Lenin's camp of the Russian party of Marxist socialism. (Ch. 28)

Book of Documents One of the earliest Chinese books, containing documents, speeches, and historical accounts about early Zhou rule. (Ch. 4)

Book of Songs The earliest collection of Chinese poetry; it provides glimpses of what life was like in the early Zhou Dynasty. (Ch. 4)

bourgeoisie The well-educated, prosperous, middle-class groups. (Ch. 24)

Boxers A Chinese secret society that blamed the country's ills on foreigners, especially missionaries, and rose in rebellion in 1900. (Ch. 26)

brahman The unchanging ultimate reality, according to the *Upanishads*. (Ch. 3)

Brahmins Priests of the Aryans; they supported the growth of royal power in return for royal confirmation of their own religious rights, power, and status. (Ch. 3)

bride wealth In early modern Southeast Asia, a sum of money the groom paid the bride or her family at the time of marriage. This practice contrasted with the dowry in China, India, and Europe, which the husband controlled. (Ch. 16)

Bushido Literally, "the way of the warrior"; the code of conduct by which samurai were expected to live. (Ch. 13)

captaincies A system established by the Portuguese in Brazil in the 1530s, whereby hereditary grants of land were given to nobles and loyal officials who bore the costs of settling and administering their territories. (Ch. 16)

caravel A small, maneuverable, three-masted sailing ship that gave the Portuguese a distinct advantage in exploration and trade. (Ch. 16)

Carolingian A dynasty of rulers that took over the Frankish kingdom from the Merovingians in the seventh century; *Carolingian* derives from the Latin word for "Charles," the name of several members of this dynasty. (Ch. 8)

caste system The Indian system of dividing society into hereditary groups whose members interacted primarily within the group, and especially married within the group. (Ch. 3)

caudillismo Government by figures who rule through personal charisma and the support of armed followers in Latin America. (Ch. 27)

Chan A school of Buddhism (known in Japan as Zen) that rejected the authority of the sutras and claimed the superiority of mind-to-mind transmission of Buddhist truths. (Ch. 7)

chattel An item of personal property; a term used in reference to enslaved people that conveys the idea that they are subhuman, like animals, and therefore may be treated like animals. (Ch. 20)

Chinggis Khan The title given to the Mongol ruler Temujin in 1206; it means Great Ruler. (Ch. 12)

chivalry A code of conduct that was supposed to govern the behavior of a knight. (Ch. 14)

Christian humanists Humanists from northern Europe who thought that the best elements of classical and Christian cultures should be combined and saw humanist learning as a way to bring about reform of the church and deepen people's spiritual lives. (Ch. 15)

Circum-Caribbean The region encompassing the Antilles as well as the lands that bound the Caribbean Sea in Central America and northern South America. (Ch. 27)

civil service examinations A highly competitive series of written tests held at the prefecture, province, and capital levels in China to select men to become officials. (Ch. 21)

class-consciousness An individual's sense of class differentiation, a term introduced by Karl Marx. (Ch. 23)

cloistered government A system in which an emperor retired to a Buddhist monastery but continued to exercise power by controlling his young son on the throne. (Ch. 13)

cocoa holdups Mass protests in Africa's Gold Coast in the 1930s by producers of cocoa who refused to sell their beans to British firms and instead sold them directly to European and American chocolate manufacturers. (Ch. 31)

Code of Manu The codification of early Indian law that lays down family, caste, and commercial law. (Ch. 3)

Cold War The post–World War II conflict between the United States and the Soviet Union. (Ch. 31)

collectivization Stalin's forcible consolidation, beginning in 1929, of individual peasant farms in the Soviet Union into large, state-controlled enterprises. (Ch. 30)

Columbian exchange The exchange of animals, plants, and diseases between the Old and the New Worlds. (Ch. 16)

Combination Acts English laws passed in 1799 that outlawed unions and strikes, favoring capitalist business owners over skilled artisans. Bitterly resented and widely disregarded by many craft guilds, the acts were repealed by Parliament in 1824. (Ch. 23)

commercial revolution The transformation of the economic structure of Europe, beginning in the eleventh century, from a rural, manorial society to a more complex mercantile society. (Ch. 14)

Common Market The European Economic Community created in 1957. (Ch. 31)

compass A tool for identifying north using a magnetic needle; it was made useful for sea navigation in Song times when placed in a protective case. (Ch. 13)

concubine A woman who is a recognized spouse but of lower status than a wife. (Chs. 13, 17)

Confucian classics The ancient texts recovered during the Han Dynasty that Confucian scholars treated as sacred scriptures. (Ch. 7)

Congress of Vienna A meeting of the Quadruple Alliance (Russia, Prussia, Austria, Great Britain) and France held in 1814–1815 to fashion a general peace settlement after the defeat of Napoleonic France. (Ch. 24)

conquistador Spanish for "conqueror"; a Spanish soldier-explorer, such as Hernán Cortés or Francisco Pizarro, who sought to conquer the New World for the Spanish crown. (Ch. 16)

conservatism A political philosophy that stressed retaining traditional values and institutions, including hereditary monarchy and a strong landowning aristocracy. (Ch. 24)

constitutionalism A form of government in which power is limited by law and balanced between the authority and power of the government, on the one hand, and the rights and liberties of the subject or citizen, on the other; it includes constitutional monarchies and republics. (Ch. 18)

consuls Primary executives in the Roman Republic, elected for one-year terms, who commanded the army in battle, administered state business, and supervised financial affairs. (Ch. 6)

Continental System A blockade imposed by Napoleon in which no ship coming from Britain or its colonies was permitted to dock at any port controlled by the French. (Ch. 22)

Copernican hypothesis The idea that the sun, not the earth, was the center of the universe. (Ch. 19)

Coptic Christianity Orthodox form of Christianity from Egypt practiced in Ethiopia. (Ch. 20)

Cossacks Free groups and outlaw armies living on the borders of Russian territory from the fourteenth century onward. In the mid-sixteenth century they formed an alliance with the Russian state. (Ch. 18)

cottage industry Manufacturing with hand tools in peasant cottages and work sheds, a form of economic activity that became important in eighteenth-century Europe. (Ch. 19)

cowrie shells Imported from the Maldives, they served as the medium of exchange in West Africa. (Ch. 20)

craft guilds Associations of artisans organized to regulate the quality, quantity, and price of the goods produced as well as the number of affiliated apprentices and journeymen. (Ch. 14)

Creoles People of European descent born in the Americas. (Ch. 22)

crossbow A powerful mechanical bow developed during the Warring States Period. (Ch. 4)

Crusades Holy wars sponsored by the papacy for the recovery of the holy city of Jerusalem from the Muslims. (Ch. 14)

Crystal Palace The location of the Great Exhibition in 1851 in London, an architectural masterpiece made entirely of glass and iron. (Ch. 23)

cuneiform Sumerian form of writing; the term describes the wedge-shaped marks made by a stylus. (Ch. 2)

daimyo Regional lords in Japan, many of whom were self-made men. (Ch. 21)

Dao The Way, a term used by Daoists to refer to the natural order. (Ch. 4)

Dawes Plan The product of the 1924 World War I reparations commission, accepted by Germany, France, and Britain, that reduced Germany's yearly reparations, made payment dependent on German economic prosperity, and granted Germany large loans from the United States to promote recovery. (Ch. 28)

debate about women An argument about women's character, nature, and proper role in society that began in the later years of the fourteenth century and lasted for centuries. (Ch. 15)

Declaration of Independence The 1776 document in which the American colonies declared independence from Great Britain and recast traditional English rights as universal human rights. (Ch. 22)

deism Belief in a distant, noninterventionist deity, shared by many Enlightenment thinkers. (Ch. 19)

democracy A type of Greek government in which all citizens administered the workings of government. (Ch. 5)

dependency theory The belief, formulated in Latin America in the mid-twentieth century, that development in some areas of the world locks other nations into underdevelopment. (Ch. 31)

détente The progressive relaxation of Cold War tensions between the United States and the Soviet Union in the late 1960s and early 1970s. (Ch. 32)

devshirme A process whereby the sultan's agents swept the provinces for Christian youths to be trained as soldiers or civil servants. (Ch. 17)

dharma The Sanskrit word for moral law, central to both Buddhist and Hindu teachings. (Ch. 3)

dhimmis A term meaning "protected peoples"; they included Jews, Christians, and Zoroastrians. (Ch. 9)

Diet of Worms An assembly of representatives from the territories of the Holy Roman Empire convened by Charles V in the city of Worms in 1521. It was here that Martin Luther refused to recant his writings. (Ch. 15)

digital divide The gap between levels of access to computing, Internet, and telecommunications between rich and poor regions and populations. (Ch. 33)

dioceses Geographic administrative districts of the church, each under the authority of a bishop and centered on a cathedral. (Ch. 8)

divine right of kings The belief propagated by absolutist monarchs in Europe that they derived their power from God and were only answerable to him. (Ch. 18)

division of labor Differentiation of tasks by gender, age, training, status, or other social distinction. (Ch. 1)

diwān An administrative unit of government through which Arab soldiers were registered during the early years of the spread of Islam. (Ch. 9)

domesticated Plants and animals modified by selective breeding so as to serve human needs; domesticated animals will behave in specific ways and breed in captivity. (Ch. 1)

Dreyfus affair A divisive case in which Alfred Dreyfus, a Jewish captain in the French army, was falsely accused and convicted of treason. The Catholic Church sided with the anti-Semites against Dreyfus; after Dreyfus was declared innocent, the French government severed all ties between the state and the church. (Ch. 24)

dynastic cycle The theory that Chinese dynasties go through a predictable cycle from early vigor and growth to subsequent decline as administrators become lax and the well-off find ways to avoid paying taxes, cutting state revenues. (Ch. 13)

economic liberalism The theory, associated with Adam Smith, that the pursuit of individual self-interest in a competitive market would lead to rising prosperity and greater social equality, rendering government intervention unnecessary and undesirable. (Ch. 19)

Eightfold Path The eight-step code of conduct set forth by the Buddha in his first sermon. (Ch. 3)

emirs Arab governors who were given overall responsibility for public order, maintenance of the armed forces, and tax collection. (Ch. 9)

empiricism A theory of inductive reasoning that calls for acquiring evidence through observation and experimentation rather than reason and speculation. (Ch. 19)

Enabling Act An act pushed through the Reichstag by the Nazis in 1933 that gave Hitler absolute dictatorial power for four years. (Ch. 30)

enclosure The controversial process of fencing off common land to create privately owned fields that increased agricultural production at the cost of reducing poor farmers' access to land. (Ch. 19)

encomienda system A system whereby the Spanish crown granted the conquerors the right to forcibly employ groups of indigenous people as laborers and to demand tribute payments from them in exchange for providing food, shelter, and instruction in the Christian faith. (Ch. 16)

endogamy The practice of marrying within a certain ethnic or social group. (Ch. 1)

enlightened absolutism Term coined by historians to describe the rule of eighteenth-century monarchs who, without renouncing their own absolute authority, took up the call to reform their governments in accordance with the rational and humane principles of the Enlightenment. (Ch. 19)

Enlightenment An intellectual and cultural movement in late-seventeenth- and eighteenth-century Europe and the wide world that used rational and critical thinking to debate issues such as political sovereignty, religious tolerance, gender roles, and racial difference. (Ch. 19)

epic poem An oral or written narration of the achievements and sometimes the failures of heroes that embodies peoples' ideas about themselves. (Ch. 2)

Epicureanism A system of philosophy based on the teachings of Epicurus, who viewed a life of contentment, free from fear and suffering, as the greatest good. (Ch. 5)

Esoteric Buddhism A sect of Buddhism that maintains that the secrets of enlightenment have been secretly transmitted from the Buddha and can be accessed through initiation into the mandalas, mudras, and mantras. (Ch. 13)

Estates General Traditional representative body of the three estates of France that met in 1789 in response to imminent state bankruptcy. (Ch. 22)

eunuchs Castrated males who played an important role as palace servants. (Ch. 7)

European Union (EU) An economic and political alliance of twelve European nations formed in 1993 that has since grown to include twenty-eight European nations. (Ch. 32)

Europe first policy The military strategy, set forth by Churchill and adopted by Roosevelt, that called for the defeat of Hitler in Europe before the United States launched an all-out strike against Japan in the Pacific. (Ch. 30)

evolution The idea, developed by Charles Darwin, that all life had gradually evolved from a common origin through a process of natural selection. (Ch. 24)

examination system A system of selecting officials in imperial China based on competitive written examinations. (Ch. 13)

existentialism The name given to a highly diverse and even contradictory philosophy that stresses the meaninglessness of existence and the search for moral values in a world of terror and uncertainty. (Ch. 28)

extraterritoriality The legal principle that exempts individuals from local law, applicable in China because of the agreements reached after China's loss in the Opium War. (Ch. 26)

Factory Act of 1833 English law that led to a sharp decline in the employment of children by limiting the hours that children over age nine could work and banning employment of children younger than nine. (Ch. 23)

fascism A movement characterized by extreme, often expansionist nationalism, anti-socialism, a dynamic and violent leader, and glorification of war and the military. (Ch. 30)

feminization of poverty The issue that those living in extreme poverty are disproportionately women. (Ch. 33)

feudalism A medieval European political system that defines the military obligations and relations between a lord and his vassals and involves the granting of fiefs. (Ch. 14)

fief A portion of land, the use of which was given by a lord to a vassal in exchange for the latter's oath of loyalty. (Ch. 14)

filial piety Reverent attitude of children to their parents extolled by Confucius. (Ch. 4)

Five Pillars of Islam The basic tenets of the Islamic faith; they include reciting a profession of faith in God and in Muhammad as God's prophet, praying five times daily, fasting and praying during the month of Ramadan, making a pilgrimage to Mecca once in one's lifetime, and contributing alms to the poor. (Ch. 9)

five-year plan Launched by Stalin in 1928 and termed the "revolution from above," its goal was to modernize the Soviet Union and generate a Communist society with new attitudes, new loyalties, and a new socialist humanity. (Ch. 30)

foot binding The practice of binding the feet of girls with long strips of cloth to keep them from growing large. (Ch. 13)

foraging A style of life in which people gain food by gathering plant products, trapping or catching small animals and birds, and hunting larger prey. (Ch. 1)

Four Noble Truths The Buddha's message that pain and suffering are inescapable parts of life; suffering and anxiety are caused by human desires and attachments; people can understand and triumph over these weaknesses; and this triumph is made possible by following a simple code of conduct. (Ch. 3)

free womb laws Laws passed across the nineteenth-century Americas that instituted a gradual form of abolition through which children born to slaves gained their freedom. (Ch. 27)

functionalism The principle that buildings, like industrial products, should serve the purpose for which they were made as well as possible. (Ch. 28)

general will A concept associated with Rousseau, referring to the common interests of all the people, who have displaced the monarch as the holder of sovereign power. (Ch. 19)

germ theory The idea that disease is caused by the spread of living organisms that can be controlled. (Ch. 24)

Ghana From the word for "war chief," the name of a large and influential African kingdom inhabited by the Soninke people. (Ch. 10)

Girondists A moderate group that fought for control of the French National Convention in 1793. (Ch. 22)

glasnost Soviet premier Mikhail Gorbachev's popular campaign for government transparency and more open media. (Ch. 32)

global warming The consensus view of an overwhelming majority of the world's scientists that hydrocarbons produced through the burning of fossil fuels have caused a greenhouse effect that has increased global temperatures over time. (Ch. 33)

Gothic The term for the architectural and artistic style that began in Europe in the twelfth century and featured pointed arches, high ceilings, and flying buttressess. (Ch. 14)

Grand Canal A canal, built during the Sui Dynasty, that connected the Yellow and Yangzi Rivers. It was notable for strengthening China's internal cohesion and economic development. (Ch. 7)

Grand Empire The empire over which Napoleon and his allies ruled, encompassing virtually all of Europe except Great Britain. (Ch. 22)

Great Leap Forward Mao Zedong's acceleration of Chinese development in which industrial growth was to be based on small-scale backyard workshops run by peasants living in gigantic self-contained communes. (Ch. 31)

great migration The mass movement of people from Europe in the nineteenth century; one reason that the West's impact on the world was so powerful and complex. (Ch. 25)

Great Mutiny / Great Revolt The terms used by the British and the Indians, respectively, to describe the last armed resistance to British rule in India, which occurred in 1857. (Ch. 26)

Great Proletarian Cultural Revolution A movement launched in 1965 by Mao Zedong that attempted to recapture the revolutionary fervor of his guerrilla struggle. (Ch. 31)

Great Wall A rammed-earth fortification built along the northern border of China during the reign of the First Emperor. (Ch. 7)

great white walls Discriminatory laws passed by Americans and Australians to keep Asians from settling in their countries in the 1880s. (Ch. 25)

Great Zimbabwe A ruined southern African city five-hundred to a thousand years old; it is considered the most impressive monument south of the Nile Valley and Ethiopian highlands. (Ch. 10)

green revolution Beginning in the 1950s, the increase in food production stemming from the introduction of high-yielding wheat, hybrid seeds, and other advancements. (Ch. 33)

gunboat diplomacy The imposition of treaties and agreements under threat of military violence, such as the opening of Japan to trade after Commodore Perry's demands. (Ch. 26)

hadith Collections of the sayings of and anecdotes about Muhammad. (Ch. 9)

Hammurabi's law code A proclamation issued by Babylonian king Hammurabi to establish laws regulating many aspects of life. (Ch. 2)

Harappan The first Indian civilization; also known as the Indus Valley civilization. (Ch. 3)

Haskalah A Jewish Enlightenment movement led by Prussian philosopher Moses Mendelssohn. (Ch. 19)

Hellenistic Literally means "like the Greek"; describes the period from the death of Alexander the Great in 323 B.C.E. to the Roman conquest of Egypt in 30 B.C.E., when Greek culture spread. (Ch. 5)

Hellenization The spread of Greek ideas, culture, and traditions to non-Greek groups across a wide area. (Ch. 5)

heresy A religious practice or belief judged unacceptable by church officials. (Chs. 8, 14)

Holocaust The attempted systematic extermination of all European Jews and other "undesirables" by the Nazi state during World War II. (Ch. 30)

hominids Members of the family Hominidae that contains humans, chimpanzees, gorillas, and orangutans. (Ch. 1)

hoplites Heavily armed citizens who served as infantrymen and fought to defend the polis. (Ch. 5)

horticulture Crop raising done with hand tools and human power. (Ch. 1)

Huguenots French Calvinists. (Ch. 15)

humanism A program of study designed by Italians that emphasized the critical study of Latin and Greek literature with the goal of understanding human nature. (Ch. 15)

iconoclastic controversy The conflict over the veneration of religious images in the Byzantine Empire. (Ch. 8)

id, ego, superego Freudian terms for the primitive, irrational unconscious (id), the rationalizing conscious that mediates what a person can do (ego), and the ingrained moral values that specify what a person should do (superego). (Ch. 28)

imam The leader in community prayer in Islam. (Ch. 9)

import substitution industrialization (ISI) The use of trade barriers to keep certain foreign products out of one's country so that domestic industry can emerge and produce the same goods. (Ch. 31)

Inca The name of the dynasty of rulers who built the largest and last indigenous empire across the Andes. (Ch. 11)

Inca Empire The vast and sophisticated Peruvian empire centered at the capital city of Cuzco that was at its peak in the fifteenth century but weakened by civil war at the time of the Spanish arrival. (Ch. 16)

indentured laborers Laborers who agreed to a term of employment, specified in a contract. (Ch. 26)

Indian Civil Service The bureaucracy that administered the government of India. Entry into its elite ranks was through examinations that Indians were eligible to take, but these tests were offered only in England. (Ch. 26)

Indian National Congress A political association formed in 1885 that worked for Indian self-government. (Ch. 26)

Indo-European languages A large family of languages that includes English, most of the languages of modern Europe, ancient Greek, Latin, Persian, Hindi, Bengali, and Sanskrit. (Ch. 2)

indulgence A document issued by the pope that substituted for earthly penance or time in purgatory. (Ch. 15)

Industrial Revolution A term first coined in the 1830s to describe the burst of major inventions and economic expansion that took place in certain industries, such as cotton textiles and iron, between 1780 and 1850. (Ch. 23)

intifada Beginning in 1987, a prolonged campaign of civil disobedience by Palestinian youth against Israeli soldiers; the Arabic word *intifada* means "shaking off." (Ch. 32)

Iron Age Period beginning about 1100 B.C.E. when iron became the most important material for weapons and tools in some parts of the world. (Ch. 2)

iron law of wages Theory proposed by English economist David Ricardo suggesting that the pressure of population growth prevents wages from rising above the subsistence level. (Ch. 23)

Jacobin club A political club during the French Revolution to which many of the deputies of the Legislative Assembly belonged. (Ch. 22)

Jainism Indian religion whose followers consider all life sacred and avoid destroying other life. (Ch. 3)

janissaries Turkish for "recruits"; they formed the elite army corps. (Ch. 17)

"Japan, Inc." A nickname from the 1970s and 1980s used to describe what some considered the unfair relationship between Japan's business world and government. (Ch. 32)

jati The thousands of Indian castes. (Ch. 12)

Java War The 1825–1830 war between the Dutch government and the Javanese, fought over the extension of Dutch control of the island. (Ch. 26)

Jesuits Members of the Society of Jesus, founded by Ignatius Loyola in 1540, whose goal was the spread of the Roman Catholic faith through schools and missionary activity. (Chs. 15, 18)

jihad Religious war waged by Muslim scholars and religious leaders against both animist rulers and Islamic states that they deemed corrupt. (Ch. 25)

junta A government headed by a council of commanders of the branches of the armed forces. (Ch. 32)

Justinian's Code Multipart collection of laws and legal commentary issued in the sixth century by the emperor Justinian. (Ch. 8)

karma The tally of good and bad deeds that determines the status of an individual's next life. (Ch. 3)

khanates The states ruled by a khan; the four units into which Chinggis divided the Mongol Empire. (Ch. 12)

khipu An intricate system of knotted and colored strings used by early Andean cultures to store information such as census and tax records. (Ch. 11)

kibbutz A Jewish collective farm, first established by Zionists in Palestine, on which each member shared equally in the work, rewards, and defense. (Ch. 29)

Kilwa The most powerful city on the east coast of Africa by the late thirteenth century. (Ch. 10)

Koumbi Saleh The city in which the king of Ghana held his court. (Ch. 10)

laissez faire A doctrine of economic liberalism advocating unrestricted private enterprise and no government interference in the economy. (Ch. 24)

Lateran Agreement A 1929 agreement in which Mussolini in Italy recognized the Vatican as an independent state and agreed to give the church heavy financial support in return for the pope's public support. (Ch. 30)

latifundios Vast landed estates in Latin America. (Ch. 27)

law of inertia A law formulated by Galileo stating that motion, not rest, is the natural state of an object and that an object continues in motion forever unless stopped by some external force. (Ch. 19)

law of universal gravitation Newton's law that all objects are attracted to one another and that the force of attraction is proportional to the object's quantity of matter and inversely proportional to the square of the distance between them. (Ch. 19)

League of Nations A permanent international organization established during the 1919 Paris Peace Conference to protect member states from aggression and avert future wars. (Ch. 28)

Legalists Political theorists who emphasized the need for rigorous laws and laid the basis for China's later bureaucratic government. (Ch. 4)

Lerdo Law An 1856 Mexican law that barred corporate landholdings. (Ch. 27)

liberalism A philosophy whose principal ideas were equality and liberty; liberals demanded representative government and equality before the law as well as such individual freedoms as freedom of the press, freedom of speech, freedom of assembly, and freedom from arbitrary arrest. (Ch. 24)

liberation theology A movement within the Catholic Church to support the poor in situations of exploitation that emerged with particular force in Latin America in the 1960s. (Ch. 31)

loess Soil deposited by wind; it is fertile and easy to work. (Ch. 4)

logographic A system of writing in which each word is represented by a single symbol, such as the Chinese script. (Ch. 4)

Long March The 6,000-mile retreat of the Chinese Communist army in 1934 to a remote region on the northwestern border of China, during which tens of thousands lost their lives. (Ch. 29)

Lucknow Pact A 1916 alliance between the Hindus leading the Indian National Congress Party and the Muslim League. (Ch. 29)

Luddites Group of handicraft workers who attacked factories in northern England in 1811 and after, smashing the new machines that they believed were putting them out of work. (Ch. 23)

madrasa A school for the study of Muslim law and religion. (Ch. 9)

Mahayana The "Great Vehicle," a tradition of Buddhism that aspires to be more inclusive. (Ch. 3)

Majlis The national assembly established by the despotic shah of Iran in 1906. (Ch. 29)

Mandate of Heaven The theory that Heaven gives the king a mandate to rule only as long as he rules in the interests of the people. (Ch. 4)

manifest destiny The doctrine that the United States should absorb the territory spanning from the original Atlantic states to the Pacific Ocean. (Ch. 27)

manorialism The economic system that governed rural life in medieval Europe, in which the landed estates of a lord were worked by the peasants under the lord's jursidiction in exchange for his protection. (Ch. 14)

March Revolution The first phase of the Russian Revolution of 1917, in which unplanned uprisings led to the abdication of the tsar and the establishment of a provisional democratic government that was then overthrown in November by Lenin and the Bolsheviks. (Ch. 28)

Marshall Plan A 1948 American plan for providing economic aid to Europe to help it rebuild after World War II. (Ch. 31)

Mauryan Empire The first Indian empire, founded by Chandragupta. (Ch. 3)

Maya A highly developed Mesoamerican culture centered in the Yucatán peninsula of Mexico. The Maya created the most intricate writing system in the Western Hemisphere. (Ch. 11)

May Fourth Movement A Chinese nationalist movement against foreign imperialists and warlord rule; it began as a 1919 student protest against the decision of the Paris Peace Conference to leave the Shandong Peninsula in the hands of Japan. (Ch. 29)

megacities Cities with populations of 5 million people or more. (Ch. 33)

megafaunal extinction Die-off of large animals in many parts of the world, 45,000–10,000 B.C.E., caused by climate change and most likely human hunting. (Ch. 1)

Meiji Restoration The 1867 ousting of the Tokugawa Shogunate that "restored" the power of the Japanese emperors. (Ch. 26)

Mein Kampf Adolf Hitler's autobiography, published in 1925, which also contains Hitler's political ideology. (Ch. 28)

mercantilism A system of economic regulations aimed at increasing the power of the state derived from the belief that a nation's international power was based on its wealth, specifically its supply of gold and silver. (Ch. 18)

Merovingian A dynasty of rulers that decisively unified the Franks under the reign of Clovis (ca. 481–511) and ruled the Frankish kingdom until the seventh century. (Ch. 8)

Mesoamerica The term used to designate the area spanning present-day central Mexico to Nicaragua. (Ch. 11)

Messiah In Jewish belief, a savior who would bring a period of peace and happiness for Jews; many Christians came to believe that Jesus was that Messiah. (Ch. 6)

Mexica The dominant ethnic group of what is now Mexico, who created an empire based on war and religion that reached its height in the fifteenth century. (Ch. 11)

Middle Passage Enslaved Africans' horrific voyage across the Atlantic to the Americas, under appalling and often deadly conditions. (Ch. 20)

middle powers Countries with significant economic influence that became increasingly assertive regional leaders after the Cold War. (Ch. 33)

migration chain The movement of peoples in which one strong individual blazes the way and others follow. (Ch. 25)

militarism The glorification of the military as the supreme ideal of the state with all other interests subordinate to it. (Ch. 28)

Mines Act of 1842 English law prohibiting underground work for all women and girls as well as for boys under ten. (Ch. 23)

Ming Dynasty The Chinese dynasty in power from 1368 to 1644; it marked a period of vibrant urban culture. (Ch. 21)

Moche A Native American culture that thrived along Peru's northern coast between 100 and 800 C.E. (Ch. 11)

modernism A variety of cultural movements at the end of the nineteenth century and beginning of the twentieth that rebelled against traditional forms and conventions of the past. (Ch. 28)

modernization The changes that enable a country to compete effectively with the leading countries at a given time. (Ch. 24)

modernization theory The belief, held in countries such as the United States in the mid-twentieth century, that all countries evolved in a linear progression from traditional to mature. (Ch. 31)

Mogadishu A Muslim port city in East Africa founded between the eighth and tenth centuries; today it is the capital of Somalia. (Ch. 10)

Monroe Doctrine An 1823 proclamation that established a U.S. sphere of influence over the Americas by opposing European imperialism on the continent. (Ch. 27)

moral economy The early modern European view that community needs predominated over competition and profit and that necessary goods should thus be sold at a fair price. (Ch. 18)

Mountain Led by Robespierre, the French National Convention's radical faction, which led the Convention in 1793. (Ch. 22)

movable type A system of printing in which one piece of type is used for each unique character. (Ch. 13)

Mozarabs Christians who adopted some Arab customs but did not convert. (Ch. 9)

Mughal A term used to refer to the Muslim empire of India, which was the largest, wealthiest, and most populous of the Islamic empires of the early modern world. (Ch. 17)

multinational corporations Business firms that operate in a number of different countries and tend to adopt a global rather than a national perspective. (Ch. 33)

Muslim League Political party founded in 1906 in colonial India that advocated for a separate Muslim homeland after independence. (Ch. 31)

mystery religions Belief systems that were characterized by secret doctrines, rituals of initiation, and sometimes the promise of rebirth or an afterlife. (Ch. 5)

Nahuatl The language of the Aztecs, which they inherited from the Toltecs. (Ch. 11)

Napoleonic Code French civil code promulgated in 1804 that reasserted the 1789 principles of the equality of all male citizens before the law and the absolute security of wealth and private property. (Ch. 22)

Nara Japan's capital and first true city; it was established in 710 and modeled on the Tang capital of Chang'an. (Ch. 7)

National Assembly French representative assembly formed in 1789 by the delegates of the third estate and some members of the clergy, the second estate. (Ch. 22)

nationalism The idea that each people had its own spirit and its own cultural unity, which manifested itself especially in a common language and history and could serve as the basis for an independent political state. (Ch. 24)

National Liberation Front The anticolonial movement in Algeria, which began a war against the French in 1954 and won independence in 1962. (Ch. 31)

NATO The North Atlantic Treaty Organization, an anti-Soviet military alliance of Western nations, formed in 1949. (Ch. 31)

Navigation Acts Mid-seventeenth-century English mercantilist laws that greatly restricted other countries' rights to trade with England and its colonies. (Ch. 18)

Nazism A movement born of extreme nationalism and racism and dominated by Adolf Hitler from 1933 until the end of World War II in 1945. (Ch. 30)

Neanderthals Group of *Homo erectus* with brains as large as those of modern humans that lived in Europe and western Asia between 200,000 and 30,000 years ago. (Ch. 1)

neocolonialism The establishment of political and economic influence over regions after they have ceased to be formal colonies. (Ch. 27)

Neo-Confucianism The revival of Confucian thinking that began in the eleventh century, characterized by the goal of attaining the wisdom of the sages, not exam success. (Ch. 13)

neoliberalism A return beginning in the 1980s to policies intended to promote free markets and the free circulation of capital across national borders. (Ch. 32)

Neolithic era Period beginning in 9000 B.C.E. during which humans obtained food by raising crops and animals and continued to use tools primarily of stone, bone, and wood. (Ch. 1)

New Culture Movement An intellectual revolution beginning in 1916 that attacked traditional Chinese, particularly Confucian, culture and promoted Western ideas of science, democracy, and individualism. (Ch. 29)

New Deal Franklin Delano Roosevelt's plan to reform capitalism in the United States through forceful government intervention in the economy. (Ch. 30)

New Economic Policy (NEP) Lenin's 1921 policy reestablishing limited economic freedom in the Soviet Union in an attempt to rebuild agriculture and industry in the face of economic disintegration. (Ch. 30)

New Imperialism The late-nineteenth-century drive by European countries to create vast political empires abroad. (Ch. 25)

New Order Hitler's program, based on the guiding principle of racial imperialism, which gave preferential treatment to the Nordic peoples above "inferior" Latin peoples and, at the bottom, "subhuman" Slavs and Jews. (Ch. 30)

Nguyen Dynasty The last Vietnamese ruling house, which lasted from 1802 to 1945. (Ch. 26)

1911 Revolution The uprising that brought China's monarchy to an end. (Ch. 26)

nixtamalization Boiling maize in a solution of water and mineral lime to break down compounds in the kernels, increasing their nutritional value. (Ch. 11)

nomads Groups of people who move from place to place in search of food, water, and pasture for their animals, usually following the seasons. (Ch. 12)

Nō theater A type of Japanese theater performed on a bare stage by one or two actors wearing brilliant brocade robes, one actor wearing a mask. The performers conveyed emotions and ideas as much through gestures, stances, and dress as through words. (Ch. 21)

oba The title of the king of Benin. (Ch. 20)

October Manifesto The result of a great general strike in Russia in October 1905, it granted full civil rights and promised a popularly elected Duma (parliament) with real legislative power. (Ch. 24)

oligarchs In Latin America, the small number of individuals and families that had monopolized political power and economic resources since the colonial era. (Ch. 27)

oligarchy A type of Greek government in which citizens who owned a certain amount of property ruled. (Ch. 5)

Olmec The earliest advanced Mesoamerican civilization. (Ch. 11)

Opium War The 1839–1842 war between the British and the Chinese over limitations on trade and the importation of opium into China. (Ch. 26)

Organization of the Petroleum Exporting Countries (OPEC) A cartel formed in 1960 by oil-exporting countries designed to coordinate oil production and raise prices, giving those countries greater capacity for economic development and greater leverage in world affairs. (Ch. 32)

Orthodox Church Another name for the Eastern Christian Church, over which emperors continued to have power. (Ch. 8)

Ottomans Ruling house of the Turkish empire that lasted from 1299 to 1922. (Ch. 17)

pagan Originally referring to those who lived in the countryside, the term came to mean those who practiced religions other than Judaism or Christianity. (Ch. 6)

Paleolithic era Period before 9000 B.C.E. during which humans used tools of stone, bone, and wood and obtained food by gathering and hunting. (Ch. 1)

Palestine Liberation Organization (PLO) Created in 1964, a loose union of Palestinian refugee groups opposed to Israel and united in the goal of establishing a Palestinian state. (Ch. 31)

palm oil A West African tropical product often used to make soap; the British encouraged its cultivation as an alternative to the slave trade. (Ch. 25)

Pan-Africanists People who, through a movement beginning in 1919, sought black solidarity and envisioned a vast self-governing union of all African peoples. (Ch. 31)

pastoralism An economic system based on herding flocks of goats, sheep, cattle, or other animals. (Ch. 1)

paterfamilias The oldest dominant male of the family, who held great power over the lives of family members. (Ch. 6)

patriarchy Social system in which men have more power and access to resources than women, and some men are dominant over other men. (Ch. 1)

patricians The Roman hereditary aristocracy, who held most of the political power in the republic. (Ch. 6)

patronage Financial support of writers and artists by cities, groups, and individuals, often to produce specific works or works in specific styles. (Ch. 15)

pax Romana The "Roman peace," a period during the first and second centuries C.E. of political stability and relative peace. (Ch. 6)

penance Ritual in which Christians asked a priest for forgiveness for sins and the priest set certain actions to atone for the sins. (Ch. 8)

peninsulares A term for natives of Spain and Portugal. (Ch. 22)

perestroika Economic restructuring and reform implemented by Soviet premier Mikhail Gorbachev that permitted an easing of government price controls on some goods, more independence for state enterprises, and the establishment of profit-seeking private cooperatives. (Ch. 32)

Permanent Mandates Commission A commission created by the League of Nations to oversee the developed nations' fulfillment of their international responsibility toward their mandates. (Ch. 29)

petrodollars The global recirculation by international banks of profits from the higher price of oil following the 1973 OPEC oil embargo. (Ch. 32)

Petrograd Soviet A counter-government to the 1917 Russian provisional government, this organization was a huge, fluctuating mass meeting of two to three thousand workers, soldiers, and socialist intellectuals. (Ch. 28)

pharaoh The title given to the king of Egypt in the New Kingdom, from a word that meant "great house." (Ch. 2)

philosophes A group of French intellectuals who proclaimed that they were bringing the light of knowledge to their fellow humans. (Ch. 19)

Phoenicians People of the prosperous city-states in what is now Lebanon who traded and founded colonies throughout the Mediterranean and spread the phonetic alphabet. (Ch. 2)

Plan de Ayala Document written by Zapatistas during the Mexican Revolution that demanded the government return all land, forests, and waters taken from rural communities. (Ch. 27)

Platonic ideals In Plato's thought, the eternal unchanging ideal forms that are the essence of true reality. (Ch. 5)

plebeians The common people of Rome, who were free but had few of the patricians' advantages. (Ch. 6)

polis Generally translated as "city-state," it was the basic political and institutional unit of ancient Greece. (Ch. 5)

politiques Catholic and Protestant moderates who sought to end the religious violence in France by restoring a strong monarchy and granting official recognition to the Huguenots. (Ch. 15)

polytheism The worship of many gods and goddesses. (Ch. 2)

popes Heads of the Roman Catholic Church, who became political as well as religious authorities. The period of a pope's term in office is called a pontificate. (Ch. 8)

Popular Front A party formed in 1936 in France that encouraged unions and launched a far-reaching New Deal–inspired program of social reform. (Ch. 30)

Porfiriato The regime of Porfirio Díaz, who presided in Mexico from 1876 to 1880 and again from 1884 to 1911. (Ch. 27)

predestination Calvin's teaching that God decided at the beginning of time who would be saved and who damned, so people could not actively work to achieve salvation. (Ch. 15)

proletariat The Marxist term for the working class of modern industrialized society. (Ch. 24)

protected people The Muslim classification used for Hindus, Christians, and Jews; they were allowed to follow their religions but had to pay a special tax. (Ch. 12)

protectorate An autonomous state or territory partly controlled and protected by a stronger outside power. (Ch. 25)

Protestant Originally meaning "a follower of Luther," this term came to be generally applied to all non-Catholic western European Christians. (Ch. 15)

Protestant Reformation A religious reform movement that began in the early sixteenth century and split the Western Christian Church. (Chs. 15, 18)

Ptolemy's *Geography* A second-century work translated into Latin around 1410 that synthesized the classical knowledge of geography and introduced latitude and longitude markings. (Ch. 16)

public sphere An idealized intellectual space that emerged in Europe during the Enlightenment. Here, the public came together to discuss important social, economic, and political issues. (Ch. 19)

Punic Wars A series of three wars between Rome and Carthage in which Rome emerged the victor. (Ch. 6)

Pure Land A school of Buddhism that taught that by calling on the Buddha Amitabha, one could achieve rebirth in Amitabha's Pure Land paradise. (Ch. 7)

Puritans Members of a sixteenth- and seventeenth-century reform movement within the Church of England that advocated purifying it of Roman Catholic elements, such as bishops, elaborate ceremonials, and wedding rings. (Ch. 18)

Qing Dynasty The dynasty founded by the Manchus that ruled China from 1644 to 1911. (Ch. 21)

Qizilbash Nomadic Turkish Sufis who supplied the early Safavid state with military troops in exchange for grazing rights. (Ch. 17)

Quechua The official language of the Incas, it is still spoken by most Peruvians today. (Ch. 11)

quinine An agent that proved effective in controlling attacks of malaria, which had previously decimated Europeans in the tropics. (Ch. 25)

Qur'an The sacred book of Islam. (Ch. 9)

reconquista A fourteenth-century term used to describe the long Christian crusade to wrest Spain back from the Muslims; clerics believed it was a sacred and patriotic mission. (Ch. 14)

Records of the Grand Historian A comprehensive history of China written by Sima Qian. (Ch. 7)

Reign of Terror The period from 1793 to 1794, during which Robespierre's Committee of Public Safety tried and executed thousands suspected of political crimes and a new revolutionary culture was imposed. (Ch. 22)

ren Humanity, the ultimate Confucian virtue. (Ch. 4)

Renaissance A French word meaning "rebirth," used to describe a cultural movement that began in fourteenth-century Italy and looked back to the classical past. (Ch. 15)

republicanism A form of government in which there is no monarch and power rests in the hands of the people as exercised through elected representatives. (Ch. 18)

revisionism An effort by various socialists to update Marxist doctrines to reflect the realities of the time. (Ch. 24)

Rig Veda The earliest collection of Indian hymns, ritual texts, and philosophical treatises, it is the central source of information on early Aryans. (Ch. 3)

Rocket The name given to George Stephenson's effective locomotive that was first tested in 1829 on the Liverpool and Manchester Railway and reached a maximum speed of 35 miles per hour. (Ch. 23)

Romanticism A movement in art, literature, and music characterized by a belief in emotional exuberance, unrestrained imagination, and spontaneity in both art and personal life. (Ch. 24)

Roosevelt Corollary A corollary to the Monroe Doctrine stating that the United States would correct what it saw as "chronic wrongdoing" in neighboring countries. (Ch. 27)

Russo-Japanese War The 1904–1905 war between Russia and Japan fought over imperial influence and territory in northeast China (Manchuria). (Ch. 26)

sacraments Certain rituals of the church believed to act as a conduit of God's grace, such as baptism. (Ch. 8)

Safavid The dynasty that ruled all of Persia and other regions from 1501 to 1722; its state religion was Shi'ism. (Ch. 17)

saints People who were venerated for having lived or died in a way that was spiritually heroic or noteworthy. (Ch. 8)

salons Regular social gatherings held by talented and rich Parisian women in their homes, where philosophes and their followers met to discuss literature, science, and philosophy. (Ch. 19)

samsara The transmigration of souls by a continual process of rebirth. (Ch. 3)

sans-culottes The laboring poor of Paris, so called because the men wore trousers instead of the knee breeches of the wealthy; the term came to refer to the militant radicals of the city. (Ch. 22)

Sanskrit India's classical literary language. (Ch. 12)

sati A practice whereby a high-caste Hindu woman would throw herself on her husband's funeral pyre. (Ch. 12)

satyagraha Loosely translated as "soul force," which Gandhi believed was the means of striving for truth and social justice through love, suffering, and conversion of the oppressor. (Ch. 29)

scholar-official class Chinese educated elite that included both scholars and officials. The officials had usually gained office by passing the highly competitive civil service examination. (Ch. 13)

Scholastics Medieval professors who developed a method of thinking, reasoning, and writing in which questions were raised and authorities cited on both sides of a question. (Ch. 14)

Senate The assembly that was the main institution of power in the Roman Republic, originally composed only of aristocrats. (Ch. 6)

sensationalism An idea, espoused by John Locke, that all human ideas and thoughts are produced as a result of sensory impressions. (Ch. 19)

separate spheres A gender division of labor with the wife at home as mother and homemaker and the husband as wage earner. (Ch. 23)

sepoys The native Indian troops who were trained as infantrymen. (Ch. 17)

serf A peasant who lost his or her freedom and became permanently bound to the landed estate of a lord. (Ch. 14)

shah Persian word for "king." (Ch. 17)

shamans Spiritually adept men and women who communicated with the unseen world. (Ch. 1)

shari'a Muslim law, which covers social, criminal, political, commercial, and religious matters. (Ch. 9)

shi The lower ranks of Chinese aristocracy; these men could serve in either military or civil capacities. (Ch. 4)

Shi'a Arabic term meaning "supporters of Ali"; they make up one of the two main divisions of Islam. (Ch. 9)

Shinto The Way of the Gods, Japan's native religion. (Ch. 7)

shogun The Japanese general-in-chief. (Ch. 13)

shore trading A process for trading goods in which European ships sent boats ashore or invited African dealers to bring traders and slaves out to the ships. (Ch. 20)

Silk Road The trade routes across Central Asia linking China to western Eurasia. (Ch. 7)

Social Darwinism The application of the theory of biological evolution to human affairs, it sees the human race as driven to ever-greater specialization and progress by an unending economic struggle that determines the survival of the fittest. (Ch. 24)

social hierarchies Divisions between rich and poor, elites and common people that have been a central feature of human society since the Neolithic era. (Ch. 1)

socialism A radical political doctrine that opposed individualism and that advocated cooperation and a sense of community; key ideas were economic planning, greater economic equality, and state regulation of property. (Ch. 24)

Sokoto caliphate Founded in 1809 by Uthman dan Fodio, this African state was based on Islamic history and law. (Ch. 25)

Solidarity Led by Lech Wałęsa, an independent Polish trade union organized in 1980 that worked for the rights of workers and political reform. (Ch. 32)

sorting A collection or batch of British goods that would be traded for a slave or for a quantity of gold, ivory, or dyewood. (Ch. 20)

sovereignty Authority of states that possess a monopoly over the instruments of justice and the use of force within clearly defined boundaries and in which private armies present no threat to central control; seventeenth-century European states made important advances toward sovereignty. (Ch. 18)

spinning jenny A simple, inexpensive, hand-power spinning machine created by James Hargreaves about 1765. (Ch. 23)

Srivijaya A maritime empire that held the Strait of Malacca and the waters around Sumatra and adjacent islands. (Ch. 12)

stateless societies African societies bound together by ethnic or blood ties rather than by being political states. (Ch. 10)

steam engines A breakthrough invention by Thomas Savery in 1698 and Thomas Newcomen in 1705 that burned coal to produce steam, which was then used to operate a pump; the early models were superseded by James Watt's more efficient steam engine, patented in 1769. (Ch. 23)

steppe Grasslands that are too dry for crops but support pasturing animals; they are common across much of the center of Eurasia. (Ch. 12)

Stoicism A philosophy, based on the ideas of Zeno, that held that people could only be happy when living in accordance with nature and accepting whatever happened. (Ch. 5)

Sudan The African region surrounded by the Sahara, the Gulf of Guinea, the Atlantic Ocean, and the mountains of Ethiopia. (Ch. 10)

sultan An Arabic word used by the Ottomans to describe a supreme political and military ruler. (Ch. 17)

Sunna An Arabic term meaning "trodden path." The term refers to the deeds and sayings of Muhammad, which constitute the obligatory example for Muslim life. (Ch. 9)

Sunnis Members of the larger of the two main divisions of Islam; the division between Sunnis and Shi'a began in a dispute about succession to Muhammad, but over time many differences in theology developed. (Ch. 9)

Swahili Meaning "People of the Coast," the term used for the people living along the East African coast and on nearby islands. (Chs. 10, 20)

Sykes-Picot Agreement The 1916 secret agreement between Britain and France that divided up the Arab lands of Lebanon, Syria, southern Turkey, Palestine, Jordan, and Iraq. (Ch. 29)

Taghaza A settlement in the western Sahara, the site of the main salt-mining center. (Ch. 20)

Taiping Rebellion A massive rebellion by believers in the religious teachings of Hong Xiuquan, begun in 1851 and not suppressed until 1864. (Ch. 26)

Tale of Genji, The A Japanese literary masterpiece about court life written by Lady Murasaki. (Ch. 13)

Tanzimat A set of radical reforms designed to remake the Ottoman Empire on a western European model. (Ch. 25)

taotie A stylized animal face commonly seen in Chinese bronzes. (Ch. 4)

tariff protection A government's way of supporting and aiding its own economy by laying high taxes on imported goods from other countries, as when the French responded to the flood of cheaper British goods in their country by imposing high tariffs on some imported products. (Ch. 23)

tax-farming Assigning the collection of taxes to whoever bids the most for the privilege. (Ch. 12)

Tenochtitlan The largest Aztec city, built starting in 1325. The Spanish admired it when they entered in 1519. (Ch. 11)

Teotihuacan The monumental city-state that dominated trade in classical era Mesoamerica. (Ch. 11)

Thermidorian reaction A reaction in 1794 to the violence of the Reign of Terror, resulting in the execution of Robespierre and the loosening of economic controls. (Ch. 22)

Thirty Years' War A large-scale conflict extending from 1618 to 1648 that pitted Protestants against Catholics in central Europe, but also involved dynastic interests, notably of Spain and France. (Ch. 18)

Tiananmen Square The site of a Chinese student revolt in 1989 at which Communists imposed martial law and arrested, injured, or killed hundreds of students. (Ch. 32)

Timbuktu Originally a campsite for desert nomads, it grew into a thriving city under Mansa Musa, king of Mali and Africa's most famous ruler. (Ch. 10)

Tokugawa Shogunate The Japanese government in Edo founded by Tokugawa Ieyasu. It lasted from 1603 to 1867. (Ch. 21)

totalitarianism A radical dictatorship that exercises complete political power and control over all aspects of society and seeks to mobilize the masses for action. (Ch. 30)

total war Practiced by countries fighting in World War I, a war in which the government plans and controls all aspects of economic and social life in order to make the greatest possible military effort. (Ch. 28)

Treaty of Guadalupe Hidalgo The 1848 treaty between the United States and Mexico in which Mexico ceded large tracts of land to the United States. (Ch. 27)

Treaty of Lausanne The 1923 treaty that ended the Turkish war and recognized the territorial integrity of a truly independent Turkey. (Ch. 29)

Treaty of Paris The 1763 peace treaty that ended the Seven Years' War, according vast French territories in North America and India to Britain and Louisiana to Spain. (Ch. 22)

Treaty of Tordesillas The 1494 agreement giving Spain everything west of an imaginary line drawn down the Atlantic and giving Portugal everything to the east. (Ch. 16)

Treaty of Verdun A treaty ratified in 843 that divided Charlemagne's territories among his three surviving grandsons; their kingdoms set the pattern for the modern states of Germany, France, and Italy. (Ch. 8)

Treaty of Versailles The 1919 peace settlement that ended World War I; it declared Germany responsible for the war, limited Germany's army to one hundred thousand men, and forced Germany to pay huge reparations. (Ch. 28)

trench warfare Fighting behind rows of trenches, mines, and barbed wire; used in World War I with a staggering cost in lives and minimal gains in territory. (Ch. 28)

tributary system A system first established during the Han Dynasty to regulate contact with foreign powers. States and tribes beyond China's borders sent envoys bearing gifts and received gifts in return. (Ch. 7)

Triple Entente The alliance of Great Britain, France, and Russia in the First World War. (Ch. 28)

Truman Doctrine The 1945 American policy of preventing the spread of Communist rule. (Ch. 31)

Tuareg Major branch of the nomadic Berber peoples who controlled the north-south trans-Saharan trade in salt. (Ch. 20)

ulama Religious scholars who interpret the Qur'an and the Sunna, the deeds and sayings of Muhammad. (Chs. 9, 17)

umma A community of people who share a religious faith and commitment rather than a tribal tie. (Ch. 9)

Valladolid debate A debate organized by Spanish king Charles I in 1550 in the city of Valladolid that pitted defenders of Spanish conquest and forcible conversion against critics of these practices. (Ch. 16)

vassal A knight who has sworn loyalty to a particular lord. (Ch. 14)

vernacular literature Literature written in the everyday language of a region rather than Latin; this included French, German, Italian, and English. (Ch. 14)

viceroyalties The name for the four administrative units of Spanish possessions in the Americas: New Spain, Peru, New Granada, and La Plata. (Ch. 16)

viziers Chief assistants to caliphs. (Ch. 17)

War Communism The application of the total-war concept to a civil conflict; the Bolsheviks seized grain from peasants, introduced rationing, nationalized all banks and industry, and required everyone to work. (Ch. 28)

Warring States Period The period of Chinese history between 403 B.C.E. and 221 B.C.E., when states fought each other and one state after another was destroyed. (Ch. 4)

Washington Consensus Policies restricting public spending, lowering import barriers, privatizing state enterprises, and deregulating markets in response to the 1980s debt crisis in Latin America. (Ch. 32)

water frame A spinning machine created by Richard Arkwright that had a capacity of several hundred spindles and used waterpower; it therefore required a larger and more specialized mill—a factory. (Ch. 23)

wergeld Compensatory payment for death or injury set in many barbarian law codes. (Ch. 8)

white man's burden The idea that Europeans could and should civilize more primitive nonwhite peoples and that imperialism would eventually provide nonwhites with modern achievements and higher standards of living. (Ch. 25)

witch-hunts Campaign against witchcraft in Europe and European colonies during the sixteenth and seventeenth centuries in which hundreds of thousands of people, mostly women, were tried, and many of them executed. (Ch. 15)

Yahweh All-powerful god of the Hebrew people and the basis for the enduring religious traditions of Judaism. (Ch. 2)

yin and yang A concept of complementary poles, one of which represents the feminine, dark, and receptive, and the other the masculine, bright, and assertive. (Ch. 4)

Young Turks Fervent patriots who seized power in the revolution of 1908, forcing the conservative sultan to implement reforms; they helped pave the way for the birth of modern secular Turkey. (Ch. 25)

yurts Tents in which the pastoral nomads lived; they could be quickly dismantled and loaded onto animals or carts. (Ch. 12)

zaibatsu Giant conglomerate firms established in Japan beginning in the Meiji period and lasting until the end of World War II. (Ch. 29)

Zen A school of Buddhism that emphasized meditation and truths that could not be conveyed in words. (Ch. 13)

Zionism The movement toward Jewish political nationhood started by Theodor Herzl. (Ch. 24)

Zoroastrianism Religion based on the teachings of Zoroaster that emphasized the individual's responsibility to choose between good and evil. (Ch. 2)

20°E 40°E 60°E 80°E 100°E 120°E 140°E 160°E 80°N

Arctic Circle 60°N

URAL MTS.

Volga R.

Ob R.

EUROPE

ALPS

GOBI

Yellow R. (Huang He)

Yangzi R.

ASIA 40°N

HIMALAYA MTS.

Mediterranean Sea

SAHARA

ARABIAN DESERT

Nile R.

Ganges R.

AFRICA

Arabian Sea

Bay of Bengal

South China Sea

Tropic of Cancer 20°N

PACIFIC OCEAN

Congo R.

INDIAN OCEAN

Equator 0°

Zambezi R.

KALAHARI DESERT

AUSTRALIA

Tropic of Capricorn 20°S

40°S

Vegetation zones

- Tundra
- Northern forest
- Temperate forest
- Temperate grassland
- Desert and dry shrub
- Mediterranean shrub
- Mountain grassland
- Tropical grassland and savanna
- Tropical forest
- Permanent ice cover

60°S

Antarctic Circle

80°S

Merry E. Wiesner-Hanks (Ph.D., University of Wisconsin–Madison) taught first at Augustana College in Illinois and since 1985 at the University of Wisconsin–Milwaukee, where she is currently UWM Distinguished Professor in the department of history. She is the Senior Editor of the *Sixteenth Century Journal*, one of the editors of the *Journal of Global History*, and the author or editor of more than thirty books, including *A Concise History of the World*. From 2017 to 2019 she is serving as the president of the World History Association.

Patricia Buckley Ebrey (Ph.D., Columbia University), professor of history at the University of Washington in Seattle, specializes in China. She has published numerous journal articles and *The Cambridge Illustrated History of China*, as well as several monographs. In 2010 she won the Shimada Prize for outstanding work of East Asian Art History for *Accumulating Culture: The Collections of Emperor Huizong*.

Roger B. Beck (Ph.D., Indiana University) is Distinguished Professor of African and twentieth-century world history at Eastern Illinois University. His publications include *The History of South Africa*; a translation of P. J. van der Merwe's *The Migrant Farmer in the History of the Cape Colony, 1657–1842*; and more than a hundred articles, book chapters, and reviews. He is a former treasurer and Executive Council member of the World History Association.

Jerry Dávila (Ph.D., Brown University) is Jorge Paulo Lemann Professor of Brazilian History at the University of Illinois. He is the author of *Dictatorship in South America*; *Hotel Trópico: Brazil and the Challenge of African Decolonization*, winner of the Latin Studies Association Brazil Section Book Prize; and *Diploma of Whiteness: Race and Social Policy in Brazil, 1917–1945*. He has served as president of the Conference on Latin American History.

Clare Haru Crowston (Ph.D., Cornell University) teaches at the University of Illinois, where she is currently professor of history and department chair. She is the author of *Credit, Fashion, Sex: Economies of Regard in Old Regime France* and *Fabricating Women: The Seamstresses of Old Regime France, 1675–1791*, which won the Berkshire and Hagley Prizes. She edited two special issues of the *Journal of Women's History*, has published numerous journal articles and reviews, and is a past president of the Society for French Historical Studies.

John P. McKay (Ph.D., University of California, Berkeley) is professor emeritus at the University of Illinois. He has written or edited numerous works, including the Herbert Baxter Adams Prize–winning book *Pioneers for Profit: Foreign Entrepreneurship and Russian Industrialization, 1885–1913*.